Hoover's Handbook of

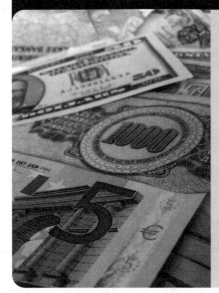

World Business

2007

HOOVERS™

A D&B COMPANY

Austin, Texas

Hoover's Handbook of World Business 2007 is intended to provide readers with accurate and authoritative information about the enterprises covered in it. Hoover's asked all companies and organizations profiled to provide information. Many did so; a number did not. The information contained herein is as accurate as we could reasonably make it. In many cases we have relied on third-party material that we believe to be trustworthy, but were unable to independently verify. We do not warrant that the book is absolutely accurate or without error. Readers should not rely on any information contained herein in instances where such reliance might cause loss or damage. The publisher, the editors, and their data suppliers specifically disclaim all warranties, including the implied warranties of merchantability and fitness for a specific purpose. This book is sold with the understanding that neither the publisher, the editors, nor any content contributors are engaged in providing investment, financial, accounting, legal, or other professional advice.

The financial data (Historical Financials sections) in this book are from a variety of sources. EDGAR Online provided selected data for the Historical Financials sections of publicly traded companies. For private companies and for historical information on public companies prior to their becoming public, we obtained information directly from the companies or from trade sources deemed to be reliable. Hoover's, Inc., is solely responsible for the presentation of all data.

Many of the names of products and services mentioned in this book are the trademarks or service marks of the companies manufacturing or selling them and are subject to protection under US law. Space has not permitted us to indicate which names are subject to such protection, and readers are advised to consult with the owners of such marks regarding their use. Hoover's is a trademark of Hoover's, Inc.

10 9 8 7 6 5 4 3 2

Publishers Cataloging-in-Publication Data
Hoover's Handbook of World Business 2007
    Includes indexes.
    ISBN 978-1-57311-116-4
    ISSN 1055-7199
    1. Business enterprises — Directories. 2. Corporations — Directories.
HF3010 338.7

Hoover's Company Information is also available on the Internet at Hoover's Online (www.hoovers.com). A catalog of Hoover's products is available on the Internet at www.hooversbooks.com.

The Hoover's Handbook series is produced for Hoover's Business Press by:

Sycamore Productions, Inc.
5808 Balcones Drive, Suite 205
Austin, Texas 78731
info@sycamoreproductions.com

Cover design is by John Baker. Electronic prepress and printing are by Von Hoffman Corporation, Owensville, Missouri.

U.S. AND WORLD BOOK SALES

Hoover's, Inc.
5800 Airport Blvd.
Austin, TX 78752
Phone: 512-374-4500
Fax: 512-374-4538
e-mail: orders@hoovers.com
Web: www.hooversbooks.com

EUROPEAN BOOK SALES

William Snyder Publishing Associates
5 Five Mile Drive
Oxford OX2 8HT
England
Phone & fax: +44-186-551-3186
e-mail: snyderpub@aol.com

Hoover's, Inc.

Founder: Gary Hoover
Interim President: Paul Pellman
EVP Customer Experience and International: Russell Secker
EVP Product and Technology: Jeffrey (Jeff) Guillot
EVP US Sales: John Lysinger
VP Acquisition Marketing: Chris Warwick
VP Advertising: Paul Rostkowski
VP Finance: Charles (Chuck) Harvey
VP Marketing: Fred Howard
VP Subscription Sales: Mel Yarbrough

EDITORIAL

Managing Editor: Margaret C. Lynch
Senior Editors: Kathleen Kelly, Laurie Najjar, Barbara Redding, Dennis Sutton
Team Leads: Larry Bills, Zack Gonzales, Lisa Goodgame, Nancy Kay, Greg Perliski, Lee Simmons
Editors: Sally Alt, Adi Anand, Adam Anderson, Alex Biesada, Joe Bramhall, James Bryant, Ryan Caione, Jason Cella, Catherine Colbert, Elizabeth Cornell, Danny Cummings, Jeff Dorsch, Bobby Duncan, Lesley Epperson, Stuart Hampton, Jim Harris, Chris Huston, Donna Iroabuchi, Jessica Jimenez, Kenny Jones, Linnea Anderson Kirgan, Julie Krippel, Anne Law, Josh Lower, John MacAyeal, Barbara Murray, Nell Newton, Kristi Park, Peter Partheymuller, David Ramirez, Melanie Robertson, Belen Rodriguez, Matt Saucedo, Amy Schein, Seth Shafer, Katherine Smith, Paula Smith, Anthony Staats, Betsy Staton, Diane Stimets, Barbara Strickland, Daysha Taylor, Vanita Trippe, Tim Walker, Kathi Whitley, Randy Williams, David Woodruff
QA Editors: Jason Cother, Carrie Geis, Rosie Hatch, Diane Lee, John Willis
Project Analyst: Tara LoPresti
Editorial Customer Advocates: Anna Porlas

HOOVER'S BUSINESS PRESS

Senior Director: Jim Currie
Distribution Manager: Rhonda Mitchell
Customer Support and Fulfillment Manager: Michael Febonio

ABOUT HOOVER'S, INC. – THE BUSINESS INFORMATION AUTHORITY™

Hoover's, a D&B company, gives its customers a competitive edge with insightful information about industries, companies, and key decision makers. Hoover's provides this updated information for sales, marketing, business development, and other professionals who need intelligence on U.S. and global companies, industries, and the people who lead them. This information, along with powerful tools to search, sort, download, and integrate the content, is available through Hoover's (www.hoovers.com), the company's premier online service. Hoover's business information is also available through corporate intranets and distribution agreements with licensees, as well as via Hoover's books. The company is headquartered in Austin, Texas.

Abbreviations

AB – Aktiebolag (Swedish)*

ADR – American Depositary Receipts

AG – Aktiengesellschaft (German)*

AFL-CIO – American Federation of Labor and Congress of Industrial Organizations

AMEX – American Stock Exchange

A/S – Aktieselskab (Danish)*

ASA – Allmenne Aksjeselskaper (Norwegian)*

ATM – asynchronous transfer mode; automated teller machine

CAD/CAM – computer-aided design/computer-aided manufacturing

CASE – computer-aided software engineering

CD-ROM – compact disc – read-only memory

CEO – chief executive officer

CFO – chief financial officer

CMOS – complementary metal-oxide semiconductor

COMECON – Council for Mutual Economic Assistance

COO – chief operating officer

DAT – digital audio tape

DOD – Department of Defense

DOE – Department of Energy

DOT – Department of Transportation

DRAM – dynamic random-access memory

DVD – digital versatile disc/digital video disc

EC – European Community

EPA – Environmental Protection Agency

EPS – earnings per share

EU – European Union

EVP – executive vice president

FCC – Federal Communications Commission

FDA – Food and Drug Administration

FDIC – Federal Deposit Insurance Corporation

FTC – Federal Trade Commission

GATT – General Agreement on Tariffs and Trade

GmbH – Gesellschaft mit beschränkter Haftung (German)*

GNP – gross national product

HDTV – high-definition television

HMO – health maintenance organization

HR – human resources

HTML – hypertext markup language

ICC – Interstate Commerce Commission

IMF – International Monetary Fund

IPO – initial public offering

IRS – Internal Revenue Service

KGaA – Kommanditgesellschaft auf Aktien (German)*

LAN – local-area network

LBO – leveraged buyout

LNG – liquefied natural gas

LP – limited partnership

Ltd. – Limited

MFN – Most Favored Nation

MITI – Ministry of International Trade and Industry (Japan)

NAFTA – North American Free Trade Agreement

Nasdaq – National Association of Securities Dealers Automated Quotations

NATO – North Atlantic Treaty Organization

NV – Naamlose Vennootschap (Dutch)*

NYSE – New York Stock Exchange

OAO – open joint stock company (Russian)

OAS – Organization of American States

OECD – Organization for Economic Cooperation and Development

OEM – original equipment manufacturer

OOO – limited liability company (Russian)

OPEC – Organization of Petroleum Exporting Countries

OS – operating system

OTC – over-the-counter

P/E – price-to-earnings ratio

PLC – public limited company (UK)*

RAM – random-access memory

R&D – research and development

RISC – reduced instruction set computer

ROA – return on assets

ROI – return on investment

SA – Société Anonyme (French)*; Sociedad(e) Anónima (Spanish and Portuguese)*

SA de CV – Sociedad Anónima de Capital Variable (Spanish)*

SEC – Securities and Exchange Commission

SEVP – senior executive vice president

SIC – Standard Industrial Classification

SpA – Società per Azioni (Italian)*

SPARC – scalable processor architecture

SVP – senior vice president

VAR – value-added reseller

VAT – value-added tax

VC – venture capitalist

VP – vice president

WAN – wide-area network

WWW – World Wide Web

ZAO – closed joint stock company (Russian)

z o.o. – z ograniczona odpowiedzialnoscia (Polish)*

* These abbreviations are used in companies' names to convey that the companies are limited liability enterprises; the meanings are usually the equivalent of *corporation* or *incorporated*.

Contents

List of Lists

Companies Profiled

Companies Profiled (continued)

About Hoover's Handbook of World Business 2007

This 14th edition of *Hoover's Handbook of World Business* is focused on its mission of providing you with premier coverage of the global business scene. Featuring 300 of the world's most influential companies based outside of the United States, this book is one of the most complete sources of in-depth information on large, non-US-based business enterprises available anywhere.

Hoover's Handbook of World Business is one of our four-title series of handbooks that covers, literally, the world of business. The series is available as an indexed set, and also includes *Hoover's Handbook of American Business*, *Hoover's Handbook of Private Companies*, and *Hoover's Handbook of Emerging Companies*. This series brings you information on the biggest, fastest-growing, and most influential enterprises in the world.

HOOVER'S ONLINE FOR BUSINESS NEEDS

In addition to the 2,550 companies featured in our handbooks, comprehensive coverage of more than 40,000 business enterprises is available in electronic format on our Web site, Hoover's Online (www.hoovers.com). Our goal is to provide one site that offers authoritative, updated intelligence on US and global companies, industries, and the people who shape them. Hoover's has partnered with other prestigious business information and service providers to bring you all the right business information, services, and links in one place.

We welcome the recognition we have received as the premier provider of high-quality company information — online, electronically, and in print — and continue to look for ways to make our products more available and more useful to you.

We believe that anyone who buys from, sells to, invests in, lends to, competes with, interviews with, or works for a company should know all there is to know about that enterprise. Taken together, this book and the other Hoover's products and resources represent the most complete source of basic corporate information readily available to the general public.

HOW TO USE THIS BOOK

This book has four sections:

1. "Using Hoover's Handbooks" describes the contents of our profiles and explains the ways in which we gather and compile our data.

2. "A List-Lover's Compendium" contains lists of the largest, fastest-growing, and most valuable companies of global importance.

3. The company profiles section makes up the largest and most important part of the book — 300 profiles of major business enterprises, arranged alphabetically.

4. Three indexes complete the book. The first sorts companies by industry groups, the second by headquarters location. The third index is a list of all the executives found in the Executives section of each company profile.

As always, we hope you find our books useful. We invite your comments via phone (512-374-4500), fax (512-374-4538), mail (5800 Airport Boulevard, Austin, Texas 78752), or e-mail (custsupport@hoovers.com).

The Editors,
Austin, Texas,
January 2007

Using Hoover's Handbooks

SELECTION OF THE COMPANIES PROFILED

The 300 profiles in this book include a variety of international enterprises, ranging from some of the largest publicly traded companies in the world — DaimlerChrysler AG, for example — to Malaysia's largest and oldest conglomerate, Sime Darby Berhad. It also includes many private businesses, such as Bertelsmann AG and LEGO, as well as a selection of government-owned entities, including the British Broadcasting Corporation and Mexico's Petróleos Mexicanos. The companies selected represent a cross-section of the largest, most influential, and most interesting companies based outside the United States.

In selecting these companies, we followed several basic criteria. We started with the global giants, including Toyota and Royal Dutch Shell, and then looked at companies with substantial activity in the US, such as Vivendi and Diageo. We also included companies that dominate their industries (e.g., Electrolux, the world's #1 producer of household appliances), as well as representative companies from around the world (one Indian conglomerate, Tata; one firm from Finland, Nokia; and two companies from Russia, OAO Gazprom and OAO LUKOIL). Companies that weren't necessarily global powerhouses but had a high profile with consumers (e.g., IKEA) or had interesting stories (Virgin Group) were included. Finally, because of their truly global reach, we added the Big Four accounting firms (even though they are headquartered or co-headquartered in the US).

ORGANIZATION

The profiles are presented in alphabetical order. You will find the commonly used name of the enterprise at the beginning of the profile; the full, legal name is found in the Locations section. For some companies, primarily Japanese, the commonly translated English name differs from the actual legal name of the company, so both are provided. (The legal name of Nippon Steel Corporation is Shin Nippon Seitetsu Kabushiki Kaisha.) If a company name starts with a person's first name (e.g., George Weston Limited), it is alphabetized under the first name. We've also tried to alphabetize companies where you

would expect to find them — for example, Deutsche Lufthansa is in the L's and Grupo Televisa can be found under T.

The annual financial information contained in the profiles is current through fiscal year-ends occurring as late as August 2006. We have included certain nonfinancial developments, such as officer changes, through December 2006.

OVERVIEW

In the first section of the profile, we have tried to give a thumbnail description of the company and what it does. The description will usually include information on the company's strategy, reputation, and ownership. We recommend that you read this section first.

HISTORY

This extended section reflects our belief that every enterprise is the sum of its history and that you have to know where you came from in order to know where you are going. While some companies have limited historical awareness and were unable to help us much and other companies are just plain boring, we think the vast majority of the enterprises in this book have colorful backgrounds. We have tried to focus on the people who made the enterprises what they are today. We have found these histories to be full of twists and ironies; they make fascinating reading.

EXECUTIVES

Here we list the names of the people who run the company, insofar as space allows. We have shown age and pay information where available, although most non-US companies are not required to report the level of detail revealed in the US.

Although companies are free to structure their management titles any way they please, most modern corporations follow standard practices. The ultimate power in any corporation lies with the shareholders, who elect a board of directors, usually including officers or "insiders" as well as individuals from outside the company. The chief officer, the person on whose desk the buck stops, is usually called the chief executive officer (CEO) in the US. In other countries, practices vary widely. In the UK, traditionally, the Managing Director performs the functions of the CEO without the title, although the use of the term CEO is on the rise there. In Germany it is customary to have two boards of directors: a managing board populated by the top executives of the company and a higher-level supervisory board consisting of outsiders.

As corporate management has become more complex, it is common for the CEO to have a "right-hand person" who oversees the day-to-day operations of the company, allowing the CEO plenty of time to focus on strategy and long-term issues. This right-hand person is usually designated the chief operating officer (COO) and is often the president of the company. In other cases one person is both chairman and president.

We have tried to list each company's most important officers, including the chief financial officer (CFO), the chief legal officer, and the chief human resources or personnel officer. For companies with US operations, we have included the names of the US CEO, CFO, and top human resources executive, where available.

The people named in the Executives section are indexed at the back of the book.

The Executives section also includes the name of the company's auditing (accounting) firm, where available.

LOCATIONS

Here we include the company's full legal name and its headquarters, street address, telephone and fax numbers, and Web site, as available. We also list the same information for the US office for each company, if one exists. Telephone numbers of foreign offices are shown using the standardized conventions of international dialing. The back of the book includes an index of companies by headquarters location.

In some cases we have also included information on the geographic distribution of the company's business, including sales and profit data. Note that these profit numbers, like those in the Products/Operations section below, are usually operating or pretax profits rather than net profits. Operating profits are generally those before financing costs (interest income and payments) and before taxes, which are considered costs attributable to the whole company rather than to one division or part of the world. For this reason the net income figures (in the Historical Financials section) are usually much lower, since they are after interest and taxes. Pretax profits are after interest but before taxes.

PRODUCTS/OPERATIONS

This section lists as many of the company's products, services, brand names, divisions, subsidiaries, and joint ventures as we could fit. We have tried to include all its major lines and all familiar brand names. The nature of this section varies by company and the amount of information available. If the company publishes sales and profit information by type of business, we have included it (in US dollars).

COMPETITORS

In this section we have listed enterprises that compete with the profiled company. This feature is included as a quick way to locate similar companies and compare them. Because of the difficulty in identifying companies that only compete in foreign markets, the list of competitors is still weighted to large international companies with a strong US presence.

HISTORICAL FINANCIALS

Here we have tried to present as much data about each enterprise's financial performance as we could compile in the allocated space. Financial data for all companies is presented in US dollars, using the appropriate exchange rate at fiscal year-end.

While the information presented varies somewhat from industry to industry, it is less complete in the case of private companies that do not release data (although we have always tried to provide annual sales and employment). The following information is generally present.

A five-year table, with relevant annualized compound growth rates, covers:
- Sales — fiscal year sales (year-end assets for most financial companies)
- Net income — fiscal year net income (before accounting changes)
- Net profit margin — fiscal year net income as a percent of sales (as a percent of assets for most financial firms)
- Employees — fiscal year-end or average number of employees
- Stock price — the fiscal year close
- P/E — high and low price/earnings ratio
- Earnings per share — fiscal year earnings per share (EPS)
- Dividends per share — fiscal year dividends per share

The information on the number of employees is intended to aid the reader interested in knowing whether a company has a long-term trend of increasing or decreasing employment. As far as we know, we are the only company that publishes this information in print format.

The numbers on the left in each row of the Historical Financials section give the month and the year in which the company's fiscal year actually ends. Thus, a company with a September 30, 2006, year-end is shown as 9/06.

In addition, we have provided in graph form a stock price history for companies that trade on the major US exchanges. The graphs, covering up to five years, show the range of trading between the high and the low price as well as the closing price for each fiscal year. For public companies that trade on the OTC or Pink Sheets or that do not trade on US exchanges, we graph net income. Generally, for private companies, we have graphed net income, or, if that is unavailable, sales.

Key year-end statistics in this section generally show the financial strength of the enterprise, including:

- Debt ratio (long-term debt as a percent of shareholders' equity)
- Return on equity (net income divided by the average of beginning and ending common shareholders' equity)
- Cash and cash equivalents
- Current ratio (ratio of current assets to current liabilities)
- Total long-term debt (including capital lease obligations)
- Number of shares of common stock outstanding
- Dividend yield (fiscal year dividends per share divided by the fiscal year-end closing stock price)
- Dividend payout (fiscal year dividends divided by fiscal year EPS)
- Market value at fiscal year-end (fiscal year-end closing stock price multiplied by fiscal year-end number of shares outstanding)
- Fiscal year sales for financial institutions.

Per share data has been adjusted for stock splits. The data for public companies with sponsored American Depositary Receipts has been provided to us by Edgar Online. Other public company information was compiled by Hoover's, which takes full responsibility for the content of this section.

In the case of private companies that do not publicly disclose financial information, we usually did not have access to such standardized data. We have gathered estimates of sales and other statistics from numerous sources.

Hoover's Handbook of

World Business

A List-Lover's Compendium

The 100 Largest Companies by Sales in
Hoover's Handbook of World Business 2007

Rank	Company	Sales ($ mil.)	Rank	Company	Sales ($ mil.)	Rank	Company	Sales ($ mil.)
1	Royal Dutch Shell	306,731	36	METRO	65,992	71	Vodafone Group	41,319
2	BP	245,486	37	Munich Re	64,419	72	Mitsubishi	41,048
3	Toyota	179,083	38	Royal Bank of Scotland	64,212	73	Fujitsu	40,746
4	DaimlerChrysler	177,395	39	Electricité de France	64,010	74	HBOS	40,631
5	TOTAL	145,229	40	Sony	63,541	75	NTT DoCoMo	40,568
6	Samsung	141,421	41	Petróleos de Venezuela	63,200	76	CNP Assurances	40,514
7	ING	130,580	42	BNP Paribas	62,164	77	EADS	40,510
8	Allianz	115,723	43	Repsol YPF	60,458	78	Nokia	40,496
9	Volkswagen	112,826	44	Nippon Life Insurance	58,885	79	Enel	40,333
10	Generali	107,213	45	France Telecom	58,567	80	Auchan	39,802
11	Crédit Agricole	105,571	46	Statoil	58,012	81	Japan Tobacco	39,439
12	HSBC Holdings	93,494	47	Hyundai	57,636	82	PETROBRAS	37,452
13	NTT	91,805	48	Deutsche Post	57,177	83	GlaxoSmithKline	37,273
14	Siemens	90,896	49	LUKOIL	55,774	84	ALDI	37,000
15	Eni	88,269	50	BMW	55,255	85	Telecom Italia	36,232
16	Carrefour	88,227	51	Fiat S.p.A.	55,127	86	Philips Electronics	36,000
17	Aviva	87,636	52	Unilever	54,413	87	Mitsui & Co.	34,982
18	Petróleos Mexicanos	87,279	53	ABN AMRO	53,965	88	BT Group	34,345
19	AXA	84,887	54	Toshiba	53,945	89	Tengelmann	33,840
20	Honda	84,218	55	AEGON	53,902	90	Sanofi-Aventis	33,771
21	Hitachi	80,451	56	Legal & General Group	53,314	91	Mitsubishi UFJ Financial Group	33,323
22	Fortis	79,165	57	Banco Santander Central Hispano	52,440	92	Nippon Steel	33,219
23	UBS	76,292	58	Royal Ahold	52,223	93	A.P. Møller - Mærsk	33,058
24	Matsushita	75,602	59	ThyssenKrupp	50,658	94	Novartis	32,526
25	Deutsche Bank	72,659	60	BASF	50,627	95	Bayer	32,432
26	Deutsche Telekom	70,595	61	Robert Bosch	49,102	96	BHP Billiton	32,153
27	Prudential	70,453	62	Renault	48,957	97	Bouygues	31,916
28	Nissan	70,087	63	RWE	47,986	98	Canon	31,911
29	Dexia	69,400	64	Barclays	47,942	99	Deutsche Bahn	31,654
30	Nestlé	69,208	65	Lloyds TSB	46,625	100	Volvo	30,238
31	Tesco	68,701	66	Telefónica	46,547			
32	Credit Suisse	68,393	67	NEC	45,650			
33	Zurich Financial Services	67,186	68	Gazprom	42,836			
34	E.ON	66,788	69	Tokyo Electric Power	41,632			
35	Peugeot	66,637	70	Saint-Gobain	41,581			

SOURCE: HOOVER'S, INC., DATABASE, DECEMBER 2006

The 100 Most Profitable Companies in
Hoover's Handbook of World Business 2007

Rank	Company	Net Income ($ mil.)	Rank	Company	Net Income ($ mil.)	Rank	Company	Net Income ($ mil.)
1	Royal Dutch Shell	26,261	36	Credit Suisse	4,447	71	Unilever	2,541
2	BP	19,642	37	Roche Holding	4,398	72	Teléfonos de México	2,516
3	HSBC Holdings	15,495	38	Allianz	4,374	73	Munich Re	2,500
4	TOTAL	13,736	39	NTT	4,262	74	Dexia	2,479
5	Toyota	11,681	40	Nokia	4,243	75	AEGON	2,468
6	UBS	10,665	41	Deutsche Post	4,222	76	BBVA	2,390
7	BHP Billiton	10,450	42	Deutsche Bank	4,180	77	L'Oréal	2,337
8	Samsung	9,483	43	POSCO	3,972	78	Lloyds TSB	2,325
9	Eni	8,981	44	AstraZeneca	3,884	79	Norsk Hydro	2,307
10	E.ON	8,771	45	BASF	3,535	80	Telecom Italia	2,297
11	ING	8,262	46	Anglo American	3,521	81	Hyundai	2,277
12	Royal Bank of Scotland	7,888	47	ABN AMRO	3,399	82	Imperial Oil	2,231
13	Banco Santander Central Hispano	7,484	48	Philips Electronics	3,397	83	Gaz de France	2,064
14	Crédit Agricole	7,086	49	Repsol YPF	3,389	84	Prudential	2,051
15	Gazprom	7,078	50	DaimlerChrysler	3,371	85	LVMH	1,975
16	BNP Paribas	6,931	51	Mittal Steel	3,365	86	Bank of Montreal	1,935
17	France Telecom	6,748	52	British American Tobacco	3,265	87	Scottish Power	1,888
18	LUKOIL	6,443	53	Aviva	3,265	88	BT Group	1,849
19	Deutsche Telekom	6,307	54	Canon	3,265	89	Electricité de France	1,829
20	AXA	6,197	55	National Australia Bank	3,250	90	Toronto-Dominion Bank	1,823
21	PETROBRAS	6,190	56	Zurich Financial Services	3,214	91	Jardine Matheson	1,820
22	Nestlé	6,075	57	Telstra	3,179	92	Generali	1,793
23	GlaxoSmithKline	5,741	58	Mitsubishi UFJ Financial Group	3,090	93	SAP	1,772
24	HBOS	5,612	59	Ericsson	3,079	94	OMV	1,772
25	Enel	5,562	60	Vivendi	3,045	95	Legal & General Group	1,763
26	Mizuho Financial	5,527	61	Royal Bank of Canada	2,970	96	Nippon Life Insurance	1,745
27	NTT DoCoMo	5,197	62	Nippon Steel	2,925	97	Centrica	1,743
28	Novartis	5,190	63	Robert Bosch	2,902	98	Mitsui & Co.	1,721
29	Honda	5,075	64	Tesco	2,744	99	Japan Tobacco	1,714
30	Barclays	5,045	65	Siemens	2,708	100	Carrefour	1,701
31	Rio Tinto	4,969	66	BMW	2,652			
32	Telefónica	4,908	67	RWE	2,642			
33	Nissan	4,752	68	Tokyo Electric Power	2,640			
34	Fortis	4,721	69	Sanofi-Aventis	2,608			
35	Statoil	4,533	70	Nomura Holdings	2,590			

SOURCE: HOOVER'S, INC., DATABASE, DECEMBER 2006

The 100 Largest Employers in
Hoover's Handbook of World Business 2007

Rank	Company	Employees	Rank	Company	Employees	Rank	Company	Employees
1	Adecco	735,284	36	Allianz	177,625	71	BNP Paribas	109,780
2	Siemens	461,000	37	Woolworths	175,000	72	Royal Dutch Shell	109,000
3	Carrefour	436,747	38	Auchan	174,584	73	Karstadt Quelle	107,130
4	Compass Group	410,074	39	Fiat S.p.A.	173,695	74	SANYO Electric	106,389
5	Gazprom	397,000	40	Toshiba	172,000	75	BMW	105,798
6	DaimlerChrysler	382,724	41	Accor	168,623	76	DENSO	105,723
7	Deutsche Post	347,607	42	Royal Ahold	167,801	77	BT Group	104,400
8	Volkswagen	344,902	43	Philips Electronics	159,226	78	KPMG	103,621
9	Sodexho Alliance	324,446	44	Sony	158,500	79	ABB	103,500
10	Hitachi	306,876	45	Fujitsu	158,491	80	GlaxoSmithKline	100,728
11	Toyota	285,977	46	Electricité de France	156,152	81	ABN AMRO	98,080
12	HSBC Holdings	284,000	47	J Sainsbury	153,300	82	Sanofi-Aventis	97,181
13	Veolia Environnement	271,153	48	George Weston	151,500	83	British American Tobacco	96,952
14	Robert Bosch	249,000	49	NEC	147,800	84	BP	96,200
15	METRO	246,875	50	Rallye	147,520	85	Bayer	93,700
16	Deutsche Telekom	243,695	51	LUKOIL	145,400	86	Lufthansa	92,303
17	SNCF	229,877	52	PricewaterhouseCoopers	142,162	87	Novartis	90,924
18	Samsung	229,000	53	Petróleos Mexicanos	139,171	88	Seiko Epson	90,701
19	Mittal Steel	224,286	54	Royal Bank of Scotland	137,000	89	IKEA	90,000
20	Unilever	223,000	55	Crédit Agricole	136,848	90	Schneider Electric	88,670
21	Securitas	217,000	56	Deloitte Touche Tohmatsu	135,000	91	Bertelsmann	88,516
22	Deutsche Bahn	216,389	57	Loblaw	134,000	92	Danone	88,184
23	Bank of China	209,265	58	VINCI	133,513	93	RWE	85,928
24	Peugeot	208,500	59	Michelin	127,319	94	PPR	84,316
25	Casino Guichard-Perrachon	208,403	60	Renault	126,584	95	Magna International	82,000
26	Telefónica	207,641	61	Wal-Mart de México	124,295	96	Koç Holding	81,926
27	France Telecom	203,008	62	Nissan	123,748	97	BASF	80,945
28	Tata Group	202,713	63	Bridgestone	123,727	98	Lafarge	80,146
29	Hutchison Whampoa	200,000	64	Canon	115,583	99	AXA	78,800
30	Saint-Gobain	199,630	65	Bouygues	115,441	100	InBev	77,000
31	NTT	199,000	66	ING	115,328			
32	Anglo American	195,000	67	Ernst & Young	114,000			
33	ThyssenKrupp	183,729	68	Barclays	113,300			
34	Tengelmann	183,050	69	EADS	113,210			
35	Coles Group	182,338	70	TOTAL	112,877			

SOURCE: HOOVER'S, INC., DATABASE, DECEMBER 2006

The 100 Fastest-Growing Companies in Five-Year Sales Growth in
Hoover's Handbook of World Business 2007

Rank	Company	Annual % Change*	Rank	Company	Annual % Change	Rank	Company	Annual % Change
1	BHP Billiton	127.0	36	Atos Origin	29.1	71	MAN	19.7
2	BBVA	108.7	37	Sinopec Shanghai Petrochemical	29.1	72	Carlsberg	19.1
3	Espírito Santo	102.5	38	Barclays	28.5	73	Japan Airlines	19.0
4	Banco Santander Central Hispano	97.3	39	Aviva	27.6	74	Royal Bank of Canada	18.8
5	Novo Nordisk	86.5	40	Ladbrokes	27.4	75	Porsche	18.3
6	Anglo American	80.6	41	Statoil	27.2	76	Bank of Montreal	18.0
7	Magna International	80.1	42	Televisa	26.8	77	Benetton Group	17.9
8	Tomkins	75.8	43	SOFTBANK	26.7	78	Mitsubishi UFJ Financial Group	17.8
9	Imperial Tobacco	74.7	44	Hutchison Whampoa	26.4	79	Tesco	17.8
10	Mittal Steel	72.8	45	A.P. Møller - Mærsk	25.5	80	Hyundai	17.6
11	Repsol YPF	63.7	46	Energias de Portugal	25.5	81	EADS	17.2
12	Rio Tinto	62.4	47	MOL	25.4	82	Alcan	17.1
13	LVMH	57.0	48	Crédit Agricole	25.2	83	Nissan	17.0
14	British Sky Broadcasting	54.7	49	AXA	25.2	84	Volvo	16.9
15	Mitsubishi	53.7	50	POSCO	24.9	85	PETROBRAS	16.5
16	Agrium	52.8	51	HSBC Holdings	24.4	86	IKEA	16.3
17	Mitsui & Co.	50.4	52	SANYO Electric	24.3	87	Telecom Italia	15.9
18	Nokia	44.8	53	Stora Enso Oyj	24.1	88	British Airways	15.9
19	Sanofi-Aventis	43.2	54	Publicis	24.0	89	Generali	15.5
20	Telefonica Chile	42.3	55	Royal Dutch Shell	23.8	90	Acer	15.2
21	TOTAL	39.5	56	TDK	23.3	91	Hitachi	15.0
22	Telefónica	39.1	57	Eni	23.0	92	Tatung	14.9
23	Infosys Technologies	39.1	58	Compass Group	23.0	93	Lloyds TSB	14.9
24	National Australia Bank	38.5	59	PKN ORLEN	22.9	94	Wal-Mart de México	14.9
25	ING	38.5	60	Koç Holding	22.5	95	FUJIFILM	14.7
26	Dexia	38.3	61	Rogers Communications	22.4	96	Electricité de France	14.7
27	Coles Group	38.2	62	Allied Irish Banks	22.3	97	Kubota	14.4
28	SABMiller	35.9	63	Formosa Plastics	21.3	98	Royal Bank of Scotland	14.3
29	Honda	35.1	64	OMV	21.3	99	YPF	14.3
30	KLM	34.8	65	HBOS	21.1	100	Adecco	14.3
31	LUKOIL	33.3	66	Woolworths	20.4			
32	Toronto-Dominion Bank	32.4	67	Inco	20.3			
33	Norsk Hydro	30.9	68	Tata Group	20.3			
34	Toyota	30.2	69	Gaz de France	20.3			
35	Wipro	29.3	70	Gazprom	19.7			

*These rates are compounded annualized increases, and may have resulted from acquisitions or one time gains. If less than 6 years of data are available, growth is for the years available.

SOURCE: HOOVER'S, INC., DATABASE, DECEMBER 2006

The 100 Fastest-Growing Companies in Five-Year Employment Growth in
Hoover's Handbook of World Business 2007

Rank	Company	Annual % Change*	Rank	Company	Annual % Change	Rank	Company	Annual % Change
1	Mittal Steel	111.0	36	HBOS	12.8	71	WPP Group	6.3
2	Novo Nordisk	55.3	37	San Miguel	12.7	72	Kubota	6.2
3	OMV	54.0	38	Sojitz	12.5	73	Nikon	6.1
4	Royal Bank of Scotland	47.5	39	Koç Holding	12.4	74	Pioneer	6.1
5	British Sky Broadcasting	42.7	40	Tatung	12.3	75	Novartis	6.0
6	Wipro	40.5	41	Atos Origin	12.1	76	Canon	5.9
7	Infosys Technologies	39.9	42	Alcan	11.9	77	Lufthansa	5.8
8	Imperial Tobacco	38.8	43	SABMiller	11.4	78	Gazprom	5.8
9	Mitsui & Co.	38.7	44	Heineken	11.2	79	Carrefour	5.7
10	Japan Airlines	37.4	45	Wal-Mart de México	10.7	80	Samsung	5.6
11	Hutchison Whampoa	32.2	46	Rogers Communications	10.6	81	Pearson	5.5
12	Millea Holdings	30.2	47	Tesco	10.5	82	PETROBRAS	5.4
13	Toyota	27.7	48	PKN ORLEN	10.3	83	Seiko Epson	5.4
14	SANYO Electric	27.2	49	Banco Santander Central Hispano	10.2	84	Air France	5.4
15	Sanofi-Aventis	27.2	50	Gaz de France	9.7	85	Auchan	5.3
16	Honda	24.6	51	Volvo	9.6	86	Repsol YPF	5.2
17	SOFTBANK	23.2	52	Kao	9.4	87	Mitsubishi	5.1
18	Telefónica	22.8	53	Allianz	9.4	88	Porsche	5.0
19	HSBC Holdings	21.0	54	Creative Technology	9.2	89	EADS	5.0
20	TDK	19.4	55	IKEA	9.2	90	Gallaher Group	5.0
21	Publicis	19.3	56	KLM	9.2	91	Robert Bosch	4.8
22	Toronto-Dominion Bank	18.7	57	Kyocera	8.9	92	Reed Elsevier	4.8
23	Stora Enso Oyj	18.6	58	Crédit Agricole	8.5	93	Centrica	4.6
24	TOTAL	18.0	59	Dexia	7.4	94	Woolworths	4.6
25	Agrium	17.9	60	Statoil	7.3	95	DENSO	4.4
26	InBev	17.6	61	Deloitte Touche Tohmatsu	7.3	96	Munich Re	4.3
27	ING	17.2	62	SAP	7.1	97	Schneider Electric	4.2
28	Allied Irish Banks	17.1	63	Virgin Group	7.0	98	Airbus	4.1
29	NTT DoCoMo	16.5	64	Ernst & Young	6.8	99	Magna International	4.0
30	Adecco	16.0	65	Dentsu	6.8	100	LUKOIL	3.9
31	Casino Guichard-Perrachon	15.6	66	Coles Group	6.6			
32	Nokia	15.5	67	Rallye	6.5			
33	Compass Group	14.2	68	BNP Paribas	6.4			
34	Hitachi	13.9	69	Hollinger	6.3			
35	Asahi Shimbun	13.8	70	CNP Assurances	6.3			

*These rates are compounded annualized increases, and may have resulted from acquisitions or one time gains. If less than 6 years of data are available, growth is for the years available.

SOURCE: HOOVER'S, INC., DATABASE, DECEMBER 2006

Forbes' 100 Largest Public Companies by Market Value

Rank	Company	Country	Market Value* ($ mil.)	Rank	Company	Country	Market Value ($ mil.)
1	ExxonMobil	US	362,530	51	Hewlett-Packard	US	93,080
2	General Electric	US	348,450	52	Banco Santander	Spain	91,340
3	Microsoft	US	279,020	53	Home Depot	US	89,530
4	Citigroup	US	230,930	54	Wachovia	US	88,420
5	BP	UK	225,930	55	Saudi Telecom	Saudi Arabia	88,310
6	Royal Dutch/Shell Group	Netherlands	203,520	56	ConocoPhillips	US	83,990
7	Procter & Gamble	US	197,120	57	United Parcel Service	US	82,850
8	HSBC Group	UK	193,320	58	Siemens Group	Germany	81,700
9	Pfizer	US	192,050	59	ING Group	Netherlands	81,430
10	Wal-Mart Stores	US	188,860	60	Time Warner	US	79,370
11	Saudi Basic Industries	Saudi Arabia	184,730	61	UnitedHealth Group	US	79,080
12	Gazprom	Russia	184,370	62	Nokia	Finland	78,100
13	Bank of America	US	184,170	63	Qualcomm	US	77,810
14	Toyota Motor	Japan	175,540	64	BNP Paribas	France	77,730
15	American International Group	US	172,240	65	Merck & Co.	US	76,620
16	PetroChina	China	172,230	66	Sumitomo Mitsui Financial Group	Japan	76,220
17	Johnson & Johnson	US	171,510	67	Barclays	UK	75,990
18	TOTAL	France	154,740	68	Telefónica	Spain	75,920
19	Altria Group	US	149,570	69	UniCredit	Italy	75,890
20	GlaxoSmithKline	UK	147,420	70	Rio Tinto	UK/Australia	74,500
21	JPMorgan Chase	US	144,130	71	AstraZeneca	UK	72,740
22	Mitsubishi UFJ Financial Group	Japan	143,010	72	E.ON	Germany	72,480
23	Berkshire Hathaway	US	133,670	73	HBOS	UK	71,250
24	Roche Group	Switzerland	127,510	74	Sprint Nextel	US	71,000
25	Chevron	US	126,800	75	Merrill Lynch	US	70,690
26	IBM	US	126,740	76	BBVA-Banco Bilbao Vizcaya	Spain	69,050
27	Novartis Group	Switzerland	125,730	77	Dell	US	69,050
28	Cisco Systems	US	124,520	78	Abbott Laboratories	US	68,000
29	Intel	US	121,190	79	Schlumberger	Netherlands	67,710
30	Sanofi-Aventis	France	119,370	80	Unilever	Netherlands/UK	67,430
31	Vodafone	UK	115,440	81	Wyeth	US	66,900
32	ENI	Italy	114,420	82	American Express	US	66,760
33	Nestlé	Switzerland	113,920	83	Deutsche Telekom	Germany	66,220
34	BHP Billiton	Australia/UK	109,130	84	AXA Group	France	66,120
35	Wells Fargo	US	107,800	85	Allianz Worldwide	Germany	65,550
36	Google	US	107,170	86	Medtronic	US	65,260
37	AT&T	US	107,040	87	LUKOIL Holding	Russia	65,120
38	Royal Bank of Scotland	UK	106,410	88	Oracle	US	64,010
39	UBS	Switzerland	105,690	89	Morgan Stanley	US	63,100
40	China Construction Bank	China	104,980	90	SAP	Germany	63,100
41	Samsung Electronics	South Korea	104,220	91	Eli Lilly & Co	US	62,850
42	PETROBRAS-Petróleo Brasil	Brazil	99,820	92	Goldman Sachs Group	US	61,770
43	Coca-Cola	US	99,780	93	Société Générale Group	France	61,450
44	PepsiCo	US	97,890	94	Nippon Telegraph and Telephone	Japan	60,380
45	China Mobile (HK)	Hong Kong/China	96,890	95	Credit Suisse Group	Switzerland	60,150
46	Electricité de France	France	94,940	96	Boeing	US	59,580
47	Mizuho Financial	Japan	93,810	97	United Technologies	US	59,310
48	Al Rajhi Bank	Saudi Arabia	93,640	98	Apple Computer	US	57,920
49	Verizon Communications	US	93,180	99	Deutsche Bank Group	Germany	57,840
50	Amgen	US	93,140	100	BellSouth	US	57,820

*As of February 28, 2006.

SOURCE: *FORBES*, MARCH 30, 2006

The *FORTUNE* Global 500

Rank	Company	Country	2005 Sales ($ mil.)
1	Exxon Mobil	US	339,938.0
2	Wal-Mart Stores	US	315,654.0
3	Royal Dutch Shell	Netherlands	306,731.0
4	BP	UK	267,600.0
5	General Motors	US	192,604.0
6	Chevron	US	189,481.0
7	DaimlerChrysler	Germany	186,106.3
8	Toyota Motor	Japan	185,805.0
9	Ford Motor	US	177,210.0
10	ConocoPhillips	US	166,683.0
11	General Electric	US	157,153.0
12	TOTAL	France	152,360.7
13	ING Group	Netherlands	138,235.3
14	Citigroup	US	131,045.0
15	AXA	France	129,839.2
16	Allianz	Germany	121,406.0
17	Volkswagen	Germany	118,376.6
18	Fortis	Belgium/ Netherlands	112,351.4
19	Crédit Agricole	France	110,764.6
20	American International Group	US	108,905.0
21	Assicurazioni Generali	Italy	101,403.8
22	Siemens	Germany	100,098.7
23	Sinopec	China	98,784.9
24	Nippon Telegraph & Telephone	Japan	94,869.3
25	Carrefour	France	94,454.5
26	HSBC Holdings	UK	93,494.0
27	ENI	Italy	92,603.3
28	Aviva	UK	92,579.4
29	International Business Machines	US	91,134.0
30	McKesson	US	88,050.0
31	Honda Motor	Japan	87,510.7
32	State Grid	China	86,984.3
33	Hewlett-Packard	US	86,696.0
34	BNP Paribas	France	85,687.2
35	PDVSA	Venezuela	85,618.0
36	UBS	Switzerland	84,707.6
37	Bank of America Corp.	US	83,980.0
38	Hitachi	Japan	83,596.3
39	China National Petroleum	China	83,556.5
40	Pemex	Mexico	83,381.7
41	Nissan Motor	Japan	83,273.8
42	Berkshire Hathaway	US	81,663.0
43	Home Depot	US	81,511.0
44	Valero Energy	US	81,362.0
45	J.P. Morgan Chase & Co.	US	79,902.0
46	Samsung Electronics	South Korea	78,716.6
47	Matsushita Electric Industrial	Japan	78,557.7
48	Deutsche Bank	Germany	76,227.6
49	HBOS	UK	75,798.8
50	Verizon Communications	US	75,111.9
51	Cardinal Health	US	74,915.1
52	Prudential	UK	74,744.7
53	Nestlé	Switzerland	74,658.6
54	Deutsche Telekom	Germany	74,061.8
55	Dexia Group	Belgium	72,814.3
55	METRO	Germany	72,814.3
57	Credit Suisse	Switzerland	72,193.5
58	Royal Bank of Scotland	UK	71,164.3
59	Tesco	UK	71,127.6
60	Peugeot	France	69,915.4
61	U.S. Postal Service	US	69,907.0
62	Altria Group	US	69,148.0
63	Zurich Financial Services	Switzerland	67,186.0
64	E.ON	Germany	66,313.2
65	Sony	Japan	66,025.6
66	Vodafone	UK	65,314.2
67	Société Générale	France	64,441.9
68	Électricité De France	France	63,434.1
69	Nippon Life Insurance	Japan	61,158.3
70	Statoil	Norway	61,032.7
71	France Télécom	France	60,932.9
72	LG	South Korea	60,574.1
73	Kroger	US	60,552.9
74	Munich Re Group	Germany	60,255.7
75	Deutsche Post	Germany	59,989.8
76	State Farm Insurance Cos.	US	59,223.9
77	Marathon Oil	US	58,958.0
78	BMW	Germany	57,973.1
79	Fiat	Italy	57,833.9
80	Hyundai Motor	South Korea	57,434.9
81	Procter & Gamble	US	56,741.0
82	ABN AMRO Holding	Netherlands	56,614.9
83	Royal Ahold	Netherlands	56,427.3
84	Repsol YPF	Spain	56,423.6
85	Legal & General Group	UK	56,384.8
86	Petrobrás	Brazil	56,324.0
87	Toshiba	Japan	56,028.0
88	Dell	US	55,908.0
89	Lloyds TSB Group	UK	55,407.0
90	ThyssenKrupp	Germany	55,260.7
91	Boeing	US	54,848.0
92	AmerisourceBergen	US	54,589.6
93	Santander Central Hispano Group	Spain	53,848.8
94	BASF	Germany	53,113.3
95	Costco Wholesale	US	52,935.2
96	Suez	France	52,742.9
97	Target	US	52,620.0
98	Morgan Stanley	US	52,498.0
99	Robert Bosch	Germany	52,207.6
100	Renault	France	51,365.1

SOURCE: *FORTUNE*, JULY 24, 2006

The *FORTUNE* Global 500 (continued)

Rank	Company	Country	2005 Sales ($ mil.)	Rank	Company	Country	2005 Sales ($ mil.)
101	Pfizer	US	51,353.0	151	CVS	US	37,006.2
102	Gazprom	Russia	50,824.4	152	Motorola	US	36,843.0
103	Barclays	UK	50,634.3	153	Indian Oil	India	36,537.0
104	Johnson & Johnson	US	50,514.0	154	Freddie Mac	US	36,526.0
105	RWE	Germany	50,346.2	155	Mitsui	Japan	36,349.3
106	Unilever	UK/Netherlands	49,580.8	156	Caterpillar	US	36,339.0
107	Sears Holdings	US	49,124.0	157	Archer Daniels Midland	US	35,943.8
108	Telefónica	Spain	48,833.3	158	Wachovia Corp.	US	35,908.0
109	CNP Assurances	France	48,474.9	159	Sanofi-Aventis	France	35,429.2
110	Merrill Lynch	US	47,783.0	160	Allstate	US	35,383.0
111	SK	South Korea	47,142.6	161	A.P. Møller - Mærsk	Denmark	35,214.7
112	MetLife	US	46,983.0	162	BT	UK	34,808.3
113	Tokyo Electric Power	Japan	46,418.3	163	Bayer	Germany	34,804.2
114	Dow Chemical	US	46,307.0	164	Seven & I Holdings	Japan	34,717.3
115	LUKOIL	Russia	46,284.0	165	Sprint Nextel	US	34,680.0
116	UnitedHealth Group	US	45,365.0	166	Sumitomo Life Insurance	Japan	34,625.7
117	Wellpoint	US	45,136.0	167	DZ Bank	Germany	34,554.5
118	Nippon Oil	Japan	45,071.2	168	Nippon Steel	Japan	34,501.8
119	Dai-ichi Mutual Life Insurance	Japan	44,597.8	169	Groupe Caisse d'Épargne	France	34,245.1
120	Petronas	Malaysia	44,280.4	170	Canon	Japan	34,091.6
121	AT&T	US	43,862.0	171	Meiji Yasuda Life Insurance	Japan	33,632.4
122	Time Warner	US	43,652.0	172	Standard Life Assurance	UK	33,452.1
123	Saint-Gobain	France	43,626.4	173	Caremark Rx	US	32,991.3
124	Goldman Sachs Group	US	43,391.0	174	Sumitomo Mitsui Financial Group	Japan	32,725.0
125	Lowe's	US	43,243.0	175	PepsiCo	US	32,562.0
126	United Technologies	US	42,725.0	176	Lehman Brothers Holdings	US	32,420.0
127	Mitsubishi	Japan	42,633.2	177	Novartis	Switzerland	32,212.0
128	NEC	Japan	42,615.4	178	Volvo	Sweden	32,183.6
129	United Parcel Service	US	42,581.0	179	Franz Haniel	Germany	32,172.5
130	EADS	Netherlands	42,503.1	180	Walt Disney	US	31,944.0
131	Nokia	Finland	42,484.5	181	Mitsubishi Electric	Japan	31,833.4
132	Enel	Italy	42,320.5	182	Prudential Financial	US	31,708.0
133	Fujitsu	Japan	42,319.4	183	Rabobank	Netherlands	31,659.3
134	Walgreen	US	42,201.6	184	Mizuho Financial Group	Japan	31,421.5
135	Groupe Auchan	France	42,073.2	185	Veolia Environnement	France	31,368.4
136	Tyco International	US	41,780.0	186	Plains All American Pipeline	US	31,177.3
137	Arcelor	Luxembourg	40,521.3	187	Sunoco	US	31,176.0
138	Wells Fargo	US	40,407.0	188	Deutsche Bahn	Germany	31,132.4
139	Albertson's	US	40,397.0	189	Best Buy	US	30,848.0
140	Microsoft	US	39,788.0	190	Northrop Grumman	US	30,721.0
141	Telecom Italia	Italy	39,764.5	191	Bouygues	France	30,548.4
142	AEON	Japan	39,480.6	192	Sysco	US	30,281.9
143	GlaxoSmithKline	UK	39,366.1	193	American Express	US	30,080.0
144	Intel	US	38,826.0	194	Millea Holdings	Japan	30,029.8
145	Royal Philips Electronics	Netherlands	38,579.1	195	BHP Billiton	Australia	29,587.0
146	Safeway	US	38,416.0	196	Anglo American	UK	29,434.0
147	Mitsubishi UFJ Financial Group	Japan	37,925.6	197	FedEx	US	29,363.0
148	Medco Health Solutions	US	37,870.9	198	Foncière Euris	France	29,308.4
149	Aegon	Netherlands	37,694.4	199	Industrial & Commercial Bank of China	China	29,167.1
150	Lockheed Martin	US	37,213.0	200	Honeywell International	US	28,862.0

Rank	Company	Country	2005 Sales ($ mil.)	Rank	Company	Country	2005 Sales ($ mil.)
201	Ingram Micro	US	28,808.3	251	Woolworths	Australia	24,035.7
202	China Mobile Communications	China	28,777.8	252	La Poste	France	24,017.5
203	J. Sainsbury	UK	28,649.0	253	AstraZeneca	UK	23,950.0
204	Roche Group	Switzerland	28,495.6	254	Landesbank Baden-Württemberg	Germany	23,943.7
205	DuPont	US	28,491.0	255	Bank Of China	China	23,860.1
206	Hon Hai Precision Industry	Taiwan	28,350.1	256	News Corp.	US	23,859.0
207	DENSO	Japan	28,160.4	257	Nippon Mining Holdings	Japan	23,615.3
208	Mittal Steel	Netherlands	28,132.0	258	Fuji Photo Film	Japan	23,560.2
209	Swiss Reinsurance	Switzerland	28,092.8	259	Hutchison Whampoa	China	23,474.8
210	New York Life Insurance	US	28,051.0	260	Compass Group	UK	23,468.7
211	Johnson Controls	US	28,019.5	261	TUI	Germany	23,364.9
212	Gaz de France	France	27,826.0	262	Federated Department Stores	US	23,347.0
213	UES of Russia	Russia	27,768.1	263	Hess	US	23,255.0
214	RAG	Germany	27,762.1	264	Delhaize Group	Belgium	23,162.0
215	Marubeni	Japan	27,732.2	265	PTT	Thailand	23,109.0
216	Coles Myer	Australia	27,408.8	266	China Southern Power Grid	China	23,105.0
217	China Life Insurance	China	27,389.2	267	Coca-Cola	US	23,104.0
218	JFE Holdings	Japan	27,365.9	268	Weyerhaeuser	US	23,000.0
219	Delphi	US	27,201.0	269	Banco Bradesco	Brazil	22,920.4
220	Hartford Financial Services	US	27,083.0	270	East Japan Railway	Japan	22,896.9
221	KDDI	Japan	27,034.1	271	Aetna	US	22,885.0
222	Norsk Hydro	Norway	27,032.8	272	KBC Group	Belgium	22,879.3
223	VINCI	France	26,991.5	273	Magna International	Canada	22,811.0
224	Samsung Life Insurance	South Korea	26,692.3	274	Sumitomo	Japan	22,799.9
225	Alcoa	US	26,601.0	275	Massachusetts Mutual Life Insurance	US	22,798.8
226	National Australia Bank	Australia	26,471.4	276	Kansai Electric Power	Japan	22,779.1
227	Manulife Financial	Canada	26,446.5	277	China Construction Bank	China	22,770.6
228	Air France-KLM Group	France	26,098.9	278	Adecco	Switzerland	22,742.7
229	SNCF	France	26,086.4	279	China Telecommunications	China	22,735.8
230	Old Mutual	UK	26,084.1	280	Endesa	Spain	22,650.7
231	Tyson Foods	US	26,014.0	281	ABB	Switzerland	22,642.0
232	George Weston	Canada	25,947.2	282	Lufthansa Group	Germany	22,446.9
233	TIAA-CREF	US	25,916.8	283	Abbott Laboratories	US	22,337.8
234	International Paper	US	25,797.0	284	Danske Bank Group	Denmark	22,336.5
235	Mazda Motor	Japan	25,788.9	285	Comcast	US	22,255.0
236	POSCO	South Korea	25,677.8	286	UniCredito Italiano	Italy	22,230.7
237	Idemitsu Kosan	Japan	25,370.0	287	Bertelsmann	Germany	22,229.5
238	Centrica	UK	25,062.7	288	PPR	France	22,075.0
239	Vivendi	France	25,061.3	289	Merck	US	22,011.9
240	Korea Electric Power	South Korea	24,841.0	290	Power Corp. of Canada	Canada	21,962.1
241	Cisco Systems	US	24,801.0	291	William Morrison Supermarkets	UK	21,939.3
242	Sharp	Japan	24,705.0	292	Deere	US	21,930.5
243	Mitsubishi Heavy Industries	Japan	24,660.8	293	Raytheon	US	21,894.0
244	HCA	US	24,455.0	294	Nationwide	US	21,832.0
245	Bridgestone	Japan	24,440.2	295	T&D Holdings	Japan	21,588.8
246	St. Paul Travelers	US	24,365.0	296	Baosteel Group	China	21,501.4
247	Bunge	US	24,275.0	297	Washington Mutual	US	21,326.0
248	Ladbrokes	UK	24,271.0	298	General Dynamics	US	21,290.0
249	Suzuki Motor	Japan	24,257.6	299	Mitsubishi Chemical Holdings	Japan	21,276.6
250	Royal Bank of Canada	Canada	24,145.6	300	SANYO Electric	Japan	21,171.3

The *FORTUNE* Global 500 (continued)

Rank	Company	Country	2005 Sales ($ mil.)
301	3M	US	21,167.0
302	Liberty Mutual Insurance Group	US	21,161.0
303	Groupama	France	21,093.8
304	Sinochem	China	21,089.0
305	Karstadt Quelle	Germany	21,004.2
306	Halliburton	US	20,994.0
307	SABIC	Saudi Arabia	20,865.5
308	Wolseley	UK	20,806.2
309	Publix Super Markets	US	20,744.8
310	Rio Tinto Group	UK	20,742.0
311	Commerzbank	Germany	20,721.0
312	AMR	US	20,712.0
313	Alcan	Canada	20,659.0
314	BellSouth	US	20,613.0
315	Tech Data	US	20,542.1
316	Electronic Data Systems	US	20,537.0
317	Poste Italiane	Italy	20,485.2
318	McDonald's	US	20,460.2
319	L.M. Ericsson	Sweden	20,311.6
320	BAE Systems	UK	20,228.3
321	Bristol-Myers Squibb	US	20,222.0
322	Cepsa	Spain	20,114.4
323	Banco Do Brasil	Brazil	19,959.9
324	Supervalu	US	19,863.6
325	Lafarge	France	19,842.5
326	Sara Lee	US	19,727.0
327	Goodyear Tire & Rubber	US	19,723.0
328	Itochu	Japan	19,592.1
329	William Hill	UK	19,530.6
330	Cendant	US	19,471.0
331	Cathay Financial Holdings	Taiwan	19,468.5
332	AutoNation	US	19,468.0
333	Japan Airlines	Japan	19,425.7
334	OMV Group	Austria	19,389.5
335	Michelin	France	19,371.6
336	Northwestern Mutual	US	19,220.8
337	Cosmo Oil	Japan	19,100.0
338	Chubu Electric Power	Japan	18,994.0
339	J.C. Penney	US	18,968.0
340	Duke Energy	US	18,944.0
341	SHV Holdings	Netherlands	18,825.7
342	Reliance Industries	India	18,773.3
343	Wyeth	US	18,755.8
344	Aisin Seiki	Japan	18,729.7
345	Mitsubishi Motors	Japan	18,725.1
346	Coca-Cola Enterprises	US	18,706.0
347	Banca Intesa	Italy	18,645.9
348	Mitsui Sumitomo Insurance	Japan	18,608.6
349	Lyondell Chemical	US	18,606.0
350	Commonwealth Bank of Australia	Australia	18,576.6
351	Countrywide Financial	US	18,536.9
352	Corus Group	UK	18,429.0
353	Gasunie Trade & Supply	Netherlands	18,311.7
354	MAN Group	Germany	18,229.7
355	Scottish & Southern Energy	UK	18,096.6
356	Sun Life Financial Services	Canada	18,087.6
357	Christian Dior	France	18,086.8
358	Koç Holding	Turkey	18,083.7
359	L'Oréal	France	18,057.6
360	Dominion Resources	US	18,041.0
361	CRH	Ireland	17,954.2
362	Bayerische Landesbank	Germany	17,896.4
363	Otto Group	Germany	17,858.6
364	Kookmin Bank	South Korea	17,853.1
365	Japan Tobacco	Japan	17,742.2
366	Sumitomo Electric Industries	Japan	17,727.7
367	Rosneft Oil	Russia	17,670.0
368	Bharat Petroleum	India	17,613.8
369	UAL	US	17,379.0
370	Constellation Energy	US	17,374.8
371	Electrolux	Sweden	17,321.2
372	Emerson Electric	US	17,305.0
373	Swiss Life	Switzerland	17,286.2
374	Vattenfall	Sweden	17,279.6
375	Rite Aid	US	17,271.0
376	Continental	Germany	17,193.6
377	Agricultural Bank of China	China	17,165.6
378	Hindustan Petroleum	India	17,106.4
379	Accenture	US	17,094.4
380	Lear	US	17,089.2
381	Hanwha	South Korea	17,068.5
382	Sompo Japan Insurance	Japan	17,059.4
383	Telstra	Australia	17,042.9
384	Nippon Yusen	Japan	17,040.2
385	Japan Post	Japan	17,000.5
386	Visteon	US	16,976.0
387	TNT	Netherlands	16,974.7
388	Mediceo Paltac Holdings	Japan	16,973.2
389	Hochtief	Germany	16,965.0
390	British American Tobacco	UK	16,947.8
391	Ricoh	Japan	16,914.7
392	San Paolo IMI	Italy	16,885.2
393	Alstom	France	16,852.6
394	National Grid	UK	16,840.5
395	CFE	Mexico	16,825.0
396	EnCana	Canada	16,801.0
397	KT	South Korea	16,748.7
398	América Telecom	Mexico	16,719.2
399	Cigna	US	16,684.0
400	Skanska	Sweden	16,678.8

Rank	Company	Country	2005 Sales ($ mil.)
401	Alliance Unichem	UK	16,668.3
402	Oil & Natural Gas	India	16,609.2
403	U.S. Bancorp	US	16,596.0
404	WestLB	Germany	16,535.9
405	BCE	Canada	16,506.4
406	Tesoro	US	16,473.0
407	Groupe Danone	France	16,455.3
408	Stora Enso	Finland	16,386.3
409	Migros	Switzerland	16,357.8
410	Banco Bilbao Vizcaya Argentaria	Spain	16,339.7
411	Alcatel	France	16,321.1
412	Occidental Petroleum	US	16,286.0
413	Express Scripts	US	16,266.0
414	Delta Air Lines	US	16,191.0
415	Itaúsa-Investimentos Itaú	Brazil	16,185.8
416	Lagardère Groupe	France	16,169.5
417	Royal Mail Holdings	UK	16,153.7
418	Akzo Nobel	Netherlands	16,153.3
419	Manpower	US	16,080.4
420	Staples	US	16,078.9
421	TJX	US	16,057.9
422	Gap	US	16,023.0
423	Australia & New Zealand Banking	Australia	15,940.4
424	Edeka Zentrale	Germany	15,916.4
425	Kimberly-Clark	US	15,902.6
426	Nippon Express	Japan	15,844.5
427	Nomura Holdings	Japan	15,835.0
428	KFW Bankengruppe	Germany	15,827.4
429	Altadis	Spain	15,790.8
430	Westpac Banking	Australia	15,715.3
431	Xerox	US	15,701.0
432	Kajima	Japan	15,679.8
433	Flextronics International	Singapore	15,566.0
434	ConAgra Foods	US	15,515.7
435	Centex	US	15,465.1
436	Canadian Imperial Bank of Commerce	Canada	15,431.9
437	Exelon	US	15,405.0
438	Taisei	Japan	15,403.5
439	Loews	US	15,363.3
440	Toronto-Dominion Bank	Canada	15,327.6
441	China Railway Engineering	China	15,293.7
442	British Airways	UK	15,188.7
443	Surgutneftegas	Russia	15,153.6
444	Finmeccanica	Italy	15,129.5
445	Samsung	South Korea	15,113.7
446	Bank of Nova Scotia	Canada	15,054.2
447	ACS	Spain	15,052.3
448	Anheuser-Busch	US	15,035.7
449	Komatsu	Japan	15,032.4
450	Carso Global Telecom	Mexico	14,956.5
451	Cemex	Mexico	14,934.5
452	Daiei	Japan	14,927.9
453	Bombardier	Canada	14,903.0
454	Quanta Computer	Taiwan	14,900.5
455	Pulte Homes	US	14,895.5
456	Henkel	Germany	14,878.5
457	Royal KPN	Netherlands	14,831.2
458	Holcim	Switzerland	14,819.5
459	Sodexho Alliance	France	14,819.0
460	Nordea Bank	Sweden	14,798.9
461	Kobe Steel	Japan	14,726.3
462	Tohoku Electric Power	Japan	14,662.1
463	COFCO	China	14,653.8
464	Eli Lilly	US	14,645.3
465	Computer Sciences	US	14,623.6
466	Iberdrola	Spain	14,585.5
467	SK Networks	South Korea	14,570.5
468	CBS	US	14,536.4
469	Schneider Electric	France	14,511.7
470	China First Automotive Works	China	14,510.8
471	Kingfisher	UK	14,483.8
472	Inbev	Belgium	14,483.3
473	Humana	US	14,418.1
474	Onex	Canada	14,395.5
475	Shanghai Automotive	China	14,365.2
476	AFLAC	US	14,363.0
477	Schlumberger	US	14,317.2
478	Whirlpool	US	14,317.0
479	Progressive	US	14,303.4
480	Office Depot	US	14,278.9
481	Friends Provident	UK	14,277.9
482	Eastman Kodak	US	14,268.0
483	AREVA	France	14,196.3
484	Scottish Power	UK	14,172.0
485	China Railway Construction	China	14,138.9
486	China State Construction	China	14,122.4
487	GUS	UK	14,118.5
488	Chubb	US	14,082.3
489	Paccar	US	14,057.4
490	United States Steel	US	14,039.0
491	Isuzu Motors	Japan	13,971.5
492	Apple Computer	US	13,931.0
493	Marks & Spencer	UK	13,909.2
494	Qwest Communications	US	13,903.0
495	Lennar	US	13,870.3
496	D.R. Horton	US	13,863.7
497	Asahi Glass	Japan	13,863.5
498	State Bank of India	India	13,755.8
499	Sumitomo Chemical	Japan	13,748.5
500	Nike	US	13,739.7

BusinessWeek's Information Technology 100

Rank	Company	Country	Revenue ($ mil.)	Rank	Company	Country	Revenue ($ mil.)
1	América Móvil	Mexico	16,108.0	51	Oracle	US	13,407.0
2	Hon Hai Precision Industry Co.	Taiwan	28,440.0	52	Nikon	Japan	6,516.7
3	High Tech Computer	Taiwan	2,242.5	53	AT&T	US	49,449.0
4	Apple Computer	US	17,306.0	54	Cisco Systems	US	27,081.0
5	SOFTBANK	Japan	9,884.3	55	L-3 Communications Holdings	US	10,386.0
6	Telefonica Moviles	Spain	21,204.3	56	Yahoo!	US	5,651.0
7	Telefónica	Spain	48,642.9	57	Wipro	India	2,290.7
8	China Mobile	Hong Kong	30,281.9	58	Advanced Micro Devices	US	5,953.1
9	Nokia	Finland	43,903.2	59	Canon	Japan	33,470.4
10	Bharti Airtel	India	2,519.8	60	Xyratex	UK	727.6
11	Motorola	US	38,695.0	61	Agilent Technologies	US	5,416.0
12	Telekomunikasi Indonesia	Indonesia	4,517.2	62	KDDI	Japan	27,288.6
13	Google	US	7,135.8	63	Acer	Taiwan	9,921.8
14	Accenture	US	17,840.8	64	LG TeleCom	Korea	3,702.0
15	Dell	US	56,738.0	65	Rogers Communications	Canada	6,796.5
16	TPV Technology	Hong Kong	5,054.0	66	SK Telecom	Korea	11,310.0
17	Inventec	Taiwan	6,198.7	67	Hoya	Japan	3,069.0
18	Wistron	Taiwan	5,138.3	68	Nextel Partners	US	1,896.7
19	Seagate Technology	US	8,856.0	69	Qualcomm	US	6,493.0
20	BT Group	UK	36,510.7	70	Yahoo! Japan	Japan	1,548.6
21	China Netcom Group (Hong Kong)	Hong Kong	10,868.8	71	MiTAC International	Taiwan	2,600.2
22	TD AMERITRADE Holding	US	1,500.1	72	Cap Gemini	France	8,929.3
23	Amazon.com	US	8,867.0	73	NVIDIA	US	2,473.6
24	Novatek Microelectronics	Taiwan	809.1	74	Texas Instruments	US	13,754.0
25	Telenor	Norway	11,348.6	75	Verizon Communications	US	79,676.0
26	Toshiba	Japan	56,555.3	76	Amkor Technology	US	2,327.6
27	Telefonos de Mexico	Mexico	14,409.7	77	Tellabs	US	1,962.5
28	E*Trade Financial	US	2,847.9	78	VTech Holdings	Hong Kong	1,022.0
29	Brightpoint	US	2,239.7	79	Lite-On Technology	Taiwan	7,096.4
30	NII Holdings	US	1,903.9	80	Cosmote Mobile Telecommunications	Greece	2,308.2
31	Quanta Computer	Taiwan	14,947.8	81	Amphenol	US	1,967.7
32	Asustek Computer	Taiwan	11,161.7	82	Jabil Circuit	US	8,694.4
33	Hutchison Telecommunications Intl.	Hong Kong	3,137.5	83	Heartland Payment Systems	US	901.5
34	Tata Consultancy Services	India	2,796.1	84	Cognizant Technology Solutions	US	989.6
35	MediaTek	Taiwan	1,647.0	85	Corning	US	4,791.0
36	Sprint Nextel	US	39,292.0	86	TDC	Denmark	8,021.9
37	Microsoft	US	42,639.0	87	Broadcom	US	3,021.1
38	Western Digital	US	4,196.2	88	Sega Sammy Holdings	Japan	4,932.4
39	SAP	Germany	10,930.4	89	Palm	US	1,511.2
40	Komag	US	754.2	90	Anixter International	US	4,041.4
41	Avaya	US	5,019.0	91	Logitech International	Switzerland	1,796.7
42	Infosys Technologies	India	2,057.0	92	Siliconware Precision Industries	Taiwan	1,356.5
43	Turkcell Iletisim Hizmetleri	Turkey	4,268.5	93	Millicom International Cellular	Luxembourg	1,137.6
44	Hewlett-Packard	US	88,885.0	94	Compal Electronics	Taiwan	8,280.3
45	Netflix	US	753.9	95	Harris	US	3,304.3
46	SanDisk	US	2,478.4	96	NIDEC	Japan	4,786.3
47	LM Ericsson	Sweden	21,038.1	97	Intuit	US	2,301.2
48	Satyam Computer Services	India	1,035.4	98	Amdocs	UK	2,268.8
49	VimpelCom	Russia	3,211.1	99	Alliance Data Systems	US	1,653.8
50	Mobile Telesystems	Russia	5,011.0	100	National Semiconductor	US	2,158.1

Note: Rank based on shareholder return, return on equity, revenue growth, and total revenue (revenue for the most recent four quarters available; most recent FY for those companies that do not report quarterly results).

SOURCE: *BUSINESSWEEK*, JULY 3, 2006

The World's 100 Largest Public Financial Companies

Rank	Company	Country	Assets* ($ mil.)	Rank	Company	Country	Assets ($ mil.)
1	Barclays	UK	1,592,415	51	Legal & General Group	UK	330,085
2	Mitsubishi UFJ Financial Group	Japan	1,582,865	52	Sanpaolo Imi	Italy	316,694
3	UBS	Switzerland	1,566,202	53	The Toronto-Dominion Bank	Canada	316,021
4	Citigroup	US	1,494,037	54	Nomura Holdings	Japan	298,145
5	BNP Paribas	France	1,489,943	55	Manulife Financial Corporation	Canada	295,526
6	HSBC Holdings	UK	1,406,944	56	Munich Re	Germany	292,975
7	Crédit Agricole	France	1,386,044	57	The Bear Stearns Companies	US	292,635
8	ING Groep	Netherlands	1,375,606	58	The Hartford Financial Services Group	US	285,557
9	The Royal Bank of Scotland Group	UK	1,345,013	59	Eurohypo Aktiengesellschaft	Germany	277,485
10	Bank of America Corporation	US	1,291,803	60	The Bank of Nova Scotia	Canada	274,887
11	Mizuho Financial Group	Japan	1,272,307	61	Bank of Montreal	Canada	254,807
12	JPMorgan Chase & Co.	US	1,198,942	62	CNP Assurances	France	248,538
13	Allianz	Germany	1,187,333	63	Commonwealth Bank of Australia	Australia	246,625
14	Deutsche Bank	Germany	1,175,116	64	Skandinaviska Enskilda Banken	Sweden	240,607
15	ABN AMRO Holding	Netherlands	1,050,654	65	Canadian Imperial Bank of Commerce	Canada	239,223
16	Credit Suisse Group	Switzerland	1,017,947	66	Crédit Industriel et Commercial	France	231,927
17	Banco Santander Central Hispano	Spain	963,051	67	National Australia Bank Limited	Australia	229,853
18	HBOS	UK	930,518	68	Australia and New Zealand Banking Group	Australia	221,707
19	Sumitomo Mitsui Financial Group	Japan	927,307	69	DEPFA BANK	Ireland	218,361
20	Morgan Stanley	US	898,523	70	U.S. Bancorp	US	209,465
21	Fortis SA/NV	Belgium	863,348	71	Svenska Handelsbanken	Sweden	203,982
22	American International Group	US	853,370	72	Berkshire Hathaway	US	198,325
23	Société Générale	France	819,885	73	Westpac Banking Corporation	Australia	197,490
24	The Goldman Sachs Group	US	706,804	74	Bank of Ireland	Ireland	195,634
25	AXA	France	684,311	75	Capitalia	Italy	181,114
26	Merrill Lynch & Co.	US	681,015	76	Erste Bank	Austria	180,796
27	General Electric Company	US	673,342	77	SunTrust Banks	US	179,713
28	Dexia	Belgium	602,526	78	Kookmin Bank	South Korea	178,508
29	HVB Group	Germany	584,479	79	Banca Monte dei Paschi di Siena	Italy	176,458
30	Commerzbank	Germany	579,535	80	Countrywide Financial Corporation	US	175,085
31	Lloyds TSB Group	UK	526,422	81	Swiss Reinsurance Company	Switzerland	166,530
32	Wachovia Corporation	US	520,755	82	Deutsche Postbank	Germany	166,134
33	Wells Fargo & Company	US	481,741	83	ERGO Versicherungsgruppe	Germany	160,079
34	MetLife	US	481,645	84	Allied Irish Banks	Ireland	158,970
35	Banco Bilbao Vizcaya Argentaria	Spain	475,891	85	Sun Life Financial	Canada	158,250
36	Aviva	UK	453,234	86	Allianz Lebensversicherungs	Germany	157,799
37	Prudential Financial	US	417,776	87	The Allstate Corporation	US	156,072
38	Lehman Brothers Holdings	US	410,063	88	Shinhan Financial Group	South Korea	155,115
39	Royal Bank of Canada	Canada	399,140	89	Woori Finance Holdings	South Korea	154,915
40	KBC Group	Belgium	385,846	90	Swedbank	Sweden	154,293
41	Danske Bank	Denmark	385,236	91	The Standard Life Assurance Company	UK	152,100
42	Assicurazioni Generali	Italy	383,718	92	The Sumitomo Trust and Banking Company	Japan	147,916
43	Nordea Bank	Sweden	376,519	93	Swiss Life Holding	Switzerland	146,319
44	Banca Intesa	Italy	374,552	94	State Bank of India	India	143,567
45	AEGON	Netherlands	372,911	95	National City Corporation	US	142,397
46	Resona Holdings	Japan	367,860	96	Old Mutual	UK	138,620
47	UniCredit	Italy	362,626	97	Millea Holdings	Japan	131,887
48	Prudential	UK	360,294	98	Assurances Générales de France	France	130,954
49	Washington Mutual	US	343,573	99	Principal Financial Group	US	127,035
50	Zurich Financial Services	Switzerland	339,612	100	Mitsui Trust Holdings, Inc.	Japan	124,886

*Assets at the latest available fiscal year-end

SOURCE: HOOVER'S INC. DATABASE, DECEMBER 2006

The World's Top 20 Electronics Companies

Rank	Company	Electronics Revenue ($ mil.)	Total Revenue ($ mil.)
1	IBM	91,134.0	91,134.0
2	Hewlett-Packard	87,901.0	87,901.0
3	Matsushita Electric Industrial	81,437.9	81,437.9
4	Samsung Electronics	57,722.0	57,722.0
5	Dell	55,908.0	55,908.0
6	Siemens	53,102.3	96,549.6
7	Hitachi	46,433.6	85,988.2
8	Sony	45,589.3	68,145.4
9	Fujitsu	44,762.2	44,762.2
10	NEC	44,744.4	44,774.4
11	Microsoft	41,359.0	41,359.0
12	Toshiba	41,300.9	57,362.4
13	Nokia	40,497.5	40,497.5
14	Intel	38,826.0	38,826.0
15	Motorola	36,843.0	36,843.0
16	Ingram Micro	28,808.3	28,808.3
17	Canon	28,696.3	31,858.3
18	Philips Electronics	27,928.0	36,001.4
19	Hon Hai Precision Industry	27,751.4	27,751.4
20	Cisco Systems	25,946.0	25,946.0

*For the four quarters ending closest to December 31, 2005

SOURCE: *ELECTRONIC BUSINESS*, AUGUST 1, 2006

The World's Top 20 Motor Vehicle and Parts Manufacturers

Rank	Company	Country	2005 Revenue ($ mil.)
1	General Motors	US	192,604
2	DaimlerChrysler	Germany	186,106
3	Toyota Motor	Japan	185,805
4	Ford Motor	US	177,210
5	Volkswagen	Germany	118,377
6	Honda Motor	Japan	87,511
7	Nissan Motor	Japan	83,274
8	Peugeot	France	69,915
9	BMW	Germany	57,973
10	Fiat	Italy	57,834
11	Hyundai Motor	South Korea	57,435
12	Robert Bosch	Germany	52,208
13	Renault	France	51,365
14	Volvo	Sweden	32,184
15	DENSO	Japan	28,160
16	Johnson Controls	US	28,020
17	Delphi	US	27,201
18	Mazda Motor	Japan	25,789
19	Bridgestone	Japan	24,440
20	Suzuki Motor	Japan	24,258

SOURCE: *FORTUNE*, JULY 24, 2006

The World's Top 20 Telecommunications Companies

Rank	Company	Country	2005 Revenue ($ mil.)
1	Nippon Telegraph & Telephone	Japan	94,869
2	Verizon Communications	US	75,112
3	Deutsche Telekom	Germany	74,062
4	Vodafone	UK	65,314
5	France Télécom	France	60,933
6	Telefónica	Spain	48,833
7	AT&T	US	43,862
8	Telecom Italia	Italy	39,765
9	BT	UK	34,808
10	Sprint Nextel	US	34,680
11	China Mobile Communications	China	28,778
12	KDDI	Japan	27,034
13	Vivendi	France	25,061
14	China Telecommunications	China	22,736
15	Comcast	US	22,255
16	BellSouth	US	20,613
17	Telstra	Australia	17,043
18	KT	South Korea	16,749
19	América Telecom	Mexico	16,719
20	BCE	Canada	16,506

SOURCE: *FORTUNE*, JULY 24, 2006

The World's Top 20 Marketing Organizations

Rank	Company	Headquarters	Revenue ($ mil.)
1	Omnicom Group	New York	10,481.1
2	WPP Group	London	10,032.2
3	Interpublic Group of Cos.	New York	6,274.3
4	Publicis Groupe	Paris	5,107.2
5	Dentsu	Tokyo	2,887.8
6	Havas	Suresnes, France	1,808.0
7	Aegis Group	London	1,577.6
8	Hakuhodo DY Holdings	Tokyo	1,364.0
9	Asatsu-DK	Tokyo	444.8
10	MDC Partners	Toronto/New York	443.5
11	Carlson Marketing Group	Minneapolis	370.0
12	Sapient Corp.	Cambridge, MA	358.4
13	Digitas	Boston	340.5
14	aQuantive	Seattle	258.4
15	Aspen Marketing Services	West Chicago, IL	229.0
16	Media Square	London	215.0
17	HealthSTAR Communications	Woodbridge, NJ	213.0
18	Cheil Communications	Seoul	210.7
19	George P. Johnson Co.	Auburn Hills, MI	193.0
20	Epsilon	Wakefield, MA	184.4

SOURCE: *ADVERTISING AGE*, April 28, 2006

The World's Top 10 Aerospace and Defense Companies

Rank	Company	Country	2005 Revenue ($ mil.)
1	Boeing	US	54,848
2	United Technologies	US	42,725
3	EADS	Netherlands	42,503
4	Lockheed Martin	US	37,213
5	Northrop Grumman	US	30,721
6	Honeywell Intl.	US	28,862
7	Raytheon	US	21,894
8	General Dynamics	US	21,290
9	BAE Systems	UK	20,228
10	Finmeccanica	Italy	15,129

SOURCE: *FORTUNE*, JULY 24, 2006

The World's Top 10 Petroleum Refining Companies

Rank	Company	Country	2005 Revenue ($ mil.)
1	Exxon Mobil	US	339,938
2	Royal Dutch Shell	UK/Netherlands	306,731
3	BP	UK	267,600
4	Chevron	US	189,481
5	ConocoPhillips	US	166,683
6	TOTAL	France	152,361
7	Sinopec	China	98,785
8	ENI	Italy	92,603
9	PDVSA	Venezuela	85,618
10	China National Petroleum	China	83,557

SOURCE: *FORTUNE*, JULY 24, 2006

The World's Top Energy Companies

Rank	Company	Country	2005 Revenue ($ mil.)
1	E.ON	Germany	66,313
2	Suez	France	52,743
3	Gazprom	Russia	50,824
4	RWE	Germany	50,346
5	Plains All American Pipeline	US	31,177
6	Gasunie Trade & Supply	Netherlands	18,312
7	Constellation Energy	US	17,375
8	AREVA	France	14,196

SOURCE: *FORTUNE*, JULY 24, 2006

The World's Top 10 Electric and Gas Utilities

Rank	Company	Country	2005 Revenue ($ mil.)
1	State Grid	China	86,984
2	Électricité De France	France	63,434
3	Tokyo Electric Power	Japan	46,418
4	Enel	Italy	42,320
5	Veolia Environnement	France	31,368
6	Gaz de France	France	27,826
7	UES of Russia	Russia	27,768
8	Centrica	UK	25,063
9	Korea Electric Power	South Korea	24,841
10	China Southern Power Grid	China	23,105

SOURCE: *FORTUNE*, JULY 24, 2006

The World's Top 10 Pharmaceutical Companies

Rank	Company	Country	2005 Revenue ($ mil.)
1	Pfizer	US	51,353
2	Johnson & Johnson	US	50,514
3	GlaxoSmithKline	UK	39,366
4	Sanofi-Aventis	France	35,429
5	Novartis	Switzerland	32,212
6	Roche Group	Switzerland	28,496
7	AstraZeneca	UK	23,950
8	Abbott Laboratories	US	22,338
9	Merck	US	22,012
10	Bristol-Myers Squibb	US	20,222

SOURCE: *FORTUNE*, JULY 24, 2006

Forbes' "Richest People in the World" by Net Worth

Rank	Name	Age	Net Worth ($ bil.)	Country	What
1	William Gates III	50	50.0	US	Microsoft
2	Warren Buffett	75	42.0	US	Berkshire Hathaway
3	Carlos Slim Helu	66	30.0	Mexico	Telecom
4	Ingvar Kamprad	79	28.0	Switzerland	IKEA
5	Lakshmi Mittal	55	23.5	UK	Steel
6	Paul Allen	53	22.0	US	Microsoft/investments
7	Bernard Arnault	57	21.5	France	LVMH
8	Prince Alwaleed Bin Talal Alsaud	49	20.0	Saudi Arabia	Investments
9	Kenneth Thomson & family	82	19.6	Canada	Publishing
10	Li Ka-shing	77	18.8	Hong Kong	Diversified
11	Roman Abramovich	39	18.2	UK	Oil
12	Michael Dell	41	17.1	US	Dell
13	Karl Albrecht	86	17.0	Germany	Supermarkets
14	Sheldon Adelson	72	16.1	US	Casinos/hotels
15	Liliane Bettencourt	83	16.0	France	L'Oréal
15	Lawrence Ellison	61	16.0	US	Oracle
17	Christy Walton	51	15.9	US	Wal-Mart
17	Jim Walton	58	15.9	US	Wal-Mart
19	S. Robson Walton	62	15.8	US	Wal-Mart
20	Alice Walton	56	15.7	US	Wal-Mart
21	Helen Walton	86	15.6	US	Wal-Mart
22	Theo Albrecht	83	15.2	Germany	Supermarkets
23	Amancio Ortega	70	14.8	Spain	Zara
24	Steven Ballmer	50	13.6	US	Microsoft
25	Azim Premji	60	13.3	India	Software
26	Sergey Brin	32	12.9	US	Google
27	Larry Page	33	12.8	US	Google
28	Abigail Johnson	44	12.5	US	Fidelity
29	Nasser Al-Kharafi & family	62	12.4	Kuwait	Construction
29	Barbara Cox Anthony	82	12.4	US	Cox Enterprises
29	Anne Cox Chambers	86	12.4	US	Cox Enterprises
32	Stefan Persson	58	12.3	Sweden	Hennes & Mauritz
33	Charles Koch	70	12.0	US	Oil, commodities
33	David Koch	65	12.0	US	Oil, commodities
35	Raymond, Thomas & Walter Kwok	—	11.6	Hong Kong	Real estate
36	Adolf Merckle	71	11.5	Germany	Pharmaceuticals
37	Sulaiman Bin Abdul Al Rajhi	86	11.0	Saudi Arabia	Banking
37	Vagit Alekperov	55	11.0	Russia	Oil/gas
37	Silvio Berlusconi	69	11.0	Italy	Media
37	Lee Shau Kee	78	11.0	Hong Kong	Real estate
41	Vladimir Lisin	49	10.7	Russia	Steel
42	Michael Otto & family	62	10.4	Germany	Retail
43	Pierre Omidyar	38	10.1	US	eBay
44	Leonardo Del Vecchio	70	10.0	Italy	Eyewear
44	Michele Ferrero & family	79	10.0	Monaco	Chocolates
44	Forrest Mars Jr.	74	10.0	US	Candy
44	Jacqueline Mars	66	10.0	US	Candy
44	John Mars	69	10.0	US	Candy
44	Viktor Vekselberg	48	10.0	Russia	Oil/gas
50	Mikhail Fridman	41	9.7	Russia	Oil/banking

SOURCE: *FORBES*, MARCH 9, 2006

Hoover's Handbook of

World Business

The Companies

ABB

You could be forgiven for thinking that ABB is short for "A Bunch of Businesses" — though the bunch is smaller than it once was. ABB (which used to be called Asea Brown Boveri) operates through two major divisions — power technologies and automation technologies — and serves a broad base of utility, industrial, and commercial customers. The power technologies division provides the power supply industry with equipment and services for transmission, distribution, and automation. The automation technologies unit offers equipment used to monitor and control processes in plants and utilities. The company has undergone extensive restructuring to focus on these two core units after years in which it overdiversified, racked up huge debts, alienated investors, and faced the threat of bankruptcy. During the early 2000s, the company pared its enormous workforce by a quarter and sold several businesses.

ABB has consolidated its remaining businesses into two areas. Its power technologies division comprises the former power technology products and utilities divisions, and its automation technologies division comprises its former automation technology products and industries divisions. The company retains an important presence in many sectors: ABB claims the largest installed base of industrial robots in the world, and has claimed that it equips and services three-quarters of all pulp and paper mills worldwide. It has taken further steps to streamline operations, for example by moving its main robotics operation from Detroit to Shanghai.

In 2006 the company ended years of litigation — and a major corporate headache — when it reached a settlement on an asbestos liability case related to a US subsidiary. As part of the settlement, ABB committed more than $1.4 billion to pay settled claims. Also in 2006 ABB voluntarily disclosed to the US Department of Justice and the SEC that the company had made payments in the Middle East that may have violated anti-bribery laws.

HISTORY

Asea Brown Boveri (ABB) was formed in 1988 when two giants, ASEA AB of Sweden and BBC Brown Boveri of Switzerland, combined their electrical engineering and equipment businesses. Percy Barnevik, head of ASEA, became CEO.

ASEA was born in Stockholm in 1883 when Ludwig Fredholm founded Electriska Aktiebolaget to manufacture an electric dynamo created by engineer Jonas Wenstrom. In 1890 the company merged with Wenstrom's brother's firm to form Allmanna Svenska Electriska Aktiebolaget (ASEA), a pioneer in industrial electrification. Early in the 1900s ASEA began its first railway electrification project. By the 1920s it was providing locomotives and other equipment to Sweden's national railway, and by the next decade ASEA was one of Sweden's largest electric equipment manufacturers. In 1962 it bought 20% of appliance maker Electrolux. ASEA created the nuclear power venture ASEA-ATOM with the Swedish government in 1968 and bought full control in 1982.

BBC Brown Boveri was formed in 1891 as the Brown, Boveri, and Company partnership between Charles Brown and Walter Boveri in Baden, Switzerland. It made power generation equipment and produced the first steam turbines in Europe in 1900. BBC entered Germany (1893), France (1894), and Italy (1903) and diversified into nuclear power equipment after WWII.

By 1988 BBC, the bigger company, had a West German network that ASEA, the more profitable company, coveted. Both had US joint ventures. In an unusual merger, ASEA (which became ABB AB) and BBC (later ABB AG) continued as separate entities sharing equal ownership of ABB. Barnevik crafted a unique decentralized management structure under which national subsidiaries were closely linked to their local customers and labor forces. In six years ABB took over more than 150 companies worldwide.

An ABB-led consortium built one of the world's largest hydroelectric plants in Iran in 1992, and in 1995 ABB merged its transportation segment into Adtranz (a joint venture with Daimler-Benz, now DaimlerChrysler) to form the world's #1 maker of trains.

Tragedy struck in 1996. Robert Donovan, CEO of ABB's US subsidiary, died in a plane crash along with Commerce Secretary Ron Brown and other executives on a trade mission. In 1997 Barnevik gave up the title of CEO, remaining as chairman (until 2001), and was succeeded by Göran Lindahl, an engineer who had worked his way up the ranks at ASEA.

In 1999 ABB acquired Elsag Bailey, a Dutch maker of industrial control systems, for about $1.5 billion, and sold its 50% stake in Adtranz to DaimlerChrysler for $472 million. ABB and France's Alstom combined their power generation businesses to form the world's largest power plant equipment maker. Also that year ABB AB and ABB AG were united under a single stock.

ABB sold its nuclear power business to BNFL for $485 million and its 50% stake in ABB Alstom Power to ALSTOM for $1.2 billion in 2000. In 2001 Lindahl resigned and Jörgen Centerman, head of the company's automation business, replaced him. With economic slowdowns occurring in the company's key markets, ABB announced plans in July 2001 to cut 12,000 jobs, or about 8% of its workforce, over 18 months. Later that year, amid rising numbers of asbestos claims against US subsidiary Combustion Engineering, ABB took a $470 million fourth-quarter charge to cover asbestos liabilities. The claims charged asbestos exposures stemming from products supplied before the mid-1970s by Combustion Engineering, which ABB had acquired in 1990.

In 2002 ABB found itself embroiled in controversy after revealing not only a record loss but also payments of large pensions to former chairman Barnevik and former chief executive Lindahl. The former executives agreed that year to return a part (about $82 million) of their pension payouts. That year ABB agreed to sell part of its financial services unit to GE Commercial Finance for $2.3 billion. The day after the company sold its structured finances unit, ABB's chief executive, Jörgen Centerman, resigned and was replaced by the chairman, Jürgen Dormann.

In 2003, as part of its settlement with asbestos plaintiffs, ABB placed Combustion Engineering into bankruptcy. ABB sold its upstream oil, gas, and petrochemicals unit to Candover Partners, 3i, and J.P. Morgan Partners for $925 million in 2004.

Sulzer CEO Fred Kindle succeeded Dormann as ABB's CEO in January 2005.

EXECUTIVES

Chairman: Jürgen Dormann, age 66, $1,139,850 pay
President and CEO: Fred Kindle, age 47, $2,417,812 pay
Executive Committee Member, Power Products Division: Bernhard Jucker, age 52
EVP, Human Resources: Gary Steel, age 54, $1,008,241 pay
EVP, Power Technologies: Peter Smits, age 55, $1,071,032 pay
CFO: Michel Demaré, age 40, $1,105,085 pay
Head of Corporate Development: Ulrich Spiesshofer, age 42, $161,777 pay
President, Global Markets and Technologies; President, ABB Inc.; Chairman, ABB India: Dinesh C. Paliwal
SVP, Sustainability Affairs: Christian Kornevall
CTO: H. Markus Bayegan
CIO: Haider Rashid
Deputy CFO and Head, Corporate Finance and Taxes: Alfred Storck
General Counsel and Head, Legal and Compliance: John G. Scriven, age 63
Executive Committee Member, Power Systems Division: Samir Brikho, age 48
Executive Committee Member, Automation Products Division: Tom Sjöekvist, age 59
Corporate Communications: Thomas Schmidt
Investor Relations: Michel Gerber, age 39
Auditors: Ernst & Young Ltd.

LOCATIONS

HQ: ABB Ltd.
   Affolternstrasse 44, 8050 Zurich, Switzerland
Phone: +41-43-317-71-11   **Fax:** +41-43-317-44-20
US HQ: 501 Merritt 7, Norwalk, CT 06058
US Phone: 203-750-2200   **US Fax:** 203-750-2263
Web: www.abb.com

ABB operates in more than 100 countries worldwide.

2005 Sales

	$ mil.	% of total
Europe	11,139	50
Asia/Pacific	5,127	23
Americas	4,231	19
Middle East & Africa	1,945	8
Total	**22,442**	**100**

PRODUCTS/OPERATIONS

2005 Sales

	$ mil.	% of total
Automation Technologies	12,161	50
Power Technologies	9,784	41
Non-core activities		
Oil, gas & petrochemicals	933	4
Building systems	421	2
Other activities	67	—
Corporate & other	733	3
Adjustments	(1,657)	—
Total	**22,442**	**100**

Major Operations and Products

Automation Technologies
   Automation products
      Instrumentation
         Actuators and positioners
         Analytical instruments
         Flowmeters
         Pressure transmitters
         Recorders and indicators
         Temperature sensors
      Low- and high-voltage motors
      Low- and medium-voltage drives
      Motor control systems
      Power electronics systems
      Wire management equipment
   Manufacturing automation
      Control systems
      Industrial robots
   Process automation
      Collaborative production management systems
      Marine propulsion equipment
      Process control systems
      Product quality sensors
      Turbochargers

Power Technologies
  High-voltage products
    Cables
    Gas-insulated switchgear
    Generator circuit breakers
  Medium-voltage products
    Circuit breakers
    Fuses
    Sensors
    Switches
    Vacuum interrupters
  Power systems
    Flexible alternating current transmission systems
      (FACTS)
    High-voltage direct current (HVDC) systems
    Power lines
  Transformers
    Converter transformers
    Distribution transformers
    Phase-shifting transformers
    Reactors
    Single-phase transformers
  Utility automation systems
    Distributed control systems
    Substation automation equipment
    Utility communication networks
Other operations
  Building systems
  Equity ventures
  Structured finance

COMPETITORS

Aker Kværner
ALSTOM
Bechtel
Cooper Industries
Emerson Electric
Endress + Hauser
Fluor
Foster Wheeler
GE
Halliburton
Hitachi
Honeywell ACS
Invensys
JGC
McDermott
Metso
Rockwell Automation
Samsung Group
Schneider Electric
Siemens AG
Technip
Toshiba
VA Technologie

HISTORICAL FINANCIALS
Company Type: Public

Income Statement
FYE: December 31

	REVENUE ($ mil.)	NET INCOME ($ mil.)	NET PROFIT MARGIN	EMPLOYEES
12/05	22,442	735	3.3%	103,500
12/04	20,721	(35)	—	102,500
12/03	18,784	(779)	—	116,500
12/02	18,295	(783)	—	139,051
12/01	23,726	(691)	—	156,865
Annual Growth	(1.4%)	—	—	(9.9%)

2005 Year-End Financials
Debt ratio: 112.9%   No. of shares (mil.): —
Return on equity: 23.3%   Dividends
Cash ($ mil.): 3,594   Yield: —
Current ratio: 1.22   Payout: —
Long-term debt ($ mil.): 3,933   Market value ($ mil.): —

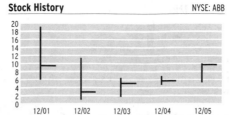

Stock History   NYSE: ABB

	STOCK PRICE ($) FY Close	P/E High	P/E Low	PER SHARE ($) Earnings	PER SHARE ($) Dividends
12/05	9.72	27	15	0.36	—
12/04	5.66	—	—	—	—
12/03	5.08	—	—	—	1.21
12/02	2.87	—	—	—	—
12/01	9.41	—	—	—	—
Annual Growth	0.8%	—	—	—	—

ABN AMRO

When the tulip bed got a little too crowded, ABN AMRO Holding decided to cultivate more exotic acreage, concentrating on Asia, the US, and the rest of Europe for much of its growth. One of the Netherlands' largest financial services firms, ABN AMRO performs retail banking services mainly in its home country, Brazil (through Banco ABN AMRO Real), and the US, where it runs LaSalle Bank in Illinois, Indiana, and Michigan, and is one of the largest foreign banks by assets. Other lines of business, which operate worldwide, include private banking, asset management, and investment banking. All told, ABN AMRO and its subsidiaries operate nearly 3,600 offices in some 60 countries.

To unify its stateside brands ABN AMRO changed the name of Standard Federal Bank in Michigan and Indiana to LaSalle Bank in 2005.

The company is reconfiguring its divisions to focus on mid-sized clients. It is cutting 2,400 jobs and doubling its back-office operations in India. Like many foreign banks, it is eyeing opportunities in Latin America, Italy, and China, the world's fastest-growing economy. The company plans to open at least 20 branches there and has signed a memorandum of agreement with Chinese securities firm Haitong Securities.

In 2006 it agreed to sell its futures and commodities trading business to UBS. It also agreed to sell its Taiwanese domestic asset management business for as much as €68 million to ING Groep. Later that year it said it would sell its property management division, Bouwfonds, to Rabobank and SNS Reaal Groep NV for €1.69 billion. It will use proceeds from that sale for its share buyback program.

ABN AMRO was caught in the fallout of the collapse of a US hedge fund run by former NYMEX head Bo Collins. The fund bet wrong on natural gas prices and the bank was left facing up to a $100 million loss. The bank also faces criminal charges in Vietnam over deals it made with Vietnamese bank Incombank.

HISTORY

ABN AMRO comes by its initials honestly. It is the product of a 1991 merger between the Netherlands' #1 and #2 banks — Algemene Bank Nederland (ABN) and Amsterdam-Rotterdam Bank (AMRO), respectively — and a final amalgamation of what were the four top banks in the Netherlands.

The Netherlands Trading Society was founded in 1824 to finance business ventures in the Dutch colonies, operating from an office in what is now Jakarta, Indonesia. The company prospered, moving into agricultural financing and commercial banking and acquiring banks in the early 1900s. Although the firm weathered WWI and the Depression, WWII was catastrophic — Germany occupied the homeland and Japan took over the Dutch East Indies.

The Netherlands Trading Society never recovered, and in 1964 it merged with Twentsche Bank (founded in 1861 as an agricultural bank) to form Algemene Bank Nederland. ABN's chief rival was AMRO, product of the 1964 merger of Amsterdam Bank and Rotterdam Bank. Founded in 1863, Rotterdam Bank financed commercial activity in the colonies before refocusing on the shipping business through Rotterdam. Amsterdam Bank was founded in 1871 by several Dutch and German banks and was the largest Dutch bank when it merged with Incasso Bank in 1948. In 1964 the new entity added the operations of Hollandsche Bank — Unie.

ABN was smaller than AMRO until it bought merchant bank Mees & Hope (1975) followed by the purchase of Chicago-based LaSalle National Bank (1979). ABN had retreated so far from its colonial roots that it was largely unscathed by the mass default of Third World banks in 1987. Instead, AMRO financed oil and gas exploration and construction on the English Channel Tunnel.

ABN and AMRO merged in 1991, and the new company turned its attention to overseas markets like the American Midwest, where LaSalle National Bank was gobbling up competitors like Talman Home Federal Savings (1991). ABN AMRO also took control of European American Bank (EAB), which had sustained heavy losses on bad real estate and Third World loans. The company bought investment banks Chicago Corp. and Alfred Berg in 1995.

Expansion brought internal oversight problems during the next few years: in 1995 Swiss banking authorities asked ABN AMRO to better police its branches there after the bank lost as much as $124 million to embezzlement. In 1997 the firm closed its diamond office after losing about $100 million to fraud.

In 1998 ABN AMRO bought Brazil's Banco Real and Bandepe banks (and then closed their European and US offices). The next year it began buying minority interests in Italian banks. Also in 1999 the company elected to become a major force in European real estate with the acquisition of Bouwfonds Nederlandse Gemeenten, the Netherlands' #5 mortgage lender. As part of this effort, it expanded its mortgage servicing portfolio with the purchase of Pitney Bowes subsidiary Atlantic Mortgage and Investment Corp.

ABN AMRO cut 150 branches in its overbanked home market (and about 10% of its Dutch workforce) in 2000. It bought the energy-derivative business of Merrill Lynch, Barclays' Dial car-leasing unit, and Alleghany Corporation's asset management unit.

In 2001 ABN AMRO sold EAB to Citigroup and bought US-based Michigan National Corporation from National Australia Bank and merged it with another Michigan holding, Standard Federal Bancorporation, to form Standard Federal Bank, one of the largest banks in Michigan. It also bought the US brokerage and corporate finance operations of Dutch rival ING Groep in a quarter-billion dollar deal.

Thailand's "one presence" rule, which prevents foreign banks from holding a major stake in a local bank while also maintaining their own branches, forced ABN AMRO to sell its majority stake in Bank of Asia to Singapore-based United Overseas Bank in 2004.

In 2005 and 2006 the company divested other businesses, such as trust, professional brokerage, and prime brokerage. It also upped stakes in other holdings and made several acquisitions.

In 2006 ABN AMRO sold its mutual fund business to Highbury Financial Inc., for $38.6 million. That year it boosted its ownership of Banca Antonveneta, a regional bank in northeastern Italy, to nearly 99% after it bought the 30% stake owned by Banca Popolare Italiana, which tried to block ABN AMRO's original takeover bid. That year the private-equity unit bought NextiraOne, a French IT services company with more than $1 billion in sales.

EXECUTIVES

Chairman, Supervisory Board: Arthur C. Martinez, age 66
Chairman, Managing Board: Rijkman W. J. Groenink, age 57
Member, Managing Board, Responsible for Business Unit Europe, Business Unit Private Clients; Chairman, Consumer Client Segment: Dolf Collee, age 54
Member, Managing Board, Responsible for Business Unit Netherlands, Business Unit Global Clients, Business Unit Asset Management, and ABN AMRO Capital: Wilco G. Jiskoot, age 56
Member, Managing Board, Responsible for Business Unit North America; Chairman, Group Business Committee (GBC): Joost Ch. L. Kuiper, age 59
CFO: Hugh Y. Scott-Barrett, age 48
SEVP; CEO, Consumer and Commercial Clients, The Netherlands: Jan Peter Schmittmann
SEVP; Head, Business Unit Latin America: Fabio C. Barbosa
SEVP; Head, Business Unit North America: Norman R. (Norm) Bobins, age 63
SEVP; CEO, Transaction Banking Group: Ann Cairns
SEVP; Head, Group Risk Management: David A. Cole
SEVP; Head, Business Unit Europe: Lex Kloosterman, age 50
Member, Managing Board, Responsible for Business Unit Latin America, Business Unit Transaction Banking, Services, and EU Affairs and Market Infrastructure: Ron Teerlink
SEVP; Head, Business Unit Global Clients: Alexandra E.J.M. Cook-Schaapveld, age 48
SEVP; Business Unit Europe; Head of Sub Region; Country Executive France; and Vice Chairman, Corporates: Pierre Fleuriot
SEVP; Head, Group Compliance and Legal: Carin Gorter
SEVP, Business Unit North America; Head of Services and HR: M. Hill Hammock
SEVP, Group Finance: Maurice B.G.M. Oostendorp
Head of Investor Relations: Richard P. Bruens
Head of Corporate Communications: Robin Boon
Global Head of Research: Michael Baptista
Auditors: Ernst & Young Accountants

LOCATIONS

HQ: ABN AMRO Holding N.V.
Gustav Mahlerlaan 10,
1082 PP Amsterdam, The Netherlands
Phone: +31-20-628-9393   **Fax:** +31-20-629-9111
US HQ: 135 S. La Salle St., Chicago, IL 60603
US Phone: 312-904-2000   **US Fax:** 312-904-2579
Web: www.abnamro.com

PRODUCTS/OPERATIONS

2005 Sales

	% of total
Interest	39
Fees & commissions	20
Trading income	11
Income of consolidated private equity holdings	16
Other	14
Total	**100**

COMPETITORS

Citigroup
Credit Suisse
Deutsche Bank
Dresdner Bank
Fifth Third
Harris Bankcorp
HSBC Holdings
ING
JPMorgan Chase
National City
Northern Trust
Société Générale

HISTORICAL FINANCIALS

Company Type: Public

Income Statement
FYE: December 31

	ASSETS ($ mil.)	NET INCOME ($ mil.)	INCOME AS % OF ASSETS	EMPLOYEES
12/05	1,050,654	3,399	0.3%	98,080
12/04	839,363	3,853	0.5%	97,276
12/03	712,651	3,917	0.5%	110,201
12/02	589,646	2,212	0.4%	107,416
12/01	537,299	1,193	0.2%	112,206
Annual Growth	18.3%	29.9%	—	(3.3%)

2005 Year-End Financials

Equity as % of assets: 3.2%
Return on assets: 0.4%
Return on equity: 10.9%
Long-term debt ($ mil.): 406,239
No. of shares (mil.): —
Dividends
Yield: 3.5%
Payout: —
Market value ($ mil.): —
Sales ($ mil.): 53,965

Stock History
NYSE: ABN

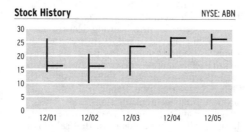

	STOCK PRICE ($) FY Close	P/E High/Low		PER SHARE ($) Earnings	Dividends
12/05	26.14	—	—	—	0.92
12/04	26.60	—	—	—	0.91
12/03	23.48	—	—	—	0.75
12/02	16.18	—	—	—	0.63
12/01	16.28	—	—	—	0.66
Annual Growth	12.6%	—	—	—	8.7%

Accor

Accor est l'hospitalité. The company is one of the world's leading hotel operators, owning or managing almost 4,000 properties in 90 countries throughout the world. It serves travelers through its upscale brands Lenôtre and Sofitel, as well as its midscale Novotel, Mercure, and Suitehotel, and economy chains Ibis and Formule 1. In North America it operates budget brands Motel 6 and Red Roof Inns. Accor also owns a 29% stake in resorts operator Club Méditerranée, and 34% of casino hotel company Groupe Lucien Barrière. In addition, Accor operates or owns stakes in several hospitality and food services; its Accor services unit provides outsourced benefits services to more than 340,000 corporate customers.

Nearly 70% of Accor's revenue comes from its hotel operations, which are anchored by its upscale and mid-market chains in Europe. Many of these hotels are either owned or operated by the company. In contrast, its US economy brands (accounting for less than 20% of sales) boast more than 1,200 properties, most of which are franchised.

Accor is focusing on expansion efforts in the Asia/Pacific region, opening hotels in China, Thailand, Indonesia, and South Korea, as well as Australia and New Zealand.

In 2006 Accor sold its 50% stake in travel services giant Carlson Wagonlit to Carlson Companies and JP Morgan affiliate One Equity Partners.

Also in 2006 veteran chairman and CEO Jean-Marc Espalioux left the company as Accor reorganized its board of directors and management structure. Gilles Pélisson, head of Bouygues Telecom (France's #3 mobile carrier controlled by conglomerate Bouygues), was named the company's new CEO.

HISTORY

Until Gérard Pélisson and Paul Dubrule built their first hotel in 1967, French hotels were generally quaint old inns or expensive luxury hotels. Pélisson and Dubrule's Novotel introduced mid-priced hotels based on the American model. The pair opened the Ibis Hotel in 1973 and bought the Mercure chain in 1975. By 1979, when it opened its first US hotel in Minneapolis, Novotel was Europe's #1 hotel chain, operating 184 hotels on four continents.

Dubrule and Pélisson married their growing hotel business to Jacques Borel International, forming publicly traded Accor in 1983. Jacques Borel had started out with one restaurant in 1957 and was Europe's #1 restaurateur by 1975, when he took over Belgium's Sofitel chain of luxury hotels. Losses in the hotel game prompted Borel to sell Sofitel to Dubrule and Pélisson in 1980, making their company one of the world's top 10 hotel operators — a list traditionally dominated by US chains. They picked up the rest of Borel's empire in 1983, launching Accor into the restaurant business.

Accor began offering packaged vacations in 1984, after buying a majority stake in Africatours (Africa's largest tour operator), then expanded into the South Pacific, Asia, and the Americas by buying Islands in the Sun (1986), Asietours (1987), and Americatours (1987).

The company opened its first budget hotels (Formule 1) in France in 1985. Accor started marketing Paquet cruises in 1986 and formed the Hotelia and Parthenon chains (Brazilian residential hotels) the next year.

Faced with a mature European market and eager to take advantage of favorable exchange rates, Accor bought Dallas-based budget chain Motel 6 (along with its high debts and poor reputation, which Accor began remedying with an expensive renovation program) in 1990. The next year Accor bought US-based Regal Inns (now part of Motel 6).

Also in 1990 Accor joined Société Générale de Belgique to buy 26.7% of Belgium's Wagons-Lits, owner of about 300 hotels in Europe, Thailand, and Indonesia, as well as restaurants, caterers, and travel agencies in Europe. After a battle involving both Belgian and EC antitrust officials, Accor was allowed to buy a majority stake of Wagons-Lits (later called Wagonlit Travel).

This buy — along with Accor's attempt to increase its share of the luxury market, the continuing burden of its US purchases, and a recession in the travel business — took a financial toll. In response, it began selling assets in 1994, ridding itself of expensive hotel real estate. The company also joined with US-based Carlson Companies to form a joint travel venture called Carlson Wagonlit Travel.

In 1997 co-chairmen Dubrule and Pélisson retired from active management and were succeeded by Jean-Marc Espalioux, formerly of Générale des Eaux (now Vivendi Universal). As part of its strategy to continue to expand internationally, Accor reached an agreement that year with the Moroccan government to develop that country's hotel industry. In 1999 Accor continued hotel acquisitions with US chain Red Roof Inns and hotels in Finland, France, the Netherlands, Poland, and Sweden.

The following year the company opened a luxury Sofitel hotel in downtown Manhattan and began developing other Sofitels in Dallas, Chicago, and Washington, DC. It also sold its EuropCar stake to Volkswagen. In 2001 the company announced plans for a 370-room Sofitel in the high-tech center of Shenyang, China. Early in 2002 Accor bought a 22% stake in Compagnie Européenne de Casinos, an operator of 24 casinos mostly in France, in a bid to buy out the company. However, after a two-month bidding war with competitor Groupe Partouche, Accor sold its stake to Partouche. The bidding war had driven up Compagnie Européenne's stock dramatically, and Accor ended up pocketing some £12 million from the sale. Also in 2002, Accor opened 261 new hotels, largely Ibis, Etap, and Mercure properties. Later that year the company acquired a 30% stake in Dorint AG, a German hotel group.

Accor acquired a 29% stake in resorts operator Club Méditerranée in 2004. Later that year it merged its casino operations with Société Hôtelière de la Chaîne Lucien Barrière and Société des Hôtels et Casinos de Deauville to form Group Lucien Barrière, with Accor holding a 30% stake in the new business. US-based investment firm Colony Capital made a $1.3 billion investment in Accor the following year.

Espalioux left the company in 2006 and Gilles Pélisson, formerly head of mobile carrier Bouygues Telecom (controlled by conglomerate Bouygues), was named the company's new CEO. Also that year Accor sold its stake in Carlson Wagonlit.

EXECUTIVES

Chairman: Serge Weinberg, age 55
CFO: Jacques Stern, age 42
CEO and Director: Gilles Pélisson
EVP Human Resources and Sustainable Development: Cathy Kopp
EVP Strategy and Hotel Development: Philippe Adam
VP Corporate Communication: Armelle Volkringer
President and CEO, Carlson Wagonlit Travel: Hubert Joly, age 47
CEO, Club Méditerranée: Henri Giscard d'Estaing, age 50
COO, Accor Asia Pacific: David Baffsky
COO, Accor Italy: Roberto Cusin
COO, Accor Latin America: Firmin António
COO, Accor North America: Georges Le Mener
COO, Accor Services: Serge Ragozin
COO, Hotels Northern Europe: Michael Flaxman
COO, Hotels Southern Europe, Middle East, and Africa; CEO, Sofitel: Yann Caillère
Corporate Secretary: Pierre Todorov
Communications and External Relations: Jacques Charbit
Coprorate Finance: Marc Vieilledent
Corporate Legal Services: Catherine Bertini
Marketing and Development, Accor Services: Thierry Gaches
Investor Relations and Financial Communication: Éliane Rouyer
Labor Relations: Gérald Ferrier
Legal Affairs: Catherine Levy
Treasury and Finance: Christian Gary
Auditors: Deloitte Touche Tohmatsu

LOCATIONS

HQ: Accor
  2, rue de la Mare-Neuve, 91021 Évry, France
Phone: +33-1-69-36-80-80   **Fax:** +33-1-69-36-79-00
US HQ: 4001 International Pkwy., Carrollton, TX 75007
US Phone: 972-360-9000   **US Fax:** 972-360-2821
Web: www.accor.com

2005 Sales

	% of total
Europe	
France	34
Other countries	34
North America	17
Latin America & Caribbean	8
Other regions	7
Total	**100**

PRODUCTS/OPERATIONS

2005 Sales

	% of total
Hotels	68
Services	8
Other	24
Total	**100**

Selected Operations

Hotels

Etap Hotel	Novotel
Formule 1	Red Roof Inn
Ibis	Sofitel
Lenôtre	Studio 6
Mercure	Suitehotel
Motel 6	

Services
  Compliance services
  Employee benefits programs
  Employee training programs
  Expense management
  Facilities management
  Family and personal assistance programs
  Relationship marketing
  Social programs

Other business units and subsidiaries
  Club Méditerranée (29%, resorts)
  Groupe Lucien Barrière (34%, casino hotels)

COMPETITORS

Best Western
Carlson Hotels
Choice Hotels
Hilton
Hilton International
Hyatt
InterContinental Hotels
Ladbrokes
Marriott
Société du Louvre
Starwood Hotels & Resorts
Wyndham

HISTORICAL FINANCIALS

Company Type: Public

Income Statement				FYE: December 31
	REVENUE ($ mil.)	NET INCOME ($ mil.)	NET PROFIT MARGIN	EMPLOYEES
12/05	9,027	394	4.4%	168,623
12/04	9,716	326	3.4%	168,619
12/03	8,571	339	4.0%	158,023
12/02	7,482	451	6.0%	157,412
12/01	6,458	420	6.5%	146,748
Annual Growth	8.7%	(1.6%)	—	3.5%

Net Income History   Euronext Paris: AC

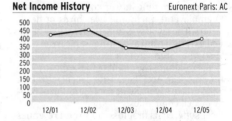

Acer

Acer's plan: divide and conquer. The company is a leading manufacturer of notebook, tablet, handheld, and desktop computers. Other Acer products include servers, storage systems, projectors, LCD televisions, digital cameras, and computer displays. The company also provides IT support services. Acer has streamlined its operations in recent years, spinning off its contract manufacturing operations (now Wistron), as well as its consumer electronics and peripherals business (now BenQ). It still holds stakes in both companies. Acer now outsources its manufacturing. It sells through resellers and distributors worldwide.

Slumping sales in a weakening computer hardware market prompted Acer's restructuring efforts. In addition to clarifying the structure of Acer's sizable operations, the separation of Acer's branded operations and Wistron serves to eliminate possible customer concerns about a conflict of interest between the two businesses. The company has made China and other Asian markets the primary target for its ongoing business, although it has also seen its market share grow considerably in European countries. Acer pulled out of the US retail market in 1999, and it now focuses on serving corporate customers through distributors in the US.

HISTORY

Acer founder and chairman Stan Shih, respected enough for his business acumen to once be considered for the premiership of Taiwan, designed that country's first desktop calculator in the early 1970s. The company's precursor, Multitech International, was launched in 1976 with $25,000 by Shih and four others who called themselves the "Gardeners of Microprocessing." In 1980 Multitech introduced the Dragon Chinese-language terminal, which won Taiwan's top design award; in 1983 it introduced an Apple clone and its first IBM-compatible PC. Multitech set up AcerLand, Taiwan's first and largest franchised computer retail chain, in 1985.

The company changed its name to Acer (the Latin word for "sharp, acute, able, and facile") in 1987 and went public on the Taiwan exchange the next year. Acer got into the semiconductor market in 1989 when it entered into a joint venture with Texas Instruments (named TI-Acer) to design and develop memory chips in Taiwan. In 1990 Acer's US subsidiary, Acer America, paid $90 million for Altos Computer Systems, a US manufacturer of UNIX systems.

During the prosperous 1980s Acer increased its management layers and slowed the decision making process. In late 1990 the company restructured, trimming its workforce by 8% (about 400 employees), including two-thirds of headquarters. The layoff was unprecedented — being asked to resign from a job in Taiwan carries a social stigma. Shih wrote a letter to all those affected, explaining the plight of the company. The following year Acer began its decentralization plan to create a worldwide confederation of publicly owned companies.

Acer suffered its first loss in 1991 on revenues of almost $1 billion, partly because of increased marketing budgets in the US and Europe and continuing investment in TI-Acer. The company bounced back in 1993, with 80% of its profit coming from that joint venture.

The Aspire PC, available in shades of gray and green, was unveiled in 1995. In 1996 the company expanded into consumer electronics, introducing a host of new, inexpensive videodisc players, video telephones, and other devices in order to boost global market share. In 1997 Acer purchased TI's notebook computer business. A slowdown in memory chip sales, plus a financial slide at Acer America, cost the firm $141 million, but Acer finished the year in the black.

Shih stepped down as president in 1998 to focus on restructuring. The company ended its venture with TI, buying TI's 33% stake and renaming the unit Acer Semiconductor Manufacturing. The company also began making information appliances, introducing a device able to play CD-ROMs via TV sets and perform other task-specific functions. Continued losses due to a highly competitive US market caused a drop in profits for 1998.

In 1999 Acer sold a 30% stake in its struggling Acer Semiconductor Manufacturing affiliate to Taiwan Semiconductor Manufacturing Corp. (TSMC completed its purchase of the remaining 70% of the business, which was renamed TSMC-Acer Semiconductor Manufacturing, the following year.) The competitive heat and the rise of under-$1,000 PCs took a toll that year when Acer cut US jobs, streamlined operations, and withdrew from the US retail market. The company intensified its focus on providing online software, hardware, and support for users, launching a digital services business and a venture capital operation to invest in promising Internet startups.

The company suffered a financial blow in 2000 when large customer IBM cancelled an order for desktop computers. Late that year, after continued losses in a slowing PC market, the company announced it would cut more jobs in the US and Germany and close an unspecified number of plants worldwide.

In 2001 the company spun off its contract manufacturing and peripherals units, and renamed them Wistron and BenQ, respectively. Acer's restructuring efforts continued the following year, when it merged with its distribution unit, Acer Sertek. (Although Sertek was the surviving entity, the company immediately revived the Acer name to maintain its stronger brand.)

In 2005 president J.T. Wang succeeded Shih as CEO.

EXECUTIVES

Chairman and CEO: J. T. Wang
President: Gianfranco Lanci
CFO: Howard Chan
Chief Quality Officer: Richard Lai
Associate Director, Investor Relations: Andrew Chang
Media Relations: Stella T.H. Chou
Auditors: KPMG Peat Marwick

LOCATIONS

HQ: Acer Inc.
9F, 88 Hsin Tai Wu Rd., Sec 1, Hsichih,
Taipei 221, Taiwan
Phone: +886-2-696-1234　　**Fax:** +886-2-696-3535
US HQ: 2641 Orchard Pkwy., San Jose, CA 95134
US Phone: 408-432-6200　　**US Fax:** 408-922-2933
Web: www.acer.com

PRODUCTS/OPERATIONS

Selected Products

Computers (desktop, handheld, notebook, server, tablet)
Digital cameras
Digital projectors
LCD televisions
Monitors (cathode-ray tube and liquid-crystal display)

COMPETITORS

Apple Computer	MEDION
Dell	NEC
eMachines	Palm
Founder Holdings	Samsung Electronics
Fujitsu	Samsung Group
Fujitsu Siemens	Sharp Electronics
Computers	Siemens AG
Gateway	Sony
Hewlett-Packard	Sun Microsystems
Hitachi	Tatung
IBM	Toshiba
Lenovo	TriGem
Matsushita	

HISTORICAL FINANCIALS

Company Type: Public

Income Statement				FYE: December 31
	REVENUE ($ mil.)	NET INCOME ($ mil.)	NET PROFIT MARGIN	EMPLOYEES
12/05	9,654	257	2.7%	6,554
12/04	7,036	219	3.1%	6,560
12/03	4,623	214	4.6%	6,368
12/02	3,070	247	8.1%	6,240
12/01	3,226	30	0.9%	—
Annual Growth	31.5%	71.9%	—	1.6%

Net Income History　　　Taiwan: ACER

Adecco

Any way you stack it, Adecco is the world's largest employment agency, serving some 150,000 clients from more than 6,600 offices worldwide. The company provides temporary staffing, permanent employee placement, project assistance, outsourcing services, and other human resources-related services. Adecco's services are managed through its six professional business lines: Adecco Finance & Legal, Adecco Engineering & Technical, Adecco Information Technology, Adecco Medical & Scientific, Adecco Sales, Marketing & Events, and Adecco Human Capital Solutions. Adding to its global staffing operations, Adecco bought German staffing firm DIS Deutscher Industrie Service in early 2006.

The deal for DIS Deutscher Industrie Service (DIS) was for $770 million, with DIS chief Dieter Scheiff eventually appointed to the Adecco CEO position in mid-2006.

Saying it wanted to focus more on its professional offerings, the company restructured in 2006 from three main divisions (Adecco Staffing, Ajilon Professional, and Lee Hecht Harrison Career Services) to six global divisions.

Chairman Klaus Jacobs owns more than 20% of the company.

HISTORY

Accountant Henri-Ferdinand Lavanchy founded Adia in 1957 when a client asked him to find someone to fill a job. The company expanded internationally in the 1960s with offices in Belgium and elsewhere in Europe and entered the US in 1972. When Adia went public in Switzerland in 1979, Lavanchy retired from active management. Martin Pestalozzi succeeded him. The US operation, Adia Services, went public in 1984.

Pestalozzi's management group was ousted when retailer Asko Deutsche Kaufhaus and Swiss investor Klaus Jacobs bought about 50% of Adia in 1991 after a scandal involving the sale of part of the company to Swiss financier (later fugitive) Werner Ray. Jacobs bought out Asko in 1993, as well as Adia's US investors, bringing US operations under company ownership again.

Adia and Ecco SA, one of the top French employment services companies, merged in 1996 to form Adecco. (Adia chairman Jacobs and Ecco chairman Philippe Foriel-Destezet began a revolving chairmanship and former Adia executive John Bowmer became CEO.) After the merger, Adecco bought ICON Recruitment (IT recruiting, Australia; 1996), Seagate Associates (outplacement consulting, New Jersey; 1997), and Massachusetts-based TAD Resources International, the largest private staffing services company in the US, in 1997. The company bought rival Olsten's staffing and IT business in 2000 to further solidify Adecco as the world's largest temporary staffing firm.

Adecco restructured around four divisions (Adecco Staffing, Ajilon Staffing and Managed Services, Career Services, and e-Recruiting and Executive Search) in 2001. In 2002 Klaus retired from the company; Bowmer became chairman and 10-year company veteran Jérôme Caille took over as CEO. Adecco sold jobpilot, an online job board, to Monster Worldwide in 2004. In 2005 the company acquired French human resources firm Altedia. Caille left the company in 2005 and Jacobs came back onboard as chairman and interim CEO. In 2006 Dieter Scheiff was named as the new CEO.

EXECUTIVES

Chairman: Klaus J. Jacobs, age 68
CEO: Dieter C. Scheiff
CFO: Jim Fredholm, age 54
CIO: Franco Gianera
Chief of Internal Audit: Michel Tcheng
Chief Legislative, Public Affairs, and CSR Officer: Enrique de la Rubia
Chief Marketing and Communication Officer: Francois Vassard
SVP Public Relations and Global Marketing Partnerships: Ian Grundy
Corporate Secretary: Hans R. Brütsch
Treasurer: Jörg Salmini
Treasury: Patrick Dobler
Vice Chairman, Adecco Spain: Luis Sanchez de Leon
CEO, Adecco USA: Ray Roe
CEO, UK and Ireland: René Schuster, age 44
CEO, LHH Career Services Division and Group Chief HR Officer: Stephen G. (Steve) Harrison
COO, Adecco USA: Joyce Russell
CFO, Adecco USA: Stephen Nolan
SVP and General Counsel, Adecco Group North America: George M. Reardon
SVP Human Resources, Adecco USA: Leo Loucas
Chief Marketing and Communications Officer: Gonzalo Fernandez-Castro
Interim General Counsel: Tundé Johnson
Head, Investor Relations: Nicole Burth Tschudi, age 33
Auditors: Ernst & Young AG

LOCATIONS

HQ: Adecco S.A.
Sägereistrasse 10, 8152 Glattbrugg, Zürich, Switzerland
Phone: +41-44-878-8888 **Fax:** +41-44-829-8888
US HQ: 175 Broad Hollow Rd., Melville, NY 11747
US Phone: 631-844-7800 **US Fax:** 631-844-7363
Web: www.adecco.com

Adecco has offices in more than 70 countries and territories.

2005 Sales

	% of total
Europe	67
North America	20
Asia/Pacific	11
Other regions	2
Total	**100**

PRODUCTS/OPERATIONS

2005 Sales

	% of total
Staffing services	88
Professional staffing	11
Career services	1
Total	**100**

COMPETITORS

Administaff	Robert Half
Gevity HR	Spherion
Kelly Services	Synergie
Manpower	TAC Worldwide
MPS	Vedior
Onet	Volt Information
Randstad	Westaff

HISTORICAL FINANCIALS

Company Type: Public

Income Statement
FYE: Sunday nearest December 31

	REVENUE ($ mil.)	NET INCOME ($ mil.)	NET PROFIT MARGIN	EMPLOYEES
12/05	21,678	537	2.5%	735,284
12/04	23,521	453	1.9%	729,635
12/03	20,199	379	1.9%	678,081
12/02	18,047	255	1.4%	679,000
12/01	16,288	(255)	—	700,000
Annual Growth	**7.4%**	**—**		**1.2%**

2005 Year-End Financials

Debt ratio: 34.1%
Return on equity: 21.8%
Cash ($ mil.): 1,004
Current ratio: 1.25
Long-term debt ($ mil.): 855
No. of shares (mil.): —
Dividends
  Yield: 1.4%
  Payout: 6.1%
Market value ($ mil.): —

Stock History

NYSE: ADO

	STOCK PRICE ($) FY Close	P/E High/Low		PER SHARE ($) Earnings	Dividends
12/05	11.54	5	4	2.77	0.17
12/04	12.65	10	6	1.69	0.14
12/03	16.11	—	—	—	0.09
12/02	9.54	—	—	—	0.13
12/01	13.50	—	—	—	0.12
Annual Growth	**(3.8%)**	**—**	**—**	**63.9%**	**9.1%**

adidas

Jesse Owens and Muhammad Ali broke records in their adidas athletic shoes. The heart of the adidas product line is athletic shoes, but the three-stripe logo appears on apparel and other jock accoutrements. Bankruptcy once had it on the ropes, but it made a comeback by shifting production to Asia and beefing up its marketing. The #2 maker of sporting goods worldwide, behind NIKE, it has inked deals with football and basketball athletes, as well as the New York Yankees. The firm won sponsorship rights to the 2008 Olympic Games in Beijing. Its purchase of Salomon, the French maker of ski and golf gear, was short-lived. It sold the unit to Amer Sports Corp. and bought Reebok in 2006 for some $3.8 billion.

Having already put its footprint on athletic shoe history and widely recognized for its exper-

tise in engineering footwear, adidas has been missing two integral components: a brand as strong and as global as Nike's and a sturdy foundation in the US market. With its acquisition of Reebok, adidas now has the traction it needs to cross both components off its wish list. To boot, adidas, through its purchase of Reebok, has greatly expanded its portfolio of licensed brands, has gotten a leg up on the urban market, and has begun to chip away at Nike's long-running status as the world's #1 footwear firm that controls more than 20% of the US athletic shoe market.

The athletic shoemaker has plans for global expansion, particularly in China where adidas aims to overtake Nike by the 2008 Beijing Olympics. The company secured a strong foothold in US professional sports in April 2006, when adidas inked an 11-year deal to be the official supplier of uniforms and other products to the National Basketball Association.

adidas makes athletic clothing and gear such as TaylorMade golf clubs and Mavic bike components. (adidas products account for nearly 80% of sales.) To return to its core competencies and focus on its more profitable apparel, footwear, and golf sectors, adidas sold its Salomon division to equipment maker Amer Sports Corp., a unit of Amer Group, in late 2005. The deal included the Arc'Teryx, Bonfire, Cliche, Mavic, and Salomon businesses. The company changed its name, as a result, in May 2006 to adidas Group.

HISTORY

adidas grew out of an infamous rift between German brothers Adi and Rudi Dassler, who created athletic shoe giants adidas and Puma. As WWI was winding down, Adi scavenged for tires, rucksacks, and other refuse to create slippers, gymnastics shoes, and soccer cleats at home. His sister cut patterns out of canvas. By 1926 the shoes' success allowed the Dasslers to build a factory. At the 1928 Amsterdam Olympics, German athletes first showcased Dassler shoes to the world. In 1936 American Jesse Owens sprinted to Olympic gold in Dassler's double-striped shoes.

Business boomed until the Nazis commandeered the Dassler factory to make boots for soldiers. Although both Rudi and Adi were reportedly members of the Nazi party, only Rudi was called to service. Adi remained at home to run the factory. When Allied troops occupied the area, Adi made friends with American soldiers — even creating shoes for a soldier who wore them at the 1946 Olympics. Rudi came home from an American prison camp and joined his brother; together they scavenged the war-torn landscape for tank materials and tents to make shoes.

Soon a dispute between the brothers split the business. Rumors circulated that Rudi resented that Adi had failed to use his American connections to help spring him from prison camp. Rudi set up his own factory facing Adi across the River Aurach. The brothers never spoke to each other again, except in court. Rudi's company was named Puma, and Adi's became adidas. Adi added a third stripe to the Dassler's trademark shoe, while Rudi chose a cat's paw in motion. Thus began one of the most intense rivalries in Europe. The children of Puma and adidas employees attended separate elementary schools, and the employees even distinguished themselves by drinking different beers.

With Adi's innovations throughout the late 1940s and 1950s (such as the replaceable-cleat soccer shoe), adidas came to dominate the world's athletic shoe market. In the late 1950s it capitalized on the booming US market, overtaking the canvas sneakers made by P.F. Flyers and Keds. The company also initiated the practice of putting logos on sports bags and clothing.

In the 1960s and 1970s, adidas continued to expand globally to maintain its dominant position. However, a flood of new competitors following the 1972 Munich Olympics and the death of Adi in 1978 signaled the end of an era. As NIKE and Reebok captured the North American market during the 1980s, adidas made one of its biggest missteps — it turned down a sneaker endorsement offer from a young Michael Jordan in 1984.

French politician and entrepreneur Bernard Tapie bought the struggling company in 1989, but he stepped down in 1992 amid personal, political, and business scandals. The following year Robert Louis-Dreyfus became CEO. He shifted production to Asia, pumped up spending on advertising, and brought in former NIKE marketing geniuses to re-establish the company's identity.

adidas became adidas-Salomon in 1997 with its $1.4 billion purchase of Salomon, a French maker of skis and other sporting goods. The company also opened its first high-profile store in Portland, Oregon, that year. In a 1998 reorganization, Louis-Dreyfus sacked Jean-Francois Gautier as Salomon's president in the wake of disappointing sales, particularly from TaylorMade Golf, Salomon's golf subsidiary.

Amid a 10% slide in revenue, several key executives decided to leave the company in 2000, including adidas America CEO Steve Wynne. Citing poor health, Louis-Dreyfus soon followed (but remained as chairman); he was replaced by the new CEO of adidas America, Ross McMullin, who soon after was diagnosed with cancer.

In 2001 Louis-Dreyfus retired as chairman and in March COO Herbert Hainer became chief executive. In early 2003 adidas was delisted from the Paris Euronext exchange due to low trading volume. The company remains listed on the Frankfurt Stock Exchange. Britain's Barclays Bank PLC became adidas' largest shareholder in 2004, raising its stake to 5.4%.

EXECUTIVES

Chairman and CEO: Herbert Hainer, age 51
Deputy Chairman, Supervisory Board: Hans Friderichs, age 74
Deputy Chairman, Supervisory Board: Fritz Kammerer, age 60
CFO: Robin Stalker, age 47
President and CEO, adidas Brand: Erich Stamminger, age 48
President and CEO, Reebok Brand: Paul Harrington
President and CEO, TaylorMade-adidas Golf: Mark King
Director, Global Operations: Glenn Bennett, age 42
President, adidas Golf: John Kawaja
President, adidas North America: Rob Langstaff, age 42
Managing Director, Central Area: Ulli Gritzhuhn
Managing Director, India: Andreas Gellner
Head of Asia/Pacific Region: Christophe Bezu, age 46
SVP, Sales, adidas America: Russ Hopcus
Chief Corporate Communications Officer: Jan Runau
Head of Investor Relations: Natalie M. Knight
Head of Global Brand Marketing, adidas Brand: Eric Liedtke
Director of Retail, adidas USA: Kerry Barnes
Director of Marketing Communications: Britt Jorgenson
Director of Sports Marketing: Kevin Wulff
General Counsel: Frank Dassler
Auditors: KPMG Deutsche Treuhand-Gesellschaft AG

LOCATIONS

HQ: adidas AG
Adi-Dassler-Strasse 1-2,
91074 Herzogenaurach, Germany
Phone: +49-9132-84-0   **Fax:** +49-9132-84-2241
US HQ: 5055 N. Greeley Ave., Portland, OR 97217
US Phone: 971-234-2300   **US Fax:** 971-234-2450
Web: www.adidas-group.com

2005 Sales

	% of total
Europe	48
North America	24
Asia	23
Latin America	5
Total	**100**

PRODUCTS/OPERATIONS

2005 Sales

	% of total
adidas	85
TaylorMade-adidas golf	10
Discontinued operations	5
Total	**100**

2005 Sales

	% of total
Footwear	45
Apparel	42
Hardware	13
Total	**100**

Selected Brands

adidas (footwear and apparel for basketball, cycling, running, soccer, and tennis)
Maxfli (golf balls and accessories)
Reebok (footwear and apparel)
TaylorMade (golf clubs, accessories)

COMPETITORS

Amer Sports	Mizuno
Benetton	New Balance
Callaway Golf	NIKE
Converse	PUMA
Fila USA	Rollerblade
Fortune Brands	Rossignol
Head	Sara Lee
Head-Tyrolia-Mares	Trek
Huffy	Under Armour
K2	Victoria's Secret Stores
K-Swiss	

HISTORICAL FINANCIALS

Company Type: Public

Income Statement

FYE: December 31

	REVENUE ($ mil.)	NET INCOME ($ mil.)	NET PROFIT MARGIN	EMPLOYEES
12/05	7,859	462	5.9%	15,935
12/04	8,836	429	4.9%	16,342
12/03	7,866	327	4.2%	15,686
12/02	6,837	240	3.5%	14,716
12/01	5,414	185	3.4%	13,941
Annual Growth	**9.8%**	**25.8%**	**—**	**3.4%**

Net Income History

OTC: ADDDY

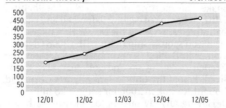

AEGON

Not only has AEGON expanded across Europe, it has also spread Transamerica. The Dutch life insurance giant is using its expertise in acquisition (US rival Transamerica was its largest catch) and consolidation to build a transnational collection of financial services businesses. Its subsidiaries operate primarily in the US, the Netherlands, and the UK, offering personal and commercial life and accident insurance, as well as retirement and savings advice and management services. Its US operations also offer life, nonmedical health, and long-term insurance, and sell annuities and other retirement products. AEGON also has banking operations in the Netherlands.

The company, which derives about 80% of its revenues from life insurance, is expanding in Asia and the Pacific including its Beijing-based insurance joint venture with the Chinese National Offshore Oil Corporation (CNOOC). AEGON also operates in the Czech Republic, Hungary, Spain, Slovakia, and Taiwan. It acquired the Polish operations of Nationwide Insurance in 2005. The following year, AEGON acquired a 49% stake in Mexican insurer Seguros Argos and announced plans to form a venture with Ranbaxy in India.

AEGON has sold its German subsidiary AEGON Lebensversicherngs-AG, which operates as MoneyMaxx, to Deutscher Ring.

Focusing on life insurance and pensions, the company has sold most of the business of its Transamerica Finance subsidiary (which had been on the market since 1999) to GE Commercial Finance; Transamerica Finance's real estate tax unit was sold to First American, and the company has sold the European trailer leasing business of Transamerica Finance to a joint venture held by Goldman Sachs and Cerberus Capital Management. AEGON has also been focusing on broadening its distribution channels, which include independent agents, brokers, direct response, workplace marketing, banks, and other financial institutions.

Vereniging AEGON, an independent trust, owns 12% of AEGON.

HISTORY

AEGON traces its roots to 1844, when former civil servant and funeral society agent J. Oosterhoff founded Algemeene Friesche, a burial society for low-income workers. The next year a similar organization, Groot-Noordhollandsche, was founded. These companies later became insurers and expanded nationwide. Meanwhile Olveh, a civil servants' aid group, was founded in 1877. The three companies merged in 1968 to form AGO Holding.

AEGON's other operations came from different traditions. Vennootschap Nederland was founded in 1858 as a *tontine* (essentially a death pool, with the survivors taking the pot) by Count A. Langrand-Dumonceau, an ex-French Foreign Legionnaire from Belgium. In 1913 the company merged with Eerste Nederlandsche, whose accident and health division had been previously spun off as Nieuwe Eerste Nederlandsche.

A year after Vennootschap was founded, C. F. W. Wiggers van Kerchem founded a similar scheme, Nillmij, in the Dutch East Indies. The government promoted Nillmij to colonial civil servants and military people, and for a while the company enjoyed a monopoly in the colony.

Nillmij's Indonesian operations were nationalized after independence in 1957, but its Dutch subsidiaries continued to operate. All insurers were hit by fast-growing postwar government social programs. As a result, industry consolidation came early to the Netherlands. In 1969 Eerste Nederlandsche, Nieuwe Eerste Nederlandsche, and Nillmij merged to form Ennia.

The shrinking Dutch insurance market forced companies to look overseas. AGO moved into the US in 1979 by buying Life Investors; by 1982 half of its sales came from outside the Netherlands. Ennia, meanwhile, expanded in Europe (it entered Spain in 1980) and the US (buying Arkansas-based National Old Line Insurance in 1981).

AGO and Ennia merged in 1983 to form AEGON. The company made more purchases at home and abroad and spent much of the rest of the decade assimilating operations.

AEGON's US units accounted for about 40% of sales in the mid-1980s, and the firm increased that figure with acquisitions. In 1986 it bought Baltimore-based Monumental Corp. (life and health insurance) and expanded the company's US penetration.

This left AEGON underrepresented in Europe, as deregulation paved the way for economic union, and social service cutbacks spurred opportunities in private financial planning in the region. So in the 1990s AEGON began buying European companies, including Regency Life (UK, 1991) and Allami Biztosito (Hungary, 1992). It formed an alliance with Mexico's Grupo Financiero Banamex in 1994. This reduced its reliance on US sales. It continued buying specialty operations in the US, particularly asset management lines.

In 1997 AEGON began to concentrate on life insurance and financial services and shed its other operations. It bought the insurance business of Providian (now part of Washington Mutual) and sold noncore lines, such as auto coverage. The next year it sold FGH Bank (mortgages) to Germany's Bayerische Vereinsbank (now Bayerische Hypotheken und Vereinsbank) and in 1999 sold auto insurer Worldwide Insurance.

That year AEGON expanded further in the US with the $9.7 billion purchase of Transamerica and bought the life and pensions businesses of the UK's Guardian Royal Exchange. In 2000 the company sold Labouchere N.V., a Dutch banking subsidiary, to Dexia. Also in 2000 AEGON acquired UK-based third-party administrator HS Administrative Services.

EXECUTIVES

Chairman of the Supervisory Board:
Dudley G. (D.G.) Eustace, age 70
Vice Chairman of the Supervisory Board: O. John Olcay, age 70
Chairman of the Executive Board: Donald J. Shepard, age 60, $6,539,240 pay
Member of the Executive Board and CFO:
Joseph B.M. Streppel, age 57, $1,148,000 pay
Member of the Executive Board and CEO, AEGON Nederland N.V.: Johan G. van der Werf, age 54, $1,334,706 pay
Member of the Executive Board:
Alexander R. Wynaendts, age 46, $1,353,654 pay
EVP, Group Legal and Compliance: Erik Lagendijk
EVP, Group Finance and Information:
Ruurd A. van den Berg
EVP, Group Treasury: C. Michiel van Katwijk

SVP, Group Business Development: Marc A. van Weede
SVP, Group Tax: Adri D. J. Verzijl
SVP, Group Risk: Tom M. P. Grondin
SVP, Group Corporate Affairs: Guy Nielsen
VP, Group Corporate Responsibility: Charles Henderson, age 43
Company Secretary: Peter Tuit
Company Secretary: J. Onno van Klinken
President and CEO, AEGON USA, Inc.:
Patrick S. (Pat) Baird, age 52
CEO, AEGON UK: Otto Thoresen, age 50
CFO, AEGON UK: Mark Laidlaw, age 40
Auditors: Ernst & Young Accountants

LOCATIONS

HQ: AEGON N.V.
AEGONplein 50,
2591 TV The Hague, The Netherlands
Phone: +31-70-344-3210   **Fax:** +31-70-347-5238
US HQ: 1111 N. Charles St., Baltimore, MD 21201
US Phone: 410-576-4571   **US Fax:** 410-347-8685
Web: www.aegon.com

AEGON operates worldwide, but primarily in the Netherlands, the UK, and the US.

PRODUCTS/OPERATIONS

Selected Subsidiaries and Affiliates

ÁB-AEGON Általános Biztosító Rt. (Hungary)
AEGON Asset Management UK plc
AEGON Bank N.V.
AEGON España S.A. (99.98%; Spain)
AEGON Financiële Diensten B.V.
AEGON International N.V.
AEGON Levensverzekering N.V.
AEGON Life Insurance (Taiwan) Inc.
AEGON NabestaandenZorg N.V.
AEGON Nederland N.V.
AEGON Schadeverzekering N.V.
AEGON Spaarkas N.V.
AEGON UK Distribution Holdings Ltd.
AEGON UK plc
AEGON USA, Inc. (US)
AEGON Vastgoed Holding B.V.
AEGON-CNOOC Life Insurance Company Ltd. (50%, insurance joint venture)
Commonwealth General Corporation (US)
First AUSA Life Insurance Company (US)
Guardian Assurance plc (UK)
Guardian Linked Life Assurance Limited (UK)
Guardian Pensions Management Limited (UK)
HS Administrative Services Limited (UK)
Life Investors Insurance Company of America (US)
Meeùs Groep B.V.
Monumental Life Insurance Company (US)
Peoples Benefit Life Insurance Company (US)
Scottish Equitable International Holdings plc (UK)
Scottish Equitable plc (UK)
Spaarbeleg Kas N.V.
Stonebridge Casualty Insurance Company (US)
Stonebridge Life Insurance Company (US)
TKP Pensioen B.V.
Transamerica Corporation (US)
Transamerica Financial Life Insurance Company, Inc (US)
Transamerica Life Canada
Transamerica Life Insurance and Annuity Company (US)
Transamerica Life Insurance Company (US)
Transamerica Occidental Life Insurance Company (US)
Veterans Life Insurance Company (US)
Western Reserve Life Assurance Co. of Ohio (US)

COMPETITORS

AIG	MetLife
Allianz	New York Life
AXA	Prudential
CIGNA	Prudential plc
Citigroup	Royal & Sun Alliance
Fortis SA/NV	Insurance
The Hartford	Swiss Life
ING	Winterthur
Legal & General Group	Zurich Financial Services
Merrill Lynch	

HISTORICAL FINANCIALS

Company Type: Public

Income Statement

	ASSETS ($ mil.)	NET INCOME ($ mil.)	INCOME AS % OF ASSETS	EMPLOYEES
12/05	372,911	2,468	0.7%	27,159
12/04	335,678	1,951	0.6%	27,446
12/03	298,455	1,923	0.6%	27,707
12/02	253,195	(2,440)	—	26,659
12/01	238,722	560	0.2%	25,663
Annual Growth	11.8%	44.9%	—	1.4%

FYE: December 31

2005 Year-End Financials

Equity as % of assets: 8.4%   Dividends
Return on assets: 0.7%   Yield: —
Return on equity: 8.8%   Payout: —
Long-term debt ($ mil.): 125,571   Market value ($ mil.): —
No. of shares (mil.): —   Sales ($ mil.): 53,902

Stock History

NYSE: AEG

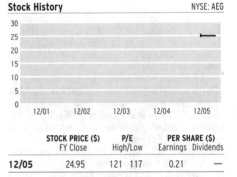

	STOCK PRICE ($) FY Close	P/E High/Low		PER SHARE ($) Earnings	Dividends
12/05	24.95	121	117	0.21	—

Agrium

It's no bull that Agrium is a top producer and marketer of fertilizers in North America. A leader in the production of nitrogen, the company operates plants in Canada, the US, and Argentina that produce mostly nitrogen (though also potash and phosphate) products. The plants have the capacity to produce more than 8 million tons of the nutrients per year. In addition to supplying wholesalers, Agrium operates more than 200 fertilizer retail outlets in the US in 21 states and more than 30 retail farm centers in South America. The company also owns 50% of Profertil, a joint venture with Spain's Repsol YPF that runs Argentina's largest nitrogen plant.

In early 2005 Agrium expanded its operations in Argentina, Bolivia, and Chile by acquiring retail businesses of United Agri Products (UAP) South America. The retail outlets focus on selling branded crop protection chemicals. It operates 33 of the retail farm centers in Argentina, four in Chile, and two in Bolivia.

Agrium expanded its retail business even more in the US by acquiring control of the outstanding Income Deposit Securities of Royster-Clark ULC and Royster-Clark Ltd in 2006. Royster-Clark is a major distributor of agricultural nutrients and seed and crop protection products in the US. Agrium also acquired two divisions of US-based Spectrum Brands' Nu-Gro subsidiary.

HISTORY

Agrium was formed in 1992 to facilitate the reorganization of Cominco's fertilizer division and to acquire the fertilizer business of the Alberta Energy Company (1993). Cominco was founded in 1896 as the Smelting and Refining Company when Fritz Heinze fired up his first smelter at Trail Creek Landing, British Columbia. Using the ores of the nearby Rossland mines, the company soon diversified into other products (such as fertilizers) and new metallurgical technologies. In 1906 the Smelting and Refining Company, the Rossland mines, and the nearby St. Eugene Mine merged to form the Consolidated Mining and Smelting Company of Canada Limited.

During WWI the Canadian government conscripted all the company's lead, zinc, and chemical production and instructed the company to make explosive-grade ammonium nitrate at its fertilizer plants. Cominco became the company's official name in 1966.

Alberta Energy was formed in 1973 to lessen Alberta's dependence on foreign oil, in response to the OPEC oil embargo. In 1989 its petrochemical division established fertilizer (ammonium nitrate) subsidiaries in the US.

Agrium was established to compete in the rapidly consolidating fertilizer market (the number of North American ammonia producers fell from 55 in 1980 to 26 at the end of 1996). The phosphate and potash industries also consolidated, albeit on a smaller scale.

Between 1993 and 1996 the company expanded its US operations by acquiring Crop Protection Services and Western Farm Service (both retail operations), AG-BIO (the phosphate-based fertilizer business of Imperial Oil), and Nu-West Industries. Agrium expanded into South America in 1995 by opening retail sales units for selling fertilizer, agricultural chemicals, and other services in the farming regions of Argentina.

In 1996 Agrium acquired Viridian, a Canadian fertilizer producer with nitrogen- and phosphate-based fertilizer plants in Alberta. Expanding its supply base, the company bought a phosphate mine in Alberta in 1997. The company also bought back 10% of its shares in 1998.

Agrium opened a phosphate rock mine in Ontario in 1999 to replace its reliance on phosphate rock imported from West Africa. In 2000 Agrium bought Unocal's nitrogen-based fertilizer operations for around $325 million. That year Agrium's Profertil nitrogen plant, a joint venture with Spain's industrial giant Repsol-YPF, began production in Argentina, but the plant was shut down by a government agency following an accidental discharge of ammonia. The plant was reopened later in 2000. Agrium also increased its nitrogen production capacity some 60% with the acquisition of Unocal's agricultural products division.

EXECUTIVES

Chairman: Frank W. Proto, age 63
President, CEO and Director: Michael M. (Mike) Wilson, $2,111,359 pay
SVP, Finance and CFO: Bruce G. Waterman, $778,645 pay
SVP, Corporate Development and Strategy: Andrew K. Mittag
SVP, Agrium; President, Wholesale: Ronald A. (Ron) Wilkinson, $652,982 pay
SVP; President, Retail: Richard L. Gearheard
SVP, General Counsel and Corporate Secretary: Leslie A. O'Donoghue
SVP, Human Resources: James M. Grossett

VP and Treasurer: Patrick J. Freeman
VP, Supply Management: Christopher W. (Chris) Tworek
Manager, Investor Relations: Christine Gillespie
Auditors: KPMG LLP

LOCATIONS

HQ: Agrium Inc.
13131 Lake Fraser Dr. SE,
Calgary, Alberta T2J 7E8, Canada
Phone: 403-225-7000   **Fax:** 403-225-7609
US HQ: 4582 S. Ulster St., Ste. 1700, Denver, CO 80237
US Phone: 303-804-4400   **US Fax:** 303-804-4482
Web: www.agrium.com

Agrium has operations in Argentina, Bolivia, Canada, Chile, and the US.

2005 Sales

	$ mil.	% of total
US	1,846	56
Canada	745	22
Argentina	222	7
Other	481	15
Total	**3,294**	**100**

PRODUCTS/OPERATIONS

2005 Sales

	$ mil.	% of total
Wholesale		
Nitrogen	1,622	47
Phosphate	313	9
Potash & other operations	265	8
Retail		
Fertilizers	626	18
Chemicals	458	13
Other products	158	5
Adjustments	(148)	—
Total	**3,294**	**100**

Subsidiaries and Affiliates

Agrium Nitrogen Company (US)
Agrium Partnership
Agrium U.S. Inc.
Agroservicios Pampeanos SA (Argentina)
Canpotex Limited (International, 33%)
Crop Production Services, Inc. (US)
Nu-West Industries, Inc. (US)
Profertil SA (50%, Argentina)
Viridian Fertilizers Ltd.
Viridian Inc.
Western Farm Service, Inc. (US)

COMPETITORS

BASF AG
CF Industries
K+S
Koch
PotashCorp
SQM
Terra Industries
Yara

HISTORICAL FINANCIALS

Company Type: Public

Income Statement

FYE: December 31

	REVENUE ($ mil.)	NET INCOME ($ mil.)	NET PROFIT MARGIN	EMPLOYEES
12/05	3,294	270	8.2%	4,719
12/04	3,001	263	8.8%	4,617
12/03	2,499	(38)	—	4,667
12/02	2,083	(39)	—	4,829
Annual Growth	16.5%	—	—	(0.8%)

2005 Year-End Financials

Debt ratio: 37.3%   No. of shares (mil.): —
Return on equity: 25.5%   Dividends
Cash ($ mil.): 300   Yield: 0.4%
Current ratio: 2.24   Payout: 5.2%
Long-term debt ($ mil.): 442   Market value ($ mil.): —

Stock History

NYSE: AGU

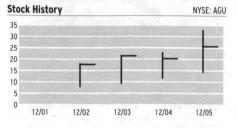

	STOCK PRICE ($) FY Close	P/E High	/Low	PER SHARE ($) Earnings	Dividends
12/05	25.62	15	7	2.12	0.11
12/04	20.25	12	6	1.89	0.11
12/03	21.39	—	—	(0.25)	0.11
12/02	17.70	—	—	(0.31)	0.17
Annual Growth	13.1%	—	—	—	(13.5%)

Air France

It's blue skies ahead for Air France, one of two main subsidiaries of Europe's leading airline company, Air France-KLM. Air France and KLM operate independently from their respective hubs in Paris and Amsterdam, but the carriers are working to coordinate their businesses. Together, they serve about 250 destinations worldwide with a fleet of some 565 aircraft. Air France offers regional as well as long-haul service, and its fleet of about 390 planes includes more than 130 devoted to regional operations. Air France and KLM extend their worldwide networks as members of the SkyTeam marketing alliance, which also includes carriers such as Alitalia, Delta Air Lines, Korean Air Lines, and Northwest Airlines.

The holding company Air France-KLM was formed when Air France bought KLM in 2004. Since the deal's completion the two airlines have managed to wring considerable savings from their combined operations. The carriers' cargo businesses have been brought together as Air France-KLM Cargo. In addition, Air France and KLM are saving money by working together on aircraft maintenance.

Along with its airline operations, Air France offers airport catering through its Servair unit and owns a 23% interest in the computer reservation system Amadeus.

HISTORY

Société Air France was founded in 1933, the product of consolidation during the adolescence of French aviation. The government that year forced a four-way merger of France's competing airlines: Air Union, Air Orient, Société Générale de Transport Aérien, and Compagnie Internationale de Navigation Aérienne.

Air France expanded during the 1930s to become one of the world's leading airlines, but its ascent was interrupted by WWII and the German occupation, during which the carrier shuttered operations.

Air France resumed flight after the war, and as the French state began nationalizing some industries to quickly rebuild the postwar economy, it took control of the airline in 1948. Renamed Compagnie Nationale Air France, the carrier enjoyed government-backed financing that allowed it to launch its expansion.

With the era of big jets dawning, Air France began adding Boeing 707s to its fleet in 1960. Then France and the UK agreed in 1962 to jointly develop a supersonic transport — the Concorde. The next year French authorities realigned France's airline industry: International flights to Africa, Australia, and the Pacific were granted to a private carrier, Union de Transports Aériens (UTA); Air France controlled the remaining international routes. The domestic market was closed to both.

Air France added more jets to its fleet in the early 1970s and launched its cargo transport services. The company began flying the Concorde in 1976. Though spiraling development costs had made the Mach 2 jetliner a debatable investment, the supersonic transport served as a symbol of national pride.

In 1987 Air France joined in creating the Amadeus computer reservation system (launched 1989). The late 1980s were boom times in the industry, with Air France scoring healthy profits. But its attempt to take control of the domestic market by buying Air Inter was challenged by UTA, which increased its Air Inter stake in opposition. The battle was resolved in 1990: Air France bought control of both airlines.

But this French consolidation came just as the Gulf War, high oil prices, and an economic downturn began to wreak havoc on airlines. Air France fell into a money-losing streak just as deregulation in Europe was about to unleash new levels of competition. The government slapped down chairman Christian Blanc's attempt to cut wages and jobs in 1993 in the face of massive strikes. The airline eventually slimmed down and achieved net profits in 1997; Blanc, however, resigned in 1997 as the state dragged its feet on privatization.

With the 1998 signing of a US-France open skies agreement, Air France boosted flights to the US and struck code-sharing deals with Delta and Continental. The government finally launched a public offering of Air France in 1999 (keeping 63%, later reduced).

To better compete with members of the Star and Oneworld global airline marketing alliances, Air France joined Delta Air Lines, AeroMéxico, and Korean Air Lines to form the SkyTeam alliance in 2000. Also that year Air France further consolidated the domestic market by acquiring or upping stakes in regional carriers Proteus Airlines, Flandre Air, and Regional Airlines.

An Air France Concorde jet crashed shortly after takeoff from Paris in 2000, killing all 109 people on board and four more on the ground. Concorde flights were grounded after the crash, but resumed the following year.

Air France fared better than most airlines in the wake of September 2001 terrorist attacks on the US. The airline curbed its expansion plans and streamlined its fleet, but did not cut back on routes or resort to layoffs to stay aloft. Instead, Air France began looking for ways to grow, and it began talks with Dutch carrier KLM in 2002. Initially the carriers discussed forming an alliance, but discussions soon developed into the merger kind. By 2003 the two carriers were looking into how to combine their respective operations and announced their intent to merge.

The European Commission threw a wrench in the deal when it launched an investigation in early 2004 into potential anti-competitive elements of the merger. The investigation could have taken months to complete and slowed the roll-out of the new airline. The Commission, however, approved the merger rather quickly when the two airlines agreed to give up 94 slots per day between their airports to ensure a competitive market amongst European airlines.

Air France shareholders approved a capital increase to facilitate the acquisition of KLM in 2004. That same year it signed a codeshare agreement with Australia's Qantas Airways.

Early in 2005 Air France became the first European airline to say it would add the new Airbus A380 super jumbo to its fleet. Also that year Air France sold its 30% stake in Air Austral to French bank Credit Agricole.

EXECUTIVES

Chairman and CEO: Jean-Cyril Spinetta, age 63
President and COO: Pierre-Henri Gourgeon, age 60
CFO: Philippe Calavia, age 58
EVP, Air France Cargo: Marc Boudier, age 56
EVP, Air France Industries: Alain Bassil, age 51
EVP, Commercial France: Christian Boireau, age 56
EVP, Flight Operations: Gilbert Rovetto, age 59
EVP, Ground Operations: Pascal de Izaguirre, age 49
EVP, International Commercial Affairs:
 Patrick Alexandre, age 51
EVP, Marketing and Network Management:
 Bruno Matheu, age 43
EVP, Social Policy: Jean-François Colin, age 58
SVP, Corporate Communications: François Brousse
SVP, Information Technology: Edouard Odier
VP, Finance: Catherine Guillouard, age 39
Secretary General: Jacques Pichot, age 59
Regional Manager, Vietnam: Louis Vergeon, age 53
Sales Manager, Vietnam: Pham Hy Thinh
Auditors: Constantin Associés; Deloitte Touche
 Tohmatsu

LOCATIONS

HQ: Air France
 45, rue de Paris, 95747 Roissy, France
Phone: +33-1-41-56-78-00   **Fax:** +33-1-41-56-56-00
US HQ: 125 W. 55th St., 2nd Fl., New York, NY 10019
US Phone: 212-830-4000   **US Fax:** 212-830-4244
Web: www.airfrance.com

COMPETITORS

Aer Lingus	Ryanair
Air Berlin	SAS
AMR Corp.	Singapore Airlines
British Airways	SNCF
Delta Air Transport	Swiss
easyJet	UAL
Iberia	Virgin Atlantic Airways
Lufthansa	Virgin Express

HISTORICAL FINANCIALS

Company Type: Subsidiary

Income Statement
FYE: March 31

	REVENUE ($ mil.)	NET INCOME ($ mil.)	NET PROFIT MARGIN	EMPLOYEES
3/04*	15,018	113	0.8%	71,654
3/03	13,696	130	0.9%	71,525
3/02	10,899	133	1.2%	70,156
3/01	10,790	370	3.4%	64,717
3/00	9,861	338	3.4%	59,190
Annual Growth	11.1%	(23.9%)	—	4.9%

*Most recent year available

2004 Year-End Financials

Debt ratio: 100.7%	Current ratio: 2.78
Return on equity: 2.4%	Long-term debt ($ mil.): 4,980
Cash ($ mil.): 402	

Net Income History

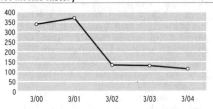

Airbus

Dare you imagine 550-800 people in one airplane? Airbus, which has moved past Boeing as the world's #1 commercial aircraft maker, is betting that airlines will love its huge double-decker A380 (maiden flight completed in 2005; due out in 2007) for hub airports. The company's current planes include single-aisle (A318, A319, A320, A321) and wide-body (A300, A310, A330, A340) models with capacities ranging from about 110 to 400 passengers.

Airbus has also announced that it will build a new mid-sized plane, the A350. Due out in 2010 and based on the A330 platform, the A350 will compete directly against Boeing's upcoming 787 Dreamliner.

European Aeronautic Defence & Space Company (EADS) owns Airbus; UK-based BAE SYSTEMS sold its 20% stake back to EADS in 2006. EADS consists of DaimlerChrysler Aerospace (Germany), Aerospatiale Matra (France), and CASA (Spain). Each company oversees part of the production; for example, aircraft wings hail from the UK, cockpits are from France, and interiors come from Germany. Airbus plants in France and Germany assemble the parts.

With the A350 — due in 2010, three years behind the 787 — the company has hedged its bets. Before the A350 announcement, Airbus had been banking on its jumbo A380 (which received brisk orders even before it was formally approved — so much so that Boeing scrapped plans for a competing plane), a steady increase in passenger air travel and air cargo transport, new flight routes, and the need for more midsized, long-range aircraft for future success.

Airbus delivered more planes than Boeing for the first time ever in 2003, 305 to 281, and repeated the feat in 2004, 320 to 285. Airbus maintained a slim lead in the orders race in 2005, racking up 1,055 orders to Boeing's 1,002; it also delivered more planes than Boeing again, 378 to 290.

Airbus CEO Noël Forgeard left to become co-CEO of EADS in mid-2005. Former Airbus chief operating officer Gustav Humbert replaced Forgeard as Airbus' CEO.

In mid-2006 Airbus announced there would be additional delivery delays of the A380 of up to six or seven months. An announcement of the delays came weeks after Forgeard had made a suspiciously timed stock transaction that netted him just over $3 million. In an effort to quell the waning confidence of investors and customers

Forgeard and Humbert resigned. Former Saint-Gobain COO Christian Streiff was named to replace Humbert. Some of Airbus' airline customers are seeking compensation for the delays, or are considering taking their business elsewhere (Boeing).

Later in 2006 EADS announced still more delays in the delivery of Airbus' first A380s. Airbus' parent company said the latest round of delays stemmed from an underestimation in June 2006 regarding the amount of work involved in the installation of electrical harnesses in the front and rear areas of the fuselage.

EADS said the first A380s would not be delivered until the second half of 2007. Deliveries for the A380 in the coming years as forecasted by EADS are: 2008 — 13 aircraft, 2009 — 25, 2010 — 45.

Along with the announcement of delivery delays, EADS outlined a recovery plan dubbed POWER8. The scheme aims to achieve €5 billion in cumulated cash savings by 2010 and €2 billion in sustainable, annual cash savings thereafter. The plan will also reduce development cycles by two years while boosting overall productivity by 20%. Airbus is also reviewing its European production sites and may announce job cuts. Additionally, the company has announced it will streamline operations by reducing its number of suppliers from 3,000 to about 500.

After the dust settled from the delay announcements, Christian Streiff stepped down as Airbus CEO with only three months under his belt. Louis Gallois, co-CEO of EADS, was named to replace him.

Late in 2006 FedEx became the first Airbus customer to cancel when it said it would not buy the 10 A380s it had ordered. Citing Airbus' repeated production delays and an urgent need for more freight capacity, FedEx said it would instead pay $3.5 billion for 15 Boeing 777s, and place an option to buy 15 more later.

HISTORY

In the 1970s three US companies, Boeing, Lockheed, and McDonnell Douglas, dominated the commercial aircraft market. France and the UK had been discussing an alliance to build competing jets since 1965, but political infighting stalled the talks. Finally, in 1969 France and West Germany committed to building the Airbus A300. Airbus Industrie was born in 1970 as a *groupement d'intérêt économique* (grouping of economic interest, a structure used by allied French vineyards). Seed money came from partners Aerospatiale Matra and Deutsche Airbus. CASA joined in 1971.

The A300 entered service with Air France in 1974, but Airbus had trouble selling it outside member countries. The following year the firm hired former American Airlines president George Warde to help market the A300 in the US. His efforts paid off when Eastern Air Lines decided to buy the A300. Also in 1975 Airbus launched the A310, a smaller, more fuel-efficient version of the A300. The UK joined the consortium in 1979.

By 1980 Airbus trailed only Boeing among the world's commercial jet makers. The A320 was introduced in 1984 — it featured a groundbreaking "fly-by-wire" system that allowed pilots to adjust the aircraft's control surfaces via a computer, helping to make it the fastest-selling jetliner in history. The firm launched the A330 and A340, larger planes designed for medium- and long-range flights, in 1987. Two

years later Airbus introduced the A321, an elongated version of the A320, and received a $6 billion order from Federal Express.

The German government sold its 20% stake in Deutsche Airbus to Daimler-Benz (now DaimlerChrysler) in 1992, giving Daimler-Benz 100% ownership of the German partner (now about 38%).

In 1993 Airbus sold only 38 planes, about one-sixth as many as Boeing. Sales rebounded in 1995, and the next year the firm won a contract worth about $5 billion to provide planes to USAir (now US Airways). The four Airbus partners agreed in 1997 to restructure the consortium as a limited liability company, possibly as a first step toward taking it public.

In 1998 Airbus won orders from Iberia Airlines and three Latin American carriers, then landed orders from longtime Boeing customers British Airways and UPS, narrowing the gap with its chief rival.

Seeking more customers in Asia, Airbus signed parts contracts with Japanese suppliers in 1999 and launched production of its A318, a 107-seat short-haul passenger jet designed to compete with Boeing's 717. Also that year Airbus won a contract worth $946 million to provide British Airways with up to 24 of its A318s. For the first time ever, the company recorded more plane orders than Boeing.

In 2000 the company said it had finally inked a deal to turn Airbus into a corporation. It also committed to producing the superjumbo A3XX and soon received 17 firm orders from Air France and Emirates Airlines. Airbus officially launched the A3XX (renamed the A380) late in 2000. Early in 2001 Airbus announced that it would become a stand-alone corporation (rather than a consortium) before the end of the year. In July Airbus Industrie was incorporated in France as Airbus S.A.S.

Faced with the drastic downturn in the commercial aviation market due to the September 11 attacks, in 2002 the company announced that it would cut full-time equivalent work hours by around 13% (equal to about 6,000 jobs) through voluntary retirement, reduction in part-time work, and cancellation of temporary contracts.

Airbus unveiled the first A380 to press and buyers in January of 2005, and the plane made its maiden test flight of nearly four hours on April 27, 2005. Late in 2005 six Chinese airlines agreed to buy 150 A320s worth about $10 billion.

EXECUTIVES

President and CEO; Co-CEO; European Aeronautic Defence and Space: Louis Gallois, age 62
COO: Fabrice Brégier, age 44
CFO: Andreas Sperl, age 59
CFO: Hans Peter Ring, age 55
EVP, Military Programmes: Juan Carlos Martinez Saiz
EVP, Human Resources: Geoff Lloyd
EVP, Operations: Karl-Heinz Hartmann, age 55
EVP, Procurement: Henri Courpron, age 43
EVP, Programmes: Tom Williams, age 54
EVP, and Head of A380 Programme: Alain Flourens, age 49
EVP, Strategy and Co-Operation: Olivier Andriès
COO, Customer and Chief Commercial Officer: John J. Leahy, age 56
Chairman, Airbus North America Holdings, Inc.: T. Allan (Allan) McArtor

SVP; General Manager, Airbus España: Manuel Hita-Romero, age 61
SVP, COO, and Head of A380 Programme: Mario Heinen, age 50
SVP; General Manager, Airbus France: Jean-Marc Thomas
SVP; General Manager, Airbus Germany: Gerhard Puttfarcken, age 60
SVP; General Manager, Airbus UK: Iain Gray, age 49
President, Airbus China: Laurence Barron, age 55
President and CEO, Airbus Japan: Glen S. Fukushima, age 57

LOCATIONS

HQ: Airbus S.A.S.
 1, Rond point Maurice Bellonte,
 31707 Blagnac, France
Phone: +33-5-61-93-33-33 **Fax:** +33-5-61-93-49-55
US HQ: 198 Van Buren St., Ste. 300, Herndon, VA 20170
US Phone: 703-834-3400 **US Fax:** 703-834-3341
Web: www.airbus.com

Airbus S.A.S. has offices in China, North America, and Singapore, and it manufactures airplanes in factories throughout Europe, with final assembly carried out in France and Germany.

PRODUCTS/OPERATIONS

Selected Aircraft
Single-aisle twin-engine jets
 A318
 A319
 A320
 A321

Superjumbo four-engine jets
 A380 (555-passenger, scheduled for delivery in 2007)

Wide-body twin-engine jets
 A300-600
 A300-600F
 A310

Wide-body two- and four-engine jets
 A330 (two-engine)
 A340 (four-engine)
 A340-500
 A340-600
 A350-800 (245-passenger, scheduled for delivery in 2010)
 A350-900 (285-passenger, scheduled for delivery in 2010)

Selected Customers
Aer Lingus
Air Canada
Air France
Alitalia
America West
American Airlines
China Southern
Delta
Federal Express
Iberia
Japan Air System
Korean Airlines
Lufthansa
Northwest
SilkAir (Singapore Airlines)
United
US Airways
Virgin Atlantic Airways

COMPETITORS

Boeing
Boeing Commercial Airplanes
Boeing UK
Bombardier
Bombardier Aerospace
Embraer
Gulfstream Aerospace
Sextant Avionique

HISTORICAL FINANCIALS

Company Type: Subsidiary

Income Statement				FYE: December 31
	REVENUE ($ mil.)	NET INCOME ($ mil.)	NET PROFIT MARGIN	EMPLOYEES
12/05	26,410	—	—	55,000
12/04	27,280	—	—	53,000
12/03	24,225	—	—	50,000
12/02	20,333	—	—	46,000
12/01	18,159	—	—	45,000
Annual Growth	9.8%	—	—	5.1%

Revenue History

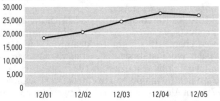

Akzo Nobel

Akzo Nobel is the world's largest paint maker, but it can do more than paint a picture. The company is among the world's largest chemical manufacturers and also is a major salt producer. Akzo Nobel is organized along three business lines. The company's coatings group makes paints, automotive finishes, and decorative coatings. Its chemical unit produces pulp and paper chemicals, functional chemicals (including flame retardants and crop nutrients), surfactants, polymers, and catalysts. A third unit, pharmaceuticals, produces contraceptives, fertility treatments, antidepressants, antipsychotics, over-the-counter drugs, and veterinary medicines. Akzo has announced plans to split off its pharmaceuticals division.

Coming off a difficult 2003, Akzo Nobel spent much of 2004 trimming down, divesting three businesses (phosphorous chemicals, catalysts, and coating resins) from its chemicals segment. The three transactions netted the company $1 billion, which it intends to use to buffer the coatings segment.

The fruits of those sell-offs came with 2005 acquisitions in Germany, France, and Switzerland. That last purchase, of Swiss Lack, made Akzo Nobel the largest paint company in Switzerland as well. The following year the company made a bigger purchase, with the acquisition of Canadian coatings maker Sico for $285 million.

Also in 2006 Akzo Nobel decided to further pare down its operations with the sale of its inks and adhesive resins business to Hexion Specialty Chemicals. The business is concentrated in Europe but has strong international operations as well.

The company's pharmaceutical business has been hurt in recent years by the end of patent protection in the US on its top-selling drug, the antidepressant Remeron. A management reorganization in the unit led to a rethinking of strategy. Akzo Nobel now actively seeks out partnerships in the manufacture and marketing of its drugs.

Early in 2006 Akzo announced plans to split off the pharmaceuticals division, called Organon. If all goes as planned, the company will float a minority share early in 2007 and then fully separate the new company — to be known as Organon Biosciences — by 2009.

HISTORY

The Akzo side of Akzo Nobel traces its roots to two companies — German rayon and coatings maker Vereinigte Glanzstoff-Fabriken (founded in 1899) and Dutch rayon maker Nederlandsche Kunstzijdebariek (founded in 1911 and known as NK or Enka). In 1928 NK built a plant near Asheville, North Carolina, in what later became the town of Enka. The two companies merged in 1929 to create Algemene Kunstzijde-Unie (AKU).

In 1967 two Dutch companies merged to form Koninklijke Zout-Organon (KZO). In 1969 KZO bought US-based International Salt and merged with AKU to form Akzo. In the 1980s Akzo focused on building its chemicals, coatings, and pharmaceuticals businesses. Akzo sold its paper and pulp business to Nobel in 1993. A few months later the company reclaimed that business when it bought Nobel.

Best remembered for the prizes that bear his name (which were first awarded in 1901 through a bequest in his will), Alfred Nobel invented the blasting cap in 1863, making it possible to control the detonation of nitroglycerin. He then persuaded Stockholm merchant J. W. Smitt to help him finance Nitroglycerin Ltd. to make and sell the volatile fluid (1864). Nobel's quest to improve nitroglycerin led to his invention of dynamite in 1867.

After Nobel's death in 1896, Nitroglycerin Ltd. remained an explosives maker, and in 1965 it changed its name to Nitro Nobel. In 1978 Swedish industrialist Marcus Wallenberg bought Nitro Nobel for his KemaNord chemical group, known afterward as KemaNobel. Within six years industrialist Erik Penser controlled both armaments maker Bofors and KemaNobel, and he merged them in 1984 as Nobel Industries.

Risky investments led Penser to ruin in 1991. His holdings, including Nobel, were taken over by a government-owned bank and conveyed into Securum, a government-owned holding company (which still owns 18% of Akzo Nobel). In 1992 Nobel spun off its consumer-goods segment.

Akzo bought Nobel in 1994. Although the company had good financial results in 1995, it faced pressure from rising costs for raw materials and a difficult foreign-exchange environment. Akzo announced major closings and layoffs — it sold its polyethylene packaging resin business and moved some clothing-grade rayon operations to Poland.

The merger between Akzo and Nobel was legally completed in 1996. That year the company introduced Puregon, a fertility drug, and Remeron, touted as a replacement for Prozac, in the US and other countries. In 1997 Akzo Nobel put most of its worst-performing segment, fibers, into a joint venture with Turkish conglomerate Sabanci. It also sold its North American salt unit to Cargill.

Akzo Nobel acquired Courtaulds (coatings, sealants, and fibers) in 1998 and changed the firm's name to Akzo Nobel UK. Akzo Nobel also bought BASF deco, the European decorative-coatings business of BASF Coatings. Akzo Nobel combined its fiber business with Akzo Nobel UK to form a new division, Acordis. Akzo Nobel then sold Acordis to investment firm CVC Capital

Partners in 1999 for $859 million (Akzo Nobel retains a minority share). Also in 1999 Akzo Nobel bought Hoechst's animal-health unit, Hoechst Roussel Vet, for $712 million. The next year the company bought Dexter Corporation's aircraft coatings business.

In 2001 Akzo Nobel sold its medical diagnostics division to French drugmaker bioMérieux-Pierre Fabre. Later that year the company picked up the vehicle refinishes business of MAC Specialty Coatings of the US. In November Akzo Nobel agreed to sell its printing inks business to a private equity firm.

CEO Cees van Lede retired in May 2003, succeeded by Hans Wijers, who immediately set about restructuring, cutting costs, and erasing debt. By the end of that year more than 3,300 jobs were cut and Akzo Nobel had sold off three big chemical units: catalysts (to Albemarle for about $750 million), coating resins, and phosphorous chemicals (to Ripplewood Holdings for another $270 million).

In late 2005 Akzo Nobel acquired a 60% stake in Egypt-based powder coatings manufacturer Coatech For Chemical Industries SAE; the new joint venture will change its name to Akzo Nobel Powder Coatings.

EXECUTIVES

Chairman, Supervisory Board: Jonkheer Aarnout Loudon, age 69
Chairman, Board of Management and CEO: G. J. (Hans) Wijers, age 55, $1,723,156 pay
Member, Board of Management and CFO: Rob Frohn, age 46, $1,107,320 pay
Member, Board of Management, Chemicals: Leif Darner, age 54, $1,107,320 pay
Member, Board of Management, Pharma; President, Organon: A.T. M. (Toon) Wilderbeek, age 56, $1,107,320 pay
SVP, Finance: Frits H. Hensel, age 62
SVP, Human Resources: Heiko Hutmacher, age 46
General Counsel: A. Jan A. J. Eijsbouts
Secretary: G.H. (Han) Jalink
Senior Group Director, Chemicals; President and Treasurer, Akzo Nobel, Inc.: Conrad S. Kent
Senior Group Director, Coatings; General Manager, Car Refinishes: M. (Rinus) Rooseboom, age 59
Senior Group Director, Pharmaceuticals: Jan H. Dopper
Corporate Information Officer: Bill Stubbins, age 50
Corporate Director, Corporate Social Responsibility and Health, Safety, and Environment: André Veneman, age 45
Director, Internal Auditing: Paul Grimmelikhuizen, age 51
Director, Corporate Strategy: Derek Welch
Auditors: KPMG Accountants N.V.

LOCATIONS

HQ: Akzo Nobel N.V.
Velperweg 76, 6800 SB Arnhem, The Netherlands
Phone: +31-26-366-4433 **Fax:** +31-26-366-3250
US HQ: 525 W. Van Buren St., Chicago, IL 60607
US Phone: 312-544-7000 **US Fax:** 312-544-7320
Web: www.akzonobel.com

Akzo Nobel has operations throughout the world.

2005 Sales

	$ mil.	% of total
Europe		
Germany	1,466.3	10
The Netherlands	1,020.9	7
UK	958.2	6
Sweden	611.2	4
Other	4,826.4	31
US & Canada	2,842.5	19
Asia	1,883.2	12
Latin America	983.1	6
Other regions	805.4	5
Total	**15,397.2**	**100**

PRODUCTS/OPERATIONS

2005 Sales and Operating Income

	Sales $ mil.	% of total	Operating Income $ mil.	% of total
Coatings	6,579.3	43	454.8	26
Chemicals	4,607.3	30	369.5	21
Organon	2,872.3	19	491.5	28
Intervet	1,295.7	8	281.9	16
Other	42.6	—	162.3	9
Total	**15,397.2**	**100**	**1,760.0**	**100**

Selected Products

Coatings
  Car refinishes
  Decorative coatings
  Industrial finishes
  Industrial products
  Marine and protective coatings
  Powder coatings

Chemicals
  Base chemicals
  Energy
  Functional chemicals
  Polymer chemicals
  Pulp and Paper chemicals
  Salt
  Surface chemistry

Pharmaceuticals
  Drugs for human health care (including oral
    contraceptives, antidepressants, and infertility
    treatments)
  Pharmaceutical ingredients
  Veterinary medicines (including antibiotics, vaccines,
    and anti-infectives)

COMPETITORS

Abbott Labs	Hempel
Alfa	Hercules
Asahi Kasei	Imperial Chemical
BASF AG	Industries
Bayer	Kemira
Bristol-Myers Squibb	Merck
Compass Minerals	Novo Nordisk
Degussa	Orica
Dow Chemical	PPG
DuPont	Rohm and Haas
Eastman Chemical	RPM
Eli Lilly	Sherwin-Williams
Ferro	Solvay
Formosa Plastics	Valspar
GlaxoSmithKline	Wyeth
H.B. Fuller	

HISTORICAL FINANCIALS

Company Type: Public

Income Statement

FYE: December 31

	REVENUE ($ mil.)	NET INCOME ($ mil.)	NET PROFIT MARGIN	EMPLOYEES
12/05	15,397	841	5.5%	61,340
12/04	17,312	1,135	6.6%	60,350
12/03	16,388	702	4.3%	66,400
12/02	14,738	902	6.1%	67,900
12/01	12,544	397	3.2%	66,300
Annual Growth	**5.3%**	**20.6%**	**—**	**(1.9%)**

2005 Year-End Financials

Debt ratio: 40.3%
Return on equity: 10.3%
Cash ($ mil.): 1,760
Current ratio: 1.79
Long-term debt ($ mil.): 3,200

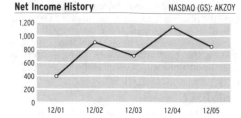

Net Income History

NASDAQ (GS): AKZOY

Alcan

Its Alcan-do attitude has helped make Alcan one of the world's largest aluminum producers, behind the US's Alcoa and just ahead of Russia's RUSAL. The company controls 13% of the world's aluminum production capacity. It mines bauxite (aluminum ore) and makes and recycles aluminum sheet, foil, wire and cable, and extrusions (doors, windows, auto parts). Alcan also generates hydroelectric power and makes aluminum-related specialty chemicals and packaging products. This decade has proved busy for Alcan. It bought Algroup in 2000, Pechiney in 2003, and spun off its aluminum rolled products unit into a public company called Novelis in early 2005.

Finally settled down following the additions of Algroup and Pechiney and the divestiture of Novelis, Alcan runs its business through four segments: Packaging, Engineered Products, Primary Metal, and Bauxite and Alumina.

Alcan's packaging segment includes aluminum, plastic, paperboard, glass, and steel products for a variety of industries. The engineered products group makes cable and wire along with composite materials. The primary metal division runs smelting operations, power generation, and manufacture of anodes and fluoride. Lastly, the bauxite and alumina unit mines bauxite and then refines it, making alumina.

The US accounts for close to a third of company sales. In early 2006 Alcan sold some of its US plastic packaging operations to Ball Corporation. The deal, for $180 million, divested three plastic bottle manufacturing facilities.

The company's purchase of VAW Flexible Packaging from Norsk Hydro ASA appreciably bolstered Alcan's packaging sector. The move was part of Alcan's strategic push to expand the global reach of its packaging business. The company also acquired a Polish flexible packaging plant that furthers its Central and Eastern European interests even more. Another move designed to increase its international business was the 2005 acquisition of the Malaysian tobacco packaging company CM Printing. The deal raised Alcan's presence in a region where many tobacco companies are ramping up production.

HISTORY

In 1886 American chemist Charles Hall and a French chemist simultaneously discovered an inexpensive process for aluminum production. Two years later Hall, with an investor group led by Captain Alfred Hunt, formed the Pittsburgh Reduction Company. It became the Aluminum Company of America (Alcoa) in 1907.

As mandated by a US antitrust divestment order, in 1928 Alcoa organized its Canadian and other foreign operations as a separate company, Aluminium Limited (which used the British spelling for *aluminum*). The new company retained close ties with Alcoa and appointed Edward Davis, brother of former Alcoa chairman Arthur Davis, its first chief executive.

After narrowly surviving the Depression, Aluminium Limited expanded globally, building plants in Asia and Europe. Aluminum demand during WWII made it the world's largest smelter by war's end.

US courts in 1950 ordered the Mellon and Davis families to end their joint ownership of Alcoa and Aluminium Limited. Both families opted to stay with Alcoa.

In 1961 the company began fabricating its own products in Oswego, New York. Aluminium Limited changed its name to Alcan in 1966. Alcan had to readjust its strategy when Guyana nationalized its raw resources in 1971. Six years later Jamaica (a major bauxite producer) acquired 70% of Alcan's assets, and the two formed joint venture Jamalcan.

David Culver became the company's CEO (the first non-Davis family member to hold the position) in 1979 and led Alcan through an early 1980s recession with a massive cost-cutting campaign. In 1989 Alcan built the world's largest aluminum beverage-can recycling plant in Berea, Kentucky.

The entrance of former Soviet republics and other Eastern Bloc countries into the international aluminum market in 1991 caused a drastic drop in aluminum prices worldwide. That year Alcan shut down 8% of its smelting capacity and began selling off less-profitable operations.

By 1994 increased global demand for aluminum and cutbacks in production spurred industrywide recovery, and Alcan's operations returned to the black for the first time in four years.

In 1998 Alcan signed a 10-year pact to supply aluminum to General Motors. As market conditions in Asia soured, Alcan reduced its ownership of Nippon Light Metal Company from 45% to about 11%. Also that year it sold Handy Chemicals Limited.

Facing tough market conditions in 1999, Alcan restructured into two divisions — primary metals (bauxite and alumina) and fabricated products (fabricated aluminum and recycling). The company also announced the sale of its alumina refinery in Ireland to Glencore International AG and agreed to acquire Pechiney and Alusuisse Lonza Group (Algroup) in a three-way merger to create Alcan-Pechiney-Algroup.

In 2000 the European Commission approved a proposed merger between Alcan and Algroup, but Alcan's plan to include Pechiney in a three-way merger had to be withdrawn because of antitrust concerns. Pechiney pulled out of the deal entirely after Alcan voted against selling its 50% stake in a German aluminum plant (Norf). Alcan acquired Algroup in a $5.3 billion deal.

Company president and CEO Jacques Bougie resigned in 2001 and was replaced by former ITT Industries CEO Travis Engen. To reflect its broader array of products, the company changed its name from Alcan Aluminium to Alcan Inc. that year.

Alcan acquired VAW Flexible Packaging from Norsk Hydro for around $545 million in 2003. Mid-year Alcan launched a hostile bid for French competitor Pechiney for roughly $3.9 billion in cash and stock. Pechiney's board members unanimously rejected Alcan's takeover bid indicating the offer was undervalued. Alcan raised its offer to $4.3 billion but Pechiney rejected that offer as well. The company countered a third time with a proposal of roughly $5 billion, which about 92% of Pechiney's shareholders accepted. Soon after, Alcan reopened its offering and gained another 7%, making its total ownership in Pechiney approximately 99%. In 2004 Alcan was granted the last remaining percentage, giving it full ownership in Pechiney.

In 2005 Alcan spun off its aluminum rolled products unit, known as Novelis, as a publicly traded company.

EXECUTIVES

Chairman: L. Yves Fortier, age 70
President, CEO, and Director: Richard B. (Dick) Evans, age 58
EVP and CFO: Michael Hanley, age 41
EVP, Corporate Development and Chief Legal Officer: David L. McAusland, age 52
SVP, Human Resources: Jean-Christophe Deslarzes, age 42
SVP, Corporate and External Affairs: Daniel Gagnier, age 60
SVP; President and CEO, Alcan Packaging: Ilene Gordon, age 53
SVP; President and CEO, Alcan Primary Metal Group: Cynthia Carroll, age 49
SVP, Alcan Inc.; President and CEO, Alcan Bauxite and Alumina: Jacynthe Côté, age 48
SVP, President and CEO, Alcan Engineered Products: Christel Bories, age 42
SVP, Alcan Inc.; President, Alcan France: Gaston Ouellet, age 64
SVP, President and CEO, Alcan Primary Metal Group: Michel Jacques, age 54
VP and Controller: Cesidio Ricci, age 41
VP and Treasurer: Rhodri J. Harries, age 42
VP, International Relations and Government Affairs: Thierry Berthoud
Corporate Secretary: Roy Millington, age 46
VP, Communications: Elizabeth Vassallucci
VP, Investor Relations: Corey B. Copeland
Chief Tax Officer: Michael O'Connor
Director, Information Technology and Corporate Services: Denis Lamontagne
Auditors: PricewaterhouseCoopers LLP

LOCATIONS

HQ: Alcan Inc.
    1188 Sherbrooke St. West,
    Montreal, Quebec H3A 3G2, Canada
Phone: 514-848-8000   **Fax:** 514-848-8115
US HQ: 8770 W. Bryn Mawr Ave., Chicago, IL 60631
US Phone: 773-399-8000
Web: www.alcan.com

Alcan operates bauxite mines in Australia, Brazil, and Ghana; alumina plants in Australia, Brazil, Canada, and the UK; and manufacturing plants or sales offices in more than 38 countries in Africa, Asia, Australia, Europe, and the Americas.

2005 Sales

	$ mil.	% of total
Europe		
France	2,244	11
Germany	1,989	10
UK	1,641	8
Switzerland	300	2
Other	3,333	16
US	5,944	29
Asia & Other Pacific	1,926	10
Canada	1,438	7
Brazil	420	2
Australia	221	1
Other	864	4
Total	**20,320**	**100**

PRODUCTS/OPERATIONS

2005 Sales

	$ mil.	% of total
Primary Metal	6,877	34
Engineered Products	6,015	30
Packaging	6,004	29
Bauxite & Alumina	1,478	7
Other	47	—
Adjustments	(101)	—
Total	**20,320**	**100**

Selected Products and Services
Fabrication Group
    Castings (automobile engine components, aluminum alloys)
    Extrusions (automobile components, doors, and windows; extrusion ingots)
    Flat-rolled products (foil and sheet)
    Flexible packaging
    Recycling
    Wire and cable
Primary Metal Group
    Alumina refining
    Aluminum activities
    Bauxite mining
    Power generation

COMPETITORS

Alcoa	Ormet
Alumina	Rio Tinto
Aluminum Corporation of China	Ryerson
Corus Group	SEPI
Hydro Aluminium	Sojitz
Imsa	Southwire
Kaiser Aluminum	Vale do Rio Doce

HISTORICAL FINANCIALS
Company Type: Public

Income Statement
FYE: December 31

	REVENUE ($ mil.)	NET INCOME ($ mil.)	NET PROFIT MARGIN	EMPLOYEES
12/05	20,320	129	0.6%	65,000
12/04	24,885	258	1.0%	82,500
12/03	13,640	77	0.6%	88,000
12/02	12,540	374	3.0%	48,100
12/01	12,626	5	0.0%	52,000
Annual Growth	**12.6%**	**125.4%**	**—**	**5.7%**

2005 Year-End Financials
Debt ratio: 55.5%
Return on equity: 1.3%
Cash ($ mil.): 181
Current ratio: 1.10
Long-term debt ($ mil.): 5,265
No. of shares (mil.): —
Dividends
Yield: 1.3%
Payout: 181.8%
Market value ($ mil.): —

Stock History
NYSE: AL

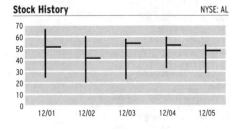

	STOCK PRICE ($) FY Close	P/E High/Low		PER SHARE ($) Earnings	Dividends
12/05	47.76	159	87	0.33	0.60
12/04	52.58	86	48	0.69	0.60
12/03	54.16	261	107	0.22	0.60
12/02	41.43	52	18	1.15	0.60
12/01	51.10	—	—	(0.01)	0.60
Annual Growth	**(1.7%)**	**—**	**—**	**—**	**0.0%**

Alcatel-Lucent

Alcatel-Lucent has found its calling. One of France's largest industrial companies, the company is a leading global supplier of high-tech equipment for telecommunications networks. Alcatel acquired rival Lucent Technologies for $11.6 billion in late 2006, forming a new organization called Alcatel-Lucent. The company provides core network switching and transmission systems for wireline and wireless networks for carriers and enterprises. Other products include cell phones, communications cable, and satellite equipment. The company also manufactures transport automation equipment and provides a wide array of services.

Former Alcatel chairman and CEO Serge Tchuruk (pronounced "cha-RUK") is chairman of the new combined company; Lucent chief Patricia Russo was named CEO. The new Alcatel-Lucent organization is made up of five business units: wireline, wireless, covergence, enterprise, and services.

The company has announced plans to sell its satellite and security holdings to Thales, which would increase its stake in the defense giant to about 22%. Alcatel-Lucent has agreed to acquire the UMTS access network assets of Nortel Networks for $320 million.

Tchuruk honed a once lumbering Alcatel with broad industrial interests into a focused telecom heavyweight. He has overseen an extensive restructuring that included the sale of noncore businesses such as electrical power, engineering, nuclear power, and defense electronics.

Alcatel bought iMagic and PacketVideo in 2003 as part of an effort to gain ground in the video networking market. It boosted its wireless equipment portfolio with the acquisition of mobile network switching products maker Spatial Wireless for $250 million in 2004. Alcatel also turned its attention to its IP routing products with the acquisitions of eDial and TiMetra that year.

HISTORY

In 1898 Pierre Azaria combined his electric generating company with three others to form Compagnie Générale d'Électricité (CGE). As one of Europe's pioneer electric power and manufacturing companies, CGE expanded operations in France and abroad through acquisitions. After the French government nationalized electric utilities in 1946, CGE diversified into the production of telecommunications equipment, consumer appliances, and electronics.

In 1970 CGE bought Alcatel, a French communications pioneer founded in 1879 that had introduced digital switching exchanges. CGE combined its telecom division with Alcatel to form CIT Alcatel.

The Mitterrand government nationalized CGE in 1982. The next year the company traded its electronics units for Thomson's communications businesses, making CGE the world's fifth-largest telephone equipment maker. Later, CGE combined Alcatel with ITT's phone equipment operations to form Alcatel NV, a Brussels-based company that started off as the world's second-largest telecom enterprise, after AT&T.

In 1987 the government sold CGE to the public. Two years later CGE and UK-based The General Electric Company, plc (GEC, now Marconi plc) combined their power systems and engineering businesses to create GEC Alsthom NV.

The company adopted the Alcatel Alsthom name in 1991 (shortened to Alcatel in 1998) and purchased the transmission equipment unit of US-based Rockwell International (now Rockwell Automation).

Turnaround specialist Serge Tchuruk, the former head of French oil giant TOTAL, was chosen to lead the company in 1995. Deregulation and intense competition in the European telecom market, along with massive writeoffs of bad investments dating back to the 1980s, led to a $5 billion loss in 1995, Alcatel's first loss and one of the largest to date by a French company. Alcatel divested nonstrategic assets and cut its workforce by more than 12,500 employees. The company bounced back with a profit in 1996.

Following the recommendation of the French government, in 1998 Alcatel, Dassault Industries, and Aerospatiale joined forces to buy part of the state's stake in defense electronics group Thomson-CSF (now Thales). Intensifying its telecommunications focus, Alcatel sold its main engineering unit (Cegelec) to GEC Alsthom in 1998 and then spun off the venture as ALSTOM. That year Alcatel bought networking specialists Packet Engines and DSC Communications to further push into the US market.

In 1999 Alcatel acquired several more US-based data network equipment makers, including Xylan and Assured Access. The next year it swapped all but 10% of its stake in nuclear power company Framatome for an additional 10% of Thomson-CSF. The company pressed further into the US that year with the purchases of Genesys Telecommunications (computer-telephony software) and Canadian equipment maker Newbridge Networks.

Alcatel changed the name of its power and communication cables business, one of the world's largest cable manufacturing operations, to Nexans in 2000. The company also sold 20% of its optical components unit to create the first European tracking stock.

In mid-2001 Alcatel spun off Nexans to the public (it sold its remaining minority stake in the company in 2004), sold its remaining stake in ALSTOM, and bought a controlling stake in its joint venture in China with Shanghai Bell. The company beefed up its line of fiber-optic products when it bought passive component maker Kymata that year.

In 2002 Alcatel sold its enterprise distribution and services operations in Europe to Platinum Equity. The company also sold several of its European manufacturing facilities to contractor Sanmina-SCI; items produced at these locations included point-to-point microwave systems and wireline network access systems.

The company added to its optical transport products for metro networks with the acquisition of startup Astral Point that year, and it announced that it would acquire privately held Telera, a US-based provider of software for making Web content accessible by phone, in order to strengthen Genesys' contact center software business. That year it sold its semiconductor business, Alcatel Microelectronics, to STMicroelectronics for about $345 million; the two companies will jointly develop chipsets for DSL networking equipment.

Alcatel in 2003 began a series of acquisitions intended to build its presence in the wireless, IP routing, and video markets. The company that year also sold its power systems unit, which comprised AEG SVS Power Supply Systems, Alcatel Converters, Harmer & Simmons, and the Saft Power Systems business lines.

EXECUTIVES

Chairman: Serge Tchuruk, age 68
CEO: Patricia F. (Pat) Russo, age 53
CFO: Jean-Pascal Beaufret, age 54
CTO: Olivier Baujard
SEVP, Integration and Chief Administrative Officer: Frank A. D'Amelio, age 48
President, Convergence Group: Marc Rouanne
President, Enterprise Group: Hubert de Pesquidoux
President, Science, Technology, and Strategy: Mike Quigley, age 52
President, Wireless Group: Mary Chan
President, Wireline Group: Michel Rahier
President, Asia/Pacific Region: Frederic Rose
President, North American Region: Cindy Christy
President, Bell Laboratories: Jeong H. Kim, age 45
President, Services Group: John A. Meyer, age 49
President, Europe and North Region: Vincent J. Molinaro
President, Integration Team: Christian Reinaudo, age 50
President, Carrier Business Group: Etienne Fouques, age 56
President, Europe and South Region: Olivier Picard
President, Caribbean and Latin America Region: Victor Agnellini
VP, Corporate Strategy: Helle Kristoffersen
VP, Corporate Human Resources and Communications: Claire Pedini
President, Iberian Regional Unit and Telefonica Group; CEO, Alcatel-Lucent España: Alfredo Redondo
General Counsel: William R. (Bill) Carapezzi Jr., age 48
Chief Marketing Officer: John P. Giere
VP, Corporate Communications: Caroline Guillaumin
VP, Investor Relations, North America: Charlotte Laurent-Ottomane
Press Contact, North America: Mary Lou Ambrus
Auditors: Deloitte & Associés

LOCATIONS

HQ: Alcatel-Lucent
54, rue La Boétie, 75008 Paris, France
Phone: +33-1-40-76-10-10   **Fax:** +33-1-40-76-14-00
US HQ: 600 Mountain Ave., Murray Hill, NJ 07974
US Phone: 908-582-8500   **US Fax:** 908-508-2576
Web: www.alcatel-lucent.com

2005 Sales

	% of total
Europe	
France	35
Germany	10
Other Western Europe	20
Other Europe	2
North America	15
Asia/Pacific	11
Other countries	7
Total	**100**

PRODUCTS/OPERATIONS

2005 Sales

	% of total
Fixed communications	39
Mobile communications	31
Private communications	30
Total	**100**

Selected Operations

Access systems
Core optical transmission equipment
Data switching and routing equipment
Enterprise networking systems
Metro optical transmission equipment
Mobile network transmission and switching equipment and software
Modems (ADSL, SHDSL)
Optical components
Optical fiber, cable, and connectivity hardware

Professional services
  Consulting
  Deployment
  Design
  Integration
  Maintenance
  Operation
  Planning
Satellite systems
Software
  Call center
  Messaging and billing
  Network management
  Operation support systems
  Service creation
Submarine systems
Telephones
Transport automation equipment
Video delivery products
Voice and multimedia switching equipment
Wireless access and transmission systems

Selected Subsidiaries and Affiliates

Alcatel SEL AG (Germany)
Alcatel USA, Inc.
Genesys Telecommunications Laboratories, Inc. (US)
Thales (9%)

COMPETITORS

3Com	Motorola
ADC Telecommunications	NEC
Avaya	Nokia
Cisco Systems	Nortel Networks
Corning	Oki Electric
DIRECTV	Panasonic Mobile
ECI Telecom	Communications
Ericsson	SAFRAN
Fujitsu	Siemens AG
Harris Corp.	telent
Hitachi	Tellabs
Juniper Networks	Toshiba

HISTORICAL FINANCIALS

Company Type: Public

Income Statement

	REVENUE ($ mil.)	NET INCOME ($ mil.)	NET PROFIT MARGIN	EMPLOYEES
12/05	15,554	903	5.8%	58,000
12/04	16,734	750	4.5%	55,718
12/03	15,782	(2,168)	—	60,486
12/02	17,350	(12,070)	—	75,940
12/01	22,811	(4,394)	—	99,314
Annual Growth	**(9.1%)**	**—**	**—**	**(12.6%)**

FYE: December 31

2005 Year-End Financials

Debt ratio: 31.6%
Return on equity: 9.2%
Cash ($ mil.): 6,099
Current ratio: 1.23
Long-term debt ($ mil.): 3,259

No. of shares (mil.): —
Dividends
  Yield: —
  Payout: —
Market value ($ mil.): —

Stock History

NYSE: ALU

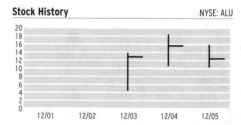

	STOCK PRICE ($) FY Close	P/E High/Low		PER SHARE ($) Earnings	Dividends
12/05	12.40	—	—	—	—
12/04	15.63	—	—	—	—
12/03	12.85	—	—	—	—
Annual Growth	**(1.8%)**				

ALDI

ALDI keeps it cheap so shoppers can, too. How has discount food retailer ALDI Group become one of the world's biggest grocery chains, running about 7,500 stores worldwide? By offering deeply discounted prices on about 700 popular food items (a typical grocery store has 25,000). No frills ALDI (short for "Albrecht Discounts") buys cheap land mostly on city outskirts, builds cheap warehouses, keeps a tiny staff, and carries mostly private-label items, displaying them on pallets rather than shelves. ALDI has 800-plus stores in 26 US states, but Germany (where ALDI has a 40% share of the grocery market) accounts for about two-thirds of sales. Brothers and co-founders Theo and Karl Albrecht own the company.

Although Spartan-like, the company's stores do sell housewares, textiles, electronic equipment, and garden supplies. But ALDI is better known for the products and services it doesn't offer, such as in-store banking, pharmacies, liquor, fresh meats and fish, and checkout newsstands. As penny-pinching as its customers, ALDI doesn't advertise and about 85% of ALDI's products are private labels. A pair of reclusive billionaires, the Albrecht brothers also own US specialty food retailer Trader Joe's, as well as a minority stake in supermarket operator Albertson's.

ALDI's discount market dominance is being challenged by its European competitors, including compatriot Lidl & Schwarz, who have emulated its low-cost operating methods while offering brand-name products, and stolen customers from ALDI. In response, ALDI has changed its private label strategy to begin offering more branded items from consumer goods makers such as Procter & Gamble and Unilever. In 2006 ALDI will increase its focus on brands and fresh produce. In a move that is likely to spark a massive price war in the German market for prepaid cellular service, ALDI recently launched its own brand of prepaid wireless phone service.

While ALDI operates in Germany, the US, and 10 other countries, it is missing out on the fast-growing markets in Eastern Europe, where it is not present. However, ALDI is growing rapidly in Australia, where it has about 100 outlets in New South Wales and Victoria, and in Ireland. The international limited-assortment grocery chain is also mulling over a move into the New Zealand market.

In the UK, where ALDI operates more than 275 stores, the discount retailer plans to open as many as 200 more outlets over the next five to seven years. The chain may also expand its Scandinavian business by opening stores in Sweden. (ALDI already does business in Denmark.)

The German discount supermarket chain entered the US market in 1976 and has grown to ring up annual sales here of about $5.0 billion. The discount grocery chain is expanding into new markets here, including Florida, where it has plans for more than 100 locations. It is also building a new regional headquarters and distribution center in Frederick, Maryland to serve its stores in the Baltimore-Washington, DC area.

HISTORY

Brothers Karl and Theo Albrecht began running their first grocery store in 1948 in the Ruhr Valley, Germany. By the late 1950s the quickly growing company ran about 350 Albrecht Discount stores in Germany, which were later abbreviated to ALDI. As business progressed in the early 1960s, Karl and Theo decided to go their separate ways and divided the company in half. (The company also introduced self-service stores at this time.) Karl began overseeing ALDI Sud (South), which would eventually encompass Australia, Austria, parts of Germany, Ireland, the UK, and the US. Brother Theo took ALDI Nord (North), which would grow to include Belgium, Denmark, France, parts of Germany, Luxembourg, and the Netherlands. (Austrian ALDI stores run under the Hofer banner.)

The firm remained notoriously private and secretive, especially following the 1971 kidnapping of Theo, who was taken by an Italian terrorist group known as the Red Brigade. He was released after the family paid the group's ransom demands.

ALDI broke US ground in 1976 when it opened its first store across the Atlantic. In 1979 the Albrecht brothers bought grocery store Trader Joe's (formerly Pronto Markets) from founder Joseph Coulombe.

The chain opened its first store in the UK in 1990 and had grown to about 250 stores there by the end of the 1990s. In 1999 Karl crossed over the Irish Sea, opening stores in Dublin and Cork. ALDI intends to dot its stores all over the Emerald Isle.

In February 2000 top cereal maker Kellogg agreed to make five cereals under ALDI's own Gletscher Krone brand. The cereals will be called Schoko Chips, Schoko Flakes, Honey Nut Flakes, Honey Balls, and White Flakes.

ALDI Sud went south literally in 2000, opening its first Australian location in Sydney. Another 100 stores were planned over the next couple of years. The company also opened stores in Spain.

In protest over a new German law imposing a mandatory deposit on aluminum cans and small bottles, ALDI stopped selling canned beer and soft drinks on January 1, 2003. To eliminate inventory the discounter cut the price of beer to as little as five cents a can at the end of 2002.

Co-founders Theo and Karl Albrecht stepped down as co-CEOs in 2003 and turned over the day-to-day operation of ALDI Sud to Ulrich Wolters and Norbert Podschlapp. Theo's son Theo Albrecht Jr. is the chief executive of ALDI Nord.

In November 2004 ALDI opened a distribution center in Scotland to support its expansion in the UK.

EXECUTIVES

Co-Chairman: Karl Albrecht, age 84
Co-Chairman: Theo Albrecht, age 81
CEO, ALDI Nord: Theo Albrecht Jr.
Co-CEO, ALDI: Norbert Podschlapp
Co-CEO, ALDI Sud: Ulrich Wolters, age 64
CFO: Dietmar Stewan
Group Managing Director, Australia: Michael Kloeters
Managing Director: Harman Wusman
President, ALDI USA: Charles Youngstrom
Divisional VP, ALDI USA: Dan Gavin
Director, Personnel: Painer Mobius
Director, Real Estate: Brian McGee
Director of Real Estate, Michigan: David Kapusansky
Director, Real Estate, Western New York: Lew Kibling

LOCATIONS

HQ: ALDI Group
Eckenbergstrasse 16, Postfach 13 01 110,
45307 Essen, Germany
Phone: +49-201-85-93-0   **Fax:** +49-201-85-93-31-9
US HQ: 1200 N. Kirk Rd., Batavia, IL 60510
US Phone: 630-879-8100   **US Fax:** 630-879-8152
Web: www.aldi.com

ALDI Group has operations in Australia, Austria, Belgium, Denmark, France, Germany, Ireland, Luxembourg, the Netherlands, Spain, the UK, and the US.

COMPETITORS

Albertsons
ASDA
AVA AG
Carrefour
Casino Guichard
Coles Myer
Co-operative Group
Costco Wholesale
Delhaize
Edeka Zentrale
E.Leclerc
Giant Eagle
ITM Entreprises
Kroger
Lidl & Schwarz Stiftung
METRO AG
Migros
Musgrave Budgens-Londis
Netto Foodstores
Publix
REWE-Zentral
Royal Ahold
Save-A-Lot Food Stores
Schlecker
SPAR Handels
SUPERVALU
Tengelmann
Tesco
Wal-Mart
Winn-Dixie
Woolworths Limited

HISTORICAL FINANCIALS
Company Type: Private

Income Statement
FYE: December 31

	ESTIMATED REVENUE ($ mil.)	NET INCOME ($ mil.)	NET PROFIT MARGIN	EMPLOYEES
12/04	37,000	—	—	—
12/03	35,000	—	—	—
12/02	32,500	—	—	—
12/01	30,000	—	—	—
12/00	27,500	—	—	—
Annual Growth	7.7%	—	—	—

Revenue History

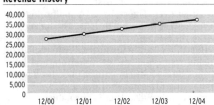

Alitalia

Alitalia – Linee Aeree Italiane is navigating its way through a major financial restructuring. Italy's leading airline, Alitalia serves more than 100 destinations worldwide from hubs in Rome and Milan with a fleet of some 175 aircraft, including those operated by regional unit Alitalia Express. Alitalia extends its network as a member of the SkyTeam code-sharing and marketing alliance, which also includes Air France, Continental Airlines, Delta Air Lines, KLM, and Northwest Airlines. As part of its restructuring, Alitalia has sold a controlling stake in its aircraft maintenance unit, Alitalia Servizi. The Italian government owns 49% of Alitalia and has agreed to sell about 25% by early 2007.

Italian state-owned holding company Fintecna took a 51% stake in Alitalia Servizi in 2005. Alitalia retains a 49% interest in the unit, which continues to work as a contractor for its former parent's airline operations.

Besides the spinoff of Alitalia Servizi, the restructuring of Alitalia has involved cost-cutting efforts, including workforce reductions. The company has also reduced its aircraft fleet, and it is working to use its planes more efficiently.

Alitalia sees itself occupying a middle ground between global mega-carriers and regional lowcost operators. It plans to continue to offer both long-haul and short-haul service and to promote its Rome and Milan hubs as natural connecting points between Western Europe and destinations in Eastern Europe, the Mediterranean, and the Middle East.

HISTORY

Alitalia got off the ground in 1946 as Alitalia Aerolinee Italiane Internazionali. The airline was 40%-owned by BEA (British European Airways, later part of British Airways) and 60%-owned by the Italian government. Alitalia was intended to be an international carrier; TWA and the Italian state set up Linee Aeree Italiane (LAI) for domestic flights.

Alitalia began flying in 1947 with a Turin-Rome-Catania route, and service to Africa and Brazil was launched from Rome in 1948. To better compete with other European carriers, Alitalia and LAI merged in 1957 and took the name Alitalia – Linee Aeree Italiane. The government bought the shares held by BEA and TWA and assigned Alitalia to IRI, the Italian state holding company. The new airline's fleet boasted 37 aircraft.

By 1960 Alitalia carried a million passengers and had introduced its first jets. By 1968 it had an all-jet fleet. The stylized "A" tailfin logo appeared a year later, and in 1970 Alitalia adopted use of the Boeing 747.

But Alitalia began losing money in the 1970s. Facing rising fuel prices, inflation, and labor strikes, it responded by cutting underused routes and buying fuel-efficient Boeing 727s.

In the early 1980s Alitalia diversified by creating Sigma (travel-related information systems) and Italiatour (tour operator). Diversification came, however, at the expense of the airline's expansion, and it began losing market share to rivals Air France and Lufthansa. In 1988 Alitalia brought in Carlo Verri from the private sector to deal with labor and structural problems. He secured labor contracts and developed aircraft financing, but his auspicious start ended with a

fatal car crash in 1989. Alitalia limped through the early 1990s with losses, aging equipment, and a reputation for poor service.

IRI hired former IBM executive Renato Riverso as chairman in 1994. With deregulation fast approaching, Alitalia penned code-sharing partnerships with Continental (1994) and Canadian Airlines (1995). In 1995 several labor strikes flared up amid talk of restructuring and cost-cutting measures. After receiving little government support, Riverso resigned in 1996. His short-lived reign laid a foundation: Labor tensions were eased with the promise of an employee-owned share in the company.

Europe's air transportation market was opened to competition in 1996 (after a long process that began in 1983). Alitalia began lowfare carrier Alitalia Team, signed on Italian regional airline Azzurra as a code-share partner the next year, and set up its own regional carrier, Alitalia Express. In 1997 it also achieved its first annual profit since 1988.

IRI reduced its stake in Alitalia to 53% in 1998, and employees got their 20% stake. Alitalia began an alliance with Dutch carrier KLM, and in 1999 Alitalia and KLM completed a "virtual merger" that unified their management structures for passenger and cargo joint ventures and allowed them to share profits. KLM ditched the partnership in 2000, however, and demanded Alitalia repay $91 million it had spent to upgrade an Italian airport. Alitalia protested KLM's termination of the alliance, and the dispute between the carriers wound up in arbitration proceedings. (Later, in 2002, A European court found KLM's reason for abandoning the deal insufficient and ordered the Dutch carrier to pay Alitalia 150 million euros.)

IRI was liquidated in 2000, and the state holding company's stake in Alitalia was transferred to the Treasury Ministry. In 2001 Alitalia said it would unload noncore assets, including its leisure division. The next year the company sold its reservation services unit, Sigma. That year the Italian government raised its stake in the airline from 53% to 62%. Alitalia posted a profit in 2002, but losses mounted the next year, and in late 2003 Alitalia cut some 1,500 jobs from its workforce of 21,000.

Early in 2004, the company was plagued with labor disputes, facing several strikes within a few weeks over a restructuring plan proposed by the board that called for a reduction of 2,700 jobs. It was forced to cancel hundreds of flights, leading to long delays and dismayed passengers.

The government then drafted its own plan for restructuring the airline, which led to the resignation of then-CEO Francesco Mengozzi. Another management shake-up occurred just months after the first when layoffs were once again put on the table. The government called for the resignations of Marco Zanichelli, who had replaced Mengozzi as CEO, and chairman Giuseppe Bonomi. The majority of the company's board of directors resigned shortly after it accepted Zanichelli's resignation. Giancarlo Cimoli, a veteran of national railroad Ferrovie dello Stato, subsequently took over as CEO.

The Italian government received approval in 2004 from the EU to grant the carrier a bridge loan of up to €400 million, which could be supplemented by private banks. In addition, the Italian government was required to reduce its stake from 62% to 49%.

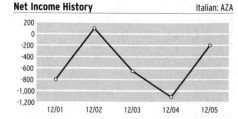

All Nippon Airways

All Nippon Airways (ANA) is Japan's second-largest carrier, behind Japan Airlines. With a fleet of more than 180 jets (mostly Boeings), ANA flies on about 140 routes in Japan and about 35 to destinations overseas. It extends its international network as a member of the Star Alliance marketing and code-sharing partnership, which includes carriers such as UAL's United Airlines and Deutsche Lufthansa. Besides passenger service, ANA's air transportation operations include cargo and mail hauling and aircraft maintenance and ground support. The company also provides international and domestic travel packages (ANA Hallo Tour and ANA Sky Holiday) and owns hotels.

Domestic passenger flights account for most of the company's air transportation business, but ANA sees international passenger service and cargo operations as its main growth areas.

The company is working to add routes between Japan and China, where it serves additional destinations via its code-sharing partnership with Air China. Another key to international growth for ANA is the expansion of Tokyo's Haneda Airport, where a fourth runway is under construction.

ANA plans to gradually add freighters to its cargo fleet, which consists of four Boeing 767-300s. Its cargo routes are focused on Asia, but also include US destinations. Much of the company's cargo service is provided through ANA & JP Express, or AJV, a joint venture with Japan Post, Nippon Express, and Mitsui O.S.K. Lines that was launched in 2006.

Also in 2006 ANA formed a hotel management joint venture with hospitality industry leader InterContinental Hotels Group (IHG). The new company, IHG ANA Hotels Group Japan, will manage ANA's 30-plus hotel properties, some under co-branding arrangements.

In addition to its air transportation, travel, and hotel businesses, ANA has interests in information services, logistics, and trading companies.

HISTORY

Two domestic Japanese air carriers that started in 1952 — Nippon Helicopter and Aeroplane Transport and Far East Airlines — consolidated operations in 1957 as All Nippon Airways (ANA).

Throughout the 1960s ANA developed a domestic route network linking Japan's largest cities — Tokyo, Osaka, Fukuoka, and Sapporo — and its leading provincial centers, including Nagoya, Nagasaki, Matsuyama, and Hakodate. During this period domestic traffic grew at an annual rate of 30% to 60%.

In 1970 the Japanese cabinet formulated routes for its major airlines, giving ANA scheduled domestic service and unscheduled international flights. That year Tokuji Wakasa became ANA's chairman, and the company began a program of diversification that led to the establishment of ANA Trading, international charter service (starting with Hong Kong), and a hotel subsidiary. Air Nippon, a regional domestic airline, was started in 1974.

The company established Nippon Cargo Airlines, a charter service set up jointly with four steamship lines, in 1978. ANA carried 19.5 million passengers that year, but its growth slowed between 1978 and 1980. High jet fuel prices caused a $45.6 million loss in 1979, but ANA rebounded a year later. In 1982 ANA opened international charter service to Guam. The company founded ANA Sports in 1984 to manage the company soccer team.

Japan deregulated air routes in 1985, allowing ANA to offer scheduled international flights. The airline offered its first regular flight from Tokyo to Guam in 1986 and soon added service to Los Angeles and Washington, DC. Flights to China, Hong Kong, and Sydney began a year later.

Between 1988 and 1990 ANA added flights to Bangkok, London, Moscow, Saipan, Seoul, Stockholm, and Vienna. In 1988 ANA bought a minority stake in Austrian Airlines and set up the domestic computer reservation system (CRS). The company's international CRS, INFINI (a joint venture with CRS co-op ABACUS), went online in 1990.

ANA started World Air Network Charter (WAC) in 1991 to serve travelers from Japan's smaller cities. That year ANA opened its first European hotel (in Vienna), was listed on the London Stock Exchange, and opened a flight school in the US for its pilots.

In 1992 ANA premiered a hotel in Beijing. In 1995 the airline announced that it would increase its international traffic by more than 30%. As part of this strategy ANA and Air Canada began a code-sharing service in 1996 between Osaka and Vancouver, and a year later ANA became the first Japanese airline to operate a Boeing 777 on an international route (between Tokyo and Beijing).

As the Asian financial crisis sent Japanese airlines to the brink, a pilot strike in 1998 dashed ANA's hopes for a 15% pay cut. To cope, ANA formed alliances with UAL's United Airlines, Lufthansa, and Brazil's VARIG. ANA extended those partnerships in 1999 by joining the global Star Alliance. To shore up its financial strength, ANA reorganized domestic routes, dropping some unprofitable ones and shifting others to its Air Nippon unit; it also announced plans to launch low-cost air service for international routes in Asia. Competition intensified when Japan fully deregulated domestic fares in 2000, sparking a fare war.

The following year ANA avoided a potentially costly strike and began working toward expanding through partnerships. However, terrorist attacks on the US caused a slump in worldwide air travel, and ANA was forced to cut back on its flights. Then ANA had to trim more routes in response to a worldwide slump in air travel in 2003 due to the SARS outbreak.

In order to develop its own cargo business, ANA sold its 27%-plus stake in Nippon Cargo Airlines to Nippon Yusen Kabushiki Kaisha in 2005.

EXECUTIVES

Chairman: Yoji Ohashi
President and CEO: Mineo Yamamoto
SEVP: Suguru Omae
SEVP: Hiromichi Toya
EVP: Kenichiro Hamada
EVP: Shinichiro Ito
EVP: Katsuhiko Kitabayashi
EVP: Shin Nagase
EVP: Koshichiro Kubo
SVP: Minoru Aimono
EVP: Masao Nakano
SVP: Osamu Asakawa
SVP: Kenkichi Honbo
SVP: Hiroyuki Ito
SVP: Katsuyori Kikuchi
SVP: Isamu Komatsu
SVP: Shinsuke Maki
SVP: Junji Onishi
SVP: Atsuro Takahashi
Auditors: Ernst & Young ShinNihon

LOCATIONS

HQ: All Nippon Airways Co., Ltd.
(Zen Nippon Kuyu Kabushiki Kaisha)
Shiodome City Center, 1-5-2 Higashi-Shimbashi,
Minato-ku, Tokyo 105-7133, Japan
Phone: +81-3-6735-1000   **Fax:** +81-3-6735-1005
US HQ: 1251 Avenue of the Americas, Ste. 820,
New York, NY 10020
US Phone: 212-840-3700   **US Fax:** 212-840-3704
Web: www.ana.co.jp

PRODUCTS/OPERATIONS

2006 Sales

	% of total
Air transportation	71
Travel services	13
Hotel operations	4
Other	12
Total	**100**

COMPETITORS

Accor
Air France-KLM
American Express
AMR Corp.
British Airways
Carlson Wagonlit
Cathay Pacific
Central Japan Railway
China Airlines
China Eastern Airlines
China Southern Airlines
Continental Airlines
Delta Air
East Japan Railway
EVA Air
Hyatt
Japan Airlines
Kintetsu Corp.
Korean Air
Northwest Airlines
Qantas
Singapore Airlines
Virgin Atlantic Airways
West Japan Railway

HISTORICAL FINANCIALS

Company Type: Public

Income Statement

FYE: March 31

	REVENUE ($ mil.)	NET INCOME ($ mil.)	NET PROFIT MARGIN	EMPLOYEES
3/06	11,640	227	2.0%	30,322
3/05	12,021	251	2.1%	29,098
3/04	11,526	234	2.0%	28,870
3/03	10,146	(236)	—	29,001
3/02	9,081	(71)	—	29,095
Annual Growth	**6.4%**	**—**	**—**	**1.0%**

Net Income History

Pink Sheets: ALNPY

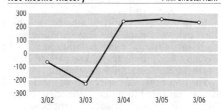

Allianz

One of the world's biggest insurers, Allianz SE (formerly Allianz AG) offers a range of insurance products and services — including life, health, and property/casualty — through some 100 subsidiaries and affiliates. The company's Allianz Global Investors unit manages private and institutional funds, and its Dresdner Bank subsidiary is one of Germany's largest banks, offering personal and corporate banking, wealth management, and business finance advisory services. In 2006 Allianz acquired the remainder of its majority-owned subsidiary Ras Holding and transformed itself into a Societas Europaea, a joint stock company that operates under European Union rules.

Both the acquisition and name change are part of the company's restructuring plans designed to sharpen its focus on European markets. Allianz had previously owned 55% of Italian insurer Ras (formerly Riunione Adriatica di Sicurtà); it bought out minority shareholders of the firm for about $7 billion.

Allianz is part of a web of interlocking German corporate ownership. It holds stakes in the country's top corporations (including Bayer and Schering), as well as 9% of the world's largest reinsurer, Munich Re (which has a 5% stake in Allianz).

The company in 2004 sold most of its Canadian property/casualty operations to ING Canada.

HISTORY

Carl Thieme founded Allianz in Germany in 1890. That year the company took part in the creation of the Calamity Association of Accident Insurance Companies, a consortium of German, Austrian, Swiss, and Russian firms, to insure international commerce.

By 1898 Thieme had established offices in the UK, Switzerland, and the Netherlands. His successor, Paul von der Nahmer, expanded Allianz into the Balkans, France, Italy, Scandinavia, and the US. After a hiatus during WWI, Allianz returned to foreign markets.

In WWII, Allianz insured Auschwitz, Dachau, and other death camps. Company documents show Allianz wasn't worried about risk at the SS troop-guarded camps. After the German defeat, the victors seized Allianz's foreign holdings, except for a stake in Spain's Plus Ultra. In the 1950s Allianz repurchased confiscated holdings in Italian and Austrian companies.

Allianz saturated the German market and began a full-scale international drive in the late 1950s and 1960s. It became Europe's largest insurer through a series of acquisitions beginning in 1973. Allianz formed Los Angeles-based Allianz Insurance in 1977.

In 1981 Allianz launched a takeover (which turned hostile) of the UK's Eagle Star insurance company. After a 1983 bidding joust with Britain's B.A.T Industries (now part of Zurich Financial Services), Allianz withdrew.

The firm consoled itself by shopping. In 1984 it won control of Riunione Adriatica di Sicurtà (Ras), Italy's second-largest insurance company. Two years later the firm bought Cornhill in the UK (on its third try). As the Iron Curtain crumbled, Allianz in 1989 acquired 49% of Hungaria Biztosito. Its *drang nach Osten* continued the next year after national reunification, when it gained control of Deutsche Versicherungs AG, East Germany's insurance monopoly. Allianz that year became the first German insurer licensed in Japan; it also bought the US's Fireman's Fund Insurance.

Natural disasters led to large claims and set the company back in 1992, the first time in 20 years it lost money from its German operations. Allianz restructured operations that year; profits surged in 1993, mostly from international business.

Allianz expanded in Mexico in 1995, forming a life and health insurance joint venture with Grupo Financiero BanCrecer (now owned by Grupo Financiero Banorte). The company set up an asset management arm in Hong Kong in 1996 with an eye to further Asian expansion, getting a license in China the next year. In 1997 after Holocaust survivors sued Allianz and other insurers for failing to pay on life policies after WWII, Allianz agreed to participate in a repayment fund.

In 1998 Allianz bought control of Assurances Générales de France; it was the white knight that prevented Assicurazioni Generali from taking the company. In 1999 Allianz said it would restructure some of its insurance operations, including spinning off its marine and aviation lines, to better compete in the multinational market. That year US subsidiary Allianz Life bought Life USA Holding. In 2000 Allianz bought 70% of PIMCO Advisors Holdings to strengthen its asset management operations. That year the company continued its push into Asia, buying a 12% stake in Hana Bank of South Korea and planning to boost its ownership of Malaysia British Assurance Life. Also in 2000, Allianz acquired Dutch insurer Zwolsche Algemeene.

Allianz remained acquisitive in 2001, buying US investment manager Nicholas-Applegate and taking a majority stake in ROSNO, one of Russia's largest insurers. Also that year, it bought a nearly 96% stake in German banking giant Dresdner and acquired the remainder the following year.

Allianz paid out claims of some $1.3 billion relating to the terrorist attacks on the World Trade Center. The company has set up a terrorism insurance unit, offering coverage primarily for companies within the European Union.

After a year of record losses (primarily due to investment losses and Dresdner's struggles), former CEO Henning Schulte-Noelle stepped down and assumed the chair post in 2003. Allianz' stock lost more than 75% of its value in 2002.

Getting out of the red, Allianz rebounded some in 2003, thanks to the upturn in the stock markets and the streamlining of its operations (the company shrunk its employee total by some 8,000 people). Allianz also raised some $5 billion to improve its capital base.

EXECUTIVES

Chairman of the Supervisory Board:
Henning Schulte-Noelle, age 64
Deputy Chairman of the Supervisory Board:
Norbert Blix, age 57
Chairman of the Management Board:
Michael Diekmann, age 51, $2,835,214 pay
Member of the Management Board (Group Finance):
Paul Achleitner, age 50, $2,090,289 pay
Member of the Management Board (Insurance Anglo Broker Markets/Global Lines): Clement B. Booth, age 52
Member of the Management Board (Europe I, P/C Sustainability Program): Enrico Tomaso Cucchiani, age 56

Member of the Management Board (Americas); Chairman, Fireman's Fund Insurance and Allianz Life Insurance Company of North America; CEO, Allianz of America: Jan R. Carendi, age 61
Member of the Management Board (Allianz Dresdner Asset Management); CEO, Allianz Global Investors: Joachim Faber, age 56, $1,795,399 pay
Member of the Management Board (Insurance Germany): Gerhard Rupprecht, age 58, $1,788,293 pay
Member of the Management Board (Group Controlling, Financial Risk Management, Accounting, Taxes, Compliance): Helmut Perlet, age 59, $1,800,136 pay
Member of the Management Board (Insurance Europe II, Sustainability Program Life Insurance): Jean-Philippe Thierry, age 58
Member of the Management Board (Banking Worldwide): Herbert Walter, age 53, $2,073,709 pay
Member of the Management Board (Insurance Growth Markets): Werner Zedelius, age 49, $1,865,272 pay
President, Allianz of America: Charles (Chuck) Kavitsky
Auditors: KPMG Deutsche Treuhand-Gesellschaft AG

LOCATIONS

HQ: Allianz SE
  Königinstrasse 28, D-80802 Munich, Germany
Phone: +49-89-3800-0   **Fax:** +49-89-3800-3425
US HQ: 777 San Marin Dr., Novato, CA 94945
US Phone: 415-899-2000   **US Fax:** 415-899-3600
Web: www.allianz.com

Allianz operates in more than 70 countries in Africa, Asia, Europe, North and South America, and the Pacific Rim.

PRODUCTS/OPERATIONS

2005 Sales

	% of total
Life/health insurance	48
Property & casualty insurance	44
Banking	6
Asset management	2
Total	**100**

Selected Holdings

Adriática de Seguros C.A. (Venezuela)
AGF Allianz Argentina Compañia de Seguros Generales S.A.
AGF Brasil Seguros S.A. (Brazil)
Allianz Cornhill Insurance plc. (UK)
Allianz Elementar Versicherung-AG (Austria)
Allianz Fire and Marine Insurance Japan Ltd.
Allianz General Insurance Malaysia Berhad p.l.c.
Allianz Individual Insurance Group LLC (US)
Allianz Insurance Company of Singapore Pte. Ltd.
Allianz Insurance Ltd. (South Africa)
Allianz Irish Life Holdings p.l.c.
Allianz Lebensversicherungs-AG
Allianz Life Insurance Company of North America (US)
Allianz México S.A. Compañía de Seguros
Allianz Nederland Groep N.V. (The Netherlands)
Allianz pojišťovna, a.s. (Czech Republic)
Allianz Subalpina Società di Assicurazioni e Riassicurazioni S.p.A. (Italy)
Allianz Tiriac Insurance S.A. (Romania)
Assurances Générales de France (61%)
Assurances Générales du Laos Ltd. (51%)
Banque AGF S.A. (France)
Deutsche Lebensversicherungs-AG
Dresdner Bank AG
ELVIA Assurances S.A. (Belgium)
ELVIA Reiseversicherungs-Gesellschaft AG (Switzerland)
Fireman's Fund Insurance Company (US)
Hungária Biztosító Rt (Hungary)
Jefferson Insurance Company of N.Y. (US)
Les Assurances Fédérales IARD (France)
Monticello Insurance Company (US)
PT Asuransi Allianz Utama Indonesia Ltd
TU Allianz Polska S.A. (Poland)
Zwolsche Algemeene Europa B.V. (The Netherlands)

COMPETITORS

AEGON
AIG
Allstate
AMB Generali
Aviva
AXA
Citigroup
ERGO
Fortis SA/NV
Generali
ING
Legal & General Group
MetLife
Millea Holdings
Mitsui Sumitomo Insurance
Munich Re
New York Life
Nippon Life Insurance
Prudential
Prudential plc
Royal & Sun Alliance Insurance
Sompo Japan Insurance
State Farm
Swiss Re
Winterthur
Zurich Financial Services

HISTORICAL FINANCIALS

Company Type: Public

Income Statement

FYE: December 31

	ASSETS ($ mil.)	NET INCOME ($ mil.)	INCOME AS % OF ASSETS	EMPLOYEES
12/05	1,187,333	4,374	0.4%	177,625
12/04	1,360,648	3,931	0.3%	162,180
12/03	1,178,011	2,819	0.2%	173,750
12/02	881,626	(1,321)	—	181,651
12/01	835,469	3,796	0.5%	179,146
Annual Growth	9.2%	3.6%	—	(0.2%)

2005 Year-End Financials

Equity as % of assets: 4.5%
Return on assets: 0.3%
Return on equity: 8.9%
Long-term debt ($ mil.): —
No. of shares (mil.): —
Dividends
Yield: 1.2%
Payout: —
Market value ($ mil.): —
Sales ($ mil.): 115,723

Stock History

NYSE: AZ

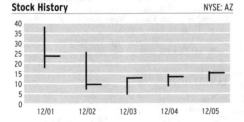

	STOCK PRICE ($) FY Close	P/E High/Low		PER SHARE ($) Earnings	Dividends
12/05	15.14	—	—	—	0.18
12/04	13.29	—	—	—	0.14
12/03	12.72	—	—	—	1.14
12/02	9.55	—	—	—	0.11
12/01	23.60	—	—	—	0.09
Annual Growth	(10.5%)	—	—	—	18.9%

Allied Irish Banks

Allied Irish Banks (AIB), one of Ireland's largest banks and private employers, is looking beyond the Emerald Isle for its proverbial pot o' gold. The company offers retail and commercial accounts and loans, life insurance, financing, leasing, pension, and trust services through some 275 branches in Ireland and another 60 in Northern Ireland, where it operates First Trust Bank. In England and Scotland, AIB focuses on commercial clients through about 40 locations. The company's capital markets division offers commercial treasury services, corporate finance, and investment banking services.

The bank's four operating divisions are divided into the following categories: AIB Bank Republic of Ireland, AIB Bank Great Britain and Northern Ireland, Capital Markets, and Poland.

The small Irish market and its inevitable ties to the UK's economy have made AIB look overseas to remain competitive. (Its home turf also faces intruders — namely European banks free to do business in the EU-opened Irish market.) The firm has positioned itself as an international bank with a presence in Eastern Europe where it owns a majority stake in Poland-based Bank Zachodni and nearly 400 branches. In the US, AIB owns more than 20% of New York-based M&T Bank. About a third of AIB's assets and pre-tax profits now come from outside of the country.

HISTORY

Allied Irish Banks was formed in 1966 by combining the "trinity" of Provincial Bank (founded 1825), The Royal Bank (founded 1836), and Munster and Leinster (founded 1885 but with origins back to the late 1600s). Both AIB and its then-larger rival, Bank of Ireland, had to consolidate in order to compete with North American banks entering Ireland. From its start, AIB sought to expand overseas, and by 1968 it had an alliance with Canada's Toronto-Dominion Bank.

In the 1970s AIB expanded its branch network to England and Scotland. The 1980s saw AIB boost its presence in the US market (it had already debuted AIB branches) with the acquisition of First Maryland Bancorp.

The Irish Parliament's Finance Act of 1986 instituted a withholding tax known as the Deposit Interest Retention Tax (DIRT) for Irish residents. Consequently (with a wink and a nod) AIB and other banks let customers create bogus nonresident accounts to avoid paying DIRT. An investigation indicated that, at one point, AIB's branch in Tralee had 14,700 non-resident accounts on its rolls — more than half the local population. After tax authorities began probing, many of the accounts in question were reclassified as "resident," and customers had to pay the taxes on them. In 1991 AIB was reprimanded, but neither the bank nor its customers have paid the remaining $100 million tax bill.

Tom Mulcahy, who integrated AIB's treasury, investment, and international banking activities, became chief executive in 1994. Mulcahy, a respected leader, envisioned AIB as an international, Ireland-based bank.

In 1995 AIB bought UK-based investment fund manager John Govett from London Pacific Group (now Berkeley Technology Limited). Mulcahy moved AIB the same year into Eastern

Europe with a stake in Poland-based Wielkopolski Bank Kredytowy (or WBK, of which it now owns 60%).

AIB was busy in 1999. It gained a toehold in Asia by entering a cross-marketing agreement with Singapore's Keppel TatLee bank, a survivor of the region's financial crisis. Liberalized Singapore banking laws allowed AIB the right to buy one-quarter of the bank by 2001. AIB also bought an 80% stake of Bank Zachodni in Poland in 1999.

That year AIB merged First Maryland Bancorp and its other US holdings into the renamed Allfirst Financial, a sizable mid-Atlantic states bank.

In 2001 AIB merged Wielkopolski Bank Kredytowy and Bank Zachodni into Bank Zachodni WBK in Poland to consolidate its power in Eastern Europe. That year Mulcahy retired but then was appointed by the Irish government to take over as chairman of troubled airline Aer Lingus.

In 2003 AIB sold troubled Maryland-based bank Allfirst Financial to M&T Bank Corporation. As part of the deal, AIB assumed ownership of more than 20% of M&T, becoming the company's largest shareholder. Under AIB's direction Allfirst grew into a major regional player with about 250 branches in Maryland, Virginia, Pennsylvania, and Washington, DC. However, AIB lost nearly $700 million from 1996 to 2002, apparently from bogus foreign exchange transactions made by rogue trader John Rusnak, who pleaded guilty to bank fraud.

EXECUTIVES

Chairman: Dermot Gleeson, age 56
Group Chief Executive and Director: Eugene J. Sheehy, age 52
Group Chief Risk Officer: Shom Bhattacharya, age 54
Group Finance Director: John O'Donnell
Managing Director, AIB Bank, Republic of Ireland: Donal Forde, age 43
Managing Director, AIB Capital Markets: Colm E. Doherty, age 47
Managing Director, AIB Group (UK) p.l.c.: Robbie Henneberry
Managing Director, AIB Poland Division: Gerry Byrne, age 49
Secretary: W. M. Kinsella
Director, Operations: Steven Meadows
Head of Corporate Relations: Catherine Burke
Head of Group Investor Relations: Alan Kelly
Head of Strategic Human Resources: Mary Toomey
Group Internal Auditor: Tony Schatzel
Auditors: KPMG

LOCATIONS

HQ: Allied Irish Banks, p.l.c.
Bankcentre, Ballsbridge, Dublin 4, Ireland
Phone: +353-1-660-0311   **Fax:** +353-1-660-9137
US HQ: 405 Park Ave., New York, NY 10022
US Phone: 212-339-8000   **US Fax:** 212-339-8008
Web: www.aibgroup.com

PRODUCTS/OPERATIONS

2005 Sales

	$ mil.	% of total
Interest	6,100.8	80
Fees & commissions	1,256.7	17
Trading income	132.7	2
Other	105.4	1
Total	**7,595.6**	**100**

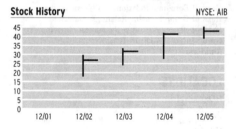
AMP Limited

AMP is on top — down under. The company is one of Australia's largest life insurance and investment management groups. Nearly 2,000 representatives sell the company's insurance and financial products, which include life insurance, retirement products, financial planning and advice, superannuation products (professionally managed retirement investment funds), banking, and investment management. The company's AMP Financial Services (AFS) division serves individual and corporate clients throughout Australia and New Zealand; AMP Capital Investors provides investment management to AFS and to other individual and institutional investors.

AMP Limited also provides retail financial services under the Hillcross, Arrive Wealth Management, and MAGNIFY brands. Its Cobalt/Gordian unit is running off the company's general insurance business. AMP Limited, which has approximately $75 billion of assets under management, claims that one in six Australians are AMP customers.

HISTORY

AMP was conceived in Sydney in 1848 by W. S. Walsh (a clergyman), Thomas Mort (a businessman), and Thomas Holt (a wool trader), who convened with two others to discuss forming a mutual life insurance company in Australia. (Many of the UK's and US's largest mutuals were also founded about this time.) The next year Australian Mutual Provident Society was born; it opened for business with a staff of two: secretary William Perry and a small boy. In its first year the company sold only 42 policies. Luckily, no one died in the first three years of operations and the company was able to build up some reserves. The company grew slowly over the next decade, appointing just two agents — in Auckland, New Zealand, and Hobart, Australia.

Sales took off with the 1860 appointment of the company's first full-time agent, Benjamin Short, who had the novel idea of actively recruiting customers and actually *selling* policies. The company opened an office in New Zealand in 1871; it opened a branch in the UK in 1908.

In the next few decades, the company helped build the Australian economy through investment of its reserves. It funded industry and infrastructure, including farming communities, as part of the South Australian Land Development Scheme. The company grew free of foreign competition, protected by regulations severely restricting the activities of foreign companies in the banking and financial industries in Australia. In 1958 the company formed AMP Fire and General Insurance (changed to AMP General in 1990).

In 1988 AMP moved abroad with the acquisition of London Life Assurance. The following year it made history with its acquisition of funds management group Pearl Assurance, then the largest takeover of a British financial firm by a foreign company.

The company founded AMP Asset Management in 1991 to manage its overseas assets. In 1995 the company expanded its international presence through a joint venture with the financial services arm of UK-based Virgin Group. The company also began offering mortgage and banking products in Australia through a new unit, Priority One.

After a careful inquiry, in 1996 AMP's board recommended demutualization; policyholders approved in 1997, and the conversion was completed the next year with the company taking the name AMP Limited. Trading got off to a rocky start, however, as the company imposed an unusual pricing mechanism by which the official initial stock price was linked to pricing activity over the first five days of trading. This was done to protect individual policyholders from typical opening-day stock gyrations, but institutional investors were unable to value their investments for several days (a technical breach of accounting rules).

AMP bought Citibank's New Zealand retail banking business and UK fund manager Henderson in 1998. The next year AMP battled to buy general insurer GIO Australia Holdings, picking up 57% after resistance to its original low-ball offer; it also bought UK mutual insurer National Provident Institution (NPI).

The company streamlined all of its investment-management operations into a single unit in 1999 and expanded Asian operations with offices in Beijing and Tokyo. In 2000 the problems arising from the GIO takeover resulted in a board shakeup; chairman Ian Burgess resigned.

Local rival Suncorp-Metway bought AMP's domestic general insurance unit in 2001, and Churchill Insurance (a subsidiary of Credit Suisse) acquired its similar operations in the UK that year.

AMP split off its UK-based operations as HHG at the end of 2003 (retaining a 10% share). HHG eventually changed its name to Henderson Group plc in 2005. AMP sold its shares in Henderson later that year.

EXECUTIVES

Chairman: Peter Mason, age 59
CEO and Director: Andrew Mohl, age 50, $2,970,286 pay
CFO: Paul Leaming, $1,435,000 pay
CIO: Lee Barnett
Managing Director, AMP Capital Investors:
　Stephen Dunne, $883,787 pay
General Manager, AMP Australian Financial Services:
　Craig Dunn, age 38, $1,608,000 pay
General Manager, Corporate and Public Affairs:
　Matthew Percival, age 50, $669,957 pay
General Manager, Human Resources and Strategy:
　Peter Hodgett, $795,482 pay
General Counsel: David Cohen, $753,883 pay
Auditors: Ernst & Young

LOCATIONS

HQ: AMP Limited
　Level 24, 33 Alfred St., Sydney 2000, Australia
Phone: +61-2-9257-5000　　**Fax:** +61-2-9257-7178
Web: www.ampgroup.com

PRODUCTS/OPERATIONS

2005 Sales

	% of total
AMP Financial Services	76
AMP Capital Investors	13
Cobalt/Gordian	11
Total	**100**

COMPETITORS

AIG
Australia and New
　Zealand Banking
Aviva
AXA Asia Pacific
Commonwealth Bank
　of Australia

Fortis SA/NV
ING
Macquarie Bank
National Australia Bank
Royal & Sun Alliance
　Insurance
St.George Bank

HISTORICAL FINANCIALS

Company Type: Public

Income Statement — FYE: December 31

	ASSETS ($ mil.)	NET INCOME ($ mil.)	INCOME AS % OF ASSETS	EMPLOYEES
12/05	62,389	590	0.9%	3,500
12/04	55,418	728	1.3%	3,464
12/03	52,596	(4,151)	—	3,961
12/02	89,190	(506)	—	11,403
12/01	88,624	353	0.4%	15,000
Annual Growth	(8.4%)	13.7%	—	(30.5%)

2005 Year-End Financials

Equity as % of assets: —
Return on assets: 1.0%
Return on equity: —

Long-term debt ($ mil.): —
Sales ($ mil.): 9,921

Net Income History — Australian: AMP

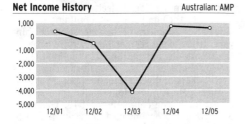

	12/01	12/02	12/03	12/04	12/05

Anglo American

Anglo American's name might be a little misleading — it's never been American. The UK-based company owns stakes in leading global producers of gold (42%, AngloGold Ashanti), platinum (75%, Anglo Platinum), and diamonds (45%, De Beers Consolidated). In addition, Anglo American has interests in paper and packaging goods (more than 20% of sales), ferrous and base metals, and industrial minerals. It also is one of the world's largest independent coal miners. The company controls assets around the world. Descendants of the founding Oppenheimer family no longer control Anglo American, although Nicky Oppenheimer, who chairs De Beers, sits on the company's board.

The company, formerly Anglo American Corporation of South Africa, moved to the UK and began trading on the London Stock Exchange in an effort to reach international investors. When it was based in South Africa, Anglo American was unable to send its money overseas (the result of boycotts connected to that country's apartheid policies), so it bulked up on South African interests. Anglo American now depends on product and geographic diversity to weather global economic turmoil.

It also seems to be capitulating to demands from the investor community and the idea that the gold industry is sufficiently different from the rest of the mining industry as to necessitate separate management. It sold its 20% stake in Gold Fields Limited to Norilsk Nickel in 2004 and disposed of a portion of its stake in gold, reducing its stake in Anglo Gold Ashanti to 42% from its former 51% in 2006. In addition, Anglo American made several other divestitures. It and partner BHP Billiton sold their joint venture, chrome miner and manufacturer Samancor, to US investment firm the Kermas Group for $469 million,

and Anglo American rid itself of subsidiary Boart Longyear, selling the mining machinery and services company in two parts for a total of $635 million. Other plans for divestiture include selling its 80% stake in Highveld Steel and ridding itself of its paper and packaging businesses.

HISTORY

In 1905 the Oppenheimers, a German family with a major interest in the Premier Diamond Mining Company of South Africa, began buying some of the region's richest gold-bearing land. The family formed Anglo American Corporation of South Africa in 1917 to raise money from J. P. Morgan and other US investors. The name was chosen to disguise the company's German background during WWI.

Under Ernest Oppenheimer the company bought diamond fields in German Southwest Africa (now Namibia) in 1920, breaking the De Beers hegemony in diamond production. Oppenheimer's 1928 negotiations with Hans Merensky, the person credited with the discovery of South Africa's "platinum arc," led to Anglo American's interest in platinum.

The diamond monopoly resurfaced in 1929 when Anglo American won control of De Beers, formed by Cecil Rhodes in 1888 with the help of England's powerful Rothschild family.

Anglo American and De Beers had become the largest gold producers in South Africa by the 1950s. They were also major world producers of coal, uranium, and copper. In the 1960s and 1970s, Anglo American expanded through mergers and cross holdings in industrial and financial companies. It set up Luxembourg-based Minorco to own holdings outside South Africa and help the company avoid sanctions placed on firms doing business in the apartheid country.

Minorco sold its interest in Consolidated Gold Fields in 1989, and in 1990 it bought Freeport-McMoRan Gold Company (US). In 1993 Minorco bought Anglo American's and De Beers' South American, European, and Australian operations as part of a swap that put all of Anglo American's non-African assets, except diamonds, in Minorco's hands. Some analysts claimed the company had moved the assets to protect them from possible nationalization by the new, black-controlled South African government. The company spun off insurer African Life to a group of black investors in 1994.

Anglo American bought a stake in UK-based conglomerate Lonrho (now Lonmin) in 1996. 1997 Anglo American made mining acquisitions in Zambia, Colombia, and Tanzania and began reorganizing its gold and diamond operations. In 1998 the company's First National and Southern Life financial units merged with Rand Merchant Bank's Momentum Life Assurers to form FirstRand. (Anglo American has divested most of its interest in FirstRand.)

The company left its homeland for London in 1999, changed its name to Anglo American plc, and wrapped up the acquisitions of many of its minority interests including Amcoal, Amgold, Amic, and Minorco.

In 2000 the company bought UK building materials company Tarmac plc and later sold Tarmac America to Greece-based Titan Cement for $636 million. That year De Beers paid $590 million for Anglovaal Mining's stake in De Beers' flagship Venetia diamond mine and $900 million for Royal Dutch Shell's Australian coal mining business. On the disposal side, Anglo American sold its 68% stake in LTA and its 14%

stake in Li & Fung, a Hong Kong trading company. Harry Oppenheimer died that year at the age of 92.

In a surprising move, in early 2001 Anglo American announced that it had formed a consortium with Central Holding (the Oppenheimer family) and Debswana Diamond to acquire De Beers. In February De Beers agreed to be acquired in a deal worth about $17.6 billion. The deal — giving Anglo American and Central Holding 45% each and Debswana a 10% stake — was completed in June 2001.

In 2002 Anglo American and Japan-based conglomerate Mitsui pooled their Australian coal resources; Anglo American owns 51% of the joint venture. The company also completed a $1.3 billion deal that year for Chilean copper assets (two mines and a smelter) formerly owned by Exxon Mobil. In 2003 the company eyed the red hot iron ore market when it acquired a controlling stake in South Africa-based iron producer Kumba Resources.

EXECUTIVES

Chairman: Sir Mark Moody-Stuart, age 66
CEO and Executive Director: Anthony J. (Tony) Trahar, age 56
Director-Elect and CEO-Elect: Cynthia Carroll, age 49
EVP, Group Human Resources and Business Development: Russell King, age 48
Director, Finance and Executive Director: René Médori, age 47, $803,427 pay
Chairman, Base Metals and Industrial Minerals and Executive Director: Simon Thompson, age 46, $942,779 pay (partial-year salary)
Chief Executive, Mondi Group and Executive Director: David Hathorn, age 43, $947,940 pay (partial-year salary)
Chairman and CEO, Ferrous Metals and Industries: Philip M. Baum, age 51
Group Technical Director and Chairman, Coal: Tony Redman, age 57
Auditors: Deloitte & Touche LLP

LOCATIONS

HQ: Anglo American plc
20 Carlton House Terrace,
London SW1Y 5AN, United Kingdom
Phone: +44-20-7968-8888   **Fax:** +44-20-7968-8500
Web: www.angloamerican.co.uk

Anglo American's operations include subsidiaries in Australia, Austria, Brazil, Canada, Chile, the Czech Republic, France, Germany, Ireland, Namibia, Peru, Poland, South Africa, Spain, the UK, and Venezuela.

2005 Sales by Origin

	% of total
Africa	
South Africa	41
Other countries	4
Europe	33
South America	13
Australia & Asia	7
North America	2
Total	**100**

2005 Sales by Destination

	% of total
Europe	46
Africa	
South Africa	18
Other countries	2
Australia & Asia	19
North America	9
South America	6
Total	**100**

PRODUCTS/OPERATIONS

2005 Sales

	$ mil.	% of total
Paper & Packaging	6,673	23
Ferrous Metals & Industries	6,030	21
Industrial Minerals	4,043	14
Base Metals	3,647	12
Platinum	3,646	12
Coal	2,766	9
Gold	2,629	9
Total	**29,434**	**100**

Selected Industries and Subsidiaries

Paper and Packaging
Frantschach Packaging AG (70%, industrial packaging, Austria)
Mondi Limited (paper and packaging, South Africa)
Mondi Packaging (Europe) SA (corrugated packaging, Luxembourg)
Neusiedler AG (graphic paper, Austria)

Ferrous Metals & Industries
Highveld Steel (79%, steel, vanadium, and ferroalloys)
Kumba Resources Limited (66%; coal, iron ore, heavy minerals; South Africa)
Scaw Metals (iron, steel, and engineering works; South Africa)
The Tongaat-Hulett Group Limited (53%; sugar, starch, aluminum; South Africa)

Industrial Minerals
Bilfinger Berger Baustoffe GmbH (construction materials, Germany)
Copebras Limitada (73%, phosphate products, Brazil)
Lausitzer Grauwacke GmbH (construction materials, Germany)
Midland Quarry Products Limited (50%, construction materials, UK)
Steetley Iberia SA (construction materials, Spain)
Tarmac France SA (construction materials, France)
Tarmac Group Limited (construction materials, UK)
Tarmac Severokamen AS (construction materials, Czech Republic)
WKSM SA (construction materials, Poland)

Base Metals
Black Mountain (copper, lead, and zinc; South Africa)
Empresa Minera de Mantos Blancos SA (copper, Chile)
Gamsberg Zinc Corporation (zinc, South Africa)
Hudson Bay Mining and Smelting Co. (copper and zinc, Canada)
Minera Loma de Níquel, CA (91%, nickel, Venezuela)
Minera Quellaveco SA (80%, copper, Peru)
Minera Sur Andes Limitada (copper, Chile)
Namakwa Sands (mineral sands, South Africa)

Diamonds
De Beers Consolidated (45%)

Platinum
Anglo Platinum Corporation Limited (75%, South Africa)

Gold
AngloGold Ashanti (42%, gold mines, South Africa)

Coal
Anglo Coal (South Africa)
Anglo Coal (Callide) Pty Limited (Australia)

COMPETITORS

ASARCO	Mitsubishi Materials
Barrick Gold	Newmont Mining
BHP Billiton	Norilsk Nickel
Brookfield	Peñoles
Cameco	Phelps Dodge
Centromin	Rio Tinto
CRH	Sappi
Freeport-McMoRan	Stora Enso Oyj
Grupo México	Teck Cominco
Hanson	Umicore
Harmony Gold	UPM-Kymmene
Impala Platinum	Vale do Rio Doce
Inco Limited	Weyerhaeuser
International Paper	Xstrata

HISTORICAL FINANCIALS

Company Type: Public

Income Statement

FYE: December 31

	REVENUE ($ mil.)	NET INCOME ($ mil.)	NET PROFIT MARGIN	EMPLOYEES
12/05	29,434	3,521	12.0%	195,000
12/04	24,930	2,913	11.7%	209,000
12/03	18,637	1,592	8.5%	193,000
12/02	15,183	1,563	10.3%	177,000
Annual Growth	**24.7%**	**31.1%**	**—**	**3.3%**

2005 Year-End Financials

Debt ratio: 29.1%
Return on equity: 14.5%
Cash ($ mil.): 4,193
Current ratio: 1.38
Long-term debt ($ mil.): 6,871

Stock History

NASDAQ (CM): AAUK

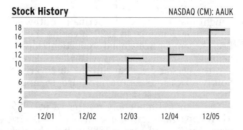

	STOCK PRICE ($) FY Close	P/E High/Low		PER SHARE ($) Earnings	Dividends
12/05	17.39	7	5	2.36	0.38
12/04	11.90	15	10	0.90	0.27
12/03	11.06	20	12	0.55	0.24
12/02	7.30	—	—	—	0.23
Annual Growth	**33.6%**	**—**	**—**	**107.1%**	**18.2%**

A.P. Møller – Mærsk

Big metal boxes mean money for A.P. Møller – Mærsk. The company's Maersk Line, one of the world's largest container shipping concerns, maintains a fleet of more than 500 containerships with an overall capacity of more than 1.3 million TEUs (twenty-foot-equivalent units). Besides containerships, the A.P. Møller – Mærsk fleet includes bulk carriers, supply and specialty ships, and tankers. The company also is a major container terminal operator, through APM Terminals. In addition, A.P. Møller – Mærsk drills for oil and gas, primarily in the North Sea, and owns one of Denmark's largest grocery and general merchandise chains. Other units build ships and shipping containers and provide air cargo services.

Maersk Line, launched as a brand in 2006, combines the operations of Maersk Sealand and Royal P&O Nedlloyd, which was acquired by A.P. Møller – Mærsk in 2005. A related business, Maersk Logistics, incorporates the operations of P&O Nedlloyd Logistics.

Among A.P. Møller – Mærsk's major oil and gas assets is a 39% stake in the Dansk Undergrunds Consortium (DUC), which is engaged in exploration and production in the Danish sector of the North Sea.

A.P. Møller – Mærsk's retail segment is led by Dansk Supermarked, Denmark's #2 supermarket chain (behind FDB). Dansk Supermarked operates stores under names such as Føtex, Bilka, and Netto in Denmark, Germany, Poland, Sweden and the UK.

HISTORY

Arnold Peter Møller and his father, sea captain Peter Mærsk Møller, founded Aktieselskabet Dampskibsselskabet Svendborg (Steamship Company Svendborg) in 1904 in Svendborg, Denmark. Their first ship, a second-hand steamer, bore on its funnel a white seven-pointed star on a blue background, which had been on Peter's first ship. Later known as the Maersk star, the logo adorned all subsequent ships of the company, as well as ships of a second company formed eight years later — Dampskibsselskabet af 1912, Aktieselskab (Steamship Company of 1912). At that point, six ships were in the Maersk fleet.

In 1917 the company began building its own ships after establishing the Odense Steel Shipyard. It launched regular liner service between the US and the Far East in 1928, calling the operation the Maersk Line. With the addition of its first tankers that year, Maersk owned 35 ships.

Mærsk Mc-Kinney Møller, A.P.'s son, became a partner in the company in 1940. That year, with Germany occupying Denmark, he fled to the US with his bride on one of the last ships out. Refusing to take orders from the Nazis, A.P. transferred control of the company to the US, where the 26-year-old Mærsk had established operations. Most of the Maersk fleet flew under British or US flags during the war, which took the life of 148 Maersk seamen and claimed 25 ships. Mærsk Mc-Kinney Møller returned to Denmark in 1947.

A.P. Møller formed the Maersk Company in 1951 in London as a shipbroker, which became one of the world's largest shipowners. The early 1960s saw A.P. Møller diversifying as it moved into oil and gas exploration and production in Denmark in 1962 and established supermarket chain Dansk Supermarked in 1964. A.P. died the next year, having run the company for more than 60 years. Prior to his death, he had created three foundations to hold most of the company's shares. His son Mærsk took command of A.P. Møller and the Maersk fleet, which contained 88 ships. Under his leadership the company expanded even further and became more international; his business savvy became apparent when he sold some of the company's tanker fleet in the 1970s, just prior to prices going down.

In 1970 A.P. Møller established domestic carrier Maersk Air. A.P. Møller began seeing its first oil production in the North Sea in 1972. The next year the company acquired its first container vessel, the *Svendborg Maersk*.

Maersk Container Industri was formed in 1991 to produce intermodal containers. That year Maersk and rival Sea-Land entered into a transpacific vessel-sharing agreement, which was expanded into a global alliance in 1995. In 1999, just months after buying South Africa's Safmarine Container Lines, Maersk bought Sea-Land's international liner services and 18 terminals. The Maersk Line and Sea-Land operations were merged to form Maersk Sealand.

In 2000 A.P. Møller planned to extend its Bilka grocery chain into southern Sweden. That year Maersk Sealand decided to shift its transshipment hub in Singapore to a Malaysian port. In 2001 Maersk Air and Scandinavian Airlines System (SAS) were together fined $45 million by the European Commission for infringing on the EC's competition rules by entering a secret deal to monopolize certain air routes in Scandinavia. As a result, Maersk Air's chairman and managing director stepped down and were replaced.

A.P. Møller, which through the years had continued to operate through two separately listed companies — Aktieselskabet Dampskibsselskabet Svendborg and Dampskibsselskabet af 1912, Aktieselskab — reorganized in 2003 and wound up with a single publicly traded company — A.P. Møller – Mærsk A/S — at its head.

A.P. Møller – Mærsk purchased the majority of Kerr-McGee's North Sea oil assets in late 2005. Also that year, the passenger transportation business of Maersk Air was sold to an Icelandic investment group.

EXECUTIVES

Chairman; Vice Chairman, Olie og Gas: Michael Pram Rasmussen, age 48
Vice Chairman: Ane Mærsk Mc-Kinney Uggla
Vice Chairman: Poul J. Svanholm
Partner and CEO; Chairman, Olie og Gas: Jess Søderberg, age 61
Partner: Tommy Thomsen, age 48
Group CFO: Søren Thorup Sørensen, age 40
Co-CEO, A.P. Møller – Mærsk A/S Container Business: Eivind Kolding, age 46
Co-CEO, A.P. Møller – Mærsk A/S Container Business: Knud E. Stubkjær, age 50
CEO, Olie og Gas: Thomas Thune Andersen, age 51
SVP, Corporate Communications: Jette Clausen
SVP and CFO, Maersk Container Business: Michael T. Jørgensen
Managing Director, Maersk España S.A.: Eric A. Sisco
Managing Director, T&W Holding and A-huset Holding: Jan Tøpholm
Managing Director: Jørn Steen Nielsen, age 49
Director, Kraks Forlag and PFA Holding: Svend-Aage Nielsen
Auditors: KPMG C. Jespersen

LOCATIONS

HQ: A.P. Møller – Mærsk A/S
 Esplanaden 50, DK-1098 Copenhagen K, Denmark
Phone: +45-3363-3363 **Fax:** +45-3363-4108
Web: www.apmoller.com

2005 Sales

	% of total
Europe	46
North and South America	24
Asia	11
Other regions	19
Total	**100**

PRODUCTS/OPERATIONS

2005 Sales

	% of total
Shipping	
Container shipping	60
Tankers & offshore	9
Oil & gas	13
Retail	12
Other	6
Total	**100**

Selected Operating Units

Container shipping
 APM Terminals
 Maersk Line
 Maersk Logistics
 Safmarine Container Lines N.V.
Tankers and offshore
 Maersk Contractors
 Maersk Supply Service
 Maersk Tankers
 Norfolkline B.V.

Oil and gas
 Maersk Olie og Gas AS Group
Retail
 Dansk Supermarked Group
Other
 Maersk Container Industri A/S (manufacturing of refrigerated shipping containers)
 Odense Staalskibsvaerft A/S Group (shipbuilding)
 Rosti A/S Group (plastics)
 Star Air A/S (air cargo transportation)

COMPETITORS

Bolloré	John Swire & Sons
BP	Mediterranean Shipping
CMA CGM	Company
COSCO Group	Mitsui O.S.K. Lines
DP World	Neptune Orient
Evergreen Marine	Norsk Hydro
FDB	NYK Line
Hanjin Shipping	Orient Overseas
Hapag-Lloyd	PSA
Hess	Singamas
Hutchison Port Holdings	SSA Marine
ICA AB	Statoil

HISTORICAL FINANCIALS

Company Type: Public

Income Statement

FYE: December 31

	REVENUE ($ mil.)	NET INCOME ($ mil.)	NET PROFIT MARGIN	EMPLOYEES
12/05	33,058	—	—	67,498
12/04	30,421	—	—	62,300
12/03	26,489	—	—	63,161
12/02	21,388	—	—	61,294
12/01	17,865	—	—	—
Annual Growth	**16.6%**	**—**		**3.3%**

Revenue History

Copenhagen: MAERSKA

Asahi Shimbun

The Asahi Shimbun Company helps the Japanese wake up informed. The company's flagship *Asahi Shimbun* is the #2 newspaper in Japan (behind *Yomiuri Shimbun*). With a daily circulation of 8 million, it is noted for its in-depth political coverage and investigative reporting. Asahi Shimbun also publishes books and magazines, including *AERA* and *Shukan Asahi*. The firm's English-language *Asahi Evening News* has been replaced by the *International Herald Times/The Asahi Shimbun*, published in cooperation with International Herald Tribune. The founding Murayama and Ueno families control Asahi Shimbun.

In addition to publishing, Asahi Shimbun operates in television broadcasting (as the largest shareholder of Asahi National Broadcasting, known as TV Asahi). The company also publishes content on the Internet.

Kotaro Akiyama replaced Shinichi Hakoshima as president of Asahi Shimbun in 2005 after a scandal involving paid editorial content in one of the company's publications. A second scandal broke later that year when a reporter for the newspaper was accused of fabricating information used in stories.

In addition to its domestic operations, Asahi Shimbun has publishing operations in several international locations, including Hong Kong, London, Los Angeles, New York, and Singapore.

HISTORY

Ryohei Murayama, the son of a wealthy merchant in Osaka, published the first issue of *Asahi Shimbun* in 1879. The four-page paper was intended to provide news in an easy-to-read format for the general public. Riichi Ueno later joined Murayama, and together in 1881 they purchased the paper outright from their backers. By 1883 it was the most widely read newspaper in Japan. It expanded to Tokyo in 1888 and became the first Japanese newspaper publisher to have foreign correspondents in Europe and the US.

A sharp critic of the government and the military, Asahi Shimbun defied the government censorship during the Rice Riots of 1918 (when housewives plundered the warehouses of rice merchants who were speculating on rice prices). The company successfully launched two weeklies in the 1920s, *Shukan Asahi* (1922) and *Asahi Graph* (1923). Its criticism of the armed forces led to a military boycott of *Asahi Shimbun* in the 1930s, culminating in an assault on its Tokyo office by army officers in 1936. Military censorship stifled the newspaper's reporting during WWII, and following the war the company's executives admitted their complicity in publishing misleading information and resigned.

Regaining its standing as the "people's organ," the company launched its English-language *Asahi Evening News* and the English-language review, *Japan Quarterly*, in the 1950s. Asahi Shimbun became the first publisher in the world to use facsimile and offset printing to publish daily newspapers in 1959.

Major investigative pieces became the hallmark of *Asahi Shimbun* in the 1970s and 1980s. The paper exposed collusion between government, big business, and the civil service, such as the Lockheed scandal involving under-the-table payments to Japanese politicians. In 1988 *Asahi Shimbun* broke the "Recruit Affair," another bribery scandal that led to the resignation of then Prime Minister Noboru Takeshita and other top politicians. Its journalistic drive continued into the 1990s, breaking the 1992 story of 500 million in kickbacks to Japanese political kingmaker Shin Kanemaru in connection to scandals centering on parcel delivery service Tokyo Sagawa Kyubin. (The news touched off a nationwide political reform movement.)

In 1995 Asahi Shimbun scored an exclusive when it was the first to beam images of the Sakhalin (Russia) earthquake around the world. SOFTBANK and News Corp. sold their shares of Asahi National Broadcasting (TV Asahi) to Asahi Shimbun in 1997 to promote future cooperation of Japanese TV programming for Japan Sky Broadcasting (JSkyB), a satellite broadcasting network started by the two heavyweights. Asahi Shimbun president Muneyuki Matsushita died in 1999 and was replaced by Shinichi Hakoshima, the company's senior managing director. The next year TV Asahi went public to finance its conversion to digital broadcasting standards. In 2001 the firm joined the *International Herald Tribune* to publish a new English-language paper to replace the *Asahi Evening News*.

Kotaro Akiyama replaced Hakoshima as president in 2005.

EXECUTIVES

President, CEO, and Director: Kotaro Akiyama, age 60
Senior Managing Director: Aihiko Bando, age 61
Senior Managing Director: Norio Utsumi
Managing Director, Advertising: Yukio Hirose, age 62
Managing Director: Fumio Ikeuchi, age 60
Managing Director and Internal Auditor:
Yasuhiro Kobayashi, age 59
Managing Director, Editorial: Shin-ichi Yoshida, age 56
Director, Sales: Ikutaro Hama, age 60
Auditors: KPMG AZSA & Co.

LOCATIONS

HQ: The Asahi Shimbun Company
5-3-2 Tsukiji, Chuo-ku, Tokyo 104-8011, Japan
Phone: +81-3-3545-0131   **Fax:** +81-3-3545-8450
US HQ: 845 3rd Ave., 11th Fl., New York, NY 10022
US Phone: 212-317-3030   **US Fax:** 212-317-3039
Web: www.asahi.com

PRODUCTS/OPERATIONS

Selected Operations

Book publishing
Magazines
AERA (news)
Ronza (business)
Shukan Asahi (news)
Newspapers
Asahi Shimbun
International Herald Times/The Asahi Shimbun
Shukan Asahi
Other investments
Asahi National Broadcasting (TV Asahi)
Daiko Advertising

COMPETITORS

Dow Jones
Fuji Television
International
 Herald Tribune
Kodansha
Nihon Keizai Shimbun
Nippon Television
Tokyo Broadcasting System
Yomiuri Shimbun

HISTORICAL FINANCIALS

Company Type: Private

Income Statement

FYE: March 31

	REVENUE ($ mil.)	NET INCOME ($ mil.)	NET PROFIT MARGIN	EMPLOYEES
3/05	5,700	179	3.1%	14,407
3/04	5,701	120	2.1%	14,122
Annual Growth	(0.0%)	49.5%	—	2.0%

2005 Year-End Financials

Debt ratio: 6.1%   Current ratio: 1.47
Return on equity: 7.3%   Long-term debt ($ mil.): 154
Cash ($ mil.): 839

Net Income History

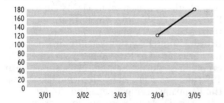

AstraZeneca

AstraZeneca's products run the gamut from A (breast cancer drug Arimidex) to Z (migraine treatment Zomig). One of the world's top pharmaceutical firms, AstraZeneca specializes in drugs for gastrointestinal, cardiovascular, and oncology therapeutic areas. The firm's biggest seller is acid reflux remedy Nexium. For matters of the heart, AstraZeneca makes hypertension and heart failure drug Atacand and cholesterol reducer Crestor. The company's oncology drugs include Nolvadex (breast cancer) and Zoladex (prostate cancer), and lung cancer growth-inhibitor Iressa. The company also makes drugs for respiratory and central nervous system conditions and pain control.

Faced with patent expirations of such top-selling drugs as Prilosec, Nolvadex, and Zestril, the company answered the challenge with several promising new drugs. Its purple Prilosec follow-up, Nexium, rocketed to the top of its offerings (gastrointestinal treatments account for more than a quarter of sales). Cholesterol medication Crestor made an impressive debut, but in 2005 the FDA ordered AstraZeneca to note on Crestor's label that the drug can cause life-threatening muscle damage to some patients, particularly those of Asian descent.

To keep new drugs coming, AstraZeneca is investing heavily in research and development in its core areas of expertise. The company's pipeline is stocked with projects such as diabetes therapy Galida. The company ceased production and clinical studies of Exanta, a stroke prevention drug. Other projects include drugs for gastrointestinal disorders, psychiatric diseases, cancer, and pain.

In 2006, AstraZeneca's Symbicort gained FDA approval as a combination asthma therapy inhaler. The drug is currently approved in 90 other countries and is expected to hit the US market in mid-2007. Later that year, Nexium was approved to treat Zollinger-Ellison Syndrome, a rare disorder that causes tumors and ulcers in the pancreas and stomach areas.

AstraZeneca's other businesses include Aptium Oncology (formerly Salick Health Care), which operates cancer treatment centers in the US, and Astra Tech, which manufactures such medical devices as urinary catheters and dental implant systems.

The company was fined $73 million by the European Commission in mid-2005 in the first case that used EU antitrust laws to punish a company for manipulating patent laws to prevent generic competition. The Commission said AstraZeneca had tried to prevent generic versions of Losec (known as Prilosec in the US) from coming to market in Denmark, Sweden, and Norway.

In a move symbolic of the company's current direction, when chief executive Sir Tom McKillop retired at the close of 2005, he was succeeded by marketing expert David Brennan. Brennan's strategy, like many in the top pharma spots, appears to be to acquire biotech companies and strengthen the pipeline that way rather than redirecting cash away from marketing and promotion. In 2006, for example, the company purchased Cambridge Antibody Technology (CAT) for about $1.3 billion, hoping that its antibody-based research would be more productive and less costly in the long run.

Asset management firm The Capital Group Companies owns almost 15% of the company.

HISTORY

AstraZeneca forerunner Imperial Chemical Industries (ICI) was created from the 1926 merger of four British chemical companies — Nobel Industries; Brunner, Mond and Company; United Alkali; and British Dyestuffs — in reaction to the German amalgamation that created I. G. Farben. ICI plunged into research, recruiting chemists, engineers, and managers and forming alliances with universities. Between 1933 and 1935, at least 87 new products were created, including polyethylene.

Fortunes declined as competition increased after WWII. In 1980 ICI posted losses and cut its dividend for the first time. In 1982 turnaround artist John Harvey-Jones shifted ICI from bulk chemicals to high-margin specialty chemicals such as pharmaceuticals and pesticides. That business became Zeneca, which ICI spun off in 1993.

The takeover specter loomed large over the company during its first year. Zeneca had several drugs in its pipeline, but it also had expiring patents on others, making them fair game for competitors. Bankrolled by its agrochemical business, Zeneca forged alliances with other pharmaceutical firms. In 1994 it entered a marketing alliance with Amersham International (now Amersham) to sell Metastron, a nuclear-medicine cancer agent. The next year Zeneca formed a joint venture with Chinese companies Advanced Chemicals and Tianli to make textile-coating chemicals.

In 1995 Glaxo was forced to sell a migraine drug candidate to complete its merger with Wellcome. Zeneca's gamble in buying the then-unproven drug (Zomig) paid off when the product gained US FDA approval two years later.

By 1997 Zeneca completed its gradual acquisition of Salick Health Care, formed to create more humane cancer treatment programs. The purchase followed a trend of large drug firms moving into managed care, which raised concerns that centers might be pressured to use their parent companies' drugs, but Zeneca maintained that Salick would remain independent except to the extent that it offered an opportunity to evaluate treatments.

In 1998 Zeneca got the FDA's OK to sell its brand of tamoxifen (Nolvadex) to women at high risk of contracting breast cancer. In 1999 it sued Eli Lilly to protect Nolvadex against Lilly's marketing claim that its osteoporosis treatment Evista reduced breast cancer risk, a use for which it was not approved.

In 1999 Zeneca completed its purchase of Sweden's Astra to form AstraZeneca. That year the firm sold its specialty chemicals unit, Zeneca Specialties, to Cinven Group and Investcorp. With its agricultural business stagnated due to crippled markets in Asia and Europe, AstraZeneca announced plans to merge the unit with the agrochemicals business of Novartis and spin it off as Syngenta. In 2000 Sweden approved ulcer drug Nexium, as well as Symbicort Turbuhaler, an asthma inhaler.

In 2001 AstraZeneca sold its genetic diversity testing services subsidiary, Cellmark Diagnostics, to Orchid Cellmark (with whom the company also announced a multi-year collaborative research agreement).

EXECUTIVES

Chairman: Louis Schweitzer, age 64, $476,000 pay
CEO and Board Member: David R. Brennan, age 52, $1,076,000 pay (partial-year salary)
Deputy Chairman: Håkan Mogren, age 61, $183,000 pay
Executive Director, Development; Board Member: John Patterson, age 58, $1,498,000 pay
CFO and Board Member: Jonathan Symonds, age 46, $1,784,000 pay
EVP, Global Marketing and Business Development: Martin Nicklasson
EVP, Discovery Research: Jan Lundberg
EVP, Human Resources: Tony Bloxham
EVP, Europe, Japan, Asia Pacific, and the Rest of the World: Bruno Angelici
EVP, North America; President and CEO, AstraZeneca US: Tony P. Zook
EVP, Operations: Barrie Thorpe
VP, Federal Government Affairs: Richard (Rich) Buckley
VP, Medical Affairs: Les Paul
VP, Public Policy: Robert Perkins
VP, Global Compensation and Benefits: Peter Brown
Chief Medical Officer: Howard Hutchinson
Auditors: KPMG Audit Plc

LOCATIONS

HQ: AstraZeneca PLC
15 Stanhope Gate,
London W1K 1LN, United Kingdom
Phone: +44-20-7304-5000   **Fax:** +44-20-7304-5151
US HQ: 1800 Concord Pike, Wilmington, DE 19803
US Phone: 302-886-3000   **US Fax:**
Web: www.astrazeneca.com

AstraZeneca's principal facilities are in Australia, Canada, France, Germany, Italy, Japan, Puerto Rico, Sweden, the UK, and the US.

2005 Sales

	$ mil.	% of total
US	10,771	45
Europe	8,463	35
Japan	1,527	6
Rest of world	3,189	14
Total	**23,950**	**100**

PRODUCTS/OPERATIONS

2005 Sales

	% of total
Gastrointestinal	
Nexium	19
Losec/Prilosec	7
Other	1
Cardiovascular	
Seloken	7
Crestor	4
Atacand	4
Plendil	2
Tenormin	2
Zestril	2
Other	2
Neurology	
Seroquel	9
Local anesthetics	3
Diprivan	2
Zomig	1
Other	1
Oncology	
Casodex	5
Zoladex	4
Arimidex	5
Iressa	1
Nolvadex	1
Respiratory & Inflammation	
Pulmicort	5
Symbicort	4
Rhinocort	2
Other	1
Infection	
Merrem	2
Other	1
Other products	3
Total	**100**

Selected Products

Gastrointestinal
  Entocort (anti-inflammatory for inflammatory bowel disease)
  Losec/Prilosec/Omepral (acid reflux disease)
  Nexium (acid reflux disease)
Cardiovascular
  Atacand (hypertension and heart failure)
  Crestor (cholesterol-lowering drug)
  Plendil (hypertension and angina)
  Seloken ZOK/Toprol-XL (beta-blocker)
  Zestril (ACE inhibitor)
Oncology
  Arimidex (breast cancer)
  Casodex (prostate cancer)
  Faslodex (breast cancer)
  Iressa (anti-tumor)
  Nolvadex (breast cancer)
  Zoladex (prostate and breast cancer)
Respiratory and Inflammation
  Accolate (asthma)
  Oxis (asthma)
  Pulmicort (anti-inflammatory)
  Rhinocort (topical nasal anti-inflammatory)
  Symbicort (anti-inflammatory and bronchodilator in one inhaler)
Neurology
  Diprivan (general anesthetic)
  Naropin (local anesthetic)
  Seroquel (schizophrenia)
  Xylocaine (local anesthetic)
  Zomig (migraines)
Infection
  Merrem/Meronem (antibiotic)

COMPETITORS

Abbott Labs
Bayer
Bristol-Myers Squibb
Elan
Eli Lilly
GlaxoSmithKline
Hoffmann-La Roche
Johnson & Johnson
Memorial Sloan-Kettering
Merck
Novartis
Pfizer
Roche
Sanofi-Aventis
Schering
Schering-Plough
Wyeth

HISTORICAL FINANCIALS

Company Type: Public

Income Statement

FYE: December 31

	REVENUE ($ mil.)	NET INCOME ($ mil.)	NET PROFIT MARGIN	EMPLOYEES
12/05	23,950	3,884	16.2%	64,900
12/04	21,960	3,051	13.9%	64,000
12/03	19,074	2,268	11.9%	60,000
12/02	17,954	2,307	12.8%	58,000
Annual Growth	10.1%	19.0%	—	3.8%

2005 Year-End Financials

Debt ratio: 3.7%
Return on equity: 11.6%
Cash ($ mil.): 6,603
Current ratio: 2.01
Long-term debt ($ mil.): 1,183
No. of shares (mil.): —
Dividends
  Yield: 2.1%
  Payout: 42.5%
Market value ($ mil.): —

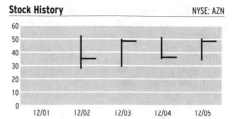

	STOCK PRICE ($) FY Close	P/E High/Low		PER SHARE ($) Earnings	Dividends
12/05	48.60	21	14	2.40	1.02
12/04	36.39	—	—	0.00	0.83
12/03	48.38	—	—	—	0.73
12/02	35.09	—	—	—	0.70
Annual Growth	11.5%	—	—	—	13.4%

Atos Origin

Atos Origin has a firm toehold on Europe's information technology (IT) services mountain. The company provides services such as facilities management, e-commerce consulting, and systems design, implementation, and integration. Atos Origin also offers data and transaction processing services, Web site hosting, and outsourcing services for such functions as customer relationship management and enterprise resource planning. Formed from the 2000 combination of Atos and Origin (the computer services division of Philips Electronics), Atos Origin targets clients in the financial services, automotive, manufacturing, and telecommunications industries.

The company acquired KPMG International's British and Dutch operations in 2002, moving the company into high-end consulting and the realm of Capgemini and IBM. In early 2004 Atos Origin acquired the SEMA Group, the IT services arm of Schlumberger, for about $1.5 billion, a purchase that significantly increased its annual revenues.

After the purchase of the SEMA Group, the company began selling business considered either geographically or commercial non-core. These have included its US-based Cellnet business and operations in the Middle East and the Nordic region. It is focusing on expanding in European markets and has looked far east to markets in India and China for future growth.

Philips is one of the company's largest clients (it had owned more than one-third of Atos Origin, but sold off its stake in 2004 and 2005); KPN is another large customer. Other customers include Vivendi, BNP Paribas, and Unilever.

HISTORY

Atos Origin's lineage is a story of mergers. The company's predecessor, Groupe Sligos, was itself the product of a merger — the 1973 union of Sliga (Crédit Lyonnais' data processing services subsidiary) with Cegos Informatique, a management systems development and consulting company started in 1962.

In 1981 Sligos debuted the first bank/retailer network switching system. It acquired Soliac,

France's largest credit card maker, in 1983. Sligos went public in 1986 and two years later acquired a majority stake in CMG (acquired by rival Logica plc to form LogicaCMG in 2002), one of France's leading computer engineering companies.

During the early 1990s Sligos focused on international growth, gaining majority interests in banking systems companies. It bought a controlling interest in Marben Group, a systems integration and networking firm, in 1993.

In 1996 Sligos joined with CyberCash, a (now-defunct) US-based transaction processing company, to develop a secure Internet payment method for the European market. It sold CMG (by then a PC retailing subsidiary) to Infopoint and its Soliac magnetic strip and smart card unit to Schlumberger.

In late 1997 Sligos merged with French IT services company Axime. (Axime was created by the 1991 merger of IT service providers FITB, Segin, and Sodinforg. Bernard Bourigeaud joined Axime that year and became its chairman and CEO in 1992.)

Following the Sligos-Axime merger the company changed its name to Atos, with Axime's Bourigeaud assuming the role of chairman. Atos spent the last half of 1997 (and the first half of 1998) reorganizing its operations around four key areas: systems integration, outsourcing, multimedia, and services.

In 1998 Atos pared off its networking services and direct marketing subsidiaries. That year the company doubled the size of its Italian operation by acquiring IT services firm Sesam from Fiat and Digital Equipment (later acquired by Compaq), and it bought French customer relationship management specialist Statilogie. Atos in 1999 bought a controlling interest in France-based Odyssée, a consulting specialist in the financial services market. The next year the company developed a joint venture with ParisBourse to offer online stock trading and electronic banking.

In 2000 the company merged with Origin, the computer services arm of Philips Electronics. Bourigeaud became chairman and CEO of the new company, named Atos Origin. In 2002 Atos Origin acquired KPMG's British and Dutch operations for $617 million. Late the same year, Philips ended up taking a sizeable write-off on its stake in Atos Origin.

In early 2004 the company acquired the IT services arm of Schlumberger for about $1.5 billion.

EXECUTIVES

Chairman: Didier Cherpitel
CEO: Bernard Bourigeaud, age 62, $2,316,491 pay
CFO: Eric Guilhou, $1,134,600 pay
Managing Director, UK, Americas, and Asia/Pacific: Xavier Flinois, $1,375,205 pay
Managing Director, France, Germany, Central Europe; Coordinator, Global Managed Operations: Dominique Illien, $1,159,000 pay
Managing Director, Netherlands, Belgium, and Luxembourg; Coordinator, Global Consulting and Global Systems Integration; Head, Marketing Communications and Public Relations: Wilbert Kieboom, $1,372,603 pay
Managing Director, Italy, Spain, Portugal, Southern Europe, South America, and Africa; Coordinator, Telecommunications Sector: Giovanni Linari, $1,228,119 pay
Managing Director, Consulting Division: Keith Rowling
Finance Director, Atos Origin UK: John Campbell
Director, Communication and Public Relations: Marie-Tatiana Collombert
Director, Investor Relations: John White

Head of Applications Maintenance Services: Patrice Dannenberg
Sales Manager, Banking and Telecom, Argentina; Business Manager, Chile: Victor Rodriguez Cubero
Manager, Public Relations: Anne de Beaumont
Manager, Public Relations: Emilie Moreau
Manager, Public Relations: Anne-Marie Capilla
Financial Communications: Bertrand Labonde
Auditors: Amyot Exco; Deloitte & Associés

LOCATIONS

HQ: Atos Origin S.A.
Tour Les Miroirs — Bâtiment C, 18, avenue d'Alsace, 92926 Paris, France
Phone: +33-1-55-91-20-00   **Fax:** +33-1-55-91-20-05
US HQ: 5599 San Felipe, Ste. 300, Houston, TX 77056
US Phone: 713-513-3000   **US Fax:** 713-403-7204
Web: www.atosorigin.com

Atos Origin has operations in more than 40 countries.

2005 Sales

	% of total
Europe, Middle East & Africa	
France	28
UK	21
Benelux	21
Germany & Central Europe	10
Italy	6
Spain	5
Other	2
Americas	4
Asia/Pacific	3
Total	**100**

PRODUCTS/OPERATIONS

2005 Sales

	% of total
Managed operations	51
Systems integration	41
Consulting	8
Total	**100**

2005 Sales By Industry Sector

	% of total
Public Sector & Utilities	26
Telecom & Media	19
Finance	19
Discrete Manufacturing	12
CPG & Retail	10
Process industries	8
Other	6
Total	**100**

Selected Services

Systems Integration
  Application and data migration
  Application lifecycle management
  Configuration management
  Enterprise architecture
  Enterprise resource planning
  eServices
  Operations design, roll-out, and support
  Systems development
Managed Operations
  Business continuity
  Data and application hosting
  IT support outsourcing
  On-demand services
  Security services
Consulting
  Business intelligence
  Business strategy
  Customer relationship management
  Enterprise security
  Financial management solutions
  Knowledge services
  Supply chain management
  Transformation management

COMPETITORS

Altran Technologies	GFI Informatique
ARES	HP Technology Solutions
Aubay	Group
BT	IBM Global Services
Bull	LogicaCMG
Capgemini	Morse
CBGI	Parity
Computacenter	Siemens Business Services
Computer Sciences Corp.	Sogeti-Transiciel
CS Communication	Sopra
Devoteam	Steria
Diagonal	TEAMLOG
Dimension Data	Triple P
EDS	Umanis
Finsiel	Unilog
Fujitsu Services	Unisys
Getronics	Xansa

HISTORICAL FINANCIALS

Company Type: Public

Income Statement				FYE: December 31
	REVENUE ($ mil.)	NET INCOME ($ mil.)	NET PROFIT MARGIN	EMPLOYEES
12/05	6,465	291	4.5%	47,684
12/04	7,232	174	2.4%	46,584
12/03	3,809	(212)	—	26,345
12/02	3,189	74	2.3%	28,602
12/01	2,691	109	4.1%	26,278
Annual Growth	**24.5%**	**27.8%**	**—**	**16.1%**

Net Income History   Euronext Paris: ATO

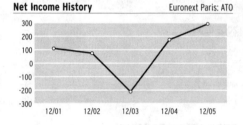

Auchan

Auchan's mammoth markets make room for more than meals. France's third-largest supermarket chain (behind Carrefour and ITM Entreprises), Auchan operates about 365 hypermarkets (French for supercenters) and 655 supermarkets in a dozen countries. France is Auchan's largest market, but it has stores throughout Europe and in China, Morocco, Russia, and Taiwan. (Auchan exited the US and Mexico markets in 2003.) Its hypermarkets carry up to 100,000 products including groceries, apparel, consumer electronics, and fast food. They also provide travel services. Auchan runs Leroy Merlin, a leading home improvement retail chain in France. The founding Mulliez family owns 85% of Auchan; employees own the rest.

The Mulliez family, one of the richest in the world, also owns Tapis Saint-Maclou, France's largest carpet company, and about 80 Kiabi clothing stores in France, Spain, and Italy.

Auchan is expanding in Europe — Poland, Hungary, Italy, and Russia — and in China and Taiwan. In Hungary, where Auchan has 10 hypermarkets (combination grocery and department stores), the French retailer plans to have up to 20 hypermarkets by 2008. Through a partnership with Morocco's ONA group, Auchan plans to open eight hypermarkets and 25 supermarkets there in the next several years. In Italy, Auchan has acquired the food retailing operations of La Rinascente for about $1.4 billion. La Rinascente has split its department store and food businesses. (Auchan already owns part of La Rinascente.)

The company's hypermarkets operate under the names Auchan, Alcampo, Marjane, and RT Mart; its supermarkets operate under various banners including Atac in France, Acima in Morocco, and Sabeco in Spain. In addition to its 665 company-owned supermarkets, another 1,500-plus supermarkets are operated as partnerships or franchises.

Auchan's Leroy Merlin home improvement chain has about 150 stores in France, Italy, and Spain. The do-it-yourself retailer plans to acquire Brico DIY stores in France, Spain, and Portugal. Other holdings include French retailers Decathlon, warehouse-style sporting goods stores, and Boulanger, a consumer electronics chain. Auchan's real estate subsidiary Immochan operates more than 300 shopping centers in 11 countries.

HISTORY

Gerard Mulliez opened his first grocery store in Roubaix, France, in 1961. Seven years later he opened a store (under the Auchan banner) in Roncq — the store was the first modern hypermarket. For the next decade Mulliez expanded his retail operations across France, opening 26 stores.

In 1967 he started an employee shareholding program. Reaching outside the grocery and basic consumer goods market, the company acquired a 50% stake in home improvement retailer Leroy Merlin in 1979.

Auchan entered the international market in 1981, opening an Alcampo hypermarket in Spain. By 1988 the company had one store in the US and a few in Italy. In 1996 Auchan opened hypermarkets in Poland, Mexico, Portugal, and Luxembourg. Also that year Auchan doubled in size by acquiring French grocery retailer Docks de France (including Mammouth hypermarkets and Atac supermarkets) and bought Pao de Acucar, which added more stores in Spain and Portugal. In 1997 it opened stores in Thailand and Argentina, followed by a hypermarket in Hungary in 1998. In 1999 Auchan opened its first store in China.

In April 2000 the company sold 407 small grocery and convenience stores to rival French food retailer Casino Guichard-Perrachon (the stores were obtained when Auchan bought Docks de France). Also in 2000 Auchan opened its second US store (also in Houston) and it bought 68% of retailer RT Mart Taiwan.

Though having announced plans for expansion into Morocco and Russia, Auchan agreed in April 2001 to sell its only hypermarket in Thailand to its rival Casino. Also in 2001 Auchan launched e-commerce sites in France and Spain and acquired Billa, a Polish chain of 11 supermarkets. Overall, the company added 44 supermarkets and 51 hypermarkets that year.

In 2002 Auchan expanded into Russia with the opening of two hypermarkets in the Moscow area.

Auchan closed its hypermarkets in Mexico and shuttered its two remaining US outlets in Houston in March 2003, citing a sharp rise in competition in the Houston area. Overall in 2003, the company opened 31 new stores (nine hypermarkets and 22 supermarkets) in Europe and two hypermarkets in Beijing and Chengdu, China.

Despite a difficult year in France and Italy, Auchan opened 23 new hypermarkets and enlarged another 17 locations in 2005. The retailer also opened its first Atak supermarket in Russia.

EXECUTIVES

Chairman and Managing Director, Hypermarkets: Christophe Dubrulle
Director, Support Services, Hypermarkets; Vice Chairman, France: Henri Mathias
Director, Finance, Hypermarkets: Xavier de Mézerac
Director, Business Development; Chairman, Innochan: Vianney Mulliez
Director, Training and Human Resources; Chairman, Hypermarkets, Poland: Phillipe Saudo
Chairman, Hypermarkets, France: Arnaud Mulliez
Managing Director, Hypermarkets, France; Chairman, Hypermarkets, Luxembourg: Philippe Baroukh
Managing Director, Hypermarkets, Luxembourg: François Remy
Chairman, Hypermarkets, Spain and Portugal: Francis Lepoutre
Managing Director, Hypermarkets, Spain: Patrick Coignard
Managing Director, Hypermarkets, Portugal: Eduardo Igrejas
Managing Director, Hungary: Jean-Paul Filliat
Chairman and Deputy Director, Italy: Benoît F. Lheureux
Managing Director, Italy: Patrick Espasa
Managing Director, Poland: François Colombié
Chairman, Hypermarkets, Hungary and Russia: Jean Mailly
Managing Director, Hypermarkets, Russia: Patrick Longuet
Chairman, Hypermarkets, Morocco: Tajeddine Guennouni
Managing Director, Hypermarkets, Morocco: Philippe Le Grignou
Chairman, Hypermarkets, China and Taiwan: Christian Clerc-Batut
Managing Director, China: Bruno Mercier
Director, Finance, Supermarkets: Philippe Delalande
Auditors: KPMG Audit

LOCATIONS

HQ: Auchan S.A.
200 rue de la Recherche,
59650 Villeneuve d'Ascq, France
Phone: +33-3-28-37-67-00   **Fax:** +33-3-20-67-55-20
Web: www.auchan.com

2005 Stores

	No.
Hypermarkets	
France	120
China	74
Spain	46
Italy (La Rinascente)	43
Poland	19
Taiwan	19
Portugal	17
Morocco	12
Hungary	10
Russia	9
Luxembourg	1
Supermarkets	
France	286
Italy (La Rinascente)	219
Spain	124
Morocco	20
Poland	14
Russia	2
Total	**1,035**

PRODUCTS/OPERATIONS

2005 Sales

	% of total
Hypermarkets	78
Supermarkets	20
Other	2
Total	**100**

COMPETITORS

Carrefour	Kingfisher
Casino Guichard	Lidl & Schwarz Stiftung
Castorama Dubois	Migros
E.Leclerc	PPR
Galeries Lafayette	Royal Ahold
Guyenne et Gascogne	Tengelmann
ITM Entreprises	Tesco
J Sainsbury	Wal-Mart

HISTORICAL FINANCIALS

Company Type: Private

Income Statement

	REVENUE ($ mil.)	NET INCOME ($ mil.)	NET PROFIT MARGIN	EMPLOYEES
				FYE: December 31
12/05	39,802	1,156	2.9%	174,584
12/04	40,983	649	1.6%	155,000
12/03	36,032	722	2.0%	156,000
12/02	28,888	306	1.1%	143,000
12/01	23,196	292	1.3%	136,000
Annual Growth	14.5%	41.0%	—	6.4%

Net Income History

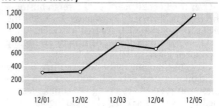

1,200					
1,000					
800					
600					
400					
200					
0	12/01	12/02	12/03	12/04	12/05

Aviva

In the consolidating European insurance industry, no acronym can last for long. Originally formed as CGNU after the merger of insurer CGU and nonlife specialist Norwich Union, this company has reinvented itself as Aviva. A major insurance force in the UK and a leading firm worldwide, Aviva offers both life and general insurance. Its long-term savings segments focuses on life insurance, pensions, unit trusts, and other products; its general insurance segment includes home, auto, and fire coverage. Financial services include international fund management.

In 2006, after a failed bid for rival Prudential plc (not to be confused with the US-based Prudential Financial) was flatly rejected, Aviva acquired US rival AmerUs Group for $2.9 billion in cash. AmerUs is now a fully-owned subsidiary of Aviva unit Aviva USA, jumpstarting Aviva's re-entry into the US market. Aviva acquired UK-based automotive-service company RAC in 2005, only to sell the vehicles solutions business off a year later to VT Group. At around the same time, the company also divested its 50% ownership in Lex Vehicle Leasing to HBOS.

As part of its strategy of exiting unprofitable insurance markets, Aviva sold its US general insurance operations to White Mountains Insurance Group. The company instead focused on smaller acquisitions in emerging markets: Aviva bought insurers in Belgium, Hungary, and the Netherlands. The company also purchased Fortis' Australian operations, making Aviva one of that country's top 10 insurers. Extending its distribution channels, Aviva has teamed up with banks all across Europe (including tie-ups with ABN AMRO and Royal Bank of Scotland).

Aviva is focused on growing its long-term savings business (including the launch of online wealth management services in the UK) and on expanding into central and eastern Europe. Having entered Russia in March 2006, Aviva hopes that a major push will gain it 10% of the Russian market by 2011. The insurer also looks to Asia for operational strategies as it moves more and more of its back-office operations to India and Sri Lanka. Aviva expects to employ as many as 7,000 offshore workers by the end of 2007. In September 2006 the company announced plans to cut 4,000 jobs in the UK and add 1,000 workers in India.

HISTORY

When insurers hiked premiums after the 1861 Great Tooley Street Fire of London, merchants formed Commercial Union Fire Insurance (CU). It opened offices throughout the UK and in foreign ports and soon added life (1862) and marine (1863) coverage.

Over the next 20 years, CU's foreign business thrived. The firm had offices across the US by the 1880s. In the 1890s CU entered Australia, India, and Southeast Asia. Foreign business eventually accounted for some 75% of CU's sales.

CU went shopping in the 20th century, adding accident insurer Palatine Insurance Co. of Manchester in 1900 and rescuing two companies ruined by San Francisco's 1906 earthquake and fire. CU recovered from the Depression with the help of a booming auto insurance market, and spent most of the 1930s and WWII consolidating operations to cut costs.

Profits suffered in the 1950s as CU faced increased competition in the US. To boost sales, it merged with both multiline rival North British and Mercantile and life insurer Northern and Employers Assurance in the early 1960s. While US business continued to lag in the 1970s, the company's European business grew.

From 1982 to 1992, CU cut its operations in the US, entered new markets (Poland, 1992; South Africa and Vietnam, 1996), and sold its New Zealand subsidiaries (1995). As competition in the UK increased, the company in 1997 reorganized and merged with General Accident in 1998.

General Accident & Employers Liability Assurance Association (GA) was formed in 1885 in Perth, Scotland, to sell workers' compensation insurance. Within a few years, GA had branches in London and Scotland. It diversified into insurance for train accidents (1887), autos (1896), and fire (1899); in 1906 its name changed to General Accident Fire and Life Assurance.

GA expanded into Australia, Europe, and Africa at the turn of the century. After WWI, the company's auto insurance grew along with car ownership. During the 1930s the company entered the US auto insurance market. WWII put a stop to GA's growth.

The company expanded after the war, forming Pennsylvania General Fire Insurance Association

(1963) and acquiring the UK's Yorkshire Insurance Co. (1967). By the 1980s about one-third of its sales came from the US.

After 1986 GA acquired some 500 real estate brokerage agencies to cross-sell its home and life insurance. To increase presence in Asia and the Pacific, the company in 1988 acquired NZI Corp., a New Zealand banking and insurance company whose failing operations cost GA millions. At the same time, new US government regulations and a series of damaging storms hammered the company.

In response GA cut costs, posting a profit by 1993. As the industry consolidated, the company bought nonstandard auto insurer Sabre (1995), life insurer Provident Mutual (1996), and General Insurance Group Ltd. in Canada (1997). Unable to compete on its own, GA merged with Commercial Union to form CGU in 1998.

After the merger, CGU added personal pension plans and entered alliances to sell insurance in Italy and India. Merger costs and exceptional losses for 1998 hit operating profits hard. In 1999 CGU upped its stake in French bank Société Générale to about 7% to help it fend off a hostile takeover attempt by Banque Nationale de Paris (now BNP Paribas).

In 2000 the company merged with rival Norwich Union to form CGNU and made plans to exit the Canadian life and the US general insurance businesses. In 2001 CGNU sold its US property/casualty operations to White Mountains Insurance.

In an attempt to strengthen its brand name, the company changed its name to Aviva in 2002. Aviva in 2004 announced plans to merge 10 life and pension subsidiaries into four, saying the move would streamline operations and save the company money. Aviva also made changes to its Asian operations in 2004, selling its general insurance business in Asia to Mitsui Sumitomo Insurance.

EXECUTIVES

Chairman: Lord Colin Sharman, age 63
Group Chief Executive and Board Member: Richard Harvey, age 55
Group Finance Director and Board Member: Andrew Moss, age 48
Group Executive Director, Aviva International; Board Member: Philip Scott, age 52
Group Executive Director, Aviva UK; Board Member: Patrick Snowball, age 55
Chief Executive, Aviva Europe: Tidjane Thiam
Chief Executive, Norwich Union; Managing Director, RAC: Simon Machell
Chief Executive, Norwich Union Life: Mark Hodges
CEO, Russia: Andrei Doubinine, age 43
Group Company Secretary: Richard Whitaker
Investor Relations Director: Charles Barrows, age 43
Director of External Affairs: Hayley Stimpson
Head of Group Media Relations: Sue Winston
Auditors: Ernst & Young

LOCATIONS

HQ: Aviva plc
St. Helen's, 1 Undershaft,
London EC3P 3DQ, United Kingdom
Phone: +44-20-7283-2000   **Fax:** +44-20-7662-2753
Web: www.aviva.com

Aviva has offices in more than 50 countries in Africa, the Asia/Pacific region, Europe, the Middle East, and North and South America.

2005 Sales

	% of total
Europe	
UK	41
Other countries	53
Other regions	6
Total	**100**

PRODUCTS/OPERATIONS

Selected Subsidiaries and Affiliates

Aseguradora Valenciana, SA de Seguros y Reaseguros (50%; Spain)
Aviva Asigurari de Viata SA (Romania)
AVIVA COFCO Life Insurance Company Limited (50%; China)
Aviva Australia Holdings Limited
  Navigator Australia Limited
  Norwich Union Life Australia Limited
  Portfolio Partners Limited (Australia
Aviva Canada Inc
  Aviva Insurance Company of Canada
Aviva Eletbiztosito Rt. (Hungary)
Aviva Hayat ve Emeklilik (Turkey)
Aviva Insurance Berhad (51%; Malaysia)
Aviva Insurance (Thai) Co. Limited (68%; Thailand)
Aviva Italia Holding SpA (Italy)
Aviva Life Insurance Company India Pvt. Limited (26%)
Aviva Life Insurance Company Limited (Hong Kong)
Aviva Limited (Singapore)
Aviva Participations SA (France)
Aviva Sigorta AS (99%; Turkey)
Aviva USA Corporation
  Aviva Life Insurance Company (US)
Aviva Vida y Pensiones, SA de Seguros y Reaseguros (50%; Spain)
Aviva zivotni pojist'ovna a.s. (Czech Republic)
Bank Nagelmackers 1747 NV (99.6%; Belgium)
Bia Galicia de Seguros y Reaseguros (50%; Spain)
The British Aviation Insurance Company Limited (38%)
Caja Espana Vida, Compania de Seguros y Reaseguros (50%; Spain)
CGNU Life Assurance Limited
CGU Bonus Limited
CGU Insurance plc
CGU International Insurance plc
CGU Underwriting Limited
Commercial Union International Life SA (Luxembourg)
Commercial Union Life Assurance Company Limited
Commercial Union Polska Towarzystwo Ubezpieczen na Zycie SA (90%; Poland)
Commercial Union Polska Towarzystwo Ubezpieczen Ogolnych SA (90%; Poland)
Commercial Union Powszechne Towarzystwo Emerytalne BPH CU WBK SA (75%; Poland)
Curepool Limited (Bermuda)
Delta Lloyd Deutschland AG (Germany)
  Berlinische Lebensversicherung AG (99.5%; Germany)
Delta Lloyd Life NV (Belgium)
Delta Lloyd NV (Netherlands)
Eurovida BNC Companhia de Seguros de Vida S.A. (50%; Portugal)
General Accident plc
General Vida Sociedad de Agencia de Seguros (25%; Spain)
Hibernian Group plc (Ireland)
  Hibernian General Insurance Limited (Ireland)
  Hibernian Investment Managers Limited (Ireland)
  Hibernian Life & Pensions Limited (Ireland)
London & Edinburgh Insurance Group Limited
Morley Fund Management International Limited
Morley Fund Management Limited
Morley Investment Services Limited
Morley Pooled Pensions Limited
Morley Properties Limited
The Northern Assurance Company Limited
Norwich Union Annuity Limited
Norwich Union Equity Release Limited
Norwich Union Healthcare Limited
Norwich Union Insurance Limited
Norwich Union Investment Funds Limited
Norwich Union Life & Pensions Limited
Norwich Union Linked Life Assurance Limited
Norwich Union Personal Finance Limited
ProCapital SA (44%; France)
RBS Life Investments Limited (49.99%)
RBSG Collective Investments Limited (49.99%)
Unicorp Vida, Compania de Seguros y Reaseguros SA (50%; Spain)

COMPETITORS

Abbey National
Allianz
AXA UK
Chubb Corp
Equity Insurance
Guardian Royal Exchange plc
Highway Insurance
Legal & General Group
Lloyd's
Lloyds TSB
Millea Holdings
Prudential plc
QBE Insurance
Royal & Sun Alliance Insurance
Standard Life
Zurich Financial Services

HISTORICAL FINANCIALS

Company Type: Public

Income Statement

FYE: December 31

	ASSETS ($ mil.)	NET INCOME ($ mil.)	INCOME AS % OF ASSETS	EMPLOYEES
12/05	453,234	3,265	0.7%	54,791
12/04	447,399	2,036	0.5%	55,872
12/03	371,012	1,687	0.5%	60,740
12/02	296,598	(857)	—	64,562
12/01	273,128	1,634	0.6%	68,107
Annual Growth	13.5%	18.9%	—	(5.3%)

2005 Year-End Financials

Equity as % of assets: —
Return on assets: 0.7%
Return on equity: —
Long-term debt ($ mil.): —
Sales ($ mil.): 87,636

Net Income History

London: AV

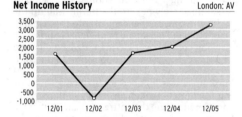

AXA

The insurance world revolves around this AXA. AXA, which started as a sleepy collection of mutual insurance companies, is today one of the world's largest insurers (alongside Allianz and ING) and a financial management powerhouse. In the US, AXA owns AXA Financial, which owns a majority of investment manager Alliance Capital Management. The company also has major subsidiaries in the UK (AXA UK, formerly Sun Life and Provincial Holdings), Australia (AXA Asia Pacific, formerly National Mutual), and Belgium (AXA Belgium, formerly Royale Belge). The companies offer life insurance; personal and commercial property and casualty insurance; reinsurance; financial services; and real estate investment services.

In 2006, AXA sold its reinsurance business, AXA RE, to Paris Re Holdings. Under the agreement, AXA retains but 5 to 10% ownership of the company.

Mutuelles AXA (a group of eight mutuals) controls AXA through its 20% stake.

Rather than trying to run a cross-border organization, AXA instead buys and builds up businesses in each country, rebranding them under the AXA name.

Through former executive chairman (now supervisory board chairman) Claude Bébéar, acquisitive AXA brought a North American style to the once-genteel practice of business in France. The company wielded its power in the bank takeover struggle that resulted in the formation of BNP Paribas.

AXA has discontinued its slumping US-based reinsurance operations (AXA Corporate Solutions Reinsurance and AXA Corporate Solutions Life Reinsurance).

In an attempt to strengthen its US retail insurance and annuity business, AXA, through subsidiary AXA Financial, bought MONY Group for some $1.5 billion. The deal was opposed by some of MONY's shareholders, but ultimately gained approval.

In 2006 AXA entered into talks with Credit Suisse to acquire the Winterthur insurance division from the latter at a cost of more than $8 billion. Switzerland-based Winterthur offers life, pension, and non-life insurance policies in about 15 countries worldwide. The acquisition would strengthen AXA's position in Eastern Europe and Asia (specifically China and Japan). The deal was approved by US antitrust authorities a few months after it was announced; AXA still must wait for additional approval from similar counterparts internationally.

HISTORY

AXA dates to the 1817 formation of regional fire insurer Compagnie d'Assurances Mutuelles contre l'incendie in Rouen, France (northwest of Paris). In 1881 France's first mutual life insurer was founded: Mutuelle Vie.

In 1946 these two operations and the younger Anciennes Mutuelles Accidents (founded 1922) were brought together by Sahut d'Izarn (general manager of Compagnie d'Assurances) as the Groupe Ancienne Mutuelle. Later members included Ancienne Mutuelle of Calvados (1946), Ancienne Mutuelle of Orleans (1950), Mutualité Générale (1953), and Participation (1954).

A long-term thinker, d'Izarn named not only his successor, Lucien Aubert, but also Aubert's successor: Claude Bébéar, a 23-year-old friend of d'Izarn's son. Never having held a job, Bébéar found the whole thing amusing and decided to try it.

Groupe Ancienne Mutuelle prospered during the 1960s, thanks to d'Izarn's disciplined management, but his technophobia kept the company from entering the computer age.

D'Izarn died in 1972. Aubert capitulated to worker demands during a series of strikes in the early 1970s; Bébéar ended a 1974 strike by threatening to use force against an employee sit-in, then ousted Aubert.

Bébéar spent the rest of the 1970s upgrading the firm's technology. During this period the company became known as Mutuelles Unies.

Bébéar then began building the firm through a series of spectacular acquisitions. In 1982 Mutuelles Unies gained control of crisis-ridden stock insurer Drouot. Two years later the company's name became AXA (which has no meaning and was chosen because it is pronounced the same in most Western languages). When another old-line insurer, Providence, went on the market, AXA went after it. Providence's management was entertaining another offer when AXA bought tiny,

inactive Bayas Tudjus, which held the right to a seat on the Providence board. Bébéar capitalized on small stockholders' dissatisfaction to spark a bidding war and used a new issue of Drouot stock in 1986 to buy Providence — France's first hostile takeover.

AXA bought lackluster US firm Equitable (now AXA Financial) in 1991, infusing $1 billion into the firm in return for the right to own up to 50% of its stock upon demutualization in 1992. AXA moved into Asia with the purchase of Australia's National Mutual in 1995.

Bébéar consolidated the operations into a global organization. In 1996 AXA bought the ailing Union des Assurances de Paris, which had done poorly since its 1994 privatization. It bought the 52% of Belgian insurer Royale Belge SA it didn't already own, as well as Belgian savings bank Anhyp in 1998.

Bébéar raised hackles when he supported the Société Générale-Paribas bank merger, then supported BNP's hostile takeover attempt of both (which garnered only Paribas). In 1999 AXA bought Guardian Royal Exchange, then sold the life and pensions business to Dutch insurer AEGON; Bébéar announced his retirement in 1999. In 2000 he stepped down from the management board but took over as chairman of the Supervisory Board.

That year AXA took control of Japan's Nippon Dantai Life Insurance. It also bought the remaining shares of AXA Financial and the 44% of AXA UK (formerly Sun Life and Provincial Holdings) it didn't already own. The next year AXA unloaded its debt-heavy subsidiary Banque Worms to Deutsche Bank.

EXECUTIVES

Chairman of the Supervisory Board: Claude Bébéar, age 71
Vice Chairman of the Supervisory Board: Jean-René Fourtou, age 67
Chairman of the Management Board and CEO: Henri de Castries, age 52, $3,582,674 pay
Member of the Management Board in charge of Transversal Operations and Projects, Human Resources, Brand and Communication: Claude Brunet, age 49, $1,522,810 pay
Member of the Management Board in charge of Finance, Control, and Strategy: Denis Duverne, age 53, $1,901,885 pay
Member of the Management Board and CEO and President, AXA Financial: Christopher M. (Kip) Condron, age 59, $5,135,362 pay
Member of the Management Board, CEO, AXA France, and Head of Large Risks, Assistance and AXA Canada: François Pierson, age 59, $1,739,621 pay
Chairman, AXA Seguros and Head of Mediterranean Region: Jean-Raymond Abat
Group CEO, Japan and Asia-Pacific Region; President of the Board of Directors, AXA RE: Philippe Donnet, age 46
Group CEO, AXA UK: Nicolas Moreau, age 41
CEO, AXA Re: Hans-Peter Gerhardt
Group CEO, AXA Asia Pacific Holdings: Andrew (Andy) Penn, age 43
CEO, AXA Investment Managers: Dominique Carrel-Billiard, age 40
Group CEO, AXA Northern Europe; CEO, AXA Royale Belge: Alfred J. (Freddy) Bouckaert, age 60
Chairman, Management Board, AXA Konzern: Eugène Teysen
Vice Chairman and CFO, AXA Financial: Stanley B. (Stan) Tulin, age 56
SVP, Group Procurement: Alain Page-Lecuyer
Regional CFO, AXA Northern Europe: Christophe Dupont Madinier

President, COO, and Director, AllianceBernstein:
Gerald M. (Jerry) Lieberman, age 59
VP, Group Communications, Brand and Sustainable
Development: Claire Dorland-Clauzel
Auditors: PricewaterhouseCoopers Audit

LOCATIONS

HQ: AXA
25 avenue Matignon, 75008 Paris, France
Phone: +33-1-40-75-57-00   **Fax:** +33-1-40-75-57-95
US HQ: 1290 Avenue of the Americas,
New York, NY 10104
US Phone: 212-314-2902   **US Fax:** 212-707-1805
Web: www.axa.com

AXA has operations in more than 60 countries in the Asia/Pacific region, Europe, and North and South America.

PRODUCTS/OPERATIONS

Selected Subsidiaries and Affiliates

Alliance Capital Management (56%; US)
ASA Portugal Life (95%)
AXA Art (91%; Germany)
AXA Asia Pacific Holdings
AXA Assicurazioni (Italy)
AXA Assistance
AXA Assurance Maroc (51%; Morocco)
AXA Assurances (Canada)
AXA Assurances (Switzerland)
AXA Aurora (Spain)
AXA Bank (91%; Germany)
AXA Bank Belgium
AXA Banque
AXA Bausparkasse (91%; Germany)
AXA Belgium
AXA China Region (52%; Hong Kong)
AXA Corporate Solutions Assurance (99%)
AXA Credit
AXA Financial (US)
AXA France Assurances
AXA Germany
AXA Insurance (96%; Japan)
AXA Insurance (Canada)
AXA Insurance (Singapore)
AXA Insurance (UK)
AXA Investment Managers (93%; US)
AXA Ireland
AXA Japan
AXA Konzern (95%; Germany)
AXA Life (52%; Singapore)
AXA Luxembourg
AXA Non-Life Insurance (Japan)
AXA Oyak (50%; Turkey)
AXA Portugal (99%)
AXA PPP Healthcare (UK)
AXA Re
AXA Real Estate Investment Managers (93%; US)
AXA Rosenberg (75%; US)
AXA Sun Life (UK)
AXA UK Holdings
AXA Verzekeringen (The Netherlands)
Compagnie Financiere de Paris
Direct Seguros (50%; Spain)

COMPETITORS

AEGON	ING
AGF	Legal & General Group
AIG	Merrill Lynch
Allianz	MetLife
CIGNA	Munich Re
Citigroup	Nationwide
Dai-ichi Mutual Life	New York Life
Fortis SA/NV	Nippon Life Insurance
Generali	Prudential
The Hartford	Sumitomo Life
Highway Insurance	

HISTORICAL FINANCIALS

Company Type: Public

Income Statement

FYE: December 31

	ASSETS ($ mil.)	NET INCOME ($ mil.)	INCOME AS % OF ASSETS	EMPLOYEES
12/05	684,311	6,197	0.9%	78,800
12/04	663,639	4,414	0.7%	76,339
12/03	566,007	4,612	0.8%	74,584
Annual Growth	10.0%	15.9%	—	2.8%

2005 Year-End Financials

Equity as % of assets: 6.2%
Return on assets: 0.9%
Return on equity: 14.7%
Long-term debt ($ mil.): 22,858
No. of shares (mil.): —
Dividends
Yield: 2.1%
Payout: 20.7%
Market value ($ mil.): —
Sales ($ mil.): 84,887

Stock History

NYSE: AXA

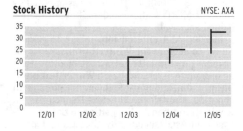

	STOCK PRICE ($) FY Close	P/E High/Low		PER SHARE ($) Earnings	Dividends
12/05	32.33	10	7	3.23	0.67
12/04	24.75	11	8	2.36	0.38
12/03	21.47	—	—	—	0.38
Annual Growth	22.7%	—	—	36.9%	32.8%

Axel Springer

The paper trail has been a path to success for Axel Springer Verlag. One of Europe's leading publishers, the company owns hundreds of newspapers and magazines throughout the continent, including *Bild* (Germany's #1 newspaper), *Die Welt*, and *Hamburger Abendblatt*. Its magazine portfolio boasts titles such as *Bild der Frau* (women's monthly), *Hörzu* (television guide), and *Sport Bild*. Axel Springer is also one of Germany's leading book publishers, owns about a dozen commercial printing plants (for company and third-party use), and has investments in on-line bookseller Buecher.de and TV production company ProSiebenSat.1. The family of the late founder owns about 50% of the firm.

Axel Springer publishes more than 150 newspapers and magazine titles in total, with distribution to about 30 countries worldwide.

Widening its reach, Springer has had success with publications in Eastern Europe and has published its first Russian magazine. The company launched a Russian edition of licensed business magazine *Forbes*. In 2005 the company announced plans to expand content and distribution of its reduced-format daily newspaper *Welt Kompakt*. Part of the reasoning behind it is to stem competition such as Sweden's Metro from getting a foothold on the dailies market.

The company has also launched a new sports daily called Sport-B.Z., which will focus primarily on soccer.

Axel Springer has attempted to acquire German cable television producer ProSiebenSat.1, of which it already owned about 12%. The deal would have changed the landscape of German media and therefore had to be closely examined by the German antitrust authority, which in the end caused the downfall of the deal. The antitrust authority told Axel Springer that it could take over ProSiebenSat.1 if the company sold off either the ProSieben or Sat.1 portions of the newly formed company. Axel Springer refused to compromise and dropped the deal altogether in early 2006.

The company has reduced its workforce by some 20% in recent years. It announced further cuts in 2007, in order to follow a consultant's recommendation to eliminate some 300 jobs over a three-year period.

HISTORY

Hinrich Springer, whose newspaper business had been closed by the Nazi government in 1941, and his son Axel launched Axel Springer Verlag in 1946 with the magazine *Nordwestdeutsche Hefte*. In 1948 the company unveiled *Hamburger Abendblatt*, which became Hamburg's best-selling newspaper by 1950. Axel Springer eventually took over the business and introduced the tabloid *Bild Zeitung* (later renamed *Bild*) in 1952. The success of the paper helped fund the company's expansion.

Axel Springer bought the daily *Die Welt* in 1953 and *Berliner Morgenpost* in 1959. The company moved its headquarters to Berlin in 1966. Fiercely supportive of the reunification of Germany, Springer built the company's headquarters immediately next to the Berlin Wall. In the 1970s the company expanded into the regional newsletter and magazine market. Axel Springer's growing control over German media did not go unnoticed, however, and opposition to the company's power was demonstrated when its Hamburg office was bombed in 1972 (the company was the target of arson again in 1998). Springer considered selling the entire company, but opted to sell several individual publications instead.

The company expanded beyond print media in 1984, investing in satellite consortium SAT.1 Satelliten Fernsehen. In 1985 it acquired stakes in cable TV and bought two Munich radio stations. After taking the company public that year, founder Axel Springer died. In 1989 German media firm KirchGruppe (since renamed TaurusGroup) began buying shares in Axel Springer Verlag.

In 1996 Axel Springer entered the Czech and Slovak newspaper markets with the purchase of a 49% stake in Dutch firm Ringier-Taurus. The company formed a joint venture in 1998 with Infoseek (later absorbed by Walt Disney Internet Group) and other partners to launch a German-language Web search service. It also bought 95% of German book publisher ECON + LIST Verlagsgesellschaft. August Fischer, former chief executive of News Corp.'s News International, was appointed chairman and CEO that year. A 1998 bid to buy UK-based media firm Mirror Group (now Trinity Mirror) proved unsuccessful.

In 1999 Axel Springer acquired stakes in several TV production companies, including a 90% interest in Schwartzkopff TV-Productions. The following year the company merged its 41%-owned TV station SAT.1 with German TV station operator Pro Sieben Media to create ProSiebenSAT.1 Media, Germany's largest commercial TV group. (Axel Springer now owns 12% of the company.)

Fischer retired at the end of 2001 and was replaced by Mathias Döpfner. The company began investing in new online ventures, including a portal built around *Bild*. TaurusGroup sold its shares in the company in 2003 to Deutsche Bank.

In 2003 it agreed to sell the paperback unit of its Ullstein Heyne List book group to Random House. The company also sold off several of its stakes in TV production companies as it seeks to focus on its main publishing unit. In 2004, it took a 49% stake in Stepstone Deutschland, a Web-based employment agency in Germany.

EXECUTIVES

Chairman: Giuseppe Vita, age 71
CEO; Head, Newspaper Division: Mathias Döpfner, age 43
Deputy Chairman of the Management Board and Head of Printing and Logistics Division: Rudolf Knepper, age 61
COO and CFO: Steffen Naumann, age 40
Head of Magazines and International Division: Andreas Wiele, age 44
Head of Investor Relations: Diana Ioana Grigoriev
Investor Relations: Claudia Thomé
Auditors: PwC Deutsche Revision AG

LOCATIONS

HQ: Axel Springer Verlag AG
  Axel-Springer-Str. 65, 10888 Berlin, Germany
Phone: +49-30-2591-0
Web: www.asv.de

2005 Sales

	% of total
Germany	84
Other countries	16
Total	**100**

PRODUCTS/OPERATIONS

2005 Sales

	% of total
Newspapers	60
Magazines	33
Printing	4
Other	3
Total	**100**

Selected Magazines

Auto Bild
Bild der Frau
Bildwoche
Computer Bild
Hörzu
Musikexpress
Popcorn
Sport Bild
TVneu
Yam!

Selected Newspapers

Berliner Morgenpost
Bild
Bild am Sonntag
B.Z.
Die Welt
Euro am Sonntag
Hamburger Abendblatt
Welt am Sonntag

Selected Electronic Media and TV Investments

Buecher.de (25%, online bookseller)
ProSiebenSat.1 Media (12%, TV group)
Schwartzkopff TV (TV production)

COMPETITORS

American Institute Of Physics	METRO AG
Bertelsmann	Metro International
Dow Jones	Modern Times Group AB
Edipresse	News Corp.
Editis	Pearson
Emap	Reed Elsevier Group
EM.TV	Reuters
Financial Times	Schibsted
Gruner + Jahr	Time
Hachette Filipacchi Médias	Georg von Holtzbrinck
IPC Group	VNU

HISTORICAL FINANCIALS

Company Type: Public

Income Statement

	REVENUE ($ mil.)	NET INCOME ($ mil.)	NET PROFIT MARGIN	EMPLOYEES
12/05	2,832	273	9.6%	10,166
12/04	3,276	201	6.1%	10,700
12/03	3,056	164	5.3%	11,694
12/02	2,910	64	2.2%	13,203
12/01	2,537	(175)	—	13,500
Annual Growth	**2.8%**	**—**	**—**	**(6.8%)**

FYE: December 31

Net Income History

German: SPR

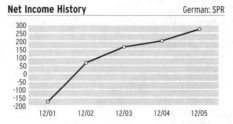

Bacardi & Company

You want proof? The folks at Bacardi Limited will pour it for you — from a bottle. One of the world's leading wine and spirits groups, Bacardi produces a dozen varieties of its rum, selling more than 200 million bottles per year in nearly 200 countries. Other brands include Bombay Sapphire gin, Martini & Rossi vermouth, Dewar's Scotch whisky, DiSaronno Amaretto, and B&B and Benedictine liqueurs. Other drinks by Bacardi include vodka, tequila, cognac, sparkling wine, and Hatuey beer. About 600 descendants of founder Facundo Bacardi y Massó own Bacardi.

Steeped in liquor lore, Bacardi claims the first Cuba Libre (rum and cola) was made with its product in 1898. Its bottles feature Bacardi's trademark bat logo, said to have been inspired by bats (an omen of good luck) that lived in the company's first distillery. To round out its white liquor portfolio, the distiller has been expanding its line of premium liquors through acquisitions, including one of Mexico's leading premium tequilas, Tequila Cazadores. It also holds distribution rights in Mexico to Brown-Forman's Jack Daniel's, Southern Comfort, and other popular brands. In 2004 Bacardi topped off its liquor offerings with the purchase of premium vodka brand Grey Goose. In 2006 the company acquired New Zealand spirits company 42 BELOW, known for its vodka, for approximately $91 million. Though a well-known family operation,

Bacardi may go public. Shareholders have approved the creation of two classes of company stock — one for family members and one for the public. While family members would maintain a controlling interest in the company, it is believed the company needs outside investment to grow its business. It has yet to actually issue any new stock. Ruben Rodriguez was replaced as chairman in 2005 by Facundo Bacardi, a great-grandson of the company's founder.

HISTORY

Facundo Bacardi y Massó immigrated to Cuba from Spain in 1830. He started in the liquor business as a rum salesman for John Nunes, an Englishman who owned a small distillery in Santiago, Cuba. In 1862 Facundo, his brother José, and a French wine merchant bought Nunes' distillery and began producing a smoother rum from a formula created by Facundo after years of trial and error. The more mixable quality of Bacardi's rum proved to be a key to its success. In 1877 Facundo passed company leadership to his sons; the eldest, Emilio, took over running the company (and spent some of his spare time in jail for his anti-Spanish activities).

Bacardi Limited struggled during the 1890s as Cuba's economy foundered. The business was thrown into even greater turmoil when revolutionary leader José Marti began what would be the final fight for Cuban independence. One of Marti's biggest supporters was Emilio, who earned another stay in jail and then exile for his sympathies. After Cuba gained its independence in 1902, Bacardi grew rapidly, getting a further boost from Prohibition as Havana became "the unofficial US saloon." (Prohibition did, however, end a venture in the US.)

The company moved into brewing in the 1920s and expanded its rum operations in the 1930s, opening a distillery in Mexico (1931) and another in Puerto Rico (1935). In 1944 it opened Bacardi Imports in the US and built up its overseas operations during the 1950s.

Amid all its success, Bacardi again became embroiled in Cuban politics during the late 1950s. Although some company leaders showed open opposition to Cuban leader Fulgencio Batista and support for Fidel Castro, others opposed Castro. As a result of the 1959 revolution, the Bacardi family was forced into exile, fleeing to the US and Europe. Castro seized Bacardi's assets in 1960. However, the expropriation was not a fatal blow since both the Mexican and Puerto Rican operations had been outearning the Cuban operations since the 1940s. Bacardi continued to enjoy explosive growth during the 1960s and 1970s. In 1977 some family members sold about 12% of the Bacardi empire to Hiram Walker.

By 1980 Bacardi was the #1 liquor brand in the US, but family squabbles and bad decisions threatened the company. Bacardi Capital, set up to manage the empire's money, lost $50 million in 1986. That year the empire's leadership started to buy up shares in Bacardi companies, including those sold to Hiram Walker and the 10% of Bacardi Corporation that had been sold to the public in 1962.

In an effort to diversify and to increase its European markets, the company bought a majority stake in Martini & Rossi in 1993. Two years later it launched Bacardi Limon, a citrus-flavored rum, and Hatuey (pronounced "ah-tway") beer. In 1996 family lawyer George Reid became president and CEO, the first nonfamily member to head the company.

Bacardi acquired the rights to the Havana Club trademark in 1997 from the Arechabala family. The move exacerbated a dispute with France's Pernod Ricard, which had partnered with the Cuban government to use the Havana Club name (the dispute lives on in the US, spearheaded by Bacardi U.S.A.). Bacardi bought the Dewar's Scotch whisky and Bombay gin brands from Diageo in 1998.

In 2000 Reid resigned and Ruben Rodriguez was appointed president and CEO. Later in the year Rodriguez added chairman to his titles when Manuel Jorge Cutillas retired. In 2000 Bacardi (along with partner Brown-Forman) also lost the bidding war for Seagram's alcoholic drinks business (Glenlivet, Sterling Vineyards, Martell Cognac) to rival bidding duo Diageo and Pernod Ricard.

In 2002 Bacardi acquired Tequila Cazadores, a leader in Mexico's Agave Reposado segment. Javier Ferran, an 18-year company veteran, left Bacardi in 2004 after serving as CEO for only about 18 months. Ferran was replaced by Andreas Gembler, a Philip Morris veteran.

Rodriguez retired in 2005 as the company's chairman. Bacardi named Facundo Bacardi, a great-grandson of the company's founder, as chairman. Rodriguez remained a board member.

EXECUTIVES

Chairman: Facundo L. Bacardi, age 38
President, CEO, and Director: Andreas Gembler, age 62
VP, Operations and Sales: Guillermo Rodriguez
VP, Packaging Global Manufacturing: Yousef Zaatar
President and CEO, Bacardi North America:
Eduardo M. Sardina
CEO, Bacardi Canada: Paul Beggan
President, Bacardi Puerto Rico: Angel Torres
Global Chief Marketing Officer: Stella David, age 42
Director, Barcardi-Martini BV Northern Europe:
Luis Bach
Director, Global Operations: Jon Grey
Director, IT: Ron Stan
Director, Marketing: Andrew Carter
Director, Trade Marketing: Brue Ray
Manager, Bacardi Global Project: Richie DiFranco
Manager, Marketing: Joe Metevier

LOCATIONS

HQ: Bacardi & Company Limited
65 Pitts Bay Rd., Pembroke HM 08, Bermuda
Phone: 441-295-4345 **Fax:** 441-292-0562
Web: www.bacardi.com

Bacardi Limited has 20 production facilities worldwide.

PRODUCTS/OPERATIONS

Selected Brands

Bacardi

8	Black	Limón
151	Carta Blanca	Select
1873	Exclusiv	Solera
Solera	Gold	Spice
Anejo	Light	

Castillo
Anejo
Gold
White
Estelar Suave
Ron Bacardi Anejo

Other Spirits and Beverages

Alcohol-based aperitif
Pastis Casanis
Pastis
Amaretto
DiSaronno Amaretto
Beer
Hatuey
Brandy
Gran Reserva Especial
Vergel
Viejo Vergel
Champagne
Charles Volner
Veuve Amiot
Cognac
Exshaw
Gaston de la Grange
Otard
Gin
Bombay
Bombay Sapphire
Bosford, Martini
Liqueur
B&B
Benedictine
China Martini
Kalyr
Nassau Royale
Low-alcohol beverage
Bacardi Breezer
Bacardi & Cola
Caribbean Classics
Martini Brand Jigger
Scotch whisky
Dewar's
Glen Deveron
William Lawson's Finest Blend
William Lawson's Scottish Gold
Sparkling wine
Grande Auguri
Martini & Rossi Asti Spumante
Montelera Riserva
Martini Brand Asti
Martini Brand Riesling
Tequila
Camino Real
Tequila Cazadores
Vodka
Eristoff
Grey Goose
Martini
Natasha
Russian Prince

COMPETITORS

Angostura
Beam Global Spirits & Wine
Blavod Extreme Spirits
Brown-Forman
Cabo Wabo
Constellation Brands
Cruzan International
Diageo
Eckes
Fortune Brands
Gallo
Heaven Hill Distilleries
Jose Cuervo
LVMH
Pernod Ricard
Rémy Cointreau
Sebastiani Vineyards
Suntory Ltd.
William Grant & Sons

HISTORICAL FINANCIALS

Company Type: Private

Income Statement

FYE: March 31

	REVENUE ($ mil.)	NET INCOME ($ mil.)	NET PROFIT MARGIN	EMPLOYEES
3/04	3,300	—	—	6,000
3/03	3,100	—	—	6,300
3/02	2,900	—	—	6,300
3/01	2,700	—	—	6,200
3/00	2,600	—	—	6,000
Annual Growth	6.1%	—	—	0.0%

Revenue History

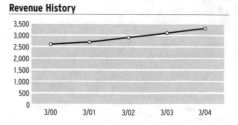

BAE SYSTEMS

BAE SYSTEMS, which helped win the Battle of Britain with its Mosquito and Spitfire fighters, is now Europe's largest defense contractor and the largest foreign player in the US defense market. BAE's offerings include avionics, military aircraft, armored vehicles, air-defense systems, missiles, artillery locators, communications and navigation systems, radar, ships, space systems, and aerospace electronics. BAE's fighter aircraft include the Harrier, Hawk, Tornado, and the next-generation Eurofighter Typhoon. The company acquired armored vehicle maker Alvis in 2004 and United Defense Industries the following year. In 2006 BEA divested its 20% stake in Airbus when it sold its shares back to EADS.

BAE has been leveraging its airborne technology know-how in its land systems and has beefed up its defense electronics operations by buying units from Lockheed Martin. The company's interest in expanding its North American operations has been spurred by the underperformance of its UK Ministry of Defence programs.

In 2005 BAE acquired — through its North American subsidiary — US-based United Defense Industries (UDI) as part of its push to get more US defense contracts. Now part of the company's BAE Systems Land and Armaments business, UDI made armored vehicles (including the Bradley Fighting Vehicle), landing craft, and weapons systems. Upon closing the UDI deal, BAE SYSTEMS North America changed its name to BAE Systems Inc.

It has also been reported that BAE is planning to sell its Atlas Elektronic GmbH unit, a German business specializing in civil and military maritime electronics. But the big news is that the company sold its Airbus stake to EADS for €2.75 billion (about $3.53 billion) in order to focus on its defense businesses — primarily in the US. Selling its Airbus stake to EADS should help fund expansion in the US defense sector.

HISTORY

Post-Wright brothers and pre-WWII, a host of aviation companies sprang up to serve the British Empire — too many to survive after the war when the empire contracted. Parliament took steps in 1960 to save the industry by merging companies to form larger, stronger entities — Hawker-Siddeley Aviation and British Aircraft Corporation (BAC).

Hawker-Siddeley, made up of aircraft and missiles divisions, was created by combining A.V. Roe, Gloster Aircraft, Hawker Aircraft, Armstrong Whitworth, and Folland Aircraft. It attained fame in the 1960s for developing the Harrier "jump jet."

BAC was formed from the merger of Bristol Aeroplane, English Electric, and Vicker-Armstrong. In 1962 it joined France's Aerospatiale to build the supersonic Concorde and became a partner in ventures to develop the Tornado and Jaguar fighters. The cost of these ventures, plus the commercial failure of the Concorde, was more than the company could bear. Realizing British aviation was again in trouble, the British government nationalized BAC and Hawker-Siddeley in 1976 and merged them in 1977 with Scottish Aviation to form British Aerospace (BAe).

BAe joined the Airbus consortium in 1979. A partial privatization of the company began in 1981 when the government sold 52% to the public (the remaining stake sold in 1985). Also in 1981 BAe announced a joint venture with Comsat General and announced that it would be the prime contractor for L-SAT-1, the European Space Agency's telecommunications satellite.

In 1987 BAe bought Steinheil Optronik (optical equipment) and Ballast Nedam Groep (civil and marine engineering). In 1990 BAe formed Ballast Nedam Construction.

BAe began to restructure its troubled regional aircraft division in 1992 by laying off thousands of workers and closing a major plant. The company sold Ballast Nedam and its corporate jet business to Raytheon and won a $7.5 billion contract from Saudi Arabia for Tornado jets in 1993. BAe sold its satellite business in 1994.

Matra BAe Dynamics, the world's third-largest maker of tactical missiles, was formed in a 1996 merger between BAe and Lagardère subsidiary Matra Hachette. BAe joined Lockheed Martin in a competition to build fighter jets for the UK and the US.

In 1998 BAe spent $454 million for a 35% stake in Swedish military jet maker Saab AB. Also in 1998 BAe bought Siemens' UK- and Australia-based defense electronics operations. In 1999 BAe bought the electronic systems defense unit of Marconi Electronic Systems (MES) for $12.7 billion (including US-based Tracor). The company changed its name to BAE SYSTEMS to remove the British influence from its name.

In 2000 BAE acquired Lockheed Martin's control-systems unit for about $510 million. The prime contractor for the UK's new Type 45 destroyer, BAE was named to build two of the first three Type 45s. Late in the year BAE spent about $1.67 billion for a group of Lockheed Martin's defense electronics businesses, including its Sanders airborne electronics unit.

BAE was selected as the prime contractor for the UK's next two aircraft carriers in 2003. In 2004, however, the Ministry of Defence took away that designation and brought in Thales to work on the carrier project.

BAE SYSTEMS took a 29% stake in Alvis, maker of the Challenger main battle tank, in August 2003. In 2004 General Dynamics made a 280 pence a share bid for Alvis; BAE topped that offer with a bid of 320 pence a share (about $650 million) and a deal was struck. BAE then combined Alvis with its RO Defence group to form a new business unit, Land Systems.

It was revealed in January 2005 that BAE was seeking buyers for its aerostructures business, which makes airframe components for such customers as Airbus, Boeing, Raytheon, and Cessna. Around the same time the Ministry of Defence selected Kellogg Brown & Root to work on the UK aircraft carrier project along with BAE and Thales. In February of 2005 BAE reduced its stake in SAAB AB from 35% to 22%.

In the summer of 2005 BAE acquired US armored vehicle maker United Defense Industries (UDI) in a deal worth about $4.2 billion. UDI was combined with BAE operations to form BAE Systems Land and Armaments.

In 2006 BAE sold its aerostructures business to Spirit AeroSystems.

EXECUTIVES

Chairman: Richard L. (Dick) Olver, age 59
CEO: Michael J. (Mike) Turner, age 57, $2,738,877 pay
COO, UK: Chris V. Geoghegan, age 52, $1,493,307 pay
COO, UK: Steven L. (Steve) Mogford, age 50, $1,524,274 pay
Group Managing Director, Customer Solutions and Support and Land Systems: Ian King
COO, US; President and CEO, BAE Systems Inc.: Mark H. Ronald, age 65, $2,131,576 pay
Group Communications Director: Charlotte Lambkin
Chief of Staff: George Mayhew
Group Finance Director: George W. Rose, age 53, $1,711,798 pay
Group Legal Director: Michael Lester, age 65, $1,839,108 pay
Group Legal Director: Phillip Bramwell, age 49
Group Marketing Director: Mike Rouse
Group Managing Director, Air Systems: Nigel Whitehead
Group Managing Director, Command/Control, Communications, Computing, Intelligence, Surveillance, and Reconnaissance: Phill Blundell
Group Managing Director, International Partnerships: Stephen Henwood
Group Managing Director, Sea Systems: Brian Phillipson
Group HR Director; Group Managing Director, Shared Services: Alastair Imrie
Group Strategic Development Director: Alison Wood, age 41
Director of Audit: Grenville Hodge
VP, Homeland Security: Harris Belman
VP and General Counsel, BAE Systems Inc.: Sheila C. Cheston
VP, Human Resources, BAE Systems Inc.: Curtis L. (Curt) Gray
Managing Director, Marketing, US: Bob Fitch
Investor Relations Director: Andrew Wrathall
Auditors: KPMG Audit Plc

LOCATIONS

HQ: BAE SYSTEMS plc
6 Carlton Gardens,
London SW1Y 5AD, United Kingdom
Phone: +44-1252-373-232   **Fax:** +44-1252-383-000
US HQ: 1601 Research Blvd., Rockville, MD 20850
US Phone: 301-738-4000   **US Fax:** 301-738-4643
Web: www.baesystems.com

BAE SYSTEMS has operations in Africa, Asia, Australia, Europe, and North America.

2005 Sales

	$ mil.	% of total
Europe		
UK	4,378.4	23
Other countries	3,394.4	18
US & Canada	7,399.5	39
Middle East	2,625.3	14
Asia & Pacific	827.5	4
Africa, Central & South America	332.0	2
Total	**18,957.1**	**100**

PRODUCTS/OPERATIONS

2005 Sales

	$ mil.	% of total
Electronics, Intelligence & Support	6,332.8	32
Programmes	4,851.5	25
Customer Solutions & Support	4,337.1	22
Land & Armaments	2,178.0	11
Integrated Systems & Partnerships	1,090.7	6
Commercial Aerospace	691.6	3
HQ and other businesses	220.3	1
Adjustments	(744.9)	—
Total	**18,957.1**	**100**

Selected Products and Services

Electronics, Intelligence, and Support
    Advanced airborne reconnaissance system
    Avionics support equipment
    Communications jamming
    Doppler navigation systems
    Laser transmitters and receivers
Programmes
    Astute class submarine
    Eurofighter Typhoon
    Hawk
    Nimrod
    Type 45 destroyers
Customer Solutions and Support
    Military services and support
Land and Armaments
    All terrain vehicles (Bv206)
    Armored personnel carriers (Warrior, Piranha)
    Battle tanks (Challenger 2)
    Naval gun system (Mk 45)
    Recovery vehicles (Beach Recovery Vehicle)
Integrated Systems and Partnerships
    Air-to-air missiles
    Combat and radar systems
    Naval sonar

COMPETITORS

Astronautics
Beretta
Boeing
Bombardier
Colt's
EADS
General Dynamics
General Dynamics UK
Glock
Honeywell International
Horstman Defence Systems
L-3 Storm
Lockheed Martin
Lockheed Martin Aeronautics
Lockheed Martin Missiles
Lockheed Martin UK
Meggitt USA
Northrop Grumman
Northrop Grumman Integrated Systems
Northrop Grumman Ship Systems
Park Air Systems
Rockwell Collins (UK)
SEPI
Smiths Group
Thales
Ultra Electronics

HISTORICAL FINANCIALS

Company Type: Public

Income Statement   FYE: December 31

	REVENUE ($ mil.)	NET INCOME ($ mil.)	NET PROFIT MARGIN	EMPLOYEES
12/05	18,957	955	5.0%	74,000
12/04	17,519	(900)	—	73,300
12/03	14,911	11	0.1%	68,400
12/02	12,953	(1,100)	—	68,100
12/01	13,119	(194)	—	70,100
Annual Growth	9.6%	—	—	1.4%

Net Income History   Pink Sheets: BAESY

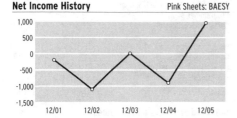

Banco Santander Central Hispano

Banco Santander Central Hispano (SCH) is the leader in the running of Spanish banks. The company offers retail banking and consumer finance in Spain, Portugal, and other parts of Europe. Subsidiaries such as Banco Santander-Chile, Banco Río de la Plata in Argentina, and Mexico's Grupo Financiero Santander Mexicano, make it a top banking group in Latin America, where it has operations in about 10 countries. Through other subsidiaries, SCH offers asset management, private banking, corporate and investment banking, and insurance. In one of Europe's largest cross-border bank mergers ever, SCH paid more than $15 billion for British bank Abbey National in 2004.

SCH owns nearly 90% of Puerto Rico's Santander BanCorp and in 2006 made its first serious foray into the US with its purchase of nearly 20% of Sovereign Bancorp, which is active in the Northeast. Later that year, the company bought 90% of US auto lender Drive Financial Services. All told, SCH has more than 60 million customers and some 10,000 locations in a dozen countries.

The company sold its 22% stake in Spanish utility Unión Fenosa to Spanish construction firm ACS for about $2.7 billion.

The Botín family has led SCH since its founding in 1857. Emilio Botín, Spain's richest man (depending on who you ask), has been chairman since 1986.

HISTORY

Banco Santander Central Hispano (BSCH) was created by the 1999 merger of Banco Santander and Banco Central Hispano (BCH).

In 1857 a group of Basque businessmen formed Banco Santander to finance Latin American trade. The emergence of Cantabria as a leading province after WWI helped the bank expand, first regionally, then nationally.

The Botín family has been closely identified with the bank for decades. Before his death in 1923, Emilio Botín served as a board member, then for a few years as chairman. The post was held by his son Emilio Botín-Sanz de Sautuola from 1950 to 1986, when *his* son Emilio Botín Ríos (known as Don Emilio) took over.

Spanish banks were spared the worst of the Great Depression (thanks to their isolation and the country's shunning the gold standard), but Spain's civil war was draining. In the early 1940s Santander expanded into Madrid and other major Spanish cities and merged with a few rivals. In the 1950s and 1960s, as interest rates were controlled and mergers halted, banks competed by building branch networks and investing overseas, particularly in Latin America. In 1965 Santander joined with Bank of America to form Bankinter (it divested most of its stake by the mid-1990s).

Tight economic controls were relaxed in the 1970s after Franco's death. Despite global recession, Santander continued to invest in Latin America through the mid-1980s.

In the late 1980s Santander prepared to compete in a deregulated Spain and Europe, forming alliances with Royal Bank of Scotland, Kemper (now part of Zurich Financial Services), and Metropolitan Life Insurance. In 1989 the bank jumpstarted competition by introducing Spain's first high-interest account.

Santander focused on home in the 1990s. Spurned by Banco Hispano Americano (BHA), Santander acquired a 60% stake in the ailing Banco Español de Crédito (Banesto); Banesto became wholly owned in 1998. The bank took a hit when Latin America plunged into an economic crisis that year. With profit margins falling, the bank merged with BCH in 1999.

BCH was formed by the 1991 merger of Banco Central and BHA. BHA was established in 1900 by investors in Latin America; Central was founded in 1919. The mixed banks offered both commercial and investment banking; they funded industrialization and investment in Latin America and became two of Spain's largest banks before the civil war.

After the war BHA sold its Latin American assets when the currency dried up, while Central used mergers and acquisitions to expand across Spain. Isolated from WWII by Franco, the two banks used their dual strategies to fund overseas investment and domestic-branch growth.

After Franco's death, the banks faced increased competition at home and abroad. Central bought BHA in 1991 to remain competitive as Spain entered the European Economic Community (now the EU) in 1992.

Following the merger, BCH trimmed 20% of its branches, fired some 10,000 employees, and sold unprofitable holdings. Focused on Latin America, the bank took small stakes in small banks. Losing its edge, BCH merged with Santander in 1999.

In 2000 BSCH focused on expanding in Europe and Latin America. Among its European moves was its alliance with Société Générale to buy investment-fund management firms, particularly in the US. In Latin America the bank bought Brazil's Banco Meridional, Banco do Estado de São Paulo (Banespa), and Grupo Financiero Serfín, Mexico's #3 bank. Critics question the $5 billion price tag BSCH paid for Banespa, charging that the formerly state-run bank was overvalued in 2001. Executive infighting saw ex-Santander chairman Emilio Botín triumph over ex-BCH chairman José María Amusátegui for control of BSCH's helm. Soon

after, the bank started doing business as simply Santander Central Hispano (SCH). The following year the bank sold off its shares of Germany's Commerzbank and France's Société Générale.

EXECUTIVES

Chairman: Emilio Botín
Second Vice Chairman and CEO: Alfredo Sáenz
Director; Chairwoman, Banesto: Ana P. Botín
Third Vice Chairman: Matías Rodríguez Inciarte
CEO, Abbey National: Francisco Gómez Roldán, age 52
Director; EVP, America: Francisco Luzón
EVP, America: Marcial Portela
EVP, America: Jesús M. Zabalza, age 47
EVP, Asset Management and Insurance: Joan-David Grimà
EVP, Communications and Research: Juan Manuel Cendoya
EVP, Europe and Consumer Lending: Juan Rodríguez Inciarte
EVP, Financial Accounting: José Manuel Tejón
EVP, Financial Management: José A. Alvarez
EVP and General Secretary: Ignacio Benjumea
EVP, Global Wholesale Banking: Gonzalo de las Heras, age 65
EVP, Internal Auditing: David Arce
EVP, Portugal: Antonio Horta Osorio
EVP, Resources and Costs: Pedro Mateache
EVP, Retail Banking: Enrique García Candelas
EVP, Risk: Teodoro Bragado
EVP and Vice-Secretary General: Juan Guitard

LOCATIONS

HQ: Banco Santander Central Hispano, S.A.
Santander Group City, Boadilla del Monte, 28660 Madrid, Spain
Phone: +34-91-659-75-17
Web: www.gruposantander.com

Banco Santander Central Hispano is mainly active in Argentina, Brazil, Chile, Colombia, Germany, Italy, Mexico, Portugal, Puerto Rico, Spain, the UK, and Venezuela.

COMPETITORS

Banco Comercial Português
Banco de la Nación
Banco do Brasil
Banco Galicia
Banco Popular
Bank of America
Bankinter
BBVA
BBVA Chile
Citigroup
Deutsche Bank
Dresdner Bank
Espírito Santo
HSBC Holdings
Itaúsa
JPMorgan Chase

HISTORICAL FINANCIALS

Company Type: Public

Income Statement   FYE: December 31

	ASSETS ($ mil.)	NET INCOME ($ mil.)	INCOME AS % OF ASSETS	EMPLOYEES
12/05	963,051	7,484	0.8%	129,196
12/04	789,304	5,377	0.7%	126,488
12/03	438,451	2,843	0.6%	103,038
12/02	345,063	2,397	0.7%	104,178
Annual Growth	40.8%	46.1%	—	7.4%

2005 Year-End Financials

Equity as % of assets: 5.4%
Return on assets: 0.9%
Return on equity: 14.3%
Long-term debt ($ mil.): 247,709
No. of shares (mil.): —
Dividends
Yield: 3.1%
Payout: —
Market value ($ mil.): —
Sales ($ mil.): 52,440

Stock History

NYSE: STD

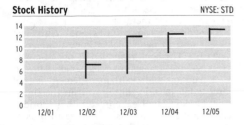

	STOCK PRICE ($) FY Close	P/E High/Low		PER SHARE ($) Earnings	Dividends
12/05	13.19	—	—	—	0.41
12/04	12.37	—	—	—	0.33
12/03	12.01	—	—	—	0.28
12/02	7.05	—	—	—	0.22
Annual Growth	23.2%	—	—	—	23.1%

Bank of China

Issuer of Great Wall credit cards, the Bank of China (BOC) is China's oldest bank and one of its top four state-owned commercial banks. BOC operates some 11,000 domestic branches and 600 offices in some 25 countries and regions. Commercial banking makes up the majority of its business, including corporate and retail banking and banking with financial institutions. The bank also provides car financing, investment banking, insurance, and credit card operations, including a joint venture with Royal Bank of Scotland (BOC owns 51%). BOC raised some $10 billion in its 2006 IPO.

It was estimated to be the world's largest IPO in six years, with foreign banks and investors scrambling for a piece. Saudi investor Prince Al-waleed bin Talal invested a $2 billion stake in the bank in what may be the first of many Chinese investments; China is the second biggest market for oil after the US.

The successful IPO is fraught with symbolism for the banking industry in China, which only recently was struggling. China has had to bail out two of the country's top banks, BOC and China Construction Bank, three times in the last six years. For decades, money in China's state banks was used to support failing state companies, leaving the banks with a mountain of bad loans.

Mostly recently, the government made a $45 billion payment to prop up both banks. The money may have been well spent as a way to make the banks profitable and attractive to foreign investment, as well as able to withstand foreign competition China promised the World Trade Organization that it would open its doors to foreigners in 2006.

Perhaps as a result of that initiative, BOC sold small commercial lender Nam Tung Bank to Morgan Stanley in 2006.

BOC is building networks with other economies. In the first move of its kind, BOC, the Korea Exchange Bank, and Japan's Sumitomo Mitsui signed an accord on foreign exchange co-operation in 2003. The agreement focuses on settlement systems and network channels, which should smooth electronic transactions among the three banks. The banks also agreed to share human and intellectual resources.

China developed a credit card system culminating in the 1986 debut of the BOC's Great Wall card. An estimated 600 million cards have been issued since then, although almost all are debit cards that draw money directly from consumers' bank accounts. BOC faces new competition from Citibank and HSBC Holdings, who now offer credit cards to the growing population of newly affluent Chinese who might adopt the credit habits of their neighbors.

In an attempt to increase its non-interest income, a BOC subsidiary in late 2006 acquired Singapore Aircraft Leasing for $965 million.

HISTORY

The Bank of China (BOC) has always had strong ties to the government of China. Established as a central bank in 1912, right after the establishment of the Provisional Government of the Republic of China, BOC became a government-chartered international exchange bank in 1928. Their first overseas branch was opened in London in 1929, leading to a global network of 34 overseas branches over the next two decades. After WWII the bank specialized in foreign exchange, supporting foreign trade and the development of China's national economy. Between 1984 and 2001 BOC issued bonds in the international capital market 27 times. In 1993, when China initiated reform in its foreign exchange system, BOC played a key role in the unification of exchange rates, foreign exchange purchases and sales, and the incorporation of foreign-funded enterprises into the foreign exchange sales system. In 1994 BOC began to transform from a specialized bank to a wider-based, state-owned commercial bank by issuing its first BOC Hong Kong dollar notes and then Macao pataca notes. The issue of both notes helped stabilize their respective markets. BOC International Holdings, a wholly owned subsidiary of BOC specializing in investment banking, was incorporated in Hong Kong in 1998. Three years later Bank of China restructured its Hong Kong operations by merging 10 of its member banks into Bank of China (Hong Kong) Limited, a locally registered bank that successfully listed on the Hong Kong Stock Exchange in July 2003.

The bank is not free of scandal. A 2002 probe into BOC's New York branch by the US Office of the Comptroller of the Currency revealed that preferential treatment was given to certain customers who had personal relationships with some members of the bank's previous management. Regulators from the US and China fined BOC $20 million for "unsafe and unsound" business practices.

In 2005 the Royal Bank of Scotland formed a consortium that bought a 10% stake in BOC. In exchange, BOC agreed to distribute the Scottish bank's credit cards and other products.

BOC went public in 2006.

EXECUTIVES

Honorary Chairperson: Chen Muhua, age 84
Honorary Vice Chairman: Chuang Shi Ping, age 95
Chairman: Xiao Gang, age 47
Vice Chairman and President: Li Lihui, age 53
Executive Director and Board Member: Hua Qingshan, age 52
EVP and Managing Director: Zhang Yanling, age 54
EVP and Managing Director: Zhou Zaiqun, age 53
Executive Director and Board Member: Li Zaohang, age 51
Assistant President: Zhu Min, age 53
Assistant President: Zhu Xinqiang, age 53
Assistant President: Wang Yongli, age 41
COO, Bank of China and BOC Hong Kong: Raymond W. H. Lee, age 55
Company Secretary: Jason C. W. Yeung, age 51
Secretary, Party Discipline Committee: Zhang Lin, age 49
Chief Credit Officer: Lonnie Dounn, age 53
Auditors: PricewaterhouseCoopers Zhong Tian CPAs Limited Company

LOCATIONS

HQ: Bank of China Limited
   (Zhongguo Yinhang Gufen Youxien Gongsi)
   1 Fuxingmen Nei Dajie, Beijing 100818, China
Phone: +86-10-6659-6688   **Fax:** +86-10-6659-3777
US HQ: 410 Madison Ave., New York, NY 10017
US Phone: 212-935-3101   **US Fax:** 212-593-1831
Web: www.bank-of-china.com

PRODUCTS/OPERATIONS

Selected Subsidiaries

Bank of China (Canada)
Bank of China Group Insurance Company Ltd.
Bank of China Group Investment Ltd.
Bank of China (Hungary) Ltd.
Bank of China International (UK) Limited
Bank of China (Kazakhstan)
Bank of China (Luxembourg) S.A.
Bank of China (Malaysia) Berhad
Bank of China (Zambia) Ltd.
Bank of China-Bangkok
Bank of China-Birmingham
Bank of China-Elusoi (Moscow)
Bank of China-Frankfurt
Bank of China-Glasgow
Bank of China-Grand Cayman
Bank of China-Hamburg
Bank of China-Haymarket
Bank of China-Ho Chi Minh City
Bank of China-Hong Kong
Bank of China-Johannesburg
Bank of China-London
Bank of China-Los Angeles
Bank of China-Luxembourg
Bank of China-Macau
Bank of China-Manchester
Bank of China-Manila
Bank of China-Melbourne
Bank of China-Milan
Bank of China-New York
Bank of China-Osaka
Bank of China-Panama
Bank of China-Paris
Bank of China-Seoul
Bank of China-Shanghai
Bank of China-Singapore
Bank of China-Sydney
Bank of China-Tibet
Bank of China-Tokyo
Bank of China-Toronto
Bank of China-Vancouver
Bank of China-West End
Bank of China-Yokohama
BOC International (China) Ltd.
BOC International Holdings Ltd.
BOC International (Singapore) Pte Ltd.
Chiyu Banking Corp. Ltd.
Nanyang Commercial Bank Ltd.

COMPETITORS

Agricultural Bank of China
Bank of East Asia
Cathay Financial Holding
China Construction Bank
China Development Bank
China Merchants Bank
China Minsheng Banking
CITIC International Financial
Hang Seng Bank
HSBC Holdings
Industrial and Commercial Bank of China
JCG Holdings
Mitsui Trust
Shanghai Pudong Development Bank

HISTORICAL FINANCIALS

Company Type: Public

Income Statement				FYE: December 31
	REVENUE ($ mil.)	NET INCOME ($ mil.)	NET PROFIT MARGIN	EMPLOYEES
12/05	22,841	—	—	209,265
12/04	18,007	—	—	181,894
12/03	15,007	—	—	188,716
12/02	15,015	—	—	192,468
12/01	17,852	—	—	201,590
Annual Growth	6.4%	—	—	0.9%

Revenue History Exchange: Hong Kong

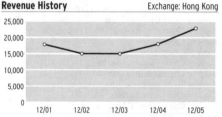

Bank of Montreal

Bank of Montreal, Canada's oldest and fourth-largest bank, has about 1,000 branches serving individuals, government agencies, institutions, and businesses large and small at home and abroad. The company, which also goes by BMO Financial Group, provides mortgages, insurance, asset management services, and mutual funds. In the US, it owns Chicago's Harris Bankcorp, which provides retail and corporate banking in the Midwest. Subsidiary BMO Capital Markets (formerly BMO Nesbitt Burns) offers brokerage, mergers and acquisitions advice, and investment and merchant banking services in Canada and the US.

Organized along operational lines (Personal and Commercial Client Group, Private Client Group, and Investment Banking Group), the company is focused on building its business through acquisitions as well as organic growth. With more than a quarter of its revenue coming from south of the border, it would like to build on its successful Harris Bank franchise. The bank has already made modest forays into Florida and Arizona.

Continuing its southward push, it bought Chicago-area community banks Lakeland Community Bank, New Lenox State Bank, and Villa Park Trust and Savings Bank, as well as Indiana-based Mercantile Bancorp. The company is now looking to expand its market area and is on the prowl for a larger US bank elsewhere in the Midwest. As part of that initiative, Harris is buying First National Bank & Trust in Indiana for $290 million.

Bank of Montreal sold US-based online brokerage Harrisdirect to E*TRADE in 2005; the company continues to operate its BMO InvestorLine online brokerage.

Bank of Montreal was the only Canadian bank to get a piece of the highly anticipated Bank of China IPO. With that success under its belt, the bank opened an investment banking office in Beijing in 2006.

HISTORY

Montreal was a key port for fur and agriculture trade by the early 1800s. To finance these activities, the Montreal Bank (Canada's first) opened in 1817. Chartered in 1822, the bank officially became Bank of Montreal. Its ties with the US were strong, and nearly 50% of its original capital came from Yanks.

When the fur trade shifted northward to Hudson Bay in the 1820s, the bank diversified. In 1832 Bank of Montreal financed Canada's first railroad, the Champlain & St. Lawrence. The bank also grew through acquisitions, including the Bank of Canada (1831) and the Bank of the People (1840). It opened a branch in New York in 1859.

Canada united in confederacy in 1867, and Bank of Montreal expanded west. During the 1860s, it became Canada's de facto central bank until the 1935 creation of the Bank of Canada. By 1914 Bank of Montreal was the nation's largest bank. It bought the British Bank of North America (1918), Merchants Bank of Canada (1922), and Molsons Bank (1925). During the Depression, however, its growth ground to a halt.

WWII pumped up Canada's economy and the company's finances. Bank of Montreal enjoyed even greater growth during the postwar boom. It began expanding internationally, particularly in Latin America. But the bank failed to capitalize on the growth of consumer and small-business lending during the 1960s and was the last major Canadian bank to issue a credit card (in 1972). In 1975 Bank of Montreal hired William Mullholland, a Morgan Stanley veteran, to run the company. Mullholland closed unprofitable branches and modernized operations.

The bank bought Chicago-based Harris Bankcorp in 1984. As Canada's banking industry deregulated, Bank of Montreal moved into investment banking, acquiring one of Canada's largest brokerage firms, Nesbitt Thomson, in 1987.

The Latin American debt crisis and the recession of the late 1980s and early 1990s hit Bank of Montreal hard. It tumbled into the red in 1989, partly because of loan defaults. The next year Matthew Barrett replaced Mullholland as chairman and began overhauling operations, focusing on consumer and middle-market business banking and on cutting costs.

By 1994 nonperforming assets were down, and Bank of Montreal began growing again. It bought brokerage Burns Fry and merged it with Nesbitt Thomson to form Nesbitt Burns, thus increasing its presence in merchant and investment banking and securities. It added to its Harris Bank network with the purchase of Suburban Bancorp. The next year Bank of Montreal expanded its private banking business for wealthy individuals; it also began targeting aboriginal Canadians.

Eyeing international growth, Bank of Montreal bought an interest in Mexico's Grupo Financiero Bancomer in 1996 (now called BBVA Bancomer; it has since sold its interest) and opened branches in Beijing (1996) and Dublin, Ireland (1997). It agreed in 1998 to merge with Royal Bank of Canada, but Canada's finance minister rejected the merger.

Barrett stepped down as CEO and chairman in 1999; the firm named F. Anthony Comper its new CEO. The bank realigned its operations to focus on retail and commercial banking, investment banking, and wealth management and cut some 2,450 jobs. Eyeing growth in the US, in 2000 Bank of Montreal agreed to buy Florida's Village Banc of Naples, as well as Seattle brokerage Freeman Welwood. Also that year subsidiary Harris Bank began offering wireless banking.

In 2001 Bank of Montreal took its southern expansion one step further when it announced it would buy the 18-branch First National Bank of Joliet (Illinois) and merge it into Harris Bank. Later, Bank of Montreal sold its stake in BBVA Bancomer to Banco Bilbao Vizcaya Argentaria.

The next year Bank of Montreal picked up online brokerage CSFBdirect and merged it into Harrisdirect; it sold its interest in Harrisdirect at the end of 2005.

EXECUTIVES

Chairman: David A. Galloway
President, CEO, and Director: F. Anthony (Tony) Comper, age 60, $2,293,650 pay
Deputy Chair and COO; Interim President and CEO, Personal and Commercial Client Group: William A. (Bill) Downe, age 54
CFO and Chief Administrative Officer: Karen E. Maidment, $1,310,082 pay (prior to promotion)
SEVP, Human Resources and Office of Strategic Management: Rose M. Patten
EVP and Global Economic Strategist: Sherry S. Cooper
EVP and Chief Risk Officer, Enterprise Risk & Portfolio Management: Robert (Bob) McGlashan
EVP and Senior Market Risk Officer: Penelope F. (Penny) Somerville
EVP Finance and Treasurer: Thomas E. (Tom) Flynn
EVP Taxation and General Counsel: Ronald B. Sirkis
Head of Investment Banking Group; President and CEO, BMO Capital Markets: Yvan J.P. Bourdeau, $2,764,890 pay (prior to promotion)
President and CEO, Personal and Commercial Banking Canada: Franklin J. (Frank) Techar, age 45
President and CEO, Private Client Group; Vice Chair, BMO Capital Markets: Gilles G. Ouellette, $16,565,250 pay
President, Québec; Chairman, BMO Capital Markets: L. Jacques Ménard, age 60
President and CEO, Technology and Solutions: Lloyd F. Darlington, age 61
SEVP and Head of National Office, Personal and Commercial Client Group: Maurice A. D. Hudon
EVP Global Private Banking: Graham T. Parsons
EVP Personal and Commercial Delivery: Pamela J. (Pam) Robertson
Vice Chair, BMO Capital Markets; Deputy Head of Investment and Corporate Banking: Frederick J. (Fred) Mifflin
Vice Chairman, Harris Bankcorp: Charles R. (Chuck) Tonge, age 54
VP Corporate Communications, BMO Financial Group and Harris Bank: Andrew (Andy) Plews
VP and Corporate Secretary: Robert V. Horte
Director Investor Relations: Steve Bonin
Auditors: KPMG LLP

HQ: Bank of Montreal
1 First Canadian Place, 100 King St. West,
Toronto, Ontario M5X 1A1, Canada
Phone: 416-867-5000 **Fax:** 416-867-6793
US HQ: 111 W. Monroe St., Chicago, IL 60603
US Phone: 312-461-2121 **US Fax:** 312-461-3869
Web: www.bmo.com

2005 Sales

	% of total
Canada	71
US	26
Other countries	3
Total	**100**

PRODUCTS/OPERATIONS

2005 Sales

	% of total
Interest	
Loans	51
Securities	12
Deposits with banks	4
Noninterest	
Securities, commissions & fees	7
Deposit & payment service charges	5
Lending, card & investment fees	9
Trading	3
Other	9
Total	**100**

2005 Assets

	% of total
Cash & equivalents	7
Securities	18
Loans	59
Derivatives	11
Other	5
Total	**100**

COMPETITORS

Bank of America
CIBC
Citigroup
JPMorgan Chase
Laurentian Bank
Northern Trust
RBC Dain Rauscher
RBC Financial Group
Scotiabank
TD Bank
Washington Mutual
Wells Fargo

HISTORICAL FINANCIALS

Company Type: Public

Income Statement

FYE: October 31

	ASSETS ($ mil.)	NET INCOME ($ mil.)	INCOME AS % OF ASSETS	EMPLOYEES
10/05	254,807	1,935	0.8%	33,785
10/04	235,936	1,840	0.8%	33,593
10/03	196,218	1,355	0.7%	33,993
10/02	163,445	869	0.5%	33,000
Annual Growth	**16.0%**	**30.6%**	**—**	**0.8%**

2005 Year-End Financials

Equity as % of assets: 4.8%
Return on assets: 0.8%
Return on equity: 16.7%
Long-term debt ($ mil.): 26,658
Sales ($ mil.): 12,935

Net Income History NYSE: BMO

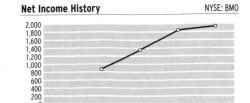

Barclays

An old hand at banking in Britain, Barclays traces its origins to the 17th century. The bank sports more than 2,000 branches in the UK and some 800 branches in Europe, Africa, Asia, Australia, and the US. Its operations include personal financial services (savings, checking, and consumer loans); corporate banking; asset management for wealthy individuals; mortgage lender Woolwich; and Barclaycard, a leading credit card issuer in Europe. US-based Barclays Global Investors is one of the world's largest institutional fund managers, while Barclays Capital handles foreign exchange, derivatives, and fixed-income business. Barclays also runs one of the UK's largest online banks, with nearly 4 million registered users.

The company entered the US credit card market when it bought Juniper Financial from Canadian Imperial Bank of Commerce (CIBC) in 2004. In a previous hook-up with CIBC, Barclays merged its Caribbean banking business with CIBC to create an 85-branch regional bank, FirstCaribbean International Bank, with each company owning 44%. In 2006 CIBC doubled its ownership by buying Barclays' stake in the bank for more than $1 billion.

Barclays has an alliance with London-based Legal & General Group to market that company's life insurance products; it sells general insurance from Aviva.

In 2006 the bank announced plans to close up 200 bank branches, consolidating its Woolwich branches into existing Barclays branches. It will retain the Woolwich mortgage brand but account holders will have to switch their accounts to Barclays.

That year the bank agreed to sell its vendor finance businesses in the UK and Germany to CIT Group. Barclays said that the sale will allow it to focus on its commercial leasing business.

Like a bad penny, Enron keeps turning up in Barclays' business. A US federal judge has reinstated Barclays as a defendant in the shareholder lawsuit that alleges several banks knowingly helped prop up the ailing energy company.

At the end of 2006 Merrill Lynch speculated that Bank of America would make a pitch for Barclays. If such a deal went through it would create the world's biggest bank.

HISTORY

Barclays first spread its wings in 1736 when James Barclay united his family's goldsmithing and banking businesses. As other family members joined the London enterprise, it became known as Barclays, Bevan & Tritton (1782).

Banking first became regulated in the 19th century. To ward off takeovers, 20 banks combined with Barclays in 1896. The new firm, Barclay & Co., began preying on other banks. Within 20 years it bought 17, including the Colonial Bank, chartered in 1836 to serve the West Indies and British Guiana (now Guyana). The company, renamed Barclays Bank Ltd. in 1917, weathered the Depression as the UK's #2 bank.

Barclays began expanding again after WWII, and by the late 1950s it had become the UK's top bank. It had a computer network by 1959, and in 1966 it introduced the Barclaycard in conjunction with Bank of America's BankAmericard (now Visa).

In 1968 the UK's Monopolies Commission barred Barclays' merger with two other big London banks, but had no objections to a two-way merger, so Barclays bought competitor Martins.

Barclays moved into the US consumer finance market in 1980 when it bought American Credit, 138 former Beneficial Finance offices, and Bankers Trust's branch network.

During the 1980s, London banks faced competition from invading overseas banks, local building societies, and other financial firms. Banking reform in 1984 led to formation of a holding company for Barclays Bank PLC.

To prepare for British financial deregulation in 1986, Barclays formed Barclays de Zoete Wedd (BZW) by merging its merchant bank with two other London financial firms. Faced with sagging profits, Barclays sold its California bank in 1988 and its US consumer finance business in 1989.

In 1990 Barclays bought private German bank Merck, Finck & Co. and Paris bank L'Européenne de Banque. The company countered 1992's bad-loan-induced losses by accelerating a cost-cutting program begun in 1989. To appease stockholders, chairman and CEO Andrew Buxton (a descendant of one of the bank's founding families) gave up his CEO title, hiring Martin Taylor (previously CEO of textile firm Courtaulds) for the post.

The company sold its Australian retail banking business in 1994, then began trimming other operations, including French corporate banking and US mortgage operations. However, it bought the Wells Fargo Nikko Investment Company to boost Asian operations.

Barclays' piecemeal sale of BZW signaled its failure to become a global investment banking powerhouse. In 1997 it sold BZW's European investment banking business to Credit Suisse First Boston, retaining the fixed-income and foreign exchange business. (Credit Suisse bought Barclays' Asian investment banking operations in 1998.)

Losses in Russia and a $250 million bailout of US hedge fund Long-Term Capital Management hit Barclays Capital in 1998. Taylor resigned that year in part because of his radical plans for the bank. Sir Peter Middleton stepped in as acting CEO; Barclays later tapped Canadian banker Matthew Barrett for the post. (Middleton also became chairman upon Buxton's retirement.)

Barclays in 1999 started a move toward online banking at the expense of traditional branches. The company announced free lifetime Internet access for new bank customers.

In 2000 the bank ruffled feathers when it announced the closure of about 170 mostly rural UK branches. Also in 2000 the company sold its Dial auto leasing unit to ABN AMRO and bought Woolwich plc. The following year Barclay's closed its own life insurance division, opting instead to sell the life insurance and pension products of London-based Legal & General Group.

After exiting the South African market in 1987 over apartheid concerns, Barclays returned in a big way in 2005, buying a majority stake (about 57%) in Absa Group, one of the country's largest retail banks. The deal also represented the largest-ever direct foreign investment there. The next year Barclays sold its South African businesses, including corporate, international retail, and commercial operations, to Absa.

EXECUTIVES

Chairman: Matthew W. (Matt) Barrett, age 62, $1,118,260 pay
Director: Marcus Agius, age 60
Deputy Chairman: Sir Nigel Rudd, age 59
Group Vice Chairman: Gary A. Hoffman, age 46
Group Chief Executive and Director: John S. Varley, age 50, $1,462,340 pay
President and Director; Chief Executive, Investment Banking and Investment Management: Robert E. (Bob) Diamond Jr., age 55
COO: Paul Idzik, age 44
Group Finance Director: Naguib Kheraj, age 42, $860,200 pay
Group Finance Director: Chris Lucas, age 45
Chief Executive, Global Retail and Commercial Banking and Director: Frederik F. (Frits) Seegers, age 47
Executive Director: David Roberts, age 44
Chief Executive, International Retail and Commercial Banking: Vittorio de Stasio, age 46
Chief Administrative Officer: Mike Foley
Group Financial Controller: Jonathon Britton
CIO: Dominic Trotta
Group Secretary: Lawrence Dickinson
Group Treasurer: Chris Grigg, age 45
General Counsel: Mark Harding
Head of Compliance and Regulatory Affairs: Mike Walters
Director of Corporate and External Affairs: Stephen Whitehead, age 39
Corporate Responsibility Director: Alistair Camp
Director of Finance: Colin Walklin
Investor Relations Director: Cathy Turner
Public Relations Director: Chris Tucker
Human Resources Director, International Retail and Commercial Banking: Allan Fielder, age 43
Auditors: PricewaterhouseCoopers

LOCATIONS

HQ: Barclays PLC
1 Churchill Place,
London E14 5HP, United Kingdom
Phone: +44-20-7116-1000
US HQ: 200 Park Ave., New York, NY 10166
US Phone: 212-412-4000
Web: www.barclays.com

Barclays has operations in 60 countries, including Australia, Botswana, Egypt, France, Germany, Ghana, Gibraltar, Hong Kong, India, Ireland, Italy, Japan, Kenya, Mauritius, Portugal, Singapore, South Africa, South Korea, Spain, Switzerland, Tanzania, Uganda, the United Arab Emirates, the UK, the US, Zambia, and Zimbabwe.

PRODUCTS/OPERATIONS

2005 Sales

	% of total
Interest	62
Fees & commissions	23
Trading income	8
Other	7
Total	**100**

COMPETITORS

Bank of New York
CIBC
Citigroup
Credit Suisse
Deutsche Bank
HBOS
HSBC Holdings
JPMorgan Chase
Lloyds TSB
Mizuho Financial
RBC Financial Group
RBS
Standard Chartered
UBS
The Vanguard Group

HISTORICAL FINANCIALS

Company Type: Public

Income Statement

FYE: December 31

	ASSETS ($ mil.)	NET INCOME ($ mil.)	INCOME AS % OF ASSETS	EMPLOYEES
12/05	1,592,415	5,045	0.3%	113,300

2005 Year-End Financials

Equity as % of assets: 2.0%
Return on assets: —
Return on equity: 16.4%
Long-term debt ($ mil.): 763,884
No. of shares (mil.): —
Dividends
Yield: 4.4%
Payout: —
Market value ($ mil.): —
Sales ($ mil.): 47,942

Stock History

NYSE: BCS

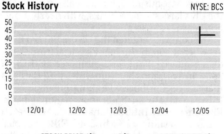

	STOCK PRICE ($) FY Close	P/E High/Low	PER SHARE ($) Earnings	Dividends
12/05	42.08	— —	—	1.85

BASF

The world is BASF's ester. BASF is the world's largest chemical company, ahead of Dow and DuPont. It has more than 100 major manufacturing facilities and does business worldwide through five business segments: plastics (including polyolefins and polystyrene), performance products (value-added chemicals, coatings, and dyes), basic chemicals (plasticizers, catalysts, solvents), oil and gas exploration and production (through subsidiary Wintershall AG), and agricultural products (additives, herbicides, and fertilizers). BASF sold Basell, its petrochemical JV with Shell, in 2005. The company acquired catalysts maker Engelhard the next year and rebranded it BASF Catalysts.

BASF uses what it calls *Verbund* strategy throughout its facilities — plants are both customers and suppliers of each other. While the company still gets more than half its sales from

Europe, it continues to expand overseas, particularly in Asia. It saw early on that the chemicals market in Asia will be the equal of that in Europe and wanted a healthy piece of the action.

Toward that end, the company has opened two Verbund sites in Asia — one in Nanjing, China and the other in Kuantan, Malaysia. The Chinese site delivered its first product in early 2005 and began operating fully in the middle of that year. It's the centerpiece and primary operation of a joint venture with Sinopec that was formed in 2000, BASF-YPC. BASF's goal is to achieve 20% of its sales and earnings from Asia by 2010. (It's currently getting about 15% from the region.)

BASF and Shell announced in late 2004 that they planned to exit the polyolefins business with the sale of Basell. The deal was finalized in 2005. Investment group Access Industries came in with the winning bid of about $5.7 billion. Also in 2005 BASF added Merck KGaA's electronic chemicals unit for nearly $500 million.

Early in 2006 BASF announced an offer to buy the former Engelhard, among the largest specialty chemicals companies in the world. BASF had met with the company's management earlier but was rebuffed. Afterward it chose to take its $4.9 billion offer directly to shareholders as a hostile takeover bid; it later raised its offer to just more than $5 billion. The increased offer did the trick; Engelhard's board agreed to the deal in mid-2006 and the company became a subsidiary of BASF.

Not long after BASF also acquired Degussa's construction chemicals business for about $3.4 billion. A further move to build up its specialties business, BASF acquired the US resins manufacturer Johnson Polymer for about $470 million. Johnson Polymer's resins are used in coatings and packaging, primarily.

HISTORY

Originally named Badische Anilin & Soda-Fabrik, BASF AG was founded in Mannheim, Germany, by jeweler Frederick Englehorn in 1861. Unable to find enough land for expansion in Mannheim, BASF moved to nearby Ludwigshafen in 1865. The company was a pioneer in coal tar dyes, and it developed a synthetic indigo in 1897. Its synthetic dyes rapidly replaced more expensive organic dyes.

BASF scientist Fritz Haber synthesized ammonia in 1909, giving BASF access to the market for nitrogenous fertilizer (1913). Haber received a Nobel Prize in 1918 but was later charged with war crimes for his work with poison gases. Managed by Carl Bosch, another Nobel Prize winner, BASF joined the I.G. Farben cartel with Bayer, Hoechst, and others in 1925 to create a German chemical colossus. Within the cartel BASF developed polystyrene, PVC, and magnetic tape. Part of the Nazi war machine, I.G. Farben made synthetic rubber and used labor from the Auschwitz concentration camp during WWII.

After the war I.G. Farben was dismantled. BASF regained its independence in 1952 and rebuilt its war-ravaged factories. Strong postwar domestic demand for basic chemicals aided its recovery, and in 1958 BASF launched a US joint venture with Dow Chemical (BASF bought out Dow's half in 1978). The company moved into petrochemicals and became a leading manufacturer of plastic and synthetic fiber.

In the US the company purchased Wyandotte Chemicals (1969), Chemetron (1979), and Inmont (1985), among others. To expand its natural gas business in Europe, in 1991 the company signed deals with Russia's Gazprom and France's Elf Aquitaine. BASF bought Mobil's polystyrene-resin business and gained almost 10% of the US market.

BASF bought Imperial Chemical's polypropylene business in 1994 and became Europe's second-largest producer of the plastic. The next year the company paid $1.4 billion for the pharmaceutical arm of UK retailer Boots.

In 1997 BASF formed a joint venture with PetroFina (now TOTAL S.A.); in 2001 the venture opened the world's largest liquid steam cracker, in Port Arthur, Texas.

In 1999 the US fined the company $225 million for its part in a worldwide vitamin price-fixing cartel (in 2001 the European Commission fined it another $260 million, bringing the total expected cost of fines, out-of-court settlements, and legal expenses to about $800 million); BASF also faced a class-action suit as a result of the scheme. That year the company moved into oil and gas exploration in Russia through a partnership agreement with Russia's Gazprom. BASF also merged its textile operations into Bayer and Hoechst's DyStar joint venture, forming a $1 billion company that is a world leading dye maker.

BASF completed its acquisition of Rohm and Haas' industrial coatings business in 2000. That year BASF expanded its superabsorbents business by paying $656 million for US-based Amcol International's Chemdal International unit.

Rather than attempt to compete in the rapidly consolidating pharmaceutical industry, in 2001 BASF sold its mid-sized Knoll Pharmaceutical unit to Abbott Laboratories for about $6.9 billion. It also announced that it was closing 10 plants and cutting about 4,000 jobs (4% of its workforce).

In 2003 BASF bought a portion of Bayer's agchem businesses for $1.3 billion when European antitrust regulators mandated the Bayer divestment following its acquisition of Aventis CropScience. BASF also acquired Honeywell Specialty Materials' engineering plastics business in exchange for its fibers division.

That year also brought chairman Jürgen Hambrecht's announcement that the company would push forward with a restructuring of its North American business. Included among the steps were job cuts of approximately 1,000 and the relocation of its North American headquarters (though remaining in New Jersey) in late 2004.

EXECUTIVES

Chairman, Supervisory Board: Jürgen F. Strube, age 65
Chairman, Board of Executive Directors:
  Jürgen Hambrecht, age 59
Vice Chairman, Board of Executive Directors:
  Eggert Voscherau, age 63
Member, Board of Executive Directors and CFO:
  Kurt W. Bock, age 47
Member, Board of Executive Directors:
  Martin Brudermüller, age 44
Member, Board of Executive Directors: John Feldmann, age 56
Member, Board of Executive Directors:
  Andreas Kreimeyer, age 50
Member, Board of Executive Directors; CEO, BASF Corp.: Klaus Peter Löbbe, age 59
Member, Board of Executive Directors:
  Stefan Marcinowski, age 52
Member, Board of Executive Directors, Agricultural Products and Fine Chemicals: Peter Oakley, age 52
President, Europe: Walter Seufert
President, Chemicals, Plastics, and Performance Products North America: Joseph (Joe) Breunig
President, Communications: Felix Gress, age 43
President, Global Human Resources: Dietmar Kokott
President, Investor Relations: Magdalena Moll
President, Legal, Taxes, and Insurance: Eckart Sünner

President, Chemicals Research and Engineering:
  Rainer Diercks
President, Corporate Engineering: Stefan Robert Deibel
President, Environment, Safety, and Energy:
  Ernst Schwanhold
President, Agricultural Products: Michael Heinz, age 41
President, Fine Chemicals: Wolfgage Büchele
President, Inorganics: Ehrenfried Baumgartner, age 53
President, Intermediates: Walter Gramlich
President, Oil and Gas; Chairman, Wintershall:
  Reinier Zwitserloot, age 57
President, Performance Chemicals: Patrick M. Prevost
President, Petrochemicals: Albert Heuser, age 50
Head of Corporate Media Relations: Michael Grabicki
Director, Investor Relations: Rolf Reinecke
Auditors: Deloitte & Touche GmbH

LOCATIONS

HQ: BASF Aktiengesellschaft
  Carl-Bosch St. 38, 67056 Ludwigshafen, Germany
Phone: +49-621-60-0   **Fax:** +49-621-60-42525
US HQ: 100 Campus Dr., Florham Park, NJ 07932
US Phone: 973-245-6000   **US Fax:** 973-895-8002
Web: www.basf.com

BASF AG has operations in more than 100 countries.

2005 Sales

	% of total
Europe	
Germany	40
Other countries	19
North America	22
Asia/Pacific	14
South America/Africa/Middle East	5
Total	**100**

PRODUCTS/OPERATIONS

2005 Sales

	% of total
Plastics	27
Performance Products	19
Chemicals	19
Oil & Gas	18
Agricultural Products & Nutrition	
Agricultural Products	8
Fine Chemicals	4
Other	5
Total	**100**

Selected Products

Plastics
  Engineering plastics
  Foams
  Polyurethane
  Polyamide and intermediates
  Styrenics
Performance Products
  Automotive coatings
  Automotive fluids
  Construction chemicals
  Decorative paints
  Industrial coatings
  Pigments
  Printing systems
  Surfactants
  Textile chemicals
Chemicals
  Inorganics (ammonia, formaldehyde, melamine, sulfuric acid, and urea)
  Intermediates
  Performance chemicals (water-based resins, etc.)
  Petrochemicals (feedstocks, industrial gases, and plasticizers)
  Specialty chemicals
Oil and Gas
  Crude oil and natural gas exploration
  Natural gas distribution and trading
Ag Products and Nutrition
  Agricultural products (fungicides, herbicides, and insecticides)
  Fine chemicals (fragrances, pharmaceutical ingredients, UV absorbers, and vitamins)

COMPETITORS

3M
Air Products
Akzo Nobel
Albemarle
Ashland
Bayer
BP
Cargill
Ciba Specialty Chemicals
Clariant
Cognis
Degussa
Dow Chemical
DSM
DuPont
Eastman Chemical
Exxon Mobil
FMC
Formosa Plastics
Henkel
Honeywell International
Huntsman Corp.
Ineos
Lanxess
LG Group
Lyondell Chemical
Mitsubishi Chemical
Monsanto
PPG
Royal Dutch Shell
SABIC
Sasol
Sony
Syngenta
TOTAL

HISTORICAL FINANCIALS

Company Type: Public

Income Statement

FYE: December 31

	REVENUE ($ mil.)	NET INCOME ($ mil.)	NET PROFIT MARGIN	EMPLOYEES
12/05	50,627	3,535	7.0%	80,945
12/04	50,817	2,522	5.0%	81,955
12/03	42,325	1,685	4.0%	87,159
12/02	34,096	1,800	5.3%	89,398
12/01	29,167	5,067	17.4%	92,545
Annual Growth	**14.8%**	**(8.6%)**	**—**	**(3.3%)**

2005 Year-End Financials

Debt ratio: 20.0%
Return on equity: 15.7%
Cash ($ mil.): 1,292
Current ratio: 1.80
Long-term debt ($ mil.): 4,361
No. of shares (mil.): —
Dividends
  Yield: 2.3%
  Payout: 30.2%
Market value ($ mil.): —

Stock History

NYSE: BF

	STOCK PRICE ($) FY Close	P/E High/Low		PER SHARE ($) Earnings	Dividends
12/05	76.48	14	11	5.69	1.72
12/04	72.02	—	—	—	1.32
12/03	55.75	—	—	—	1.25
12/02	38.22	15	10	3.10	0.92
12/01	37.91	6	3	8.41	1.37
Annual Growth	**19.2%**	—	—	**(9.3%)**	**5.9%**

Bayer

You could get a headache trying to name all of Bayer's products. The company, which created aspirin in 1897, makes health care products (diagnostic equipment and pharmaceuticals), agricultural products (crop protection and animal health), and specialty materials (plastics and synthetic rubber). It operates in the US through Bayer Corporation.

Bayer has reorganized, spinning off its divisions and becoming a management holding company. It also has separated its former chemicals subgroup, which was spun off as a publicly traded company called Lanxess in early 2005. In 2004 Bayer bought Roche's consumer health unit for nearly $3 billion and in 2006 spent nearly $20 billion for pharmaceutical giant Schering.

Besides its line of Bayer aspirins, the company's best-known brands include Alka-Seltzer and One-A-Day vitamins. Bayer spends about 10% of revenues on R&D, with much of that money going to fuel advances in its health care unit. The success of drugs such as Cipro, Levitra, and Avalox (used to treat infectious diseases) has prompted the company to expand its biotechnology and genetic research efforts.

In late 2003 Bayer announced that it would spin off the chemicals business (combined with parts of Bayer MaterialScience) to Bayer shareholders in 2005; the new company is called Lanxess. Afterward Bayer planned to concentrate on its core businesses: HealthCare, CropScience, and MaterialScience.

The Roche deal created one of the top three non-prescription drugs companies in the world, combining Bayer's aspirin, Alka-Seltzer, and Midol brands with Roche's Aleve pain relievers, among others.

That acquisition falls in step with Bayer's intention to focus its health care group on becoming the world's #1 OTC drug company, and part of that process is to divest noncore assets.

The early 2006 offer to buy Schering came as the German pharmaceuticals maker (the world's #1 maker of birth control) was fending off a hostile takeover attempt by rival Merck. Bayer will remain the parent company, with the pharmaceuticals unit re-named Bayer-Schering Pharmaceuticals and headquartered in Berlin. Bayer plans to pay for the acquisition through a combination of equity, debt financing, and the sale of two Bayer MaterialScience subsidiaries, Wolff Walsrode and H.C. Starck. (The latter was sold in late 2006 to private investors Advent International and Carlyle Group for about $1.6 billion.) Upon integration of Schering, Bayer HealthCare will be by far the largest unit of the parent company, supplanting Bayer MaterialScience.

While in the process of doing that, though wholly unrelated according to Bayer, the company agreed to sell the Diagnostics unit of Bayer HealthCare to Siemens for about $5.3 billion. Also that year Bayer HealthCare agreed to acquire the Western OTC cough and cold drug business of Topsun Science and Technology, a Chinese drugmaker for about $150 million.

HISTORY

Friedrich Bayer founded Bayer in Germany in 1863 to make synthetic dyes. Research led to such discoveries as Antinonin (synthetic pesticide, 1892), aspirin (1897), and synthetic rubber (1915).

Under Carl Duisberg, Bayer allegedly made the first poison gas used by Germany in WWI. During the war the US seized Bayer's US operations and trademark rights and sold them to Sterling Drug.

In 1925 Bayer, BASF, Hoechst, and other German chemical concerns merged to form I.G. Farben Trust. Their photography businesses, combined as Agfa, also joined the trust. Between wars Bayer developed polyurethanes and the first sulfa drug, Prontosil (1935).

During WWII the trust took over chemical plants of Nazi-occupied countries, used slave labor, and helped make Zyklon B gas used to kill people at Auschwitz. At war's end Bayer lost its 50% of Winthrop Laboratories (US) and Bayer of Canada (to Sterling Drug). The 1945 Potsdam Agreement called for the breakup of I.G. Farben, and Bayer AG emerged in 1951 as an independent company with many of its original operations, including Agfa.

After rebuilding in West Germany, Bayer AG and Monsanto formed a joint venture (Mobay, 1954); Bayer AG later bought Monsanto's share (1967). In the 1960s the company offered more dyes, plastics, and polyurethanes, and added factories worldwide. Agfa merged with Gevaert (photography, Belgium) in 1964; Bayer AG retained 60%. Over the next 25 years it acquired Miles Labs (Alka-Seltzer, US, 1978), the rest of Agfa-Gevaert (1981), Compugraphic (electronic imaging, US, 1989), and Nova's Polysar (rubber, Canada, 1990).

Bayer AG integrated its US holdings under the name Miles in 1992 (renamed Bayer Corporation in 1995). It regained US rights to the Bayer brand and logo in 1994 by paying SmithKline Beecham $1 billion for the North American business of Sterling Winthrop.

Bayer AG formed a joint venture with Swiss rival Roche Holding in 1996 to market over-the-counter Roche drugs in the US. In 1997 Bayer, Baxter International, Rhône-Poulenc Rorer, and Green Cross agreed to a $670 million settlement over blood products that infected thousands of hemophiliacs with HIV during the 1980s.

In 1998 the company sold the food-ingredients arm of its Haarmann & Reimer unit to Tate & Lyle. Bayer bought US-based Chiron's diagnostics operations for $1.1 billion, created a North American joint venture with Crompton & Knowles' seed-treatment unit, and formed a research alliance with Millennium Pharmaceuticals (giving Bayer a 14% stake in Millennium).

Bayer, Hoechst, and BASF merged their textile activities in 1999 to form the world's largest dye-making company. The next year Bayer boosted its polyurethane business by paying $2.5 billion for US-based Lyondell Chemical's polyols unit.

In 2001 the company had to recall Baycol (known as Lipobay in Europe), its popular cholesterol-lowering drug that has been linked to more than 100 deaths worldwide. In a bid to bolster its agrochemical business, Bayer acquired Aventis CropScience in 2002 for about $5 billion plus $2 billion in debt.

In mid-2003 the company, along with partner GlaxoSmithKline, launched Levitra, its rival to Pfizer's $1 billion-earning Viagra.

EXECUTIVES

Chairman, Supervisory Board: Manfred Schneider, age 67
Vice Chairman, Supervisory Board: Thomas de Win, age 48
Chairman, Management Board: Werner Wenning, age 60, $2,728,019 pay
Member, Management Board, Finance: Klaus Kühn, age 54, $1,487,420 pay
Member, Board of Management, Innovation, Technology and Environment: Wolfgang Plischke, age 54
Member, Management Board, Strategy and Human Resources: Richard Pott, age 53, $1,487,420 pay
Member, Management Board, Innovation, Technology, and Environment: Udo Oels, age 62, $1,487,420 pay
Member, Management Board; President and CEO, Bayer Corporation: Attila Molnar, age 58
Chairman, Management Board, Bayer CropScience: Friedrich Berschauer, age 56
Chairman, Management Board, Bayer MaterialScience: Hagen Noerenberg, age 59
Chairman and CEO, Bayer HealthCare: Arthur J. Higgins, age 50
Managing Director, Bayer Business Services: Andreas Resch, age 53
Managing Director, Bayer Technology Services; CTO, Bayer Corporation: Achim Noack, age 47
Managing Director, Bayer Industry Services: Jürgen Hinz, age 60
Head of Investor Relations: Alexander Rosar
Member, Supervisory Board: Gregor Jüsten, age 58
Auditors: PricewaterhouseCoopers AG

LOCATIONS

HQ: Bayer AG
Bayerwerk, Gebäude W11, Kaiser-Wilhelm-Allee, 51368 Leverkusen, Germany
Phone: +49-214-30-1   **Fax:** +49-214-30-66328
US HQ: 100 Bayer Rd., Pittsburgh, PA 15205
US Phone: 412-777-2000   **US Fax:** 412-777-2034
Web: www.bayer.de

Bayer operates primarily in Canada, France, Germany, Japan, the UK, and the US.

2005 Sales

	% of total
Europe	43
North America	27
Asia/Pacific	17
Latin America/Africa/Middle East	13
Total	**100**

PRODUCTS/OPERATIONS

2005 Sales

	% of total
MaterialScience	
Systems	24
Materials	15
HealthCare	
Pharmaceuticals & Biological Products	15
Consumer Care	8
Diabetes Care & Diagnostics	8
Animal Health	3
CropScience	
Crop Protection	18
Environmental Science & BioScience	4
Adjustments	5
Total	**100**

Selected Operations and Products

MaterialScience
Cellulose products (Wolff Walsrode)
Coatings
Colorants
Plastics
Polyurethanes
Specialty metals (H. C. Starck)

HealthCare
   Diagnostics (laboratory products)
   Pharmaceuticals
      Pharmaceutical research and development
      Consumer care products (over-the-counter drugs)
CropScience
   BioScience (biotechnology and seeds)
   Crop protection (insecticides and herbicides)
   Environmental Science (lawn care and non-
      agricultural pesticides)

Selected Brands
Adalat (cardiovascular medication)
Alka-Seltzer (analgesic and antacid)
Aspirin (analgesic)
Cipro (antibiotic)
Dralon (acrylic staple fiber)
Glucometer (blood sugar monitor)
Levitra (impotence drug)
Makrolon (polycarbonate resin)
One-A-Day (vitamins)

COMPETITORS

3M	Henkel
Abbott Labs	Imperial Chemical
Akzo Nobel	Industries
AstraZeneca	Johnson & Johnson
BASF AG	Merck
Baxter	Merck KGaA
Boehringer Ingelheim	Mitsubishi Chemical
Bristol-Myers Squibb	Monsanto
Degussa	Norsk Hydro
Dow Chemical	Novartis
DSM	Pfizer
DuPont	Rhodia
Eastman Chemical	Sanofi-Aventis
Eli Lilly	Schering-Plough
E.ON	Syngenta
GlaxoSmithKline	

HISTORICAL FINANCIALS
Company Type: Public

Income Statement
FYE: December 31

	REVENUE ($ mil.)	NET INCOME ($ mil.)	NET PROFIT MARGIN	EMPLOYEES
12/05	32,432	1,572	4.8%	93,700
12/04	40,602	891	2.2%	113,825
12/03	35,872	(1,815)	—	118,280
12/02	32,172	1,339	4.2%	122,600
12/01	25,639	709	2.8%	116,900
Annual Growth	6.1%	22.0%	—	(5.4%)

2005 Year-End Financials
Debt ratio: 58.2%
Return on equity: 9.7%
Cash ($ mil.): 4,426
Current ratio: 1.83
Long-term debt ($ mil.): 8,510
No. of shares (mil.): —
Dividends
   Yield: 6.0%
   Payout: 96.5%
Market value ($ mil.): —

Stock History
NYSE: BAY

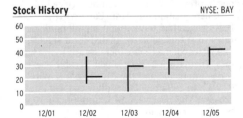

	STOCK PRICE ($) FY Close	P/E High/Low		PER SHARE ($) Earnings	Dividends
12/05	41.76	17	12	2.59	2.50
12/04	33.98	28	19	1.21	0.47
12/03	29.41	—	—	—	0.80
12/02	21.65	—	—	—	0.64
Annual Growth	24.5%		—	114.0%	57.5%

BBVA

It's not Cortez revisited, but Banco Bilbao Vizcaya Argentaria (BBVA), one of Spain's top banks (with Santander Central Hispano), is conquering Latin America, where it operates in about 10 countries in the region through subsidiaries Banco Bilbao Vizcaya Argentaria, Chile and BBVA Banco Francés in Argentina. With some 7,500 offices in more than 30 countries, it offers retail, corporate, and institutional banking; investment banking; asset management; insurance; and Internet banking. BBVA also operates in Europe, mainly Portugal, France, and Italy. It's expanding in the US with acquisitions of Texas banks Texas Regional Bancshares for more than $2 billion and State National Bancshares Inc. for $480 million.

The deals give BBVA more of the lucrative business transacted between the US and Mexico and access to the exploding Spanish-speaking market in the US. They follow on its 2005 acquisition of Laredo National Bancshares (LNB). LNB is part of a new US unit that will focus on money transfers to Latin American countries. BBVA also set up a private equity fund that will invest in US-based Hispanic-owned small and medium-sized enterprises with annual sales between $25 million and $500 million.

HISTORY

Banco Bilbao Vizcaya Argentaria (BBVA) is the progeny of the 2000 merger of Banco Bilbao Vizcaya (BBV) and Argentaria, Caja Postal y Banco Hipotecario. BBV formed when Banco de Bilbao and Banco de Vizcaya merged in 1988, while Argentaria, Caja Postal y Banco Hipotecario coalesced from the 1991 merger of six government-owned banks.

In 1857 a group of Basque businessmen banded together to offer loans and other banking services to businesses. The bank — eventually Banco de Bilbao — helped fund the region's industrialization. Its first foray beyond the Basque region was Paris, not Madrid, in 1902. It later entered London, Madrid, and other major European cities.

Franco's rise to power and the isolation of WWII deterred industrial growth. In protectionist Spain, Bilbao bought 16 banks between 1941 and 1943 and formed a unit to focus on US and Latin American partnerships.

In the 1960s Bilbao reorganized and formed a unit focused on industrial growth. It rolled with the punches as banking rules continued to change in the 1970s and 1980s. The bank expanded consumer services, began issuing credit cards (1971), and bought banks that couldn't cope with changing regulations.

To compete in financially deregulated Europe, Spain's overpopulated banking industry began to consolidate in the early 1990s. After #3 Bilbao failed to take over #2 Banco Español de Crédito, it merged with regional rival Banco de Vizcaya.

Formed in 1901 by Basque merchants, Banco de Vizcaya expanded through purchases and had some 200 branches by 1935, including offices in Europe's leading cities. During the post-WWII bust, it bought weaker banks and invested in Spain's industrial complex.

In the 1960s and 1970s, Vizcaya added industrial banking, insurance, personal investment management, and leasing. The bank refocused on international growth, opening branches in London, Mexico City, New York, and other cities. It entered consumer banking and became another participant in the branch race; by 1980 Vizcaya had some 900 offices. Looking to be a strong player in deregulated Europe, the bank merged with Bilbao in 1988; together, the two banks had nearly 3,400 branches.

The merger almost unraveled after Vizcaya chair Pedro Toledo (set to lead the new bank with Bilbao chair José Ángel Sánchez Asiain) died in 1989. The two banks fought over Toledo's replacement until the Bank of Spain suggested in 1990 Bilbao executive Emilio Ybarra y Churruca become the only chair.

Until 1992 government regulations and strong unions prevented BBV from cutting some 5,000 jobs and 600 branches. After Europe's 1992 deregulation, the company targeted Latin America, buying banks in Mexico and Peru (1995); Argentina, Colombia, and Venezuela (1996); and Brazil and Chile (1997). The merger of rivals Banco Santander and Banco Central Hispanoamericano in 1999 prompted BBV to merge with Argentaria in 2000.

After the merger, BBVA teamed with top Spanish telecom Telefónica to develop online banking services. The duo later bought first-e, one of Europe's first Internet-only banks, and merged it with BBVA's Uno-e online bank to form UnoFirst. BBVA bought 30% of Grupo Financiero Bancomer, Mexico's #2 bank, and merged it into its existing Mexican bank, Grupo Financiero BBV-Probursa; the resulting Grupo Financiero BBVA-Bancomer is the country's largest bank. The bank completed the renaming of its subsidiaries to reflect their position as BBVA subsidiaries in 2002.

In 2004 BBVA bought the 40% of Mexico's BBVA Bancomer that it did not already own. To finance about half of the approximately $4 billion bid, the company issued 195 million new shares.

The next year BBVA tried to buy the rest of Italian bank Banca Nazionale del Lavoro (BNL) (it already owned 15%). However, Italian regulatory bodies nixed the deal and BNP Paribas bought BNL.

EXECUTIVES

Chairman and CEO: Francisco González Rodríguez, age 61
President, COO, and Director: José Ignacio Goirigolzarri Tellaeche, age 52
Company Secretary and Director: José Maldonado Ramos, age 53
CFO: Manuel González Cid
Managing Director, Americas: Vitalino M. Nafría Aznar
Managing Director, BBVA Foundation: Rafael Pardo
Managing Director, Business Development: Manuel Castro
Managing Director, Corporate Relations: José Ignacio Wert
Managing Director, Human Resources and General Services: Ángel Cano Fernández
Managing Director, Innovation and Development: Javier Bernal
Managing Director, Retail Banking, Spain and Portugal: Julio López Gómez
Managing Director, Risk Management: Manuel Méndez del Río
Managing Director, Systems and Operations: Ignacio Sánchez-Asiaín Sanz
Managing Director, Wholesale and Investment Banking: José María Abril Pérez
Director, Communications and Image: Javier Ayuso
Head of the Office of the Chairman: José Sevilla Álvarez
General Counsel: Eduardo Arbizu Lostao
Auditors: Deloitte SL

LOCATIONS

HQ: Banco Bilbao Vizcaya Argentaria, S.A.
   Plaza San Nicolás, 4, 48005 Bilbao, Vizcaya, Spain
Phone: +34-944-875-555   **Fax:** +34-944-876-161
US HQ: 1345 Avenue of the Americas, 45th Fl.,
   New York, NY 10105
US Phone: 212-728-1500   **US Fax:** 212-333-2906
Web: www.bbv.es

PRODUCTS/OPERATIONS

2005 Sales

	% of total
Interest income	58
Commissions & fees	17
Insurance	14
Gains on financial assets	10
Other	1
Total	**100**

2005 Assets

	% of total
Cash & equivalents	3
Government debt securities	6
Due from credit institutions	7
Debentures & other debt securities	20
Other investments	4
Net loans	55
Other	5
Total	**100**

Selected Subsidiaries

Administradora de Fondos de Pensiones Provida
Administradora de Fondos Para el Retiro-Bancomer, S.A. de C.V.
Banco Bilbao Vizcaya Argentaria (Portugal), S.A.
Banco Bilbao Vizcaya Argentaria Puerto Rico, S.A.
Banco Continental, S.A.
Banco de Crédito Local, S.A.
Banco Granahorrar, S.A.
Banco Provincial S.A.Banco Universal
BBVA Banco Francés, S.A.
BBVA Bancomer, S.A. de C.V.
BBVA Chile, S.A.
BBVA Colombia, S.A.
BBVA Factoring E.F.C., S.A.
BBVA Ireland Public Limited Company
BBVA Paraguay, S.A.
BBVA Privanza Bank (Jersey) Ltd.
BBVA Renting, S.A.
BBVA Seguros, S.A.
BBVA Switzerland
Finanzia, Banco de Credito, S.A.
Hipotecaria Nacional, S.A. de C.V.
Laredo National Bancshares Inc.
Pensiones Bancomer, S.A. de C.V.
Seguros Bancomer
Uno-e Bank, S.A.

COMPETITORS

ABN AMRO
Banamex
Banco Comercial Português
Banco de la Nación
Banco do Brasil
Banco Galicia
Banco Popular
Banco Río de la Plata
Banco Zaragozano
Bankinter
Banorte
Barclays
Credit Suisse
DEPFA BANK
Deutsche Bank
Espírito Santo
HSBC Holdings
JPMorgan Chase
SCH
Société Générale
Unibanco
Wells Fargo

HISTORICAL FINANCIALS

Company Type: Public

Income Statement

FYE: December 31

	ASSETS ($ mil.)	NET INCOME ($ mil.)	INCOME AS % OF ASSETS	EMPLOYEES
12/05	475,891	2,390	0.5%	94,681
12/04	431,761	4,223	1.0%	84,117
Annual Growth	10.2%	(43.4%)	—	12.6%

2005 Year-End Financials

Equity as % of assets: 6.3%
Return on assets: 0.5%
Return on equity: 7.7%
Long-term debt ($ mil.): 69,257
No. of shares (mil.): —
Dividends
   Yield: 2.8%
   Payout: —
Market value ($ mil.): —
Sales ($ mil.): 27,381

Stock History

NYSE: BBV

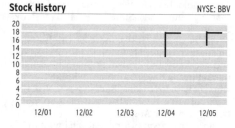

	STOCK PRICE ($) FY Close	P/E High/Low	PER SHARE ($) Earnings	Dividends
12/05	17.85	—	—	0.50
12/04	17.74	—	—	0.42
Annual Growth	0.6%	—	—	19.0%

BCE

BCE is the Biggest Communications Enterprise in Canada. The company (BCE actually stands for Bell Canada Enterprises) owns Bell Canada, the incumbent provider of long-distance and local access in Ontario and Quebec. Bell Canada also owns stakes in local phone companies across the nation (including 53% of Aliant), as well as wireless carrier Bell Mobility. Other BCE services include Internet access, data and e-commerce services, and satellite communications. BCE owns 20% of Bell Globemedia, which includes broadcaster CTV, Internet portal Sympatico, and *The Globe and Mail* newspaper (it reduced its Globemedia stake from 68% in a 2006 ownership restructuring of the unit).

BCE has announced plans to drop its holding company structure. It will turn Bell Canada into an income trust, to be called Bell Canada Income Fund. Boards of directors have approved the new structure but shareholders must vote on the change.

Bell Canada operates more than 13 million local access lines and provides wireless services to nearly 5 million customers. It also provides dial-up Internet access (nearly 1 million subscribers) and broadband Internet access (to 1.5 million), as well as direct-to-home satellite TV (1.4 million customers).

The company has teamed up with Aliant to create a regional telecom services provider. BCE is contributing Bell Canada's regional wireline operations in Ontario and Quebec and its 63% stake in Bell Nordiq. BCE also is acquiring Aliant Mobility and Aliant's DownEast Communications retail outlets. The new carrier, which will be formed as a consolidated income trust, will have more than 3 million local access lines and 400,000 broadband Internet subscribers with operations in six provinces including Atlantic Canada, Ontario, and Quebec. Aliant is contributing its wireline operations. BCE will control the new operator.

Reaching for the sky, units Telesat and TMI Communications provide satellite services. Bell ExpressVu has more than 1.3 million direct-to-home satellite TV customers. BCE took full ownership of Internet portal Sympatico in 2002, acquiring the 29% formerly held by Lycos. Bell Canada and ExpressVu have teamed up with Microsoft to develop Internet protocol TV (IPTV). The company's Ventures division handles investments in other telecom and media firms, including troubled Bell Canada International, which held interests in telecom and cable TV providers in Latin America. BCE is dismantling 62%-owned Bell Canada International.

HISTORY

Alexander Graham Bell experimented with the telephone in his native Canada before moving to the US in the mid-1870s. His father sold his Canadian patent rights to National Bell Telephone (which became AT&T Corp.), which combined with Canada's Hamilton District Telegraph to form Bell Telephone Company of Canada. Known as Bell Canada, it received a charter in 1880 and settled in Montreal. By 1882 it had 40 exchanges. AT&T owned 48% of the company in 1890, but by 1925 Canadians owned 95% of Bell Canada. (AT&T severed all ties in 1975).

As telecommunications needs grew, the company began buying smaller exchanges (1954). It acquired a 90% stake in telecom equipment maker Northern Electric in 1957 and the rest in 1964. After Bell Canada reduced the stake in 1973, Northern became Northern Telecom in 1976 (now Nortel Networks). Bell Canada also invested in a satellite joint venture (Telesat, 1970) and formed Bell Canada International (BCI) to provide international telecom consulting (1976).

In 1983, responding to proposed legislation that would have calculated manufacturing profits in phone rate formulas, Bell created Bell Canada Enterprises (renamed BCE in 1988) as a holding company to separate unregulated businesses from phone carriers. BCE branched out with stakes in gas pipelines (1983) and real estate (1985) but dropped out of the ventures to focus on its core telecom business (1989). It began providing wireless phone service in 1985.

As deregulation rolled into Canada in the 1990s, Bell Canada had to maintain high long-distance rates to subsidize its regulated local service. In 1993 it was denied a rate increase and took a large loss. That year it bought stakes in cable operator Jones Intercable and the UK's Cable & Wireless (C&W). In 1994 regulators allowed local rate increases. The next year BCE announced 10,000 jobs cuts and began offering Internet access.

BCE took a loss in 1997, writing down assets in preparation for full competition. Also that year it floated part of BCI, following contracts for cellular systems in Brazil and India. BCE began staging a comeback in 1998 when it sold its shares in Jones Intercable and C&W. It made new investments, including 100% of Telesat Canada, a part of fONOROLA's fiber network, and more than 40% of computer consulting firm CGI

Group. Insider Jean Monty (who had steered Nortel's turnaround) became CEO.

Through an alliance with MCI WorldCom (now WorldCom), the company gained access to a global network in 1999. Also that year Ameritech (now part of AT&T Inc., formerly SBC Communications) bought a 20% stake in Bell Canada, which snapped up the 35% of its wireless subsidiary that it didn't already own and a 20% stake in Manitoba Telecom Services (it sold its stake in MTS in 2004).

In 2000 Bell Canada spun off nearly all of its 40% Nortel stake to shareholders. That year it bought broadcaster CTV, and went on to buy global broadband services provider Teleglobe in a $5 billion stock deal. BCE combined its broadcasting and Internet portal assets with Thomson's *The Globe and Mail* newspaper to form a new company, Bell Globemedia, in 2001 (Thomson sold its stake in 2003).

A lack of demand for its broadband services forced BCE to reconsider the value of its Teleglobe unit. In 2002 BCE discontinued long-term funding for Teleglobe, which began working to restructure its debt under bankruptcy protection. As 2002 ended Teleglobe was sold to a unit of Ernst & Young, the court-appointed creditors' monitor.

The company in 2004 sold its 64% stake in e-commerce firm BCE Emergis in a spin-off to shareholders. It also sold its Bell Canada directories business to Kohlberg Kravis Roberts & Co. and a unit of the Ontario Teachers' Pension Plan. In the deal, valued at C$3 billion, BCE kept a 10% stake in the new company. BCE then used the proceeds from this sale to buy back the 16% of Bell Canada owned by Texas-based AT&T Inc. (formerly SBC Communications). It also bought the 40% of Bell West it did not own.

EXECUTIVES

Chairman: Richard J. (Dick) Currie, age 68
President, CEO, and Director; CEO, Bell Canada: Michael J. Sabia, age 53
CFO, BCE and Bell Canada: Siim A. Vanaselja
EVP Communications and Marketing Services, BCE and Bell Canada: Peter Daniel
EVP and Chief Strategy Officer: Mark R. Bruneau
EVP and Chief Corporate Officer: Lawson A. W. Hunter, age 60
EVP; Group President, Corporate Performance and National Markets, Bell Canada: Stephen G. Wetmore, age 52, $633,278 pay (prior to promotion)
SVP Taxation: Barry W. Pickford
SVP and Treasurer: Michael T. Boychuk, age 49
SVP, Audit and Risk Management: Mahes S. Wickramasinghe
SVP; President, BCE Corporate Services Inc.: Alain Bilodeau
VP and Controller: Karyn A. Brooks
VP Programming and Content, Bell ExpressVu: Alison Green
Group President, Systems and Technology, Bell Canada: Eugene Roman
President and CEO, Bell Globemedia; CEO, CTV Inc.: Ivan Fecan
CEO, Bell Mobility and Bell Distribution, Bell Canada: Robert Odendaal
President and CEO, Telesat Canada: Daniel S. (Dan) Goldberg, age 41
President, BCE Ventures: William D. (Bill) Anderson, age 55
President and COO, Bell Canada: George A. Cope, age 44
Chief Legal Officer, BCE and Bell Canada: Martine Turcotte
Chief Talent Officer, BCE and Bell Canada: Léo W. Houle, age 59
Corporate Secretary, BCE and Bell Canada: Patricia A. Olah, age 48
Auditors: Deloitte & Touche LLP

LOCATIONS

HQ: BCE Inc.
1000, rue de La Gauchetière Ouest, Ste. 3700, Montreal, Quebec H3B 4Y7, Canada
Phone: 514-870-8777   **Fax:** 514-870-4385
Web: www.bce.ca

PRODUCTS/OPERATIONS

2005 Sales

	% of total
Bell Canada	
Local & access	28
Data	21
Wireless	16
Long-distance	11
Video	5
Terminal sales & other	9
Bell Globemedia	8
Telesat	2
Total	**100**

2005 Sales

	% of total
Bell Canada	
Residential	40
Business	31
Aliant	10
Other Bell Canada	9
Other BCE	10
Total	**100**

Selected Subsidiaries and Affiliates

Bell Canada Holdings Inc.
  Aliant (53%, local phone service, Atlantic Canada)
  Bell Canada (telecommunications services)
  Bell Conferencing (teleconferencing services)
  Bell Distribution Inc. (retail outlets)
  Bell ExpressVu L.P. (direct-to-home satellite TV)
  Bell Mobility Inc. (wireless phone and paging)
  Bell Nordiq Group (income fund administrator)
  Bell West Inc. (competitive local-exchange carrier)
  Connexim (outsourcing and professional services)
  Expertech (75%, installation of telecom networks)
  NorthernTel L.P. (63%, local phone service, Ontario)
  Northwestel Inc. (local phone service, northwestern Canada)
BCE Ventures
  Bell Canada International (BCI, 62%, telecom investments outside Canada)
  Telesat Canada (satellite communications)
Bell Globemedia (20%, broadcast, print, and Internet services)
  CTV Inc. (broadcast TV)
  The Globe and Mail (newspaper)

COMPETITORS

Canada Payphone
Cancom
CanWest Global Communications
COGECO Inc.
MTS Allstream
Persona
Primus Telecommunications
Quebecor
Rogers Communications
Rogers Telecom
Shaw Communications
Sprint Nextel
TELUS
Time Warner
Vonage
Yak Communications

HISTORICAL FINANCIALS

Company Type: Public

Income Statement

FYE: December 31

	REVENUE ($ mil.)	NET INCOME ($ mil.)	NET PROFIT MARGIN	EMPLOYEES
12/05	16,392	1,669	10.2%	60,001
12/04	15,936	1,315	8.3%	61,739
12/03	14,725	1,264	8.6%	64,054
12/02	12,541	(2,942)	—	66,266
Annual Growth	9.3%	—	—	(3.3%)

2005 Year-End Financials

Debt ratio: 102.9%
Return on equity: 16.5%
Cash ($ mil.): 311
Current ratio: 0.65
Long-term debt ($ mil.): 10,398

No. of shares (mil.): —
Dividends
  Yield: —
  Payout: —
Market value ($ mil.): —

Stock History

NYSE: BCE

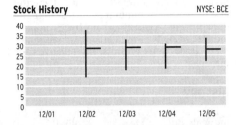

	STOCK PRICE ($) FY Close	P/E High/Low		PER SHARE ($) Earnings	Dividends
12/05	27.87	20	13	1.67	—
12/04	28.92	22	14	1.35	—
12/03	28.90	25	14	1.31	—
12/02	28.50	—	—	(3.87)	—
Annual Growth	(0.7%)	—	—	—	—

Benetton Group

If Benetton had a theme song, it could be "We Are the World." Italy's largest clothing maker, The Benetton Group pushes a global attitude in its ads while dressing customers in 120 countries through more than 5,100 franchised Benetton stores, department stores, and megastores. Benetton's clothing — primarily casual knitwear and sportswear for men, women, and children — bears labels such as United Colors of Benetton and Sisley (nearly 20% of sales). Not content with selling sunglasses, watches, clothes, and shoes, Benetton once branched out into sporting goods, but withdrew to hone in on its clothing division. The Benetton family, through Edizione Holding, owns about 67% of Benetton.

The Italian clothing manufacturer began looking for a new CEO following the abrupt resignation of Silvano Cassano in November 2006. (Concurrently, CFO Pier Francesco Facchini also resigned.)

The company's controversial ads, a mix of provocative images and political stances (bloody soldiers, death-row inmates, a priest and a nun kissing), have won a following as well as a fair share of critics. Benetton has since parted ways with the agency responsible for the shocking campaign.

Despite its global outlook, nearly 85% of Benetton Group's sales come from Europe, which is plagued by a sluggish economy. Consequently, Benetton is looking to new markets for growth in Asia (China, India, and South Korea), Eastern Europe, and the Mediterranean (Greece, Spain, and Turkey). Benetton plans to open about 40 stores in China this year (including flagship stores in Beijing and Shenzhen), and would like to have as many as 200 stores there by 2008. The Italian retailer also recently formed a joint venture with Turkey's Boyner Group to boost sales in that country. Benetton is also focusing on attracting younger customers to its stores. To that end, the retailer has expanded its low-priced collections of denim, polo shirts, and sweatshirts.

Benetton also operates two companies that manufacture textiles for the apparel and fashion industries, including its own apparel business.

The group's multimedia enterprises fall under the Fabrica umbrella, which Benetton describes as a "communication research and development center," that the company founded in 2000. Fabrica produces films, funds avant-garde music projects, and publishes the magazine *Colors*.

HISTORY

Luciano Benetton began selling men's clothing while still in his teens in post-WWII Treviso, Italy. His younger, artistic sister, Giuliana, knitted colorful and striking sweaters for a small, local clientele. In 1955 the two pooled their skills. Giuliana sold Luciano's accordion and a younger brother's bicycle, raising enough money to purchase a knitting machine. Luciano then marketed her moderately priced sweaters.

Demand for their clothes grew, and the pair did so well that 10 years later they built a factory in Ponzano, near Treviso. Siblings Gilberto and bicycleless Carlo joined the business, and the first Benetton store opened in Belluno, in the Alps, in 1968. By 1975 Benetton had 200 stores in Italy and had set up headquarters in a 17th-century villa. In 1979 the company opened five stores in the US.

Through the early to mid-1980s, the company averaged one store opening a day; Benetton was the first Western retailer to enter Eastern Europe. The company's controversial advertising program began in 1984 with ads depicting such provocative images as then-president Ronald Reagan with AIDS lesions.

When it went public in 1986, Benetton had almost 600 stores in the US. That year it established a factory in the US. In the late 1980s Edizione Holding, the family's investment firm, also bought a hotel chain and ski equipment maker Nordica.

Benetton began losing US market share in the late 1980s. Competition from The Limited and The Gap hurt and overexpansion brought complaints from franchisees that the stores were cannibalizing each other's sales. (In New York City there were seven stores on Fifth Avenue alone.) In the early 1990s The Gap established stores in the already-mature European market, and Benetton began looking for new markets.

Edizione increased its investments, acquiring 80% of Prince Manufacturing, a US maker of tennis equipment, and bought a 50% interest in the TWR group, a racecar manufacturer. The company formed Benetton Legs in 1991 to produce and sell pantyhose in Europe.

In 1995 Benetton won its second lawsuit against German retailers who refused to pay for merchandise because they said sales had been hurt by the company's shock advertising. The next year it opened a United Colors of Benetton megastore on Fifth Avenue in New York City, the first to combine Edizione's clothing, sporting goods, and accessories under one roof.

Benetton bought Edizione's sports equipment and apparel collection, Benetton Sportsystem, and renamed the division Playlife in 1998. Benetton began selling the sporting goods through specialty sports stores and a new chain of Playlife megastores.

Trying to win back US consumers, Benetton in 1998 cut a deal to sell Benetton USA-brand clothing in Sears, Roebuck & Co. stores. In early 2000, however, Sears yanked the Italian goods from its store after customers complained about Benetton's anti-death penalty ad campaign. Soon after, Benetton and controversial ad man Oliviero Toscani parted ways. Benetton's ads are now produced by an ad agency Toscani founded.

In 2001 Carlo Gilardi stepped down as joint managing director and Luigi de Puppi (former CEO of Electrolux Zanussi) was named his successor. Just weeks before its 2003 shareholders meeting, the company announced that de Puppi would step down since his mandate to clear out of Benetton's ailing sports divisions was completed with sales of Rollerblade, Nordica, and tennis racket and sportswear maker Prince.

In May 2005 Alessandro Benetton, son of Chairman Luciano Benetton, was named deputy chairman of the company's board, a title he now shares with his uncle Carlo. The Italian apparel maker teamed up with America's largest toymaker Mattel to launch a new line of clothing called "Barbie Loves Benetton." The Barbie-inspired brand appeared in stores in September 2005.

In November 2006 CEO Silvano Cassano resigned abruptly after having completed a three-year reorganization plan, according to the company. Concurrently, CFO Pier Francesco Facchini also resigned his post. Cassano will remain on the board of the company.

EXECUTIVES

Chairman: Luciano Benetton, age 71
Deputy Chairman: Alessandro Benetton, age 42
Deputy Chairman: Carlo Benetton, age 62
COO: Biagio Chiarolanza, age 44
CIO: Adolfo Pastorelli, age 50
CFO: Emilio Foà
Benneton Group Marketing and Strategy Director: Maximo Ibarra
Art Director, United Colors of Benetton: Joel Berg
Chairman and Editorial Director, Colors Magazine: Kurt Andersen
CEO, Benetton India: Madhu Kumar
Director of Media and Corporate Communication: Federico Sartor
Sales and Marketing Manager, North and Central America: Paola Ugolini
Head of Investor Relations: Mara Di Giorgio
Senior Investor Relations: Barbara Ferrante
Investor Relations: Giada De Mattia
Chief of Human Resources: Andrea Negrin, age 43
Tax, Legal, and Corporate Affairs Officer; Secretary: Pierluigi Bortolussi, age 57
IT Manager: Mike Wainwright
Auditors: PricewaterhouseCoopers SpA

LOCATIONS

HQ: Benetton Group S.p.A.
  Villa Minelli, 31050 Ponzano Veneto, Treviso, Italy
Phone: +39-0422-519111   **Fax:** +39-0422-969501
US HQ: 601 5th Ave., 11th Fl., New York, NY 10017
US Phone: 212-593-0290   **US Fax:** 212-371-1438
Web: www.benetton.com

Benetton Group sells its products in more than 120 countries.

2005 Sales

	% of total
Europe	84
Asia	12
The Americas	4
Total	**100**

2005 Stores

	No.
Europe	
Italy	2,167
Other countries	1,930
Asia	726
The Americas	288
Other regions	38
Total	**5,149**

PRODUCTS/OPERATIONS

2005 Sales by Brand

	% of total
Benetton	74
Sisley	19
Playlife	1
Killer Loop	1
Other	5
Total	**100**

Selected Brands

Casual wear
  Sisley (higher-fashion men's and women's clothing)
  United Colors of Benetton

Sportswear
  Killer Loop (snowboarding clothing)
  Playlife (sporty leisure wear)

Selected Products

Baby products
Dresses
Handbags
Hats
Knitwear
Perfume
Shirts
Shoes
Socks
Sportswear
Sunglasses
Underwear
Watches

COMPETITORS

Abercrombie & Fitch	Lands' End
Aéropostale	Levi Strauss
American Eagle Outfitters	Limited Brands
AnnTaylor	Liz Claiborne
Burberry	Marks & Spencer
C&A	Maxeda
Calvin Klein	Mossimo
Cortefiel	Nautica Enterprises
Esprit Holdings	NIKE
French Connection	Polo Ralph Lauren
Gap	Quiksilver
H&M	Tommy Hilfiger
Inditex	Warnaco Group
J. Crew	Wet Seal

HISTORICAL FINANCIALS

Company Type: Public

Income Statement

				FYE: December 31
	REVENUE ($ mil.)	NET INCOME ($ mil.)	NET PROFIT MARGIN	EMPLOYEES
12/05	2,230	114	5.1%	7,978
12/04	2,405	146	6.1%	7,424
12/03	2,362	159	6.7%	6,949
12/02	2,126	69	3.2%	7,162
Annual Growth	1.6%	18.3%	—	3.7%

2005 Year-End Financials

Debt ratio: 41.7%
Return on equity: 7.4%
Cash ($ mil.): 233
Current ratio: 2.44
Long-term debt ($ mil.): 608

No. of shares (mil.): —
Dividends
Yield: 2.7%
Payout: —
Market value ($ mil.): —

Stock History

NYSE: BNG

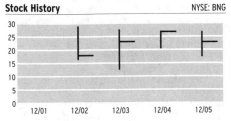

	STOCK PRICE ($) FY Close	P/E High/Low		PER SHARE ($) Earnings	Dividends
12/05	22.90	—	—	—	0.62
12/04	26.76	—	—	0.00	0.67
12/03	23.07	—	—	—	0.81
12/02	17.90	—	—	—	0.55
Annual Growth	8.6%	—	—	—	4.1%

Bertelsmann

Bertelsmann is so big, it needs space in the bookcase, CD rack, and magazine stand. One of the world's top media firms, Bertelsmann has publishing, music, and broadcasting operations in nearly 60 countries. It owns #1 trade book publisher Random House and 50% of #2 music firm Sony BMG Music Entertainment. It also has a 75% stake in magazine publisher Gruner + Jahr, owns 90% of RTL Group, Europe's #1 TV broadcaster, and owns media services firm arvato. In addition, Bertelsmann owns several book and music clubs and e-tail channels. Carl Bertelsmann founded the company in 1835. His descendants, the Mohn family own 23% of the company, and the Bertelsmann Foundation owns the rest.

Investment firm Groupe Bruxelles Lambert exchanged its 30% stake in RTL for a quarter interest in Bertelsmann in 2001 with the understanding that Bruxelles could demand a Bertelsmann IPO by 2006, ending the German media giant's longtime status as a private company. The Mohn family has long opposed taking Bertelsmann public, but former CEO Thomas Middelhoff convinced them that the benefit of gaining control over RTL versus bringing in an outside investor was worth the risk. But in mid-2002 the plan backfired when the board unexpectedly fired Middelhoff citing differences of opinion in the company's direction. He was replaced by arvato's chairman Gunter Thielen. In mid-2006 Bruxelles announced its intention to pursue the IPO, and the Mohns scraped up $5.7 billion to instead buy out the investment firm's interest.

Shortly after his arrival, Thielen embarked on a major selloff of the company's non-core Internet operations, opting to focus on e-commerce assets that made sense when paired with Bertelsmann's traditional book and music holdings.

Bertelsmann hoped to strengthen its position in the music industry with the 2004 creation of Sony BMG Music Entertainment, a 50-50 joint venture with consumer electronics and media giant Sony. The company is now the world's second largest music firm, behind Universal Music. Since its inception, however, Sony BMG has been distracted by costly integration, internal squabbling, and departures from the executive suite, and as a result has lost some market share to Universal. Also weighing on the business, a European Union court decided in 2006 that regulators had failed to study the merger of Sony Music Entertainment and BMG Entertainment sufficiently and ruled that the companies would need to resubmit the merger for approval.

Following its buyout of Bruxelles, Bertelsmann agreed to sell its BMG Music Publishing unit to Vivendi for about $2.1 billion. The #3 music publisher (behind EMI Music Publishing and Warner/Chappell Music) controls the rights to more than a million songs and collects royalties for the use of those compositions in film, television shows, and commercials. It was not part of the Sony BMG merger and continues to be a solid performer for Bertelsmann. Vivendi, which owns #1 music business Universal Music Group, plans to merge the publishing business with its own Universal Music Publishing Group to create a new leader in the industry.

HISTORY

Carl Bertelsmann founded his publishing company C. Bertelsmann Verlag in Gütersloh, Germany, in 1835. The company primarily published hymnals and religious materials, expanding into newspapers during the 1860s. Heinrich Mohn, a fourth-generation descendant, took over the company in 1921 and expanded its operations to include popular fiction, which helped Bertelsmann expand to more than 400 employees by 1939.

During WWII the company published books and propaganda material for the German army, but was closed by the Nazi government in 1944 as it was not considered important to the war effort. (The company had maintained for decades it was closed because it produced religious materials, but contrary evidence was uncovered in 2000 by historians working at the behest of the company.) After WWII Mohn's son, Reinhard (who had been captured by the Allies and interned in a Kansas POW camp), returned to Germany determined to rebuild the company.

Bertelsmann boosted book sales by launching book clubs in Germany during the 1950s and bought Germany's UFA (TV and film production) in 1964. It took a minority interest in publisher Gruner + Jahr in 1969, taking a controlling stake in 1973. In the US, Bertelsmann bought 51% of Bantam Books in 1977 (and the rest in 1981) and Arista Records in 1979. In 1986 it took control of Doubleday Publishing and bought RCA Records (forming Bertelsmann Music Group the next year). Mohn transferred substantial nonvoting shares in the company to the Bertelsmann Foundation in 1993.

The company teamed up with AOL in 1995 to form AOL Europe, and with Luxembourg broadcaster CLT it launched CLT-Ufa in 1997. Bertelsmann acquired book publisher Random House the next year. The company also took a 50% stake in online bookseller barnesandnoble.com (retaining nearly 40% after an IPO in 1999). Thomas Middelhoff became chairman and CEO in 1998. In 1999 Reinhard Mohn transferred his controlling shares in the company to Bertelsmann Verwaltungsgesellschaft, a firm controlled by Bertelsmann executives and the Mohn family.

In 2000 Bertelsmann announced that it would sell its half-interest in AOL Europe back to AOL (now part of Time Warner) by mid-2002; it also spun off Lycos Europe (retaining 27%, now about 20%). It later merged CLT-Ufa with Pearson TV to form RTL Group. (Bertelsmann got a 37% stake.)

Bertelsmann bought Groupe Bruxelles Lambert's 30% stake in RTL Group in 2001. As part of the deal Bruxelles gained a 25% stake in Bertelsmann with the understanding that it would be able to float its interest to the public in four years. Bertelsmann combined RTL's Ufa Sports unit with French sports-rights company Jean-Claude Darmon in exchange for a 40% stake in the combined company, now called Sportfive. Later that year it bought Pearson's 22% stake in RTL Group.

The company's board fired Middelhoff in 2002 citing disagreements over the direction of the company. He was replaced by Gunter Thielen, chairman of Bertelsmann's arvato business unit.

In 2004, Bertelsmann combined BMG with Sony Music to create Sony BMG Music Entertainment, a joint venture with Sony that is now the world's #2 music company.

EXECUTIVES

Honorary Chairman: Reinhard Mohn, age 85
Chairman of the Supervisory Board: Dieter H. Vogel, age 65
Chairman of the Executive Board and CEO: Gunter Thielen, age 64
CFO: Thomas Rabe, age 39
Chairman and CEO, Random House: Peter W. Olson, age 56
Chairman, arvato: Harmut Ostrowski, age 48
Chairman, BMG US; Chairman and CEO, J Records: Clive Davis, age 73
Chairman, Gruner + Jahr: Bernd Kundrun, age 49
Chairman, Sony BMG Music Entertainment: Andrew R. (Andy) Lack, age 59
Vice Chairman, RTL Group: Martin Taylor
CEO, DirectGroup Bertelsmann: Ewald Walgenbach, age 47
CEO, RTL Group: Gerhard Zeiler, age 51
CEO, Sony BMG Music Entertainment: Rolf Schmidt-Holtz, age 58
Board Member; EVP Corporate Development, Random House; President, Random House Ventures: Richard Sarnoff, age 47
Auditing: Klaus-Peter Blobel
Controlling and Strategic Planning: Günther Grüger
Corporate Center, New York: Rob Sorrentino
Corporate Communications: Jasmine Borhan, age 41
Corporate Network: Ralf Schremper
Financial Reporting, Accounting, and Taxes: Wolfgang Wiedermann
Human Resources: Immanuel Hermreck, age 36
Legal Department: Urlich Koch
Media Technology: Johannes Mohn, age 56
Mergers and Acquisitions: Kay Krafft, age 35
Treasury and Finance: Roger Schweitzer
Auditors: KPMG Deutsche Treuhand-Gesellschaft AG

LOCATIONS

HQ: Bertelsmann AG
Carl-Bertelsmann-Strasse 270,
D-33311 Gütersloh, Germany
Phone: +49-5241-80-0   **Fax:** +49-5241-80-9662
US HQ: 1540 Broadway, Ste. 24, New York, NY 10036
US Phone: 212-782-1000   **US Fax:** 212-782-7600
Web: www.bertelsmann.de

Bertelsmann has operations worldwide.

PRODUCTS/OPERATIONS

2005 Sales

	$ mil.	% of total
RTL Group	6,054.9	28
arvato	5,170.1	24
Gruner + Jahr	3,108.0	14
DirectGroup	2,823.7	13
BMG	2,520.5	11
Random House	2,165.1	10
Adjustments	(655.2)	—
Total	**21,187.1**	**100**

Selected Operations

arvato (media services)
DirectGroup Bertelsmann (book and music clubs, e-commerce)
Gruner + Jahr (75%, magazine and newspaper publishing)
Random House (book publishing)
RTL Group (90%, broadcasting, radio, Internet, television production)
Sony BMG Music Entertainment (50%, music publishing)

COMPETITORS

Advance Publications
Amazon.com
Axel Springer
Disney
Editis
Hachette Filipacchi Médias
Hearst
IWCO Direct
Lagardère
McGraw-Hill
News Corp.
Pearson
PRIMEDIA
Reed Elsevier Group
Schibsted
Sony
Time Warner
Universal Music Group
Verlagsgruppe Georg von Holtzbrinck
Virgin Group
VNU
Warner Music
Wolters Kluwer

HISTORICAL FINANCIALS

Company Type: Private

Income Statement

FYE: December 31

	REVENUE ($ mil.)	NET INCOME ($ mil.)	NET PROFIT MARGIN	EMPLOYEES
12/05	21,187	1,233	5.8%	88,516
12/04	23,210	1,408	6.1%	76,266
12/03	21,089	193	0.9%	73,221
12/02*	19,193	973	5.1%	80,632
6/01	17,011	824	4.8%	82,162
Annual Growth	5.6%	10.6%	—	1.9%

*Fiscal year change

Net Income History

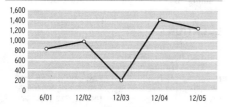

BHP Billiton

Two heads — or headquarters — are better than one. Aussie minerals and oil company BHP Limited acquired UK miner Billiton plc in 2001. The result is a two-headquartered, dual-listed company that is run as a single entity with the same board of directors and management. The Melbourne side is BHP Billiton Limited; the London side is BHP Billiton Plc; collectively they're known as BHP Billiton. The company ranks among the world's top producers of iron ore and coal (thermal and metallurgical) and is a major producer of petroleum products such as crude oil and natural gas. Other units produce aluminum, base metals, diamonds, manganese, and stainless steel. BHP Billiton has operations on six continents.

BHP Billiton is experiencing eyebrow-raising growth thanks in part to high commodity prices and the emerging Asian economies. China, for example, represented 17% in 2006, up from 10% two years prior. Due to the strong demand, BHP Billiton has increased production of iron ore, coking coal, and manganese. On the petroleum side, the company is continuing to acquire oil and gas exploration leases in the Gulf of Mexico.

With Anglo American, BHP Billiton had a South African joint venture called Samancor. In early 2005 the two companies sold Samancor's chrome mining and manufacturing business to the Kermas Group for $469 million.

In mid-2005 BHP Billiton acquired 100% of the shares in metals and minerals company WMC Resources, which had been the subject of much takeover speculation and the target of the Swiss mining heavyweight Xstrata. BHP Billiton opened talks with WMC's board and made an offer for the Australian company in early 2005. Its offer of $7.3 billion surpassed Xstrata's and was accepted and endorsed by the WMC board. The addition of WMC added significantly to BHP Billiton's copper, nickel, and uranium operations.

HISTORY

In 1883 Charles Rasp, a boundary rider for the Mt. Gipps sheep station, believed valuable ore lay in the Broken Hill outcrop in New South Wales, Australia. He gathered a few young speculators, and The Broken Hill Proprietary Company (BHP) was incorporated in 1885. BHP immediately found a massive lode of silver, lead, and zinc. None of the founders knew how to run a mine, so they recruited US engineers William Patton and Herman Schlapp. From the beginning, labor and management clashed. The founding directors set up the head office in Melbourne, far from the mine, and gambled with gold sovereigns in the boardroom. But the miners worked in dangerous conditions. An 1892 labor strike was the first of BHP's bitter strikes.

In 1902 the new general manager, Guillaume Delprat, invented a flotation process that recovered valuable metals from iron ore waste. Delprat also foresaw a future in steel, although Australia had no steel industry. BHP commissioned the Newcastle steelworks in 1915 and soon became the country's largest steel producer. BHP's 1935 purchase of Australian Iron and Steel, its only competitor, gave it a virtual steel monopoly, while high tariffs protected it from outside competition. Its exhausted Broken Hill mine was closed that year.

In the 1960s BHP got into oil when it partnered with Esso Standard, the Australian subsidiary of Standard Oil of New Jersey, for offshore exploration. In 1967 the partners found oil in the Bass Strait, which soon supplied 70% of Australia's petroleum. In the 1960s and 1970s, BHP began expanding its iron ore, manganese, and coal interests. Meanwhile, public opposition mounted to BHP's market power and labor practices, and in 1972 the government took steps to limit BHP's power, removing some subsidies and tax breaks.

The weak steel market of the 1970s and 1980s caused BHP to lay off almost a third of its steelworkers in 1983, but with government intervention, BHP radically improved its steel productivity. In 1984 BHP bought Utah International's mining assets from General Electric (including Chile's rich Escondida copper mine). In 1986 corporate raider Robert Holmes à Court took a run at BHP; BHP decided to become an international mining company to prevent further raids. Its acquisitions in the late 1980s included ERG Inc. and Monsanto Oil (combined into BHP Americas), Aquila Steel, and Pacific Refining in Hawaii.

A peace deal with Holmes à Court gave BHP about 37% of Foster's Brewing, but in 1992 BHP took a $700 million write-down after Foster's stock declined. BHP also bought Arizona-based Magma Copper in 1996, but plunging world copper prices forced a $420 million write-down.

With new worries over Asia's economic troubles, BHP soon was struggling. In 1997 BHP sold most of its stake in Foster's, and three senior executives resigned. In 1998 the company unloaded Pacific Refining, which was acquired by Tesoro Petroleum for about $275 million.

As BHP's woes continued, CEO John Prescott resigned; Paul Anderson was recruited from Duke Energy to succeed Prescott. In 1999 D. R. Argus took over as chairman, replacing Jeremy Ellis. In a restructuring move, the company sold its engineering, power, insurance and information technology businesses in 1999 and 2000. BHP began to sell $2 billion worth of steel operations (including its long product unit, OneSteel). In 2000 the company shortened its official name to BHP Limited.

BHP acquired Billiton in 2001, forming BHP Billiton Ltd. and BHP Billiton plc. The combined BHP Billiton had sales of almost $20 billion and a market capitalization approaching $30 billion. In addition, BHP paid $436 million for Dia Met Minerals, which owned 29% of Canada's only producing diamond mine, Ekati.

Also in 2001 BHP Billiton and Alcoa combined their North American metals distribution businesses as joint venture Integris Metals (subsequently sold and integrated into Ryerson). In order to focus on its minerals and oil and gas operations, in 2002 BHP Billiton spun off its steel business as BHP Steel. After a revolving door of CEOs during the past five years, BHP named Charles Goodyear to the position after the ouster of Brian Gilbertson in early 2003.

EXECUTIVES

Chairman: Don R. Argus, age 68
CEO and Director: Charles W. (Chip) Goodyear, age 48
Executive President and Director:
Miklos (Mike) Salamon, age 50
Executive President: Robert W. (Bob) Kirkby, age 58
CFO: Alex Vanselow, age 43

Director; Group President, Carbon Steel Materials:
Christopher J. (Chris) Lynch, age 52
Director; Group President, Non-Ferrous Businesses:
Marius Kloppers, age 44
Group President, Energy: Philip S. (Phil) Aiken, age 57,
$1,691,455 pay
Group President, Energy: J. Michael (Mike) Yeager,
age 53
President and COO, Western Australia Iron Ore:
Ian R. Ashby, age 48
President, Aluminium: Graeme Hunt, age 49
President, Base Metals: Diego Hernandez, age 57
President, Diamonds and Specialty Products:
Alberto Calderon, age 46
President, Energy Coal: Mahomed Seedat, age 50
President, Gas and Power: Rebecca A. McDonald, age 54
President, Manganese: Peter Beaven, age 39
President, Metallurgical Coal: David (Dave) Murray,
age 51
President, Stainless Steel Materials: Chris Pointon,
age 58
President, Marketing: Tom Schutte, age 41
**VP, Investor Relations and Communications (UK and
US):** Mark Lidiard
Chief Human Capital and Excellence Officer:
Marcus P. Randolph, age 50
Chief Legal Counsel and Head of External Affairs:
John Fast, age 56, $1,387,362 pay
Special Advisor and Head of Group Secretariat:
Karen J. Wood, age 50
Auditors: KPMG Audit Plc

LOCATIONS

HQ: BHP Billiton
180 Lonsdale St., Melbourne 3000, Australia
Phone: +61-1300-55-4757   **Fax:** +61-3-9609-3015
US HQ: 1360 Post Oak Blvd., Ste. 150,
Houston, TX 77056
US Phone: 713-961-8500   **US Fax:** 713-961-8400
Web: www.bhpbilliton.com

BHP Billiton primarily has production operations in
Africa, Australia, and South America. It maintains
corporate offices in Houston, Johannesburg, London,
Melbourne, and Santiago.

2006 Sales

	$ mil.	% of total
Asia		
China	5,294	17
Japan	2,959	9
South Korea	1,689	9
Other	2,496	8
Europe	10,027	31
Australia	3,507	11
North America	2,344	7
Southern Africa	1,426	4
South America	729	2
Other	682	2
Total	**32,153**	**100**

PRODUCTS/OPERATIONS

2006 Sales

	$ mil.	% of total
Base Metals	10,294	27
Carbon Steel Materials	9,760	25
Petroleum	5,876	14
Aluminum	5,084	13
Energy Coal	3,319	9
Stainless Steel Materials	2,955	8
Diamonds & Specialty Products	1,263	3
Other	548	1
Adjustments	(6,946)	—
Total	**32,153**	**100**

Selected Divisions

Base metals
  Cathode
  Copper
  Gold
  Lead
  Silver
  Zinc
Carbon steel materials
  Iron ore
  Manganese
  Metallurgical coal
Petroleum
  Crude oil
  Ethane
  LPG
  Natural gas
Aluminum
  Alumina
  Aluminum
Energy coal
Stainless steel materials
  Cobalt
  Ferrochrome
  Nickel
Diamonds and specialty products
  Diamonds

COMPETITORS

Alcan	Koch
Alcoa	Marathon Oil
Aluminum Corporation of	Newmont Mining
China	Nippon Steel
Anglo American	Norsk Hydro
BP	Ormet
Chevron	Phelps Dodge
Codelco	Repsol YPF
ConocoPhillips	Rio Tinto
Corus Group	Royal Dutch Shell
Exxon Mobil	ThyssenKrupp
Freeport-McMoRan	TOTAL
Inco Limited	Xstrata

HISTORICAL FINANCIALS

Company Type: Holding company

Income Statement				FYE: June 30
	REVENUE ($ mil.)	NET INCOME ($ mil.)	NET PROFIT MARGIN	EMPLOYEES
6/06	32,153	10,450	32.5%	33,184

BMW

Bayerische Motoren Werke (better known as
BMW) is one of Europe's top automakers. BMW's
car offerings include sedans, coupes, convert-
ibles, and sport wagons in the 3 Series, 5 Series,
6 Series, and 7 Series model groups. Other models include the M3 coupe and convertible; the X5
sport utilities; and the Z4 roadster. In addition to
its BMW automobiles, the company's operations
include motorcycles (K 1200 GT, R 1200 GS, and
R 1150 R models, among others), the MINI automotive brand, Rolls-Royce Motor Cars, and
software (softlab GmbH). BMW's motorcycle division also offers a line of motorcycling apparel
such as leather suits, gloves, and boots.

After a record-setting year in 2004, 2005 was
a bit more challenging for BMW as automotive
profits were down nearly 6% due mainly to high
raw materials costs and intense global competition. Motorcycle sales, in the doldrums in 2004,
have improved, however. BMW financial services
operations also enjoyed a brisk business in 2005.

High oil prices have driven up costs for plastics, and steel prices also remain high. To offset
these conditions, BMW is working closely with
its suppliers to lower the cost of components
while keeping innovation and quality high.

BMW has opened up a joint-venture in China
(with local partner Brilliance China Automotive
Holdings Ltd.) for production of BMWs for that
market. The company is also looking out for opportunities in Eastern Europe as nations there
join the European Union. BMW is also working
to set up a manufacturing and dealer presence
in India to bolster its Asian strategy as Asia is the
fastest-growing geographical segment of the automotive market.

In late 2006 BMW announced it would introduce a hydrogen-burning version of its 7-Series
sedan in April of 2007. The new 7-Series will be
capable of burning hydrogen as well as gasoline. When in hygrogen mode its only emission
is water vapor. Due to the new sedan's high
price, it will only be available for lease to select
BMW customers. BMW is also working on fuel
cell-powered cars, but is launching the hydro-
gen/gasoline 7-Series first as it is more practi-
cal for the near-term.

Germany's Quandt family controls BMW.

HISTORY

BMW's logo speaks to its origin: a propeller in
blue and white, the colors of Bavaria. In 1913
Karl Rapp opened an aircraft-engine design shop
near Munich. He named it Bayerische Motoren
Werke (BMW) in 1917. The end of WWI brought
German aircraft production to a halt, and BMW
shifted to making railway brakes until the 1930s.
BMW debuted its first motorcycle, the R32, in
1923, and the company began making automobiles in 1928 after buying small-car company
Fahrzeugwerke Eisenach.

In 1933 BMW launched a line of larger cars.
The company built aircraft engines for Hitler's
Luftwaffe in the 1930s and stopped all auto and
motorcycle production in 1941. BMW chief Josef
Popp resisted and was ousted. Under the Nazis,
the company operated in occupied countries,
built rockets, and developed the world's first production jet engine.

With its factories dismantled after WWII, BMW
survived by making kitchen and garden equipment. In 1948 it introduced a one-cylinder motorcycle, which sold well as cheap transportation
in postwar Germany. BMW autos in the 1950s
were large and expensive and sold poorly. When
motorcycle sales dropped, the company escaped
demise in the mid-1950s by launching the Isetta,
a seven-foot, three-wheeled "bubble car."

Herbert Quandt saved the enterprise in 1959 by
buying control for $1 million. Quandt's BMW fo-
cused on sports sedans and released the first of
the "New Range" of BMWs in 1961. Success of the
niche enabled BMW to buy automaker Hans Glas
in 1966.

In the 1970s BMW's European exports soared,
and the company set up a distribution subsidiary
in the US. The company also produced larger
cars that put BMW on par with Mercedes-Benz.

Rapid export growth in the US, Asia, and Australia continued in the 1980s, but Japanese bikes
and poor demand hurt motorcycle sales. The
launch of the company's luxury vehicles in 1986

heated up the BMW-Mercedes rivalry. US sales peaked that year and fell 45% by 1991. However, in 1992 BMW outsold Mercedes in Europe for the first time and became the first European carmaker to operate a US plant since Volkswagen pulled out in 1988.

BMW teamed with the UK's Rolls-Royce aerospace firm in 1990 to make jet engines for planes that included executive business-travel jets such as the Gulfstream V.

The company bought UK carmaker Rover from British Aerospace and Honda in 1994 and introduced a cheaper vehicle, the four-wheel-drive Discovery.

BMW offered to buy the luxury Rolls-Royce auto unit (including the Bentley) from UK-based Vickers in 1998, but lost out when Volkswagen (VW) countered with a higher offer. Also in 1998 BMW was hit by a class-action lawsuit brought by Holocaust survivors seeking compensation for their work as slave laborers during WWII.

In mid-1998 BMW began cutting jobs at its money-losing Rover unit. As Rover's plants continued their downward trend in 1999, BMW's board forced out chairman Bernd Pischetsrieder, who spearheaded the Rover acquisition in 1994. The UK later pledged to help pay for renovations at Rover's Longbridge plant to save about 14,000 jobs and prevent it from moving operations to Hungary.

The company in 2000 sold its Land Rover SUV operations to Ford in a deal worth about $2.7 billion. Also that year BMW handed over its Rover Cars operations and MG brand to the Phoenix Consortium, a UK-based group led by former Rover CEO John Towers.

In 2001 BMW launched its MINI brand in the UK; other European markets soon followed. BMW brought the MINI Cooper to US shores in 2002. The following year BMW took control of the Rolls-Royce brand from Volkswagen, and began making Rolls-Royce Phantoms in Goodwood in the south of England.

Despite selling the operations of Rover in 2000, BMW still retained the rights to the brand. In 2006 BMW agreed to sell the Rover brand to an unidentified buyer at an undisclosed price, although Dow Jones Newswires reported the buyer was Shanghai Automotive Industry Corp. and the price was nearly $21 million. That deal, however, was derailed a month later when Ford Motor said it would exercise its right of first refusal agreement with BMW and take control of the brand for about $11 million.

EXECUTIVES

Chairman, Supervisory Board: Joachim Milberg, age 63
Chairman of the Board of Management:
 Norbert Reithofer, age 50
Member, Management Board, Finance: Stefan Krause
Member, Management Board, Research, Development and Purchasing: Klaus Draeger, age 49
Member, Management Board, Human Resources and Industrial Relations Director: Ernst Baumann
Member, Management Board, Production:
 Frank-Peter Arndt, age 50
Member, Management Board, Sales and Marketing:
 Michael Ganal
SVP and Member, Supervisory Board: Anton Ruf
SVP: Friedrich Eichiner
VP, Brand Management, MINI: Kay Segler
VP, Central Marketing and Brand Management, BMW:
 Torsten Müller-Oetvoes
Managing Director, BMW Group Middle East:
 Guenther Seemann
Managing Director, BMW Asia Pte Ltd: Roland Kruger
Chairman and CEO, BMW Financial Services:
 John Christman
President, India: Peter Kronschnabl

General Manager: Felix Toelke
General Manager: Christoph von Tschirschnitz
Director of Design: Chris Bangle
Regional Director, China: Christoph Stark
Regional Director, Europe: David Barry Panton
Regional Director, Germany: Ludwig Willisch
Regional Director, USA; Chairman and CEO, BMW of North America: Tom Purves
General Counsel: Dieter Löchelt
Head of Corporate Communications: Bill McAndrews
Auditors: KPMG Deutsche Treuhand-Gesellschaft AG

LOCATIONS

HQ: Bayerische Motoren Werke AG
 Petuelring 130, D-80788 Munich, Germany
Phone: +49-89-382-0 **Fax:** +49-89-382-2-44-18
US HQ: 300 Chestnut Ridge Rd.,
 Woodcliff Lake, NJ 07677
US Phone: 201-307-4000 **US Fax:** 201-307-4095
Web: www.bmw.com

The BMW Group operates globally, with 23 production and assembly plants in seven countries.

2005 Sales

	$ mil.	% of total
Europe		
Germany	13,028.5	24
Other countries	20,448.1	37
The Americas	13,690.5	25
Africa, Asia & Oceania	8,087.6	14
Total	**55,254.7**	**100**

PRODUCTS/OPERATIONS

2005 Sales

	$ mil.	% of total
Automobiles	54,313.1	82
Financial services	11,142.0	16
Motorcycles	1,448.4	2
Adjustments	(11,648.8)	—
Total	**55,254.7**	**100**

Selected Products

Automobiles
 BMW models

1 Series	7 Series
Hatchback	750i Sedan
3 Series	750Li Sedan
325Ci Convertible	760i Sedan
325Ci Coupe	760Li Sedan
325i Sedan	M Models
325xi Sedan	M3 Convertible
325xi Sports Wagon	M3 Coupe
330Ci Convertible	M5 Sedan
330Ci Coupe	M6 Coupe
330i Sedan	X3 Models
330xi Sedan	X3 3.0i
5 Series	X5 Models
525i Sedan	X5 3.0i
525xi Sedan	X5 4.4i
530i Sedan	X5 4.8is
530xi Sedan	Z4 Models
530xi Sports Wagon	Z4 Coupe
550i Sedan	Z4 Roadster 3.0i
6 Series	Z4 Roadster 3.0si
650i Convertible	
650i Coupe	

MINI
 MINI Cooper
 MINI Cooper Convertible
 MINI Cooper S
 MINI Cooper S Convertible
Rolls-Royce
 Phantom

Motorcycles

Enduro	Sport
F 650 GS	K 1200 S
F 650 Dakar	R 1200 S
HP 2 Enduro	Sport Touring
R 1200 GS	K 1200 GT
R 1200 Adventure	R 1200 ST
Naked	Touring
F 650 CS	K 1200 LT
K 1200 R	R 1200 CL
R 1150 R	R 1200 RT
R 1150 R Rockster	

COMPETITORS

DaimlerChrysler	Nissan
Ducati	Peugeot
Fiat	Renault
Ford	Saab Automobile
General Motors	Suzuki Motor
Harley-Davidson	Toyota
Honda	Ultra Motorcycle
Kawasaki Heavy Industries	Volkswagen
Mazda	Yamaha

HISTORICAL FINANCIALS

Company Type: Public

Income Statement

FYE: December 31

	REVENUE ($ mil.)	NET INCOME ($ mil.)	NET PROFIT MARGIN	EMPLOYEES
12/05	55,255	2,652	4.8%	105,798
12/04	60,473	3,031	5.0%	105,972
12/03	52,122	2,444	4.7%	104,342
12/02	44,316	2,117	4.8%	101,395
12/01	34,071	1,653	4.9%	97,275
Annual Growth	**12.8%**	**12.5%**	**—**	**2.1%**

2005 Year-End Financials

Debt ratio: 99.2%   Current ratio: 0.96
Return on equity: 12.1%   Long-term debt ($ mil.): 19,932
Cash ($ mil.): 1,920

Net Income History

German: BMW

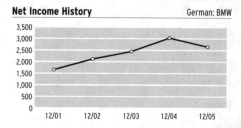

BNP Paribas

No Napoleon complex here. One of Europe's largest banks, BNP Paribas operates some 2,200 retail branches in France and has operations in nearly 90 other countries. The company and its many subsidiaries specialize in retail banking, corporate and investment banking, and asset management. Other activities include private banking (BNP Paribas Banque Privée), real estate financing (UCB), private equity (BNP Paribas Capital), and insurance (Cardif Assurance Vie and Natio Assurance, a joint venture with AXA). BNP Paribas also controls consumer lender Cetelem, online brokerage Cortal Consors, and property management firm Klépierre.

BNP Paribas bought 98% of Italy's Banca Nazionale del Lavoro (BNL) in 2006; it plans to buy the remaining shares of BNL and to delist the Italian bank. The acquisition, valued at some $11 billion, was one of more than a dozen global buys BNP Paribas made in 2005 and 2006. Others included acquisition of a 51% stake in UkrSibbank, one of Ukraine's leading banks; it also made deals in the US, China, the Netherlands, and Turkey. BNP Paribas is focused on growing its international retail banking operations, particularly in the US, where it owns BancWest (the parent of Bank of the West and First Hawaiian Bank). It expanded there with its purchases of Community First Bankshares in 2004 and Commercial Federal Corporation in 2005. Additional US acquisitions, however, are not imminent: The bank said in 2006 that it intended to take a break from further buys in the States. However, Europe appears to be fair game: BNP and Italian bank Unicredito are rumored to be looking at buying Landesbank Berlin from Bankgesellschaft Berlin. Through its BNP Paribas Immobilier unit, the company also offers a wide range of real estate services through such subsidiaries as Atisreal (commercial real estate advisory services), BNP Paribas REIM (real estate investment management), Comadim (property management), and Meunier (property development).

HISTORY

BNP Paribas Group's predecessor Banque Nationale de Paris (BNP) is the progeny of two state banks with parallel histories; each was set up to jump-start the economy after a revolution in 1848.

For a century, Paris-based Comptoir National d'Escompte de Paris (CNEP) bounced between private and public status, depending on government whim. It was the #3 bank in France from the late 19th century through the 1950s.

Banque National pour le Commerce et l'Industrie (BNCI) started in Alsace, a region that was part of Germany from the Franco-Prussian War until WWI. BNCI served as an economic bridge between Germany and France, which had to give the bank governmental resuscitation during the Depression. By the 1960s BNCI had passed CNEP in size.

French leader Charles de Gaulle expected banking to drive post-WWII reconstruction, and in 1945 CNEP and BNCI were nationalized. In 1966 France's finance minister merged them and they became BNP. That year the company started an association with Dresdner Bank of Germany, under which the two still operate joint ventures, primarily in Eastern Europe.

By 1993 privatization was again in vogue, and BNP was cut loose by the government. It expanded outside France to ameliorate the influences of the French economy and government. Even before it was privatized, BNP was involved in such politically charged actions as the bailout of OPEC money repository Banque Arabe and the extension of credit to Algeria's state oil company Sonatrach.

The privatized BNP looked overseas in the late 1990s. In 1997 alone, it won the right to operate in New Zealand, bought Laurentian Bank and Trust of the Bahamas, took control of its joint venture with Egypt's Banque du Caire, and opened a subsidiary in Brazil.

BNP bought failed Peregrine Investment's Chinese operations in 1998. That year the bank also expanded in Peru, opened an office in Algeria, opened a representative office in Uzbekistan, set up an investment banking subsidiary in India,

and bought Australian stock brokerage operations from Prudential.

After a decade of globe-trotting, BNP brought it on home in 1999 and set off a year of tumult in French banking. As France's other two large banks (Société Générale and Paribas) made plans to merge, BNP decided it would absorb both banks as a means to get a bigger chunk of the to-be-privatized Crédit Lyonnais and to protect France from Euro-megabank penetration by creating the globe's largest bank.

Executives at Société Générale (SG) had other ideas, forming a cartel called "Action Against the BNP Raid." Meanwhile, BNP tried to boost to controlling stakes its holdings in the two banks. (In Europe's cross-ownership tradition, the target banks also owned part of BNP.) France's central bank tried unsuccessfully to negotiate a deal (the government supported the triumvirate merger). A war of words was played out in the media, and finally shareholders had to vote on the proposals. In the end, BNP won control of Paribas, but not SG. As BNP prepared to integrate a reluctant Paribas into its operations, regulators ordered BNP to relinquish its stake in SG. The newly merged company was dubbed BNP Paribas Group.

In 2000 BNP Paribas and Avis Group launched a fleet-management joint venture. BNP also bought 150 shopping centers from French retailer Carrefour and the 40% of merchant bank Cobepa that it didn't already own. In 2001 BNP Paribas took full control of US-based BancWest.

The company bought United California Bank from UFJ Holdings (now part of Mitsubishi UFJ Financial Group) in 2002.

EXECUTIVES

Chairman: Michel Pébereau, age 64, $829,010 pay
Vice Chairman: Jean-Louis Beffa, age 65
President, CEO, and Director: Baudouin Prot, age 55, $933,623 pay
Co-COO: Georges Chodron de Courcel, age 56, $582,281 pay
Co-COO: Jean Clamon, age 54, $538,856 pay
Head of Asset Management and Services: Alain Papiasse, age 49
Head of Compliance: Vivien Lévy-Garboua, age 57
Head of Corporate and Investment Banking: Jacques d'Estais
Head of French Retail Banking: Jean-Laurent Bonnafé
Head of Group Development and Finance: Philipe Bordenave
Head of Group Human Resources: Bernard Lemée
Head of Human Resources: Frédéric Lavenir
Head of Group Information Systems: Hervé Gouëzel
Head of International Retail Banking and Financial Services: Pierre Mariani, age 49
Head of BNP Paribas Capital: Amaury de Seze, age 60
Head of Research and Strategy: Patrick Mange
Managing Director, Head of Foreign Exchange Options, North America: Andrew Goldberg
Director, Customer Equity Finance Trading: Matthew Flannery
Head, European Corporate Group: Ligia Torres
Auditors: Barbier Frinault & Autres; Mazars & Guérard; PricewaterhouseCoopers Audit

LOCATIONS

HQ: BNP Paribas
16, boulevard des Italiens, 75009 Paris, France
Phone: +33-1-40-14-45-46   **Fax:** +33-1-40-14-69-73
US HQ: 787 7th Ave., New York, NY 10019
US Phone: 212-841-3000
Web: www.bnpparibas.com

2005 Sales

	% of total
Europe	
France	56
Other countries	22
Americas	15
Asia/Oceania	4
Other regions	3
Total	**100**

PRODUCTS/OPERATIONS

2005 Sales

	% of total
Interest	46
Commission income	13
Net gain on financial instruments	8
Net gain on available-for-sale financial assets	2
Other	31
Total	**100**

2005 Net Banking Income By Business Segment

	% of total
Retail banking	
International retail banking & financial services	28
French retail banking	24
Corporate & investment banking	
Advisory & capital markets	17
Financing	12
Asset management & services	16
Other	3
Total	**100**

COMPETITORS

ABN AMRO	Generale de Belgique
Banco Popular	HSBC Holdings
Bank of America	JPMorgan Chase
Barclays	Natixis
BBVA	Société Générale
Caisses d'Epargne	UBS
Citigroup	U.S. Bancorp
Crédit Agricole	Wells Fargo
Deutsche Bank	

HISTORICAL FINANCIALS

Company Type: Public

Income Statement

	ASSETS ($ mil.)	NET INCOME ($ mil.)	INCOME AS % OF ASSETS	EMPLOYEES
12/05	1,489,943	6,931	0.5%	109,780
12/04	1,235,699	6,367	0.5%	94,900
12/03	982,917	4,721	0.5%	89,100
12/02	744,485	3,454	0.5%	87,700
12/01	731,047	3,559	0.5%	85,000
Annual Growth	**19.5%**	**18.1%**	**—**	**6.6%**

FYE: December 31

2005 Year-End Financials

Equity as % of assets: —   Long-term debt ($ mil.): —
Return on assets: 0.5%   Sales ($ mil.): 62,164
Return on equity: —

Net Income History

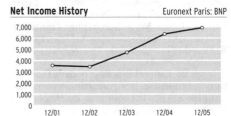

Euronext Paris: BNP

Bombardier

Bombardier makes the goods to get people moving. Its Bombardier Aerospace subsidiary is the world's #3 maker of civil aircraft behind Boeing and Airbus; the #1 regional aircraft maker (Canadair, de Havilland), ahead of Embraer; and one of the two largest makers of business jets (Challenger, Learjet), just behind Gulfstream. Its Bombardier Transportation division — which added DaimlerChrysler's Adtranz rail systems unit in 2001 — is the world's largest railway equipment maker. The company has sold its recreation vehicle business, which made Ski-Doo and Lynx snowmobiles, ATVs, and Sea-Doo personal watercraft. The Bombardier family controls Bombardier.

After announcing that it would sell units that can't generate 30% growth earnings per share, Bombardier sold its Recreational Products group (which previously accounted for about 10% of sales) in December 2003. It also agreed to sell its inventory finance division, which provides equipment financing, to GE Commercial Finance for $2.4 billion ($1.4 billion in cash and $1 billion in assumed liabilities).

The company is focusing on its aerospace operations, which account for just over half of sales (down from 65% in 2001); and its transportation operations, which account for about 40% of sales. Bombardier's rail operations became the largest producer of railway equipment in the world — ahead of ALSTOM and Siemens AG — when the company acquired DaimlerChrysler's Adtranz rail systems unit.

On the aerospace front, Bombardier cut thousands of jobs in response to the plunge in commercial aircraft demand in 2002 and 2003. As things began looking up in 2004, however, Bombardier announced that it was considering building a family (C Series) of 100- to 130-seat jets that would compete directly with Boeing and Airbus. Early in 2005 the company's board approved the larger C Series planes, but it deferred its final decision; in 2006 Bombardier announced that it would focus instead on 80- to 100-seat passenger planes. Sales of business jets increased nearly 70% in 2004.

Meanwhile, Bombardier is interested in pursuing international growth outside of North America and Western Europe. The company is also in the midst of restructuring its Transportation segment; the changes are expected to cut about 4,000 jobs. The Bombardier family owns more than 50% of Bombardier.

HISTORY

Bombardier got its start in the 1920s when mechanic Joseph-Armand Bombardier began converting old cars into snowmobiles. He founded L'Auto-Neige Bombardier Limited in 1942 to make commercial snow vehicles. In 1959 Bombardier introduced the first personal snowmobile, the Ski-Doo.

At age 27, Laurent Beaudoin became the company's president in 1966. Bombardier went public in 1969. When the bottom dropped out of the snowmobile business due to the energy crisis in 1973, Beaudoin diversified, and in 1974 Bombardier won its first mass-transit contract to build Montreal subway cars. Expanding further into mass transportation, Bombardier merged with MLW-Worthington Limited, a builder of diesel engines and diesel-electric locomotives. In 1978 the company became Bombardier Inc.

During the 1980s Bombardier continued to diversify. It expanded into military vehicles and became the leading supplier to the North American rail transit industry. The company entered the European railcar market in 1986, the same year it acquired Canadair, Canada's largest aerospace company, from the national government.

Founded in 1920 as the aircraft division of Canadian Vickers, Canadair became a separate company producing military and civilian aircraft in 1944. Acquired by Electric Boat (which became part of General Dynamics) in 1947, it was nationalized by the Canadian government in 1976. In 1978 Canadair introduced its Challenger 600 business jet, which became a major seller.

Bombardier began development of a commuter aircraft, the Canadian Regional Jet (a 50-seat derivative of the Challenger), in 1989.

In 1990 the company bought US-based Learjet and its service centers, and two years later it acquired a stake in de Havilland, a regional aircraft maker, which it jointly owns with the Province of Ontario. The company bought German railroad-equipment maker Waggonfabrik Talbot in 1995.

In 1996 Amtrak selected an international consortium headed by Bombardier to produce high-speed trains, electric locomotives, and train-maintenance facilities. Also that year the Global Express business jet made its first flight.

Bombardier doubled the size of its European operations in 1998 by buying German railcar maker Deutsche Waggonbau. In 1999 Bombardier announced the launch of its all-new business jet, the eight-passenger Continental.

The company sold its 50% stake in Shorts Missile Systems to Thomson in 2000. Also that year Bombardier landed a $817 million contract to supply Spanish carrier Air Nostrum with 44 planes. It also inked a $2 billion deal to make 94 regional jets for Delta Air Lines; the Delta order includes options for an additional 406 aircraft through 2010.

To start off 2001, Bombardier signed a deal with SkyWest worth about $1.4 billion for 64 Canadair regional jets. It was also selected by a bankruptcy court as winning bidder for Outboard Marine's Evinrude and Johnson outboard marine engine assets. Completing an agreement made the year before, Bombardier acquired DaimlerChrysler's Adtranz rail systems unit for about $725 million, making it part of its Bombardier Transportation division. In September the company announced that it would take a charge of about $600 million and lay off about 10% of its aerospace workforce (it also said that it would cut another 7% of that workforce if demand did not grow).

In 2002 Bombardier sought about $870 million in damages from DaimlerChrysler over the Adtranz deal, claiming that the level of equity in Adtranz was overstated and that the costs related to third-party contracts were higher than stated at the time of the deal. Late in 2002 Bombardier temporarily suspended business jet production. Bombardier divested its Recreational Products unit in December 2003.

CEO Paul Tellier resigned in December 2004 amid rumored boardroom differences with Laurent Bombardier, who assumed the CEO duties.

EXECUTIVES

Chairman and CEO: Laurent Beaudoin, age 67
Vice Chairman: J.R. André Bombardier
Vice Chairman: Jean-Louis Fontaine
SVP and CFO: Pierre Alary, $814,104 pay
SVP and Treasurer: François Lemarchand
SVP, Strategy and Corporate Audit Services and Risk Assessment: Richard C. Bradeen
SVP and General Counsel: Daniel Desjardins
SVP, Public Affairs: John Paul MacDonald
SVP: Carroll L'Italien, $791,490 pay
Corporate Secretary: Roger Carle
EVP, President, and COO, Bombardier Aerospace: Pierre Beaudoin, $1,330,000 pay
President and COO, Bombardier Capital: Brian Peters
EVP and President, Bombardier Transportation: André Navarri, age 57, $1,701,404 pay
COO, Bombardier Transportation: Wolfgang Toelsner
Director, Investor Relations: Shirley Chénier
Auditors: Ernst & Young LLP

LOCATIONS

HQ: Bombardier Inc.
   800 René-Lévesque Blvd. West,
   Montreal, Quebec H3B 1Y8, Canada
Phone: 514-861-9481   **Fax:** 514-861-7053
Web: www.bombardier.com

Bombardier's principal production facilities are located in Canada, the UK, and the US.

2006 Sales

	$ mil.	% of total
The Americas		
US	5,810	39
Canada	825	6
Other countries	649	4
Europe		
UK	1,573	11
Germany	1,529	10
France	707	5
Italy	387	3
Spain	346	2
Switzerland	250	2
The Netherlands	245	2
Sweden	205	1
Austria	174	1
Other countries	641	4
Asia/Pacific		
Japan	219	2
China	196	1
Other countries	899	6
Other regions	71	1
Total	**14,726**	**100**

PRODUCTS/OPERATIONS

2006 Sales

	% of total
Aerospace	55
Transportation	45
Total	**100**

Selected Operations

Aerospace
   Amphibious aircraft
      Canadair-415 turboprop
   Business aircraft
      Canadair SE
      Challenger 604
      Continental
      Global Express
      Learjet 31A, 45, 60
   Defense services
      Flying training
      Military aircraft technical service
      Special defense products (Unmanned Aerial Vehicle)
   Regional aircraft
      CRJ 200
      CRJ 700
      CRJ 900
      Q100
      Q200
      Q300
      Q400

Transportation
- Freight cars
- Locomotives for passenger trains
- Monorails
- Rapid-transit cars
- Single-level and bi-level railcars
- Subway cars
- Trams
- Tram-trains
- Turbotrains
- Vehicles with tilting systems

Bombardier Capital
- Aircraft and industrial equipment financing and leasing
- Consumer financing
- Inventory financing
- Mortgage financing
- Ski industry financing

COMPETITORS

Airbus
ALSTOM
BMW
Boeing
Brunswick
Cessna
Cirrus Design
Eclipse Aviation
Embraer
Fiat
Gulfstream Aerospace
Lockheed Martin
NetJets
Northrop Grumman
Polaris Industries
Raytheon
Safire
Siemens AG
Suzuki Motor
Textron
Trinity Industries
Yamaha

HISTORICAL FINANCIALS

Company Type: Public

Income Statement

FYE: January 31

	REVENUE ($ mil.)	NET INCOME ($ mil.)	NET PROFIT MARGIN	EMPLOYEES
1/06	14,726	249	1.7%	55,922
1/05	15,839	(85)	—	59,550
1/04	16,025	(67)	—	64,600
1/03	15,482	(403)	—	70,411
1/02	13,614	246	1.8%	74,879
Annual Growth	2.0%	0.3%	—	(7.0%)

Net Income History

Toronto: BBD.B

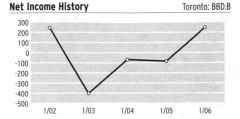

Bouygues

Bouygues (pronounced "bweeg") is très beeg in construction, property development, road work, media, and telecommunications. The group runs more than 40 subsidiaries and affiliates in 80 countries, including Colas (road construction) and Bouyges Construction. The company has increased its stake in Bouygues Telecom (France's #3 mobile phone carrier) to 90%, and it also owns around 40% of TF1 (France's #1 TV channel). Chairman Martin Bouygues and his brother Olivier, sons of the company's founder, together own about 18% of Bouygues through holding company SCDM.

Bouyges's Colas subsidiary, which provides road construction and maintenance internationally, accounts for about 40% of sales, Construction services through Bouyges Construction generate about 23% of sales. Other construction subsidiaries include ETDE (power and data transmission networks construction) and Bouyges Immobilier (property management). The construction division has been expanding in Western Europe, especially the UK and the Netherlands, while slowing down in the Asia/Pacific region.

The group's media holdings include a stake in Société Télévision Française 1 (TF1), France's oldest and leading TV channel. TF1 owns 66% of TPS, France's second-largest satellite operator. Bouygues also has been steadily upping its stake in Bouygues Telecom and it has increased its stake in ALSTOM, a builder of rail cars, seagoing vessels, and power plants, to 23%. Bouyges has promised not to try to increase its control over the company nor to sell the stake for at least three years.

HISTORY

With $1,700 in borrowed money, Francis Bouygues, son of a Paris engineer, started Entreprise Francis Bouygues in 1952 as an industrial works and construction firm in the Paris region of France. Within four years his firm had expanded into property development.

By the mid-1960s Bouygues had entered the civil engineering and public works sectors and developed regional construction units across France. In 1970 it was listed on the Paris stock exchange. Four years later the company established Bouygues Offshore to build oil platforms.

In 1978 the firm built Terminal 2 of Paris' Charles de Gaulle airport. Three years later it won the contract to construct the University of Riyadh in Saudi Arabia (then the world's largest building project at 3.2 million sq. ft.), which was completed in 1984. That year Bouygues acquired France's #3 water supply company, Saur, and power transmission and supply firm ETDE.

Expansion continued in 1986 with the purchase of the Screg Group, which included Colas, France's top highway contractor. The next year the company led a consortium to buy 50% of newly privatized network Société Télévision Française 1 (TF1), France's leading TV channel. Bouygues became the largest shareholder with a 25% stake (increased to 40% by 1999). In 1988 the company began building the Channel Tunnel (completed in 1994) and moved into its new ultramodern headquarters, dubbed Challenger, in Saint-Quentin-En-Yvelines, outside Paris.

After rumors of failing health, Francis Bouygues resigned as chairman in 1989. His youngest son, Martin, took over as chairman and

CEO, although the patriarch, called France's "Emperor of Concrete," remained on the board until his death in 1993.

Despite fears that the group would suffer without its founder's leadership, Bouygues continued to grow with the 1989 acquisition of a majority interest in Grands Moulins de Paris, France's largest flour milling firm (sold in 1998). In 1990 it purchased Swiss construction group Losinger.

The company entered the telecom industry in 1993 with a national paging network and added a mobile phone license a year later. In 1996 the group listed 40% of Bouygues Offshore's shares on the New York and Paris stock exchanges. Also that year it launched mobile phone operator Bouygues Telecom and entered a partnership with Telecom Italia.

By 1999 Bouygues Telecom had reached 2 million customers, and Bouygues bought back a 20% share held by the UK's Cable and Wireless to increase its stake to nearly 54%. That year Bouygues Offshore bought Norwegian engineering firm Kvaerner, and the group spun off its construction sector, creating Bouygues Construction.

After word circulated that Deutsche Telekom wanted to acquire the group's telecom unit, Bouygues became the target of takeover rumors. Francois Pinault, France's richest businessman, became Bouygues' largest non-family shareholder when he increased his stake to 14% (since reduced to about 2%). Pinault's biggest rival, Bernard Arnault, upped his stake to more than 9% of the group, fueling speculation of a battle over control of the board.

In 2001 the company pulled out of France's auction for a third-generation wireless license and remained the only European incumbent mobile carrier without a major domestic investment in 3G technology. The next year the company agreed to buy Telecom Italia's stake in Bouygues Telecom, increasing Bouygues' ownership in the mobile operator from 54% to more than 65%. In 2002 the company sold its 51% stake in oil field platform construction unit Bouygues Offshore to Italian oil services group Saipem, which announced plans to bid for the remaining shares.

However, talks with German utility giant E.ON over the sale of Bouygues' Saur subsidiary failed that year, after E.ON decided to focus instead on its electricity and gas operations.

In 2005, Bouygues was more successful when it sought to sell Saur piecemeal. It sold several divisions of the subsidiary (Coved, Saur France, Saur International, and Stereau) to French private equity firm PAI Partners but retained the African and Italian (Sigesa-Crea) divisions of the firm.

In 2006 Bouygues bought the French government's stake in ALSTOM for $2.5 billion. The deal was approved on the condition that it not try to control the company for at least three years.

EXECUTIVES

Chairman and CEO: Martin Bouygues, age 54, $2,300,000 pay
Deputy CEO and Director: Olivier Poupart-Lafarge, age 64, $2,300,000 pay
Director: Michel Derbesse, age 71
Deputy CEO and Director: Olivier Bouygues, age 56, $1,932,000 pay
EVP, Information Systems and New Technologies and Director: Alain Pouyat, age 62, $1,702,000 pay
EVP, Telecommunications and New Activities; Chairman and CEO, Bouygues Telecom: Philippe Montagner, age 63
SVP, Cash Management and Finance: Lionel Verdouck, age 56

SVP, Human Resources and Administration:
Jean-Claude Tostivin, age 59
Director; Chairman and CEO, Bouygues Construction:
Yves Gabriel, age 56, $1,912,500 pay
Director; Chairman and CEO, Bouygues Immobilier:
François Bertière, age 56
Director; Chairman and CEO, Colas: Alain Dupont,
age 66, $2,300,000 pay
Director; Chairman and CEO, TF1: Patrick Le Lay,
age 64, $2,136,000 pay
Corporate Secretary: Jean-François Guillemin, age 53
CEO, Saur: Hervé Le Bouc
Group Corporate Communications Director:
Blandine Delafon
Press Department: Justine Welcomme
Press Department: Stéphanie Beauvais
Investor Relations: Anthony Mellor
Auditors: Ernst & Young Audit; Mazars & Guérard

LOCATIONS

HQ: Bouygues SA
1, avenue Eugène Freyssinet,
78061 Saint-Quentin-en-Yvelines, France
Phone: +33-1-30-60-23-11   **Fax:** +33-1-30-60-48-61
Web: www.bouygues.fr

PRODUCTS/OPERATIONS

2005 Sales

	% of total
Colas	39
Bouygues Construction	24
Telecommunications	19
TFI	10
Bouygues Immobilier	6
Other	2
Total	**100**

Selected Subsidiaries and Affiliates

Construction and Roads
  Bouygues Bâtiment SA (99.9%)
  Bouygues Construction SA (99.9%)
  Bouygues Immobilier Group
  Colas SA (96%)
  ETDE SA (99.9%)
Telecoms
  Bouygues Telecom SA (89.5%)
  Télévision Française 1 SA (TF1, 43%)
  Télévision Par Satellite SNC (TPS, 66%)

COMPETITORS

Alarko	Foster Wheeler
AMEC	France Telecom
Autostrade	Halliburton
AWG plc	HOCHTIEF
Balfour Beatty	Hyundai
Bechtel	MWH Global
Bilfinger Berger	Severn Trent
Bovis Lend Lease	SFR
CANAL+	Skanska
CSCEC	SNEF
Dragados	SUEZ
EIFFAGE	SUEZ Environnement
FCC Barcelona	Technip
Fluor	VINCI

HISTORICAL FINANCIALS

Company Type: Public

Income Statement

FYE: December 31

	REVENUE ($ mil.)	NET INCOME ($ mil.)	NET PROFIT MARGIN	EMPLOYEES
12/05	31,916	1,229	3.9%	115,441
12/04	31,920	1,170	3.7%	113,300
12/03	27,391	565	2.1%	124,300
12/02	23,317	698	3.0%	121,604
12/01	18,135	305	1.7%	125,034
Annual Growth	**15.2%**	**41.7%**	**—**	**(2.0%)**

Net Income History   Euronext Paris: EN

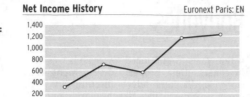

BP

BP is also BO (Big Oil). It is the world's second largest integrated oil concern, behind Exxon Mobil. The company, which was formed in 1998 from the merger of British Petroleum and Amoco, grew by buying Atlantic Richfield Company. BP has proved reserves of 18.3 billion barrels of oil equivalent, including large holdings in Alaska. BP is the largest oil and gas producer in the US and also a top refiner, processing 2.8 billion barrels of crude oil per day. BP operates about 28,500 gas stations worldwide, including 15,900 in the US. With the success of its BP Solar International subsidiary, BP has created BP Alternative Energy (hydrogen, solar, and wind power generation) with an initial investment of $1.8 billion.

Outside of the US, BP has significant production activities in Canada, the Gulf of Mexico, the North Sea, Trinidad, and now India. The company has announced plans for a joint venture with the India-based Hindustan Petroleum to build a $3 billion refinery in the city of Bhatinda. BP has also dedicated $615 million to develop two fields in the Gulf of Suez through its joint venture with Egyptian General Petroleum. It has agreed to purchase nearly a quarter (23%) of China Aviation Oil, a jet fuel importer.

In 2003 BP agreed to sell some of its mature oil and gas assets in the US and the North Sea (including its Forties field, where oil was discovered in 1970) to Apache for $1.3 billion, as part of a strategy to focus on more profitable production assets. Also in 2003 BP, the Alfa Group, and Access-Renova combined their Russian oil assets to create TNK-BP, one of Russia's largest oil companies.

In 2004 the company sold its minority stakes in Chinese entities Sinopec and PetroChina. It also announced plans to sell its one-third stake in Singapore Refining Company.

In 2006 the company sold its remaining producing properties on the Outer Continental Shelf of the Gulf of Mexico to Apache Corporation for $845 million. That year BP agreed to sell its 28% stake in the Shenzi field in the Gulf of Mexico to Repsol for $2.2 billion. It also acquired a $1 billion stake in Rosneft.

In 2006 the discovery of corrosion in a major oil pipeline forced BP to close down part of its Prudhoe Bay oilfield (which represents 8% of daily US crude production) for several weeks.

That year the company also announced plans to invest $3 billion to reconfigure its Whiting Refinery in Indiana to process Canadian heavy crude oil.

Also in 2006 Rosneft and BP agreed to team up to develop energy projects in Russia's Arctic.

HISTORY

Today's BP (formerly BP Amoco) was born on two sides of the Atlantic. In the US, Amoco emerged from Standard Oil Trust, organized by John D. Rockefeller in 1882. In 1886 he bought Lima (Ohio) oil, a high-sulfur crude, anticipating the discovery of a sulfur-removing process. Such a process was, indeed, patented in 1887, and in 1889 Standard organized Standard Oil of Indiana, which later established such innovations as company-owned service stations and a research lab at the refinery.

Overseas, British Petroleum (BP) was a twinkle in the eye of English adventurer William D'Arcy, who began oil exploration of Persia in 1901. In 1908, bankrolled by Burmah Oil, D'Arcy's firm was the first to strike oil in the Middle East. D'Arcy and Burmah Oil formed Anglo-Persian Oil in 1909, and the British government took a 51% stake in 1914.

Back in the US, Standard was broken up into 34 independent oil companies in 1911. Standard Oil of Indiana kept its oil refining and US marketing operations. In 1925 it added a few Mexican and Venezuelan firms, including Pan American Petroleum and Transport, which held half of American Oil Co., known for Amoco antiknock gasoline. It began Amoco Chemicals in 1945.

Anglo-Persian took the BP name in 1954 and bought its own Standard Oil: After making a strike in Alaska in 1969, BP swapped Alaskan reserves for a 25% interest (later upped to 55%) in Standard Oil of Ohio (SOHIO). BP also struck North Sea oil in 1970. But falling oil and copper prices in the mid-1980s and a dry hole in the Beaufort Sea hurt earnings. Under Robert Horton, SOHIO sold off units. BP also bought livestock feed producer Purina Mills (1986, sold 1998) and the rest of SOHIO (1987).

Standard Oil of Indiana had its own problems, including being kicked out of Iran after the Islamic revolution and causing a major oil spill off the French coast in 1978. The firm, which became Amoco in 1985, bought Canada's Dome Petroleum in 1988, making it the largest private owner of North American gas reserves, but the big purchase proved hard to swallow.

In 1992 Amoco hurled itself into overseas oil exploration. It was the first foreign oil company to explore the Chinese mainland. But by 1995 production was down. That year John Browne, often compared to Rockefeller, became BP's CEO. In 1996 the British government sold its remaining stake in BP.

As oil prices tumbled in 1998, BP merged with Amoco in a $52 billion deal that formed BP Amoco. The new oil major agreed the following year to buy US-based Atlantic Richfield in a deal that closed in 2000. BP Amoco sold ARCO's Alaskan properties to Phillips (later ConocoPhillips) for $7 billion to gain regulatory approval for the purchase.

Its stake in Siberian oil fields was nearly taken away in a controversial 1999 bankruptcy sale before BP Amoco and Russia's Tyumen Oil agreed to cooperate. In 2000 BP Amoco and Shell Oil sold their stakes in Altura Energy to Occidental Petroleum for $3.6 billion. Also that year BP Amoco bought motor-oil maker Burmah Castrol for $4.7 billion.

The company adopted BP as its main worldwide brand in 2000, and it officially shortened its name the next year.

In 2001 BP agreed to swap control of its stake in German natural gas supplier Ruhrgas, plus $1.6 billion in cash and $950 million in assumed debt, to German utility giant E.ON for a majority interest in Veba Oel, owner of Germany's largest gas station chain. The agreement allowed BP to take full ownership of Veba Oel in 2002. To recoup some of its investment, BP (with E.ON's consent) sold Veba Oel's exploration and production operations to Petro-Canada.

That year BP increased it stake in Russian oil and gas producer Sidanco from 10% to 25%.

In 2003 BP sold its Boqueron field and Desarrollo Zulia Occidental assets, both located in Venezuela, to Europe's Perenco. In late 2005 BP sold its petrochemical unit, Innovene, to INEOS for a reported $9 billion.

EXECUTIVES

Chairman: Peter D. Sutherland, age 60
Deputy Chairman: Sir Ian M. G. Prosser, age 62
Group Chief Executive and Executive Director:
Lord E. John P. Browne, age 58
Group Executive Officer and Executive Director:
Iain C. Conn, age 43, $1,498,468 pay
CFO and Executive Director: Byron E. Grote, age 58, $3,480,369 pay
EVP, Group Chief of Staff, Group Managing Director, and Executive Director: David C. Allen, age 51, $1,567,284 pay
EVP; Chief Executive, Refining and Marketing; Managing Director; and Executive Director:
John A. Manzoni, age 46, $1,498,468 pay
Chief Executive, Exploration and Production; Managing Director; and Executive Director:
Anthony B. (Tony) Hayward, age 49, $1,532,876 pay
EVP and Group General Counsel: Peter B. P. Bevan, age 62
EVP, Human Resources: Sara (Sally) Bott, age 57
EVP and Deputy CEO, Exploration and Production Segment: Andrew G. Inglis, age 47
Company Secretary: David J. Jackson, age 53
EVP, Gas, Power, and Renewables, and Integrated Supply and Trading: Vivienne Cox, age 47
Chairman and President, BP America:
Robert A. (Bob) Malone, age 54
President and CEO, BP Energy Company:
Cameron Byers, age 46
President, BP Exploration (Alaska) Inc.: Steve Marshall
President, BP Alternative Energy North America:
Robert Lukefahr
Chief Executive, Petrochemicals: Ralph C. Alexander, age 50
Chief Scientist: Steven E. Koonin
Head of Investor Relations: Fergus MacLeod
Project Manager, BP Clean Fuels: Brad Johnson
US Press Office: Neil Chapman
VP, Investor Relations: Peter Hall
Auditors: Ernst & Young

LOCATIONS

HQ: BP p.l.c.
1 St. James's Square,
London SW1Y 4PD, United Kingdom
Phone: +44-20-7496-4000 **Fax:** +44-20-7496-4630
US HQ: 28100 Torch Pkwy., Warrenville, IL 60555
US Phone: 630-821-2222 **US Fax:** 630-836-5513
Web: www.bp.com

2005 Sales

	$ mil.	% of total
US	101,190	31
Europe		
UK	95,375	29
Other countries	72,972	22
Other regions	60,314	18
Adjustments	(84,365)	—
Total	**245,486**	**100**

PRODUCTS/OPERATIONS

2005 Sales

	$ mil.	% of total
Refining & marketing	213,465	69
Exploration & production	47,210	16
Gas, power & renewables	25,557	8
Other businesses & corporate	21,295	7
Adjustments	(62,041)	—
Total	**245,486**	**100**

Major Operations

Refining and Marketing
 Marketing
 Refining
 Supply and trading
 Transportation and shipping
Exploration and Production
 Field development
 Gas processing and marketing
 Oil and gas exploration
 Pipelines and transportation
  Alyeska Pipeline Service Co. (47%)
   Trans Alaska Pipeline System
   Valdez terminal
Gas and Power
 Natural gas marketing and trading
 Natural gas liquids
Chemicals
 Chemical intermediates
 Feedstock
 Performance products
 Polymers
Other
 Coal mining
 Solar power

COMPETITORS

Apache	Huntsman
Ashland	ICI American
BASF AG	Imperial Oil
Bayer	Koch
BG Group	Lyondell Chemical
BHP Billiton	Norsk Hydro
Cargill	Occidental Petroleum
Chevron	PDVSA
Chevron Stations	PEMEX
Dow Chemical	PETROBRAS
DuPont	Royal Dutch Shell
Eni	Shell Aviation
Exxon Mobil	Sinclair Oil
Hercules	Sunoco
Hess	TOTAL

HISTORICAL FINANCIALS

Company Type: Public

Income Statement

FYE: December 31

	REVENUE ($ mil.)	NET INCOME ($ mil.)	NET PROFIT MARGIN	EMPLOYEES
12/05	245,486	19,642	8.0%	96,200
12/04	285,059	15,731	5.5%	102,900
12/03	232,571	13,143	5.7%	103,700
12/02	180,186	8,397	4.7%	115,250
12/01	175,389	4,164	2.4%	110,150
Annual Growth	**8.8%**	**47.4%**	**—**	**(3.3%)**

2005 Year-End Financials

Debt ratio: 16.4%   No. of shares (mil.): —
Return on equity: 24.3%   Dividends
Cash ($ mil.): 12,818   Yield: 3.3%
Current ratio: 1.04   Payout: 37.7%
Long-term debt ($ mil.): 13,926 Market value ($ mil.): —

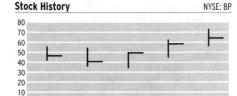

	STOCK PRICE ($) FY Close	P/E High/Low		PER SHARE ($) Earnings	Dividends
12/05	64.22	13	10	5.55	2.09
12/04	58.40	—	—	—	1.66
12/03	49.35	—	—	0.00	1.53
12/02	40.65	—	—	—	1.41
12/01	46.51	—	—	—	1.29
Annual Growth	**8.4%**	**—**	**—**	**—**	**12.8%**

Bridgestone

Although stone bridges may be increasingly rare, Bridgestone can help most vehicles traverse almost any type of terrain. Bridgestone is the world's largest tire maker, but in addition to supplying tires to most major car manufacturers, the company also makes tires for heavy equipment (off-road and mining vehicles) and aircraft. Non-tire products include building materials (roof tiles), sporting goods (golf balls), industrial rubber products (conveyor belts and automotive hoses), marine components (dredging hoses, marine fenders, oil booms, and silt barriers), and switches.

Demand for tires is growing on a worldwide basis and Bridgestone's increased 2005 sales and profits reflect that demand. In industrialized regions demand is shifting to high-performance and oversized tires. Meanwhile Bridgestone has increased production in emerging markets such as China, Thailand, and Eastern Europe.

Despite increased sales and profits, high materials costs posed a challenge to Bridgestone in 2005 and the company is predicting a tougher environment in the future. To keep these issues from creating roadblocks, Bridgestone is keeping a close eye on its costs, while maintaining its vertical integration model (from rubber plantation to tire retailer) that has made it the world's #1 tire producer.

Late in 2006 Bridgestone announced that it would purchase Bandag Inc., an Iowa-based tire retreader and provider of tire services through a network of 900 or so franchised dealers. The acquisition is being made through Bridgestone's Bridgestone Americas Holding subsidiary. The deal is valued at about $1.05 billion.

HISTORY

In 1906 Shojiro Ishibashi and his brother Tokujiro assumed control of the family's clothing business. They focused on making *tabi,* traditional Japanese footwear, and in 1923 began working with rubber for soles. In 1931 Shojiro formed Bridgestone (Ishibashi means "stone bridge" in Japanese) to make tires, and during that decade the company began producing auto tires, airplane tires, and golf balls. Bridgestone followed the Japanese military to occupied territories, where it built plants. The company's headquarters moved to Tokyo in 1937.

Although Bridgestone lost all of its overseas factories during WWII, its Japanese plants escaped damage. The company began making bicycles in 1946 and signed a technical assistance pact with Goodyear five years later, enabling Bridgestone to import badly needed technology. In the 1950s and 1960s, Bridgestone started making nylon tires and radials and again set up facilities overseas, mostly elsewhere in Asia. The company benefited from the rapid growth in Japanese auto sales in the 1970s. Shojiro died at age 87 in 1976.

In 1983 Bridgestone bought a plant in LaVergne, Tennessee, from tire maker Firestone. Five years later Bridgestone topped Italian tire maker Pirelli's bid and bought the rest of Firestone for $2.6 billion, valuing the tire manufacturer at a lofty 26 times its earnings. Bridgestone/Firestone (now Bridgestone Americas Holding) became Bridgestone's largest subsidiary. Harvey Firestone had founded his tire business in 1900 and expanded with the auto industry in the US. In the 1920s he leased 1 million acres in Liberia for rubber plantations and established a chain of auto supply and service outlets. After WWII Firestone started making synthetic rubber and automotive components, expanded overseas, and acquired US tire producers Dayton Tire & Rubber and Seiberling.

At the time of Firestone's purchase, General Motors (GM) dropped it as a supplier. Bridgestone/Firestone compensated for this loss in volume by selling more tires through mass-market retailers. It began selling tires to GM's Saturn Corporation in 1990.

The following year new Bridgestone/Firestone chairman Yoichiro Kaizaki moved to cut production costs, alienating union workers. He became company head in 1993. During the early 1990s Bridgestone bought Colonial Rubber Works, a US roofing material manufacturer, and America Off The Road Company, which makes tires for heavy equipment. To improve its distribution, in 1992 Bridgestone renamed its 1,550 North American MasterCare auto service centers "Tire Zone at Firestone" and took the unheard-of step of selling rival Michelin's tires. It expanded operations in Brazil, Indonesia, Mexico, Thailand, and the US the next year.

Bridgestone's US operations have been plagued with problems, such as disputes with the United Rubber Workers (URW) union. Tensions rose in 1995 when the company hired 2,300 permanent replacement workers during a plant strike. In 1996, after URW members had become part of United Steelworkers of America, the two sides approved a new contract.

In 1997 Bridgestone built a South Carolina plant to help reduce Japanese imports. Although sales remained almost steady that year, net profit dropped nearly 50% when a change in accounting caused the company to write off costs associated with its Firestone purchase.

Expanding its markets, Bridgestone opened a retail outlet in Moscow in 1999 and acquired a radial tire plant in China from South Korea's Kumho Industrial Company in 2000. That year the company recalled approximately 6.5 million Firestone ATX, ATX II, and Wilderness AT tires after dozens of incidents where the tires came apart at road speeds. The affected tires have been used on light trucks and SUVs since 1990, many of them as original equipment on the Ford Ex-

plorer. Not long after the recall, Bridgestone/Firestone chairman and CEO Masatoshi Ono retired and was replaced by John Lampe. The fallout and ensuing blame-game (improper inflation guidelines/unstable vehicle vs. faulty tires) virtually ended Bridgestone's 95-year relationship with Ford (Bridgestone still does business with Ford outside the Americas).

In 2001, while revealing that it would face its first loss since listing 30 years ago, Bridgestone announced that it would close the Decatur, Illinois, plant at which many of the recalled tires were made. The plant employed about 1,500 workers. Later in the year the company announced that it would recall an additional 3.5 million tires at a cost of nearly $30 million.

Near the end of 2001 Bridgestone announced it would inflate its beleaguered Bridgestone/Firestone subsidiary with $1.3 billion in cash. In early 2003 the company's US subsidiary changed its name from Bridgestone/Firestone Americas Holding to Bridgestone Americas Holding.

In 2005 Bridgestone purchased the Indonesian rubber plantations business (Goodyear Sumatra Plantations) of Goodyear Tire & Rubber for about $62 million.

EXECUTIVES

Chairman, President, and CEO: Shoshi Arakawa, age 61
Vice Chairman and CFO, Bridgestone Americas Holding, Inc.: Shoji Mizuochi
VP and Senior Officer, Administration and Motorsport, and Chief Compliance Officer: Tomoyuki Izumisawa
VP and Senior Officer, Diversified Products; Director, Chemical Division and Director: Yasuo Asami
VP and Senior Officer, Original Equipment and Director: Tatsuya Okajima
VP and Senior Officer, Replacement Tire Sales and Director: Giichi Miyakawa
VP and Senior Officer, Tire Production and Distribution and Safety, Quality, and Environment and Director: Masaharu Oku
VP and Officer; Chairman, President, and CEO, Bridgestone Europe NV/SA: Takashi Urano
VP and Senior Officer; Chairman and President, Bridgestone (China) Investment Co., Ltd.: Hiromichi Odagiri
VP and Officer, Brand Management and Product Planning: Hideki Yokoyama
VP, Chief Compliance Officer, and Senior Officer, Corporate Administration and Director: Tomuyuki Izumisawa
VP and Officer, General Affairs, Legal Affairs and Corporate Communications: Masayuki Okabe
VP and Officer, International Tire Business Operations; Director, Americas and Europe Operations Division, International Tire Administration Division: Kiyoshi Nomura
VP and Officer, Safety, Quality, and Environment: Hiroshi Yamaguchi
VP; Vice Chairman and President, Bridgestone Americas Holding, Inc.: Asahiko (Duke) Nishiyama
VP and Officer; Research and Development and Intellectual Property: Shigehisa Sano
VP, Senior Technology Officer, and Director: Osamu Inoue, age 57
Director; Chairman, President, and CEO, Bridgestone Americas Holding, Inc.: Mark A. Emkes, age 53
Auditors: Deloitte Touche Tohmatsu

LOCATIONS

HQ: Bridgestone Corporation
10-1, Kyobashi 1-chome, Chuo-ku,
Tokyo 104-8340, Japan
Phone: +81-3-3567-0111   **Fax:** +81-3-3535-2553
US HQ: 535 Marriott Dr., Nashville, TN 37214
US Phone: 615-937-1000   **US Fax:** 615-937-3621
Web: www.bridgestone.co.jp

Bridgestone operates more than 150 tire factories and diversified products plants worldwide.

2005 Sales

	$ mil.	% of total
Japan	9,861.2	36
The Americas	9,824.0	36
Europe	3,113.2	12
Other regions	4,224.5	16
Adjustments	(4,189.3)	—
Total	**22,833.6**	**100**

PRODUCTS/OPERATIONS

2005 Sales

	$ mil.	% of total
Tires	18,298.0	79
Diversified products	4,791.5	21
Adjustments	(255.9)	—
Total	**22,833.6**	**100**

Selected Products

Tires and Tubes
  Agricultural machinery
  Aircraft
  Buses
  Cars
  Commercial vehicles
  Construction and mining vehicles
  Monorails
  Motorcycles
  Race cars
  Scooters
  Trucks

Diversified Products (Chemical and Industrial Products)
  Belts
  Building materials
  Ceramic foam
  Flexible polyurethane foam products
  Hoses
  Industrial rubber products
  Marine products
  Office equipment components
  Thermal insulating polyurethane foam
  Vibration-isolating and noise-insulating materials

Sporting Goods
  Bicycles
  Golf balls
  Golf clubs
  Tennis goods

COMPETITORS

3M
Acushnet
Armstrong Holdings
Brunswick
Callaway Golf
Continental AG
Cooper Tire & Rubber
Goodyear
Huffy
K2
Kumho Tire
Marangoni
Michelin
Sime Darby
Sumitomo Rubber
TBC

HISTORICAL FINANCIALS

Company Type: Public

Income Statement

				FYE: December 31
	REVENUE ($ mil.)	NET INCOME ($ mil.)	NET PROFIT MARGIN	EMPLOYEES
12/05	22,834	—	—	123,727
12/04	23,439	—	—	113,699
12/03	21,512	—	—	108,315
12/02	18,962	—	—	106,846
12/01	16,270	—	—	104,700
Annual Growth	**8.8%**	**—**	**—**	**4.3%**

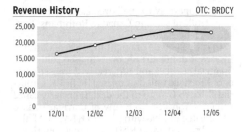

Revenue History OTC: BRDCY

British Airways

A member of the royal family of European airlines, British Airways (BA) serves about 150 destinations in some 75 countries from hubs at London's Heathrow and Gatwick airports. The carrier operates a fleet of more than 280 aircraft, consisting mainly of Airbus and Boeing jets. BA extends its network via code-sharing relationships, chiefly with AMR's American Airlines and other members of the Oneworld global marketing alliance, such as Cathay Pacific Airways, Iberia, and Qantas. (Code-sharing allows airlines to sell tickets on one another's flights and thus offer passengers additional destinations.) Among Europe's flag carriers, BA is outranked only by the combined Air France-KLM and by Deutsche Lufthansa.

Network airline, or long-haul, passenger and cargo operations account for more than 90% of BA's sales. The company also offers regional service, both within the UK and between the UK and continental Europe, through BA Connect. The former British Airways CitiExpress was renamed BA Connect in 2006 in conjunction with price cuts and service revisions intended to help the airline better compete with up-and-coming low-fare carriers.

Looking ahead, BA is preparing to shift the bulk of its operations to a new terminal under construction at Heathrow. Terminal 5, scheduled to be completed by 2008, is seen as a major step up from the carrier's current facilities both for customers and employees.

In advance of the move, BA announced plans in March 2006 to achieve £450 million in cost savings over two years. At the same time, the carrier is working to boost margins by selling more tickets through its Web site and selling more premium services on long-haul flights.

In 2006 BA was a target of an investigation by US and UK government agencies into alleged price-fixing by passenger airlines. Two company officials, commercial director Martin George and communications head Iain Burns, were placed on leave and then resigned in connection with the inquiry.

HISTORY

British Airways has a jet trail winding back to 1916 and its biplane-flying ancestor, Aircraft Transport and Travel, which in 1919 launched the world's first daily international air service (between London and Paris). Concerned about subsidized foreign competition, British authorities in 1924 merged Aircraft Transport and Travel successor Daimler Airways with other fledgling British carriers — British Air Marine Navigation, Handley Page, and Instone Air Line — to form Imperial Airways.

Imperial pioneered routes from London to India (1929), Singapore (1933), and — in partnership with Qantas Empire Airways — Australia (1934). Competition on European routes emerged in the 1930s from upstart British Airways; in 1939 the government, troubled by the threat to Imperial, nationalized and merged the two airlines to form British Overseas Airways Corporation (BOAC).

After WWII, BOAC continued as the UK's international airline, but state-owned British European Airways (BEA) took over domestic and European routes. In 1972 the government combined the duo to form British Airways (BA).

BA and Air France jointly introduced supersonic passenger service in 1976 with the Concorde — a PR victory that contributed to years of losses. Colin Marshall became CEO in 1983 and reduced manpower and routes.

In 1987 the government sold BA to the public, and the airline bought chief UK rival British Caledonian. Hoping to become a globe-spanning carrier, in 1992 BA tried to gain a 44% stake in USAir (which became US Airways). American Airlines, United, and Delta strongly objected, demanding equal access to UK markets. BA settled for a 25% stake, the maximum foreign ownership allowed by US law, in 1993. It also bought 25% of Qantas.

That year BA settled a libel suit brought by UK competitor Virgin Atlantic Airways, which accused BA of waging a smear campaign against it. The settlement cost BA about $5 million, and Virgin Atlantic followed with a $1 billion antitrust suit in the US (dismissed in 1999). In 1994 BA paid out $4 million to settle yet another Virgin Atlantic suit, this one claiming BA had done sloppy maintenance on Virgin aircraft. BA also sold British Caledonian.

In 1996 Marshall turned over the CEO job to Bob Ayling, who had joined BA in 1985. BA and American Airlines agreed to coordinate prices and schedules and to share market data for their transatlantic routes. Though the deal met regulatory obstacles from the start, in 1997 BA sold its stake in US Airways. BA and American also took the lead in forming the Oneworld global alliance (which took effect in 1999).

The next year BA launched low-fare European carrier Go. In 1999 BA and American all but abandoned plans for their comprehensive transatlantic linkup after US regulators denied antitrust immunity. Ayling resigned in 2000, and Marshall stepped in as temporary CEO before Rod Eddington, a veteran of Cathay Pacific and Ansett, was appointed. Also that year BA took a 9% stake in Iberia and sold its interest in France's Air Liberté.

BA grounded its Concordes in 2000 (flights resumed in 2001), three weeks after the crash of an Air France Concorde outside Paris in which 113 people were killed. The airline put its no-frills carrier Go up for sale that year, and in 2001 sold the airline to venture capital firm, 3i Group. Also in 2001 BA and American announced plans to once again seek regulatory approval for a code-sharing partnership.

That year BA laid off 5,200 employees as a result of decreased demand for air travel after the terrorist attacks in New York and Washington, DC. The layoffs were on top of 1,800 job cuts the airline made earlier in the year, reducing BA's workforce by 10%.

BA's long-negotiated transatlantic alliance with American Airlines received tentative approval from the US Department of Transportation in 2002. But the airlines chose to abandon the deal rather than accept regulators' terms, which called for BA and American to give up more landing slots at London's Heathrow airport than they were willing to relinquish. The next year the carriers won approval for an extensive code-sharing agreement that did not include routes between London and US cities.

2003 also saw the retirement of the BA's Concorde fleet, a longtime symbol of the airline's transatlantic dominance.

BA sold its 19% stake in Qantas in 2004 to help cut down on its debt. Eddington stepped down as CEO in 2005, and former Aer Lingus chief Willie Walsh was named to replace him.

EXECUTIVES

Chairman: Martin F. Broughton, age 59
Chief Executive: William M. (Willie) Walsh, age 44
CFO: Keith Williams, age 50
CIO: Paul Coby, age 49
Secretary and Head of Risk Management:
  Alan Buchanan, age 47
Director, Brands and Marketing: Kelly Reed
Director, Engineering: Alan McDonald, age 55
Director, Flight Operations: Lloyd Cromwell Griffiths, age 61
Director, Ground Operations, UK and Overseas:
  Geoff Want, age 53
Director, Investments and Alliances:
  Roger Paul Maynard
Director, People: Neil Robertson, age 52
Director, Planning: Robert Boyle, age 40
Area Cargo Manager, India and Nepal, British Airways World Cargo: Mat Burton
Area Commercial Manager, Japan and Korea, British Airways World Cargo: Rory Black
Commercial Manager, Southern Region, British Airways World Cargo: Ian Barrigan
Regional Commercial Manager, Asia Pacific, British Airways World Cargo: Chris Chan
General Counsel: Robert Webb, age 56
Auditors: Ernst & Young

LOCATIONS

HQ: British Airways Plc
  Waterside, Harmondsworth,
  London UB7 0GB, United Kingdom
Phone: +44-870-850-8503   **Fax:** +44-20-8759-4314
US HQ: 75-20 Astoria Blvd., Jackson Heights, NY 11370
US Phone: 347-418-4000
Web: www.british-airways.com

2006 Sales

	% of total
Europe	
UK	49
Other countries	14
The Americas	19
Africa, Middle East & Indian sub-continent	10
Asia/Pacific & Australia	8
Total	**100**

PRODUCTS/OPERATIONS

2006 Sales

	% of total
Passenger	80
Cargo	6
Other (including fuel surcharges)	14
Total	**100**

2006 Sales by Service Type

	% of total
Network airline	93
Regional airline	4
Other	3
Total	**100**

COMPETITORS

Air France-KLM
All Nippon Airways
Delta Air
easyJet
Japan Airlines
Lufthansa
Northwest Airlines
Ryanair
SAS
Singapore Airlines
UAL
Virgin Atlantic Airways

HISTORICAL FINANCIALS

Company Type: Public

Income Statement			FYE: March 31	
	REVENUE ($ mil.)	NET INCOME ($ mil.)	NET PROFIT MARGIN	EMPLOYEES
3/06	14,814	258	1.7%	49,957
3/05	14,681	673	4.6%	50,326
3/04	13,744	723	5.3%	51,939
3/03	12,108	(202)	—	57,014
3/02	11,863	(184)	—	61,460
Annual Growth	5.7%	—	—	(5.0%)

2006 Year-End Financials

Debt ratio: 156.2%
Return on equity: 6.7%
Cash ($ mil.): 4,245

Current ratio: 1.71
Long-term debt ($ mil.): 6,267

Net Income History   NYSE: BAB

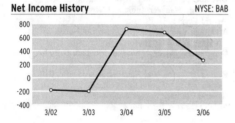

British American Tobacco

When people pick up smoking, British American Tobacco (BAT) picks up steam. Spun off in the reorganization of B.A.T Industries, BAT is the world's #2 tobacco firm (behind Marlboro maker Altria Group) with about 15% of the market. It sells nearly 855 billion cigarettes in more than 190 countries. BAT's international cigarette brands include Dunhill, Kent, Lucky Strike, and Pall Mall. It also makes loose tobacco and regional cigarette brands. Its former US unit, Brown & Williamson (Kool and GPC cigarettes), merged with R.J. Reynolds Tobacco (RJRT) in 2004. Companies controlled by South African billionaire Anton Rupert own about 28% of BAT.

BAT owns 42% of Reynolds American, which was created by the Brown & Williamson/RJRT merger. Not surprisingly, BAT now looks to emerging markets in South Korea, Vietnam, and Nigeria for growth. In early 2005, the tobacco company ruled out speculation that it was eyeing Gallaher or Altadis, saying it was considering a smaller buy.

Moreover, BAT would like to build a factory in China, the world's top tobacco market, and would move its Asian headquarters to Hong Kong if that were to happen. Meanwhile, it's scaling back in the UK and Canada. In 2004 it closed a manufacturing plant in Darlington, cutting about 500 jobs. In 2005 it closed the doors on a Southampton, UK, plant and eliminated some 530 positions (and more than 65 in Ireland). Its subsidiary, Imperial Tobacco Canada (not affiliated with the UK's Imperial Tobacco), cut almost 850 jobs after closing a Montreal plant and other Canadian facilities. Imperial Tobacco says it controls about 60% of the Canadian cigarette market.

In response to health concerns and lawsuits brought against the tobacco industry in the US, BAT is test-marketing a Swedish product called snus, a pasteurized tobacco product that resembles a small teabag. BAT plans to market it in South Africa under the Peter Stuyvesant brand and in Sweden under the Lucky Strike brand as more than 100 times less harmful than cigarettes.

HISTORY

After a year of vicious price-cutting between Imperial Tobacco (UK) and James Buchanan Duke's American Tobacco in the UK, Imperial counterattacked in the US. To end the cigarette price war in the UK, the firms created British American Tobacco (BAT) in 1902. The truce granted Imperial the British market, American the US market, and they jointly owned BAT in the rest of the world.

With Duke in control, BAT expanded into new markets. In China it was selling 25 billion cigarettes a year by 1920. When the Communist revolution ended BAT's operations in China, the company lost more than 25% of its sales (although China later reemerged as a major export market for the company's cigarettes).

A 1911 US antitrust action forced American to sell its interest in BAT and opened the US market to the company. BAT purchased US cigarette manufacturer Brown & Williamson in 1927 and continued to grow through geographical expansion until the 1960s. In 1973 BAT and Imperial each regained control of its own brands in the UK and Continental Europe. Imperial sold the last of its stake in BAT in 1980.

Fearing that mounting public concern over smoking would limit the cigarette market, BAT acquired nontobacco businesses; it changed its name to B.A.T Industries in 1976. The acquisitions of retailers Saks (1973), Argos (UK, 1979), Marshall Field (1982), and later, insurance firms, diversified the company's sales base. After a 1989 hostile takeover bid from Sir James Goldsmith, it sold its retail operations, and retained its tobacco and financial services.

In 1994 B.A.T acquired the former American Tobacco for $1 billion. In 1997 the company acquired Cigarrera de Moderna (with 50% of Mexico's cigarette sales) and formed a joint venture with the Turkish tobacco state enterprise, Tekel.

B.A.T's tobacco operations were spun off in 1998 as British American Tobacco (BAT). The financial services operations were merged with Zurich Insurance in a transaction that created two holding companies: Allied Zurich (UK) and Zurich Allied (Switzerland). With the changes, Martin Broughton became chairman of BAT.

The company in 1999 paid $8.2 billion to buy Dutch cigarette company Rothmans International (Rothmans, Dunhill) from Switzerland's Compagnie Financiere Richemont and South Africa's Rembrandt Group — both controlled by

Anton Rupert. With the purchase, BAT received a controlling stake in Canada's Rothmans, Benson & Hedges (RBH).

In early 2000 BAT bought the 58% of Canada's Imasco it didn't already own. Imasco sold off its financial services and BAT received Imasco's Imperial Tobacco unit (not related to the UK's Imperial Tobacco Group) in the deal. (Formerly called Imperial Tobacco Company of Canada, Imasco was created in 1908 with help from BAT.) BAT also unloaded its share of RBH via a public offering.

In 2001 BAT bought the 40.5% of its BAT Australasia subsidiary (formed in 1999 through the Rothmans merger) it didn't already own. Broughton announced that year that the Chinese government had approved development plans that would allow the company to build a factory in China. The company also announced it would build the first foreign-owned cigarette factory in South Korea, at that time the world's #8 tobacco market.

Increasing its Latin American regional presence, BAT purchased a controlling stake in Peru's top tobacco company, Tabacalera Nacional, and several of its suppliers in 2003. However, two months later BAT said it would not make the million-dollar investment in the company. The announcement came soon after Peru raised taxes on cigarettes. By the end of the year, BAT had purchased tobacco manufacturer Ente Tabacchi Italiani S.p.A. from the Italian government. In 2004, BAT sold the distribution end of its Italian business to Compañía de Distribución Integral Logista.

EXECUTIVES

Chairman: Jan P. du Plessis, age 52
Deputy Chairman: Rt. Hon. Kenneth H. Clarke, age 64
CEO and Director: Paul Adams, age 51
COO and Director; Director, America/Pacific: Antonio Monteiro de Castro, age 60
Director, Finance and Director: Paul Rayner, age 50
Director, Africa & Middle East: Nicandro Durante
Director, Asia/Pacific: John Daly, age 48
Director, Corporate and Regulatory Affairs: Michael Prideaux, age 54
Director, Human Resources: Rudi Kindts, age 47
Director, Europe: Ben Stevens, age 45
Director, Latin America and Caribbean: Flávio de Andrade, age 56
Director, Legal and General Counsel: Neil Withington, age 48
Director, Marketing: Jimmi Rembiszewski, age 54
Director, Operations and IT: Peter Taylor, age 52
Director, US: Susan M. Ivey, age 47
Legal Director, BAT Nigeria: Flora Okereke
EVP, Consumer and Trade Marketing, R.J. Reynolds Tobacco Co.: Gavin D. Little, age 38
Manager, UK Social Reporting Manager: Nicky Donnelly
Head, Investor Relations: Ralph Edmondson
Head, Science and Regulation: Christopher Procter
Auditors: PricewaterhouseCoopers LLP

LOCATIONS

HQ: British American Tobacco p.l.c.
    Globe House, 4 Temple Place,
    London WC2R 2PG, United Kingdom
Phone: +44-20-7845-1000   **Fax:** +44-20-7240-0555
Web: www.bat.com

2005 Sales

	% of total
Europe	37
Asia/Pacific	19
Latin America	17
Africa & Middle East	15
America/Pacific	12
Total	**100**

PRODUCTS/OPERATIONS

Selected International Cigarette Brands

Barclay
Benson & Hedges (Asia/Pacific, Middle East, Africa)
Capri
Carlton
Dunhill
John Player Gold Leaf
Kent
Kool
Lucky Strike
Misty
Pall Mall
Peter Stuyvesant
Player's
Rothmans
State Express 555
Viceroy
Winfield

Selected Regions and Brands

Argentina (Jockey Club)
Asia/Pacific (Holiday)
Australia (Stradbroke)
Canada (du Maurier)
Europe (Golden American)
Finland (North State)
Germany (HB)
Hungary (Sopianae)
India (Wills)
Indonesia (Ardath)
Ireland (Carrolls)
Latin America (Belmont, Derby, Free, Hollywood)
Mexico (Boots)
Peru (Hamilton)
Poland (Jan III Sobieski)
Russia (Yava Gold)
South Africa (Courtleigh)
Switzerland (Parisienne)
US (GPC)
Uzbekistan (Xon)

Selected Other Products and Brands

Cigars (Dunhill, Mercator, Schimmelpenninck)
Fine cut tobaccos (Ajja, Belgam, Javaanse Jongens,
  Samson, Schwarzer Krauser)
Pipe tobaccos (Captain Black, Clan, Dunhill, Erinmore)

COMPETITORS

Altadis	Santa Fe Natural Tobacco
Carolina Group	Swedish Match
Gallaher	Swisher International
Imperial Tobacco	Tiedemanns
Japan Tobacco	Universal Corporation
Philip Morris International	Vector
Reemtsma	

HISTORICAL FINANCIALS

Company Type: Public

Income Statement — FYE: December 31

	REVENUE ($ mil.)	NET INCOME ($ mil.)	NET PROFIT MARGIN	EMPLOYEES
12/05	16,043	3,265	20.4%	96,952
12/04	65,982	2,115	3.2%	90,249
12/03	45,553	1,122	2.5%	86,941
Annual Growth	(40.7%)	70.6%	—	5.6%

Net Income History — AMEX: BTI

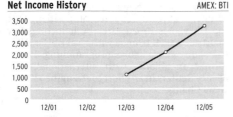

British Broadcasting

The dominant broadcaster in the UK, British Broadcasting Corporation (BBC) operates several public TV channels, a 24-hour cable news channel, digital channels, national and digital radio networks, and an online news service. The BBC World Service broadcasts radio programming in more than 30 languages and is the sole source of news in some parts of the world. Subsidiary BBC Worldwide offers international TV channels (BBC Prime, BBC America), program distribution, and magazine publishing. In addition, the company (often called The Beeb) operates a number of Web sites.

Established by royal charter, the BBC (once fondly referred to by Brits as "Auntie" for its prudish image) is governed by a 12-member board appointed by the queen. It derives 75% of its sales from annual mandatory license fees paid by TV set owners in the UK. In early 2005, the government seriously re-examined the role of the company in the widest-ever review of the BBC. Although the UK renewed the BBC's royal charter until 2016, it demanded that the company restructure its management operations by replacing the board of governors with a more independent body that does not also run the BBC's day-to-day management. The new body, called the BBC Trust, will begin governing when the current charter expires at the end of 2006.

Michael Grade, the BBC's chairman, stepped down in 2006 to take on the role of executive chairman at rival network ITV plc, which offered a much larger pay package. His decision left the BBC shocked, as Grade had been overhauling the company and would have led the new BBC Trust. He also abandoned the BBC at a crucial point in its negotiations with the government over licensing fees.

The BBC's growing involvement in commercial ventures has prompted public grumbling that the broadcaster is straying from its public service role. It increased license fees to fund a move into digital television, which also drew fire. To prove that it is serious about controlling costs, the company is cutting 3,800 jobs, or 19% of its workforce, over a three year period (the cuts began in 2005). The BBC also launched a new children's channel as a way to profitably expand the broadcaster's operations.

HISTORY

Established as the British Broadcasting Company Limited in 1922, the BBC was founded by a group of radio manufacturers aiming to block any single manufacturer from grabbing a broadcasting monopoly. Under general manager John Reith, BBC radio programming grew to include news, cultural events, sports, and weather. A burgeoning social and cultural presence led to its re-establishment in 1927 under a new royal charter. The organization was renamed the British Broadcasting Corporation, and the charter ensured it would remain outside the control of the British Parliament.

By 1935 BBC radio had reached about 95% of the British population. TV broadcasting debuted the next year, but the cost of TV sets limited audience numbers to about 20,000. Those who could afford a TV got to see the coronation of King George VI and Wimbledon. TV broadcasting would be short-lived, however: Beginning in 1939 and throughout WWII, the signal

was blacked out when the transmitter proved a good aircraft direction finder.

Although TV screens went dark, BBC radio served a vital role during WWII. Its broadcasts to occupied territories and the airing of Prime Minister Winston Churchill's wartime speeches elevated the BBC's reputation as a news broadcaster.

BBC TV transmission resumed in 1946. The 1953 broadcast of the coronation of Queen Elizabeth II helped launch the television age of the 1950s. In 1955 commercial broadcaster Independent Television Network became the BBC's first rival for viewers. The BBC introduced its second public TV channel (BBC Two) in 1964. By 1969 both BBC One and BBC Two were broadcasting in color.

The corporate culture of the BBC during the 1970s and 1980s was dominated by financial upheaval. Budget cuts combined with growing competition prompted the formation of a committee to review the BBC's financing alternatives. Although the committee's 1986 report did not permit commercial advertising on the BBC, it did lead to more flexibility in funding.

Sir John Birt was appointed the BBC's director general in 1992, and the reorganization and cost-cutting program he instituted fueled the debate over the company's move toward commercialization. Through BBC Worldwide, the BBC inched away from its public service roots. In 1997 the BBC privatized its domestic TV and radio transmission business and launched a 24-hour cable news channel. UKTV (a commercial TV joint venture with Flextech) also went on the air that year. In 1998 the BBC began digital broadcasts. It teamed with Discovery Communications to launch BBC America, a US cable channel, and teamed with Scottish Power to provide free Internet access.

In 1999 Greg Dyke, who had been chief executive of Pearson Television, was named to succeed Birt, who left in January 2000. Shortly after Dyke took the reins, he announced a massive restructuring of the organization designed to cut costs (eliminating hundreds of jobs), foment more partnerships with private entities, and increase the amount spent on programming. In 2001 the BBC received approval for five digital radio and four digital TV channels. Dyke announced that he would explore privatizing parts of the company, such as its magazine and book operations.

In 2002 the company started commercial subsidiary BBC Broadcast, which offers channel management services. (The BBC sold that business in 2005.) Both Dyke and chairman Gavyn Davies resigned from the BBC in 2004 following a British judge's ruling that a controversial BBC story accusing Prime Minister Tony Blair of exaggerating Iraq's weapons of mass destruction capabilities was riddled with errors. Television executive Michael Grade became chairman, and former Channel Four CEO Mark Thompson became the new director general.

The BBC started 2005 with a renewal of its royal charter that will keep the company in business until 2016. However, the UK government has demanded that it abolish its board of governors with a more independent body that is not also responsible for the BBC's day-to-day managment.

In 2006 the BBC suffered a blow when Grade left the organization to head commercial broadcasting firm ITV.

EXECUTIVES

Acting Chairman: Anthony Salz, age 56
Director General: Mark Thompson, age 49, $609,000 pay
Deputy Director-General: Mark Byford, age 48, $770,599 pay
COO: Caroline Thompson
Group Finance Director: Zarin Patel, $310,000 pay
CTO: John Varney
Acting Chair, BBC Trust: Chitra Bharucha
CEO, BBC Worldwide: John Smith, age 48, $727,112 pay
Managing Director, BBC Magazines: Peter S. Phippen
COO and Finance Director, BBC New Media and Technology: Sharmila Nebhrajani
Director BBC People: Steve Kelly
Director BBC Radio and Music: Jenny Abramsky, age 60, $539,246 pay
Creative Director; Director Drama, Entertainment, and CBBC: Alan Yentob, age 59
Director Global News: Richard Sambrook, age 50
Director Governance: Nicholas Kroll, age 50
Director Marketing, Communications, and Audiences: Tim Davie, age 38, $473,145 pay (partial-year salary)
Director Nations and Regions: Pat Loughrey
Director Future Media and Technology: Ashley Highfield, age 41, $296,000 pay
Director News: Helen Boaden
Director Policy, Strategy, Legal, and Distribution: Caroline Thomson, age 49, $525,329 pay
Director Sport: Roger Mosey
Director BBC Vision: Jana Bennett, age 48, $587,952 pay
Director Operations and Rights, BBC Vision: Bal Samra
Head of Human Resources and Development, BBC Vision: Lesley Swarbrick
Auditors: KPMG LLP; PricewaterhouseCoopers LLP

LOCATIONS

HQ: British Broadcasting Corporation
Broadcasting House, Portland Place, London W1A 1AA, United Kingdom
Phone: +44-20-7580-4468   **Fax:** +44-20-7765-1181
US HQ: 7475 Wisconsin Ave., Ste. 110, Bethesda, MD 20814
US Phone: 301-347-2233   **US Fax:** 301-656-8591
Web: www.bbc.co.uk

PRODUCTS/OPERATIONS

Selected Television Operations
BBC America (US cable channel)
BBC Four (digital channel focusing on culture and the arts)
BBC Japan (Japan cable channel)
BBC News 24 (24-hour news programming)
BBC One (news and entertainment programming)
BBC Parliament (unedited coverage of the Parliament)
BBC Prime (international entertainment programming)
BBC Three (digital channel featuring youth-oriented programming)
BBC Two (entertainment and informational programming)
CBBC (children's digital channel)
CBeebies (children's digital channel)

Selected Radio Operations
1Xtra (digital channel aimed at hip-hop audiences)
6 Music (music, music news, and documentary programming)
BBC 7 (speech-based digital service)
BBC Asian Network (broadcasts in English to Asian audiences in the UK)
BBC World Service (news and information in 33 languages)
Radio 1 (news and music programming)
Radio 2 (news and music programming)
Radio 3 (classical, jazz, and world music programming)
Radio 4 (news, educational, dramatic, and documentary programming)
Radio 5 Live (news and sports radio programming)
Five Live Sports Extra (digital channel focusing on live sports events)

Selected BBC Worldwide Magazines
BBC Good Food
BBC History
BBC Music
BBC Wildlife
Easy Gardening
It's HOT!
Radio Times
Top Of The Pops

Selected Subsidiaries and Units
BBC Resources (broadcast facilities)
BBC Online (Internet site)
BBC Worldwide Limited (oversees international operations)

Regional Operations
BBC Northern Ireland (radio and television)
BBC Scotland (radio and television)
BBC Wales (radio and television)

COMPETITORS

BSkyB	Liberty Media
CanWest	PBS
Channel 4	Pearson
Daily Mail	RTL Group
Emap	Scottish Radio
Flextech	SMG (UK)
Future	Time Warner
GCap Media	Yorkshire-Tyne Tees
ITV	Television

HISTORICAL FINANCIALS
Company Type: Government-owned

Income Statement
FYE: March 31

	REVENUE ($ mil.)	NET INCOME ($ mil.)	NET PROFIT MARGIN	EMPLOYEES
3/06	6,967	6	0.1%	25,377
3/05	7,205	(354)	—	27,264
3/04	6,766	(454)	—	27,632
3/03	5,559	(495)	—	27,148
3/02	4,823	(23)	—	25,568
Annual Growth	9.6%	—	—	(0.2%)

Net Income History

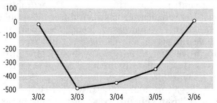

British Sky Broadcasting

The lofty British Sky Broadcasting Group (BSkyB) is the UK's #1 pay-TV provider. BSkyB distributes entertainment, news, and sports programming that reach more than 16 million homes in the UK and Ireland, including the more than 8 million subscribers to its digital direct-to-home (DTH) satellite service. Responding to the success of Freeview in the UK, BSkyB quietly introduced its own free-to-air TV service, in hopes of capturing some of that growing market. The company also has rolled out Sky Broadband, a broadband Internet access services offered free to existing customers. Rupert Murdoch's News

Corp. owns 38% of BSkyB, and Rupert's son James Murdoch is CEO.

BSkyB also offers interactive TV services. In late 2006 the company acquired a nearly 18% stake in ITV (formerly Granada), a leading European TV broadcasting and production company, in a deal valued at about $2 billion. In addition, BSkyB holds broadcast rights to the leading football (soccer) leagues in England and Scotland, and has minority stakes in several clubs. It also resells fixed-line phone service, and it has acquired Easynet, which allows BSkyB to offer a triple play of TV, phone, and broadband services. While about 75% of the company's revenues come from its DTH satellite customer base, BSkyB also wholesales some of its channels to competing pay TV provider NTL.

To boost brand awareness, BSkyB broadcasts three channels — Sky News, Sky Sports News, and Sky Travel — over Freeview, a free-to-air TV service jointly owned by the BBC, BSkyB, and Crown Castle. With millions of untapped homes in the UK, the company is hoping increased exposure will bring in more subscriber revenue.

In order to compete with the very popular Freeview, BSkyB has quietly introduced its own free-to-air satellite TV offering. With the purchase of a set of reception equipment, customers have access to about 200 TV and radio channels with no subscription fees. The company also offers a high definition TV (HDTV) service.

HISTORY

Australian-born media czar Rupert Murdoch, after taking control of several British newspapers, moved into satellite TV service in the UK in 1989 when his News Corp. holding company started Sky Network Television. Broadcasting SkyTV's four channels via satellites owned by the Luxembourg-based Astra group allowed Murdoch to avoid restrictions of the British Broadcasting Act, which prohibited owners of national newspapers from owning more than 20% of a TV company.

In 1990 a consortium of companies, including Chargeurs, Granada, and Pearson, set up rival service British Satellite Broadcasting. The rivals faced a consumer market slow to adapt to new technology and a shrinking advertising base caused by an economic recession; both companies posted huge losses (SkyTV's weekly losses grew to more than $20 million in 1990). In the wake of such financial hemorrhaging, the firms merged that year and became British Sky Broadcasting (BSkyB), a slimmer operation with five channels. The small stake held by Chargeurs was later transferred to its Pathé communications unit.

In 1993 BSkyB teamed up with US media group Viacom to produce a Nickelodeon channel (children's programming) for the UK market. Then the firm allied with home shopping channel QVC to launch QVC UK (BSkyB sold its stake in the company in 2004). By the end of 1993, more than 3 million UK homes were receiving BSkyB's programs.

BSkyB sold about 20% of itself to the public in 1994, dropping News Corp.'s stake from 50% to 40%. That year it reinforced its position as the top UK sports broadcaster by launching Sky Sports 2. BSkyB teamed with rival BBC in 1995 to acquire more sports programming. It also formed an alliance with international news agency Reuters in an effort to strengthen its Sky News Channel.

In 1996 BSkyB announced a joint venture with Kirch Gruppe (now TaurusHolding) to sell digital TV in Germany, but the deal later fell through. In 1997 BSkyB began developing digital satellite TV and interactive services in the UK through British Interactive Broadcasting, a joint venture with British Telecommunications (now BT Group), HSBC Holdings, and Matsushita Electric Industrial. (The service, Sky Digital, was launched in 1998 and offers subscribers about 150 channels.)

Managing director Sam Chisholm and his deputy, David Chance, resigned in 1997, opening the door for Murdoch's 29-year-old daughter, Elisabeth, to take a greater role at BSkyB. (She left the company in 2000.) Mark Booth (formerly with Murdoch's Japanese Sky Broadcasting) became CEO. BSkyB launched digital pay-per-view TV in the UK in 1997.

In 1999 the government blew the whistle on BSkyB's plan to buy UK soccer team Manchester United for $1 billion, saying it would have reduced competition in soccer broadcasting. (BSkyB retained its minority stake in the team.)

Fox/Liberty Networks CEO Tony Ball replaced Booth as CEO in 1999 after Booth was named to head a News Corp.-backed new media company. French conglomerate Vivendi (now Vivendi Universal) bought Pathé's stake in BSkyB, along with those of Granada and Pearson, and Rupert Murdoch took over as chairman of BSkyB, replacing Pathé's Jerome Seydoux. Vivendi announced in 2000 that it would sell its BSkyB stake to clear regulatory hurdles in its bid to acquire Canada's Seagram and take over the Universal entertainment group. That year BSkyB paid $1 billion for a 24% stake (which was then sold off in 2002) in Germany's KirchPayTV.

News Corp. in 2000 spun off its satellite holdings, including BSkyB, to form a new company, Sky Global Networks. That same year BSkyB completed the transition to an all-digital network and acquired both British Broadcasting Limited, which operates the OpenTV interactive service, and Sports Internet Group, a sports-related Web site operator.

Ball stepped down as CEO in 2003. In November of the same year, eyebrows were raised when Rupert Murdoch's son James was brought in to fill the CEO spot. At least in part because he was only 30 years old at the time, there were many grumblings about nepotism.

The company scored big points when it acquired exclusive broadcasting rights to the Premier League football games in 2003, but the deal prompted the European Commission to scrutinize the situation as a possible violation of European competition rules.

EXECUTIVES

Chairman: K. Rupert Murdoch, age 75, $81,911 pay
Deputy Chairman: Lord Jacob Rothschild, age 70
CEO and Director: James R. Murdoch, age 33, $3,518,190 pay
CFO and Director: Jeremy Darroch, age 44, $1,948,536 pay
COO: Mike Darcey, age 41
CTO: Didier Lebrat, age 46
Managing Director, Channels and Services: Dawn Airey, age 45
Managing Director, Customer Group: Brian Sullivan
Managing Director, Sky Media: Nick Milligan, age 45
Managing Director, Sky Sports: Vic Wakeling, age 63
Company Secretary: David (Dave) Gormley, age 43

Group Director Engineering and Platform Technology: Alun Webber, age 40
Group Director for Communications and Brand Marketing: Matthew Anderson
Director, IT and Strategy: Jeff Hughes, age 35
Director for People and Organisational Development: Beryl Cook, age 45
Head of Public Affairs: Martin Le Jeune
Head of Regulatory Affairs: Michael Rhodes, age 42
General Counsel: James Conyers, age 41
Strategic Adviser, Technology: Robin Crossley, age 47
Auditors: Deloitte & Touche LLP

LOCATIONS

HQ: British Sky Broadcasting Group plc
Grant Way, Isleworth,
London TW7 5QD, United Kingdom
Phone: +44-20-7705-3000   **Fax:** +44-20-7705-3453
Web: www.sky.com

PRODUCTS/OPERATIONS

2006 Sales

	$ mil.	% of total
Subscribers		
DTH	5,728.6	76
Cable	406.9	6
Advertising	621.2	8
Sky Active	165.3	2
Sky Bet	67.2	1
Other	544.8	7
Total	**7,534.0**	**100**

Selected Channels

The Amp (music programming)
Artsworld
Flaunt (music programming)
Scuzz (music programming)
Sky Box Office (pay-per-view programming)
Sky Cinema (classic cinema programming)
Sky Movies
Sky News
Sky One (general entertainment programming)
Sky Sports
Sky Travel (travel programming)
Sky Vegas Live (interactive entertainment)

Selected Subsidiaries and Affiliates

Attheraces Holdings Limited (50%, broadcast horse racing and related services)
British Interactive Broadcasting Holdings Limited (interactive TV services)
British Sky Broadcasting Limited (pay-TV broadcasting)
British Sky Broadcasting SA (satellite transponder leasing, Luxembourg)
The History Channel (UK) (50%, history programming)
MUTV (33%, Manchester United football channel)
National Geographic Channel UK (50%, natural history and adventure programming)
Nickelodeon UK (50%, children's programming)
Paramount UK (25%, comedy programming)
Sky In-Home Service Limited (supply, installation, and maintenance of satellite TV receiving equipment)
Sky News Australia Channel Pty Limited (33%, 24-hour news)
Sky Subscribers Services Limited (satellite broadcasting support services)
Sky Television Limited (holding company)
Sky Ventures Limited (joint ventures holding company)

COMPETITORS

BBC
Channel 4
Flextech
ITV
NTL
RTL Group
SMG (UK)
UnitedGlobalCom
Yorkshire-Tyne Tees Television Holdings

HISTORICAL FINANCIALS

Company Type: Public

Income Statement

FYE: June 30

	REVENUE ($ mil.)	NET INCOME ($ mil.)	NET PROFIT MARGIN	EMPLOYEES
6/06	7,534	1,001	13.3%	11,216
6/05	7,427	1,041	14.0%	9,958
6/04	6,608	784	11.9%	9,500
6/03	5,384	472	8.8%	9,132
6/02	4,469	(2,250)	—	9,083
Annual Growth	**13.9%**	**—**	**—**	**5.4%**

2006 Year-End Financials

Debt ratio: 268.0%   Current ratio: 1.49
Return on equity: 70.1%   Long-term debt ($ mil.): 3,694
Cash ($ mil.): 2,670

Net Income History

NYSE: BSY

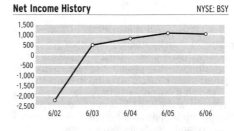

BT Group

Once upon a time, BT Group rivals could have fit into one of the company's signature red phone booths. Though competition has taken a toll, BT Group still wears the crown as the UK's leading telecommunications carrier. Formerly known as British Telecommunications, the BT Group offers local and long-distance phone service through nearly 30 million access lines (20 million residential and more than 8 million business connections). It also provides Internet access and other data services. In a major reorganization, BT Group has turned itself into a holding company. Ordered to upgrade and open its domestic networks, it has split its UK fixed-line network operations into separate wholesale and retail businesses.

BT Group operates primarily in the UK, but the BT Group empire stretches into other parts of Western Europe and across the pond to North America. BT Group has expanded its information communications technology (ICT) services offered to multi-site corporations in the US. It has signed its largest IT services deal to date, valued at $3 billion over eight-and-a-half years, with the Reuters Group.

To expand its global professional services offerings, the company has made several purchases in 2006 including US-based Counterpane Internet Security, a provider of managed networked security services that was founded by CTO Bruce Schneier. Schneier is recognized as a leading security technologist and acknowledged expert on cryptology. He is notable as the model for the lead character in the popular novel "The Da Vinci Code."

It has acquired Infonet, a leading provider of corporate managed voice and data network services. The company, renamed BT Infonet, is part of the BT Global Services unit. It also has expanded its multi-protocol label switching (MPLS) capacity in North America. BT Group also has acquired SkyNet Systems, a provider of Internet protocol-based LAN systems.

BT is refocusing its other international holdings to concentrate on Europe. It acquired Fiat's Italian telecom subsidiary Atlanet in early 2006 and later that year BT bought Fiat's Brazilian telecom business Telexis.

Once the UK's leading wireless telecoms operator, BT Group has reentered that market through its BT Mobile unit, wireless services marketed by the parent company using the Vodafone Group network. BT Group had countered mounting debt woes in 2001 with the spin-off of its wireless businesses (named O2), including its UK operations.

HISTORY

In 1879 the British Post Office (now known as Royal Mail and formerly Consignia) got the exclusive right to operate telegraph systems. When private firms tried to offer phone service, the government objected, arguing in court that its telegraph monopoly was imperiled. The courts agreed, and the Post Office was empowered to license private phone companies, collect a 10% royalty, and operate its own systems.

The private National Telephone Company emerged as the leading phone outfit, competing with the Post Office. When National's license expired in 1911, the Post Office took over and became the monopoly phone company. In 1936 the phone system introduced its familiar red public call offices (phone booths), designed for King George V's jubilee.

Under a 1981 law, telecommunications operations were split off from the Post Office and placed under the new British Telecommunications (BT). The government also allowed competitor Mercury Communications (Formerly One 2 One and now known as T-Mobile (UK)) to compete. The Thatcher government soon called for BT's privatization.

After the Telecommunications Act of 1984, BT went public in one of the largest UK stock offerings in history. The act set up the regulatory Office of Telecommunications (OFTEL). The next year Cellnet, BT's joint venture with Securicor, launched its mobile phone network. To become a multinational concern, BT bought control of Canadian phone equipment maker Mitel (1986, sold in 1992) and 20% of firm McCaw Cellular (1989, sold to AT&T in 1994).

In 1990 the British government opened the UK to more phone competition and BT responded with improvements to its network and a workforce reduction. The government sold almost all of its remaining shares in BT in 1993. The next year the company bought a 20% stake in MCI, the #2 US long-distance carrier, and the two formed Concert, a joint venture to compete in the international arena. BT's 1996 attempt to buy Cable and Wireless failed when the company asked for more than BT was willing to pay.

In 1998 BT bought the remaining 25% stake in Concert and found a new US partner in AT&T; the two agreed in 1999 to merge most of their international operations in a $10 billion global joint venture that took the Concert name (but after repeated losses the two parent companies dismantled the venture in 2002).

Also in 1999 BT expanded in continental Europe, Latin America (a 20% stake in IMPSAT), Asia (with AT&T, a 30% stake in Japan Telecom),

and the US, where it bought systems integration firm Syntegra (USA) (formerly Control Data Systems and now part of BT Americas) and Yellow Book USA. At home UK regulators ordered the company to upgrade its UK phone network and open it to rivals by 2001.

BT bought Ireland's Esat Telecom in 2000. That year the government sold its remaining stake in BT. Also that year, BT bought Telenor's stake in VIAG Interkom; early the next year it took full ownership of the German mobile phone company.

BT Group countered increasing competition and mounting debt woes through restructuring that included the 2001 spin-off of its domestic and international wireless businesses, combined under the mmO2 brand (formerly BT Wireless), which included BT Cellnet, a leading UK mobile phone operator. The decision left BT Group as the only top-tier European telecom firm without a wireless network.

To further its restructuring, the company in 2002 sold its Yellow Pages unit, Yell, to two buyout firms, (Hicks, Muse, Tate & Furst (now HM Capital Partners) and Apax Partners.

In 2002 BT dismantled Concert, its failed business telecom services joint venture with AT&T that combined most of the companies' international operations. The company also sold its 26% stake in France's Cegetel to Vivendi Universal. It also has unloaded other noncore assets including its 21% stake in Hong Kong wireless carrier SmarTone Telecommunications in its continuing effort to reduce debt.

EXECUTIVES

Chairman: Sir Christopher Bland, age 68, $500,000 pay
Deputy Chairman: Maarten A. van den Bergh, age 64
Chief Executive and Director:
 Bernardus J. (Ben) Verwaayen, age 54, $2,787,991 pay
Group Finance Director and Director: Hanif Lalani, age 44, $1,352,664 pay
Group Strategy Director and Regional Director, London: Clive R. Ansell
Chief Executive, BT Global Services, and Director:
 Andy Green, age 50, $1,690,830 pay
Chief Executive, BT Retail and Director:
 Ian P. Livingston, age 41
Chief Executive, BT Wholesale, and Director:
 Paul Reynolds, age 49, $1,119,215 pay
Chief Executive, BT Exact: Al-Noor Ramji, age 52
Chief Executive, BT Infonet: José A. Collazo, age 60
CEO, Openreach: Steve Robertson
CTO: Matthew W. (Matt) Bross, age 45
CIO: J.P. Rangaswami
Futurologist: Ian Pearson
Company Secretary: Larry Stone, age 49
President, BT International: François Barrault, age 44
Managing Director, BT Openworld: Duncan Ingram
Managing Director, Products and Enterprises, BT Retail: Steve Andrews
Director, Customer Contact Centre, BT Retail:
 Carol Borghesi
President, Global Telecom Markets: Karsten Lereuth
VP, BT Global Sales and Account Management:
 Kevin Ackling
Chief Human Resources Officer, BT Global Services:
 Alan Davis, age 50
Auditors: PricewaterhouseCoopers LLP

LOCATIONS

HQ: BT Group plc
 BT Centre, 81 Newgate St.,
 London EC1A 7AJ, United Kingdom
Phone: +44-20-7356-5000　　**Fax:** +44-20-7356-5520
US HQ: 350 Madison Ave., New York, NY 10017
US Phone: 646-487-7400　　**US Fax:** 646-487-3370
Web: www.btplc.com

2006 Sales

	$ mil.	% of total
Europe		
UK	29,746.4	87
Other countries	3,344.1	10
Americas	1,103.5	3
Asia & Pacific	151.4	—
Total	**34,345.4**	**100**

PRODUCTS/OPERATIONS

2006 Sales

	$ mil.	% of total
Business		
Major corporate	12,109.1	35
Other business	4,090.3	12
Consumer	9,321.2	27
Wholesale	8,793.2	26
Other	31.6	—
Total	**34,345.4**	**100**

2006 Sales

	% of total
BT Retail	32
BT Wholesale	35
BT Global Services	33
Total	**100**

Selected Operating Units

BT Exact (research, technology, and information technology (IT) operations)
BT Global Services (formerly BT Ignite, international data and IP (Internet protocol) services)
　BT Infonet (BT Global Services operations in the US)
　BT International (BT Global Services operations in Europe, the Americas, and the Asia Pacific regions, and BT Group's international sales and marketing operations)
　Syntegra (business transformation and change management services)
BT Retail (consumer communications services and products)
　BT Broadband (high-speed Internet access)
　BT Openworld (Internet access and portal services)
BT Wholesale (carrier-level network and communications services and products)
Openreach (local network services)

COMPETITORS

Accenture
AT&T
Bush Telegraph
Cable & Wireless
COLT Telecom
Deutsche Telekom AG
Euphony Communications
France Telecom
Integrated Communications
KPN
NTL
O2
PTV
T-Com
Telecom Italia
Telefónica
Verizon
Virgin Mobile
Wanadoo UK
Xfone

HISTORICAL FINANCIALS

Company Type: Public

Income Statement

FYE: March 31

	REVENUE ($ mil.)	NET INCOME ($ mil.)	NET PROFIT MARGIN	EMPLOYEES
3/06	34,345	1,849	5.4%	104,400
3/05	35,314	2,437	6.9%	102,100
3/04	34,541	1,613	4.7%	99,900
3/03	32,123	6,511	20.3%	104,700
Annual Growth	2.3%	(34.3%)	—	(0.1%)

2006 Year-End Financials

Debt ratio: —
Return on equity: —
Cash ($ mil.): 4,174
Current ratio: 0.71
Long-term debt ($ mil.): 15,336

Net Income History

NYSE: BT

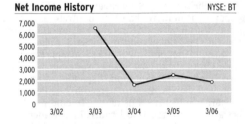

	3/02	3/03	3/04	3/05	3/06

Cable and Wireless

Telegraph cables and short-wave radio have given way to webs of optical fiber and satellites, but Cable and Wireless nonetheless promotes its famous name like never before. The company has been rerouting its corporate strategy and is taking on the business world's data needs, focusing on the demand for business data and Internet services and exiting the residential broadband market. It undertook a reorganization in 2006 that split its operations into two distinct units — its UK businesses and its international operations. The UK unit also includes the fixed-line operations of the former Energis Communications, which Cable and Wireless acquired in late 2005.

In line with its decision to discontinue residential services, the company is selling its broadband services provider Bulldog Communications.

The company's international division serves customers in dozens of countries with wireless and fixed-line voice and data services. The company has its primary operations in the Caribbean, Europe, the Middle East, and the Americas.

Cable and Wireless intended to rid itself of noncore holdings and to invest in the development of IP (Internet protocol) networks and Web hosting facilities, but overcapacity in the market forced the company to withdraw from many fronts and refocus on its UK operations and those in the Caribbean.

Cable and Wireless has expanded its operations in the UK with the 2005 acquisition of Energis Communications, a deal valued at £647 million ($1.1 billion). It had acquired Bulldog Communications the year before in a deal valued at nearly £19 million.

HISTORY

British cable and telegraph veteran John Pender began Eastern Telegraph in 1872. When Pender died in 1896, Eastern and associated companies owned one of every three miles of telegraph cable on the planet.

As the new century began, telecommunications expanded to include the wireless radio communications promoted by inventor Guglielmo Marconi, head of the UK's Marconi Wireless Telegraph. After WWI, the industry grew in importance, and, partly to counter a threat from a new US company called ITT, UK companies, including Marconi Wireless and Eastern Telegraph, joined in 1929 to form Cable and Wireless (C&W).

C&W began providing telegraph and telephone services in the UK's far-flung colonies, from Hong Kong to the Philippines to the Cayman Islands. It was nationalized in 1947, and in the 1950s C&W began losing franchises in former colonies or had local governments strip it of its monopolies.

The Thatcher government returned C&W to private ownership in 1985. C&W began building a network of undersea fiber-optic cables and satellites to link the Caribbean, Hong Kong, Japan, the UK, and the US. To complete the task, C&W assembled the world's largest commercial fleet of cable ships.

C&W joined British Petroleum (BP) and Barclays Merchant Bank in 1982 to form Mercury Communications as a rival to giant British Telecommunications (BT, now BT Group). C&W bought out BP and Barclays in 1984. The next year Mercury won the right to interconnect with BT.

As the 1990s began, C&W was adrift. In 1993 C&W and U S WEST's cable unit (later MediaOne) launched a digital cellular service — One 2 One — in the UK, but overall C&W wasn't making much headway in Europe. In 1996 merger talks with BT to build the world's largest telecom company failed. At this low point, Dick Brown, an American, was named C&W's CEO. Under Brown's direction C&W disposed of underperforming assets and created Cable & Wireless Communications (CWC) by combining Mercury with cable firms NYNEX CableComms, Bell Cablemedia, and Videotron.

When the UK handed over Hong Kong to China in 1997, C&W — in a bid to get access to the mainland market — sold a stake in Hong Kong Telecom to China Telecom. When MCI agreed to merge with WorldCom in 1998, C&W bought MCI's Internet business in a major step toward its emerging data-centric strategy. The company later sold the US dial-up business to Prodigy and the remaining data hosting and services operations later became C&W USA Inc.

Hong Kong Telecom became Cable & Wireless HKT in 1999. Brown left that year and was succeeded by Graham Wallace, former boss of CWC. C&W won a bidding war with NTT for Japan's International Digital Communications (now Cable & Wireless IDC). But selling was generally the order of the day: C&W sold its Global Marine undersea-cable operations to Global Crossing and struck a deal (which closed in 2000) to sell its UK consumer phone and cable TV business to rival NTL. It also sold One 2 One for about $11 billion to Deutsche Telekom.

In 2000 C&W announced plans to build a fiber-optic network in Japan. It took an 11% stake in Japanese ISP Garnet Connections and continued to acquire European ISPs. That year the company completed the sale of Cable & Wireless HKT, Hong Kong's dominant telecom carrier, to Pacific Century CyberWorks (now called PCCW).

C&W sold its controlling interest in Cable & Wireless Optus, and in 2001 Optus was acquired by Singapore Telecommunications. Also that year Cable and Wireless bought US-based Digital Island, and in 2002 it completed the acquisition of assets from bankrupt Exodus Communications. But the Exodus purchase proved unwise and the company cut 30% of its workforce from C&W Global, its Internet unit. The company cut jobs in Europe and sold some operations in that region, including businesses offering domestic-only services in Belgium, the Netherlands, Russia, Sweden, and Switzerland. Cable and Wireless also sold its 14% stake in Hong Kong operator PCCW.

Cable and Wireless purchased bankrupt PSINet's Japan unit in 2002. It also teamed up with Alcatel to lay a new transatlantic cable for Internet traffic.

The company in 2003 announced that it would exit the US market. It sold its bankrupt US operations, which included Cable & Wireless Internet Services and Cable & Wireless USA, to SAVVIS in 2004 as part of this strategy. Later that year Cable and Wireless bought Monaco Telecom from Vivendi Universal as part of an effort to expand its presence in Europe.

EXECUTIVES

Chairman: Richard D. Lapthorne, age 62
Group Deputy Chairman and Chairman, International: Rt. Hon. George Robertson, age 59
Executive Deputy Chairman: Robert O. (Rob) Rowley, age 56
Group Managing Director and Chairman, UK Division: John Pluthero, age 41
Group Managing Director and CEO, International: Harris Jones III, age 43
Group Managing Director, Central and Finance Director: Tony Rice
Executive Director, Human Resources: George Battersby, age 59
General Counsel and Company Secretary: Nick Cooper
Chief Executive, Bulldog Communications Ltd.: Emanuele Angelidis, age 40
Chief Executive, UK: Jim Marsh
President, Cable & Wireless US: Rob Breuche
Group Head, Media Communications: Steve Double
Director, Investor Relations: Ashley Rayfield
Manager, Investor Relations: Craig Thornton
Auditors: KPMG Audit Plc

LOCATIONS

HQ: Cable and Wireless plc
Lakeside House, Cain Road,
Bracknell RG12 1XL, United Kingdom
Phone: +44-1908-845-000   **Fax:** +44-20-7315-4460
Web: www.cw.com

Cable and Wireless has principal operations in the Caribbean, the Channel Islands, Macao, Monaco, Panama, and the UK.

2006 Sales

	% of total
Europe	
UK	63
Monaco	4
Caribbean	17
Panama	9
Macao	4
Other regions	3
Total	**100**

PRODUCTS/OPERATIONS

Selected Subsidiaries and Affiliates

Bahrain Telecommunications Company B.S.C. (Batelco, 20%)
Bulldog Communications Limited (UK)
Cable & Wireless Americas Operations, Inc. (US)
Cable & Wireless (Barbados) Limited (81%)
Cable & Wireless (Cayman Islands) Limited
Cable & Wireless Guernsey Ltd. (Channel Islands)
Cable & Wireless Jamaica Limited (82%)
Cable & Wireless Panama S.A. (49%)
Cable & Wireless UK (formerly Cable & Wireless Communications Mercury)
Companhia de Telecomunicações de Macau S.A.R.L. (CTM, 51%)
Dhivehi Raajjeyge Gulhun Private Limited (Dhiraagu, 45%, Maldives)
Monaco Telecom S.A.M. (49%)
Telecommunications Services of Trinidad and Tobago Limited (TSTT, 49%)

COMPETITORS

AT&T
BT
BT Infonet
Bush Telegraph
Check Communications
Deutsche Telekom AG
Equant
France Telecom
Global Crossing
Level 3 Communications
NTT
Verizon

HISTORICAL FINANCIALS

Company Type: Public

Income Statement

FYE: March 31

	REVENUE ($ mil.)	NET INCOME ($ mil.)	NET PROFIT MARGIN	EMPLOYEES
3/06	5,619	304	5.4%	14,325

Cadbury Schweppes

Drop a melted Cadbury chocolate bar on your favorite white shirt? Not to worry, Schweppes club soda will get it right out. A leading global confectioner, Cadbury Schweppes is also the world's #3 soft-drink producer, after The Coca-Cola Company and PepsiCo. Its beverage brands are sold mainly in North America and Western Europe and include 7 UP (US only), A&W Root Beer, Canada Dry, Dr Pepper, and Hawaiian Punch. It also makes Mott's apple products and Clamato juice. The company's confections are the market leaders in the UK. Along with the famous Cadbury Créme Egg, its candy brands include Trebor and Bassett. Cadbury Schweppes' gum brands include Bubbas, Trident, and Dentyne. Cadbury Schweppes' US candy brands — which include Cadbury, Peter Paul, and York — are licensed to The Hershey Company.

Cadbury's UK division, Cadbury Trebor Bassett, has one of the strongest confectionery brands in Dairy Milk. In other countries, the firm markets its powerful Cadbury name with regional brands. Its purchase of Pfizer's consumer business, Adams, brought with it Bubblicious,

Certs, Chiclets, Dentyne, Halls, and Trident to the company's roster.

In 2006 the company sold its European beverage business to a group of private investors managed by The Blackstone Group and Lion Capital for $2.2 billion in cash. The European unit's sales are concentrated in France, Germany, and Spain, but has operations in such far-flung places as the Middle East and northern and western Africa. The sale did not include Cadbury's US drinks business. Brands involved include Schweppes, Orangina, Oasis, Apollinaris, and La Casera. Cadbury will continue to own Dr Pepper, 7 UP, and Snapple.

That year Cadbury sold its South African soft drink business, Bromor Foods, and purchased Dan Products, South Africa's leading chewing gum company. It also paid $353 million to buy out The Carlyle Group's 53% stake in Dr Pepper/Seven Up Bottling Group (now called Cadbury Schweppes Bottling Group) and took full control of the US bottler.

Bowing to the public's growing concern about childhood obesity, in 2006 Cadbury, along with Coca-Cola, Pepsi, and the American Beverage Association agreed to sell only water, unsweetened juice, and low-fat milks to public elementary and middle schools in the US. As for high schools, the agreement calls for no sugary sodas to be sold and one-half of the offered drinks to be water, diet sodas, lemonade, or iced tea.

Because a batch of chocolate was contaminated with waste water from a leaking pipe at its Marlbrook, England, plant in January 2006, Cadbury recalled 1 million chocolate bars in Britain and Ireland in June 2006. Traces of salmonella were found in some of the products produced with the contaminated batch. The UK's Foods Standards Agency questioned the company's delay in announcing the contamination and recall.

HISTORY

Cadbury Schweppes is the product of a merger between two venerable British firms: Schweppes, the world's first soft-drink maker, and Cadbury, a candy confectionery. Schweppes began in 1783 in London, where Swiss national Jacob Schweppe first sold his artificial mineral water. The company introduced a lemonade in 1835 and tonic water and ginger ale in the 1870s. Beginning in the 1880s Schweppes expanded worldwide. In the 1960s it diversified into food products.

John Cadbury opened a coffee and tea shop in Birmingham, England, in 1824. He sold cocoa for drinking, which proved so popular that in 1831 he began making cocoa and was producing 15 varieties of chocolates by 1841.

The companies merged in 1969. Under Dominic Cadbury (great-grandson of founder John), Cadbury Schweppes acquired Peter Paul (Mounds, Almond Joy) in 1978 while increasing beverage sales in Europe and Asia. In 1982 it acquired applesauce and juice maker Duffy-Mott.

The company sold its noncandy and nonbeverage businesses in 1986. It then acquired Canada Dry, the rights to Sunkist soda, and 34% of Dr Pepper (reduced to 18% when Dr Pepper merged with Seven Up in 1988).

Fatigued by Mars' and Hershey's US dominance, Cadbury Schweppes signed a licensing agreement with Hershey in 1988, ending its direct involvement in the US candy market. The company added the Orange Crush and Hires brands in 1989, and it acquired candy makers Trebor and Bassett and the noncola soft-drink operations of Source Perrier in 1990.

The Camelot Group, a UK consortium that includes Cadbury Schweppes, was picked in 1994 to operate the UK's National Lottery. Cadbury Schweppes bought the rest of Dr Pepper/Seven Up for $2.5 billion in 1995, and became the world's #3 soft-drink company. John Sunderland was appointed CEO of Cadbury Schweppes in 1996 and named executive chairman in 2003. Todd Stitzer succeeded Sunderland as Cadbury's CEO that same year.

Cadbury Schweppes and The Carlyle Group investment firm created American Bottling through acquisitions in 1998. In 1999 Cadbury Schweppes and Carlyle bought the Dr Pepper Bottling Company of Texas for $691 million, combining it with American Bottling to form Dr Pepper/Seven Up Bottling Group, of which Cadbury owns a minority interest.

In 1999 Cadbury Schweppes sold its beverage operations in more than 160 countries (excluding Australia, Continental Europe, and the US) to The Coca-Cola Company for $973 million.

In 2000 the company acquired Snapple Beverage Group from Triarc Companies in a deal worth about $1.45 billion. Expanding further into soft drinks, the firm agreed to buy Pernod Ricard's soft-drink businesses (including the Orangina and Yoo-Hoo brands) in Continental Europe, North America, and Australia in 2001 for about $640 million.

The next year the company bought Nantucket Allserve (Nantucket Nectars) from Ocean Spray Cranberries. Later in 2002 Cadbury and Nestlé made a joint $10.5 billion bid for Hershey but Hershey subsequently called the sale off. In 2003 Cadbury Schweppes completed its purchase of Pfizer Inc.'s Adams confectionery business for $4.2 billion.

In 2005 Cadbury bought UK organic chocolate maker, Green & Black's and sold Holland House cooking wines. It also agreed to buy Tahincioglu Holdings' 30% share of Kent (Turkey's second-largest confectionery and gum maker), thus upping its stake in Kent to 95%.

EXECUTIVES

Chairman: Sir John M. Sunderland, age 60, $6,043,765 pay
Deputy Chairman: Roger M. Carr, age 59
CEO and Director: Todd Stitzer, age 54, $1,347,073 pay
CFO and Director: Ken Hanna, age 52, $892,888 pay
VP, Government Affairs: Deborah L. Louison
Chief Human Resources Officer and Director: Robert J. (Bob) Stack, age 55, $720,848 pay
Chief Legal Officer: Henry (Hank) Udow
CIO: Christine Connolly
Chief Science and Technology Officer: David MacNair
Chief Executive, Bebidas de Espana: Patrick Falgas
President and CEO, Americas Beverages: Gilbert M. (Gil) Cassagne
President and CEO, Americas Confectionery; President, Cadbury Adams USA: James R. (Jim) Chambers
President and CEO, Asia/Pacific: Rajiv Wahi
President and CEO, Europe Beverages: Marie-Bernard Trannoy, age 61
President and CEO, Europe, Middle East, and Africa Confectionery: Matt Shattock
President, Global Supply Chain: Steve Driver
President, Snapple Distributing Company: Jack Belsito
Group Secretary: Hester Blanks, age 53
Director, Finance Confectionary UK: James Reed
Director, Investor Relations and Finance Global Commercial: Sally Jones
Director, Sales: Louise Cook
Head of Group Public Relations: Dora McCabe
Auditors: Deloitte & Touche LLP

LOCATIONS

HQ: Cadbury Schweppes plc
25 Berkeley Sq., London W1J 6HB, United Kingdom
Phone: +44-20-7409-1313 **Fax:** +44-20-7830-5200
US HQ: 5301 Legacy Dr., Plano, TX 75024
US Phone: 972-673-7000 **US Fax:** 972-673-7980
Web: www.cadburyschweppes.com

Cadbury Schweppes' confections are sold in more than 190 countries. Cadbury Schweppes sells beverages in nine countries and licenses the sale of its beverages in about 20 others.

2005 Sales

	% of total
Europe, Middle East, Africa	36
Americas Beverages	27
Americas Confectionery	19
Asia/Pacific	18
Total	**100**

PRODUCTS/OPERATIONS

Selected Brand Names

Beverages
7 UP (US, Puerto Rico)
A&W Root Beer
Canada Dry
Clamato
Cottee's (Australia)
Country Time (licensed, US)
Crush
Crystal Light (licensed, US)
Diet Rite
Dr Pepper (Australia, Canada, Mexico, US)
Hawaiian Punch
Mauna La'i
Mistic (fruity beverages)
Mott's
Nantucket Nectars
Nehi
RC Cola
Schweppes
Snapple
Solo (Australia)
Spring Valley (Australia)
Squirt
Stewart's (sodas)
Sunkist (licensed)
Sun Valley Squeeze
Wave (Australia)
Welch's (licensed, US)
WhipperSnapple
YooHoo
Confections
Bassett
Beldent
Bouquet d'Or (France)
Butterkist (UK)
Cadbury
Cadbury Creme Egg
Cadbury Dairy Milk
Carambar (France)
Certs
Elegan
Fuzzy Peach
Halls
Jelibon (Turkey)
Kent (Turkey)
La Pie Qui Chante (France)
Maynards (UK)
Peter Paul
Piasten (Germany)
Picnic
Poulain (France)
Red Tulip (Australia)
Sour Patch Kids
Swedish Fish
Trebor
Turbo (Turkey)
Wedel (Poland)
York

Chewing gum
Bazooka
Beldent
Bubbalicious
Bubbas
Chiclets
Clorets
Dentyne
Hollywood
Relax
STIMOROL
Trident
V6

COMPETITORS

Altria	National Beverage
Associated British Foods	National Grape Cooperative
Britvic	Nestlé
Campbell Soup	Northern Foods
Coca-Cola	Ocean Spray
Cott	PepsiCo
CSM	PepsiCo International
Ferolito, Vultaggio	Pernod Ricard
Heinz	Russell Stover
Hershey	See's Candies
Jelly Belly Candy	Thorntons
Jones Soda	Tootsie Roll
Kellogg	Virgin Group
Lindt & Sprüngli	Wrigley
Mars	

HISTORICAL FINANCIALS

Company Type: Public

Income Statement

FYE: Saturday nearest December 31

	REVENUE ($ mil.)	NET INCOME ($ mil.)	NET PROFIT MARGIN	EMPLOYEES
12/05	11,219	1,008	9.0%	58,581
12/04	12,934	827	6.4%	58,442
12/03	11,435	662	5.8%	55,799
Annual Growth	(1.0%)	23.4%	—	2.5%

2005 Year-End Financials

Debt ratio: 66.4%
Return on equity: 13.3%
Cash ($ mil.): 769
Current ratio: 1.08
Long-term debt ($ mil.): 5,283
No. of shares (mil.): —
Dividends
Yield: 2.4%
Payout: 46.7%
Market value ($ mil.): —

Stock History

NYSE: CSG

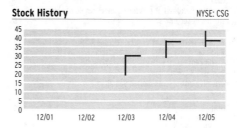

	STOCK PRICE ($) FY Close	P/E High/Low		PER SHARE ($) Earnings	Dividends
12/05	38.29	22	18	1.95	0.91
12/04	37.70	21	16	1.82	0.88
12/03	29.89	23	15	1.31	0.77
Annual Growth	13.2%	—	—	22.0%	8.7%

Canadian Imperial Bank of Commerce

Canadian Imperial Bank of Commerce (CIBC) is both Canadian and imperial when it comes to growing its business. CIBC's more than 1,000 branches offer a range of consumer and business services, including deposits, loans, brokerage, and mutual funds. It operates in two main segments: CIBC Retail Markets (consumer and small business banking, credit cards, wealth management) and CIBC World Markets (corporate banking, securities, foreign exchange trading). Operating units within its business lines include trust and custody services provider CIBC Mellon (a joint venture with Mellon Financial) and retail brokerage CIBC Wood Gundy.

To build its customer base, which stands at some 11 million, the bank is focusing on its core banking operations, targeting small businesses and retail customers.

In 2004 and again in 2006, CIBC was sued by creditors of Internet telecommunications company Global Crossing, stating that the bank had engaged in insider trading to the tune of $2 billion. Creditors demanded a return of the proceeds. CIBC denied the claims.

CIBC took a hit in 2005 when it agreed to pay some $2.4 billion in an investor class-action suit to resolve claims that the company helped notorious energy trader Enron to conceal losses. The next year two units of the bank agreed to pay $17.4 million to investors in ill-fated telecom Global Crossing.

Also that year the company divested its student lending subsidiary, EDULINX.

Elsewhere, CIBC and UK bank Barclays each owned around 44% of FirstCaribbean International Bank; in 2006 CIBC bought out Barclays' stake for more than $1 billion.

HISTORY

In 1858 Bank of Canada was chartered; Toronto financier William McMaster bought the charter in 1866 when investors failed to raise enough money to open it and changed the name to Canadian Bank of Commerce.

Canadian Bank of Commerce opened in 1867, bought the Gore Bank of Hamilton (1870), and expanded within seven years to 24 branches in Ontario, as well as Montreal and New York. Led by Edmund Walker, the bank spread west of the Great Lakes with the opening of a Winnipeg, Manitoba, branch in 1893 and joined the Gold Rush with branches in Dawson City, Yukon Territory, and Skagway, Alaska, in 1898.

As the new century began, the bank's purchases spanned the breadth of Canada, from the Bank of British Columbia (1901) to Halifax Banking (1903) and the Merchants Bank of Prince Edward Island (1906). More buys followed in the 1920s; the bank's assets peaked in 1929 and then plunged during the Depression. It recovered during WWII.

In 1961 Canadian Bank of Commerce merged with Imperial Bank of Canada to become Canadian Imperial Bank of Commerce. Imperial Bank was founded in 1875 by Henry Howland; it went west to Calgary and Edmonton and became known as "The Mining Bank." It bought Barclays Bank (Canada) in 1956.

As the energy and agriculture sectors declined in the early 1980s, two of CIBC's largest borrowers, Dome Petroleum and tractor maker Massey-Ferguson, defaulted on their loans. Deregulation opened investment banking to CIBC, which in 1988 bought a majority share of Wood Gundy, one of Canada's largest investment dealers; CIBC also purchased Merrill Lynch Canada's retail brokerage business.

In 1992 CIBC added substantially to its loss reserves (resulting in an earnings drop of 98%) to cover real estate losses from developer Olympia & York and others. This launched more cost-cutting as the company reorganized by operating segments.

Deregulation allowed CIBC to begin selling insurance in 1993; the company built a collection of life, credit, personal property/casualty, and nonmedical health companies.

In 1996 the bank formed Intria, a processing and technical support subsidiary. The next year CIBC Wood Gundy became CIBC World Markets, and CIBC bought securities firm Oppenheimer & Co. and added its stock underwriting and brokerage abilities to CIBC World Markets.

In 1998, increasing foreign competition prompted CIBC and Toronto-Dominion to plan a merger (as did Royal Bank of Canada and Bank of Montreal); the government halted both plans citing Canada's already highly concentrated banking industry.

Spurned, the bank overhauled its operations to spark growth in the late 1990s. To cut costs it eliminated some 4,000 jobs and sold its more than $1 billion real estate portfolio. It teamed with the Winn-Dixie (1999) and Safeway (2000) supermarket chains to operate electronic branches in the US. The firm scaled back its disappointing international operations and began selling its insurance units.

In 2000 CIBC created Amicus as a holding company for CIBC World Markets' retail electronic banking business. The following year the bank sold its merchant card services business to US-based Global Payments.

In 2002 the company snagged US-based Merrill Lynch's Canadian retail brokerage, asset management, and securities operations, renaming it CIBC Asset Management Inc. That same year CIBC merged its Caribbean banking business with that of UK-based Barclays to create FirstCaribbean Bank.

The next year CIBC sold the Oppenheimer private client and asset-management divisions to Fahnestock Viner (now Oppenheimer Holdings).

It sold Juniper Financial, a Delaware-based credit card issuer, to Barclays for some $293 million in 2004.

EXECUTIVES

Chairman: William A. Etherington, age 64
President, CEO, and Director:
  Gerald T. (Gerry) McCaughey, age 48, $630,046 pay
SEVP, Administration, Technology, and Operations:
  Ron A. Lalonde
Vice Chairman and CIO: Michael D. (Mike) Woeller
SEVP and CFO: Tom D. Woods, $339,800 pay
SEVP, CIBC Retail Markets: Sonia A. Baxendale, $344,856 pay
SEVP and Chief Risk Officer: Steven R. McGirr, age 49, $269,009 pay
SEVP, Corporate Development; Deputy Chairman and Managing Director, CIBC World Markets:
  Richard E. Venn, age 55
SEVP; Chairman and CEO, CIBC World Markets:
  Brian G. Shaw, age 51, $269,009 pay

EVP and Chief Privacy Officer: Pankaj Puri
EVP, CIBC Retail Markets: John D. Orr
EVP and Controller: Bruce Renihan
EVP, Credit and Investment Risk Management:
  P. Kenneth M. (Ken) Kilgour
EVP and General Counsel, Legal and Regulatory Compliance: Michael G. Capatides
EVP, Global Operations: Malcolm Eylott
EVP, Retail Distribution, CIBC Retail Markets:
  Ted R. Cadsby
EVP, Technology and Operations: Mike J. Boluch
EVP, Technology Infrastructure: Grant C. Westcott
EVP and Treasurer: Michael G. Horrocks
EVP, Wealth Management: Victor Dodig
SVP and Chief Accountant: Francesca Shaw
SVP, Communications and Public Affairs:
  Stephen J. Forbes
VP and Corporate Secretary: Michelle Caturay
VP, Investor Relations: John P. Ferren
Ombudsman: Donna R. MacCandlish
Auditors: Ernst & Young LLP

LOCATIONS

HQ: Canadian Imperial Bank of Commerce
  Commerce Court,
  Toronto, Ontario M5L 1A2, Canada
Phone: 416-980-2211   **Fax:** 416-980-5028
US HQ: 425 Lexington Ave., New York, NY 10017
US Phone: 212-856-4000   **US Fax:** 212-667-4590
Web: www.cibc.com

PRODUCTS/OPERATIONS

2005 Sales

	% of total
Interest	
Loans	41
Securities	17
Deposits with banks	2
Noninterest	
Commissions on securities transactions	5
Trading revenue	4
Deposit & payment fees	4
Underwriting & advisory fees	4
Mutual fund fees	4
Investment securities gains	3
Other	16
Total	**100**

2005 Assets

	% of total
Cash & equivalents	4
Trading securities	19
Securities borrowed or purchased under resale agreements	7
Investment securities	5
Loans	
Residential mortgages	28
Personal	10
Credit card	2
Business & government	11
Derivative instruments market valuation	7
Other	7
Total	**100**

COMPETITORS

Bank of America	JPMorgan Chase
Bank of New York	Lehman Brothers
Barclays	Merrill Lynch
Bear Stearns	Mizuho Financial
BMO Financial Group	Morgan Stanley
Citigroup	National Bank of Canada
Credit Suisse	RBC Financial Group
Deutsche Bank	Scotiabank
Goldman Sachs	TD Bank
HSBC Holdings	UBS Financial Services

HISTORICAL FINANCIALS

Company Type: Public

Income Statement

FYE: October 31

	ASSETS ($ mil.)	NET INCOME ($ mil.)	INCOME AS % OF ASSETS	EMPLOYEES
10/05	239,223	176	0.1%	37,308
10/04	239,268	1,783	0.7%	37,281
10/03	216,797	1,677	0.8%	36,630
10/02	177,724	114	0.1%	42,552
Annual Growth	10.4%	15.5%	—	(4.3%)

2005 Year-End Financials

Equity as % of assets: 2.9%   Long-term debt ($ mil.): 17,797
Return on assets: 0.1%   Sales ($ mil.): 15,975
Return on equity: 2.3%

Net Income History

NYSE: CM

10/01	10/02	10/03	10/04	10/05

Canon

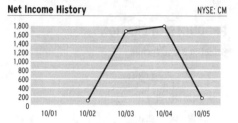

Canon is still banging away at the document reproduction market. The company makes printers and other computer peripherals for home and office use. Its other well-known lines include copiers, fax machines, and scanners. Canon's optical segment features products used in such diverse applications as semiconductor manufacturing equipment, television broadcast lenses, and devices used for eye examinations. Canon still operates its original camera business, which makes digital cameras, camcorders, liquid-crystal display projectors, lenses, and binoculars.

Canon's imaging products, its largest segment, include printers, copiers, scanners, and multifunction devices for the consumer and enterprise markets. Canon sells branded products and supplies partners such as Hewlett-Packard that resell under their own brands. The company is targeting color office products for growth in this segment.

Perhaps still best known for its cameras, Canon has seen its photographic business drop to about 20% of revenues. However, the company is a leader in the digital camera market, where it is concentrating on high-end single lens reflex (SLR) devices.

Canon has teamed with Toshiba to develop surface-conduction electron-emitter display (SED) products, an alternative to liquid-crystal display (LCD) and plasma technologies.

Canon adheres to the *kyosei* philosophy (living and working together for the common good), which stresses respect for local cultures and customs and more local control of subsidiaries. The company, which generates about two-thirds of its revenues outside of Japan, continues to emphasize its product development and marketing efforts in Europe and the US.

HISTORY

Takeshi Mitarai and a friend, Saburo Uchida, formed Seiki Kogaku Kenkyusho (Precision Optical Research Laboratory) in Tokyo in 1933 to make Japan's first 35mm camera. In 1935 the camera was introduced under the brand name Kwanon (the Buddhist goddess of mercy) — but later renamed Canon. In response to a pre-World War II military buildup, the company made X-ray machines for the Japanese.

In 1947 the company became Canon Camera Company as the brand name gained popularity. Canon opened its first overseas branch — in New York — in 1955. It diversified into business equipment by introducing the first 10-key electronic calculator (1964) and a plain-paper photocopier (1968) independent of Xerox's patented technology. Canon dropped "Camera Company" from its name in 1969.

The company invented the "liquid dry" copying system, which uses plain paper and liquid developer, in 1972. It failed to produce new cameras and was surpassed by Minolta as Japan's top camera exporter. Sales were sluggish in the early 1970s, and in 1975 Canon suspended dividends for the first time since World War II.

At that time Canon's managing director, Ryuzaburo Kaku, convinced Mitarai that the company's problems stemmed from indecisive leadership and weak marketing. Kaku turned Canon around, unleashing the electronic AE-1 in a media blitz that in 1976 included the first-ever TV commercials for a 35mm camera. With automated features, the AE-1 appealed to the clumsiest photographers. Its success catapulted Canon past Minolta as the world's #1 camera maker.

In 1979 Canon introduced the first copier to use a dry developer. As the copier market matured in the early 1980s, Canon shifted to making other automated office equipment, including laser printers and fax machines.

Mitarai died in 1984. Minolta the next year again displaced Canon as the world's #1 camera maker, when it introduced a fully automated model. But Canon came back in 1987 with the electronic optical system (EOS) auto-focus camera, which returned the company to preeminence in 1990. That year the company initiated an ink cartridge recycling program. Canon teamed up with IBM in 1992 to produce portable PCs. In 1993 Takeshi Mitarai's son Hajime, who had joined Canon in 1974, was named president and began expanding product development.

In 1995 Canon introduced the world's first color ferroelectric liquid-crystal display designed to replace cathode-ray tubes in computer and TV screens as the industry standard. When Hajime died that year, cousin Fujio Mitarai, a 34-year Canon employee who served as the head of Canon U.S.A. in the 1980s, was named president and CEO. In 1996 the company made Canon Latin America a direct subsidiary of Canon U.S.A., with the *kyosei* idea that regionalized control would make the subsidiary more efficient.

Canon stopped making PCs in 1997. The next year the company unveiled its Hyper Photo System, which combines a scanner, PC server, and printer to produce photo prints, and expanded its copier remanufacturing operations. In 1999, after 16 years of production, Canon stopped making optical memory cards. The company also opened a research and development facility in the US.

In 2000 Canon and Toshiba began working together to develop technology for flat-panel displays. Canon expanded its line of digital cameras

in 2001; the company's sales in that segment almost doubled that year.

The next year the company announced that it would merge two of its office equipment subsidiaries, Copyer and Canon Aptex, in an effort to improve operating efficiency.

EXECUTIVES

Chairman and CEO: Fujio Mitarai, age 71
President and COO: Tsuneji Uchida, age 65
Senior Managing Director; Group Executive, Finance and Accounting: Toshizo Tanaka, age 66
Director; Chief Executive, Chemical Products Operations: Haruhisa Honda, age 58
Senior Managing Director; Group Executive, Corporate Intellectual Property and Legal HQ: Nobuyoshi Tanaka, age 60
Managing Director; Group Executive, Corporate Strategy and Development: Kunio Watanabe, age 62
Managing Director; Group Executive, General Affairs HQ: Akiyoshi Moroe, age 62
Senior Managing Director; Chief Executive, Optical Products HQ: Junji Ichikawa, age 63
Managing Director; President and CEO, Canon U.S.A.: Yoroku Adachi, age 58
Senior Managing Director: Hajime Tsuruoka, age 63
Managing Director; Chief Executive, Peripheral Products: Yasuo Mitsuhashi, age 57
Managing Director; Group Executive, Production Management HQ; Group Executive, Global Environment Promotion HQ: Hironori Yamamoto, age 62
Director; EVP, Canon USA: Ryoichi Bamba, age 60
Director; Deputy Chief Executive, Image Communication Products: Tomonori Iwashita, age 56
Director, Group Executive, Device Technology Development: Shigeyuki Matsumoto, age 56
Director; Chief Executive, Inkjet Products: Katsuichi Shimizu, age 60
Director; Group Executive, L Printer Business Promotion: Toshio Honma, age 57
Director; Group Executive, Global Procurement HQ: Masahiro Ohsawa, age 59
Director; Group Executive, Human Resource Management and Organization HQ; Group Executive, Information and Communications Systems HQ: Keijiro Yamazaki, age 58
Director: Tetsuro Tahara, age 57
Auditors: Ernst & Young ShinNihon

LOCATIONS

HQ: Canon Inc.
30-2, Shimomaruko 3-chome, Ohta-ku, Tokyo 146-8501, Japan
Phone: +81-3-3758-2111　　**Fax:** +81-3-5482-5135
US HQ: 1 Canon Plaza, Lake Success, NY 11042
US Phone: 516-328-5000　　**US Fax:** 516-328-5069
Web: www.canon.com

2005 Sales

	% of total
Europe	32
Americas	30
Japan	26
Other regions	12
Total	**100**

PRODUCTS/OPERATIONS

2005 Sales

	% of total
Business machines	67
Cameras	23
Optical & other	10
Total	**100**

Selected Products

Business Machines
　Business information
　　Document scanners
　　Fax machines
　　Handy terminals

Computer peripherals
　Consumables
　Printers (bubble jet and laser)
　Scanners
Office imaging
　Consumables
　Office
　Personal
Camera segment
　Cameras
　　Digital
　　Film
　Lenses
　Liquid-crystal display projectors
　Video camcorders
Optical
　Broadcasting equipment
　Digital radiography
　Encoders
　Eye care systems
　Medical imaging systems
　Semiconductor production equipment
　Transceivers

COMPETITORS

Agfa
ASML
Eastman Kodak
Epson
Fuji Xerox
Fujifilm
Fujitsu
Hewlett-Packard
Hitachi
IBM
Konica Minolta
Kyocera
Lexmark
Matsushita
NEC
Nikon
Océ
Océ Imagistics
Oki Electric
Olympus
Pentax
Philips Electronics
Polaroid
Ricoh
SANYO
Sharp
Sony
Toshiba
Victor Company of Japan
Xerox

HISTORICAL FINANCIALS

Company Type: Public

Income Statement

FYE: December 31

	REVENUE ($ mil.)	NET INCOME ($ mil.)	NET PROFIT MARGIN	EMPLOYEES
12/05	31,911	3,265	10.2%	115,583
12/04	33,638	3,330	9.9%	108,257
12/03	29,742	2,564	8.6%	102,567
12/02	24,697	1,602	6.5%	97,802
12/01	22,098	1,274	5.8%	93,620
Annual Growth	9.6%	26.5%	—	5.4%

2005 Year-End Financials

Debt ratio: 1.0%　　　　　　No. of shares (mil.): —
Return on equity: 15.0%　　Dividends
Cash ($ mil.): 8,544　　　　　Yield: 1.4%
Current ratio: 2.28　　　　　Payout: 22.0%
Long-term debt ($ mil.): 230　Market value ($ mil.): —

	STOCK PRICE ($) FY Close	P/E High/Low		PER SHARE ($) Earnings	Dividends
12/05	39.22	16	13	2.45	0.54
12/04	36.17	15	12	2.50	0.37
12/03	31.76	—	—	—	0.28
12/02	24.57	—	—	—	0.14
12/01	23.37	30	17	0.95	0.11
Annual Growth	13.8%	—	—	26.7%	48.9%

Capgemini

Technology and outsourcing are the twin pillars of this business. Capgemini is one of the world's leading providers of systems integration and consulting services, with operations in more than 30 countries. It offers enterprise systems development and implementation, as well as analysis and consulting services to help businesses choose the technology best suited to their needs. It also offers a range of business process outsourcing (BPO) services in such functional areas as customer relationship management (CRM), finance, human resources, and supply chain management. Capgemini also provides traditional management consulting services.

In 2006 Capgemini expanded its financial services and insurance offerings when it agreed to buy global information technology (IT) services firm Kanbay International in a cash deal valued at $1.25 billion. Kanbay International is especially strong in the financial services sector, a large chunk of the global IT market. It also has significant presence in India as well as in the US.

Also in 2006 the company transferred its European Networking Infrastructure Services (NIS) unit to UK-based incumbent telecoms carrier BT Group. The move expands the NIS operations through BT's network. About 250 Capgemini employees transferred to BT Group in the transaction.

Reorganization efforts in 2004 (including a name change from Cap Gemini Ernst & Young) helped focus the company along the functional lines of consulting, outsourcing, and technology services. Its Sogeti-Transiciel division provides support and consulting to smaller customers through local offices, primarily in Europe. As a result, local professional services and outsourcing have become Capgemini's growth areas as the company diversifies its revenue base.

Like other consultancies, the firm was hit hard by the long technology downturn, but the effects were felt especially hard at Capgemini in part because of its 2000 acquisition of Ernst & Young's consulting arm. Both chairman Serge

Kampf and CEO Paul Hermelin came under fire for pursuing the $11 billion deal, but under their leadership Capgemini has weathered the storm and emerged as a more streamlined company.

HISTORY

Serge Kampf founded software house Sogeti in 1967 in Grenoble, France. He had an economics degree and had held a variety of jobs — from selling bakery ovens and computers to working for the French national telephone company. Frustrated as an executive with French computer company Groupe Bull, he resigned and started Sogeti.

Believing the future of information technology (IT) would be in support rather than hardware, Kampf focused on providing computer services to companies outside Paris that were being overlooked by his larger competitors. He was immediately successful, and three years later opened a Paris branch. In 1973 Kampf changed the focus of the company, abandoning the more specialized activities of data processing for general consulting, software, and technical assistance.

Cap Gemini Sogeti was created two years later by merging Sogeti with two French software service companies, C.A.P. (Computerized Applications Programming, started in 1962) and Gemini (1969). At first it operated as a "body shop," a loose organization of freelance programmers offering temporary help to computer users. It set up a consulting team in the US in 1978 and began a series of US acquisitions that led to the formation of Cap Gemini America (1981).

The company acquired a 42% stake in French competitor Sesa in 1982; six years later it bought the rest as part of a new strategy to become a global operator with a range of services. Cap Gemini Sogeti's 1990 purchase of Hoskyns Group, the UK's largest computer services company, was just one of a string of acquisitions aimed at fulfilling that goal. (Over a five-year period, it bought 22 European and American companies for $1.1 billion.) To raise money for his international expansion plans, Kampf sold 34% of the company to German carmaker Daimler-Benz (now DaimlerChrysler) in 1991.

As Cap Gemini Sogeti expanded around the world, its decentralized network of operations rarely shared business or expertise. In 1993, on the heels of its first loss, the company launched a restructuring program that set up seven strategic business areas with dual regional and segment roles and modified product lines. Cap Gemini Sogeti returned to profitability in 1995.

The mid-1990s brought more than a dozen partnerships, including deals with French chemical conglomerate Rhône-Poulenc (now Sanofi-Aventis, 1995) and British Steel (now Corus Group, 1996). Also in 1996 the company launched its year 2000 date fixing software. It completed the reorganization, creating holding company Cap Gemini, and moved its corporate headquarters to Paris.

In 1997 Daimler-Benz sold its stake (then 24%) in Cap Gemini to Compagnie Générale d'Industrie et de Participations (CGIP, now controlled by Wendel Investissement). The next year Cap Gemini bought the UK finance and commerce arm of AT&T. The company sold its UK training unit in 1999 to focus its UK operations on IT services. Expanding further into the US that year, the company bought telecommunications specialist Beechwood.

In 2000 Cap Gemini solidified its US presence with the $11 billion purchase of the consulting business of Ernst & Young, changing its name to Cap Gemini Ernst & Young. Geoff Unwin took over as CEO that year; Kampf remained as chairman.

Stung by a slowdown in IT spending (primarily in the US), in 2001 the company announced it was cutting 5,400 jobs. Later that year Unwin announced his retirement as CEO, and was succeeded by COO Paul Hermelin. In 2002 another 5,500 jobs (about 10% of its workforce) were cut, mainly in its telecom and financial services units. The appointment of Alexandre Haeffner as COO launched major managerial restructuring.

In 2004 the company simplified its name to Capgemini as part of an overall reorganization effort. Soon after, the company's struggling US division got a shot in the arm when it signed a 10-year, $3.5 billion business and computer consulting services with power company TXU Corp. Capgemini also acquired consulting firm Transiciel (now Sogeti-Transiciel).

Capgemini sold its North American health care consulting practice in 2005 to Accenture for about $175 million. Later that year, however, COO Pierre Danon, credited with helping to turn around Capgemini's North American operations, was fired after news leaked he was seeking the CEO position at hotelier Accor.

EXECUTIVES

Chairman: Serge Kampf, age 72
Vice Chairman: Ernest-Antoine Sellière
CEO and Director: Paul Hermelin, age 49
CFO: Nicolas Dufourcq
Managing Director, Central and Southern Europe and Consulting Services Global Coordination: Antonio Schnieder
Managing Director, France and Technology Services Global Coordination: Philippe Donche-Gay
Managing Director, Northern Europe and Asia Pacific: Henk W. Broeders, age 54
Managing Director, Local Professional Services; Chairman, Sogeti-Transiciel: Luc-François Salvador
Managing Director, Outsourcing Services: Paul Spence
CEO, Capgemini Americas, and Director: Terrence R. (Terry) Ozan, age 60
CEO, India: Baru S. Rao
President, Asia Pacific: Paul Thorley
General Secretary and Human Resources: Alain Donzeaud
General Manager, Capgemini North America: Salil Parekh
Group Director of Communication: Philippe Grangeon
Group Director of Strategy: Pierre-Yves Cros
Global Financial Services Leader: Bertrand Lavayssière
Global Manufacturing, Retail & Distribution Leader: Bernard Helders
Global Marketing Manager and Global Energy & Utilities Leader: Colette Lewiner
Global Sales and Alliances Manager: Patrick Nicolet
Head of Investor Relations: Manuel Chaves d'Oliveira, age 42
Head of Press Relations: Sylvie Haurat, age 42
Auditors: PricewaterhouseCoopers; KPMG S.A.

LOCATIONS

HQ: Capgemini
    Place de l'Etoile, 11, rue de Tilsitt,
    75017 Paris, France
Phone: +33-1-47-54-50-00   **Fax:** +33-1-47-54-50-86
US HQ: 750 7th Ave., Ste. 1800, New York, NY 10019
US Phone: 212-314-8000   **US Fax:** 212-314-8001
Web: www.capgemini.com

Capgemini has operations in more than 30 countries.

2005 Sales

Europe	% of total
UK	25
France	24
Benelux	14
Central Europe	6
Nordic countries	6
Southern Europe	4
North America	20
Asia/Pacific	1
Total	**100**

PRODUCTS/OPERATIONS

2005 Sales

	% of total
Outsourcing	38
Technology services	33
Local professional services	16
Consulting	13
Total	**100**

Selected Services

Application management
Customer relationship management
Enterprise resource planning
Finance and employee transformation
Information technology consulting
Knowledge management
Management consulting
Outsourcing
Program management
Software development
Strategy consulting
Supply chain management
Systems integration
Training

COMPETITORS

Accenture	EDS
Affiliated Computer	Fujitsu Services
Services	Getronics
Atos Origin	HP Technology Solutions
Bain & Company	IBM Global Services
BearingPoint	Infosys
Booz Allen	LogicaCMG
Bull	McKinsey & Company
Capita	Perot Systems
CGI Group	Tata Consultancy
Computer Sciences Corp.	Unisys
Deloitte Consulting	Wipro Technologies
Dimension Data	

HISTORICAL FINANCIALS

Company Type: Public

Income Statement

FYE: December 31

	REVENUE ($ mil.)	NET INCOME ($ mil.)	NET PROFIT MARGIN	EMPLOYEES
12/05	8,236	167	2.0%	61,036
12/04	8,581	(490)	—	59,324
12/03	7,222	(247)	—	49,805
12/02	7,386	(539)	—	52,683
12/01	7,455	135	1.8%	57,760
Annual Growth	**2.5%**	**5.5%**	**—**	**1.4%**

Net Income History

Euronext Paris: CAP

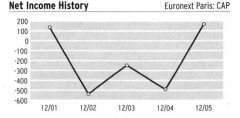

Carlsberg

If any company has thirst quenching down to a science, it's Carlsberg A/S, the owner of Carlsberg Breweries. In addition to the worldwide brewing operations of its flagship subsidiary, Carlsberg A/S also operates the Carlsberg Research Center, which houses 80 beer brewing laboratories. In 2004 the group acquired Swedish conglomerate Orkla's 40% stake in Carlsberg Breweries and the Germany-based beer brewer and distributor Holsten-Brauerei. Carlsberg has more than 90 production sites in 50 countries. The group is controlled by the Carlsberg Foundation, established in 1876 by founder J.C. Jacobsen.

Although most of the company's revenue comes from the sale of Carlsberg beers, the group also sells the Tuborg brand. Tuborg is one of the best-selling beers in Norway. Carlsberg also has a 50/50 joint venture, Baltic Beverages Holding (BBH), with UK brewer Scottish & Newcastle. Baltika Breweries, which is controlled by BBH, plans to merge with three other brewers in 2006 to make it the largest brewer in Russia.

Carlsberg's soft drink sales are generated mainly from licenses to produce drinks from Coca-Cola and Pepsi, but the company also produces regional beverages. In Denmark, Norway, and Sweden, Carlsberg produces leading brands of mineral water. It has divested its mineral water operations in Switzerland. Its portfolio also includes a number of local brands, such as Feldschlösschen (Sweden), Okocim (Poland), Pripps (Sweden), Ringnes (Norway), Koff (Finland), and Tetley's (the UK).

In addition to its beverage operations, the group is also involved to a lesser extent in property development and sales, primarily in Denmark. The company announced in 2006 that it expected to cut 400 jobs in the UK and it is closing its Valby brewery in Copenhagen.

Carlsberg is expanding through its Baltic Beverages Holding unit and other Eastern European businesses and through acquisitions in China and Germany.

A generally declining beer market in Western Europe, however, has prompted Carlsberg's decision to close about half of its breweries there.

HISTORY

Carlsberg stems from the amalgamation of two proud Danish brewing concerns. Captain J. C. Jacobsen founded the first of these in Copenhagen; his father had worked as a brewery hand before acquiring his own small brewery in 1826. Studious and technically minded, J. C. inherited the brewery in 1835. He opened the Carlsberg Brewery (named for his son Carl) in 1847 and exported his first beer (to the UK) in 1868. J. C. established the Carlsberg Foundation in 1876 to conduct scientific research and oversee brewery operations.

Carl, who conflicted with his father over brewery operations, opened a new facility (New Carlsberg) adjacent to his dad's in 1881. Both men bestowed gifts upon their city, such as a church, an art museum, a royal castle renovation, and Copenhagen Harbor's famous Little Mermaid statue. Father and son willed their breweries to the foundation, which united them in 1906.

Tuborgs Fabrikker was founded in 1873 by a group of Danish businessmen who wanted to establish a major industrial project (including a brewery) at Tuborg Harbor. Philip Heyman headed the group and in 1880 spun off all operations but the brewery.

Carlsberg and Tuborg became Denmark's two leading brewers. After WWII, both began marketing their beers outside the country. Between 1958 and 1972 they tripled exports and established breweries in Europe and Asia. Both brewers' desire to grow internationally influenced their decision to merge, which they did in 1969 as United Breweries.

During the 1980s the firm diversified, forming Carlsberg Biotechnology in 1983 to extend its research to other areas. It strengthened its position in North America through licenses with Anheuser-Busch (1985) and John Labatt (1988). United Breweries reverted to the old Carlsberg name in 1987.

Carlsberg and Allied-Lyons (which became Allied Domecq before being acquired by Pernod Ricard in 2005) combined their UK brewing, distribution, and wholesaling operations under the name Carlsberg-Tetley (now Carlsberg UK) in 1992, creating the UK's third-largest brewer (behind Bass and Courage).

The firm teamed up with India's United Breweries in 1995 to distribute Carlsberg beer on the subcontinent. Bass acquired Allied's 50% of Carlsberg-Tetley in 1996 but sold its stake to Carlsberg in 1997 upon orders from regulators. Also in 1997 Carlsberg and Coca-Cola set up Coca-Cola Nordic Beverages to bottle and distribute soft drinks in Nordic countries. That year Poul Svanholm retired after 25 years as CEO; he was replaced by Jørn Jensen.

Carlsberg acquired a 60% stake in Finnish brewer Sinebrychoff in 1998. Carlsberg then sold a 60% stake in Vingaarden to Finland's Oy Rettig (1999), sold its remaining 43% share of the Tivoli amusement park to Danish tobacco group Skandinavisk Tobakskompagni (2000), and reduced its 64% holding in Royal Scandinavia to 28% (2000). Carlsberg bought the beverage operations of Swedish firm Feldschlösschen Hürlimann in 2000 and agreed to combine brewing businesses with Norway-based Orkla in a deal worth $1.5 billion; Carlsberg Breweries was formed in February 2001 after both agreed to divest several brands and distribution rights to gain regulatory approval.

Carlsberg stopped production at Coca-Cola Nordic Beverages (the company still exists but has no operations) in 2001 because of conflicts with Orkla's Pepsi bottling contracts in Sweden and Norway; Carlsberg and Coca-Cola continued to produce and sell Coke in Denmark and Finland. In 2002 Carlsberg sold 32% of its Lithuanian brewery to Russia's Baltic Beverage Holding, a joint venture between Carlsberg and Scottish & Newcastle. That year Carlsberg also signed an agreement giving Carib Brewery Ltd., part of the ANSA McAl Group, the rights to brew and distribute Carlsberg Beer in selected areas of the Caribbean.

In January 2003 Carlsberg Breweries acquired an additional 27.5% stake in Pirinsko Pivo, a Bulgarian brewery, bringing its overall ownership to 94.5%. That same month it purchased the Chinese brewer Kunming in southeast China. Carlsberg bought a second Chinese brewer, Dali, in June 2003.

Chairman: Prof. Povl Krogsgaard-Larsen
EVP and CFO; CFO, Carlsberg Breweries: Jørn P. Jensen, age 42
CEO: Nils S. Andersen
EVP, Eastern Europe: Jørgen Buhl Rasmussen, age 50
SVP, Asia, Malawi, Balkan, and Export and Licence: Jesper Bjørn Madsen
SVP, Sales and Marketing: Alex Myers
SVP, Supply Chain and Procurement: Kasper Madsen
SVP, UK, Switzerland, Italy, and Portugal: Lars Fellman
VP, Business Development and Projects: Geir Nesheim
VP, Carlsberg Properties: Orla Kristensen
VP, Controlling: Morten Leth
VP, Corporate Communications: Anne-Marie Skov
VP, Group Accounting: Jan Rasmussen
VP, Human Resources: Vibeke Frank
VP, Legal Counseling: Ulrik Andersen
VP, Treasury and Risk Management: Jørgen Andersen
Chairman, Carlsberg Sweden: Paul Bergqvist, age 60
CEO, Carlsberg Sweden: Stig Sunde, age 42
Director, Export, Licence, and Duty Free: Thomas K. Jakobsen
Human Resources Director, Carlsberg Danmark: Thomas Kolber
Manager, Investor Relations: Mikael Bo Larsen
Auditors: KPMG; PricewaterhouseCoopers

LOCATIONS

HQ: Carlsberg A/S
1, Valby Langgade, DK-2500 Valby, Denmark
Phone: +45-3327-2727   **Fax:** +45-3327-4850
Web: www.carlsberg.com

2005 Sales

	% of total
Western Europe	70
Eastern Europe	
Baltic Beverages Holding	17
Other Eastern European operations	9
Asia	4
Total	**100**

COMPETITORS

Heineken
InBev
SABMiller
Scottish & Newcastle

HISTORICAL FINANCIALS

Company Type: Public

Income Statement

FYE: December 31

	REVENUE ($ mil.)	NET INCOME ($ mil.)	NET PROFIT MARGIN	EMPLOYEES
12/05	8,213	176	2.1%	30,000
12/04	6,596	87	1.3%	31,703
12/03	5,838	161	2.8%	31,531
12/02	5,015	143	2.8%	28,466
12/01	4,082	142	3.5%	27,368
Annual Growth	19.1%	5.6%	—	2.3%

Net Income History

Copenhagen: CARC

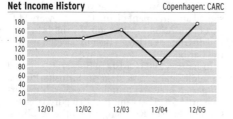

Carrefour

At the junction of groceries, merchandise, and services, you'll find Carrefour (which means "crossroads"). The world's second-largest retailer (behind Wal-Mart), Carrefour operates more than 12,000 stores under some two dozen names, including hypermarkets (Carrefour), supermarkets (Champion), convenience stores (Shopi, Marché Plus), discount stores (Dia, Ed), and cash-and-carry stores (Promocash) in about 30 countries in Europe, Latin America, and Asia. France accounts for nearly half of the retailer's sales. Carrefour secured its spot as the #1 European retailer (based on sales) when it merged with food retailer Promodès early in 2000 and raised its banner over those stores.

Carrefour is an originator of hypermarkets — huge department store and supermarket combinations that sell food, clothing, electronics, and household appliances, among other items, at a discount. It is consolidating many of its banners under the Carrefour name for hypermarkets and Champion for supermarkets.

The French retail giant is in the express lane toward growth. Unable to build new stores in its homeland due to regulations protecting smaller stores, Carrefour expands through acquisitions at home and abroad. Between 2006 and 2008 the company plans to open 100 hypermarkets; almost half of the openings will be in Asia, with an emphasis on China. Brazil, Italy, and Turkey will also account for a large number of new stores. All of the new stores will be outside of France.

Carrefour is China's largest foreign retailer (ahead of Wal-Mart), with about 300 hypermarkets, supermarkets, and discount stores in some 20 cities.

Closer to home, Carrefour is in the midst of an expansion drive in Italy, where it is already the second-largest retailer via subsidiary Carrefour Italia. It's also expanding in Poland where it has agreed to acquire the Polish operations (some 180 supermarkets and 15 hypermarkets) of Dutch grocer Royal Ahold. Previously, Carrefour purchased a dozen Hypernova hypermarkets in Poland from the Dutch chain. The French firm is expanding in Cyprus and Turkey as well.

Carrefour has about 885 hypermarkets, supermarkets, and discount stores in Latin America (including the 110-plus store Norte grocery chain in Argentina, and about 370 outlets in Brazil where it continues to expand), and about 425 outlets in seven Asian countries, including China, South Korea, and Taiwan. In South Korea, where Carrefour holds a relatively weak market position, the retailer has agreed to sell its 32 stores to local fashion retailer E.Land for about $1.9 billion.

The retailer launched its own mobile phone service, Carrefour Mobile, at all 218 of its hypermarkets in France in late 2006. Rival Auchan launched a similar product earlier in the year.

The Halley family owns about 20% of Carrefour's shares.

HISTORY

Although its predecessor was actually a supermarket opened by Marcel Fournier and Louis Defforey in a Fournier's department store basement in Annecy, France, the first Carrefour supermarket was founded in 1963 at the intersection of five roads (Carrefour means "crossroads"). That year Carrefour opened a vast store, dubbed a hypermarket by the media, in Sainte-Genevieve-des-Bois, outside Paris.

The company opened outlets in France and moved into other countries, including Belgium (1969), Switzerland (1970 — the year it went public), Italy and the UK (1972), and Spain (1973). Carrefour stepped up international expansion during the mid-1970s after French legislation limited its growth within the country.

Carrefour exported its French-style hypermarkets to the US (Philadelphia) in 1988. Scant advertising, limited selection, and a union strike led Carrefour to close it US operations in 1993. Carrefour opened its first hypermarket in Taiwan in 1989. The next year it formed Carma, a 50-50 joint venture with Groupama, to sell insurance. Carrefour paid over $1 billion for two rival chains (the bankrupt Montlaur chain and Euromarche) in 1991.

Daniel Bernard replaced Michel Bon, the hard-charging expansion architect, in 1992 after a 50% drop in first-half profits. A year later Carrefour partnered with Mexican retailer Gigante to open a chain of hypermarkets in Mexico. (In 1998 Carrefour bought Gigante's share of the joint venture.) In 1996 the company bought a 41% stake in rival GMB (Cora hypermarket chain) and sold its 11% stake in US warehouse retailer Costco (it now owns 20% of Costco UK). The next year Carrefour allowed 16 hypermarkets owned by Guyenne et Gascogne, Coop Atlantique, and Chareton to operate under the Carrefour name. It expanded into Poland in 1997 and the Czech Republic in 1998.

Its biggest acquisition (at that time) came in 1998 when Carrefour acquired French supermarket operator Comptoirs Modernes (with about 800 stores under the Stoc, Comod, and Marché Plus flags).

In 1999 Carrefour announced a deal even bigger than the one for Comptoirs Modernes — a $16.3 billion merger with fellow French grocer Promodès, which operated more than 6,000 hypermarkets, supermarkets, convenience stores, and discount stores in Europe. Paul-Auguste Halley and Leonor Duval Lemonnier founded Promodès in Normandy, France, in 1961.

In 2000 Carrefour bought Belgian retailer GB (about 500 stores). In 2003 it entered the Scandinavian market through a franchise partnership and supply agreement with Norwegian grocer NorgesGruppen. In late 2003, Carrefour's discount chain Ed acquired 44 Treff Marche shops in France from German retailer Edeka.

In 2004 Carrefour opened its first Champion supermarket in Beijing. In September it entered Norway with six Meny Champion discount supermarkets in Oslo, in partnership with Norway's NorgesGruppen.

In February 2005 Luc Vandevelde, the former chairman of troubled British retailer Marks and Spencer, succeeded Daniel Bernard as nonexecutive chairman of Carrefour. Concurrently, ex-CFO José-Luis Duran was named CEO. In November the French retailer acquired full ownership of three of its Chinese hypermarket joint ventures from its local partners: Kunming Department Store Co., a unit of China's Kunming Sinobright (Group) Co.; Hunan Yiyou Commercial Trade Co.; and Xinjiang Grandscape Investment Co.

In July 2006 Carrefour acquired 98% of the share capital and 99% of the voting rights of Hyparlo, which operates stores under the Carrefour banner in France and Romania.

EXECUTIVES

Chairman: Luc Vandevelde, age 55
Chairman, Management Board: José-Luis Duran, age 40
Management Board Member, Human Resources, Communications, Legal, Quality and Risks, International Partnerships, and Convenience France: Jacques Beauchet, age 54
Management Board Member, Dia, Food Sales and Organization, Systems, and Supply Chain: Javier Campo, age 50
Management Board Member, Sales, Italy, Spain, Belgium, and Other European Countries: José Maria Folache, age 45
Management Board Member, Hypermarkets: Guy Yraeta, age 53
Operational Director, Latin America: Eric Uzan, age 46
Operational Director, Supermarkets, France: Thierry Garnier, age 39
Operational Director, Spain: Gilles Petit
Operational Director, Other European Countries: Gilles Roudy
Operational Director, Dia Europe: Javier de la Pena
Operational Director, Italy: Didier Fleury
Operational Director, Convenience and Cash & Carry, France: Gérard Dorey
Operational Director, Other Asian Countries: Noël Prioux
Operational Director, Dia Spain: Ricardo Curras
Operational Director, Belgium: Marc Oursin
CEO, China: Éric Legros
Manager, Grocery Sales: Juan Cubillo
Managing Director, Asia: Philippe Jarry
Managing Director, Supermarkets Group: Philippe Pauze
General Counsel and Secretary: Etienne van Dyck
Media Relations: Christian d'Oléon
Investor Relations Contact: David Shriver
Auditors: KPMG Audit; Deloitte & Associés

LOCATIONS

HQ: Carrefour SA
6, avenue Raymond Poincaré, 75016 Paris, France
Phone: +33-1-53-70-19-00   **Fax:** +33-1-53-70-86-16
Web: www.carrefour.com

Carrefour has operations in about 30 countries, including Argentina, Bahrain, Belgium, Brazil, China, Colombia, Cyprus, Dominican Republic, Egypt, France, Greece, Indonesia, Italy, Malaysia, Martinique, Oman, Poland, Portugal, Qatar, Romania, Saudi Arabia, Singapore, South Korea, Spain, Switzerland, Taiwan, Thailand, Tunisia, Turkey, and the United Arab Emirates.

2005 Stores

	No.
Europe	
France	3,831
Other countries	6,681
Latin America	885
Asia	424
Partner countries (franchised)	207
Total	**12,028**

2005 Sales

	% of total
Europe	
France	48
Other countries	38
Asia	8
Latin America	6
Total	**100**

PRODUCTS/OPERATIONS

2005 Stores

	No.
Hard discount stores	5,451
Supermarkets	2,455
Hypermarkets	926
Other stores	3,196
Total	**12,028**

2005 Sales

	% of total
Hypermarket	59
Supermarket	18
Hard discount	8
Other	15
Total	**100**

Selected Operations and Banners

Hypermarkets
  Carrefour
Supermarkets
  Champion
  GB
  Globi
  GS
  Marinopoulos
  Norte
  Super GB
  Super GS
  Unic
Hard discount stores
  Dia
  Ed
  Minipreco
Other stores
  Cash-and-carry stores
  Docks Market
  Promocash
  Puntocash
Convenience stores
  8 à Huit
  Di per Di
  GB Express
  Marché Plus
  Proxi
  Shopi

Other Operations

Carfuel (petroleum products)
Comptoirs Modernes (supermarkets)
Costco UK (20%, warehouse club)
Erteco (hard-discount stores)
Financiera Pryca (46%, consumer credit, Spain)
Fourcar B.V. (investments, The Netherlands)
GlobalNetXchange (Internet-based supply exchange joint venture)
Immobiliere Carrefour (real estate)
Ooshop (online shopping)
Prodirest (catering)
Providange (auto centers)
S2P (60%, consumer credit)

COMPETITORS

AEON
ALDI
Auchan
Brasileira de Distribuição
Casino Guichard
Dairy Farm International
Delhaize
Disco
Edeka Zentrale
E.Leclerc
Eroski
Falabella
Galeries Lafayette
Generale Supermercati
Globex Utilidades
ITM Entreprises
Ito-Yokado
La Rinascente
Lidl & Schwarz Stiftung
Marui
METRO AG
Migros
Primisteres Reynoird
Rallye
REWE-Zentral
Royal Ahold
SHV Holdings
Tengelmann
Tesco
Wal-Mart

HISTORICAL FINANCIALS

Company Type: Public

Income Statement

FYE: December 31

	REVENUE ($ mil.)	NET INCOME ($ mil.)	NET PROFIT MARGIN	EMPLOYEES
12/05	88,227	1,701	1.9%	436,747
12/04	99,119	1,892	1.9%	430,695
12/03	88,474	2,045	2.3%	419,040
12/02	72,035	1,440	2.0%	396,662
12/01	61,551	1,121	1.8%	382,821
Annual Growth	**9.4%**	**11.0%**	**—**	**3.3%**

Net Income History

Euronext Paris: CA

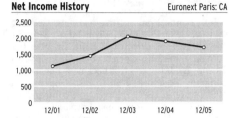

	12/01	12/02	12/03	12/04	12/05

Casino Guichard-Perrachon

You won't hit the jackpot at Casino Guichard-Perrachon, but odds are you'll go home with the groceries. The company owns and operates 9,300-plus hypermarkets (mostly Géant), supermarkets (Casino, Franprix, and Monoprix, to name a few), restaurants (Casino Cafétéria), convenience stores, and discount stores (Leader Price). Casino is the #1 convenience store operator in France (primarily Petit Casino, but other banners include Vival and Spar). Most of its stores are in France, but it has more than 2,000 outlets in a dozen countries worldwide, including Brazil, Mexico, Thailand, and the US (where Casino owns about 53% of the Smart & Final warehouse grocery chain). France's Rallye SA owns about 50% of Casino.

Nearly 60% of Casino's sales are made at home in France. The company's 125 Géant hypermarkets (warehouse-style stores that sell groceries and other merchandise) contribute about 40% of revenues, with supermarkets and convenience stores a close second. Casino is France's fifth-largest supermarket company. Casino Cafétéria operates about 245 eating places in varying size and cuisines, including Poncholito (Tex-Mex) and La Pastaria (Italian). Casino is also active in e-commerce (Caly-online).

Casino has an option until the end of 2008 to increase to 51% the 38% stake it purchased in 2002 in Dutch supermarket operator Laurus.

Price competition from discounters has hurt Casino and rival Carrefour as French shoppers eschew their traditional hypermarkets and supermarkets for discount stores. Flat sales preceded the abrupt departure of CEO Pierre Bouchut who was replaced by Casino's chairman and controlling shareholder Jean-Charles Naouri. Taking on both jobs, Naouri said, will accelerate decision making.

Casino is shoring up its balance sheet through a plan to dispose of non-core assets by the end of 2007. To that end, Casino has said it may sell its equity stake in Smart & Final and the French supermarket operator spun off its property company Mercialys. Following the IPO, Casino holds a 75% stake in Mercialys. Casino has sold its Polish hypermarkets to METRO AG and its Leader Price supermarkets there to Britain's Tesco for a total of about $1.2 billion.

The French retailer also owns a majority stake in Vindémia, an operator of supermarkets and hypermarkets in Asia and Africa.

HISTORY

Frenchman Geoffroy Guichard married Antonia Perrachon, a grocer's daughter, in 1889 in Saint-Etienne, France. Three years later Geoffroy took over his father-in-law's general store (a converted "casino" or musical hall). In 1898 the company became Société des Magasins du Casino. By 1900, when it became a joint stock company, Casino had 50 stores; it opened its 100th store in 1904. That year the company introduced its first private-label product: canned sardines. In 1917 Guichard named his two sons, Mario and Jean, as managers.

By WWI there were about 215 branches, more than 50 in Saint-Etienne. From 1919 to the early 1920s the company opened several factories to manufacture goods such as food, soap, and perfumes. In 1925 the elder Guichard retired, leaving the day-to-day operations of Casino to his two sons. (Geoffroy died in 1940.) WWII took a heavy toll on the company: About 70 Casino stores were leveled and another 450 were damaged.

The company began opening cafeterias in 1967, and in 1976 it formed Casino USA to run them. Casino USA bought an interest in the California-based Thriftimart volume retailer in 1983, renaming the company after Thriftimart's Smart & Final warehouse stores.

Casino grew by acquiring companies across France, including CEDIS (16 hypermarkets, 116 supermarkets, and 722 smaller stores in eastern France; 1985) and La Ruche Meridionale (18 hypermarkets and 112 supermarkets in southern France, 1990). Casino bought nearly 300 hypermarkets and supermarkets from Rallye SA in 1992, giving Rallye about 30% of the company. The company opened its first hypermarket in Warsaw, Poland, in 1996.

Rival Promodès made a roughly $4.5 billion hostile takeover bid for Casino in 1997. Guichard family members voted against the Promodès offer, instead backing a $3.9 billion friendly offer from Rallye (increasing their stake to nearly 50%). Casino also launched a massive counterattack — buying more than 600 Franprix and Leader Price supermarket stores from food manufacturer TLC Beatrice and acquiring a 21% stake in hypermarket chain Monoprix. Promodès withdrew its bid four months later.

Casino expanded internationally in the late 1990s, acquiring stakes in food retailers in Argentina (Libertad), Uruguay (Disco), Colombia (Almacenes Exito SA), Brazil (Companhia Brasileira de Distribuicao), and Thailand (Big C, the country's largest retailer). It also opened its first hypermarket in Taichung, Taiwan.

Expansion in France included a joint venture (called Opera), formed in 1999 with retailer Cora SA to buy food and nonfood goods for the Casino and Cora stores, and the acquisition of 100 convenience stores (converted to the Petit Casino banner) in southwest France from retailer Guyenne et Gascogne.

Casino acquired 100 Proxi convenience stores in southeast France in 2000 from Montagne (most became Vival franchises) and more than 400 convenience stores (Eco Service and others) from Auchan. In July 2002, Casino bought a 38% stake in Laurus NV, its financially troubled Dutch rival. Laurus operates nearly 2,000 supermarkets in the Netherlands, Spain, and Belgium. (Soon after, Casino sold Laurus's unprofitable stores in Spain and Belgium.)

Chief executive Pierre Bouchut unexpectedly left Casino in March 2005. Jean-Charles Naouri, the company's chairman and controlling shareholder, replaced him. In May Casino took joint control of Brazil's leading food retailer, Companhia Brasileira de Distribuição, along with the family of Abilio Diniz. Previously, Casino held a minority stake in the supermarket chain. Casino spun off some of its shopping center assets in an October IPO for part of its real estate assets in France, including shopping mall properties adjacent to its hypermarket and supermarkets, as well as the land under its cafeterias.

In January 2006 Casino increased its stake in Colombia's biggest retailer Exito to nearly 39%. The company in July sold its 19 hypermarkets in Poland to METRO AG, its German rival, for about $1.1 billion as part of its asset disposal program. In September Casino sold its 50% stake in its Taiwanese subsidiary, Far Eastern Geant, to its joint venture partner Far Eastern Department Stores.

EXECUTIVES

Chairman and CEO: Jean-Charles Henri Naouri, age 57
Executive Deputy Managing Director, French Operations and Group Marketing: Jacques-Edouard Charret
Executive Deputy Managing Director, Finance and Administration: Jacques Patrice Marie Joseph Tierny
Deputy Managing Director, European Hypermarkets (France and Poland): Daniel Sicard
Human Resources Director: Thierry Bourgeron, age 53
Director, Planning and Strategy: Hervé Daudin
Merchandise and Supply Chain: Jean-Michel Duhamel
Neighbourhood Stores and Supermarkets Director: François Duponchel
Real Estate and Expansion Director: Jacques Ehrmann
Non-food Activities Director: Joël Luc Albert Mornet
Deputy Managing Director, European Supermarkets (France and the Netherlands), and Restaurants: Jean-Brice Hernu, age 52
Director, Business Development, Asia: Christian P. Couvreux, age 53
Director, Finance: Pascal Announ, age 40
President and CEO, Smart & Final: Etienne Snollaerts, age 50
Director, Asian and Indian Ocean region (Thailand, Taiwan, Vietman, Reunion Island, Madagascar, Mauritius, and Mayotte): André Mercier
Director, Business Development and Real Estate: Daniel Pain
Director, Customer Care: Philippe Marxgut
Director, Latin American region (Argentina, Uruguay, Venezuela, Brazil, and Colombia): Francis André Mauger
Director, Financial Communications: Marc Maillet
Director, Financial Communications: Rhomas Rault
International Activities Director: Xavier Desjobert
Auditors: Bernard Roussel; Ernst & Young Audit

LOCATIONS

HQ: Casino Guichard-Perrachon S.A.
24, rue de la Montat, 42008 Saint-Etienne, France
Phone: +33-4-77-45-31-31   **Fax:** +33-4-77-45-38-38
Web: www.casino.fr

Casino Guichard-Perrachon has operations in France and about a dozen other countries (Argentina, Brazil, Colombia, Mexico, the Netherlands, Poland, Taiwan, Thailand, Uruguay, the US, Venezuela, and Vietnam).

2005 Sales

	% of total
France	58
Latin America	19
Netherlands	10
North America	5
Asia	4
Indian Ocean	2
Poland	2
Total	**100**

2005 Stores

	No.
France	
Petit Casino	2,098
Vival	1,348
Spar	787
Franprix	622
Corners, Relais, Shell, Elf & others	582
Leader Price	421
Casino	360
Monoprix-Prisunic	303
Casino Cafétéria	247
Géant	126
Affiliates & other	269
Netherlands	700
Brazil	556
US	236
Poland	288
Colombia	99
Mexico	13
Venezuela	67
Argentina	61
Thailand	50
Uruguay	48
Indian Ocean	43
Taiwan	14
Vietnam	3
Total	**9,341**

PRODUCTS/OPERATIONS

Selected Operations

Banque du Groupe Casino (financial services)
Big C (68%, Thailand and Vietnam)
Caly-online (40%, online services)
Cdiscount (51%; discount-priced books, CDs, DVDs, CD Roms, videos online)
C-mesCourses (40%, Internet grocery shopping)
C-online (40%, shopping hub for stores and services)
Casino (supermarkets)
Casino Cafétéria (restaurants, cafeterias, catering)
Casino Enterprise (non-food operations)
Casino USA (99.7%, with a 57% stake in Smart & Final)
Cativen (58%)
Cada (supermarkets in Venezuela)
Companhia Brasileira de Distribuição (34%)
Barateiro (discount stores in Brazil)
Eletro (specialty shops in Brazil)
Extra (hypermarkets in Brazil)
Pão de Açúcar (supermarkets in Brazil)
Sendas (supermarkets in Brazil)
Disco (50%, supermarkets in Uruguay)
Devoto (48%, supermarkets in Uruguay)
Eco Service (convenience stores)
Exito (39%, supermarkets in Colombia)
Franprix (70%, supermarkets)
Géant (hypermarkets)
Imagica (photo and digital imaging processing)
Komogo (multimedia specialist in PCs, software and video games, telephony, books)
Leader Price (70%, supermarkets)
Les Chais Beaucairos (wine production, bottling, and sales)
Libertad (hypermarkets in Argentina)
Monoprix (49%, supermarkets)
Opera (50%, joint-purchasing venture with Cora SA)
Petit Casino (convenience stores)
Spar (convenience stores)
Vival (convenience stores)

COMPETITORS

ALDI
A.P. Møller - Mærsk
Auchan
Carrefour
Costco Wholesale
E.Leclerc
Groupe Flo
Guyenne et Gascogne
IGA
ITM Entreprises
Kingfisher
METRO AG
Migros
Primisteres Reynoird
Royal Ahold
Tesco
Wal-Mart

HISTORICAL FINANCIALS

Company Type: Public

Income Statement

	REVENUE ($ mil.)	NET INCOME ($ mil.)	NET PROFIT MARGIN	EMPLOYEES
12/05	27,009	836	3.1%	208,403
12/04	31,603	666	2.1%	212,603
12/03	28,848	618	2.1%	206,760
12/02	23,957	467	1.9%	115,757
12/01	19,473	336	1.7%	106,736
Annual Growth	**8.5%**	**25.6%**	**—**	**18.2%**

Net Income History

Euronext Paris: CO

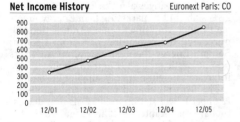

CASIO COMPUTER

CASIO COMPUTER wants a watch on every arm and a handheld computer in every pocket. The company makes a wide range of electronics for consumers, including calculators, cell phones, digital cameras, portable TVs, watches, and musical keyboards. CASIO COMPUTER also manufactures computing and communications devices, like PDAs, and electronic cash registers. The company likes to seek superlatives in its products: the G-Shock watch (1983) boasted that it was the toughest (able to survive a fall from a three-story building), and the EXILIM camera (2002) claimed to be the world's thinnest (roughly the size of a credit card). The three younger brothers of late founder Tadao Kashio continue to run CASIO COMPUTER.

CASIO COMPUTER generates most of its sales from consumer electronic products (calculators, digital cameras, and electronic dictionaries) while the rest of revenues are derived from electronic components. To combat sluggish consumer electronics sales, the company is focusing on three primary product categories: digital cameras, electronic dictionaries, and cell phones.

The company launched a joint venture with Hitachi in 2004; the new business unit, Casio Hitachi Mobile Communications Co., produces mobile phone handsets.

HISTORY

In 1942 Tadao Kashio started a Tokyo-based machine shop, Kashio Manufacturing. His brother, Toshio, later joined him. After reading about a 1946 computing contest in which an abacus bested an electric calculator, Toshio, an inventor, wrote a note to himself: "Abacus is human ability; calculator is technology." In 1950 he began developing a calculator. The other Kashio brothers — Yukio, a mechanical engineer, and Kazuo, who took over sales — joined the company in the 1950s.

The brothers incorporated in 1957 as CASIO COMPUTER, an anglicization of the family name. That year the company launched its first product, an electric calculator featuring an innovative floating decimal point display; it was the first Japanese-built electric calculator. CASIO COMPUTER took advantage of new transistor technology to create electronic calculators, and in 1965 it introduced the first electronic desktop calculator with memory. The company began exporting to the US in 1970.

In the 1970s only CASIO COMPUTER and Sharp emerged as significant Japanese survivors of the fierce "calculator war." CASIO COMPUTER's strategy of putting lots of new functions on a proliferation of small models and selling them at rock-bottom prices worked not only with calculators but with digital watches as well. The company introduced its first digital watch in 1974 and went on to dominate that market.

CASIO COMPUTER expanded its product line into electronic music synthesizers (1980), pocket TVs (1983), and thin-card calculators (1983). Determined to break away from the production of delicate timepieces, CASIO COMPUTER introduced shock-resistant (G-Shock) digital watches in 1983. In the mid-1980s sales were hurt by a rising yen and stiff price competition from developing Asian nations. The company responded by releasing sophisticated calculators for such specialized users as architects and insurance agents. To offset the effects of the yen's heightened value in the late 1980s, CASIO COMPUTER moved manufacturing to Taiwan, Hong Kong, South Korea, California, and Mexico. Kazuo Kashio was named president in 1988.

In 1990 CASIO COMPUTER established CASIO COMPUTER Electronic Devices to sell LCDs and chip-on-film components. In 1991 the company acquired a capital interest in Asahi, a producer of communications equipment and light electrical appliances. CASIO COMPUTER moved much of its production overseas in 1994, primarily to Thailand and Malaysia, after the high yen contributed to a nearly 28% drop in exports.

The company introduced its first digital camera in 1995. The next year CASIO COMPUTER launched its CASSIOPEIA handheld PC, and in 1997 it entered the US pager market. In 1998 the company formed subsidiary CASIO Soft to develop Microsoft-based software for handheld PCs and other mobile devices.

In 2000 the company restructured its management system, and cut expenses (particularly research and development). The following year it instituted a three-year plan designed to strengthen its digital imaging, mobile networking, and electronic components businesses.

EXECUTIVES

Chairman: Toshio Kashio
President and CEO: Kazuo Kashio
EVP and Representative Director: Yukio Kashio
Managing Director: Fumitsune Murakami
Managing Director: Yoshio Ono
Managing Director: Yozo Suzuki
Managing Director: Akinori Takagi
Director: Akira Kashio
Director: Atsushi Mawatari
Director: Tadashi Takasu
Director: Kouichi Takeichi
Director: Susumu Takashima
Corporate Officer: Harunori Fukase
Corporate Officer: Ichiro Ohno
Corporate Officer: Naomitsu Satoh
Corporate Officer: Eiichi Takeuchi
Corporate Officer: Tomimoto Umeda
Corporate Officer: Atsushi Yazawa
Corporate Officer: Osamu Ohno
Corporate Officer: Yuichi Masuda
Corporate Officer: Isamu Shimozato
Corporate Auditor: Hironori Daitoku
Corporate Auditor: Yoshinobu Yamada
Corporate Auditor: Takeshi Honda
Auditors: KPMG AZSA & Co.

LOCATIONS

HQ: CASIO COMPUTER CO., LTD.
(Casio Keisanki Kabushiki Kaisha)
6-2, Hon-machi 1-chome, Shibuya-ku,
Tokyo 151-8543, Japan
Phone: +81-3-5334-4111
US HQ: 570 Mount Pleasant Ave., Dover, NJ 07801
US Phone: 973-361-5400   **US Fax:** 973-537-8910
Web: www.casio.co.jp

CASIO COMPUTER has subsidiaries in Canada, China, France, Germany, Hong Kong, India, Japan, Malaysia, Mexico, Singapore, South Korea, Taiwan, Thailand, the UK, and the US.

2006 Sales

	% of total
Asia	
Japan	59
Other countries	17
Europe	14
North America	10
Total	**100**

PRODUCTS/OPERATIONS

2006 Sales

	% of total
Electronics	82
Electronic components	18
Total	**100**

Selected Products

Electronics
  Consumer products
    Calculators
    Digital cameras
    Electronic dictionaries
    Electronic musical instruments
    Label printers
  Mobile Network Solutions
    Cell phones
    Pocket PCs
  System Equipment
    Electronic cash registers
    Office computers
    Printers
    Data projectors
  Timepieces
    Analog watches
    Clocks
    Digital watches

Electronic Components and Other Products
  Electronic components
    Bump processing consignments
    Carrier tape
    LCDs
    TCP assembly and processing consignments
  Other
    Factory automation
    Molds
    Toys

COMPETITORS

Canon	Ricoh
Fujitsu	Roland
Hewlett-Packard	Samsung Group
Hitachi	SANYO
IBM	Seiko
Matsushita	Sharp
Motorola	Sony
NEC	Timex
Nikon	Toshiba
Palm	Yamaha
Philips Electronics	

HISTORICAL FINANCIALS
Company Type: Public

Income Statement
FYE: March 31

	REVENUE ($ mil.)	NET INCOME ($ mil.)	NET PROFIT MARGIN	EMPLOYEES
3/06	4,935	202	4.1%	12,673
3/05	5,198	200	3.9%	12,140
3/04	4,956	134	2.7%	12,929
3/03	3,676	47	1.3%	12,691
3/02	2,881	(188)	—	14,670
Annual Growth	14.4%	—	—	(3.6%)

Net Income History
Exchange: Tokyo

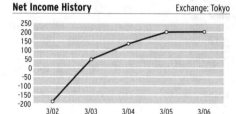

Centrica

Centrica is centered on energy. The UK's largest gas supplier, Centrica serves 11.1 million households under the British Gas brand. It also serves 5.9 million residential electricity customers, and it supplies electricity and gas to 909,000 businesses. Other operations include gas and electricity production, wholesale energy marketing, international retail energy marketing, drain cleaning services, and appliance sales. Expanding geographically, the company has acquired Dutch reseller Oxxio BV, and a 51% stake in Belgian generator SPE SA (which it agreed to boost to 76% in 2006). Its growing Direct Energy unit (aka Centrica North America) supplies gas and power to residential customers in Canada and the US.

In 2005 the company sold its One.Tel telecom interest to Carphone Warehouse for about $273 million in order to focus more on its energy businesses.

Centrica's natural gas production interests — the company has proven and probable reserves of 2.6 trillion cu. ft. — account for about 25% of its supply. The company is expanding its gas production operations in the UK and North America to support its supply businesses; it also has gas storage operations.

Through its aggressive acquisition strategy in North America, Centrica has gained some 5.1 million retail power and gas supply customers, including more than 800,000 in the purchase of two Texas retail electric providers from American Electric Power and 1 million through the purchase of Canadian Utilities' retail businesses. These companies have been grouped together under the firm's Centrica North America division (Direct Energy).

Centrica has also acquired Electricity Direct, a UK commercial retail supplier serving nearly 1 million customers. The company has entered continental Europe by investing in Belgium energy supplier Luminus, and it has entered the Spanish retail market. Centrica has purchased several power plant interests in the UK to support its supply business, and it is buying plants in North America as well. It has also agreed to pay Kerr-McGee more than half a billion dollars for stakes in North Sea natural gas fields.

The company has completed the sale of its Goldfish financial services operations to partner Lloyds TSB, and it has sold its Automobile Association business to equity firms CVC and Permira for $3.2 billion.

HISTORY

William Murdock invented gas lighting in 1792. In 1812 the Gas Light and Coke Company of London was formed as the world's first gas supplier to the public, and by 1829 the UK had 200 gas companies.

In the second half of the 19th century, the gas industry began looking for new uses for the fuel. Gas stoves were introduced in 1851, the geyser water heater was invented in 1868, and in 1880 the first gas units to heat individual rooms were developed.

Gas companies countered the emerging electricity industry by renting gas stoves at low prices and installing gas fittings (stove, pipe, and lights) in poor homes with no installation charges or deposits. By 1914 the UK had 1,500 gas suppliers.

The electricity industry soon made major strikes against the gas industry's dominance. In 1926 the government began reorganizing the fragmented electricity supply industry, building a national power grid and establishing the Central Electricity Generating Board to oversee it.

The gas industry was nationalized in 1949, and 1,050 gas suppliers were brought under the control of the British Gas Council. Still, the gas industry was losing. Supplying gas was more expensive than generating electricity: Gas was seen as a power supply of the past. The Gas Council sought to change that image through an aggressive marketing campaign in the 1960s, touting gas as a modern, clean fuel. Other factors played a part in its re-emergence: The Clean Air Act of 1956 steadily reduced the use of coal for home heating, liquefied natural gas was discovered in the North Sea, and OPEC raised oil prices in the 1970s. When natural gas was introduced, most of the old gasworks were demolished, and the British Gas Council (which became the British Gas Corp. in 1973) set about

converting, free of charge, every gas appliance in the UK to natural gas.

As Margaret Thatcher's government began privatizing state industries, the British Gas Corp. was taken public in 1986. Freed from government control, British Gas expanded its international exploration and production activities. When the US gas industry began deregulating, British Gas formed joint venture Accord Energy in 1994 with US gas trader Natural Gas Clearinghouse (now NGC) to sell gas on the wholesale market.

With the opening of the UK gas-supply market (which began regionally in 1996 and went nationwide in 1998), British Gas split into two public companies to avoid a conflict of interest between its supply business and its monopoly transportation business. In 1997 it spun off Centrica, the retail operations, and BG (now BG Group), which received the transportation business and the international exploration and production operations.

The UK electricity supply market began opening up to competition in 1998, and Centrica won 750,000 UK electricity customers, most of them also gas customers. In 1999 it bought the Automobile Association, which provided roadside service to motorists and sells insurance, from AA members. In 2000 Centrica began offering telecom services in the UK.

Centrica moved into North America in 2000 by purchasing two Canadian companies: natural gas retailer Direct Energy Marketing and gas production company Avalanche Energy. It gained a 28% stake in US marketing firm Energy America through the Direct Energy transaction and purchased the remaining 72% from US firm Sempra Energy the next year. Continuing its non-domestic strategy, Centrica bought a 50% interest in Belgium energy supplier Luminus.

The firm purchased 60% of the 1,260-MW Humber Power station in 2001, its first domestic power plant interest. It also acquired the UK operations of Australia's One.Tel, and it bought Enron's European retail supply business, Enron Direct, for $137 million.

In 2002 Centrica purchased the retail energy services business of Canadian pipeline company Enbridge for $637 million. Later that year Centrica acquired 200,000 retail customer accounts in Ohio and Pennsylvania from NewPower.

EXECUTIVES

Chairman: Roger M. Carr, age 59
Chief Executive: W. Sam H. Laidlaw, age 50
Group Finance Director and Managing Director, Europe: Phillip K. (Phil) Bentley, age 47
CIO: Peter Brickley
Director Corporate Strategy, Development, and M&A: Mark Crosbie
Group General Counsel and Company Secretary: Grant Dawson
CEO, North America: Deryk I. King
Director Corporate Affairs: Catherine May
Managing Director, British Gas Business: Ian Peters
Managing Director, Centrica Energy and Director: Jake Ulrich
Group Director, Human Resources: Anne Minto
Managing Director, British Gas Home Services: Chris Weston
Director Investor Relations: Kieran McKinney
Director Media Relations: Andrew Hanson
Finance Director, Centrica Energy: Andrew Le Poidevin
Energy Director, British Gas: Lois Hedg-Peth
Auditors: PricewaterhouseCoopers LLP

LOCATIONS

HQ: Centrica plc
Millstream, Maidenhead Road,
Windsor SL4 5GD, United Kingdom
Phone: +44-1753-494-000   **Fax:** +44-1753-494-001
Web: www.centrica.co.uk

Centrica has operations in Belgium, the Netherlands, Canada, Spain, the UK, and the US.

PRODUCTS/OPERATIONS

Selected Subsidiaries and Affiliates

British Gas Services Limited (installation and servicing of gas heating systems)
British Gas Trading Limited (energy supply)
Centrica Business Services (British Gas Business, commercial energy supply)
  Electricity Direct (UK) Ltd (retail energy supply)
Centrica Energía SL (Luseo Energía, retail energy supply, Spain)
Centrica Energy Management Group (industrial sales and wholesaling, gas production, and energy trading)
  Accord Energy Limited (wholesale energy trading)
  Centrica Resources Limited (gas production)
  Hydrocarbon Resources Limited (gas production)
Centrica North America (retail energy supply)
  CPL Retail Energy LP (energy sales, US)
  Direct Energy LP (energy sales, US)
  Direct Energy Marketing Limited (energy sales, Canada)
  Energy America LLC (energy sales, US)
  WTU Retail Energy LP (energy sales, US)
Centrica Storage Holdings Limited (gas storage)
Luminus N.V. (50%, retail energy supply, Belgium)
Oxxio BV (energy supply, The Netherlands)

COMPETITORS

AGL Resources	npower
British Energy	Scottish and Southern
Calor	Energy
Community Energy	Scottish Power
EDF Energy	STASCO
Electrabel	TNP Enterprises
E.ON Ruhrgas	United Utilities
E.ON UK	Viridian Group
Gasunie	Western Power
Gaz de France	Distribution
Green Mountain Energy	

HISTORICAL FINANCIALS

Company Type: Public

Income Statement

FYE: December 31

	REVENUE ($ mil.)	NET INCOME ($ mil.)	NET PROFIT MARGIN	EMPLOYEES
12/05	23,136	1,743	7.5%	35,410
12/04	35,255	2,662	7.6%	43,414
12/03	31,880	889	2.8%	42,573
12/02	22,960	767	3.3%	38,051
12/01	18,299	469	2.6%	31,550
Annual Growth	6.0%	38.9%	—	2.9%

Net Income History

Pink Sheets: CPYYY

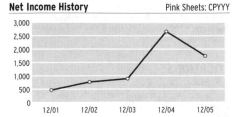

Club Méditerranée

Hobbled by a reputation that has become passe, Club Méditerranée (popularly known as Club Med) is struggling to revamp its 1970s "sea, sex, and sun" image and overcome recent losses. With more than 1 million guests annually, the company has 150 leisure operations in more than 40 countries, including about 120 resort villages, 12 villas, a cruise ship operation, and a French tour operator. Nearly 60% of its visitors come from Europe. Former chairman Philippe Bourguignon, who breathed life into Euro Disney, returned Club Med to profitability and tried new concepts such as Club Med World recreational centers. Worldwide hotel operator Accor owns about 29% of the company.

The series of global natural disasters occurring in 2005 and 2006 (tsunamis, hurricanes, and terrorist attacks) have had a palpable impact on Club Med's operations. As a result, the company had to shut down five resorts and villages in addition to coping with its customers perception of the overall psychological risks of tourism. In 2005, the company launched an initiative to reposition its brand as more elegant and refined. The following year, it announced it was spending more than $100 million through 2008 to renovate and upgrade its villages and resorts. The company has also relied heavily on sharing resources, skill sets, and taking advantage of synergies with its primary shareholder, Accor, in order to increase revenue and stay profitable.

In 2004 Accor acquired its 29% equity interest in Club Med, including the 21% from Exor and 8% from Caisse des Depots et Consignations. The acquisition made Accor the core shareholder in Club Méditerranée.

HISTORY

Belgian diamond cutter Gérard Blitz dreamed up the Club Méditerranée concept as an escape from the post-WWII doldrums in Europe. In 1950 he convened a gathering of charter members on the island of Majorca, where the group slept in tents, cooked their own food, and had a great deal of fun. The Club Med philosophy was born — vacation villages in exotic locations, combining low prices and simple amenities with community spirit and entertainment.

Frenchman Gilbert Trigano, who provided the tents for that first gathering, came on board as managing director of the company in 1954 and launched a major expansion drive. Polynesian-style huts replaced the tents at the newly opened location in Greece in 1954, and in 1956 the company set up its first ski resort in Leysin, Switzerland. Club Méditerranée was incorporated the following year.

The Rothschild Group was the company's main shareholder from 1961 until 1988, providing the capital for much of Club Méditerranée's expansion. The company went public in 1966.

Club Méditerranée expanded into the cruise line business during the late 1960s, but surly crews and the outbreak of the Arab-Israeli War in 1967 scuttled plans. In the late 1960s Club Méditerranée gained a foothold in the US, opening an office in New York and a hotel in Northern California. In the 1970s the company became one of the biggest leisure groups in France through a series of mergers and acquisitions. The 1970s and 1980s also saw the company hone its freewheeling, anything-goes image.

Club Med, Inc., was set up in New York in 1984 to handle the company's business in the Americas and Asia. Trigano relaunched the cruise line concept in 1990. Club Méditerranée's expansion came to a crashing halt in 1991 as the company suffered its first-ever loss. Political unrest in its prime tourist locations plagued operations, leading in 1993 to a major loss and Trigano's resignation (though he remained as a director). His son Serge took over as chairman that year and set about cutting costs. Lawsuits plagued the company in 1996 — one involving the fatal crash of a Club Med plane, the other involving a blackface minstrel show.

Board members looking to turn around losses created a new position for Serge Trigano in 1997 and replaced him as chairman with Philippe Bourguignon, who had helped revive Euro Disney. To boost profits, the company sold its *Club Med 1* cruise ship, as well as other assets that were outside the scope of its core resort business. It also phased out its lower-priced Club Aquarius resorts as part of its efforts to refocus on a single brand. But Club Med suffered record losses in 1997, and Trigano and his father later resigned.

With its restructuring plan in full swing in 1998, Club Med made its way back into the black. The company began renovating its village resorts and consolidating and centralizing its administrative offices. Club Med also implemented a new advertising campaign in 1998 and announced plans to open new ski resorts in the US and Canada, as well as Club Med at Paris Bercy, a recreational center in Paris. In 1999 Club Med bought French travel company Jet Tours Holding.

In 2000 it branched into e-commerce through its creation of Internet subsidiary Club Med On Line. It also purchased its third US village in 2000 in Crested Butte in Colorado. Club Med branched into the body building business in 2001 when it purchased Gymnase Club, a chain of 200 fitness clubs since renamed Club Med Gym.

However, the company closed 17 of its resorts (12 just for the winter) following September 11, 2001, to help cut costs in a diminished market for tourism. Amid losses for a second consecutive year, Bourguignon resigned in 2002.

EXECUTIVES

Chairman and CEO: Henri Giscard d'Estaing, age 50
EVP and CFO: Michel Wolfovski
SVP Development, Construction, and Assets Management: Bertrand Julien-Laferrière
SVP Human Resources: Olivier Sastre
President and CEO, Club Med Americas: Cedric Gobilliard
President, Jet Tours, Club Med Discovery, and Oyyo: Laurence Berman
SEVP, Europe: François Salamon
SVP Sales and Transportation, Club Med North America: Paula Hayes
Director Marketing: Sabina Wehring
Director Sales and Marketing, Club Med Mexico: Robert Cao
Commercial Director, Club Med Sales Canada: Brenda Kyllo
Public Relations Manager, Club Med Americas: Kate Moeller
Press Contact, Worldwide: Thierry Orsoni
Auditors: Cogerco-Flipo; Ernst & Young Audit

LOCATIONS

HQ: Club Méditerranée S.A.
11 rue Cambrai, 75019 Paris, France
Phone: +33-1-53-35-35-53 **Fax:** +33-1-53-35-32-01
Web: www.clubmed.com

Club Méditerranée has operations in about 40 countries.

2005 Sales

	% of total
Europe	
France	37
Other countries	22
Americas	12
Asia	8
Jet tour operations	18
Other	3
Total	**100**

Selected Club Med Resort Locations

Australia	Mauritius
Bahamas	Mexico
Croatia	Montenegro
Cuba	Morocco
Dominican Republic	New Caledonia
Egypt	Portugal
France	Saint Lucia
French West Indies	Saint Martin
Greece	Senegal
Haiti	Spain
Indonesia	Switzerland
Israel	Thailand
Italy	Tunisia
Ivory Coast	Turkey
Japan	Turks and Caicos
Malaysia	US
Maldives	

PRODUCTS/OPERATIONS

Selected Brands

Club Med
Club Med Business
Club Med Cruises
Club Med Discovery
Club Med Gym
Club Med Voyages
Club Med World
Jet Tours

COMPETITORS

Carlson	Rank
Carnival	Royal Caribbean Cruises
ClubCorp	Sandals Resorts
Disney	Société du Louvre
Hilton	Sol Meliá
Hyatt	Starwood Hotels & Resorts
Kerzner International	TUI
Marriott	Vail Resorts

HISTORICAL FINANCIALS

Company Type: Public

Income Statement

FYE: October 31

	REVENUE ($ mil.)	NET INCOME ($ mil.)	NET PROFIT MARGIN	EMPLOYEES
10/05	1,915	5	0.3%	20,333
10/04	2,004	(54)	—	18,694
10/03	1,914	(109)	—	20,333
10/02	1,758	(61)	—	22,518
10/01	1,829	(63)	—	25,150
Annual Growth	**1.2%**	**—**	**—**	**(5.2%)**

Net Income History

OTC: CLMDY

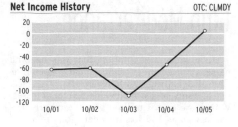

CNP Assurances

Running to the post office and bank? Buy some insurance while you're out. CNP Assurances is France's top personal life insurer. In addition to life insurance and other savings products, it sells health, death and disability, and other personal risk coverage and pensions. CNP sells its products primarily through La Poste, the French postal service, and La Caisse Nationale des Caisses d'Epargne, the state savings banks; together these two channels account for about 75% of CNP's sales. These partners are also shareholders in the company, together owning about 35%. Another French paragovernmental organization, Caisse des Dépôts et Consignations, owns more than 35%.

CNP's savings products, including life insurance, account for nearly 80% of premiums; personal risk products such as long-term-care, death and disability, and loan insurance make up about 15%.

The firm has distribution deals with France's Treasury and its civil service mutual insurance companies, and such financial institutions as Mutualité Française, the umbrella organization for France's mutual health insurers. CNP has been gradually moving abroad, taking stakes in neighboring countries' leading insurers (primarily in Portugal) as they are privatized.

CNP also controls Caixa Seguros in Brazil. The company's holdings in Argentina were slammed by the economic depression in that country, but CNP is restructuring them for future profitability. The insurer is also working to launch a joint venture with China's postal service.

HISTORY

CNP Assurances traces its origins to three government insurance entities established in the mid-19th century. Caisse nationale d'assurance en cas d'accident ("accident insurance") was formed in 1868. Caisse nationale d'assurance en cas de décès ("death and disability insurance") was formed in 1848, while Caisse de retraite pour la vieillesse ("retirement pensions") followed two years later. These two organizations were merged in 1949, forming Caisse nationale d'assurance sur la vie. Ten years later it was merged with the government's accident insurance bureau to form Caisse Nationale de Prévoyance ("provident society"). CNP was put under the domain of the French government's investment banking arm, Caisse des Dépôts et Consignations (CDC).

Over the years CNP earned a reputation for specializing in certain risks, introducing a variety of life and personal risk insurance and pension and savings products. During the 1980s the company

enjoyed a healthy growth rate around 20% annually as more French individuals and companies began investing in insurance products.

In 1987 CNP became a national public establishment, making it independent from, though still owned by, the government. The next year the company teamed with Centre National des Caisses d'Epargne et de Prévoyance (now La Caisse Nationale des Caisses d'Epargne or Caisses d'Epargne) to form Ecureuil-Vie, a joint venture to sell CNP's insurance and savings products in the national savings banks. That year it partnered with Portugal's Caixa Geral de Depósitos to create new products.

In the early 1990s CNP was among several entities the government announced it would privatize. To prepare for the change, the company reorganized and became CNP Assurances; the government sold a large chunk of the firm to CDC, La Poste, and Caisses d'Epargne, reducing its stake to 42%. During this time CNP passed rival Union des Assurances de Paris (now part of AXA) to become France's top life insurer.

Privatization lurched along until 1995, when it was put on hold for elections; the Socialist government that came to power was less enthusiastic about the sale of government assets than its predecessor. The process hit another snag two years later when some workers protested, fearing they'd lose their status as civil servants and the perks associated with it. Also in 1997 CNP became the major shareholder of Polish life insurer Polisa-Zycie when it raised its stake from 26% (purchased 1996) to 46%. By 1998 privatization was back on track, and the government sold a 22% stake in CNP to the public. CDC, La Poste, and Caisses d'Epargne raised their interests to their current levels. Before the year's end, CNP bought majority stakes in Portuguese insurers Global and Global Vida.

Expansion abroad continued in 1999 when CNP announced plans to set up operations in China. That year it teamed with the UK's Prudential for cobranded insurance products. In 2000 the company extended its selling arrangement with Caisses d'Epargne to 2005. In 2001 CNP moved into the Brazilian market with the purchase of 51% of insurer Caixa Seguros. In 2003 it sold off its share of Italian bancassurance company Carivita.

EXECUTIVES

Chairman: Edmond Alphandéry
Vice Chairman: Jean-Paul Bailly, age 60
CEO: Gilles Benoist, age 60
CFO: Antoine Lissowski
Director, International Operations:
Xavier Larnaudie-Eiffel
Director, Management and Innovation: Jean-Pierre Walbaum, age 60
Director, Partnerships and Business Development: Gérard Ménéroud, age 59
Personnel Director: Dominique Pagant
Secretary to the Advisory Board: Hugues de Vauplane
Investor Relations Officer: Brigitte Molkhou
Auditors: KPMG Audit; Mazars & Guérard; Calan Ramolino & Associés

LOCATIONS

HQ: CNP Assurances SA
4 place Raoul Dautry, 75716 Paris, France
Phone: +33-1-42-18-88-88   **Fax:** +33-1-42-18-86-55
Web: www.cnp.fr

CNP Assurances has operations in Europe and South America.

2004 Premium Sales

	% of total
Europe	
France	96
Other countries	1
Latin America	3
Total	**100**

PRODUCTS/OPERATIONS

2004 Sales

	% of total
Premiums	72
Investment income	27
Other	1
Total	**100**

2004 Premium Sales By Channel

	% of total
Savings banks	40
French Post Office	36
Mutual insurers & local authorities	7
Companies	5
Financial institutions	5
Foreign subsidiaries	4
French Treasury	3
Total	**100**

2004 Premium Sales By Segment

	% of total
Savings	75
Pensions	9
Loan insurance	8
Personal risk insurance	6
Health insurance	1
Property & casualty	1
Total	**100**

Selected Subsidiaries and Affiliates

Age d'Or Expansion
Assurbail (99%, property leasing)
Assurposte (50%, insurance)
Caixa assessoria (52%, services, Brazil)
Caixa capitalização s/a (26%, insurance, Brazil)
Caixa Consorcio S/A (52%, insurance, Brazil)
Caixa Seguros (52%, insurance, Brazil)
Caixa vida e previdência s/a (51%, insurance, Brazil)
Cantis (50%)
CDC Ixis Asset Management (20%, finance company)
Cegape (42%)
CNP Caution
CNP IAM (insurance)
CNP Immobilier (property)
CNP International (reinsurance)
CNP Seguros de Vida (76%, insurance, Argentina)
Ecureuil vie (50%, insurance)
Filassistance (50%)
Fongépar (49%)
Forestière CDC (50%)
Gespré Europe (40%)
Global (84%, insurance, Portugal)
Global Vida (84%, insurance, Portugal)
GPM Assurances SA (33%)
Informatique CDC (30%)
Investissement Trésor Vie (insurance)
Parc de Monfort (50.8%)
Préviposte (insurance)
Previsol AFPJ (30%, insurance, Argentina)
Previsol Seguros de Retiro (30%, insurance, Argentina)
Previsol Seguros de Vida (30%, insurance, Argentina)
Provincia Seguros de Vida (40%, insurance, Argentina)
Sicac (property)

COMPETITORS

AGF
Allianz
AXA
BNP Paribas
Crédit Agricole
Eureko
Groupama
ING

HISTORICAL FINANCIALS

Company Type: Public

Income Statement

FYE: December 31

	ASSETS ($ mil.)	NET INCOME ($ mil.)	INCOME AS % OF ASSETS	EMPLOYEES
12/04*	248,538	858	0.3%	4,501
12/03	210,022	731	0.3%	3,998
12/02	161,479	599	0.4%	3,982
12/01	128,722	518	0.4%	—
12/00	124,628	439	0.4%	—
Annual Growth	**18.8%**	**18.2%**	**—**	**6.3%**

*Most recent year available

2004 Year-End Financials

Equity as % of assets: 3.0%
Return on assets: 0.4%
Return on equity: 12.4%
Long-term debt ($ mil.): —
Sales ($ mil.): 40,514

Net Income History

Euronext Paris: CNP

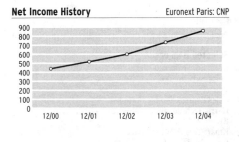

Coles Group

Coles Group (formerly Coles Myer) is a top dingo among Australian retailers. The company is one of the country's largest retailers, with 2,500-plus supermarkets and other stores throughout Australia and New Zealand. Coles sells apparel and general merchandise through the discount chains Target, Kmart, and Officeworks. (Coles holds the rights from Kmart and Target to use the Kmart and Target names in Australia and New Zealand, although it is discontinuing its relationship with Kmart.) The company is restructuring its Bi-Lo food, liquor, and fuel business and converting it to the Coles brand. Coles sold its Myer department store chain in mid-2006. It changed its name in November 2006 to Coles Group Ltd. to reflect the Myer sale.

Coles has rejected as too low a $13.7 billion offer for the company from a consortium of investors led by US buyout firm Kohlberg Kravis Roberts & Co.

In another swipe at Woolworths, which sells gasoline at its supermarkets to drive business, Coles has forged a discount fuel alliance with Royal Dutch Shell to become the operator of Shell's network of 584 service stations in Australia. The Shell deal has sparked a fuel price war with Woolworths. However, competition authorities are giving the Coles-Shell tie-up another look, and could scuttle the deal.

The retailer has expanded throughout Australia by acquiring supermarket (Franklins), liquor (Theo's Liquor and Mr Corks), and hotel operators (Hedley Hotel Group), and converting the outlets to its own banners. In 2006 Coles acquired Hedley Hotel Group; entailed in the deal, beyond the more than 36 hotels, was more than 100 bottle shops and more than 15 1st Choice

Liquor Superstores in Queensland, Australia's fastest-growing state. Previously in Queensland Coles spent about $100 million on 11 new stores and remodeled 15 others in 2004. Overall, the retailer plans to add about 200 stores by 2007.

The company boosted its holdings in Queensland in late 2006 when it acquired Mr Corks Liquor Group for $51 million and folded the operation into its Coles Myer Liquor Group unit. Comprising 35 hotels, 102 retail liquor stores, and sites for some 17 1st Choice Liquor Superstores, the Mr Corks buy gives Coles a hefty leg up in Queensland, one of the fastest-growing liquor markets in Australia.

Coles became Australia's #1 online seller of groceries in 2003 when it acquired ShopFast.

HISTORY

After studying US and UK chain-store retailing, including the five-and-dime stores of S. S. Kresge, George James Coles opened his first "3d, 6d, and 1/-" discount variety store in 1914 in a working-class neighborhood of Collingwood, Australia. Coles expanded to a larger store five years later. With the formation of G. J. Coles & Coy in 1921, Coles spent the 1920s and 1930s opening stores in other Australian cities. The company went public in 1927.

Following WWII the firm embarked on a major acquisition binge. Coles & Coy bought Selfridges (Australasia — New South Wales, 1950), F&G Stores (Victoria, 1951), and Penneys (Queensland, 1956). The company expanded into food retailing in 1958 with the purchase of the 54-store John Connell Dickins chain. A year later it acquired Beilby's of South Australia and, in 1960, the Matthews Thompson group of 265 outlets in New South Wales.

Coles & Coy opened its first major discount store, Colmart, in 1968 and opened its first Kmart the following year through a joint venture with S. S. Kresge. In 1978 it bought out the renamed Kmart Corporation's interest in return for stock.

The company bought several liquor store chains in 1981, including Liquorland and Mac the Slasher (converted to the Liquorland banner). Coles & Coy began opening Super K food and general merchandise stores in 1982. Two years later it bought Katies, a women's apparel chain with 117 stores, of Melbourne.

Coles & Coy became Coles Myer in 1986 when it merged with the Myer Emporium chain. Founded in 1900 by Sidney Myer, the company went public in 1925 and began opening Target stores in 1970. At the time of the merger, Myer was Australia's #3 retailer and largest department store chain, with 56 department stores, 68 Target stores, 122 Fosseys variety stores, and 45 Country Road stores (spun off in 1987).

In 1987 Coles Myer entered discount food retailing with the acquisition of 25 Bi-Lo supermarkets. The next year it moved outside Australia when it opened a Kmart in Auckland, New Zealand. Coles Myer shares were listed on the New York Stock Exchange in 1988. In 1989 Myer Direct, the company's new direct mail order business, was established by Myer Stores.

In 1993 Coles Myer repurchased the 21.5% stake owned by Kmart while continuing to use the Kmart name in Australia and New Zealand.

When finance director Philip Bowman was fired in 1995, he sued the company for wrongful dismissal. Bowman claimed he was investigating a 1990 transaction that cost the company $18 million while indirectly benefiting chairman

Solomon Lew by the same amount. The deal resulted in Lew's ouster as chairman, though he stayed on the board. Bowman's suit was settled for $1.1 million. In 1997 former chairman and CEO Brian Quinn was found guilty of conspiring to defraud Coles Myer of $3.5 million (used to pay for renovations to his Melbourne home) and sentenced to four years in prison.

In 1997 and 1998 Coles Myer started a dozen concept stores, including Myer Megamart (furniture and electronics), Target Home (home furnishings), and Essentially Me (health and beauty items). The trend continued in 1999 with let's eat (a combination restaurant and grocery).

In 2001 the company sold its Myer Direct online business. John Fletcher became CEO in 2001 following the retirement of Dennis Eck. Under Fletcher, Coles Myer began in 2002 its biggest restructuring in more than a decade, but met resistance from dissident board member and former executive chairman Solomon Lew. (Following a messy public brawl over the future direction of the company, Lew, Coles Myer's largest shareholder, was voted off the board.) Stan Wallis' five-year stint as chairman came to an end prematurely when he was replaced by director Rick Allert.

Coles Myer bought the Australian operations of Office Depot in 2003. It also acquired Australia's biggest online food retailer, ShopFast.

In June 2006 Coles Myer sold 61 Myer department stores to Newbridge Capital and its US parent, Texas Pacific Group, for about $1 billion to better focus on regaining market share from rival Woolworths.

EXECUTIVES

Chairman: Richard H. (Rick) Allert, age 63
Managing Director, CEO, and Director:
John E. Fletcher, age 54, $2,887,620 pay
CFO: Fraser MacKenzie, $928,771 pay
Chief Officer, Corporate and Property Services:
Tim Hammon, $914,882 pay
Managing Director, Operations, Supermarkets:
Peter Merritt
Managing Director, Officeworks: Joe Barberis
Managing Director, Target: Launa Inman, $707,373 pay
Managing Director, Kmart: Larry Davis, $1,597,353 pay
CIO: Peter Mahler
Group General Manager, Corporate Affairs:
Pamela Catty
Group General Manager, Human Resources: Ian Clubb
General Manager, Supermarket Marketing: Tom Lemke
Group General Manager, Supply Chain: Andrew Potter
Group General Manager, Risk and Internal Audit:
Fiona Bennett
**Group General Manager, Marketing and Managing
Director, Coles Express and Coles Myer Liquor Group:**
Mick McMahon
Auditors: PricewaterhouseCoopers

LOCATIONS

HQ: Coles Group Limited
800 Toorak Rd., Tooronga, Victoria 3146, Australia
Phone: +61-3-9829-3111   **Fax:** +61-3-9829-6787
Web: www.colesgroup.com.au

2005 Sales

	% of total
Australia	99
New Zealand	1
Total	**100**

PRODUCTS/OPERATIONS

2005 Stores

	No.
Food, liquor & fuel	
Coles Myer Liquor Group	669
Coles Express	597
Coles	505
Bi-Lo	214
Target	255
Kmart	232
Officeworks	95
Myer	61
Megamart	9
Total	**2,637**

2005 Sales

	% of total
Food, liquor & fuel	68
Kmart	11
Target	9
Myer	8
Officeworks	3
Megamart	1
Total	**100**

Selected Banners

Bi-Lo Supermarkets
Coles Supermarkets
Coles Online
Coles Express Service Stations
Harris Technology
Kmart
Kmart Tyre & Auto Service
Liquorland
Liquorland Direct
Megamart
Officeworks
Shopfast
Target
Theo's Liquor
Vintage Cellars

COMPETITORS

ALDI	Harris Scarfe Holdings
Barbeques Galore	Harvey Norman Holdings
Body Shop	InterTAN
Esprit Holdings	Metcash
Foodland Associated	Woolworths Limited

HISTORICAL FINANCIALS

Company Type: Public

Income Statement

FYE: Last Sunday in July

	REVENUE ($ mil.)	NET INCOME ($ mil.)	NET PROFIT MARGIN	EMPLOYEES
7/05	27,696	388	1.4%	182,338
7/04	22,897	337	1.5%	176,108
7/03	17,929	295	1.6%	162,414
7/02	13,756	166	1.2%	164,272
Annual Growth	26.3%	32.6%	—	3.5%

2005 Year-End Financials

Debt ratio: 36.8%
Return on equity: 16.7%
Cash ($ mil.): 334

Current ratio: 1.09
Long-term debt ($ mil.): 918

Net Income History

Pink Sheets: CMYRF

	7/01	7/02	7/03	7/04	7/05

Compass Group

Look in almost any direction and you'll likely see a foodservice operation run by this company. Compass Group is the world's largest foodservice company with operations in more than 90 countries. It provides hospitality and foodservice for a variety of businesses and such public sector clients as cultural institutions, hospitals, and schools. It also offers vending services, as well as catering and consessions services for a number of events and sports venues. Its foodservice brands include Chartwells, Crothall, and Rail Gourmet. In addition, Compass is a franchisee of such well-known chains as Burger King, Pizza Hut, and Sbarro.

The company has been aggressive in seeking out new contracts to extend its concessions and hospitality business throughout the world. In the UK it has renewed relationships with Prudential and the UK National Health Service, while in the rest of Europe it struck new deals with Alcatel (now Alcatel-Lucent) in Germany and Bouygues Arc de Seine in France. In North America, Compass has inked deals to provide corporate foodservice to telecommunications giant AT&T as well as institutional services to the University of Pennsylvania (through its Morrison Management Specialists unit).

Strategic acquisitions have also been important to the company's global expansion. In 2006 Compass acquired High Food Services, a vending and cafeteria operator with locations in Maryland and Pennsylvania. It also acquired the 51% of upscale restaurateur and concessionaire Levy Restaurants it didn't already own for about $250 million. Meanwhile, the company sold a 75% stake in its US quick-casual sandwich chain, Au Bon Pain, back to its management in 2005. The following year Compass sold its travel hospitality businesses for more than $3 billion, including UK motorway operator Moto and US-based Creative Host Services. Sydney-based Macquarie Bank bought the UK motorway business while EQT Partners (part of Sweden's Investor AB) acquired the rest of the operation, which also included Select Service Partner.

Compass is also going through a transformation in its executive ranks as chairman Francis Mackay departed in 2006 and was replaced by Centrica CEO Roy Gardner. Compass CEO Michael Bailey also stepped down; he was replaced by Richard Cousins, formerly chief executive of building materials manufacturer BPB.

HISTORY

Compass Group was formed in 1987 when management bought out the catering business of London-based food and spirits giant Grand Metropolitan (now Diageo) for $260 million. The company went public the next year, listing on the London Stock Exchange. Gerry Robinson, CEO at the time, left in 1991 to take a position with British TV programming giant Granada Group (renamed ITV plc in 2004), where he helped that company diversify into foodservice operations. Finance director Francis Mackay took over as CEO.

Believing that real growth in the catering industry could come from size and economies of scale, Mackay orchestrated a $2.5 billion acquisition plan over the next five years. In 1992 Compass bought Traveller's Fare (now Upper Crust), a railway caterer, from British Rail. The company expanded into airports the following year with the acquisition of Scandinavian Airlines System's catering operations. Then in 1994 Compass bought Canteen Corporation, the US's third-largest vending and foodservice company.

Compass achieved its goal of becoming the world's largest caterer in 1995 with the acquisition of France's Eurest International, putting it ahead of Sodexho and Granada. Mackay calmed London investors nervous about the pace of Compass' acquisitions by selling off its hospital management operations and paying lip service to focusing on organic growth. Later that year Compass was awarded the world's largest foodservice contract, a $250-million, five-year deal with IBM.

By 1996 the company seemed to have forgotten all about organic growth, buying Service America, and then Daka International and France's SHRM in 1997. The next year Compass solidified its position in the airport markets with a five-year licensing deal for use of the T.G.I. Fridays brand, joining Taco Bell, Pizza Hut, Burger King, and Harry Ramsden's fish and chip shops in Compass' quiver of branded airport outlets.

In 1999 CEO Mackay became group chairman, leaving the reins to Compass' chief of North American operations, Michael Bailey. The company's US acquisitions quickly paid off that year with a contract to serve 90% of the food venues at the 2002 Winter Olympics in Salt Lake City. In 2000 the company merged with UK hospitality giant Granada Group (the combined firm became Granada Compass), which then spun off its media operations as a separate company, Granada Media. Late that year it bought Boston-based bakery/café chain Au Bon Pain.

The new company got a quick divorce in 2001 when Granada Compass decided to demerge and make Compass Group public again. Compass Group later sold the Le Meridien hotel operations it gained from the Granada merger to Nomura International for nearly $3 billion. (The firm kept the Travelodge chain but sold it in 2003.) The company then began making purchases, including Morrison Management Specialists for $563 million, the 66% it didn't already own in Selecta Group, UK vending machine company Vendepac, and health-care services management company Crothall Services. Compass lost seven operating sites during the September 11 terrorist attacks on the World Trade Center. Late in 2001 Compass strengthened its presence in Japan with the $277 million acquisition of Seiyo Food Systems, that country's #2 foodservices group.

In 2002 Compass signed arguably the industry's largest contract ever, a $200 million a year deal to feed Chevron employees around the world. In 2003 the company sold its Travelodge motel business and Little Chef diners to private equity firm Permira for $1.14 billion, a 5% discount to the asking price. Compass became the first non-Chinese company to provide food in stations and on trains operated by the Shanghai Railway Administration in 2004. In addition, the firm bought Creative Host Services in 2004.

In 2005, Compass sold a 75% stake in Au Bon Pain back to a management group, retaining a 25% interest in the quick-casual chain. The following year it sold its travel hospitality businesses, including Creative Host and UK motorway operator Moto, to private investors for more than $3 billion.

EXECUTIVES

Chairman: Sir Roy A. Gardner, age 60
Group Chief Executive and Director:
Richard J. Cousins, age 46
Group Finance Director and Director: Andrew Martin, age 46, $419,000 pay
CEO, Business and Industry Operations: Chris Copner
CEO, Americas Division, and CEO, North America and Director: Gary R. Green
CEO, Compass Group UK & Ireland Ltd.:
Ian El-Mokadem, age 38
CEO, Emerging Markets: Alain F. Dupuis, age 60
Director, Corporate Affairs: Paul Kelly
Director, Corporate Policy and Communications:
Michael Young
Director, Reward Group: David Walker
Auditors: Deloitte & Touche LLP

LOCATIONS

HQ: Compass Group PLC
Compass House, Guildford Street, Chertsey, Surrey KT16 9BQ, United Kingdom
Phone: +44-1932-573-000   **Fax:** +44-1932-569-956
US HQ: 2400 Yorkmont Rd., Charlotte, NC 28217
US Phone: 704-329-4000   **US Fax:** 704-329-4160
Web: www.compass-group.com

Compass Group's food catering and concession services operate in more than 90 countries.

2005 Sales

	% of total
Europe	
UK	23
France	8
Germany	4
Italy	3
Spain	3
Switzerland	2
The Netherlands	2
Other countries	8
North America	32
Japan	4
Australia	2
Other regions	9
Total	**100**

PRODUCTS/OPERATIONS

2005 Sales

	% of total
Business & industry	36
Travel concessions	14
Healthcare	13
Education	11
Sports & leisure	10
Defense, offshore & remote	8
Vending	8
Total	**100**

Selected Operating Units

Canteen Vending (vending machines)
Chartwells (education foodservices)
Eurest (workplace foodservice contracts)
FLIK (upscale foodservices)
Letheby & Christopher (sporting and leisure events)
Medirest (health care services)
Morrison Management Specialists (health care foodservice)
Restaurant Associates (sporting and leisure events)
Scolarest (education foodservices)
Selecta (vending machines)

COMPETITORS

Albert Abela
ARAMARK
Centerplate
Delaware North
Elior
Rentokil Initial
Sara Lee Foodservice
Sodexho Alliance
SYSCO

HISTORICAL FINANCIALS

Company Type: Public

Income Statement

FYE: September 30

	REVENUE ($ mil.)	NET INCOME ($ mil.)	NET PROFIT MARGIN	EMPLOYEES
9/05	22,391	2	0.0%	410,074
9/04	21,176	324	1.5%	402,375
9/03	18,806	307	1.6%	412,574
9/02	16,574	347	2.1%	392,352
9/01	12,839	215	1.7%	344,830
Annual Growth	**14.9%**	**(69.8%)**	**—**	**4.4%**

2005 Year-End Financials

Debt ratio: 113.4%
Return on equity: 0.0%
Cash ($ mil.): 560
Current ratio: 0.85
Long-term debt ($ mil.): 4,567

Net Income History

London: CPG

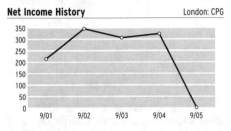

Creative Technology

Creative Technology wants PC audiophiles to be entertained. The firm is a leading maker of digital entertainment products, including portable audio players (Zen), PC sound cards (Sound Blaster), and digital cameras. Creative also makes modems and CD and DVD drives for PCs. Subsidiaries include Cambridge Soundworks (PC speakers), 3Dlabs, Creative Labs, and E-MU/ENSONIQ (audio chips and electronic musical instruments). Creative's top customers include computer manufacturers Dell, Gateway, and Hewlett-Packard. Co-founder and CEO Sim Wong Hoo owns about 30% of Creative.

Competitive pricing is key to Creative's marketing strategy, particularly in the portable audio market where it runs into the dominant presence of Apple's iPod. The company uses low-cost manufacturing at its own facilities in China and Malaysia and through subcontractors in those countries and Singapore.

The firm has been shifting its focus in recent years. Sales of personal entertainment products represented a third of Creative's sales in 2004. In 2006, however, sales of the same products generated 65% of its overall revenue. During the same period, Creative's audio and speakers operations decreased to both 13% in 2006 revenue while the firm ramped up its operations in Europe, surpassing sales in the Americas.

To cater to customers' needs in the fickle personal niche of the digital entertainment products market, Creative has beefed up product offerings and shuttered underperforming units. In late 2005 Creative released a high-end addition to its Zen line; with 30GB of storage the Zen Vision:M features music, video, and photo capabilities. Also, Creative announced in 2006 that its 3Dlabs unit will refocus its smaller graphics operation on the portable handheld device market rather than the professional workstation graphics market. To this end, the company purged staff.

HISTORY

In 1981 Sim Wong Hoo (chairman and CEO) and Ng Kai Wa (later joined by Chay Kwong Soon) used a $6,000 stake to found Creative Technology as an engineering services company. It began making Apple II clones for the Chinese market in 1984; two years later it started producing PC clones. From 1983 to 1988 most of Creative's revenues came from PCs.

With stiff competition in the PC market, Sim shifted Creative's focus to sound cards and other PC enhancements. The company introduced its first Sound Blaster audio card in 1989; Sound Blaster soon became the industry standard. That year Creative launched PJS, an artificial intelligence-based Chinese-language operating system, and Views, a complementary word processor and desktop publisher with a more than 70,000-character alphabet. Also in 1989 Tandy (now RadioShack) ordered a large supply of Game Blasters — a sound card targeted at gamers — for its 8,000 Radio Shack stores, giving Creative a strong foothold in the US.

In 1991 Creative launched the first of its market-dominating upgrade kits, the Sound Blaster Multimedia Upgrade Kit, a software package bundled with a high-performance CD-ROM drive and a set of software applications. The company went public in 1992.

The growing popularity of multimedia products was music to Creative's ears. More computers were selling with sound cards and multimedia capabilities pre-installed, so the company signed deals to supply manufacturers including Compaq and Dell. Creative also diversified: In 1993 it acquired ShareVision Technology (videoconferencing products) and E-MU Systems (digital sound production systems).

The company also tried its hand at communication products. In 1994 it acquired modem maker Digicom (now Broadxent). The next year it released Phone Blaster, which combined voice mail, e-mail, and fax transmission functions.

Cracks began to show in Creative's progress in 1995. The slowing of the sound board market caused a steep drop in profits and prompted the company to restructure and refocus on sound products. Ng resigned that year, and Chay left in 1996. Creative introduced Graphics Blaster add-on graphics accelerator cards and signed a deal for Samsung to build its CD-ROM drive products that year.

Opting to add new technology quickly through acquisitions, in 1997 Creative bought speaker maker Cambridge Soundworks; ENSONIQ, manufacturer of audio chips and electronic musical instruments (now part of E-MU/ENSONIQ); and the NetMedia Group of core logic chipset maker OPTi. In 1998 the company acquired Silicon Engineering, a maker of communications, multimedia, and storage integrated circuits. In 1999 Creative debuted the Nomad MP3 player, which played digitally encoded music downloaded from PCs.

Sharp declines in Creative's Internet investments and the broader electronics market led the company to restructure its operations in 2001. Creative closed a factory, cut its staff by 10%, wrote off substantial losses in its investment portfolio, and recentered its operations on its core lines of digital audio products.

In 2002 the company acquired graphics chip maker 3Dlabs in a deal worth about $105 million. Years later, in 2006, Creative whittled away at 3Dlabs' operations and refocused the graphics unit on the portable handheld device market.

EXECUTIVES

Chairman and CEO: Sim Wong Hoo, age 51
CFO: Ng Keh Long, age 47
President, 3Dlabs: C. Hock Leow, age 52
President, Creative Labs: Craig McHugh
Director, Corporate Communications:
 Phil O'Shaughnessy
Director, Product Marketing: Brad Anderson
Senior Brand Manager, Portable Media: Lisa O'Malley
Auditors: PricewaterhouseCoopers

LOCATIONS

HQ: Creative Technology Ltd.
 31 International Business Park, Creative Resource,
 609921, Singapore
Phone: +65-6895-4000   **Fax:** +65-6895-4999
US HQ: 1901 McCarthy Blvd., Milpitas, CA 95035
US Phone: 408-428-6600   **US Fax:** 408-428-6611
Web: www.creative.com

Creative Technology has production and distribution facilities in China, Ireland, Malaysia, Singapore, and the US.

2005 Sales

	$ mil.	% of total
The Americas	522	43
Europe	469	38
Asia/Pacific	233	19
Total	**1,224**	**100**

PRODUCTS/OPERATIONS

2005 Sales

	$ mil.	% of total
Personal digital entertainment	769	63
Speakers	176	14
Audio	166	14
Other	113	9
Total	**1,224**	**100**

Selected Products

Personal digital entertainment
 MP3 players (Zen)
Audio
 Digital sampling systems
 Electronic musical instruments
 Sound cards and chipsets (Sound Blaster)
Speakers (Cambridge Soundworks)
Graphics and video
 2-D/3-D graphic accelerator cards (3D Blaster line)
 Desktop digital camera (Video Blaster WebCam)
 PC digital video disk (DVD) players (Encore)
Multimedia upgrade kits (sound card, drive, speakers,
 software)
Communications
 Bridging and routing devices
 Modems (internal and external)
 Wireless modems
Other
 Rewritable CD drives (Blaster CD-RW)

COMPETITORS

Altec Lansing Technologies
Apple Computer
Archos
ATI Technologies
Bose
Boston Acoustics
Canon
CASIO COMPUTER
Dell
D-Link
Eastman Kodak
ESS Technology
Guillemot
Harman International
Intel
Iomega
Logitech
Motorola
NVIDIA
Philips Electronics
Reigncom
Sony
Toshiba
USRobotics
Yamaha
Zoom Technologies

HISTORICAL FINANCIALS

Company Type: Public

Income Statement

	REVENUE ($ mil.)	NET INCOME ($ mil.)	NET PROFIT MARGIN	EMPLOYEES
6/05	1,224	1	0.0%	7,780
6/04	815	134	16.5%	4,700
6/03	702	23	3.3%	3,900
6/02	806	(20)	—	4,300
6/01	1,229	(130)	—	5,000
Annual Growth	(0.1%)	—	—	11.7%

FYE: June 30

2005 Year-End Financials

Debt ratio: 36.0%   Current ratio: 2.79
Return on equity: 0.1%   Long-term debt ($ mil.): 209
Cash ($ mil.): 187

Net Income History   NASDAQ (GS): CREAF

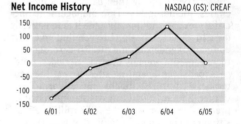

Crédit Agricole

The name suggests a country farmer's credit union, but Crédit Agricole's scope is much greater. France's largest bank, Crédit Agricole owns a 25% stake each in about 40 regional banks, which in turn own more than half of Crédit Agricole. It offers retail and business banking, lending, and deposit services at more than 9,000 locations throughout the country, including those of subsidiary Le Crédit Lyonnais (LCL), which it acquired in 2003. Crédit Agricole is also involved in investment banking and capital markets (through its Calyon unit), in addition to insurance, leasing, factoring, and asset management.

Formed in 2004, Calyon is the combination of corporate and investment bank Crédit Agricole Indosuez and LCL's corresponding activities. LCL now focuses exclusively on retail banking.

Crédit Agricole acquired Euler Hermes' 49% stake in Eurofactor, the European factoring group, in late 2004. The following year, the bank merged its previously existing factoring subsidiary, Transfact, into Eurofactor. Crédit Agricole's Sofinco subsidiary, one of the leading consumer finance companies in France, has about 100 locations.

Outside of France, Crédit Agricole has partnerships with Italy's Banca Intesa and Banco Espírito Santo in Portugal; the company plans to acquire some 650 branches in Italy from Banca Intesa for some $7.5 billion. It also acquired more than 70% of Emporiki Bank of Greece. However, the bank dropped plans to bid for UK lender Alliance & Leicester after determining the returns wouldn't be worth it.

Crédit Agricole is active in Africa, the Middle East, and Southeast Asia as well.

HISTORY

In the mid-1800s France's farmers were suffering from crop failures and a lack of credit. The government tried to meet the credit crunch without much success until in 1894 it created an agricultural credit company, Crédit Agricole, that was tax-exempt and provided state-subsidized farm loans (a monopoly it enjoyed until 1989). Five years later the government established the regional banks as intermediaries between it and the local banks. By the turn of the century, Crédit Agricole's three-tiered structure was in place.

The first 30 years of the 20th century were a time of growth for the bank. The government allowed Crédit Agricole to expand its lending to include long-term personal loans to encourage the growth of rural farming (1910) and loans to businesses involved in other industries (1919). The bank survived WWI and the drop in farm production largely through government support. After the war Crédit Agricole funded rural electrification and other infrastructure.

After WWII the bank grew as it issued loans to finance the modernization of France's farms. In 1959 the government allowed Crédit Agricole to begin writing mortgages; expansion of the bank's operations continued in the 1960s as it was permitted to broaden its lending scope and create subsidiaries, including one to finance individual investments (Union d'Etudes et d'Investisements). In 1967 it began keeping deposits (before it had transferred them to the French Treasury) and used the assets to fuel its national growth.

The early 1970s saw the bank continue to expand its lending operations. Its diversification came under fire from both the government, which wanted the bank to focus on agriculture, and rival banks, which resented their tax-exempt competitor. Crédit Agricole expanded beyond France in the mid-1970s, offering mainly agricultural loans and funds to export firms. It opened its first international office in Chicago in 1979.

In the early 1980s the government continued to allow Crédit Agricole to broaden its lending scope but at a price: The bank lost its tax-exempt status. It continued diversifying; it established such subsidiaries as Predica (life insurance, 1986) and bought stakes in two brokerage firms (1988). As the 1980s closed, Crédit Agricole became a mutual company when the government sold 90% of the bank to the regional banks.

In 1991 the last restrictions on Crédit Agricole's lending were removed, and the bank began transforming itself into a financial services firm. It expanded its lending operations around the world and added subsidiaries offering a variety of financial services. In 1996 it bought Banque Indosuez (which became Crédit Agricole Indosuez), fueling its growth in international wholesale banking. In the late 1990s the bank sought partnerships to expand its operations.

Its expansion was slowed by financial turmoil in Russia and Asia, and the bank closed its emerging markets business. The next year Crédit Agricole teamed with Spain's Banco Bilbao Vizcaya Argentaria and Commercial Bank of Greece as part of its plans to expand its presence in the Mediterranean and southern Europe; it already owned sizable stakes in Italy's Banca Intesa (now IntesaBci) and major banks in Lebanon, Morocco, and Portugal.

In 2000 the bank bought a majority share in Poland-based Europejski Fundusz Leasingowy, but declined an offer to become the controlling shareholder of fellow French bank Crédit Lyonnais, which it eventually acquired in 2003. Crédit Agricole went public on the Euronext Paris Exchange at the end of 2001.

Under pressure from the US government, Crédit Lyonnais admitted in 2003 to illegally acquiring Executive Life, the Californian insurance company, in the early 1990s. Crédit Lyonnais agreed to pay a fine of nearly $772 million to avoid criminal prosecution. It was also allowed to keep its US banking license.

EXECUTIVES

Chairman: René Carron, age 64
CEO; Chairman, Crédit Lyonnais: Georges Pauget, age 58
Deputy CEO and Head of Corporate and Investment Banking; Chairman and CEO, Calyon:
Edouard Esparbès
Group CFO and Group Chief Risk Management Officer: Gilles de Margerie
Head of Bank Operations Information Systems: Aline Bec
Head of Regional Banks and Private Equity: Jérôme Brunel
Head of Asset Management: Thierry Coste
Head of Management Control and Planning, Subsidiaries and Affiliates and Head of Strategy and Development: Marc Ghinsberg
Head of General Secretariat: Gilles Guitton
Head of International Retail Banking and Investment Capital: Jean-Frédéric de Leusse
Head of Operations and Logisitics: Bernard Michel
Head of Specialised Financial Services; Chairman and CEO, Sofinco: Patrick Valroff
General Manager, Italy: Ariberto Fassati
Head of Risk Management and Permanent Controls: Alain Strub
Head of Development, France: Jacques Lenormand
CEO, Crédit Lyonnais: Christian Duvillet, age 56
CEO, Fédération Nationale du Crédit Agricole: Jean-Yves Rossi
General Secretary, Crédit Lyonnais: Agnés de Clermont Tonnerre
Auditors: Barbier Frinault & Autres; PricewaterhouseCoopers Audit

LOCATIONS

HQ: Crédit Agricole S.A.
91-93 Boulevard Pasteur, 75015 Paris, France
Phone: +33-1-43-23-52-02   **Fax:** +33-1-43-23-34-48
Web: www.credit-agricole-sa.fr

COMPETITORS

ABN AMRO	Dresdner Bank
BNP Paribas	GE Money Bank
Caisses d'Epargne	Generale de Belgique
Citigroup	HSBC Holdings
Commerzbank	Société Générale
Credit Suisse	UBS
Deutsche Bank	

HISTORICAL FINANCIALS

Company Type: Public

Income Statement   FYE: December 31

	ASSETS ($ mil.)	NET INCOME ($ mil.)	INCOME AS % OF ASSETS	EMPLOYEES
12/05	1,386,044	7,086	0.5%	136,848
12/04	1,244,848	5,414	0.4%	135,502
12/03	986,568	1,288	0.1%	96,500
12/02	530,043	1,115	0.2%	96,500
12/01	438,530	945	0.2%	96,000
Annual Growth	33.3%	65.5%	—	9.3%

2005 Year-End Financials

Equity as % of assets: —   Long-term debt ($ mil.): —
Return on assets: 0.5%   Sales ($ mil.): 105,571
Return on equity: —

Net Income History   Pink Sheets: CRARF

Credit Suisse

Credit Suisse Group is the #2 financial services firm in Switzerland, behind UBS. After a reorganization that began in 2005, in which the company merged with its Credit Suisse First Boston subsidiary, Credit Suisse is divided into three segments: investment banking, private banking, and asset management. Its investment banking operations, formerly Credit Suisse First Boston (CSFB), operates from nearly 70 locations in more than 30 countries. Its asset management offices can be found in 18 countries. The company also offers retail banking in Switzerland through about 215 branches. It is selling its life and nonlife insurance subsidiary Winterthur to insurance giant AXA for nearly $10 billion.

A Winterthur sale has been on Credit Suisse's agenda for a while, as the bank seeks to divest noncore operations. Originally it was seeking a spinoff of at least part of the subsidiary, but that idea went in favor of a quick sale.

Credit Suisse's CEO duties had been split between John Mack (who also ran CSFB) and Oswald Grübel, with Walter Kielholz, former CEO of Swiss Re, as chairman. But the company's board of directors, disenchanted with the two-CEO system (Mack was based in New York City, while Grübel is in Zurich), decided not to renew Mack's contract when it expired in July 2004.

Credit Suisse is combining four private banks and one securities dealer into a single entity, called Clariden Leu. The company hopes to save $78 million by combining the businesses. It is also expanding its investment banking and asset management operations in Singapore, in part to take advantage of the city's lower costs compared to Hong Kong and Tokyo. Elsewhere in Asia the bank bought a 30% stake in Korean firm Woori Asset Management. The firm will be renamed Woori Credit Suisse Asset Management and will be the fourth-largest asset management firm in South Korea.

In fallout from the Enron collapse, the bank agreed to pay $90 million to the company to settle claims that it helped the energy trader commit fraud.

Credit Suisse, along with General Electric and American International Group, is buying London City Airport. Credit Suisse and GE together will hold a 50% stake in the airport, which serves about 2 million travelers a year; AIG will own the other half.

HISTORY

In 1856, shortly after the creation of the Swiss federation, Alfred Escher opened Credit Suisse (CS) in Zurich. Primarily a venture capital firm, CS helped fund Swiss railroads and other industries. It later opened offices in Italy and helped establish the Swiss Bank Corporation.

CS shifted its focus to commercial banking in 1867 and sold most of its stock holdings. By 1871 it was Switzerland's largest bank, buoyed by the nation's swift industrialization. In 1895 CS helped create the predecessor of Swiss utility Electrowatt. Foreign activity grew in the 1920s. A run on banks in the Depression forced CS to sell assets at a loss and dip into reserves of unreported retained profits.

Trade declined in WWII, but neutrality left Switzerland's institutions intact and made it a major banking center, partly due to CS's role as a conduit for the Nazi's plundered gold. Foreign exchange and gold trading became important activities for CS after WWII. Mortgage and consumer credit acquisitions fueled domestic growth in the 1970s.

In 1978 the bank took a stake in US investment bank First Boston and, with it, formed London-based Credit Suisse-First Boston (CSFB). CS created 44%-owned holding company Credit Suisse First Boston to own First Boston, CSFB, and Tokyo-based CS First Boston Pacific.

The stock market crash of 1987 led a damaged First Boston to merge with CSFB the next year. In 1990 CS (renamed CS Holding) injected $300 million into CSFB and shifted $470 million in bad loans from its books, becoming the first foreign owner of a major Wall Street investment bank.

In the early 1990s CS Holding strengthened its insurance business with a Winterthur Insurance alliance. In 1993 and 1994 acquisitions helped it gain share in its overbanked home market.

In 1996 CS Holding reorganized as Credit Suisse Group and grew internationally, including further merging the daredevil US investment banking operations into Credit Suisse's more staid and relationship-oriented corporate banking. It bought Winterthur (Switzerland's #2 insurer) in 1997, as well as Barclays' European investment banking business.

Credit Suisse and other Swiss banks came under fire in 1996 for refusing to relinquish assets from Jewish bank accounts from the Holocaust era and for gold trading with the Nazi regime. In 1997 the banks agreed to establish a humanitarian fund for Holocaust victims. A stream of lawsuits by American heirs and boycott threats from US states and cities led in 1998 to a tentative $1.25 billion settlement (unpopular in Switzerland), with Credit Suisse on the hook for about a third of that.

CS in 1998 expanded its investment banking by buying Brazil's Banco de Investimentos Garantia; it also moved to expand US money management operations by allying with New York-based Warburg Pincus Asset Management. By 1999 that joint venture — which was to give the investment firm access to CS's mutual fund distribution channels in Europe and Asia — had morphed into CS's $650 million purchase of Warburg Pincus Asset Management.

Japan revoked the license of the company's financial products unit for obstructing an investigation (the harshest penalty ever given to a foreign firm at the time); it also accused the company of helping 60 others hide losses and cover up evidence.

In 2000 the company decided to allow searches of Holocaust-era accounts. The next year, as a part of its European expansion, Credit Suisse acquired Spanish broker and asset manager General de Valores y Cambios.

Under CEO Lukas Mühlemann, the company expanded Credit Suisse First Boston when it bought US investment firm Donaldson, Lufkin & Jenrette in 2000, and renamed it Credit Suisse First Boston (USA). The collapse of Credit Suisse's share price, along with what proved to be an over-ambitious acquisition strategy, brought about the downfall of Mühlemann, who was pressured out by shareholders in 2002.

In 2005 Credit Suisse merged with its Credit Suisse First Boston subsidiary, creating a global Credit Suisse brand, and in 2006 reorganized into three distinct operating segments — investment banking, private banking, and asset management, along with insurance.

EXECUTIVES

Chairman: Walter B. Kielholz, age 54
Vice Chairman: Peter Brabeck-Letmathe, age 62
Vice Chairman: Hans-Ulrich Doerig, age 66
CEO: Oswald J. Grübel, age 63
COO: Urs Rohner, age 47
CFO: Renato Fassbind, age 50
Chairman, Bank Leu, Bank Hofmann, and BGP Banca di Gestione Patrimoniale; CEO, Private Banking, Credit Suisse: Walter Berchtold, age 44
Head of Integration; Executive Vice Chairman, Credit Suisse First Boston: Richard E. Thornburgh, age 54
CEO, Bank Leu: Hans Nützi
CEO, Clariden Bank: F. Bernard Stalder
CEO, Credit Suisse Asset Management: David J. Blumer
CEO, Investment Banking and CEO, Credit Suisse First Boston; President and CEO, Credit Suisse Americas: Brady W. Dougan, age 46
CEO, Winterthur: Leonhard H. Fischer, age 43
President, Credit Suisse First Boston and CSFB Private Equity: Brian D. Finn, age 45
CEO, Credit Suisse Switzerland, and Head of Private and Business Banking Switzerland, Credit Suisse: Ulrich Körner, age 44
Chairman and CEO, Asia Pacific, Credit Suisse First Boston: Paul Calello, age 45
CEO, Credit Suisse Europe, Middle East, and Africa: Michael G. Philipp, age 53

Chief Risk Officer: D. Wilson Ervin, age 45
Group Chief Communications Officer: Charles Naylor
Chief of Staff: Philip Hess
Head of Economic Research: Alois Bischofberger
Group Chief Accounting Officer: Rudolph A. Bless
Head of Group Legal and Compliance: David P. Frick
Head of Human Resources: Timothy S. Gardner
Corporate Secretary: Béatrice Fischer
Head of Human Resources, Credit Suisse: Denise Stüdi
Auditors: KPMG Klynveld Peat Marwick Goerdeler SA

LOCATIONS

HQ: Credit Suisse Group
Paradeplatz 8, 8070 Zurich, Switzerland
Phone: +41-44-212-16-16 **Fax:** +41-44-333-25-87
US HQ: 11 Madison Ave., New York, NY 10010
US Phone: 212-325-2000 **US Fax:** 212-325-6665
Web: www.credit-suisse.com

2005 Sales

	% of total
Europe	
Switzerland	36
Other countries	36
Americas	23
Asia/Pacific/Africa	5
Total	**100**

PRODUCTS/OPERATIONS

2005 Sales

	% of total
Interest & dividend income	46
Insurance premiums	23
Commissions & fees	16
Trading revenues	8
Gains from investment securities	2
Other	5
Total	**100**

COMPETITORS

ABN AMRO
Barclays
Bear Stearns
Citigroup
Citigroup Global Markets
Deutsche Bank
Goldman Sachs
HSBC Holdings
Merrill Lynch
Mitsubishi UFJ Financial Group
Mizuho Financial
Nomura Securities
UBS
UBS Financial Services

HISTORICAL FINANCIALS

Company Type: Public

Income Statement				FYE: December 31
	ASSETS ($ mil.)	NET INCOME ($ mil.)	INCOME AS % OF ASSETS	EMPLOYEES
12/05	1,017,947	4,447	0.4%	63,523
12/04	962,996	4,975	0.5%	60,532
12/03	808,769	620	0.1%	60,477
12/02	740,889	(3,208)	—	78,457
Annual Growth	11.2%	—	—	(6.8%)

2005 Year-End Financials

Equity as % of assets: 3.1%
Return on assets: 0.4%
Return on equity: 13.9%
Long-term debt ($ mil.): 119,294
No. of shares (mil.): —
Dividends
Yield: 1.6%
Payout: —
Market value ($ mil.): —
Sales ($ mil.): 68,393

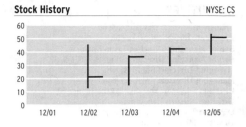

	STOCK PRICE ($) FY Close	P/E High/Low		PER SHARE ($) Earnings	Dividends
12/05	50.95	—	—	—	0.80
12/04	42.19	10	7	4.20	0.37
12/03	36.33	—	—	—	0.05
12/02	21.28	—	—	(2.01)	1.34
Annual Growth	33.8%	—	—	—	(15.8%)

Dai Nippon Printing

A leading commercial printer, Dai Nippon Printing (DNP) has diversified well beyond the business of putting ink on paper. The company still produces books and magazines, promotional materials, and business forms, and it has added items such as CD-ROMs and smart cards to the mix. DNP's Lifestyle and Industrial Supplies segment makes decorative materials for use in fixtures and furniture, along with packaging for consumer products. The company's electronics products include photomasks used in the manufacture of integrated circuits and color filters for liquid crystal displays. In addition, DNP owns about 60% of Hokkaido Coca-Cola Bottling.

Like other printing companies, DNP is working to market itself as a complete provider of information communications services, offering clients marketing and promotional support, communications software, and cross-media services.

In its Lifestyle and Industrial Supplies business, DNP wants to make its products and manufacturing processes more environmentally friendly.

Electronics has been the company's fastest-growing business. Because it makes both products related to the inside (photomasks) and outside (displays) of high-tech equipment, DNP believes it is well-positioned for additional growth.

HISTORY

In 1876 Shueisha, the predecessor to Dai Nippon Printing (DNP), was established in central Tokyo. As the only modern printing firm in Japan, it was well-positioned to attract the business of the emerging newspaper and book industries. The company originally used a movable-type hand printer, but became the first private industry to use steam power in Japan when it updated its presses in 1884.

Following Japanese victories over China and Russia at the turn of the century, Japan embarked on a period of military and economic expansion. This was matched by a growing demand for printing. In 1927 Japan published 20,000 book titles and 40 million magazines. The country's first four-color gravure printing system was inaugurated the following year. In 1935 Shueisha changed its name to Dai Nippon Printing following its merger with Nisshin Printing.

The 1930s and 1940s were lean times for printers; Japan's repressive military government suppressed publishers and banned books. WWII devastated the publishing industry, along with the rest of the Japanese economy, but the publishing industry recovered soon after the end of the war. DNP was assisted in its recovery by government contracts; in 1946 it was designated by the Ministry of Finance to print 100-yen notes. In 1949 the company entered the securities printing business, and in 1951 it expanded into packaging and decorative interiors production. DNP reemerged in 1958 as Japan's largest printing firm.

In 1963 DNP followed Toppan in setting up an office in Hong Kong. Both Hong Kong and Singapore had become havens for Shanghai printing entrepreneurs who had emigrated in the face of the Communist takeover of China in 1949. These cities became centers for low-cost, high-quality color printing for British and American book publishers. In 1973 DNP overtook R. R. Donnelley as the world's largest printer. The next year the company set up a subsidiary in the US, DNP (America), Inc.

DNP moved into the information processing business in the 1980s, developing a credit card-sized calculator in 1985, a digital color printer system in 1986, and a Japanese-language word processor in 1987. The company launched Hi-Vision Static Pictures in 1989 to market a process that converted data into a form used by high-definition TV. In 1990 DNP bought a controlling stake in Tien Wah Press, the #1 printer in Singapore.

The next year DNP completed the first construction stage of its Okayama plant, dedicated to information media supplies (mainly transfer ribbons for color printers). The second stage, specializing in interior decorative materials, was completed in 1993.

In 1994 the company launched its Let's Go to an Amusement Park! virtual reality software system. Two years later DNP produced an integrated circuit card for about a tenth of current costs, giving it a major competitive edge in the magnetic card market.

In 1999 the company began selling CD-ROMs online through subsidiary TransArt. The following year Dai Nippon formed partnerships or joint ventures with Toshiba (to develop printed circuit boards), Microsoft (to develop Windows-based smart cards), and Numerical Technologies (to develop advanced phase-shifted photomasks). In 2002 the company joined with Toshiba and Takara to develop and promote a lightweight educational computer called an Ex-Pad.

EXECUTIVES

Chairman, President, and CEO: Yoshitoshi Kitajima
Senior Managing Director: Mitsuhiko Hakii
Senior Managing Director: Satoshi Saruwatari
Senior Managing Director: Koichi Takanami
Senior Managing Director: Masayoshi Yamada
Senior Managing Director: Kosaku Mori
Senior Managing Director: Osamu Tsuchida
Senior Managing Director: Teruomi Yoshino
Senior Managing Director: Yoshinari Kitajima
Auditors: Meiji Audit Corporation

LOCATIONS

HQ: Dai Nippon Printing Co., Ltd.
(Dai Nippon Insatsu Kabushiki Kaisha)
1-1-1, Ichigaya Kagacho, Shinjuku-ku,
Tokyo 162-8001, Japan
Phone: +81-3-3266-2111   **Fax:** +81-3-5225-8239
US HQ: 335 Madison Ave., 3rd Fl., New York, NY 10017
US Phone: 212-503-1850   **US Fax:** 212-286-1493
Web: www.dnp.co.jp/index_e.html

PRODUCTS/OPERATIONS

2006 Sales

	% of total
Information Communication	43
Lifestyle & Industrial Supplies	32
Electronics	20
Beverages	5
Total	**100**

Selected Products and Services

Information Communication
  Bank notes
  Books
  Business forms
  Catalogs
  CD-ROMs and DVDs
  Direct mail
  Magazines
  Plastic cards
  Promotional publications
Lifestyle and Industrial Supplies
  Decorative materials
  Packaging
Electronics
  Color filters for liquid crystal displays
  Photomasks
  Projection TV screens
  Shadowmasks for color TVs

COMPETITORS

3M
Cookson Group
Graphic Packaging
Hitachi
LG.Philips LCD
Photronics
Quad/Graphics
Quebecor World
R.R. Donnelley
Siemens AG
Taiwan Semiconductor
Toppan Printing

HISTORICAL FINANCIALS

Company Type: Public

Income Statement

FYE: March 31

	REVENUE ($ mil.)	NET INCOME ($ mil.)	NET PROFIT MARGIN	EMPLOYEES
3/06	12,820	—	—	35,596
3/05	13,249	—	—	34,514
3/04	15,658	—	—	34,514
3/03	10,922	—	—	35,182
3/02	9,891	—	—	34,868
Annual Growth	6.7%	—	—	0.5%

Revenue History

Pink Sheets: DNPCF

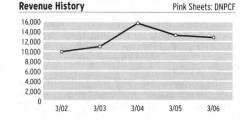

Daiei

Japan's economic woes put The Daiei on a diet. One of Japan's largest and most troubled retailers, Daiei (pronounced die-ay) operates about 1,000 stores through its subsidiaries and franchisees. Its retail businesses include supermarkets (Maruetsu), discount stores, department stores, and specialty shops. Daiei, which diversified haphazardly during the 1980s, came close to bankruptcy due to its massive debts and failure to innovate; it brought in new management and implemented a restructuring plan that included closing nearly 2,000 stores. The plan has yet to pay off. Trading company Marubeni owns about 45% of Daiei and has selected Japan's AEON to help it rebuild the company.

After closing so many stores and nearly completing its three-year restructuring plan (with the help of the Japanese government), the company has begun slowly opening stores in its core supermarket group and increasing its credit card offerings. Daiei also announced plans to open 100 grocery stores in the Tokyo and Kinki areas by 2011.

In addition to store closures, Daiei has exited the convenience store market (selling Japan's second-largest chain, LAWSON), the electronics business, and the restaurant business. It also sold its department store subsidiary Printemps Ginza and its Fukuoka hotel and baseball park, along with the Fukuoka Hawks baseball team.

The Industrial Revitalization Corp. of Japan (IRCJ), the government agency formed to turn around struggling Japanese companies, ended its long involvement with Daiei in mid-2006 when it sold its one-third stake in the company to Marubeni for about $609 million. Marubeni then chose AEON, Japan's largest supermarket chain, over Wal-Mart to help it remake Daiei and possibly acquire a stake in the once-dominant retailer.

The private equity firm Advantage Partners owns nearly 25% of Daiei.

HISTORY

Daiei founder Isao Nakauchi narrowly escaped death and the law before launching his first Daiei corner drugstore. As a Japanese soldier serving in the Philippines in WWII, he came under heavy fire but survived. He later thanked sloppy American engineering (the bombs that fell near him did not explode) for his survival. After the war he and his brother made a fortune selling penicillin above the legal price; his brother was arrested for his part in the dealings.

Nakauchi launched his Housewives' Store Daiei in Osaka in 1957 at the depth of the post-Korean War depression. The low prices of a discount drugstore appealed to hard-pressed consumers, and the success of the first store prompted Nakauchi to open others in the Osaka area. He also took advantage of the depression at the wholesale level, buying up surplus goods from cash-strapped manufacturers.

In 1958 the company opened in Sannomiya and introduced the concept of the discount store chain to Japan. Over the next three decades, Daiei diversified its offerings while staying focused on its "for the customers" philosophy, i.e., very low prices.

The company expanded into Tokyo in 1964 with the purchase of Ittoku and opened its first suburban store in 1968 near Osaka. By 1972

Daiei was not only a nationwide chain, it was also Japan's #1 supermarket operator (with 75 stores) and #2 retailer. In 1974 the company overtook Mitsukoshi to become Japan's top retailer. A year later Daiei opened its first convenience store, Lawson.

Showing an increasing interest in sourcing from international businesses, Daiei teamed up with J. C. Penney (1976) and Marks and Spencer (1978) for retailing and Wendy's and Victoria Station (both in 1979) for restaurants. The retailer entered the US market in 1980 with the purchase of Holiday Mart, a three-store discount chain in Hawaii. It also set up its first purchasing office there.

Daiei entered the hotel business in 1988 by winning the contract for a $2.2 billion recreation center in Fukuoka. In 1992 the company opened the first American-style membership warehouse in Japan (Kobe), Kuo's Wholesale Membership Club. That year Daiei acquired 42% of major retailer Chujitsuya. The company launched private-label products in 1994. Also that year Daiei merged with retail affiliates Chujitsuya, Uneed Daiei, and Dainaha, establishing Japan's first nationwide network of stores.

When Japan lifted a 50-year ban on holding companies in 1997, Daiei was the first to take advantage of the relaxed laws, forming K.K. Daiei Holding Corporation to oversee its non-retail businesses. The company was hit hard in 1997 and 1998 as Japan's consumer spending slowed just as many of its stores were undergoing renovation. In response, in 1998 Daiei began selling real estate assets, restructuring operations, and closing unprofitable stores.

In 1999 Tasdasu Toba became president, replacing founder Nakauchi, who remained chairman of Daiei. In early 2000 trading company Mitsubishi Corp. purchased a 20% stake in convenience store chain Lawson (Daiei and subsidiaries would retain about 75% of the company). Daiei later closed four of its poorly performing restaurant chains, including Victoria Station and Sbarro Japan.

Amid allegations of an insider trading scandal, Toba resigned as president and Nakauchi resigned as chairman and CEO in 2000. Hiroshige Sasaki, a former managing director, became acting president and Kunio Takagi was named to replace him as the head of Daiei in 2001. Daiei further reduced its stake in Lawson to about 21%. In early 2002 Daiei was rescued by a bank-led bailout and the company announced a three-year restructuring plan that included 60 store closures and reducing its workforce by about 5,000 employees. The state-run Development Bank of Japan announced a new $480 million funding plan in October 2002 to aid Daiei in its restructuring. To that end, Daiei closed 60 unprofitable stores and refurbished others in the hope of engineering a turnaround.

In May 2004 five of the 15 members of the company's board of directors, including chairman Jiro Amagai, left the board. In October Daiei's next chairman — Heihachiro Yoshino — and president Kunio Takagi both announced their resignations, just days after Daiei's lenders forced the struggling retailer to seek a government bailout. Takagi assumed the largely symbolic post of chairman of the company. He was succeeded as president by Toshio Hasumi.

In 2005 AEON, operator of JUSCO supermarkets, and Wal-Mart bid for stakes in Daiei, but lost out to Marubeni, with the IRCJ's approval.

EXECUTIVES

Chairman: Fumiko Hayashi, age 60
President: Toru Nishimi, age 58
Senior Managing Director: Takao Endoh
Senior Managing Director: Shinji Seino, age 53
Managing Director: Shinji Kiyono
Managing Director: Tadahiro Tsuchiya
CFO and Director: Yoshiaki Takahashi, age 51
Director: Mitsuru Hazeyama
Director: Takayuki Itoh, age 52
Director: Mikio Kinohara
Director: Kunio Nishimoto, age 57
Director: Hiroyuki Ogawa
Director: Masahiro Ohta, age 53
Director, Sales Planning: Masakazu Satoh, age 53
Director: Kazuo Takahashi
Corporate Auditor: Satoru Kita
Corporate Auditor: Osamu Satoh, age 59
Corporate Auditor: Kenjuro Yamamoto, age 57
Director: Keiji Nakamae
Director: Akira Minami
Corporate Auditor: Eisuke Nagai
Auditors: Deloitte Touche Tohmatsu

LOCATIONS

HQ: The Daiei, Inc.
4-1-1, Minatojima Nakamachi, Chuo-ku,
Kobe 650-0046, Japan
Phone: +81-78-302-5001   **Fax:** +81-3-3433-9226
US HQ: 801 Kaheka St., Honolulu, HI 96814
US Phone: 808-973-6600   **US Fax:** 808-941-6457
Web: www.daiei.co.jp

The Daiei operates retail locations throughout Japan and maintains purchasing offices in China and the US.

PRODUCTS/OPERATIONS

2005 Sales

	% of total
Retail	83
Finance	7
Development	2
Other	8
Total	**100**

COMPETITORS

AEON
Carrefour
Costco Wholesale
Daimaru
Fast Retailing
Isetan
Ito-Yokado
Keiyo Company
Marui
Matsuzakaya
Mitsukoshi
MYCAL
Seiyu
Takashimaya
Tokyu Department Store
Uny
Wal-Mart

HISTORICAL FINANCIALS

Company Type: Public

Income Statement			FYE: Last day in February	
	REVENUE ($ mil.)	NET INCOME ($ mil.)	NET PROFIT MARGIN	EMPLOYEES
2/05	17,465	(4,869)	—	—
2/04	18,124	165	0.9%	—
2/03	18,623	1,147	6.2%	—
Annual Growth	(3.2%)	—	—	—

2005 Year-End Financials

Debt ratio: —
Return on equity: —
Cash ($ mil.): 1,983

Current ratio: 0.56
Long-term debt ($ mil.): 3,213

Net Income History NASDAQ (CM): DAIEY

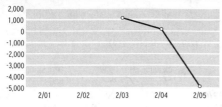

DaimlerChrysler

DaimlerChrysler is proud of its German-American heritage. Formed by the $37 billion acquisition of Chrysler by Germany's Daimler-Benz in 1998, the company makes about 4.6 million vehicles a year. Chrysler's brands include Dodge, Jeep, and, of course, Chrysler vehicles; the Mercedes Car Group includes Mercedes, Maybach (ultra-luxury vehicles), and smart (mini cars). DaimlerChrysler's Freightliner unit is the US's #1 heavy-truck maker, and through such brands as Fuso, Mercedes-Benz, and Sprinter, Daimler-Chrysler is the world's leading manufacturer of commercial vehicles.

The carmaker has about a 22% stake in EADS, the European aerospace and defense consortium (and plans to reduce its stake to about 15% in 2007).

Although it is looking to the emerging markets of Korea, Taiwan, and particularly China to make up for maturing markets in the US and Europe, DaimlerChrysler has made significant changes in its manufacturing relationships in Asia by selling its stakes in Korea's Hyundai Motor and Japan's Mitsubishi Motors. With Hyundai DaimlerChrysler saw it could still cooperate on products without holding an equity stake. Mitsubishi's credibility problems resulting from years of defects and ensuing cover-ups soured the relationship, and after only five years DaimlerChrysler just wanted out of a bad marriage.

One upshot of the Mitsubishi quagmire was that DaimlerChrysler ended up with an 85% stake in Mitsubishi Fuso Truck & Bus Corporation (MFTBC) — as well as about $200 million in cash — in the settlement. MFTBC is a significant part of DaimlerChrysler's commercial vehicles strategy.

While DaimlerChrysler may not be thriving, it is not on life-support either. Dieter Zetsche has replaced the embattled Jürgen E. Schrempp as chairman of the management board. (Zetsche had presided over a fairly impressive renaissance at Chrysler Group.) To turn things around, Mercedes Car Group is eliminating 8,500 German jobs. The company is also cutting 6,000 white-collar jobs across its organization. The move is aimed at finally consummating the Daimler and Chrysler marriage by creating more engineering- and technology-sharing programs between the two.

Mercedes Car Group, which had been having problems with quality and slipping market share, started to show signs of recovery in the second half of 2005 after the launch of four new models.

DaimlerChrysler is spending $1.56 billion to revamp the division's beleaguered smart brand. Smart's forfour model is being scrapped, and 300 jobs are on the block. The company has finally decided it will bring the smart fortwo minicar to the US beginning in 2008.

At the Chrysler Group, DaimlerChrysler had some product-based momentum going, but by mid-2006 started to falter. Excitment over earlier successes (beginning with the bold Chrysler 300 redesign) was replaced with concern over record high gasoline prices. Sales of Chrysler's gas guzzling SUVs and pickups fell though the floor. Although Chrysler said it expects deliveries to recover in 2007, it announced a 2006 third-quarter loss of $1.5 billion. The company said it was working on a plan to wring about $1,000 out of every Chrysler division vehicle.

In December 2006 Chrysler announced it had signed an agreement with Chinese manufacturer Chery Automobile to fill the need for a small car in the Chrysler lineup. The Chrysler/Chery cars, based on modifications to an existing Chery model, will carry the Dodge, Chrysler, or Jeep nameplate. They will be sold in the US and Europe, but will also be used to make gains in developing markets.

Deutsche Bank and the government of Kuwait, both shareholders of former Daimler-Benz, own 10% and 7% of DaimlerChrysler, respectively. Oil rich Dubai, a member of the United Arab Emirates, became DaimlerChrysler's third-largest shareholder late in 2004 when it bought a 1% stake in the company.

HISTORY

Former Buick president and GM VP Walter Chrysler was hired to get Maxwell Motor Car Company out of receivership in 1920. He became president in 1923 and introduced the Chrysler car the next year. He renamed the company for himself in 1925. The company acquired Dodge (1928) and introduced the low-priced Plymouth and the more luxurious DeSoto. Chrysler retired in 1935.

While other carmakers made style modifications, Chrysler kept the same models from 1942 until 1953. It lost market share and for several decades misjudged customer demands in the 1960s by introducing small cars before their time and in the 1970s by holding on to large-car production.

Facing bankruptcy, Chrysler negotiated $1.5 billion in loan guarantees from the US government and brought in former Ford president Lee Iacocca as CEO in 1978. By 1983 it had repaid its loans, seven years ahead of schedule. The company introduced the first minivan in 1984.

Iacocca was replaced by GM's head of European operations, Robert Eaton, in 1992. Chrysler sold most of its aerospace and defense holdings in 1996 and sold off Pentastar Electronics and the Dollar Thrifty Group the next year.

Chrysler's acquirer, Daimler-Benz, was formed by the merger of two German motor companies — Daimler and Benz — in 1926. Daimler-Benz bought Auto Union (Audi) in 1958 (sold to Volkswagen in 1966). The company's Mercedes cars gained notoriety and sales expanded worldwide in the 1970s.

Daimler-Benz diversified in the 1980s, buying aerospace, heavy truck (Freightliner), and consumer and industrial electrical companies. Although diversification continued, sales slowed. Losses at its aerospace unit forced Daimler-Benz into the red in 1995. Also that year the company

and ABB Asea Brown Boveri formed joint venture Adtranz, the #1 train maker in the world, and Jürgen Schrempp became chairman of the management board (CEO).

In 1998 Daimler-Benz acquired Chrysler. DaimlerChrysler rolled both companies' financial services units into DaimlerChrysler Interservices (DEBIS) and acquired the remaining shares of Adtranz in 1999. North American influence in the company began to fade in 2000 with the exit of US management, including co-chairman Robert Eaton.

In 2000 DaimlerChrysler agreed to buy a controlling $2.1 billion stake (34%) in Mitsubishi Motors (later upped to 37% when it acquired 3.3% from Volvo). It took a minority stake in South Korea-based Hyundai Motor (sold in 2004). DaimlerChrysler bought Canada-based truck maker Western Star Holdings for $456 million and paid about $473 million for the 79% of Detroit Diesel (heavy-duty truck engines) that it didn't already own. The company also agreed to sell its rail systems unit, Adtranz, to Bombardier (completed in 2001 for about $1.1 billion).

Also in 2000, in an effort to turn things around at its money-losing Chrysler division, James Holden was replaced with Dieter Zetsche, who immediately began making personnel changes. Days after Zetsche was installed, billionaire investor Kirk Kerkorian filed an $8 billion lawsuit seeking to undo the 1998 Daimler-Benz/Chrysler merger on grounds that portraying the deal as a "merger of equals" was misrepresentative. Zetsche announced early in 2001 that Chrysler would eliminate almost 26,000 North American jobs over three years (largely through retirement and attrition).

Late in 2004 DaimlerChrysler received Chinese regulatory approval to build cars in China with joint venture partner Beijing Automotive Industry Holding Co. Ltd. (BAIC).

Early in 2005 the problems with Mitsubishi came to a head when it was revealed that known defects at subsidiary Mitsubishi Fuso Truck & Bus Corporation (MFTBC) had been covered up since 1974. A deal was struck whereby Daimler-Chrysler got Mitsubishi Motors' 20% in MFTBC, reducing Mitsubishi Motors' stake to zero. Late in 2005 DaimlerChrysler sold its remaining 12% stake in Mitsubishi Motors to Goldman Sachs, marking the end of the companies' previous co-operation. Goldman Sachs sold all but .01% of the stake on the open market the following day.

Also in 2005, Zetsche replaced Schrempp as chairman of the management board.

In 2006 DaimlerChrysler formed a joint venture with Chinese Fujian Motor Industry Group and Taiwanese China Motor Corporation for the manufacture of the Mercedes-Benz Sprinter and Vito vans for the Chinese market.

EXECUTIVES

Deputy Chairman of the Supervisory Board:
Erich Klemm, age 51
Chairman of the Board of Management and Head of Mercedes Car Group: Dieter Zetsche, age 51
Member of the Board of Management; President and CEO, Chrysler Group: Thomas W. LaSorda, age 52
Member of the Board of Management; COO, Chrysler Car Group: Eric R. Ridenour, age 46
Member of the Board of Management, Truck Group:
Andreas Renschler, age 48
Member of the Board of Management, Corporate Development: Rüdiger Grube, age 55
Member of the Board of Management, Finance and Controlling/Financial Services: Bodo Uebber, age 47

Member of the Board of Management, Global Procurement and Supply: Thomas W. (Tom) Sidlik, age 56

Member of the Board of Management, Human Resources and Labor Relations Director: Günther Fleig, age 57

Member of the Board of Management, Research and Mercedes Car Group Development: Thomas Weber, age 52

SVP and CIO: Susan J. (Sue) Unger

Chairman of the Board of Management, DaimlerChrysler Services AG: Juergen H. Walker, age 57

President and CEO, DaimlerChrysler Services North America LLC: Klaus Entenmann, age 50

EVP Commercial Vehicle Division and Head of Mercedes-Benz Vans Business Unit: Rolf Bartke, age 58

EVP Design, Mercedes Car Group: Peter Pfeiffer

SVP Global Brand Marketing, Chrysler Group: George E. Murphy, age 51

SVP Human Resources, Chrysler Group: Nancy A. Rae, age 50

VP and General Counsel: Gerd T. Becht, age 54

VP Sales Strategy and Dealer Operations: Michael Manley, age 42

VP Communications, Chrysler Group: Jason Vines

Auditors: KPMG Deutsche Treuhand-Gesellschaft AG

LOCATIONS

HQ: DaimlerChrysler AG
   Epplestrasse 225, 70546 Stuttgart, Germany
Phone: +49-711-17-0   **Fax:** +49-711-17-94022
US HQ: 1000 Chrysler Dr., Auburn Hills, MI 48326
US Phone: 248-576-5741   **US Fax:** 248-576-4742
Web: www.daimlerchrysler.com

DaimlerChrysler has 105 manufacturing facilities worldwide.

2005 Sales

	% of total
Americas	
US	45
Other countries	9
European Union	
Germany	14
Other countries	18
Asia	8
Other regions	6
Total	**100**

PRODUCTS/OPERATIONS

2005 Sales

	% of total
Chrysler Group	32
Mercedes Car Group	32
Commercial vehicles	26
Financial services	9
Other	1
Total	**100**

Selected Divisions and Models

Chrysler Group
   Chrysler
      300 M
      Aspen
      Crossfire
      Pacifica
      PT Cruiser
      Sebring convertible
      Sebring coupe
      Sebring sedan
      Town & Country

Dodge
   Caliber
   Caravan
   Charger
   Dakota
   Durango
   Grand Caravan
   Magnum
   Neon
   Nitro
   Ram Pickup
   Sprinter van
   SRT-4
   Stratus coupe
   Stratus sedan
   Viper
Jeep
   Commander
   Compass
   Grand Cherokee
   Liberty
   Wrangler
Mercedes Car Group
   Maybach
   Mercedes-Benz
   smart
Commercial Vehicles Division
   Freightliner
   Mercedez-Benz
   Mitsubishi Fuso Truck and Bus
   Setra
   Sterling Trucks
   Western Star Trucks

COMPETITORS

ALSTOM
AM General
BMW
Boeing
Fiat
Ford
Fuji Heavy Industries
General Motors
Honda
Isuzu
Land Rover
MAN
Mazda
Navistar
Nissan
PACCAR
Peugeot
Renault
Saab Automobile
Saturn
Scania
Siemens AG
Suzuki Motor
Toyota
Volkswagen
Volvo

HISTORICAL FINANCIALS

Company Type: Public

Income Statement

FYE: December 31

	REVENUE ($ mil.)	NET INCOME ($ mil.)	NET PROFIT MARGIN	EMPLOYEES
12/05	177,395	3,371	1.9%	382,724
12/04	192,319	3,338	1.7%	384,723
12/03	171,870	564	0.3%	362,063
12/02	156,838	4,947	3.2%	365,571
12/01	137,151	(589)	—	372,470
Annual Growth	**6.6%**	**—**	**—**	**0.7%**

2005 Year-End Financials

Debt ratio: 121.9%
Return on equity: 7.6%
Cash ($ mil.): 14,979
Current ratio: 1.03
Long-term debt ($ mil.): 52,645

No. of shares (mil.): —
Dividends
   Yield: 3.8%
   Payout: 68.9%
Market value ($ mil.): —

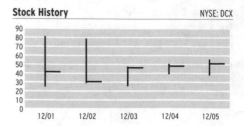

Stock History   NYSE: DCX

	STOCK PRICE ($) FY Close	P/E High/Low		PER SHARE ($) Earnings	Dividends
12/05	51.03	20	14	2.80	1.93
12/04	48.05	15	12	3.31	1.82
12/03	46.22	85	48	0.55	1.61
12/02	30.65	16	6	4.90	0.88
12/01	41.67	—	—	(0.59)	2.08
Annual Growth	**5.2%**	**—**	**—**	**—**	**(1.9%)**

Danone

You say Danone, I say Dannon; let's call the whole thing one of the largest dairy food and water producers in the world. Groupe Danone is a global leader in cultured dairy products (including yogurt, cheese, and dairy desserts). The company's Evian, Volvic, Aqua, and other water brands make it #2 worldwide in bottled water (behind Nestlé). It owns the internationally distributed LU biscuit brand. In addition, Danone has dozens of regional brands, including the US's Dannon yogurt. The company is organized around three core activities: fresh dairy products, water, and biscuits.

Acquisitions are a significant part of the company's growth plan. Danone has vigorously snapped up leading home and office water delivery companies around the globe.

Joint ventures have also been part of the company's strategy to expand into new geographic markets. It has become the leading supplier of fresh dairy products in Poland through what was originally a joint venture with a state-owned company. Finding that local milk was of poor quality, Danone arranged to supply farmers with better feeds and deduct the cost from their payments. The result was higher quality milk for which the farmers were paid higher than average.

In 2006 Danone sold AMOY Asian sauce and frozen-foods business to Ajinomoto and New Zealand biscuit maker Griffins Food to investment firm Pacific Equity Partners. Due to slow sales for its chilled products and competition from lower-priced brands, that year Danone introduced Senjà (a soy-based yogurt) in France. It acquired Egyptian fresh dairy products company Olait (which it renamed Danone Dairy Egypt) and Algerian bottled water company Tessala. On the Asian front, Danone acquired 22% of fruit-drink company Hhina Hui Yuan Juice and 51% of Wahaha.

HISTORY

In 1965 Antoine Riboud replaced his uncle as chairman of family-run Souchon-Neuvesel, a Lyons, France-based maker of glass bottles. Antoine quickly made a mark in this field — he merged the firm with Boussois, a major French flat-glass manufacturer, creating BSN in 1966.

Antoine enlarged BSN's glass business and filled the company's bottles by acquiring well-established beverage and food concerns. In 1970 BSN purchased Brasseries Kronenbourg (France's largest brewer), Société Européenne de Brasseries (another French brewer), and Evian (mineral water, France). The 1972 acquisition of Glaverbel (Belgium) gave BSN 50% of Europe's flat-glass market. The next year BSN merged with France's Gervais Danone (yogurt, cheese, Panzani pasta; founded in 1919 and named after founder Isaac Carasso's son Daniel). This moved the company into pan-European brand-name foods.

Increasing energy costs depressed flat-glass earnings, so the company began divesting its flat-glass businesses. In the late 1970s it acquired interests in brewers in Belgium, Spain, and Italy.

BSN bought Dannon, the leading US yogurt maker (co-founded by Daniel Carasso, who had continued making Danone yogurt in France until WWII), in 1982. It established a strong presence in the Italian pasta market by buying stakes in Ponte (1985) and Agnesi (1986). BSN also purchased Generale Biscuit, the world's #3 biscuit maker (1986), and RJR Nabisco's European cookie and snack-food business (1989).

In a series of acquisitions starting in 1986, BSN took over Italy and Spain's largest mineral water companies and several European pasta makers and other food companies. Adopting the name of its leading international brand, BSN became Groupe Danone in 1994.

Antoine's son, Franck, succeeded him as chairman in 1996 and restructured the company to focus on three core businesses: dairy, beverages (specifically water and beer), and biscuits.

By 1997 Danone had begun shedding non-core grocery products. The company simultaneously stepped up acquisitions of dairy, beer, biscuit, and water companies in developing markets. The 1998 purchase of AquaPenn Spring Water for $112 million doubled its US water-bottling production capacity. Danone in 1999 completed a merger and subsequent sale of part of its BSN Emballage glass-packaging unit to UK buyout firm CVC Capital Partners for $1.2 billion; Danone retained 44% ownership.

Thirsty for the #2 spot in US bottled water sales, Danone gulped down McKesson Water (the #3 bottled water firm in the US after Nestlé and Suntory) for $1.1 billion in 2000. Also that year Danone's joint venture Finalrealm (which includes several European equity firms), along with with Burlington Biscuits, Nabisco, and HM Capital Partners (then called Hicks, Muse, Tate & Furst), acquired 87% of leading UK biscuit maker United Biscuits. Danone then bought Naya (bottled water, Canada) and sold its brewing operations (#2 in Europe) to Scottish & Newcastle for more than $2.6 billion.

During 2001 Danone announced restructuring would shutter two LU biscuit plants and eliminate about 1,800 jobs; the move met with strikes and legal battles. That same year, having been bumped to the #2 spot in the US yogurt market (after General Mills' Yoplait brand), Danone acquired 40% of Stonyfield Farm, the #4 yogurt brand in the US and ultimately came to own 85% of the company.

In 2002 the company struck a deal handing Coca-Cola the distribution and marketing of Evian in North America, and formed a joint venture with Coke to distribute its lower-end water brands. Antoine Ribaud died that same year, at the age of 83.

Long after its departure from brewing, in 2004 Danone was fined €1.5 million for forming a beer distribution cartel along with Heineken in 1996. In 2005 Danone and Coca-Cola ended their 2002 water-distribution joint venture, with Coke buying out Danone's 49% share for about $100 million.

In 2005 Danone got out of the brewing business altogether, with the sale of its 33% stake in Spanish brewer Mahou. It sold its HP Foods Group, including Amoy, Lea & Perrins, and HP sauce brands, to Heinz and its biscuits businesses in the UK and Ireland. That year it sold its US home and officer water-delivery company, DS Waters of America to investment firm Kelso & Company. Danone also increased its ownership of Russian dairy and beverage company Wimm-Bill-Dann Foods to almost 10%.

EXECUTIVES

Chairman and CEO: Franck Riboud, age 51, $2,943,625 pay
Vice Chairman and Directeur Général Délégué: Jacques Vincent, age 60, $1,829,293 pay
EVP, Finance, Strategy, and Information Systems and CFO: Antoine Giscard d'Estaing, age 45
EVP, Asia/Pacific and Director: Emmanuel Faber, age 42, $1,144,102 pay
EVP, Beverages: Thomas Kunz, age 48
EVP, Biscuits and Cereal Products: Georges Casala, age 64
EVP, Fresh Dairy Products and Director: Bernard Hours, age 49
EVP, Human Resources: Franck Mougin, age 48
EVP, Research and Development: Sven Thormahlen, age 49
Chairman, Asia/Pacific: Simon Israël, age 52
President and General Manager, Argentina: Francisco Camacho
President and General Manager, Evian North America: Eric Leventhal
Secretary General: Philippe Loïc Jacob, age 41
Auditors: PricewaterhouseCoopers

LOCATIONS

HQ: Groupe Danone
 17, Boulevard Haussmann, 75009 Paris, France
Phone: +33-1-44-35-20-20   **Fax:** +33-1-42-25-67-16
US HQ: 100 Hillside Ave., Greenburgh, NY 10603
US Phone: 914-872-8400
Web: www.danonegroup.com

2005 Sales

	% of total
Europe	63
Asia	17
Other countries	20
Total	**100**

PRODUCTS/OPERATIONS

2005 Sales

	% of total
Fresh dairy products	55
Beverages	27
Biscuits	18
Total	**100**

Selected Products and Brands

Biscuits
 Argentina (Bagley)
 Czech Republic, Slovakia (Opavia)
 International (Britannia, Danone, LU, Vitalinea)
 Russia (Bolshevik)

Bottled Water
 Argentina (Villa del Sur)
 Asia/Pacific (Aqua)
 Canada (Crystal Springs, Evian, Labrador, Naya)
 China (Wahaha)
 France (Badoit, Salvetat, Arvie)
 International (Evian, Volvic)
 Mexico (Bonafont)
 Spain (Font Vella)
 Turkey (Hayat)
 US (Dannon, Evian)

Fresh Dairy
 Africa (Clover)
 Argentina (La Serenissima, Ser)
 China (Bright Dairy, Wahaha)
 France (Danone, Senjà)
 International (Actimel, Danone)
 Japan (Danone, Yakult)
 Latin America (Corpus, La Serenisima, Mastellone)
 US (Activia, Dannon, Stonyfield Farm)

COMPETITORS

Arla Foods	Leche Pascual
Bahlsen	Nestlé
Biscuits Gardeil	Nestlé Waters
Coca-Cola	Owens-Illinois
Culligan	Parmalat
Dairy Crest	PepsiCo
Fonterra	PepsiCo International
Friesland Foods	Pepsi-Cola North America
General Mills	Saint-Gobain
Glacier Water Services	Sodiaal
Glanbia	Sparkling Springs Water
Kellogg Snacks	Suntory Ltd.
Kerry Group	United Biscuits
Kraft Foods	Vermont Pure
Lactalis	

HISTORICAL FINANCIALS

Company Type: Public

Income Statement				FYE: December 31
	REVENUE ($ mil.)	NET INCOME ($ mil.)	NET PROFIT MARGIN	EMPLOYEES
12/05	15,426	1,581	10.3%	88,184
12/04	18,692	544	2.9%	89,449
12/03	16,489	1,036	6.3%	88,607
12/02	14,210	1,489	10.5%	92,209
Annual Growth	**2.8%**	**2.0%**	**—**	**(1.5%)**

2005 Year-End Financials

Debt ratio: —
Return on equity: 25.2%
Cash ($ mil.): 3,603
Current ratio: 1.34
Long-term debt ($ mil.): —

No. of shares (mil.): —
Dividends
 Yield: 1.4%
 Payout: 4.6%
Market value ($ mil.): —

Stock History

NYSE: DA

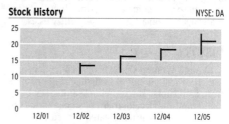

	STOCK PRICE ($) FY Close	P/E High/Low		PER SHARE ($) Earnings	Dividends
12/05	21.04	4	3	6.34	0.29
12/04	18.44	60	49	0.31	0.25
12/03	16.25	—	—	—	0.22
12/02	13.35	—	—	—	0.17
Annual Growth	**16.4%**	**—**		**1,945.2%**	**19.5%**

Deloitte Touche Tohmatsu

This company is "deloitted" to make your acquaintance, particularly if you're a big business in need of accounting services. Deloitte Touche Tohmatsu (now doing business simply as Deloitte) is one of accounting's Big Four, along with Ernst & Young, KPMG, and PricewaterhouseCoopers. Deloitte offers traditional audit and fiscal-oversight services to a multinational clientele. It also provides human resources and tax consulting services, as well as services to governments and international lending agencies working in emerging markets. (China and India are important markets.) Units include Deloitte & Touche (the US accounting arm) and Deloitte Consulting. Consulting services account for 25% of Deloitte's sales.

Deloitte spent the 1980s and 1990s pursuing a strategy of using accountants and consultants in concert to provide seamless service in auditing, accounting, strategic planning, information technology, financial management, and productivity. Deloitte Consulting became Deloitte's fastest-growing line, offering strategic and management consulting, in addition to information technology and human resources consulting services. Increasingly, though, Deloitte and its peers came under fire for their combined accounting/consulting operations; regulators and observers wondered whether accountants could maintain objectivity when they were auditing clients for whom they also provided consulting services. Criticism mounted after Enron's collapse capsized Arthur Andersen and put the entire accounting industry under scrutiny. (Deloitte picked up new business and members in Andersen's wake.) Deloitte in 2002 announced it would spin off its consulting business, becoming the last of the big accountants to do so; a year later it called off the split, citing a weakened market for consulting, among other woes. Deloitte was in the headlines again in late 2003, when auditing client Parmalat filed for bankruptcy in the midst of a $12 billion financial scandal, then dropped Deloitte as its auditor. Parmalat sued Deloitte in 2004, claiming its auditing procedures were inadequate and should have uncovered the fraud at Parmalat earlier. In 2006 the company's UK arm announced plans to integrate its Swiss counterpart. (Deloitte is an umbrella organization over partnerships that generally operate on a country-by-country basis.)

HISTORY

In 1845 William Deloitte opened an accounting office in London, at first soliciting business from bankrupts. The growth of joint stock companies and the development of stock markets in the mid-19th century created a need for standardized financial reporting and fueled the rise of auditing, and Deloitte moved into the new field. The Great Western Railway appointed him as its independent auditor (the first anywhere) in 1849.

In 1890 John Griffiths, who had become a partner in 1869, opened the company's first US office in New York City. Four decades later branches had opened throughout the US. In 1952 the firm partnered with Haskins & Sells, which operated 34 US offices.

Deloitte aimed to be "the Cadillac, not the Ford" of accounting. The firm, which became Deloitte Haskins & Sells in 1978, began shedding its conservatism as competition heated up; it was the first of the major accountancy firms to use aggressive ads.

In 1984 Deloitte Haskins & Sells tried to merge with Price Waterhouse, but the deal was dropped after Price Waterhouse's UK partners objected.

In 1989 Deloitte Haskins & Sells joined the flamboyant Touche Ross (founded 1899) to become Deloitte & Touche. Touche Ross's Japanese affiliate, Ross Tohmatsu (founded 1968) rounded out the current name. The merger was engineered by Deloitte's Michael Cook and Touche's Edward Kangas, in part to unite the former firm's US and European strengths with the latter's Asian presence. Cook continued to oversee US operations, with Kangas presiding over international operations. Many affiliates, particularly in the UK, rejected the merger and defected to competing firms.

As auditors were increasingly held accountable for the financial results of their clients, legal action soared. In the 1990s Deloitte was sued because of its actions relating to Drexel Burnham Lambert junk bond king Michael Milken, the failure of several savings and loans, and clients' bankruptcies.

Nevertheless, in 1995 the SEC chose Michael Sutton, the firm's national director of auditing and accounting practice, as its chief accountant. That year Deloitte formed Deloitte & Touche Consulting to consolidate its US and UK consulting operations; its Asian consulting operations were later added to facilitate regional expansion.

In 1997, amid a new round of industry mergers, rumors swirled that a Deloitte and Ernst & Young union had been scrapped because the firms could not agree on ownership issues. Deloitte disavowed plans to merge and launched an ad campaign directly targeted against its rivals.

The Asian economic crisis hurt overseas expansion in 1998, but provided a boost in restructuring consulting. In 1999 the firm sold its accounting staffing service unit (Resources Connection) to its managers and Evercore Partners, citing possible conflicts of interest with its core audit business. Also that year Deloitte Consulting decided to sell its computer programming subsidiary to CGI Group, and Kangas stepped down as CEO to be succeeded by James Copeland; the following year Kangas ceded the chairman's seat to Piet Hoogendoorn.

In 2001 the SEC forced Deloitte & Touche to restate the financial results of Pre-Paid Legal Services. In an unusual move, Deloitte & Touche publicly disagreed with the SEC's findings.

The accountancy put some old trouble to bed in 2003 when it agreed to pay $23 million to settle claims it had been negligent in its auditing of failed Kentucky Life Insurance, a client in the 1980s. Later that year the UK's High Court found Deloitte negligent in audits related to the failed Barings Bank; however, the ruling was considered something of a victory for the accountancy because it essentially cleared Deloitte of the majority of charges against it and effectively limited its financial liability in the matter. Copeland retired from the global CEO's office that year and handed the reins over to Bill Parrett, who had formerly served as managing director for the US and the Americas.

EXECUTIVES

Chairman: Piet Hoogendoorn
CEO; Senior Partner, US; and Director: William G. (Bill) Parrett, age 60
President: Jean-Paul Picard
CFO: Jeffrey P. Rohr
Chief Information Officer: Wolfgang Richter
Global Managing Partner, Innovation and Investment; Managing Partner, Germany and Regional Managing Partner, Europe/Middle East/Africa: Wolfgang Grewe
Regional Managing Partner, Japan, and Director: Shuichiro Sekine
Regional Managing Partner, North America; Global Managing Partner, Brand and Eminence: Colin Taylor
Global Managing Partner, Financial Advisory Services: Ralph G. Adams
Global Managing Partner, Audit: Stephen Almond
Managing Partner, Human Resources; and Director: Libero Milone
Global Managing Partner, Regulatory and Risk: Jeffrey K. (Jeff) Willemain
Global Managing Partner, Consulting: Paul D. Robinson
Chairman, Deloitte & Touche LLP, and Director: Sharon L. Allen, age 54
CEO, Deloitte & Touche LLP, and Director: James H. (Jim) Quigley, age 54
Global Managing Partner, Clients & Markets, and Director: Jerry P. Leamon
Global Managing Partner, Tax & Legal Services: Alan Schneier
Global Managing Director; Chairman, Global Management Committee; and Director: John P. Connolly
Managing Director, Finance and Administration: S. Ashish Bali
Global Managing Director, Human Resources and Managing Director, Global Office: James H. (Jim) Wall
General Counsel: Joseph J. Lambert

LOCATIONS

HQ: Deloitte Touche Tohmatsu
   1633 Broadway, New York, NY 10019
Phone: 212-489-1600   **Fax:** 212-489-1687
Web: www.deloitte.com

Deloitte Touche Tohmatsu operates through about 670 offices in nearly 150 countries.

2006 Sales

	% of total
Americas	52
Europe/Middle East/Africa	38
Asia/Pacific/Japan	10
Total	**100**

PRODUCTS/OPERATIONS

2006 Sales

	% of total
Audit	49
Consulting	22
Tax	21
Financial advisory services	8
Total	**100**

Selected Products and Services

Audit
   Auditing services
   Global offerings services
   International financial reporting conversion services
Consulting
   Enterprise applications
   Human capital
   Outsourcing
   Strategy and operations
   Technology integration
Enterprise Risk Services
   Capital markets
   Control assurance
   Environment and sustainability
   Internal audit
   Regulatory consulting
   Security services

Financial Advisory
    Corporate finance
    Forensic services
    Reorganization services
    Transaction services
Tax
    Comprehensive tax solutions
    Corporate tax
    European Union services
    Indirect tax
    International assignment services
    International tax
    Mergers and acquisitions
    Research and development credits
    Tax technology solutions
    Transfer pricing

COMPETITORS

Accenture	H&R Block
BDO International	KPMG
Booz Allen	Marsh & McLennan
Boston Consulting	McKinsey & Company
Capgemini	PricewaterhouseCoopers
EDS	Towers Perrin
Ernst & Young	Watson Wyatt
Grant Thornton	

HISTORICAL FINANCIALS

Company Type: Partnership

Income Statement				FYE: May 31
	REVENUE ($ mil.)	NET INCOME ($ mil.)	NET PROFIT MARGIN	EMPLOYEES
5/06	20,000	—	—	135,000
5/05	18,200	—	—	121,283
5/04	16,400	—	—	115,000
5/03	15,100	—	—	119,237
5/02	12,500	—	—	98,000
Annual Growth	12.5%	—	—	8.3%

Revenue History

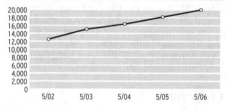

DENSO

The parts are greater than the whole for DENSO CORPORATION's carmaker customers. A leading Japanese parts manufacturer, DENSO produces auto components for most of the world's major automakers. Products include automotive air conditioners, spark plugs, antilock brake system controls, and windshield wipers. DENSO's Intelligent Transport Systems segment makes car navigation systems and electronic toll collection systems. Subsidiary DENSO Wave makes bar-code readers, factory automation robots, and programmable logic controllers. Former parent Toyota Motor now owns about 23% of DENSO.

In 2005 almost two-thirds of DENSO's sales came from customers in its native Japan, and the company felt it was a little too reliant on its home market. In 2006 DENSO reduced its dependence on its home market, with Japan accounting for just over 50% of sales. This progress was in no small part due to increasing its presence in China and Europe.

DENSO's plan for China is to develop products tailored to the Chinese market while establishing a supply network there. In 2006 DENSO added four new Chinese production facilities that make navigation systems, air conditioner compressors, instrument panels, and oil filters.

While Europe is a fully matured car market, DENSO sees opportunity there because it has a relatively small market share. DENSO also notes that Europe has a low installation rate for air conditioners and automotive diesel common rail systems (which reduce pollution) — two product categories where DENSO is a major player. After losing money in Europe for six years, DENSO's European operations returned to profitability in 2006.

Nonetheless, DENSO will continue to reap the benefits of being closely tied to Toyota as that company has already outpaced Ford and DaimlerChrysler and now has its sites set on General Motors.

HISTORY

Originally the in-house parts supplier for Toyota Motor, Nippondenso Co. (the predecessor to DENSO) was spun off by Toyota in 1949 because Toyota no longer wanted the burden of the unit's troubled financial performance. Nippondenso remained dependent upon Toyota for sales, and members of the company's controlling family, the Toyodas, remained involved in management. Nippondenso established a technological partnership with Germany's Robert Bosch in 1953.

As part of its plan to become a major supplier to North American carmakers, in 1966 Nippondenso established a sales office in Chicago and branch offices in Los Angeles and Detroit. It then turned to Europe, establishing a branch office in Stuttgart, Germany, in 1970. The following year the company established its first overseas subsidiary, Nippondenso of Los Angeles (now DENSO Sales California). In 1972 the company established three more foreign subsidiaries, in Australia, Canada, and Thailand. A European subsidiary (now DENSO Europe) was established in the Netherlands in 1973.

Nippondenso began consignment production for what is now known as Asmo Co., a maker of electric motors, in 1978. In 1984 the company joined with Allen Bradley Co. (US) to develop factory automation equipment. That year the predecessor to DENSO Manufacturing Michigan, one of the company's largest international subsidiaries, was established. Nippondenso expanded into Spain in 1989 by opening a plant in Barcelona.

In 1990 the company formed NDM Manufacturing (now DENSO Manufacturing UK), a joint venture (25%-owned) with Magneti Marelli of Italy, for the manufacture of automotive air conditioning and heating systems. The following year Nippondenso and AT&T formed a joint venture for the development of integrated circuit (IC) cards.

Nippondenso established several Chinese manufacturing joint ventures during the mid-1990s. In 1994 the company was recognized by the *Guinness Book of Records* as the maker of the world's smallest car, the DENSO Micro Car.

The company changed its name to DENSO CORPORATION in 1996. In 1999 DENSO acquired the rotating machines business of Magneti Marelli of Italy. The next year DENSO agreed to buy out Magneti Marelli's share in the companies' automotive air conditioning and heating joint venture (deal completed in 2001).

In 2001 DENSO ceased production of wireless phones in order to focus on making onboard car information systems. Also in 2001 the company merged its industrial equipment subsidiaries (bar code scanners and factory automation robots), and spun them off as majority-owned subsidiary DENSO Wave.

DENSO joined forces with Robert Bosch GmbH in 2003 to form a joint venture for the development of car navigation and multimedia systems.

EXECUTIVES

Chairman: Hiromu Okabe
Vice Chairman: Akihiko Saito
President and CEO: Koichi Fukaya
EVP: Takao Inukai
EVP: Kazuo Matsumoto
EVP: Shinro Iwatsuki
EVP: Oyuki Ogawa
Senior Managing Director: Masatoshi Ano
Senior Managing Director: Mitsuharu Kato
Senior Managing Director: Michio Fukuzaki
Senior Managing Director: Hiromi Tokuda
Senior Managing Director: Mineo Hanai
VP, DENSO International America: Bill Foy
Auditors: Deloitte Touche Tohmatsu

LOCATIONS

HQ: DENSO CORPORATION
    1-1, Showa-cho, Kariya, Aichi 448-8661, Japan
Phone: +81-566-25-5511   **Fax:** +81-566-25-4860
US HQ: 24777 Denso Dr., Southfield, MI 48086
US Phone: 248-350-7500   **US Fax:** 248-213-2337
Web: www.denso.co.jp

DENSO has manufacturing facilities in Argentina, Australia, Brazil, Canada, China, the Czech Republic, Germany, Hungary, India, Indonesia, Italy, Japan, Malaysia, Mexico, the Netherlands, the Philippines, Poland, Portugal, Saudi Arabia, South Africa, South Korea, Spain, Taiwan, Thailand, Turkey, the UK, the US, and Vietnam.

2006 Sales

	$ mil.	% of total
Japan	19,465.3	60
Americas	5,871.5	18
Europe	3,597.6	11
Asia & Oceania	3,360.0	11
Adjustments	(5,180.8)	—
Total	**27,113.6**	**100**

PRODUCTS/OPERATIONS

2006 Sales

	$ mil.	% of total
Automotive		
Thermal systems	8,775.7	33
Powertrain control systems	6,521.8	24
Electronic systems	4,139.6	15
Electric systems	3,102.6	11
Small motors	1,911.1	7
Intelligent transport systems (ITS)	1,283.0	5
Other automotive	346.4	1
Industrial systems & consumer products	597.5	2
Other products	435.9	2
Total	**27,113.6**	**100**

Selected Products

Automotive
  Thermal systems
    Air conditioning systems
    Air purifiers
    Cooling fans
    Cooling modules
    Front end modules
    Oil coolers
    Radiators
    Truck refrigeration units
  Powertrain control systems
    Diesel engine management systems
    Gasoline engine management systems
    Transmission control components
  Electronic systems
    Car security systems
    Instrument clusters
    Integrated climate control panels
    Rear and corner sonars
    Remote keyless entry controllers
    Smart keys
  Electric systems
    ABS actuators
    Airbag sensors
    Alternators
    Electric power steering motors
    Starters
  Small motors
    Power window motors
    Windshield washer systems
    Windshield wiper systems
  Intelligent transport systems (ITS)
    Car navigation systems
    Data communications modules
Industrial Systems and Environmental Systems
  Bar code readers
  Factory automation robots
  Refrigeration and air conditioning products

COMPETITORS

Adept Technology
Aisin Seiki
APM Automotive
COFIDE
Delphi
Honda
IWKA
Key Safety Systems
Linamar
Motorola
Nissan
Robert Bosch
Symbol Technologies
Visteon

HISTORICAL FINANCIALS

Company Type: Public

Income Statement

FYE: March 31

	REVENUE ($ mil.)	NET INCOME ($ mil.)	NET PROFIT MARGIN	EMPLOYEES
3/06	27,114	—	—	105,723
3/05	26,034	—	—	104,183
3/04	24,256	—	—	95,461
3/03	19,465	—	—	89,380
3/02	18,102	—	—	86,639
Annual Growth	10.6%	—	—	5.1%

Revenue History

Pink Sheets: DNZOY

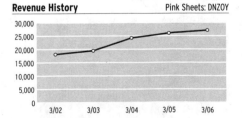

Dentsu

Unlike Godzilla, Dentsu is one monster that doesn't leave Japan in ruins. One of the largest advertising conglomerates in the world, Dentsu is the #1 ad firm in Japan. Its numerous agencies operate in 27 countries and provide creative services for more than 6,000 clients, although sales outside Japan only account for a small percentage of revenue. Dentsu also offers a host of other services, including public relations, media and event planning, and market research. The company has expanded its operations in Asia through a partnership with US-based Young & Rubicam and owns a 15% stake in ad conglomerate Publicis Groupe. The company completed its IPO on the Tokyo Stock Exchange in late 2001.

As Japan's largest ad conglomerate Dentsu controls more than 30% of Japan's advertising market. While Dentsu has outdistanced its closest domestic rivals, Hakuhodo and Asatsu-DK, the company has designs on becoming a global powerhouse on par with ad conglomerates such as WPP Group and Omnicom, but currently less than 10% of Dentsu's revenues are generated outside of Japan.

Dentsu's strategy for international expansion has been varied and somewhat unfocused; in addition to its partnership with Young & Rubicam, the company owns a handful of US ad agencies and a 15% stake in Publicis (as a result of its investment in Bcom3). Dentsu's future growth plans include expanding its operations in Asia (particularly in China) using the Dentsu brand, and maintaining a grip in the US and Europe through its partnership with Publicis.

Dentsu has organized itself along four business lines representing the company's current position and the lines it would like to grow. Advertising services comprise the bulk of Dentsu's operations, while specialized marketing services, e-solutions services, and overseas operations represent Dentsu's growth objectives.

HISTORY

Seeing a need for a Japanese wire service, Sino-Japanese war correspondent Hoshiro Mitsunaga founded Telegraphic Service Co. in 1901. Mitsunaga let newspapers pay their wire service bills with advertising space, which his advertising agency, Japan Advertising (also founded in 1901) resold. He merged the two companies as Nihon Denpo-Tsushin Sha (Japan Telegraphic Communication Company) in 1907. Known as Dentsu for short (the name was officially changed in 1955), the company gained Japanese rights to the United Press wire in 1908 and began extracting even more favorable advertising rates from its clients.

With its mix of content and advertising, Dentsu became a leading Japanese communications business. But in 1936 Japan's government consolidated all news services into its propaganda machine, Domei, taking half of Dentsu's stock. During WWII, all of Japan's advertising agencies were combined into 12 entities. Following the war, US occupation forces dismantled Domei, and its 50% holding in Dentsu stock was transferred to two new press agencies, Kyodo and Jiji.

Hideo Yoshida, who became president of Dentsu in 1947, began the task of rebuilding the company, currying favor by employing the sons of politicians and business leaders. He also helped build the television industry in Japan by investing in start-up broadcasters. Their gratitude translated into preferential treatment for Dentsu, leading to its decades-long domination of Japanese TV advertising.

By 1973 Dentsu had become the world's largest advertising agency, but the company's growth stalled with the slowing Japanese economy. Slow to expand overseas, foreign billings accounted for just 7% of revenues in 1986 (and despite growth initiatives the company has yet to make lasting progress in this area). The next year Saatchi & Saatchi passed Dentsu as the world's #1 advertising group. Young & Rubicam/Dentsu later joined with Havas' Eurocom to form HDM Worldwide (named after Havas, Dentsu, and Y&R's Marsteller).

Dentsu rebounded with Japan's economic boom in the late 1980s, but the company continued to struggle abroad. Eurocom pulled out of HDM Worldwide in 1990, and the newly named Dentsu, Young & Rubicam Partnerships reorganized to focus on North America, Asia, and Australia. Dentsu joined with Collett Dickenson Pearce to maintain its presence in Europe after HDM's demise. Restructuring in 1996 created several new units, including one to focus on the Olympics, and in 1997 the company set up the Interactive Solution Center to focus on digital media.

The company agreed to buy UK ad agency Harari Page in 1998 and announced plans for its own public offering. Dentsu took a 20% stake in Bcom3 (formerly BDM) in 2000, the new advertising holding company formed by the merger of The Leo Group and MacManus Group. It also formed a Japanese Internet services joint venture with US consulting company marchFIRST. After marchFIRST's demise Dentsu gained full ownership of the company and renamed it DentsuFUSE.

The following year Dentsu reorganized its US and European units and purchased US ad firm Oasis International Group and became a publicly listed company in late 2001.

EXECUTIVES

President and CEO: Tateo Mataki, age 67
EVP: Ko Matsumoto
EVP: Tetsu Nakamura
EVP: Tatsuyoshi Takashima
CEO, Dentsu Holdings: Toyo Shigeta
Deputy General Manager, Dentsu Chubu:
  Mitsuro Shibata
Senior Managing Director: Isao Maruyama
Senior Managing Director: Hiromori Hayashi
Managing Director: Kimiharu Matsuda
Managing Director: Ryuichi Mori
Managing Director: Haruyuki Takahashi
Managing Director: Itsuma Wakasugi
Executive Director: Toyohiko Yamonouchi
Director, Accounting Division, Finance, and Accounting Headquarters: Shoichi Nakamoto
Director, Creative Group Management Division:
  Kazuo Arai
Executive Director: Kunihiko Tainaka
Executive Project Manager, International Headquarters: Takeshi Mori
Senior Manager, Corporate Communications Division:
  Yukihiro Oguchi
Auditors: KPMG

LOCATIONS

HQ: Dentsu Inc.
1-8-1, Higashi-shimbashi, Minato-ku,
Tokyo 105-7001, Japan
Phone: +81-3-6216-5111   **Fax:** +81-3-5551-2013
US HQ: 488 Madison Ave., 23rd Fl., New York, NY 10022
US Phone: 212-829-5120   **US Fax:** 212-829-0009
Web: www.dentsu.com

Dentsu has offices in 31 cities in Japan and 41 cities in 27 countries.

PRODUCTS/OPERATIONS

Selected Operations

Creative Associates
DentsuFUSE (Internet services)
Dentsu Kosan Service (management services)
Dentsu Management Services
Dentsu Music Publishing
Dentsu Public Relations
Dentsu Research
Dentsu TEC
Dentsu Young & Rubicam (50%, advertising)

COMPETITORS

Asatsu-DK
Grey Global
Hakuhodo
Havas
Interpublic Group
Omnicom
Publicis
Video Research
WPP Group

HISTORICAL FINANCIALS

Company Type: Public

Income Statement				FYE: March 31
	REVENUE ($ mil.)	NET INCOME ($ mil.)	NET PROFIT MARGIN	EMPLOYEES
3/06	3	264	9,414.3%	15,337
3/05	2,903	358	12.3%	14,530
3/04	2,750	214	7.8%	14,245
3/03	2,359	(39)	—	13,623
3/02	2,216	204	9.2%	12,167
Annual Growth	(81.1%)	6.6%	—	6.0%

Net Income History

Exchange: Tokyo

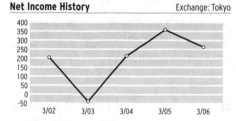

Deutsche Bahn

Deutsche Bahn gets passengers and freight from Punkt A to Punkt B. Its freight transport and logistics division moves more than 265 million tons of rail cargo annually and includes leading logistics providers Stinnes and Schenker. The railway's long-distance, regional, urban passenger transport divisions carry more than 1.7 billion passengers yearly throughout Germany and into neighboring countries. Deutsche Bahn also operates bus services in Germany. Other divisions manage the company's train stations and provide track infrastructure services. Deutsche Bahn, owned by the German government, is one of Europe's largest transportation providers.

Freight transportation and logistics operations, under the DB Logistics umbrella, have surpassed passenger transportation to become Deutsche Bahn's largest business segment. The company strengthened its logistics business in 2006 by acquiring US-based freight forwarder BAX Global, which is being integrated into Schenker.

Deutsche Bahn hopes to grow by taking advantage of its ability to combine logistics and transportation offerings for its customers. If the integration of BAX Global proceeds successfully, additional acquisitions are likely.

Solid results posted by Deutsche Bahn for the first half of 2006 renewed talk of an IPO. Privatization has been under discussion for years but has run into financial and political roadblocks. Key questions include whether the rail transportation and logistics operations should be separated and whether rail infrastructure should be part of a private company or remain under state control. An offering could come as soon as 2008, insiders predict.

HISTORY

In 1989 the Federal Cabinet of West Germany adopted a resolution to set up an independent government railway commission. That year the wall between East Germany and West Germany came down, and the two nations were united into the Federal Republic of Germany in 1990.

In 1993 the cabinet endorsed a railway reform plan submitted by the federal minister of transport, and later that year the plan won approval from the German Parliament and the Federal Council. Deutsche Bahn was then established in 1994 to unify Germany's western (Deutsche Bundesbahn) and eastern (Deutsche Reichsbahn) railway systems as a public company. The Federal Republic of Germany was sole shareholder.

The next year Deutsche Bahn created a subsidiary, DBKom, to offer telecom services in competition with Deutsche Telekom. In 1996 a consortium led by German conglomerate Mannesmann bought a 50% stake in DBKom. By 1997 Deutsche Bahn had been transformed from a government department into a registered company and split into four operating units: tracks, freight, local passenger services, and intercity passenger services. That year Deutsche Bahn also bought Lufthansa's 33% stake in tour operator Deutsches Reisebüro (DER), giving it full ownership of the company as well as DER's 20% stake in tour group TUI.

Trouble came in 1998: Deutsche Bahn sent its 59 first-generation high-speed InterCityExpress (ICE) trains for inspections after one of the trains crashed and killed 98 passengers. Investigators believed a broken wheel caused the crash.

Deutsche Bahn and French state-owned railway SNCF announced plans in 1999 to develop a high-speed train capable of traveling up to 320 km (198 miles) per hour. Also that year Hartmut Mehdorn, credited with turning around printing equipment manufacturer Heidelberger Druck and DaimlerChrysler's aerospace unit, became Deutsche Bahn's new CEO. Tasked with improving the railway's punctuality, Mehdorn pledged to make Deutsche Bahn more efficient by cutting losses and raising productivity. That year the company sold its stake in TUI to conglomerate Preussag and its DER unit to supermarket giant Rewe.

In 2000 the company's DB Cargo unit and Dutch rail freight company N.S. Cargo formed a new group, Railion (joined by Danish State Railways' freight unit DSB Gods in 2001). Also in 2000, Germany's transport minister postponed plans to float Deutsche Bahn after it posted losses for the first time since 1994.

Hoping to take advantage of Deutsche Bahn's financial troubles, Connex, then a subsidiary of French conglomerate Vivendi, offered in 2001 to acquire Deutsche Bahn's long-distance express passenger trains. But Mehdorn refused the offer, saying the company did not want to give up its long-distance traffic. Deutsche Bahn did agree in 2001 to form a railway telematics (communications system) joint venture with Mannesmann Arcor, a company controlled by Vodafone. The agreement called for Deutsche Bahn to keep its 18% stake in Arcor but lose its minority veto rights, which Deutsche Bahn had used earlier that year to block an Arcor IPO.

The company in 2002 bought the 65% stake in logistics provider Stinnes held by E.ON. The next year it took full ownership of Stinnes.

In 2004 Deutsche Bahn partnered with two UK companies, Stagecoach Group and Virgin Group, to bid on UK rail franchises. Deutsche Bahn withdrew from the venture before the bidding got very far, however. Later that year Deutsche Bahn and Russian Railways announced plans to form a joint venture for freight transport.

Deutsche Bahn sold its 83% stake in bus unit Deutsche Touring GmbH to Eurosur SA of Spain for an undisclosed amount in 2005.

EXECUTIVES

Chairman of the Supervisory Board: Werner Müller
Deputy Chairman of the Supervisory Board:
Norbert Hansen
Chairman of the Management Board and CEO:
Hartmut Mehdorn
CFO: Diethelm Sack
Economic and Political Affairs, Management Board:
Otto Wiesheu
Infrastructure and Services, Management Board:
Stefan Garber
Integrated Systems Rail, Management Board:
Roland Heinisch
Personnel, Management Board: Margret Suckale
Marketing and Political Relations, Management Board:
Klaus Daubertshäuser
Passenger Transport, Management Board:
Karl-Freidrich Rausch
Transport and Logistics, Management Board:
Norbert Bensel, age 58
Chairman of the Management Board, DB Netz:
Volker Kefer
Head of Purchasing: André Zeug, age 50
Auditors: PwC Deutsche Revision AG

LOCATIONS

HQ: Deutsche Bahn Aktiengesellschaft
Potsdamer Platz 2, D-10785 Berlin, Germany
Phone: +49-30-297-0   **Fax:** +49-30-297-6-19-19
Web: www.db.de

2005 Sales

	% of total
Europe	
Germany	76
Other countries	18
Asia/Pacific region	3
North America	2
Other regions	1
Total	**100**

PRODUCTS/OPERATIONS

2005 Sales

	% of total
Transport & logistics	49
Passenger transport	45
Infrastructure & services	5
Other	1
Total	**100**

COMPETITORS

Air Berlin
Air France
British Airways
DHL
Expeditors
FedEx
Geodis
GeoLogistics
KLM
Kuehne + Nagel
Lufthansa
National Express Group
Panalpina
SNCF
UPS Supply Chain Solutions
Veolia Environnement

HISTORICAL FINANCIALS

Company Type: Government-owned

Income Statement   FYE: December 31

	REVENUE ($ mil.)	NET INCOME ($ mil.)	NET PROFIT MARGIN	EMPLOYEES
12/05	31,654	724	2.3%	216,389
12/04	35,314	246	0.7%	233,657
12/03	33,539	(733)	—	250,913
12/02	19,584	(475)	—	250,690
12/01	15,533	(360)	—	214,371
Annual Growth	19.5%	—	—	0.2%

Net Income History

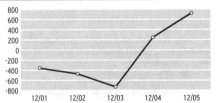

Deutsche Bank

One of the largest banks in the world, Deutsche Bank offers retail banking services in Germany; its investment bank and asset management business spans Europe, the Pacific Rim, and the Americas. The bank's three operating segments are Corporate and Investment Banking, Private Clients and Asset Management, and Corporate Investments. It has nearly 1,600 locations worldwide, more than half of those in Germany. As part of its focus on retail banking and asset management Deutsche Bank acquired Bankgesellschaft Berlin AG, the parent of Berliner Bank, for $856 million to expand its footprint at home. In the US Deutsche Bank owns investment bank Deutsche Bank Alex. Brown and mutual fund manager DWS Scudder.

The latter is part of Deutsche Asset Management, which oversees more than $700 billion for institutional and retail investors worldwide. Deutsche Bank is expanding the DWS mutual fund business across continental Europe. It is also expanding its asset management business in the UK with the acquisition of Tilney Group from Bridgepoint Capital for around £350 million. The move is perhaps an attempt to counter an overall slowdown of its business in the UK and reverse attrition: The bank had sold some of its asset management business there to Aberdeen Asset Management.

Its Corporate and Investment Banking segment, including New York-based Deutsche Bank Securities, performs all manner of capital markets and corporate banking services, including securities underwriting, trading, and research; mergers and acquisition advisory; and trust and cash management.

To boost its lending operations in the US, the company is buying MortgageIT for some $430 million. Deutsche Bank is building its already-massive real estate investment and management business through acquisitions such as RREEF in the US, but it sold its nearly 38% stake in mortgage bank Eurohypo, which specializes in commercial property across Europe and in the US, to Commerzbank.

Deutsche Bank is taking giant steps to increase its retail operations at home. In addition to its acquisition of Bankgesellschaft Berlin AG, Deutsche Bank also acquired around 100 Norisbank branches from rival DZ Bank for €420 million.

HISTORY

Georg von Siemens opened Deutsche Bank in Berlin in 1870. Three years later the firm opened an office in London and was soon buying other German banks. In the late 1800s Deutsche Bank helped finance Germany's electrification (carried out by Siemens AG) and railroad construction in the US and the Ottoman Empire. Von Siemens ran the bank until his death in 1901.

The bank survived post-WWI financial chaos by merging with Disconto-Gesellschaft and later helped finance the Nazi war machine. After the war, the Allies split the company into 10 banks; it became extinct in Soviet-controlled East Germany.

The bank was reassembled in 1957 and primarily engaged in commercial banking, often taking direct interests in its customers. It added retail services in the 1960s. In 1975, to prevent

the shah of Iran from gaining a stake in Daimler-Benz (now DaimlerChrysler), the bank bought 29% of that company.

The firm opened an investment banking office in the US in 1971 and a branch office in 1978. In the 1980s it expanded geographically, buying Bank of America's Italian subsidiary (1986) and UK merchant bank Morgan Grenfell (1989); it also moved into insurance, creating life insurer DB Leben (1989).

Terrorists killed chairman Alfred Herrhausen, a symbol of German big business, in 1989. After German reunification in 1990, successor Hilmar Kopper oversaw the bank's reestablishment in eastern Germany.

In 1994 Deutsche Bank bought most of ITT's commercial finance unit. That year the company suffered scandal when real estate developer Jurgen Schneider borrowed more than DM1 billion and disappeared; he was later found and returned to Germany.

The company grew its global investment banking operations in 1995 under its Morgan Grenfell subsidiary. Corporate culture clashes prompted Deutsche Bank to take greater control of the unit and restructure it in 1998.

Deutsche Bank's global aspirations suffered a setback in 1998 when losses on investments in Russia trimmed its bottom line. Still trying to put WWII behind it, the bank accepted responsibility for its wartime dealing in gold seized from Jews but has rejected liability to compensate victims of Nazi forced labor who toiled in industrial companies in which it holds stakes.

In 1999 the bank acquired Bankers Trust. Despite a decision to divest its industrial portfolio, in 1999 the company bought Tele Columbus, the #2 cable network in Germany, and Piaggio, the Italian maker of the famed Vespa motor scooter. On the banking front, Deutsche Bank bought Chase Manhattan's Dutch auction business and sought a foothold in Japan through alliances with Nippon Life Insurance and Sakura Bank (now part of Sumitomo Mitsui Banking).

In 2001 Deutsche Bank eliminated 2,600 jobs worldwide and realigned its businesses into two divisions. Deutsche Bank also bought Banque Worms from French insurer AXA.

Looking for a steady supply of cash, in 2001 Deutsche Bank's Morgan Grenfall Private Equity bought 3,000 English pubs owned by UK-based conglomerate Whitbread plc. In 2002 more shuffling of the executive board members allowed Deutsche Bank to grow in the international Anglo-American style, rather than as a domestic player.

In 2004 Deutsche Bank acquired Berkshire Mortgage (now Deutsche Bank Berkshire Mortgage), one of the top multifamily residential lenders in the US. The next year it bought Russian financial services company United Financial Group and combined its depositary business with its own.

The year 2006 was a bad year for the company from a public relations standpoint. Fallout from former chairman Rolf Breuer's remarks regarding the financial stability of banking client Kirch Holding led to a shakeup in the executive suite and the board that year. Later, UK financial regulators charged the bank a $11.1 million fine for market misconduct related to trading activity in 2004. In the US, the IRS investigated the bank for allegedly abusive tax shelters.

The bank also took a public relations hit when its CEO, Josef Ackermann, went on trial for illegal bonuses during his tenure at Mannesmann.

EXECUTIVES

Spokesman of the Board of Managing Directors and Chairman of the Group Executive Committee:
Josef Ackermann, age 58, $9,928,875 pay
Vice Chairman: Caio Koch-Weser
COO: Hermann-Josef Lamberti, age 49, $3,703,750 pay
CFO: Anthony Di Iorio, age 62
Chairman of the Supervisory Board: Clemens Börsig, age 57
Chief Risk Officer: Hugo Banziger, age 50
Chief Administrative Officer: Tessen von Heydebreck, age 59
Global Head of Compliance: Henry Klehm
Global Head of Convertible Bond Trading, Global Markets: Andy McDonnell
Global Head of Deutsche Asset Management: Kevin Parker
Global Head of Emerging Markets: Pablo Calderini
Managing Director and Head of Group Accounting: Martin Edelmann
Head of Global Banking: Michael Cohrs
Head of Private Wealth Management: Pierre de Weck, age 56
Head of Regional Management Worldwide; Chairman of the Management Committee, Germany:
Jürgen Fitschen
Head of Global Markets: Anshu Jain, age 42
Head of Global Transaction Banking:
Werner Steinmueller
Head of Strategic Equity Transactions Group:
Serge Marquie
Head of Private and Business Clients: Rainer Neske
Head of Equity and Fixed Income Investments:
Rami Hayek
Head of Private Wealth Management, US:
Thomas (Tom) Bowers
Head of US Private Bank: Patrick Campion
General Counsel: Hans-Dirk Krekeler
Auditors: KPMG Deutsche Treuhand-Gesellschaft AG

LOCATIONS

HQ: Deutsche Bank AG
Taunusanlage 12,
60262 Frankfurt am Main, Germany
Phone: +49-69-910-00   **Fax:** +49-69-910-34-225
US HQ: 60 Wall St., New York, NY 10005
US Phone: 212-250-2500   **US Fax:** 212-797-0291
Web: www.deutsche-bank.de

PRODUCTS/OPERATIONS

2005 Sales

	% of total
Interest	
Trading assets	32
Loans	13
Central bank funds sold & securities purchased under resale agreements	19
Securities borrowed	8
Other	5
Noninterest	
Commissions & fees	19
Gains on securities for sale	2
Other	2
Total	**100**

COMPETITORS

ABN AMRO	HVB Group
Bankgesellschaft Berlin	Intuit
Barclays	JPMorgan Chase
BNP Paribas	KfW
Charles Schwab	Lehman Brothers
Citigroup	Merrill Lynch
Citigroup Global Markets	Mizuho Financial
Commerzbank	Morgan Stanley
Cortal Consors	National Australia Bank
Credit Suisse	Rabobank
Dresdner Bank	SCH
DZ BANK	Société Générale
E*TRADE Financial	TD Bank
Goldman Sachs	UBS
HSBC Holdings	

HISTORICAL FINANCIALS

Company Type: Public

Income Statement

FYE: December 31

	ASSETS ($ mil.)	NET INCOME ($ mil.)	INCOME AS % OF ASSETS	EMPLOYEES
12/05	1,175,116	4,180	0.4%	63,427
12/04	1,146,189	3,373	0.3%	65,417
12/03	1,009,098	1,714	0.2%	67,682
12/02	794,984	416	0.1%	77,442
Annual Growth	13.9%	115.8%	—	(6.4%)

2005 Year-End Financials

Equity as % of assets: 3.0%
Return on assets: 0.4%
Return on equity: 11.8%
Long-term debt ($ mil.): 218,130
No. of shares (mil.): —

Dividends
Yield: 2.2%
Payout: 26.1%
Market value ($ mil.): —
Sales ($ mil.): 72,659

Stock History

NYSE: DB

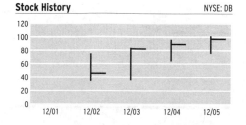

	STOCK PRICE ($) FY Close	P/E High	P/E Low	PER SHARE ($) Earnings	PER SHARE ($) Dividends
12/05	96.87	12	9	8.23	2.15
12/04	89.01	21	14	4.53	1.45
12/03	82.21	28	13	2.90	1.53
12/02	45.43	112	53	0.66	0.95
Annual Growth	28.7%	—	—	131.9%	31.3%

Deutsche Post

Deutsche Post has grown out of its mailbox. Through its DHL unit, the company is one of the world's leading providers of express delivery and logistics services, and those businesses account for more than half of the company's sales. Deutsche Post still handles the mail in Germany, delivering an average of 72 million letters per working day. In addition to traditional postal operations, the company provides mail process outsourcing at home and abroad. Majority-owned Deutsche Postbank offers financial services. The German government controls a 35% stake in Deutsche Post.

In its effort to move beyond mail, Deutsche Post has gained control of express delivery and logistics operations across Europe and in the US. The company completed its purchase of UK-based logistics provider Exel in December 2005.

To eliminate overlaps in its operations, Deutsche Post has united its parcel and express delivery services (DHL and Euro Express) and logistics services (Danzas and Exel) under the DHL brand.

HISTORY

The German postal system was established in the 1490s when German emperor Maximilian I ordered a reliable and regular messenger service to be set up between Austria (Innsbruck, where the emperor had his court) and the farther reaches of his Holy Roman Empire: the Netherlands, France, and Rome. The von Tassis (later renamed Taxis) family of Italy was responsible for running the network. Family members settled in major cities across Europe to expand the postal business.

Although the family operated what was officially an exclusively royal mail service, by the early 1500s the company was also delivering messages for private patrons. In 1600 a family member who served as general postmaster was authorized to collect fees for private mail deliveries. By the early 19th century, Thurn and Taxis, as the company was then called, was the leading postal service in the Holy Roman Empire, serving more than 11 million people.

The dissolution of the Holy Roman Empire, prompted by Napoleon's military adventures, led to the creation of a federation of 39 independent German states. Thurn und Taxis had to make agreements with members of the separate states, including Austria and Prussia. After Austria's defeat in 1866 by Prussia, the confederation was dissolved and all Thurn und Taxis postal systems were absorbed by Prussia. When Bismarck's Prussian-led German Reich was established in 1870, the new postal administration (Reichspostverwaltung) began issuing postage stamps valid across Germany.

After Germany was defeated in WWII and split into two nations in 1949, two postal systems were established: Deutsche Post (East Germany) and Deutsche Bundespost (West Germany). The fall of the Berlin Wall in 1989 preceded a reunion of the two German states in 1990. That year Deutsche Post, led by chairman Klaus Zumwinkel, was integrated into Deutsche Bundespost. The merger resulted in losses and a huge backlog of undelivered mail. Zumwinkel initiated the company's first steps to recovery by cutting 140,000 jobs.

The heavy costs of reunification (it was 1994 before Deutsche Bundespost posted a profit again) prompted the German government to set the postal system on a course toward full privatization. In 1995 the postal system was restructured as Deutsche Post AG and placed under the management of executives from the private sector.

In 1998 a new postal law reaffirmed Deutsche Post's monopoly on traditional letter delivery until 2002. However, other special mail delivery options (such as same-day delivery of letters) were granted to private companies. That year Deutsche Post acquired shares in parcel delivery companies in Europe and the US, including a stake of nearly 25% in DHL. In 1999 it acquired Deutsche Postbank, the former retail banking arm of Deutsche Bundespost, as part of a strategy to make it more attractive for an IPO.

Continuing its buying spree, Deutsche Post grabbed Swiss-based logistics giant Danzas Holding, Swedish freight forwarder ASG, and the distribution and logistics unit of Dutch transport group Royal Nedlloyd. Undeterred by a European Commission probe into whether it received improper state subsidies, Deutsche Post added more units in 2000, including US-based airfreight forwarder Air Express International, which was integrated into Danzas. It also acquired New York-based QuickMAIL.

The German government sold a minority stake in Deutsche Post to the public in 2000. (Further share sales followed, and by 2006, the government had reduced its stake in Deutsche Post to about 35%.)

In 2002 Deutsche Post took full ownership of DHL and the next year (through DHL) paid about $1 billion for the ground delivery network of US-based Airborne.

Deutsche Post sold a minority stake in Deutsche Postbank in an IPO in 2004.

EXECUTIVES

Chairman, Supervisory Board: Jürgen Weber, age 65
Chairman, Board of Management: Klaus Zumwinkel, age 61, $3,194,252 pay
Member of the Board of Management, Express Americas, Asia, and EMA: John P. Mullen, age 51
Member of the Board of Management, Finance: Edgar Ernst, $2,028,096 pay
Member of the Board of Management, Financial Services: Prof. Wulf von Schimmelmann, age 58, $2,028,848 pay
Member of the Board of Management, Logistics and Corporate Services: Frank Appel, age 45, $1,679,153 pay
Member of the Board of Management, LOGISTICS: John Murray Allan
Member of the Board of Management, Mail: Hans-Dieter Petram, $2,129,502 pay
Member of the Board of Management, Personnel: Walter Scheurle, $1,417,845 pay
EVP, Global Network Management, Deutsche Post World Net: Christoph Mueller
Executive Director, DHL Exel Supply Chain, Americas and Asia/Pacific: Bruce A. Edwards, age 50
Executive Director, DHL Exel Supply Chain, Europe, Middle East, and Africa: John Pattullo
Executive Director, DHL Global Forwarding: Chris Fahy
Auditors: PricewaterhouseCoopers

LOCATIONS

HQ: Deutsche Post AG
Charles-de-Gaulle-Str. 20, 53113 Bonn, Germany
Phone: +49-228-182-0   **Fax:** +49-228-182-7099
Web: www.dpwn.de

2005 Sales

	% of total
Europe	
Germany	50
Other countries	25
Americas	15
Asia/Pacific	8
Other regions	2
Total	**100**

PRODUCTS/OPERATIONS

2005 Sales

	% of total
Express	40
Mail	27
Logistics	18
Financial services	15
Total	**100**

COMPETITORS

Commerzbank	HSBC Holdings
Con-way Inc.	HVB Group
Deutsche Bank	Kuehne + Nagel
DZ BANK	La Poste
Erste Bank	Poste Italiane
Expeditors	Royal Mail
FedEx	Stinnes
Finland Post	TNT
Geodis	UPS
Hays	US Postal Service

HISTORICAL FINANCIALS
Company Type: Public

Income Statement   FYE: December 31

	REVENUE ($ mil.)	NET INCOME ($ mil.)	NET PROFIT MARGIN	EMPLOYEES
12/05	57,177	4,222	7.4%	347,607
12/04	60,743	2,166	3.6%	346,410
12/03	51,739	1,643	3.2%	341,572
12/02	44,295	691	1.6%	371,912
12/01	30,963	1,402	4.5%	321,369
Annual Growth	**16.6%**	**31.7%**	**—**	**2.0%**

Net Income History   German: DPW

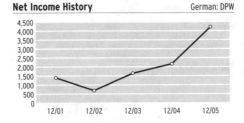

Deutsche Telekom

Operating the *autobahn* on the global information superhighway, Deutsche Telekom is the #1 telecom company in Europe and one of the largest in the world. The company's T-Com unit provides fixed-line network access services and Deutsche Telekom is still Germany's #1 fixed-line phone operator, with about 50 million access lines. T-Mobile International serves wireless phone customers and the company's majority-owned T-Online unit, with 14 million customers, is one of Europe's leading ISPs. The T-Systems division specializes in IT services. The German government has reduced its stake in the company to about 15%. German state-owned development bank KfW owns about 17%. In 2006 US-based investment firm The Blackstone Group acquired a nearly 5% stake in the company.

Deutsche Telekom announced plans to buy out minority shareholders in T-Online and reintegrate the online service into its T-Com unit. After delays due to litigation caused by complaints by T-Online shareholders, the company received a favorable court ruling and reintegrated the business, which it says is crucial to combating a loss of wireline service customers.

The company's T-Com division provides access to the traditional fixed-line telecommunications network, including domestic and international long-distance, data transmission, carrier services, and the sales and lease of customer premise equipment. It also operates through holdings in Eastern Europe. T-Online provides dial-up and broadband Internet access as well as Internet portal services primarily in Germany but also through subsidiaries in France, Spain, and elsewhere in Europe.

The T-Mobile division includes Deutsche Telekom's T-Mobile Deutschland unit, one of that country's leading wireless telecom providers (along with Vodafone's German network) serving more than 26 million subscribers. T-Mobile International also includes T-Mobile USA (with

more than 13 million subscribers), as well as wireless operations in Austria, the Czech Republic, Russia, Poland, and the UK. The company has boosted its T-Mobile USA holdings through the acquisition in 2005 of wireless networks serving California and Nevada from Cingular Wireless. The deal, valued at $2.5 billion, included the end of an agreement in which the two companies used each other's networks.

T-Systems International provides information and communications technology services worldwide to businesses, organizations, and government agencies with national and international operations, mostly German-based multinational customers.

HISTORY

Deutsche Telekom was formed by the 1989 separation of West Germany's telecommunications services from the nation's postal system. Dating back to the 15th century (when the Thurn und Taxis private postal system was created for German principalities), the service expanded to cover Austria, France, the Netherlands, and most of Germany by the 1850s. After the 1866 Austro-Prussian War, it became part of the North German Postal Confederation. When the German Empire was formed in 1871, the postal operation became the Deutsche Reichspost (later the Bundespost). Shortly thereafter, the newly invented telephone was introduced in Germany.

Post-WWI inflation shook the Bundespost, and the government allowed it to try new organizational structures. A 1924 law allowed the state-run service to operate as a quasi-commercial company. Hitler came to power in 1933, and the postal service became an instrument of Nazi surveillance. After WWII occupation forces began rebuilding Germany's badly damaged infrastructure. In 1947 the American-British zone returned postal authority to Germans, and in 1949 the USSR established the state of East Germany.

Only by the 1960s did West Germany's postal and phone services meet modern standards. Privatization of the Bundespost became a political cause when many complained about the monopoly's cost and inefficiency. Efforts to privatize the agency (named Deutsche Telekom in 1989) intensified with the 1990 German reunification. But faced with updating the antiquated phone system of the former East Germany, political opposition to taking Deutsche Telekom public faded.

The company began operating T-D1, its mobile phone network, in 1992, and the next year it launched T-Online, now Germany's largest online service provider. In 1996 Deutsche Telekom finally went public and raised more than $13 billion in Europe's largest IPO. It also launched Global One with France Telecom and Sprint; as part of the partnership, Deutsche Telekom took a 10% stake in Sprint.

In 1998 European Union (EU) member countries opened their phone markets to competition, and Deutsche Telekom's long-distance market share quickly eroded. Under EU pressure, in 1999 Deutsche Telekom said it would sell its cable network, which it divided into nine regional units. In 2000 the company sold its stake in Global One to France Telecom, as did Sprint. (In the fallout from the unwinding of the Global One partnership, Deutsche Telekom in 2001 sold its stake in Sprint PCS and sold its interest in France Telecom the next year.)

Later in 2000 Deutsche Telekom agreed to pay $5.3 billion for a controlling stake in Daimler-Chrysler's Debis Systemhaus information technology services unit. It also launched an IPO of its Internet subsidiary, T-Online.

T-Mobile International moved into the US mobile phone market in 2001 with the acquisitions of VoiceStream Wireless and Powertel, now known as T-Mobile USA. The German government's stake in Deutsche Telekom decreased by 17% largely to accommodate US regulators for the VoiceStream and Powertel acquisitions.

With competition flourishing in Germany, Deutsche Telekom worked hard to lose its bureaucratic image and reposition itself as a slimmer, customer-friendly organization. To cut costs and eliminate debt, it reduced its workforce by 22,000 jobs, or 9%, over two years.

As the company's share price slumped amid the general telecom industry downturn, CEO Ron Sommer was forced to resign in July 2002.

Until 2003 Deutsche Telekom was Germany's #1 cable provider through the company's six regional cable TV operations, which it sold for $1.87 billion to a group of US investors that included Apax Partners, the Goldman Sachs Group, and Providence Equity Partners. The deal represented a substantial discount from a 2001 agreement to sell the cable networks to US-based Liberty Media for about $5 billion. But German regulatory authorities blocked that sale. Deutsche Telekom had previously sold controlling stakes in three other regional networks.

EXECUTIVES

Chairman of the Supervisory Board: Klaus Zumwinkel, age 61
Deputy Chairman of the Supervisory Board: Franz Treml
Chairman of the Management Board and CEO: René Obermann, age 43
Member of the Management Board, Deputy CEO, Head of Finance and Controlling (CFO), and Acting Head of Human Resources: Karl-Gerhard Eick, age 52
Member of the Management Board, Head of Business Customers, and CEO, T-Systems: Lothar Pauly, age 47, $457,991 pay (partial-year salary)
Member of the Management Board, Head of Product Development & Innovation, and CEO, T-Mobile: Hamid Akhavan
Member of the Management Board, Head of Sales and Services in Germany, and CEO, T-Com: Timotheus Hottges
President and CEO, T-Mobile USA: Robert P. Dotson, age 46
Head of Group Corporate Communications; EVP, Corporate Communications, T-Mobile: Philipp Schindera
Auditors: Ernst & Young Wirtschaftsprüfungsgesellschaft

LOCATIONS

HQ: Deutsche Telekom AG
    Friedrich-Ebert-Allee 140, 53113 Bonn, Germany
Phone: +49-228-181-4949   **Fax:** +49-228-181-94004
US HQ: 600 Lexington Ave., 17th Fl.,
    New York, NY 10022
US Phone: 212-424-2900   **US Fax:** 212-424-2989
Web: www.deutschetelekom.com

Deutsche Telekom operates primarily in Germany, but it holds interests in operations worldwide.

2005 Sales

	% of total
Europe	
Germany	57
Other countries	22
North America	20
Other regions	1
Total	**100**

PRODUCTS/OPERATIONS

2005 Sales

	% of total
Mobile communications	48
Broadband & fixed networks	36
Business customers	15
Other	1
Total	**100**

Operating Divisions

T-Com (fixed-line network voice and data services)
T-Mobile (mobile communications services and equipment sales)
T-Systems (data communications and systems services for large business customers)
T-Online (Internet services)

Selected Subsidiaries and Affiliates

Deutsche Telekom Immobilien und Service GmbH (DeTe Immobilien, facility management services provider)
Deutsche Telekom Network Projects and Services GmbH
GMG Generalmietgesellschaft mbH (group leasing and rental business operations)
HT-Hrvatske telekomunikacije d.d. (Hrvatski Telekom HT, 51%, telecommunications services, Croatia)
MagyarCom Holdings GmbH (holding company)
    Magyar Telekom Telecommunications PLC (formerly MagyarTávközlési Rt., or MATÁV, 59%, telecommunications services, Hungary)
Slovak Telecom, a.s. (formerly Slovenské Telekomunikácie a.s., 51%, telecommunications services, Slovakia)
T-Mobile International AG (wireless telecommunications services)
    CMobil B.V. (92%, holding company)
        T-Mobile Czech Republic a.s. (formerly RadioMobil, 61%, wireless telecommunications services)
    Polska Telefonia Cyfrowa Sp. z o.o. (PTC, 49%, wireless telecommunications services, Poland)
    T-Mobile Deutschland GmbH (formerly Deutsche Telekom MobilNet GmbH, or DeTeMobil, wireless telecommunications services)
    T-Mobile Global Holding GmbH
        T-Mobile Holdings Ltd. (T-Mobile UK, formerly One 2 One Personal Communications Ltd., wireless telecommunications services)
        T-Mobile Netherlands B.V. (formerly BEN Nederland, wireless telecommunications services)
    T-Mobile Global Holding Nr. 2 GmbH
        T-Mobile Austria GmbH (formerly max.mobil.Telekommunikation Service GmbH, wireless telecommunications services)
    T-Mobile USA, Inc. (formerly VoiceStream Wireless Corporation, wireless telecommunications services, US)
        Powertel, Inc. (T-Mobile USA)
T-Online International AG (Internet services)
T-Systems Business Services GmbH (information technology)
T-Systems Enterprise Services GmbH (information technology)

COMPETITORS

AOL	mobilcom
Belgacom	NTT
BT	SFR
Cable & Wireless	Siemens AG
COLT Telecom	Swisscom
EDS	TDC
France Telecom	Tele2
Hungarian Telephone and Cable	Telecom Italia
	Telefónica
IBM	Telekom Austria
KPN	Telenor
Lagardère	TeliaSonera
Metromedia	Vodafone

HISTORICAL FINANCIALS

Company Type: Public

Income Statement

FYE: December 31

	REVENUE ($ mil.)	NET INCOME ($ mil.)	NET PROFIT MARGIN	EMPLOYEES
12/05	70,595	6,307	8.9%	243,695
12/04	78,972	3,157	4.0%	244,645
12/03	70,116	3,655	5.2%	248,519
12/02	60,931	(23,165)	—	255,969
Annual Growth	5.0%	—	—	(1.6%)

2005 Year-End Financials

Debt ratio: 75.7%
Return on equity: 9.9%
Cash ($ mil.): 7,403
Current ratio: 0.67
Long-term debt ($ mil.): 43,049
No. of shares (mil.): —
Dividends
    Yield: 3.8%
    Payout: 42.3%
Market value ($ mil.): —

Stock History

NYSE: DT

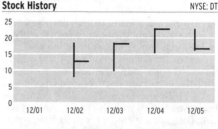

	STOCK PRICE ($) FY Close	P/E High/Low		PER SHARE ($) Earnings	Dividends
12/05	16.63	15	11	1.49	0.63
12/04	22.68	—	—	—	—
12/03	18.13	—	—	—	—
12/02	12.70	—	—	—	0.27
Annual Growth	9.4%	—	—	—	32.6%

Dexia

When Belgian burgs need backing and French cities need to get situated, they turn to Dexia Group. The Franco-Belgian bank is a leader in municipal finance in Europe, with the majority of the market in Belgium and almost half in France. Subsidiary Dexia Crediop is a prominent local government finance company in Italy. Dexia Group also offers retail banking through nearly 1,100 branches in Belgium and Luxembourg and provides asset management, insurance, and fund administration services. The group has offices throughout Europe and in North America, Asia, and Australia.

Other units include Banque Internationale à Luxembourg and Banque Artesia Nederlands. Dexia is selling the latter with its 10 branches in the Netherlands to GE Commercial Finance. US-based Financial Security Assurance Holdings insures bonds and other securities. Dexia combined its institutional investor services operations with those of the Royal Bank of Canada in a joint venture called RBC Dexia Investor Services in 2006.

Dexia found egg on its face after the late-2004 collapse of its acquisition talks with Italian bank Sanpaolo IMI. Dexia, however, remained on the lookout for acquisition targets and in 2006 acquired some 75% of Turkey's DenizBank, which offers retail and commercial banking, as well as public finance, in one of Europe's fastest-growing markets.

HISTORY

Dexia, which is Greek for both "right" and "treaty," is the product of the Maastricht Treaty of 1991, which called for full economic union within the European Economic Community.

Dexia's earliest antecedent, the still-powerful Caisse des Dépôts et Consignations (CDC), was formed in 1816 by the restored French monarchy to manage funds for institutions and government entities. It used the funds to finance public infrastructure projects.

In 1860 the Belgian government formed Crédit Communal de Belgique (known to Flemings as Gemeentekrediet) to provide banking services, particularly loans, to local governments.

Both banks were state-owned until the 1990s. In 1987 CDC, under fire for being too powerful, separated its savings and asset management functions from municipal lending, packaging the latter into Crédit Local, of which it sold 20% in 1991 (CDC now owns 12%). While France was beginning to deal with its chaotic banking system, Belgium was content with its bewildering array of specialty banks until the move toward European economic union forced it to reduce its national debt, which stood at 137% of GDP in 1993. Part of the solution was to offload debt through privatization, so in 1996 Belgium floated Crédit Communal.

As European banks began to consolidate, both Crédit Communal and Crédit Local began looking for ways to grow. Crédit Local made acquisitions in Germany and the UK, and Crédit Communal linked with Banque Internationale a Luxembourg (BIL, formed in 1856 to help finance industrial development throughout Europe).

In 1996 the two companies agreed on a merger modeled on Fortis, a cross-border pairing of insurers AG 1824 (Belgian) and AMEV (Dutch). Dexia spent 1997 assimilating its operations, but not streamlining them: Both companies retained their full management and directorial rosters. Dexia made acquisitions in Spain and Italy and began adding new services, including debt security underwriting; deposit, accounting, and cash management services; and asset management (using BIL as the nucleus for asset management offerings).

In 1999 Dexia expanded its asset management services into Asia and South America and increased its interest in BIL from about 60% to 99%. It also abandoned its unusual ownership structure, merging Dexia France and Dexia Belgium into a single Belgian holding company.

In 2000 the company announced it would jointly develop Europweb's financial Web site, called Ze Project. That year it bought US bond insurer Financial Security Assurance Holdings. It also boosted its private banking operations with the purchase from Aegon N.V. of Dutch bank Labouchere.

In 2001 Dexia bought Artesia Banking Corp., a large, privately held Belgian financial services company. The move bolstered Dexia's already notable size in Belgium. During the merger, Dexia closed about 30% of its branches, bringing its total down from 1,500 to about 1,000. In 2002 Dexia announced plans to reduce staff through attrition. It closed down its venture capital division in the same year.

EXECUTIVES

Chairman of the Management Board: Pierre Richard, age 63
Chairman and Managing Director: Axel Miller, age 40
Vice Chairman: Jacques Guerber, age 56
Member of Management Board and CFO: Rembert von Lowis, age 52
Deputy CFO and Director: Xavier de Walque, age 41
Member of the Management Board and Head of Treasury and Financial Markets; Chairman of the Management Board of Dexia Bank Nederland: Dirk Bruneel, age 55
Member of the Management Board and Group Chief Operations and Technology Officer: Claude Piret
Head of Group Human Resources and Internal Communications: Bernard-Franck Guidoni-Tarissi
Chief Compliance Officer: Jean-Noël Lequeue
Director of Communication: Françoise Lefebvre
Director of Financial Communication and Investor Relations: Robert Boublil
Auditors: PricewaterhouseCoopers Reviseurs d'Entreprises SCCRL; Mazars & Guérard

LOCATIONS

HQ: Dexia NV/SA
  Square de Meeûs, 1, 1000 Brussels, Belgium
Phone: +32-2-213-57-00   **Fax:** +32-2-213-57-01
US HQ: 350 Park Ave., New York, NY 10022
US Phone: 212-826-0100   **US Fax:** 212-688-3101
Web: www.dexia.com

Dexia Group has operations in Australia, Austria, Belgium, Canada, the Cayman Islands, Denmark, France, Germany, Hong Kong, Ireland, Israel, Italy, Japan, Luxembourg, Mexico, the Netherlands, Portugal, Singapore, Slovakia, Spain, Sweden, Switzerland, the UK, and the US.

COMPETITORS

AXA
BNP Paribas
Crédit Agricole
DEPFA BANK
Deutsche Bank
Fortis SA/NV
ING
KBC
Natixis
Sanpaolo IMI
Société Générale

HISTORICAL FINANCIALS

Company Type: Public

Income Statement

	ASSETS ($ mil.)	NET INCOME ($ mil.)	INCOME AS % OF ASSETS	FYE: December 31 EMPLOYEES
12/05	602,526	2,479	0.4%	24,418
12/04	530,807	2,417	0.5%	19,503
12/03	439,179	1,796	0.4%	23,865
12/02	367,803	1,362	0.4%	20,723
12/01	311,230	1,263	0.4%	21,460
Annual Growth	18.0%	18.4%	—	3.3%

2005 Year-End Financials

Equity as % of assets: —   Long-term debt ($ mil.): —
Return on assets: 0.4%   Sales ($ mil.): 69,400
Return on equity: —

Net Income History

Euronext Brussels: DX

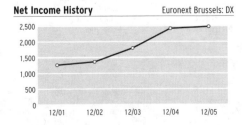

Diageo

Diageo's holiday parties must be the talk of the town. Formed by the 1997 merger of alcoholic beverage giant Guinness with food and spirits company Grand Metropolitan, Diageo is the world's largest producer of alcoholic drinks. Its beers and distilled spirits include Guinness Stout, Harp Lager, Johnnie Walker Scotch, José Cuervo tequila, Tanqueray gin, and Smirnoff vodka. Diageo helps stock bars and shelves in 200 countries around the globe. The company gained the Captain Morgan, Crown Royal, and VO Canadian brands through its purchase of Seagram's drinks business from Vivendi (formerly Vivendi Universal).

Diageo also owns 34% of Moët Hennessy. In a rebranding move to emphasize the Diageo name, the company scrapped its Guinness/UDV unit and folded those operations into its premium drinks division. As a result, Diageo ceased brewing Guinness in the UK and handles that country's demand for the dark brew from its St. James's Gate brewery in Dublin, Ireland. As many as 90 people lost their jobs as a result of the consolidation.

HISTORY

Diageo — from the Latin word for "day" and the Greek word for "world" — was born from Guinness and GrandMet's 1997 merger to fight flat liquor sales and spirited competitors.

Guinness began business in 1759 when Arthur Guinness leased a small brewery in Dublin, Ireland. Guinness began specializing in porters in 1799. Managed by the third generation of Guinnesses, the company went public as a London-based firm in 1886.

In the 1950s managing director Hugh Beaver was credited with conceiving the *Guinness Book of World Records*. During the 1970s Guinness bought more than 200 companies, with disappointing results. Guinness refocused on brewing and distilling operations in the late 1980s by selling noncore businesses and acquiring firms such as Schenley (Dewar's). In 1988 and 1989 it bought 24% of LVMH Moët Hennessy Louis Vuitton (later exchanged for 34% of LVMH's wine and spirits business). More acquisitions followed in the 1990s, capped by Guinness' 1997 announcement of its $19 billion merger with Grand Metropolitan.

GrandMet was established by Maxwell Joseph. In 1931 he began acquiring properties for resale, but WWII slowed his progress. He started buying hotels in 1946, and by 1961 GrandMet had gone public.

Diversification began in 1970 with the purchases of catering firms, restaurants, and betting shops. In the early 1970s, in what was the largest British takeover up to that time, GrandMet bought brewer Truman Hanburg, followed by Watney Mann, which owned International Distillers & Vintners, makers of Bailey's, Bombay Gin, and J&B.

GrandMet looked overseas through the 1970s, taking over the Liggett Group, a US cigarette maker (sold in 1986) whose Paddington unit was the US distributor of J&B Scotch. In 1987 it bought Heublein (Smirnoff, Lancers, José Cuervo). Two years later it bought The Pillsbury Company (Burger King and Green Giant) in a hostile takeover.

When Diageo was created, the companies and brands were divided among four divisions: The Pillsbury Company, Burger King, Guinness, and United Distillers & Vintners.

In 2000 COO Paul Walsh, a former Pillsbury CEO, took over as CEO of both Diageo and its newly combined alcoholic beverage division, Guinness/UDV. Also that year Diageo, along with fellow wine and spirits producer Pernod Ricard, agreed to pay $8.2 billion to Vivendi Universal (now just Vivendi) for the Seagram's drinks business that holds several brands, including Crown Royal, VO Canadian whiskies, and Sterling Vineyards.

In 2001 Diageo sold its Guinness World Records business to media company Gullane Entertainment for $63 million. That year the company also completed its sale of Pillsbury to General Mills. After months of wrangling with the FTC, Diageo finally won regulatory approval for the Seagram's drinks purchase in late 2001.

In May 2002 Diageo completed the sale of its Malibu rum brand to Allied Domecq for about $796 million; the deal also sealed Diageo's ownership of the Captain Morgan rum brand, as Allied Domecq agreed to drop a lawsuit involving Captain Morgan. Later in 2002 Diageo discontinued marketing its Captain Morgan Gold rum drink in the US because of disappointing sales.

Also in 2002 Diageo sold Burger King for $1.5 billion to a group composed of Texas Pacific Group, Bain Capital, and Goldman Sachs Capital Partners. Diageo's decision to sell its Pillsbury unit and its Burger King business (the #2 burger chain, after McDonald's) was part of the company's new focus on its spirits, wine, and beer businesses. The Pillsbury divestiture gave the company a 33% stake in General Mills (Diageo sold nearly half of its shares in October 2004). Also in 2002, Diageo and Pernod Ricard, which together own rights to the Seagram's brand, sold Seagram's line of nonalcoholic mixers to The Coca-Cola Company.

In 2003 Diageo and Jose Cuervo said they would jointly sell Don Julio and Tres Magueyes tequilas. Diageo also joined with Heineken to purchase 30% of InBev's Nambia Breweries in southern Africa. The brewery will make Heineken and Beck's beer.

Diageo said in September 2003 that it would launch a low-alcohol version of its highly popular Baileys Irish Cream. Known as Baileys Glide, the drink still is made with Irish whiskey, but Diageo said it would be manufactured in Germany. Also in September Diageo reopened the George Dickel distillery in Tullahoma, Tennessee. That same year Diageo cut 150 jobs from its Guinness operation amid declining sales of the well-known stout.

In 2005 Diageo and Heineken formed a partnership for the production and distribution of Guinness in Russia. The company also acquired The Chalone Wine Group in 2005 for about $260 million. It added the winery into Diageo's current US wine operations, which are organized under Diageo Chateau & Estate Wines. It also acquired Netherlands distiller Ursus Vodka for an undisclosed amount and added Bushmills Irish whiskey to its stable, with the purchase of the brand from Pernod Ricard for $363 million. It also agreed to stay out of any negotiations regarding the takeover of Allied Domecq. (In 2005 Pernod Ricard acquired Alllied Domecq.)

EXECUTIVES

Chairman: Lord James Blyth of Rowington, age 66, $989,720 pay
CEO and Director: Paul S. Walsh, age 51
CFO and Director: Nicholas C. (Nick) Rose, age 48
President and CEO, North America: Ivan M. Menezes, age 47
CEO, Diageo Korea: Song Duck-young
SVP, Public Policy: Carolyn Panzer
VP, Corporate Relations: Virginia Sanchez
VP, Global Marketing Smirnoff: Barry Sheridan
VP, Smirnoff: Pamela Bower-Nye
Chairman, Diageo Ireland, and Global Brand Director, Guinness: Brian Duffy
President, Diageo Europe: Andrew Morgan, age 50
President, Diageo-Guinness USA: Jim Young
President, Diageo International: Stuart R. Fletcher, age 49
President, Global Marketing, Sales and Innovation: Robert M. (Rob) Malcolm, age 54
President, Global and North American Marketing, Smirnoff and Captain Morgan: James Thompson
Corporate Information Officer: Yvonne Harrison
Director, Investor Relations: Catherine James
Director, Human Resources: Gareth Williams, age 53
General Counsel: Timothy D. (Tim) Proctor, age 56
Company Secretary: Susanne Bunn, age 47
Auditors: KPMG Audit Plc

LOCATIONS

HQ: Diageo plc
  8 Henrietta Place,
  London W1G 0NB, United Kingdom
Phone: +44-20-7927-5200   **Fax:** +44-20-7927-4600
US HQ: 801 Main Ave., Norwalk, CT 06851
US Phone: 203-229-2100   **US Fax:** 203-229-8901
Web: www.diageo.co.uk

Diageo has operations in more than 50 countries and sells its products in more than 200. Production takes place in Canada, Ireland, Italy, the UK, and the US.

2006 Sales

	% of total
Europe	40
North America	31
International	29
Total	**100**

PRODUCTS/OPERATIONS

Selected Divisions and Brands

Beer
  Guinness (Draught, Draught Bitter, Draught Extra Cold, Extra Stout, Foreign Extra)
  Harp lager
  Kaliber (nonalcoholic)
  Kilkenny Irish beer
  Malta (nonalcoholic)
  Red Stripe lager
  Smithwick's ale
Wine and Spirits
  American whiskey (Seagram's 7)
  Canadian whiskey (Crown Royal, Seagram's VO)
  Champagne (Moët & Chandon)
  Cognac (Hennessy)
  Gin (Gilbey's, Gordon's, Tanqueray)
  Irish whiskey (Bushmills)
  Liqueur (Baileys Original Irish Cream, Godiva Original Chocolate)
  Rum (Bundaberg, Captain Morgan, Myers)
  Scotch whisky (Bell's, J&B, Johnnie Walker, Seagram's 7, White Horse)
  Single-malt whiskies (Cragganmore, Dalwhinnie, Glenkinchie, Lagavulin, Oban, Talisker)
  Specialty spirits (Pimms)
  Tequila (Don Julio, José Cuervo outside Mexico, Cuervo Clasico, Tres Magueyes)
  Vodka (Smirnoff, Tanqueray Sterling, Ursus)
  Wine (Blossom Hill, Beaulieu Vineyard, Le Piat d'Or, Sterling Vineyards)

Selected Subsidiaries

The Chalone Wine Group, Ltd. (US)
General Mills (7%, US)
Gleneagles Hotel (golf resort)
Moët Hennessy, SNC (France)
The Old Bushmills Distillery Company Limited (UK)
Ursus Vodka Holding NV (The Netherlands)

COMPETITORS

AmBev
Angostura
Anheuser-Busch
Asahi Breweries
Asia Pacific Breweries
Bacardi
Beam Global Spirits & Wine
Blavod Extreme Spirits
Brown-Forman
Cabo Wabo
Campari
Carlsberg A/S
Constellation Brands
Edrington
FEMSA
Fortune Brands
Foster's
Future Brands
Gallo
Grupo Modelo
Heaven Hill Distilleries
Heineken
InBev
Kirin Brewery Company
Lion Nathan
Martini & Rossi
Maxxium
Miller Brewing
Molson Coors
Paramount Distillers
Pernod Ricard
Rémy Cointreau
SABMiller
Sapporo
Scottish & Newcastle
Scottish Courage
Sidney Frank Importing
Skyy
Sleeman Breweries
V&S
Yuengling & Son

HISTORICAL FINANCIALS

Company Type: Public

Income Statement

	REVENUE ($ mil.)	NET INCOME ($ mil.)	NET PROFIT MARGIN	EMPLOYEES	FYE: June 30
6/06	17,625	3,569	20.2%	22,619	
6/05	16,308	2,653	16.3%	22,966	
6/04	15,864	3,073	19.4%	23,720	
6/03	15,105	716	4.7%	38,955	
6/02	17,293	3,915	22.6%	62,124	
Annual Growth	0.5%	(2.3%)	—	(22.3%)	

2006 Year-End Financials

Debt ratio: 90.6%   Current ratio: 1.45
Return on equity: 27.5%   Long-term debt ($ mil.): 7,409
Cash ($ mil.): 1,270

Net Income History
NYSE: DEO

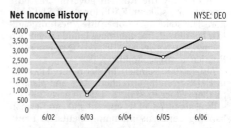

EADS

DaimlerChrysler Aerospace (DASA, Germany), Aerospatiale Matra (France), and Construcciones Aeronáuticas SA (CASA, Spain) combined to form the European Aeronautic Defence and Space Company (EADS). EADS is Europe's largest aerospace firm; worldwide it trails only Boeing. EADS' largest holding is Airbus (BAE SYSTEMS sold its 20% stake in Airbus back to EADS in 2006), which has surpassed Boeing as the world's leading maker of large commercial aircraft. Other operations include helicopters (Eurocopter), business and military jets (46% of Dassault Aviation and 43% of Eurofighter), satellites (Astrium), missiles (38% of MBDA), and commercial satellite launch systems (about 29% of Arianespace).

Airbus, which accounts for about two-thirds of EADS' sales, had been gaining on rival Boeing for years and finally surpassed Boeing in both plane orders and deliveries in 2003. For the future, Airbus is banking on its new super-jumbo A380 jet and the mid-size, long-range A350. The A380 will carry up to 800 people in a double-decker configuration; the A350 (a head-to-head competitor with Boeing's 787 Dreamliner) will seat about 250 and is expected in 2010.

EADS shares took a pounding in 2006 on Airbus' announcement that deliveries of the A380 would be delayed by six or seven months due to manufacturing glitches. A group of EADS shareholders soon cried foul and filed suit when it was revealed that co-CEO Noël Forgeard and five other EADS directors exercised stock options weeks before an internal investigation into the delays was launched. Two weeks later Forgeard resigned. Louis Gallois, former chairman of Société Nationale des Chemins de Fer Français (SNCF), France's state railway company, was named to replace him. EADS said the first A380s would not be delivered until the second half of 2007 and said the delays would lead to losses totaling more than $3.5 billion until 2010.

Along with the announcement of delivery delays, EADS outlined a plan to reduce development cycles by 2 years while boosting overall productivity by 20%. Airbus is also reviewing its European production sites and may announce job cuts.

In the midst of delivery woes and management shake-outs one bright spot emerged when the Pentagon gave EADS a $1.3 billion contract for 322 US Army light utility helicopters. The deal marks EADS' first big US military contract.

DaimlerChrysler owns about 22% of EADS; the French government (SOGEPA), France-based Lagardère, BNP Paribas, and AXA together own about 30%; Spain's state-owned SEPI owns 5.5%. BAE SYSTEMS sold its 20% stake in Airbus back to EADS in late 2006 for about €2.75 billion (about $3.53 billion).

In 2006 Russian bank Vneshtorgbank (100% controlled by the Russian government) purchased a 5% stake in EADS for about $1.17 billion. The stake does not entitle Vneshtorgbank to a board seat, but the move could strengthen cooperation between EADS and the re-emerging Russian aerospace industry.

Also in 2006 DaimlerChrysler reduced its stake in EADS from 30% to about 22% and plans to further reduce its stake to 15% in early 2007 by selling about 7% of its current stake to German banking concerns including Deutsche Bank, Commerzbank, WestLB, and state-owned KfW.

HISTORY

The short life of the European Aeronautic Defence and Space Company — EADS — is overshadowed by the long history of its components and by the obstacles overcome to cement the deal: The French and the Germans historically aren't overly fond of each other, so how did it come to pass that Germany's DaimlerChrysler Aerospace (DASA) and France's Aerospatiale Matra put aside their differences to band together with Spain's Construcciones Aeronáuticas SA (CASA)?

The US aerospace sector in the 1990s saw many companies consolidate, scrambling to make their way in the post-Cold War era. Boeing, the largest aerospace company in the world, got that way by acquiring a slew of operations, including Rockwell International's aerospace and defense operations (1995) and most importantly, McDonnell Douglas in a $16 billion deal (1997). In the same era, defense giant Lockheed merged with Martin Marietta (1995) and acquired Loral (1997). These US companies had it relatively easy — they all paid taxes to Uncle Sam, but acquisition deals in Europe were stymied by concerns over national security and privatization because much of Europe's defense industry was government-owned.

Spurred into action by their US rivals, in 1997 DASA and British Aerospace (now BAE SYSTEMS) — partners in Airbus — began merger talks. Fearful of being left out in the cold, France's government-owned Aerospatiale — another Airbus partner — began talks to merge with Matra, a French defense company controlled by Lagardère. Weeks after the Aerospatiale-Matra deal was announced in 1998, the chairman of DASA's parent company, Jürgen Schrempp, met with Lagardère's CEO, Jean-Luc Lagardère, and proposed a three-way deal. It never occurred and in 1999 the BAE SYSTEMS and DASA deal fell through as well.

Later that year Schrempp and Lagardère met again and laid the groundwork for a merger between DASA and Aerospatiale Matra. Less than three weeks after the Aerospatiale-Matra merger was completed, Lagardère found himself pitching the DASA/Aerospatiale Matra merger idea to a stunned French government (which still held a 48% stake in Aerospatiale Matra). Marathon negotiations ensued. Late in the year Spain's Construcciones Aeronáuticas SA (CASA) agreed to become part of EADS.

In 2000 EADS went public and Airbus announced that it would abandon its consortium structure in favor of incorporation. The next year EADS began pushing for a consolidation of army and naval equipment manufacturing among EU countries similar to the aerospace consolidation that created EADS. For Airbus, the long-sought switch from consortium to corporation finally occurred in July 2001 when Airbus S.A.S. was incorporated.

In October of 2004 EADS agreed to acquire US defense electronics maker Racal Instruments as part of its plan to increase defense sales in the US. In December of 2004 EADS and BAE SYSTEMS gave Airbus the greenlight to build the A350, a plane that competes directly with Boeing's upcoming 787 Dreamliner. A few months later, in February of 2005, EADS was given preferred bidder status for the UK's Royal Air Force aerial refueling tanker contract. The program is expected to be worth about $25 billion.

In 2006 EADS acquired Sofrelog of France, a provider of maritime monitoring systems.

EXECUTIVES

Co-Chairman: Manfred Bischoff, age 63
Co-Chairman: Arnaud Lagardère, age 45
Co-CEO and Director: Thomas Enders, age 47
President and CEO Airbus; Co-CEO; European Aeronautic Defence and Space: Louis Gallois, age 62
COO for Marketing, Strategy and Global Development: Jean-Paul Gut, age 44
CFO, EADS and Airbus: Hans Peter Ring, age 55
President and CEO, Eurocopter: Lutz Bertling, age 44
Head, Human Resources: Jussi Itävuori, age 51
Chairman and CEO, EADS North America: Ralph D. Crosby Jr., age 58
CEO, EADS Space: François Auque, age 49
Head, Military Transport Aircraft: Francisco Fernández Sáinz, age 60
Head, Defence and Security Systems Division: Stefan Zoller, age 48
Chief Technical Officer: Jean J. Botti, age 49
Head, Mergers and Acquisitions: Boris L. Zaïtra
Head, Corporate Communications: Christof Ehrhart, age 40
Auditors: KPMG Accountants N.V.; Ernst & Young Accountants

LOCATIONS

HQ: European Aeronautic Defence and Space Company EADS N.V.
Le Carré, Beechavenue 130-132,
1119 PR Schiphol-Rijk, The Netherlands
Phone: +31-20-655-4800
Web: www.eads-nv.com

2005 Sales

	$ mil.	% of total
Europe		
France	4,158.1	10
Germany	3,831.2	10
UK	3,176.3	8
Spain	1,204.4	3
Other countries	3,702.1	9
North America	10,689.5	26
Asia/Pacific	9,159.4	23
Middle East	2,202.8	5
Latin America	763.9	2
Other countries	1,622.5	4
Total	**40,510.2**	**100**

PRODUCTS/OPERATIONS

2005 Sales

	$ mil.	% of total
Airbus	26,266.6	62
Defence & Security Systems	9,870.0	24
Eurocopter	3,802.8	9
Military Transport Aircraft	903.6	2
Other	1,367.9	3
Adjustments	(1,700.7)	—
Total	**40,510.2**	**100**

Selected Operations and Interests

Business aircraft (Dassault Aviation, 45.8%)
Commercial airplanes (Airbus)
Helicopters (Eurocopter SAS)
Jet fighters (Dassault Aviation, 46.3%; Eurofighter, 43%)
Missile systems (MBDA, 37.5%)
Satellites (Astrium)

COMPETITORS

AgustaWestland
BAE SYSTEMS
Boeing
Bombardier
E'Prime Aerospace
LMCSS
Lockheed Martin
Northrop Grumman
Orbital Sciences
Raytheon
Textron

HISTORICAL FINANCIALS

Company Type: Public

Income Statement

FYE: December 31

	REVENUE ($ mil.)	NET INCOME ($ mil.)	NET PROFIT MARGIN	EMPLOYEES
12/05	40,510	—	—	113,210
12/04	43,322	—	—	110,662
12/03	37,823	—	—	109,135
12/02	31,339	—	—	103,967
12/01	27,281	—	—	102,967
Annual Growth	**10.4%**	—	—	**2.4%**

Revenue History

Euronext Paris: EAD

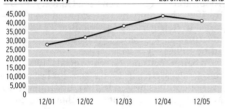

Electricité de France

While France has been slow to open its own doors to competition in the utilities industry, state-owned Electricité de France (EDF) has been quick to expand into global deregulated markets. One of the world's top electric utilities (as well as one of the last major state-owned energy monopolies in Europe), EDF has a generating capacity of more than 100,000 MW and provides power to 27 million French customers. Internationally, the company has interests in electric and gas utilities that serve 15 million customers, and it operates power plants that generate 20,000 MW of capacity in Europe, Africa, the Americas, Asia, and the Middle East. EDF launched an IPO in November 2005, selling as much as 15% of the company.

EDF agreed to acquire Edison SpA (Italy's second-largest power group) in partnership with Italian utility company AEM SpA in 2005 for an estimated $15.4 billion.

Nuclear plants provide more than 60% of EDF's domestic power supply; other sources include hydroelectric and fossil-fueled plants. The company is also developing renewable energy facilities. Making use of its extensive experience, especially in developing nuclear power, EDF builds power plants and provides plant management and consulting services worldwide.

Subsidiary EDF Trading markets electricity, natural gas, coal, and oil throughout Europe. The company's 34%-owned Dalkia unit (Veolia Environnement — formerly Vivendi Environnement — owns 66%) offers energy management and industrial services.

EDF is investing aggressively abroad, including in the liberalized markets of its European neighbors. The firm has grouped its UK retail energy supply operations under the EDF Energy brand; the division serves 5 million customers. EDF also has major utility operations in Germany (EnBW), Italy (EDF Energia Italia and Edison), and Latin America (Light and Edenor).

The company's expansion efforts have spurred criticism since it has been relatively intransigent in opening its own market. However, deregulation of 70% of the French market took effect in July 2004, and full competition is scheduled for 2007. Between 2000 and 2004, only 30% of the market was deregulated, just more than the percentage required by European Union (EU) rulings.

EDF is auctioning off capacity rights to some of its domestic generation facilities to comply with EU regulations; it is also working to create partnerships with other European utilities (including Enel and Electrabel) to allow more access to the French market. To further privatize the industry, the company will divest 49% of its newly formed transmission management firm RTE.

HISTORY

The French government nationalized hundreds of regional private firms to form Electricité de France (EDF) in 1946 as part of an effort to rebuild the nation's badly shaken post-war economy. This was a marked difference from the notoriously complex and inefficient pre-war electrical industry.

By the 1950s EDF had taken advantage of the centralized control and developed massive hydroelectric projects. Hydroelectric power would account for more than 70% of EDF's power.

But in France as elsewhere, hydro wasn't enough to keep up with the growing demand for electricity, and fossil fuels became an increasingly important power source. Then came the oil shortages of the 1970s, and France — with limited domestic supplies of oil and gas — began searching for alternatives to fossil-fueled plants. Nuclear power was determined to be the answer.

The government moved to invest billions of dollars in developing its relatively small nuclear power production facilities. Muddled with Malthusian predictions of power shortages and a preoccupation with having enough energy to be self-reliant, France found its nuclear operations left the government with more energy than it could use and more debt than it wanted. The company began to build a cable connecting the Continent to the UK in 1981. With the power grids of the two countries connected in 1986, EDF was finally able to start exporting its power to the Brits.

The 1990s brought with them deregulation. EDF fought to keep the UK-France grid closed to other energy sellers. After the government forbade the utility from diversifying into areas other than electricity in 1995, the company turned its attention to foreign investment, especially in Latin America.

The company faced increasing deregulatory pressures from without in the late 1990s. The newly formed European Union required open competition from member states. Begrudgingly and behind schedule, EDF opened about 30% of its market to competition in 2000.

Other members of the EU complained that EDF was trying to play it both ways: It was making aggressive acquisitions in the UK liberalized market (it bought London Electricity in 1999) while resisting a competition-enabling breakup or even allowing a foreign competitor to buy a stake in the French market.

EDF in 2001 expanded its stake in Italy's Montedison, a conglomerate with substantial energy holdings, by forming a consortium (Italenergia) with Italian automaker Fiat and some Italian banks to wrest control of Montedison from Italian bank MEDIOBANCA. Although the

consortium owns 94% of Montedison, EDF has only 2% of voting rights. (Montedison changed its name to Edison in 2002.)

EDF also purchased a 35% interest in German utility Energie Baden-Württemberg in 2001, and it merged its energy services unit with Dalkia, a unit of Vivendi Environnement (now Veolia Environnement), taking a 34% stake in Dalkia (which will eventually be increased to 50%). EDF subsidiary London Electricity agreed to buy $2.4 billion in UK assets from TXU Europe that year, including a 2,000 MW power plant, TXU's Eastern Electricity distribution unit, and its interest in TXU/EDF joint venture 24seven; the deals were completed in 2001 and 2002.

In 2002 EDF increased its stake in Brazilian utility Light Serviços de Eletricidade to 88% by swapping Light's interest in Sao Paulo utility Eletropaulo for AES's 24% interest in Light. Later that year EDF purchased UK electric and gas utility SEEBOARD (1.9 million customers) from US utility AEP in a $2.2 billion deal.

EXECUTIVES

Chairman and CEO: Pierre Gadonneix, age 63
SEVP and CFO: Daniel Camus, age 50
SEVP and Chief Human Resources Officer: Yann Laroche, age 57
SEVP, Customers: Jean-Pierre Benqué, age 54
SEVP, Generation: Bernard Dupraz
SEVP, International Businesses: Bruno Lescoeur, age 48
SEVP, Regulated Operations: Michel Francony
EVP, Development: Robert Durdilly
EVP, Local Development and Distribution: Pierre Bart, age 53
EVP, Americas: Fernando Ponasso, age 50
EVP, Asia Pacific: Hervé Machenaud, age 52
EVP, Continental Europe: Marc Boudier, age 47
EVP, Western Europe, Middle East, and Africa: Michel Crémieux, age 53
CEO, Dalkia: Olivier Barbaroux, age 49
CEO, EDF Energy: Vincent de Rivaz
CEO, R.T.E.: André Merlin, age 60
Corporate Secretary: Marie-Hélène Poinssot
Head of Communications and Public Affairs: Philippe Méchet
Auditors: Deloitte Touche Tohmatsu; Ernst & Young Audit; Mazars & Guérard

LOCATIONS

HQ: Electricité de France
22-30, avenue de Wagram, 75382 Paris, France
Phone: +33-1-40-42-22-22   **Fax:** +33-1-40-42-79-40
Web: www.edf.fr

2004 Sales

	% of total
Europe	
France	63
Other countries	33
Other regions	4
Total	**100**

PRODUCTS/OPERATIONS

2004 Generation Mix

	% of total
Nuclear	74
Fossil-fueled	17
Hydroelectric	9
Total	**100**

HISTORICAL FINANCIALS

Company Type: Public

Income Statement

FYE: December 31

	REVENUE ($ mil.)	NET INCOME ($ mil.)	NET PROFIT MARGIN	EMPLOYEES
12/04*	64,010	1,829	2.9%	156,152
12/03	56,382	1,076	1.9%	167,000
12/02	50,685	504	1.0%	171,995
12/01	36,066	745	2.1%	162,491
12/00	32,403	716	2.2%	117,249
Annual Growth	18.6%	26.4%	—	7.4%

*Most recent year available

2004 Year-End Financials

Debt ratio: 119.1%
Return on equity: 7.7%
Cash ($ mil.): 4,306
Current ratio: 1.00
Long-term debt ($ mil.): 28,538

Net Income History

Euronext Paris: EDF

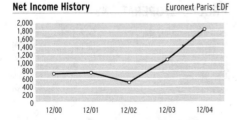

Electrolux

AB Electrolux has a hunting license for dust bunnies. The world's #1 producer of household appliances cranks out washing machines, stoves, refrigerators, and freezers under the AEG, Electrolux, Eureka, Frigidaire, and Zanussi names. Electrolux is also the world's #1 maker of vacuum cleaners, including the Electrolux and Eureka brands. Electrolux is a presence in the commercial market as well, making products such as foodservice and laundry equipment (Electrolux, Zanussi brands), chainsaws and lawn and garden equipment (Husqvarna and Jonsered brands, which the company plans to spin off), and diamond tools (Dimas and Diamant Boart brands). Electrolux's products are sold in about 90 countries.

Household appliances account for most of Electrolux's sales.

Citing production costs, Electrolux closed its Swedish factory in 2005, moving manufacturing to Hungary. Additional plant closures include its cooker factory in France and facilities in Michigan and Texas. The company announced in 2005 that it would relocate many of its North American and European plants to Asia, Mexico, and Eastern Europe; the company also announced the divestment of its Indian operations. It also terminated its partnership with Toshiba by 2006 to cut down on the number of product lines it is marketing worldwide.

The company's Husqvarna unit is buying lawn mower maker Dixon Industries, a subsidiary of Blount. The deal, which is expected to close by August 2006, allows Husqvarna to launch production of Dixon's ZTR brand mowers and add-on items in Nebraska.

Through Investor AB — which also has stakes in Saab and other multinational companies — the Wallenberg family controls about 26% of Electrolux's voting power.

HISTORY

Swedish salesman Axel Wenner-Gren saw an American-made vacuum cleaner in a Vienna, Austria, store window in 1910 and envisioned selling the cleaners door-to-door, a technique he had learned in the US. Two years later he worked with fledgling Swedish vacuum cleaner makers AB Lux and Elektromekaniska to improve their existing designs. The two companies merged to form AB Electrolux in 1919. When the board of the new company balked at Wenner-Gren's suggestion to mass-produce vacuum cleaners, he guaranteed Electrolux's sales through his own sales company.

In the 1920s the company used the "Every home — an Electrolux home" slogan as Wenner-Gren drove his sales force on and launched new sales companies in Europe and North and South America. He scored a publicity coup by securing the blessing of Pope Pius XI to vacuum the Vatican, gratis, for a year. By the end of the 1920s, Electrolux had purchased most of Wenner-Gren's sales companies (excluding Electrolux US) and had gambled on refrigerator technology and won. By buying vacuum cleaner maker Volta (Sweden, 1934), it gained retail distribution.

Despite the loss of Eastern European subsidiaries during WWII, the company did well until the 1960s, when it backed an unpopular refrigeration technology. Swedish electrical equipment giant ASEA, controlled by Marcus Wallenberg, bought a large stake in Electrolux in 1964, and in 1967 he installed Hans Werthén as chairman. Werthén slashed overhead and sold the company's minority stake in Electrolux US to Consolidated Foods. (The US Electrolux business was taken private in 1987.)

Since 1970 Electrolux has bought more than 300 companies (many of them troubled appliance makers), updated their plants, and gained global component manufacturing efficiencies. Acquisitions included National Union Electric (Eureka vacuum cleaners, US, 1974), Tappan (appliances, US, 1979), Zanussi (appliances, industrial products; Italy; 1984), White Consolidated Industries (appliances, industrial products; US; 1986), and Lehel (refrigerators, Hungary, 1991). By 1996 the company had acquired a 41% interest in Refrigeração Paraná, Brazil's #2 manufacturer of appliances. (Electrolux owned it all by 1998.)

To better focus on its "white goods" (washers, refrigerators, etc.), in 1996 Electrolux began selling noncore businesses. In 1997, under new CEO Michael "Mike the Knife" Treschow, the company launched a restructuring plan involving the closing of about 25 plants and the elimination of more than 12,000 jobs, mostly in Europe. The plan worked: Electrolux's profits more than quadrupled in 1998. Also that year the company launched a joint venture in India with Voltas Limited, forming that country's largest refrigerator manufacturer.

Electrolux acquired the European operations of chainsaw maker McCulloch in 1999. To strengthen its Asian presence, Electrolux teamed up with Toshiba for future collaboration on household appliances. Also that year the company said it would sell its vending machine unit and professional refrigeration business. That year AB Electrolux agreed to buy the major appliance business of E-mail Ltd., Australia's top household appliance maker.

In January 2002 it finalized the sale of its leisure appliance operations — mostly refrigerators for recreational vehicles — to private equity firm EQT Northern Europe. In April 2002 Electrolux CEO Michael Treschow resigned (but remained as a director) and was replaced by board member Hans Stråberg. The firm acquired Diamant Boart International, a world-leading manufacturer and distributor of diamond tools and related equipment, in June 2002.

As part of a restructuring effort to combat the effects of diminishing consumer demand and higher material costs, Electrolux cut nearly 5,000 jobs (about 6% of its workforce) during 2003.

Electrolux relaunched its flagship brand of vacuum cleaners in North America during 2004, having bought the rights from long-unaffiliated vacuum maker Electrolux LLC (now Aerus). Also that year former CEO Michael Treschow reappeared in a leadership position, assuming the role of chairman.

EXECUTIVES

Chairman: Michael Treschow, age 62
Deputy Chairman: Peggy Bruzelius, age 56
President, CEO, and Director: Hans Stråberg, age 48
CFO: Fredrik Rystedt, age 42
Head of Electrolux Major Appliances Europe: Magnus Yngen
Head of Group Staff Communication and Branding: Lars Göran Johansson
Head of Group Staff Human Resources and Organizational Development: Harry de Vos, age 48
Head of Group Staff Legal Affairs and Secretary: Cecilia Vieweg

Head of Pricing Program and Regional Administrative
  Officer: Lilian Fossum, age 43
VP, Investor Relations and Financial Information:
  Peter Nyquist
Head of Outdoor Products; President and CEO,
  Husqvarna: Bengt Andersson
Head of Professional Indoor Products: Detlef Münchow
Head of Major Appliances North and Latin America:
  Keith R. McLoughlin
Head of Major Appliances Asia Pacific:
  Claes Johan Bygge
Head of Marketing Services, Outdoor Division:
  Rachael Thomson
Head of Communications and Investor Relations,
  Electrolux Outdoor: Åsa Stenqvist
Director, Brand and Marketing, Major Appliances, UK:
  Andy Mackay
Chairman, Electrolux Deutschland: Klaus Wuhrl
Auditors: PricewaterhouseCoopers AB

LOCATIONS

HQ: AB Electrolux
  S:t Göransgatan 143, Stockholm, Sweden
Phone: +46-8-738-6000   Fax: +46-8-656-7461
Web: www.electrolux.com

2005 Sales

	% of total
Europe	46
North America	40
Asia/Pacific	9
Latin America	5
Total	**100**

PRODUCTS/OPERATIONS

2005 Sales

	% of total
Indoor products	78
Outdoor products	22
Total	**100**

Selected Products and Brands

Consumer durables
  Indoor products
    Floorcare products (Electrolux, Eureka, AEG)
    Core A (AEG, Electrolux, Eureka, Frigidaire,
      Simpson, Volta, Westinghouse, Zanussi)
  Outdoor products (Electrolux, Flymo, Husqvarna,
    Partner, McCulloch, Poulan, Poulan Pro, Weed
    Eater)
Professional products
  Indoor products
    Foodservice equipment (Dito, Electrolux, Molteni,
      Zanussi Professional)
    Laundry equipment (Electrolux)
  Outdoor products
    Chainsaws (Husqvarna, Jonsered)
    Diamond tools (Diamant Boart, Dimas, Partner
      Industrial)
    Lawn and Garden Equipment (Husqvarna, Jonsered)

COMPETITORS

Ali
BISSELL
BSH Bosch und Siemens Hausgeräte
Enodis
Franke
GE Consumer & Industrial
Gree Electrical Appliances
Haier Group
Hobart
Indesit
LG Electronics
Philips Electronics
Royal Appliance
Samsung Group
SEB
Stihl
Toro
Whirlpool
WinWholesale

HISTORICAL FINANCIALS

Company Type: Public

Income Statement

FYE: December 31

	REVENUE ($ mil.)	NET INCOME ($ mil.)	NET PROFIT MARGIN	EMPLOYEES
12/05	16,274	191	1.2%	69,523
12/04	18,267	422	2.3%	72,382
12/03	17,135	674	3.9%	77,140
12/02	15,232	607	4.0%	83,347
12/01	12,868	351	2.7%	85,749
Annual Growth	**6.0%**	**(14.2%)**	**—**	**(5.1%)**

2005 Year-End Financials

Debt ratio: 21.0%   Current ratio: 1.41
Return on equity: 5.7%   Long-term debt ($ mil.): 662
Cash ($ mil.): 687

Net Income History

Pink Sheets: ELUXY

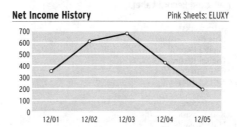

EMI Group

EMI's business is keeping music fans entertained. EMI Group is the #3 major record company (behind Universal Music Group and Sony BMG) in terms of worldwide sales. Its recorded music segment, EMI Music, distributes CDs, videos, and other music formats primarily through imprints Capitol, EMI Records, and Virgin, which together sport a roster of pop artists such as The Beastie Boys, Norah Jones, and Lenny Kravitz. Its EMI Music Publishing division, the world's largest music publishing business, handles the rights to more than a million songs. In 2006 EMI offered $4.2 billion to buy Warner Music Group (WMG), but the bid was rejected. It is reportedly in talks with private equity firms about a possible takeover.

In 2005 EMI released hits from top-selling artists Coldplay, Robbie Williams, Gorillaz, the Rolling Stones, and Keith Urban. EMI Music Publishing, meanwhile, has continued to expand with increasing sales coming from synchronization revenue (licensing music for use in movies, television, and advertising) and performance fees. Publishing accounts for more than 20% of EMI's revenue.

To improve its financial performance, the company is particularly focused on selling more music through digital channels, such as Apple Computer's iTunes and downloadable ring tones licensed to telecommunications carriers. However, the real challenge remains for EMI and its labels, particularly Capitol Records and Virgin in the US, to build a more robust stable of artists and generate more hit album releases. To that end, the company brought in former Atlantic Records chief Jason Flom to run Virgin, replacing Matt Serletic.

In 2006 EMI bet that a merger with Warner Music Group (WMG) would be the best way to compete with Apple and other online music firms (a deal would create a company worth an estimated $7 billion). Not impressed with EMI's proposed offer, WMG determined it was not in the best interests of its shareholders. WMG subsequently made a $4.6 billion counter-bid for EMI, which EMI promptly rejected. EMI and Warner have tried to combine twice before 2006, but efforts were thwarted by European regulators. In summer 2006 EMI announced it had abandoned its plans for a WMG deal.

Reports have surfaced that EMI is in preliminary talks over a private-equity takeover deal that could be worth about $3.9 billion.

HISTORY

Electric & Musical Industries (EMI) was established in 1931 as a successor to a 19th-century gramophone producer. It gradually expanded operations to produce everything from radar systems during WWII to the first television system for the BBC. In 1955 the company bought Los Angeles-based Capitol Records (founded in 1942), which featured such artists as Frank Sinatra and Nat "King" Cole. EMI became a major force in the entertainment industry over the next decades, topping off a string of acquisitions with the purchase of Associated British Picture Corporation in 1969.

EMI suffered through the 1970s with money-losing films and the PR sting of signing the outrageous punk group The Sex Pistols in 1976. (The company canceled its contract with the band in 1978.) The struggling firm was bought by appliance and electronics giant Thorn Electrical Industries (founded by Jules Thorn as the Electrical Lamp Service Company in 1928) for $356 million in 1979. Renamed THORN EMI the next year, the conglomerate lacked strategic focus and continued to suffer losses. Colin Southgate was tapped as CEO in 1985 and streamlined its operations to four business sectors. THORN EMI acquired 50% of Chrysalis Records in 1989, and the next year it added Filmtrax music publishing (UK). Also in 1990 the company's HMV stores unit opened its first US superstore in New York City.

In 1992 the company acquired Virgin Records from founder Richard Branson for $960 million. The purchase boosted EMI's US market share and made it one of the world's top music companies. THORN EMI sold its lighting division the next year, and in 1995 it bought UK bookstore business Dillons (later merged with and re-branded Waterstone's).

In 1996 EMI and Thorn split into separately traded companies to maximize the value of its disparate assets; however, share prices plunged when profits failed to materialize. The next year EMI paid $132 million for 50% of Berry Gordy's Jobete companies and its 15,000-song Motown catalog.

To focus more on music and less on retail, EMI transferred its HMV and Dillons chains to HMV Media Group, a joint venture with Advent International, in 1998. That year EMI Music head James Fifield resigned with a healthy buyout package after Southgate scotched a succession plan that would have made Fifield CEO. The following year Eric Nicoli, former CEO of United Biscuits, was tapped as Southgate's replacement.

Seeking a bigger presence on the Internet, the company bought an equity stake in music Web site Musicmaker.com in 1999. It also bought music publisher Windswept Pacific for $200 million. The following year the company sold its stake in Musicmaker.com for a hefty profit and later agreed to merge its music operations into a joint venture with Time Warner's Warner Music Group. Its deal with Warner was scrapped, however, to appease European regulators examining the merger of Time Warner and AOL. EMI opened negotiations with Bertelsmann, but the talks broke off in 2001 (again due to pressure from regulators). Also that year, EMI formed online distribution venture MusicNet with Time Warner, BMG, and RealNetworks. (The partners sold their online venture to Baker Capital for about $30 million in 2005.)

EMI's ill-fated five-record contract with pop diva Mariah Carey was a huge embarrassment for the firm. After Carey's first EMI album, *Glitter*, sold a meager 500,000 copies in 2001, the company bought out Carey's deal for $28 million. It subsequently laid off about 20% of its workforce, cut 400 acts from its roster, and took a $340 million charge for the year. Ken Berry, CEO of the EMI Recorded Music division, left the company that year and was replaced by Alain Levy, a former PolyGram executive.

In 2002 the company acquired Mute, a leading European independent record company, for $33.5 million. Also that year it sold off its remaining stake in HMV. EMI turned the tables on an earlier suitor in 2003, making an offer to buy Time Warner's music business. However, the company was outbid by former Vivendi Universal executive Edgar Bronfman, Jr., and Thomas H. Lee Partners.

EXECUTIVES

Chairman: Eric L. Nicoli, age 54, $2,759,059 pay
Deputy Chairman: John Gildersleeve, age 61
CFO and Director: Martin Stewart, age 42, $1,796,034 pay
SVP and Financial Controller: Prescott Price
SVP Content Protection: Richard Cottrell
SVP Human Resources: Avery Duff
SVP Industry and Government Affairs: Victoria Bassetti
SVP Information Technology and CIO: James Anderson
VP Legal Affairs: David Widd
VP Marketing: Leonor Villanueva
VP National Sales: Gregg Vickers
VP Operations: Reiner Kirsten
VP Sales: Al Andruchow
Director; Chairman and CEO, EMI Music: Alain M. J. I. Levy, age 59, $6,031,716 pay
Chairman and Co-CEO, EMI Music Publishing: Martin N. Bandier, age 63, $5,860,549 pay
Chairman and CEO, EMI Music Asia: Norman Cheng
Chairman and CEO, EMI Music Latin America: Marco Bissi
Chairman and CEO, EMI Music UK and Ireland: Tony Wadsworth
Chairman and CEO, Virgin Records America: Jason Flom
Vice Chairman, EMI Music; Chairman and CEO, EMI Music North America: David Munns
President and CEO, Capitol Records: Andrew (Andy) Slater
President and CEO, Capitol Records Nashville: Mike Dungan
President and CEO, Continental Europe, EMI Music Publishing: Peter Ende
Director; President and Co-CEO, EMI Music Publishing: Roger Faxon, age 58
Secretary and Group General Counsel: Charles P. Ashcroft
Auditors: Ernst & Young LLP

LOCATIONS

HQ: EMI Group plc
27 Wrights Ln., London W8 5SW, United Kingdom
Phone: +44-20-7795-7000   **Fax:** +44-20-7795-7296
Web: www.emigroup.com

EMI Group has operations in more than 50 countries.

2006 Sales

	$ mil.	% of total
Europe		
UK	606	17
Other countries	1,096	30
North America	1,129	31
Asia/Pacific	589	16
Latin America	147	4
Other regions	51	2
Total	**3,618**	**100**

PRODUCTS/OPERATIONS

2006 Sales

	$ mil.	% of total
Recorded music	2,888	80
Music publishing	730	20
Total	**3,618**	**100**

Selected Record Labels

Angel Records
Astralwerks
Blue Note Records
Capitol Records Nashville
Capitol Records US
EMI Christian Music
EMI Classics
EMI Music UK
EMI Records
EMI Televisa Records
Mute Records
Narada
Parlophone
Priority Records
Toshiba-EMI (55%-owned)
Virgin Records

COMPETITORS

Sony BMG
Universal Music Group
Warner Music

HISTORICAL FINANCIALS

Company Type: Public

Income Statement

				FYE: March 31
	REVENUE ($ mil.)	NET INCOME ($ mil.)	NET PROFIT MARGIN	EMPLOYEES
3/06	3,618	—	—	6,312
3/05	3,650	—	—	6,672
3/04	3,872	—	—	7,996
3/03	3,424	—	—	8,088
3/02	3,487	—	—	9,270
Annual Growth	**0.9%**	**—**	**—**	**(9.2%)**

Revenue History

London: EMI

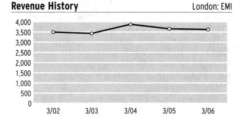

Enel

Arrivederci, monopolio! Italy's largest electric utility, Enel, has given up its monopoly status and raced into the deregulating power marketplace. Enel distributes electricity to nearly 30 million Italian customers and has some 42,200 MW of primarily fossil-fueled and hydroelectric generating capacity in the country. Enel also owns gas distribution businesses, and it has renewable and international power generation assets. Other operations include information technology, real estate, and engineering and construction services. The Italian government owns about a third of Enel.

Enel hasn't just been sipping cappuccino while competitors rush in: The company has moved to become a multi-utility. It has grown to become Italy's second-largest gas distributor (after Italgas), with almost 2 million customers. It also purchased France Telecom's 27% stake in Wind Telecomunicazioni, for $1.4 billion in 2003, making the unit a wholly owned subsidiary; Enel had flirted with the idea of taking Wind public but instead sold a majority stake to the Egypt-based Weather Investments consortium in 2005, which has the backing of Orascom Telecom's chairman and CEO, Naguib Sawiris.

Internationally, Enel has built and acquired independent power plants, primarily in Europe and the Americas. The company has also divested noncore assets, including some real estate holdings and most of its water distribution operations, to focus on its energy operations, and it is also moving back into the nuclear power field.

Italy's Bersani Decree, passed in 1999, required Enel to divest 25% of its capacity and turn over a portion of its municipal distribution networks to local governments to enhance competition in the country's power market. Enel has completed the required generation asset sales, reducing its capacity by 15,000 MW. Enel has also reduced its customer count by approximately 1 million through municipal distribution asset sales, and it has transferred management of the national transmission grid to an independent government-owned operator, Gestore della Rete di Trasmissione Nazionale (GRTN).

Italian regulators required that Enel divest 80% of its Terna subsidiary, which holds the company's power transmission assets, by 2007. Enel spun off 50% of the unit in an IPO in 2004. The following year it divested another 44%, and the company reduced its holding to about 5% by January 2006. Grid management and operational functions were also transferred from GRTN back to Terna.

The Italian government, which floated 32% of the utility in 1999, began the second round of Enel's privatization process in 2003 by selling a 7% stake to Morgan Stanley for more than $2.3 billion. In 2004 the government further reduced its stake by nearly 20% through a public offering of shares. Italy's Ministry of Economy and Finance directly owns approximately 21% of the company, and it owns another 10% indirectly, through the government-controlled bank, Cassa Depositi e Prestiti.

HISTORY

Italy's energy consumption doubled in the 1950s as the country experienced a period of rapid industrialization and urbanization. A tight-knit oligopoly controlled the electric power industry and included Edison, SADE, La Centale, SME, and Finelettrica. The economic boom pushed into the 1960s, and the Italian government created Enel (Ente Nazionale per l'Energia Elettrica) in 1962 to nationalize the power industry. In 1963 Enel began gradually buying some 1,250 electric utilities. About 160 municipal utilities and the larger independents, such as Edison, were left out of the takeover.

The company spent the late 1960s and early 1970s connecting Italy's unwieldy transmission network and building new power plants, including the La Spezia thermoelectric plant (600 MW). Construction costs, coupled with the high prices Enel was required to pay for its takeover targets, caused the utility to become steeped in debt. The Arab oil embargoes of the early 1970s made matters worse, and the Italian government helped Enel with an endowment in 1973.

The energy crisis also prompted Enel to build its first nuclear power plant, Caorso, which came on line in 1980. However, nuclear power was short-lived in Italy: After the 1986 Chernobyl accident, a national referendum forced Enel to deactivate its nukes in 1987. The firm also stepped up its development of renewable energy sources in the 1980s.

Meanwhile, Enel opened its Centro Nazionale de Controllo (CNC) in Rome in 1985 to supervise Italy's power grid. The next year the company turned its first profit.

To begin disassembling Enel's monopoly, the Italian government in 1992 opened the power generation market to outside producers and converted Enel into a joint stock company (with the state holding all of the shares). Following the European Union's 1997 directive to deregulate Europe's power industry, Enel unbundled its utility activities and began trimming its staff. Italy's Bersani Decree (passed in 1999) outlined the restructuring process: Enel was ordered to divest 15,000 MW of its generating capacity, a state-controlled operator was set up to oversee Italy's grid, and large users were allowed to choose their own suppliers.

In response, Enel began to diversify in 1998. It started Wind Telecomunicazioni, a joint venture with France Telecom and Deutsche Telekom. (Deutsche Telekom sold its stake to the other partners in 2000.) Wind began offering fixed-line and mobile telecom services to corporations in 1998 and extended the services to residential users the next year. Enel also began building water infrastructure to serve local distributors and purchased three water operations in southern Italy.

Also in 1999 the government floated 32% of Enel in one of the world's largest IPOs at the time. Enel bought fixed-line telephone company Infostrada from Vodafone in 2001 and sold its 5,400-MW Elettrogen generation unit to Spain's Endesa for $2.3 billion. In 2002 Enel sold its 7,000-MW Eurogen generation unit to a consortium backed by Fiat and Électricité de France for $2.6 billion. Also that year Infostrada was merged into Wind Telecomunicazioni to create one of Italy's top telecom companies. Also in 2002 Enel purchased Camuzzi Gazometri's gas distribution business (Italy's second-largest) from Mill Hill Investments, and it bought Endesa's Viesgo unit (2,400 MW of generating capacity and 500,000 power customers) for about $1.8 billion.

Enel sold its final generation divestment company, Interpower (2,600 MW), to a consortium of utilities (including Belgian utility Electrabel and Italian utility ACEA) in 2003.

EXECUTIVES

Chairman: Piero Gnudi
CEO, General Manager, and Director: Fulvio Conti, age 58
CTO: Francesco Emiliani
Head of Finance Department: Claudio Machetti
Head of Corporate Affairs and Secretary: Claudio Sartorelli, age 59
Head of Accounting: Luciana Tarozzi, age 60
Head of Audit: Antonio Cardani, age 55
Head of Communication: Gianluca Comin, age 42
Head of Generation and Energy Management; Chairman, Enel Produzione S.p.A.: Sandro Fontecedro, age 60
Head of Human Resources: Paolo Ruzzini, age 53
Head of Information and Communication Technology: Alessandro Bufacchi, age 58
Head of International Affairs: Andrea Brentan, age 56
Head of Legal Affairs: Salvatore Cardillo, age 55
Head of Purchasing: Salvatore Sardo, age 52
Head of Regulatory and Institutional Affairs: Massimo Romano, age 45
Head of Sales, Infrastructure, and Networks: Vincenzo Cannatelli, age 52
Head of Telecommunications; CEO, Wind Telecomunicazioni: Tommaso Pompei, age 62
Head of Transmission; CEO and Managing Director, Terna: Sergio Mobili, age 64
Investor Relations Manager: Luca Torchia
Media Relations Manager: Gerardo Orsini
International Press Officer: Roberta Vivenzio
Auditors: KPMG S.p.A.

LOCATIONS

HQ: Enel S.p.A.
Viale Regina Margherita, 137, 00198 Rome, Italy
Phone: +39-06-8305-1   **Fax:** +39-06-8305-3771
Web: www.enel.it

Enel provides utility services in Italy, has independent power production and distribution operations in other European countries and in the Americas, and has other operations in Africa and Asia.

PRODUCTS/OPERATIONS

2005 Sales

	% of total
Sales, infrastructure & networks	54
Generation & energy management	37
Services & other activities	4
Corporate	5
Total	**100**

Selected Subsidiaries and Affiliates

Sales, Infrastructure, and Networks
  Electra de Viesgo Distribucion SL (electricity distribution and sale, Spain)
  Enel Distribuzione SpA (electricity distribution)
  Enel Energia SpA (electricity sales)
  Enel Gas SpA (gas sales)
  Enel.si — Servizi Integrati SpA (engineering and energy services)
  Enel Sole Srl (formerly So.l.e. — Società luce elettrica SpA, public lighting)
  Viesgo Energia SL (electricity and gas sales, Spain)

Generation and Energy Management
  Conphoebus SpA (renewable energy-related services)
  Enel Green Power International SA (electricity from renewable resources, Luxembourg)
  Enel Latin America LLC (formerly EGI LLC, renewable electricity generation)
  Enel North America Inc. (formerly CHI Energy, renewable electricity generation, US)
  Enel Produzione SpA (electricity generation)
  Enel Trade SpA (fuel trading and logistics, electricity sales)
  Enel Union Fenosa Renovables SA (80%, renewable electricity generation, Spain)
  Maritza East III Power Holding BV (electricity generation, Bulgaria)
  Viesgo Generaciòn SL (electricity generation and sales, Spain)
Services and Other Activities
  Enel.NewHydro Srl (water distribution)
  Enelpower SpA (power-related engineering and construction)

COMPETITORS

ABB	Hidrocántabrico
ACEA	IBERDROLA
Acque Potabili	International Power
AEM	Italgas
Edison	Risanamento
Electricité de France	RWE
Endesa	SUEZ-TRACTEBEL
Eni	Telecom Italia
E.ON	Unión Fenosa
ERG S.p.A.	Vodafone Omnitel

HISTORICAL FINANCIALS

Company Type: Public

Income Statement

	REVENUE ($ mil.)	NET INCOME ($ mil.)	NET PROFIT MARGIN	EMPLOYEES
12/05	40,333	5,562	13.8%	51,778
12/04	49,786	1,407	2.8%	61,898
12/03	39,325	2,984	7.6%	64,770
12/02	32,088	1,467	4.6%	71,204
Annual Growth	7.9%	55.9%	—	(10.1%)

FYE: December 31

2005 Year-End Financials

Debt ratio: 62.2%
Return on equity: 26.3%
Cash ($ mil.): 1,238
Current ratio: 0.95
Long-term debt ($ mil.): 12,987

No. of shares (mil.): —
Dividends
  Yield: 6.1%
  Payout: —
Market value ($ mil.): —

Stock History

NYSE: EN

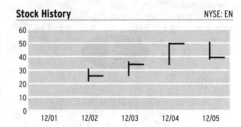

	STOCK PRICE ($) FY Close	P/E High/Low		PER SHARE ($) Earnings	Dividends
12/05	39.27	—	—	—	2.39
12/04	49.44	—	—	—	3.19
12/03	34.15	—	—	—	1.50
12/02	25.65	—	—	—	1.30
Annual Growth	15.3%	—	—	—	22.5%

Energias de Portugal

If you're from Portugal, you plug into EDP - Energias de Portugal (formerly EDP - Electricidade de Portugal), the state-controlled holding company for utilities that generate, transmit, and distribute electricity. EDP's distribution unit serves 5.9 million customers in Portugal. The company also has stakes in Brazilian power distributors that serve another 3 million customers, and it owns a controlling stake in Spanish utility Hidrocantábrico. Other EDP operations include telecommunications, information technology, gas distribution, utility metering and billing services, engineering, water and wastewater projects, and real estate management.

EDP has a combined generating capacity of more than 7,900 MW from its domestic hydroelectric, fossil-fueled, and wind-driven plants; the company also has a 30% stake in Portugal's national transmission grid operator, Rede Eléctrica Nacional (REN), a 40% stake in TURBOGÁS - Produtora Energética, S.A. (the company behind the construction of gas power station Tapada do Outeiro), and a 27% stake in PORTUGEN - Energia, S.A (which is in charge of operating Tapada do Outeiro).

Branching out across the peninsula, EDP has boosted its interest in Hidrocantábrico from 40% to 96% by purchasing German utility Energie Baden-Württemberg's 35% stake, as well as Spanish banks Cajastur (17%) and Cáser's (4%) stakes. Capitalizing on its language and cultural connections to Brazil, EDP has also been increasing its Brazilian investments, as well as investing in other Latin American companies.

For diversification at home, EDP jumped into the telecommunications arena. It owns 56% of Onitelecom (ONI), which provides fixed-line voice and Internet services. (In 2006, however, the company agreed to sell its stake in ONI). The company is increasing its investments in the Portuguese gas distribution market.

The Portuguese government, which controls 21% of EDP, has been under fire by the European Commission for creating a golden share that allows the state to veto decisions by the utility. The government is reducing its stake in EDP, but it does not plan to sell its entire interest in the company.

In 2005 the government did, however, decide that it would not renew the contracts of CEO Talone or chairman Sanchez. Antonio Mexia was named CEO the following year.

HISTORY

EDP - Energias de Portugal has its roots in the several power enterprises that sprouted throughout the country during the infancy of electricity. The first recorded event in Portugal's electrification was the import of six voltaic arc lamps in 1878. The nation's first large-scale project saw the light in 1893 when the city of Braga was illuminated by the Sociedade de Electricidade do Norte de Portugal.

Electricity grew throughout the 1900s in the form of municipal concession contracts for distribution and government-licensed power plants. Large-scale power stations were not in effect in Portugal until after 1947, when Companhia Nacional de Electricidade was formed to interconnect the small generating systems dotting the nation. From the 1950s to mid-1970s, new companies were formed to bring electricity to various parts of Portugal.

The original Electricidade de Portugal was founded in the wake of a leftist revolution during the 1970s in Portugal. In what became known as the Captain's Revolution, military officers overthrew the Portuguese government, which had been a dictatorship since 1933. The new government, dominated by Marxists, nationalized Portugal's industries, including its generation, transmission, and distribution companies, in 1975. The next year the Portuguese government created Electricidade de Portugal to unify the recently nationalized companies.

A new Social Democrat government came to power in 1987 and decided to denationalize Portuguese industry, including EDP. The company reorganized into four major sectors in 1994: production, headed by its CPPE subsidiary, and transmission, distribution, and services, led by its REN subsidiary, which operated the national grid, four regional utilities, and 10 services units. EDP was the holding company.

Seeking opportunities opened up by the privatization of Brazil's state-owned electricity distributor, EDP joined a consortium with Spain's Endesa and Chile's Chilectra to buy 70% of Rio de Janeiro distributor CERJ in 1996. The next year EDP gained a license to help build a hydro plant in Brazil. By 1998 the Endesa-led consortium had gained control of another Brazilian distributor, Coelce.

The Portuguese government floated 30% of EDP in 1997, raising $1.76 billion. In a joint venture with the UK's PowerGen and Germany's Siemens, EDP formed Turbogás to operate a power plant that would produce 20% of Portugal's electricity.

In 1998 EDP forged an alliance with Spain's Iberdrola and bought 80% of Guatemalan utility EEGSA. That year EDP and São Paulo utility CPFL gained control of São Paulo distributor Bandeirante. In 1999 EDP acquired stakes in two other Brazilian distributors. It also joined the UK's Thames Water to develop projects in Portugal, Chile, and Brazil and bought 45% of Chilean water and sewage company Essel. (EDP exchanged its stake in Essel for Thames Water's interest in the Portuguese joint venture in 2002.) The Portuguese state reduced its stake in EDP to about 50% in 1999.

Stepping up its telecommunications activities in 2000, EDP made its telecom unit, Onitelecom (ONI), fully operational and agreed to share a fiber-optic network on the Iberian Peninsula with Spain's Iberdrola. That year the Portuguese government acquired a majority stake in EDP's REN unit. Also in 2000, EDP combined its four power distribution utilities into one unit (EDP Distribuição).

In 2001 EDP and Spanish savings bank Cajastur jointly bid to buy Hidrocantábrico, one of Spain's leading utilities. EDP won control of 20% of Hidrocantábrico, while German utility Energie Baden-Württemberg (EnBW) won control of 60%. The following year, after a fierce bidding war, the two companies agreed that EDP would control the majority share (40%), while EnBW would own only 35%.

The company changed its name from EDP - Electricidade de Portugal to EDP - Energias de Portugal in 2004.

EXECUTIVES

CFO and Director: Rui M. Horta e Costa, age 44
CEO: Antonio Mexia
Head of Business Analysis: Carlos Alves Pereira, age 39
Head of Communication and Image:
Horácio M. Piriquito Casimiro, age 43
Head of Energy Planning: António J. Silva Coutinho, age 36
Head of Environment: António M. Neves de Carvalho, age 55
Head of Financial Management:
Magda Abdool Magid Vakil, age 42
Head of Human Resources:
Eugénio A. Purificação Carvalho, age 51
Head of Information Systems: José A. Abreu Aguiar, age 56
Head of Internal Audit: Vitor M. Silva Leitão, age 51
Head of Investor Relations:
Pedro M. Carreto Pires João, age 35
Head of Legal Affairs and General Secretary:
António P. Alfaia de Carvalho, age 59
Head of Planning and Control, Consolidation, and Tax:
Miguel Ribeiro Ferreira, age 37
Head of Quality: Paula Pinto Fonseca, age 43
Head of Regulation and Tariffs:
Maria J. Mano Pinto Simões, age 44
Head of Risk Management:
António M. Ramos Silva Vidigal, age 55
Head of Brazil Articulation: Joaquim P. Macedo Santos, age 51
Head of Gas Project: José M. Ferrari Bigares Careto, age 42
Head, Information Systems Office:
Luís Pedro Ferraz Flores, age 42
Head, Pension Fund Office:
Luís Manuel da Costa Veloso, age 43
Head, Quality Office:
Ana Paula Pinto da Fonseca Morais, age 44
General Manager and Secretary:
António Manuel Barreto Pita de Abreu, age 55
Auditors: PricewaterhouseCoopers

LOCATIONS

HQ: EDP - Energias de Portugal, S.A.
Praça Marquês de Pombal, 12,
1250-162 Lisbon, Portugal
Phone: +351-21-001-2500   **Fax:** +351-21-002-1403
Web: www.edp.pt

EDP - Energias de Portugal has operations in Brazil, Cape Verde, Guatemala, Macao, Portugal, and Spain.

2005 Sales

	% of total
Portugal	62
Spain	22
Brazil	16
Total	**100**

PRODUCTS/OPERATIONS

2005 Sales

	% of total
Electricity	93
Gas	6
Steam, ashes & other	1
Total	**100**

Selected Subsidiaries and Affiliates

Bandeirante Energia S.A. (96%, electricity distribution, Brazil)
Companhia de Electricidade de Macau, S.A. (21%, electricity distribution)
Companhia de Electricidade do Estado do Rio de Janeiro (CERJ, 8%, electricity distribution, Brazil)
Edinfor Sistemas Informáticos, S.A. (information technology)
EDP Distribuição (electricity distribution)
EDP Produção (electricity generation)
  Companhia Portuguesa de Produção de Electricidade, S.A. (CPPE, electricity generation)
  EDP Energia (electricity marketing and trading)
  Novas Energias, S.A. (ENERNOVA, alternative renewable-energy plants)

Empresa de Electricidade da Guatemala, S.A. (EEGSA, 17%, electricity distribution)
Empresa Energética de Mato Grosso Sul S.A. (Enersul, 36%, electricity distribution, Brazil)
Espirito Santo Centrais Elétricas S.A. (Escelsa, 55%, electricity distribution, Brazil)
Hidroeléctrica Del Cantábrico, S.A. (Hidrocantábrico, 96%, electricity and gas distribution, Spain)
Onitelecom Infocomuniçoes (ONI, 56%, telecommunications)
Rede Eléctrica Nacional, S.A. (REN, 30%, national transmission grid operator)

COMPETITORS

AES
Cemig
Electrabel
Electricité de France
ELETROBRÁS
Endesa
Enel
E.ON
IBERDROLA
Jazztel
Portugal Telecom
RWE
Unión Fenosa
Vodafone Portugal

HISTORICAL FINANCIALS

Company Type: Public

Income Statement

FYE: December 31

	REVENUE ($ mil.)	NET INCOME ($ mil.)	NET PROFIT MARGIN	EMPLOYEES
12/05	10,954	1,313	12.0%	—
12/04	9,853	326	3.3%	16,057
12/03	8,762	625	7.1%	17,618
12/02	6,718	315	4.7%	12,833
Annual Growth	17.7%	61.0%	—	11.9%

2005 Year-End Financials

Debt ratio: 157.2%
Return on equity: 20.5%
Cash ($ mil.): 1,020
Current ratio: 0.66
Long-term debt ($ mil.): 10,350

No. of shares (mil.): —
Dividends
Yield: 3.4%
Payout: 28.8%
Market value ($ mil.): —

Stock History

NYSE: EDP

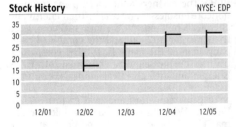

	STOCK PRICE ($) FY Close	P/E High	P/E Low	PER SHARE ($) Earnings	PER SHARE ($) Dividends
12/05	30.87	9	7	3.61	1.04
12/04	30.23	21	17	1.45	0.94
12/03	26.37	—	—	—	0.86
12/02	16.80	—	—	—	0.88
Annual Growth	22.5%	—	—	149.0%	5.7%

Eni

It's not teeny, it's Eni — and it's huge. One of Italy's largest companies, Eni operates in the oil and natural gas, petrochemicals, and oil field services industries and has expanded into power generation. Its main subsidiaries and affiliates are EniPower (power generation), Italgas (natural gas transmission), Saipem (oil field services), pipeline operator Snam Rete Gas, and Snamprogetti (contracting, engineering). As one of the world's leading oil enterprises, Eni has proved reserves of more than 6.84 billion barrels of oil equivalent, most of it in Italy and in Africa. The Italian government owns about 30% of Eni but is considering selling the holding.

The company's oil and gas holdings and exploration and production efforts extend into more than 30 countries on five continents. Eni has expanded outside its traditional bases of Africa and Italy, with ventures in the Americas, the Asia/Pacific region, Europe, and the Middle East.

In response to the opening up of Italy's energy markets, Eni is increasing its natural gas holdings and adding electricity generating power units. In 2003 Eni acquired Fortum's Norwegian oil and gas business (Fortum Petroleum) for $420 million.

HISTORY

Although the Italian parliament formed Ente Nazionale Idrocarburi (National Hydrocarbon Agency) in 1953, Enrico Mattei is the true father of Eni. In 1945 Mattei, a partisan leader during WWII, was appointed northern commissioner of Agip, a state-owned petroleum company founded in 1926 by Mussolini, and ordered to liquidate the company. Mattei instead ordered the exploration of the Po Valley, where workers found methane gas deposits in 1946.

When Eni was created in 1953, Mattei was named president. His job was to find energy resources for an oil-poor country. He initiated a series of joint ventures with several Middle Eastern and African nations, offering better deals than his large oil company rivals, which he dubbed the Seven Sisters.

Mattei didn't stick to energy: By the time he died in a mysterious plane crash in 1962, Eni had acquired machinery manufacturer Pignone, finance company Sofid, Milan newspaper *Il Giorno*, and textile company Lane Rossi. Eni grew during the 1960s, partly because of a deal made for Soviet crude in 1958 and a joint venture with Esso in 1963. It also expanded its chemical activities.

By the early 1970s losses in Eni's chemical and textile operations, the oil crisis, and the Italian government's dumping of unprofitable companies on Eni hurt its bottom line. Former finance minister Franco Reviglio took over in 1983 and began cutting inefficient operations. EniChem merged with Montedison, Italy's largest private chemical company, in 1988, but clashes between the public agency and the private company made Montedison sell back its stake in 1990. Eni became a joint stock company in 1992, but the government retained a majority stake.

Franco Bernabe took over Eni following a 1993 bribery scandal and began cutting noncore businesses. The Italian government began selling Eni stock in 1995. In 1996 Eni signed on to develop Libyan gas resources and build a pipeline to Italy. A year later the company merged its Agipa exploration and production subsidiary into its main operations. Eni also took a 35% stake in Italian telecom company Albacom (which has since been sold to British Telecom Group).

The government cut its stake in Eni from 51% to 38% in 1998. That year Vittorio Mincato, a company veteran, succeeded Bernabe as CEO. In 1999 Eni and Russia's RAO Gazprom, the world's largest natural gas production firm, agreed to build a controversial $3 billion natural gas pipeline stretching from Russia to Turkey. Eni agreed to invest $5.5 billion to develop oil and gas reserves in Libya; it also sold interests in Saipem and Nuovo Pignone, as well as some of its Italian service stations.

In 2000 Eni paid about $910 million for a 33% stake in Galp, a Portuguese oil and gas company that also has natural gas utility operations. Also that year Eni bought British-Borneo Oil & Gas in a $1.2 billion deal, and in 2001 it paid $4 billion for UK independent exploration and production company LASMO, topping a bid by US-based Amerada Hess.

The Italian government sold off another 5% of Eni in 2001, reducing its stake to about 30%, and announced that it was considering selling its entire investment. In an effort to reduce noncore holdings, the company sold property management subsidiary Immobiliare Metanopoli to Goldman Sachs. Also that year Eni sold a minority stake in its gas pipeline unit, Snam Rete Gas, to the public.

In 2002 Eni entered discussions to acquire Enterprise Oil, but lost out to a rival bid from Royal Dutch Shell. Later that year Eni's oil field services unit Saipem gained control of Bouygues Offshore.

EXECUTIVES

Chairman: Roberto Poli, age 67
Managing Director and CEO: Paolo Scaroni, age 59
Group SVP Health, Safety, and Environment: Fabrizio D'Adda, age 63
Group SVP Supply Operations: Vittorio Giacomelli, age 64
Group SVP Legal Affairs: Carlo Grande, age 64
Group SVP Administration: Roberto Jaquinto, age 63
Group SVP Finance and CFO: Marco Mangiagalli, age 56
Group SVP Strategies and International Relations: Leonardo Maugeri, age 41
Group SVP Public Affairs and Communication: Eugenio Palmieri, age 58
Group SVP Human Resources: Renato Roffi, age 58
CTO; Chairman, Snamprogetti: Luigi Patron, age 65
General Manager Exploration and Production Division: Stefano Cao, age 54
General Manager Gas and Power Division: Luciano Sgubini, age 65
General Manager Refining and Marketing Division: Angelo Taraborrelli, age 57
Manager, Corporate Communications: Luciana Santaroni
Corporate Communications: Domenico Negrini
Group SVP Supply Operations: Amedeo Santucci
Auditors: PricewaterhouseCoopers SpA

LOCATIONS

HQ: Eni S.p.A.
Piazzale Enrico Mattei 1, 00144 Rome, Italy
Phone: +39-06-5982-1   **Fax:** +39-06-5982-2141
US HQ: 666 Fifth Ave., New York, NY 10103
US Phone: 212-887-0330   **US Fax:** 212-246-0009
Web: www.eni.it

Eni's subsidiaries have operations in more than 70 countries in Africa, Asia, Europe, the Middle East, and North and South America.

2005 Sales

	% of total
Europe	
Italy	44
Other EU countries	27
Other countries	7
The Americas	8
Africa	7
Asia	6
Other regions	1
Total	**100**

PRODUCTS/OPERATIONS

2005 Sales

	% of total
Refining & marketing	36
Gas & power	25
Exploration & production	24
Petrochemicals	7
Oil field services & engineering	6
Corporate & financial	1
Other	1
Total	**100**

Major Subsidiaries and Affiliates

EniPower SpA (power generation)
Italgas SpA (natural gas supply)
Saipem SpA (43%; oil field services)
Snam Rete Gas SpA (50.07%; gas pipeline)
Snamprogetti SpA (contracting and engineering)

COMPETITORS

AEM	Exxon Mobil
Anonima Petroli Italiana	Hellenic Petroleum
Ashland	Hess
BASF AG	Koch
Bayer	Lyondell Chemical
BG Group	Marathon Oil
BP	Norsk Hydro
Chevron	Occidental Petroleum
Chiyoda Corp.	PDVSA
ConocoPhillips	PEMEX
Dow Chemical	PETROBRAS
DuPont	Royal Dutch Shell
Edison	Sunoco
E.ON	TOTAL
ERG S.p.A.	

HISTORICAL FINANCIALS

Company Type: Public

Income Statement

FYE: December 31

	REVENUE ($ mil.)	NET INCOME ($ mil.)	NET PROFIT MARGIN	EMPLOYEES
12/05	88,269	8,981	10.2%	72,258
12/04	81,427	8,734	10.7%	71,497
12/03	65,799	7,906	12.0%	76,521
12/02	51,369	5,548	10.8%	80,655
Annual Growth	**19.8%**	**17.4%**	**—**	**(3.6%)**

2005 Year-End Financials

Debt ratio: 20.6%
Return on equity: 21.2%
Cash ($ mil.): 3,085
Current ratio: 1.11
Long-term debt ($ mil.): 8,562

No. of shares (mil.): —
Dividends
  Yield: 4.3%
  Payout: 58.8%
Market value ($ mil.): —

Stock History

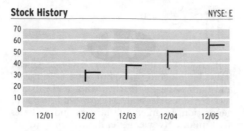

NYSE: E

	STOCK PRICE ($) FY Close	P/E High	P/E Low	PER SHARE ($) Earnings	PER SHARE ($) Dividends
12/05	55.78	15	12	4.03	2.37
12/04	50.34	15	11	3.40	1.32
12/03	37.99	11	8	3.33	1.25
12/02	31.40	—	—	—	1.07
Annual Growth	**21.1%**	**—**	**—**	**10.0%**	**30.4%**

E.ON

E.ON is on track to transform itself from a conglomerate into a multi-utility. Subsidiary E.ON Energie is one of Germany's top two power companies (running neck and neck with RWE), with some 11.6 million electricity, natural gas, and water customers in Central Europe; the unit also has about 27,800 MW of electric generating capacity and serves energy customers throughout continental Europe. Other utility subsidiaries include E.ON UK, US-based LG&E Energy, and E.ON Nordic. The company has completed its controversial acquisition of Ruhrgas (now E.ON Ruhrgas), Germany's #1 natural gas supplier. E.ON has also made a bid to acquire Endesa S.A., Spain's largest electric utility, for a reported $47.3 billion.

To raise cash for acquisitions (such as its $830 million purchase of Caledonia Oil and Gas), and to comply with US regulations on ownership of utilities, E.ON has sold off some high-profile businesses. It has sold its Veba Oel subsidiary, which explores for and produces oil and gas and operates the Aral service station chain (Germany's largest), to UK-based BP. The company has also sold its stakes in aluminum manufacturer VAW, metals distributor Klöckner, silicon wafer manufacturer MEMC, and logistics provider Stinnes. E.ON has sold its majority stake in chemical maker Degussa (and plans to further decrease its interest in the firm). In addition, the company has completed the sale of its 16% stake in Bouygues Telecom to Bouygues S.A.

E.ON was formed in 2000 from the merger of Germany's VEBA and VIAG conglomerates.

HISTORY

VEBA (originally Vereinigte Elektrizitats-und Bergwerks AG) was formed in 1929 in Berlin to consolidate Germany's state-owned electricity and mining interests. These operations included PreussenElektra, an electric utility formed by the German government in 1927; Hibernia, a coal mining firm founded in 1873; and Preussag, a mining and smelting company founded in 1923.

In the 1930s VEBA produced synthetic gasoline (essential to the German war machine) from coal at its Hibernia plant. In 1938 the company and chemical cartel I. G. Farben set up Chemische Werke Hüls to make synthetic rubber. After WWII, VEBA's assets in western Germany were transferred to the government, and several executives were arrested. Preussag was spun off in 1959.

In 1965 the government spun off VEBA to the public. That year the company entered trading and transportation by buying Stinnes, one of West Germany's largest industrial companies. In 1969 VEBA transferred its coal mining interests to Ruhrkohle and a few years later moved into oil exploration and development. The company shortened its name to VEBA in 1970.

The West German government sold its remaining stake in VEBA in 1987. In a changed regulatory environment, large investors were able to accumulate big portions of stock, and their dissatisfaction with the company's lackluster results made it a takeover target. In response, new chairman Ulrich Hartmann began cutting noncore businesses and reducing staff.

In 1990 VEBA began accumulating mobile communications, networking, and cable TV companies. It allied with the UK's Cable and Wireless (C&W) in 1995 to develop a European mobile phone business, but in 1997 C&W sold its interest to VEBA (as part of the deal, VEBA gained a 10% stake in C&W, which it sold in 1999). In anticipation of the 1998 deregulation of the German telecom market, VEBA and RWE merged their German telecom businesses in 1997.

VEBA acquired a 36% stake in Degussa, a specialty chemicals company, in 1997; two years later Degussa merged with Hüls to form a separately traded chemical company called Degussa-Hüls, in which VEBA took a 62% stake. VEBA sold a 30% stake in Stinnes to the public in 1999. The company's telecom venture sold its fixed-line telephone business, its cable TV unit, and its stake in mobile phone operator E-Plus.

These moves, however, were just the prelude to a bigger deal: a $14 billion merger agreement between VEBA and fellow German conglomerate VIAG. The partners announced plans to dump noncore businesses and beef up their energy and chemicals holdings. VEBA and VIAG completed their merger in 2000, and the combined company adopted the name E.ON. The companies' utilities businesses were combined into E.ON Energie, and their chemicals units were brought together as Degussa.

To gain regulatory approval to form E.ON, VEBA and VIAG agreed to sell their stakes in German electric utilities Bewag and VEAG and coal producer LAUBAG. E.ON sold its VEAG and LAUBAG interests, along with semiconductor and electronics distribution units, in 2000 and sold Bewag in 2001.

That year E.ON agreed to buy UK electricity generator Powergen (now E.ON UK), and it announced plans to sell off nonutility operations, including Degussa and Veba Oel. Later that year E.ON agreed to swap a 51% stake in Veba Oel for BP's 26% stake in German natural gas supplier Ruhrgas (now E.ON Ruhrgas). E.ON also sold Klöckner to UK steel trader Balli and sold its stake in silicon wafer maker MEMC to buyout firm Texas Pacific Group.

In 2002 E.ON sold its VAW Aluminum unit to Norwegian conglomerate Norsk Hydro in a $2.8 billion deal. Regulators moved to prevent E.ON from acquiring BP's stake in Ruhrgas in 2002, but BP agreed to pay for the Veba Oel stake in cash if necessary, and the swap was completed later that year. E.ON also acquired Vodafone and ThyssenKrupp's stakes in Ruhrgas in 2002, and it sold its remaining stake in Veba Oel to BP.

Also in 2002 E.ON completed its purchase of Powergen for about $8 billion, and it sold its 65% stake in logistics company Stinnes to German railroad operator Deutsche Bahn. In late 2002, E.ON acquired the UK energy supply and generation businesses of TXU Europe in a $2.5 billion deal.

The following year E.ON swapped its majority stake in chemical maker Degussa with coal group RAG for RAG's 18% interest in Ruhrgas. It completed its acquisition of Ruhrgas by purchasing the combined 40% stake held by Royal Dutch Shell, Exxon Mobil, and TUI (formerly Preussag). It also sold subsidiary Viterra's energy services unit (gas and water meters) to CVC Capital Partners.

EXECUTIVES

Honorary Chairman: Klaus Liesen, age 73
Chairman of the Supervisory Board: Ulrich Hartmann, age 68
Deputy Chairman of the Supervisory Board: Hubertus Schmoldt, age 61
Chairman of the Board of Management and CEO; Chairman, E.ON Energie, E.ON Ruhrgas, E.ON UK, and RAG: Wulf H. Bernotat, age 58
Member of the Board of Management, Finance, Accounting, Taxes, and Information Technology and CFO: Erhard Schipporeit, age 57
Member of the Board of Management, Controlling and Corporate Planning, Mergers and Acquisitions, and Legal Affairs; Chairman, Viterra: Hans Michael Gaul, age 64
Member of the Board of Management, Downstream Business; CEO, E.ON Energie: Johannes Teyssen, age 47
Member of the Board of Management, Upstream Business; CEO, E.ON Ruhrgas: Burckhard Bergmann, age 63
Member of the Board of Management, Human Resources, Infrastructure and Services, Procurement, and Organization: Manfred Krüper, age 65
EVP Corporate Communications: Peter Blau
EVP Investor Relations: Kiran Bhojani
EVP: Gert von der Groeben
EVP: Heinrich Montag
EVP: Rolf Pohlig
EVP: Hans Gisbert Ulmke
VP External Relations: Josef Nelles
VP Investor Relations: Mark C. Lewis
Human Resources: Gabriele Blank
Human Resources Development: Detlef Hartmann
Auditors: PwC Deutsche Revision AG

LOCATIONS

HQ: E.ON AG
    E.ON-Platz 1, 40479 Düsseldorf, Germany
Phone: +49-211-4579-0   **Fax:** +49-211-4579-501
US HQ: 220 W. Main St., Louisville, KY 40232
US Phone: 502-589-1444   **US Fax:** 502-627-3629
Web: www.eon.com

2005 Sales

	% of total
Europe	
Germany	60
Other European Union countries	5
Other	31
US	4
Total	**100**

PRODUCTS/OPERATIONS

2005 Sales

	% of total
Central Europe	42
Pan-European Gas	30
UK	18
Nordic	6
US Midwest	4
Total	**100**

Selected Divisions, Subsidiaries, and Affiliates

Central Europe (E.ON Energie AG; integrated electricity and downstream gas)
Pan-European Gas (E.ON Ruhrgas AG; upstream and midstream gas)
UK (E.ON UK plc; integrated energy)
Nordic (E.ON Nordic, E.ON Finland, and E.ON Sverige; integrated energy)
US Midwest (E.ON U.S. LLC; regulated energy)
    LG&E Energy LLC (natural gas and electric utility, US)
Degussa AG (43%, chemicals)

COMPETITORS

AGIV	Eni
BASF AG	EVN
Bayer	France Telecom
Deutsche Telekom AG	Nuon
Dow Chemical	RWE
DuPont	SUEZ
Electricité de France	UES of Russia
EnBW	Unión Fenosa
Endesa	Vattenfall
Enel	Vattenfall Europe Berlin

HISTORICAL FINANCIALS

Company Type: Public

Income Statement

	REVENUE ($ mil.)	NET INCOME ($ mil.)	NET PROFIT MARGIN	EMPLOYEES
				FYE: December 31
12/05	66,788	8,771	13.1%	75,173
12/04	60,576	5,874	9.7%	69,710
12/03	53,589	5,854	10.9%	66,549
12/02	37,871	2,911	7.7%	107,856
Annual Growth	**20.8%**	**44.4%**	—	**(11.3%)**

2005 Year-End Financials

Debt ratio: —
Return on equity: 17.9%
Cash ($ mil.): 17,904
Current ratio: 46.85
Long-term debt ($ mil.): —
No. of shares (mil.): —
Dividends
    Yield: 2.3%
    Payout: 5.9%
Market value ($ mil.): —

Stock History

NYSE: EON

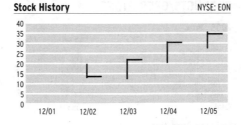

	STOCK PRICE ($) FY Close	P/E High	P/E Low	PER SHARE ($) Earnings	PER SHARE ($) Dividends
12/05	34.52	3	2	13.31	0.79
12/04	30.33	10	7	2.98	0.62
12/03	21.81	—	—	—	0.51
12/02	13.64	—	—	—	0.37
Annual Growth	**36.3%**	—	—	**346.6%**	**28.8%**

Ericsson

Ericsson has a way without wires. The company is the world's leading maker of wireless telecom infrastructure equipment. Network operators and service providers use Ericsson's antennas, transmitters, and other wireless infrastructure gear to build and expand networks. The company's other products include corporate networking gear, cable, defense electronics, and software for mobile messaging and commerce. Ericsson is also a top seller of cell phones through Sony Ericsson, a joint venture with Sony. The company is controlled by two groups, Investor AB, the investment vehicle for the Wallenberg family, and AB Industrivärden, which wield 19% and 13% of the voting power respectively.

To offset the impact of plummeting sales caused by the depressed global telecom market, Ericsson has undergone an extensive reorganization of its product groups and geographic divisions. The company has expanded its professional services business, which now accounts for more than one quarter of its systems segment sales, to take up some of the slack in equipment sales.

Ericsson, which builds products around all the major wireless standards, continues to focus on upgrading carrier networks to the third generation (3G) primarily in Western Europe, Latin America, and the US. To that end, it has increased shipments of products based on interim GPRS technology (an enhancement of the leading GSM standard) to bridge the gap between existing 2G and emerging 3G networks.

Ericsson has combined its mobile phone handset business with that of consumer product expert Sony into a 50%-owned joint venture called Sony Ericsson Mobile Communications. The pair hopes that the endeavor will help them to gain ground on industry leaders Nokia, Motorola, Samsung, and Siemens for a larger share of the cell phone market. However, the company has begun pulling out of the code division multiple access (CDMA) business after failing to gain substantial ground against Lucent Technologies (now Alcatel-Lucent) and Nortel Networks. Ericsson shut down the US headquarters for its CDMA business, located in San Diego, cutting 250 jobs.

In an effort to expand its telecom network equipment business, Ericsson has acquired certain telecom hardware assets from troubled Marconi, now known as telent. The deal, valued at about $2.1 billion, boosts Ericsson's ability to compete in an increasingly tough global telecoms marketplace.

HISTORY

Lars Magnus Ericsson opened a telegraph repair shop in Stockholm in 1876, the same year Alexander Graham Bell applied for a US patent on the telephone. Within two years Ericsson was making telephones. His company grew rapidly, supplying equipment first to Swedish phone companies and later to other European companies. In 1885 Ericsson crafted a combination receiver-speaker in one handset.

In 1911 Ericsson and SAT, the Stockholm telephone company, merged under the Ericsson banner. The company adopted its present name in 1926. In 1930 international financier Ivar "The Match King" Kreuger, owner of the Swedish Match Co., won control of Ericsson. His triumph was short-lived. Krueger committed suicide in 1932 and one of his creditors, Sosthenes Behn's ITT, took over.

ITT in 1960 sold its interest in Ericsson to the top Swedish industrialist family, the Wallenbergs. In 1975 Ericsson introduced its computer-controlled exchange, called AXE. Buoyed by AXE's success, the company unveiled the "office of the future" in the early 1980s, diversifying into computers and office furniture.

However, Ericsson's timing was off: The demand for office automation never materialized and profits plunged. Electrolux chairman Hans Werthen was recruited to split his time between the two companies and rescue Ericsson. The company sold its computer business to Nokia in 1988 and refocused on telephone equipment. It dusted off its aging AXE system for the burgeoning cellular market and quickly won key contracts.

The company and aircraft maker Saab merged their military aviation electronics operations as Ericsson Saab Avionics in 1996. (It was dissolved in 1998.) In 1998 manager Sven-Christer Nilsson was appointed CEO. He reorganized the company and laid off 14,000 workers.

After Ericsson fought bitterly with rival QUALCOMM over wireless standards and patents, the companies settled in 1999, agreeing to push for the standardization of third-generation technology based on QUALCOMM's code-division multiple access technology. As a part of the deal, Ericsson purchased QUALCOMM's infrastructure business. To expand its Internet offerings, Ericsson bought Internet router maker Torrent and Internet telephony company Touchwave.

By mid-1999 Nilsson was pushed out for moving too slowly on restructuring plans and was replaced as CEO by chairman Lars Ramqvist, who put many of the duties on president Kurt Hellström. Hellström immediately set out to simplify the company's managerial and accounting structure, trim its workforce and slow-growth businesses, and push new phone models to market.

The next year Ericsson sold noncore businesses including its private radio systems, power supply, and equipment shelter operations. The company also agreed to develop a standard for secure wireless transactions with Nokia and Motorola and formed a joint venture with Web router maker Juniper to sell routers for mobile Internet applications.

Fierce competition, an industrywide slowdown in handset sales, and manufacturing glitches led Ericsson to outsource the manufacture of its phones to Flextronics and form a joint venture (Sony Ericsson Mobile Communications) with Sony to link the development and marketing of their handsets in 2001. Ericsson also sold its direct enterprise sales and service unit, outsourced IT operations in Europe to EDS, and cut more than 20,000 jobs that year. Hellström became CEO in 2001.

Chairman Ramqvist became honorary chairman in 2002; Electrolux CEO Michael Treschow was named as the acting chairman. Ericsson announced 20,000 more layoffs in 2002. That year the company sold its semiconductor unit to Infineon for about $380 million.

Ericsson sold its optoelectronic components business in early 2003. Hellström retired later that year and Carl-Henric Svanberg, former CEO of Assa Abloy, was appointed as company president and CEO.

EXECUTIVES

Chairman: Michael Treschow, age 62
Deputy Chairman: Marcus Wallenberg, age 50
President, CEO, and Director: Carl-Henric Svanberg, age 54
EVP, CFO, and Head of Group Function Finance: Karl-Henrik Sundström, age 45
EVP and General Manager, Business Unit Access: Kurt Jofs, age 47
EVP, Group Function Sales and Marketing: Bert Nordberg, age 49
EVP and General Manager, Business Unit Systems: Björn Olsson, age 49
EVP and General Manager, Business Unit Global Services: Hans Vestberg, age 40
EVP and Head of Sales and Marketing, Sony Ericsson: Jan Wäreby
SVP, CTO, and General Manager, Research and Development: Håkan Eriksson, age 44
SVP, Group Function Communications: Henry Sténson
SVP, Group Function Human Resources and Organization: Marita Hellberg, age 50
SVP, Group Function Legal Affairs: Carl Olof Blomqvist
SVP, Group Function Operational Excellence: Joakim Westh, age 44
VP and General Manager, Market Unit North America: Angel Ruiz
VP, Communications, Ericsson Inc. (Americas): Kathy Egan
VP, Investor Relations: Gary Pinkham
Head of Media Relations: Åse Lindskog
Auditors: PricewaterhouseCoopers AB

LOCATIONS

HQ: Telefonaktiebolaget LM Ericsson
Torshamnsgatan 23, Kista,
SE-164 83 Stockholm, Sweden
Phone: +46-8-719-0000   **Fax:** +46-8-18-40-85
US HQ: 6300 Legacy Dr., Plano, TX 75024
US Phone: 972-583-0000   **US Fax:** 972-669-8860
Web: www.ericsson.com

2005 Sales

	$ mil.	% of total
Western Europe		
Sweden	768.0	4
Other countries	4,503.8	24
Central & Eastern Europe,		
Middle East & Africa	5,021.5	26
Asia/Pacific		
China	1,451.1	8
Other countries	2,499.2	13
North America		
US	2,250.5	12
Other countries	192.1	1
Latin America	2,397.7	12
Total	**19,083.9**	**100**

PRODUCTS/OPERATIONS

2005 Sales

	$ mil.	% of total
Equipment sales		
Delivery-type contracts	13,556.0	71
Construction-type contracts	2,264.1	12
Service sales	2,951.1	15
Licenses	312.7	2
Total	**19,083.9**	**100**

Selected Operations

Mobile systems
  Antennas
  Complete network service hardware platforms
  Fixed cellular terminals
  Microwave and high-speed electronics
    Circuit board
    Interconnect products
    Passive components
    Semiconductor devices
  Point-to-point and point-to-multipoint microwave systems
  Radio base station controllers
  Routers
  Wireless broadband systems

Services
  Consulting
  Customer management
  Network design, integration, management, and migration
  Product support
  Staff training and education
Fixed systems
  ATM and IP routers
  Circuit switching hardware platforms (AXE)
  IP switching hardware platforms (ANS)
Other
  Defense electronics
    Modular airborne computers
    RADAR systems
    Secure wireless communications systems
  Enterprise products
    Business communication and call center software
    Network access routers
    PBX systems (BusinessPhone, MD110, WebSwitch)
    Telephones and terminals
    Wireless LAN systems
  Software
    Billing
    Customer management
    Network and transmission management
    Service provisioning

COMPETITORS

Accenture	Motorola
Alcatel-Lucent	NEC Electronics
BenQ	Nokia
Cisco Systems	Nortel Networks
EDS	QUALCOMM
Flextronics	Samsung Electronics
IBM	Sharp
LG Electronics	Siemens Communications

HISTORICAL FINANCIALS

Company Type: Public

Income Statement

FYE: December 31

	REVENUE ($ mil.)	NET INCOME ($ mil.)	NET PROFIT MARGIN	EMPLOYEES
12/05	19,084	3,079	16.1%	56,055
12/04	19,981	2,178	10.9%	50,534
12/03	16,260	(1,463)	—	51,583
12/02	16,739	(2,279)	—	64,621
12/01	22,159	(2,350)	—	85,000
Annual Growth	**(3.7%)**	**—**		**(9.9%)**

2005 Year-End Financials

Debt ratio: 13.6%
Return on equity: 23.8%
Cash ($ mil.): 10,245
Current ratio: 1.93
Long-term debt ($ mil.): 1,783

Stock History

NASDAQ (GS): ERIC

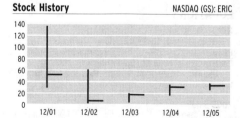

	STOCK PRICE ($) FY Close	P/E High/Low		PER SHARE ($) Earnings	Dividends
12/05	34.40	196	146	0.19	0.25
12/04	31.49	—	—	—	—
12/03	17.70	—	—	—	—
12/02	6.74	—	—	—	—
12/01	52.20	—	—	—	—
Annual Growth	**(9.9%)**			**—**	**—**

Ernst & Young

Accounting may actually be the *second*-oldest profession, and Ernst & Young is one of the oldest practitioners. Ernst & Young is also one of the world's largest accounting firms (third in revenue of the Big Four behind PricewaterhouseCoopers and Deloitte Touche Tohmatsu) with some 700 offices in 140 countries, offering auditing and accounting services. The firm also provides legal services and services relating to emerging growth companies, human resources issues, and corporate transactions (mergers and acquisitions, IPOs, and the like). Ernst & Young has one of the world's largest tax practices, serving multinational clients that have to comply with multiple local tax laws.

After spending decades building their consultancies, the big accountancies have all moved toward shedding them, because of internal and regulatory pressures, as well as the perceived conflict of interest in providing auditing and consulting services to the same clients. Ernst & Young was the first to split off its consultancy, selling it in 2000 to what is now Cap Gemini Ernst & Young.

Ernst & Young, which gained an impressive amount of weight in former rival Andersen's diaspora, has also boosted its legal services, assembling some 2,000 lawyers in dozens of countries.

But the firm has faced Andersen-style trouble of its own as client suits against auditors have become more common in the wake of corporate scandals at Enron and other troubled companies. Both Avis Budget Group, Inc (formerly Cendant) and HealthSouth have sued Ernst & Young in connection with alleged accounting missteps. As a result, the accounting firms are seeking help from Washington to protect themselves from the threat of litigation and ending up like Andersen.

In 2005 Ernst & Young's UK arm emerged victorious from a torrid legal battle with insurer Equitable Life, which in 2003 had sued the accountancy for professional negligence related to work performed when Ernst & Young was its auditor.

In 2005 Ernst & Young and its rivals enjoyed a fee bonanza fueled by changes in international accounting standards required by passage of the Sarbanes-Oxley Act in the US. Growth in the firm's tax business was less robust.

HISTORY

In 1494 Luca Pacioli's *Summa di Arithmetica* became the first published text on double-entry bookkeeping, but it was almost 400 years before accounting became a profession.

In 1849 Frederick Whinney joined the UK firm of Harding & Pullein. His ledgers were so clear that he was advised to take up accounting, which was a growth field as stock companies proliferated. Whinney became a name partner in 1859 and his sons followed him into the business. The firm became Whinney, Smith & Whinney (WS&W) in 1894.

After WWII, WS&W formed an alliance with Ernst & Ernst (founded in Cleveland in 1903 by brothers Alwin and Theodore Ernst), with each company operating on the other's behalf across the Atlantic.

Whinney merged with Brown, Fleming & Murray in 1965 to become Whinney Murray. In 1979 Whinney Murray, Turquands Barton Mayhew (also a UK firm), and Ernst & Ernst merged to form Ernst & Whinney.

But Ernst & Whinney wasn't done merging. Ten years later, when it was the fourth-largest accounting firm, it merged with #5 Arthur Young, which had been founded by Scotsman Arthur Young in 1895 in Kansas City. Long known as "old reliable," Arthur Young fell on hard times in the 1980s because its audit relationships with failed S&Ls led to expensive litigation (settled in 1992 for $400 million).

Thus the new firm of Ernst & Young faced a rocky start. In 1990 it fended off rumors of collapse. The next year it slashed payroll, even thinning its partner roster. Exhausted by the S&L wars, in 1994 the firm replaced its pugnacious general counsel, Carl Riggio, with the more cost-conscious Kathryn Oberly.

In the mid-1990s Ernst & Young concentrated on consulting, particularly in software applications, and grew through acquisitions. In 1996 the firm bought Houston-based Wright Killen & Co., a petroleum and petrochemicals consulting firm, to form Ernst & Young Wright Killen. It also entered new alliances that year, including ones with Washington-based ISD/Shaw, which provided banking industry consulting, and India's Tata Consulting.

In 1997 Ernst & Young was sued for a record $4 billion for its alleged failure to effectively handle the 1993 restructuring of the defunct Merry-Go-Round Enterprises retail chain (it settled for $185 million in 1999). On the heels of a merger deal between Coopers & Lybrand and Price Waterhouse, Ernst & Young agreed in 1997 to merge with KPMG International. But Ernst & Young called off the negotiations in 1998, citing the uncertain regulatory process they faced.

In 1999 the firm reached a settlement in lawsuits regarding accounting errors at Informix and Avis Budget Group, Inc. and sold its UK and southern African trust and fiduciary businesses to Royal Bank of Canada (now RBC Financial Group).

In 2000 Ernst & Young became the first of the (then) Big Five firms to sell its consultancy, dealing it to France's Cap Gemini Group for about $11 billion. The following year the UK accountancy watchdog group announced it would investigate Ernst & Young for its handling of the accounts of UK-based The Equitable Life Assurance Society. The insurer was forced to close to new business in 2000 because of massive financial difficulties.

Ernst & Young made headlines and gave competitors plenty to talk about in 2002 when closely held financial records were made public during a divorce case involving executive Rick Bobrow (who in 2003 abruptly retired as global CEO after just a year on the job).

Also in 2002 the firm allied with former New York City mayor Rudy Giuliani to launch a business consultancy bearing the Giuliani name. Ernst & Young later helped the venture to build its investment banking capabilities by selling its corporate finance unit (as well as its stake in Giuliani Partners) to that firm in 2004.

EXECUTIVES

Chairman and CEO; Chairman for the Americas:
James S. (Jim) Turley, age 51
COO: Paul J. Ostling
Global Vice Chair Strategy, Communications, and Regulatory Affairs: Beth A. Brooke
Chairman Global Financial Services Group:
Robert W. (Bob) Stein
Global Managing Partner, Quality and Risk Management: Sue Frieden
Global Managing Partner, Client Service and Accounts:
Thomas P. (Tom) McGrath

CFO and Global Managing Partner, Finance and Infrastructure: Jeffrey H. (Jeff) Dworken
Global Managing Partner, People: Pierre Hurstel
Global Vice Chair, Assurance and Advisory Business Services (AABS): Christian Mouillon
Global Vice Chair, Tax: Sam Fouad
Global Vice Chair, Transaction Advisory Services (TAS):
Dave Read
Global Vice Chair Technology, Communications, and Entertainment: Stephen E. Almassy
Global Vice Chair, Strategic Growth Markets:
Gregory Ericksen
Global Director, Automotive: Mike Hanley
Global Director, Business Risk Services:
Thomas (Tom) Bussa
Global Director, Insurance Industry Services:
Peter Porrino
Managing Partner Transaction Advisory Services:
Francis Small
Country Leader, Americas — US: John Ferraro

LOCATIONS

HQ: Ernst & Young International
5 Times Square, New York, NY 10036
Phone: 212-773-3000   **Fax:** 212-773-6350
Web: www.eyi.com

Ernst & Young International has approximately 700 offices in 140 countries.

PRODUCTS/OPERATIONS

Selected Services

Assurance and Advisory
  Actuarial services
  Audits
  Accounting advisory
  Business risk services
  Internal audit
  Real estate advisory services
  Technology and security risk services
Emerging Growth Companies
  Corporate finance services
  Mergers and acquisitions advisory
  Operational consulting
  Strategic advisory
  Transactions advisory
Human Capital
  Compensation and benefits consulting
  Cost optimization and risk management
  Transaction support services
Law
  Corporate and M&A
  Employment
  Finance
  Information technology services
  Intellectual property
  International trade and anti-trust
  Litigation and arbitration
  Real estate
Tax
  Global tax operations
  Indirect tax
  International tax
Transactions
  Capital management
  Corporate development advisory
  Financial and business modeling
  M&A advisory
  Post-deal advisory
  Strategic finance
  Transaction management
  Valuation

COMPETITORS

Baker Tilly International
BDO International
Deloitte
Grant Thornton International
Horwath International
IBM
KPMG
Moore Stephens International
Moores Rowland
PKF International
PricewaterhouseCoopers

HISTORICAL FINANCIALS

Company Type: Partnership

Income Statement

FYE: June 30

	REVENUE ($ mil.)	NET INCOME ($ mil.)	NET PROFIT MARGIN	EMPLOYEES
6/06	18,400	—	—	114,000
6/05	16,902	—	—	106,650
6/04	14,547	—	—	100,601
6/03	13,136	—	—	103,000
6/02	10,124	—	—	87,206
Annual Growth	16.1%	—	—	6.9%

Revenue History

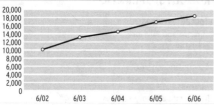

Espírito Santo

Espírito Santo Financial Group (ESFG) wields its earthly powers via two main entities: Banco Espírito Santo and Companhia de Seguros Tranquilidade, one of Portugal's top insurance firms. Its BES Investimento offers investment banking; ESAF Activos Financeiros is a fund management firm. ESFG's other holdings include stockbroker Espírito Santo Dealer (formerly ESER). Although most of its operations are in Portugal, ESFG has banking, insurance, and financial services interests in other European countries, Africa, Brazil, the Caribbean, and the US, where it owns Espírito Santo Bank of Florida. Entities associated with the founding Espírito Santo family are ESFG's major shareholders.

ESFG sells the lion's share of Tranquilidade's insurance, pension, and investment products through its bank offices, which also provide consumer and business banking services.

In 2006 the company announced that French banking giant Crédit Agricole will buy its Tranquilidade Vida and Espírito Santo Seguros units for €200 million.

HISTORY

The Espírito Santo financial empire traces its roots to a bank founded by José Maria de Espírito Santo Silva in Lisbon in 1884. After WWI, Portugal underwent a major banking expansion, and in 1920 the Espírito Santo family established Banco Espírito Santo, which grew rapidly thanks to postwar expansion and speculation.

After José Maria's oldest son, José, fled the bank and the country in scandal, his brother, Ricardo, led the massive growth of both the bank and the family's fortune. During the 1930s the Espírito Santos acquired a major interest in insurance company Tranquilidade, and in 1937 Banco Espírito Santo merged with Banco Comercial de Lisboa (founded 1875) to create Banco Espírito Santo e Comercial de Lisboa.

The family's fortunes were aided by dictator Antonio de Oliveira Salazar, who came to power in 1933. During WWII, Salazar declared Portugal neutral, and the country became a sanctuary for many of Europe's elite, who brought the Espírito Santos business and contacts.

The Espírito Santo empire was fostered by Salazar's postwar protectionist policies. Banco Espírito Santo became one of Portugal's largest banks and Tranquilidade one of its largest insurance companies. The family also acquired large coffee, sugar, and palm-oil plantations in Portugal's colonies Angola and Mozambique. At their peak, the Espírito Santo holdings were valued at $4 billion.

But the family's fortunes turned with political upheaval in Portugal during the 1970s. In 1974 the military overthrew Salazar's successor, Marcelo Caetano. A year later the leftist government nationalized Portugal's major corporations, including Banco Espírito Santo and Tranquilidade.

The family fled to London and pooled their savings to create a new company in Luxembourg, Espírito Santo Financial Holding (ESFH). In the late 1970s they got a banking license in Brazil and later set up a fund management company in Switzerland and banks in Miami and Paris. The family's name attracted business and investors.

The Portuguese government reprivatized financial services organizations in 1986. That year ESFH and France's Crédit Agricole opened Banco Internacional de Crédito in Portugal. After raising money on the Eurobond market, ESFH bought back control of Tranquilidade in 1990. A year later the company and a group of investors, including Crédit Agricole, reacquired control of Banco Espírito Santo.

In 1993 ESFH reduced its interest in Banco Internacional de Crédito to 47% (it regained 100% control in 1997). Since then the company has concentrated on Portugal. In the early 1990s recession rocked the economy — and the company. But in the mid-1990s, despite poor commercial demand, consumer-related services rebounded.

ESFH expanded its commercial banking network in 1995 and 1996. In 1997 the company and Brazil's Monteiro Aranha bought more than 60% of that country's Banco Boavista. ESFH also dropped "Holding" in favor of "Group," and the next year ESFG, in a vote of confidence in Brazil, moved to raise its holdings in Banco Boavista.

In 1999, amid a flurry of speculation about Spanish/Portuguese banking mergers, the company agreed to buy a majority interest in Spanish brokerage Benito y Monjardin. The company also moved to bolster its asset management operations by inking a deal to buy Portugal-based fund manager Gescapital.

In 2000 ESFG bought the majority stake of French credit institution Via Banque from BNP Paribas (it acquired the rest of Via Banque in 2001). The next year ESFG, in conjunction with Portugal Telecom, launched Banco Electrónico de Serviço Total (Banco Best) as a technologically integrated banking, investment, and brokerage service.

EXECUTIVES

Chairman and President:
Ricardo Espírito Santo Silva Salgado, age 61
Vice Chairman:
José Manuel Pinheiro Espírito Santo Silva, age 60
Director: Manuel de Magalhães Villas-Boas, age 60
SVP: José Carlos Cardoso Castella, age 56
SVP: Erich Dähler, age 53
SVP: Jean-Luc Schneider, age 53
Secretary: Teresa de Souza
Auditors: KPMG

LOCATIONS

HQ: Espírito Santo Financial Group, S.A.
231 Val des Bons Malades,
2121 Luxembourg-Kirchberg, Luxembourg
Phone: +352-434-945   **Fax:** +352-434-9454
US HQ: 320 Park Avenue, 29th Fl., New York, NY 10022
US Phone: 212-702-3400   **US Fax:** 212-750-3888
Web: www.esfg.com

Espírito Santo Financial Group has operations in Angola, Brazil, the Cayman Islands, China, France, Ireland, Luxembourg, Macao, Panama, Portugal, Spain, Switzerland, the UK, and the US.

PRODUCTS/OPERATIONS

Selected Subsidiaries

Banco Espírito Santo de Investimento SA (Portugal)
Banco Espírito Santo do Oriente SA (BES-ORIENTE, Macao)
Banco Espírito Santo SA (BES, Portugal)
BES Investimento do Brasil
Besleasing e Factoring (Portugal)
Compagnie Bancaire Espírito Santo (Switzerland)
Crediflash (Portugal)
Cia. de Seguros Tranquilidade SA (insurance, Portugal)
ES Capital (Portugal)
ESAF — Espírito Santo Activos Financeiros (Portugal)
Espírito Santo Activos Financeiros SGPS,SA (holding company, Portugal)
Espírito Santo Bank Ltd. (US)
Espírito Santo Dealer

COMPETITORS

Banco Comercial Português
Banco de Comercio e Industria
Banco Portugues do Atlantico
BBVA
BNP Paribas
Citigroup
Crédit Agricole
Credit Suisse
Deutsche Bank
Itaúsa
JPMorgan Chase
Merrill Lynch
SCH
Société Générale
UBS
Zurich Financial Services

HISTORICAL FINANCIALS

Company Type: Public

Income Statement

FYE: December 31

	ASSETS ($ mil.)	NET INCOME ($ mil.)	INCOME AS % OF ASSETS	EMPLOYEES
12/04*	68,900	72	0.1%	6,669

*Most recent year available

Fiat S.p.A.

The country that gave us Sophia Loren and Leonardo da Vinci also gave us century-old Fiat and its plethora of auto offerings, which range from compacts and sedans such as the Fiat Seicento to its Alfa Romeo and Ferrari sports cars (56%). Having sold some noncore businesses, Fiat's refined focus is on cars, CNH Global agricultural and construction equipment, and Iveco commercial vehicles. Other operations include Magneti Marelli (auto components), Teskid (15%, engine parts), and Comau (industrial automation). Fiat has sold its interests in publishing and aerospace. The founding Agnelli family, through holding company IFIL Investments, owns about 30% of Fiat.

After several wrong turns on the road back to profitability, Fiat is starting to make some progress. The company has sold its entire 5.1% stake in GM to an unnamed investment bank for nearly $1.2 billion in order to raise cash (GM took a 20% stake in Fiat Auto in 2000). Fiat then announced it would cut 12,300 jobs (6.9% of its worldwide workforce) over a three-year period and close 12 factories in hopes of being profitable by 2006. Most of the cuts have come at CNH Global, Iveco, and Fiat Auto. The company also sold its Fiat Avio aviation division as well as its publishing operations to raise cash. All of Fiat's effort paid off. 2005 marked the first time in five years that Fiat managed to make a profit — a whole year ahead of schedule.

A provision of the 2000 deal that gave GM 20% (later reduced to 10%) of Fiat Auto also gave the Italian automaker the option to force GM to buy the remaining 90% as early as 2004 (or as late as 2009). The "put option" was later backed off by Fiat to 2005 (or as late as 2010). GM claimed the put was rendered invalid when Fiat Auto restructured and GM's stake was reduced to 10%. Fiat insisted GM's claim was false. After a month of very private negotiations early in 2005 GM finally agreed to pay Fiat $2 billion to settle the dispute, and thereby avoid having to buy Fiat Auto.

Fiat (Fiat S.p.A. not Fiat Auto) has bought the unprofitable Maserati nameplate back from Ferrari. The company hopes that combining the operations of Maserati and Alfa Romeo will create economic and commercial synergies. Maserati has returned to US shores via Fiat's Ferrari stores and Fiat plans to reintroduce the Alfa Romeo brand to the US by 2007.

In 2006 Fiat together with India's Tata Motors announced the two companies would form a joint venture in India to build passenger cars, engines, and transmissions. The move enhances the existing alliance between the two companies. At full capacity the venture is expected to build 100,000 cars and 250,000 engines and transmissions annually. The two companies are also exploring an expansion of the agreement that would include operations in South America where Fiat has a sound footing.

HISTORY

Ex-cavalry officer Giovanni Agnelli founded Fabbrica Italiana di Automobili Torino (Fiat) in 1899. Between 1903 and 1918 the automaker expanded into trucks, rail cars, aviation, and tractors. Protected by tariffs, Fiat became Italy's dominant auto company.

WWII boosted Fiat's fortunes, but bombs damaged many of its plants. With US support, Fiat rebuilt and survived by exporting and by building plants abroad. As growth in Italy resumed, Fiat began making steel and construction equipment.

After the European Community forced Italy to lower tariffs in 1961, Fiat lost market share, although foreign sales helped offset its woes. Giovanni Agnelli II (the founder's grandson) became chairman in 1966. Fiat then bought high-end Italian carmakers Lancia and Ferrari in 1969.

The company formed Fiat Auto S.p.A. in 1979, bringing together the Fiat, Lancia, Autobianchi, Abarth, and Ferrari lines. The next year Cesare Romiti became managing director and cut 23,000 jobs and broke union influence at Fiat. The company closed its unprofitable US car operations in 1983. Fiat and British Ford combined their truck operations in 1986, and Fiat also bought Alfa Romeo that year.

In 1989 Fiat purchased 49% of luxury carmaker Maserati (it bought the rest in 1993). Fiat and Ford merged their farm and construction equipment divisions in 1991 to form Fiat subsidiary New Holland (renamed CNH Global in 1999). After posting its biggest loss in 1993, Fiat restructured.

Slow car sales in Italy prompted Fiat to temporarily lay off about 74,000 workers in 1996, and chairman Agnelli stepped down. In 1997 Agnelli's successor, Romiti, and financial director Paolo Mattioli were convicted of falsifying records and illegally financing political parties. They were barred from employment at Fiat.

Paolo Fresco, former vice chairman of General Electric, replaced Romiti as head of Fiat in 1998. Challenged with slumping car sales in Italy and South America, the company sold its chemicals and telecom businesses. Fiat's New Holland subsidiary bought agricultural and construction equipment maker Case Corporation for around $4.3 billion and changed its name to CNH Global in 1999. Also that year Fiat began making light commercial trucks in China with Yuejin Motor.

To expand its auto business outside Europe, Fiat agreed in 2000 to trade a 20% stake in its car unit for a 5.1% stake in GM. That year ALSTOM agreed to buy a 51% stake in Fiat's rail unit (Fiat Ferrovia). Also in 2000 the company's bid (with a consortium including Electricite de France) of about $5.5 billion for control of agro-energy group Montedison was accepted.

As 2002 came to a close, Fiat announced it would lay off as many as 5,600 workers, and it sold its entire stake in GM to an unnamed investment bank for nearly $1.2 billion. Gianni Agnelli, Fiat's honorary chairman and grandson of the company's founder, died at the age of 81 in early 2003. Later that year Fiat sold its Fiat Avio aviation unit to The Carlyle Group and Italian defense group Finmeccanica for about $1.8 billion.

Fiat chairman Umberto Agnelli died in late May of 2004, plunging the company into management chaos. When the board named Ferrari and Maserati chairman Luca Cordero di Montezemolo chairman of Fiat instead of Fiat CEO Giuseppe Morchio, Morchio suddenly quit. The company quickly named turnaround specialist Sergio Marchionne as Fiat S.p.A.'s fifth CEO in two years.

Early in 2005, after a messy divorce from General Motors, Fiat replaced the CEO of beleaguered Fiat Auto, Hebert Demel, with Fiat CEO Sergio Marchionne, marking the first time since 1899 that a single person ran both the Fiat holding company and Fiat Auto. Marchionne also became the fourth executive to run Fiat Auto in a little more than three years.

EXECUTIVES

Chairman; Chairman and CEO, Ferrari:
Luca Cordero di Montezemolo, age 59
Vice Chairman: John Philip Elkann, age 30
CEO; CEO, Fiat Auto and Director: Sergio Marchionne, age 54
SVP, Business Development and Strategies:
Ferruccio Luppi, age 56
SVP, Communications: Simone Migliarino, age 58
SVP, Institutional Relations: Ernesto Auci, age 60
SVP, International Relations: Giorgio Frasca, age 64
SVP, Fiat Group Human Resources, and Ferrari Human Resources and General Secretary Department:
Mario Mairano, age 55
Corporate Security and Chairman, Sirio S and Consorzio Orione: Augusto Ambroso, age 61
Senior Counsel: Roberto Russo, age 46
Chief Audit Executive and Compliance Officer:
Mauro Di Gennaro, age 44
CEO, Elasis S.c.p.A.: Nevio Di Giusto, age 53
CEO, Magneti Marelli: Eugenio Razelli, age 55
CEO, Maserati; COO, Alfa Romeo: Karl-Heinz Kalbfell, age 64
CEO, ITEDI and CEO and General Manager, Publikompass: Angelo Sajeva, age 52
CEO, Fiat Finance and Group Treasurer:
Maurizio Francescatti, age 43
CEO; Tofas Turk Otomobil Fabrikasi A S:
Ali Aydin Pandir
CEO, CNH Global N.V.: Harold D. Boyanovsky, age 61
CEO; Fiat Powertrain Technologies: Alfredo Altavilla, age 41
President and CEO, Comau S.p.A.: Daniele Pecchini, age 55
President and CEO, Iveco S.p.A.: Paolo Monferino, age 59
President and CEO, Teksid S.p.A.: Riccardo Tarantini, age 57
VP Communications and Institutional Relations, Fiat Auto: Roberto Zuccato
Auditors: Deloitte & Touche S.p.A.

LOCATIONS

HQ: Fiat S.p.A.
250 Via Nizza, 10126 Turin, Italy
Phone: +39-011-006-1111 **Fax:** +39-011-006-3798
Web: www.fiatgroup.com

2005 Sales

	% of total
Europe	
Italy	28
Other countries	40
North America	13
Mercosur	9
Other regions	10
Total	**100**

PRODUCTS/OPERATIONS

2005 Sales

	% of total
Fiat Auto	38
Agricultural & construction equipment (CNH)	22
Trucks & commercial vehicles (Iveco)	18
Components (Magneti Marelli)	8
Fiat Powertrain Technologies	4
Production systems (Comau)	3
Ferrari	2
Metallurgical products (Teskid)	2
Services (Business Solutions)	1
Maserati	1
Other	1
Total	**100**

EXECUTIVES

Chairman: Comte Maurice Lippens, age 63, $390,819 pay
Vice Chairman: Jan J. Slechte, age 69, $162,249 pay
CEO: Jean-Paul Votron, age 55
Deputy CEO, COO, and Board Member:
  Herman Verwilst, age 59
CFO: Gilbert Mittler, age 57
Managing Director, Investment: Jozef De Mey, age 63
Managing Director, Insurance: Peer van Harten, age 44
**Managing Director, Merchant, Corporate, and Private
  Banking:** Filip Dierckx, age 51
Managing Director, Risk: Karel De Boeck, age 57
Managing Director, Retail Banking: Jos Clijsters, age 56
CIO: Alain Deschênes, age 47
Chief Strategy Officer: Lex Kloosterman, age 50
General Manager, Communications: Adrian Martorana,
  age 47
Chief Risk Officer: Luc Henrard, age 49
**Chief, Institutional Relations and Chairman, Fortis
  Investments:** Joop Feilzer, age 57
General Manager, Corporate Social Responsibility:
  Eric Bouwmeester, age 49
Secretary: Ingrid Loos, age 44
Counsel to the Chairman: Michel van Pée, age 60
Human Resources Director: Michel Deboeck
Director, Investor Relations: Robert ter Weijden, age 40
Auditors: PricewaterhouseCoopers Reviseurs
  d'Entreprises SCCRL

LOCATIONS

HQ: Fortis SA/NV
  Rue Royale 20, 1000 Brussels, Belgium
Phone: +32-2-510-52-11   **Fax:** +32-2-510-56-30
US HQ: 1 Chase Manhattan Plaza, New York, NY 10005
US Phone: 212-859-7000   **US Fax:** 212-859-7034
Web: www.fortis.com

Fortis has operations in dozens of countries worldwide.

2005 Sales

	% of total
Europe	
Benelux	87
Other countries	7
US	3
Asia	3
Total	**100**

PRODUCTS/OPERATIONS

2005 Sales

	% of total
Interest income	74
Insurance premiums	14
Income related to investments for unit-linked products	4
Fee & commission income	3
Other	5
Total	**100**

2005 Sales

	% of total
Insurance	
Insurance Belgium	26
Insurance International	18
Insurance Netherlands	13
Banking	
Retail banking	21
Merchant banking	12
Commercial & private banking	10
Total	**100**

Selected Subsidiaries, Affiliates, and Operating Units

Alpha Credit
Altradius Factoring
Ardanta
Banque de La Poste (joint venture between
  Fortis Bank and the Belgian Post Office)
CaiFor
De Amersfoortse
Direktbank
Dryden Wealth Management
Europeesche Verzekeringen

Falcon Life
FB Insurance
Fintro (formerly Crédit à l'Industrie)
Fortis AG
Fortis ASR
Fortis Assurances
Fortis Bank
Fortis Banque Luxembourg
Fortis Corporate Insurance
Fortis Haitong (49%)
Fortis Insurance Limited
Fortis Intertrust
Fortis Securities
International Card Services
Mayban Fortis
Millenniumbcp Fortis
Muang Thai-Fortis
O'Connor & Co.
Taiping Life
Versiko (25%)
Von Essen KG Bankgesellschaft

COMPETITORS

ABN AMRO
AEGON
AGF
Allianz
AMP Limited
AXA
Bear Stearns
Citigroup
Deutsche Bank
Dexia
Eureko
Generali
Goldman Sachs
ING
KBC
Merrill Lynch
Nippon Life Insurance
Rabobank

HISTORICAL FINANCIALS

Company Type: Public

Income Statement

FYE: December 31

	ASSETS ($ mil.)	NET INCOME ($ mil.)	INCOME AS % OF ASSETS	EMPLOYEES
12/05	863,348	4,721	0.5%	41,162
12/04	778,364	4,581	0.6%	49,468
12/03	656,783	2,758	0.4%	54,000
12/02	509,131	557	0.1%	69,000
12/01	427,815	2,302	0.5%	66,210
Annual Growth	**19.2%**	**19.7%**	**—**	**(11.2%)**

2005 Year-End Financials

Equity as % of assets: —
Return on assets: 0.6%
Return on equity: —
Long-term debt ($ mil.): —
Sales ($ mil.): 79,165

Net Income History

Euronext Brussels: FOR

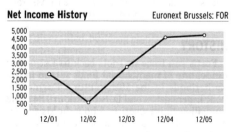

Foster's Group

Foster's Group may boast that "Foster's is Australian for beer," but it's wine that now is accounting for much of the company's bottom line. Foster's distributes its beers and wines in about 150 countries. Its Carlton and United Breweries (CUB) division is Australia's #1 brewer, producing beers such as Foster's Lager and Victoria Bitter. Its Foster's Wine States Americas (formerly Beringer Blass Wine Estates) division makes the Mildara Blass wine brands (Wolf Rothbury, Blass, Yellowglen). Beringer Blass also produces the Beringer, Stag's Leap, Meridian, and other wine brands. In 2005 Foster's Group acquired Australian winemaker Southcorp.

In addition to beer, Foster's sells pre-mixed cocktails, bourbon, cider, scotch, and vodka. In the US, the company sells beer through its 50%-owned Foster's USA unit. In 2005 Foster's acquired a total of 91% of its rival premium winemaker Southcorp. It announced a bid to take over all of Southcorp, offering $4.14 per share. Foster's then upped its bid to $4.26 per share (or $2.48 billion) and despite the objections of Southcorp's CEO (who later resigned), the winemaker's board accepted the offer. The merger, which added such brands as Lindemans, Penfolds, and Rosemount wines to Foster's portfolio, created one of the world's biggest global wine companies.

The company has put two of its Australian wineries, acquired during its takeover of Beringer Blass Wine Estates, up for sale: Jamiesons Run (sold in 2006 to Coonawarra Developments) and Rothbury Estate (sold in 2006 to Michael Hope). It sold loss-making Shanghai Brewery to Suntory in 2006. The selling price was not disclosed. The company has also decided to sell its Wine Clubs and Services businesses.

In 2006 the company restructured into three regional divisions: Foster's Australia, Asia and Pacific; Foster's Americas; and Foster's Europe, Middle East and Africa (EMEA).

HISTORY

Upon finding that Australia's only beers were English-styled ales served at room temperature, American emigrants W. M. and R. R. Foster built a lager brewery near Melbourne in 1888 and gave customers ice to chill their Foster's Lager. The brothers began exporting in 1901 when Australians left to serve in the Boer War in South Africa. Carlton and United Breweries Proprietary (CUB) was formed in 1907 when the brothers merged their operations with five other breweries, including Victoria and Carlton.

Over the years CUB acquired stakes in trading company Elder Smith Goldsbrough Mort and Henry Jones (IXL), a diversified food company owned by John Elliott. Faced with a takeover, in 1981 Elder Smith was merged into Henry Jones, forming Elders IXL. CUB became that firm's largest stockholder, with 49%, in 1983. Elders bought the rest of CUB in 1984.

Elders expanded internationally with its purchases of UK's Courage Breweries (1986) and Canada's Carling O'Keefe Breweries (1987). In 1989 Carling O'Keefe and Molson formed a joint venture, Molson Breweries. To fight possible takeover attempts, that year Harlin Holdings (led by Elliott) offered to buy a 17% stake of Elders from two companies, but regulators forced the firm to extend its offer to all shareholders. As a result, Harlin ended up with more than 55% of

Elders. The deal saddled Elders with debt, and in 1990 the company began selling its non-brewing assets. Also that year Elliott resigned as chairman and CEO, and Elders changed its name to Foster's Brewing Group.

Foster's purchased the brewing interests of Grand Metropolitan (now Diageo) in 1991. Elliott's investment firm went bankrupt in 1992 and Australian conglomerate Broken Hill Proprietary (BHP), which also owned 19% of Elders, assumed control of its shares. (BHP sold its stake in 1997.) Also in 1992 Molson Breweries chief Ted Kunkel became CEO. He wrote off over $2 billion in non-brewing assets that were still on the books and sold 10% of the brewer's interest in Molson.

In 1995 Foster's sold its UK brewing operations to Scottish & Newcastle. The next year it entered the wine business, buying Mildara Blass and Rothbury Wines, and in 1997 it entered the Australian wine club business with the purchase of Cellarmaster Wines. The next year Foster's bought wine clubs Bourse du Vin International (the Netherlands) and 51% of Germany's Heinrich Maximilian Pallhuber (later acquiring the rest).

Also in 1998 Foster's sold its Canadian brewing interests — 50% of Molson Breweries and 25% of Coors Canada — to The Molson Companies (but retained a 25% interest in Molson USA). In July 1998 Foster's acquired the Austotel Trust hotel chain from Brierly Investments, making it the largest operator of hotels in Australia.

Subsidiary Mildara Blass acquired the US direct wine marketer Windsor Vineyards in 2000; also subsidiary Cellarmaster Wines bought a 25% interest in online wine retailer Wine Planet (increased in mid-2001 to about 90%). Foster's bought Beringer Wine Estates, a leading California winery, for about $1.2 billion. Wine profits for Foster's doubled in the year following the company's 2000 purchase of Beringer.

In 2001 Foster's renamed its wine division Beringer Blass Wine Estates, merging the Beringer and Mildara Blass wine businesses. That year the company dropped "Brewing" from its official name, becoming Foster's Group Limited. In 2002 Beringer Blass Wine Estates agreed to buy the Carmenet brand from Napa-based Chalone Wine Group (now part of Diageo Chateau & Estate Wines Company). In 2002 sales of wine surpassed those of the company's beers for the first time.

Foster's spun off its Australian Leisure and Hospitality group in November 2003, which included pubs, liquor shops, and interests in hotels and real estate development. That division became a separate company known as the Australian Leisure & Hospitality Group Ltd.

In 2004 Foster's said it would expand sales in Russia by distributing through Baltika Breweries, owned by a subsidiary of Carlsberg and Scottish & Newcastle. It also changed the name, Beringer Blass Wine Estates, to Foster's Wine Estates Americas.

In 2006 Foster's sold its namesake brand in Europe to Scottish & Newcastle, broadening its earlier 1995 deal to include European countries other than the UK.

EXECUTIVES

Chairman: Frank J. Swan, age 62
CEO and Board Member: Trevor O'Hoy
CFO: Peter F. Scott
SVP, Chief Counsel, and Company Secretary: Martin Hudson, age 59
SVP, Strategy and Business Development, and Managing Director, Wine Clubs and Services: Neville Fielke
SVP, Human Resources: Ben Lawrence
VP, Investor Relations: Chris Knorr
President, North America: Scott A. Weiss
Director, External Communications: Lisa Keenan
Managing Director, Foster's Australia, Asia, and Pacific: Jamie Odell, age 48
Managing Director, Europe, the Middle East, and Africa: Peter Jackson
Managing Director, Foster's Brewing International: Richard W. Scully
Auditors: PricewaterhouseCoopers

LOCATIONS

HQ: Foster's Group Limited
   77 Southbank Blvd.,
   Southbank, Victoria 3006, Australia
Phone: +61-3-9633-2000   **Fax:** +61-3-9633-2002
US HQ: 11921 Freedom Dr., Ste. 550, Reston, VA 20190
US Phone: 703-904-4321   **US Fax:** 703-904-4336
Web: www.fostersgroup.com

Foster's Group distributes beer in more than 155 countries and has operations in the Asia Pacific, Europe, and the US.

2006 Sales

	% of total
Australia	55
Americas	34
Europe	9
Asia and Pacific	2
Total	**100**

PRODUCTS/OPERATIONS

2006 Sales

	% of total
Beer	52
Wine	48
Total	**100**

2006 Sales

	% of total
Carlton & United Beverages	57
Wine Trade	37
Wine clubs & services	3
Foster's Brewing International	3
Total	**100**

Selected Products and Brands

Beer
Carlton (Cold Filtered Bitter, D-Ale, Diamond Draft, Draught, Lager, Light, Light Bitter, Midstrength, Sterling)
Carlton and United Premium Dry
Cascade (Bitter, Diet, Draught, Four Seasons, Lager, Light Bitter, Pale Ale, Premium, Premium Light, Stout, Tiger Head)
Crown Lager
Foster's (Extra Lager, Ice, Lager, Light, LightIce, Special Bitter)
Matilda Bay (Bitter, Draught, Pilsner, Premium)
Melbourne Bitter
Powers (Bitter, Gold, Ice, Light)
Redback (Hefeweitzen, Light, Original)
Reschs (Dinner Ale, Draught, Pilsner, Real Bitter, Smooth Black Ale)
sub zero (non-beer alcoholic soda)
Victoria Bitter

Imported Beer
Asahi
Corona Extra
Guinness (Bulk & Pack)
Harp Lager
Heineken Lager
Hoegaarden (Forbidden Fruit, White)
Kilkenny Ale
Kronenbourg — 1664
Leffe (Blonde, Radieus, Vieille Cuvee)
Miller Genuine Draft
Moosehead
Negra Modelo
Stella Artois

Wines
Australian
   Greg Norman Estates
   Jamiesons Run
   The Rothbury Estate
   Saltram
   Southcorp
      Lindemans
      Penfolds
      Rosemount Estate
   Wolf Blass
   Yellowglen
California
   Beringer
   Chateau St. Jean
   Chateau Souverain
   Etude
   Meridian Vineyards
   Stags' Leap
   St. Clement
Chilean
   Dallas-Conte, Vina Tarapaca
Italian
   Catello di Gabbiano
New Zealand
   Matua Valley
Spirits
   Black Douglas
   Cougar
   Karloff

Selected Affiliates and Subsidiaries

Bourse du Vin International (wine club, Netherlands)
Carlton and United Breweries Limited
Cellarmaster Wines Pty. Ltd. (wine club)
The Continental Spirits Company
Foster's USA (49.9%, beer distribution, US)
Foster's Wine Estates Americas (wine)
Heinrich Maximilian Pallhuber (wine club, Germany)
Southcorp Ltd (wine, Australia)
Wine Planet (Internet wine retailer, US)

COMPETITORS

Accor	Lion Nathan
Anheuser-Busch	LVMH
Asahi Breweries	Marriott
Asia Pacific Breweries	Molson Coors
Boston Beer	Pabst
Carlsberg	Peerless Importers
Constellation Brands	Premier Pacific
Coors Brewers	Ravenswood Winery
Diageo	SABMiller
FEMSA	San Miguel
Gallo	Scottish & Newcastle
Gambrinus	Starwood Hotels & Resorts
Geerlings & Wade	Terlato Wine
Heineken	Trinchero Family Estates
InBev	Tsingtao
Kendall-Jackson	V&S
Kirin Brewery Company	Wine Group

HISTORICAL FINANCIALS

Company Type: Public

Income Statement

FYE: June 30

	REVENUE ($ mil.)	NET INCOME ($ mil.)	NET PROFIT MARGIN	EMPLOYEES
6/06	3,737	851	22.8%	5,851
6/05	3,025	713	23.6%	10,300
6/04	2,696	551	20.5%	9,300
6/03	3,155	309	9.8%	13,400
6/02	2,576	319	12.4%	12,950
Annual Growth	9.7%	27.8%	—	(18.0%)

Net Income History

Pink Sheets: FBRWY

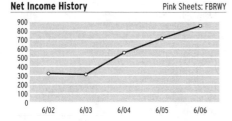

France Telecom

France Telecom hopes it can do for telecommunications services what its countrymen have done for wine: make it the product of choice. The company provides consumer and business fixed-line and wireless voice and data services. Its Orange mobile phone unit has 21 million subscribers in France, another 35 million in other European countries, and more than 63 million subscribers worldwide. France Telecom has nearly 50 million fixed-line customers. It also has acquired the 46% of data network operator Equant it did not yet own; it took full ownership of Orange and Wanadoo, a European directory publisher and ISP, in 2004. The French government has reduced its stake in the company from 56% to about 41%.

France Telecom is restructuring its operations, renaming all services under the Orange brand except for its domestic wireline operations and wireline business in Poland. It has also created a new division called Orange Business Services that combines Equant's international IP communications services and its information technology (IT) business with other enterprise businesses. And it has created a subsidiary devoted to investing in rights to French and other European films, following a trend in the telecom to bring TV and movies to mobile phone and other personal devices. The company also is divesting its cable network operations.

France Telecom had previously brought together its mobile phone operations under the umbrella of its Orange unit, which is France's #1 mobile phone company (Orange is also #2 behind Vodafone in the UK market). The wireless subsidiary also has minority stakes in wireless phone operators throughout Europe and in the Middle East. Through its Orange unit, France Telecom has agreed to acquire an 80% stake in Spain's Auna, which owns 98% of Spanish mobile carrier Retevisión Móvil, operating as Amena. The deal is valued at €6.4 billion.

The company also has acquired the 46% of data network Equant it did not own in a deal valued at $735.9 million. In late 2006 France Telecom agreed to acquire a 54% controlling stake in security network specialist Silicomp, subject to regulatory approval.

To alleviate some of its debt burden, France Telecom cut 28,500 jobs in 2003 and 2004, and has said it will eliminate another 8,000 jobs in 2005. It has sold its 54% stake in directories business PagesJaunes Groupe to Kohlberg Kravis Roberts & Co. in a deal valued at about $4.2 billion.

A change in French law that took effect on the first day of 2004 allows the government to decrease its stake in France Telecom to below 50%.

HISTORY

Shortly before he abdicated, King Louis Philippe laid the groundwork for France's state-owned telegraphic service. Established in 1851, the operation became part of the French Post Office in the 1870s, about the time Alexander Graham Bell invented the telephone. The French government licensed three private companies to provide telegraph service, and during the 1880s they merged into the Société Générale de Téléphones (SGT). In 1883 the country's first exchange was initiated in Rheims. Four years later an international circuit was installed connecting Paris and Brussels. The government nationalized SGT in 1889.

By the turn of the century France had more than 60,000 phone lines, and in 1924 a standardized telephone was introduced. Long-distance service improved with underground cabling, and phone exchanges in Paris and other leading cities became automated during the 1930s.

WWII proved a major setback to the French government's telephone operations, Direction Générale des Télécommunications (DGT), because a large part of its equipment was destroyed or damaged. For the next two decades France lagged behind other nations in telephony infrastructure development. An exception to this technological stagnation was Centre National d'Etudes des Télécommunications (CNET), the research laboratory formed in 1944 that eventually became France Telecom's research arm.

In 1962 DGT was a key player in the first intercontinental television broadcast, between US and France, via a Telstar satellite. The company began to catch up with its peers when it developed a digital phone system in the mid-1970s. In 1974 CNET was instrumental in the launch of France's first experimental communications satellite. In another technological advance, DGT began replacing its paper directories with the innovative Minitel online terminals in 1980.

The French government created France Telecom in 1988. In 1993 France Telecom and Deutsche Telekom (DT) teamed up to form the Global One international telecommunications venture, and Sprint joined the next year. Global One was formally launched in 1996. Also that year France Telecom began providing Internet access, though Minitel still reigned as the country's top online service.

In 1997 the government sold about 20% of France Telecom to the public. With Europe's state telephone monopolies ending in 1998, France Telecom reorganized and brought prices in line with those of its competitors.

In 2000 France Telecom paid $4.3 billion to DT and Sprint to take full ownership of Global One, and it paid $3.6 billion for a 29% stake in

Germany's MobilCom (it sold all but 1% of its MobilCom stake in 2005 to Texas Pacific Group). Later in 2000 France Telecom snatched up UK mobile phone operator Orange in a $37.5 billion cash and stock deal after Vodafone was forced to divest the company before merging with Mannesmann.

France Telecom also invested $4.5 billion in UK cable operator NTL and sold its stake in Mexican telecom giant Telmex. In 2001 the company sold its 49.9% stake in Noos, France's #1 cable TV operator, and it made plans to sell its stake in Sprint, which it had acquired when Global One was formed.

To reduce debt, France Telecom sold its Dutch cable unit, Casema, to a group led by US private equity firms Providence Equity Partners and Carlyle Group in a deal valued at €665 million.

As it struggled in 2002 to deal with its still burdensome debt, including its stake in troubled MobilCom, CEO Michel Bon resigned. Turnaround specialist Thierry Breton, who was credited with salvaging THOMSON multimedia, became Bon's successor. The company then received a €9 billion loan from the French government and Breton's new management team set out to reduce the nearly €70 billion debt. It announced plans to reduce the number of workers by 22,000, or about 16% of the company's workforce, over three years.

EXECUTIVES

Chairman and CEO: Didier Lombard, $1,268,345 pay
Member of the Group Management Committee, Group Transformation and French Operations: Louis-Pierre Wenes, age 57
Member of the Group Management Committee, Group Finance and Spanish Operations: Gervais Pellissier, age 46
Member of the Group Management Committee, Enterprise Communication Services: Barbara Dalibard, age 47
Member of the Group Management Committee; CEO, Orange S.A., UK and International Operations: Sanjiv Ahuja, age 50
Member of the Group Management Committee, Group Strategic Marketing and Product Factory: Georges Penalver, age 49
Member of the Group Management Committee, Group Networks and Information Systems: Jean-Philippe Vanot, age 54
Member of the Group Management Committee, Group Human Resources: Olivier Barberot, age 51
Member of the Group Management Committee and Group General Secretary: Jean-Yves Larrouturou, age 44
CEO, PagesJaunes Groupe: Michel Datchary
EVP, International Division, and TOP Program: Jean-Paul Cottet, age 51
EVP, Group Globalization and Cohesiveness: Michel Davancens, age 57
SVP and Group CTO: Marc Fossier, age 49
SVP, External Communications: Marc Meyer, age 47
SVP, Financial Rebalancing and Value Creation: Stéphane Pallez, age 46
SVP, Human Resources: Guy-Patrick Cherouvrier
SVP, Regulatory Affairs: Jacques Champeaux, age 58
SVP, Research and Development: Pascal Viginier, age 48
SVP, Content Aggregation: Patricia Langrand, age 41
Communications Director: Caroline Mille
Press Contact: Nilou du Castel
Auditors: Ernst & Young Audit; Deloitte & Associés

LOCATIONS

HQ: France Telecom
6, place d'Alleray, 75505 Paris, France
Phone: +33-1-44-44-22-22 **Fax:** +33-1-44-44-95-95
US HQ: 225 Liberty St., Ste. 4301, New York, NY 10281
US Phone: 212-332-2100
Web: www.francetelecom.com

France Telecom has investments and operations in more than 75 countries worldwide.

2005 Sales

	% of total
Europe	
France	58
UK	13
Poland	9
Spain	3
Other countries	9
Other regions	8
Total	**100**

PRODUCTS/OPERATIONS

2005 Sales

	% of total
Personal Communication Services (PCS)	43
Home Communication Services (HCS)	41
Enterprise Communication Services (ECS)	14
Directories	2
Total	**100**

Selected Operations

Operational Divisions
  Enterprise Communication Services (communication
    services to companies)
  Home Communication Services (residential
    communication services, especially fixed-line
    broadband)
  Personal Communication Services (communication
    services for individuals using mobile devices)
  Sales and Services France (domestic product
    distribution)
  International (management of international holdings
    except for subsidiaries of Orange, Wanadoo, and
    Equant)
Performance Divisions
  Networks, Carriers, and IT (management of networks
    and carriers services and information systems)
  Technology and Innovation (research and
    development)
  Sourcing (management of purchasing and operational
    and investment expenditure)
  TOP Program (plan for improved operational
    performance)
  Content Aggregation (management of partnerships
    with content providers and development of related
    technology platforms)
Support

COMPETITORS

AT&T	Level 3 Communications
Belgacom	NCR
Bouygues	Neuf Cegetel
BT	O2
Cable & Wireless	SFR
CANAL+	Tele2
Carrier1	Telecom Italia
COLT Telecom	Telefónica
CompleTel	Tiscali
Deutsche Telekom AG	T-Mobile International
EDS	T-Online
Hewlett-Packard	Unisys
Hutchison Whampoa	Verizon
IBM Global Services	Vodafone

HISTORICAL FINANCIALS

Company Type: Public

Income Statement

FYE: December 31

	REVENUE ($ mil.)	NET INCOME ($ mil.)	NET PROFIT MARGIN	EMPLOYEES
12/05	58,567	6,748	11.5%	203,008
12/04	64,341	4,037	6.3%	206,524
12/03	57,914	6,678	11.5%	218,523
12/02	48,892	(21,742)	—	243,573
Annual Growth	**6.2%**	**—**	**—**	**(5.9%)**

2005 Year-End Financials

Debt ratio: 324.2%
Return on equity: 64.0%
Cash ($ mil.): 5,095
Current ratio: 0.50
Long-term debt ($ mil.): 50,498

No. of shares (mil.): —
Dividends
  Yield: 2.3%
  Payout: —
Market value ($ mil.): —

Stock History

NYSE: FTE

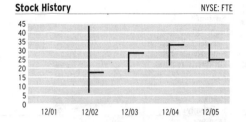

	STOCK PRICE ($) FY Close	P/E High/Low		PER SHARE ($) Earnings	Dividends
12/05	24.84	—	—	—	0.58
12/04	33.08	224	147	0.15	0.29
12/03	28.59	—	—	—	2.74
12/02	17.77	—	—	—	0.84
Annual Growth	**11.8%**	**—**	**—**	**—**	**(11.6%)**

FUJIFILM

FUJIFILM Holdings (formerly Fuji Photo Film) enjoys accentuating the negatives. As Japan's top photographic film and paper producer, FUJIFILM leads the film market on its home turf. It has hammered away at rival Eastman Kodak's lead in the US, and the two are now virtually tied globally. However, FUJIFILM understands more keenly the changes wrought by digital technology. It makes a range of digital imaging products, floppy disks, medical imaging products, office automation systems, and industrial films and chemicals. FUJIFILM Holdings has operations in Europe, Australia, Asia, and North and South America, although most of its sales come from Japan.

The company adopted a new holding company structure and changed its name to FUJIFILM Holdings in October 2006.

Like its rival Kodak, Fuji is choosing to invest more in digital technologies and less in traditional film. To that end, the company acquired Santa Clara, California-based Dimatix, a maker of inkjet printer parts, in July 2006. To meet increasing demand from consumers for digital images, Fuji has adopted what it calls "hybrid imaging" to combine its expertise in imaging with the latest electronics, such as flat-panel displays and camera-equipped cell phones. In fact, the company has designed lenses for use in cell phones.

Fuji, like Kodak, is also expanding into medical sales. In 2006 it announced plans to acquire the remaining shares of Fuji Medical Systemes France S.A. (a medical imaging products distributor) and buy TSR Holding S.A. (a medical equipment service and maintenance supplier).

The company has entered into a joint venture partnership with SVA Electron Co. of China to make color filters used in thin film transistor liquid crystal displays, which are widely used in computer monitors and flat-screen televisions.

Fuji acquired a majority of Arch Chemicals' Microelectronic Materials business in late 2004. The purchase included manufacturing and R&D locations in North America, Asia, and Europe, as well as Arch's 49% share of joint venture company FujifilmArch Co. in Japan. Fuji has also entered the nucleic acid extraction market with its tabletop DNA/RNA isolation system.

Through a joint venture with Xerox, Fuji generates some 40% of its revenues from sales of printers and office copiers.

HISTORY

Mokichi Morita, president of Japan's leading celluloid maker (Dainippon Celluloid Company, founded 1919), decided to start making motion picture film in the early 1930s. Movies were becoming popular in Japan, but there was no domestic film supplier. Working with a grant from the government, Dainippon Celluloid established Fuji Photo Film Co., an independent company, in 1934 in Minami Ashigara Village, near Mount Fuji.

At first the company had trouble gaining acceptance in Japan as a quality film producer. However, German emulsion specialist Dr. Emill Mauerhoff helped Fuji overcome its product deficiencies, producing black-and-white photographic film (1936) and the first Japanese-made color film (1948). In the meantime Fuji added 35mm photographic film, 16mm motion picture film, and X-ray film to its product line. By the early 1940s the company was operating four factories and a research laboratory in Japan. Its first overseas office, opened in Brazil in 1955, was followed by offices in the US (1958) and Europe (1964).

Fuji continued to expand its product line, adding magnetic tape in 1960. Two years later it formed Fuji Xerox, a Japanese joint venture with Xerox, to sell copiers in Japan and the Pacific Rim. It operated as a private-label film supplier in the US and did not market its products under its own brand name until 1972.

International marketing VP Minoru Ohnishi became Fuji's youngest president in 1980 at age 55. To decrease dependence on Japanese film sales, he built sales in the US (agreeing to sponsor the 1984 Los Angeles Olympics, after Eastman Kodak refused to, was key) and pumped money into the production of videotapes, floppy disks, and medical diagnostic equipment. Fuji introduced Fujicolor Quicksnap, the world's first 35mm disposable camera, in 1986. It began establishing manufacturing operations in the US two years later.

The company created the FUJIFILM Microdevices subsidiary to produce image-processing semiconductors in 1990. In 1992 Fuji scientists completed a crude artificial "eye" (a possible forerunner of more efficient eyes for robots). The following year it launched the Pictrostat instant print system, which produces color prints in one minute from photos, slides, and objects.

Fuji was forced to temporarily raise US prices in 1994 after Kodak accused it of illegally dumping its photographic paper exported to the US. But Fuji skirted the problem in 1995 by making the paper at its US plant. That year Kodak asked for economic sanctions against Fuji and the Japanese government, saying that the government encouraged Fuji to use exclusive contracts to control film distribution, thus keeping Kodak from selling film in many stores. (The case was rejected by the World Trade Organization in 1997.)

The firm unveiled the Advanced Photo System (co-developed with Kodak and three other companies) in 1996, combining conventional photography with digital-image processing and printing technology. Also that year Fuji bought six off-site wholesale photofinishing plants from Wal-Mart (the #1 US provider of photofinishing services) and won contracts to provide supplies to all of Wal-Mart's in-store one-hour photo labs.

In 1997 it chopped film prices in the US and began making film at its US plant. In 1999 Fuji introduced a high-quality image sensor for digital cameras (Super CCD) and Instax, an instant picture camera. Fuji and Sony launched HiFD, a floppy disk with 140 times the storage capacity of traditional disks, in early 2000. Fuji later announced plans to develop more efficient, low-cost ink jet printers through an alliance with Xerox and Sharp Corp.

In March 2001 Fuji acquired half of Xerox's 50% stake in the companies' Fuji Xerox joint venture. In 2002 the company acquired Japanese film processing company Jusphoto Co. and in 2003 purchased additional shares of Process Shizai Co., renaming it Fujifilm Graphic Systems Co., Ltd.

It recently bought Sericol from Saratoga Partners for $230 million and Avecia Inkjet for $260 million.

The company adopted a new holding company structure and changed its name to FUJIFILM Holdings in October 2006.

EXECUTIVES

President, CEO, and Director: Shigetaka Komori
EVP, CFO, and Director: Toshio Takahashi
SVP and Director: Hisatoyo Kato
VP: Hisamasa Abe
SVP and Director: Shinpei Ikenoue
Corporate Auditor: Keiichi Inuzuka
VP: Koji Kamiyama
VP: Yasutomo Maeda
VP: Akio Mitsui
SVP and Director: Kohtaro Nakamura
VP: Noboru Sasaki
SVP and Director: Tadashi Sasaki
VP: Shigehisa Shimizu
VP: Tsutomu Sugisaki
VP: Nobuhira Takagi
VP: Yuzo Toda
VP; President and CEO, FUJIFILM U.S.A.: Taizo Mori
VP: Shigehiro Nakajima
VP: Kozo Sato
VP: Tadashi Ogawa
VP: Yoshiyuki Uchiyama
VP: Yasushi Miyaoka
Corporate Auditor: Masahiro Miki
Corporate Auditor: Kiichiro Furusawa
President, Fuji Xerox; Director: Toshio Arima
VP: Masahiro Kosaka
VP: Takeshi Higuchi
VP: Nobuhisa Sekiguchi
VP: Kouichi Tamai
VP: Toshiaki Suzuki
VP: Nobuaki Inoue
Corporate Auditor: Daisuke Ogawa
Auditors: Ernst & Young; Ernst & Young ShinNihon

LOCATIONS

HQ: FUJIFILM Holdings Corporation
26-30, Nishiazabu 2-chome, Minato-ku,
Tokyo 106-8620, Japan
Phone: +81-3-3406-2111 **Fax:** +81-3-3406-2173
US HQ: 200 Summit Lake Dr., Valhalla, NY 10595
US Phone: 914-789-8100   **US Fax:** 914-789-8295
Web: home.fujifilm.com

2006 Sales

	% of total
Japan	50
Americas	21
Europe	14
Other regions	15
Total	**100**

Production Bases

China
  Sanhe
  Shanghai
  Shenzhen
  Suzhou
Europe
  Germany (Kleve)
  Netherlands (Tilburg)
  UK (Hertfordshire)
Japan
  Ashigara
  Ebina
  Fujinomiya
  Odawara
  Taiwa
  Yoshida-Minami
US
  Illinois
  South Carolina

PRODUCTS/OPERATIONS

2006 Sales

	% of total
Document solutions	41
Information solutions	33
Imaging solutions	26
Total	**100**

Selected Products

Document Solutions
  Digital color printers
  Digital photo printers
  Photographic papers, equipment, and chemicals
Imaging Solutions
  Electronic imaging systems
    Digital cameras and batteries
    Image scanners
    Photo players
    Photo-video imagers
  Magnetic products
    Audio tapes
    Professional videocassettes
    Videocassettes
  Motion picture films
  Optical products
    Compact cameras
    Instant cameras
    Professional cameras
  Photo lab equipment
  Photographic films
    Amateur
    Instant
    One-time
    Professional
Information Solutions
  Data storage media
    CD-Rs
    Data storage tape
    DVD-Rs
    Floppy disks
    Magnetic disks
    Zip disks

Graphic systems
  Chemicals
  Electronic imaging equipment
  Films
  Pre-sensitized plates
LCD materials
  Cellulose triacetate films
  CV films
  Photosensitive color transfer films
  Wide view films
Medical imaging products
  Computed radiography systems
  DRI-CHEM analytical systems
  Endoscopes
  Medical X-ray imaging products
Miscellaneous industrial materials and equipment
  Bio-imaging analyzers
  Industrial chemicals
  Industrial X-ray imaging products
  Lenses and optical equipment
Office automation systems
  Carbonless copying papers
  Electronic filing systems
  Heat-sensitive papers
  Microfilming systems

COMPETITORS

Agfa
Canon
Concord Camera
Datapulse Technology
Eastman Kodak
EFI
Hewlett-Packard
Imation
Iomega
Konica Minolta
Kyocera
Mitsubishi Paper Mills
Nikon
Olympus
Pentax
Philips Electronics
Polaroid
Ricoh
Sony
Veutron

HISTORICAL FINANCIALS

Company Type: Public

Income Statement

FYE: March 31

	REVENUE ($ mil.)	NET INCOME ($ mil.)	NET PROFIT MARGIN	EMPLOYEES
3/06	22,684	315	1.4%	75,845
3/05	23,500	786	3.3%	75,638
3/04	24,237	779	3.2%	73,164
3/03	20,908	405	1.9%	72,633
3/02	18,102	613	3.4%	72,569
Annual Growth	5.8%	(15.4%)	—	1.1%

Net Income History

NASDAQ (CM): FUJI

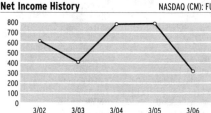

Fujitsu

Fujitsu Limited's supply of high-tech offerings seems almost limitless. The company provides products ranging from computers and electronic components to air conditioners and barcode scanners to customers worldwide. Fujitsu's computer products include PCs (it competes with NEC for #1 in Japan), servers, storage systems, and peripherals. It also provides consulting, systems integration, and other IT services (it is one of the top IT services firms in the world). Other lines include a wide range of software, telecom transmission equipment, consumer electronics, and semiconductors. Fujitsu also owns one of Japan's top Internet service providers, Nifty.

Fujitsu's technology services operations generate the largest portion of its revenue. In addition to consulting and outsourcing, it provides systems integration, migration, and optimization services. Fujitsu IT Holdings (formerly Amdahl) and Fujitsu Services (formerly ICL) are among the company's key IT services subsidiaries. Fujitsu's software offerings include customer relationship management (CRM), supply chain management (SCM), and enterprise resource planning (ERP) applications.

Fujitsu's Ubiquitous Products division is responsible for products that range from handheld and notebook PCs, to mobile phones, to disk drives, servers, and mainframes. Fujitsu and Sun Microsystems have partnered to jointly develop their UNIX-based servers; Fujitsu also offers Linux and Windows-based servers. Fujitsu and Germany's Siemens combined most of their European computer operations to form Fujitsu Siemens Computers. In addition to computers, Fujitsu's hardware products include enterprise and telecom networking equipment, mobile phones, and disk drives. Fujitsu has teamed up with Cisco to develop networking equipment.

Fujitsu has also pursued a partnership strategy in the electronic components sector, where it has targeted flash memory for devices such as cell phones and digital cameras and system-on-a-chip (SOC) circuits as growth areas. Fujitsu formed a joint venture with AMD called FASL (now Spansion) that manufactures flash memory. Other partners include Lattice Semiconductor and Transmeta. A company formed with Hitachi, Fujitsu Hitachi Plasma Display, develops plasma display panels for televisions, but early in 2005 Fujitsu agreed to sell most of its stake to Hitachi. Fujitsu sold its liquid crystal display (LCD) business, Fujitsu Display Technologies, to Sharp.

HISTORY

Siemens and Furukawa Electric created Fuji Electric in 1923 to produce electrical equipment. Fuji spun off Fujitsu, its communications division, in 1935. Originally a maker of telephone equipment, Fujitsu produced antiaircraft weapons during WWII. After the war it became one of four major suppliers to state-owned monopoly Nippon Telegraph and Telephone (NTT) and continued to benefit from Japan's rapid economic recovery in the 1950s and 1960s.

With encouragement from Japan's Ministry of International Trade and Industry (MITI), Fujitsu developed the country's first commercial computer in 1954. MITI erected trade barriers to protect Japan's new computer industry and in the early 1960s sponsored the production of mainframe computers, directing Fujitsu to develop the central processing unit. The company expanded into semiconductor production and factory automation in the late 1960s. Its factory automation business was spun off as Fujitsu Fanuc in 1972.

Fujitsu gained badly needed technology when it bought 30% of IBM-plug-compatible manufacturer Amdahl in 1972. By 1979 Fujitsu had passed IBM to become Japan's #1 computer manufacturer. In Europe, Fujitsu entered into computer marketing ventures with Siemens (1978) and UK mainframe maker ICL (1981). In the US it teamed with TRW to sell point-of-sale systems (1980), assuming full control of the operation in 1983. Fujitsu released its first supercomputer in 1982.

Fujitsu bought 80% of ICL (from the UK's Standard Telephones & Cables) in 1990 for $1.3 billion. In 1993 it formed a joint venture with Advanced Micro Devices to make flash memory products.

The company doubled its share of Japan's PC market in 1995 to more than 18% and the next year expanded its PC business globally. In 1997 Fujitsu paid about $878 million for the 58% of Amdahl it didn't already own. The next year it bought the 10% of ICL it didn't own. Fujitsu's 1998 earnings suffered from a slump in the semiconductor market, Amdahl-related expenses, and a weak Asian economy.

Also in 1998 Naoyuki Akikusa, son of a former NTT president, became head of Fujitsu. He began trimming some operations while ramping up the company's Internet activities. Fujitsu in 1999 became full owner of online services provider Nifty Serve, making it Japan's largest Internet service provider. It merged Nifty with the operations of another ISP called InfoWeb. Also that year Siemens and Fujitsu combined their European computer operations in a 50-50 joint venture (Fujitsu Siemens Computers) as one part of a larger global alliance. A restructuring of Fujitsu's semiconductor operations caused losses for 1999.

Akikusa's reorganization continued in 2000. Fujitsu overhauled its server business (subsidiary Amdahl ceased production of IBM-compatible mainframes) and accelerated production of flash memory. Responding to a global slump in its markets, in 2001 Fujitsu announced that it would cut more than 16,000 jobs — about 10% of its workforce — to control costs. Soon after, it announced the cutting of an additional 4,500 jobs.

In 2002 Fujitsu moved to outsource its semiconductor test and assembly operations when it agreed to sell its Kyushu Fujitsu Electronics subsidiary to Amkor Technology; the deal was terminated, however, when Amkor and Fujitsu were unable to agree to terms.

Fujitsu formed an alliance with Cisco late in 2004 to jointly develop networking equipment.

EXECUTIVES

Chairman: Naoyuki Akikusa
President: Hiroaki Kurokawa
EVP, Corporate Center: Masamichi Ogura
EVP, Electronic Devices Business: Toshihiko Ono
EVP, Financial Solutions Business Group:
  Yoshifumi Mita
EVP, Global Business Group and Products Business Operations Group: Kyung-Soo Ahn
EVP, Government and Public Solutions Business Group: Yasuaki Ara
EVP, Industries and Distribution Solutions Business Group: Shinichi Hasegawa
EVP, IT Services Business Group: Yoshihisa Nagano
EVP, Products Business; President, Products Business Operations Group: Chiaki Ito
EVP, Products Business Operations Group:
  Junichi Murashima
EVP, System Products Business Group:
  Takashi Nakamura
EVP, Telecom, Utility and Media Industries Business Group: Kazuo Miyata
EVP, Telecom, Utility and Media Industries Business Group: Kazuya Wada
Auditors: Ernst & Young ShinNihon

LOCATIONS

HQ: Fujitsu Limited
  Shiodome City Center, 1-5-2, Higashi-Shimbashi,
  Minato-ku, Tokyo 105-7123, Japan
Phone: +81-3-6252-2220   **Fax:** +81-3-6252-2783
US HQ: 1250 E. Arques Ave., Sunnyvale, CA 94085
US Phone: 408-746-6200   **US Fax:** 408-746-6260
Web: www.fujitsu.com

Fujitsu Limited has offices in more than 60 countries.

2006 Sales

	% of total
Japan	67
Europe	14
The Americas	8
Asia, Australasia & others	11
Total	**100**

PRODUCTS/OPERATIONS

2006 Sales

	% of total
Technology Solutions	57
Ubiquitous Product Solutions	20
Device Solutions	14
Other	9
Total	**100**

Selected Products and Services

Technology Solutions
  System platforms
    Network products
    System products
  Services
    Infrastructure services
    Systems integration
Ubiquitous Product Solutions
  Hard disk drives
  Mobile phones
  PCs
Device Solutions
  Electronic components
  LSI devices

COMPETITORS

Alcatel-Lucent	NEC
Canon	Nokia
Cisco Systems	Nortel Networks
Dell	NTT DATA
EDS	Oki Electric
Epson	Oracle
Ericsson	Philips Electronics
Fujifilm	Ricoh
Hewlett-Packard	Samsung Electronics
Hitachi	SANYO
IBM	Seagate Technology
Infineon Technologies	Sharp
Intel	Siemens AG
Matsushita	Sony
Maxtor	STMicroelectronics
Micron Technology	Sun Microsystems
Microsoft	Texas Instruments
Mitsubishi Electric	Toshiba
Motorola	Unisys

HISTORICAL FINANCIALS
Company Type: Public

Income Statement
FYE: March 31

	REVENUE ($ mil.)	NET INCOME ($ mil.)	NET PROFIT MARGIN	EMPLOYEES
3/06	40,746	583	1.4%	158,491
3/05	44,284	297	0.7%	150,970
3/04	45,123	471	1.0%	156,169
3/03	38,529	(1,019)	—	157,044
3/02	37,748	(2,884)	—	170,111
Annual Growth	1.9%	—	—	(1.8%)

Net Income History
OTC: FJTSY

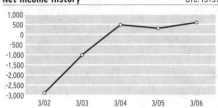

Gallaher Group

When the smoke finally settles over London, Gallaher Group helps kick it up again. The #2 UK cigarette company with about 40% of that country's cigarette market, Gallaher makes tobacco products and sells them in Asia, continental Europe, Ireland, Russia and other former Soviet republics, and the UK. Its premium cigarettes include top UK brands Benson & Hedges and Silk Cut; mid-priced brands include Berkeley; and low-priced brands include Dorchester and Mayfair. Gallaher also makes Hamlet cigars, Amber Leaf hand-rolled tobacco, and Condor pipe tobacco.

Although most of its sales come from cigarettes, Gallaher also controls nearly half of the UK cigar market and a third of all UK sales of hand-rolled tobacco.

Gallaher was spun off in 1997 from Fortune Brands, the result of a flurry of tobacco-related lawsuits in the US. Gallaher and other firms are fighting the European Union's ban on tobacco advertising (scheduled to start in 2006). The company has a European joint venture with R.J. Reynolds and seeks new international markets for its products by also partnering with Indonesian tobacco maker Sampoerna International to sell the ST Dupont Paris luxury cigarette brand in Russia. Gallaher is one of several companies, including British American Tobacco, interested in expanding its share of Chinese smokers, who puff 1.7 trillion cigarettes every year.

The company is involved in some health-related lawsuits from smokers, but to date no court has ordered it to pay damages.

In early 2005 Gallaher announed plans to curb its European production operations, including the closure of facilities in Austria, and reduce production of cigars and cigarettes at two other factories, resulting in a loss of 250 jobs.

The company is looking into expanding its distribution further into Russia, China, and Africa. At the same time, it has announced its intention to acquire Cita, the tobacco company based in the Canary Islands. Cita is one of Spain's biggest cigar-makers and is owned partly by the Zamorano family and partly by French/Spanish tobacco group Altadis.

HISTORY

Tom Gallaher started his business making and selling pipe tobacco in Londonderry, Ireland, in 1857. By 1873 he had moved his business to Belfast. By 1888 Gallaher was making cigarettes (which had become popular) and flake tobacco. That year Gallaher opened its first London office. The firm was incorporated as Gallaher Limited in 1896. In 1908 it bought Ireland's entire tobacco crop. Gallaher died in 1927.

In 1955 Gallaher bought the UK and Ireland units of cigarette firm Benson & Hedges. Richard Benson and William Hedges launched their firm in England in 1873; they pioneered selling tobacco in sealed tins for freshness. In 1877 Queen Victoria endorsed Benson & Hedges with her Royal Warrant. As more women began smoking in the early 1900s, Benson & Hedges made specialized cigarettes for them, including some with floral designs.

Gallaher bought J. Wix and Sons (Kensitas cigarettes) from American Tobacco in 1962 for a Gallaher stake. American Tobacco had increased its stake to 67% by 1968; it renamed itself American Brands in 1970 as it added nontobacco products.

Diversifying in the 1970s, Gallaher bought Dollond & Aitchison Group (optical services/products, 1970), created retail franchise Marshell Group (tobacco and confectionery concessions, 1971), and bought TM Group (Vendepac and other cigarette and snack vending machines, 1973) and Forbuoys (tobacco, sweets, and newspapers stores; 1973). In 1974 it expanded to Italy through Dollond & Aitchison. American Brands controlled 100% of Gallaher by 1975.

The company continued its acquisitions in the 1980s, including NSS Newsagents in 1986 (550 stores, combined with the 450-store Forbuoys subsidiary). By 1987 Gallaher was the #1 UK tobacco manufacturer. In 1990 the firm acquired Scotland's Whyte and Mackay Distillers.

During the early 1990s Gallaher expanded to France, Spain, and Greece. In 1993 it cut 15% of its workforce, blaming cigarette taxes for lower sales. Gallaher had become Ireland's #1 tobacco firm by 1994.

When parent American Brands sold US subsidiary American Tobacco to British American Tobacco Industries (B.A.T) in 1994, Gallaher sold B.A.T its Silk Cut rights outside Europe in exchange for a manufacturing deal. To focus on tobacco and distilling, Gallaher sold Dollond & Aitchison that year and the next year sold its other noncore units (including Forbuoys and TM Group). It also closed several plants during this period.

Twelve people sued Gallaher and rival Imperial Tobacco in 1996, alleging the firms continued using tar in cigarettes after discovering its link to cancer; the suit was abandoned after the statute of limitations expired.

As US tobacco-related litigation skyrocketed, in 1997 American Brands renamed itself Fortune Brands and spun off Gallaher Group, which floated on the London Stock Exchange in May of that year — the first time a UK firm demerged from a US parent. In 1998 it began exporting to China.

In 1999 Gallaher bought the UK tobacco business of RJR Nabisco (the Dorchester and Dickens & Grant brands and distribution of Camel and More). In a sign of tobacco's fall from favor, the Royal Palace withdrew Queen Victoria's 122-year-old endorsement of Benson & Hedges.

Gallaher entered 2000 with new CEO Nigel Northridge. In August the company bought Russian cigarette maker and distributor Liggett-Ducat from Vector Group for about $400 million. In mid-2001 Gallaher bought 41% of Austria Tabak (90% domestic market share) for more than $700 million and increased its share to more than 99% by the end of the year.

Gallaher announced 430 job cuts in Austria and the UK in May 2003.

EXECUTIVES

Chairman: John Gildersleeve, age 61
Deputy Chairman: Sir Graham J. Hearne, age 68
CEO and Board Member: Nigel Northridge, age 50, $2,486,724 pay
Group Operations Director and Board Member: Nigel Dunlop, age 50, $1,067,115 pay
Group Finance Director and Board Member: Mark Rolfe, age 47, $1,233,527 pay
Group Commercial Director and Board Member: Neil England, age 52
Chief Marketing Officer: Yann Tardif, age 45
Group Commercial Director and Board Member: Stewart Hainsworth, age 37, $652,000 pay
Managing Director, UK: Barry Jenner, age 48
Director, Group Human Resources: Mike Griffiths, age 48
Director, Investor Relations: Claire Jenkins, age 43
Head of Business Development: Suhail Saad, age 51
Head of Corporate Affairs: Jeff Jeffery, age 59
Company Secretary and General Counsel: Tom Keevil, age 44
Head of Group Human Resources Strategy: Neil Hayward, age 41
Group Financial Controller: Jon Moxon, age 42
Group Corporate Affairs Manager: Michelle McKeown, age 38
Managing Director, Northern Europe: Marc-Antoine Bailby
Managing Director, Asia/Pacific: Luke Falvey, age 42
Managing Director, Central Europe: Stefan Fitz, age 40
Managing Director, Developing Markets: Richard Johnson, age 35
Managing Director, CIS: Jason Konken, age 38
Managing Director, Middle East and Indian Sub-continent: Paul Murden, age 44
Head of Corporate Communications and Corporate Affairs, Europe: Helmut Dumfahrt, age 43
International Corporate Affairs Manager: Andy Williams
Group Treasurer: Peter Whent, age 51
Head of Group Legal: Suzanne Wise, age 44
Auditors: PricewaterhouseCoopers LLP

LOCATIONS

HQ: Gallaher Group Plc
Members Hill, Brooklands Road,
Weybridge, Surrey KT13 0QU, United Kingdom
Phone: +44-1932-859777 **Fax:** +44-1932-832792
Web: www.gallaher-group.com

2005 Sales

	% of total
UK	46
Other EU & Turkey	39
Former Soviet republics	1
Scandinavia & other regions	14
Total	**100**

PRODUCTS/OPERATIONS

Selected Products and Brands

Cigarettes
  Benson & Hedges (in UK)
  Berkeley
  Blend
  Club
  Dickens & Grant
  Dorchester
  Level
  Mayfair
  Memphis
  Milde Sorte
  Novost
  St. George
  Silk Cut
  Sovereign
  ST Dupont
  Sterling
Cigars
  Hamlet
Tobacco
  Amber Leaf
  Condor
  Old Holborn

COMPETITORS

Altadis
British American Tobacco
Carolina Group
Imperial Tobacco
Japan Tobacco
Philip Morris International
Swedish Match
Taiwan Tobacco & Wine
TCHIBO Holding

HISTORICAL FINANCIALS

Company Type: Public

Income Statement

FYE: December 31

	REVENUE ($ mil.)	NET INCOME ($ mil.)	NET PROFIT MARGIN	EMPLOYEES
12/05	14,135	516	3.7%	11,100
12/04	15,634	653	4.2%	11,000
12/03	10,037	334	3.3%	10,212
12/02	13,512	504	3.7%	9,602
Annual Growth	1.5%	0.8%	—	5.0%

2005 Year-End Financials

Debt ratio: 417.8%
Return on equity: 88.0%
Cash ($ mil.): 435
Current ratio: 0.78
Long-term debt ($ mil.): 2,753
No. of shares (mil.): —
Dividends
  Yield: 3.8%
  Payout: 0.7%
Market value ($ mil.): —

Stock History

NYSE: GLH

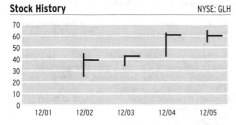

	STOCK PRICE ($) FY Close	P/E High/Low		PER SHARE ($) Earnings	Dividends
12/05	60.16	0	0	314.56	2.30
12/04	60.71	0	0	207.20	2.17
12/03	42.54	—	—	0.00	1.82
12/02	39.20	14	8	3.11	1.56
Annual Growth	15.3%	—	—	365.9%	13.8%

Gaz de France

If the Tour de France followed the path of Gaz de France, bikers would ride through Africa, Asia, all the Americas, and most of Europe. The state-owned company's main operation is the distribution of natural gas to more than 8,900 communities (or 76% of the population) in France; it also serves some 4 million customers abroad. Gaz de France also explores for and produces natural gas; operates gas transmission, storage, and trading businesses; offers energy-related construction and heating, ventilation, and air-conditioning (HVAC) services; runs cogeneration facilities; and supplies fuel for natural gas-powered buses. In 2006 the company agreed to buy international utility services provider Suez.

The merger between Gaz de France and Suez will catapult the new company into a leading position regarding energy and environmental services. It is expected to rank as the #5 producer of electricity overall and emerge as the leader of energy services in Europe.

The French government launched an initial public offering in late June 2005, raising as much as $5 billion. The government sold about 22% of Gaz de France, using the majority of the money to help pay for future European expansion. The rest of the money is expected to pay off state debts.

With operations or assets in more than 30 countries, Gaz de France is gearing up in preparation for Europe's liberalization of the gas industry. The company has been acquiring gas distribution companies outside of France, and its Cofathec unit, which provides energy-related services, has also expanded its market share through acquisitions.

Gaz de France has reserves of 670 million barrels of oil equivalent, more than 70% of which comes from natural gas. The company has nearly doubled its reserves through the acquisition of natural gas assets, primarily in the North Sea. Gaz de France produces about 10% of the gas it sells, and it plans to increase its production to 15% of gas sales.

HISTORY

Gaz de France was founded in 1946 by the French government to consolidate the more than 500 (mostly coal-fired) gas works that had existed before WWII. From 1949 on, Gaz de France focused on upgrading gas plants and local transmission networks. Its first long-distance pipeline was built in 1953, linking Paris to the Lorraine coal gas fields. With the development of the Lacq gas field in southwestern France, annual gas sales increased by 300% between 1957 and 1962.

By 1965 nearly half of the French population was supplied with natural gas. Spurred on by the loss of its Algerian colony, which held major oil and gas assets, the French government pushed for new gas supplies to supplement its Lacq resources. Gaz de France was able to secure a contract with Algerian natural gas supplier Sonatrach in 1965, and in 1967 it signed an import contract with Dutch supplier Gasunie. The company also diversified in the 1960s, helping to build a natural gas liquefaction plant in Algeria and a receiving terminal in Le Havre. It also helped pioneer gas storage engineering.

Following the price shock of the Arab oil embargo of the early 1970s, Gaz de France stepped

up its search for alternative suppliers, including contracts with Russia's largest gas producer Soyouzgazexport (in 1976, 1980, and 1984) and four separate Norwegian producers, Efofisk (1977), Stafjord (1985), Heimdal (1986), and Gullfaks (1987). The company also renewed contracts with its Dutch and Algerian suppliers.

During the 1990s Gaz de France expanded its international operations as deregulation in the industry accelerated. In 1994 the company gained a foothold in eastern Germany's gas sector by buying gas production and storage company Erdgas Erdol GmbH (EEG). Three years later Gaz de France acquired Italian heating and related services firm Agip Servizi and was awarded a joint venture contract to distribute gas in Berlin in 1997 and in the suburbs of Mexico City in 1998.

Through contracts for North Sea oil and gas with Elf Aquitaine (now owned by TOTAL FINA ELF), British-Borneo, and Ruhrgas in 1999, the company increased its natural gas supplies. It also established new gas supply contracts with Nigeria and Qatar.

For the first time in its history, Gaz de France became an offshore field operator in 2000 by acquiring exploration and production company TransCanada International Netherlands and a 39% stake in Noordgastransport BV, an offshore gas pipeline operator.

In 2001, through the purchase of a 10% interest in Petronet LNG, Gaz de France embarked on a project to import liquefied natural gas from Qatar to India.

EXECUTIVES

Chairman and CEO: Jean-François Cirelli, age 48
SEVP Infrastructure and Resources: Yves Colliou, age 58
SEVP Upstream Activities Worldwide: Jean-Marie Dauger, age 52
CFO: Philippe Jeunet
SVP Human Resources: Philippe Saimpert
SVP International: Pierre Clavel
VP Audit and Risks: Georges Bouchard
VP Communication: Raphaële Rabatel, age 42
VP Investments and Acquisitions: Emmanuel Hedde
VP Support Functions: Philippe Charbaut
VP Market Development and Sales: Jean-Pierre Piollat
VP Strategy: Stéphane Brimont
Secretary: Jean Abiteboul
Chairman and CEO, GDF International: Jacques Deyirmendjian, age 61
Chairman and CEO, Cogac; Chairman, Cofathec: Bernard Leblanc
Head of Investor Relations: Valérie Duval
Auditors: Ernst & Young Audit; Mazars & Guérard

LOCATIONS

HQ: Gaz de France
  23, rue Philibert Delorme, 75840 Paris, France
Phone: +33-1-47-54-77-25   **Fax:** +33-1-42-54-70-45
Web: www.gazdefrance.com

Gaz de France has operations in more than 20 countries, including Algeria, Argentina, Austria, Belgium, Canada, Egypt, France, Germany, Hungary, India, Italy, the Ivory Coast, Mexico, the Netherlands, Norway, Poland, Portugal, Russia, Slovakia, Spain, the UK, Ukraine, Uruguay, and the US.

2005 Sales

	% of total
Europe	
France	75
Other countries	24
Other regions	1
Total	**100**

PRODUCTS/OPERATIONS

2005 Sales

	% of total
Energy supply & services	87
Infrastructures	13
Total	**100**

COMPETITORS

BG Group	Gasunie
Centrica	Gazprom
Electricité de France	Italgas
Eni	ITERA
Gas Natural SDG	SUEZ-TRACTEBEL

HISTORICAL FINANCIALS

Company Type: Public

Income Statement

FYE: December 31

	REVENUE ($ mil.)	NET INCOME ($ mil.)	NET PROFIT MARGIN	EMPLOYEES
12/05	26,521	2,064	7.8%	52,958
12/04	24,728	1,507	6.1%	38,251
12/03	20,895	1,230	5.9%	38,101
12/02	15,246	3,831	25.1%	37,853
12/01	12,756	789	6.2%	25,357
Annual Growth	**20.1%**	**27.2%**	**—**	**20.2%**

Net Income History

Euronext Paris: GAZ

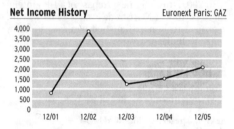

Gazprom

Gazprom, Russia's largest company, produces 94% of the country's natural gas, controls 25% of the world's reserves, and is also the world's largest gas producer. The company is engaged in gas exploration, processing, transport, and marketing. It operates Russia's domestic gas pipeline network and delivers gas to countries of the former Soviet Union and Europe. Gazprom relies heavily on Western exports and partnerships. It also holds stakes in Russian financial institutions and a polypropylene plant, and has its own telecom network. The Russian government increased its stake in Gazprom from 38% to 51% for a reported $6 billion. Gazprom has acquired a 73% stake in Sibneft for a reported $11 billion.

Millhouse Capital, a holding company controlled by Russian oligarch Roman Abramovich, sold the majority stake in Sibneft (also known as Siberian Oil Company), Russia's fifth-largest oil company. The deal is widely expected to further the Russian government's influence in the energy sector. Gazprom has announced plans to acquire another 20% of Sibneft from YUKOS, once that company's stock is unfrozen.

Gazprom, which evolved from the natural gas ministry of the former Soviet Union, accounts for about 25% of Russia's tax revenues.

Exports to Europe are critical to Gazprom, burdened by debt because of the insolvency of Russian consumers and hordes of nonpaying customers. Gazprom holds strategic partnerships with Western energy companies, including Germany's E.ON Ruhrgas, which owns almost 4% of the company's shares. Other partners include Royal Dutch Shell, Eni of Italy, and Finland's Fortum. In addition, Gazprom has announced a deal with German chemical conglomerate BASF that grants BASF minority shares in both the proposed North Europe Gas Pipeline and the West Siberia field that will feed it.

Gazprom had announced plans in 2004 to acquire Rosneft (effectively giving the Russian government control of Gazprom), though the deal was complicated by Rosneft's acquisition of the Yugansk assets acquired from YUKOS. In 2005 Gazprom abandoned plans to merge with Rosneft and set its sights on Sibneft in an effort to add significant oil operations to its business.

In 2006 Gazprom signed long-term contracts for gas deliveries with Austrian energy giant OMV.

That year Royal Dutch Shell agreed to give control of the $22 billion Sakhalin-2 project in Russia's Far East to Gazprom.

HISTORY

Following the breakup of the Soviet Union in the early 1990s, one of the first priorities of the Russian government was to move some state monopolies toward a free-market economic system. A presidential decree in 1992 moved the company toward privatization by calling for the formation of a Russian joint-stock company to explore for and produce gas, gas condensates, and oil; provide for gas processing; operate gas wells; and build gas pipelines and storage facilities. By 1993 the government had converted its natural gas monopoly, Gazprom, into a joint-stock company.

The new Gazprom was 15%-owned by Gazprom workers and 28% by people living in Russia's gas-producing regions. The state retained about a 40% share (boosted to 51% in 2003). The company inherited all of the export contracts to Western and Central Europe of the Commonwealth of Independent States.

Thanks to the power of Viktor Chernomyrdin (Gazprom's former Soviet boss and gas industry minister, who became Russia's prime minister in 1992), the company was able to enjoy large tax breaks and maintain its role as a monopoly — even as other industries were being more deeply privatized. However, the privatization of Gazprom was later attacked as being manipulated to profit the company's top management, including Chernomyrdin. Top managers were rumored to have each received 1%-5% of shares — holdings potentially worth $1.2 billion-$10 billion each.

Needing to raise cash, in 1996 Gazprom offered 1% of its stock to foreigners, the first sale of stock to foreign investors. In 1997 Gazprom and Royal Dutch/Shell formally became partners. That year Gazprom began building its Blue Stream pipeline across the Black Sea to Turkey. Italian group Eni helped back the project and became a partner by 1999.

In 1998 Gazprom acquired a stake in Promstroibank, Russia's fourth-largest financial institution. German energy powerhouse Ruhrgas acquired a 3% stake in Gazprom in 1998, which it increased to nearly 4% the next year. Also in 1999 Gazprom started building its Yamal-Europe pipeline, which was to stretch to Germany for exports to Europe.

The next year an attempt by Gazprom to muscle into Hungary's chemicals sector by offering cheaper raw materials was blocked by Hungary's TVK and Borsodchem and their allies. Also in 2000 Gazprom became embroiled in a politically controversial issue when it called for the country's leading private media holding group, Media-MOST, to sell shares to the gas giant in order to settle millions of dollars of debt. Because Media-MOST held NTV television, a major critic of Russian President Vladimir Putin, the deal was alleged to have been directed by the Kremlin. A government probe into the deal was later ordered.

The alignment of Gazprom's board changed in 2000 after the annual shareholder's meeting. For the first time in Gazprom's history, company managers did not have a majority of seats. A new chairman, Dmitri Medvyedev, second in command to Putin, was elected to replace Chernomyrdin. In 2001 the board fired CEO Rem Vyakhirev and replaced him with deputy energy minister Alexei Miller, a Putin ally.

Gazprom owned a significant stake in Russian independent television channel NTV, which in 2002 it sold in order to focus on its core energy businesses.

EXECUTIVES

Chairman, Board of Directors:
Dmitri Anatolievich Medvedev, age 41
Deputy Chairman, Board of Directors; Chairman, Management Committee: Alexei Borisovich Miller, age 44
Director; Deputy Chairman and Head of Administration, Management Committee:
Mikhail Leonidovich Sereda, age 36
Deputy Chairman, Management Committee and Chief Accountant: Elena Alexandrovna Vasilyeva, age 47
Director; Deputy Chairman, Management Committee:
Alexander Georgievich Ananenkov, age 53
Deputy Chairman, Management Committee; President, Gazprom Neft: Alexander Nikolaevich Ryazanov, age 52
Deputy Chairman, Management Committee; General Director, Security Service, Gazprom, Moscow:
Sergei Konstantinovich Ushakov, age 54
Deputy Chairman, Management Committee and Head of Finance and Economics Department:
Andrei Vyacheslavovich Kruglov, age 37
Deputy Chairman, Management Committee; Director General, Gazexport Ltd.:
Alexander Ivanovich Medvedev, age 51
Deputy Chairman, Management Committee:
Alexander Nikolaevich Kozlov, age 53
Member, Management Committee; Head of Investment and Construction Department; Director General, Gazkomplektimpex Ltd.: Valery Alexandrovich Golubev, age 54
Member, Management Committee; Head of Gas Department, Gas Condensate and Oil Production:
Vasily Grigorievich Podyuk, age 60
Member, Management Committee; Head of Strategic Development Department: Vlada Vilorikovna Rusakova, age 52
Member, Management Committee; Head of Marketing and Processing of Gas and Liquid Hydrocarbons Department; Ltd Director General, Mezhregiongaz:
Kirill Gennadievich Seleznev, age 32
Member, Management Committee; Head of Asset Management and Corporate Relations Department:
Olga Petrovna Pavlova, age 53
Member, Management Committee; Head of Gas Transportation, Underground Storage and Utilization Department: Bogdan Vladimirovich Budzulyak, age 60
Member, Management Committee; Head of Legal Department: Konstantin Anatolievich Chuichenko, age 41
Member, Management Committee; Head of Relationships with Regional Authorities of the Russian Federation Department:
Viktor Vasilievich Ilyushin, age 59
Auditors: ZAO PricewaterhouseCoopers Audit

LOCATIONS

HQ: OAO Gazprom
16 Nametkina St., 117997 Moscow V-420, Russia
Phone: +7-495-719-30-01   **Fax:** +7-495-719-83-33
Web: www.gazprom.ru

OAO Gazprom operates Russia's extensive gas pipeline system and delivers natural gas to 25 countries in Europe and the former Soviet Union.

PRODUCTS/OPERATIONS

Selected Subsidiaries

Gazprom Finance B.V.
OOO Astrakhangazprom
OOO Bashtransgaz
OOO Burgaz
OOO Dagestangazprom
OOO Ecological and Analytical Center of the Gas Industry
OOO Gazexport
OOO Gazflot
OOO Gazkomplektimpex
OOO Gaznadzor
OOO Gazobezopasnost
OOO Gazpromavia
OOO Gazprominvestholding
OOO Gazpromokhrana
OOO Gazpromrazvitiye
OOO Gaztorgpromstroy
OOO Gazsvyaz
OOO Informgaz
OOO IRTsGazprom
OOO Kavkaztransgaz
OOO Kubangazprom
OOO Lentransgaz
OOO Mezhregiongaz
OOO Mostransgaz
OOO Nadymgazprom
OOO Nadymstroygazdobycha
OOO NIIGazekonomika
OOO Novourengoy GCC
OOO Noyabrskgazdobycha
OOO Orenburggazprom
OOO Permtransgaz
OOO Podzemgazprom
OOO Samaratransgaz
OOO Servicegazprom
OOO Severgazprom
OOO Surgutgazprom
OOO Surgutstroygaz
OOO Szhizhenny gas
OOO Tattransgaz
OOO Tomsktransgaz
OOO TyumenNIIgiprogaz
OOO Tyumentransgaz
OOO Ulyanovskgazservice
OOO Uraltransgaz
OOO Urengoygazprom
OOO VNIIgaz
OOO Volgogradtransgaz
OOO Volgotransgaz
OOO Yamburggazdobycha
OOO Yugtransgaz
ZAO Yamalgazinvest

COMPETITORS

BP
E.ON Ruhrgas
Gasunie
ITERA
LUKOIL
Rosneft
Sakhalin Energy
Surgutneftegas
Tatneft

HISTORICAL FINANCIALS

Company Type: Public

Income Statement

FYE: December 31

	REVENUE ($ mil.)	NET INCOME ($ mil.)	NET PROFIT MARGIN	EMPLOYEES
12/05	42,836	7,078	16.5%	397,000
12/04	36,395	7,227	19.9%	332,800
12/03	28,867	5,841	20.2%	299,717
12/02	19,216	3,807	19.8%	295,487
12/01	19,287	3,290	17.1%	310,700
Annual Growth	22.1%	21.1%	—	6.3%

2005 Year-End Financials

Debt ratio: 20.8%
Return on equity: 8.0%
Cash ($ mil.): 2,541
Current ratio: 4.10
Long-term debt ($ mil.): 21,399

Net Income History

Russian: GAZP

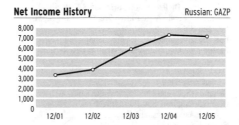

Generali

Italy's largest insurance company (and one of the largest in Europe), Assicurazioni Generali writes insurance for risks as varied as space launches and corporate package policies. Some 175 companies make up the Generali group, which also holds interests in many more companies. About 100 of the core companies are involved primarily in insurance (including life, accident, health, motor, fire, marine/aviation, and reinsurance); the rest concentrate on other financial services and real estate. Generali is noted for being a leading insurer of satellite and space missions, which it has been covering since 1964. In more earthbound realms, the company targets individuals and small to mid-sized businesses.

Italy, France, and Germany are Generali's largest markets. The insurer has entrenched itself in Germany, after acquiring a controlling interest in one of the country's largest insurers, AMB Generali (formerly Aachener und Munchener), and establishing an alliance with Commerzbank.

In 2006 Generali acquired a 65% stake in rival Toro Assicurazioni at a cost of nearly $5 billion (€3.85 billion) and is in the process of buying the remaining shares of the company. The purchase locks up Generali's leading position in both the life and non-life sectors. It also helps Generali shore up its market share regionally, and helps discourage a hostile takeover by the acquisitive AXA. With its place in Western Europe cemented, the company has begun to probe Eastern Europe and China as areas for investment and growth.

Generali shareholders include Italy's secretive and powerful MEDIOBANCA (14%), as well as Banca d'Italia and Unicredito (each about 4%).

HISTORY

Assicurazioni Generali was founded as Assicurazioni Generali Austro-Italiche in 1831 by a group of merchants led by Giuseppe Morpurgo in the Austro-Hungarian port of Trieste. Formed to provide insurance to the city's bustling trade industry, the company offered life, marine, fire, flood, and shipping coverage. That year Morpurgo established what he intended to be Generali's headquarters in Venice. (While the company maintained offices in both cities, Trieste ultimately won out.)

By 1835 Generali had opened 25 offices in Central and Western Europe; it had also expelled Morpurgo. The firm moved into Africa and Asia in the 1880s. In 1900 Generali began selling injury and theft insurance. In 1907 Generali's Prague office provided the young, experimental writer Franz Kafka his first job. (He found it disagreeable and quit after a few months.)

During WWI, the firm's Venice office pledged allegiance to Italy, while the office in Trieste (still part of Austria-Hungary) stayed loyal to the Hapsburgs. After the war Trieste was absorbed by the new Italian republic. Under Edgardo Morpurgo, Generali expanded further in the 1920s, managing 30 subsidiaries and operating in 17 countries. As fascist Italy aligned itself with Germany in the 1930s, adoption of anti-Semitic laws caused Morpurgo and a number of other high-ranking Jewish employees to flee the country. In 1938 Generali moved its headquarters to Rome (but moved them back to Trieste after WWII).

The firm maintained steady business both before and during Nazi occupation in WWII; in 1945, however, the Soviets seized all Italian properties in Eastern Europe, including 14 Generali subsidiaries. In 1950 Generali invaded the US market, offering shipping and fire insurance and reinsurance. Generali established a cooperative agreement with Aetna Life and Casualty (now Aetna Inc.) in 1966, further cementing its US connections.

In 1988 Generali tried to acquire French insurer Compagnie du Midi. Foreshadowing Generali's later dealings with Istituto Nazionale delle Assicurazioni (INA), Midi escaped Generali's grasp through a merger with AXA. As the Iron Curtain frayed in 1989, Generali formed AB Generali Budapest through a joint venture with a Hungarian insurer. In 1990 the firm opened an office in Tokyo. By 1993 Generali had become Italy's largest insurer.

In 1997 the firm was accused, along with other major European insurers, of not paying on policies of Holocaust victims. (It moved to settle claims in 1999.)

The company focused on the German and Swiss markets in 1998, acquiring controlling interests in insurer AMB Aachener und Munchener (now AMB Generali) and in Banca della Svizzera Italiana. Also that year Generali and Commerzbank established an alliance that gave the companies more access to each other's markets.

In 1999 Generali succeeded in a hostile takeover of INA, its largest domestic competitor. The move pre-empted INA's proposed merger with San Paolo IMI, which would have knocked Generali to second place among the country's insurers.

Avoiding violation of the EU's antitrust laws in connection with the INA acquisition, the company sold four subsidiaries (including Italian insurers Aurora and Navale) in 2000.

In 2002 Generali rolled together three securities investments firms — Altinia, Ina Sim, and Prime Consult Sim — into Banca Generali.

EXECUTIVES

Chairman: Antoine Bernheim, age 82
Deputy Chairman: Gabriele Galateri di Genola, age 59
Managing Director and Board Member: Sergio Balbinot, age 48
Managing Director and Board Member: Giovanni Perissinotto, age 53
General Manager, Italian Operations: Fabio Buscarini
Secretary and Deputy General Manager, Legal, Corporate Affairs, and Privacy: Vittorio Rispoli
General Manager: Raffaele Agrusti, age 49
Deputy General Manager, Corporate Development and Risk Management: Mel Carvill
Deputy General Manager: Aldo Minucci
CEO and Director General, Genertel: Davide Passero
Chief Executive, AMB Generali Holding: Walter Thiessen
Chairman and CEO, Generali France: Claude Tendil, age 59
CEO, Generali Holding Vienna: Karl Stoss, age 48
CEO, Generali Switzerland: Alfred Leu
CEO, Migdal: Izzy Cohen
General Manager, Generali Espana: Monica Mondardini
Head, Commercial Area, Italian Operations: Claudio Cominelli
Head, Non Life, Italian Operations: Adrian Bruno Trevisan
Head, Special Risks, Italian Operations: Claudio Campana
Assistant General Manager, Consolidation and Control: Benoit Jaspar
Assistant General Manager, Human Resources: Lodovico Floriani
Assistant General Manager, Finance: Amerigo Borrini
Accounting: Cristina Morgan
Corporate Communications: Mauro Giusto
Tax: Stefano Meroi
Auditors: PricewaterhouseCoopers SpA

LOCATIONS

HQ: Assicurazioni Generali SpA
Piazza Duca degli Abruzzi, 2, 34132 Trieste, Italy
Phone: +39-040-671-111 **Fax:** +39-040-671-600
US HQ: 1 Liberty Plaza, New York, NY 10006
US Phone: 212-602-7600 **US Fax:** 212-616-6399
Web: www.generali.com

Assicurazioni Generali has operations in 40 countries including Argentina, Austria, Belgium, Brazil, China, Colombia, Croatia, the Czech Republic, Ecuador, France, Germany, Greece, Guatemala, Hong Kong, Hungary, Ireland, Israel, Italy, Mexico, the Netherlands, Panama, Peru, the Philippines, Poland, Portugal, Romania, Slovakia, Slovenia, Spain, Switzerland, Thailand, Turkey, the UK, and the US.

PRODUCTS/OPERATIONS

Selected Subsidiaries and Affiliates

Aachener und Münchener Lebensversicherung Aktiengesellschaft (Germany)
Aachener und Münchener Versicherung Aktiengesellschaft (Germany)
Adriavita S.p.A.
AdvoCard Rechtsschutzversicherung AG (Germany)
Alleanza Assicurazioni S.p.A.
Allgemeine Immobilien-Verwaltungs-Gesellschaft A.I.V. (Austria)
Altegia S.A. (France)
Am Prudence S.A. (France)
AMB Generali Asset Managers Kapitalanlagegesellschaft mbH (Germany)
AMB Generali Holding AG (Germany)
ASSITALIA — Le Assicurazioni d'Italia S.p.A.
Banca BSI Italia S.p.A.
Banca Generali S.p.A.
Banca Svizzera Italiana SA (Switzerland)
Banco Vitalicio De España (Spain)
Central Krankenversicherung AG (Germany)
Continent Holding S.A. (France)
Cosmos Lebensversicherungs-AG (Germany)
Cosmos Versicherung Aktiengesellschaft (Germany)
Deutsche Bausparkasse Badenia AG (Germany)
Dialog Lebensversicherungs-AG (Germany)

ENVIVAS Krankenversicherung AG (Germany)
Europ Assistance — Companhia Portuguesa de Seguros de Assistencia S.A. (Portugal)
Europ Assistance (Ireland) Ltd.
Europ Assistance (Suisse) S.A. (Switzerland)
Europ Assistance Belgium
Europ Assistance France S.A. (France)
Europ Assistance G.M.B.H. (Austria)
Europ Assistance Holding (France)
Europ Assistance Holdings Ltd. (UK)
Europ Assistance Magyarország Kft. (Hungary)
Europ Assistance Nederland (The Netherlands)
Europ Assistance Polska SP. Z.O.O. (Poland)
Europ Assistance RU (Russia)
Europ Assistance s.r.o. (Czech Republic)
Europai Utazasi Biztosito RT. (Hungary)
Europäische Reiseversicherung-AG (Austria)
Europ-Assistance España (Spain)
Europ-Assistance Italia S.P.A.
Europ-Assistance Luxembourg
Europ-Assistance Versicherungs-AG (Germany)
Europeenne De Protection Juridique S.A. (France)
F.A.T.A. — Fondo Assicurativo Tra Agricoltori S.p.A.
Finagen S.p.A.
Fortuna Investment AG (Switzerland)
Fortuna Rechtsschutz-Versicherungs-Gesellschaft (Switzerland)
G.G.L. S.p.A.
Genagricola S.P.A.
Generali (Schweiz) Holding (Switzerland)
Generali Asigurari S.A. (Romania)
Generali Assurances iard (France)
Generali Assurances vie (France)
Generali Bank AG (Austria)
Generali Belgium S.A.
Generali Dommages (France)
Generali Epargne (France)
Generali España, Holding De Entidades De Seguros, S.A. (Spain)
Generali Finance B.V. (The Netherlands)
Generali Finances S.A. (France)
Generali France S.A. (France)
Generali Hellas A.E.A.Z. Property and Casualty Insurance Co. (Greece)
Generali Holding Vienna AG (Austria)
Generali International Ltd. (Guernsey)
Generali Life Hellenic Insurance Company A.E. (Greece)
Generali Lloyd AG (Germany)
Generali Luxembourg S.A.
Generali Osiguranje D.D. (Croatia)
Generali PanEurope Limited (Ireland)
Generali Personenversicherungen (Switzerland)
Generali Poist'ovna A.S. (Slovakia)
Generali Pojistovna a.s. (Czech Republic)
Generali Portfolio Management Limited (Guernsey)
Generali Powszechne Towarzystwo Emerytalne S.A. (Poland)
Generali Protection Vie S.A. (France)
Generali Rueckversicherung A.G. (Austria)
Generali Schadeverzekering Mij N.V. (The Netherlands)
Generali Servizi S.r.l.
Generali Sigorta A.S. (Turkey)
Generali Towarzystwo Ubezpieczen S.A. (Poland)
Generali Versicherung AG (Austria)
Generali Versicherung AG (Germany)
Generali Verzekeringsgroep NV (The Netherlands)
Generali Vida Companhia de Seguros S.A. (Portugal)
Generali Worldwide Group (Guernsey)
Generali Zavarovalnica d.d. (Slovenia)
Generali Zivotno Osiguranje D.D. (Croatia)
Generali Zycie Towarzystwo Ubezpieczen S.A. (Poland)
Generali-Providencia Biztosito RT. (Hungary)
GeneraliVoyages.com (France)
Genertel S.p.A.
Gruppo Generali Immobiliare Spa
Ina Vita S.p.A.
Interunfall Versicherung Aktiengesellschaft (Austria)
La Estrella, S.A. De Seguros Y Reaseguros (Spain)
La Federation Continentale S.A. (France)
La Venezia Assicurazioni S.p.A.
L'equité (France)
Luxembourg
Middlesea Insurance p.l.c. (Malta)
Prudence Vie (France)
Risparmio Assicurazioni S.p.A.
UMS Generali Marine S.p.A.
Uni One Assicurazioni S.p.A.

Uni One Vita S.p.A.
Union Generale Du Nord (France)
Volksfürsorge Deutsche Krankenversicherung AG (Germany)
Volksfürsorge Deutsche Lebensversicherung AG (Germany)
Volksfürsorge Deutsche Sachversicherung AG (Germany)

COMPETITORS

AGF	ING
AIG	Lloyd Adriatico
Allianz	Milano Assicurazioni
AXA	Ras Holding
ERGO	Swiss Re
Eureko	UniCredit
FonSai	Unipol
Fortis SA/NV	Zurich Financial Services

HISTORICAL FINANCIALS

Company Type: Public

Income Statement

FYE: December 31

	ASSETS ($ mil.)	NET INCOME ($ mil.)	INCOME AS % OF ASSETS	EMPLOYEES
12/04*	383,718	1,793	0.5%	58,000
12/03	326,115	1,274	0.4%	60,638
12/02	246,014	(791)	—	59,753
12/01	203,417	974	0.5%	58,445
12/00	206,202	1,342	0.7%	57,443
Annual Growth	16.8%	7.5%	—	0.2%

*Most recent year available

2004 Year-End Financials

Equity as % of assets: 3.3%   Long-term debt ($ mil.): 1,841
Return on assets: 0.5%   Sales ($ mil.): 107,213
Return on equity: 13.7%

Net Income History

Italian: G

George Weston

George Weston Limited fuels Canadians through those long winters. More than 85% of the company's sales come from its 63%-owned Loblaw Companies Limited, Canada's largest supermarket operator (with more than a dozen chains such as Loblaws, Provigo, and Zehrs) and the country's largest wholesale food distributor. The rest comes from Weston Foods, with operations in Canada and the US that focus on fresh-baked goods, frozen dough, and other bakery products. (Its Interbake Foods division is a major supplier of Girl Scout cookies in the US.) Weston Foods also has dairy operations. Chairman and president W. Galen Weston owns about 63% of the company, which was founded by his grandfather in 1882.

Subsidiary George Weston Bakeries produces baked goods under the Arnold, Entenmann's, Freihofer's, Thomas', and Wonder brand names, among others.

Both Loblaw and Weston Foods face challenges resulting from changing consumer preferences concerning what to eat and where to shop. Loblaw is up against increased competition from non-traditional rivals, such as Wal-Mart Canada, which are claiming a growing share of the retail grocery market. An increased focus on health and diet has hurt Weston Foods's sales of white-flour based products and sweet goods. As a result Weston Foods is shifting its product mix more toward whole grain products.

A new bakery in the midwestern US is expected to begin production of bread and English muffins by the end of 2006.

The food-processing segment is also expanding its bakery and biscuit operations through acquisitions; its purchase of Bestfoods Baking has made it one of the top bakeries in the US. However, it has sold noncore operations, including its forest products business, canned seafood business (Conners), and fisheries operations in Chile. In 2005 the company sold its Heritage Salmon subsidiary, thus exiting the unprofitable fisheries business entirely.

HISTORY

A baker's apprentice, George Weston began delivering bread in Toronto with a single horse in 1882. He added the Model Bakery in 1896 and began making cookies and biscuits in 1908.

Upon George's death in 1924, his son Garfield gained control of the company and took it public as George Weston Limited in 1928. Having popularized the premium English biscuit in Canada, Garfield acquired bakeries in the UK to make cheap biscuits (uncommon at the time). He grouped the bakeries as a separate public company called Allied Bakeries in 1935 (it later became Associated British Foods and is still controlled by the Weston family).

Expansion-minded Garfield led the company into the US with the purchase of Associated Biscuit in 1939. By the late 1930s George Weston was making cakes, breads, and almost 500 kinds of candy and biscuits.

During the 1940s the company made a number of acquisitions, including papermaker E.B. Eddy (1943; sold 1998 to papermaker Domtar, giving it a 20% stake in Domtar), Southern Biscuit (1944), Western Grocers (1944, its first distribution company), and William Neilson (1948, chocolate and dairy products).

In 1953 it acquired a controlling interest in Loblaw Groceterias, Canada's largest grocery chain. George Weston continued its acquisitions during the 1950s and 1960s, adding grocer National Tea and diversifying into packaging (Somerville Industries, 1957) and fisheries (British Columbia Packers, 1962; Conners Bros., 1967).

By 1970, when Garfield's son Galen became president, the company's holdings were in disarray. Galen brought in new managers, consolidated the food distribution and sales operations under Loblaw Companies Limited, and cut back on National Tea (which shrank from over 900 stores in 1972 to 82 in 1993). When Garfield died in 1978, Galen became chairman.

Ever since Galen, a polo-playing chum of Prince Charles, was the target of a failed kidnapping attempt by the Irish Republican Army in 1983, the family has kept a low public profile.

George Weston became the #1 chocolate maker in Canada with its purchase of Cadbury Schweppes' Canadian assets in 1987. The 1980s concluded with a five-year price war in St. Louis

among its National Tea stores, Kroger, and a local grocer. This ultimately proved fruitless, and Loblaw sold its US supermarkets in 1995, ending its US retail presence. As part of its divestiture of underachieving subsidiaries, the company sold its Neilson confectionery business back to Cadbury Schweppes in 1996 and sold its chocolate products company in 1998.

In early 1998 Loblaw set its sights on Quebec, buying Montreal-based Provigo. Other George Weston acquisitions in the late 1990s included Oshawa Foods' 80-store Agora Foods franchise supermarket unit in eastern Canada and its Field-fresh Farms dairy business, the frozen-bagel business of Quaker Oats, Pennsylvania-based Maier's Bakery, and Bunge International's Australian meat processor, Don Smallgoods. It also sold its British Columbia Packers fisheries unit.

Early in 2001 George Weston surprised analysts when it won Unilever's Bestfoods Baking Company (Entenmann's, Oroweat) with a bid of $1.8 billion. The company reduced its stake in Loblaw by 2% and sold its Connors canned seafood business to fund the purchase, which was completed in July 2001. To help pay down debt, in early 2002 the company sold its Orowheat business in the western US to Mexican bread giant Grupo Bimbo for $610 million.

In 2003, Weston's food distribution business introduced about 1,500 private label products.

In 2004 Weston sold its fisheries operations in Chile at a loss for about $20 million. In September of that year the company purchased Quebec-based Boulangerie Gadoua Ltée, a family-owned baking business.

The company restructured its US biscuit operations and opened a new fresh bakery plant in Orlando, Florida in 2005 as part of its push to increase its business in the southeastern US.

EXECUTIVES

Chairman and President: W. Galen Weston, age 65
Deputy Chairman: Allan L. Leighton, age 53
CFO: Richard P. (Rick) Mavrinac, age 53
EVP, Secretary, and General Counsel: Gordon A. M. Currie, age 47
SVP, Labour Relations: Roy R. Conliffe, age 55
SVP, Finance: Louise M. Lacchin, age 48
SVP; President and CEO, President's Choice Bank: Donald G. (Don) Reid, age 56
SVP, Corporate Development: Robert G. Vaux, age 57
SVP, Investor Relations and Public Affairs: Geoffrey H. (Geoff) Wilson, age 50
VP, Assistant Secretary: Robert A. Balcom, age 44
VP, Risk Management and Internal Audit Services: Manny Difilippo, age 46
VP, Taxation: J. Bradley Holland, age 42
VP, Legal Counsel: Michael N. Kimber, age 50
VP, Corporate Systems: Kirk W. Mondesire, age 45
VP, Pension and Benefits: Lucy J. Paglione, age 46
VP and Controller: Rolando Sardellitti, age 38
VP and Treasurer: Lisa R. Swartzman, age 35
Controller, Planning and Analysis: Patrick MacDonell, age 36
President, Loblaw Companies: A. Mark Foote
President, Weston Foods US: Gary J. Prince, age 54
President, Weston Foods Canada: Ralph A. Robinson, age 57
President, Interbake Foods: Raymond A. Baxter, age 61
Senior Director, Environmental Affairs: Walter H. Kraus, age 43
Auditors: KPMG LLP

LOCATIONS

HQ: George Weston Limited
22 St. Clair Ave. East,
Toronto, Ontario M4T 2S7, Canada
Phone: 416-922-2500   **Fax:** 416-922-4395
Web: www.weston.ca

George Weston Limited's Loblaw Companies operates in Canada, and its Weston Foods divisions operate in Canada and the US.

2005 Sales

	% of total
Canada	90
US	10
Total	**100**

PRODUCTS/OPERATIONS

2005 Sales

	% of total
Loblaw	86
Weston Foods	14
Total	**100**

2005 Weston Foods Sales

	% of total
Fresh bakery	50
Frozen bakery	14
Fresh-baked sweet goods	14
Dairy	12
Biscuit	10
Total	**100**

Operating Divisions

Food Distribution (selected Loblaw banners)
   Atlantic Superstore
   Extra Foods
   Fortinos
   Loblaws
   Maxi
   Maxi & Co.
   no frills
   Provigo
   The Real Canadian Superstore
   The Real Canadian Wholesale Club
   SuperValu
   valu-mart
   Your Independent Grocer
   Zehrs Markets
Food Processing (selected units)
   George Weston Bakeries Inc. (fresh-baked goods, US)
   Interbake Foods Inc. (cookies and crackers, US)
   Maplehurst Bakeries, Inc. (frozen bakery products, US)
   Neilson Dairy (milk processor)
   Ready Bake Foods Inc. (frozen bakery products)
   Stroehmann Bakeries, LC (fresh-baked goods, US)
   Weston Bakeries Limited (fresh-baked goods)
   Weston Fruitcake Company

COMPETITORS

Bimbo
Bridgford Foods
Campbell Soup
Canada Safeway
Flowers Foods
IGA
Interstate Bakeries
Jim Pattison Group
Kellogg Snacks
Lanes Biscuits
Maple Leaf Foods
METRO
Otis Spunkmeyer
Sobeys
Tasty Baking
Wal-Mart Canada

HISTORICAL FINANCIALS
Company Type: Public

Income Statement				FYE: December 31
	REVENUE ($ mil.)	NET INCOME ($ mil.)	NET PROFIT MARGIN	EMPLOYEES
12/05	26,897	599	2.2%	151,500
12/04	24,732	355	1.4%	148,000
12/03	22,553	612	2.7%	145,860
12/02	17,406	438	2.5%	142,850
12/01	15,499	366	2.4%	139,000
Annual Growth	14.8%	13.1%	—	2.2%

Net Income History   Toronto: WN

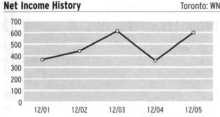

GlaxoSmithKline

GlaxoSmithKline (GSK) calms your nerves and helps you breathe easier. One of the top five pharmaceutical firms in the world, GSK's top sellers include central nervous system therapies, respiratory drugs, and anti-infectives. The company's top product is asthma medication Advair, which combines two of the company's other products, Flovent and Serevent, to form a single, twice-daily treatment. Other bestsellers include herpes treatment Valtrex, antidepressants Paxil and Wellbutrin, migraine therapy Imitrex, and antibiotic Augmentin. The company's consumer products include Tums for sour stomachs and cold sore fighter Abreva.

For smokers looking to kick the habit, GSK offers several cessation products like Commit, NicoDerm, and Nicorette. Other consumer products include rehydration beverage Lucozade, Sensodyne toothpaste, and denture care brands Poligrip, Polident, and Corega. In a move to expand its consumer product line, GSK purchased CNS, the maker of Breathe Right nasal strips, for $566 million.

The firm takes almost half its revenues from the US, and maintaining US patent protection for its bestsellers can make or break its future. The company lost patent protection for Paxil in 2003 (sales continue to plummet year-on-year and fell some 42% in 2005), and in a late 2004 partnership with Watson Pharmaceuticals, it launched a generic version of Wellbutrin SR. Biovail, the drugmaker that licensed the antidepressant to GSK, is fighting to keep generics of Wellbutrin XL, an extended-release version of the drug, off the market.

To alleviate these losses, GSK's development efforts include 140 different projects in the clinical stage of development. Drug candidates nearing the end of the development stage include an HIV protease inhibitor and therapies for high cholesterol, type 2 diabetes, lupus, and Alzheimer's disease. Seven therapies filed for approval in 2006 — including human papillomavirus vaccine Cervarix (developed with Merck) and Tykerb,

an orally administered breast cancer treatment. Eight other drugs entered Phase III of trials in 2006. New drug releases include Requip, which treats restless leg syndrome (RLS); enlarged prostate treatment Avodart; and osteoporosis drug Bonviva. Additionally, the company acquired the research operations of Pliva, Eastern Europe's largest pharmaceutical maker (the remainder of which was bought by Barr Pharmaceuticals in 2006); its specialty is research into macrolide antibiotics (it developed blockbuster antibiotic Zithromax, sold by Pfizer).

GlaxoSmithKline opened 2007 with monumental news: it has entered the most expensive licensing deal in pharmaceutical history with Genmab. The deal is worth $2.1 billion and involves co-development of a human monoclonal antibody for treatment of lymphocytic leukemia and follicular non-Hodgkin's lymphoma. In addition, the antibody, known as ofatumumab, is being tested for efficacy in treating rheumatoid arthritis. GSK will also help to bring the products to market.

GSK has been growing its vaccine production capabilities exponentially over the last couple of years, starting with its 2005 acquisition of Corixa. That purchase gained the company a factory engaged in producing Monophosphoral Lipid A, a key ingredient in a number of the company's vaccine and vaccine-related products. Later its acquisition of ID Biomedical, a Canadian vaccine producer, bolstered GSK's influenza vaccine production capability. The company also increased its flu vaccine capacity five-fold by building a new production facility in Dresden, Germany, a $633 million production facility in France, and a vaccine plant in Singapore.

Continuing its research expansion phase, in 2006 GSK announced plans to acquire private biotech Domantis Ltd, which specializes in laboratory-engineered monoclonal antibodies. The addition, which will cost the company more than $450 million, will nearly double the size of GSK's research capabilities.

Fall of 2005 saw the sale of the company's US dermatology business (part of GlaxoSmithKline Consumer Healthcare) to the PharmaDerm division of ALTANA; products involved in the deal include Alcovate, Cutivate, Emgel, Oxistat, and Temovate. In 2006 GSK sold its unbranded generic drug businesses in Spain and Italy to India's pharma giant Ranbaxy.

In 2006 the FDA approved GSK's drug Hycamtin for use in conjunction with cisplatin-based chemotherapy for the treatment of late-stage cervical cancer. Hycamtin is the first drug approved to treat persistent, recurrent, or incurable cervical cancer; it was approved a decade ago for use against ovarian cancer, and two years later to treat small-cell lung cancer. The drug prolongs the lives of patients but does not cure the cancer; it can also lower white blood cell counts.

A second breakthrough came later in 2006, when GSK announced it had potentially developed a vaccine against Avian Bird Flu. Part of the significance of this particular vaccine is the size of the dose per individual: the vaccine requires a very small amount of the treatment to inoculate against the disease. The vaccine is set on a fast-track for approval in Europe and the US and is expected to be ready for market by 2007. GSK has pledged that, in the case of a pandemic outbreak of the disease, it will collaborate with its European rivals to produce vaccinations en masse.

In September 2006 GSK settled a tax dispute with the IRS for $3.1 billion, the largest single tax payment in IRS history, over international profit allocation in taxes filed by Glaxo Wellcome (prior to the 2001 Glaxo Wellcome/SmithKline Beecham merger) from 1989 through 2000. The payment also includes taxes owed from 2001 through 2005.

HISTORY

Englishman Joseph Nathan started an import-export business in New Zealand in 1873. He obtained the rights to a process for drying milk and began making powdered milk in New Zealand, selling it as baby food Glaxo.

Nathan's son Alec, sent to London to oversee baby food sales in Britain, increased Glaxo's name recognition by publishing the Glaxo Baby Book, a guide to child care. After WWI the company began distribution in India and South America.

In the 1920s Glaxo launched vitamin D-fortified formulations. It entered the pharmaceutical business with its 1927 introduction of Ostelin, a liquid vitamin D concentrate, and continued to grow globally in the 1930s, introducing Ostermilk (vitamin-fortified milk).

Glaxo began making penicillin and anesthetics during WWII; it went public in 1947. A steep drop in antibiotic prices in the mid-1950s led Glaxo to diversify; it bought veterinary, medical instrument, and drug distribution firms.

In the 1970s the British Monopolies Commission quashed both a hostile takeover attempt by Beecham and a proposed merger with retailer and drugmaker Boots. Glaxo launched US operations in 1978.

In the 1980s Glaxo shed nondrug operations to concentrate on pharmaceuticals. A 1981 marketing blitz launched antiulcer drug Zantac (to vie with SmithKline's Tagamet) in the US, where Glaxo's sales had been small. The company boosted outreach by contracting to use Hoffmann-La Roche's sales staff. The Zantac sales assault gave Glaxo leadership in US antiulcer drug sales.

Under CEO Sir Richard Sykes, Glaxo in 1995 made a surprise bid for UK rival Wellcome. Founded in 1880 by Americans Silas Burroughs and Henry Wellcome to sell McKesson-Robbins' products outside the US, Burroughs Wellcome and Co. began making its own products two years later. By the 1990s the company, which fostered Nobel Prize-winning researchers, led the world in antiviral medicines. Its primary drug products were Zovirax (launched 1981) and Retrovir (1987).

Though an earlier bid by Glaxo had been rejected, Sykes won the takeover with backing from Wellcome Trust, Wellcome's largest shareholder.

In 1997 the company formed a new genetics division, buying Spectra Biomedical and its gene variation technology. That year the company pulled diabetes drug Romozin (Rezulin in the US) from the UK market over concerns that it caused liver damage.

Glaxo in 1998 ended its joint venture with Warner-Lambert (begun 1993), selling its former partner the Canadian and US marketing rights to acid blocker Zantac 75.

In 1999 Glaxo trimmed its product line, pulling hepatitis treatment Wellferon because of slow sales and selling the US rights to several anesthesia products. It also cut some 3,400 jobs (half from the UK). Also that year Glaxo threatened to leave the UK after the National Health

Service opted not to cover antiflu inhalant Relenza, claiming the drug is not cost-effective.

The FDA in 2000 approved Glaxo's Lotronex for irritable bowel syndrome, but several hospitalizations linked to the drug prompted the FDA to ask the company to withdraw it from the US market. Later that year Glaxo completed its merger with former UK rival SmithKline Beecham to create GlaxoSmithKline (GSK); Jean-Pierre Garnier took over as CEO.

Although GSK has largely escaped the flurry of patent worries afflicting other druggernauts, in 2001 a US court declared invalid three patents protecting Augmentin from generics until 2017 and opened the door for cheaper rivals.

GSK returned European and international marketing rights for erectile dysfunction drug Levitra back to its developer, Bayer HealthCare, in late 2004 after it, umm, failed to perform. (It still markets the drug with Schering-Plough in the US.)

EXECUTIVES

Chairman: Sir Christopher Charles (Chris) Gent, age 57
CEO and Director: Jean-Pierre (JP) Garnier, age 58, $4,394,000 pay
CFO and Director: Julian Heslop, age 52, $894,608 pay
SVP and General Counsel: Rupert Bondy
SVP, Centre of Excellence for External Drug Discovery: Maxine Gowen, age 48
SVP, Corporate Communications and Community Partnerships: Duncan Learmouth
SVP, Drug Discovery: Patrick Vallance
SVP, Corporate Communications and Community Partnerships: Jennie Younger
SVP, Human Resources: Daniel (Dan) Phelan
SVP, Medicines Development: Allan Baxter, age 55
SVP, Procurement: Joe Meier
VP, Advertising and Promotion Services: Tom Laughery
VP, Anti-Infective, Metabolic, and Endocrine Marketing: Brian A. Lortie
VP, Corporate Media Relations: Nancy Pekarek
VP, External Advocacy: Mike Pucci
VP, Procurement Global Systems and Operations: R. Gregg Brandyberry
VP, Trade, Pharmacy Sales, and Operations: John Fish
Chairman, Research and Development and Director: Moncef Slaoui, age 46
Vice Chairman, Pharmaceuticals: Robert A. (Bob) Ingram, age 64
President, Consumer Healthcare, North America: George Quesnelle
President, Pharmaceutical Operations: David M. Stout, age 52
President, US Pharmaceuticals: Chris Viehbacher
CIO: Ford Calhoun
Company Secretary: S. M. Bicknell
Public Relations: Bernadette King
Auditors: PricewaterhouseCoopers LLP

LOCATIONS

HQ: GlaxoSmithKline plc
980 Great West Rd., Brentford,
London TW8 9GS, United Kingdom
Phone: +44-20-8047-5000   **Fax:** +44-20-8047-7807
US HQ: 1 Franklin Plaza, Philadelphia, PA 19101
US Phone: 215-751-4000   **US Fax:** 215-751-3233
Web: www.gsk.com

2005 Pharmaceutical Sales

	% of total
North America	
US	49
Canada	2
Europe	
France	5
UK	4
Italy	4
Germany	3
Spain	3
Poland	1
Other countries	9
Asia/Pacific	
Japan	5
Other countries	7
Latin America	4
Middle East & Africa	4
Total	**100**

PRODUCTS/OPERATIONS

2005 Pharmaceutical Sales

	% of total
Respiratory	27
Central nervous system	18
Anti-virals	14
Anti-bacterials	8
Metabolic	8
Vaccines	7
Cardiovascular & urogenital	7
Oncology & emesis	5
Other	6
Total	**100**

2005 Consumer Health Care Sales

	% of total
Over-the-counter medicines	
Analgesics	12
Smoking control	11
Gastrointestinal	8
Dermatological	6
Natural wellness support	5
Respiratory tract	5
Oral care	32
Nutritional health care	21
Total	**100**

Selected Products

Pharmaceuticals
  Anti-bacterials
  Anti-virals
  Cardiovascular treatments
  Central nervous system disorder treatments
  Metabolic and gastrointestinal treatments
  Oncology and emesis treatments
  Respiratory treatments
  Vaccines
Consumer Products
  Over-the-Counter Medicines
    Abreva (cold sores)
    Abtei (vitamins and nutritional supplements)
    Citrucel (laxative)
    Commit (smoking-cessation)
    Contac (respiratory product)
    Nicabate/NicoDerm CQ/NiQuitin CQ (smoking-cessation)
    Nicorette (smoking-cessation)
    Panadol (analgesic)
    Tums (antacid)
    Zovirax (cold sores)
  Oral Care
    Aquafresh (toothpaste and toothbrushes)
    Dr Best (toothbrushes)
    Macleans (toothpaste)
    Odol (toothpaste)
    Polident (denture cleaner)
    Poli-Grip (denture adhesive)
    Sensodyne (toothpaste)
  Nutritional Healthcare
    Horlicks (milk-based malted food and chocolate drinks)
    Lucozade (glucose energy drink)
    Ribena (line of juice drinks rich in vitamin C)

COMPETITORS

Abbott Labs	Hoffmann-La Roche
Amgen	Johnson & Johnson
AstraZeneca	Merck
Barr Pharmaceuticals	Mylan Labs
Bayer	Novartis
Bristol-Myers Squibb	Novo Nordisk
Chiron	Pfizer
Elan	Sanofi-Aventis
Eli Lilly	Schering-Plough
Genentech	Wyeth

HISTORICAL FINANCIALS

Company Type: Public

Income Statement

FYE: December 31

	REVENUE ($ mil.)	NET INCOME ($ mil.)	NET PROFIT MARGIN	EMPLOYEES
12/05	37,273	5,741	15.4%	100,728
12/04	39,224	5,264	13.4%	100,019
12/03	38,266	4,325	11.3%	100,919
12/02	34,033	695	2.0%	106,166
Annual Growth	3.1%	102.2%	—	(1.7%)

2005 Year-End Financials

Debt ratio: 15.5%   No. of shares (mil.): —
Return on equity: 9.2%   Dividends
Cash ($ mil.): 9,007   Yield: 3.0%
Current ratio: 1.39   Payout: 72.2%
Long-term debt ($ mil.): 9,127   Market value ($ mil.): —

Stock History

NYSE: GSK

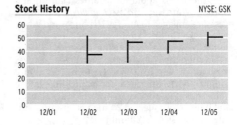

	STOCK PRICE ($) FY Close	P/E High/Low		PER SHARE ($) Earnings	Dividends
12/05	50.48	25	21	2.12	1.53
12/04	47.39	27	22	1.74	1.60
12/03	46.62	20	13	2.42	1.29
12/02	37.46	—	—	—	1.16
Annual Growth	10.5%	—	—	(6.4%)	9.7%

Hanson

Breaking rocks in the hot sun is no punishment for building materials company Hanson PLC. The company's Hanson Building Products and Hanson Aggregates operations in the US and the UK produce aggregates, ready-mixed concrete, bricks, and concrete pipe and building products. Other operations include quarries, marine dredging, and recycling. Hanson also has operations in Europe, Asia, and Australia, but the US and the UK account for most sales. The company is what's left of the Hanson Group — a huge industrial conglomerate that was broken into four publicly traded enterprises involving tobacco, coal, chemicals, and building materials.

Hanson has been meeting recent challenges by simplifying its operations. The company has divided its business structure into four regions, with

North America as its largest region. In 2003 Hanson disposed of certain noncore operations in Singapore, India, Indonesia, Germany, and the US. Of course, Hanson continues to look for acquisitions within the fragmented building-products industry, especially in high-growth markets.

Its North America operations, formerly Hanson Building Materials America, was divided into Hanson Building Products North America and Hanson Aggregates North America in 2003. The company beefed up its Hanson Australia unit with the acquisition of Pioneer International. Hanson also has a 25% stake in Cement Australia Holdings with Rinker Group and Holcim. Its European unit operates a marine dredging business in a joint venture with Tarmac.

Hanson continued to grow through acquisitions in 2004, spending more than $150 million on a nine new businesses. At the same time, the company sold its Thailand operations and some non-core US operations. Hanson also pledged to spend £200 million-£300 million on acquisitions in 2005; it actually spent £343 million.

In 2006 Hanson acquired US-based aggregates producer Material Service from General Dynamics for about $300 million.

Mike Welton became chairman in 2005 after Christopher Collins retired.

HISTORY

In the 1950s and 1960s, James Hanson and Gordon White were British *bon vivants*. Hanson was once engaged to Audrey Hepburn, and White dated Joan Collins. However, they later became better known as sharp businessmen.

Through the Wiles Group, a fertilizer business they took over in 1965, Hanson and White sought poorly managed companies in mature industries at low prices. Within 10 years Hanson and White had collected 24 such businesses with sales in excess of $120 million.

Perceiving an antibusiness attitude in the UK, White formed a New York subsidiary, Hanson Industries, in 1973. He made his first American purchase in 1974, buying Seacoast (animal feed). Other purchases in hot dogs, shoes, and batteries followed, including conglomerate US Industries in 1984. That year the company acquired leading UK brick maker London Brick.

In bitterly fought hostile takeovers in 1986, Hanson acquired SCM (Smith-Corona office equipment, Glidden Paints, Durkee's Famous Foods, SCM Chemicals) and Imperial Group (cigarettes, beer, food, hotels, restaurants). It acquired US cement maker Kaiser Cement in 1987. The company changed its name to Hanson PLC that year.

Hanson acquired Peabody (coal) in 1990 and Beazer PLC, a UK construction firm with extensive US holdings, a year later. During 1992 the company sold a number of assets; the next year it bought Quantum Chemicals (propane distribution) for $3.4 billion. Hanson took Beazer Homes (home building materials, US) public in 1994, retaining 30%.

In 1995 the company spun off some of its US operations as U.S. Industries and sold its 62% stake in Suburban Propane, a major US propane distributor. It also reorganized Beazer's US operations as Cornerstone Construction & Materials. In addition, Hanson merged its Butterley Brick and London Brick into one company, Hanson Brick. Also in 1995 founder White died.

The Hanson conglomerate began to split up its operations in 1996, creating four separate public companies focused on chemicals (Millennium Chemicals), tobacco (Imperial Tobacco), energy (Energy Group PLC), and building materials and equipment (Hanson PLC). In 1997 Cornerstone Construction & Materials acquired Concrete Pipe and Products. Founder James Hanson retired as chairman that year.

Joining the consolidation of the US building-materials sector, Hanson bought six US firms in 1998 — HG Fenton (aggregates and ready-mix concrete), Becker Minerals (aggregates), Condux (concrete pipe), Gifford-Hill American (aggregates), and Nelson & Sloan (aggregates and ready-mix concrete). That year the company paid $155 million to settle environmental liabilities inherited when it purchased Koppers Company in 1991.

In 1999 Hanson sold Grove Worldwide — a world-leading maker of cranes and materials-handling equipment — to Robert Bass' investment firm, Keystone, and also sold its 24% stake in Westralian Sands (titanium and zircon, Australia).

Hanson acquired Pioneer International, a giant Australian concrete and aggregate company, for about $2.5 billion in 2000. Smaller acquisitions during the year included US concrete pipe and products makers Joelson Taylor, Cincinnati Concrete Pipe, and Milan Concrete Products.

In late 2000 Hanson acquired Davon, another US-based concrete and aggregate company. In early 2001 the company sold its waste management division, part of Hanson Quarry Products Europe, to Waste Recycling Group. Hanson's 2001 acquisitions included Centennial Pipe and Products, a major Canadian pipe maker (from LaFarge), as well as businesses in Mexico, Spain, and the UK.

Early in 2002 Andrew Dougal retired as CEO and was replaced by Alan Murray. Hanson added to its US operations midyear with the purchase of Choctaw Inc. (concrete pipes, corrugated steel pipes, and precast concrete structures) from Amatek Holdings Ltd. That year it sold its 50% stake in North Texas Cement Co. In 2003 Hanson acquired US-based aggregates company Better Materials for $150 million. It also sold various operations in Singapore, India, Indonesia, and Germany as part of its streamlining plan.

The company bought US brick manufacturer Athens Brick in 2004. Founder Lord Hanson died the same year. Early in 2005 Hanson spent about $122 million on UK-based Marshalls Clay Products and $225 million on Thermalite (lightweight concrete blocks).

EXECUTIVES

Chairman: Mike W. Welton, age 59, $282,146 pay
CEO: Alan J. Murray, age 52, $1,954,375 pay
Finance Director: Pavi S. Binning, age 46
Legal Director: Graham Dransfield, age 54, $844,716 pay
President, Hanson Aggregates North America: James Kitzmiller
President, Hanson Building Products North America: Richard Manning
Managing Director, Continental Europe: Justin Read
Managing Director, Hanson Building Products UK: David J. Szymanski, age 50
Managing Director, Hanson Continental Europe & Asia: Patrick O'Shea
Chief Executive, Hanson Australia: Leslie (Les) Cadzow
Corporate and Investor Relations: Carol Ann Walsh
Secretary: Paul D. Tunnacliffe
Auditors: Ernst & Young LLP

LOCATIONS

HQ: Hanson PLC
1 Grosvenor Place,
London SW1X 7JH, United Kingdom
Phone: +44-20-7245-1245   **Fax:** +44-20-7235-3455
US HQ: 1333 Campus Pkwy., Neptune, NJ 07753
US Phone: 732-919-9777   **US Fax:** 732-919-1149
Web: www.hansonplc.com

Hanson has operations in 17 countries including Australia, Belgium, Canada, the Czech Republic, China, France, Germany, Indonesia, Israel, Malaysia, Mexico, the Netherlands, Singapore, Spain, Thailand, the UK, and the US.

2005 Sales

	% of total
North America	
Hanson Aggregates	26
Hanson Building Products	20
UK	
Hanson Aggregates	22
Hanson Building Products	10
Australia & Asia/Pacific	
Hanson Australia	13
Hanson Asia/Pacific	3
Hanson Continental Europe	6
Total	**100**

PRODUCTS/OPERATIONS

Selected Products

Aggregates
Asphalt
Cement
Clay brick
Clay pavers
Concrete products
Crushed rock
Marine aggregates
Ready-mix concrete
Recycled aggregates

Selected Operations

North America
Hanson Aggregates North America
Hanson Building Products North America
Hanson Brick & Tile
Hanson Pipe & Products
UK
Hanson Aggregates UK
Midland Quarry Products (joint venture with Tarmac)
Hanson Building Products UK
Continental Europe and Asia
Hanson Continental Europe & Marine
United Marine Holdings (joint venture with Tarmac)
Hanson Asia Pacific
Australia
Hanson Australia
Cement Australia Holdings (25%, with Rinker Group and Holcim)
Pioneer Road Services (joint venture with Shell Australia)

COMPETITORS

Aggregate Industries	HeidelbergCement
Aggregate Industries UK	Holcim
Boral	Italcementi
BPB	Lafarge
Castle Cement	Martin Marietta Materials
CBR	Readymix
CEMEX	Rinker Group
CRH	Saint-Gobain
CSR Limited	Siam Cement
Dyckerhoff	Taiheiyo Cement
FCC Barcelona	Tarmac
FLSmidth	Ube
Foster Yeoman	Vulcan Materials
Franz Haniel	

HISTORICAL FINANCIALS

Company Type: Public

Income Statement

FYE: December 31

	REVENUE ($ mil.)	NET INCOME ($ mil.)	NET PROFIT MARGIN	EMPLOYEES
12/05	6,394	798	12.5%	24,100
12/04	6,674	373	5.6%	27,400
Annual Growth	(4.2%)	113.9%	—	(12.0%)

2005 Year-End Financials

Debt ratio: 38.1%	No. of shares (mil.): —
Return on equity: 15.2%	Dividends
Cash ($ mil.): 1,864	Yield: 4.1%
Current ratio: 1.40	Payout: 2.5%
Long-term debt ($ mil.): 1,999	Market value ($ mil.): —

Stock History

NYSE: HAN

	STOCK PRICE ($) FY Close	P/E High	P/E Low	PER SHARE ($) Earnings	PER SHARE ($) Dividends
12/05	54.90	12	9	4.52	2.27
12/04	42.93	13	10	3.33	1.53
Annual Growth	27.9%	—	—	35.7%	48.4%

HBOS

Formed in 2001 when UK-based financial services company Halifax acquired Bank of Scotland, HBOS is happy to be one of the BMOC, as one of the UK's top financial services companies and its #1 mortgage lender. HBOS' offerings include retail banking, corporate banking, insurance, investments, and treasury and asset management. Among the members of the HBOS family are Bank of Scotland (Ireland), credit insurer St. Andrew's Group, and UK-based life insurance and financial services provider St. James's Place (60% owned). Asset management unit Clerical Medical Investment Group serves retail and institutional clients. HBOS Australia oversees Bank of Western Australia (WestBank) and St. Andrew's Australia.

HBOS — combining Halifax's Yorkshire origins and Bank of Scotland's Scottish roots — immediately created a strong contender against such London city slickers as Barclays, Lloyds TSB, and HSBC. The company hopes to capitalize upon its network of branches, agencies, and real estate agencies, using the organization to cross-sell its various financial and insurance products. Chief executive James Crosby, who led the company through the Halifax-Bank of Scotland merger, retired in 2006. COO Andy Hornby was tapped to replace Crosby. Also in 2006, HBOS acquired from Aviva the 50% of Lex Vehicle Leasing that it didn't already own. The combination of the Lex Vehicle Leasing operations with those of the Bank of Scotland makes HBOS the UK's top vehicle leasing company.

That same year HBOS agreed to sell its 90% stake in US-based Drive Financial — a provider of subprime auto loans — to Banco Santander Central Hispano.

HISTORY

Necessity was the mother of incorporation for HBOS. As urbanization sped up in the mid-19th century, housing shortages led to the rise of building societies, cooperatives that bought land and built houses for their members. Increased demand for urban housing led to the formation of the Halifax Permanent Building and Investment Society in 1853. Because it was a permanent society, members could retain membership in the cooperative after their houses had been built, receiving interest on their invested money.

Initially Halifax kept to its namesake hometown in West Yorkshire, but it eventually expanded with a branch in nearby Huddersfield in 1862. The society got some competition at home in 1871 with the debut of the similarly named Halifax Equitable Benefit Building Society. By 1888 Halifax Permanent was able to offer paid-up shares for the first time to members who had finished paying for their houses. The company's first top officer, Jonas Taylor, died after 50 years of service; he was replaced by Enoch Hill in 1903.

By 1913 Halifax Permanent was the largest building society in the UK. Its lead position was reinforced with the 1928 acquisition of Halifax Equitable; the new company became known simply as the Halifax Building Society. Sir Enoch Hill (having been knighted during his four decades at Halifax) died in 1942.

The Building Societies Act of 1986 allowed Halifax to offer banking and financial services.

In 1995 the company merged with Leeds Permanent Building Society. That company's home office became the center for Halifax's financial services operations. Halifax's move into financial services continued with the 1996 acquisition of fund manager Clerical Medical. That year it also established a general insurance subsidiary.

Halifax shuffled off its mutual coil in 1997, converting to stock ownership and instantaneously becoming the eighth-largest publicly traded company in the UK.

Flush with $5 billion from the flotation, Halifax stayed on the acquisition prowl in 1998, outbidding Royal Bank of Scotland for UK mutual banker Birmingham Midshires. It denied rumors that it would buy the UK's top insurer (Prudential plc) or its #2 bank (Barclays).

Halifax launched a reorganization in 1999 to consolidate acquired operations, cut operational costs, and reemphasize customer services. It sold off about 200 of its smaller real estate agencies and invested $150 million to develop online and telephone banking. Halifax also launched an online stock trading service: ShareXpress. That year the company announced it would no longer pursue debtors whose houses had been repossessed more than six years hence but still had leftover debt.

In 2000 the company announced plans for its Internet-based bank. It also bought St. James's Place Capital, whose wealthy clientele would provide Halifax with cross-selling opportunities. The following year Halifax bought the fund management business, sales force, and computer systems of the troubled UK mutual insurer The Equitable Life Assurance Society. Halifax bought Edinburgh-based Bank of Scotland in 2001 to become HBOS plc.

EXECUTIVES

Chairman: Lord Dennis Stevenson, age 60
Deputy Chairman: Sir Ronald (Ron) Garrick, age 65
Group Executive Director: Andy Hornby, age 39
Chief Executive, Corporate Banking and Director: Peter Cummings, age 50
Chief Executive, Strategy and International Operations and Director: Colin Matthew, age 55
Group Finance Director: Phil Hodkinson, age 48
Director; Chief Executive, Insurance & Investment Group: Jo Dawson, age 44
Head of Marketing: Philip Hanson
Finance Director, Insurance and Investment Division: Steven J. (Steve) Colsell, age 40
Head of Customer Strategy: Gerald Mclarnon
Head of Media Relations: Mark Hemingway
Head of Retail and Director: Benny Higgins
Head of Risk: Dan Watkins
General Manager, Group Communications: Shane O'Riordain
Director of Human Resources: David Fisher
Director of Investor Relations: Charles Wycks
CEO, HBOS Australia: David S. Willis, age 49
Operations Director, Retail Division: Shaun Doherty, age 48
Auditors: KPMG Audit Plc

LOCATIONS

HQ: HBOS plc
The Mound, Edinburgh EH1 1YZ, United Kingdom
Phone: +44-870-600-5000
Web: www.hbosplc.com

2005 Sales

	% of total
UK	94
Other countries	6
Total	**100**

PRODUCTS/OPERATIONS

2005 Sales

	% of total
Net investment income related to insurance & investment business	38
Net interest income	27
Net earned premiums on insurance contracts	19
Fees & commission income	9
Change in value of in-force long term assurance business	1
Net trading income	1
Other operating income	5
Total	**100**

2005 Sales By Business Segment

	% of total
Insurance & Investment	56
Retail	23
Corporate	13
International	6
Treasury & Asset Management	2
Total	**100**

Selected Subsidiaries

The Governor and Company of the Bank of Scotland
   Bank of Scotland (Ireland) Ltd
   CAPITAL BANK plc
   HBOS Australia Pty Ltd
      Bank of Western Australia Ltd
   HBOS Treasury Services PLC
Halifax plc
Halifax Share Dealing Ltd
HBOS Insurance & Investment Group Ltd
   Clerical Medical Investment Group Ltd
   Halifax General Insurance Services Ltd
   Halifax Investment Fund Managers Ltd
   Halifax Life Ltd
   Insight Investment Management Ltd
   St Andrew's Insurance plc
   St. James's Place plc (formerly St. James's Place Capital plc, 60%)

COMPETITORS

Abbey National
Alliance & Leicester
Barclays
Commonwealth Bank of Australia
HSBC Holdings
Lloyds TSB
National Australia Bank
Prudential plc
RBS
Woolwich

HISTORICAL FINANCIALS

Company Type: Public

Income Statement

	ASSETS ($ mil.)	NET INCOME ($ mil.)	INCOME AS % OF ASSETS	EMPLOYEES
12/05	930,518	5,612	0.6%	71,985
12/04	853,077	5,888	0.7%	69,243
12/03	726,118	4,359	0.6%	67,458
12/02	569,513	3,073	0.5%	63,982
12/01	453,111	2,432	0.5%	62,848
Annual Growth	19.7%	23.3%	—	3.5%

FYE: December 31

2005 Year-End Financials

Equity as % of assets: —
Return on assets: 0.6%
Return on equity: —
Long-term debt ($ mil.): —
Sales ($ mil.): 40,631

Net Income History

London: HBOS

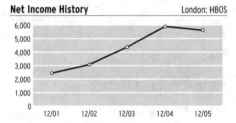

Heineken

Smaller brewers might be green with envy. Heineken, a global brewing giant, sells its namesake beer in the easily recognized green bottles in just about every country on the planet. The company's other global brands include Amstel and Murphy's — national and regional brands include Buckler (Europe), Quilmes (Argentina), Moretti (Italy), Tiger (Asia's leading regional brew), Zagorka (Bulgaria), and Bochkaryov (Russia). Heineken also distributes soft drinks and other nonalcoholic beverages. Heineken has interests in more than 115 breweries and continues to acquire more worldwide. The founding Heineken family owns 50% of Heineken Holding, which owns 50% of Heineken.

Heineken is the #2 imported beer in the US (behind Grupo Modelo's Corona, which tapped the #1 spot after nearly 65 years of Heineken dominance). The company is choosing to invest in expanding its role in the US market and introduced a new beer for the US market in 2006: Heineken Premium Light.

The company introduced a new portable draught beer system called DraughtKeg. Some 20 glasses can be dispensed from the mini keg. Heineken's BeerTender system, which keeps kegs fresh for several weeks once they have been tapped, also continued to grow in sales.

About 75% of Heineken's sales are in Europe, where it has solidified its base by buying breweries in Central Europe, Italy, Spain, and Russia. However, the company has had to shut down more than 30 breweries in recent years, mostly in Europe, as part of a cost-reduction program.

Political unrest has impeded Heineken's growth in Africa. However, it joined with Diageo to purchase 30% of InBev's Namibia Breweries in southern Africa and formed a joint venture with Kenya-based East Africa Breweries to introduce Heineken's products in Kenya and Uganda. It also has plans to increase its presence in South Africa.

HISTORY

Every Sunday morning Gerard Heineken's mother was appalled by crowds of drunken Dutchmen who had consumed too much gin the night before. Heineken, who wanted his mother's financial backing, insisted that drunkenness would decrease if people drank beer instead of gin and pointed out that there were no good beers in Holland. His strategy worked. In 1863 Heineken's mother put up the money to buy De Hooiberg (The Haystack), a 271-year-old brewery in Amsterdam.

Gerard proved his aptitude for brewing and within 10 years had established a brewery in Rotterdam. He named the business Heineken in 1873 and launched the company's lucrative foreign trade by exporting beer in 1876 to France. (By the 1950s half the beer brewed by the company was for export.) The company perfected a yeast strain (Heineken A-yeast) in 1886 that is still in use today.

In 1917 Gerard's son Dr. Henri Pierre Heineken inherited the firm and expanded operations to the US. Making a voyage to that country, Henri Pierre met Leo van Munching, a ship's bartender who displayed a remarkable knowledge of beer. Recognizing van Munching's talent, Henri Pierre hired him as Heineken's US importer. Prohibition killed the US operations, although the company entered new markets elsewhere; after repeal, Heineken was the first foreign beer to re-enter the US market.

After WWII, Henri Pierre sent his son, Alfred, to learn the business under van Munching, who had created a national distribution system in the US. Alfred succeeded his father in 1953 and stepped down in 1989.

Heineken bought the Amstel Brewery in Holland (founded 1870) in 1968. Two years later it became a producer of stout through the acquisition of James J. Murphy in Cork, Ireland. Facing a consolidation of the European market, Heineken launched a campaign in the 1980s to expand its European beer operations, purchasing breweries in France, Greece, Ireland, Italy, and Spain.

In 1991 Heineken bought the van Munching US import business and a majority interest in Hungarian brewer Komaromi Sorgyar, its first Eastern European investment. Two years later Karel Vuursteen was appointed chairman.

The firm cut more than 1,300 jobs in 1993 and sold its spirits and wine operations the next year. In 1995 Heineken began a major spending spree, acquiring Interbrew Italia and 66% of Zlaty Bazant, the largest Slovakian brewery and maltworks (it acquired the rest in 1999).

To boost its sales in Poland, in 1998 Heineken raised its stake in brewer Zaklady Piwowarskie W. Zywcu (Zywiec) to 75%, bought a minority stake in Brewpole, and merged the companies to create the largest Polish brewer. That year Heineken bought about 25% of Pivara Skopje, the largest brewery in Macedonia. In 1999 the company bought about 18% of Israel's leading brewer, Tempo (Goldstar and Maccabee beers).

In 2000 Heineken bought 99% of Spanish brewer Cruzcampo, most of it from Diageo. Cruzcampo later merged with Heineken's Spanish brewer El Águila to create Heineken España.

In 2002 vice president Anthony Ruys replaced Vuursteen as CEO. Heineken also gained EU approval that year to buy a stake in German brewer Karlsberg. Also in 2002 Heineken agreed to buy stakes in two Central American breweries: Costa Rica's Florida Ice and Farm Company (FIFCO) and Nicaragua's Consorcio Cervecero Centroamericano S.A. (COCECA). The company later purchased Russian brewer Bravo International (which changed its name to Heineken Brewery in 2003). Heineken also bought a controlling stake in Egyptian brewer Al Ahram Beverages Co. in 2002. Ak Agram produces Fayrouz, a nonalcoholic beer favored by Muslims.

In 2003 Heineken purchased Austrian brewer BBAG Österreichische Brau-Beteiligungs-AG for $1.7 billion. It combined its regional operations with BBAG, creating Brau Union AG. In 2004 Heineken entered a joint venture with Lion Nathan Limited to sell its flagship brand in Australia. Heineken also began an aggressive push into Russia, purchasing Sobol Beer LLC in West Siberia and the Volga and Shikhan breweries. In 2004 it joined its Chinese operations with those of Asia Pacific Breweries to form Heineken Asia Pacific Breweries China (HAPBC); and that year HAPBC bought an approximate 21% stake in China's Kingway Brewery Holding.

In order to compete with competitors' low-calorie, low-carb beers, in 2005 the company introduced Heineken Premium Light in select markets in the US market. Also in 2005 the company formed a partnership with Diageo to produce and distribute Guinness in Russia. It also acquired approximately 91% of German brewer Würzburger Hofbräu AG.

EXECUTIVES

Chairman, Supervisory Board: Cees (C.J.A.) van Lede
Vice Chairman, Supervisory Board: Jan Maarten (J.M.) de Jong
CEO and Chairman, Executive Board: Jean François van Boxmeer, age 45, $869,276 pay (prior to title change)
CFO and Member, Executive Board: René Hooft (D.R.) Graafland, age 51, $869,276 pay
President, Africa & Middle East and Member, Executive Committee: Thom de Man, age 58
President, Americas; Member, Executive Committee: Massimo von Wunster, age 49
President, Asia/Pacific and Member, Executive Committee: Siep Hiemstra, age 51
President, Central and Eastern Europe and Member, Executive Committee: Nico Nusmeier, age 45
President, Western Europe and Member, Executive Board: Didier Debrosse, age 50
CEO, Heineken Italy: Massimo von Wunster
CEO, Heineken Russia: Roland Pirmez
Group Director, Business Development: Mark Koster
Interim Group Director, Commercial and Member, Executive Committee: Peter van Campen, age 42
Group Director, Control and Accounting and Member, Executive Committee: Floris Van Woerkom, age 43
Group Director, Corporate Relations and Member, Executive Committee: Sean O'Neill, age 43
Group Director, Human Resources and Member, Executive Committee: Frans van der Minne, age 58
Group Director, Legal Affairs: Steven van Maassakker
Group Director, Supply Chain and Member, Executive Committee: Marc Gross, age 47
Director, Investor Relations: Jan van de Merbel
Auditors: KPMG Accountants N.V.

LOCATIONS

HQ: Heineken N.V.
Tweede Weteringplantsoen 21,
1017 ZD Amsterdam, The Netherlands
Phone: +31-20-523-9239   **Fax:** +31-20-626-3503
US HQ: 360 Hamilton Ave., Ste. 1103,
White Plains, NY 10601
US Phone: 914-681-4100   **US Fax:** 914-681-1900
Web: www.heinekeninternational.com

Heineken has more than 115 breweries in more than 65 countries.

2005 Sales

	% of total
Western Europe	47
Central & Eastern Europe	25
The Americas	15
Africa & the Middle East	9
Asia/Pacific	4
Total	**100**

PRODUCTS/OPERATIONS

2005 Sales

	% of total
Beer	75
Soft drinks	12
Wines & spirits	8
Other	5
Total	**100**

Selected Brands

33 Export	Maccabee
ABC Stout	Moretti
Aguila	Murphy's
Alfa	Paulaner
Amstel	Piton
Buckler	Presidente
Cruzcampo	Prestige
Desperados	Primus
Fayrouz (alcohol-free)	Quilmes
Fischer	Santa Fe
Golden Brau	Schneider
Guinness (licensed)	Silva
Hacker-Pschorr	Summer
Havannah	Star
Heineken	Stella
Ichnusa	Tiger
Kaiser	Victoria
Kaliber	Vos
Karlsburg	Warka
Kingway	Wieckse Witte
Kriska	Zagorka
Loewenbrau (licensed)	

COMPETITORS

AmBev	Grolsch
Anheuser-Busch	Grupo Modelo
Asahi Breweries	InBev
Bavaria S.A.	Kirin Brewery Company
Boston Beer	Lion Nathan
Carlsberg	Mendocino Brewing
Cervecerías Unidas	Miller Brewing
Constellation Brands	Molson Coors
Diageo	SABMiller
FEMSA	San Miguel
Foster's	Scottish & Newcastle
Gambrinus	Taiwan Tobacco & Wine

HISTORICAL FINANCIALS

Company Type: Public

Income Statement

FYE: December 31

	REVENUE ($ mil.)	NET INCOME ($ mil.)	NET PROFIT MARGIN	EMPLOYEES
12/05	12,786	—	—	64,305
12/04	13,647	—	—	61,732
12/03	11,617	—	—	61,271
12/02	10,788	—	—	48,237
12/01	8,515	—	—	40,025
Annual Growth	**10.7%**	**—**	**—**	**12.6%**

Revenue History

Pink Sheets: HINKY

Henkel

Henkel is focusing on home and hearth. The company sold its chemical operations (Cognis and joint venture Henkel-Ecolab), fertilizer and plant care business (Substral), and adhesive products businesses to focus on its branded laundry, home care, cosmetics, and toiletries products. Its 2004 purchase of The Dial Corporation fuels its expansion into these US market segments. Most of Henkel's operations are centered in Europe, where the company is a leading maker of toiletries, cosmetics, detergents, and cleansers. It sold its adhesives and surface care preparation products division, Henkel Technologies, in mid-2006. Relatives of the founding Henkel family control the company.

Henkel bought US-based Dial Corporation (Dial soap, Purex laundry products, Renuzit air fresheners) in March 2004 for $2.9 billion in cash. The deal gave Henkel a greater presence in the US and allows Henkel to compete with consumer products giants Procter & Gamble (P&G) and Unilever.

With the P&G and Gillette merger deal (completed in October 2005), P&G was forced to find a buyer for its overlapping deodorant brands to get past antitrust regulators. That bode well for Henkel. In 2006 Henkel's Dial added the Right Guard, Soft & Dri, and Dry Idea brands previously owned by P&G and Gillette for about $420 million. Henkel's acquisition places the company in the top three suppliers in the US deodorants market. And paring down its food units, Henkel sold Dial's Armour-branded products (Treet, Vienna sausages), corn starch, and boxed pizza to Pinnacle Foods Group in 2006 for $183 million.

In October 2004 Henkel and US bleach giant Clorox agreed to a deal (in the form of an asset swap) that dissolved Henkel's nearly 30% stake in Clorox. The $2.8 billion transaction involved Henkel's purchase of Clorox's 20% stake in Henkel Iberica, a joint venture between the two in Portugal and Spain. Henkel also bought Clorox's

stake in a pesticide company as part of the transaction and added Combat insecticides and Soft Scrub bathroom cleaner to its brand portfolio.

To strengthen its foothold in the electronics market in China, Henkel in late 2005 bought a majority stake in Huawei Electronics Co. Ltd., a manufacturer of epoxy molding compounds for semiconductors.

HISTORY

In 1876 Fritz Henkel, a chemical plant worker, started Henkel & Cie in Aachen, Germany, to make a universal detergent. He moved the business to Düsseldorf in 1878 and launched Henkel's Bleaching Soda, one of Germany's first brand-name products. In the 1880s the company began making water glass, an ingredient of its detergent, which differs from soap in the way it emulsifies dirt. Henkel debuted Persil, a detergent that eliminated the need for rubbing or bleaching clothes, in 1907. Persil became a leading detergent in Germany.

Henkel set up an Austrian subsidiary in 1913. In response to a postwar adhesives shortage, the company started making glue for its own packaging and soon became Europe's leading glue maker. Henkel began making cleansers with newly developed phosphates in the late 1920s.

When Fritz died in 1930, Henkel stock was divided among his three children. In the 1930s the company sponsored a whaling fleet that provided fats for its products, and by 1939 the firm had 16 plants in Europe.

During WWII Henkel lost most of its foreign plants and made unbranded soap in Germany. After the war it retooled its plants, branched out into personal care products, and competed with Unilever, Procter & Gamble, and Colgate-Palmolive for control of the German detergent market. (By 1968 Henkel dominated, with close to a 50% share.)

In 1960 Henkel bought its first US company, Standard Chemicals (renamed Henkel Corp. in 1971). Konrad Henkel, who took over in 1961, modernized the company's image by making changes in management structure and marketing techniques. Henkel patented a substitute for environmentally harmful phosphates, acquired 15% of Clorox in 1974, and bought General Mills' chemical business in 1977.

Henkel, owned at the time by 66 family members, went public with nonvoting shares in 1985. It bought US companies Nopco (specialty chemicals) and Parker Chemical (metal surface pretreatment) in 1987 and Emery, the #1 US oleochemicals maker, in 1989.

In 1991 Henkel formed a partnership with Ecolab (of which it owned 24% — later expanded to 50%); acquired interests in Hungary, Poland, Russia, and Slovenia; and introduced Persil in Spain and Portugal. In 1994 Henkel expanded into China and bought 25% of a Brazilian detergent maker.

The company's 1995 acquisition of Hans Schwarzkopf GmbH made Henkel the #1 hair-coloring manufacturer in Germany. In 1997 Henkel paid $1.3 billion for US adhesive giant Loctite, its biggest purchase to date. Henkel pushed into the US toiletries market in 1998 by paying $93 million for DEP and creating a new subsidiary, Schwarzkopf & DEP Inc.

Henkel picked up Yamahatsu Sangyo, a Japanese maker of hair colorants, in 2000. The company sold its Substral unit (fertilizer and plant care) to Scotts Company (now Scotts Miracle-Gro). In 2001 Henkel bought TOTAL's metal-treatment chemicals business. In addition, the company sold its Cognis specialty chemicals unit to private equity funds Schroeder Ventures and Goldman Sachs Capital Partners for about $2.2 billion. Also in 2001 Henkel also said it would cut 2,500-3,000 jobs (about 5% of its workforce) over the next two years. That year the company also sold its stake in joint venture Henkel-Ecolab to Ecolab for about $430 million.

In March 2003 Henkel bought a 7% stake in German hair-care company Wella. Later that year Henkel purchased a majority stake in La Luz S.A., a Central American manufacturer and marketer of detergents and household cleaners. (Henkel entered the Latin American detergents market via Mexico in 2000.)

Henkel strengthened its adhesives business in Russia and North, Central, and Eastern Europe when it acquired Makroflex from YIT Construction Ltd. in July 2003. Makroflex, located in Finland and Estonia, develops, makes, and sells sealants and insulation materials for the construction industry.

In 2004 Henkel acquired Alberto-Culver's Indola European professional hair care business.

In June 2006 the company sold its rubber-to-substrate bonding and rubber coating business to North Carolina-based LORD Corporation.

EXECUTIVES

Chairman of the Supervisory Board: Albrecht Woeste, age 70
Chairman of the Management Board; President and CEO: Ulrich Lehner, age 60
Vice Chairman: Winfried Zander, age 51
Management Board, Cosmetics/Toiletries: Hans Van Bylen, age 45
Management Board, Consumer and Craftsman Adhesives; Chairman, Henkel Consumer Adhesives: Alois Linder, age 59
Management Board, Finance: Lothar Steineback, age 58
Management Board, Henkel Technologies; Chairman, Henkel Corp., USA: Jochen Krautter, age 64
Management Board, Human Resources, Purchasing, Information Technologies, and Infrastructure Services: Kasper B. Rorsted, age 43
Management Board, Laundry and Home Care: Friedrich Stara, age 57
VP, Corporate Communications: Ernst Primosch
VP, Corporate Development, Henkel Merger Corporation: Helmut Nuhn
VP, Henkel Merger Corporation: Kenneth R. Pina
Operating Management, Home Care/MENA/Asia Pacific/Central America, Laundry and Home Care: Alain Bauwens
President, CFO, and Director, Henkel Corporation; President and Director, Henkel of America: John E. Knudson
President and CEO, The Dial Corporation: Bradley A. (Brad) Casper
Operating Management, Research/Technology: Wolfgang Gawrisch
Operating Management, Research and Development, Technologies: Ramón Bacardit
Corporate Communications, Business and Finance: Lars Witteck
Operating Management, Human Resources: Dirk-Stephan Koedijk
Auditors: KPMG Deutsche Treuhand-Gesellschaft AG

LOCATIONS

HQ: Henkel KGaA
 Henkelstrasse 67, D-40191 Düsseldorf, Germany
Phone: +49-211-797-0   **Fax:** +49-211-798-2484
US HQ: 2200 Renaissance Blvd., Ste. 200, Gulph Mills, PA 19406
US Phone: 610-270-8100   **US Fax:** 610-270-8104
Web: www.henkel.com

2005 Sales

	% of total
Europe, Africa & Middle East	62
North America	23
Asia/Pacific	8
Latin America	5
Corporate	2
Total	**100**

PRODUCTS/OPERATIONS

2005 Sales

	% of total
Laundry & home care	34
Henkel Technologies	27
Cosmetics/toiletries	22
Adhesives	15
Corporate	2
Total	**100**

Selected Products

Adhesives
 Consumer and craftsmen adhesives
  Adhesive tapes
  Building chemicals
  Ceiling, wall covering, and tile adhesives
  Coatings
  Contact adhesives
  Correction rollers
  Cyanoacrylates
  Flooring adhesives
  Glue rollers
  Glue sticks
  Home-decoration products
  Polyurethane foam fillers
  PVC pipe adhesives
  Roofing products
  Sealants
  Wallpaper pastes
  Wood glues
 Engineering adhesives
  Assembly adhesives
  High-performance sealants
  Reactive sealants
  Sealing systems
 Industrial and packaging adhesives
  Adhesives for nonwovens
  Adhesives for the wood-processing industry
  Bookbinding adhesives
  Cigarette adhesives
  Laminating adhesives
  Leather board
  Packaging and labeling adhesives
  Pressure-sensitive adhesives
  Rubber-to-metal bonding agents
  Shoe adhesives
  Wood adhesives
Cosmetics and Toiletries
 Bath and shower products
 Dental care and oral hygiene products
 Deodorants
 Hair colorants
 Hair salon products
 Hairstyling and permanent-wave products
 Perfumes and fragrances
 Shampoos and conditioners
 Skin care products
 Skin creams
 Toilet soaps
Detergents and Household Cleansers
 Bath and toilet cleansers
 Dishwashing products
 Fabric softeners
 Floor and carpet care products
 Furniture and kitchen care products
 Glass cleaners
 Heavy-duty detergents
 Household cleansers
 Plant care products
 Scouring agents
 Shoe care and laundry conditioning products
 Specialty detergents

Industrial and Institutional Hygiene and Surface Technologies
 Industrial and Institutional Hygiene
  Products, appliances, equipment, systems, and services for cleaning, laundry, maintenance, sanitizing, and disinfecting
 Surface Technologies
  Antifreeze agents and corrosion inhibitors for automotive cooling systems
  CFC substitutes for cleaning applications
  Cleaning products
  Corrosion inhibitors
  Corrosion-protection waxes
  Dispersion adhesives
  Elastomer sealants
  Epoxide structural adhesives
  Hotmelt adhesives
  Lubricants
  Polyurethane adhesives
  Process control and metering equipment
  Products and applications for the chemical surface treatment of metals and metal substitutes
  Products for conversion processing
  PVC and polyacrylate plastisols
  Specialty products for the automotive industry

COMPETITORS

3M
Alticor
Avon
Bayer
Beiersdorf
Church & Dwight
Colgate-Palmolive
Dow Chemical
Estée Lauder
H.B. Fuller
Johnson & Johnson
Kimberly-Clark
L'Oréal
Playtex
Procter & Gamble
Reckitt Benckiser
Sara Lee
S.C. Johnson
Shiseido
Unilever

HISTORICAL FINANCIALS

Company Type: Public

Income Statement

FYE: December 31

	REVENUE ($ mil.)	NET INCOME ($ mil.)	NET PROFIT MARGIN	EMPLOYEES
12/05	14,181	912	6.4%	52,565
12/04	14,448	2,367	16.4%	49,947
12/03	11,844	651	5.5%	48,628
12/02	10,121	456	4.5%	48,638
12/01	11,569	445	3.8%	59,995
Annual Growth	**5.2%**	**19.7%**	**—**	**(3.3%)**

Net Income History

German: HENKY

Hitachi

Hitachi, which means "risen sun," is looking for a new dawn of profits from its galaxy of businesses. The company is a world-leading maker of powerful, corporate transaction-oriented mainframes, as well as semiconductors, PCs, and other information system and telecommunications technologies. Hitachi also makes elevators and escalators, industrial robots and control systems, and power plant equipment. The company's power and industrial systems unit is its biggest revenue producer. Other products include metals, wire, and cable. Hitachi's consumer goods range from TVs to refrigerators and washing machines; the company also has operations in financial services, property management, and transportation.

Decreased demand for PC components and weakness in the telecom sector hurt Hitachi in the early 21st century, and the company is working to cut costs and reduce debt. It also hopes to combine packages of information services with more of its products.

The company has agreed with General Electric to link their businesses in nuclear energy. GE will buy an equity stake of around 20% in Hitachi's existing nuclear energy business, while Hitachi will invest in GE Nuclear Energy, a unit of GE Energy. Hitachi and GE were selected in mid-2006 to build two nuclear reactors outside of Houston, a $5.2 billion project.

Hitachi has offered to take control of Clarion, a manufacturer of audio and navigation systems for motor vehicles. In 2000 the company established a joint venture with Clarion, HCX, and in 2004 Hitachi became Clarion's largest shareholder, buying nearly 15% of the company. Hitachi offered to increase its ownership to just over 50%, spending more than ¥23 billion (about $194 million or €154 million). Hitachi sees the acquisition strengthening its position in the car information systems market. If Clarion shareholders respond enthusiastically to Hitachi's offer, Hitachi could be on the hook for nearly ¥56 billion (more than $466 million or €371 million) in purchasing Clarion shares.

HISTORY

Namihei Odaira, an employee of Kuhara Mining in the Japanese coastal city of Hitachi, wanted to prove that Japan did not have to depend on foreigners for technology. In 1910 he began building electric motors in Kuhara's engineering and repair shop. Japanese power companies were forced to buy Odaira's generators when WWI made imports scarce. Impressed, they reordered, and in 1920 Hitachi (meaning "risen sun") became an independent company.

During the 1920s acquisitions and growth turned Hitachi into a major manufacturer of electrical equipment and machinery. In the 1930s and 1940s, Hitachi developed vacuum tubes and light bulbs and produced radar and sonar for the Japanese war effort. Postwar occupation forces removed Odaira and closed 19 Hitachi plants. Reeling from the plant closures, war damage, and labor strife, Hitachi was saved from bankruptcy by US military contracts during the Korean War.

In the 1950s Hitachi became a supplier to Nippon Telegraph and Telephone (NTT), the state-owned telecommunications monopoly. Japan's economic recovery led to strong demand for the company's communications and electrical equipment. Hitachi began mass-producing home appliances, radios, TVs, and transistors. The group spun off Hitachi Metals and Hitachi Cable in 1956 and Hitachi Chemical in 1963.

With the help of NTT, the Ministry of International Trade and Industry, and technology licensed from RCA (bought by General Electric in 1986), Hitachi produced its first computer in 1965. Hitachi built factories in Southeast Asia and started manufacturing integrated circuits.

Hitachi launched an IBM-compatible computer in 1974. The company sold its computers in the US through Itel until 1979, when Itel was bought by National Semiconductor, and afterward through National Semi's National Advanced Systems (NAS) unit. In 1982 FBI agents caught Hitachi staff buying documents allegedly containing IBM software secrets. Settlement of a civil lawsuit required Hitachi to make payments to IBM for eight years as compensation for the use of IBM's software.

When in the late 1980s the rising Japanese yen hurt exports, Hitachi focused on its domestic market and invested heavily in factory automation. But a recession at home caused earnings to fall. In 1988 the company and Texas Instruments joined in the costly development and production of 16-megabyte dynamic random-access memory (DRAM) semiconductors. In 1989 Hitachi bought 80% of NAS, giving it direct control of its US distribution.

Despite its rivalry with IBM, in 1991 Hitachi began to resell IBM notebook PCs under its own name in Japan. Tokyo police in 1997 began investigating Hitachi, charging that the company and others had paid off a corporate racketeer. A slump in semiconductor prices, coupled with the Asian economic turmoil, hurt Hitachi in 1998. Etsuhiko Shoyama became president the next year, replacing Tsutomu Kanai, who became chairman. Hitachi posted its then-worst loss in history in 1999; the firm combined some subsidiaries and announced layoffs.

Hitachi teamed with Sun Microsystems in 2002 in a multibillion-dollar storage software distribution and cross-licensing agreement. The company also formed a joint venture with IBM for Hitachi to acquire IBM's disk drive operations, which was launched the following year as Hitachi Global Storage Technologies.

In 2003 the company unveiled a finger vein authentication system, for use in confirming user identities. It sold its Hitachi Printing Solutions subsidiary to Ricoh in 2004. Hitachi also announced plans for an LCD television joint venture with Toshiba and Matsushita Electric in 2004, and a plasma television joint venture with Matsushita Electric in 2005. It collaborated with NEC again on forming a joint venture, ALAXALA Networks, to make backbone routers and switches for communications networks. Hitachi took a 60% interest in ALAXALA.

In early 2005 Hitachi launched a computer server systems business in North America as part of Hitachi America.

Etsuhiko Shoyama, president and CEO of Hitachi since mid-2003, became chairman and CEO of the company in early 2006. EVP Kazuo Furukawa was promoted to president and COO at the same time.

EXECUTIVES

Chairman and CEO: Etsuhiko Shoyama, age 70
President and COO: Kazuo Furukawa, age 60
EVP; General Manager of Compliance Division: Takashi Hatchoji, age 59
EVP; Chief Hitachi Group Headquarters: Takashi Miyoshi, age 59
EVP; General Manager, Research and Development Group: Michiharu Nakamura, age 64
EVP; Chief Executive for North America, CEO of Hitachi Global Storage Technologies, Inc.: Hiroaki Nakanishi, age 60
EVP; General Manager, Information Business Group: Isao Ono
SVP; President and CEO, Automotive Systems Group: Taiji Hasegawa, age 59
SVP; General Manager of Corporate Marketing Group, Group-wide Strategic Sales Office, Customer Satisfaction Promotion Center, General Manager of Corporate Export Regulation Division: Tadahiko Ishigaki, age 60
SVP; General Manager, Research and Development Group: Junzo Kawakami, age 62
SVP; Hitachi Group Companies Management Assistance, and President and Director of Hitachi Displays, Ltd.: Kazuhiro Mori, age 60
SVP; President and CEO, Urban Planning and Development Systems Group, General Manager of Motor Power Systems Division: Kunihiko Ohnuma, age 60
SVP, Power Systems Business, Production Technology, Power Technology: Shozo Saito, age 61
SVP; President, CEO, and Chief Technology Officer, Information and Telecommunication Systems Group: Manabu Shinomoto, age 58
SVP and Chief Executive, Europe: Sir Stephen Gomersall, age 58
SVP; CEO and Chief Innovation Officer for China: Minoru Tsukada, age 59
VP; Human Capital, and General Manager of Secretarial Office and Head Office Business Support Division: Shinjiro Kasai, age 60
VP, Marketing and Sales, and Deputy General Manager: Steven King
Director, Marketing, Hitachi America: Colin Bruce
Auditors: Ernst & Young ShinNihon

LOCATIONS

HQ: Hitachi, Ltd.
(Hitachi Seisakusho Kabushiki Kaisha)
4-6, Kanda-Surugadai, Chiyoda-ku,
Tokyo 101-8010, Japan
Phone: +81-3-3258-1111   **Fax:** +81-3-3258-2375
US HQ: 50 Prospect Ave., Tarrytown, NY 10591
US Phone: 914-332-5800   **US Fax:** 914-332-5555
Web: www.hitachi.com

Hitachi has primary operations in China, France, Japan, the Netherlands, Singapore, the UK, and the US.

2006 Sales

	% of total
Asia	
Japan	70
Other countries	15
North America	9
Europe	5
Other regions	1
Total	**100**

PRODUCTS/OPERATIONS

2006 Sales

	% of total
Power & industrial systems	25
Information & telecommunication systems	21
High-functional materials & components	15
Digital media & consumer products	12
Electronic devices	11
Financial services	5
Logistics, services & other	11
Total	**100**

Selected Products and Services

Power and industrial systems
  Air-conditioning equipment
  Automotive equipment
  Construction machinery
  Elevators
  Environmental control systems
  Escalators
  Hydroelectric power plants
  Industrial machinery and plant construction
  Nuclear power plants
  Rolling stock
  Thermal power plants
Information and telecommunication systems
  Computer peripherals
  Fiber-optic components
  Mainframes
  PCs
  RAID storage systems
  Servers
  Software
  Switches
  Systems integration
High-functional materials and components
  Cables
  Carbon products
  Chemical products
  Components
  Copper products
  Electrical insulating materials
  Fine ceramics
  Magnetic materials
  Malleable cast-iron products
  Printed circuit boards
  Specialty steels
  Synthetic resins
  Wires
Electronic devices
  LCDs
  Medical electronics equipment
  Memories
  Multi-purpose semiconductors
  Semiconductor manufacturing equipment
  System LSIs
  Testing and measurement equipment
Digital media and consumer products
  Batteries
  Fluorescent lamps
  Information storage media
  Kitchen appliances
  LCD projectors
  Mobile phones
  Optical storage drives
  Refrigerators
  Room air conditioners
  TVs
  VCRs
  Videotapes
  Washing machines
Financial services
  Insurance services
  Leasing
  Loan guarantees
Logistics, services, and other
  General trading
  Property management
  Transportation

COMPETITORS

Alcatel-Lucent	NEC
ALSTOM	Nippon Steel
Applied Materials	Nokia
Canon	Nortel Networks
Dell	Oki Electric
Ericsson	Philips Electronics
Fluor	Samsung Group
Fujitsu	SANYO
GE	Sharp
Hewlett-Packard	Siemens AG
IBM	Sony
Intel	TDK
Johnson Controls	Texas Instruments
Kyocera	Toshiba
Matsushita	Truly International
McDermott	Unisys
Micron Technology	United Technologies
Mitsubishi Electric	Whirlpool
Motorola	

HISTORICAL FINANCIALS

Company Type: Public

Income Statement

FYE: March 31

	REVENUE ($ mil.)	NET INCOME ($ mil.)	NET PROFIT MARGIN	EMPLOYEES
3/06	80,451	317	0.4%	306,876
3/05	83,952	479	0.6%	323,072
3/04	82,008	151	0.2%	306,876
3/03	67,992	231	0.3%	320,528
3/02	60,224	(3,629)	—	306,989
Annual Growth	7.5%	—	—	(0.0%)

2006 Year-End Financials

Debt ratio: 56.6%
Return on equity: 1.5%
Cash ($ mil.): 6,979
Current ratio: 1.23
Long-term debt ($ mil.): 12,057

Net Income History

NYSE: HIT

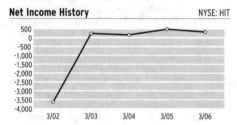

Hollinger

Hollinger makes headlines as one of the largest newspaper groups in the world. It operates through a 19% ownership stake (70% voting interest) in Sun Times Media Group, which publishes more than 200 daily, non-daily, trade, and specialty titles, primarily in the Chicago area. Sun Times Media owns the *Chicago Sun-Times*, as well as a large number of community newspapers. The company also controls some commercial real estate in Canada. Embattled former chief Conrad Black had controlled about 78% of the company through private holding company Ravelston. (Black resigned from Ravelston in 2005.)

Hollinger has been significantly paring down operations in recent years in an effort to focus on its larger newspapers. The company sold most of its Canadian newspapers in 2000, but kept a 50% stake in the *National Post* until

2002, when it sold out to partner CanWest. The company sold its remaining Canadian assets in 2006. It also sold many of its US community papers and in 2004 sold *The Jerusalem Post* for $13 million to Israeli publisher Mirkaei Tikshoret Group.

Mainly, however, the company has been embroiled in a mess involving Black, its former CEO. In 2003 its Hollinger International (now Sun Times Media), announced it was evaluating strategic alternatives and made a number of management changes, including the removal of Black as CEO after the discovery of certain unauthorized payments (more than $400 million, according to a special committee report) to him and other executives.

The SEC announced an investigation into the controversial payments and has filed civil-fraud charges against Black and former president and COO David Radler. Radler and Mark Kipnis, the company's former legal counsel, have been indicted in federal court on seven counts of fraud. Radler is cooperating with investigators and has pleaded guilty to one count of mail fraud. Black has pleaded not guilty to the charges.

Black's plan to sell his share of Hollinger International to British billionaires, the Barclay brothers, was blocked by a US judge in 2004. Press Acquisitions Limited, a group controlled by the Barclay brothers, won the bidding ($1.3 billion) for Hollinger International's London newspaper group including *The Daily Telegraph*. Hollinger lost a challenge to the bid (arguing that a vote of shareholders is required for the deal's completion) and the deal closed in 2004.

Black was court-ordered to pay Hollinger International nearly $30 million, which he later paid. A lawsuit filed by Hollinger International accused Black and other company executives of violating racketeering laws and asked for more than $1.2 billion in damages. A judge dismissed the racketeering suit in fall 2004, but left the possibility open for the company to refile. Hollinger International filed new charges later in 2004 against Black and another company executive, accusing them of breaching their fiduciary duty. Black ran into more problems in 2005 when Hollinger Inc. sued him and others for more than $525 million, charging a multitude of misappropriations and other misconduct.

In 2005, irate shareholders demanded a change in the board of directors, complaining about the direction of the company and the levels of fees the board members were paid. The company agreed to increase the number of board members to seven, comprised of five new members and two remaining members.

HISTORY

A born entrepreneur, Conrad Black bought his first share of stock (in General Motors) at age 8. Some of his early childhood deals weren't quite so constructive: He was expelled from a private school at age 14 for selling exams and was kicked out of one law school after spending all his time playing the stock market.

Black entered publishing in 1969 when he and Peter White founded Sterling Newspapers and bought the *Sherbrooke Record*. The two added to their flagship with a group of small daily papers in British Columbia, Quebec, and Prince Edward Island. In 1975 Black bought his father's 22% of the Ravelston Corporation, which owned Argus, a company formed in 1945 by E. P. Taylor to invest in breweries, malting and bottling operations, and a chemical business. Black took control of the company in the late 1970s by obtaining a loan through Sterling.

After assuming the leadership of Argus (through Ravelston), Black sold off chunks of the company to refine its holdings to key businesses. The company adopted the Hollinger name (left over from Argus' early investment in Hollinger Consolidated Gold Mines) in 1985 and gained control of struggling newspaper *The Daily Telegraph* (London), which it turned around by cutting staff and modernizing. In 1989 the firm purchased Jerusalem Post Publications.

Hollinger continued to acquire and restore struggling companies in the 1990s. It bought a stake in Southam in 1992 and in 1994 acquired the Sun-Times Company, publisher of the *Chicago Sun-Times*.

Hollinger purchased two daily and 12 non-daily papers in 1995 from Armadale, a closely held Canadian firm. That year it sold its interests in the Telegraph Group, Southam, and John Fairfax (an Australian publisher) to subsidiary Hollinger International.

In 1996 Hollinger International assumed full control of the Telegraph Group and increased its stake in Southam to about 51%. It sold most of its John Fairfax holdings to New Zealand-based Brierley Investments. Hollinger International finally bought all of Southam in 1999. That year Hollinger combined the smaller publications of Southam, Sterling Newspapers, and UniMedia into Hollinger Canadian Newspapers (in which it holds an 87% stake).

In 2000 the firm decided to sell off hundreds of its Canadian and American community newspapers and trade magazines in order to concentrate on its larger papers. It sold 13 of its larger Canadian daily newspapers, 136 community newspapers, and a 50% stake in the *National Post*, to CanWest Global Communications for $3.5 billion. (CanWest purchased the rest of the *National Post* in 2002.) It also sold off most of its US community papers. In late 2000 the company bought Copley's Fox Valley Press newspapers in Chicago. In 2001 Black announced that Hollinger would join with a small group of investors to launch a new New York City daily paper in 2002 called the *New York Sun* aimed at a conservative audience. (The *Sun* debuted in April 2002.)

After a scandal involving unauthorized payments, Black stepped down as CEO and chairman of Hollinger International in 2003. He resigned from Hollinger Inc. in 2004. Another problem arose in 2004 when it was discovered that the *Chicago Sun-Times* and the *Daily Southtown* had inflated their circulation numbers for several years. Advertisers filed lawsuits against the company; advertisers pay rates based on circulation. The company agreed to a class action settlement in which it would pay $7.7 million and give away $7.3 million in advertising to settle the suits. Paul Carroll, a director on the company's board, was named president and CEO in 2005, but his employment was terminated later that same year.

EXECUTIVES

Chairman: Stanley M. Beck, age 71
Chief Restructuring Officer: Randall C. (Randy) Benson, age 46
VP and Group Corporate Controller:
Frederick A. Creasey, age 51
Treasurer: Tatiana Samila
Auditors: KPMG LLP

LOCATIONS

HQ: Hollinger Inc.
10 Toronto St., Toronto, Ontario M5C 2B7, Canada
Phone: 416-363-8721 **Fax:** 416-364-2088
US HQ: 401 N. Wabash Ave., Ste. 740, Chicago, IL 60611
US Phone: 312-321-2299 **US Fax:** 312-321-0629
Web: www.hollingerinc.com

COMPETITORS

Dow Jones
Gannett
Hearst
New York Times
News Corp.
Quebecor
Tribune
Washington Post

Honda

According to Honda, you might be in your *Element* if you buy a *Ridgeline*. Honda is Japan's #3 automaker (after Toyota and Nissan) and the world's largest motorcycle producer. The company's car models include the Accord, CR-V, Civic, Element, and Ridgeline as well as gasoline-electric hybrid versions of the Civic and Accord. Honda's line of motorcycles includes everything from scooters to superbikes. The company also makes a line of ATVs and personal watercraft. Honda's power products division makes commercial and residential-use machinery (lawn mowers, snowblowers), portable generators, and outboard motors.

Honda is enjoying brisk motorcycle sales, particularly in Asia where motorcycles are a popular mode of transportation. The company has announced plans to build a $1 million motorcycle production facility in Argentina to keep up with the growing demand in South America. In North America, Europe, and at home in Japan, Honda has introduced new models of sport bikes. Honda has also completed the conversion of its entire motorcycle lineup to cleaner-burning four-stroke engines.

On the automotive side, Honda gained market share in the US through its entry to the light truck segment with the Ridgeline pickup. In Europe Honda is capitalizing on the popularity of diesel models, and in China the company is selling a lot of cars as the Honda brand grows in popularity. Sales have been flat in Japan, but Honda responded by tightening up its domestic sales organization.

Going forward, Honda is planning on modest growth, primarily in the US and China, but believes growth will be tempered by increasing fuel and raw materials costs as well as fluctuations in foreign currency exchange rates.

To keep its Asian motorcycle momentum rolling Honda is striving to remain competitive on price while expanding manufacturing capacity at facilities in India, China, and the Philippines. In Europe the company plans to keep delivering on the sport bikes that are popular there.

Based on the Ridgeline's success, Honda's automotive business in the US will see the introduction of additional light truck models, as well as a re-vamping of the stalwart Civic. Honda also introduced the Fit in early 2006 aimed at capturing young, new, and hopefully loyal, Honda customers. While the passenger car market in the US is waning, Honda is confident it can maintain and even grow its share of that market segment. As part of this scheme Honda has ceased production of the slow-selling Insight hybrid (September 2006). Honda plans to replace the Insight with a less expensive hybrid in 2009.

The automotive market in China is slowing, however the potential for growth is still enormous. Honda introduced a revamped Civic to China in 2006 and planned to grow overall capacity. The company is also targeting Indonesia and India for sales growth with the Jazz and Fit models that have been hits in those markets.

HISTORY

Soichiro Honda spent six years as an apprentice at Tokyo service station Art Shokai before opening his own branch of the repair shop in Hamamatsu in 1928. He also raced cars and in 1931 received a patent for metal spokes that replaced wood in wheels.

Honda started a piston ring company in 1937. During WWII the company produced metal propellers for Japanese bombers. When bombs and an earthquake destroyed most of his factory, Honda sold it to Toyota in 1945.

In 1946 Honda began motorizing bicycles with war-surplus engines. When this proved popular, Honda began making engines. The company was renamed Honda Motor Co. in 1948 and began producing motorcycles. In 1949 Soichiro Honda hired Takeo Fujisawa to manage the company so Honda could focus on engineering. Honda's innovative overhead valve design made its early 1950s Dream model a runaway success. In 1952 the smaller Cub, sold through bicycle dealers, accounted for 70% of Japan's motorcycle production.

Funded by a 1954 public offering and Mitsubishi Bank, Honda expanded capacity and began exporting. American Honda Motor Company was formed in Los Angeles in 1959, accompanied by the slogan "You meet the nicest people on a Honda" in a campaign crafted to counter the stereotypical biker image. Honda added overseas factories in the 1960s and began producing light-weight trucks, sports cars, and minicars.

The company began selling its tiny 600 model in the US in 1970, but it was the Civic, introduced in 1973, that first scored with the US car market. Three years later Honda introduced the Accord, which featured an innovative frame adaptable for many models. In 1982 Accord production started at the company's Ohio plant.

Ex-Honda engineer Nobuhiko Kawamoto was named president in 1990, a year before Soichiro Honda died. Kawamoto cut costs and continued to expand the company internationally. That year the Big Three US automakers (GM, Ford, and Chrysler), clamoring for trade sanctions against Japanese carmakers, threw Honda out of the US carmakers' trade association.

In 1997 Honda bought Peugeot's plant in Guangzhou, China, and boosted its US vehicle production by opening an all-terrain vehicle (ATV) plant in South Carolina in 1998. American Honda agreed in 1998 to pay $330 million to settle a class-action lawsuit filed by 1,800 dealers who accused Honda of delivering popular models only to dealers who paid bribes (18 executives from American Honda were convicted). That year Hiroyuki Yoshino, an engineer with US management experience, succeeded Kawamoto as CEO.

In 1999 Honda and GM agreed to a deal in which Honda would supply low-emission V6 engines and automatic transmissions to GM, while Isuzu, a GM affiliate, would supply Honda with diesel engines. In 2000 Honda announced that its super low-emission engine (as called for by US regulators) would make its mass-market debut in 2001, well ahead of competitor versions.

Honda announced in 2001 that it would introduce diesel-powered vehicles in Europe by 2003. Later that year Honda's R&D unit set up a solar-powered hydrogen production station in California as part of its efforts to develop renewable-energy fuel cell vehicles.

In 2006 Honda announced it would enter the aviation market with the introduction of what Honda CEO Takeo Fukui called the "Honda Civic of the sky." Honda said it would begin taking orders for the six-passenger, twin-engine Honda-Jet in late 2006, although the planes won't be available until about 2010.

EXECUTIVES

President, CEO, and Director: Takeo Fukui, age 62
EVP and Director; COO, Business Management Operations: Satoshi Aoki, age 60
Senior Managing Director; President and Director, American Honda Motor Co.; President and Director, Honda North America, Inc.: Koichi Kondo, age 59
Senior Managing Director; COO, Motorcycle Operations: Minoru Harada, age 59
Senior Managing Director; COO, Production Operations; Risk Management Officer; General Supervisor, Information Systems: Koki Hirashima, age 60
Senior Managing Director; President, Honda R&D Co., Ltd.: Motoatsu Shiraishi, age 60
Senior Managing Director; COO, Regional Operations (Asia and Oceania); President and Director, Asian Honda Motor Co., Ltd.: Satoshi Toshida, age 59
Senior Managing Director; COO, Regional Operations (China); President of Honda Motor (China) Investment Co. Ltd.: Atsuyoshi Hyogo, age 57
Senior Managing Director; General Supervisor, Purchasing Policy and Quality: Michiyoshi Hagino, age 62
Senior Managing Director, Government and Industrial Affairs; COO, Regional Sales Operations (Japan); Chief Officer of Driving Safety Promotion Center in Regional Sales Operations (Japan): Satoshi Dobashi, age 59
Managing Director; President and Director, Honda Motor Europe Ltd., COO, Regional Operations (Europe, Middle East and Africa): Shigeru Takagi, age 54
Senior Managing Director and Corporate Auditor: Hiroshi Okubo, age 61
Managing Director; COO, Automobile Operations: Hiroshi Kuroda, age 58
Managing Director; COO, Customer Service Operations: Akira Takano, age 57
Managing Director; COO, Purchasing Operations: Toru Onda, age 57
Managing Director and Compliance Officer: Mikio Yoshimi, age 59
Managing Officer; President and Director, Honda of America Mfg., Inc.: Akio Hamada
Auditors: KPMG

LOCATIONS

HQ: Honda Motor Co., Ltd.
(Honda Giken Kogyo Kabushiki Kaisha)
2-1-1 Minami-Aoyama, Minato-ku,
Tokyo 107-8556, Japan
Phone: +81-3-3423-1111   **Fax:** +81-3-5412-1515
US HQ: 540 Madison Ave., 32nd Fl.,
New York, NY 10022
US Phone: 212-355-9191   **US Fax:** 212-813-0260
Web: world.honda.com

2006 Sales

	$ mil.	% of total
North America	46,439	55
Asia		
Japan	14,399	17
Other countries	9,226	11
Europe	8,580	10
Other regions	5,574	7
Total	**84,218**	**100**

PRODUCTS/OPERATIONS

2006 Sales

	$ mil.	% of total
Automobiles	68,040	81
Motorcycles	10,420	12
Power products & other	3,150	4
Financial services	2,608	3
Total	**84,218**	**100**

Selected Models and Productions

Car and Truck Models
  Accord (coupe, sedan)
  Accord Hybrid Sedan
  Acura (MDX, RDX, RL, RSX, TL, TSX)
  Civic (coupe, sedan)
  Civic GX
  Civic Hybrid
  Civic Si
  CR-V (SUV)
  Element
  Fit
  Odyssey (minivan)
  Pilot (SUV)
  Ridgeline (pickup)
  S2000 (roadster)
Motorcycle Models
  CBR600F4i
  FourTrax (ATV)
  Gold Wing
  Interceptor
  Nighthawk
  Rebel
  Shadow Spirit 750
  Silver Wing (scooter)
  ST1300
  ST1300 ABS
  Valkyrie
Power Products
  Commercial mowers
  Engines
  Lawn mowers
  Marine motors
  Portable generators
  Pumps
  Snowblowers
  Tillers
  Trimmers

COMPETITORS

Black & Decker	Kia Motors
BMW	Land Rover
Briggs & Stratton	Mazda
Brunswick	Nissan
Caterpillar	Peugeot
DaimlerChrysler	Renault
Deere	Saab Automobile
Exmark Manufacturing	Suzuki Motor
Fiat	Textron
Ford	Toro
Fuji Heavy Industries	Toyota
General Motors	Triumph Motorcycles
Harley-Davidson	Volkswagen
Isuzu	Volvo
Kawasaki Heavy Industries	Yamaha Motor

HISTORICAL FINANCIALS

Company Type: Public

Income Statement

FYE: March 31

	REVENUE ($ mil.)	NET INCOME ($ mil.)	NET PROFIT MARGIN	EMPLOYEES
3/06	84,218	5,075	6.0%	144,785
3/05	80,446	4,522	5.6%	137,827
3/04	75,912	4,318	5.7%	131,600
3/03	66,163	3,541	5.4%	126,900
Annual Growth	8.4%	12.7%	—	4.5%

2006 Year-End Financials

Debt ratio: 45.5%
Return on equity: 15.5%
Cash ($ mil.): 6,352
Current ratio: 1.16
Long-term debt ($ mil.): 15,972

Net Income History

NYSE: HMC

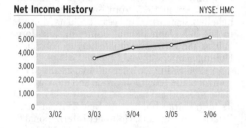

Hopewell Holdings

Hopewell Holdings springs eternal in the mind of its founder and chairman, Sir Gordon Wu. Undeterred by the collapse of several projects in the wake of the Asian economic crisis, Wu has good reason to be hopeful about the future of his real estate and infrastructure development company as the market stabilizes. Hopewell has extensive holdings in real estate in Hong Kong (including Hopewell Centre and Panda Hotel) and is a major infrastructure developer. The company built toll roads and bridges, primarily in mainland China, but has spun off its Hopewell Highway Infrastructure Limited subsidiary (HHI) as a public company. It retains a majority stake (75%).

Although its property and hotel businesses are concentrated mainly in Hong Kong, where it gets most of its sales, Hopewell has worked on infrastructure projects (toll roads and bridges) primarily in China's fast-growing Guangdong province. Mainland toll roads had been one of Hopewell's primary operations, contributing heavily to its earnings. However, the group decided to spin off its mainland infrastructure projects to finance a controversial bridge that would link Hong Kong with Macao and Zhuhai on China's Pearl River delta.

One of the first companies outside China to invest in that country's infrastructure projects, Hopewell has been involved in building in China since the 1970s. In addition to the Hopewell Centre and Panda Hotel, the group's Hong Kong holdings include the Hongkong International Trade and Exhibition Centre, Mega Tower Hotel, and Nova Taipa Gardens. The group also operates the China Hotel in Guangzhou, the capital of Guangdong in southern China. And it is constructing a property development project in Huadu, Guangzhou called the Hopewell New

Town, which will consist of apartment units, townhouses, and commercial facilities.

A downturn in the economies of Europe, Japan, and the US has caused a decrease in customers for the group's hotel operations, but Hopewell has seen a substantial growth in visitors from the mainland. And the group's toll road business in the Pearl River Delta has helped bridge the company over an economic slump.

Asian economic instability, coupled with a few missteps in the region, has cost the company dearly. Hopewell had to halt construction on a 1,320-MW power plant in Indonesia after it was 80% complete. The company has disposed of its interest in the power station. In addition, the Thai government canceled Hopewell's participation in the Bangkok Elevated Road and Train System (BERTS) project after several delays, changes, and rising costs.

HISTORY

Sir Gordon Wu's Hopewell Holdings empire grew from humble beginnings. His father started out as a Hong Kong taxi owner and driver and helped finance Gordon's first-class education — he received an engineering degree from Princeton University.

On his return to Hong Kong in 1962, Wu took a job in the government's land department. He later left to help his father develop a property business. When his father retired in 1969, custom forbade Wu Sr. from handing the company over to Gordon, the seventh of nine children. Instead, he liquidated the firm and guaranteed a $2.5 million loan to his son to start a property company of his own.

By 1972 Wu's company was large enough to be listed on the Hong Kong Stock Exchange as Hopewell Holdings Limited. But his American-style "can-do" approach gained him some enemies. He took on the Hong Kong government after it banned him from building a towering headquarters in central Hong Kong — and won. The result was the 66-floor Hopewell Centre.

While visiting nearby Guangzhou in China to promote a hotel project in the early 1980s, Wu spotted opportunity in the region's frequent power outages. Realizing that the province would boom in the 1980s and 1990s, Wu dropped the hotel idea and persuaded China to let him build a power plant. By 1987 the 700-MW plant was on line.

Other major Chinese infrastructure projects followed, including contracts for two more power stations in Guangdong province and a contract to build China's first modern highway, a six-lane toll road linking the cities of Guangzhou and Hong Kong. Wu attributed his success in negotiating with the Chinese authorities to 11 years of lobbying and consuming gallons of *mao tai* (a very potent liquor served at formal dinners in China).

In 1990 Wu gained a contract with the Thai government for a mass transit system, the Bangkok Elevated Road and Train System (BERTS) project. But the project was soon delayed, first by political unrest and then by bureaucratic red tape.

Hopewell spun off 40% of its power subsidiary, Consolidated Electric Power Asia (CEPA), in 1993. The sale helped fund other projects, including the Guangdong toll road and a power plant in the Philippines. But the Philippines project ran into problems in 1995: Although the plant was completed, the local electric utility refused to take the power. That year Wu set the company up for another fall when he pledged $100 million to Princeton. (The Asian economic crisis forced him to postpone the pledge in 1999, by which time he had given only a third of the amount.)

By late 1995 Hopewell was hemorrhaging money. The Asian financial contagion of 1997-98 didn't help matters. In 1998 the elevated train project in Bangkok was halted by the Thai government, and Hopewell lost its $153 million stake in Peregrine Investment Holdings when the Hong Kong-based firm collapsed. Hopewell also stopped work on a major Indonesian power plant that it was building in a venture. The firm fell into the red in 1998.

That year, however, the company gained a contract to help build a toll road in southern China, and in 1999 it won another contract for a toll road in the Philippines. In fiscal 1999 Hopewell regained profitability, although it lost its listing on the Hong Kong index in 2000. In 2002 the company made plans to spin off its major toll road, the Guangzhou-Shenzhen Superhighway, and to rebid for the BERTS project. Also that year Sir Gordon stepped down from his duties as managing director but remained chairman of the group.

In 2003 the company listed its Hopewell Highway Infrastructure Limited subsidiary, which held most of its mainland-China transportation infrastructure interests, on the Hong Kong stock exchange. It also divested its interest in the Tanjung Jati B power project in Indonesia.

EXECUTIVES

Honorary Chairman: James M. H. Wu
Chairman: Sir Gordon Y. S. Wu, age 68
Vice Chairman and Managing Director: Eddie P. C. Ho, age 71
Deputy Managing Director: Josiah C. L. Kwok, age 52
Deputy Managing Director; Managing Director, Hopewell Highway Infrastructure Limited: Thomas J. Wu, age 32
Executive Director, Finance: Robert V. J. Nien, age 57
Executive Director: Albert K. Y. Yeung, age 53
Executive Director: David Y. G. Lui, age 59
Executive Director: Andy L. M. Cheung, age 38
Executive Director: Eddie W. C. Ho Jr., age 35
Company Secretary: Peter Y. W. Lee
Executive Director: Barry C. T. Mok, age 47
Auditors: Deloitte Touche Tohmatsu

LOCATIONS

HQ: Hopewell Holdings Limited
64th Fl., Hopewell Centre, 183 Queen's Rd. East, Wan Chai, Hong Kong
Phone: +852-2528-4975   **Fax:** +852-2865-6276
Web: www.hopewellholdings.com

Hopewell Holdings operates primarily in Asia, including China, Hong Kong, Indonesia, the Philippines, and Thailand.

2006 Sales

	% of total
Hong Kong	76
China & Macao	24
Total	**100**

PRODUCTS/OPERATIONS

2006 Sales

	% of total
Hotel operations, restaurant & catering	40
Property letting, agency & management	36
Infrastructure project investments	12
Property development	12
Total	**100**

Selected Subsidiaries

HH Finance Limited (loan financing)
Hopewell Centre Management Limited (property management)
Hopewell China Development (Superhighway) Limited (98%, investment in superhighway project)
Hopewell Construction Company, Limited (construction, project management, and investments)
Hopewell Food Industries Limited (restaurant operations)
Hopewell Guangzhou-Zhuhai Superhighway Development Limited (investment in superhighway project)
Hopewell Housing Limited (property agents and investment holding)
Hopewell Property Management Company Limited (building and car park management)
Hopewell Shunde Roads Limited (investment in highway systems project)
International Trademart Company Limited (property investment and operation of trademart)
Kowloon Panda Hotel Limited (hotel owernship and operations)

COMPETITORS

ABB
AES
ALSTOM
Bechtel
Fluor
Foster Wheeler
GE
Hutchison Whampoa
Jardine Matheson
Marriott
McDermott
Peter Kiewit Sons'
Siemens AG
Sime Darby
Swire Pacific

HISTORICAL FINANCIALS

Company Type: Public

Income Statement

	REVENUE ($ mil.)	NET INCOME ($ mil.)	NET PROFIT MARGIN	EMPLOYEES
6/06	120	335	279.3%	1,200
6/05	87	214	245.1%	1,110
6/04	84	186	222.4%	1,057
6/03	103	79	77.3%	1,100
6/02	145	44	30.0%	1,123
Annual Growth	**(4.7%)**	**66.5%**	**—**	**1.7%**

FYE: June 30

Net Income History

OTC: HOWWY

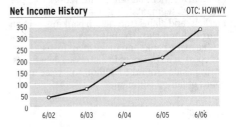

HSBC Holdings

HSBC would be a real alphabet soup if the company's name reflected its geographic diversity. HSBC Holdings has surpassed Citigroup as the largest bank in the world by assets and is active throughout the UK and Europe, North and South America, Hong Kong and the Pacific Rim, Australia, the Middle East, and Africa. All told, HSBC has more than 9,800 offices in nearly 80 countries, providing consumer and commercial banking services, credit cards, asset management, private banking, securities trading, insurance, and leasing. US operations, which include HSBC USA, got a boost with the 2003 purchase of consumer lender Household International (now HSBC Finance).

In 2004 HSBC acquired The Bank of Bermuda, as well as Marks and Spencer Financial Services (aka M&S Money), one of the UK's leading credit card issuers. It bought US credit card company Metris the following year.

Founded in Hong Kong in 1865, the company is targeting Asia for growth. In 2005 the company joined forces with Global Payments to provide merchant processing services in that part of the world; HSBC owns some 44% of the joint venture. In addition, the company bought a 70% stake in investment bank Dar es Salaam, becoming one of the first foreign banks to operate in Iraq after Saddam Hussein banned them from operating there some 35 years ago. HSBC also made the largest-ever investment at the time by a foreign bank in a Chinese bank when it bought almost 20% of Bank of Communications in 2004.

The company also owns all or parts of The Hongkong and Shanghai Banking Corporation, HSBC Bank Canada, HSBC France (formerly CCF), and Hong Kong's Hang Seng Bank. In Central and South America it operates primarily in Argentina, Brazil, and Mexico, but expanded in the region with its nearly $1.8 billion purchase of Panama-based banking group Banistmo, which also has operations in other Central American nations.

While not a major player in investment banking like many of its peers, HSBC is trying to grow its business. That may be easier said than done, considering many of its competitors are already entrenched in the industry. The company shook up its investment banking unit, reorganizing it into three segments — global banking, global markets, and global transaction banking — in an effort to jump-start the business.

Like many banks and investment firms, HSBC has boosted its business in distressed debt funds, setting aside around $1 billion to invest in the bonds of failing companies.

HISTORY

Scotsman Thomas Sutherland and other businessmen in 1865 opened the doors to Hongkong & Shanghai Bank, financing and promoting British imperial trade in opium, silk, and tea in East Asia. It soon established a London office and created an international branch network emphasizing China and East Asia. It claims to have been the first bank in Thailand (1888).

War repeatedly disrupted, but never demolished, the bank's operations. During WWII the headquarters were temporarily moved to London. (They moved back on a permanent basis in 1991.) The bank's chief prewar manager, Sir Vandeleur Grayborn, died in a Japanese POW camp. After the Communists took power in China in 1949, the bank gradually withdrew; by 1955 only its Shanghai office remained, and it was later closed. The bank played a key role in Hong Kong's postwar growth by financing industrialists who fled there from China.

In the late 1950s Hongkong & Shanghai Bank's acquisitions included the British Bank of the Middle East (founded 1889; now The Saudi British Bank) and Mercantile Bank (with offices in India and Southeast Asia). In 1965 the company bought 62% of Hang Seng, Hong Kong's #2 bank. It also added new subsidiaries, including Wayfoong (mortgage and small-business finance, 1960) and Wardley (investment banking, Hong Kong, 1972).

In the late 1970s and into the 1980s, China began opening to foreign business. The bank added operations in North America to capitalize on business between China and the US and Canada. Its acquisitions included Marine Midland Bank (US, 1980), Hongkong Bank of Canada (1981), 51% of treasury securities dealer Carroll McEntee & McGinley (US, 1983), most of the assets and liabilities of the Bank of British Columbia (1986), and Lloyds Bank Canada (1990).

Following the 1984 agreement to return Hong Kong to China, Hongkong & Shanghai Bank began beefing up in the UK, buying London securities dealer James Capel & Co. (1986) and the UK's #3 bank, Midland plc (1992). In 1993 the company formed London-based HSBC Holdings and divested assets, most notably its interest in Hong Kong-based Cathay Pacific Airways.

HSBC then began expanding in Asia again, particularly in Malaysia, where its Hongkong Bank Malaysia became the country's first locally incorporated foreign bank. The company returned to China with offices in Beijing and Guangzhou. It also added new European branches.

Latin American banks acquired in 1997 were among the non-Asian operations that cushioned HSBC from the worst of 1998's economic crises. Nonetheless, The Hong Kong Monetary Authority took a stake in the bank to shore up the stock exchange and foil short-sellers.

In 1999 China's government made HSBC a loan for mainland expansion. That year the company was foiled in its attempt to buy South Korea's government-owned Seoulbank, but did buy the late Edmond Safra's Republic New York Corporation and his international bank holding company, Safra Republic Holdings (it negotiated a $450 million discount on the $10 billion deal after a Japanese probe of Republic's securities division caused delays).

In 2000 the company unveiled several online initiatives, including Internet ventures with Cheung Kong (Holdings) and Merrill Lynch, and bought CCF (then called Crédit Commercial de France). However, HSBC's plans to buy a controlling stake in Bangkok Metropolitan Bank fell through before the year's end.

In 2001 HSBC agreed to pick up Barclays Bank's fund management operations in Greece. Later, in response to the slowing economy, it froze the salaries of 14,000 employees. Argentina's 2001 peso devaluation cost the company half a billion dollars in currency conversion losses alone. Total charges pertaining to Argentina equaled more than $1 billion that year.

EXECUTIVES

Group Chairman: Stephen K. Green, age 57
Deputy Chairman: The Baroness Dunn, age 66
Deputy Chairman: Sir Brian Moffat, age 67
Group CEO: Michael F. Geoghegan, age 53
Group COO and Group Managing Director: David H. Hodgkinson, age 55
Group Finance Director and Executive Director: Douglas J. Flint, age 50
Group Managing Director; Chairman and CEO, HSBC France: Charles-Henri Filippi, age 52
Group Managing Director; CEO, HSBC Bank plc: Dyfrig John, age 56
Group Managing Director; President and CEO, HSBC Bank Brasil — Banco Multiplo: Youssef A. Nasr, age 51
Group Managing Director; CEO, HSBC North America; Chairman and CEO, HSBC Finance: Siddharth N. (Bobby) Mehta, age 48
Group Managing Director; Executive Director, HSBC Bank, HSBC USA, and HSBC Bank USA: Stuart T. Gulliver, age 47
Group Company Secretary: R. G. Barber, age 54
Group General Manager, Global e-business: R. J. Arena, age 57
Group General Manager; CEO, Group Private Banking: C. C. R. Bannister, age 47
Group General Manager, Legal and Compliance: R. E. T. Bennett, age 54
Group General Manager; Chairman, HSBC Bank Canada: Martin J. G. Glynn, age 54
Group Executive, HSBC North America Holdings; Vice Chairman, HSBC Finance: Sandra L. (Sandy) Derickson, age 52
Group General Manager and Group Chief Accounting Officer: R. C. Picot, age 47
Group General Manager, Human Resources: J. C. S. Rankin, age 63
Global CEO, HSBC Asset Management: Alain Dromer
Auditors: KPMG Audit Plc

LOCATIONS

HQ: HSBC Holdings plc
8 Canada Sq., London E14 5HQ, United Kingdom
Phone: +44-20-7991-8888 **Fax:** +44-20-7992-4880
US HQ: 452 5th Ave., New York, NY 10018
US Phone: 212-525-5000 **US Fax:** 716-730-3030
Web: www.hsbc.com

PRODUCTS/OPERATIONS

2005 Sales

	% of total
Interest income	66
Net fee income	16
Net trading income	6
Net earned insurance premiums	6
Other	6
Total	**100**

Selected Subsidiaries

Asia/Pacific
  Hang Seng Bank Limited (62%, Hong Kong)
  The Hongkong and Shanghai Banking Corporation Limited (Hong Kong)
  HSBC Investments (Taiwan) Limited
  HSBC Bank Australia Limited
  HSBC Bank Malaysia Berhad
  HSBC Insurance (Asia) Limited (Hong Kong)
Europe
  HFC Bank Limited
  HSBC Asset Finance (UK) Limited
  HSBC Investments (UK) Limited
  HSBC Bank A.S. (Turkey)
  HSBC Bank Malta p.l.c. (70%)
  HSBC Bank plc
  HSBC France
  HSBC Guyerzeller Bank AG (Switzerland)
  HSBC Insurance Brokers Limited
  HSBC Investment Bank plc
  HSBC Life (UK) Limited
  HSBC Private Bank (Suisse) S.A. (Switzerland)
  HSBC Private Bank (UK) Limited
  HSBC Trinkaus & Burkhardt KGaA (78%, Germany)

Latin America
  HSBC Bank Argentina S.A
  HSBC Bank Brasil S.A. — Banco Múltiplo
  HSBC La Buenos Aires Seguros SA (Argentina)
  HSBC Mexico S.A.
  HSBC Seguros (Brasil) S.A. (98%)
  Máxima S.A. AFJP (60%, Argentina)
Middle East and Africa
  British Arab Commercial Bank Limited (46%)
  HSBC Bank Egypt S.A.E. (95%)
  HSBC Bank Middle East Limited
  The Saudi British Bank (40%, Saudi Arabia)
North America
  The Bank of Bermuda Limited
  HSBC Bank Canada
  HSBC Bank USA
  HSBC Finance Corporation
  HSBC North America Holdings Inc.
  HSBC Securities (USA) Inc
  HSBC Technology & Services (USA) Inc.
  HSBC USA Inc.

COMPETITORS

Bank of America
Bank of China
Barclays
CIBC
Citigroup
Credit Suisse
Deutsche Bank
HBOS
Hutchison Whampoa
JPMorgan Chase
Lloyds TSB
Mizuho Financial
RBC Financial Group
RBS
Standard Chartered
UBS

HISTORICAL FINANCIALS
Company Type: Public

Income Statement
FYE: December 31

	ASSETS ($ mil.)	NET INCOME ($ mil.)	INCOME AS % OF ASSETS	EMPLOYEES
12/05	1,406,944	15,495	1.1%	284,000
12/04	1,266,365	12,506	1.0%	253,000
12/03	1,012,023	7,231	0.7%	232,000
12/02	762,967	4,900	0.6%	192,000
Annual Growth	22.6%	46.8%	—	13.9%

2005 Year-End Financials

Equity as % of assets: 6.6%
Return on assets: 1.2%
Return on equity: 16.9%
Long-term debt ($ mil.): 274,667
No. of shares (mil.): —
Dividends
Yield: 4.3%
Payout: 261.4%
Market value ($ mil.): —
Sales ($ mil.): 93,494

Stock History
NYSE: HBC

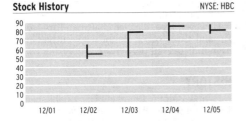

	STOCK PRICE ($) FY Close	P/E High/Low		PER SHARE ($) Earnings	Dividends
12/05	80.47	65	59	1.32	3.45
12/04	85.14	—	—	—	3.15
12/03	78.82	—	—	—	3.42
12/02	54.98	—	—	—	2.47
Annual Growth	13.5%	—	—	—	11.8%

Hutchison Whampoa

Hutchison Whampoa has a hand in just about everything in Hong Kong. The company, one of Hong Kong's oldest *hongs* (trading companies), has extensive holdings in retailing (A.S. Watson & Co), ports, energy (Hongkong Electric, Husky Energy), telecommunications (3G mobile phone and paging services), and infrastructure (power plants, toll roads, and construction materials). In addition, Hutchison Whampoa owns hotels and a sizable portfolio of Hong Kong properties. Outside Hong Kong, the company has operations in 50-plus countries, including China and elsewhere in the Asia/Pacific region, as well as in Europe and the Americas. Hutchison Whampoa is controlled by Li Ka-shing, one of the world's wealthiest men.

Hutchison Whampoa's retail and manufacturing subsidiary, A.S. Watson & Co. (ASW), accounts for more than a third of revenues. Operations include supermarkets (Park'N Shop), health and beauty stores (Watson's Your Personal Store, Drogas, Kruidvat), 70 Fortress electrical appliance stores in Hong Kong, soft drink and water bottling operations, and wine retailing (Watson's Wine Cellar). Already the world's largest operator of health and beauty stores (by store count) with outlets throughout Europe and Asia, ASW has expanded its health and beauty business with the acquisition of the French retail perfume chain Marionnaud Parfumeries and the 120-door The Perfume Shop chain in the UK.

With about 250 berths in 40-plus ports, Hutchison Port Holdings (HPH) is one of the world's biggest container terminal operators. HPH operates in 21 countries and operates five of the eight busiest container ports in the world, including three key ports on Britain's east coast and ports on both ends of the Panama Canal. In addition to owning a controlling interest in Hongkong International Terminals, which handles traffic passing through Hong Kong's container port, HPH has large investments in terminal operations in southern China. HPH is expanding in China, most recently through a deal with Shanghai International Port Group that gives it access to four more berths, bringing the number of berths it manages there to 17.

Hutchison Whampoa is a leading competitor in mobile telecommunications offering wireless service to some 8 million customers throughout Australia, Europe, and Hong Kong. Subsidiary company Hutchison Telecommunications International Limited (HTIL) provides mobile phone networks and data services in nine markets in Asia, the Middle East, and Africa.

Hutchison Whampoa has strong connections to the Chinese government, thanks to its rags-to-riches chairman, Li, who has spent years building business relationships inside China. His Cheung Kong (Holdings) Limited is a substantial shareholder in Hutchison Whampoa.

HISTORY

Hongkong and Whampoa Dock was the first registered company in Hong Kong. The enterprise was founded in 1861 when it bought dry docks in Whampoa (near present-day Guangzhou, China) after the kidnapping and disappearance of the docks' owner, John Couper, during the Second Opium War (1856-60). It bought docks in Hong Kong in 1865.

Founded in 1880 by John Hutchison, Hutchison International became a major Hong Kong consumer goods importer and wholesaler. It took control of Hongkong and Whampoa Dock and in A.S. Watson (drugstores, supermarkets, soft drinks) during an acquisition spree in the 1960s. The purchases entailed a complex web of deals that fell apart in the mid-1970s. To save Hutchison International, the Hongkong & Shanghai Bank took a large stake in the company and brought in Australian turnaround specialist Bill Wyllie. Wyllie slashed expenses, sold 103 companies in 1976, and bought the rest of Hongkong and Whampoa Dock in 1977. The company became Hutchison Whampoa that year.

In a surprise move, in 1979 Hongkong & Shanghai Bank sold its 23% stake in Hutchison to Cheung Kong Holdings: Cheung Kong founder Li Ka-shing, who began his career at age 14 by selling plastic flowers, became the first Chinese to control a British-style *hong*. Wyllie left in 1981.

In the 1980s Hutchison redeveloped its older dockyard sites, which had become prime real estate. The company's International Terminals unit grew with Hong Kong's container traffic into the world's largest privately owned container terminal operator. In the 1980s the firm diversified into energy (buying stakes in utility Hongkong Electric and Canada-based Husky Oil) and precious metals and mining. It also moved into telecommunications, buying Australian paging and UK mobile telephone units in 1989.

The following year the *hong* launched the AsiaSat I satellite in a venture with Cable & Wireless (C&W) and China International Trust & Investment. More acquisitions followed, including European mobile phone businesses and telecom equipment makers. In 1996 the firm reorganized its Hong Kong telecom operations into Hutchison Telecommunications. In 1999 the company and C&W sold their stakes in AsiaSat.

In 2001 Hutchison Whampoa sold its 18% stake in US-based mobile phone operator VoiceStream to Deutsche Telekom for $5.1 billion in cash and stocks. The next year its A.S. Watson Group bought the Netherlands-based health-and-beauty retail chain Kruidvat Group, which operates about 1,900 stores in six European countries.

In 2004 the company sold the remaining 20% stake in its joint venture in China with household-products-giant Procter & Gamble to P&G for $1.8 billion. Also in 2004 Hutchison Whampoa's fixed-line telecommunications group acquired Vanda Systems, and became a listed company on the Hong Kong Stock exchange under the new name Hutchison Global Communications Holdings (HGCH). In October the company combined its 52% stake in HGCH with its interests in the 2G cellular businesses under a single parent company Hutchison Telecommunications International Limited (HTIL) and took HTIL public on the Hong Kong and New York stock exchanges. In the interim, in June Hutchison Whampoa's retail arm, the A.S. Watson Group, acquired a leading health and beauty chain in Latvia and Lithuania, Drogas, marking its entry into the Baltic region. Drogas has 59 stores in Latvia and 24 outlets in Lithuania. In August Watson acquired a 40% stake in German health and beauty chain Rossmann, which operates more than 1,100 stores throughout Germany, Hungary, Poland, and the Czech Republic.

EXECUTIVES

Chairman: Li Ka-shing, age 77
Deputy Chairman and Executive Director:
Victor T.K. Li, age 41
Group Managing Director and Executive Director:
Canning K.N. Fok, age 55
Deputy Group Managing Director and Executive Director: Susan M.F. Chow Woo, age 52
Group Finance Director and Executive Director:
Frank J. Sixt, age 54
Executive Director; Deputy Chairman, Hutchison Harbour Ring; Director, Hutchison Telecommunications Australia: Dominic K.M. Lai, age 52
Executive Director: George C. Magnus, age 70
Executive Director: Kam Hing Lam, age 59
Company Secretary: Edith Shih, age 53
General Manager, Human Resources: Mary Tung
Group Managing Director, HPH: John E. Meredith
Group Managing Director, A.S. Watson & Co.:
Ian F. Wade, age 66
Managing Director, Fortress: Peter J. Dove
Auditors: PricewaterhouseCoopers

LOCATIONS

HQ: Hutchison Whampoa Limited
Hutchison House, 22nd Fl., 10 Harcourt Rd.,
Hong Kong
Phone: +852-2128-1188   **Fax:** +852-2128-1705
Web: www.hutchison-whampoa.com

Hutchison Whampoa operates in Hong Kong and China. It has other diversified holdings in more than 50 countries worldwide, including Australia, Austria, the Bahamas, Canada, Denmark, France, Germany, Ghana, India, Indonesia, Ireland, Israel, Italy, Japan, Latvia, Macao, Myanmar, Panama, the Philippines, Singapore, Sri Lanka, Sweden, Switzerland, Taiwan, Thailand, Turkey, and the UK.

2005 Sales

	% of total
Europe	41
Hong Kong	20
Asia & Australia	18
Americas & other	13
China	8
Total	**100**

PRODUCTS/OPERATIONS

2005 Sales

	% of total
Retail & manufacturing	37
Telecommunications — 3 Group	16
Ports & related services	12
Hutchison Telecommunications International	11
Energy	9
Infrastructure	7
Finance & investments	4
Property & hotels	4
Total	**100**

Selected Subsidiaries and Affiliates

Retail and Manufacturing
A. S. Watson & Co., Limited (Hong Kong)
A/S Drogras (Latvia)
Dirk Rossmann GmbH (40%, Germany)
Fortress Limited (Hong Kong)
Guangzhou Watson's Food and Beverage Company Limited (China)
Kruidvat Retail B.V. (Netherlands)
Marionnaud Parfumeries SA (France)
Nuance-Watson (Singapore) Pte Ltd. (Singapore)
Park'N Shop Limited (supermarkets, Hong Kong)
Savers Health and Beauty Limited (UK)
Superdrug Stores plc (UK)
The Perfume Shop Limited (UK)
Watson's Personal Care Stores (Taiwan) Co., Limited

Telecommunications and E-commerce
3 Italia S.p.A. (95%, 3G mobile multimedia services)
Hutchison 3G UK Ltd. (3G mobile multimedia services)
Hutchison Telecommunications (Australia) Limited (58%, holding company and telecommunications)
Hutchison Telecommunications (Hong Kong) Limited (70%)

Ports and Related Services
Hongkong International Terminals Limited (67%, container terminal operating)
Hongkong United Dockyards Limited (50%, ship retail and general engineering)
Shanghai Mingdong Container Terminal Limited (50%, China)
Yantian International Container Terminals Limited (48%, China)

Energy
Hongkong Electric Holdings Limited (33%, utility)
Husky Energy Inc. (35%, oil and gas investment, Canada)

Infrastructure
Cheung Kong Infrastructure Holdings Limited (85%, holding company, Hong Kong)

Finance and Investments
Hutchison Whampoa (Europe) Limited (consulting services, UK)
TOM Group Limited (24%, Internet portal, Hong Kong)

Property and Hotels
Harbour Plaza Hotel Management (International) Limited (50%, Hong Kong)
Hutchison Properties Limited (holding company, Hong Kong)

COMPETITORS

Alliance Boots	Orange
AT&T	Orient Overseas
BT	PCCW
Cable & Wireless	PSA
Carrefour	Road King
China Mobile	Schlecker
China Unicom	Sime Darby
Dairy Farm International	SkyTel Corp.
Deutsche Telekom AG	Sprint Nextel
DP World	Swire Pacific
France Telecom	Verizon
Hopewell Holdings	Wharf
Jardine Matheson	

HISTORICAL FINANCIALS

Company Type: Public

Income Statement

FYE: December 31

	REVENUE ($ mil.)	NET INCOME ($ mil.)	NET PROFIT MARGIN	EMPLOYEES
12/05	23,553	—	—	200,000
12/04	17,309	—	—	182,000
12/03	13,514	—	—	172,653
12/02	9,645	—	—	117,843
12/01	7,879	—	—	77,253
Annual Growth	31.5%	—	—	26.8%

Revenue History

Pink Sheets: HUWHY

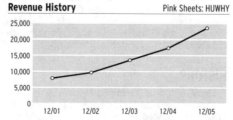

Hyundai

Hyundai Motor has been selling cars in the US since 1986, but it only started selling its heavy trucks stateside in 1998. South Korea's #1 car-maker, Hyundai produces 14 models of cars, SUVs, and minivans, as well as trucks, buses, and other commercial vehicles. The company reestablished itself as South Korea's leading carmaker in 1998 by acquiring a 51% stake in Kia Motors (since reduced to about 43%). Hyundai's exports include the Accent and Sonata, while its Korean models include the Atos subcompact. The company also manufactures machine tools for factory automation and material-handling equipment.

With Hyundai's home market in South Korea stagnating, the company is looking to key overseas markets for growth. Hyundai's targets are North America, Europe, China, and India.

To increase its presence in the US, Hyundai completed construction of a new manufacturing plant, Hyundai Motor Manufacturing Alabama, in 2005. The new plant will build about 300,000 cars per year.

Hyundai is also expanding in China. Since opening its first Chinese plant in 2002, Hyundai has doubled its production in that country. The company plans to have a 20% share of the Chinese market by 2010. To that end the automaker has signed a $1.2 billion deal to form a joint venture with Guangzhou Motor Group, giving Hyundai access to the commercial-vehicle market in China.

To keep pace with markets in Europe, Hyundai has chosen the Czech Republic for the site of a $1.2 billion manufacturing complex.

In India Hyundai is the second-best-selling brand after domestic player Maruti Udyog. This is no small feat as the Korean company only entered the market in the mid-1990s. Hyundai's operations in India are also key to the company's future throughout southwest Asia.

In 2006 Hyundai chairman Chung Mong-Koo was indicted and arrested on charges that he embezzled Hyundai company cash to create a slush fund which he used to finance bribes for Korean government officials in exchange for corporate favors. After two months of incarceration Chung was released from jail on $1.04 million bail.

Under Korean law, if convicted Chung could face a life sentence, but a long sentence is said to be unlikely. During his trial Chung admitted some wrongdoing when he said "I admit to my guilt, to some extent." Chung's son, Kia Motors boss Chung Eui Sun, had been under investigation, but prosecutors have indicated he would not be indicted.

However, Hyundai vice chairman Kim Dong-Jin and three other Hyundai executives have been indicted but not arrested.

HISTORY

Hyundai Motor Company was established in 1967, and it initially began manufacturing cars and light trucks through a technology collaboration with Ford's UK operations. By the early 1970s Hyundai was ready to build cars under its own nameplate. The company debuted the subcompact Hyundai Pony in 1974 at Italy's annual Turin Motor Show.

The Pony was an instant domestic success and soon propelled Hyundai to the top spot among South Korea's carmakers. During the mid-1970s the company began exporting the Pony to El Salvador and Guatemala.

By the 1980s Hyundai was ready to shift into high gear and begin high-volume production in anticipation of penetrating more overseas markets. The company began exporting to Canada in 1983.

Hyundai introduced the Hyundai Excel in 1985. That year the company established its US subsidiary, Hyundai Motor America. By 1986 Hyundai was exporting Excels for sale in the US. Sales of the Excel soared the next year, so Hyundai decided to build a factory in Bromont, Quebec.

But by the time the factory was finished in 1989, consumers were tiring of the aging compact car and the quality problems that came with it. Hyundai closed the plant after just four years of operation.

The company introduced its first sports car, the Scoupe, in 1990. The following year it developed the first Hyundai-designed engine, called the Alpha. Two years later the carmaker unveiled its second-generation proprietary engine, the Beta.

By 1998 Hyundai was beginning to feel the pinch of the Asian economic crisis as domestic demand dropped drastically. However, the decrease in Korean demand was largely offset by exports. That year Hyundai took a controlling stake in Korean competitor Kia Motors.

In hopes of increasing its share of the Asian automotive market, DaimlerChrysler took a 10% stake in Hyundai in 2000 (sold in 2004). The deal included the establishment of a joint venture to manufacture commercial vehicles, as well as an agreement among Hyundai, DaimlerChrysler, and Mitsubishi Motors to develop small cars for the global market.

In 2001 Hyundai decreased its stake in Kia Motors to about 46%.

The following year DaimlerChrysler announced it would exercise its option to take a 50% stake in Hyundai's heavy-truck business.

In 2004 Hyundai CEO Kim Dong-Jin was indicted in South Korea on charges that he violated campaign finance laws and engaged in managerial negligence. The charges stemmed from a general crackdown on campaign finance violations, during which more than a dozen members of South Korea's parliament were either indicted or detained. Later in 2004 Kim was convicted of the charges against him and sentenced to a suspended two-year jail term.

In 2006 Hyundai's legal woes persisted when two executives were arrested as part of a Korean bribery investigation. The pair are accused of creating a slush fund that was allegedly used to fund a lobbyist that sought favors for Hyundai from the Korean government. Officials are also investigating whether the slush fund was created at the behest of Hyundai chairman Chung Mong-Koo.

The following week state prosecutors in Korea arrested Chung Mong-Koo. Authorities alleged Chung indeed embezzled up to $106 million of Hyundai money to create the slush fund. His son Chung Eui-Sun, president of Kia Motors, was also investigated, but the state did not seek to detain him. Some weeks later the elder Chung was indicted, although the specific charges were not disclosed.

EXECUTIVES

Chairman and Co-CEO: Chung Mong-koo
Vice Chairman and Co-CEO: Kim Dong-Jin
President, Manufacturing: Jeon Cheon-Soo
President, Hyundai Motor America: Ok Suk (Owen) Koh
Auditors: Deloitte HanaAnjin LLC

LOCATIONS

HQ: Hyundai Motor Company
(Hyundai Jadongcha Chusik Hoesa)
231 Yangjae-dong, Seocho-gu,
Seoul 137-938, South Korea
Phone: +82-2-3464-1114
US HQ: 10550 Talbert Ave., Fountain Valley, CA 92728
US Phone: 714-965-3000   **US Fax:** 714-965-3001
Web: www.hyundai-motor.com

Hyundai Motor has major manufacturing plants in China, India, North America, and South Korea, and R&D centers in Europe, Japan, and North America.

PRODUCTS/OPERATIONS

Selected Models

Commercial vehicles
  Aero Town (medium bus)
  Cargo Truck (large truck)
  County (small bus)
  H 1 Truck (light commercial vehicle)
  H 120 Truck (medium truck)
  HD 65/HD72 (small truck)
  HD 250 (refrigerated van truck)
Passenger cars
  Accent (sedan)
  Atos Prime (subcompact)
  Centennial (luxury sedan)
  Elantra (sedan)
  Getz (compact sedan)
  Grandeur (sedan)
  H-I Van
  Matrix (compact SUV)
  Santa Fe (SUV)
  Sonata (sedan)
  Terracan (SUV)
  Tucson (SUV)
  Trajet (SUV)

COMPETITORS

DaimlerChrysler	Mazda
Fiat	Nissan
Ford	NUMMI
General Motors	Peugeot
GM Daewoo	Renault
Honda	Toyota
Ingersoll-Rand	Volkswagen
Isuzu	

HISTORICAL FINANCIALS

Company Type: Public

Income Statement

FYE: December 31

	REVENUE ($ mil.)	NET INCOME ($ mil.)	NET PROFIT MARGIN	EMPLOYEES
12/05	57,636	2,277	3.9%	68,000
12/04	50,695	1,610	3.2%	51,000
12/03	38,995	1,486	3.8%	51,471
12/02	40,111	1,196	3.0%	49,855
12/01	30,108	870	2.9%	50,000
Annual Growth	17.6%	27.2%	—	8.0%

Net Income History

Exchange: Korea

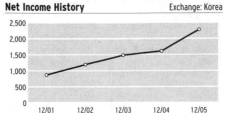

What are the chances of untangling the Agnelli web of holdings? Pretty IFI. Controlled by the wealthy Agnelli family through parent firm Giovanni Agnelli and C., holding company IFI — Istituto Finanziario Industriale owns stakes in a variety of enterprises. These holdings include a more than 60% stake in sister company Ifil Investments. Through Ifil, the company owns about 30% of automotive giant Fiat (which the Agnellis founded and still control), 60% of one of Italy's top soccer clubs, Juventus, and a majority of Sequana Capital, which owns European paper makers ArjoWiggins and Antalis. Ifil also holds shares of companies involved in tourism (Alpitour) and resorts and hotels (Turismo&Immobiliare).

In 2006 IFI sold its nearly 30% stake in Luxembourg-based Exor Group, which has holdings in French wine (Greysac), packaging (17% of US-based Graphic Packaging), and telecommunications (7% of Hong Kong's Distacom).

HISTORY

Istituto Finanziario Industriale (IFI) was formed by Giovanni Agnelli in 1927 as a family "safe" for his stakes of various industrial businesses. Automaker Fiat immediately became and remains the centerpiece of IFI's holdings.

Fiat benefited from Mussolini's protectionist policies in the 1930s, but Agnelli remained a liberal. During WWII, when Axis defeat appeared imminent, Agnelli slowed war production and put Italian resistance members on his payroll. At the end of the war, Fiat executives — unable to wait for the Marshall Plan — traveled to the US to seek reconstruction loans.

Upon Agnelli's death in 1945, ownership of IFI passed to his Agnelli and Nasi family heirs. In 1958 IFI gained control of Finanziaria di Partecipazioni (Ifil), another industrial holding company.

Ten years later IFI formed Infint (renamed EXOR Group in 1994) to manage IFI's foreign shares. Also in 1968 IFI stock was offered to the public to fund company expansion. The Agnelli and Nasi families' shares decreased throughout the 1970s and 1980s as more capital was sought.

The 1970s saw IFI dispose of non-core holdings, such as Società Assicuratrice Industriale, in order to cut debt.

IFI and Ifil bought back shares of Fiat in the 1980s while Ifil began to invest more widely. Parent company Giovanni Agnelli e C. S.a.p.az. (G.A. e C.), controlled solely by the Agnelli and Nasi families, formed in 1987 and bought IFI.

In 1997 IFI and Ifil reacted to the privatization and competition rocking the once-static world of Italian financial holdings. The companies invested in Istituto Bancario San Paolo di Torino (now San Paolo IMI) and spun off cement maker Unicem.

In 1999 G.A. e C. and IFI upped their stakes in EXOR Group. Two years later IFI sold its stake in the Rockefeller Center to T. Speyer & Crown. In 2003 the junior Giovanni Agnelli died; Umberto Agnelli died in 2004.

EXECUTIVES

Chairman: Gianluigi Gabetti, age 81
Deputy Chairman: Pio Teodorani-Fabbri
General Manager: Virgilio Marrone, age 60
Auditors: Deloitte & Touche S.p.A.

LOCATIONS

HQ: IFI - Istituto Finanziario Industriale S.p.A.
Corso Matteotti, 26, 10121 Turin, Italy
Phone: +39-011-509-0266   **Fax:** +39-011-535-600
Web: www.gruppoifi.com

PRODUCTS/OPERATIONS

Selected Holdings
Ifil (64%)
Alpitour (tourism)
Fiat (30%)
Juventus F.C. S.p.A. (60%)
Sanpaolo IMI (5%)
Sequana Capital (53%, France)

COMPETITORS

Bastogi
Gemina
Investor
Italmobiliare
Mittel
Wendel Investissement

HISTORICAL FINANCIALS

Company Type: Public

Income Statement				FYE: December 31
	REVENUE ($ mil.)	NET INCOME ($ mil.)	NET PROFIT MARGIN	EMPLOYEES
12/05	6,475	801	12.4%	18,458
12/04	70,762	160	0.2%	179,790
12/03	67,165	(163)	—	192,550
12/02	63,717	(842)	—	209,141
12/01	55,968	145	0.3%	198,764
Annual Growth	(41.7%)	53.2%	—	(44.8%)

Net Income History   Italian: IFP

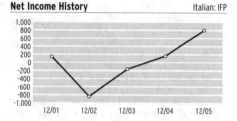

IKEA

How Swede it is. One of the world's top furniture retailers, IKEA International sells Scandinavian-style home furnishings and other housewares in nearly 240 stores in 34 countries. To cut transportation costs, IKEA uses flat packaging; customers assemble the products at home. The company designs its own furniture, which is made by about 1,300 suppliers in more than 50 countries. IKEA's stores feature playrooms for children and Swedish cuisine restaurants. It also sells by mail order and online. An acronym for founder Ingvar Kamprad and his boyhood home, Elmtaryd, Agunnaryd, IKEA began operating in Sweden in 1943. It is owned by Kamprad's Netherlands-based charitable foundation, Stichting Ingka.

If you're looking for fussy furniture in neutral tones, IKEA is not the place for you. Known for its use of bold colors and creative product names

(a Ticka alarm clock, a Ringo stool), the company sells furniture and other household items, including dinnerware, pillows, lighting, and rugs. Recently the company has focused on outfitting bedrooms and kitchens.

IKEA plans to open two dozen new stores in fiscal 2007. The Swedish furniture retailer recently opened its first store in Japan — the world's second-largest consumer market after the US — with a second store slated to open in Tokyo in 2007. Longer term, IKEA plans to open up to six stores in the Kanto (Tokyo) region and four to six outlets in the Kansai (Kobe and Osaka) regions of the country. (A previous foray into the Japanese market back in the 1970s was a flop.)

China is also on IKEA's list for expansion. The company operates four stores there and plans to open several more over in the coming years. IKEA is under pressure from cheaper Chinese household goods suppliers there. IKEA operates more than 25 stores in the US, and plans to add three to five stores a year here.

To house all its furniture, the Swedish furniture king has begun selling prefabricated homes in Sweden, Norway, Finland, and Denmark. The company's BoKlok prefab houses are available in two styles: single-family villas (available only in Sweden), and two-story timber-frame buildings containing six apartments. To date, IKEA has sold more than 2,500 homes and aims to double sales by 2008.

IKEA, Sweden's largest food exporter, is replacing its non-organic offerings with organic fare, including cheese, coffee, and jams.

HISTORY

At the age of 17, Ingvar Kamprad formed his own company in Sweden in 1943, peddling fish, vegetable seeds, and magazines by bicycle. He called the company IKEA, an acronym for his name and the village in which he grew up (Elmtaryd, Agunnaryd). Four years later he added the newly invented ballpoint pen to his product assortment and started a mail-order catalog.

In 1950 Kamprad added furniture and housewares to his mail-order products, and in 1953 he bought a furniture factory and opened a small showroom. The showroom was a hit with price-conscious Swedes and was replaced by the first official IKEA store in 1958. The first store outside Sweden was established in 1963 in Norway. Two years later the company opened its flagship store in Stockholm, a 150,000-sq.-ft. marvel whose round design was inspired by the Guggenheim Museum in New York. The store featured a nursery, a restaurant, a bank, and parking spaces for 1,000 cars. By 1969 two more stores were opened in Sweden and another in Denmark.

A fire badly damaged the Stockholm store in 1973, but the subsequent fire sale pulled in more shoppers than the store's grand opening. That year IKEA expanded beyond Scandinavia, opening stores in Switzerland and Germany. In 1976 it opened its first store outside Europe, in Canada, and during the late 1970s and early 1980s, it entered Australia, the Canary Islands, Hong Kong, Iceland, Kuwait, Saudi Arabia, and Singapore. To avoid questions of succession after his death, Kamprad in 1980 transferred ownership of the company to a charitable foundation. IKEA opened its first US store, in Philadelphia, in 1985. Anders Moberg was named president of IKEA in 1986. By 1991 there were seven outlets in the US and 95 total in 23 countries. IKEA began its push into Eastern Europe two years later, but at the same time struggled with eco-

nomic downturns in its major markets, Germany and Scandinavia.

Kamprad's reluctant announcement that he had associated with pro-Nazi groups in the 1940s and 1950s brought a torrent of bad press. The revelation prompted IKEA to reconsider opening a store in Israel, believing the Israeli government would not sanction the investment. Instead, Jewish groups claimed the company was deliberately avoiding the country. IKEA agreed in 1995 to open an Israeli store and finally granted a license for a franchise to Blue Square — Israel Ltd. in 1997.

That year IKEA announced plans to build about 20 plants over five years in the Baltics, Bulgaria, and Romania, a move designed to reduce its dependence on contract manufacturers and nearly double its own manufacturing capacity. Also in 1997 it began offering prefab housing in Sweden with construction firm Skanska.

IKEA opened its largest store (400,000 sq. ft.) outside Europe in Chicago in 1998 and announced plans to open more stores in Russia, China, and Eastern Europe. In 1999 Anders Dahlvig was named group president, replacing Moberg, who left to take a position with retailer Home Depot. In 2000 the company opened its first store in Moscow, with plans for more Russian locations.

In 2001 IKEA stated plans to open 60 to 70 more store locations in Europe, North America, and Asia over the next five years. Since June 2002 IKEA has run its own freight trains between depots in Sweden and Germany, and the company plans to extend its rail services to Italy and Poland and to double its rail transport of goods to 40% by 2006. In December 2002 IKEA Netherlands received a letter with a bomb threat and temporarily shut down 10 of its retail locations. Explosives were discovered in two stores in the Netherlands and detonated; two IKEA employees were minimally injured. Federal authorities confirmed that the motive behind the attacks was extortion.

In 2004 IKEA opened its first store in Portugal and stores in Russia outside the metro areas of Moscow and St. Petersburg. The Swedish home furnishings group opened 18 new stores in fiscal year 2005 (15 in Europe and three in North America). The following year IKEA added 16 new stores worldwide, including its first in Japan in April 2006.

EXECUTIVES

Group President: Anders Dahlvig
Group VP: Hans Gydell
Senior Adviser: Ingvar Kamprad
Global Design Chief: Lars Engman
President, IKEA North America: Pernille Spiers-Lopez, age 46
CEO, IKEA Food Service: Jan Kjellman
President, Swedwood North America: Bengt Danielsson
Regional Manager, Mid-Europe: Peter Høgsted
Creative Director, IKEA North America: Mats Nilsson
Property Director, UK: Scott Cordrey
Global Information Manager: Marianne Barner
Human Resources Manager: Lars Gejrot

LOCATIONS

HQ: IKEA International A/S
Box 640, SE 25 106 Helsingborg, Sweden
Phone: +46-42-267-100   **Fax:** +46-42-132-805
US HQ: 496 W. Germantown Pike,
Plymouth Meeting, PA 19462
US Phone: 610-834-0180   **US Fax:** 610-834-0872
Web: www.ikea.com

2006 Sales

	% of total
Europe	80
North America	17
Asia & Australia	3
Total	**100**

PRODUCTS/OPERATIONS

2006 Stores

	No.
Company-owned	210
Franchised	27
Total	**237**

Selected Products

Armchairs
Bath accessories
Bath suites
Bean bags
Bed linens
Beds and bedroom suites
Bookcases
Boxes
CD storage
Ceiling lamps
Children's furniture
Clocks
Coffee tables
Cookware
Cord management
Desk accessories
Dining tables and chairs
Dinnerware
Entertainment units
Floor lamps
Frames
Instruments for children
Kitchen organizers
Kitchen units
Leather sofas
Lighting
Mattresses
Mirrors
Office chairs and suites
Posters
Rugs
Sofas and sofa beds
Spotlights
Stools
Table lamps
Toy storage
TV cabinets and stands
Utility storage
Video storage
Wall shelves and systems
Wardrobe units
Window treatments

COMPETITORS

ASDA	Jennifer Convertibles
Bassett Furniture	John Lewis
Bed Bath & Beyond	Kmart
Bombay Company	La Rinascente
Container Store	Linens 'n Things
Euromarket Designs	METRO AG
Eurway	Otto
Galiform	Pier 1 Imports
Gruppo Coin	Pier Import Europe
Harvey Norman Holdings	Restoration Hardware
Home Retail	Rooms To Go
Horten	Wal-Mart
Hulsta-Werke Huls	Williams-Sonoma

HISTORICAL FINANCIALS

Company Type: Private

Income Statement

FYE: August 31

	REVENUE ($ mil.)	NET INCOME ($ mil.)	NET PROFIT MARGIN	EMPLOYEES
8/06	22,194	—	—	104,000
8/05	18,089	—	—	90,000
8/04	15,425	—	—	84,000
8/03	12,409	—	—	80,000
8/02	11,779	—	—	75,500
Annual Growth	**17.2%**	—	—	**8.3%**

Revenue History

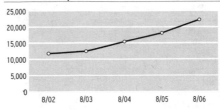

Imperial Chemical

Empire may not be such a popular word any longer, but Imperial Chemical Industries (ICI) is still among the chemical royalty. Its specialty products group consists of National Starch and Chemical (industrial adhesives, starch), Quest (fragrance and flavors). Its paint offerings include the Alba, Dulux, and Glidden brands. ICI's regional and industrial chemicals segment (subsidiaries in Argentina, India, and Pakistan) makes explosives, soda ash, sulfur-related products, and fibers. The company sold a part of its specialties unit, Uniqema (a maker of natural and synthetic lubricants and personal care products), to Croda for $750 million in 2006. It also agreed to sell its Quest unit to Givaudan for $2.3 billion.

ICI set out in 2003 to identify growth opportunities within its portfolio and direct investment accordingly. Thus came the sale of Quest's food ingredients business and National Starch's emulsion polymers unit to Celanese. Also the company has followed the rest of the world into Asia and China in particular, expanding ICI Paints' sales and marketing operations throughout the region and opening two manufacturing plants for National Starch in 2004.

The company has broken out its businesses into two groups, those it is choosing to grow aggressively (North American paints, flavors and fragrances, and all of its Asian businesses) and those it is trying to make more efficient if not grow larger (specialty chemicals, paints in Europe and Latin America). The sale of Uniqema and Quest allows ICI to concentrate on its chosen growth units and to reinvest the proceeds of the divestitures into those divisions.

HISTORY

Imperial Chemical Industries (ICI) began in 1926 when four British chemical companies (Nobel Industries; Brunner, Mond and Company; United Alkali; and British Dyestuffs) merged to compete with German cartel I. G. Farben. The most-famed ICI predecessor, Nobel Industries, was created as the British arm of Alfred Nobel's explosives empire. Nobel mixed nitroglycerin with porous clay to make dynamite. In 1886 he created the London-based Nobel Dynamite Trust to embrace British and German interests. After Nobel's death in 1896, the empire unraveled, and WWI severed the German and UK components of the Nobel firm. The British arm became Nobel Industries (1920).

In 1929 ICI and American chemical company DuPont signed a patents-and-process agreement to share research information. Around the same time it focused on research and between 1933 and 1935 created some 87 new products, including polyethylene.

After WWII the cartel club began to disband. The US government won antitrust sanctions against the DuPont-ICI alliance in 1952, and ICI faced new competition from the sundered components of I. G. Farben (Bayer, BASF, Hoechst). ICI added foreign operations in the 1960s, but fortunes declined, and in 1980 it posted losses and cut its dividend for the first time.

The company recruited turnaround artist John Harvey-Jones in 1982. He cut layers of decision making, reorganized along product lines, and added non-UK directors to the board. ICI also shifted production from bulk chemicals such as soda and chlorine to high-margin specialty chemicals such as pharmaceuticals and pesticides.

Harvey-Jones bought 100 companies between 1982 and his retirement in 1987. ICI expanded in the US market by purchasing Beatrice's chemical operations (1985) and Glidden paints (1986).

ICI sold its nylon business to DuPont in 1992 and spun off its pharmaceutical and agricultural operations as Zeneca the next year. It opened its first plant in China, a paint factory, in 1994 and named 30-year Unilever veteran Charles Miller Smith its new CEO in 1995.

In 1997 ICI bought Unilever's specialty chemicals unit in a deal worth about $8 billion. The same year it picked up Canada-based St. Clair Paint & Wallpaper. ICI then sold its polyester resin and intermediates operations (1997) and film business (1998) to Dupont for around $2 billion. In 1998 ICI paid $560 million for specialty chemicals maker Acheson Industries. ICI's attempts to reduce debt from the Unilever purchase stumbled when W. R. Grace & Co. terminated its deal to buy ICI's Crosfield silicas and catalysts business and DuPont and NL Industries backed out of the $1 billion purchase of ICI's titanium dioxide business.

Still saddled with debt, ICI sold a rash of companies in 1999: its utilities and services division to Enron for about $500 million; its polyurethanes and titanium-dioxide businesses and some petrochemicals businesses to US-based Huntsman for about $2.8 billion (though it kept a 30% stake, which it then sold back to Huntsman in 2003); its industrial coatings and auto refinish businesses in the Americas and Europe, and Germany-based coatings business to PPG Industries for $684 million; and its acrylics division (raw materials such as methylacrylates and value-added products such as Lucite and Perspex) to Belgium-based Ineos Acrylics (which has since become Lucite International) for $833 million.

Continuing to divest in 2000, ICI sold paint distribution network Master Distribution to Lafarge SA. The next year ICI sold its giant plant in Runcorn, UK, to Ineos Chlor. Despite the money brought in from all the sell-offs, ICI was threatened with its debt rating being reduced to junk bond status. In response, the company raised about $1.15 billion in a share offering in order to reduce debt. It also sold its 30% stake in Huntsman ICI Chemicals back to Utah-based Huntsman for nearly $500 million, which it then used to pay down more of its debt in 2003.

EXECUTIVES

Chairman: Peter B. Ellwood, age 62
CEO: John D. G. McAdam, age 58
EVP, Mergers & Acquisitions, General Counsel, and Company Secretary: Andy Ransom
EVP, Uniqema: Leonard J. (Len) Berlik, age 57
EVP, Regional and International Business: David Gee, age 56
EVP, Human Resources: Rolf Deusinger, age 47
CFO: Alan J. Brown, age 48
Chairman and CEO, ICI Paints: David Hamill, age 47
Chairman and CEO, National Starch and Director: William H. Powell, age 60
Chairman and Chief Executive, Quest International: Charles F. Knott, age 50
SVP, Technology: Graeme D. Armstrong, age 43
VP, Investor Relations and Corporate Communications: John Dawson
Chief Press Officer: John Edgar
Director, Corporate Communications: Regina Kilfoyle
Auditors: KPMG Audit Plc

LOCATIONS

HQ: Imperial Chemical Industries PLC
20 Manchester Sq.,
London W1U 3AN, United Kingdom
Phone: +44-20-7009-5000   **Fax:** +44-20-7009-5001
US HQ: 10 Finderne Ave., Bridgewater, NJ 08807
US Phone: 908-685-5000   **US Fax:** 908-685-5005
Web: www.ici.com

Imperial Chemical Industries has more than 200 manufacturing facilities on six continents.

2005 Sales

	% of total
North America	32
Europe	
UK	15
Other countries	22
Asia	22
Latin America	7
Other regions	2
Total	**100**

PRODUCTS/OPERATIONS

2005 Sales

	% of total
Paints	40
National Starch	32
Uniqema	11
Quest	10
Regional & Industrial	7
Total	**100**

International Businesses

Paints
  Packaging coatings (for food and drink cans)
  Paints (Devoe, Dulux, Inca, Glidden)
National Starch
  Adhesives
  Electronic and engineering materials
  Specialty starches
  Specialty synthetic polymers

Quest (flavors and fragrance)
Regional and Industrial Chemicals
  ICI Argentina
    Sulfur-related chemicals
    Wine chemicals
  ICI India
    Adhesives
    Catalysts
    Explosives
  ICI Pakistan
    Fibers
    Soda ash

COMPETITORS

3M
Akzo Nobel
BASF AG
BASF Catalysts
Ciba Specialty Chemicals
Clariant
Degussa
Dow Chemical
Dow Corning
DSM
DuPont
Eastman Chemical
Ferro
Frutarom
H.B. Fuller
Hercules
Honeywell Specialty Materials
International Flavors
Millennium Chemicals
Mitsubishi Chemical
PPG
Rhodia
Rohm and Haas
RPM
Sherwin-Williams

HISTORICAL FINANCIALS

Company Type: Public

Income Statement

FYE: December 31

	REVENUE ($ mil.)	NET INCOME ($ mil.)	NET PROFIT MARGIN	EMPLOYEES
12/05	10,001	358	3.6%	31,910
12/04	10,858	202	1.9%	33,300
12/03	10,431	(295)	—	35,030
12/02	9,830	14	0.1%	36,660
Annual Growth	**0.6%**	**191.8%**	**—**	**(4.5%)**

2005 Year-End Financials

Debt ratio: 49.7%
Return on equity: 9.1%
Cash ($ mil.): 950
Current ratio: 1.01
Long-term debt ($ mil.): 1,719

No. of shares (mil.): —
Dividends
  Yield: 2.4%
  Payout: —
Market value ($ mil.): —

Stock History

NYSE: ICI

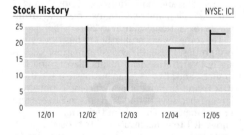

	STOCK PRICE ($) FY Close	P/E High/Low		PER SHARE ($) Earnings	Dividends
12/05	22.79	—	—	—	0.56
12/04	18.43	—	—	—	0.49
12/03	14.32	—	—	—	0.46
12/02	14.39	—	—	—	0.74
Annual Growth	**16.6%**	**—**	**—**	**—**	**(8.9%)**

Imperial Oil

Imperial Oil, Canada's largest oil company, holds sway over a vast empire of oil and gas resources. It has proved reserves of 634 million barrels of oil and 744 billion cu. ft. of natural gas. Imperial is one of Canada's top natural gas producers, the #1 refiner and marketer of petroleum products, and a major supplier of petrochemicals. It sells petroleum products, including gasoline, heating oil, and diesel fuel, under the Esso name and other brand names. Most of the company's production comes from fields in Alberta and the Northwest Territories. Imperial also owns 25% of Syncrude Canada, which operates the world's largest oil sands development. Exxon Mobil owns about 70% of Imperial.

The oil company sells gasoline to motorists at 2,000 Esso service stations (700 company-owned or leased) across Canada. At Cold Lake, Alberta, the company uses steam to recover very heavy crude and related products from oil sands deposits, through its participation in the Syncrude Project. Management is seeking to boost production from its plentiful oil sands holdings; its research laboratories in Ontario and Alberta are focused on developing technology for finding better ways to recover heavy oil.

Imperial's petroleum products and chemicals business operates four refineries and has an extensive network of wholesale outlets (in addition to its gas station chain) in every region of Canada. The company's chemicals segment operates a manufacturing plant in Sarnia, Ontario, and a number of distribution centers across Canada.

Imperial has reduced employment and closed service stations to stay competitive; it also is selling noncore assets and underperforming units (including refineries).

In 2002 Imperial worked out a deal to offer the popular Tim Hortons brand of soups and sandwiches at its Esso stations across Canada.

HISTORY

London, Ontario, boomed from the discovery of oil in the 1860s and 1870s, but when the market for Canadian kerosene became saturated in 1880, 16 refiners banded together to form the Imperial Oil Company.

The company refined sulfurous Canadian oil, nicknamed "skunk oil" for its powerful smell. Imperial faced tough competition from America's Standard Oil, which marketed kerosene made from lighter, less-odorous Pennsylvania crude. Guided by American expatriate Jacob Englehart, Imperial built a better refinery and hired a chemist to develop a process to clean sulfur from the crude.

By the mid-1890s Imperial had expanded from coast to Canadian coast. Cash-starved from its expansion, the company turned to old nemesis Standard Oil, which bought controlling interest in Imperial in 1898. That interest is today held by Exxon Mobil.

After the turn of the century, Imperial began producing gasoline to serve the new automobiles. The horseless carriages were spooking the workhorses at the warehouse where fuel was sold, so an Imperial manager in Vancouver opened the first Canadian service station in 1907. The company marketed its gas under the Esso banner borrowed from Standard Oil.

An Imperial crew discovered oil in 1920 at Norman Wells in the remote Northwest Territories. In 1924 a subsidiary sparked a new boom with a gas well discovery in the Turner Valley area northeast of Edmonton. But soon Imperial's luck ran as dry as the holes it was drilling; it came away empty from the next 133 consecutive wells. That string ended in 1947 when it struck oil in Alberta at the Leduc No. 1. To get the oil to market, Imperial invested in the Interprovincial Pipe Line from Alberta to Superior, Wisconsin.

In 1964 the company began research to extract bitumen from the oil sands in Cold Lake, Alberta. During the 1970s oil crisis, Imperial continued to search for oil in northern Canada. It found crude on land near the Beaufort Sea (1970) and in its icy waters (1972). The company formed its Esso Resources Canadian Ltd. subsidiary in 1978 to oversee natural resources production.

In 1989 Texaco (acquired by Chevron in 2001), still reeling from a court battle with Pennzoil, sold Texaco Canada to Imperial. To diminish debt and comply with regulators, Imperial agreed to sell some of Texaco Canada's refining and marketing assets in Atlantic Canada, its interests in Interhome Energy, and oil and gas properties in western Canada.

Imperial reorganized in 1992, centralizing several units, and in 1993 closed its refinery at Port Moody, British Columbia. It sold most of its fertilizer business in 1994; disposed of 339 unprofitable gas stations in 1995; and the next year closed down Canada's northernmost oil refinery at Norman Wells.

In 1997 Imperial announced an ambitious program to expand Syncrude's oil sands bitumen upgrading plant. In 1998 Exxon agreed to buy Mobil, which had substantial Canadian oil assets. In 1999 Canada pre-approved the potential merger of Imperial Oil and Mobil Canada. Later that year Exxon completed its purchase of Mobil to form Exxon Mobil.

In the face of public pressure for cleaner gasoline (Imperial had been implicated by government tests as Canada's "dirtiest" oil producer), Bob Peterson (who stepped down as CEO in 2002) told shareholders in 2000 that he did not agree with the theory of global warming. Activities at its Mackenzie Gas Project were halted in 2005 due to what Imperial termed as "insufficient progress."

EXECUTIVES

Chairman, President, and CEO:
Timothy J. (Tim) Hearn, age 61, $1,715,200 pay
SVP, Finance and Administration, Controller, and Director: Paul A. Smith, age 52, $507,706 pay
SVP, Resources Division and Director: Randy L. Broiles, age 48, $299,500 pay
VP, General Counsel, and Corporate Secretary: Brian W. Livingston
VP and Treasurer: John F. Kyle, age 63, $408,789 pay
VP, Human Resources: Robert F. Lipsett, age 59, $462,118 pay
Auditors: PricewaterhouseCoopers LLP

LOCATIONS

HQ: Imperial Oil Limited
237 4th Ave. SW, Calgary, Alberta T2P 3M9, Canada
Phone: 800-567-3776   **Fax:** 800-367-0585
Web: www.imperialoil.ca

Imperial Oil's exploration and development are conducted primarily in Alberta and the Northwest Territories. It owns two refineries in Ontario, and one each in Alberta and Nova Scotia. It also operates a chemical plant in Ontario.

PRODUCTS/OPERATIONS

2005 Sales

	% of total
Petroleum products	78
Natural resources	17
Chemicals	5
Total	**100**

COMPETITORS

Abraxas Petroleum	Lyondell Chemical
Ashland	Marathon Oil
Barnwell Industries	Murphy Oil
BHP Billiton	Occidental Petroleum
BP	PDVSA
Canadian Natural	PEMEX
ConocoPhillips	PETROBRAS
Devon Energy	Petro-Canada
Dominion Resources	Pioneer Natural Resources
DuPont	Royal Dutch Shell
EnCana	Suncor
Eni	Sunoco
Hunting	Talisman Energy
Husky Energy	TOTAL
Koch	

HISTORICAL FINANCIALS

Company Type: Public

Income Statement

FYE: December 31

	REVENUE ($ mil.)	NET INCOME ($ mil.)	NET PROFIT MARGIN	EMPLOYEES
12/05	24,208	2,231	9.2%	5,100
12/04	18,649	1,704	9.1%	6,100
12/03	14,842	1,317	8.9%	6,300
12/02	10,732	770	7.2%	6,460
12/01	10,842	782	7.2%	6,740
Annual Growth	22.2%	30.0%	—	(6.7%)

2005 Year-End Financials

Debt ratio: 15.3%
Return on equity: 40.8%
Cash ($ mil.): 1,425
Current ratio: 0.97
Long-term debt ($ mil.): 872
No. of shares (mil.): —
Dividends
Yield: 0.7%
Payout: 12.0%
Market value ($ mil.): —

Stock History

AMEX: IMO

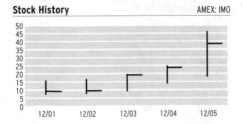

	STOCK PRICE ($) FY Close	P/E High/Low		PER SHARE ($) Earnings	Dividends
12/05	38.47	21	8	2.17	0.26
12/04	23.72	13	7	1.91	0.23
12/03	19.18	17	8	1.16	0.21
12/02	9.57	24	12	0.68	0.18
12/01	9.29	—	—	—	0.18
Annual Growth	42.7%	—	—	47.2%	9.6%

Imperial Tobacco

The UK's #1 cigarette maker (ahead of Gallaher Group), Imperial Tobacco Group has traded up to an even bigger throne. The company's purchase of German tobacco firm Reemtsma (Davidoff and West cigarettes) nearly doubled its size and made it the world's #4 tobacco company. Imperial's brands include Lambert & Butler, the UK's #1 cigarette, as well as Castella cigars, and Amphora and St Bruno pipe tobacco. Its Drum brand is the #1 hand-rolling tobacco worldwide, and Rizla is a top cigarette paper. Acquisitions in Australia and New Zealand have assured Imperial's presence in emerging markets.

Imperial Tobacco also looks to open new markets in China, where it signed a 10-year deal to produce and sell cigarettes. Imperial also is expanding to new markets in Africa. Despite global expansion, the UK still rings up nearly a majority of its sales. Imperial controls nearly 45% of the UK market.

Like rivals British American Tobacco and Gallaher, Imperial was spun off from a conglomerate eager to distance itself from increasingly problematic tobacco operations (it was part of Hanson until that group's 1996 four-way split). It's speculated that Altadis, owner of the world's largest cigar operation, and Imperial Tobacco might merge their operations.

In early 2005 Imperial restructured its European production, resulting in the closure of its operations in Dublin, Ireland, and nearly 100 job cuts. At around the same time, the company braced itself for the first round of class-action lawsuits directed at Canadian tobacco companies, in which subsidiary Imperial Tobacco Canada was named.

Later the same year the company announced further restructuring measures, which included moving production of about 10 billion cigarettes, distributed in Eastern Europe, from Germany to Poland; though production in Germany has been consolidated, it will not cease. Instead, that facility will move from Berlin to Hannover, and will feed the habits of the German smoking populous. It also announced the transfer of production from its Treforest, Wales, production facility to Wilrijk, Belgium. All told, more than 350 jobs were lost in the closures.

On the acquisitions side, Imperial Tobacco bought Swedish snus manufacturer Skruf in September 2005; months later brought the company's acquisition of Norwegian tobacco product distributor Gunnar Stenberg.

HISTORY

Imperial Tobacco Group was formed in 1901 to fight American Tobacco's invasion of the UK. American Tobacco had become the dominant US tobacco company partly by using a large cash reserve to undercut competitors. When it bought UK tobacco and cigarette factory Ogden's that year, 13 UK tobacco firms responded by registering as The Imperial Tobacco Company. The firms (including Wills, Lambert & Butler, and John Player & Sons) continued to make and sell their products separately.

As expected, American Tobacco cut prices, and Imperial fought back, acquiring the Salmon & Cluckstein tobacco shop chain and offering bonuses to retailers that sold its products. When Imperial threatened US expansion in 1902, American Tobacco surrendered: It gave Ogden's to Imperial and halted its Ireland and Great Britain business in exchange for Imperial's pledge to stay out of the US (except for buying tobacco leaf). The two formed the British American Tobacco Company (BAT) to sell both firms' cigarettes overseas. But when American Tobacco split into four companies in 1911 and sold its BAT interest, the agreement was modified to let Imperial sell some of its brands in the US.

By the 1950s Imperial controlled more than 80% of the UK tobacco market, but its share decreased during the 1960s due to competition from Gallaher Group (Benson & Hedges). Imperial diversified, buying companies such as Golden Wonder Crisps snack food (1961) and the Courage & Barclay brewery (1972).

In 1973 BAT and Imperial agreed that each firm would control its own brands in the UK and Continental Europe. Imperial sold the last of its stake in BAT in 1980. Conglomerate Hanson Trust paid $4.3 billion for Imperial in a 1986 hostile takeover. Hanson reduced Imperial's tobacco brands from more than 100 to five brand families (a move that decreased its UK market share to 33% by 1990). It also sold Imperial's drinks unit, including Courage and John Smith beer, to Elders IXL (now Foster's Brewing). Between 1986 and 1993 Hanson cut Imperial's tobacco operations from five factories and 7,500 employees to three factories and 2,600 employees; it also sold Imperial's restaurant and food operations.

As UK cigarette consumption dropped, Imperial began expanding overseas in 1994. By 1996 exports had risen to 15% of sales. That year Gareth Davis became CEO of Imperial.

Facing further declining UK cigarette sales and a government tax hike, Imperial bought the world's #1 cigarette paper brand, Rizla (1997), and Sara Lee's cut-tobacco unit, Douwe Egberts Van Nelle (1998), which it renamed Van Nelle Tabak. That acquisition added Drum hand-rolling tobacco and Amphora pipe tobacco to Imperial's brands. In 1999 the company added a bevy of Australian and New Zealand brands (Horizon, Brandon, Flagship, Peter Stuyvesant) from BAT.

In 2000 Imperial acquired paper maker EFKA (Germany, Canada) and tobacco maker Baelen (Belgium). That year Imperial tripled its cigarette vending operations by acquiring Mayfield Vending (27,000 UK locations).

Imperial expanded operations in Africa in 2001 with the acquisition of 75% of Tobaccor. It also began distributing the Marlboro brand in the UK. The company bought 90% of Reemtsma in 2002; the deal at the time was valued at $5.1 billion.

In 2004, Imperial cut 940 jobs as it closed manufacturing plants in Hungary, Slovakia, and Slovenia. The company shifted production to Germany and Poland. More cuts arrived in 2005 with the closing of a plant in Dublin.

EXECUTIVES

Chairman: Derek C. Bonham, age 62
Joint Vice Chairman: Anthony Alexander, age 65
Joint Vice Chairman: Iain Napier, age 56
CEO and Director: Gareth Davis, age 56, $2,256,001 pay
Finance Director: Robert (Bob) Dyrbus, age 53, $1,431,150 pay
Corporate Affairs Director and Director: Frank A. Rogerson, age 53, $560,000 pay
Manufacturing Director and Director: David Cresswell, age 61, $987,000 pay
Sales and Marketing Director and Board Member: Graham Blashill, age 58
Director of Finance and Planning: Alison Cooper, age 38

Group Human Resources Director: Kathryn Brown, age 49
Company Secretary: Matthew Phillips, age 35
Regional Director, Southern Central European Region: Zsolt Totos
Head, Corporate Communications: Jacqueline Smithson
Deputy Company Secretary: Trevor Williams, age 42
Assistant Company Secretary: Christopher Deft
Group Media Relations Executive: Simon Evans
Group Media Relations Manager: Alex Parson
Investor Relations Manager: Nicola Tate
Auditors: PricewaterhouseCoopers LLP

LOCATIONS

HQ: Imperial Tobacco Group PLC
Upton Rd., Bristol BS99 7UJ, United Kingdom
Phone: +44-117-963-6636   **Fax:** +44-117-966-7405
Web: www.imperial-tobacco.com

Imperial Tobacco Group operates about 32 factories in Africa, Canada, Europe, New Zealand, and the UK.

2005 Sales

	% of total
Europe	
UK	40
Germany	24
Other countries	14
Other regions	22
Total	**100**

PRODUCTS/OPERATIONS

Selected Products and Brands

Cigarettes
 Bastos
 Cabinet
 Davidoff (flagship brand)
 Drum (roll-your-own tobacco)
 Embassy
 Excellence
 Golden Virginia (launched in the UK in 1877)
 Horizon
 John Player (Blue, Special)
 Lambert & Butler (discount brand)
 Prima
 Regal
 Richmond (discount brand)
 Rizla (rolling paper)
 Route 66 (American blend sold in France, Belgium, and Eastern Europe)
 R1
 Superkings
 West (sold in more than 100 countries)
Cigars
 Cadena
 Castella
 Classic
 Panama
Rolling Paper and Tobacco
 Amphora
 Drum
 Rizla (rolling paper)
 St Bruno

COMPETITORS

Altadis
Altria
British American Tobacco
Gallaher
General Cigar
Gudang Garam
Japan Tobacco
JT International
Philip Morris International
Rothmans
Skandinavisk Tobakskompagni
Swedish Match
Swisher International
Tiedemanns
UST

HISTORICAL FINANCIALS

Company Type: Public

Income Statement

	REVENUE ($ mil.)	NET INCOME ($ mil.)	NET PROFIT MARGIN	EMPLOYEES
			FYE: Saturday nearest September 30	
9/05	19,840	1,199	6.0%	14,428
9/04	3,739	670	17.9%	15,633
9/03	5,335	827	15.5%	16,804
9/02	12,951	467	3.6%	11,440
Annual Growth	**15.3%**	**36.9%**	**—**	**8.0%**

2005 Year-End Financials

Debt ratio: 157.3%   Current ratio: 0.83
Return on equity: 45.8%   Long-term debt ($ mil.): 5,012
Cash ($ mil.): 451

Net Income History   NYSE: ITY

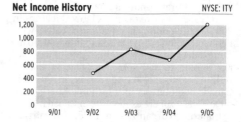

InBev

InBev NV/SA knows a good beer is timeless. With origins that date back to 1366 it has a collection of more than 200 global beers brands. The company outranks all others as the world's largest brewer by volume thanks to an ambitious merger in 2004 with the world's #5 brewer, Brazil's Companhia de Bebidas das Américas (AmBev). InBev operates facilities in more than 30 countries, producing lagers, premium beers, and specialty brews that are sold in 140 countries. InBev's flagship brands include Beck's Brahma, Leffe, Skol, and Stella Artois.

InBev was created through the 2005 merger of Interbrew and AmBev, which now serves as InBev's headquarters in the Americas. The merger resulted in a series of transactions between Interbrew subsidiary Labatt and Mexico's FEMSA. By creating InBev, Interbrew gave up interest in distributing FEMSA beer brands in the US. In return, Interbrew retained full control of the US division of Labatt. InBev has merged Labatt U.S.A. with what was Beck's North America to create InBev USA. In 2006 the company agreed to pay some $1 billion to increase its stake in Quinsa, an Argentine brewer, to 90% from 57%.

In addition to expanding in Latin America through AmBev, InBev is looking to emerging markets for growth, particularly in the Asian sector. InBev owns the brewing operations of Malaysia's Lion Group and a controlling interest in the KK Group, both of which brew popular beers in China. It also owns a controlling interest in Chinese brewers Zhejiang Shiliang Brewery Company Ltd. and Hunan Debier Brewery Company Ltd. In South Korea, InBev has a majority stake in Oriental Brewery. In 2006 the company acquired a Chinese brewer Fujian Sedrin.

Saying it intended to concentrate on import brands in the US market, in 2006 the company sold subsidiary InBev USA's domestic beer brand Rolling Rock to Anheuser-Busch for $82 million. Later in the year InBev and A-B struck an additional deal for A-B to serve as the exclusive distributor for some of its European brands, such as Beck's, Bass, and Stella Artois.

Chairman Pierre Jean Everaert became honorary chairman of the board in May 2006. He was succeeded as chairman by director Peter Harf.

HISTORY

Monks at the Leffe Abbey in Belgium were brewing beer as early as 1240, and surviving records from 1366 mention Belgium's Den Horen brewery. Belgian master brewer Sebastien Artois (best known for his Stella Artois lager) took over Den Horen in 1717. In 1853 the Piedboeuf family founded a brewery at Liege and established the Jupiler lager. Albert Van Damme assumed management of that brewery in 1920.

Over the years, the Artois and Piedboeuf families took over or established operations both in and outside Belgium. Direct descendants (the clans de Spoelberch, Van Damme, and de Mevius) of the two families were still managing the companies in 1987 when they decided the key to survival in the fragmented European beer market was to merge.

Artois-Piedboeuf-Interbrew acquired the Hoegaarden brewery in Belgium in 1989. The company changed its name to Interbrew three years later, acquired another Belgian brewery (Belle-Vue), and bought stakes in breweries in Bulgaria, Croatia, and Hungary. In 1995 Dommelsche Bierbrouwerij bought Allied Breweries Nederland, an Allied Domecq subsidiary, and Interbrew acquired the Oranjeboom breweries in the Netherlands.

The company purchased John Labatt Ltd. for $2 billion in 1995. As a result of the deal, Interbrew gained control of Latrobe Brewing (Rolling Rock beer, US), 22% of Mexico's FEMSA Cerveza (increased to 30% in 1998), the Toronto Argonauts football team, 90% of the Toronto Blue Jays (it sold an 80% stake in the baseball team to cable firm Rogers Communications in 2000) and various broadcast properties.

Interbrew sold many noncore assets, including Lehigh Valley Dairies (US) and John Labatt Retail (pubs, UK), in 1996. Also that year the company established joint ventures in the Dominican Republic and the US (to import Mexican beers through FEMSA).

In 1998 Interbrew paid $250 million for 50% of the Doosan Group's Oriental Brewery, South Korea's second-largest brewer, and bought a majority stake in Russian brewer Rosar. The next year Interbrew combined its Russian operations with Sun Brewing, forming Russian brewer Sun-Interbrew. It then bought Korea's Jinro-Coors Brewery for about $378 million. Hugo Powell was later named CEO of Interbrew.

Interbrew bought Britain's third-largest brewer, Whitbread Beer Company, in 2000 for $590 million. Having gained a foothold in the UK market, the company then bought Bass Brewers from Bass PLC in 2000 for more than $3 billion. Interbrew went public on the Euronext (Brussels) exchange in 2000.

In 2001 Baron Paul De Keersmaeker retired as chairman and was replaced by Pierre Jean Everaert. That year the company took an 80% stake in Germany's 10th-largest brewer, Diebels. Interbrew also sold Carling, which controls about 18% of the UK beer market, to Coors for $1.7 billion, after being ordered to remedy unfair competition advantages related to the Bass Brewers purchase.

John Brock, former Cadbury Schweppes COO, became CEO of Interbrew in 2003. That year it sold a minority stake of its Namibian Breweries in southern Africa to Diageo and Heineken.

In 2004 Interbrew purchased a 70% stake in Chinese brewer Zhejiang Shiliang, which gave Interbrew nearly a 50% market share in China's Zhejiang province. Later that year, Interbrew changed its name to InBev following its merger with Brazilian brewer AmBev.

Exiting the Slovenian market, InBev sold its stake in Pivovarna Union to Pivovarna Lasko in 2005. That year it acquired Russian premium brewer Tinkoff and sold its stake in soft-drink company Bremer Erfrischungsgetränke to Coca-Cola. It also sold its minority stake in Spanish brewer Damm. At year end Carlos Brito, formerly zone president for the company's North American operations, succeeded John Brock as CEO of InBev.

EXECUTIVES

Chairman: Peter Harf, age 60
CEO: Carlos Brito, age 46
CFO: Felipe Dutra, age 41
SVP, External Growth: Gauthier de Biolley
VP, External Growth and Market Development: Simon Thorpe
VP, Export and Licenses Asia Pacific: Ben Cheng
VP, Investor Relations: Patrick Verelst
Marketing Director: Devin Kelly
Zone President, Latin America: Luiz Fernando Zeigler de Saint Edmond, age 40
Zone President, North America: Miguel Nuno da Mata Patrício
Zone President, Western Europe: Stéfan Descheemaeker, age 46
President and CEO, InBev USA: Doug Corbett
President, InBev Central Europe: Philipp Vandervoort
President, InBev France: Sabine Sagaert
President, Interbrew UK: Colin Pedrick, age 52
CTO: André Weckx, age 53
CIO and Chief Services Officer: Claudio Garcia, age 38
Chief Commercial Officer: Steve Cahillane, age 38
Chief Legal Officer: Sabine Chalmers
Chief People Officer: Peter Vrijsen, age 52
Chief Strategy and Business Development Officer: Jo Van Biesbroeck
Manager, Investor Relations: Philip Ludwig
Manager, Public Affairs and External Communications: Lian Verhoeven
Auditors: Klynveld Peat Marwick Goerdeler

LOCATIONS

HQ: InBev NV/SA
 Brouwerijplein 1, 3000 Leuven, Belgium
Phone: +32-16-24-71-11 **Fax:** +32-16-24-74-07
US HQ: 101 Merrit 7, Norwalk, CT 06856
US Phone: 203-750-6600 **US Fax:** 203-750-6699
Web: www.inbev.com

2005 Sales

	% of total
Latin America	34
Western Europe	32
North America	15
Central & Eastern Europe	13
Asia/Pacific	6
Total	**100**

PRODUCTS/OPERATIONS

Selected Brands

Global flagship brands
 Beck's
 Brahma
 Stella Artois
Global specialty brands
 Cuvée
 Hoegaarden
 Leffe
Licensed brands
 Absolut Cut
 Budweiser
 Castelmaine
 Murphy's
Local brands
 Bass
 Boddingtons
 Kokanee
 Labatt
 Liber
 Löwenbräu
 Staropramen
 Tennet's
 Zhujiang

COMPETITORS

Anchor Brewing	Grupo Modelo
Anheuser-Busch	Heineken
Asahi Breweries	Holsten-Brauerei
Asia Pacific Breweries	Kirin Brewery Company
Big Rock Brewery	Miller Brewing
Blaue Quellen Mineral	Molson Coors
Boston Beer	Pyramid Breweries
Brau und Brunnen	Radeberger Gruppe
Carlsberg	Redhook Ale
CBR Brewing	SABMiller
Central European Distribution	San Miguel
Constellation Brands	Sapporo
Diageo	Scottish & Newcastle
FEMSA	Suntory Ltd.
Foster's	Tsingtao
Gambrinus	Vidrala
Grolsch	Yanjing
	Yuengling & Son

HISTORICAL FINANCIALS

Company Type: Public

Income Statement				FYE: December 31
	REVENUE ($ mil.)	NET INCOME ($ mil.)	NET PROFIT MARGIN	EMPLOYEES
12/05	13,804	1,660	12.0%	77,000
12/04	11,687	981	8.4%	74,694
12/03	8,842	634	7.2%	50,000
12/02	7,328	490	6.7%	35,044
12/01	6,469	618	9.6%	37,617
Annual Growth	20.9%	28.0%	—	19.6%

Net Income History   Euronext Brussels: INBS

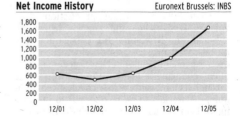

Inco

Inco turns nickel into gold. The company is the world's #2 producer of nickel (after Russian giant Norilsk Nickel), which is used primarily for manufacturing stainless steel and batteries. Inco also mines and processes copper, gold, cobalt, and platinum group metals. It makes nickel battery materials and nickel foams, flakes, and powders for use in catalysts, electronics, and paints. Sulphuric acid and liquid sulphur dioxide are made as byproducts. The company's mining and processing operations are in Canada, Indonesia, and the UK. In 2006 the Brazilian iron ore miner Companhia Vale do Rio Doce (CVRD) acquired 76% of Inco in a deal that values the entire company at $19 billion.

The Canadian mining industry has undergone much turmoil in 2006. To begin with, Canadian zinc miner Teck Cominco offered to buy Inco in 2006 for about $16 billion. Teck Cominco had approached Inco the previous fall but had been turned down in favor of Inco's previously proposed acquisition of Falconbridge. Had Teck been successful in its attempt, Inco would have had to call off the deal to buy Falconbridge. In response to Teck Cominco's move, Inco raised its offer price for Falconbridge by $1.7 billion. Xstrata apparently wanted to get in on the action, too, because in 2006 it made a counter offer to buy Falconbridge that valued the company at $18 billion. It eventually won out.

Inco and Falconbridge had been looking for a way out of the Xstrata/Teck Cominco situations and seemed to have found it in the middle of 2006 when they announced they would combine with copper company Phelps Dodge. However, Xstrata's persistence, and a considerably raised offer, in its pursuit of Falconbridge scuttled those plans.

Further complicating the matter, CVRD entered the picture with a $19 billion cash offer for Inco of its own later in the summer of 2006. While the offer price wasn't necessarily any higher than Phelps Dodge's or Teck Cominco's, CVRD's all-cash offering trumped the other two, which relied more heavily on those companies' burgeoning stock. In response, both Teck Cominco and Phelps Dodge pulled out of the running not long after CVRD announced its intentions. CVRD won control of Inco in late 2006 and extended its offer in an attempt to acquire 100% of the company. The Brazilian giant is looking to make Inco its foothold in North America and plans to build on those holdings. Inco will change its name to CVRD Inco upon completion of the offer; its entire board (except CEO Scott Hand) resigned after the deal got done.

In late 2005 Inco began production at its Voisey's Bay nickel and copper deposit in Labrador and Newfoundland, Canada. Its Goro nickel-cobalt project is in development (startup is expected in 2006) in New Caledonia.

The company is making inroads into China through its joint venture in Inco Advanced Technology Materials (82% ownership) to produce nickel foam for use in rechargeable batteries. In 2005, Inco acquired a large stake in another nickel foam producer, Shenyang Golden Champower New Materials.

HISTORY

In 1883 a Canadian Pacific Railway blacksmith discovered copper and nickel deposits in the Sudbury Basin. Two companies — the Orford Nickel and Copper Company and the Canadian Copper Company — tried to exploit the ore but couldn't separate the copper from the nickel. Nickel was all but worthless at the time. In 1890 Orford, led by Robert Thompson, patented a process to separate the two metals just as the US Navy was beginning to use a nickel-steel alloy for armaments.

Enter financier J. P. Morgan, architect of U.S. Steel. With Morgan's help Orford and Canadian Copper combined with five smaller companies in 1902 to form New Jersey-based International Nickel Company. In 1916 the company formed a Canadian subsidiary, International Nickel Company of Canada.

Sales plummeted after WWI, and in a 1928 restructuring, the Canadian subsidiary became the parent company. In 1929 International Nickel gained control of the world's nickel output when it bought Mond Nickel, a British metals refiner. By the 1950s the company accounted for 85% of noncommunist production.

Oil crises and inflation decreased demand for metals and battered International Nickel during the 1970s and early 1980s. In 1974 the company bought ESB Ray-O-Vac, the world's largest battery maker (sold in the early 1980s). Two years later the company shortened its name to Inco Limited.

Inco suffered from lack of demand for its metals until 1986. Then-CEO Donald Phillips cut employees and boosted productivity at Inco's mines and refineries. Demand for stainless steel rose in the late 1980s; Inco's sales more than doubled from 1987 to 1989.

Metal prices declined again in the early 1990s in response to a North American recession and entry of former Iron Curtain countries into the metals markets. With a worldwide surplus, Inco cut nickel production. The company also reorganized. In 1991 it merged its gold interests with Consolidated TVX Mining (in 1993 it sold its 62% interest in TVX).

As the US economy recovered and new Asian markets developed, exploration activities revved up with new ore discoveries in 1994 and 1995. In 1995 Inco bought a 25% share of the copper, cobalt, and nickel rights to rich deposits at Voisey's Bay in Newfoundland and Labrador; the following year it bought the remaining rights along with their holder, mining company Diamond Fields (the total cost was $3.2 billion).

Inco also unloaded some of its nonmining businesses. The company spun off Doncasters (aircraft components) in 1997. About 4,700 miners went on strike that year, cutting the company's nickel production by more than half. As rising worldwide nickel production drove prices down in 1998, the company reduced its workforce by more than 1,400.

In 1999 Inco entered into joint ventures with Dowa Mining of Japan to search for copper, zinc, silver, and gold in Indonesia and Turkey. That year the company shut down its Manitoba nickel production facility for several months over a contract dispute with labor.

Inco started building a nickel-cobalt mining and refining facility on the French island of New Caledonia in 2000 (expecting to begin production in 2007). The company continued negotiations throughout 2001 with the governments of Canada, Labrador, and Newfoundland, and an agreement was reached in mid-2002. Inco eventually began construction and development of its Voisey's Bay nickel project in 2003; it began production in 2005.

EXECUTIVES

President and CEO, CVRD Inco and Director: Scott M. Hand, age 64
President and COO: Peter C. Jones, age 58
COO, CVRD Inco: Mark Cutifiani, age 47
EVP and CFO: Robert D. J. (Bob) Davies, age 56
EVP, Technical Services: Ronald C. (Ron) Aelick, age 57, $865,648 pay
EVP, Corporate Affairs: Stuart F. Feiner, age 58
EVP, Marketing: Peter J. Goudie, age 57, $1,078,618 pay
VP and CIO: Subhash (Subi) Bhandari, age 61
VP and Comptroller: Ronald A. Lehtovaara, age 55
VP and Treasurer: Stephanie E. Anderson, age 44
VP, Business Development — Asia: John B. Jones, age 63
VP, Capital Projects and Engineering: Edward H. Bassett, age 59
VP, Environment and Health: William A. Napier, age 51
VP, Exploration: S. Nicholas Sheard, age 56
VP, Human Resources: Mark J. Daniel, age 59
VP, Inco Special Products: William B. Kipkie, age 60
VP, Public and Government Affairs: Bruce R. Drysdale, age 39
VP, Research and Development: Anthony O. (Tony) Filmer
VP, Taxation: Gary G. Kaiway, age 57
President, Asia/Pacific: Logan W. Kruger, age 55, $884,917 pay
Chairman Nominee: Roger Agnelli, age 46
Auditors: PricewaterhouseCoopers LLP

LOCATIONS

HQ: Inco Limited
145 King St. West, Ste. 1500,
Toronto, Ontario M5H 4B7, Canada
Phone: 416-361-7511   **Fax:** 416-361-7781
US HQ: Park 80 West, Plaza 2, Saddle Brook, NJ 07663
US Phone: 201-368-4800   **US Fax:** 201-368-4858
Web: www.inco.com

Inco Limited's core subsidiaries operate mines and facilities in Canada, China, Indonesia, Japan, New Caledonia (in the southwest Pacific), South Korea, Taiwan, and the UK. The company also operates in the US and has exploration activities in Australia, Brazil, Canada, China, Greenland, and Finland.

2005 Sales

	$ mil.	% of total
North America		
US	1,434	32
Canada	231	5
Asia		
China	617	14
Japan	610	13
Indonesia	175	4
UK	724	16
Other regions	727	16
Total	**4,518**	**100**

PRODUCTS/OPERATIONS

2005 Sales

	$ mil.	% of total
Primary nickel	3,655	82
Copper	463	10
Precious metals	267	6
Cobalt	57	1
Other	76	1
Total	**4,518**	**100**

Selected Products

Cobalt
Copper
Nickel (including intermediates)
Precious metals
  Gold
  Iridium
  Palladium
  Platinum
  Rhodium
  Ruthenium
  Silver
Special products (foams, flakes, powders, oxides, and
  nickel-coated graphite and carbon fibers)
Other
  Liquid sulfur dioxide
  Sulfuric acid

Selected Subsidiaries and Affiliates

I.E.L. Holdings (UK)
  Inco Europe Limited (UK)
Inco TNC Limited (67%, Japan)
Goro Nickel S.A.S (71%, France)
Monticello Capital (Barbados) Limited
  Inco Asia Limited (Barbados)
P.T. International Nickel Indonesia Tbk (61%, Indonesia)
Voisey's Bay Nickel Company Limited (Newfoundland
  and Labrador)

COMPETITORS

Anglo American	Outokumpu
ASARCO	Phelps Dodge
BHP Billiton	Rio Tinto
Eramet	Southern Copper
Newmont Mining	Special Metals
Nippon Mining	Stillwater Mining
Norilsk Nickel	Umicore

HISTORICAL FINANCIALS

Company Type: Public

Income Statement

FYE: December 31

	REVENUE ($ mil.)	NET INCOME ($ mil.)	NET PROFIT MARGIN	EMPLOYEES
12/05	4,518	628	13.9%	11,707
12/04	4,326	479	11.1%	10,973
12/03	2,578	(129)	—	10,478
12/02	2,161	(2,119)	—	10,534
Annual Growth	27.9%	—	—	3.6%

2005 Year-End Financials

Debt ratio: 82.0%
Return on equity: 24.3%
Cash ($ mil.): 958
Current ratio: 2.09
Long-term debt ($ mil.): 2,377
No. of shares (mil.): —
Dividends
  Yield: 0.6%
  Payout: 10.5%
Market value ($ mil.): —

Stock History

Pink Sheets: INCLF

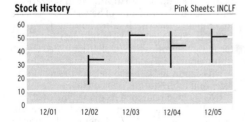

	STOCK PRICE ($) FY Close	P/E High/Low		PER SHARE ($) Earnings	Dividends
12/05	50.50	19	11	2.87	0.30
12/04	44.00	18	9	2.99	—
12/03	51.65	—	—	(0.81)	—
12/02	33.38	—	—	(11.73)	—
Annual Growth	14.8%	—	—	—	—

Infosys Technologies

IT normally means information technology, but in the case of this company it could also stand for Indian technology. Infosys Technologies is one of India's leading technology consulting firms with operations in more than 15 countries. The company provides software development and engineering through a network of development centers in Asia and North America. It also provides data management, systems integration, project management, support, and maintenance services. In addition, its Progeon subsidiary offers business process outsourcing (BPO) services and US-based Infosys Consulting provides strategic consulting.

Infosys has rapidly expanded its presence in international markets, especially in North America which now accounts for about 65% of sales. In 2004 it launched Infosys Consulting to capture additional business in the US. The company has also added operations in China and Australia and continues to eye opportunities in Asia, Africa, and Latin America.

For India, Infosys has been a beacon of success as one of the country's fastest-growing and most admired businesses. Its main campus, called Infosys City, resembles many modern American technology facilities, sporting such features as a gymnasium, a sauna, a pool hall, a mini golf course, several tennis courts, and even its own power generators. Infosys was one of the first companies in India to offer employees stock options.

Leading the way has been chairman Narayana Murthy, who founded Infosys with six friends and $250 borrowed from their wives. Murthy is also a generous philanthropist who has made improving social welfare in India a major goal. Despite being one of India's wealthiest men (he owns almost 7% of Infosys), Murthy lives a modest life: his wife often drives him to the bus stop, where he boards a company bus to work.

HISTORY

After receiving a master's degree in electrical engineering from one of India's highly regarded Institutes of Technology (Kanpur) in the 1960s, Narayana Murthy left for France and a job developing software for the air traffic control system at Paris' Charles de Gaulle airport.

During college Murthy had developed the belief that communism was the answer to his country's problems with poverty and corruption, a stance that was fortified during his time spent with Paris leftists in the 1970s. But while hitchhiking back to India in 1974, Murthy's Marxist sympathies eroded quickly after he was jailed in Hungary for allegedly disclosing state secrets while talking with Austrian tourists on a train. Murthy became a socialist at heart but capitalist in practice, setting out on a mission to create wealth rather than redistribute poverty.

That mission officially began in 1981, when Murthy convinced six fellow software engineers to start their own company. Infosys was founded that year with $250 in capital (mostly borrowed from their wives) and no idea of what it would sell. From the beginning Murthy looked for business outside of India, where he was able to sell multinational corporations such as Reebok and Nordstrom customizable, inexpensive software. But a lack of reputation and government regulations made business difficult for Infosys during

the 1980s — it took nine months just to get the company's first telephone line, and three years to import new computers. Infosys opened its first US office in 1987.

Many of the government regulations that had kept India's economy stagnant were lifted when reform swept the country in 1991. But this also opened the door for companies such as IBM (which had been asked to leave in 1977) and Digital Equipment (later acquired by Compaq) to enter India and lure away its best engineers. While no Indian company had ever done this before, Murthy initiated a stock option plan and other perks to retain his employees. Infosys went public in 1993. Morgan Stanley swooped in to salvage the under-subscribed IPO in a move that would later reap millions when Infosys' stock began to soar.

In 1995 Infosys lost its biggest customer, General Electric, which had accounted for more than 20% of sales. Murthy took it as a lesson to never let one client or product drive more than 10% of a business. Infosys responded quickly by inking big deals with Xerox, Levi Strauss, and Nynex. By 2003, the company's biggest customer accounted for only about 6% of revenues. The company grew rapidly in the mid-1990s by signing short-term pilot projects that it was able to leverage into more extensive contracts for managing mainframe upgrades, designing custom software, and implementing e-commerce systems.

In the late 1990s Infosys established offices in Canada, Japan, and the UK to better market its offshore development capabilities. The move paid off — by the end of fiscal 1999 sales had reached $121 million. That year Infosys became the first Indian company to list its shares on Nasdaq, an offering timed perfectly with the surge in demand for technology stocks. Infosys' market cap ballooned to more than $17 billion in 2000.

The company that year inked a long-term pact with Microsoft to dedicate more than 1,200 engineers to build e-commerce, financial services, and customer relationship management applications for the software giant.

Not immune to the slowing economy, Murthy saw his wealth drastically decrease in 2001; he lost more than $100 million due to Infosys' declining share value. In 2002 Murthy stepped down from the daily management of the company; co-founder Nandan Nilekan took over as CEO while Murthy, who remained chairman, adopted the new title chief mentor. That same year, Infosys launched a new subsidiary, Progeon, to provide business process outsourcing services.

EXECUTIVES

Chairman and Chief Mentor: N. R. Narayana Murthy, age 59, $75,280 pay
President, CEO, and Managing Director:
  Nandan M. Nilekani, age 51, $75,280 pay
Deputy Managing Director and COO; Head of Customer Service and Technology: S. (Kris) Gopalakrishnan, age 51, $75,280 pay
CFO and Company Secretary: V. Balakrishnan, age 41, $94,708 pay
Director, Human Resources and Director:
  T. V. Mohandas Pai, age 47, $143,238 pay
Director and Head of Information Systems, Quality and Productivity, and Communication Design Group:
  Krishnaswamy Dinesh, age 51, $75,280 pay
Director and Head of Global Accounts and Asia Pacific:
  Srinath Batni, age 51, $131,185 pay
Director and Head of Worldwide Sales and Customer Delivery: S. D. Shibulal, age 51, $224,566 pay

SVP Accounts and Administration: U. Ramadas Kamath, age 44
SVP Commercial and Facilities: H. R. Binod, age 42
SVP Global Alliances: John K. Conlon
SVP Infosys Leadership Institute: Girish G. Vaidya, age 55
SVP Quality and Productivity: Satyendra Kumar, age 51
Corporate Counsel: Roopa P. Doraswamy, age 34
CEO and Managing Director, Infosys Consulting: Stephen R. (Steve) Pratt
CEO and Managing Director, Infosys Technologies (Australia): Gary Ebeyan
CEO and Managing Director, Infosys Technologies (Shanghai): James Lin
Public Relations, North America: Peter McLaughlin
Auditors: KPMG LLP; Bharat S. Raut & Co.

LOCATIONS

HQ: Infosys Technologies Limited
   Electronics City, Hosur Road,
   Bangalore, Karnataka 560 100, India
Phone: +91-80-2852-0261   **Fax:** +91-80-2852-0362
US HQ: 6607 Kaiser Dr., Fremont, CA 94555
US Phone: 510-742-3000   **US Fax:** 510-742-3090
Web: www.infosys.com

Infosys Technologies has operations in Australia, Belgium, Canada, China, France, Germany, India, Italy, Japan, Mauritius, the Netherlands, Sweden, Switzerland, the United Arab Emirates, the UK, and the US.

2006 Sales

	$ mil.	% of total
North America	1,394	65
Europe	528	25
India	38	2
Other regions	192	8
Total	**2,152**	**100**

PRODUCTS/OPERATIONS

2006 Sales

	$ mil.	% of total
Financial services	775	36
Telecommunications	354	16
Manufacturing	299	14
Retail	219	10
Other	505	24
Total	**2,152**	**100**

Selected Services

Custom application development
Information technology consulting
Maintenance and production support
Package evaluation and implementation
Software re-engineering
Other services
   Business process management
   Engineering
   Infrastructure management
   Management consulting
   Operations and business process consulting
   Systems integration
   Testing

COMPETITORS

Accenture	Keane
BearingPoint	LogicaCMG
Capgemini	Oracle
Cognizant Tech Solutions	Patni Computer Systems
Computer Sciences Corp.	Perot Systems
Deloitte Consulting	SAP
EDS	Satyam
HP Technology Solutions	Tata Consultancy
Group	Wipro Technologies
IBM Global Services	

HISTORICAL FINANCIALS

Company Type: Public

Income Statement

FYE: March 31

	REVENUE ($ mil.)	NET INCOME ($ mil.)	NET PROFIT MARGIN	EMPLOYEES
3/06	2,152	555	25.8%	52,700
3/05	1,592	419	26.3%	36,800
3/04	1,063	270	25.4%	25,700
3/03	754	195	25.9%	15,940
3/02	545	165	30.2%	10,740
Annual Growth	**41.0%**	**35.5%**	**—**	**48.8%**

2006 Year-End Financials

Debt ratio: —
Return on equity: 35.9%
Cash ($ mil.): 1,059
Current ratio: 7.22
Long-term debt ($ mil.): —

Net Income History

NASDAQ (GS): INFY

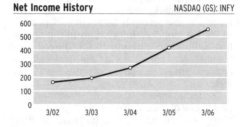

ING

ING Groep is a hybrid of bank*ing,* insur*ing,* and asset-manag*ing* services. One of the world's largest insurers, its operations are focused on Asia/Pacific, the Benelux countries, Central Europe, and North America. Key products include life insurance, pensions, retirement services, and non-life insurance. Its banking operations include wholesale and retail banking and mortgage lending in Europe. The company's ING Direct business offers online retail banking for individuals in Australia, Austria, Canada, France, Germany, Italy, Spain, the UK, and the US. ING provides asset management for individuals and institutional investors through both its insurance and banking businesses.

ING has taken aim at becoming a financial services player in all four corners of the world. While its Asian operations are already strong, the company considers China, India, and Thailand as sites for its future growth. ING has taken a majority stake in India's Vysya Bank and has set up joint banking ventures in Australia and China. During 2005 it also acquired a 20% stake in the Bank of Beijing as part of a strategic alliance. However, back in Europe, the company has announced that it intends to sell its 83% stake in Germany's mortgage bank Deutsche Hypothekenbank AG.

The company also has an aging population in its sights, and considers retirement planning and pensions as sources of future growth.

HISTORY

ING Groep's roots go back to 1845 when its earliest predecessor, the Netherlands Insurance Co., was founded. The firm began expanding geographically; in 1903 it added life insurance. In 1963 it merged with the century-old Nationale

Life Insurance Bank to form Nationale-Nederland (NN). Over the next three decades, the company grew primarily through acquisitions in Europe, North America, and Australia. In 1986 NN became the first European life insurance company to be licensed in Japan.

Another predecessor, the Rijkspostspaarbank, was founded in 1881 to provide Dutch citizens with simple post office savings accounts. In 1918 the Postcheque-en Girondienst (giro) system was established to allow people to use vouchers drawn on their savings accounts to pay bills. This system became the main method of settling accounts (instead of bank checking accounts).

Rijkspostspaarbank and Postcheque merged in 1986 to become Postbank. Postbank merged in 1989 with the Nederlandse Middenstandsbank (founded 1927) to become NMB Postbank. The vast amounts of cash tied up in the post office savings and giro systems fueled NMB's business.

In 1991, as the Europe economic union became a reality, and barriers between banking and insurance began to fall, NN merged with NMB Postbank to form Internationale Nederland Groep (ING). ING began cutting costs, shedding redundant offices and unprofitable operations in both its segments. In the US, where insurance and banking were legally divided, the company "debanked" itself in order to keep its more lucrative insurance operations (but retained the right to provide banking services to those operations).

In the 1990s ING sought to increase its investment banking and finance operations. In 1995 it took over UK-based Barings Bank (personal banker to the Queen of England) after Nicholas Leeson, a trader in Barings' Singapore office, lost huge sums of money in derivatives trading. The acquisition gave the firm a higher profile but cost more than anticipated and left it embroiled in lingering legal actions.

In 1996 ING bought Poland's Bank Slaski (it had first entered Poland in 1994). The next year it expanded its securities business by acquiring investment bank Furman Selz, doubled its US life insurance operations by purchasing Equitable of Iowa, and listed on the NYSE. In 1998 ING's acquisition strategy again involved Europe and North America: It bought Belgium's Banque Bruxelles Lambert and Canadian life insurer Guardian Insurance Co. (from Guardian Royal Exchange, now part of AXA UK).

In 1999 ING turned eastward, kicking off asset management operations in India and buying a minority stake in South Korea's HC&B (formerly Housing & Commercial Bank). In 2000 the company bulked up its North American operations with the purchase of 40% of Savia SA, a Mexican insurance concern. It also bought US firm ReliaStar Financial in a $6 billion deal and Charterhouse Securities from CCF (then called Crédit Commercial de France).

ING acquired US-based Aetna's financial services and international divisions.

ING in 2004 realigned its management structure, dividing the company's operations into six business lines: Insurance Americas, Insurance Europe, Insurance Asia-Pacific, Wholesale Banking, Retail Banking, and ING Direct. ING boosted its North American insurance operations with the acquisition of Allianz's Canadian property and casualty operations. The company struggled with investment banking arm ING Barings. The unit was reorganized and streamlined for cost-savings purposes, but ultimately was put on the block. Its Asian equities operations were sold to Macquarie Bank in 2004. Barings Private Equity Partners unit was sold to its management. The

Barings investment management operations were sold to MassMutual in 2005 while Northern Trust bought up its fund administration, trust, and custody operations.

ING sold most of ING BHF-Bankin to Sal. Oppenheim during 2004. The next year ING turned over its US life reinsurance operations to Scottish Re and sold subsidiary Life Insurance Company of Georgia to Jackson National Life.

In 2006 the company sold off its UK brokerage business, Williams de Broë, to The Evolution Group.

EXECUTIVES

Chairman, Supervisory Board:
Cornelius A. J. (Cor) Herkströter, age 69
Vice Chairman, Supervisory Board:
Eric Bourdais de Charbonnière, age 67
CEO and Chairman, Executive Board: Michel Tilmant, age 54, $3,326,699 pay
CFO and Vice Chairman, Executive Board: Cees Maas, age 59, $1,780,003 pay
Executive Board, CFO, and Chief Risk Officer:
Dick Harryvan, age 53
Executive Board, Retail Banking: Eli P. Leenaars, age 45, $1,585,777 pay
Executive Board, ING Retail US Financial Services:
Jacques de Vaucleroy, age 44
Executive Board Member, Wholesale Banking:
Eric Boyer de la Giroday, age 54, $2,125,818 pay
Executive Board, Retail Division ING Netherlands:
Hans van der Noordaa, age 45
Global Head of Pensions; CEO, ING Central Europe Insurance: Tom Kliphuis, age 41
Head of UK Region: Igno van Waesberghe
CEO, ING Asia/Pacific: Jacques Kemp
Executive Board, ING U.S. Financial Services:
Thomas J. (Tom) McInerney, age 49
Chief Investment Officers, ING Investment Management, Europe: Maes van Lanschot
Auditors: Ernst & Young Accountants

LOCATIONS

HQ: ING Groep N.V.
ING House, Amstelveenseweg 500,
1081 KL Amsterdam, The Netherlands
Phone: +31-20-541-5411   **Fax:** +31-20-541-5497
US HQ: 5780 Powers Ferry Rd. NW, Atlanta, GA 30327
US Phone: 770-980-5100   **US Fax:** 770-980-3301
Web: www.ing.com

ING Groep operates in more than 50 countries in Africa, Asia, Europe, North America, the Pacific Rim, and South America.

2005 Sales

	% of total
Americas	
North America	37
Latin America	4
Europe	
Netherlands	24
Belgium	7
Other countries	8
Asia/Pacific	
Asia	18
Australia	1
Other regions	1
Total	**100**

PRODUCTS/OPERATIONS

2005 Sales

	% of total
Premium income	64
Investment income	15
Interest from banking operations	13
Commissions	5
Other	3
Total	**100**

2005 Sales

	% of total
Insurance Americas	39
Insurance Europe	23
Insurance Asia/Pacific	19
Wholesale banking	8
Retail banking	8
ING Direct	3
Total	**100**

Selected Products and Services

Personal Finance
  Checking accounts
  Individual insurance (life, health, property/casualty)
  Individual loans (lines of credit, mortgage loans)
  Private banking
  Savings and investment products
Corporate and Institutional Clients
  Cash management
  Corporate insurance (group benefits and pensions; general insurance)
  Corporate lending
  Debt capital markets
  Debt markets (fixed income products)
  Employee benefits
  Equities
  Equity capital markets and IPOs
  Equity derivatives
  Foreign exchange
  Institutional asset management
  Interest rate derivatives
  Leasing (equipment, automobiles)
  Mergers and acquisitions advisory
  Money market products
  Real estate (development, management, financing)
  Research
  Securities services
  Securitization
  Structured finance
  Structured products
  Trust services

COMPETITORS

ABN AMRO
AEGON
AGF
AIG
AIG American General
Allianz
Allstate
AXA
Barclays
Bear Stearns
Chubb Corp
CIGNA
Citigroup
CNP Assurances
Credit Suisse
Deutsche Bank
Deutsche Bundesbank
Dexia
Fortis SA/NV
General Re
Generali
Goldman Sachs
The Hartford
HSBC Holdings
HVB Group
KBC
Legal & General Group
Lehman Brothers
Lloyd's
Merrill Lynch
MetLife
Prudential
Prudential plc
Royal & Sun Alliance Insurance
Swiss Life
UBS
Zurich Financial Services

HISTORICAL FINANCIALS

Company Type: Public

Income Statement

FYE: December 31

	ASSETS ($ mil.)	NET INCOME ($ mil.)	INCOME AS % OF ASSETS	EMPLOYEES
12/05	1,375,606	8,262	0.6%	115,328
12/04	1,195,822	9,001	0.8%	113,039
12/03	989,431	5,666	0.6%	115,218
12/02	799,343	(10,092)	—	113,060
Annual Growth	**19.8%**	**—**	**—**	**0.7%**

2005 Year-End Financials

Equity as % of assets: 3.6%
Return on assets: 0.6%
Return on equity: 17.0%
Long-term debt ($ mil.): 453,740
No. of shares (mil.): —
Dividends
  Yield: 3.0%
  Payout: —
Market value ($ mil.): —
Sales ($ mil.): 130,580

Stock History

NYSE: ING

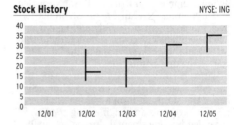

	STOCK PRICE ($) FY Close	P/E High/Low	PER SHARE ($) Earnings	Dividends
12/05	34.82	— —	—	1.04
12/04	30.25	— —	—	0.94
12/03	23.41	— —	—	0.83
12/02	16.84	— —	—	0.68
Annual Growth	**27.4%**	**— —**	**—**	**15.2%**

Invensys

Invensys maintains a broad inventory of ways to keep its customers in control. The company operates through six units: Controls (used in industrial equipment, HVAC systems, and appliances), Process Systems (automation technology for the energy and chemical industries), Rail Systems (signalling, communication, and control systems for railroads and subways), APV (valves for food, beverage, and dairy plants), Wonderware (industrial automation software), and Eurotherm (industrial monitoring systems). Invensys operates in more than 60 countries throughout the world. Its customers include BP, China Light and Power, Bayer, Eli Lilly, Corus, Pilkington, and Bombardier.

Formed by Siebe's 1999 purchase of BTR, Invensys fell on hard times in the first half of the 2000s. Faced with a faltering economy — and steadily declining sales and profits since its formation — Invensys cut jobs and costs and divested much of what had constituted its business. Its annual sales in 2005 were just over a third of what they were in 1999.

Among the things to go: its energy storage, sensor systems, flow control, metering, and power supply businesses. Late in 2005 Invensys sold that power supply business, which comprises a majority-owned JV called Densei-Lambda, to TDK for $235 million. The next year it sold the US and Asia/Pacific operations of Invensys Building Systems to Schneider Electric for nearly $300 million.

By 2006, the company had announced solid progress in its turnaround plans, to the point that it said it would seek out small acquisitions to help fuel its growth.

HISTORY

Immigrant Austrian artillery officer Augustus Siebe founded Siebe in London in 1819. A lifelong inventor, Siebe's creations included breechloading rifles, carbon arc lamps, the world's first diving suit, and early ice-making machines.

From the 1890s to the early 1970s, Siebe made a name for itself in marine engineering and as a maker of breathing apparatuses, developing products such as submarine escape and diving equipment for Britain's Royal Navy. General Dynamics veteran Barrie Stephens took over management of the struggling Siebe in 1963. Stephens cut costs, restructured, terminated half the workforce, and in the late 1960s, started making acquisitions.

With its 1972 purchase of European safety equipment specialist James North & Sons, Siebe began transforming from a marine-based engineer to a controls and engineering company. It expanded into continental Europe and in 1982 moved into North America with the purchase of Tecalemit (garage equipment).

Included in the Tecalemit buy were two healthy electronic controls businesses, which Stephens tried, but failed, to sell. When Siebe acquired CompAir (compressed air) in 1985 (sold 2002), the deal included three pneumatic controls companies. Without trying, Siebe had established a controls presence. That segment was strengthened further in 1986 when it bought Robertshaw (appliance controls, US). The following year's additions of US concerns Ranco and Barber-Colman added automotive, industrial, and commercial building controls.

In 1990 Siebe hit the jackpot with the $650 million acquisition of Foxboro, which had developed a UNIX-based system capable of controlling entire oil refineries and automobile plants. With the Foxboro purchase, Siebe's control business began to seriously challenge Honeywell.

Mid-to-late-1990s acquisitions included AVP (food and drinks industry equipment), Wonderware (factory application software), Eurotherm (temperature controls), and Electronic Measurement (industrial power supply). To offset costs associated with these acquisitions, Siebe began restructuring in 1998 and sold its North Safety Products Business (personal safety and life support products) to Norcross Safety Products.

In 1999 Siebe acquired engineering rival BTR plc in a $6 billion deal that nearly tripled Siebe's size; the combined company changed its name to BTR Siebe and later to Invensys. Also that year the company sold more than a dozen businesses, including its automotive and aerospace operations. It also sold 90% of its Paper Technology Group to investment firm Apax Partners in a deal valued at about $800 million. Invensys' 1999 acquisitions included Best Power (uninterruptible power supplies), purchased from industrial products maker SPX for around $240 million.

Invensys formed a pact with Microsoft in early 2000 to develop standards for connecting home appliances to the Internet. Later that year the company gained control of Netherlands-based Baan Company, a near-bankrupt maker of software that allows manufacturers to manage their internal operations, in a $709 million deal.

Early in 2002 Invensys sold its energy storage business for $425 million. That May the company reorganized and sold its flow control business to US-based Flowserve Corporation for $535 million. Invensys also sold its Invensys Sensor Systems business to Honeywell for $415 million in cash. In late 2003 Invensys agreed to sell its metering business for about $650 million. The following year Invensys sold its Powerware subsidiary (uninterruptible power supplies and power management systems) to Eaton for $560 million.

EXECUTIVES

Chairman: Martin Jay, age 66
CEO and Director: Ulf Henriksson, age 43
CFO and Director: Steve Hare
SVP, Human Resources: Paula Larson
SVP and General Counsel: Victoria Hull
President, Invensys Controls: Chan W. Galbato, age 43
President, Invensys Rail Systems: James Drummond
President, APV: Haluk Durudogan
President, Eurotherm: Peter Tompkins
Acting President, Invensys Process Systems:
  Ken Brown
VP, Corporate Communications: Steve Devany
Secretary: John Clayton
Manager, Investor Relations: Nina Delangle
Auditors: Ernst & Young LLP

LOCATIONS

HQ: Invensys plc
  Portland House, Stag Place,
  London SW1E 5BF, United Kingdom
Phone: +44-20-7834-3848   **Fax:** +44-20-7834-3879
US HQ: 33 Commercial St., Foxborough, MA 02035
US Phone: 508-543-8750   **US Fax:** 508-543-2735
Web: www.invensys.com

Invensys has major subsidiaries in Australia, Brazil, Denmark, Japan, Luxembourg, the Netherlands, Spain, the UK, and the US.

2006 Sales

	% of total
Europe	
UK	13
Other countries	29
North America	39
Asia/Pacific	12
South America	4
Africa & Middle East	3
Total	**100**

PRODUCTS/OPERATIONS

2006 Sales

	$ mil.	% of total
Controls	1,356	29
Process Systems	1,254	27
Rail Systems	755	16
APV	676	14
Eurotherm	206	4
Discontinued operations	446	10
Adjustments	(26)	—
Total	**4,667**	**100**

COMPETITORS

ABB	Parker Hannifin
Emerson Electric	Rockwell Automation
Endress + Hauser	SICK
FWMurphy	Siemens AG
GE	SPX
Honeywell International	Tomkins
Johnson Controls	

HISTORICAL FINANCIALS

Company Type: Public

Income Statement

FYE: March 31

	REVENUE ($ mil.)	NET INCOME ($ mil.)	NET PROFIT MARGIN	EMPLOYEES
3/06	4,667	—	—	28,434
3/05	5,491	—	—	36,365
3/04	7,104	—	—	43,602
3/03	7,898	—	—	48,867
3/02	9,939	—	—	73,005
Annual Growth	**(17.2%)**	—	—	**(21.0%)**

Revenue History

Pink Sheets: IVNYY

ISUZU

Tokyo-based Isuzu has said "Sayonara" to SUVs and "Konichiwa" to commercial trucks. These days Isuzu's only passenger car offerings are a few remaining Ascender SUVs and its line of compact pickups. Isuzu is in the process of transforming itself into one of the world's top makers of light-, medium-, and heavy-duty trucks (N Series, F Series, and C&E Series, respectively); it also makes diesel engines and buses. Isuzu's formal exit from the SUV vehicle class came in 2006 when the last Ascender left a General Motors assembly line. After a recapitalization scheme, GM's stake in the company was reduced from 49% to 8%. GM sold its remaining Isuzu stake in 2006.

In the summer of 2002 Isuzu announced a revised three-year business plan. To avoid bankruptcy, Isuzu asked its creditor banks to forgive ¥100 billion (about $750 million) in debt in exchange for stakes in the company. As part of the plan, GM wrote off its entire stake in Isuzu, and re-infused the ailing carmaker with $84 million. The deal resulted in a recapitalized Isuzu and reduced GM's stake to 8%. As part of the scheme GM boosted its stake in US-based joint venture DMAX Ltd., and took a stake in Isuzu's wholly owned Polish unit. To reduce its workforce, Isuzu offered voluntary retirement to about 3,700 workers.

The plan seems to be working. Isuzu's emphasis on becoming a worldwide player in commercial vehicles and engines is evident by the diminishing number of passenger models available in the US. The i-350 and i-280 pickups are the only passenger models that Isuzu still manufactures for sale in the US. The once popular Rodeo and Axiom SUVs have been discontinued.

Now that Isuzu has ensured its survival, it is focused on growth in foreign markets. The company plans to utilize the vast dealer network of its old pal GM to expand in Latin America, South Africa, and the Middle East.

While Isuzu has been recovering, GM has been floundering. Staggering 2005 losses of more than $10 billion are forcing it to stage a fire sale of its stakes in other carmakers. Early in 2006 GM sold its 8% stake in Isuzu to entities including Mitsubishi Corporation, ITOCHU Corporation, and Mizuho Corporate Bank.

As 2006 wound near its close, Toyota Motor picked up a 5.9% stake in Isuzu Motors from Mitsubishi Corporation and ITOCHU Corporation. The two companies plan to cooperate on engine technologies.

HISTORY

After collaborating on car and truck production for 21 years, Tokyo Ishikawajima Shipbuilding and Engineering and Tokyo Gas and Electric Industrial formed Tokyo Motors, Inc., in 1937. The partners began producing the A truck (1918) and the A9 car (1922) under licenses from Wolseley (UK).

Tokyo Motors made its first truck under the Isuzu nameplate in 1938. It spun off Hino Heavy Industries in 1942. By 1943 the company was selling trucks powered by its own diesel engines, mostly to the Japanese military.

By 1948 the company was Japan's premier maker of diesel engines. It was renamed Isuzu (Japanese for "50 bells") in 1949. With generous public- and private-sector financing and truck orders from the US Army during the Korean War, Isuzu survived and refined its engine- and truck-making prowess. A pact with the Rootes Group (UK) enabled Isuzu to enter automaking. Beginning in 1953, Isuzu built Rootes' Hillman Minx in Japan.

Despite its strong reputation as a truck builder, Isuzu suffered financially, and by the late 1960s its bankers were shopping the company around to more stable competitors. GM, after witnessing rapid Japanese progress in US and Asian auto markets, bought about 34% of Isuzu in 1971. During the 1970s Isuzu launched the popular Gemini car and gained rapid entry to the US through GM, exporting such vehicles as the Chevy Luv truck and the Buick Opel.

As exports to GM waned, Isuzu set up its own dealer network in the US in 1981. That year GM CEO Roger Smith told a stunned Isuzu chairman Toshio Okamoto that Isuzu lacked the global scale GM was seeking. Smith asked Okamoto for help in buying a piece of Honda. After Honda declined and GM settled for 5% of Suzuki, Isuzu extended its GM ties, building the Geo Storm and establishing joint production facilities in the UK and Australia.

Despite a high-profile advertising campaign featuring Joe Isuzu, the company suffered in the 1980s in its efforts to gain any kind of significant share of the US passenger car market. Post-1985 yen appreciation hurt exports. Subaru-Isuzu Automotive, a joint venture with Fuji Heavy Industries, initiated production of Rodeos in Lafayette, Indiana, in 1989.

After Isuzu lost nearly $500 million in 1991 and 1992, it called on GM for help. GM responded by sending Donald Sullivan, a strategic business planning expert, to become Isuzu's #2 operations executive.

Isuzu signed a joint venture with Jiangxi Automobile Factory and ITOCHU in 1993 to build light-duty trucks in China. In 1994 Nissan and Isuzu agreed to cross-supply vehicles.

Isuzu weathered a public relations storm in 1996 when *Consumer Reports* magazine claimed that the top-selling Trooper sport utility vehicle was prone to tip over at relatively low speeds. Isuzu dismissed the report as unscientific, and

the National Highway Traffic Safety Administration sided with the automaker. In 1997 the company sued the magazine for defamation. (Isuzu lost the case in 2000.)

The next year GM and Isuzu announced a joint venture to make diesel engines in the US. Also in 1998 Isuzu announced restructuring plans that included cutting 4,000 jobs and reducing the number of its domestic marketing subsidiaries. In 1999 GM boosted its stake in Isuzu to 49%. Isuzu also agreed to form a joint venture with Toyota to manufacture buses.

Amid mounting losses and pressure from GM, Isuzu announced a management shake-up in 2001 that included naming GM chairman John Smith Jr. as special advisor and installing Randall Schwarz (GM truck group) as vice president. Days later Isuzu announced its "Isuzu V plan," its sweeping cost-savings scheme that included job cuts and the closure of one factory.

The Isuzu V plan was revised in 2002 when the company announced GM would write off its entire stake while infusing Isuzu with about $84 million. Near the close of 2002 Isuzu agreed to sell its 49% stake in carmaking joint venture Subaru-Isuzu Automotive Inc. to Fuji Heavy Industries (FHI). When the deal was completed in January 2003, FHI renamed the company Subaru of Indiana Automotive Inc.

EXECUTIVES

President and Representative Director: Yoshinori Ida
EVP and Representative Director: Basil N. Drossos
EVP and Director: Hiroshi Suzuki
EVP and Director: Shigeki Toma
Senior Executive Officer: Fujio Anzai
Senior Executive Officer: Shunichi Satomi
Senior Executive Officer: Akira Shinohara
Senior Executive Officer: Takashi Urata
Executive Officer: Masanori Katayama
Executive Officer: Shigeji Nakamori
Executive Officer: Yukio Narimatsu
Executive Officer: Masaru Odajima
Executive Officer: Shinichi Ohoka
Executive Officer: Takafumi Ozawa
Executive Officer: Hakaru Shibata
Executive Officer: Yasuaki Shimizu
Executive Officer: Ryozo Tsukioka
Executive Officer: Makoto Ushiyama
Executive Officer: Tsutomu Yamada
Standing Corporate Auditor: Michio Kamiya
Standing Corporate Auditor: Shigeaki Wakabayashi
Standing Corporate Auditor: Koji Yamaguchi
Corporate Auditor: Susumu Tsuchida
Corporate Auditor: Yasuharu Nagashima
Auditors: Ernst & Young ShinNihon

LOCATIONS

HQ: Isuzu Motors Limited
(Isuzu Jidosha Kabushiki Kaisha)
26-1, Minami-oi 6-chome, Shinagawa-ku,
Tokyo 140-8722, Japan
Phone: +81-3-5471-1141 **Fax:** +81-3-5471-1043
US HQ: 13340 183rd Street, Cerritos, CA 90702
US Phone: 562-229-5000 **US Fax:** 562-229-5463
Web: www.isuzu.co.jp

2006 Sales

	$ mil.	% of total
Japan	8,224.6	61
Asia	3,514.3	26
North America	1,405.8	11
Other regions	307.4	2
Total	**13,452.1**	**100**

PRODUCTS/OPERATIONS

Selected Vehicles and Brands
Buses
  Erga heavy-duty bus
  Erga Mio medium-duty bus
Commercial Vehicles
  Heavy-duty trucks (C&E Series)
  Light-duty trucks (N Series)
  Medium-duty trucks (F Series)
Pickups
  D-MAX pickup
  i-280 Extended Cab
  i-350 Crew Cab
Sport Utility Vehicles and Minivans
  Ascender
  Axiom
  MU-7
  Panther

COMPETITORS

China Yuchai	Kubota
Cummins	Navistar
DaimlerChrysler	Oshkosh Truck
Fiat	PACCAR
Ford	Scania
General Motors	Volkswagen
Hino Motors	Volvo

HISTORICAL FINANCIALS

Company Type: Public

Income Statement

FYE: March 31

	REVENUE ($ mil.)	NET INCOME ($ mil.)	NET PROFIT MARGIN	EMPLOYEES
3/06	13,452	—	—	7,371
3/05	13,887	—	—	19,600
3/04	13,540	—	—	18,130
3/03	11,260	—	—	20,690
3/02	12,045	—	—	26,234
Annual Growth	**2.8%**	—	—	**(27.2%)**

Revenue History

OTC: ISUZF

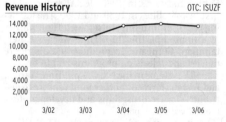

ITOCHU

If you drive it, eat it, fly it, or wear it, there's a good chance this company is involved with it. ITOCHU Corporation is a leading Japanese *sogo shosha* (general trading company), along with Mitsui & Co. and Mitsubishi, with business interests in such diverse areas as aerospace, equipment manufacturing, food distribution, and textiles. It also has interests and operations in chemicals, energy and mining, and financial services. The conglomerate has more than 150 offices in about 80 countries but operates through more than 500 subsidiaries and affiliated companies around the world.

ITOCHU is focused on expanding its businesses in consumer-oriented products, such as textiles and food distribution, and in natural resource development, both of which have historically been the strongest performing sectors for the company. It is also investing in its growing financial services and real estate operations, while creating new businesses in such markets as health care, senior care, and travel. Geographically, ITOCHU is increasing its involvement in China and North America; its domestic operations account for about 60% of revenue.

HISTORY

Chubei Itoh was only 18 when he organized his own wholesale linen business, C. Itoh & Co., in 1858. As Japan opened to foreign trade in the 1860s, the company prospered and was one of Osaka's largest textile wholesalers by the 1870s. C. Itoh established a trade office in San Francisco in 1889.

By 1919 C. Itoh had trading offices in New York, Calcutta, Manila, and four cities in China. Although it was not one of the *zaibatsu* (industrial groups) that flourished in Japan during the period between the world wars, C. Itoh benefited from the general increase in trade.

In 1941 C. Itoh was merged with two other trading companies, Marubeni and Kishimoto, into a new company, Sanko Kabushiki Kaisha. C. Itoh and Marubeni were separated in 1949. C. Itoh supplied UN troops with provisions during the Korean War; profits were used to diversify into petroleum, machinery, aircraft, and automobiles.

After the oil crisis of 1973 demonstrated Japan's vulnerability to oil import disruptions, C. Itoh actively participated in the development of petroleum production technology. To prevent the failure of Japan's 10th-largest trading company, Ataka, the Japanese government arranged a merger in 1977, making C. Itoh the third-largest *sogo shosha*.

The company established Japan Communications Satellite (JCSAT) with Mitsui and Hughes Communications in 1985. JCSAT launched its first two satellites in 1989 and 1990. The following year C. Itoh and Toshiba joined Time Warner in a limited partnership, Time Warner Entertainment Company, to produce and distribute movies and television programs and to operate cable TV systems in the US. C. Itoh, Time Warner, and Toshiba formed another joint venture to distribute Warner Bros. films and develop amusement parks in Japan.

C. Itoh changed its name to ITOCHU, a transliteration of its Japanese name, in 1992. After sales dropped the next year, ITOCHU began selling poorly performing subsidiaries, reducing its investment portfolio by more than one-third.

In 1996 the company formed an alliance with US oil company Atlantic Richfield to buy Coastal Corp.'s western US coal operations, and it took a stake in a massive project led by Amoco and British Petroleum to develop oil and gas deposits in the Caspian Sea. That year PerfecTV! (a joint venture with Sumitomo and other Japanese companies) began satellite broadcasting. Also in 1996 ITOCHU bought stakes in the Asia Broadcasting and Communications Network, a satellite communications company.

To help cover its losses from the Asian currency crisis, the company sold 40% of its stake in Time Warner in 1998; in 1999 ITOCHU sold its remaining stake. ITOCHU also sold lowperforming real estate investments and laid plans to divest about one-third of its subsidiaries.

Two of ITOCHU's agricultural subsidiaries were liquidated in 2000. The company also sought out partnerships in order to offset costs incurred in new ventures: it joined with Japan's other top trading companies and Brazil's Petrobras to develop oil fields in South America. And in response to the rapid consolidation of Japan's steel industry, ITOCHU and Marubeni agreed to integrate their steel operations in 2001 to better compete.

In 2002 ITOCHU formed a partnership with Bally International to expand the European fashion brand's presence in Japan. In 2004 the company sold its interest in Utah-based Canyon Fuel Co. to Arch Coal, Inc. for $112 million, and dissolved its subsidiary, ITOCHU Coal International Inc. Also that year, the company formed a joint venture with Ishimori Shotaro Pro Inc. to establish Ishimori Entertainment, which produces movies, television programs, and publications based on Shotaro Ishimori titles, including the popular MASKED RIDER.

ITOCHU established a fund with Turner Broadcasting to finance Japanese animation in 2005. It also acquired two US medical-device-distribution companies, Products for Surgery and Flanagan Instruments, marking ITOCHU's first step into that market.

EXECUTIVES

Co-Chairman: Uichiro Niwa
Co-Chairman, President, and CEO: Eizo Kobayashi
Co-Vice Chairman; Chief Officer, Kansai District Operation: Makoto Kato
Co-Vice Chairman: Sumitaka Fujita
EVP; COO, Textile Division: Etsuro Nakanishi
EVP and COO: Akira Yokota
Senior Managing Director; CFO, Chief Administration Officer, and Chief Compliance Officer: Toshihito Tamba
Senior Managing Director; President, Food Company: Kouhei Watanabe
Senior Managing Director; President, Aerospace, Electronics, and Multimedia Company: Shigeki Nishiyama
Managing Director; President, Finance, Realty, Insurance, and Logistics Services Company: Akira Kodera
Manging Director; President, Food Company: Shigeharu Tanaka
Managing Director; President, Chemicals, Forest Products & General Merchandise Company: Yosuke Minamitani
Managing Director; President, Machinery Company: Takanobu Furuta
Managing Director; President, Textile Company: Masahiro Okafuji
Managing Director; President, Energy, Metals & Minerals Company: Yoichi Kobayashi
Managing Director; President, Finance, Realty, Insurance & Logistics Services Company: Takao Shiomi
Managing Director; President, Machinery Company: Jiro Takemori
Executive Officer; Deputy Chief Corporate Planning Officer and General Manager, International Operations Division: Masahiro Nakagawa
Executive Officer; President and CEO, ITOCHU International Inc.: Yoshio Akamatsu
General Manager, Human Resources Division: Tetsushi Ishizuka
Auditors: Deloitte Touche Tohmatsu

LOCATIONS

HQ: ITOCHU Corporation
(Itochu Shoji Kabushiki Kaisha)
5-1, Kita-Aoyama 2-chome, Minato-ku,
Tokyo 107-8077, Japan
Phone: +81-3-3497-2121   **Fax:** +81-3-3497-4141
US HQ: 335 Madison Ave., Bank of America Plaza, 22nd, 23rd, and 24th Fls., New York, NY 10017
US Phone: 212-818-8000   **US Fax:** 212-818-8543
Web: www.itochu.co.jp

2006 Sales

	% of total
Japan	60
US	22
Australia	5
Other countries	13
Total	**100**

PRODUCTS/OPERATIONS

2006 Trading Transactions

	% of total
Energy, metals & minerals	27
Food	20
Chemicals, forest products & general merchandise	19
Machinery	14
Textiles	8
Aerospace, electronics & multimedia	7
Finance, real estate, insurance & logistics services	2
Other	3
Total	**100**

2006 Trading Profit

	% of total
Food	20
Textiles	17
Aerospace, electronics & multimedia	16
Chemicals, forest products & general merchandise	16
Energy, metals & minerals	10
Machinery	10
Finance, real estate, insurance & logistics services	6
Other	5
Total	**100**

COMPETITORS

ADM	Mitsui
Altria	Nestlé
Balli	Nippon Steel
Dow Chemical	Nippon Television
Exxon Mobil	NTT
Fluor	Samsung Group
Hutchison Whampoa	Sharp
Kanematsu	Sojitz
Klöckner	Sumitomo
LG Group	Tokyo Broadcasting System
Lockheed Martin	TOMEN
Marubeni	TOTAL
Matsushita	Unilever
Mitsubishi Corporation	

HISTORICAL FINANCIALS

Company Type: Public

Income Statement

FYE: March 31

	REVENUE ($ mil.)	NET INCOME ($ mil.)	NET PROFIT MARGIN	EMPLOYEES
3/06	6,075	1,234	20.3%	42,967
3/05	5,865	723	12.3%	40,890
3/04	5,262	(302)	—	40,737
3/03	4,723	168	3.5%	39,109
3/02	4,364	228	5.2%	36,529
Annual Growth	**8.6%**	**52.6%**	**—**	**4.1%**

Net Income History

OTC: ITOCY

ITV

With operations in television broadcasting and production, pay and digital TV, and television leasing, ITV plc (formerly Granada) has the channels covered. The company owns 11 of the UK's Independent Television 1 (ITV1, a national broadcast network) stations. ITV plc also owns sister digital channels ITV2, ITV3, ITV4, and ITV News and has stakes in pay-TV channels and Internet ventures. Its ITV Production division produces some 3,500 hours of programming for ITV and other broadcasters and maintains a library of 35,000 hours of television programs and 1,500 movie titles. In 2004 ITV licensees Granada and Carlton combined operations to form ITV plc.

The company's productions range from drama specials (Agatha Christie's *Marple*) to serialized soaps (*Coronation Street*), and from news to reality programs (*I'm A Celebrity. Get Me Out Of Here!*) The company is planning to expand through boosting its production business, increasing its channel offerings, and building on non-advertising revenue. ITV in 2005 restructured its divisions to align with these goals; several boardroom changes were made at that time.

A strategy to boost the company's content-based offerings also came into focus in 2005, when ITV launched several Internet services and acquired Friends Reunited, a popular community-building Web site. The successes of ITV's newer ventures have helped to offset declining ratings and advertising losses at ITV1.

In 2006, an investment group including Apax Partners and Blackstone Group made an unsuccessful offer to acquire a controlling stake in ITV. BSkyB took a nearly 18% stake in the company for about $2 billion in late 2006. Popular as a merger target, the company later rejected a buyout offer of $9 billion from NTL. NTL has abandoned its plan to buy ITV.

In a major coup, ITV hired away Michael Grade from rival the BBC in late 2006. Grade, who had been the BBC's chairman, will serve as executive chairman beginning in 2007.

HISTORY

Granada (now ITV) traces its roots to the Edmonton Empire, a northern London theater built by Alexander Bernstein in 1906. After Bernstein died in 1922, his sons Cecil and Sidney set up a chain of movie theaters during the 1920s and incorporated their business as Granada Theatres Ltd. in 1934. Granada went public the next year. Between 1936 and 1938 it opened a cinema every three months.

In 1955 Granada was granted a TV broadcasting license for the north of England. Changing its name to Granada Group Ltd. in 1957, the company began diversifying in the late 1950s. Granada first got into the TV rental business and later started Granada Motorway Services. By 1967 Granada was operating more than 200 TV-rental showrooms nationwide and later expanded into North America. Sidney Bernstein resigned in 1979, and his nephew Alex took over as chairman.

During the 1980s the company's TV production arm gained international acclaim with shows like *Brideshead Revisited* (1981) and *The Jewel in the Crown* (1984). In 1986 it fended off a hostile bid from rival leisure company The Rank Organisation (now The Rank Group). By the end of the 1980s, Granada had disposed of its theater operations and invested in startup British Satellite Broadcasting (later British Sky Broadcasting) in 1990. Overextended and facing a recession, Granada sold its bingo businesses in 1991.

That year chief executive Derek Lewis resigned and Irish-born Gerry Robinson took over. The former chief of catering giant Compass Group, Robinson fired nearly all of the senior management during his first year. Under his acquisitive management, Granada bought the Sutcliffe Group, a major catering firm, from cruise operators P & O for $500 million in 1993 and the next year acquired London Weekend Television for $150 million.

Robinson replaced Bernstein as chairman in 1996, and Granada TV head Charles Allen was appointed as chief executive. Buying Forte for $6.1 billion that year added hotel operations and Little Chefs restaurants. In 1997 the company bought the 73% of Yorkshire Tyne Tees Television it did not already own in a deal valued at about $1.1 billion. The next year Granada's digital TV joint venture ON Digital (with Carlton Communications) began broadcasting. (The venture was later renamed ITV Digital and was shut down in 2002.)

In 1999 the company disposed of its stake in BSkyB and acquired fish and chips chain Harry Ramsden's. A proposed merger between rivals Carlton and United News & Media (now United Business Media) that year threatened Granada's dominance in UK television. In 2000 Granada proposed its own merger with either company, temporarily derailing the deal. (It was all moot anyway when Carlton and United canceled their deal after it raised too many competition concerns.) Later that year the company purchased hospitality firm Compass Group and spun off its media business as Granada Media, retaining about 83% of the new TV company.

In early 2001 Allen took on the title of chairman and Steve Morrison took over as chief executive. Shortly after completing the deal, in 2001 the fickle company de-merged by placing its hospitality assets back into Compass Group (which is a public firm again) and absorbing its stake in Granada Media. Granada Compass then changed its name to Granada plc. Morrison left as CEO in 2002.

The company jumped back on the merger train in 2004 when it purchased rival Carlton Communications and changed its name to ITV plc. Also that year, ITV acquired BSkyB's 49.5% stake in Granada Sky Broadcasting, which had been formed as a Granada International and BSkyB joint venture in 1996.

Allen left as CEO in 2006. The company later named Michael Grade, BBC chairman, as executive chairman beginning in 2007.

EXECUTIVES

Chairman: Sir Peter A. Burt, age 62, $344,080 pay
Deputy Chairman: Sir George Russell, age 71
Executive Chairman: Michael Grade, age 63
Interim CEO and Director: John Cresswell, age 45
Commercial Director: Graham Parrot, age 53
Commercial Director: Ian McCulloch
Communications Director: Brigitte Trafford

Finance Director, Group Finance and Strategy:
 Neil Canetty-Clarke
Strategy Director: Ben McOwen Wilson, age 35
Director Treasury: Charles van der Welle
Director Television: Simon Shaps
Head, ITV Play: William Van Rest
Acting Head, ITV Worldwide: William Medlicott
CEO, ITV Regions and News: Clive Jones, age 57
Commercial Development Director, ITV Consumer:
 Jane Marshall
Finance Director, ITV Broadcasting: Mike Green, age 44
Finance Director, ITV News Group: Mike Fegan
Director Consumer, ITV: Jeff Henry
Director Production, ITV: John Whiston, age 47
Director Sales, ITV: Gary Digby
Head of Investor Relations: Georgina Blackburn
Company Secretary: James Tibbitts
Auditors: KPMG Audit Plc

LOCATIONS

HQ: ITV plc
 London Television Centre, Upper Ground,
 London SE1 9LT, United Kingdom
Phone: +44-20-7620-1620   **Fax:** +44-20-7261-3520
Web: www.itvplc.com

2005 Sales

	% of total
UK	94
Other countries	6
Total	**100**

COMPETITORS

BBC
BSkyB
Channel 4
Daily Mail
Flextech
Liberty Media International
NTL
PTV
RTL Group
SMG (UK)
Vivendi
Zone Vision

HISTORICAL FINANCIALS
Company Type: Public

Income Statement				FYE: December 31
	REVENUE ($ mil.)	NET INCOME ($ mil.)	NET PROFIT MARGIN	EMPLOYEES
12/05	3,745	389	10.4%	5,952
12/04	3,955	268	6.8%	6,262
12/03*	5,245	(420)	—	4,316
9/02	2,228	(590)	—	4,696
9/01	3,602	(194)	—	30,797
Annual Growth	1.0%	—	—	(33.7%)

*Fiscal year change

Net Income History

London: ITV

J Sainsbury

J Sainsbury is getting its trolley back on track. The UK's third-largest grocery retailer (after Tesco and ASDA) operates the long-struggling Sainsbury's Supermarkets chain — 455 supermarkets in the UK (accounting for about 85% of sales). The supermarkets get about 50% of their sales from private-label products. In addition to supermarkets, the company operates nearly 300 convenience stores under the Sainsbury's Local, Bells and Jacksons banners. Sainsbury also owns 55% of Sainsbury's Bank (in a joint venture with Scottish bank HBOS) and a property development company. Sainsbury sold its US business, Shaw's Supermarkets, to Albertsons in 2004. Sainsbury family trusts hold about 22% of the company's shares.

Stiff competition from price-chopping rivals Tesco and Wal-Mart-owned ASDA has eroded Sainsbury's market share to less than 15% of the UK grocery market. Sainsbury lost its #1 title to Tesco in 1995, and was kicked out of second place by ASDA in mid-2003. However under CEO Justin King, who was hired in 2004 to reverse Sainsbury's slide, the grocery chain has clawed its way back recently to tie with ailing ASDA for second place.

While Sainsbury has benefited from missteps at ASDA, its revival has also been helped by acquisitions. Sainsbury has purchased 23 stores from Wm Morrison. (Sainsbury used funds from the sale of Shaw's to Albertsons to acquire the stores.) The food retailer is also making a big push into the rapidly consolidating UK convenience store market.

Concentrating on its struggling grocery business, the company sold its 280-outlet UK-based Homebase home and garden supply superstores. King, formerly head of food at Marks and Spencer, capitalized on the sale of Shaw's to shake up the company's management team. To that end, King pushed out supermarket boss Stuart Mitchell and assumed his responsibilities.

To bolster its non-food offering, the grocery retailer has launched its own line of houseware and cookware products and is tripling the number of in-store banks in its supermarkets.

HISTORY

Newlyweds John James and Mary Ann Sainsbury established a small dairy shop in their London home in 1869. Customers flocked to the clean and efficient store, a far cry from most cluttered and dirty London shops. They opened a second store in 1876. By 1914, 115 stores had been opened, and the couple's sons had entered the business.

During WWI the company's stores established grocery departments to meet demand for preserved products, such as meat and jams, which were sold under the Sainsbury's label.

Mary Ann died in 1927 and John James the next year. Son John Benjamin, wholly devoted to the family business, took charge. (He is reported to have said on his deathbed, "Keep the stores well lit.") In the 1930s he engineered the company's first acquisition, the Thoroughgood stores.

Sales dropped by 50% during WWII, and some shops were destroyed by German bombing. Under third-generation leader Alan John Sainsbury, the company opened its first self-service store in 1950 in Croydon. The 75,000-sq.-ft. store opened in 1955 in Lewisham was considered to be the largest supermarket in Europe.

J Sainsbury went public in 1973. It established a joint venture with British Home Stores in 1975, forming the Savacentre hypermarkets (the company bought out its partner in 1989).

Sainsbury partnered with Grand Bazaar Innovation Bon Marche, of Belgium, in 1979 to establish Homebase, a do-it-yourself chain. (It bought the remaining 25% in 1996 and then sold the company in 2001, retaining only 18%.)

By 1983 most of Sainsbury's 229 stores were clustered in the south of England. A mature market and stiff competition forced the company to look elsewhere — both overseas and close to home. It began buying out US-based Shaw's Supermarkets in New England and in 1984 opened its first Scottish hypermarket. By 1987 the grocer owned 100% of Shaw's, which had 60 stores in Massachusetts, Maine, and New Hampshire.

In 1994 the company purchased a $325 million stake in Maryland-based Giant Food. The following year it bought 12 supermarkets in Connecticut from Dutch retailer Royal Ahold and entered Northern Ireland.

A year later the company opened Sainsbury's Bank. Royal Ahold bought Giant Food, including Sainsbury's 20% stake, in 1998. David Sainsbury — a great-grandson of the founders — retired as chairman in 1998 to pursue politics, marking the first time a Sainsbury had not headed up the company in its more-than-a-century history.

As a cost-cutting effort in 1999, Sainsbury cut 2,200 jobs, more than half in management. Also that year Sainsbury bought the 53-store Star Markets chain of Massachusetts, merging it into its Shaw's operations. In March 2000 Sir Peter Davis took over as CEO of Sainsbury's Supermarkets, replacing David Bremner.

In 2001 Sainsbury acquired 19 Grand Union stores in the US (17 of which were converted to the Shaw's banner), and opened 25 new stores in the UK. In January 2004, the grocery chain acquired Swan Infrastructure (an Accenture affiliate), the company that ran its information technology systems, for about $1 billion.

Yielding to shareholder anger, Sainsbury withdrew Sir Ian Prosser as chairman designate one week after announcing his appointment in February 2004. Justin King (formerly of Marks and Spencer) joined Sainsbury as its CEO in March 2004, succeeding Sir Peter Davis who became chairman of the board. In April Sainsbury sold JS USA Holdings, which operated 203 Shaw's and Star Markets stores in New England, to US grocery chain Albertson's in a deal worth about $2.4 billion. Davis stepped down as chairman one year ahead of schedule and following a prolonged dispute with investors that culminated in a fight over his compensation.

Philip Hampton (former finance director of Lloyds TSB, BT Group, and BG Group) joined Sainsbury as its new chairman on July 19, 2004. In September Sainsbury agreed to pay ex-chairman Davis £2.6 million despite shareholder protests in July that forced the grocery retailer to withdraw a similar offer. At that time Lord Levene of Portsoken and Keith Butler-Wheelhouse, both non-executive directors of the company and members of the remuneration committee, resigned from the board.

In October 2004, Sainsbury said it was writing off £140 million against information technology systems and an another £120 million linked to ineffective supply chain equipment as a result of a huge infrastructure investment program, instituted by ex-chairman Davis, that failed.

EXECUTIVES

Chairman: Philip Hampton, age 52, $512,885 pay
CEO and Director: Justin King, age 44, $1,290,000 pay
CFO and Director: Darren Shapland, age 39, $441,000 pay
Managing Director, Sainsbury's To You: Toby Anderson
Acting CEO, Sainsbury's Bank plc: Jim Kinloch
Company Secretary: Tim Fallowfield, age 41
Managing Director, Bells Stores and Jacksons Stores: Angus Oughtred
Brand Communications Director: Helen Buck
Buying Director, Tu: Adrian Mountford
Director, Supermarket Finance: Jonny Mason
Change Director: Hamish Elvidge, age 51
Customer Services Director: Gwen Burr, age 44
Fresh Food Director, Sainsbury's Supermarkets: Ian Merton
General Merchandise Director: Penny Teale
Human Resources Director: Imelda Walsh, age 41
Information Technology Director: Angela Morrison
Product Development Director: Jean-Paul Barat
Property Director: Peter Baguley
Retail Director: Ken McMeikan, age 39
Head of Group Legal Services: David Thurston
Head of Investor Relations: Lynda Ashton
Head of Public Affairs: Erica Zimmer
Auditors: PricewaterhouseCoopers LLP

LOCATIONS

HQ: J Sainsbury plc
33 Holborn, London EC1N 2HT, United Kingdom
Phone: +44-20-7695-6000   **Fax:** +44-20-7695-7610
Web: www.j-sainsbury.co.uk

PRODUCTS/OPERATIONS

2006 Sales

	% of total
Food retailing	98
Sainsbury's Bank	2
Total	**100**

2006 Stores

	No.
Sainsbury's Supermarkets	455
Convenience stores	297
Total	**752**

Store Formats

Sainsbury's at Bells Stores (convenience stores)
Sainsbury's Central (convenience stores averaging 10,000 sq. ft. and 6,500 product lines)
Sainsbury's Local (convenience stores averaging 3,000 sq. ft. and 2,500 product lines)
Sainsbury's Supermarkets (full-service supermarkets averaging 20,000-30,000 sq. ft. and 17,000 product lines)
Superstores (full-service supermarkets averaging 30,000-50,000 sq. ft. and 26,000 product lines, plus amenities such as restaurants, dry cleaners, and gasoline stations)

Selected Subsidiaries

Bells Stores Ltd. (food retailing)
Jacksons Stores Ltd. (convenience)
JB Beaumont Ltd. (convenience)
Sainsbury's Bank plc (55%, financial services)
SL Shaw Ltd. (convenience)

COMPETITORS

ALDI	METRO AG
Alliance Boots	Musgrave Budgens-Londis
ASDA	Netto Foodstores
Co-operative Group	One Stop Stores
Costcutter Supermarkets	Somerfield
First Quench	Tesco
John Lewis	Wm Morrison
Marks & Spencer	Supermarkets

HISTORICAL FINANCIALS

Company Type: Public

Income Statement

	REVENUE ($ mil.)	NET INCOME ($ mil.)	NET PROFIT MARGIN	EMPLOYEES
3/06	27,938	101	0.4%	153,300
3/05	28,949	(98)	—	154,900
3/04	31,296	723	2.3%	180,200
3/03	27,433	715	2.6%	174,500
3/02	24,466	519	2.1%	174,700
Annual Growth	3.4%	(33.6%)	—	(3.2%)

FYE: March 31

Net Income History

OTC: JSNSY

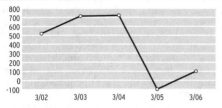

Japan Airlines

Japan Airlines Corporation (also known as The JAL Group) is the Land of the Rising Sun's largest carrier. Acting through Japan Airlines International, its primary operating company, the carrier serves more than 170 cities in some 35 countries and operates more than 270 mostly jet aircraft. Japan Airlines also carries air cargo, operates a low-fare domestic airline, provides maintenance and ground-support services, and owns the international chain of Nikko hotels. The company has agreed to join the Oneworld global marketing alliance, a group counting such members as UAL Corporation's American Airlines and British Airways, by 2007.

Although it's been courted by Oneworld for years, Japan Airlines had long refused to join a global marketing alliance. Instead, it has signed code-sharing agreements with about 20 carriers, including American, Air France, and Iberia. The airline signaled a turnaround in its policy, however, with the June 2006 announcement that it would join Oneworld and continue present code-sharing agreements. Japan Airlines will be the alliance's third largest member after American and British Airways.

Competition has been growing, with the deregulation wave making its way to Japan's shores. However, the previous merger of the two airlines gave the group a better grasp on domestic routes. It also expanded the group's presence in China, a rapidly growing new market.

Like other airlines, however, Japan Airlines is struggling to keep profits aloft over rising jet fuel prices. It has announced plans to discontinue low-profit international routes and cut nearly 6,000 jobs by mid-2007, among other measures, to compensate for the higher cost of fuel. Nonetheless, Japan Airlines has ordered about 60 planes worth $5.3 billion from Boeing.

Japan Airlines Corporation was created as a result of the 2002 merger of Japan's #1 airline, Japan Airlines (JAL), and Japan Air Systems (the country's #3 airline) in order to boost domestic coverage. Both carriers operated separately as Japan Airlines International (JAL International) and Japan Airlines Domestic (JAL Domestic) until October 2006, when they were integrated into a single operating company. Japan Airlines International emerged as the surviving entity, with Japan Airlines continuing to function as the group's holding company.

HISTORY

After WWII Japan was not allowed to form its own airline until the end of US occupation in 1951. That year a group of bankers led by Seijiro Yanagito founded Japanese Air Lines (JAL). JAL was essentially a revival of the prewar Nihon Koku Kabushiki Kaisha (Japan Air Transport Company), the national airline created by the Japanese government in 1928 and dissolved by the Allies in 1945. Since the Allied Peace Treaty forbade the airline to use Japanese flight crews, it leased both pilots and equipment from Northwest. In 1953 the airline was reorganized as Japan Airlines, with the government and the public owning equal shares.

Under Yanagito, who ran the airline until 1961, JAL expanded quickly, opening a transpacific route from Tokyo to San Francisco in 1954 and extending regional service to Hong Kong in 1955, Bangkok in 1956, and Singapore in 1958. A polar route from Tokyo to London and Paris gave the airline a foothold in Europe in 1961. Service to Moscow began in 1967, and that year JAL formed Southwest Airlines (now Japan TransOcean Air) to serve the islands of Japan.

In 1974 JAL suspended flights to Taipei, the mainstay of Chinese nationalists, in favor of new service to Beijing and Shanghai. Japan Asia Airways, a new subsidiary, resumed flights to Taipei the next year.

JAL ran into problems in the early 1980s: in 1982 a mentally unstable pilot crashed a plane into Tokyo Bay, killing 24; and in 1985 a JAL 747 crashed into a mountainside, killing all but four of the 524 on board. The worst single-plane accident in history, the disaster led to the resignation of most of JAL's top executives.

Facing a strong US currency in 1985, JAL signed an 11-year, $3 billion aircraft contract with Boeing, set at a fixed exchange rate of 184 yen per dollar. But the contract would haunt the airline in the 1990s, denying JAL the benefit of a weakened dollar that would fall below 100 yen.

The government sold its stake in JAL to the public in 1987. With air transport no longer nationalized, overseas routes were opened to the company's longtime domestic rival, All Nippon Airways (ANA).

In 1992 JAL reported its first loss ($100 million) since privatization, the result of high labor costs and the expansion of its fleet and facilities. With Japan sliding into recession, the company announced a five-year, $4.8 billion belt-tightening program.

Falling short of those cost-cutting goals, in 1993 JAL announced it would close half its North American offices, suspend recruitment, and freeze salaries. It also signed an agreement with ANA to share some aircraft maintenance costs. Traffic increased in 1994, but JAL was forced to cut prices to meet lower competing fares.

In 1995 JAL hooked up with American Airlines to connect computer reservation systems and act as agents for each other's cargo businesses. But JAL's losses continued, and chairman Susumu Yamaji and president Akira Kondo resigned in 1998. That year the airline announced job cuts, restructured routes, and launched low-cost domestic carrier JAL Express.

JAL finally posted a profit again in 1999. It also added Alitalia and Iberia Airlines as code-sharing partners and reduced its stake in delivery giant DHL from 26% to 6%. JAL came under renewed pressure in 2000, when government deregulation of domestic fares sparked a price war.

The next year demand for international travel slumped in the wake of the September 11 terrorist attacks on the US. In response, JAL had to modify its route structure, which included reducing several flights and modifying its code-sharing agreement with American Airlines.

In 2002 JAL merged with Japan's #3 carrier Japan Air Systems and created a new holding company called Japan Airlines System to operate the two airlines. In 2004 the company was reorganized under the JAL/Japan Airlines brand, which includes Japan Airlines Domestic and Japan Airlines International. However, Japan Airlines integrated the Japan Airlines International and Japan Airlines Domestic brands in 2006. As a result, Japan Airlines International emerged as the surviving entity, with Japan Airlines continuing to function as the group's holding company.

EXECUTIVES

Chairman: Toshiyuki Shinmachi
President and CEO: Haruka Nishimatsu
Managing Director, SVP and Deputy General Manager, Corporate Safety and SVP, Environmental Affairs: Takenori Matsumoto
SVP, Public Relations: Nobuyoshi Sera
SVP and Deputy General Manager, Corporate Planning and SVP, Brand Management: Fumio Tsuchiya
SVP: Shunji Kono
SVP: Ken Moroi, age 78
SVP: Shinobu Shimizu, age 75
Senior Executive Officer and General Manager, Corporate Affairs and VP, Executive Secretariat Office: Sumio Yasunaga
Senior Executive Officer, Marketing Strategy and Research, Corporate Planning, and Corporate Affairs, and VP Strategic Policy and Research: Hideyuki Kanenari
Executive Officer, Associated Business: Kimio Hiroike
Executive Officer, IT Strategy and Planning: Shunichi Saito
Auditors: Ernst & Young ShinNihon

LOCATIONS

HQ: Japan Airlines Corporation
(Nippon Koku Kabushiki Kaisha)
2-4-11, Higashi-Shinagawa, Shinagawa-ku, Tokyo 140-8605, Japan
Phone: +81-3-5769-6098
US HQ: 655 5th Ave., New York, NY 10022
US Phone: 212-310-1318
Web: www.jal.co.jp

2006 Sales

	% of total
Japan	91
Other	9
Total	**100**

PRODUCTS/OPERATIONS

2006 Sales

	% of total
Air transportation	69
Travel services	17
Airline-related business	7
Card & lease operations	1
Other	6
Total	**100**

2006 Sales

	% of total
Passenger	
Domestic	30
International	31
Cargo	
Domestic	2
International	9
Other	28
Total	**100**

Selected Subsidiaries

Airport Ground Service Co., Ltd.
AXESS International Network Inc. (75%, computer reservation system)
JAL Express Co., Ltd. (domestic regional carrier)
JAL Logistics Inc. (cargo services)
JAL Royal Catering Co., Ltd. (51%, in-flight catering)
JALPAK Co., Ltd. (78%, package tours)
JALways Co., Ltd. (low-fare carrier)
Japan Asia Airways Co., Ltd. (regional services)

COMPETITORS

Accor
ACE Aviation
Air France
All Nippon Airways
British Airways
Carlson
Central Japan Railway
China Airlines
China Eastern Airlines
Continental Airlines
Delta Air
Dragonair
East Japan Railway
Evergreen Marine
Garuda Indonesia
Hyatt
Kintetsu Corp.
KLM
Korean Air
Lufthansa
Northwest Airlines
Singapore Airlines
Skymark
Thai Airways
UAL
Virgin Atlantic Airways
West Japan Railway

HISTORICAL FINANCIALS

Company Type: Public

Income Statement

FYE: March 31

	REVENUE ($ mil.)	NET INCOME ($ mil.)	NET PROFIT MARGIN	EMPLOYEES
3/06	18,704	(402)	—	53,010
3/05	19,804	280	1.4%	53,010
3/04	18,286	(839)	—	54,053
3/03	17,385	97	0.6%	54,885
Annual Growth	2.5%	—	—	(1.2%)

Net Income History

Exchange: Tokyo

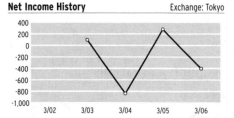

	3/02	3/03	3/04	3/05	3/06

Japan Tobacco

Japan Tobacco has plenty to puff about. The company controls more than 70% of the cigarette market in a country where about half of the male population smokes. Japan Tobacco is the world's #3 tobacco company, after Altria and British American Tobacco. The company's JT International unit sells Camel, Salem, and Winston brands outside the US. Japan Tobacco also operates in the foods, pharmaceuticals, agribusiness, engineering, and real estate industries. A state-owned monopoly until 1985, the Japanese Finance Ministry now owns half of the company.

In a country where the average smoker burns through a pack each day, Japan Tobacco makes nine of the nation's top 10 brands, including such favorites as Mild Seven, Caster, and Seven Stars. Two new brands, Icene Super Cooling Menthol and LUCIA Citrus Fresh Menthol are being touted as producing less odor and smoke than conventional brands. Japan Tobacco has expanded into 70 markets worldwide through its JT International unit. The company also is expected to bid for a government-run tobacco firm in Turkey.

The company closed 13 of its 25 manufacturing plants and six of its 30 sales branches by March 2006 as part of an effort to increase profits. These reductions slashed as many as 4,000 jobs from company payrolls, as demand for cigarettes, partly depressed by higher taxes, continues to decline. Japan Tobacco is also using its own line of premium smokes to fill the gap left in the product line by the absence of Marlboro cigarettes. The company's deal with Philip Morris to sell Marlboro lapsed in 2005.

HISTORY

In 1898, roughly 325 years after tobacco was introduced in Japan, the nation's Ministry of Finance formed a bureau to monopolize its production to fund military and industrial expansion.

During WWII, Japan's tobacco leaf imports from North and South America grew scarce and led to cigarette rationing. In 1949 the government began operating the tobacco production bureau as a business: the Japan Tobacco and Salt Public Corporation (in 1905 the bureau also became responsible for a salt monopoly).

The company launched Hope, the first Japanese-made filter cigarette, in 1957, and it became the world's best seller a decade later. In 1972 it began printing mild packaging "warnings": "Be careful not to smoke excessively for your health."

Japan Tobacco and Salt began selling Marlboro cigarettes licensed from Philip Morris in 1973. The Mild Seven brand (its current bestseller) went on sale in 1977; it became the world's #1 cigarette in 1981 but dropped to #2 (behind Marlboro) in 1993.

When its tobacco monopoly ended in 1985, the government established the firm as Japan Tobacco (a government-owned joint stock company). As competition from foreign imports increased, the firm came up with new means of making yen. It formed Japan Tobacco International (cigarette exports mainly to the US and Southeast Asia), moved into agribusiness and real estate operations, and, in 1986, created JT Pharmaceutical. In 1987 cigarette import tariffs ended, and importers lowered prices to match the company's; its sales and market share subsequently declined. During the late 1980s it intro-

duced HALF TIME beverages and its first low-tar cigarettes (Mild Seven Lights is now the world's #1 light cigarette).

In 1992 Japan Tobacco bought its first overseas production facility, Manchester Tobacco (closed in 2001). Former Ministry of Finance official Masaru Mizuno became CEO that year — and soon took up smoking. Also in 1992 the company and Agouron Pharmaceuticals agreed to jointly develop immune system drugs; in 1994 they added antiviral drugs. The government sold about 20% of the firm's stock to the public in 1994 and 13% in 1996. The firm began operating Burger King restaurants in Japan in 1996. Japan Tobacco bought Pillsbury Japan in 1998.

Japan Tobacco in 1999 paid nearly $8 billion for R.J. Reynolds International, the international tobacco unit of what was then RJR Nabisco. The company then renamed the unit, which has operations in 70 countries worldwide, JT International. It also bought the food products division of Asahi Chemical, Torii Pharmaceutical from Asahi Breweries, and the Unimat vending machine company.

Slowing sales prompted Japan Tobacco to announce in 2000 that it would reduce its workforce by 6,100 by 2005. Company exec Katsuhiko Honda became CEO that year (Mizuno remained as chairman) and said he'd push the government to sell its stake. Honda retired in 2006. In February 2001 the company announced plans to sell parts of its OTC drugs and health care businesses to Nichiiko Pharmaceutical to concentrate on prescription drugs. It also intended to sell all 25 of its Burger King outlets. In May Mizuno stepped down as chairman and was replaced by Takashi Ogawa.

In December 2001 Japan's Ministry of Finance recommended that it cut its holdings in the company from 66% to 50%; it would also allow the company to sell additional shares, which could further dilute the government's stake to as little as 33%. In 2002 Japan Tobacco completed the sale of its 25 Burger King outlets and its OTC drug business.

In January 2004 the company unveiled six new brands: Mild Seven One Menthol Box, Bitter Valley, Fuji Renaissance, Fuji Renaissance 100's, Hi-Lite Menthol, and BB Slugger. An added brand, Hope Menthol, currently being tested in the marketplace, also will see expanded availability. Japan Tobacco's Canadian subsidiary filed for bankruptcy protection in August 2004 following a billion-dollar smuggling claim by the Canadian government. Canada said that the company owed $1.4 billion in Canadian back taxes for allegedly smuggling cigarettes in 1998 and 1999.

Japan Tobacco in 2005 ended its agreement with Philip Morris to produce and sell Marlboro cigarettes.

EXECUTIVES

Chairman: Yoji Wakui
President, CEO, and Representative Director: Hiroshi Kimura, age 52
Executive Deputy President; CFO; Assistant to CEO in Compliance and Food Business; and Representative Director: Takao Hotta
Executive Deputy President; Assistant to CEO in Planning, CSR, HR and Operational Review and Business Assurance: Kazuei Obata
Executive Deputy President; President, Tobacco Business; Assistant to CEO in Vending Machinery; and Representative Director: Ichiro Kumakura
Executive Deputy President; Assistant to CEO in Communications, General Administration and Legal; and Representative Director: Ryoichi Yamada

EVP; President, Food Business; and Director: Mutsuo Iwai
EVP; President, Pharmaceutical Business; and Director: Noriaki Okubo
EVP and Chief Legal Officer: Ryuichi Shimomura
EVP; Head of Central Pharmaceutical Research Institute; and Chief Scientific Officer, Pharmaceutical Business: Shigeo Ishiguro
EVP and Head of Corporate, Scientific, and Regulatory Affairs, Tobacco Business: Seiki Sato
EVP and Head of Manufacturing General Division, Tobacco Business: Kenji Iijima
EVP and Head of Sales, General Division, Tobacco Business: Zenjiro Watanabe
EVP and Head of Tobacco Business Planning Division, Tobacco Business: Mitsuomi Koizumi
SVP and Chief Communications Officer: Masakazu Shimizu
SVP and Chief Human Resources Officer: Yoshiyuki Murai
SVP and Chief General Affairs Officer: Kazuhiro Nishino
SVP and Chief Strategy Officer: Sadao Furuya
President and CEO, JTI: Pierre de Labouchere
Auditors: Deloitte Touche Tohmatsu

LOCATIONS

HQ: Japan Tobacco Inc.
(Nihon Tabako Sangyo)
2-1, Toranomon 2-chome, Minato-ku,
Tokyo 105-8422, Japan
Phone: +81-3-3582-3111   **Fax:** +81-3-5572-1441
Web: www.jti.co.jp

Japan Tobacco operates 25 tobacco factories in Japan.

PRODUCTS/OPERATIONS

2006 Sales

	% of total
Tobacco	
Japan	73
Other countries	19
Foods	6
Pharmaceuticals	1
Other	1
Total	**100**

Selected Cigarette Brands

BB Slugger
Bitter Valley
Cabin and Cabin Mild
Camel (outside the US)
Caster and Caster Mild
Frontier
Fuji Renaissance
Hi-Lite Menthol
Hope Menthol
Icene Super Cooling Menthol
LUCIA Citrus Fresh Menthol
Mild Seven (regular, Lights, Super Lights)
Salem (outside the US)
Seven Stars
Winston (outside the US)

Selected Divisions and Operations

Agribusiness
Beverage business
Engineering
Food business
Pharmaceuticals
Real estate
Tobacco

COMPETITORS

Ajinomoto	Mitsubishi Chemical
Altadis	Nestlé
Asahi Breweries	Nisshin Seifun Group
British American Tobacco	Philip Morris International
Coca-Cola	Reemtsma
Gallaher	Suntory Ltd.
Imperial Tobacco	Unilever
Kraft Foods International	Vector

HISTORICAL FINANCIALS

Company Type: Public

Income Statement

FYE: March 31

	REVENUE ($ mil.)	NET INCOME ($ mil.)	NET PROFIT MARGIN	EMPLOYEES
3/06	39,439	1,714	4.3%	31,476
3/05	43,371	582	1.3%	32,640
3/04	43,782	(72)	—	39,243
3/03	37,483	628	1.7%	38,628
3/02	34,259	278	0.8%	39,387
Annual Growth	**3.6%**	**57.6%**	**—**	**(5.5%)**

Net Income History

Exchange: Tokyo

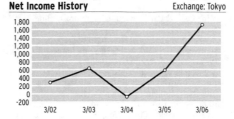

Jardine Matheson

The British no longer govern Hong Kong, but don't tell Jardine Matheson Holdings (JMH), which governs the many interests of its affiliate Jardine Strategic Holdings; one of the oldest of the Hong Kong *hongs* (diversified trading companies) and one of the few still in British hands. JMH's subsidiaries include Jardine Pacific and Jardine Motors Group, Asian supermarket operator Dairy Farm, and Hongkong Land, which owns prime real estate in Hong Kong. Other businesses include financial services, hotels (Mandarin Oriental), construction, and transport services. Members of the Keswick family, descendants of the co-founder William Jardine, control JMH and Jardine Strategic through a complex ownership structure.

JMH owns about 80% of Jardine Strategic, while Jardine Strategic owns more than 50% of JMH. (The cross shareholding between the two companies is designed to repel takeovers. JMH created Jardine Strategic in 1986 in an anti-takeover transaction.)

JMH also has numerous investments in China and throughout Asia. The company has diversified geographically, but the Asia/Pacific region is where the money is — more than three-quarters of the company's revenues come from that part of the world. To maintain its footing in the region's uncertain economic times, JMH is working to control costs. The company is also buying up additional shares in its affiliates, and focusing on building its businesses in Southeast Asian countries including Indonesia, Malaysia, and Singapore. Dairy Farm is growing rapidly in China and Hong Kong through supermarkets, convenience and health and beauty stores, and restaurants. Through Jardine Cycle & Carriage the group now owns more than 50% of carmaker Astra International of Indonesia, making it a subsidiary of the

group. Jardine Motors is expanding its Mercedes-Benz network in Southern China and developing its Hyundai passenger car business in Hong Kong. In the UK it is going upmarket.

Across the Pacific, Jardine Matheson is expanding its Mandarin Oriental hotel business with eight hotels under development and about 30 in operation.

HISTORY

Scotsmen William Jardine and James Matheson met in Bombay in 1820. In 1832 they founded Jardine, Matheson in Canton, the only Chinese city then open to foreigners. The company started shipping tea from China to Europe and smuggling opium from India to China. In 1839 Chinese authorities tried to stop the drug trade, seizing 20,000 chests of opium, 7,000 of them Jardine's. Jardine persuaded Britain to send gunboats to China, precipitating the First Opium War. China lost the war and ceded Hong Kong to Britain in 1842.

Jardine moved to Hong Kong and resumed trading opium. The Second Opium War (1856-60) resulted in the opening of 11 more ports and the legalization of opium imports. Jardine flourished and later branched into the more legitimate fields of brewing, textiles, banking, insurance, and sugar. It formed Hongkong Land (HKL), a real estate company; introduced steamships to China; and built the country's first railroad line (1876). The company earned the sobriquet "the Princely *Hong*" because of its high-society officers with free-spending habits.

The Sino-Japanese War and WWII shut the company down. In 1945, with China gripped by civil war, Jardine reopened in Hong Kong. Attempts to re-establish operations in China ended in 1954 after the Communist takeover. The company went public in 1961 and was run during the 1960s by members of the Keswick family. Henry Keswick was succeeded by *Taipan* (big boss) David Newbigging in 1972.

The cost incurred in an acquisition program begun in the 1970s made Jardine a takeover target by 1980. Newbigging defended the company by erecting a bulwark of crossholdings of it and HKL stock. The resulting debt pushed Jardine to the brink of bankruptcy, forcing it to sell assets.

Simon Keswick — Henry's younger brother — succeeded Newbigging in 1984 and reorganized the company, making investments in Mercedes-Benz distributorships and fast-food franchises that helped turn Jardine around. As the UK and China negotiated the transfer of Hong Kong to Chinese control, Keswick moved Jardine's legal home to Bermuda. Jardine continued to be plagued by takeover attempts, however, particularly by Li Ka-shing, who was assisted by China's investment organization, CITIC. In a 1986 anti-takeover transaction, the company created Jardine Strategic Holdings to hold interests in HKL and its spin-offs. When the Chinese army put down student demonstrations in Beijing two years later, Keswick called the Chinese government "a thuggish, oppressive regime."

To increase its holdings outside of Hong Kong, Jardine bought 26% of Trafalgar House in 1993 but sold its stake in the troubled British conglomerate in 1996, which contributed to lower profits. Jardine delisted five of its companies from the Hong Kong stock exchange in 1994. Continuing to expand geographically, the company acquired 20% of India's Tata Industries and bought London's Hyde Park Hotel in 1996.

Hong Kong was returned to China in 1997, and in a display of public fence-mending, Chinese Vice Premier Zhu Rongji welcomed Jardine's participation in mainland ventures. But Jardine's stormy relationship with China continued even as Jardine's profits dropped during the Asian economic crisis. In 1999 China closed down Jardine's Beijing and Guangzhou brokerage offices (and banned the two chief China officers from the business for life), claiming that Jardine was engaging in unauthorized activities.

In 2000 Jardine sold its minority holdings in UK-based investment firm Robert Fleming Group. That year and again in 2001 the Keswicks — Simon and his brother Henry — turned back attempts by US-based Brandes Investment Partners, which owns about 10% of Jardine, to seize control of the company. In 2004 Mandarin Oriental opened new hotels in New York and Washington, DC.

In 2005 JMH acquired a 20% stake in Rothschilds Continuation, a holding company with financial services interests, including investment bank N M Rothschild & Sons.

Managing Director Percy Weatherall retired in March 2006. (He also be stepped down as managing director of group companies Jardine Strategic Holdings, Hongkong Land, Dairy Farm International, and Mardarin Oriental at that time.) Weatherall was succeeded by Anthony Nightingale, chairman of Jardine Cycle & Carriage, Jardine Motors, Jardine Pacific, and MCL Land.

EXECUTIVES

Chairman: Henry Keswick, age 64
Managing Director; Chairman, Jardine Cycle & Carriage, Jardine Motors Group, and Jardine Pacific: Anthony J. L. Nightingale
CFO: James Riley
Chairman, Dairy Farm, Hongkong Land, and Mandarin Oriental, and Director: Simon Keswick, age 61
Chairman, Jardine Matheson China: Y.K. Pang
Group Head of Human Resources: Ritchie Bent
CEO, Jardine Pacific: Benjamin William (Ben) Keswick
Group Taxation Manager: Betty Chan
Group General Counsel: Jonathan Gould
Group Audit Controller: Eric van der Hoeven
Group Treasurer: Simon Dixon
Group Strategy Director: Mark Greenberg
Group Financial Controller: P. M. Kam
Group Corporate Secretary and Director, Group Corporate Affairs: Neil M. McNamara
Group Legal Manager: Jonathan Collins
Group Managing Director, Jardine Cycle & Carriage: Adam Phillip Charles Keswick
Company Secretary: C.H. Wilken
Auditors: PricewaterhouseCoopers LLP

LOCATIONS

HQ: Jardine Matheson Holdings Limited
48th Fl., Jardine House, Hong Kong
Phone: +852-2843-8288   **Fax:** +852-2845-9005
Web: www.jardines.com

2005 Sales

	$ mil.	% of total
Southeast Asia	6,026	51
Hong Kong & China	3,509	29
Europe	1,737	14
Northeast Asia	563	5
North America	94	1
Total	**11,929**	**100**

PRODUCTS/OPERATIONS

2005 Sales

	$ mil.	% of total
Dairy Farm	4,749	40
Astra	2,590	22
Jardine Motors Group	2,078	17
Jardine Cycle & Carriage	1,087	9
Jardine Pacific	1,024	9
Mandarin Oriental	399	3
Other	2	—
Total	**11,929**	**100**

Major Subsidiaries and Affiliates

Astra International (automobile distribution and manufacturing, financial and IT services, heavy machinery)
Jardine Cycle & Carriage Ltd (63%, motor trading, Singapore)
Dairy Farm International Holdings Ltd (78%, supermarkets, health and beauty and home furnishings stores, and restaurants)
Hongkong Land Holdings Ltd (44%, real estate)
Jardine Lloyd Thompson plc (30%, insurance and brokerage, London)
Jardine Motors Group Holdings Ltd. (auto distribution, sales, and service; China, Hong Kong, Macau, and the UK)
Jardine Pacific Holdings Ltd. (transport services, engineering and construction, restaurants, and IT services)
Jardine Strategic Holdings Ltd. (80%, holding company)
Mandarin Oriental International Ltd. (74%, hotels)

COMPETITORS

Accor
Carrefour
Cheung Kong Holdings
Chevalier
China Resources Enterprise
Daiei
Hopewell Holdings
HSBC Holdings
Hutchison Whampoa
Hyatt
ITOCHU
Kumagai Gumi
Marriott
Marubeni
McDonald's
Royal Ahold
Samsung Group
Seiyu
Sime Darby
Swire Pacific
Tesco

HISTORICAL FINANCIALS

Company Type: Public

Income Statement

FYE: December 31

	REVENUE ($ mil.)	NET INCOME ($ mil.)	NET PROFIT MARGIN	EMPLOYEES
12/05	11,929	1,820	15.3%	110,000
12/04	8,970	947	10.6%	100,000
12/03	8,452	181	2.1%	105,000
12/02	7,398	352	4.8%	110,000
12/01	9,413	115	1.2%	130,000
Annual Growth	**6.1%**	**99.5%**	**—**	**(4.1%)**

Net Income History

Singapore: JARD

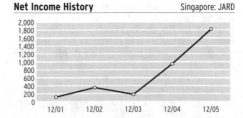

Kao

More than a century after Kao affixed a lunar logo to its name, Japanese consumers still think the company's products hang the moon. Kao (pronounced "cow") is Japan's #1 maker of personal care, laundry, and cleaning products. Its brands include Attack (#1 laundry detergent in Japan), Bioré (skin care), Family Kyukyutto (dishwashing detergent), Asience (shampoo), Laurier (sanitary napkins), Merries (disposable diapers), and ALBLANC (cosmetics). The company also makes cooking oils and fatty chemicals, printer and copier toner products, and plastics used in products such as sneaker soles.

Although popular in Japan, Kao is striving to attain the international scope of rivals like Procter & Gamble (P&G) and Unilever. Subsidiaries Kao Professional Salon Services and Guhl Ikebana make hair care products in Europe, and its Kao Brands subsidiary makes skin care products, including Jergens brand items, in North America. To bring new products to market, Kao invests heavily in research and development.

Kao brought its fat-reducing Econa cooking oil to the US in early 2003. Introduced in Japan in 1999, Econa is marketed as Enova in the US through a joint venture with Archer Daniels Midland Co.

HISTORY

Tomiro Nagase founded the Kao Soap Company in 1887; shortly afterward, he began selling bars under the motto, "A Clean Nation Prospers." Kao's longtime rivalry with Procter & Gamble (P&G) was foreshadowed when it adopted a moon trademark in 1890 strikingly similar to the one chosen by P&G eight years earlier.

Kao moved into detergents in the 1940s. In the 1960s the company struck upon an idea that would vertically integrate it and set it apart from other consumer products manufacturers: It set up a network of wholesale distributors ("hansha") who sell only Kao products. The hansha system improved distribution time and cut costs by eliminating middlemen.

Yoshio Maruta, one of several chemical engineers to run Kao, took over as president in 1971. Maruta presented himself as more Buddhist scholar than corporate honcho; during his 19 years at the top, he gave the company a wider vision through his emphasis on creativity and his insistence on an active learning environment. To encourage sharing of ideas, the company used open conference rooms for meetings and anyone interested could attend and participate in any meeting.

Under Maruta, Kao launched a string of successful products in new areas in the 1980s. In 1982 the company introduced its Sofina cosmetics line, emphasizing the line's scientific basis in a break from traditional beauty products marketing. The next year its Super Merries diapers (with a new design that reduced diaper rash) trounced P&G's Pampers in Japan. Its popular Attack laundry detergent (the first concentrated laundry soap) led the market within six months of its 1987 debut.

Seeking a way to enter the US market, Kao bought the Andrew Jergens skin care company — based in Cincinnati, as is P&G — in 1988. (It also purchased a chemical company to supply the materials to make Jergens' products.) P&G and

Unilever braced themselves for the new competition, but Kao didn't deliver, releasing products like fizzy bath tablets that didn't sell well in a nation of shower-takers. In 1989 it bought a 75% interest in Goldwell, a German maker of hair care and beauty products sold through hair stylists. (By 1994 Kao owned all of Goldwell, which is now called Kao Professional Salon Services.)

In the mid-1980s Kao built a name for itself in the floppy disk market and became the top producer of 3 1/2-in. floppy disks in North America by 1990. However, competition crowded the field and drove the price of disks down. In 1997 the company stopped production of floppy disks in the US.

Chemical engineer Takuya Goto took over as president that year. Kao looked to other Asian markets and the US for potential consumers and found a willing audience in the US for its Bioré face strips. In 1998 Kao purchased Bausch & Lomb's skin care business, gaining the Curel and Soft Sense lotion brands.

In 2000 Kao established a joint venture with Novartis to make baby foods and over-the-counter drugs such as stomach medicines and other pain relief drugs. In 2001 Kao lost out on its offer for Clairol to P&G. Also in 2001 it formed a joint venture with Archer Daniels Midland to produce an anti-obesity diacylglycerol oil (used in margarine, cooking oil, salad dressing, and mayonnaise) and in 2002 began marketing it in the US under the brand name Enova. That year Kao dissolved its OTC-medicine-manufacturing joint venture with Novartis and renamed its Sofina cosmetics brand Prestige Cosmetics. Additionally in 2002 Kao acquired John Frieda Professional Hair Care through Andrew Jergens. (Andrew Jergens became Kao Brands in 2004.)

In 2004 Goto became chairman and Motoki Ozaki was promoted from president of the Global Fabric and Home Care division to president and CEO. The same year Kao broke off talks to purchase Kanebo.

EXECUTIVES

Chairman: Takuya Goto
President, CEO, and Director: Motoki Ozaki
SEVP, Corporate Functions and Director: Toshio Hoshino
EVP, VP, Legal and Compliance, Global and Global Communications; Director: Shunichi Nakagawa
EVP, President, International Business, Consumer Products and Director: Norihiko Takagi
EVP, President, Global Consumer Products and Director: Hiroshi Kanda
SVP, Global Production and Engineering; Director: Takuo Goto
VP, Global Accounting and Finance; Director: Shinichi Mita
VP, Global Production and Engineering: Yoshitaka Nakatani
VP, Global Marketing Service: Yoshiiku Hirai
VP, Global Human Capital Development: Yasushi Aoki
President and CEO, Kao Cosmetics and Director: Toshio Takayama
President, Chemical Company and Director: Toshihide Saito
President and CEO, Kao Hanbai; Director: Tatsuo Takahashi
President, Global Prestige Cosmetics; Director: Masato Hirota
President and CEO, Kao Brands: William J. (Bill) Gentner

President, Global Personal Care, Skin Care and Hair Care: Masumi Natsusaka
President, Global Health Care: Takuji Yasukawa
President, Global Fabric and Home Care: Shigeru Koshiba
President, Global Research and Development; Director: Toshiharu Numata
President and CEO, Kao Corporation Shanghai: Shinichirou Hiramine
Auditors: Deloitte Touche Tohmatsu

LOCATIONS

HQ: Kao Corporation
14-10 Nihonbashi Kayabacho, 1-chome, Chuo-ku, Tokyo 103-8210, Japan
Phone: +81-3-3660-7111   **Fax:** +81-3-3660-8978
Web: www.kao.co.jp

Kao sells its products primarily in Asia but also in Australia, Europe, North America, and South Africa.

2006 Sales

	% of total
Asia & Oceania	
Japan	73
Other countries	11
Europe	11
North America	9
Adjustments	(4)
Total	**100**

PRODUCTS/OPERATIONS

2006 Sales

	% of total
Consumer products	72
Chemical products	22
Prestige cosmetics	9
Adjustments	(3)
Total	**100**

Selected Products

Fatty chemicals and edible oils (fatty acids, fatty alcohols, fatty amines, glycerin)
Hygiene and bath products (sanitary napkins, disposable diapers, bath additives)
Laundry and cleaning products (laundry detergents, laundry finishers, kitchen and other household detergents, fabric softeners)
Personal care products and cosmetics (soap, body cleansers, shampoos, conditioners, hair care products, cosmetics and skin care products, toothpastes, toothbrushes)

Selected Brand Names

Attack (laundry detergent)
Ban (deodorant)
Bioré (skin care)
Bub (shower gel)
Econa (cooking oil)
Family Kyukyutto (dishwashing detergent)
Jergens (skin care)
Laurier (sanitary napkins)
Merries (disposable diapers)
Quickle Wiper (electrostatic duster)

COMPETITORS

Alticor
Colgate-Palmolive
Johnson & Johnson
Kanebo
Kimberly-Clark
Lion Corporation
Nisshin Oillio
Pfizer
Procter & Gamble
Revlon International Corporation
Shiseido
Unicharm
Unilever

HISTORICAL FINANCIALS

Company Type: Public

Income Statement

FYE: March 31

	REVENUE ($ mil.)	NET INCOME ($ mil.)	NET PROFIT MARGIN	EMPLOYEES
3/06	8,259	605	7.3%	29,908
3/05	8,711	671	7.7%	19,143
3/04	8,544	619	7.2%	19,330
3/03	7,220	521	7.2%	19,807
3/02	6,325	454	7.2%	19,923
Annual Growth	**6.9%**	**7.4%**	**—**	**10.7%**

Net Income History

Exchange: Tokyo

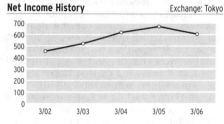

Karstadt Quelle

Seems like unification has caught on in Germany. Karstadt Quelle is the product of a merger between Germany's biggest department store group, Karstadt, and #1 mail-order firm, Quelle. It operates about 90 department stores (Karstadt, Hertie, Wertheim, Alsterhaus, and KaDeWe) and 30-plus sports shops. Karstadt Quelle is also a leader in travel services and has expanded into real estate and financial services. Schickedanz-Holding, owned by the Riedel and Herl families, has a stake of more than 50% in Karstadt Quelle. Stung by weak consumer spending in its home country and a global trend away from department stores, Karstadt Quelle is in the midst of a protracted attempt to restructure its business.

Under the leadership of Thomas Middelhoff, who joined the company in 2005, Karstadt Quelle has paid down some $5.9 billion in debt and worked to streamline its corporate structure, speed up the refurbishment of its Karstadt department stores, and boost sagging catalog sales. The company sold about 75 of its smaller Karstadt Kompakt department stores as well as the Golf House, Runners Point, SinnLeffers, and Wehmeyer specialty store chains. To date, the company has laid off some 25,000 workers, or about a quarter of its workforce.

While Karstadt's department store business has improved, the mail-order business is still losing money. As a result, the department-store-to-mail order conglomerate in late 2006 put its mail order business, Neckermann, up for sale (or possibly a public offering) and also announced plans to sell its mail-order business in France, Spain, and Portugal run by Quelle. The Dutch and Belgian units of Quelle will close. The divestments will focus the company's mail-order efforts on the larger German and Russian markets.

Under the Quelle and Neckermann brands, the company mails out 730 million catalogs per year all over Europe. Those are supplemented by nearly 180 specialty catalogs, which cover women's fashion, baby products, kitchenware, and children's clothing, among other things.

Previous divestments included the group's 82% stake in Karstadt Coffee back to Starbucks Corporation, as well as portions of its department store and logistics business and shipping and mail-order delivery operations to Deutsche Post for more than $500 million.

Continuing its restructuring, the retailer has announced plans to sell another €600 million worth of real estate, including its headquarters building in Essen, by the end of 2006.

With a whopping 50% of the department store market, Karstadt Quelle is prevalent in Germany.

The service companies of Karstadt Quelle provide consulting, information, financial, and travel services. With airline operator Deutsche Lufthansa, Karstadt Quelle shares a 50/50 joint venture in Thomas Cook AG, making it the #3 travel services company in the world (behind American Express and Carlson Wagonlit) and the second-largest in Europe (after TUI).

In 2005 the Schickedanz family increased its share in the company to about 58%, adding to speculation that the family has plans to split up the company and sell off separate parts.

HISTORY

In 1881 Rudolph Karstadt opened a store in Mecklenburg, Germany, selling candy, apparel, and fabric. His store was one of Germany's first department stores; it offered separate departments for merchandise and offered low, fixed prices and cash-only sales. In 1885 Theodor Althoff took control of his mother's haberdashery, wool, and linen shop in Westfalen, Germany. He adopted the same business model as Karstadt.

Rudolph Karstadt AG was founded in 1920 and soon merged with Althoff's business. Six years later Karstadt founded EPA Einheitspreis, an American-style discount store. The company grew rapidly, reaching 89 outlets in 1929. But overexpansion and a worldwide depression hurt Karstadt, and it found itself in financial trouble by 1931. With the help of a bank consortium, the company restructured that year.

Karstadt operated 67 stores in 1939, but by the end of WWII, only 45 remained in West Germany and most were heavily damaged. (The company lost the remainder to East Germany and the Iron Curtain.) Postwar economic reform and reconstruction boosted personal incomes; as a result, Karstadt's sales rose too. In 1948 the retailer was accepted into "Interkontinentale Warenhausgruppe" (the "Intercontinental Department Store Group").

In 1971 Karstadt and mail-order firm Quelle founded travel firm TransEuropa-Reisen, which became KS-Touristik-Beteiligungs in 1972. (Karstadt sold its share in 1976.)

In 1976 Karstadt became a major shareholder in Germany's third-largest mail-order company, Neckermann Versand, which was restructured into a public limited company. The next year Karstadt upped its stake to 51% of Neckermann Versand, and it controlled virtually all of the company by 1984. (Neckermann Versand travel subsidiary NUR Neckermann+Reisen became NUR Touristik in 1982.) Karstadt also founded Runners Point in 1984.

The company in 1988 opened a distribution center in Unna, Germany. When the wall came down, bringing trade barriers with it, Karstadt established cooperation agreements with 10 Centrum and four Magnet department stores in the former East Germany. The same sort of agreement was set up with GUM department store in Moscow in 1992.

Karstadt opened Optic Point Warenhandelsgesellschaft in 1993 and acquired Hertie Waren- und Kaufhaus in 1994, making it by far Germany's largest department store group. Retail group Schickedanz bought 20% of Karstadt in 1997. A year later Karstadt formed travel group C&N Touristic with Lufthansa.

In 1999 the company purchased mail-order company Quelle from Schickedanz-Holding and became Karstadt Quelle, one of Europe's largest retailers. Amidst European retail industry consolidation in 2000, C&N Touristic bought Thomas Cook from rival Preussag AG (now TUI) and took on the Thomas Cook name. The move made it the second-largest travel company in Europe and #3 in the world.

In 2001 Karstadt Quelle's major restructuring plan included almost 4,000 job cuts. The company's 2004 plan to divest 77 of its Karstadt stores and to sell all of its specialty shops was rejected by trade union officials, whose concern is the nearly 30,000 jobs that may be lost.

In April, 2005, CEO Christoph Achenbach resigned abruptly in the midst of the company's restructuring. Achenbach had served as CEO for only 10 months. A month later, Thomas Middelhoff, formerly of media giant Bertelsmann, joined the struggling company and accelerated its reorganization.

EXECUTIVES

CEO: Thomas Middelhoff, age 53
CFO and Head of Mail Order Division: Harald Pinger, age 45
Head and Director, Corporate Communications: Jörg Howe
Director, Corporate Communications: Thomas Diehl
Director, Foreign Offices, Logistics, Personnel, Environment and Corporate Policy, and Synergies: Helmut Merkel, age 55
Director, Human Resources: Matthias Bellmann, age 52
Director, Investor Relations: Detlef Neveling
Director, Logistics and IT, Neckermann Versand and Quelle AG: Ulrich Wiggers
Director, Marketing and Sales, Neckermann Versand and Quelle AG: Gebhard Stammler
Director, Sales and Marketing: Thomas Freude
Director, Specialty Mail Order, Neckermann Versand and Quelle AG: Leo Günther Kraftsik
Director, Technology and Consumer Durables, Neckermann Versand and Quelle AG: Michael Badke
Director, Textile, Neckermann Versand and Quelle AG: Helmut Klier
Group Secretary: Sylvia Ehlert
Head of Public Relations: Stephanie Venus
Chairman and CEO, Thomas Cook: Thomas Holtrop, age 52
Finance Director and Controller, Quelle: Georg Michael Zupancic, age 45
Auditors: BDO Deutsche Warentreuhand AG

LOCATIONS

HQ: Karstadt Quelle AG
Theodor-Althoff-Strasse 2, D-45133 Essen, Germany
Phone: +49-20-17271   **Fax:** +49-20-1727-5216
Web: www.karstadtquelle.com

Karstadt Quelle has operations in Austria, Belgium, Croatia, France, Germany, Montenegro, the Netherlands, Poland, Serbia, Spain, and Switzerland.

2005 Sales

	% of total
Western Europe	93
Eastern Europe	7
Total	**100**

PRODUCTS/OPERATIONS

2005 Sales

	% of total
Mail order	42
Retail stores	29
Thomas Cook (tourism)	24
Real estate	3
Services	2
Total	**100**

Selected Operations

Mail Order
 Neckermann
 Quelle

Department Stores
 Alsterhaus
 Hertie
 KaDeWe
 Karstadt
 Wertheim

Specialty Retail
 LeBuffet (restaurants)
 Schaulandt/Schürmann and WOM World of Music (multimedia)

Services
 INTELLIUM (information technology)
 KarstadtQuelle Bank (financial services)
 Quelle Versicherungen (insurance)
 Thomas Cook Tourism Group (50% joint venture)

Real Estate
 KARSTADT Immobilien

COMPETITORS

American Express
AVA AG
C&A
Carlson Wagonlit
Carrefour
Douglas Holding
Edeka Zentrale
H&M
Lidl & Schwarz Stiftung
METRO AG
Otto
TUI

HISTORICAL FINANCIALS

Company Type: Public

Income Statement

	REVENUE ($ mil.)	NET INCOME ($ mil.)	NET PROFIT MARGIN	EMPLOYEES
12/05	18,765	(375)	—	107,130
12/04	18,342	(2,225)	—	120,891
12/03	19,167	135	0.7%	100,956
12/02	16,575	170	1.0%	104,536
12/01	14,232	208	1.5%	112,141
Annual Growth	**7.2%**	**—**	**—**	**(1.1%)**

FYE: December 31

2005 Year-End Financials

Debt ratio: —
Return on equity: —
Cash ($ mil.): 837
Current ratio: 1.12
Long-term debt ($ mil.): 3,568

Net Income History

German: KAR

Kingfisher

Home improvement is netting the big catch in retail these days, and Kingfisher is angling for it. Kingfisher operates nearly 650 home improvement stores in about a dozen countries in Europe, where it is the largest DIY retailer, and Asia. The company's do-it-yourself (DIY) portfolio includes B&Q stores in the UK, and Castorama in France, Italy, Poland, and now Russia. Kingfisher's other DIY stores include Brico Dépôt in France and Spain and 50%-owned Koçtas in Turkey. Kingfisher sold its chain of about 700 Superdrug stores (even though it was the UK's #2 drugstore chain, behind Boots The Chemists) in 2001, and it spun off its Woolworths and other general merchandise stores in a public offering in August 2001.

Kingfisher also owns 21% of Hornbach Holding, the parent company of German DIY warehouse retailer Hornbach-Baumarkt with about 125 stores across Europe. Kingfisher is growing quickly in China where it operates 48 B&Q stores (the Beijing B&Q is the world's biggest) and plans to operate 75 stores in that country by 2009.

To reverse a slump in DIY sales in the UK, Kingfisher plans to remodel 110 of its biggest B&Q warehouse stores there.

Most recently the company entered Russia with a single Castorama store, but plans to add 50 stores there under the Castorama banner. To that end, Kingfisher has appointed a former IKEA executive, Peter Partma, as the country manager for Castorama Russia. Kingfisher also plans to increase its Polish store count to more than 60 by 2009.

The company is also looking to expand its considerable acreage within the UK, with plans to expand its building-trade-oriented chain that would bring its French Brico into the country as well as digging in deeper with Screwfix.

In 2005 The Home Depot announced that it was considering a buyout of the company, but added provisions including the requirement that the company sell off its loss-making French Castorama business. This, in combination with a recent investment by Warren Buffett, through Berkshire Hathaway insurance subsidiary Geico, has led to rumors that the company is seeking suitors.

HISTORY

The beginning of Kingfisher is directly tied to the former US Woolworth chain (now Foot Locker). With the success of F.W. Woolworth general merchandise stores in the US, founder Frank Woolworth expanded overseas, first to Canada, then in 1909 to Liverpool, England. By 1914 Woolworth's UK subsidiaries had 31 stores.

Growing quickly, the company went public in 1931, with its US parent retaining a 53% stake. It spent most of the postwar years rebuilding bombed stores and had 762 stores by 1950.

In 1967 the company opened its first Woolco Department Store, modeled after the US Woolco stores of its parent. However, other retailers had cut into sales, and by 1968 it lost its place as Britain's leading retailer to Marks and Spencer. In 1973 it opened Shoppers World, a catalog showroom. It made its first takeover in 1980, buying B&Q, a chain of 40 do-it-yourself stores.

An investment group acquired Woolworth in 1982 using the vehicle Paternoster Stores. (The US parent sold its stake in Woolworth.) The company, renamed Woolworth Holdings, closed unprofitable Woolworth stores and sold its Shoppers World stores in 1983 and its Ireland Woolworth stores in 1984. It also acquired Comet, a UK home electronics chain, and continued to expand B&Q.

Two years later all of its F.W. Woolworth stores were renamed Woolworths, and food and clothing lines were abandoned. Also in 1986 the company sold its Woolco stores and bought record and tape distributor Record Merchandisers (later renamed Entertainment UK). The next year Woolworth Holdings acquired Superdrug, a chain of 297 discount drugstores. Adding to its Superdrug chain, in 1988 the company acquired and integrated two UK pharmacy chains: 110-store Tip Top Drugstores and 145-store Share Drug.

To reflect its growing diversity of businesses, the company was renamed Kingfisher in 1989. Also that year it bought drug retailer Medicare, with 86 stores. Expanding further into electronics, in 1993 Kingfisher acquired Darty, with 130 stores. Adding music retail to music distribution, that year the firm founded Music and Video Club (MVC).

In 1998 Kingfisher increased its presence in France by taking control of electronics chain BUT. It also merged its B&Q chain with the do-it-yourself stores of France's Castorama in 1998 and gained a 55% stake in the new group.

In 2001 Kingfisher sold its Superdrug chain to Kruidvat, a Dutch health and beauty group. It spun off Woolworths Group the same year in a public offering. With Woolies went electronic entertainment companies EUK, MVC, VCI, and Streets Online. Also in 2001 Kingfisher bought 25% plus one share of the unlisted ordinary voting shares of Germany's Hornbach Holding, a family-owned group that owns 80% of one of Germany's leading DIY chains, Hornbach-Baumarkt.

In 2002 Kingfisher acquired the remainder of Castorama and bought 17.4% of Hornbach's listed non-voting preference shares (which with the 2001 purchase represents a 21.2% stake in Hornbach). Kingfisher additionally bought 5.5% of the ordinary shares of Hornbach-Baumarkt.

CEO Geoffrey Mulcahy stepped down in 2002 and was replaced by Gerry Murphy, formerly CEO for Carlton (now ITV plc), in 2003. Kingfisher sold its 20 retail parks for $1.1 billion to a consortium that includes real estate firms Pillar Property and Capital & Regional Properties the same year. Also in 2003 Kingfisher sold ProMarkt, with about 190 stores in Germany, to its former owners, Michael and Matthias Wegert.

To focus on DIY, Kingfisher floated its electrical businesses as a new company, Kesa Electricals, in 2003. Kingfisher sold two home improvement chains that year. Réno-Dépôt, which operates about 20 home-improvement stores in Canada, was sold to RONA. NOMI, with about 40 stores in Poland, was acquired by Enterprise Investors.

In June 2005 the company acquired its biggest competitor in Asia, OBI Asia, which added about a dozen stores in China and its first outlet in South Korea.

In February 2006, Kingfisher entered its 11th market, Russia, with its first Castorama store there. In May Sir Francis Mackay retired as chairman of the company and was succeeded by Peter Jackson.

EXECUTIVES

Chairman: Peter J. Jackson, age 59
Deputy Chairman: Daniel Bernard, age 60
Deputy Chairman: John Nelson, age 59
CEO and Director: Gerry Murphy, age 51, $1,756,512 pay
Group Finance Director and Director: Duncan Tatton-Brown, age 41, $747,292 pay
Group Commercial Director: Paul Worthington, age 43
Group Human Resources Director: Tony Williams, age 48
Group Property Director: Terry Hartwell, age 49
Group Strategy, Development and Planning Director: Régis Schultz, age 37
Group Communications Director: Ian Harding, age 41
CEO, B&Q and Director: Ian Cheshire, age 47, $1,015,260 pay
CEO, Castorama France: Phillippe Tible, age 54
CEO, UK Trade: George Adams, age 49
CEO, B&Q Asia: Steve Gilman, age 49
CEO, Brico Dépôt: Patrick Langlade, age 58
Director of Governance and Corporate Services: Helen Jones, age 50
Managing Director, Screwfix: John Allan
Head, External Communications: Nigel Cope
Head, Investor Relations: Loraine Woodhouse
Auditors: PricewaterhouseCoopers LLP

LOCATIONS

HQ: Kingfisher plc
3 Sheldon Sq., Paddington,
London W2 6PX, United Kingdom
Phone: +44-20-7372-8008   **Fax:** +44-20-7644-1001
Web: www.kingfisher.co.uk

2006 Sales

	% of total
UK	52
France	34
Other countries	14
Total	**100**

2006 Stores

	No.
UK	324
France	175
China	48
Poland	30
Italy	26
Taiwan	20
Ireland	7
Spain	7
Turkey	7
Russia	1
South Korea	1
Total	**646**

PRODUCTS/OPERATIONS

Selected Operations

B&Q (UK, Ireland, China, Taiwan)
B&Q Home (South Korea)
Brico Dépôt (France, Spain)
Castorama (France, Italy, Poland, Russia)
Koçtas (50%, Turkey)
Screwfix Direct (UK)

COMPETITORS

BMB Buildbase
Focus
Grafton Group
Homebase
METRO AG
MPS Builders and Merchants
Saint-Gobain Building Distribution
Tengelmann
Travis Perkins
Wolseley

HISTORICAL FINANCIALS

Company Type: Public

Income Statement

FYE: January 31

	REVENUE ($ mil.)	NET INCOME ($ mil.)	NET PROFIT MARGIN	EMPLOYEES
1/06	14,155	—	—	75,500
1/05	14,447	—	—	70,811
1/04	15,981	—	—	81,096
1/03	17,735	—	—	99,879
1/02	15,893	—	—	119,002
Annual Growth	(2.9%)	—	—	(10.8%)

Revenue History

London: KGF

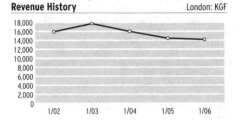

Kirin Brewery

You might say this company makes good luck beer. Named for a unicorn that is a symbol of good fortune, Kirin Brewery Company is the #2 beer maker in Japan (behind Asahi Breweries), with a portfolio of brands that includes Kirin Lager and Ichiban Shibori, as well as Kirin Tanrei happo-shu (low-malt) beer. The company also makes chu-hi, an alcoholic fruit drink, and it distributes such third party brands as Chivas Regal and Franzia. In addition to its alcoholic beverages, Kirin markets coffee drinks, mineral water, and tea drinks, as well as health supplements and pharmaceutical products. The company is part of the Mitsubishi *keiretsu*.

In addition to its domestic beer production, Kirin has stakes in several brewers serving international markets. It has a 45% stake in Lion Nathan, a leading brewer in Australia, and it has a 20% stake in San Miguel Corporation, the leading food and beverage company in the Philippines. It also owns Zhuhai Kirin Brewery and has a small stake in Dalian Daxue Brewery, both of which serve markets in China. Kirin sells its beer in the US through a partnership with Anheuser-Busch. (Under the reciprocal deal, Kirin brews Budweiser beer in Japan.) It also owns soft drink bottler Coca-Cola Bottling Co. of Northern New England.

Kirin is looking to new categories of beer to expand its business, including low-malt happoshu beverages, as well as a new no-malt brand called Nodogoshi. It also has high hopes for its diversified business interests in pharmaceuticals and agricultural products. The company's therapeutic products include treatments for renal anemia and leucopenia, while in the development pipeline are treatments for kidney cell cancer and other kidney diseases. In the US, Kirin's majority-owned Hematech is working to genetically engineer cows capable of producing human antibodies, while its Gemini Science subsidiary is helping to develop a treatment for the influenza A virus. Other businesses are involved

in dairy production, commercial flower growing, and dietary supplements.

Koichiro Aramaki, who led the company's diversification into pharmaceuticals and other business stepped down as president in 2006, turning the leadership over to managing director Kazuyasu Kato. (Aramaki remains as chairman and CEO.) Under its new leadership, Kirin plans to reorganize its businesses in 2007 under a new holding company called Kirin Holdings with separate subsidiaries overseeing beverage production and pharmaceuticals.

HISTORY

American William Copeland went to Yokohama, Japan, in 1864 and five years later established the Spring Valley Brewery, the first in Japan, to provide beer for foreign nationals. Lacking funds to continue the brewery, Copeland closed it in 1884. The next year a group of foreign and Japanese businessmen reopened it as Japan Brewery. The business created the Kirin label in 1888 and was soon profitable.

The operation was run primarily by Americans and Europeans at first, but by 1907 Japanese workers had filled the ranks and adopted the Kirin Brewery Company name. Sales plummeted during WWII when the government limited brewing output. After the war, the US occupation forces inadvertently assisted Kirin when they split Dai Nippon Brewery (Kirin's main competitor) into two companies (Asahi and Sapporo Breweries) while leaving Kirin intact. The company became Japan's leading brewer during the 1950s.

During the 1970s it introduced several soft drinks and in 1972 branched into hard liquor through a joint venture with Seagram (Kirin-Seagram). The firm bought several Coca-Cola bottling operations in New England and Japan in the 1980s. Kirin also entered the pharmaceuticals business, in part through a joint venture with US-based Amgen. In 1988 the brewer signed an agreement with Molson to produce Kirin beer for the North American market. In 1989 Kirin bought Napa Valley's Raymond Vineyards.

In 1991 Kirin formed a partnership to market Tropicana drinks in Japan. It also entered an alliance with Sankyo (Japan's #2 drug company) in 1991 to market Kirin's medication for anemia, which it had developed with Amgen.

Chairman Hideyo Motoyama resigned in 1993 after four company executives were arrested for allegedly paying a group of racketeers who had threatened to disrupt Kirin's annual meeting. Joint venture Kirin-Amgen won the rights to make thrombopoietin (TPO), a blood platelet growth stimulator, in 1995.

Yasuhiro Satoh became president of Kirin in 1996. The brewer moved into China that year through an agreement with China Resources (Shenyang) Snowflake Brewery. To brew its beers in the US, the company formed Kirin Brewery of America, also in 1996.

In response to losing market share to Asahi, Kirin cut its workforce in 1998 and introduced Tanrei, a cheaper, low-malt beer that quickly captured half its market. Building on its presence in China, Kirin bought 45% of brewer Lion Nathan (based in Australia and New Zealand) for $742.5 million that year. It became a licensed brewer of Anheuser-Busch in 1999.

Like other Japanese brewers, Kirin struggled against dwindling demand for its most expensive brews in 2000. Koichiro Aramaki was named president of the company the following year and

began to expand and diversify Kirin's operations to overcome slow growth domestically. In 2002 the company bought 15% of Philippine food and drink giant San Miguel for about $530 million. It also boosted ties with beverage giant Pernod Ricard by purchasing 32% of SIFA, a French food services firm, for an estimated $155 million. (The deal gave Kirin a 3% indirect interest in Pernod Ricard.) In 2002 Kirin also formed Flower Season Ltd., a joint venture with Dole Food Company to sell flowers to Japanese retailers. Also in 2002 Kirin launched its new Pure Blue brand of "shochu" distilled liquor.

Kirin said in 2003 it planned to sell Four Roses Kentucky Straight Bourbon in the US with the help of Southern Wine & Spirits of America. The brand had been sold exclusively as an export since 1959. Kirin purchased the Four Roses brand from Diageo.

In 2006 Aramaki stepped down as president (he remained chairman) and turned the reins over to managing director Kazuyasu Kato.

EXECUTIVES

Chairman and CEO: Koichiro Aramaki
President and COO: Kazuyasu Kato
Managing Executive Officer: Akira Negami
Managing Executive Officer: Shozo Sawada
Managing Executive Officer: Takeshi Shigenaga
Managing Executive Officer: Kazuhiro Sato
Managing Executive Officer: Takeshi Shimazu
SVP, Pharmaceutical Division: Ken Yamazumi
VP, Pharmaceutical Research Laboratories: Junichi Koumegawa
President, Agribio Business Division: Yoshiyuki Matsushima
President, International Beer Division: Hitoshi Oshima
President, Nutrient Food and Feed Division: Yoshihiko Kitamura
President, Pharmaceutical Division: Katsuhiko Asano
General Manager, Corporate Communications Department: Hideo Mori
General Manager, Marketing Department, Sales and Marketing Division: Hitoshi Maeda
General Manager, Personnel Department: Tomohiro Mune
General Manager, Research and Development Department: Kazuo Yoshioka
Auditors: Asahi & Co.; KPMG AZSA & Co.

LOCATIONS

HQ: Kirin Brewery Company, Limited
  10-1 Shinkawa 2-chome, Chuo-ku,
  Tokyo 104-8288, Japan
Phone: +81-3-5540-3411 **Fax:** +81-3-5540-3547
US HQ: 2400 Broadway, Ste. 240,
  Santa Monica, CA 90404
US Phone: 310-829-2400 **US Fax:** 310-829-0424
Web: www.kirin.co.jp

2005 Sales

	% of total
Asia/Pacific	
Japan	82
Other countries	13
Other regions	5
Total	**100**

PRODUCTS/OPERATIONS

2005 Sales

	% of total
Alcoholic beverages	46
Soft drinks	28
Pharmaceuticals	5
Other	21
Total	**100**

Selected Products

Alcoholic beverages
  Kirin Chu-hi Hyoketsu (alcoholic fruit drink)
  Kirin Lager Beer
  Kirin Nodogoshi (no malt beer)
  Tanrei (happo-shu beer)
  Third-party brands
    Chivas Regal
    Four Roses
    Franzia
    Lanson
    J.P. Chenet
Soft drinks
  Gogono-Kocha (tea)
  Kirin Alkali-Ion-no-Mizu (mineral water)
  Kirin Fire (coffee drink)
  Kirin Nuda (sparkling water)
  Nama-cha (tea)
  Volvic (mineral water)
Pharmaceuticals
  ESPO
  GRAN
  PHOSBLOCK Tablets
  Rocaltrol Injection
Other
  Agricultural products
  Commercial flower production
  Dairy products
  Health and dietary supplements

COMPETITORS

Anheuser-Busch	Miller Brewing
Asahi Breweries	Molson Coors
Asia Pacific Breweries	Nippon Beet Sugar
Carlsberg	Novartis
Chugai	Pabst
Diageo	Pepsi Bottling
FEMSA	Red Bull
Foster's	SABMiller
Gallo	Sapporo
Heineken	Snow Brand Milk
InBev	Suntory Ltd.
ITOCHU	Taiwan Tobacco & Wine
Kokubu & Co.	Takara
LVMH	Tsingtao
Mercian	Yanjing

HISTORICAL FINANCIALS

Company Type: Public

Income Statement

FYE: December 31

	REVENUE ($ mil.)	NET INCOME ($ mil.)	NET PROFIT MARGIN	EMPLOYEES
12/05	13,824	434	3.1%	22,089
12/04	16,052	476	3.0%	22,160
12/03	14,912	302	2.0%	22,852
12/02	9,486	271	2.9%	23,070
Annual Growth	13.4%	17.0%	—	(1.4%)

Net Income History

OTC: KNBWY

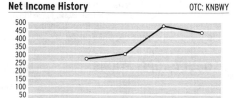

KLM

The legendary Flying Dutchman sails on alone, but KLM Royal Dutch Airlines is part of Air France-KLM, Europe's largest airline company. KLM and Air France operate from their respective hubs in Amsterdam and Paris as independent carriers, but they are working to coordinate their businesses. Combined, the airlines serve about 250 destinations worldwide with a fleet of about 565 aircraft.

KLM operates more than 175 planes, including about 50 used for its Cityhopper regional operations. It also owns charter carrier Transavia. Air France and KLM extend their worldwide networks as members of the SkyTeam marketing alliance, which also includes carriers such as Alitalia, Delta Air Lines, Korean Air Lines, and Northwest Airlines.

Air France acquired KLM and formed the Air France-KLM holding company in 2004, and since then efforts to achieve cost savings by combining aspects of the carriers' operations have exceeded expectations. Air France and KLM have integrated parts of their aircraft maintenance units, and the carriers' freight operations have been brought together as Air France-KLM Cargo.

In their core passenger transportation businesses, the airlines have maintained some duplicate destinations, but they have been working to shift routes and to streamline redundant systems.

Air France-KLM owns 98% of the economic rights and 49% of the voting rights of KLM. The balance of the voting rights are held by Dutch foundations (43%) and the Dutch government (6%); other shareholders own the remainder of the economic and voting rights. The complex shareholding structure is a temporary arrangement that was necessary to preserve air traffic rights for KLM until 2007; eventually, Air France-KLM is expected to own 100% of the economic and voting rights of KLM.

HISTORY

Flight lieutenant Albert Plesman founded Koninklijke Luchtvaart Maatschappij voor Nederland en Kolonien (Royal Airline Company for the Netherlands and Colonies) in The Hague in 1919. Queen Wilhelmina granted the honorary title of *koninklijke* (or royal), and Dutch businessmen financed the venture. Early passengers — who flew in an open cockpit with the pilot — were issued leather jackets, goggles, gloves, and parachutes.

Under Plesman's leadership KLM established service between Amsterdam and London, Copenhagen, Brussels, and Paris in the early 1920s. The airline initiated the longest air route in the world, from Amsterdam to Indonesia, in 1928 and extended its European network in the years before WWII. Hitler's occupation of Holland shut down KLM's European operations in 1940; the Germans imprisoned Plesman from 1940 to 1942, bombing or confiscating two-thirds of KLM's planes.

After the war Plesman quickly re-established commercial service, using 47 US military surplus airplanes, and in 1946 KLM became the first continental European airline to offer scheduled service from Europe to the US. Plesman died in 1953, and KLM began trading on the NYSE in 1957.

KLM established NLM Dutch Airlines in 1966 (renamed Cityhopper in 1976) to provide commuter flights within the Netherlands. The airline addressed overcapacity problems in the 1970s by converting the rear portions of its 747s to cargo space.

In 1988 KLM bought 40% of Dutch charter airline Transavia (increased to 80% in 1991) and began looking for partners to help it compete in key markets. It bought 10% of Covia Partnership, owner and operator of United Airlines' Apollo computer reservation system (1988), and invested in Wings Holdings, a company formed to buy Northwest Airlines (1989). In 1991 KLM bought 35% of Air Littoral, a French regional airline, and 40% of ALM Antillean Airlines.

Airline deregulation in Europe spawned numerous efforts to develop strategic relationships. A deal giving KLM and British Airways 20% each of Belgium's national airline, Sabena, fell apart in 1990, and KLM-British Airways merger talks collapsed in early 1992. In 1994, when Northwest recovered from four straight losses, KLM bought brewer Foster's 6% stake in the airline.

American Airlines and British Airways invited KLM in 1996 to join a proposed alliance, which would combine transatlantic flights and marketing. However, the plan would have required KLM to sell its Northwest stake. That year KLM executed a buyback of about 13% of KLM stock from the Dutch government; it also took a 25% stake in Kenya Airways.

In 1998 KLM sold back its 19% stake in Northwest Airlines for about $1.1 billion, while forming a strategic partnership with the carrier. The deal resolved a feud stemming from KLM's attempt to increase its Northwest stake to 25%.

In 2000 KLM's low-fare European service, buzz, began service from its hub at London's Stansted airport. However, KLM's potential merger with British Airways was called off that year.

The airline cut back its flights in the wake of the September 11, 2001, terrorist attacks on the US in anticipation of reduced demand for transatlantic service.

By early 2002, KLM was involved in talks with Air France over forming an alliance. Those discussions, which had begun informally as early as 1999, soon turned to talks of a merger, and by late 2003 the two carriers began negotiating a plan to form Europe's largest airline company.

Before it found its European partner, the Dutch carrier was relying on KLM Cityhopper to cover smaller markets and counting on gaining a better foothold in Europe through its low-fare carrier, buzz. But KLM was unable to turn a profit with buzz, and it chose instead to sell the low-fare carrier to Ryanair in 2003.

The European Commission initiated an investigation in potential anti-competition elements of the Air France-KLM deal in 2004, potentially delaying the rollout of the new airline giant. To appease regulators, the airlines had to give up crucial slots at some of Europe's busiest hubs. Their cooperation paid off, and the commission approved the transaction on the condition the airlines give up 94 slots per day to ensure a competitive environment. The deal — officially, an acquisition of KLM by Air France — was completed in 2004.

Chairman, Supervisory Board: Kornelis J. (Kees) Storm, age 64
President and CEO: Leo M. van Wijk, age 60
Managing Director and COO: Peter F. Hartman, age 55
CFO: Frederic Gagey
Managing Director, Air France KLM:
  Cees van Woudenberg, age 58
SVP, Corporate Communications: Peter Elbers, age 41
SVP, Marketing and Brand: Bart Vos
VP, Revenue Management: Martin van der Zee
VP, Revenue Management, KLM Northwest:
  Barry ter Voert
Secretary: Barbara C.P. van Koppen
Auditors: KPMG Accountants N.V.

LOCATIONS

HQ: KLM Royal Dutch Airlines
  (Koninklijke Luchtvaart Maatschappij N.V.)
  Amsterdamseweg 55,
  1182GP Amstelveen, The Netherlands
Phone: +31-20-649-9123   **Fax:** +31-20-649-2324
Web: www.klm.nl

PRODUCTS/OPERATIONS

Selected Subsidiaries and Affiliates

Kenya Airways Ltd. (26%)
KLM Cityhopper bv (regional airline)
Martinair Holland nv (50%, international cargo and
  passenger airline)
Transavia Airlines bv (charters and scheduled holiday
  service)

COMPETITORS

ACE Aviation
Aer Lingus
Air Berlin
All Nippon Airways
AMR Corp.
Austrian Airlines
British Airways
Czech Air
Delta Air Transport
easyJet
Iberia
Lufthansa
Ryanair
SAS
Singapore Airlines
Swiss
UAL
US Airways
Virgin Atlantic Airways
Virgin Express

HISTORICAL FINANCIALS

Company Type: Subsidiary

Income Statement

FYE: March 31

	REVENUE ($ mil.)	NET INCOME ($ mil.)	NET PROFIT MARGIN	EMPLOYEES
3/06	8,695	333	3.8%	30,164
3/05	8,317	118	1.4%	27,983
3/04	7,154	29	0.4%	31,182
Annual Growth	**10.2%**	**237.9%**	**—**	**(1.6%)**

Net Income History

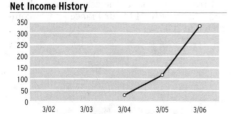

Koç Holding

In Turkey, Koç (pronounced "coach") class equals first class. Led by its automotive businesses, Koç Holding is Turkey's top industrial conglomerate. The company's Tofas unit, a joint venture with Fiat, is Turkey's leading carmaker; Koç's joint venture with Ford Motor sells imported Ford models. Other businesses include supermarkets (Migros), large household appliances (Arçelik), and energy (distribution of liquefied petroleum gas). Subsidiaries engage in food production, construction, international trading, and hospitality and tourism. Koç also operates banking, securities brokerage, and insurance businesses. The Koç family, Turkey's wealthiest dynasty, controls the company.

Koç is looking far across the Bosphorus for growth. With a goal modeled on its success at home, Koç intends to enter every household in Europe with at least one product and one day take in 50% of its revenue from outside Turkey.

In January 2006 Koç and Royal Dutch Shell together acquired the Turkish government's 51% stake in oil refiner TÜPRAS for more than $4 billion. The next month, however, Turkey's Council of State — the country's top administrative court — blocked the sale after the Petrol-Is oil workers' union lodged a complaint.

HISTORY

In 1917, 16-year-old Vehbi Koç and his father opened a small grocery store in Ankara, Turkey. With the fall of the Ottoman Empire after WWI, Turkey's capital was moved to Ankara, which was then only a village. The Koçs recognized an opportunity and expanded into construction and building supplies, winning a contract to repair the roof of the Turkish parliament building. By age 26, Koç was a millionaire.

Ford Motor made Koç its Turkish agent in 1928. In 1931 Mobil Oil and Koç entered an exclusive agreement to search for oil in Turkey. The company incorporated in 1938 as Koç Ticaret Corporation, the first Turkish joint stock company with an employee stock-ownership program.

Despite Turkey's neutrality in WWII, the fighting disrupted Koç's business. The nation became isolationist after the war and restricted foreign concerns to selling through local agents; Koç benefited from importing foreign products.

General Electric and Koç entered a joint venture in 1946 to build Turkey's first lightbulb factory. In 1955 Koç set up Arçelik, the first Turkish producer of refrigerators, washing machines, and water heaters; Türk Demir Döküm, the first Turkish producer of radiators and, later, auto castings; and Turkay, the country's first private producer of matches. In 1959 Koç constructed Turkey's first truck assembly plant (Otosan).

Other firsts followed in the 1960s as the company leveraged its size and government influence to attract more ventures. These included a tire factory (with Uniroyal), a cable factory (with Siemens), production of electric motors and compressors (with GE), and the production of Anadol, the first car to be made entirely in Turkey (by Otosan, under license from Ford). In 1974 Koç expanded into retailing with the purchase of Migros, Turkey's largest chain of supermarkets.

The Turkish military imposed martial law in 1980 and restricted foreign exchange payments, forcing Koç to limit its operations. In 1986, a

year after foreign companies were allowed to export products directly to Turkey, Koç and American Express started Koç-Amerikan Bank (which Koç bought out and renamed Koçbank in 1992). In the late 1980s Vehbi's only son, Rahmi, took over the company's leadership. Vehbi Koç died in 1996.

Auto sales fell sharply in 1996 as buyers awaited the country's entry into the European Union's customs union. In an effort to offset market risks, Koç forged a number of alliances in 1997. It participated in a British-Canadian-Turkish consortium that was building a large power plant in central Turkey.

Reflecting a greater willingness to open the company to foreign investors, Koç announced plans to offer $250 million in shares in a public offering in 1998, but it soon canceled the offering because of market volatility. A year later, the company completed an auto plant in Samarkand, Uzbekistan, to build Otoyol-Iveco buses and trucks.

Koç entered into a joint venture — Koç Finansal Hizmetler — with Unicredito Italiano in 2002 in an effort to further consolidate its financial holdings.

EXECUTIVES

Honorary Chairman: Rahmi M. Koç, age 75
Chairman: Mustafa V. Koç
Vice Chairman: Temel K. Atay, age 65
Vice Chairman: Suna Kiraç, age 65
CEO: F. Bülend Özaydinli
Auditing Group President: Ali Tark Uzun
Corporate Communications and Foreign Relations President: Hasan Bengü, age 57
Construction Group President: Bülent Bulgurlu, age 58
Energy Group President: Erol Memioǝlu, age 52
Financial Services Group President: Rüsdü Saraçoglu
Food/Retailing and Tourism Group President:
  Ömer Bozer
Information Technologies Group President: Ali Y. Koç, age 39
Other Automotive Companies Group President:
  Selçuk Gezdur
General Secretary: Tahsin Saltik
Human Resources Director: Neslihan Tözge
Accounting Manager: Emine Alangoya
Governmental Affairs Coordinator: Ömer Tunç Koyuncu
Legal Affairs: Kemal Erol
Auditors: PricewaterhouseCoopers

LOCATIONS

HQ: Koç Holding A.S.
  Nakkastepe Azizbey Sokak No. 1, Kuzguncuk,
  34674 Istanbul, Turkey
Phone: +90-216-531-00-00   **Fax:** +90-216-531-00-99
Web: www.koc.com.tr

Koç Holding has operations in Algeria, Austria, Azerbaijan, Bahrain, Bulgaria, China, France, Germany, Hong Kong, Iraq, Ireland, Italy, Kazakhstan, Macedonia, the Netherlands, Poland, Romania, Russia, Spain, Switzerland, the UK, the US, and Uzbekistan.

PRODUCTS/OPERATIONS

2005 Sales

	% of total
Consumer durables	26
Automotive	23
Energy	20
Food & retailing	15
Financial	10
Other	6
Total	**100**

Core Businesses

Automotive
Construction and mining
Durable goods
Energy
Financial services
Food and retailing
International trade
New business development
Tourism and services

COMPETITORS

Caterpillar	Renault
Electrolux	Robert Bosch
Honda	Sabanci
International Power	Siemens AG
Opel	Yazicilar

HISTORICAL FINANCIALS

Company Type: Public

Income Statement

FYE: December 31

	REVENUE ($ mil.)	NET INCOME ($ mil.)	NET PROFIT MARGIN	EMPLOYEES
12/05	18,168	—	—	81,926
12/04	16,624	—	—	59,513
12/03	11,152	—	—	53,985
12/02	6,828	—	—	50,019
12/01	4,901	—	—	39,866
Annual Growth	38.8%	—	—	19.7%

Revenue History

Istanbul: KCHOL

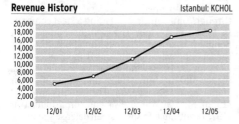

Komatsu

Like a sumo wrestler, Komatsu can throw a lot of weight around. The diversified company is the world's #2 construction equipment maker, behind Caterpillar. Komatsu makes building and mining equipment ranging from bulldozers and wheel loaders to dump trucks and debris crushers. Komatsu also makes industrial machinery such as laser-cutting machines and sheet-metal presses. Its electronics division produces LCD manufacturing equipment and silicon wafers; a civil engineering and construction division makes prefabricated structures and offers contracting and real-estate sales and leasing services. Other products include generators, armored vehicles, diesel engines, and computer software.

Komatsu means "little pine tree" in Japanese.

Its largest segment, construction and mining equipment, generates more than 70% of the company's sales. Komatsu has recieved numerous orders for its large press business and is increasing manufacturing capacity to meet demand.

The worldwide demand for mining equipment also remains robust. To take advantage of the upswing Komatsu plans to steadily expand its production capacity, both at home and abroad. The company is also expecting operations in China and the former Soviet Union to grow.

HISTORY

Komatsu's roots reach back to the Takeuchi Mining Company, founded in Japan in 1894. The company grew during WWI, and in 1917 it created an in-house ironworks to make machine tools and mining equipment. The ironworks was separated in 1921 to create Komatsu Manufacturing.

The firm grew into one of Japan's major makers of machine tools and pumps by adding new products to its line. Komatsu introduced its first metal press in 1924 and in 1931 made Japan's first crawler-type farm tractor. Komatsu began making high-grade casting and specialty steel materials in 1935.

During WWII Komatsu made munitions and bulldozers for the Japanese Navy. After the war it began making construction machinery and industrial vehicles as Japan rebuilt its infrastructure. The company began building diesel engines in 1948. Komatsu continued to expand during the 1950s. In 1952 it began producing motor graders, which became its first construction equipment to be exported (to Argentina) in 1955.

During the 1960s Komatsu entered joint ventures with US manufacturers, including Cummins Engine (1961), Bucyrus Erie (1963), and International Harvester (now Navistar, 1965). Komatsu established its first overseas subsidiary, Komatsu Europe, in Belgium in 1967 and introduced the world's first radio-controlled bulldozer.

The company changed its name to Komatsu Limited in 1970. International expansion continued as subsidiaries were established in the US, Brazil and Germany (1970), Singapore (1971), and Panama (1972). Komatsu began making bulldozers in Mexico (1976) and opened an Australian subsidiary (1978).

In the 1980s Komatsu pushed further into the US market, going head-to-head with Caterpillar. A strong dollar helped Komatsu undercut Caterpillar's prices by as much as 30%. In 1986 the company opened its first US factory in Chattanooga, Tennessee. In 1988 it merged American construction equipment-making operations with those of Dresser Industries, creating Komatsu Dresser.

Komatsu partnered with semiconductor giant Applied Materials in 1993 and entered the LAN market the next year with a print server and two types of hubs. The company expanded its construction equipment operations outside Japan in the mid-1990s, when it formed a joint venture in Vietnam and opened plants in China. Demand for construction equipment in Japan plunged soon after.

In 1997 Komatsu set up a joint venture with India's Larsen & Toubro to make hydraulic excavators. A semiconductor industry downturn prompted Komatsu to close some of its US silicon wafer operations in 1998.

Hammered by low demand for construction equipment in Japan (down nearly 80% over three years), Komatsu recorded its first loss in fiscal 1999 and closed plants. The company backed out of its joint venture with Applied Materials, selling its stake back to Applied Materials for $87 million in cash. Former GM manager Keith Sheldon was hired to overhaul the company's ailing global finances and prepare the company for stock listing on the New York Stock Exchange. In March 2000 the company sold its machine vision systems business to Cognex Corporation. Komatsu reached profitability in fiscal 2001 thanks to a new growth strategy focused on its construction and mining equipment businesses. Later the same year — as the economy swooned — Komatsu announced that it expected losses and was cutting about 2,200 jobs in Japan.

Komatsu's reorganization plans launched during the last quarter of 2001 carried over through 2002 and 2003. The company implemented its new growth strategy for the construction and mining equipment business, reduced fixed costs, and restructured its electronics business. In 2003 the company showed an increase of 5.2% in consolidated net sales over the previous year. That year the company decided to dissolve its Komatsu Metal Ltd. subsidiary.

Also in 2003 Komatsu acquired KONE Corporation's Partek Forest AB and Partek Forest Holdings (collectively known as Partek Forest); the additions became a part of Komatsu Forest AB.

In 2005 the company sold a 75% stake in its US subsidiary Advanced Silicon Materials to the Norwegian company Renewable Energy Corporation. Advanced Silicon makes polycrystalline silicon for use in semiconductors. The company makes nearly $140 million in annual sales.

EXECUTIVES

Chairman: Toshitaka Hagiwara, age 66
President, CEO, and Director: Masahiro Sakane, age 65
Senior Executive Officer; President, Construction and Mining Equipment Marketing Division, Regional Director of Japan, Asia and Pacific, and China: Kunio Noji, age 60
Senior Executive Officer; President, Defense Systems Division: Shigeki Fujimori
Senior Executive Officer; President, Development Division and President, Engines and Hydraulics Business Division, Supervising Research and Development Operations: Kunihiko Komiyama, age 61
Senior Executive Officer; President, Production Division: Susumu Isoda
Senior Executive Officer; General Manager Corporate Planning Supervising External Corporate Affairs, Structural Reorganization, Compliance, Safety and Environment, Electronics, and Human Resources and Director: Masahiro Yoneyama, age 60
Senior Executive Officer; Supervising CSR, General Affairs, Corporate Communications, and Investor Relations: Munenori Nakao
Senior Executive Officer and CFO: Kenji Kinoshita
Senior Executive Officer; General Manager, Corporate Planning; and Director: Yasuo Suzuki, age 58
Senior Executive Officer; President, Construction and Mining Equipment Marketing Division; and Director: Yoshinori Komamura, age 58
Executive Officer; President, Overseas Marketing, Construction and Mining Equipment Marketing Division: Taizo Kayata
Executive Officer; President, Research Division: Masao Fuchigami
Executive Officer; VP, Construction and Mining Equipment Marketing Division; President, Product Support Division: Mamoru Hironaka
Executive Officer; VP, Development Division; General Manager, Product Planning: Nobukazu Kotake
Executive Officer; President, Construction and Mining Equipment Strategy Division: Masaji Kitamura
Executive Officer; Osaka Plant Manager, Production Division: Nobutsugu Ohira
Executive Officer; President, Industrial Machinery Division: Koji Yamada
Executive Officer; General Manager, Human Resources: Masakatsu Hioki
Chairman and CEO, Komatsu America: David W. (Dave) Grzelak
Auditors: KPMG AZSA & Co.

LOCATIONS

HQ: Komatsu Ltd.
2-3-6 Akasaka, Minato-ku, Tokyo 107-8414, Japan
Phone: +81-3-5561-2687   **Fax:** +81-3-3505-9662
US HQ: 1701 W. Golf Rd., Rolling Meadows, IL 60008
US Phone: 847-437-5800   **US Fax:** 847-437-5814
Web: www.komatsu.com

Komatsu has subsidiaries and affiliates in Australia, Belgium, Brazil, Canada, China, Egypt, France, Germany, Ghana, Hong Kong, India, Indonesia, Iran, Italy, Kenya, Malaysia, Mexico, Mongolia, Myanmar, the Netherlands, Norway, Pakistan, the Philippines, Poland, Russia, Saudi Arabia, Singapore, South Africa, Spain, Taiwan, Thailand, Turkey, the United Arab Emirates, the UK, the US, and Vietnam.

2006 Sales

	$ mil.	% of total
Asia		
Japan	4,597.6	31
China	819.7	6
Other countries	2,068.4	14
Americas	4,191.2	28
Europe	2,106.7	14
Middle East & Africa	1,008.9	7
Total	**14,792.5**	**100**

PRODUCTS/OPERATIONS

2006 Sales

	$ mil.	% of total
Construction & mining equipment	11,222.5	76
Industrial machinery & vehicles	2,608.8	18
Electronics	961.2	6
Total	**14,792.5**	**100**

Products and Services

Construction and mining equipment
Backhoe loaders
Crawler dozers
Crawler excavators
Diesel engines and power generators
Dump trucks
Forest machines
Hydraulic equipment
Mini excavators
Minimal swing radius excavators
Mobile crushers/recyclers
Motor graders
Skid steer loaders
Vibratory rollers
Wheel excavators
Wheel loaders

Industrial machinery, vehicles, and other
Crankshaft millers
Forging presses
Forklift trucks
Gardening tools and hobby engines
Large presses
Press brakes
Recycling plants
Shears
Small and medium-sized presses

Electronics
Excimer laser
LAN peripheral equipment
Mobile tracking and communication terminals
Monosilane gas
Network information terminals
Semiconductor manufacturing-related thermoelectric devices
Silicon wafers
Thermoelectric modules
Vehicle controllers

COMPETITORS

Barloworld	Metso Minerals
CAMECO Industries	Mitsubishi Heavy
Caterpillar	Industries
CLARK Material	Mitsubishi Materials
CNH	Mitsui
Comau	Nisshinbo
Cymer	RAG
Deere	Rasa
Deere-Hitachi	Shin-Etsu Handotai
Furukawa	Sumitomo
Harnischfeger	Terex
JLG Industries	Toyota
Kubota	Victor L. Phillips

HISTORICAL FINANCIALS

Company Type: Public

Income Statement

FYE: March 31

	REVENUE ($ mil.)	NET INCOME ($ mil.)	NET PROFIT MARGIN	EMPLOYEES
3/06	14,793	977	6.6%	34,597
3/05	13,597	552	4.1%	33,008
3/04	11,438	255	2.2%	31,635
3/03	9,093	25	0.3%	30,666
3/02	7,810	(608)	—	30,760
Annual Growth	**17.3%**	**—**	**—**	**3.0%**

2006 Year-End Financials

Debt ratio: 31.3%
Return on equity: 20.0%
Cash ($ mil.): 599

Current ratio: 1.38
Long-term debt ($ mil.): 1,668

Net Income History

OTC: KMTUY

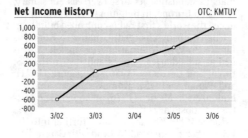

Koor Industries

Once a socialist vision, now a model of capitalism, Koor Industries is Israel's leading holding company. Koor's core businesses have been its holdings in agrochemicals (Makhteshim-Agan), defense electronics (Elisra Electronics Group), and telecommunications equipment (ECI Telecom, ECTel, and Telrad Networks). The company's venture capital arm has invested in enterprises including Chiaro Networks and Mysticom. Koor Industries also has operations in tourism, real estate, and trade. IDB Holding Corp. subsidiary Discount Investment Corporation (DIC) owns 30% of Koor. The company was founded to provide employment for Jewish refugees during WWII.

Claridge Israel, a unit of Canadian billionaire Charles Bronfman's investment firm, owned 30% of the group before selling its stake to DIC in mid-2006. Earlier in the year DIC agreed to buy 35% of Koor Industries from the Bronfman family and chairman Jonathan Kolber (whose entire stake will be sold at the end of 2006). IDB had already owned 10% of the company, so this purchase will give it a 45% stake in Koor. Bronfman

and six other Koor Industries directors resigned from the board upon the sale of Claridge's stake.

Koor's general strategy for its agrochemical business is based upon timing the commercial release of the generic equivalent products that it develops to coincide with the expiration of patents for similar existing products.

While Koor's bread and butter is its chemical business, the company is attempting to build up its export-based businesses, which include its telecom equipment and defense electronics units. To this end, the company's investment arm has distributed venture capital primarily to communications-oriented hardware and software developers. The company invests in telecommunications businesses through its ECI Telecom, Telrad Networks, and ECTel holdings.

HISTORY

Koor Industries is an offshoot of Solel Boneh, a construction company formed in 1924 in British Palestine by the Histadrut Labour Federation. Solel Boneh founded Koor in 1944 to build factories to provide employment for Jewish refugees arriving during WWII.

An Arab attack quickly followed Israel's creation in 1948. Israel prevailed, but the threat of future conflicts spurred development of its defense industry. In 1952 Koor teamed with a Finnish firm to create Soltam, an Israeli artillery manufacturer. The previous year, it had diversified into telecommunications equipment with Telrad.

Koor continued to expand and diversify through joint ventures, creating a steel company in 1954 and Alliance Tire & Rubber in 1955 (it bought full control of Alliance in 1983). Koor and the Israeli government founded Tadiran (defense electronics, 1962), and Koor acquired chemical maker Makhteshim (1963) and food processor Hamashbir Lata (1970). The Sinai campaign (1956), Six-Day War (1967), and Yom Kippur War (1973) continued to spur Israeli defense spending. However, with Histadrut's emphasis on socialist aims, Koor never became very profitable. Successful subsidiaries were offset by money-losers.

The company was hurt in the 1980s by a government program that cut subsidies and lowered trade barriers. Inflation damaged Koor's global competitiveness. With the help of junk bond guru Michael Milken, Koor raised $105 million in a 1986 debt issue. That year, however, Koor posted its first loss in 20 years, and losses widened in 1987. Benjamin Gaon became CEO in 1988 and began restructuring the heavily indebted company, which by then had about 130 units. He kept closing plants, but the company incurred a loss in 1988 and a record $369 million deficit in 1989. Gaon negotiated a new arrangement with creditors in 1991.

By 1992 Gaon's cost cutting had begun to pay off, and the company returned to profitability. Histadrut sold out in 1995, severing a link to Koor's socialist past. That year the company raised nearly $120 million in an international IPO, and Northern Telecom (now Nortel Networks) acquired 20% of Telrad (sold back to Koor in 2000).

Koor continued divesting assets to focus on its core businesses. ITT Sheraton International took a 50% stake in Koor Tourism in a 1996 alliance to manage hotels in Israel, and Henkel bought 50% of Koor's detergent operations. Discontinued operations included Beep-A-Call (wireless paging, 1995), Gamda Trade (food retail, 1996), and TAMI (food industry, 1997).

In 1995 Gaon sowed the seeds for his departure by selling a controlling stake in Koor to the Shamrock Group, a Disney family investment firm. Disagreements with Gaon over Koor's strategy led Shamrock to sell its stake in 1997 to Claridge Israel, an investment fund controlled by Canadian billionaire Charles Bronfman. Jonathan Kolber, then CEO of Claridge Israel, replaced Gaon in 1998.

Kolber made plans to increase exports and focus on Koor's telecom equipment, defense electronics, and agrochemicals segments, while scaling back in construction materials. In 1998 Koor bought a stake in Israel's ECI Telecom, which merged with Tadiran Telecom in 1999. Koor also dumped several non-core assets (including cable TV, energy, and software services units), raising more than $360 million. It then sold its 50% stake in cement group Mashav.

Koor joined with Nortel Networks in 2000 to launch Nortel Networks Israel to deliver high-performance Internet products to carrier and enterprise customers. The restructuring of the Elisra Group (formerly the Elisra-Tadiran Group) was completed in 2001. The next year Koor sold a 30% stake in Elisra Electronics Systems to government-owned Israel Aircraft Industries.

The company reorganized the operations of ECI Telecom in part by divesting its wireless networking equipment unit in 2002 so that ECI could focus more closely on core wireline products. In 2003 Nortel took over Koor Industries' 28% stake in Nortel Networks Israel.

As part of a long-term strategy, the company sold its 32% stake in military communications systems manufacturer Tadiran Communications to shareholders of Israeli international defense electronics company Elbit Systems in 2005. Elbit Systems also acquired Koor's stake in Elisra Electronic Systems.

Claridge sold its stake in 2006 and Kolber resigned as CEO and became chairman.

EXECUTIVES

Chairman: Jonathan B. Kolber, age 45
CEO: Raanan Cohen
President: Danny Biran, age 64
VP: Aaron Zuker, age 61
General Counsel and Corporate Secretary: Shlomo Heller, age 63
EVP: David (Didi) Paz
Corporate Controller: Michal Yageel
SVP and CFO: Ran Maidan, age 35
VP Investor Relations: Fiona Darmon
Director Corporate Development; Managing Director, Koor Corporate Venture Capital: Jackie Goren, age 39
Auditors: Somekh Chaikin

LOCATIONS

HQ: Koor Industries Ltd.
   14 Hamelacha St., Park Afek,
   Rosh Ha'Ayin 48091, Israel
Phone: +972-3-900-8333   **Fax:** +972-3-900-8334
Web: www.koor.com

2005 Sales

	% of total
North America	52
Israel	32
Europe	11
Africa	2
Asia & Australia	2
South America	1
Total	**100**

PRODUCTS/OPERATIONS

2005 Sales

	% of total
Tourism	53
Telecommunication	46
Other	1
Total	**100**

Selected Subsidiaries and Affiliates

Agrochemicals
   Makhteshim-Agan Industries Ltd. (34%)
Defense electronics
   BVR Systems (46%)
   Spectralink
Telecommunications equipment
   ECI Telecom Ltd. (31%)
   Nortel Networks Israel (28%)
   Telrad Networks
Venture capital investments
   Koor Corporate Venture Capital
Other
   Knafaim-Arkia Holdings (28%, flight and tourism operator)
   Koor Trade
   Sheraton-Moriah Israel (55%, hotels)

COMPETITORS

Alcatel-Lucent
Ampal-American Israel
Clal Industries
DIRECTV
Dow AgroSciences
DuPont Agriculture & Nutrition
Elron
GE
Gilat Satellite
Harris Corp.
The Israel Corporation
Lucent
NEC
Oryx Technology
Philips Electronics
Raytheon
Rockwell Automation
Siemens AG
Toshiba

HISTORICAL FINANCIALS

Company Type: Public

Income Statement

	REVENUE ($ mil.)	NET INCOME ($ mil.)	NET PROFIT MARGIN	EMPLOYEES
12/05	345	77	22.3%	2,318
12/04	2,135	26	1.2%	6,559
12/03	1,767	(24)	—	6,328
12/02	1,527	(164)	—	6,899
12/01	1,618	(569)	—	7,297
Annual Growth	(32.1%)	—	—	(24.9%)

FYE: December 31

2005 Year-End Financials

Debt ratio: 80.5%
Return on equity: 16.2%
Cash ($ mil.): 191
Current ratio: 1.90
Long-term debt ($ mil.): 437
No. of shares (mil.): —
Dividends
   Yield: —
   Payout: —
Market value ($ mil.): —

Stock History

NYSE: KOR

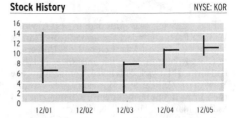

	STOCK PRICE ($) FY Close	P/E High/Low		PER SHARE ($) Earnings	Dividends
12/05	10.99	—	—	—	—
12/04	10.56	—	—	—	—
12/03	7.74	—	—	(0.31)	—
12/02	2.10	—	—	—	—
12/01	6.51	—	—	—	—
Annual Growth	14.0%				

KPMG

Businesses all over the world count on KPMG for accounting. KPMG is the smallest, yet most geographically dispersed of accounting's Big Four, which also includes Deloitte Touche Tohmatsu, Ernst & Young, and PricewaterhouseCoopers. KPMG, a cooperative that operates as an umbrella organization for its member firms, has organized its structure into three operating regions: the Americas; Asia/Pacific; and Europe, Middle East, Africa. Member firms' offerings include audit, tax, and advisory services; KPMG focuses on clients in such industries as financial services, consumer products, government, health care, information, communications, and entertainment. KPMG has discontinued its KLegal International network.

After much regulatory pressure, KPMG separated its accounting and consulting operations; it sold a chunk of the consulting business to networking equipment maker Cisco Systems, then took it public and sold off its shares in 2002. The consulting unit, which in 2002 changed its name to BearingPoint, acquired KPMG's Austrian, German, and Swiss consulting businesses.

A run-in with the US government over questionable tax shelters characterized as abusive (costing the US more than $1 billion in tax revenues) led to a shakeup in the US firm's tax services unit in 2004 and the payment of a $456 million penalty in mid-2005. While KPMG appears to have headed off an indictment of the firm, eight former KPMG executives have been indicted and charged with conspiracy in connection with the tax shelters.

Lawsuits over KPMG's work for other former clients hit the accountancy's pocketbook. In 2003 KPMG agreed to pay $125 million to settle a dispute regarding work for Rite Aid. The next year, KPMG's Belgian and US units agreed to a $115 million settlement regarding now-defunct Lernout & Hauspie Speech Products.

KPMG's UK and German operations in 2006 announced they would merge to form KPMG Europe, which will continue to operate under the KPMG International umbrella. The move is seen as the first step in a plan to unite KPMG's European units into a single firm.

HISTORY

Peat Marwick was founded in 1911, when William Peat, a London accountant, met James Marwick during an Atlantic crossing. University of Glasgow alumni Marwick and Roger Mitchell had formed Marwick, Mitchell & Company in New York in 1897. Peat and Marwick agreed to ally their firms temporarily, and in 1925 they merged as Peat, Marwick, Mitchell, & Copartners.

In 1947 William Black became senior partner, a position he held until 1965. He guided the firm's 1950 merger with Barrow, Wade, Guthrie, one of the US's oldest firms, and built its consulting practice. Peat Marwick restructured its international practice as PMM&Co. (International) in 1972 (renamed Peat Marwick International in 1978).

The next year several European accounting firms led by Klynveld Kraayenhoff (the Netherlands) and Deutsche Treuhand (Germany) began forming an international accounting federation. Needing an American member, the European firms encouraged the merger of two American firms founded around the turn of the century, Main Lafrentz and Hurdman Cranstoun. Main Hurdman & Cranstoun joined the Europeans to form Klynveld Main Goerdeler (KMG), named after two of the member firms and the chairman of Deutsche Treuhand, Reinhard Goerdeler. Other members were C. Jespersen (Denmark), Thorne Riddel (Canada), Thomson McLintok (UK), and Fides Revision (Switzerland).

Peat Marwick merged with KMG in 1987 to form Klynveld Peat Marwick Goerdeler (KPMG). KPMG lost 10% of its business as competing client companies departed. Professional staff departures followed in 1990 when, as part of a consolidation, the firm trimmed its partnership rolls.

In the 1990s the then-Big Six accounting firms all faced lawsuits arising from an evolving standard holding auditors responsible for the substance, rather than merely the form, of clients' accounts. KPMG was hit by suits stemming from its audits of defunct S&Ls and litigation relating to the bankruptcy of Orange County, California (settled for $75 million in 1998). Nevertheless KPMG kept growing; it expanded its consulting division with the acquisition of banking consultancy Barefoot, Marrinan & Associates in 1996.

In 1997, after Price Waterhouse and Coopers & Lybrand announced their merger, KPMG and Ernst & Young announced one of their own. But they called it quits the next year, fearing that regulatory approval of the deal would be too onerous. The creation of PricewaterhouseCoopers (PwC) and increasing competition in the consulting sides of all of the Big Five brought a realignment of loyalties in their national practices. KPMG Consulting's Belgian group moved to PwC and its French group to Computer Sciences Corporation. Andersen nearly wooed away KPMG's Canadian consulting group, but the plan was foiled by the ever-sullen Andersen Consulting group (now Accenture) and by KPMG's promises of more money. Against this background, KPMG sold 20% of its consulting operations to Cisco Systems for $1 billion. In addition to the cash infusion, the deal allowed KPMG to provide installation and system management to Cisco's customers.

Even while KPMG worked on the IPO of its consulting group (which took place in 2001), it continued to rail against the SEC as it called for relationships between consulting and auditing organizations to be severed. In 2002 KPMG sold its British and Dutch consultancy units to France's Atos Origin.

In 2003 the SEC charged US member firm KPMG L.L.P. and four partners with fraud in alleged profit inflation at former client Xerox in the late 1990s. (In April 2005 the accounting firm paid almost $22.5 million, including a $10 million civil penalty, to settle the charges.)

KPMG exited various businesses around the globe during fiscal 2004, including full-scope legal services and certain advisory services, to focus on higher-demand services.

EXECUTIVES

Chairman: Michael D. V. (Mike) Rake, age 58
CEO: Michael P. (Mike) Wareing
Chairman, Asia Pacific Region; Senior Partner, China and Hong Kong, SAR: John B. Harrison
Chairman and CEO, KPMG LLP: Timothy P. (Tim) Flynn, age 48
Chairman, Europe, Middle East and Africa Region; Chairman, The Netherlands: Ben van der Veer
Senior Partner, KPMG UK: John Griffith-Jones
CEO, KPMG UK: Colin Cook
Chairman, Germany: Rolf Nonnenmacher
Vice Chairman: Ruth Anderson
Vice Chairman and Managing Partner, Global Markets: Alistair Johnston
Vice Chairman: Philip Wallace
Vice Chairman: Derek Zissman
General Counsel: Tom Wethered

LOCATIONS

HQ: KPMG International
Burgemeester Rijnderslaan 10,
1185 MC Amstelveen, The Netherlands
Phone: +31-20-656-7890   **Fax:** +31-20-656-7700
US HQ: 345 Park Ave., New York, NY 10154
US Phone: 212-758-9700   **US Fax:** 212-758-9819
Web: www.kpmg.com

KPMG International has offices in nearly 145 countries.

2005 Sales

	$ mil.	% of total
Europe, Middle East, South Asia & Africa	8,100	52
Americas	5,670	36
Asia/Pacific	1,920	12
Total	**15,690**	**100**

PRODUCTS/OPERATIONS

2005 Sales

	$ mil.	% of total
Audit services	7,810	50
Advisory services	4,710	30
Tax services	3,170	20
Total	**15,690**	**100**

2005 Sales by Customer Type

	$ mil.	% of total
Financial services	3,860	28
Industrial markets	3,480	22
Information, communications & entertainment	3,280	22
Infrastructure, government & health care	3,110	15
Consumer markets	1,960	13
Total	**15,690**	**100**

Selected Services

Audit services
  Financial statement audit
  Internal audit services
Tax services
  Corporate and business tax
  Global tax
  Indirect tax
  Personal tax

Advisory services
  Audit support services
  Financial risk management
  Information risk management
  Process improvement
  Regulatory and compliance

Selected Industry Specializations

Consumer markets
  Consumer products
  Food and beverage
  Retail
Industrial markets
  Chemicals and pharmaceuticals
  Energy and natural resources
  Industrial and automotive products
Financial services
  Banking
  Insurance
Infrastructure, government, and health care
  Building, construction, and real estate
  Funding agencies
  Government
  Healthcare
  Transportation
Information, communications, and entertainment
  Business services
  Communications
  Electronics
  Media
  Software

COMPETITORS

Aon
Bain & Company
Baker Tilly International
BDO International
Booz Allen
Deloitte
Ernst & Young
Grant Thornton International
H&R Block
Hewitt Associates
Marsh & McLennan
McKinsey & Company
PricewaterhouseCoopers
Towers Perrin
Watson Wyatt

HISTORICAL FINANCIALS

Company Type: Partnership

Income Statement

FYE: September 30

	REVENUE ($ mil.)	NET INCOME ($ mil.)	NET PROFIT MARGIN	EMPLOYEES
9/05	15,690	—	—	103,621
9/04	13,440	—	—	93,983
9/03	12,160	—	—	93,470
9/02	10,720	—	—	98,000
9/01	11,700	—	—	103,000
Annual Growth	7.6%	—	—	0.2%

Revenue History

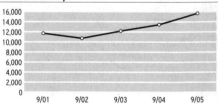

KPN

Spawned from one of the Old World's state-owned postal and telephone monopolies — Dutch PTT — Koninklijke KPN (also known as Royal KPN) faces a new world of technology and competition. In the Netherlands, the company has 7.7 million fixed-line phone customers. Its mobile division, KPN Mobile, has more than 14.7 million subscribers in the Netherlands, Germany, and Belgium. Through its ownership of several European ISPs, KPN also provides Internet access to 1.5 million customers, and it offers business network services and data transport throughout Western Europe. The Dutch government had cut its stake in KPN to 8% and given up its "golden share" veto rights. It sold its remaining stake in 2006.

The company has agreed to sell its international voice wholesale business, KPN Global Carrier Services, to VoIP carrier iBasis. The deal gives KPN a 51% stake in iBasis and is seen as a leap toward KPN's strategy of becoming an "All IP" carrier. KPN remains the dominant telecom operator in the Netherlands, a position improved with its 2005 acquisition of wireless telecom operator Telfort. KPN also is extending its European data communications network, including the purchase of some assets from KPNQwest, its failed joint venture with US-based Qwest Communications that operated a pan-European data communications network with connections to North America.

KPN Mobile, in which Japanese wireless operator NTT DoCoMo has taken a 15% stake, has mobile phone operations in Belgium, Germany, and the Netherlands, and it is introducing NTT DoCoMo's i-mode mobile multimedia services to these markets. KPN also has acquired HubHop, a wireless Internet (Wi-Fi) services provider, and Freeler, a small ISP in the Netherlands. To expand its IP-based services it has acquired Dutch telecom firm Enertel from Greenfield Capital in a deal valued at €10 million. KPN also has introduced a no-frills wireless service called simyo for customers in Germany.

Up-and-down economic conditions and the company's sizable debt (due largely to paying high prices for advanced wireless phone licenses) have led KPN to seek the sale of many of its international holdings, including its stakes in US-based Infonet, Ireland's eircom, Czech phone company Ceský Telecom, and Hungarian mobile phone operator Pannon GSM. It also sold KPN Belgium and its Belgian ISP, Planet Internet Belgium. The company also has said it will cut up to 8,000 jobs through the year 2010 and focus on broadband Internet business for growth.

KPN finds itself facing challenges in its Dutch market. Opta, the Dutch telecom regulator, dealt the company a blow by proposing that KPN's competitors must be given room to offer fixed-line subscriptions to customers, a revenue source dominated by KPN.

HISTORY

Koninklijke KPN is a descendant of the Dutch PTT — a traditional European state-owned postal, telegraph, and telephone monopoly. The PTT traces its roots to the 1700s, when Dutch provinces began taking over postal operations from cities. Under Napoleonic rule in 1799, mail delivery was organized under one national service.

In 1877 postal and telegraph services were assigned to the new ministry for water, commerce, and industry. The operation became an independent administration, called Postal Services and Telegraphy (P&T), in 1893.

The telephone made its Dutch debut in 1881 with Netherlands Bell Telephone, and several private operators and the P&T soon entered the business. After building its first local phone exchange in 1911, the P&T became the Staats Bedrijf der Posterijen, Telegraphie & Telephony (PTT) in 1928. In 1941 during the Nazi occupation, all independent phone operators were folded into the PTT.

After WWII, business began to boom for the PTT, which had fully automated its phone systems by 1962. Despite inflation and the government's practice of siphoning off PTT funds in the 1970s, the company stuck to a course of investment and new services. It launched a packet data network in 1982 and an analog mobile phone network in 1985.

Following years of debate, the PTT became an independent corporation called PTT Nederland NV in 1989, but the state was its only shareholder. Momentum had been building within Europe for liberalizing telecom services, and the door was opened to competition for some postal and telecom services. Fearing competition from the likes of British Telecom (now BT Group), PTT joined Sweden's Televerket (renamed Telia in 1993) to form Unisource, a global communications provider. Swisscom joined Unisource in 1993, and AT&T began working with the venture the next year.

Meanwhile, KPN launched a digital GSM (global system for mobile communications) mobile phone network in 1994, and Dutch mobile use began to take off. The company, now called Koninklijke PTT Nederland NV (or KPN; *Koninklijke* means "royal"), launched its long-awaited IPO that year; the state sold a 30% share. Also in 1995 the firm began offering Internet access.

KPN's mail delivery and logistics businesses were finally spun off in 1998 as TNT Post Group (KPN had bought express carrier TNT in 1996). The company began to focus squarely on telecom and adopted the name Royal KPN. AT&T abandoned the unsuccessful Unisource venture that year, and the others decided to sell its assets. Wireless subsidiary KPN Mobile was formed in 1999 and took a 77% interest in German GSM operator E-Plus (BellSouth bought the remaining 23%, then sold it to KPN in 2002).

KPN announced it would take KPN Mobile public in 2001 and entered merger talks with Belgacom, Belgium's leading telecom company, but the companies could not come to terms.

Also in 2001 KPN raised $4.6 billion in a public offering that reduced the Dutch government's stake in the company to 35%. The next year the company dissolved KPNQwest, its bankrupt joint venture formed in 1999 with US-based Qwest Communications, which operated a pan-European data communications network with connections to North America.

Also in 2002 KPN began searching for a buyer for its stake in the European wireless services joint venture with NTT DoCoMo and Hutchison Whampoa (formed in 2000). The next year the company sold its directory unit to private equity firm 3i Group and investment bank Veronis Suhler Stevenson Partners in a deal valued at $503 million. Also in 2003 the company sold its 16% stake in Ukrainian Mobile Communications for $55 million to Mobile Telesystems of Russia.

EXECUTIVES

Chairman of the Supervisory Board:
A. H. J. (Ton) Risseeuw, age 70
Vice Chairman of the Supervisory Board:
Dudley G. (D.G.) Eustace, age 70
Chairman of the Management Board and CEO:
A. J. (Ad) Scheepbouwer, age 62, $2,372,504 pay
Member of the Board of Management and CFO:
Marcel H. M. Smits, age 45, $626,007 pay
CEO, BASE: Libor Voncina
CEO, E-Plus: Michael Krammer, age 45
COO, Fixed Division: Eelco Blok
Head of Investor Relations: Jantiene T. Klein Roseboom
COO, KPN Mobile The Netherlands: Marco Visser, age 43
Operations Manager, Fixed Division: Cees P. Bosman
Senior Investor Relations Officer:
Catrien H. van Buttingha Wichers
Business Developments and Strategy Manager, Fixed Division: J. Wildeboer
Finance Manager, Fixed Division: S. van Schilfgaarde
Consumer Market Manager, Fixed Division:
M. Buitelaar
Carrier Services Manager, Fixed Division:
J. F. E. Farwerck
Auditors: PricewaterhouseCoopers Accountants N.V.

LOCATIONS

HQ: Koninklijke KPN N.V.
Maanplein 5, 2516 CK The Hague, The Netherlands
Phone: +31-70-343-43-43   **Fax:** +31-70-332-44-85
US HQ: 494 8th Ave., 23rd Fl., New York, NY 10001
US Phone: 212-560-9898   **US Fax:** 212-560-0770
Web: www.kpn.com

Koninklijke KPN N.V. operates primarily in Belgium, Germany, and the Netherlands.

PRODUCTS/OPERATIONS

2005 Sales

	% of total
Fixed Division	
Business	21
Consumer	20
Wholesale & Operations	12
Mobile Division	
E-Plus	23
The Netherlands	17
Base	5
Other	2
Total	**100**

Selected Subsidiaries and Affiliates

KPN EnterCom
  KPN EnterCom Solutions B.V. (voice and data business communications)
  Telecom Management B.V. (management of integrated business communications services)
KPN Mobile Holding B.V.
  KPN Mobile N.V. (85%, mobile telecommunications)
    BASE N.V./S.A. (mobile telecommunications, Belgium)
    E-Plus Mobilfunk GmbH & Co KG (mobile telecommunications, Germany)
    Hutchison 3G UK Holdings Ltd. (15%, mobile telecommunications)
    KPN International B.V.
    KPN Mobile The Netherlands B.V.
KPN Telecom B.V.
  Infonet Services Corporation (18%, data network operator, US)
  Proclare (10%)
KPN Telecommerce B.V.
  KPN Consumer Internet and Media Services B.V.
    Planet Media Group N.V.
    SNT Group N.V.
    XS4ALL Holding B.V.
KPN Vastgoed & Facilities B.V.
Volker Wessels Netwerk Bouw B.V. (45%)

HISTORICAL FINANCIALS

Company Type: Public

Income Statement

FYE: December 31

	REVENUE ($ mil.)	NET INCOME ($ mil.)	NET PROFIT MARGIN	EMPLOYEES
12/05	14,137	1,627	11.5%	29,286
12/04	16,512	2,837	17.2%	31,116
12/03	16,207	(4,709)	—	32,736
12/02	13,402	(15,837)	—	38,118
Annual Growth	1.8%	—	—	(8.4%)

2005 Year-End Financials

Debt ratio: 147.6%
Return on equity: 20.1%
Cash ($ mil.): 1,229
Current ratio: 0.63
Long-term debt ($ mil.): 9,767
No. of shares (mil.): —
Dividends
Yield: 4.2%
Payout: 67.7%
Market value ($ mil.): —

Stock History

NYSE: KPN

	STOCK PRICE ($) FY Close	P/E High/Low		PER SHARE ($) Earnings	Dividends
12/05	10.04	16	13	0.62	0.42
12/04	9.56	8	6	1.17	0.18
12/03	7.71	—	—	—	—
12/02	6.42	—	—	—	—
Annual Growth	16.1%	—	—	(47.0%)	133.3%

Kubota

Kubota is an old hand when it comes to turning Japanese soil. The Osaka-based company, which dates to 1890, is Japan's top maker of tractors and farm equipment such as rice transplanters and combine harvesters. It also leads the nation in the production of iron ductile pipe used in water-supply systems. Kubota, a diversified enterprise, makes industrial castings (ductile tunnel segments), PVC pipe, building materials (siding, cement roofing, and prefabricated houses), waste-recycling plants, and agricultural and industrial engines. In addition, the company builds water- and sewage-treatment plants, and it makes vending machines for cigarettes and beverages.

Fiscal 2006 marked the end of a two-year medium-term management strategy which saw Kubota reorganize its businesses, cut thousands of jobs, and reduce costs throughout the company in an effort to streamline its operations and return to profitability.

The plan seems to have worked as the company reported the highest level of operating income in its history for fiscal 2006. To keep up the momentum Kubota is focusing on two keys areas: overseas expansion and restructuring its pubic works businesses.

Specifically, Kubota wants to expand its engine and machinery businesses by introducing new products, increasing production capacity, and growing its marketing network. In its well-established European and North American markets Kubota is focused on wringing savings out of its operations by tightening its supply chain. Meanwhile the company is also busy establishing a stronger manufacturing and marketing footprint in emerging markets, primarily China and Thailand. To meet increased overseas demand, Kubota is also investing in production capacity expansion both at home and abroad.

Public works spending in Japan continues to decline and Kubota's pipe, valve, industrial castings, and engineering services segments have all been hard hit. In response Kubota has made efforts to reduce costs at its pipe and valve business. However, the engineering business for public works contracts continues to flounder in the midst of reduced domestic demand and stiff competition. The company has chosen to deemphasize its public works businesses and focus instead on overseas expansion of its successful engines and equipment businesses.

HISTORY

The son of a poor farmer and coppersmith, Gonshiro Oode left home in 1885 at age 14 and moved to Osaka to find work. He began as an apprentice at the Kuro Casting Shop, where he learned about metal casting. He saved his money and in 1890 opened Oode Casting.

Oode's shop grew rapidly, thanks to the industrialization of the Japanese economy and the expansion of the iron and steel industries. One of Oode's customers, Toshiro Kubota, took a liking to the hardworking young man, and in 1897 Kubota adopted him. Oode changed his own name to Kubota and also changed the name of his company to Kubota Iron Works.

Kubota made a number of technological breakthroughs in the early 1900s, including a new method of producing cast-iron pipe (developed in 1900). The company became the first to make the pipe in Japan, and it continued to grow as the country modernized its infrastructure.

Kubota began making steam engines, machine tools, and agricultural engines in 1917, and it also began exporting products to countries in Southeast Asia. In 1930 Kubota restructured and incorporated. It continued to add product lines, including agricultural and industrial motors.

Although WWII brought massive destruction to Japan, the peacetime that followed created plenty of work for Kubota's farm equipment and pipe operations as the country rebuilt. By 1960 the company was Japan's largest maker of farm equipment, ductile iron pipe, and cement roofing materials. That year Kubota introduced the first small agricultural tractor in Japan.

Over the next three decades, Kubota expanded its products and its geographic reach. The company created subsidiaries in Taiwan (1961), the US (1972), Iran (1973), France (1974), and Thailand (1977). It also made a major push into the US high-tech industry during the 1980s with the 44% purchase of supercomputer graphics company Ardent (1985). Two years later Kubota bought disk company Akashic Memories, and in 1989 it formed a joint venture with disk drive maker Maxtor to build optical storage products.

While loading up on high-tech operations, Kubota also expanded its lower-tech core businesses in the US. The company opened its first US manufacturing plant in 1989 in Georgia to make front-end loader attachments, and in 1990 it bought a 5% interest in Cummins Engine.

The next year Kubota took over the operations of struggling Stardent Computers; however, Kubota was unable to revive the graphic workstation business and dissolved its Kubota Graphics subsidiary in California in 1994.

In 1995 Kubota formed subsidiary Kubota Biotech to develop and sell biotechnological products such as biological insecticides. The next year Kubota launched a rice-cultivation machine for use in large fields.

Kubota gave its unprofitable computer hard disk business the boot in 1997 with the sale of Akashic Memories and the management buyout of subsidiary Maxoptix (computer memory storage drives). In 1998 the company formed a joint venture in China to make cast-steel products, and the following year it established a subsidiary there to make combine harvesters.

With its sales decreasing in response to Japan's economic slowdown, in 2000 Kubota implemented a three-year cost-cutting strategy. It began cutting its workforce by about 13% and jettisoning unprofitable businesses. The company's net sales increased in 2001, the result in part of its introduction of sub-compact tractors to the US the previous year. Kubota continued slimming down in 2002, exiting its Kubota Concrete (concrete piles) and Kubota House (pre-manufactured housing) businesses.

EXECUTIVES

President and Representative Director: Daisuke Hatakake, age 65
EVP and Representative Director: Moriya Hayashi, age 62
Executive Managing Director: Yoshihiro Fujio, age 62
Executive Managing Director: Toshihiro Fukuda, age 61
Executive Managing Director: Yasuo Masumoto, age 59
Managing Director: Yoshiharu Nishiguchi, age 59
Managing Director: Eisaku Shinohara, age 59
Managing Director: Nobuo Izawa, age 58
Managing Director: Yoshihiko Tabata, age 60
Managing Director: Kazunobu Ueta, age 59
Director and President, Kubota Tractor Corporation: Tetsuji (Mike) Tomita, age 56
Director: Tokuji Ohgi, age 59
Director: Morimitsu Katayama, age 58
Director: Nobuyuki Toshikuni, age 55
Director: Hirokazu Nara, age 58
Director: Masayoshi Kitaoka, age 56
Director: Masatoshi Kimata, age 55
Director: Nobuyo Shioji
Director: Takeshi Torigoe
Director: Satoru Sakamoto
Director: Hideki Iwabu
Auditors: Deloitte Touche Tohmatsu

LOCATIONS

HQ: Kubota Corporation
2-47, Shikitsuhigashi 1-chome, Naniwa-ku, Osaka 556-8601, Japan
Phone: +81-6-6648-2111 **Fax:** +81-6-6648-3862
US HQ: 2715 Ramsey Rd., Gainesville, GA 30501
US Phone: 770-532-0038 **US Fax:** 770-532-9057
Web: www.kubota.co.jp

Kubota has primary manufacturing facilities in Japan, and it has subsidiaries and affiliates in the Americas, Asia, Australia, Europe, and the Pacific Rim region.

2006 Sales

	$ mil.	% of total
Japan	5,633.0	63
North America	2,334.0	26
Other regions	1,016.3	11
Total	**8,983.3**	**100**

PRODUCTS/OPERATIONS

2006 Sales

	$ mil.	% of total
Internal Combustion Engine & Machinery	5,630.6	63
Pipes, Valves & Industrial Castings	1,621.4	18
Environmental Engineering	944.3	10
Other	787.0	9
Total	**8,983.3**	**100**

Selected Products

Internal Combustion Engine and Machinery
  Ancillary tools and implements for agriculture
  Carriers
  Cleaning and vending machines for rice
  Combine harvesters
  Construction machinery
  Cooperative facilities for rice seedlings
  Dairy and stock raising facilities
  Engines
  Farm facilities
  Farm facilities
  Farm machinery
  Gardening facilities
  Gasoline and diesel engines for farming and industrial
    purposes
  Harvesters
  Implements and attachments for farm equipment
  Lawn and garden equipment
  Mini-excavators
  Multipurpose warehouse
  Outdoor power equipment
  Power tillers
  Reaper binders
  Rice driers
  Rice mill plants
  Rice transplanters
  Tillers
  Tractors
  Welders
  Wheel loaders
Pipes, Valves, and Industrial Castings
  Cargo oil pipes
  Cast steel products
  Cast-iron soil pipes
  Castings
  Castings for engines
  Castings for machinery
  Ductile iron pipes
  Ductile tunnel segments
  Filament winding pipes
  G-columns
  G-piles
  Pipes
  Plastic valves
  Polyethylene pipes
  Polyvinyl chloride pipes and fittings
  Reformer tubes
  Rolls for steel mills
  Spiral welded steel pipes
  Suction roll shells for paper industry
Environmental Engineering
  Amusement fountains
  Solid waste treatment plants
  Water and sewage treatment plants

Other
  Air-conditioning equipment
  CAD systems
  Cement siding materials
  Colored cement roofing materials
  Condominiums
  Crushing plants
  Dioxins decomposition systems
  Grinding mills
  Industrial waste treatment plants
  Irrigation and water supply systems
  Landfill leachate treatment facilities
  Nightsoil treatment plants
  Photovoltaic shingles
  Pipe-laying work
  Pumps
  Pyrolysis gasification and melting furnaces
  Refuse incineration and melting plants
  Repair and maintenance works for sewage treatment
    and refuse incineration plants
  Scales
  Septic tanks
  Sewage sludge incineration and melting plants
  Sewage treatment plants
  Submerged membrane systems for night-soil and
    wastewater purification
  Vending machines
  Waste pulverizing plants
  Waste recycling plants
  Water purification facilities
  Water treatment plants
  Weighing and measuring control systems

COMPETITORS

AGCO	Isuzu
Caterpillar	Komatsu
CNH	Lafarge
Crane	Marubeni-Komatsu
Deere	Nippon Steel
Fiat	Sekisui House
Fuji Electric	Toro
Ishikawajima-Harima	Toyota

HISTORICAL FINANCIALS

Company Type: Public

Income Statement   FYE: March 31

	REVENUE ($ mil.)	NET INCOME ($ mil.)	NET PROFIT MARGIN	EMPLOYEES
3/06	8,983	693	7.7%	23,049
3/05	9,189	1,102	12.0%	22,916
3/04	8,776	110	1.3%	22,198
3/03	7,718	(67)	—	22,834
Annual Growth	**5.2%**	**—**	**—**	**0.3%**

2006 Year-End Financials

Debt ratio: 25.1%
Return on equity: 14.3%
Cash ($ mil.): 785
Current ratio: 1.47
Long-term debt ($ mil.): 1,299

Net Income History   NYSE: KUB

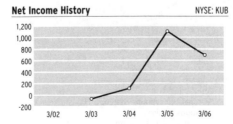

Kyocera

Don't confuse Kyocera's ceramics with teacups and pottery. The company, which began producing technical ceramics nearly half a century ago, makes a wide range of components and fine ceramic products — including capacitors, fiber-optic connectors, and semiconductors — primarily for customers in the electronics industry. Besides its ceramics and other electronic components, the company makes various types of finished electronics products, including cell phones, office equipment such as photocopiers and fax machines, and digital and film cameras.

Kyocera was hit hard in the early 21st century by weak demand for electronics and telecommunications gear, as more than 80% of its business came from customers in the information technology and telecom markets. In response, the company has worked to diversify its customer base by developing products for new markets, such as components for the automotive industry.

Kyocera has also expanded its manufacturing operations in China and consolidated operations elsewhere to cut costs. The company has operations in the Americas, Asia, and Europe; Japan accounts for 40% of sales.

Telecom giant KDDI provides approximately 8% of Kyocera's sales; Kyocera owns about 13% of KDDI.

Japan Trustee Services Bank and The Master Trust Bank of Japan each own nearly 7% of Kyocera. The Bank of Tokyo-Mitsubishi UFJ holds around 5% of the company. Morgan Stanley Japan has an equity stake of nearly 5%.

HISTORY

Born to a poor Japanese family in 1932, Kazuo Inamori never quite fit the mold. He went to work for Shofu Industries (ceramic insulators) in the mid-1950s, but quit three years later and started Kyoto Ceramic with seven colleagues in 1959. Their first product was a ceramic insulator for cathode-ray tubes. In the late 1960s the company developed the ceramic package for integrated circuits (ICs) that has made it a world-class supplier.

Kyoto Ceramic started manufacturing in the US in 1971. A few years later the company began to diversify its interests when it ventured into artificial gemstones (Crescent Vert, 1977) and dental implants (New Medical, 1978). In 1979 Inamori bought control of failing Cybernet Electronics (Japanese citizens-band radio maker), using it to move Kyoto Ceramic into the production of copiers and stereos.

The company merged five subsidiaries in 1982, forming Kyocera Corporation. The 1983 acquisition of Yashica moved it into the production of cameras and other optical equipment. That year Kyocera ran into trouble. At the time Nippon Telegraph and Telephone (NTT) was the only legal supplier of phones in Japan, and when Kyocera started marketing cordless phones without the required approval, the government forced it to recall the phones.

The government abolished NTT's monopoly in 1984, and Kyocera joined 24 other companies to form Daini-Denden ("second phone company") — now KDDI. In 1988 Inamori set up Kyocera regional offices in Asia, Europe, and the US. The company bought Elco (electronic connectors, US) in 1989 and AVX (multilayer ceramic capacitors, US) in 1990.

In order to diversify further, Kyocera entered into a series of alliances in the 1990s that included partnerships with Canon to produce video and electronic optical equipment, with Carl Zeiss (Germany) to make cameras and lenses, and with Cirrus Logic to make chips for a cordless phone project.

The company's Guangdong-based optical instrument joint venture began making cameras and lenses for the Chinese market in 1996. The next year Inamori went into partial retirement. In 1998 the company took over failed copier maker Mita Industrial, which had been a major buyer of Kyocera's electronic components.

In 1999 Kyocera acquired Golden Genesis (solar electric systems, US) and changed the company's name to Kyocera Solar. In the same year Kyocera's product line grew even more diverse as it entered the health food market and began selling mushroom products in Japan. Kyocera purchased the wireless phone business of QUALCOMM in early 2000.

Also in early 2000 the company's acquisition of failed copier maker Mita Industrial (which changed its name to Kyocera Mita Corporation) was approved. The deal included the forgiveness (by Mita's creditors) of most of Mita's debt and a cash infusion in Kyocera Mita by Kyocera.

Kyocera transferred its printer business to Kyocera Mita in 2002. Later that year the company made Toshiba Chemical Corporation a wholly owned subsidiary, changing its name to Kyocera Chemical Corporation.

Expanding its operations in China, Kyocera in 2003 created a sales company, Kyocera (Tianjin) Sales and Trading Corporation, and established a subsidiary to make solar-power modules, Kyocera (Tianjin) Solar Energy Co., Ltd. Also that year the company made Kinseki Ltd., a manufacturer of artificial crystals and related products, a wholly owned subsidiary, later called Kyocera Kinseki Corporation. In 2003 Kyocera also acquired the surface laminar circuitry (SLC) business of IBM Japan and formed a new subsidiary, Kyocera SLC Technologies Corporation.

The following year, the company folded its organic material components business into Kyocera SLC Technologies and manufacturing of crystal-related components was transferred to Kyocera Kinseki. Kyocera SLC Components Corporation was established as a manufacturer of buildup substrates. Also in 2004 Japan Medical Materials Corporation was set up as a joint venture between Kyocera and Kobe Steel, with Kyocera taking a 77% equity interest.

In 2005 Kyocera Solar Europe was established in the Czech Republic to assemble solar modules. Also that year Kyocera Wireless outsourced production of its mobile handsets to Flextronics International, eliminating nearly 1,600 manufacturing jobs in Mexico and the US.

EXECUTIVES

Chairman Emeritus: Kazuo Inamori, age 74
Chairman, Kyocera Mita and Director: Koji Seki, age 68
Chairman and CEO: Yasuo Nishiguchi, age 63
Vice Chairman and CFO: Masahiro Umemura, age 62
President, COO, and Director: Makoto Kawamura, age 56
President, Kyocera Chemical and Director: Noboru Nakamura, age 62
President, Kyocera Communication Systems and Director: Naoyuki Morita, age 64
President, Kyocera ELCO and Director: Yuzo Yamamura, age 64

President, Kyocera International and Director: Rodney N. Lanthorne, age 61
President, Kyocera Kinseki and Director: Isao Kishimoto, age 62
President, Kyocera Optec and Director: Michihisa Yamamoto, age 64
President, Kyocera Tianjin Sales and Trading and Director: Hisao Hisaki, age 60
President and CEO, AVX Corporation and Director: John S. Gilbertson, age 62
Senior Managing Executive Officer: Isao Yukawa
Managing Executive Officer: Takashi Itoh
Managing Executive Officer: Tetsuo Kuba
Managing Executive Officer: Tatsumi Maeda
Managing Executive Officer: Osamu Nomoto
Managing Executive Officer: Hisashi Sakumi
Managing Executive Officer: Eiichi Toriyama
Managing Executive Officer: Tsutomu Yamori
Auditors: ChuoAoyama PricewaterhouseCoopers

LOCATIONS

HQ: Kyocera Corporation
6 Takeda Tobadono-cho, Fushimi-ku, Kyoto 612-8501, Japan
Phone: +81-75-604-3500   **Fax:** +81-75-604-3501
US HQ: 8611 Balboa Ave., San Diego, CA 92123
US Phone: 858-576-2600   **US Fax:** 858-569-9412
Web: www.kyocera.co.jp

Kyocera has operations in Australia, Brazil, China, the Czech Republic, France, Germany, Hong Kong, India, Indonesia, Israel, Italy, Japan, Malaysia, Mexico, the Netherlands, Singapore, South Korea, the UK, and the US.

2006 Sales

	$ mil.	% of total
Asia/Pacific		
Japan	4,060	40
Other countries	1,698	17
US	2,168	21
Europe	1,576	16
Other regions	596	6
Total	**10,098**	**100**

PRODUCTS/OPERATIONS

2006 Sales

	$ mil.	% of total
Electronic Device Group	2,219	22
Information Equipment Group	2,131	21
Telecommunications Equipment Group	1,957	19
Semiconductor Parts Group	1,156	11
Applied Ceramic Products Group	1,005	10
Fine Ceramic Parts Group	593	6
Optical Equipment Group	128	1
Others	1,068	10
Adjustments	(159)	—
Total	**10,098**	**100**

Selected Products

Electronic Equipment
  Information equipment
    Copy machines
    Facsimile machines
    Page printers (Ecosys)
  Optical instruments
    Compact zoom cameras
    Digital cameras
    SLR cameras and lenses
  Telecommunications equipment
    Cellular handsets
    Personal Handyphone System (PHS) products (base stations handsets)
    Wireless local loop systems

Fine Ceramics
  Applied Ceramic Products Group
    Cutting tools (Ceratip)
    Dental and orthopedic implants (Bioceram)
    Jewelry and applied ceramic products (Crescent Vert)
    Solar energy products
  Fine ceramic parts
    Ceramic substrates
    Fiber-optic network components
    OA equipment components
    Parts for semiconductor fabrication equipment
  Semiconductor parts
    Ceramic dual-in-line packages (Cerdips)
    Metalized products
    Multilayer packages
    Organic packages
Electronic Devices
  Capacitors
  High-frequency modules
  Thin-film products
  Timing devices (TCXOs, VCOs)

COMPETITORS

Apple Computer	Nokia
Canon	NTT
Ericsson	Oki Electric
Fujifilm	Palm
Fujitsu	Philips Electronics
Hewlett-Packard	Ricoh
Hitachi	RIM
IBIDEN	Saint-Gobain
IBM	Samsung Electronics
Lexmark	SANYO
LG Electronics	Seiko
Lucent	Sharp
Matsushita	Sony
Molex	TDK
Motorola	Toshiba
Murata Manufacturing	Tyco
NEC	UTStarcom
NGK INSULATORS	Xerox

HISTORICAL FINANCIALS

Company Type: Public

Income Statement

FYE: March 31

	REVENUE ($ mil.)	NET INCOME ($ mil.)	NET PROFIT MARGIN	EMPLOYEES
3/06	10,098	596	5.9%	61,468
3/05	11,034	429	3.9%	58,559
3/04	10,969	655	6.0%	57,870
3/03	9,066	349	3.8%	49,420
Annual Growth	**3.7%**	**19.5%**	**—**	**7.5%**

2006 Year-End Financials

Debt ratio: 2.6%
Return on equity: 5.4%
Cash ($ mil.): 3,323
Current ratio: 2.43
Long-term debt ($ mil.): 285

Net Income History

NYSE: KYO

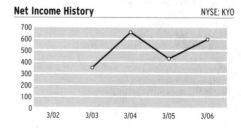

Ladbrokes

Ladbrokes will take that bet — on anything from sports to politics to unique speculations. Ladbrokes (formerly Hilton Group) makes odds online, over the phone, and at its more than 2,500 bookmaking shops in the UK, Ireland, and Belgium. The company's online gaming operations include a leading sportsbook that offers wagering on a host of international sporting events and boasts more than 2 million registered users from 200 countries. It also operates one of Europe's top poker sites and a host of online casino games. In addition, Ladbrokes runs such poker events as Ladbrokes Poker Million and Ladbrokes Poker Cruise.

Ladbrokes had previously been involved in the hotel business, owning the rights to the Hilton brand outside the US. In 2006 the company sold its hotel operations to US-based Hilton Hotels for $5.7 billion and subsequently changed its name to reflect its focus on gaming. With more than than 400 Hilton, Conrad, and Scandic hotels in 80 countries, the hospitality business had accounted for about 15% of the company's revenue.

Even before the sale to Hilton Hotels was announced, the company had been paring its hospitality holdings, selling 15 UK hotels and announcing plans for additional UK and international disposals, including a Sydney hotel that had its refurbishment completed in 2005.

Having shed its hotel business, Ladbrokes is working to expand its gaming operations and take advantage of new opportunities within the UK gaming market. The company hopes to see increased wagering in 2007 when new regulations in the 2005 Gambling Act take effect, allowing betting parlors to be open in the evenings during the winter. Ladbrokes is also eyeing a bid for one of 17 new casino gaming licenses. Already the company has opened a casino at the London Paddington Hilton, its first foray into casino operations since selling several gaming properties in 2000.

Ladbrokes online operations continue to perform well, but a renewed stance against online gaming in the US could impinge on the company's growth. In 2006 the US enacted laws restricting the banking industry from processing payments to offshore gaming businesses making it difficult, if not illegal, for US citizens to bet on sporting events or wager in online poker games with international gaming businesses.

HISTORY

Ladbrokes traces its roots to the village of Ladbroke in central England, where Arthur Bendir, a local racehorse trainer, set up a partnership in 1886 to take bets on horse races. Although off-track betting was illegal, betting on credit was allowed for wealthier members of society. The partnership, Ladbroke and Co., moved to London in 1900 and established itself as a quality credit betting shop in the city's plush West End. Bendir sold the business in 1957 to the Stein family. In 1960 the government legalized cash betting and Ladbroke began to expand. Cyril Stein became chairman in 1966 and took the company public the next year as the Ladbroke Group. It had 109 off-track betting shops in operation; by 1971 it had 660.

Stein pushed to diversify the company into real estate and casinos during the 1970s, and in 1973 Ladbroke bought three hotels. In the late 1970s the company suffered a major setback when its casino ventures in London were closed down and it was found guilty of violating gaming laws. The firm abandoned the casino business in 1979. In 1984 the company bought the Belgian Le Tierce betting shop chain and broke into the US market in 1985 with the acquisition of the Detroit Race Course (sold 1998). In 1987 Ladbroke beat out competitors to buy the 91-hotel Hilton International chain from Allegis Corporation for more than $1 billion. The deal made Ladbroke one of the world's top hotel operators.

Stein retired as chairman in 1994 and was replaced by John Jackson. Peter George, who had been with the company since 1963, was appointed chief executive. That year the company re-entered the casino business, paying $75 million for three London casinos. Though Ladbroke's property and retail division suffered in the 1990s, the hotel chain continued to expand; by 1995 there were 160 in operation. In 1997 Ladbroke entered into a sales and marketing alliance with US-based Hilton Hotels to promote the Hilton brand throughout the world. The next year Ladbroke acquired #3 betting shop operator Coral from leisure group Bass (which later split into Mitchells & Butlers and InterContinental Hotel Group). However, UK regulators later forced the company to sell the chain. (A venture capital company backed by Morgan Grenfell Private Equity bought it for about $655 million.)

With its $2 billion acquisition of Stakis in 1999, Ladbroke gained 55 hotels and 20 casinos in the UK and Ireland, as well as the LivingWell health club chain. Stakis' CEO, David Michels, became head of Hilton International. Ladbroke changed its name to Hilton Group that year. In 2000 Peter George resigned from the company and was replaced by Michels. That year Hilton Group sold its casino operations for $373 million to Gala Group. In 2001 the company bought the Scandic Hotel chain for about $885 million. Also that year Jackson retired as chairman and was replaced by Ian Robinson. The company fully returned to its betting roots in 2006, selling its hospitality operations to Hilton Hotels and changing its name back to Ladbrokes.

EXECUTIVES

Chairman: Sir Ian Robinson, age 63, $356,347 pay
CFO and Director: Rosemary Thorne, age 53
CEO and Director: Christopher (Chris) Bell, age 48, $1,034,361 pay
Head of Public Relations: Ciaran O'Brien
HR Director, Ladbrokes Worldwide: Ros Barker
Director, Corporate Development: Roger Devlin
SVP Development, Europe and Africa: Patrick Fitzgibbon
Trading Director, Ladbrokes Worldwide: Mike O'Kane
Managing Director, Remote Betting and Gaming: John O'Reilly
Director, Group Corporate Affairs: Alex Pagett
CEO, Vernons: Steve Roberts
Managing Director, European Retailing: Alan Ross
Finance Director, Ladbrokes Worldwide: Andy Scott
Head of Group Human Resources and Legal Services: Bryan Taker
Director, Human Resources: Nicola Jeffries
Commercial Director, e-gaming: David Briggs, age 35
Head of Investor Relations: Julian Arlett
Secretary: Michael J. Noble
Head of Marketing, UK Retail: Michael (Mike) Simpkin
Auditors: Ernst & Young

LOCATIONS

HQ: Ladbrokes plc
  Imperial House, Imperial Drive, Rayners Lane, Harrow, London HA2 7JW, United Kingdom
Phone: +44-20-8868-8899   **Fax:** +44-20-8868-8767
Web: www.ladbrokesplc.com

2005 Sales

	% of total
UK	86
Europe & Africa	9
Nordic	3
Americas	1
Middle East & Asia/Pacific	1
Total	**100**

PRODUCTS/OPERATIONS

2005 Sales

	% of total
Gaming	
Retail betting	74
Other	12
Hotels	14
Total	**100**

COMPETITORS

365 Media
888 Holdings
Camelot
Gala Group
Paddy Power
PartyGaming
Rank
Sporting Index
Sportingbet
Stanley Leisure
Victor Chandler
William Hill
Zetters

HISTORICAL FINANCIALS

Company Type: Public

Income Statement

FYE: December 31

	REVENUE ($ mil.)	NET INCOME ($ mil.)	NET PROFIT MARGIN	EMPLOYEES
12/05	19,789	570	2.9%	50,991
12/04	22,909	502	2.2%	51,890
12/03	15,878	199	1.3%	49,187
12/02	8,788	156	1.8%	51,637
12/01	6,039	208	3.4%	55,413
Annual Growth	**34.5%**	**28.7%**	**—**	**(2.1%)**

Net Income History

OTC: HLTGY

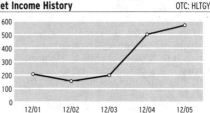

Lafarge

There's nothing abstract about Lafarge. The company, the world's #1 maker of cement (ahead of Holcim) and roofing products, #2 in aggregates and concrete, and #3 in gypsum, is a giant in the building materials industry. Cement accounts for more than 45% of sales. Lafarge manufactures aggregates and concrete, roofing (concrete and clay tiles, ceramic chimney systems; it may sell this division), and gypsum products (wallboard, plasters, insulation). It has operations in some 75 countries worldwide; Western Europe accounts for about 40% of sales, but acquisitions are expanding Lafarge's presence in Asia and other emerging markets. Lafarge recently boosted its stake in Lafarge North America to 92%.

Groupe Bruxelles Lambert SA holds 15% of Lafarge and may be planning to buy a controlling stake in the company.

Lafarge has agreed to sell its topflight roofing business to PAI Partners for nearly €2 billion. After the deal, it will buy a 35% stake in the business. Lafarge will use proceeds from the deal to concentrate on its more lucrative cement business.

Intent on strengthening its position as a world leader in construction materials, Lafarge continues to grow through acquisitions, especially in emerging markets such as Asia and Africa. Such emerging markets account for about 33% of sales. The company expanded in China in 2003 with the purchase of a stake in Chongqing Cement and has been focusing much attention on the fast-growing Asian market. Lafarge expects that construction growth in developing countries will far exceed the sector's growth in developed areas. On the downside, business in such regions is typically more risky.

Lafarge's plant in Aceh, Indonesia, was destroyed by the tsunami that devastated the country in December 2004. The company is fighting to maintain its market share in the area by shipping cement in from Malaysia and still faces fallout from the disaster.

HISTORY

Auguste Pavin de Lafarge started a small lime kiln along the Rhone river in 1831. By the turn of the century, the company's markets included the Americas and Asia, and in 1919 the company was incorporated as Chaux et Ciments du Lafarge et de Teil.

During the 1920s the company began producing portland cement, which could harden under water. It then capitalized on the Depression by buying failing cement companies.

The Lafarge family withdrew from the business in 1959, and the company began to grow through borrowing. That led to Lafarge's 1970 merger with Canada Cement, Canada's dominant cement maker. Lafarge's next big move in North America was the 1981 takeover of General Portland, a major US cement maker. The two companies, Lafarge Canada Cement and General Portland, were then merged, creating Lafarge Corporation. (Lafarge maintains a 52% stake in the publicly traded subsidiary.)

Current chairman Bertrand Collomb joined Lafarge in 1975 and became head of the company in 1989. Since taking over, Collomb has expanded the company's operations from 12 countries to more than 70.

Lafarge has grown through acquisitions, most notably the 1997 $3.7 billion purchase of Redland, a major UK roofing and aggregate company. Deals in 1999 included the acquisition of India-based Tisco's cement plants. The company also bought the remaining shares of Lafarge Braas GmbH that year, the holding company that houses its European roofing operations.

Lafarge's 2000 takeover bid for UK-based Blue Circle Industries failed, but it acquired a 23% stake in Blue Circle. In early 2001 Lafarge sold most of its specialty products business to Advent International and CVC Capital Partners for $747 million. Lafarge received a one-third stake in the new company being formed from the divisions, called MATERIS. Lafarge acquired the 77% of Blue Circle that it didn't already own for about $3.6 billion that July. The following year the company bought cement plants in Central Europe (Slovenia and Serbia-Montenegro).

In late 2002 the European Union fined Lafarge $248 million for its role in an alleged building materials price-fixing cartel. The next year Lafarge divested Lafarge Florida (part of Lafarge North America) and MATERIS (formerly part of its specialty products division).

The tsunami that stuck Asia in December 2004 destroyed Lafarge's $220 million cement plant in Aceh, Indonesia, and killed about a third of the employees there. Lafarge's plant was the only cement plant in the region.

EXECUTIVES

Chairman; Chairman, Lafarge Corporation: Bertrand P. Collomb, age 63
Vice Chairman: Bernard L.M. Kasriel, age 60, $842,064 pay
Vice Chairman: Jacques Lefèvre, age 67
CEO and Director: Bruno Lafont, age 49, $470,640 pay
EVP and CFO: Jean-Jacques Gauthier, age 46
COO, Co-President, Cement: Michel Rose, age 63, $555,864 pay (prior to title change)
EVP, Central Europe: Yves de Clerck, age 62
EVP, Human Resources and Organization: Christian Herrault, age 54
EVP, President, Aggregates & Concrete: Jean-Charles Blatz, age 61
EVP, President, Gypsum: Isidoro Miranda, age 46
EVP, President, Roofing: Jean-Christophe Barbant
EVP, Strategy and Development: Jean Desazars
EVP, Western Europe and Morocco: Jean Carlos Angulo, age 55
EVP, Co-President, Cement: Ulrich Glaunach, age 48
Group EVP, Co-President, Cement: Guillaume Roux
EVP, President and CEO, Lafarge North America: Philippe R. Rollier, age 63
Director Investor Relations: Yvon Brind'Amour, age 47
SVP, Group Sustainable Development and Public Affairs: Olivier Luneau
VP Group External Communications: Stéphanie Tessier
Head Media Relations: Louisa Pearce-Smith
Auditors: Deloitte & Associés

LOCATIONS

HQ: Lafarge S.A.
   61, rue des Belles Feuilles, 75116 Paris, France
Phone: +33-1-44-34-11-11   **Fax:** +33-1-44-34-12-00
US HQ: 12950 Worldgate Dr., Ste. 500,
   Herndon, VA 20170
US Phone: 703-480-3600   **US Fax:** 703-796-2215
Web: www.lafarge.com

Lafarge has operations in about 75 countries around the world.

2005 Sales

	% of total
Europe	
Western Europe	39
Central & Eastern Europe	6
North America	28
Africa	9
Asia/Pacific	9
Latin America	5
Mediterranean	4
Total	**100**

PRODUCTS/OPERATIONS

2005 Sales

	% of total
Cement	47
Aggregates & concrete	34
Roofing	10
Gypsum	9
Total	**100**

Selected Products

Cement
   Cements (marine, oil well, silica fume, slag, white)
   Hydraulic binders (road surfacing and natural lime)
   Masonry cements

Aggregates and Concrete
   Asphalt
   Crushed rock
   Gravel
   Industrial sand
   Precast concrete
   Ready-mix concrete

Roofing
   Chimneys
   Clay roof tiles
   Concrete roof tiles
   Roofing components

Gypsum
   Industrial plasters
   Plaster block
   Plasters
   Wallboard

COMPETITORS

Aggregate Industries	Italcementi
Ashland	Mitsui Mining
Boral	Readymix
Cementos Portland	Saint-Gobain
Valderrivas	Siam Cement
CEMEX	Sika
Ciments Français	Sumitomo Osaka Cement
CRH	Taiheiyo Cement
Dyckerhoff	Tarmac
FLSmidth	Titan Cement
Hanson	Uralita
Hanson Aggregates UK	USG
HeidelbergCement	Vicat
Holcim	Wienerberger
Holcim Apasco	

HISTORICAL FINANCIALS

Company Type: Public

Income Statement				FYE: December 31
	REVENUE ($ mil.)	NET INCOME ($ mil.)	NET PROFIT MARGIN	EMPLOYEES
12/05	18,914	1,299	6.9%	80,146
12/04	19,697	1,347	6.8%	77,075
12/03	15,656	1,044	6.7%	75,338
12/02	14,054	457	3.3%	77,547
Annual Growth	10.4%	41.7%	—	1.1%

2005 Year-End Financials

Debt ratio: 65.5%
Return on equity: 11.0%
Cash ($ mil.): 2,171
Current ratio: 1.30
Long-term debt ($ mil.): 8,132
No. of shares (mil.): —
Dividends
  Yield: 2.4%
  Payout: 7.1%
Market value ($ mil.): —

Stock History

NYSE: LR

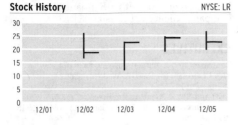

	STOCK PRICE ($) FY Close	P/E High/Low		PER SHARE ($) Earnings	Dividends
12/05	22.52	3	3	7.56	0.54
12/04	24.15	—	—	—	0.52
12/03	22.37	—	—	—	1.54
12/02	18.72	—	—	—	0.42
Annual Growth	6.4%	—	—	—	8.7%

Lagardère

Lagardère is flying high with its mix of media and missiles. The company's primary holdings include publisher Hachette Filipacchi Médias (*Elle* and *Premier*) and a minority stake in #3 aerospace firm European Aeronautic Defence and Space Company (EADS), which produces defense and weapon systems, military aircraft, satellites and space systems, and commercial aircraft. Lagardère's other media holdings include book publishing (Hachette Livre), Internet content (Lagardère Active), and satellite TV (34%-owned CanalSatellite).

Adding even more pages to its book operations, in 2006 Lagardère bought Time Warner Book Group, the fifth biggest US book publisher, for $544 million and renamed it Hatchette Book Group USA. Hachette Livre was catapulted from fifth to third-largest book publisher in the world as a result of the Time Warner Book acquisition.

Eager to continue further growth for this segment, Lagardère has been studying a number of possible acquisitions. The company bought the assets of Vivendi Universal Publishing (VUP), with the exception of the Houghton Mifflin educational subsidiary, from troubled media giant Vivendi. To get past antitrust authorities, Lagardère sold 60% of VUP, which it renamed Editis, to Wendel Investissement. To fund further acquisitions, the firm also decreased its stake in T-Online International. It also announced that it will halve its stake in EADS, from its current 15% to 7.5%, in 2009.

The company is also beginning to leverage its established print brands across other mediums such as television and the Internet through Lagardère Active. Lagardère is busy concentrating on its media operations; it has launched Gulli, a French children's television channel, and plans to acquire a 20% stake in Canal Plus France, which is being created by the merger of the Canal+ Group and Television Par Satellite (TPS), a rival in satellite television.

Lagardère has expanded its retailing business through its purchase of 16 French Virgin Megastores from Richard Branson's Virgin Group. Chairman Arnaud Lagardère owns about 7% of the company (and controls some 9% of its votes) through Lagardère Capital & Management.

HISTORY

Jean-Luc Lagardère began his rise to industrial titan when he joined French aerospace contractor Dassault as an engineer in the 1950s. He was tapped to be president and CEO of military equipment manufacturer Mécanique Aviation TRAction (Matra) in 1963, where he pushed the firm to branch out into electronics, space systems, and automobiles during the 1970s. Lagardère turned his focus to the media world in 1981 when he joined with Filipacchi Médias to acquire control of venerable French publishing firm Hachette.

Started by schoolteacher Louis Hachette in 1826, the publishing firm first catered to the textbook market and later began producing general trade books and travel guides. It became involved in the newspaper business in the 1920s and launched fashion magazine *Elle* in 1945. A diversification strategy in the 1970s proved disastrous, however, leading to Lagardère's takeover.

The engineer-turned-entrepreneur launched international spinoffs of Hachette's magazines, including a successful US *Elle* in 1985 in partnership with media maven Rupert Murdoch. In the late 1980s Hachette invested in radio broadcasting, bought US magazine distributor Curtis Circulation, and acquired Spanish encyclopedia publisher Salvat. Meanwhile, Matra launched its Espace minivan in 1983 (marketed by Renault). In 1988 Hachette acquired encyclopedia publisher Grolier for $1.1 billion and later bought out Murdoch's share of *Elle*.

In 1990 Hachette bought a 25% stake in money-losing French TV network La Cinq. The station collapsed a year later, leaving Hachette with a $643 million write-off. To cover the huge debt, Lagardère merged Matra with Hachette in 1993 under the holding company that now bears his name. Its Matra division acquired British Aerospace's satellite division the next year and Hachette expanded its North American distribution business in 1995. Two years later Filipacchi Médias and Hachette Filipacchi Press merged to form Hachette Filipacchi Médias.

With French industry decreasing its reliance on defense business, Lagardère merged its Matra unit with Aerospatiale, France's state-owned aerospace firm, in 1999. Not long after, the new Aerospatiale Matra agreed to merge with Germany's DaimlerChrysler Aerospace and Spain's Construcciones Aeronauticas to form European Aeronautic Defence and Space Company (EADS). Completed the following year, the merger created the world's #3 aerospace company. (Lagardère retained a minority stake in the venture.)

Later in 2000 Lagardère sold Grolier to Scholastic Corp. for about $400 million and bought the rest of Hachette Filipacchi Médias from its minority shareholders. The same year Jean-Luc Lagardère escaped a 1988 fraud charge when a judge ruled that the time limit for prosecution had expired. To begin leveraging its media assets, the company created multimedia unit Lagardère Active in 2001.

Jean-Luc Lagardère died in 2003 of a rare neurological disease. Also that year the company exited the automotive design business with the sale of its Matra subsidiary.

EXECUTIVES

Chairman; Chairman and CEO, Lagardère Media; and Chairman, EADS: Arnaud Lagardère, age 45
Deputy Chairman and COO: Philippe Camus, age 55
COO: Pierre Leroy
EVP Human Relations and Communications: Thierry Funck-Brentano
EVP and CFO: Dominique D'Hinnin
EVP, EADS International: Jean-Paul Gut, age 45
COO, Lagardère Media: Jean-Luc Allavena
Chairman and CEO, Hachette Distribution Services: Jean-Louis Nachury
Chairman and CEO, Hachette Filipacchi Médias: Gérald de Roquemaurel
Chairman and CEO, Hachette Livre: Arnaud Nourry
Group Director, HFM — Lagardère Active; Executive Chairman, Hachette Filipacchi Médias and Lagardère Active: Didier Quillot, age 46
Co-CEO, EADS: Thomas Enders, age 47
Co-CEO, EADS: Noël Forgeard, age 59
Auditors: Barbier Frinault & Autres; Mazars & Guérard

LOCATIONS

HQ: Lagardère SCA
4 rue de Presbourg, 75016 Paris, France
Phone: +33-1-40-69-16-00 **Fax:** +33-1-40-69-21-31
US HQ: 1633 Broadway, 45th Fl., New York, NY 10019
US Phone: 212-767-6753 **US Fax:** 212-767-5635
Web: www.lagardere.fr

2005 Sales

	% of total
Europe	
France	30
Other EU countries	34
Other countries	4
North America	15
Asia/Pacific	11
Middle East	3
Other regions	3
Total	**100**

PRODUCTS/OPERATIONS

2005 Sales

	% of total
Lagardère Media	62
EADS	38
Total	**100**

Selected Operations

Lagardère Media
  Editis (book publishing)
  Hachette Distribution Services (newspaper and magazine distribution)
  Virgin Megastores (entertainment retail stores)
  Hachette Filipacchi Médias (magazine publishing)
  Hachette Livre (book publishing)
    Hodder Headline
  Lagardère Active
    CanalSatellite (34%, satellite broadcasting)
    Lagardère Active Broadband (Internet and new media)
    Lagardère Active Broadcasting (99%, radio broadcasting)
    Lagardère Thématiques
High Technology
  European Aeronautic Defence and Space Company (15%)
    Aeronautics
    Airbus
    Defense and civil systems
    Military transport aircraft
    Space systems
Magazines
  Car & Driver
  Elle
  Entrevue
  Paris Match
  Premiere
Radio Stations
  Europe 1 Communication (news and talk radio)
  Europe 2 (pop music)
  RFM (oldies)

COMPETITORS

Advance Publications	Lockheed Martin
Axel Springer	Meredith
BAE SYSTEMS	Modern Times Group AB
Bertelsmann	Northrop Grumman
Boeing	NRJ
Dawson Holdings	Pearson
Emap	PRIMEDIA
Hearst	Textron

HISTORICAL FINANCIALS

Company Type: Public

Income Statement

FYE: December 31

	REVENUE ($ mil.)	NET INCOME ($ mil.)	NET PROFIT MARGIN	EMPLOYEES
12/05	16,026	831	5.2%	48,245
12/04	19,065	521	2.7%	46,947
12/03	16,404	419	2.6%	43,009
12/02	14,474	(305)	—	45,826
12/01	11,777	546	4.6%	46,337
Annual Growth	8.0%	11.1%	—	1.0%

Net Income History

Euronext Paris: MMB

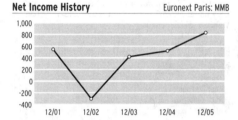

Legal & General Group

Generally speaking, Legal & General Group is one of the UK's biggest life insurers. The holding company's subsidiaries provide groups and individuals with life, health, property, auto, and liability lines of insurance. The firm is a major provider of investment services, including fund management, unit trusts, and individual savings accounts, or ISAs. Legal & General also provides mortgage loans and has real estate (Legal & General Estate Agencies) and venture capital (Legal & General Ventures) operations. In the US, the company does business as Banner Life Insurance Company and William Penn Life Insurance Company of New York.

The company's primary market is the UK, where it has deals with UK-based Bradford & Bingley, Alliance & Leicester, and Barclays to expand its product offerings and boost its distribution channels.

Legal & General is known for conservative, prudent growth. Longer-living pensioners, as well as the general slump in the global equities market, have impacted the company's bottom line. Although Legal & General is focusing on its core domestic market, it has expanded in France, Germany, and the Netherlands. Legal & General's fund management unit is one of the UK's largest pension funds managers.

HISTORY

The Legal in Legal & General's name comes from its founding mission — to provide life insurance to members of the legal profession. The company was started in 1836 by six lawyers as the Legal & General Life Assurance Society; its first customer, solicitor Thomas Smith, ill-manneredly died four years later after paying less than 200 pounds on a 1,000-pound policy.

Throughout that century and into the next, the company made loans to individuals and corporations; it also moved into real estate. After struggling under claims during WWI and the 1918 flu pandemic, it moved into fire and accident coverage in 1920. It opened membership to nonlawyers in 1929. The company took over the UK operations of the US firm Metropolitan Life (MetLife) in 1933.

In 1934 Legal & General bought Gresham Life Assurance and Gresham Fire and Accident, to gain a presence in Australia. During WWII the company was hit hard by German air attacks, both physically (it had to relocate away from London for a time) and at the bottom line.

The postwar years were a time of expansion as the company moved into South Africa and also broadened its operations at home. In 1949 it moved into marine insurance and in 1956 inaugurated life insurance in Australia.

The company began expanding its product offerings in the 1970s with managed pension funds and retail unit trusts. It established a direct sales force for life and pensions in 1977. The company also formed alliances with several European insurance companies and sold its Gresham life subsidiary. In 1979 it formed Legal & General Group Limited as a holding company for its now-separate insurance, international, and investment management operations.

In 1981 Legal & General bought US auto insurer GEICO's two-thirds interest in Government Employees Life Insurance Company, changing the subsidiary's name to Banner Life. Three years later it bought the Dutch operations of Unilife Assurance and created a subsidiary in the Netherlands. Despite all this activity, however, the company's performance during the 1980s was poor, and it brought in David Prosser (who became CEO in 1991) to goose its asset management operations.

In 1989 the company bought William Penn Life Insurance from Continental Corp. and opened its first real estate agency — just in time for the real estate market crash. Legal & General and other mortgage guarantee insurers were also squeezed by the resulting increase in mortgage default rates as homebuyers were caught between high interest rates and high unemployment.

The company formed a joint venture with Woolwich Building Society to provide Woolwich customers with insurance products in 1995. The next year it followed the insurance industry trend by establishing a bank of its own.

With each succeeding merger of its rivals, Legal & General became the target of rumors about its own fate. The company has remained adamantly independent, with Prosser claiming that Legal & General could instead benefit by picking up business left behind by the new entities.

In 1998 the British insurance industry was stung by scandalous revelations regarding improper pension sales in the late 1980s and early 1990s. Legal & General set aside about $1 billion to compensate victims; it also sold its Australian operations. In 1999 banking company National Westminster and Legal & General talked takeover,

but the deal fell through. (NatWest was eventually bought by Royal Bank of Scotland.)

In 2001 Legal & General announced a deal with UK-based Barclays to provide the bank's customers with life insurance and pension products. In 2002 Legal & General extended its marketing agreement with UK financial services company Alliance & Leicester.

EXECUTIVES

Chairman: Rob J. Margetts, age 59, $520,074 pay
Vice Chairman: Sir David A. Walker, age 66, $167,579 pay
CEO and Board Member: Tim Breedon, age 47
Group Director, Retail Distribution: Kate Avery, age 45, $770,480 pay
Group Director, Finance: Andrew Palmer, age 52, $1,024,738 pay
Group Director, UK Operations: Robin Phipps, age 55, $1,097,934 pay
Group Director, Product and Corporate: John Pollock, age 47, $568,229 pay
Director, Healthcare: Chris Rolland
Chief Executive of Legal & General Investment Management (LGIM): Peter Chambers
Insurance Business Development Director: Peter Richmond
Marketing Director, General Insurance: Garry Skelton
Head of Legal: Geoffrey Timms
Head of Publicity and Press Relations: John Morgan, age 51
Company Secretary: David W. Binding
Systems Actuary: Anant Chavda
Head of Sales, Healthcare: Patricia Matthews
Auditors: PricewaterhouseCoopers LLP

LOCATIONS

HQ: Legal & General Group Plc
Temple Court, 11 Queen Victoria St.,
London EC4N 4TP, United Kingdom
Phone: +44-20-7528-6200 **Fax:** +44-20-7528-6222
US HQ: 1701 Research Blvd., Rockville, MD 20850
US Phone: 301-279-4800 **US Fax:** 301-294-6960
Web: www.legalandgeneralgroup.com

Legal & General Group operates primarily in the UK, but also in France, Germany, the Netherlands, and the US.

PRODUCTS/OPERATIONS

2005 Sales

	% of total
Life & pensions	83
Investment management	12
General insurance	1
Other	4
Total	**100**

Selected Subsidiaries and Affiliates

Alliance & Leicester Life Assurance Company Ltd (long-term insurance)
Arlington Business Parks Partnership (56%)
Banner Life Insurance Company Inc (long-term insurance, US)
Bracknell Regeneration Limited Partnership (50%)
Chenas Finance SA (69%, Luxembourg)
Europe Loisirs SA (83%, Luxembourg)
First British American Reinsurance Company (US)
Gresham Insurance Company Limited (90%)
Hayley Conference Centres Holdings Limited (41%)
HMG Holdings Limited (65%)
Industrial Property Investment Fund (25%)
Legal & General (France) SA (long-term insurance)
Legal & General (Portfolio Management Services) Limited (investment management)
Legal & General (Unit Trust Managers) Limited
Legal & General Assurance (Pensions Management) Limited (long-term insurance)

Legal & General Assurance Society Limited (long-term and general insurance)
Legal & General Bank (France) SA (financial services)
Legal & General Estate Agencies Limited
Legal & General Finance Plc (treasury operations)
Legal & General Insurance Limited (general insurance)
Legal & General Investment Management Limited
Legal & General Nederland Levensverzekering Maatschappij NV (long-term insurance, Netherlands)
Legal & General Property Limited (property management)
Legal & General Resources Limited (provision of services)
Legal & General Ventures Limited (venture capital management)
Leisure Fund Limited Partnership (49.49%)
Moliflor Loisirs Participations SAS (50.08%, France)
Performance Shopping Centre Limited Partnership (50%)
Trident Components Group Limited (49.16%)
Vue Entertainment Holdings Limited (31%)
William Penn Life Insurance Company of New York Inc (long-term insurance, US)

COMPETITORS

AEGON
AIG
Alliance & Leicester
Allianz
AMVESCAP
Aviva
AXA
Guardian Royal Exchange plc
ING
Lincoln National (UK)
Lloyds TSB
Prudential plc
Resolution
Royal & Sun Alliance Insurance
Royal London Mutual
Standard Life

HISTORICAL FINANCIALS

Company Type: Public

Income Statement

FYE: December 31

	ASSETS ($ mil.)	NET INCOME ($ mil.)	INCOME AS % OF ASSETS	EMPLOYEES
12/05	330,085	1,763	0.5%	9,273
12/04	292,079	894	0.3%	8,807
12/03	222,126	718	0.3%	8,547
12/02	171,125	(289)	—	8,873
12/01	157,114	(277)	—	8,453
Annual Growth	20.4%	—	—	2.3%

2005 Year-End Financials

Equity as % of assets: —
Return on assets: 0.6%
Return on equity: —
Long-term debt ($ mil.): —
Sales ($ mil.): 53,314

Net Income History

Pink Sheets: LGGNY

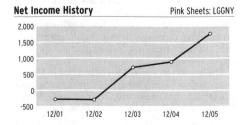

LEGO

Toy blocks are the building blocks of success at LEGO. Since 1949 LEGO Holding (aka LEGO Group) has made more than 200 billion of its interlocking toys, keeping little hands busy worldwide. In a nod to kids' high-tech skills, it offers LEGO kits to build PC-programmable robots (such as its Mindstorms line), and its top seller, BIONICLE, features an evolving story line on the Internet and various merchandising opportunities. The group also owns LEGO retail outlets in the US and Europe. Due to a slump in toy sales and subsequent losses, the group has sold its theme parks and is closing factories and cutting staff. Vice chairman Kjeld Kirk Kristiansen is LEGO's majority shareholder.

The word LEGO is derived from the Danish words for "play well," and children have been doing so with the company's familiar building blocks for years. To boot, LEGO toys were named the Toy of the Century by *FORTUNE* magazine in 1999. Despite the accolades, the company has experienced sales slumps and has been working to improve its performance in the past few years with other product additions such as the widely successful *Harry Potter* and *Bob the Builder* lines, as well as forming alliances with the NHL, the NBA, and NIKE.

As part of its reorganization strategy, LEGO has been shifting much of its production operations, which have been in Denmark, Switzerland, and the US, to lower-cost countries in 2006. To that end, LEGO has announced plans to outsource its toy-brick production to plants operated by electronics manufacturer Flextronics in the Czech Republic and Mexico. The shift eliminates some 1,200 jobs in Enfield, Connecticut, and Denmark over the next three years.

LEGO also produces television shows, educational materials, and merchandise including books, video games, and computer game software. In late 2003 LEGO and Miramax Film Corp. debuted (on DVD and video) *BIONICLE: Mask of Light* — a 3-D animated film based on the BIONICLE toy line. It has strengthened its licensing agreement with book publisher Scholastic, giving the company the rights to publish a wide variety of materials based on LEGO's intellectual properties.

LEGO's legal tussle with rival MEGA Brands (formerly Mega Bloks) continued after the Canadian Supreme Court issued its decision in 2005 giving LEGO the right to appeal the verdict of the Canadian Federal Court of Appeal. The original suit claimed Mega Bloks infringed upon LEGO's intellectual property by passing off its micro bricks as LEGO bricks. However, LEGO lost on its appeal later that year.

HISTORY

Ole Kirk Christiansen opened a carpentry shop in 1916 in Denmark and in 1932 began making carved wooden toys. Two years later Ole held a contest among his employees to name the company, from which came LEGO (a combination of two Danish words, "leg" and "godt," meaning "play well"). A fire destroyed the LEGO factory in 1942, but the company quickly resumed manufacturing.

The availability of quality plastic following WWII prompted the company to add plastic toys to its line. The predecessor to the common

LEGO block was invented in 1949; called Automatic Binding Bricks, they fit on top of each other but did not snap together.

After hearing criticism that no company made a comprehensive toy system, in 1954 Ole's son Godtfred assembled a list of 10 product criteria for LEGO's toys, including that they have lots of compatible components. Deciding that the Automatic Binding Bricks had the most potential, the firm launched the first LEGO playset in 1955. It introduced the "stud and tube" snaptogether building block in 1958. LEGOs were soon one of the most popular toys in Europe. When a second fire in 1960 destroyed its warehouse for wooden toys, the company ceased production of wooden items in favor of plastics.

Luggage-maker Samsonite began manufacturing and distributing LEGOs in the US in 1961 under license. LEGO's first LEGOLAND park, built from 42 million LEGO blocks, opened in Billund, Denmark, in 1968. (A UK park followed in 1996, a California park in 1999, and one in Germany in 2002.) By 1973, after relatively lackluster US sales, Samsonite opted not to renew its license, and the LEGO Company set up a sales and production facility in Connecticut. US sales increased tenfold by 1975.

Aiming for the preteen market, the company introduced the more-complex LEGO Technic model sets in 1977 and the popular LEGOLAND Space playset two years later. However, LEGO hit a bump when its patent for the LEGO brick expired in 1981 and a slew of knockoffs flooded the market.

In 1999 Godtfred died; his son, Kjeld, who changed the spelling of Christiansen to Kristiansen, succeeded him.

In the 1990s growth of the video game industry far outpaced the growth of the construction toys market, and LEGO suffered. With profits shrinking, in 1998 the company reversed its tradition of avoiding commercial tie-ins; it snapped together an agreement to produce building kits and figures based on the popular *Star Wars* movies and Walt Disney's Winnie the Pooh. However, those events came too late to prevent LEGO from suffering its first loss since the 1930s. The company began cutting up to 10% of its workers in 1999.

To build up its interactive, electronic, and educational toy development, LEGO bought smart toys developer Zowie Intertainment in 2000, marking the first time the company purchased another toy maker. In 2001, LEGO inked a deal to create children's online games and activities for software giant Microsoft Corporation. However, amid another periodic slump in sales LEGO announced in 2001 it would cut 500 jobs and discontinue some noncore products.

Facing record losses for 2003, LEGO announced in early 2004 significant changes to both its strategy and management structure. The company refocused on its core LEGO brick product and brand, and downsized its top leadership structure from 14 members to nine. In October co-owner Kjeld Kirk Kristiansen resigned as the company's CEO, but remained on the board as vice chairman. Joergen Vig Knudstorp, SVP of corporate affairs, was named as his replacement. Later that year the company changed its name from LEGO Company to LEGO Group.

The company divested its 44% stake in playground equipment manufacturer KOMPAN in 2004. The next year it sold its LEGOLAND parks, which featured LEGO sculptures, rides, and exhibits, to the Blackstone Group. It also sold a Swiss tool factory, Lego Werkzeugbau Steinhausen, in 2005.

EXECUTIVES

Chairman: Mads Øvlisen, age 66
Vice Chairman: Kjeld Kirk Kristiansen
CEO: Jørgen Vig Knudstorp
EVP and COO, Operations: Jesper Ovesen, age 46
EVP, Community, Education, and Direct:
  Lisbeth Valther Pallesen
EVP, Corporate Center: Christian Iversen
EVP, Global Supply Chain: Iqbal Padda
EVP, Markets and Products: Mads Nipper
SVP, Global Supply Chain: Lars Altemark
President, LEGO Systems: Søren Torp Laursen
Head, Legal Services: Poul H. Nielsen
Head, Corporate Communications: Charlotte Simonsen
Senior Producer, LEGO Virtual (Web Division):
  Leah Weston
Manager, Marketing, Bionicle: Lars Kaae
Brand Manager, LEGO MINDSTORMS: Joanna Gale
VP, LEGO Brand Retail, US: Matt Harker
National Sales and Marketing Manager, New Zealand:
  Matthew Ott
Controller, LEGO Systems, US: Christian Bidstrup
Director, Global Licensing, LEGO Systems, US:
  Stephanie Lawrence
**Director, Global Marketing Communications, LEGO
  Systems, US:** Lars Norman Andersen
**Director, Brand Relations and Integration, LEGO
  Systems, US:** Charles McLeish
Senior Global Manager, Marketing, LEGO Direct:
  Alex Algermissen
Senior Brand Relations Manager, LEGO Americas:
  Michael McNally
**Senior Manager, Strategic Alliances and Promotions,
  LEGO Systems, US:** Heather Kashner
Auditors: PricewaterhouseCoopers

LOCATIONS

HQ: LEGO Holding A/S
  Aastvej 1, DK-7190 Billund, Denmark
Phone: +45-79-50-60-70   **Fax:** +45-75-33-27-25
US HQ: 555 Taylor Rd., Enfield, CT 06083
US Phone: 860-763-3211   **US Fax:** 860-763-6680
Web: www.lego.com

LEGO Holding operates in more than 30 countries worldwide.

PRODUCTS/OPERATIONS

Selected Products

Alpha Team
BIONICLE
CLIKITS (fashion design system for girls)
Discovery Kids
Dora the Explorer
Harry Potter
Knights Kindom
LEGO BABY toys
LEGO Belville toys (for girls)
LEGO *Bob the Builder*
LEGO City
LEGO Creator sets
LEGO Designer
LEGO Duplo
LEGO Factory
LEGO Mindstorms
LEGO Quatro
LEGO Racers
LEGO Star Wars
LEGO Technic
Orient Expedition
Spiderman 2
Spybotics
Trains
X-Pod

COMPETITORS

Apple Computer	Mega Brands
Corgi International	Namco Bandai
Discovery Toys	Parc Paradisio
Disney	Playmobil
Hasbro	SMOBY
Hershey Entertainment	Sony
JAKKS Pacific	StarParks
K'NEX Industries	Toy Quest
Mattel	VTech Holdings

HISTORICAL FINANCIALS

Company Type: Private

Income Statement

FYE: December 31

	REVENUE ($ mil.)	NET INCOME ($ mil.)	NET PROFIT MARGIN	EMPLOYEES
12/05	1,117	80	7.2%	6,643
12/04	1,229	(289)	—	7,294
12/03	1,213	(138)	—	8,298
12/02	1,612	60	3.7%	8,297
12/01	1,266	51	4.0%	7,247
Annual Growth	(3.1%)	11.9%	—	(2.2%)

Net Income History

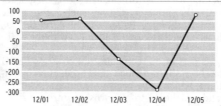

Lloyd's

After a lot of R&R (reconstruction and renewal), Lloyd's (aka Lloyd's of London) is back at work as the world's leading insurance exchange. Not an insurance company, it regulates about 60 syndicates with more than 40 managing agents, which are made up of corporate underwriters and wealthy individuals that transact insurance business worth billions in premiums each year. Also part of the picture are Lloyd's brokers, which bring business to the market. Lloyd's is a top conduit for aviation and marine insurance, as well as specialty insurance, such as policies covering art and jewelry or protecting against acts of terrorism.

The wealthy individuals it serves are called Names but their number has been dropping since the 1980s and is down to some 2,000.

Gross premiums written, for the entire Lloyd's market as a whole, total more than $24 billion (£14 billion). Reinsurance adds up to about 30% of that, with the next biggest chunks coming from third-party liability insurance (23%) and fire and other property damage (20%). Business in the US accounts for about a third of premiums written, followed by the UK, with a quarter.

Despite its overhaul, Lloyd's tradition of specialty lines has hampered its ability to compete against global insurance firms offering more comprehensive service. Encouraged by Lloyd's to consolidate, some syndicates, infused with capital from corporate-owned managing agencies that enables them to completely underwrite a contract, are turning into full-service insurance companies. Corporate underwriters, such as ACE Limited and Berkshire Hathaway's General Re, now account for most of Lloyd's capital backing, where Names once dominated.

Lloyd's is catching up to its rivals, particularly bargain-rate insurers who entered the offshore markets in the early 1990s. Catastrophic losses in recent years have forced them to raise their prices, making the Lloyd's market competitive again. But Lloyd's corporation is taking cost-cutting steps such as outsourcing operations ranging from data processing and catering to facilities management.

In another attempt to renew itself, Lloyd's has unveiled plans to replace its current accounting system and stop accepting capital from traditional Names. The company is lobbying for changes in the regulatory practices of the Names, most significantly the shift to a franchise system. Lord Peter Levene, the former Mayor of London, has assumed the chairman's post. Despite Levene's inexperience in the insurance industry, critics feel his government experience is the change needed to jumpstart the Lloyd's market.

HISTORY

In 1688 Edward Lloyd opened Lloyd's Coffee House near London's docks. Maritime insurance brokers and underwriters met at Lloyd's, which offered a comfortable venue for exchanging shipping information. The loose association of brokers began publishing shipping newspaper *Lloyd's List* in 1734 (sold 1996).

The coffeehouse attracted people who used insurance as a cover for gambling — members who "insured" the gender of the transvestite Chevalier d'Eon began Lloyd's tradition of specialty insurance.

In 1871 Parliament enacted the Lloyd's Act, which formed Lloyd's Corporation to oversee the activities of the underwriting syndicates (made up of Names with unlimited personal liability). In the 1880s the market began covering nonmarine risks. By 1900 Lloyd's members wrote 50% of the world's nonlife insurance. Prompt claims payment after the 1906 San Francisco earthquake boosted the market's image in the US. After WWI, Lloyd's members began writing automotive, credit, and aviation insurance.

In 1981 and 1982 a syndicate managed by Richard Outhwaite wrote contracts on the future liabilities of old insurance contracts with claims (many with environmental exposure) still pending.

That decade Lloyd's attracted new Names: the merely well-off — highly paid people without great wealth — who pledged assets were often overvalued in the 1980s boom. Exercising little oversight, Lloyd's let syndicates close their books on pending claims by reinsuring them repeatedly through new syndicates financed by neophyte Names.

The boom's end coincided with a rise in US environmental claims covered by insurance contracts such as those written by Outhwaite. When Names with reduced net worth balked at paying claims, Lloyd's faced disaster. From 1991 to 1994, the number of syndicates fell by half and premium rates increased. In 1993, with billions in claims and many Names refusing to pay or suing their syndicates for not disclosing the risks, Lloyd's imposed new underwriting and reporting rules, took control of most syndicates' back-office functions, and brought in capital by finally admitting corporate members (mostly foreign insurers).

Lloyd's reached a multibillion-pound settlement with most of its Names in 1996. It also required its active investors to help finance a new insurance company, Equitas, to cover old liabilities (billions in claims are still outstanding). In 1997 Lloyd's sought to increase the number of broker members. The next year, amid regulatory disagreements with Singapore's government and a faltering Asian economy, it called off plans to open an exchange branch there. In 1999 Lloyd's began cutting its operating costs. It also began bolstering its Central Fund with insurance rather than cash and admitted the captive insurer of pharmaceuticals powerhouse SmithKline Beecham (now GlaxoSmithKline) into its marketplace.

In 2000, as litigation dragged on over whether a recalcitrant group of Names owed Lloyd's more than £50 million for claims, the corporation continued to trim costs by selling property. That year the US became Lloyd's single largest market for the first time in the company's 300-year history.

After the insurer was hit hard by the attacks on the World Trade Center, resulting in £3.1 billion in losses, another first occurred: It issued an annual report to publicly document the heavy deficits.

EXECUTIVES

Chairman: Lord Peter Levene, $1,074,820 pay
Deputy Chairman: John Coldman, age 58
Deputy Chairman: Bronislaw E. (Bronek) Masojada, age 43
Acting Chief Executive; Director, Finance and Risk Management: Luke Savage
Chief Executive: Richard Ward, age 48
CIO: Chris Rawson
Director, Franchise Performance: Rolf Tolle, $1,354,119 pay
Director, Legal and Compliance and General Counsel: Sean McGovern
Director, Operations: Steve Quiddington
Director, Worldwide Markets: Julian James
President, Lloyd's America: Wendy Baker
Head, Change Management and Human Resources: Steven Haasz
Head, Strategy and Business Planning: Stuart Degg
Auditors: Ernst & Young LLP

LOCATIONS

HQ: Society of Lloyd's
1 Lime St., London EC3M 7HA, United Kingdom
Phone: +44-20-7327-1000   **Fax:** +44-20-7327-5599
US HQ: The Museum Office Bldg., 25 W. 53rd St., 14th Fl., New York, NY 10019
US Phone: 212-382-4060   **US Fax:** 212-382-4070
Web: www.lloyds.com

Lloyd's syndicates operate in about 190 countries.

COMPETITORS

AGF
AIG
Allianz
Aon
Aviva
AXA
Chubb Corp
Citigroup
General Re
ING
Markel
Marsh & McLennan
Millea Holdings
Munich Re
Swiss Re
Zurich Financial Services

HISTORICAL FINANCIALS
Company Type: Insurance society

	REVENUE ($ mil.)	NET INCOME ($ mil.)	NET PROFIT MARGIN	EMPLOYEES
Income Statement				FYE: December 31
12/04	348	94	26.9%	587
12/03	238	(31)	—	582
12/02	207	(7)	—	589
12/01	208	85	41.0%	825
12/00	218	177	81.1%	1,176
Annual Growth	12.3%	(14.7%)	—	(15.9%)

2004 Year-End Financials

Debt ratio: 0.0%   Current ratio: 1.94
Return on equity: 52.0%   Long-term debt ($ mil.): 0
Cash ($ mil.): 127

Net Income History

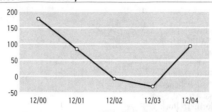

Lloyds TSB

Don't confuse Lloyds TSB with that *other* Lloyd's in The City. Unrelated to the world-renowned Lloyd's of London insurance exchange, Lloyds TSB is near the top of the UK's banking industry. In addition to consumer and commercial banking operations, Lloyds TSB is a leading home mortgage lender through its Cheltenham & Gloucester unit and boasts a burgeoning insurance and investment business through subsidiary Scottish Widows that accounts for a substantial portion of its sales. Lloyds TSB owns approximately 2,100 locations in England, Scotland, and Wales. Lloyds also offers banking, financing, venture capital, and other services to multinational companies in the UK and overseas.

To augment its auto lending operations, it offers car sales online and over the phone.

Not content to stay with its 3% share of the London foreign-exchange market, Lloyds TSB Group has decided to offer more investment services, such as derivatives, securitizations, and private placements, to its large corporate client base. In fact, the company hopes to increase the ratio of product and service sales to corporate clients from 10%-20% of current bank income to about 70%. It also may sell Scottish Widows as the subsidiary has been the subject of many takeover rumors.

Although international business once comprised about 20% of the bank's total revenue, Lloyds TSB divested operations in France, Argentina, Brazil, Colombia, Guatamala, Honduras, and Panama. Lloyds TSB sold National Bank of New Zealand to Australia and New Zealand Bank Group in 2003. Offices can still be found, however, throughout Europe, the Middle East, Asia, and the Americas, and in 2006 it opened its first office in China. That year the bank also returned to Brazil.

The bank has come under fire for its decision to outsource around 200 jobs to India.

HISTORY

In 1765 John Taylor and Sampson Lloyd II founded Taylors and Lloyds bank in Birmingham, England; five years later their sons opened a London agent. In 1852 the last Taylor involved with the bank died. In 1865 the bank converted to joint stock form and became Lloyds Banking Company Ltd. Over the next half century, it grew by merging with some 50 banks, becoming one of England's largest banks by the turn of the century.

Despite the post-WWI roller-coaster economy, the bank acquired Capital and Counties Bank (1918, bringing foreign connections); Fox, Fowler & Company (1921); and Cox & Company (1923). During both wars, deposits grew while lending dropped. After WWII, growth was hampered by high inflation.

Lloyds added branches and products in the 1960s. By 1971 it had branches in 43 countries. It moved into insurance (1972), home mortgages (1979), real estate agency services (1982), and merchant banking (1986).

In 1987 Latin American bank defaults pummeled Lloyds. Refocusing on domestic operations, the bank sold overseas subsidiaries (including Lloyds Bank Canada in 1990) and acquired 58% of life insurer Abbey Life (1988) and Cheltenham & Gloucester Building Society (1994). HSBC outbid Lloyds for Midland Bank in 1992; Lloyds bought TSB Group in 1995.

TSB Group evolved from the trustee savings banks (TSBs) formed in the 1800s. By 1860 there were 600 such banks, mainly in northern England and Scotland. During WWI many TSBs consolidated or closed. By WWII about 100 remained, and the mergers continued.

In the 1960s TSBs began offering checking accounts and trust services. Loans, credit cards, and other services came in 1973. In 1986 the four remaining TSBs (TSB Channel Islands, TSB England and Wales, TSB Northern Ireland, and TSB Scotland) agreed to merge and go public in order to gain equal footing with stock banks. TSB Group was born.

Flush with cash from its offering, TSB group defied the late 1980s recession to buy Target Group (life insurance, sold 1993), Hill Samuel (merchant banking), and other units; the purchases sent TSB sprawling.

As debt rose in the 1990s, TSB Group refocused on banking and insurance. TSB and Lloyds merged in 1995, linking their geographically complementary branch networks to fend off competition.

After the merger, Lloyds TSB focused on loans and insurance and dabbled in consumer finance, including the sale and delivery of big-ticket items (cars, large appliances). Returning overseas, it bought the consumer finance unit of Brazil's Banco Multiplic.

In late 1997 and 1998, the bank overhauled its operations to eliminate redundancies and began rebranding under one green and blue banner. In 1999 Lloyds TSB bailed out Abbey Life, which had nearly been bankrupted by the cost of settling pension mis-selling claims.

The bank in 2000 bought Scottish Widows to boost its fund management services. It sold the Abbey Life name and its new business to Zurich Financial Services' Allied Dunbar; Abbey Life will continue to service existing business for Lloyds. Also that year, Lloyds TSB bought consumer and auto finance unit Chartered Trust from Standard

Chartered. After a yearlong battle to buy London-based mortgage lender Abbey National the UK government, in 2001, blocked the merger attempt because of concerns for the consumer.

Earlier in 2001 Lloyds TSB closed Bahamas-based subsidiary British Bank of Latin America because of alleged money-laundering links revealed in a US Senate report.

Lloyds TSB's asset finance operations bought First National Vehicle Holdings and Abbey National Vehicle Finance from Abbey National plc in 2002. The division also acquired Chartered Trust and Dutton-Forshaw Group, a car dealership.

Commerzbank unit Comdirect Bank sold its UK subsidiary, Comdirect Ltd, to Lloyds TSB unit Executive Services Group in 2004.

In 2005 the bank struggled under the weight of bad debt, in part because of Scottish Widows. The insurance arm was still trying to get out from under the pension mis-selling claims that had plagued it and the industry in 2003.

In 2006 the bank raised eyebrows when it said it was going to maintain its current aircraft lending portfolio rather than expand it, at a time when rivals were seeking to enter the business.

EXECUTIVES

Chairman: Sir Victor Blank, age 63
Group Chief Executive and Director: J. Eric Daniels, age 54, $1,591,370 pay
Deputy Group Chief Executive and Director: Michael E. Fairey, age 57, $1,732,443 pay
Group Finance Director: Helen A. Weir, age 43, $942,779 pay
Group Executive Director, Human Resources: Frans Hijkoop
Group Executive Director, Insurance and Investments: Archie G. Kane, age 54, $848,157 pay
Group Executive Director, UK Retail Banking and Director: Teresa A. (Terri) Dial, age 56, $934,177 pay
Group Executive Director, Wholesale and International Banking: G. Truett Tate, age 56, $1,002,038 pay
Company Secretary: Alastair J. Michie
Chief Risk Director: Carol Sergeant
Managing Director, Financial Markets: Mark Preston
Head of Credit Trading, Financial Markets: Paul Lewitt
Managing Director, Retail Distribution: Neil Berkett, age 50
Regional Director, Midlands and East: Phil Whitby
Director, Investor Relations: Michael D. Oliver
Director, Telephony Operations: Martin Dodd
Auditors: PricewaterhouseCoopers LLP

LOCATIONS

HQ: Lloyds TSB Group plc
25 Gresham St.,
London EC2V 7HN, United Kingdom
Phone: +44-20-7626-1500 **Fax:** +44-20-7489-3484
Web: www.lloydstsbgroup.co.uk

In addition to offices in the UK, the Channel Islands, and the Isle of Man, Lloyds TSB Group has operations in Argentina, Belgium, Brazil, China, Colombia, Dubai, Ecuador, Gibraltar, Hong Kong, Luxembourg, Malaysia, Monaco, the Netherlands, Paraguay, Singapore, Spain, Switzerland, Tokyo, and Uruguay.

PRODUCTS/OPERATIONS

2005 Assets

	% of total
Loans & advances to customers	56
Trading securities	19
Securities available for sale	5
Derivative financial instruments	2
Loans & advances to banks	10
Investment property	1
Other assets	7
Total	**100**

Selected Subsidiaries

The Agricultural Mortgage Corporation PLC
Black Horse Limited (consumer credit, leasing, and related services)
Cheltenham & Gloucester plc
Lloyds TSB Asset Finance Division Limited
Lloyds TSB Bank (Jersey) Limited
Lloyds TSB Bank plc
Lloyds TSB Commercial Finance Limited
Lloyds TSB General Insurance Limited
Lloyds TSB Insurance Services Limited
Lloyds TSB Leasing Limited
Lloyds TSB Life Assurance Company Limited
Lloyds TSB Private Banking Limited
Lloyds TSB Scotland plc
Scottish Widows Annuities Limited
Scottish Widows Investment Partnership Group Limited
Scottish Widows plc

COMPETITORS

Abbey National
Alliance & Leicester
AMVESCAP
Aviva
AXA UK
Barclays
HBOS
HSBC Holdings
Legal & General Group
MasterCard
Northern Rock
Prudential plc
RBS
Standard Life
Woolwich

HISTORICAL FINANCIALS

Company Type: Public

Income Statement

FYE: December 31

	ASSETS ($ mil.)	NET INCOME ($ mil.)	INCOME AS % OF ASSETS	EMPLOYEES
12/05	526,422	2,325	0.4%	66,797
12/04	542,527	2,905	0.5%	69,985
12/03	446,685	5,746	1.3%	71,609
12/02	408,142	2,809	0.7%	79,537
Annual Growth	**8.9%**	**(6.1%)**	**—**	**(5.7%)**

2005 Year-End Financials

Equity as % of assets: 3.6%
Return on assets: 0.4%
Return on equity: 11.3%
Long-term debt ($ mil.): 88,802
No. of shares (mil.): —

Dividends
 Yield: 7.5%
 Payout: 617.1%
Market value ($ mil.): —
Sales ($ mil.): 46,625

Stock History

NYSE: LYG

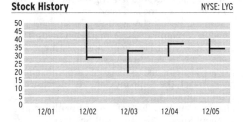

	STOCK PRICE ($) FY Close	P/E High/Low		PER SHARE ($) Earnings	Dividends
12/05	33.80	96	76	0.41	2.53
12/04	36.79	137	109	0.27	2.44
12/03	32.55	—	—	—	2.21
12/02	28.59	—	—	—	2.03
Annual Growth	**5.7%**	**—**	**—**	**51.9%**	**7.6%**

Loblaw

When grocery shopping in Canada, it's difficult to escape the long arm of Loblaw. Loblaw Companies Limited is the market share leader among Canadian supermarket operators. Its corporate, franchised, and associated banners fly over more than 1,500 stores. Trade names include Loblaws, Atlantic SaveEasy, Extra Foods, Fortinos, No Frills, Provigo, Your Independent Grocer, and Zehrs Markets, to name just a few. Its stores offer more than 7,000 private-label products, including its President's Choice brand (featuring financial services, as well as traditional and organic grocery fare). Loblaw is also Canada's largest wholesale food distributor. Parent company George Weston owns about 63% of Loblaw's voting shares.

In turn, Loblaw's former chairman W. Galen Weston owns more than 62% of George Weston.

Overall, Loblaw has about a one-third share of Canada's grocery market. To stay atop the food chain in the face of Wal-Mart Canada, the north-of-the-border counterpart of US retail giant Wal-Mart Stores, Loblaw has been building new, bigger stores to replace older, smaller formats, and many of the company's large stores feature a pharmacy, photo shop, and financial services (some even include a fitness center). The grocery chain has stocked up on nonfood offerings too, including DVD players, and is launching its own line of apparel called "Joe Fresh," after fashion designer Joseph Mirman. It is also aggressively expanding its low-price Real Canadian Superstore format, which numbers nearly 90 stores. (The chain is already well established in western Canada.) The retailer has cut jobs (more than 600 in Ontario), wages, and benefits for workers at its new superstores and lowered prices to better compete with Wal-Mart Canada and Wal-Mart-owned SAM'S CLUB, which recently entered Ontario, Canada's largest retail market. In an effort to streamline its supply chain, Loblaw has announced plans to shutter six warehouses in Ontario and Quebec over the next three years. The closures will result in the loss of about 1,400 jobs.

Following a growing retail trend already well established in France, the UK and US, Loblaw is adding gas stations at some of its grocery store locations. The company also plans to sell some products over the Internet through eBox.com, a delivery company.

HISTORY

Canadian Garfield Weston, CEO of a family business specializing in bakery goods, bought shares in Loblaw Groceterias, a Chicago-based food distributor, in the 1940s and 1950s. George Weston Limited controlled a majority interest by 1953 and incorporated the company as Loblaw Companies Limited three years later.

Over the next four decades, the Weston family transformed the distributor into an expansion vehicle through which George Weston acquired other food distributors and wholesalers across Canada and the midwestern US, at a rate of almost one a year into the 1960s. George Weston acquired National Grocers of Ontario in 1955, a stake in US-based retailer National Tea in 1956, British Columbia wholesaler Kelly Douglas & Co. in 1958, Maritime-based Atlantic Wholesalers in 1960, and Canadian supermarket chain Zehrmart in 1963.

Despite the restructuring of George Weston's operations in the 1970s, during which time many of its subsidiaries were consolidated, Garfield was persuaded by his son Galen not to sell Loblaw. When Garfield died in 1978, Galen became chairman of George Weston and Loblaw.

Loblaw went on a buying spree in 1982, acquiring Golden Dawn Foods, Star Supermarkets, and Wittington Leaseholds. It also acquired the remainder of National Tea.

After the Irish Republican Army tried to kidnap Galen in 1983, the Weston family started keeping a low public profile. Loblaw bought 26 St. Louis stores from Kroger in 1986.

Major union problems dogged the company in the 1980s and 1990s. In the early 1980s Loblaw attempted to gain union support for its supermarket expansion in Winnipeg, Canada, by matching the Manitoba Food and Commercial Workers Union's wage contract with competitor Safeway. In return the company demanded a six-year, no-strike, no-lockout arrangement. Shortly after the deal was signed, employees of SuperValu accused the parent company of violating a number of contract agreements. Eventually the sides came to terms.

Labor unrest broke out again in 1993 in New Orleans when Loblaw engaged the United Food and Commercial Workers Union in a 34-week strike. The union finally conceded to Loblaw's original offer aimed at gaining parity in labor costs with other nonunionized food chains in the area.

In 1995 the company sold its 89 US supermarkets to St. Louis-based Schnuck Markets for around $354 million, and it sold its New Orleans stores, thereby divesting the last of its National Tea assets. By 1996 Loblaw no longer had any stores operating in the US, and it shifted its focus to Canadian expansion, adding about 50 new locations. Also that year a new labor agreement was signed, ending labor unrest and wage pressures from the company's heavily unionized workforce (79% of employees).

In 1997 Loblaw set its sights on conquering Quebec, where it had no significant presence, and strengthening Ontario. It began by opening its own stores, then took a giant leap forward in 1998 when it bought Montreal-based Provigo for $1.1 billion (it sold about 50 Ontario stores as part of the deal). Loblaw then bought Agora Foods and its chain of 80-plus stores (mostly under the IGA banner) and three warehouses in eastern Canada from Oshawa Group.

Richard Currie, Loblaw's president for 24 years and the man credited with molding the company into the multi-billion-dollar company it has become, stepped down in late 2000; he was replaced by Loblaw veteran John Lederer.

In August 2002 the company became the target of at $68 million class action lawsuit following a hepatitis A health scare at one of its Toronto stores. In 2003 Loblaw walked away from a potential deal to acquire the legendary Maple Leaf Gardens that would have turned the hockey shrine into a grocery store.

Loblaw moved its corporate headquarters to Brampton, Ontario in 2005.

In September 2006 John Lederer resigned from the company and was replaced as president by Mark Foote, who joined the company in April 2006 as EVP of general merchandise. Concurrently, it was announced that Galen G. Weston would succeed his father W. Galen Weston as chairman of Loblaw's board.

EXECUTIVES

Chairman: Galen G. Weston, age 32
Deputy Chairman: Allan L. Leighton, age 53
President and Chief Marketing Officer: A. Mark Foote
EVP, Real Estate: David K. Bragg, age 56
EVP; President, Western Operation and General Merchandise Sourcing and Procurement: David R. Jeffs, age 47, $1,016,771 pay
EVP, Treasury, Tax, Risk Management, and Investor Relations: Richard P. (Rick) Mavrinac, age 53, $206 pay
EVP, Information Technology, Food Sourcing, and Procurement: Paul D. Ormsby, age 54
EVP, Financial Control and Reporting, Human Resources, and Loss Prevention: Stephen A. Smith, age 48, $635,482 pay
EVP, Supply Chain: Peter McMahon
EVP: Frank Rocchetti
SVP, Secretary, and General Counsel: Robert A. Balcom, age 44
SVP, Labour Relations: Roy R. Conliffe, age 55
SVP, Finance: Louise M. Lacchin, age 48
SVP, Financial Control: Franca Smith, age 42
SVP, Investor Relations and Public Affairs: Geoffrey H. (Geoff) Wilson, age 50
VP, Risk Management and Strategic Initiatives: Manny Difilippo, age 46
VP, Taxation: J. Bradley Holland, age 42
VP and Legal Counsel: Michael N. Kimber, age 50
VP, Real Estate Development: George D. Seslija, age 50
VP and Treasurer: Lisa R. Swartzman, age 35
VP, Legal Counsel, Compliance and Regulatory Affairs, Privacy and Ethics Officer: David G. Gore, age 35
Auditors: KPMG LLP

LOCATIONS

HQ: Loblaw Companies Limited
1 President's Choice Circle,
Brampton, Ontario L6Y 5S5, Canada
Phone: 905-459-2500   **Fax:** 905-861-2206
Web: www.loblaw.com

2005 Supermarkets and Superstores

	No.
Québec	252
Ontario	169
Alberta	67
British Columbia	41
Nova Scotia	36
Saskatchewan	34
Manitoba	24
New Brunswick	22
Newfoundland & Labrador	16
Prince Edward Island	5
Northwest Territories	3
Yukon	1
Total	**670**

PRODUCTS/OPERATIONS

2005 Stores

	No.
Maxi	97
Loblaws	95
The Real Canadian Superstore	88
Provigo	81
Extra Foods	78
Cash & Carry & Presto	57
Zerhs Markets	52
Atlantic Superstore	51
The Real Canadian Wholesale Club	37
Maxi & Cie	15
Dominion (in Newfoundland & Labrador)	14
Other corporate banners	5
Total	**670**

2005 Stores

	No.
Franchised & associated banners	874
Corporate	670
Total	**1,544**

COMPETITORS

7-Eleven
Canada Safeway
Costco Wholesale Canada
Couche-Tard
Jean Coutu
Jim Pattison Group
Katz Group
METRO
SAM'S CLUB
Shoppers Drug Mart
Sobeys
Wal-Mart Canada

HISTORICAL FINANCIALS

Company Type: Public

Income Statement

FYE: Saturday nearest December 31

	REVENUE ($ mil.)	NET INCOME ($ mil.)	NET PROFIT MARGIN	EMPLOYEES
12/05	23,842	640	2.7%	134,000
12/04	21,754	803	3.7%	130,000
12/03	19,480	653	3.4%	126,000
12/02	14,639	462	3.2%	122,000
12/01	13,504	354	2.6%	119,000
Annual Growth	**15.3%**	**16.0%**	**—**	**3.0%**

2005 Year-End Financials

Debt ratio: 71.3%
Return on equity: 13.4%
Cash ($ mil.): 786

Current ratio: 1.17
Long-term debt ($ mil.): 3,597

Net Income History

Toronto: L

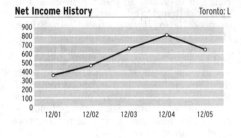

Lonmin

At Lonmin, all that glitters is not gold — platinum is more precious to the company these days. The company is the world's #3 platinum producer (after Anglo Platinum and Impala Platinum), with an annual production of more than 900,000 ounces. Applications for platinum include catalytic converters for vehicles and jewelry. Its Lonmin Platinum, or Lonplats, unit mines platinum group metals (PGMs, including platinum, palladium, and rhodium) through two South African companies: Western Platinum and Eastern Platinum. In addition to its Australian PGM investments, Lonmin has exploration activities in North America, South Africa, and Tanzania. Prudential plc has a 14% stake in the company.

Lonmin has decided to concentrate primarily on its PGM operations and says it intends to up its platinum production to more than 1.1 million ounces per year starting in 2010. To that end, the company has added smelter capacity and sunk new shafts in South Africa. The company has been selling off its non-platinum assets, including its gold assets in politically troubled Zimbabwe. It exited the gold business completely in

2004 when Lonmin sold its interests in gold properties to AngloGold Ashanti. The company also divested its holdings in coal-mining, hotel, and insurance businesses.

Looking to expand its operations in South Africa, the company made a successful $190 million offer for Southern Platinum in 2005 and another offer for AfriOre the following year.

HISTORY

Founded in 1909 as the London & Rhodesian Mining & Land Company to acquire mining rights in Zambia and Zimbabwe, the company later expanded into real estate, ranching, and agriculture. In 1961 Roland "Tiny" Rowland traded his Rhodesian assets for a 48% interest in the company and managing directorship.

Rowland then bought the Beira oil pipeline (southern Rhodesia to Mozambique) in 1961, changed its name to Lonrho in 1963, and shut down the pipeline in 1965 when economic sanctions were imposed against Rhodesia after white settlers declared independence. Rowland also bought a major interest in the Ashanti gold fields of Ghana in 1968.

In 1973 a group of directors tried to oust Rowland, claiming he had bribed African leaders and violated Rhodesian sanctions. A British inquiry cleared him but found that he had made questionable payments. Lonrho bought Volkswagen and Audi distributors in the UK in 1975, Princess Hotels in 1979, and the *Observer* newspaper in 1981. His attempt to buy retailer House of Fraser (owner of Harrod's) was frustrated by the British Mergers and Monopolies Commission in 1985.

Back in Africa, where Tanzania had nationalized Lonrho's operations (1978), Rowland continued his politically incorrect dealings through the 1980s. He helped the Marxist government of Mozambique manage its agricultural resources and increased Lonrho's South African holdings despite sanctions against the government's policy of apartheid.

Weakened by debt and low commodity prices, Lonrho began shedding assets in the late 1980s. In 1992 Rowland sold a third of the Metropole Hotel chain to Libya and accepted a loan from Colonel Gadhafi. Lonrho's stock plummeted, attracting the attention of German financier Dieter Bock, who bought about 18% of the company. Bock and Rowland were co-CEOs for about a year until Bock won control of the board. Rowland was forced out of management in 1994. Rowland, angered by Bock's plan to dismember the company, sold his 6% of the firm in 1995 but remained a frequent critic of its new management. In 1996 EU regulators rejected Bock's plan to spin off Lonrho's mining operations.

Bock resigned as CEO in 1996 and sold his 18% interest in Lonrho to South African titan Anglo American. Nicholas Morrell assumed the CEO position that year. Lonrho sold its Metropole Hotel chain to Stakis (UK) for $533 million that year, as well, and sold its Lonrho Sugar operations in 1997. Sir John Craven took the helm as chairman as the company continued to restructure. Anglo sold its 26% stake in Lonrho to JCI in 1997. The next year the deal was restructured so that Anglo kept a 7% stake in Lonrho. In 1998 Lonrho bought Tavistock (a JCI coal operation) and divested its Lonrho Africa division, Hondo Oil & Gas, and Princess Hotels.

The company changed its name to Lonmin in 1999 and made a failed attempt to increase its interests in the Ashanti gold mines. Having decided to focus on platinum production that year,

Lonmin sold its Duiker and Tweefontein coal operations for $209 million to Switzerland-based commodity house Glencore International in 2000. The company sold its interests in its hotel and insurance businesses that year, as well. With restructuring completed, Nick Morrell stepped down as CEO to become director of Cardew & Co., a London PR firm, and Edward Haslam, a lifelong mining executive, took his place.

Lonmin was able to bounce back from a major smelting furnace fire in early 2003 by recommissioning a stand-by facility. The company also sold its 12% stake in the Munni Munni project that year. Lonmin, which owned a substantial stake in Ashanti Goldfields, received cash and a small stake (which it sold) in new company AngloGold Ashanti, upon the merger of Ashanti and AngloGold in 2004. Bradford Mills replaced Edward Haslam as CEO in 2004.

EXECUTIVES

Chairman: Sir John A. Craven, age 65, $352,500 pay
Chief Executive and Director: Bradford A. (Brad) Mills, age 51, $1,632,123 pay
CFO and Director: John N. Robinson, age 51, $765,750 pay
Chief Strategic Officer and Director: Ian P. Farmer, age 43, $702,331 pay
VP, Business Development: Jack Jones
VP, Finance: Mark Jarvis
VP, Business Development — Technical: Geoff Fenner
VP, Human Capital: Lee Johnson
VP, Exploration and Business Development: Chris Davies
VP, Investor Relations: Alexandra Shorland-Ball
VP, Marketing: Fraser King
Chief Information Officer: Karel van Zyl
General Manager, Investor Relations Manager and Internal Communications: Teresa Heritage
Company Secretary: Rob C. Bellhouse, age 39
Auditors: KPMG Audit Plc

LOCATIONS

HQ: Lonmin Plc
  4 Grosvenor Place,
  London SW1X 7YL, United Kingdom
Phone: +44-20-7201-6000   **Fax:** +44-20-7201-6100
Web: www.lonmin.com

Lonmin has mining and exploration activities in North America, Tanzania, and South Africa.

PRODUCTS/OPERATIONS

2005 Sales by Destination

	% of total
Americas	33
Asia	31
Europe	19
South Africa	16
Zimbabwe	1
Total	**100**

Selected Mining and Refining Operations

Incwala Resources Ltd. (25%, PGMs, South Africa)
Lonmin Platinum (Lonplats, 82%)
  Eastern Platinum Ltd. (PGMs, South Africa)
  Western Metal Sales Limited
  Western Platinum Ltd. (PGMs, South Africa)

COMPETITORS

African Rainbow Minerals	Impala Platinum
Anglo Platinum	Inco Limited
Aquarius Platinum	Norilsk Nickel
Barrick Gold	North American Palladium
BHP Billiton Plc	Rio Tinto
Gold Fields	Stillwater Mining

HISTORICAL FINANCIALS

Company Type: Public

Income Statement

	REVENUE ($ mil.)	NET INCOME ($ mil.)	NET PROFIT MARGIN	EMPLOYEES
9/05	1,128	163	14.5%	22,402
9/04	1,030	195	18.9%	20,931
9/03	779	74	9.5%	20,668
9/02	697	185	26.5%	24,071
9/01	866	274	31.6%	26,829
Annual Growth	6.8%	(12.2%)	—	(4.4%)

FYE: September 30

2005 Year-End Financials

Debt ratio: 62.8%   Current ratio: 0.91
Return on equity: 21.0%   Long-term debt ($ mil.): 510
Cash ($ mil.): 11

Net Income History   Pink Sheets: LNMIY

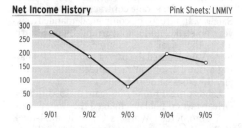

L'Oréal

L'Oréal's success is built on a strong foundation. The world's largest beauty products company, it creates makeup, perfume, and hair and skin care items. Its brands include L'Oréal and Maybelline (mass-market), Lancôme (upscale), and Redken and SoftSheen/Carson (retail and salon). L'Oréal, which bought Dallas-based SkinCeuticals, also conducts cosmetology and dermatology research. With about half of its sales generated outside Europe, L'Oréal has focused on acquiring brands in those markets.

Liliane Bettencourt, daughter of the firm's founder, and her family indirectly control L'Oréal. Nestlé owns a large stake. The Bettencourts and Nestlé have been indirect owners of L'Oréal through the Gesparal holding company for some 30 years. In 2004 L'Oréal shareholders approved a reorganization that would dissolve the holding company and restructure L'Oréal. The proposal gave Bettencourt, then 82, and her family a direct 27.5% stake and 28.6% of the voting rights. Nestlé received a 26.4% direct share and 27.5% in voting rights. In early 2004 Bettencourt's inherited share of L'Oréal was valued at $12.7 billion. (She ranked 11th, with $18.8 billion, on *Forbes* magazine's 2004 billionaire list.)

Another change, announced in early 2005, shook up what has been in place at the company for nearly two decades. Chairman and CEO Lindsay Owen-Jones, who turned 60 in March 2006 and has logged a lengthy, impressive career at L'Oréal, tapped Jean-Paul Agon to run the firm as its chief executive beginning April 2006. Owen-Jones held the posts of chairman and CEO for 18 years. He began his career at L'Oréal in 1969; Agon joined L'Oréal in 1978. Both men have similar management styles — most notably demanding of others and themselves — but the industry will likely miss the charisma and lust for life that Owen-Jones has exhibited in his work and personal lives. (He traded racing Formula One cars on a Grand Prix track to racing sailboats — to relax.)

Consumer brands such as GARNIER, L'Oréal, Maybelline, and Softsheen/Carson make up about half of the company's cosmetic sales. However, well-known luxury brands, including Lancôme, Ralph Lauren, and Giorgio Armani, continue to gain popularity.

L'Oréal expanded its Active Cosmetics division (with existing brands Vichy, La Roche-Posay, and Inneov) by folding SkinCeuticals into the operation in 2005. The acquisition opened doors for L'Oréal in the dermatology arena, which caters to high-end spas and plastic surgeons. In 2005 it purchased Sara Lee Corporation's suncare brand Delial and folded it into its GARNIER portfolio to give L'Oréal a leg up in Southern Europe solar protection. And in 2006 it folded Sanoflore, maker of certified organic cosmetics, into its Active Cosmetics unit.

Expanding aggressively into the Asian market, L'Oréal acquired Chinese skin care brand Mininurse in late 2003; the next year it purchased Yue-Sai, a mass-market Chinese makeup and skin care brand, and its Shanghai manufacturing plant from Coty.

To boost its research and safety efforts and move the company into alternative methods for animal testing of its products, L'Oréal acquired SkinEthic in 2006 through its Episkin subsidiary. The company, based in Nice, France, produces and markets human epidermal and epithelial tissues for in vitro test applications.

L'Oréal also acquired UK-based The Body Shop International in 2006. L'Oréal will run the unit as a separate business and retain its current management, including founder Anita Roddick who remains on the company's board. The number of Body Shop stores could more than double to 5,000 shops worldwide under L'Oréal's ownership.

L'Oréal funds more than 2,800 scientists on three continents who file about 500 patents a year. Of note is the company's creation of UV-absorbing makeup and test models of human skin.

HISTORY

Parisian Eugène Schueller, a chemist by trade, invented the first synthetic hair dye in 1907. Schueller quickly found a market for his products with local hairdressers and in 1909 established L'Oréal to pursue his growing hair products operation. The company's name came from its first hair color, Auréole (French for "aura of light").

L'Oréal expanded to include shampoos and soaps, all under the watchful direction of the energetic Schueller, who was known to taste hair creams to ensure that they were made up of the exact chemical composition that he required. In the 1920s the company began advertising on the radio (before its French competitors).

Demand for L'Oréal's products intensified after WWII. In 1953 the company formed licensee Cosmair to distribute its hair products to US beauty salons, and Cosmair soon offered L'Oréal's makeup and perfume as well. (Cosmair became L'Oréal USA in 2000.) When Schueller died in 1957, control of L'Oréal passed to right-hand man François Dalle. Dalle carried L'Oréal's hair care products into the consumer market and overseas and sold its soap units in 1961.

The company went public in 1963; Schueller's daughter, Liliane Bettencourt, retained a majority interest. Diversification came in 1965 with the acquisition of upscale French cosmetics maker Lancôme. L'Oréal entered the pharmaceuticals business in 1973 by purchasing Synthélabo. Bettencourt traded nearly half of her L'Oréal stock for a 3% stake in Swiss food producer Nestlé in 1974. L'Oréal purchased a minority stake in the publisher of French fashion magazine *Marie Claire* three years later.

During the 1980s L'Oréal vaulted from relative obscurity to become the world's #1 cosmetics company, largely through acquisitions. These included Warner Communications' cosmetics operations (Ralph Lauren and Gloria Vanderbilt brands, 1984), Helena Rubinstein (US beauty products, 1988), Laboratories Pharmaeutiques Goupil (1988), and its first major investment in Lanvin (1989). Englishman Lindsay Owen-Jones became CEO in 1988.

Chairman Jacques Correze died in 1991 during an investigation into his Nazi war activities. (He had served five years in prison.) In 1994 the company purchased control of Cosmair from Nestlé and Bettencourt. It acquired two generic drug companies in 1995: Lichtenstein Pharmazeutica in Germany and Irex in France. That year L'Oréal became the #2 US cosmetics maker (behind Procter & Gamble, maker of Cover Girl and Max Factor) by buying #3 Maybelline for $508 million.

L'Oréal then added subsidiaries in Japan and China (1996) and in Romania and Slovenia (1997). In 1998 L'Oréal's 57%-owned Synthélabo subsidiary merged with Elf Aquitaine's pharmaceuticals unit, Sanofi. L'Oréal retained a 19.5% stake in the newly formed pharmaceuticals group, Sanofi-Synthélabo.

In 2000 L'Oréal acquired family-owned prestige cosmetics company Kiehl's Since 1851 and salon products maker Matrix Essentials (from Bristol-Myers Squibb). In 2001 L'Oréal sold its stakes in Lanvin SA (to Harmonie SA) and *Marie Claire* (to Holding Evelyne Prouvost).

Expanding its leadership in the professional hair salon products market in 2002, L'Oréal subsidiary L'Oréal USA acquired Artec Systems Group and its brands, including Artec Color Deposit System, Kiwi, Purehair, and Textureline.

EXECUTIVES

Chairman: Lindsay Owen-Jones, age 60
Vice Chairman: Jean-Pierre Meyers
CEO: Jean-Paul Agon, age 49
EVP, Administration and Finance: Christian Mulliez, age 45
EVP, Corporate Communications and External Affairs: Béatrice Dautresme
EVP, Human Resources: Geoff Skingsley
EVP, Production and Technology: Marcel Lafforgue
EVP, Research and Development: Jean-François Grollier
Managing Director, Africa: Alain Evrard
Managing Director, Luxury Products Division: Marc Menesguen, age 49
President, Consumer Products: Patrick Rabain
President, Luxury Products: Gilles Weil
President, Professional Products: Jean-Jacques Lebel
President and CEO, L'Oréal USA: Laurent Attal, age 47
SVP and General Manager, Lancôme: Dalia Chammas
Director of International Development, Yue-Sai: Arnaud de Fontgalland
Director of Strategic Development, Luxury Products: Marc Dubrule
Director of International Financial Communications: François Archambault
Director of International Press Relations: Mike Rumsby
Director of Investor Relations: Caroline Millot
Auditors: PricewaterhouseCoopers Audit

LOCATIONS

HQ: L'Oréal SA
41, rue Martre, 92117 Clichy, France
Phone: +33-1-47-56-70-00 **Fax:** +33-1-47-56-80-02
US HQ: 575 5th Ave., New York, NY 10017
US Phone: 212-818-1500 **US Fax:** 212-984-4538
Web: www.loreal.com

PRODUCTS/OPERATIONS

Selected Operations

Consumer Products
  Gemey
  Laboratoires GARNIER
  L'Oréal
  Maybelline
  SoftSheen/Carson
Cosmetics
  Active Cosmetics
  La Roche-Posay
  Vichy
Luxury Products
  Biotherm
  Cacharel (fragrances only)
  Giorgio Armani (fragrances only)
  Guy Laroche (fragrances only)
  Helena Rubinstein
  Kiehl's
  Lancôme
  Paloma Picasso (fragrances only)
  Ralph Lauren (fragrances only)
  Shu Uemura
Pharmaceuticals and Dermatology
  Tri-Luma
  Innéov Firmness
  RozexMetvix
Professional Products
  Artec
  Inne
  Kérastase
  L'Oréal Professionnel
  Matrix
  Redken

Selected Subsidiaries

Carson/Soft Sheen Products
Galderma
L'Oréal USA
The Laboratoires Inneov
Sanofi-Synthélabo

COMPETITORS

Alberto-Culver
Alticor
Avon
Bath & Body Works
BeautiControl Cosmetics
Chanel
Clarins
Diamond Products
Estée Lauder
Gillette
Hoffmann-La Roche
Intimate Brands
Johnson & Johnson
LVMH
Mary Kay
Merle Norman
Modern Organic Products
Novartis
Nu Skin
Perrigo
Procter & Gamble
Puig Beauty & Fashion
Revlon
Shiseido
Unilever
Yves Saint-Laurent Groupe

HISTORICAL FINANCIALS

Company Type: Public

Income Statement				FYE: December 31
	REVENUE ($ mil.)	NET INCOME ($ mil.)	NET PROFIT MARGIN	EMPLOYEES
12/05	17,211	2,337	13.6%	52,403
12/04	19,824	4,946	24.9%	52,081
12/03	17,609	1,872	10.6%	50,500
12/02	14,975	1,526	10.2%	50,491
12/01	12,171	1,089	8.9%	49,150
Annual Growth	9.0%	21.0%	—	1.6%

Net Income History   OTC: LORLY

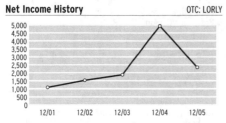

Lufthansa

Deutsche Lufthansa is Europe's #2 airline company, behind the combined Air France-KLM. With its regional subsidiaries, the German carrier operates more than 430 aircraft from hubs in Frankfurt and Munich. It serves more than 400 destinations in about 100 countries, including those served by code-sharing partners. (Code-sharing enables airlines to sell tickets on one another's flights and thus extend their networks.) Lufthansa's partners include fellow members of the Star Alliance such as UAL's United Airlines. The company's Lufthansa Cargo unit is a leading global airfreight carrier; Lufthansa also has interests in aircraft maintenance, catering, information technology, and leisure travel businesses.

Passenger transportation accounts for about 65% of the company's sales, and Lufthansa hopes to grow in that area by building on one of its greatest strengths: its extensive international route network. The carrier views China, India, and Eastern Europe — places where it has already established a foothold — as particularly promising expansion opportunities.

To facilitate international expansion, and to respond to the acquisition of KLM by Air France, Lufthansa in 2005 agreed to buy Swiss International Air Lines. (The ownership transfer has been delayed by questions of international air traffic rights; for now, a holding company 51%-owned by a Switzerland-based foundation and 49%-owned by Lufthansa controls SWISS.) The carriers already have begun coordinating their schedules, and they expect to achieve significant cost savings by integrating key cargo and purchasing functions. SWISS is to continue to operate under its own brand, however, and the carrier's Zurich headquarters will be a third major hub for the Lufthansa group.

The company's logistics segment, led by Lufthansa Cargo, accounts for about 15% of overall sales. Lufthansa Cargo operates a fleet of about 20 freighters; the unit also sells cargo space on

Lufthansa passenger flights and on those of regional subsidiaries and alliance partners.

Lufthansa Technik is the flagship of the company's maintenance, repair, and overhaul business. Not only an in-house service business, it serves carriers worldwide. Similarly, catering unit LSG Sky Chefs (part of LSG Lufthansa Service Holding) generates revenue for the parent company by working for rival airlines, as well.

In addition, Lufthansa owns 50% of leisure travel giant Thomas Cook AG (German retailer Karstadt Quelle owns the other half), along with a minority stake in the Amadeus travel reservations service.

HISTORY

The Weimar government created Deutsche Luft Hansa (DLH) in 1926 by merging private German airlines Deutscher Aero Lloyd (founded 1919) and Junkers Luftverkehr (formed in 1921 by aircraft manufacturer Junkers Flugzeugwerke). DLH built what would become Europe's most comprehensive air route network by 1931. It served the USSR through Deruluft (formed 1921; dissolved 1941), an airline jointly owned by DLH and the Soviet government. In 1930 DLH and the Chinese government formed Eurasia Aviation Corporation to develop air transport in China.

DLH established the world's first transatlantic airmail service from Berlin to Buenos Aires in 1934 and went on to develop air transport throughout South America. The outbreak of WWII ended operations in Europe, and the Chinese government seized Eurasia Aviation in 1941. Klaus Bonhoeffer, head of DLH's legal department, led an unsuccessful coup against the Nazi leadership and was executed in 1945. Soon afterward all DLH operations ceased.

In 1954 the Allies allowed the recapitalization of Deutsche Lufthansa. The airline started with domestic routes, returned to London and Paris (1955), and then re-entered South America (1956). In 1958 it made its first nonstop flight between Germany and New York and initiated service to Tokyo and Cairo. Meanwhile, it started a charter airline with several partners in 1955. Lufthansa bought out its partners in 1959 and renamed the unit Condor two years later.

The carrier resumed service behind the Iron Curtain in 1966 with flights to Prague. The stable West German economy helped Lufthansa maintain profitability through most of the 1970s.

The reunification of Germany in 1990 ended Allied control over Berlin airspace, allowing Lufthansa, which had bought Pan Am's Berlin routes, to fly there under its own colors for the first time since the end of WWII. The company began seeking international partners in 1991, but that year European air travel suffered its first-ever slowdown, forcing Lufthansa into the red for the first time since 1973.

The company restructured in 1994 into a group of new business units: Lufthansa Technik, Lufthansa Cargo, and Lufthansa Systems. In 1995 the carrier began to face increased domestic competition from Deutsche BA, a British Airways affiliate.

The airline formed a code-sharing agreement with Air Canada in 1996. In 1997 the Star Alliance was formed, and Lufthansa signed a pact with Singapore Airlines. That year the German government sold its remaining 38% stake in Lufthansa. In 1998 Lufthansa and All Nippon Airways formed a code-sharing alliance, and

Condor was combined with Karstadt's tour company NUR Touristic to form C&N Touristic. (After buying UK-based travel operator Thomas Cook in 2000, C&N Touristic changed its name to Thomas Cook in 2001.)

In a plan to gain more access to London's Heathrow Airport, Lufthansa took a 20% stake in British Midland, which was admitted into the Star Alliance in 2000 along with Mexicana Airlines. In 2001 the airline bought the 52% of Texas-based Sky Chefs it did not already own and formed a new unit, LSG Sky Chefs International, to hold its catering operations.

Lufthansa said goodbye to its 24% stake in delivery firm DHL when it sold its share to Deutsche Post in 2002.

In early 2005 Swiss International Air Lines agreed to be acquired by Lufthansa. As the first step in a lengthy and complicated transition process, Lufthansa created a Swiss holding entity named AirTrust through which all Swiss International Air Lines shares were held. Lufthansa then took an initial 11% stake in the newly created company, which was increased to 49% by mid-2006.

EXECUTIVES

Chairman and CEO; CEO, Lufthansa German Airlines: Wolfgang Mayrhuber, age 59

CFO: Stephan Gemkow, age 46

Chief Officer Aviation Services and Human Resources; Interim Chairman and CEO, Lufthansa Cargo AG: Stefan Lauer, age 51

Chairman, Lufthansa Systems Group GmbH: Wolfgang F. W. Gohde

Chairman, Lufthansa Technik AG: August-Wilhelm Henningsen

Chairman, Thomas Cook AG: Thomas Holtrop, age 52

CEO, Finance, Human Resources, Information Management, and Corporate Functions, LSG Lufthansa Service Holding AG: Walter Gehl

Airlines, Thomas Cooke AG: Ralf Teckentrup

Finance and Human Resources, Lufthansa Cargo AG: Roland Busch, age 42

Finance and Human Resources, Thomas Cook AG: Heinz-Ludger Heuberg

Finance, Lufthansa Technik AG: Peter Jansen, age 52

Human Resources, Lufthansa Technik AG: Wolfgang Warburg, age 64

Human Resources and Services, Lufthansa German Airlines: Carsten Spohr

Inflight Service Solutions, LSG Lufthansa Service Holding AG: Jochen Müller

Marketing and Sales, Lufthansa Cargo AG: Andreas Otto

Marketing and Sales, Lufthansa German Airlines: Thierry Antinori

Marketing and Sales, Lufthansa Systems GmbH: Gunter Küchler

Director Public Affairs, The Americas: Natalie A. Hartman

Auditors: PwC Deutsche Revision AG

LOCATIONS

HQ: Deutsche Lufthansa AG
Von-Gablenz-Strasse 2-6,
D-50679 Cologne 21, Germany
Phone: +49-0221-826-3992   **Fax:** +49-0221-826-3646
US HQ: 1640 Hempstead Tpke., East Meadow, NY 11554
US Phone: 516-296-9200   **US Fax:** 516-296-9838
Web: www.lufthansa.com

2005 Sales

	% of total
Europe	62
North America	16
Asia/Pacific	15
Middle East	3
Africa	2
Central & South America	2
Total	**100**

PRODUCTS/OPERATIONS

2005 Sales

	% of total
Passenger transportation	64
Logistics	15
Catering	10
Maintenance, repair & overhaul	10
Information technology services	1
Total	**100**

COMPETITORS

AAR	Deutsche Bahn
Aer Lingus	easyJet
Air Berlin	Gate Gourmet
Air France-KLM	Iberia
Alitalia	Japan Airlines
AMR Corp.	Northwest Airlines
Aviall	Qantas
British Airways	Ryanair
Continental Airlines	TIMCO Aviation
Delta Air	Virgin Atlantic Airways
Delta Air Transport	Virgin Express

HISTORICAL FINANCIALS

Company Type: Public

Income Statement

FYE: December 31

	REVENUE ($ mil.)	NET INCOME ($ mil.)	NET PROFIT MARGIN	EMPLOYEES
12/05	21,394	537	2.5%	92,303
12/04	23,140	551	2.4%	90,673
12/03	20,029	(1,235)	—	93,246
12/02	17,788	751	4.2%	94,135
12/01	14,784	(561)	—	87,975
Annual Growth	**9.7%**	**—**	**—**	**1.2%**

Net Income History

Pink Sheets: DLAKY

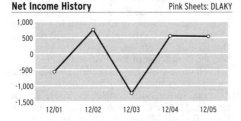

LUKOIL

Most Russians look to LUKOIL for their oil and gas needs. Russia's #1 integrated oil company produces, refines, and sells oil and oil products; it accounts for 19% of Russia's crude oil production. LUKOIL has proved reserves of more than 20.3 billion barrels of oil equivalent. The company has operations in 60 regions in Russia and 25 other countries and owns eight refineries and a total of 5,830 gas stations (including 2,000 gas stations in the US). LUKOIL moved into the US by buying Getty Petroleum Marketing. That year the Russian government sold its remaining 7.6% stake in LUKOIL to Conoco-Phillips, which announced plans to increase its stake to 20% by 2008. ConocoPhillips currently owns about 16%.

LUKOIL, Russia's second-largest company behind natural gas monopoly Gazprom, is trying to transform itself from a top-heavy, bureaucratic enterprise into a decentralized, entrepre-neurial company with hopes of competing in free markets.

The company explores for oil and gas in Azerbaijan, Egypt, Iraq, Kazakhstan, and other areas in the Middle East and Central Asia. It operates four refineries in Russia, one in Ukraine, one in Bulgaria, and one in Romania, and owns a gas stations network in Russia, the Baltic states, Central and Eastern Europe, and the US. More than three-quarter's of LUKOIL's sales are outside of Russia.

With an appetite for expansion, the company is upping its production with refinery acquisitions, and is investing heavily in new oil patches, such as the Caspian Sea. In 2005 LUKOIL acquired Finland-based Oy Teboil AB and Suomen Petrooli Oy, affiliated refined oil products companies, for an undisclosed amount. LUKOIL also acquired Nelson Resources, which has oil and gas interests in Western Kazakhstan, for about $2 billion.

In 2006 the company acquired Marathon Oil's assets in Khanty-Mansiysk Autonomous Region — Yugra of Western Siberia for $787 million.

HISTORY

LUKOIL was formed from the combination of three major state-owned oil and gas exploration companies — Langepasneftegaz, Uraineftegaz, and Kogalymneftegaz — that traced their origins to the discovery of oil in western Siberia in 1964. More than 25 years later, after the Soviet Union broke up, the oil and gas sector was one of the first industries marked for privatization.

In 1992 the government called for Langepasneftegaz, Uraineftegaz, and Kogalymneftegaz to merge, and LUKOIL was created the next year. (The LUK of LUKOIL comes from the initials of the three companies.) Russian president Boris Yeltsin appointed Siberian oil veteran Vagit Alekperov as the company's first president. The Russian government also formed several other large integrated oil companies, including Yukos, Surgutneftegaz, Sidanco, and Sibneft.

LUKOIL went public on the fledgling Russian Trading System in 1994. The next year the company absorbed nine other enterprises, including oil exploration companies Astrakhanneft, Kaliningradmorneftegaz, and Permneft. That year LUKOIL became the first Russian oil company to set up an exploration and production trading arm. In 1996 LUKOIL acquired a 41% stake in *Izvestia*, Russia's major independent newspaper.

Chevron and LUKOIL, with seven other oil and gas companies and three governments, agreed in 1996 to build a 1,500-kilometer pipeline to link the Kazakhstan oil fields to world markets.

In 1997 LUKOIL became the first Russian corporation to sell bonds to international investors, and the government sold 15% of its stake in the company. That year LUKOIL's 50%-owned Nexus Fuels unit opened its first gas stations located in the parking lots of US grocery stores (the partnership dissolved and Nexus went bankrupt in 2000).

LUKOIL began a partnership with Conoco (later ConocoPhillips) in 1998 to develop oil and natural gas reserves in Russia's northern territories. LUKOIL also acquired 51% of Romania's Petrorel refinery. In 1999 it acquired control of refineries in Bulgaria and Ukraine and in a petrochemical firm in Saratov. It also acquired oil company KomiTEK in one of Russia's largest mergers.

The government sold a 9% stake in LUKOIL to a Cyprus-based unit, Reforma Investments, held in part by LUKOIL's "boss of bosses," Vagit Alekperov (gained at the bargain price of $200 million). Critics cited the sale as Yeltsin's bid to gain Alekperov's political support.

The company announced the first major oil find in the Russian part of the Caspian Sea in 2000, and formed a joint venture (Caspian Oil Company) with fellow Russian energy giants Gazprom and Yukos to exploit resources in the Caspian. The next year LUKOIL acquired more than 1,300 gas stations on the East Coast of the US when it bought Getty Petroleum Marketing.

That year LUKOIL also acquired Bitech, a Canadian oil exploration and production firm with operations in the Republic of Komi in the Russian Federation. In 2002 the company sold its oil service business, a move that cut its overall workforce by some 20,000 and resulted in savings of $500 million annually.

EXECUTIVES

Chairman: Valery Grayfer
President and Director: Vagit Y. Alekperov
First VP Exploration and Production and Director: Ravil U. Maganov
First VP Economics and Finance: Sergei P. Kukura
First VP Refining, Marketing, and Distribution: Dmitri Tarasov
VP and Head of the Main Division of General Affairs, Corporate Security, and Communications: Anatoly A. Barkov
VP and Head of the Main Division of Oil and Gas Production and Infrastructure: Dzhevan K. Cheloyants
VP and Head of the Main Division of Strategic Development and Investment Analysis: Leonid A. Fedun
VP and Head of the Main Division of Treasury and Corporate Financing: Alexander K. Matytsyn
VP and Head of the Main Division of Capital Construction and Corporate Agencies: Serik Rakhmetov
VP and Head of the Main Division of Control and Internal Audit: Vagit S. Sharifov
VP and Head of the Main Division of Sales and Supplies: Yury Storozhev
Head of the Main Division of Legal Support: Ivan Masliaev
Head of the Main Division of Human Resources: Anatoly Moskalenko
Chief Accountant: Lyubov Khoba
Secretary of the Board of Directors and Head of the Board's Office: Evgueni Havkin
Auditors: ZAO KPMG

LOCATIONS

HQ: OAO LUKOIL
11 Sretenski Blvd., 101 000 Moscow, Russia
Phone: +7-495-928-9841   **Fax:** +7-495-916-0020
Web: www.lukoil.com

LUKOIL operates in 60 regions within Russia and in 25 other countries.

2005 Sales

	$ mil.	% of total
Russia		
European Russia	8,656	16
Western Siberia	250	—
Other countries	46,868	84
Total	**55,774**	**100**

PRODUCTS/OPERATIONS

2005 Sales

	$ mil.	% of total
Refining, marketing & distribution	53,064	95
Chemicals	1,628	3
Exploration & production	1,047	2
Other	35	—
Total	**55,774**	**100**

Selected Subsidiaries

Refining, supplies, marketing, and transportation
  Getty Petroleum Marketing
  OAO LUKOIL Ukhtaneftepererabotka (refining)
  OOO LUKOIL Volgogradneftepererabotka (refining)
  OOO LUKOIL Volgogradnefteprodukt (marketing)
  OOO LUKOIL Vologdanefteprodukt (marketing)

Exploration and production
  OAO KomiTEK
  OOO LUKOIL Astrakhanmorneft
  OOO LUKOIL Kaliningradmorneft
  OOO LUKOIL Nizhnevolzhskneft
  OOO LUKOIL Permneft
  OOO LUKOIL Western Siberia
  ZAO LUKOIL Perm

Other
  LUKOIL International GmbH
  OAO LUKOIL Arktic Tanker (shipping)
  ZAO LUKOIL Neftekhim (petrochemicals)

COMPETITORS

Ashland	PETROBRAS
BP	Rosneft
Exxon Mobil	Royal Dutch Shell
Imperial Oil	Sibneft
Norsk Hydro	Surgutneftegas
Occidental Petroleum	Tatneft
PDVSA	TOTAL
PEMEX	YUKOS

HISTORICAL FINANCIALS

Company Type: Public

Income Statement

FYE: December 31

	REVENUE ($ mil.)	NET INCOME ($ mil.)	NET PROFIT MARGIN	EMPLOYEES
12/05	55,774	6,443	11.6%	145,400
12/04	33,845	4,248	12.6%	—
12/03	22,299	3,701	16.6%	14,000
12/02	15,449	1,843	11.9%	130,000
12/01	13,562	2,109	15.6%	130,000
Annual Growth	42.4%	32.2%	—	2.8%

Net Income History

Pink Sheets: LUKOY

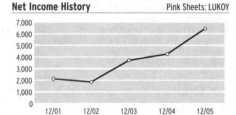

LVMH

LVMH Moët Hennessy Louis Vuitton is the world's largest luxury goods company, with brands that are bywords for the good life and everything showy. LVMH makes wines and spirits (Dom Pérignon, Moët & Chandon, Veuve Clicquot, and Hennessy), perfumes (Christian Dior, Guerlain, and Givenchy), cosmetics (Bliss, Fresh, and BeneFit), fashion and leather goods (Donna Karan, Givenchy, Kenzo, and Louis Vuitton), and watches and jewelry (TAG Heuer, Ebel, Chaumet, and Fred). LVMH's retail division includes Sephora cosmetics stores, Le Bon Marché Paris department stores, and 61% of DFS Group (duty-free shops). Chairman Bernard Arnault and his family own 48% of LVMH.

The company has been focusing on controlling as much of its distribution as possible. LVMH has more than 1,500 retail outlets, including 280-plus Vuitton stores, some 150 DFS Group duty-free shops, Le Bon Marché, and hundreds of designer boutiques. Its Sephora self-serve cosmetics and fragrance chain boasts nearly 500 stores worldwide.

Competition in the UK from department stores and upscale retailers, though, has been more difficult than the firm had anticipated. LVMH exited the UK altogether in mid-2005 by closing all nine of its Sephora shops.

Though the company denies rumors that it wants to unload DFS and Sephora, it has sold its teen-targeted Hard Candy and Urban Decay cosmetics brands. LVMH shed several of the less productive of its 50 brands in 2003, including auction house Phillips, de Pury & Luxemborg and fashion brand Michael Kors. In 2004, Bliss spas was sold off, followed in 2005 by fashion design house Christian Lacroix SNC.

The company nonetheless maintains one eye on growth. In 2005 LVMH was the winning bidder for whisky-maker Glenmorangie PLC, for which it paid £300 million. In 2006 the company announced that its star brand, Louis Vuitton, had the most potential for growth and that Sephora could become a "little Vuitton."

In early 2004 LVMH won a landmark lawsuit against Morgan Stanley, alleging that the firm had used biased research in misstatements about the financial health of LVMH that caused damage to the company's image. The presiding Parisian court ordered Morgan Stanley to pay 100 million euros (about $38 million) in damages. Morgan Stanley appealed the ruling later that year.

In 2005 Japanese designer Kenzo Takada filed a lawsuit in Paris alleging that LVMH, which owns Kenzo SA, does not have the right to use the brand name in any language. Takada, who is suing for 18.4 million euros (or about $24.4 million at the time of the filing), says he has had the right to use his first and last names since 1996. LVMH says that the designer was given the right to use his full name in Latin letters under certain circumstances.

HISTORY

Woodworker Louis Vuitton started his Paris career packing dresses for French Empress Eugenie. He later designed new types of luggage, and in 1854 he opened a store to sell his designs. In 1896 Vuitton introduced the LV monogram fabric that the company still uses. By 1900 Louis Vuitton had stores in the US and England, and by WWI Louis' son, Georges, had the world's largest retail store for travel goods.

Henry Racamier, a former steel executive who had married into the Vuitton family, took charge in 1977, repositioning the company's goods from esoteric status symbols to designer must-haves. Sales soared from $20 million to nearly $2.5 billion within a decade. Concerned about being a takeover target, Racamier merged Louis Vuitton in 1987 with Moët Hennessy (which made wines, spirits, and fragrances) and adopted the name LVMH Moët Hennessy Louis Vuitton.

Moët Hennessy had been formed through the 1971 merger of Moët et Chandon (the world's #1 champagne maker) and the Hennessy Cognac company (founded by Irish mercenary Richard Hennessy in 1765). Moët Hennessy acquired rights to Christian Dior fragrances in 1971.

Racamier tried to reverse the merger when disagreements with chairman Alain Chevalier arose. Racamier invited outside investor Bernard Arnault to increase his interest in the company. Arnault gained control of 43% of LVMH and became chairman in 1989. Chevalier stepped down, but Racamier fought for control for another 18 months and then set up Orcofi, a partner of cosmetics rival L'Oréal.

LVMH increased its fashion holdings with the purchases of the Givenchy Couture Group (1988), Christian Lacroix (1993), and Kenzo (1993). The company also acquired 55% of French media firm Desfosses International (1993), Celine fashions (1996), the Château d'Yquem winery (1996), and duty-free retailer DFS Group (1996). Next LVMH bought perfume chains Sephora (1997) and Marie-Jeanne Godard (1998). In 1998 LVMH integrated the Paris department store Le Bon Marché, which was controlled by Arnault.

LVMH accumulated a 34% stake in Italian luxury goods maker Gucci in early 1999 and planned to buy all of it. Fellow French conglomerate Pinault-Printemps-Redoute (PPR) later thwarted LVMH by purchasing 42% of Gucci.

Through its LV Capital unit, in 1999 LVMH began acquiring stakes in a host of luxury companies, including a joint venture with fashion company Prada to buy 51% of design house Fendi (LVMH bought Prada's 25.5% stake for $265 million in November 2001). It has since upped its Fendi stake to about 70%. LVMH later added the Ebel, Chaumet, and TAG Heuer brands to its new watch division.

In 2000 LVMH bought Miami Cruiseline Services, which operates duty-free shops on cruise ships, auction house L'Etude Tajan, and 67% of Italian fashion house Emilio Pucci. In late 2000 LVMH acquired Gabrielle Studio, which owns all Donna Karan licenses. In 2001 the company bought Donna Karan International.

LVMH in 2001 began marketing De Beers diamond jewelry in a 50-50 joint venture with the diamond powerhouse. Also in 2001, LVMH prompted the investigation of a Dutch court into the PPR-Gucci alliance, but later that year sold its stake in Gucci to PPR for $806.5 million.

In 2002 LVMH ceased trading on the Brussels and Nasdaq exchanges to concentrate on its Euronext investors. In 2003 the company sold Canard-Duchene to the Alain Thienot Group. LVMH opened its biggest store — a four-story emporium on New York's Fifth Avenue — in 2004. A few months later, the company added whisky-maker Glenmorangie PLC to its subsidiary roster. LVMH also made its debut in the South African market in October 2004, opening its first sub-Saharan boutique in Johannesburg.

EXECUTIVES

Chairman and CEO: Bernard Arnault
Vice Chairman: Antoine Bernheim, age 82
Group Managing Director: Antonio (Toni) Belloni
Advisor to the Chairman: Patrick Houel
Adviser to the Chairman: Pierre Godé
Adviser to the Chairman: Patrick Ouart
Adviser to the Chairman, Group EVP of Synergies, and President, LVMH Italy: Concetta Lanciaux
Finance Director: Jean-Jacques Guiony
Development and Acquisitions, Managing Director, Groupe Arnault: Nicolas Bazire

Executive Committee, Fashion and Leather Goods:
Yves Carcelle
Executive Committee, Perfumes and Cosmetics:
Patrick Choël, age 63
Executive Committee, LV Capital: Daniel Piette, age 61
Executive Committee, Operations: Bernard Rolley
Executive Committee, Strategy and Operations:
Pierre-Yves Roussel
Executive Committee, Travel Retail:
Edward (Ed) Brennan
President, LVMH Watch & Jewelry Worldwide:
Philippe Pascal
Executive Committee, Wines and Spirits Group:
Christophe Navarre
Executive Committee, Selective Retailing:
Pierre Letzelter
**President and CEO, LVMH Watch and Jewelry Division
North America:** Daniel Lalonde
**SVP, Public Relations and Communications, North
America:** Katherine Ross
Director: Jean-Marc Loubier
General Secretary: Marc-Antoine Jamet
Auditors: Ernst & Young Audit; Deloitte & Associés

LOCATIONS

HQ: LVMH Moët Hennessy Louis Vuitton SA
22 avenue Montaigne, 75008 Paris, France
Phone: +33-1-44-13-22-22   **Fax:** +33-1-44-13-21-19
US HQ: 19 E. 57th St., New York, NY 10022
US Phone: 212-931-2000   **US Fax:** 212-931-2903
Web: www.lvmh.com

2005 Sales

	% of total
Europe	
France	15
Other countries	20
Asia	
Japan	15
Other countries	16
US	27
Other regions	7
Total	**100**

PRODUCTS/OPERATIONS

2005 Sales

	% of total
Fashion & leather goods	33
Selective retailing	25
Wines & spirits	22
Perfumes & cosmetics	16
Watches & jewelry	4
Total	**100**

Selected Brands and Operations

Fashion and leather goods
  Berluti
  Celine
  Christian Lacroix
  Donna Karan
  Emilio Pucci
  Fendi
  Gabrielle Studio (Donna Karan label)
  Givenchy
  Kenzo
  Loewe
  Louis Vuitton
  Marc Jacobs
  Thomas Pink
Retailing
  DFS Group
  La Samaritaine
  Le Bon Marché
  Miami Cruiseline Services (duty-free shops)
  Sephora

Fragrances and cosmetics
  Aqua di Parma
  BeneFit
  Bliss
  Fresh
  Guerlain
  Kenzo Parfums
  Make Up For Ever
  Marc Jacobs Fragrances
  Parfums Christian Dior
  Parfums Givenchy
Spirits and wines
  10 Cane
  Belvedere
  Canard-Duchêne
  Chandon Estates
  Château d'Yquem
  Dom Pérignon
  Hennessy
  Krug
  Mercier
  Moët & Chandon
  MountAdam
  Newton
  Ruinart
  Veuve Clicquot
Watches and jewelry
  Chaumet
  De Beers
  Ebel
  Fred
  Omas
  TAG Heuer
  Zenith
Media (Desfosses International Group)
  Investir
  La Tribune
  Radio Classique

COMPETITORS

Armani	L'Oréal
Avon	MacAndrews & Forbes
Bacardi	Oscar de la Renta
Brown-Forman	Polo Ralph Lauren
Calvin Klein	PPR
Chanel	Prada
Douglas Holding	Puig Beauty & Fashion
Eckes	Rémy Cointreau
Escada	Richemont
Estée Lauder	Shiseido
Galeries Lafayette	Swatch
Gallo	Taittinger
Gianni Versace	Tiffany
Hermès	Unilever
Hugo Boss	Vera Wang
Inditex	Yves Saint-Laurent Groupe
Kirin Brewery Company	

HISTORICAL FINANCIALS

Company Type: Public

Income Statement

FYE: December 31

	REVENUE ($ mil.)	NET INCOME ($ mil.)	NET PROFIT MARGIN	EMPLOYEES
12/05	16,474	1,975	12.0%	61,088
12/04	17,218	1,378	8.0%	59,840
12/03	15,015	908	6.0%	56,386
12/02	13,304	583	4.4%	56,591
Annual Growth	**7.4%**	**50.2%**	**—**	**2.6%**

Net Income History

Euronext Paris: MC

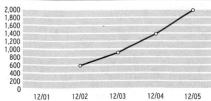

Magna International

Through its various subsidiaries and divisions Magna International makes just about everything you might need to put together a car, minivan, or truck. Magna Steyr, Magna's largest division, offers niche vehicle production services in Europe. Intier Automotive makes seats, instrument and door panels, closures, and sound insulation. Cosma International makes metal auto body systems. MAGNA Powertrain offers transaxles, transmission systems, and engine parts. Decoma International offers exterior trim, and Magna Donnelly makes automotive mirrors and engineered glass products. Other operations include Magna Car Top Systems.

Chairman Frank Stronach and his daughter (former CEO) Belinda, control Magna.

While most large North American auto parts suppliers are shrinking to survive, Magna is growing to thrive. The company has already surpassed Visteon to become North America's second-largest parts maker. Once Delphi emerges from Chapter 11, Magna will likely surpass it too.

Magna has re-thought its strategy of spinning off its automotive subsidiaries. The company's decentralized structure had initially been aimed at fostering teamwork and an entrepreneurial spirit among management and workers. However, recognizing that North America's auto industry is in crisis, Magna moved in 2005 to circle the wagons and re-centralize its operations in order to take better advantage of competitive opportunities.

Clever acquisitions have also helped steer Magna's growth. The company picked up New Process Gear from DaimlerChrysler in 2004 to enhance its MAGNA Powertrain offerings. In early 2006 Magna added car tops to its extensive line of automotive component offerings when it completed the purchase of CTS Fahzeug-Dachsysteme GmbH from Porsche.

Later in 2006 Magna hinted that it might enter the automotive parts retail market by offering aftermarket replacement parts and accessories — possibly under the Magna brand name. The company is also exploring the potential of expanding Magna Steyr's niche-vehicle manufacturing operations to include a manufacturing site in North America and/or Eastern Europe. Magna Steyr's current operations are situated in Austria. Also in 2006 Magna moved to increase Magna Steyr's North American presence with the purchase of Porsche's Michigan-based Porsche Engineering Services Inc.

Going for a drive of a different kind, Magna acquired the Fontana Golf and Sports Club from spinoff Magna Entertainment in 2006. The country club is located in Oberwaltersdorf, Austria.

HISTORY

Magna International is rooted in a tool and die shop founded by Franck Stronach and friend Tony Czapka in Ontario, Canada, in 1957. Austrian-born Stronach immigrated to Canada in 1954. By the end of 1957, the business, called Multimatic, had 10 employees. Multimatic delved into car parts when it landed a contract in 1960 to make sun visor brackets for a General Motors division in Canada. As a hobby, Stronach bought his first racing horse the next year.

To go public, in 1969 Multimatic underwent a reverse merger with Magna Electronics, a publicly traded maker of components for aerospace, defense, and industrial markets. (Stronach retained control of the company.) Annual sales reached $10 million that year. The company expanded its automotive operations during the early 1970s by adding more stamped and electronic components. Magna was renamed Magna International in 1973.

With sales increasing steadily among its auto parts businesses, Magna sold its aerospace and defense business (now part of Heroux-Devtek) in 1981. The new Magna consisted of five distinct automotive divisions that made seat tracks, door latches, electronic components, and other auto parts. During the 1980s the company expanded by adding factories and product lines. It also capitalized on carmakers' penchants for outsourcing labor and bypassing unions. By 1987, when sales reached $1 billion, the company was producing systems for every area of the automobile. Stronach didn't spend all his time on cars, however. He had opened restaurants, tried various publishing ventures (which failed), and even made an unsuccessful run for a Canadian parliament seat in 1988.

Aggressive expansion during the 1980s eventually caught up with the company, and in 1989 Magna began to restructure, selling assets to pay off its debt. The company also was bailed out, in part, by two of its principal customers — General Motors and Chrysler. Having recovered somewhat, Magna began acquiring small auto parts companies in Europe in 1992.

Magna expanded its European presence with the purchase of Austria-based Steyr-Daimler-Puch in 1998, adding about $1 billion in annual sales. The deal steered Magna into the auto assembly business. Stronach also added Santa Anita Park to his holdings that year. In late 1999 the company's racetrack interests were spun off as Magna Entertainment, with Magna retaining a 78% stake. Stronach's horse, Red Bullet, won the 2000 Preakness. Later that year Magna sold its 50% stake in Webasto Sunroofs to the privately owned German auto parts maker Webasto AG.

Early in 2001 Stronach's daughter Belinda was named VC and CEO. The company then prepared to spin off Magna Steyr and Intier as public companies. Intier was spun off later in 2001.

In 2002 Magna acquired rival automotive mirror maker Donnelly Corp. in a stock-and-debt deal worth $320 million. The company divested its stake in Magna Entertainment in 2003.

Early in 2004 Belinda Stronach stepped down as president, CEO, and director in order to make a bid for the leadership of Canada's new Conservative Party. Her father, Magna chairman Frank Stronach, assumed the role of interim president. Ms. Stronach's bid for the leadership of the Conservative Party was not successful. Mr. Stronach ran the company until 2005 when Magna adopted a co-CEO management structure with Donald Walker and Siegfried Wolf at the helm.

In May of 2004 Magna and DaimlerChrysler announced that Magna would buy DaimlerChrysler's drivetrain manufacturing subsidiary New Venture Gear for about $435 million. After approval by the European Commission the following September, New Venture Gear was acquired by a newly created joint venture called New Process Gear, with Magna holding an 80% interest and DaimlerChrysler holding 20% until 2007, when Magna will buy out DaimlerChrysler's stake.

EXECUTIVES

Chairman: Frank Stronach, age 73
Co-CEO; President and CEO, Intier Automotive Inc.: Donald R. Walker, age 60
Co-CEO: Siegfried Wolf, age 47, $4,286,790 pay
Executive Vice Chairman; Chairman and CEO, Tesma International Inc.: Manfred Gingl
President: Mark T. Hogan, age 55
EVP and CFO: Vincent J. Galifi, age 45
EVP: Jeffrey O. Palmer
EVP, Corporate Development: Peter Koob
EVP, Global Human Resources: Marc Neeb
EVP, Operations: Tom Skudutis
EVP, Special Projects and Secretary: J. Brian Colburn
SVP, Corporate Affairs: Keith J. Stein
VP and Controller: Patrick W.D. McCann
VP, Core Projects: Cameron Hastings
VP, Internal Audit: Roland B. Nimmo
VP, Investor Relations: Louis Tonelli
VP, Marketing: Stephen I. Rodgers
VP, Public Affairs: Kevin Gallagher
Chairman and CEO, Magna Donnelly: Carlos E. Mazzorin
President and CEO, Decoma International, Inc.: Alan J. Power
President, Cosma International: Horst Prelog
Managing Director, China: Keith Lomason
Auditors: Ernst & Young

LOCATIONS

HQ: Magna International Inc.
337 Magna Dr., Aurora, Ontario L4G 7K1, Canada
Phone: 905-726-2462 **Fax:** 905-726-7164
US HQ: 600 Wilshire Dr., Troy, MI 48084
US Phone: 248-729-2400 **US Fax:** 248-729-2410
Web: www.magnaint.com

Magna International has manufacturing facilities in Austria, Brazil, Belgium, Canada, China, the Czech Republic, France, Germany, Italy, Mexico, Poland, Slovakia, South Korea, Spain, Turkey, the UK, and the US.

2005 Sales

	$ mil.	% of total
North America		
Canada	6,513	27
US	5,714	24
Mexico	1,123	5
Europe		
UK	918	4
Other EU	8,714	37
Other countries	580	2
Other regions	209	1
Adjustments	(960)	—
Total	**22,811**	**100**

PRODUCTS/OPERATIONS

2005 Sales

	$ mil.	% of total
Complete vehicle assembly	4,110	18
Interior & seating systems	4,047	18
Metal body systems	3,657	16
Powertrain & drivetrain systems	3,505	15
Exterior systems	2,888	13
Mirrors & electronic systems	1,418	6
Closure systems	1,213	5
Tooling, engineering & other	1,973	9
Total	**22,811**	**100**

2005 Sales by Customer

	$ mil.	% of total
DaimlerChrysler	5,642	25
General Motors	5,605	25
BMW	4,011	17
Ford Motor	3,364	15
Other	4,189	18
Total	**22,811**	**100**

Selected Operation and Products/Services

Cosma International Inc.
Body systems
Chassis systems
Design and engineering
Finishing
Metal forming technologies
Stampings

Decoma International Inc.
Body side systems
Front and rear bumper systems
Greenhouse systems
Lighting systems
Polymeric glazing systems
Sealing systems
Top systems
Vehicle enhancement packages

Intier Automotive
Carpets, acoustic, and cargo management systems
Closure and latching systems
Cockpit systems
Electro-mechanical systems
Glass moving systems
Overhead systems
Seating hardware systems
Seating systems
Sidewall systems
System module technologies

MAGNA Powertrain
Automatic overdrives
Differentials
Engine systems
Power take-offs
Transaxles
Transfer cases
Transmission systems

Magna Steyr
Complete vehicle manufacturing
OEM engineering

COMPETITORS

Aisin Seiki	Haldex
AISIN World Corp.	Hella
American Axle & Manufacturing	Johnson Controls
ArvinMeritor	Lacks Enterprises
Benteler Automotive	Lear
BorgWarner	Linamar
Calsonic Kansei	Plastic Omnium
Collins & Aikman	Prodrive
Dana	Robert Bosch
Delphi	Tenneco
DENSO	Textron
DESC	ThyssenKrupp
Dura Automotive	ThyssenKrupp Budd
Eaton	Torotrak
Faurecia	Tower Automotive
Ficosa	Toyota Auto Body
Gentex	Trico Products
GKN	Valeo
Guide Corporation	Visteon
	ZF Friedrichshafen

HISTORICAL FINANCIALS

Company Type: Public

Income Statement

FYE: December 31

	REVENUE ($ mil.)	NET INCOME ($ mil.)	NET PROFIT MARGIN	EMPLOYEES
12/05	22,811	639	2.8%	82,000
12/04	20,653	668	3.2%	81,000
12/03	15,345	483	3.1%	75,000
12/02	12,971	505	3.9%	73,000
Annual Growth	**20.7%**	**8.2%**	**—**	**4.0%**

2005 Year-End Financials

Debt ratio: 10.7% No. of shares (mil.): —
Return on equity: 10.8% Dividends
Cash ($ mil.): 1,682 Yield: 1.8%
Current ratio: 1.50 Payout: 25.8%
Long-term debt ($ mil.): 700 Market value ($ mil.): —

	STOCK PRICE ($) FY Close	P/E High/Low		PER SHARE ($) Earnings	Dividends
12/05	84.00	17	10	5.90	1.52
12/04	98.57	17	10	6.87	1.48
12/03	80.05	22	9	5.02	1.02
12/02	79.01	20	8	5.42	1.70
Annual Growth	2.1%	—	—	2.9%	(3.7%)

MAN

This venerable old MAN still shows considerable strength. MAN Aktiengesellschaft (founded in 1845) and its subsidiaries manufacture a variety of heavy equipment ranging from commercial vehicles to diesel engines for ships. MAN is one of Europe's largest truck makers as well as a leading supplier of equipment for newspaper printing presses and industrial compressors and turbines. The company also makes components for rocket launchers and space transport systems, and it provides trading and industrial services. Additionally, MAN is a top manufacturer of equipment used to process plastics and metals. MAN is bidding to acquire rival Scania to improve its competitive position in truck manufacturing.

Scania has rejected MAN's unsolicited bid, valued at €10.3 billion ($12.9 billion) in cash and stock. Renault has agreed to sell its stake in Scania to MAN; with that stake and shares acquired on the open market, MAN has gained control over about 14% of the voting rights in Scania. Volkswagen, which holds 34% of Scania's voting rights, initially opposed MAN's bid for the Swedish truck manufacturer and bought a 15% equity stake in MAN. VW, however, seems open to the idea of combining the truck operations of MAN, Scania, and VW under friendly, negotiated circumstances, and stated that it would consider selling its stake in Scania to MAN if other shareholders warm to the hostile bid.

In an effort to streamline its operations to better compete within the European Union market, MAN has restructured its organization under two main division headings: Manufacturing (commercial vehicles, printing machines, diesel engines, and turbomachines) and Services (industrial and financial services). It plans to expand its operations in China, India, and Russia in the years ahead.

The company has gathered its information technology functions into one central organization, MAN IT Services, to provide IT services across the corporate group.

MAN has sold MAN TAKRAF Fördertechnik to Germany's VTC Industrieholding. TAKRAF Fördertechnik, acquired by MAN in 1994, builds equipment, systems, and complete facilities for open-pit mining, harbor and crane technology, and bulk cargo handling.

The company has sold MAN Roland Druckmaschinen, its printing press business, to a new venture put together by Allianz Capital Partners for €624 million (about $790 million). MAN kept a 35% equity stake in the business following the transaction.

Although MAN's reach is global, Europe accounts for more than two-thirds of sales. The company's commercial vehicle division accounts for about half of its revenues.

HISTORY

MAN grew out of a company started by Carl August Reichenbach and Carl Buz, who leased an engineering plant in Augsburg, Germany, in 1844. Reichenbach, whose uncle had invented the flatbed printing press, began producing printing presses in 1845. On the same premises, Buz began manufacturing steam engines and industrial drive systems, and he soon added rotary printing presses, water turbines, pumps, and diesel engines. In 1898 the company took the name MAN (Maschinenfabrik Augsburg-Nurnberg) after merging with a German engineering company of the same name.

Another German heavy-industry company, Gutehoffnungshutte Aktienverein AG (GHH, with roots stretching to 1758), bought a majority interest in MAN in 1921. Through acquisitions and internal growth MAN emerged from the world wars as one of Germany's major heavy-industry companies, with added interests in commercial vehicles, shipbuilding, and plant construction. By 1955 MAN's commercial vehicles were a major division destined to dominate the company's sales; MAN moved the division's headquarters to Munich that year.

During the 1970s an overseas recession caused the sales of some operations to slump, although MAN's commercial vehicles and printing-equipment businesses held steady. When economic hardship reached Europe in the 1980s, MAN sought markets outside its home region, especially targeting Asia, the Middle East, and the US. Late in the decade the company dropped its less-profitable products (lifts, pumps, heavy cranes) and began licensing more of its technology and subcontracting out more work. MAN moved its corporate headquarters to Munich in 1985 and merged with GHH in 1986.

After a fast start in the 1990s, Europe's economy again faltered, taking a toll on the company's sales. MAN's profits slumped in fiscal 1994. It laid off about 10% of its workforce between 1993 and 1995. As the economy recovered, so did MAN, and by fiscal 1998, its stagnant profits had rebounded.

Early in 2000 MAN purchased truck makers ERF Holdings (UK) and STAR (Poland). Later that year MAN picked up ALSTOM's diesel engine business. MAN acquired the Neoplan bus-making business of Gottlob Auwarter GmbH in 2001, as well as the turbomachinery business of Sulzer AG of Switzerland. After discovering accounting irregularities that year, the company suspended the CEO (John Bryant) and CFO (Klaus Wagner) of the newly acquired ERF. In 2002 the company began implementing its Truck Generation A (TG-A) technology into all of its commercial vehicles. In 2003, MAN sold its 51% stake in SMS AG.

In 2005 MAN group sold off its MAN Wolffkran subsidiary to private investors. The business sells and rents tower cranes, a.k.a. cherry pickers, for the building industry; the sale was part of the company's effort to pare down its operations to what are considered to be its core divisions. It also restructured its financial services division to prepare it for expansion; the company was renamed MAN Finance International and will finance activities in seven countries, including France, Germany, Italy, and Spain.

EXECUTIVES

Chairman of the Supervisory Board: Volker Jung, age 67
Deputy Chairman of the Supervisory Board: Gerlinde Strauss-Wieczorek
Chairman of the Executive Board: Rudolf Rupprecht, age 65
Chairman: Håkan Samuelsson, age 53
Member of the Executive Board, Controlling: Philipp J. Zahn
Member of the Executive Board, Diesel Engines: Hans-Jürgen Schulte
Member of the Executive Board, Industrial Services; Chairman, Ferrostaal: Matthias Mitscherlich, age 56
Member of the Executive Board, Finances: Ferdinand Graf von Ballestrem, age 61
Member of the Executive Board, Printing Machines: Gerd Finkbeiner, age 47
Member of the Executive Board, Technology; Chairman, MAN Technologie: Wolfgang Brunn, age 61
Chairman, MAN B&W Diesel: Fritz Pape, age 63
Chairman, MAN Roland Druckmaschinen: Ingo Koch
Chairman, MAN Turbomaschinen: Jürgen Maus, age 60
Chairman, Schwäbische Hüttenwerke: Lothar Hauck
Member of Executive Board, Controlling: Karlheinz Hornung, age 55
Press Speaker: Wieland Schmitz
Investor Relations Director: Ulf Steinborn
Auditors: BDO Deutsche Warentreuhand AG

LOCATIONS

HQ: MAN Aktiengesellschaft
Ungererstrasse 69, D-80805 Munich, Germany
Phone: +49-89-36098-0   **Fax:** +49-89-36098-250
Web: www.man.de

MAN has manufacturing facilities in Austria, Germany, Mexico, Poland, South Africa, Turkey, and the UK.

2005 Sales

	% of total
Europe	
Germany	26
Other European Union	34
Other countries	8
Americas	14
Asia	13
Africa	4
Australia & Oceania	1
Total	**100**

PRODUCTS/OPERATIONS

2005 Sales

	% of total
Commercial vehicles	49
Industrial services	19
Printing systems	12
Diesel engines	11
Turbomachines	5
Other	4
Total	**100**

Selected Subsidiaries and Products

Deggendorfer Werft und Eisenbau
  Autoclaves
  Condensers
  Dump barges
  Floating dredgers
  Gas coolers
  Heat exchangers
  Pilot reactors
  Pressure vessels
  Tube reactors
  Salt bath-cooled reactors

Ferrostaal
  Facility construction and contracting
  Industrial equipment and systems
  Steel trading and logistics

MAN B&W Diesel
  Diesel engines for locomotives, marine propulsion,
    and power plants
  Exhaust gas turbochargers
  Power turbines

MAN Nutzfarzeuge
  Buses and coaches
  Components
    Axles
    Cabs
    Cast parts
    Pressed parts
    Tools
    Transfer cases
  Diesel engines for automobiles, boats, and power
    generation
  Gas Motors
  Transport logistics and fleet management
  Trucks (6 to 50 tons gross weight)

MAN Roland Druckmaschinen (35% owned)
  Digital-based printing systems
  Sheet-fed offset printing presses
  Web-fed offset printing presses

MAN Technologie
  Space transport propulsion components and systems

MAN Turbomaschinen GHH BORSIG
  Industrial compressors
  Industrial turbines

RENK
  Automatic transmissions for tracked vehicles
  Bearings
  Couplings
  Industrial gear units
  Marine gear units
  Test systems

Schwäbische Hüttenwerke
  Brake discs
  Castings
  Chilled cast iron rolls
  Industrial pumps
  Sintered parts

COMPETITORS

ALSTOM	ITT Corporation
ArvinMeritor	Kawasaki Heavy Industries
Baldwin Technology	Koenig & Bauer
Cummins	Mitsubishi Heavy
DaimlerChrysler	Industries
Dana	Navistar
DEUTZ	PACCAR
Federal-Mogul	Renault
Fiat	Scania
GE Energy	Sumitomo Heavy
GEA Group	Industries
Goss International	TUI
Hanjin Heavy Industries	Voith
Heidelberg	Volvo

HISTORICAL FINANCIALS

Company Type: Public

Income Statement

FYE: December 31

	REVENUE ($ mil.)	NET INCOME ($ mil.)	NET PROFIT MARGIN	EMPLOYEES
12/05	17,375	547	3.1%	60,000
12/04	20,388	420	2.1%	61,259
12/03	18,854	285	1.5%	64,158
12/02	16,812	142	0.8%	75,054
12/01	14,439	134	0.9%	77,606
Annual Growth	4.7%	42.2%	—	(6.2%)

2005 Year-End Financials

Debt ratio: 10.4%
Return on equity: 14.0%
Cash ($ mil.): 1,207
Current ratio: 1.17
Long-term debt ($ mil.): 398

Net Income History

German: MAN

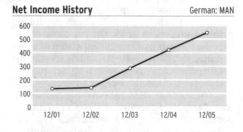

Marks and Spencer

The sun now sets on Marks and Spencer (M&S). The department stores sell mid-priced clothing, food, and household items under the company's famous private label, the "very British" St Michael brand (found on items ranging from tweed jackets to marmalade). One of the UK's largest sellers of clothing, it has sold off most overseas operations in order to salvage its 450 M&S stores in the UK. The company got rid of more than 220 Brooks Brothers clothing stores in the US and Asia (to Retail Brand Alliance, 2001) as well as its Kings Super Markets chain in the US in 2006, and 18 M&S stores in France (to Galeries Lafayette, 2001). M&S owns stores in Ireland and Hong Kong and operates about 200 franchise stores.

M&S has finally sold its US supermarket chain, Kings Super Markets, to a pair of New York-based private equity firms and a former supermarket executive for about $61.5 million. Previously, New York grocer Gristede's had offered to pay $120 million for Kings, but in 2003 M&S announced it wasn't selling.

More than 90% of the company's sales are made in the UK. Food accounts for about 50% of M&S's (Marks & Sparks in Cockney rhyming slang) UK business. Of that, M&S's new "Eat Well" line of healthier foods is expected to account for about 40% of total food sales by year-end 2006. The company has about 145 Simply Food outlets around the UK, including a pilot program to put Simply Food stores in railway stations and motorway service areas.

M&S has taken a number of steps to defend its UK apparel business, which has suffered from stiff competition over the past several years. It recently upgraded its women's Classic range and launched a petite line. The company has pared its menswear offering from eight brands to three

(Autograph, Blue Harbour, and Collezione). The clothing retailer has also launched a new underwear collection for men and women. Building on the success of its Per Una clothing line, M&S launched Per Una Due (designed by high-street legend George Davies), an edgy clothing line targeted at women in their late teens to early 30s. In 2005 M&S bought the Per Una brand from designer George Davies for about £126 million.

Overall, M&S has about a 10% share of the UK clothing and footwear market and is the leading lingerie retailer in Britain with more than 25% of the market.

The company made plans in 2006 to open up to 30 franchised stores in the Baltic countries, Bulgaria, Ukraine, and Dubai.

Lord Burns, a former chairman of Abbey National, took up the post of chairman in July 2006 after joining Marks and Spencer as deputy chairman in 2005. Burns succeeds interim chairman Paul Myners, who took over from Luc Vandevelde when Vandevelde and chief executive Roger Holmes left the company in 2004.

HISTORY

Fleeing anti-Semitic persecution in Russian Poland, 19-year-old Michael Marks immigrated to England in 1882. Eventually settling in Leeds, Marks eked out a meager existence as a traveling peddler until he opened a small stall at the town market in 1884. Because he spoke little English, Marks laid out all of his merchandise and hung a sign that read, "Don't Ask the Price, It's a Penny," unaware at the time that self-service would eventually become the retailing standard. His methods were so successful that he had penny bazaars in five cities by 1890.

Finding himself unable to run the growing operation alone, Marks established an equal partnership with Englishman Tom Spencer, a cashier for a local distributor, forming Marks and Spencer in 1894. By the turn of the century, the company had 36 branches. Following the deaths of Spencer (1905) and Marks (1907), management of the company did not return to family hands until 1916, when Marks' 28-year-old son Simon became chairman.

Marks and Spencer broke with time-honored British retailing tradition in 1924 by eliminating wholesalers and establishing direct links with manufacturers. In 1926 the firm went public, and two years later it launched its now famous St Michael brand. The company turned its attention to pruning unprofitable departments to concentrate on goods that had a rapid turnover. In 1931 the Marks & Spencer stores (M&S) introduced a food department that sold produce and canned goods.

The company sustained severe losses during WWII, when bombing damaged approximately half of its stores. Marks and Spencer rebuilt, and in 1964 Simon's brother-in-law Israel Sieff became chairman. The company expanded to North America a decade later by buying three Canadian chains: Peoples (general merchandise, sold 1992), D'Allaird's (women's clothing, sold 1996), and Walker's (clothing shops, converted to M&S). Sieff's son Marcus Sieff became chairman in 1972. It opened its first store in Paris in 1975.

Derek Rayner replaced Marcus Sieff as chairman in 1984, becoming the first chairman hired from outside the Marks family since 1916. Under Rayner, Marks and Spencer moved into financial services by launching a charge card in 1985. The company purchased US-based Kings Super Markets and Brooks Brothers (upscale clothing stores) in 1988. Rayner retired in 1991, and CEO Richard Greenbury became chairman. During the 1990s M&S opened new stores in Germany, Hong Kong, Hungary, Spain, and Turkey.

In 1997 it paid Littlewoods $323 million for 19 UK stores, which it converted to M&S. Greenbury, facing criticism that the company was too slow to expand and embrace new ideas, in 1999 was succeeded as CEO by handpicked heir Peter Salsbury. That year, continued poor sales led Marks and Spencer to cut 700 jobs and close its 38 M&S stores in Canada, and part ways with its clothing supplier of 30 years, William Baird. Chairman Luc Vandevelde took over as CEO in September, when Salsbury resigned.

Unhappy with the company's direction and its departure from older values, Marks and Spencer board members Sir David Sieff (the last remaining founder member), Sir Ralph Robins, and Sir Michael Perry left the board in July 2001. Marks and Spencer sold Brooks Brothers to Retail Brand Alliance for $225 million (a loss from the $750 million the company paid for it in 1988) in 2001. In 2002 Vandevelde — who is credited with masterminding the M&S turnaround — announced he would give up his role as CEO and hand the reins to managing director Roger Holmes. Vandevelde became the company's part-time chairman in 2003.

In 2004 both Vandevelde and Holmes left M&S. Stuart Rose, formerly head of Arcadia, was named CEO; non-executive board member Paul Myners was named interim chairman.

EXECUTIVES

CEO and Director: Stuart A. Rose, age 57, $3,665,127 pay
Group Finance Director and Director: Ian Dyson, age 43, $1,047,180 pay
Executive Director, Marketing, e-Commerce, and Store Design and Development, and Director: Steven Sharp, age 55, $561,859 pay
Group Secretary and Head of Corporate Governance: Graham Oakley, age 48
Business Unit Director, Womenswear, Girlswear, and Babywear: Kate Bostock, age 50
Business Unit Director, Menswear, Boyswear, Schoolwear, and Children's Nightwear: Andrew Skinner, age 40
Director, Lingerie and Sleepwear: Matthew (Matt) Hudson, age 38
Director, General Merchandise Planning: Andrew Moore, age 49
Director, Food: Guy Farrant, age 45
Director, Home: Steve Rowe, age 39
Director, Retail Operations: Anthony Thompson, age 42
Director, Human Resources: Keith Cameron, age 59
Director, Information Technology: Darrell Stein, age 39
Director, International and UK Outlets: Richard Wolff, age 49
Director, General Merchandise Supply Chain and Logistics: Simon Ratcliffe
Director, Sourcing: Glen Tinton, age 44
Director, Communications: Flic Howard-Allen, age 46
Corporate Finance and Group Reporting Director: Paula Hay-Plumb
Corporate Press Manager: Sue Sadler
Auditors: PricewaterhouseCoopers LLP

LOCATIONS

HQ: Marks and Spencer Group p.l.c.
Waterside House, 35 N. Wharf Rd.,
London W2 1NW, United Kingdom
Phone: +44-20-7935-4422   **Fax:** +44-20-7487-2679
Web: www.marksandspencer.com

2006 UK Stores

	No.
England	388
Scotland	35
Wales	18
Northern Ireland	10
Total	**451**

PRODUCTS/OPERATIONS

2006 Sales

	% of total
UK	
Food	47
Clothing	42
Home	4
Other countries	7
Total	**100**

COMPETITORS

Arcadia
ASDA
Benetton
Berwin & Berwin
Burberry
Carrefour
Debenhams
Fortnum & Mason
Gap
H&M
Harrods
Harvey Nichols
House of Fraser
J Sainsbury
John Lewis
Kingfisher
Littlewoods
Mothercare
New Look
NEXT
Pret A Manger
Primark
Somerfield
Tesco
T.K. Maxx
Topshop
Zara

HISTORICAL FINANCIALS

Company Type: Public

Income Statement				FYE: March 31
	REVENUE ($ mil.)	NET INCOME ($ mil.)	NET PROFIT MARGIN	EMPLOYEES
3/06	13,564	910	6.7%	65,000
3/05	14,921	1,103	7.4%	70,550
3/04	15,157	1,008	6.7%	70,101
3/03	12,713	756	5.9%	67,133
3/02	11,598	218	1.9%	69,899
Annual Growth	**4.0%**	**42.9%**	**—**	**(1.8%)**

Net Income History   Pink Sheets: MAKSY.PK

Matsushita

Matsushita Electric Industrial, one of the world's top consumer electronics makers, may have an unfamiliar name, but its brands are recognizable: Panasonic, Quasar, Technics, and JVC, to name a few. Its AVC Networks sector produces TVs, VCRs, CD and DVD players, PCs, cellular phones, and fax machines. Matsushita also sells components (batteries, electric motors, displays, semiconductors), home appliances (washing machines, vacuum cleaners), and factory automation equipment (industrial robots, welding equipment). The Matsushita group includes about 380 consolidated companies around the globe; its products are sold worldwide.

Matsushita (whose founder's name means "lucky man under the pine tree") also makes products sold around the world under the National and Victor brands. Its top revenue generator, the AVC Networks segment, accounts for about 45% of sales.

China is becoming a more important manufacturing center for Matsushita; the company is shifting its low-end product manufacturing to China (due primarily to lower production costs), with more expensive products being made in Japan and Southeast Asia. However, the company is planning to build a large manufacturing plant in China. The plant, which will produce home appliances, will primarily serve the Chinese market.

The company is merging its resources with other companies in order to launch new technologies, particularly in the consumer home electronics segment. It became a member of the Blu-ray Disc Founders (along with Sony and Samsung) to promote the Blu-ray optical disc format as the standard for next-generation optical storage media — succeeding the DVD format. (Matsushita launched a Blu-ray compatible DVD recorder that can record 4-1/2 hours of programming.)

The fast-growing flat-screen television market has become a new focus for Matsushita; with its PDP (plasma display panel) and liquid crystal display (LCD) products, the company's Panasonic brand was the top PDP manufacturer in 2005. In September 2004 it began to build a large-scale PDP plant with textile-maker Toray; the plant is expected to boost the company's production to 4.5 million units by 2007. It is building an LCD plant with electronics partners Hitachi and Toshiba (a joint venture called IPS Alpha Technology), giving Matsushita an increased supply of LCD panels for its TVs.

The company is accelerating its chip-making operations, viewing semiconductors as a key ingredient in product innovation.

HISTORY

Grade school dropout Konosuke Matsushita took $50 in 1918 and went into business making electric plugs (with his brother-in-law, Toshio Iue, founder of SANYO). His mission, to help people by making high-quality, low-priced conveniences while providing his employees with good working conditions, earned him the sobriquet, "god of business management." Matsushita Electric Industrial grew by developing inexpensive lamps, batteries, radios, and motors in the 1920s and 1930s.

During WWII the Japanese government ordered the firm to build wood-laminate products for the military. Postwar occupation forces prevented Matsushita from working at his firm for four years. Thanks to unions' efforts, he rejoined his namesake company shortly before it entered a joint venture with Dutch manufacturer Philips in 1952. The following year it moved into consumer goods, making televisions, refrigerators, and washing machines and later expanding into high-performance audio products. Matsushita bought a majority stake in Victor Company of Japan (JVC, originally established by RCA Victor) in 1954. Its 1959 New York subsidiary opening began Matsushita's drive overseas.

Sold under the National, Panasonic, and Technics names, the firm's products were usually not cutting-edge but were attractively priced. Under Masaharu Matsushita, the founder's son-in-law who became president in 1961, the company became Japan's largest home appliance maker, introducing air conditioners, microwave ovens, stereo components, and VCRs in the 1960s and 1970s. JVC developed the VHS format for VCRs, which beat out Sony's Betamax format.

Matsushita built much of its sales growth on new industrial and commercial customers in the 1980s. The company expanded its semiconductor, office and factory automation, auto electronics, audio-visual, housing, and air-conditioning product offerings that decade. Konosuke died in 1989.

The next year Matsushita joined the Japanese stampede for US acquisitions, buying Universal Studios' then-owner, MCA. In 1993 Yoichi Morishita was named president and the company acquired Philips' stake in their joint venture. Two years later, when cultural incompatibility depressed MCA's performance, Matsushita sold 80% of the company (now Universal) to liquor mogul Seagram, resulting in a fiscal 1996 loss. That same year Matsushita pushed the technology envelope, introducing the first DVD player.

Declining sales forced the firm to rethink its strategy; it began a multiyear restructuring, including a buildup in parts of Asia with cheaper labor and job cuts. In 1997 the downside of Matsushita's move into emerging Asian markets became apparent as many Southeast Asian countries suffered currency crises.

A lagging market led Matsushita to close its North American semiconductor operations in late 1998. In June 2000 Yoichi Morishita became chairman and Kunio Nakamura took the reigns as president of Matsushita. The next December, following a year with a three-fold increase in expenditures on chip-making ($1.2 billion), the company began making chips for cell phones, digital cameras, and digital TVs.

In early 2002 Matsushita announced plans to turn around its financial slump by cutting 13,000 local jobs (through early retirement) and trimming directors' salaries.

In April 2002 Matsushita buddied up with Chinese home appliance manufacturer TCL Holdings; the move was intended to help Matsushita increase its presence in China's growing consumer electronic market.

EXECUTIVES

Honorary Chairman: Masaharu Matsushita, age 94
Chairman: Kunio Nakamura, age 67
Vice Chairman: Masayuki Matsushita, age 61
President and Director: Fumio Ohtsubo, age 61
EVP Corporate Marketing and Corporate Sales Strategy and Director: Kazuo Toda, age 65
EVP and Director; President, Panasonic Automotive Systems Company: Takami Sano, age 63

Senior Managing Director, Technology, Device Technology, and Environmental Technology and Director; President, Semiconductor Company: Susumu Koike, age 61
Senior Managing Director, Finance and Accounting and Director: Tetsuya Kawakami, age 64
Senior Managing Director, Home Appliances and Director; President, Matsushita Home Appliances Company: Yoshitaka Hayashi, age 60
Managing Director, Facility Management, Quality Assurance and Environmental Affairs and Director: Hidetsugu Otsuru, age 63
Managing Director, Planning and Director: Toshihiro Sakamoto, age 60
Managing Director, Corporate Communications and Director; Vice Chairman, Showroom Strategic Committee: Takahiro Mori
Managing Director, Personnel, General Affairs, and Social Relations and Director: Shinichi Fukushima, age 58
Director; President, Panasonic System Solutions Company: Masaki Akiyama
Director, Corporate Legal Affairs: Mikio Ito
Director; Deputy Chief, Overseas Operations and Director, Global Strategy Research Institute: Ikusaburo Kashima
Executive Officer; Director, Corporate Management for North America; Chairman, Panasonic Corporation of North America: Yoshihiko (Yoshi) Yamada
Auditors: KPMG AZSA & Co.

LOCATIONS

HQ: Matsushita Electric Industrial Co., Ltd.
(Matsushita Denki Sangyo Kabushiki Kaisha)
1006 Oaza Kadoma, Kadoma,
Osaka 571-8501, Japan
Phone: +81-6-6908-1121   **Fax:** +81-6-6908-2351
US HQ: 1 Rockefeller Plaza, Ste. 1001,
New York, NY 10020
US Phone: 212-698-1365   **US Fax:** 212-698-1369
Web: matsushita.co.jp

2006 Sales

	% of total
Japan	57
North & South America	11
Europe	9
Asia & other regions	23
Total	**100**

PRODUCTS/OPERATIONS

2006 Sales

	% of total
AVC Networks	38
MEW & PanaHome	17
Components & devices	13
Home appliances	12
JVC	7
Other	13
Total	**100**

Selected Segments and Products

AVC Networks
  Audio equipment (home, broadcast)
  Camcorders
  CD and mini-disc players
  Computer drives (CD-ROM, DVD-ROM/RAM)
  Computers (PCs)
  Digital cameras
  DVD players and recorders
  Fax machines
  Memory cards
  Photocopiers
  Printers
  Telephones
  TVs (color, LCD, plasma display)
  VCRs

MEW and PanaHome
  Automation controls
  Beauty and personal care products
  Condominiums
  Detached housing
  Electronic and plastic materials
  Health-enhancing products
  Home amenity and security systems
  Home remodeling
  Interior furnishings
  Land lots for housing
  Lighting products
  Medical and nursing care facilities
  Modular kitchens
  Rental apartment housing
  Residential real estate
  Wiring devices
Components and devices
  Batteries (dry, rechargeable)
  Displays (CRTs, LCDs, PDPs)
  Electric motors
  General components (capacitors, resistors, printed
    circuit boards)
  Magnetic recording heads
  Semiconductors
Home appliances
  Air conditioners and purifiers
  Dishwashers
  Dryers
  Fans
  Irons
  Microwave ovens
  Refrigerators
  Vacuum cleaners
  Water heaters
  Washing machines
JVC (Victor Company of Japan)
  Camcorders
  Car audio equipment
  CD radio cassette recorders
  DVD players and recorders
  Karaoke systems
  Stereo equipment
  TVs
  VCRs
  Video projectors

Selected Brands

JVC
National
Panasonic
Quasar
Technics
Victor

COMPETITORS

Apple Computer
BSH Bosch und Siemens Hausgeräte
Canon
Dell
Duracell
Eastman Kodak
Electrolux
Fujitsu Siemens Computers
GE Consumer & Industrial
Haier Group
Hewlett-Packard
IBM
Intel
Konica Minolta
LG Electronics
Motorola
NEC
Nokia
Olympus
Philips Electronics
Samsung Electronics
Sharp
Sony
THOMSON
Truly International
Tyco Electronics
Whirlpool

HISTORICAL FINANCIALS

Company Type: Public

Income Statement

FYE: March 31

	REVENUE ($ mil.)	NET INCOME ($ mil.)	NET PROFIT MARGIN	EMPLOYEES
3/06	75,602	1,313	1.7%	334,402
3/05	81,037	544	0.7%	334,752
3/04	72,547	400	0.6%	290,493
3/03	62,193	(162)	—	288,324
3/02	52,299	(3,233)	—	297,196
Annual Growth	9.7%	—	—	3.0%

2006 Year-End Financials

Debt ratio: 7.0%
Return on equity: 4.0%
Cash ($ mil.): 14,749

Current ratio: 1.53
Long-term debt ($ mil.): 2,245

Net Income History

NYSE: MC

Mazda

Having outrun an ailing Mitsubishi, Mazda Motor Corporation is now Japan's fourth-largest automaker behind Toyota, Nissan, and Honda. Mazda makes cars, minivans, pickup trucks, and commercial vehicles. Models sold by Mazda in the US include sedans (Mazda 3, Mazda 6), mini-vans (MPV), sports cars (Miata, RX-8), and pickup trucks (B-Series). Mazda has added a crossover SUV to its lineup with the introduction of the CX-7. Operating from two Japanese and 18 international manufacturing plants, Mazda sells its vehicles in some 140 countries. Ford Motor owns a controlling 33% of Mazda.

Mazda is profitable — a condition of which Ford is no doubt envious. The company has turned itself around in the last few years despite a weak North American market. In fact, Mazda sold more cars in Europe in 2005 than it did in North America — a fact that would have been hard to imagine just a few years ago.

To stay on track Mazda will introduce 16 new models by 2007. In the US, currently the company's toughest market, Mazda plans to offer new SUV crossover vehicles as the country's fascination with large SUVs wanes in response to higher fuel prices. In Europe Mazda plans to offer new models that feature diesel engines, a feature favored by European drivers. At home in Japan Mazda is bringing new minivans to market while revamping its dealer network.

In conjunction with its partner Ford, Mazda has made huge gains in China. In 2001 it sold 6,000 cars; in 2004, it sold 96,000; and in 2005 it sold 130,000. By 2010 Mazda wants to sell 300,000 cars in China. It plans to do this by introducing more models, building cars in China, and shoring up its Chinese dealer network.

In 2006 Mazda purchased 15% of Ford's joint venture with Chinese partner Changan Automotive. The venture, formerly called Changan Ford Automobile, was renamed Changan Ford Mazda Automobile. Ford now controls 35% of the venture; Changan Automobile holds a 50% stake.

HISTORY

Ingiro Matsuda founded cork producer Toyo Cork Kogyo in Hiroshima in 1920. The company changed its name to Toyo Kogyo in 1927 and began making machine tools. Impressed by Ford trucks used in 1923 earthquake-relief efforts, Matsuda had the company make a three-wheel motorcycle/truck hybrid in 1931.

The second Sino-Japanese War forced Toyo Kogyo to make rifles and cut back on its truck production. Although the company built a prototype passenger car in 1940, the outbreak of WWII refocused it on weapons. The August 1945 bombing of Hiroshima killed more than 400 Toyo Kogyo workers, but the company persevered, producing 10 trucks that December. By 1949 it was turning out 800 per month.

The company launched the first Mazda, a two-seat minicar, in 1960. The next year Toyo Kogyo licensed Audi's new rotary engine technology. After releasing a string of models, the company became Japan's #3 automaker in 1964. Toyo Kogyo introduced the first Mazda powered by a rotary engine, Cosmo/110S, in 1967, followed by the Familia in 1968.

The company grew rapidly and began exporting to the US in 1970. However, recession, high gas prices, and concern over the inefficiency of rotary engines halted growth in the mid-1970s. Sumitomo Bank bailed out Toyo Kogyo. The company shifted emphasis back to piston engines but managed to launch the rotary engine RX-7 in 1978.

Ford's need for small-car expertise and Sumitomo's desire for a large partner for its client led to Ford's purchase of 25% of Toyo Kogyo in 1979. The company's early 1980s GLC/323 and 626 models were sold as Fords in Asia, Latin America, and the Middle East.

Toyo Kogyo changed its name to Mazda Motor Corporation in 1984. ("Mazda" is loosely derived from Matsuda's name, but the carmaker has never discouraged an association with the Zoroastrian god of light, Ahura Mazda.) The company opened a US plant in 1985, but a strong yen, expensive increases in production capacity, and a growing number of models led to increased overhead, soaring debt, and shrinking margins. By 1988 Mazda had begun to focus on sporty niche cars; it launched the hot-selling Miata in 1989.

The company faced more problems with the early 1990s recession. In 1992 Mazda introduced a new 626 model. That year Mazda also sold half its interest in its Flat Rock, Michigan, plant to Ford. As the yen, development costs, and prices for its cars in the US all rose, sales in the US fell. In 1993 Mazda reorganized subsidiary Mazda of America by cutting staff.

Ford sank $481 million into Mazda in 1996, increasing its stake to 33%. That year the Ford-appointed former EVP of Mazda, Henry Wallace, became Mazda's president, making history as the first non-Japanese to head a major Japanese corporation. In 1997 Wallace resigned to become CFO of Ford's European operations, and former Ford executive James Miller replaced him. That year Mazda consolidated four US operations into Mazda North American Operations.

Restructuring continued in 1998 as Mazda consolidated some European operations and closed a plant in Thailand. In 1999 Mazda sold its credit division to Ford and its Naldec auto parts unit to Ford's Visteon unit. It announced plans to sell its stake in South Korean carmaker Kia Motors. Later in the year, another American, Ford's Mark Fields, took over as president.

In 2000 Mazda recalled 30,000 MPV minivans (year 2000) to fix a powertrain control module and asked owners of all year 2000 MPVs to bring in their vehicles for front-bumper reinforcement. Mazda also announced plans to close about 40% of its North American dealership outlets over the next three years.

In 2001 Mazda completed a program to assume direct control over distribution in some European markets including France, Italy, Spain, and the UK.

EXECUTIVES

Representative Director and Chairman: Hisakazu Imaki
Representative Director and Vice Chairman: John G. Parker, age 58
Senior Managing Executive Officer, CFO and Director: David E Friedman
EVP, Corporate Liaison, Purchasing, and Director: Mutsumi Fujiwara
EVP: Robert J. Graziano, age 47
Senior Managing Executive Officer, China Business and Director: Kiyoshi Ozaki
Senior Managing Executive Officer, Corporate Communications and Liaison, IT Solutions, Assistant to the CFO and Director: Ryoichi Hasegawa
Senior Managing Executive Officer, Marketing, Sales, and Customer Service and Director: Daniel T. Morris
Senior Managing Executive Officer, Secretariat, Personnel and Human Development, Internal Auditing, and Director: Takashi Yamanouchi
Senior Managing Executive Officer, Production and Business Logistics: Masaharu Yamaki
Managing Executive Officer, Domestic Marketing, Sales, and Customer Service: Masazumi Wakayama
Managing Executive Officer, Research and Powertrain Development: Nobuhiro Hayama
Managing Executive Officer, Research and Development: Seita Kanai
Managing Executive Officer; President and CEO, Mazda Motor Europe GmbH: James M. Muir
Managing Executive Officer; President and CEO, Mazda Motor of America (Mazda North American Operations): James J. (Jim) O'Sullivan
Managing Executive Officer; Overseas Sales and Customer Service: Malcolm D. Gough
Managing Executive Officer; Corporate Affairs, Risk Management, CSR and Mazda Hospital: Masaki Kanda
Executive Officer; General Manager, Overseas Sales Division: Yuji Nakamine
Executive Officer; General Manager, Personnel and Human Resources Development Division: Minoru Mitsuda
Auditors: KPMG AZSA & Co.

LOCATIONS

HQ: Mazda Motor Corporation
(Matsuda Jidosha Kabushiki Kaisha)
3-1, Shinchi, Fuchu-cho, Aki-gun,
Hiroshima 730-8670, Japan
Phone: +81-82-282-1111   **Fax:** +81-82-287-5190
US HQ: 10 Corporate Park, Ste. 200, Irvine, CA 92606
US Phone: 949-727-1990   **US Fax:** 949-752-2130
Web: www.mazda.co.jp

Mazda Motor Corporation has production facilities in 16 countries. Its sales and service network includes 1,660 dealers, sales, and service outlets in Japan and more than 5,000 in other countries.

2006 Sales

	$ mil.	% of total
Japan	10,317.7	42
North America	7,002.8	28
Europe	5,573.2	23
Other regions	1,936.5	7
Total	**24,830.2**	**100**

PRODUCTS/OPERATIONS

Selected Models

B-Series (pickup)
CX-7 (crossover SUV)
Mazda 3 (hatchback sedan)
Mazda 5 (minivan)
Mazda 6 (sport sedan)
MAZDASPEED
MX-5 Miata (roadster)
MPV (van)
RX-8 (sports car)
Tribute (SUV)

Selected Subsidiaries and Affiliates

AutoAlliance International, Inc. (50%, US)
Mazda Australia Pty. Ltd.
Mazda Motor Logistics Europe NV (Belgium)
Mazda Motor of America, Inc. (93%, US)

COMPETITORS

BMW
DaimlerChrysler
Fiat
Ford
Fuji Heavy Industries
General Motors
Honda
Isuzu
Kia Motors
Nissan
Peugeot
Renault
Saab Automobile
Suzuki Motor
Toyota
Volkswagen

HISTORICAL FINANCIALS

Company Type: Public

Income Statement

FYE: March 31

	REVENUE ($ mil.)	NET INCOME ($ mil.)	NET PROFIT MARGIN	EMPLOYEES
3/06	24,830	—	—	36,626
3/05	25,063	—	—	35,680
3/04	27,604	—	—	35,627
3/03	19,730	—	—	36,184
3/02	15,794	—	—	37,824
Annual Growth	**12.0%**	**—**	**—**	**(0.8%)**

Revenue History

Exchange: Tokyo

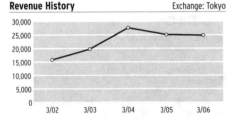

METRO

A ride on this METRO could be a shopper's delight. The company, Germany's largest retailer, owns and operates more than 2,100 wholesale stores, supermarkets, hypermarkets, department stores, and Media Markt and Saturn consumer electronics stores. Two-thirds of its shops are in Germany but METRO also has stores in 29 other countries. Store banners include Metro Cash & Carry wholesale outlets, Extra supermarkets, Real hypermarkets, and Galeria Kaufhof department stores. METRO also runs restaurants in its department stores and hypermarkets and offers advertising and insurance to its retail chains. Nearly 60% of METRO is owned by founder Otto Beisheim, Franz Haniel & Cie, and the Schmidt-Ruthenbeck family.

Germany's hostile retail environment has apparently convinced Wal-Mart Stores to abandon the German market. The world's largest retailer has agreed to sell the last of its 85 stores there to METRO, which will convert the outlets to its Real hypermarket banner. METRO also plans to acquire 19 Géant stores in Poland from France's Casino Guichard-Perrachon.

Due to the lackluster retail economy in its home country, the German retail giant's growth is being driven by its international operations. (Sales outside Germany have overtaken those in the company's home market for the first time.)

METRO is investing heavily in Eastern Europe and in Asia, where China is a focus on expansion. METRO is speeding up its expansion in China, where it operates about 30-plus stores in 27 cities. The German retailer plans to double its cash-and-carry stories in China, its most promising new market, by the end of the decade.

The German retailer opened its first Metro Cash & Carry wholesale stores in Moscow and Moldavia in 2004, and expanded into Serbia in 2005. New markets include Sweden (Media Markt) in 2006, and Pakistan (Metro Cash & Carry) in 2007.

In late 2005, METRO took its DIY home improvement chain Praktiker Bau- und Heimwerkermärkte, public in an IPO.

HISTORY

METRO SB-Grossmarkte was founded by Otto Beisheim in the German town of Mulheim in 1964. A wholesale business serving commercial customers, it operated under the name METRO Cash & Carry. Three years later Beisheim received backing from the owners of Franz Haniel & Cie (an industrial company founded in 1756) and members of the Schmidt-Ruthenbeck family (also in wholesaling). This allowed METRO to expand rapidly in Germany and, in 1968, into the Netherlands under the name Makro Cash & Carry via a partnership with Steenkolen Handelsvereeniging (SHV). During the 1970s the company expanded its wholesaling operations within Europe and moved into retailing.

METRO's foray into retailing was aided during the next decade by the acquisition of department store chain Kaufhof AG. By the 1980s the rise of specialty stores had many department stores on the defensive, and Kaufhof's owners sold it to METRO and its investment partner, Union Bank of Switzerland.

As METRO's ownership interest in Kaufhof rose above 50%, the chain began converting some of its stores from department stores into fashion and sporting goods sellers. Kaufhof began acquiring a stake in computer manufacturer and retailer Vobis in 1989. In 1993 METRO, now operating as METRO Holding AG, acquired a majority interest in supermarket company Asko Deutsche Kaufhaus, which owned the Praktiker building materials chain. The reclusive Beisheim retired from active management the following year.

To cut costs and prepare for expansion into Asia, in 1996 METRO Holding merged its German retail holdings — Kaufhof; Asko; another grocery operation, Deutsche SB Kauf; and its German cash-and-carry operations — into one holding company, METRO AG. The new subsidiary purchased 58 Wirichs home improvement centers in Germany that year to complement its Praktiker chain.

In 1998 METRO bought the 196-store Makro self-service wholesale chain from Dutch-based SHV. METRO also added to its German food operations by acquiring the 94-store German Allkauf hypermarket chain and then by purchasing the 20-store Kriegbaum hypermarket chain.

Hans-Joachim Korber became METRO's CEO in 1999. In 2000 the company transferred 290 hypermarkets and department stores in Germany, Greece, Hungary, Luxembourg, and Turkey to a joint venture company (51% owned by Westdeutsche Landesbank) to raise cash for the expansion and remodeling of its wholesale outlets. Expanding on the Internet, METRO acquired control of German e-commerce business Primus Online.

In 2001 METRO AG redistributed all of its shares held by METRO Holding AG to its top three shareholders for tax purposes. At the end of the year, the first two Cash & Carry stores in Russia and one in Croatia opened.

In 2002 METRO sold its entire stake in Primus Online to Beisheim Holding Schweiz AG. Overall in 2002 METRO opened 61 stores — 53 of which were Metro Cash & Carry outlets — including new stores in China, Bulgaria, and Russia (one each), and Vietnam (two outlets). In 2003 the company opened its first store in St. Petersburg (its fourth in Russia). In July, a third Metro Cash and Carry store opened in Vietnam. The German retailer opened a global sourcing headquarters in Hong Kong in September that covers all markets outside the European Union.

As part of its international expansion plan, in October 2003 METRO opened the first of two cash and carry distribution centers in Bangalore, India. In December 2003, METRO sold its 49% stake in Divaco in a buyout led by Divaco's management. Divaco was originally founded together with financial investors as a joint venture with the objective of optimally divesting non-core METRO Group activities.

Gunther Hulse stepped down as chairman of METRO's supervisory board for personal reasons in June 2004. Hulse was succeeded by Theo Siegert, a member of the management board of Franz Haniel & Cie, a German wholesale drug distribution company. The German retailer added two new nations to its roster in 2004: Russia and Moldova.

In 2005 the company added more than 100 new stores and completed the initial public offering of its Praktiker home improvement chain. Following the IPO Metro retained a 40% stake in its former subsidiary. It sold the remainder of its shares, less 5%, in April 2006.

In February 2006 Theo Siegert stepped down as chairman of the supervisory board and was succeeded by Eckhard Cordes.

EXECUTIVES

Chairman: Eckhard Cordes, age 56
Vice Chairman: Klaus Bruns
Chairman and CEO, Management Board:
Hans-Joachim Körber, age 60
CFO: Thomas Unger, age 46
**Director of Purchasing, Imports, Advertising, and
Catering:** Stefan Feuerstein
EVP, Human Resources and CIO: Zygmunt Meirdorf,
age 54
Managing Director and Country Manager, India:
Harsh Bahadur
General Director, Metro Cash and Carry, Russia:
Andrea F. Martinelli
General Director, Metro Cash and Carry, Vietnam:
James Scott
COO, Asia-Pacific: Heinrich Birr
**Manager, Procurement, Logistics, Advertising, and
Dinea:** Franz Muller, age 45
Head of Quality Assurance: Hans-Jürgen Matern
Auditors: Fasselt-Mette & Partner GmbH

LOCATIONS

HQ: METRO AG
Schlüterstrasse 1, 40235 Düsseldorf, Germany
Phone: +49-211-6886-0   **Fax:** +49-211-6886-2178
Web: www.metro.de

METRO AG operates more than 2,100 stores in 30
countries, primarily in Europe, but also in China, India,
Japan, Moldova, Morocco, Russia, Turkey, Ukraine, and
Vietnam.

2005 Sales

	% of total
Germany	47
Rest of Western Europe	32
Eastern Europe	19
Africa & Asia	2
Total	**100**

PRODUCTS/OPERATIONS

2005 Sales

	% of total
Cash & carry	50
Consumer electronics	24
Food retail	18
Department stores	6
Other	2
Total	**100**

Selected Operations

Retail
Makro
Metro Cash & Carry (wholesale stores)
Food
Extra (supermarkets)
Real (hypermarkets)
Nonfood Specialty Stores
Media Markt (consumer electronics)
Saturn (consumer electronics)
Department Store
Galeria Kaufhof

Other Operations

Dinea-Gastronomie (restaurants/catering)
METRO MGE Einkauf (purchasing)
METRO MGI Informatik (IT services)
METRO Real Estate Management (construction services)
METRO Werbegesellschaft (advertising)
METRO Online AG (Internet retailer)
MGB METRO Buying Group Hong Kong Ltd.
(purchasing, Asia and Non-European Union countries)

COMPETITORS

ALDI	Lidl & Schwarz Stiftung
AVA AG	Maxeda
Carrefour	REWE-Zentral
Casino Guichard	Royal Ahold
Edeka Zentrale	Tengelmann
Karstadt	Wal-Mart

HISTORICAL FINANCIALS

Company Type: Public

Income Statement

FYE: December 31

	REVENUE ($ mil.)	NET INCOME ($ mil.)	NET PROFIT MARGIN	EMPLOYEES
12/05	65,992	769	1.2%	246,875
12/04	76,942	1,128	1.5%	261,438
12/03	67,272	623	0.9%	252,037
12/02	54,004	464	0.9%	235,283
12/01	43,867	296	0.7%	230,848
Annual Growth	**10.7%**	**27.0%**	**—**	**1.7%**

Net Income History

German: MEO

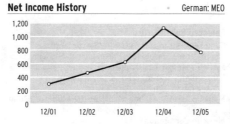

Michelin

The Michelin Man (whose name, by the way, is
Bibendum) produces more than 190 million tires
a year — pity the Michelin Woman. Compagnie
Générale des Établissements Michelin sells about
36,000 products, including tires, wheels, and
inner tubes used on passenger cars and trucks,
aircraft, bicycles, and agricultural vehicles. Included in Michelin's stable of tires are brands recognized all over the world (BF Goodrich and
Uniroyal), as well as more regional lines (Kleber
in Europe and Warrior in China). Other company
products include travel publications such as road
maps and travel guides. A vertically integrated
corporation, Michelin owns rubber plantations
and factories around the globe.

Michelin is banking on Asia — a region that
accounts for nearly 30% of the global tire market. India's truck market has grown to half the
size of Europe's, and China is poised to surpass
Japan as the third-largest market for automobiles (behind the US and Europe). China also
boasts nearly a 30% share of the global truck
tire market. Other emerging markets include
Eastern Europe, South America, and Russia.

Despite high materials costs, the company is
also doing well in the developed markets of
North America, Europe, and Japan by focusing
on high-margin specialty tires such as high performance, winter, and 4x4 tires. In these markets
Michelin has experienced double-digit growth
— margins that outperform market norms.

Co-Managing Partner Edouard Michelin,
youngest son of patriarch François Michelin and

the fourth generation of Michelins in the business, was killed in a boating accident in May
2006. Edouard's father, along with partner René
Zingraff, control the company.

The company's other Co-Managing partner,
Michel Rollier, now leads Michelin.

HISTORY

After toying with making rubber balls,
Edouard Daubrée and Aristide Barbier formed a
partnership in Clermont-Ferrand, France, in
1863 and entered the rubber business in earnest.
Both men soon died, but Barbier in-law André
Michelin, a successful businessman, took over
the company in 1886. André recruited his
brother, Edouard, a Parisian artist, to run the
company, and in 1889 it was renamed Compagnie Générale des Établissements Michelin.

That year Edouard found that air-filled tires
made bicycling more comfortable. But pneumatic tires were experimental and, because they
were glued to the rims, required hours to
change. In 1891 Edouard made a detachable bicycle tire that took only 15 minutes to change.

The Michelins promoted their tires by per-
suading cyclists to use them in long-distance
races where punctures were likely. They demonstrated the applicability of such tires for cars in
an auto race in 1895. In 1898 André commented
that a stack of tires would look like a man if it
had arms, a notion that led to the creation of
Bibendum, the Michelin Man. André launched
the *Michelin Guide* for auto tourists in 1900.

Expansion followed as Michelin opened a
London office (1905) and began production in
Italy (1906) and the US (in New Jersey in 1908).
Innovations included detachable rims and spare
tires (1906), tubeless tires (1930), treads (1934),
and modern low-profile tires (1937). During
the Depression, Michelin closed its US plant
and accepted a stake in Citroën, later converted
into a minority stake in Peugeot, in lieu of payment for tires.

Michelin patented radial tires in 1946. Expansion was largely confined to Europe in the 1950s
but, thanks to radials, increased worldwide in
the 1960s. Sears began selling Michelin radials
in 1966. Radials took hold during the 1970s, and
Michelin returned to manufacturing in the US,
opening a plant in South Carolina in 1975.

Expanding aggressively (Michelin opened or
bought a plant every nine months from 1960 to
1990), the company went into the red when economic conditions dipped in the early 1980s and
in 1990 and 1991. The company's $1.5 billion pur-
chase of Uniroyal Goodrich in 1990 contributed
to the latter losses but improved Michelin's position in the US, the world's largest auto market.

In response to the losses, Michelin attacked its
bloated infrastructure and reinvented itself along
nine product lines (according to tire/vehicle type
plus travel, suspension, and primary product
manufacturing). It also consolidated facilities
and cut about 30,000 jobs. The company continued to focus on R&D, bringing out new high-
performance tires such as its "green" tire
designed to help cars save fuel.

Michelin bought a majority interest in a Polish tire maker in 1995, and the next year it
bought 90% of Taurus, a Hungarian firm that
produces most of that country's rubber. Michelin joined German competitor Continental in
1996 to make private-label tires for independent
distributors. The next year Michelin introduced
a run-flat tire — capable of traveling 50 miles

after a puncture — for the automotive aftermarket. The company acquired Icollantas, a Colombian tire group with two factories in Bogotá and Cali, in 1998.

After leading the company for more than 40 years, patriarch François Michelin stepped down in 1999, leaving his youngest son, Edouard, in charge. Almost immediately, Edouard announced a restructuring that would cut 7,500 jobs in Europe, including almost 2,000 in France. The company benefited somewhat from Firestone's recall woes in 2000, but Michelin still faced rising material costs and difficult market conditions.

The European Commission fined Michelin nearly $20 million in 2001, claiming the company engaged in anticompetitive behavior by abusing its dominant position in Europe. In 2003 Michelin and TRW Automotive created EnTire Solutions, a joint venture, to develop a tire pressure monitoring system. Michelin announced a licensing agreement in 2004 for Toyo Tire to make, sell, and promote PAX system tires (run-flat tires).

EXECUTIVES

Chairman of the Supervisory Board:
Eric Bourdais de Charbonnière, age 67
Managing Partner: Michel Rollier, age 62
Member of the Group Executive Council, Tourist Services, ViaMichelin, Supply Chain, and IT Systems: Michel Caron
Member of the Group Executive Council, Passenger Car and Light Truck, Competition: Thierry Coudurier
Member of the Group Executive Council, Asia: Hervé Coyco
Member of the Group Executive Council, Europe, Euromaster, Head of Marketing and Sales Performance: Eric de Cromières
Member of the Group Executive Council, North America, TCI: Jim Micali
Member of the Group Executive Council, Technology Center and Industrial Performance: Didier Miraton
Member of the Group Executive Council, Personnel Department, Environment and Prevention: Jean Moreau
Member of the Group Executive Council, Truck, Africa/Middle-East: Pete Selleck
Member of the Group Executive Council, Finance Department, Legal Services, and Plans and Results; CFO: Jean-Dominique Senard
Member of the Group Executive Council, Agricultural, Aircraft, 2-Wheel, Earthmover, Wheels, Components, South America, Purchasing: Bernard Vasdeboncoeur
CEO, Euromaster: Eric Van Geel
Secretary of the Group Executive Council: Patrick Oliva
Investor Relations: Eric Le Corre
Auditors: PricewaterhouseCoopers Audit

LOCATIONS

HQ: Compagnie Générale des Établissements Michelin
23, place des Carmes-Déchaux,
63040 Clermont-Ferrand, France
Phone: +33-4-73-32-20-00   **Fax:** +33-45-66-15-53
US HQ: 1 Parkway South, Greenville, SC 29615
US Phone: 864-458-5000   **US Fax:** 864-458-6359
Web: www.michelin.com

Michelin has more than 70 manufacturing facilities in 19 countries, six rubber plantations in Brazil and Nigeria, and offices in more than 170 countries.

2005 Sales

	$ mil.	% of total
Europe	9,076.5	49
North America	6,558.6	36
Other regions	2,828.1	15
Total	**18,463.2**	**100**

PRODUCTS/OPERATIONS

2005 Sales

	$ mil.	% of total
Passenger car & light truck tires	10,209.8	55
Truck tires	6,006.8	33
Other	2,246.6	12
Total	**18,463.2**	**100**

Selected Products and Services

Agricultural tires
Aircraft tires
Earthmover tires
Passenger car and light-truck tires
Suspension systems
Travel publications
Truck tires
Two-wheel tires

Selected Brands

BF Goodrich
Euromaster
Kleber
Michelin
Riken
Taurus
Uniroyal

Selected Subsidiaries

Compagnie Financière Michelin (Switzerland)
Manufacture Française des Pneumatiques Michelin
Michelin Aircraft Tire Company (US)
Michelin Americas Research & Development Corporation (US)
Michelin Asia-Pacific Import-Export (HK) Limited (Hong Kong)
Michelin Corporation (US)
Michelin North America, Inc. (US)
Michelin Gummi Compagni A/S (Denmark)

COMPETITORS

Avalon Travel Publishing
Bandag
Bridgestone
Continental AG
Cooper Tire & Rubber
Fieldens
Goodyear
Kumho Tire
Sime Darby
Sumitomo Rubber
Toyo Tire & Rubber
Vredestein
Watts Industrial Tyres
Yokohama Rubber

HISTORICAL FINANCIALS

Company Type: Public

Income Statement

FYE: December 31

	REVENUE ($ mil.)	NET INCOME ($ mil.)	NET PROFIT MARGIN	EMPLOYEES
12/05	18,463	—	—	127,319
12/04	21,400	—	—	126,474
12/03	19,292	—	—	127,210
12/02	16,398	—	—	126,285
12/01	13,973	—	—	127,467
Annual Growth	**7.2%**	**—**	**(0.0%)**	

Revenue History

Euronext Paris: ML

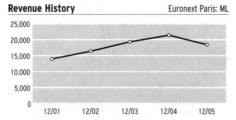

Millea Holdings

Thoroughly modern Millea Holdings showed that even though Tokio Marine and Fire Insurance was old it could learn new tricks. Japan's oldest and largest property/casualty insurance company, Tokio Marine merged with Nichido Fire and Marine to create Tokio Marine & Nichido Fire Insurance. The merger created the largest insurance sales network in Japan, and operates as a subsidiary of Millea Holdings. Through Tokio Marine & Nichido and other subsidiaries, Millea Holdings provides marine, fire, property/casualty, personal accident, and auto insurance. The company also offers asset management and pensions plans. Millea Holdings is allied with the Mitsubishi industrial group.

Millea has found that niches can be helpful. It has expanded its lines to include such products as Lady Guard, insurance for women that covers the costs of damage caused by stalkers, and Diabetes Casualty Insurance to cover diabetes-related care and prevention. Nonetheless, auto insurance, the company's main line of business, still accounts for more than half of its property and casualty insurance sales.

Acquisitions are another part of the company's strategy for growth. In April 2006 the company announced an agreement to acquire Asia General Holding (AGH) and its life insurance companies The Asia Insurance Company and The Asia Life Assurance Society Limited which operate in Singapore and Malaysia. The acquisition is a leisurely one: Tokio Marine & Nichido Fire is steadily acquiring chunks of AGH, while that company sheds its non-insurance related assets.

Its 2005 acquisition of Real Seguros S.A. allowed the company to bring its life insurance products to Brazil.

Outside of insurance, the company has determined that the elderly and infirm can benefit from its services. Tokio Marine & Nichido Samuel Co. offers both institutional and in-home nursing care services.

HISTORY

After the US forced Japan to open to trade in 1854, Western marine insurers began operating there. In 1878 Japan's government organized backers for a Japanese marine insurance firm. Tokio Marine and Fire was founded the next year.

Tokio grew quickly, insuring trading companies like Mitsubishi and Mitsui; it soon had offices in London, Paris, and New York. Increased competition in the 1890s forced it to curtail its foreign operations and begin using brokers in most other countries.

Victory in the Russo-Japanese War of 1904-05 buoyed the country, but the economy slowed as it demobilized. Businesses responded by forming cooperative groups known as *zaibatsu*. Tokio Marine and Fire was allied with the Mitsubishi group.

Before WWI, Tokio expanded by adding fire, personal accident, theft, and auto insurance, and it continued to buy foreign sales brokers. Japan's insurance industry consolidated in the 1920s, and the company bought up smaller competitors. The 1923 Tokyo earthquake hit the industry hard, but Tokio's new fire insurance operations had little exposure.

Most of Tokio Marine's foreign operations were seized during WWII. In 1944 Tokio merged with Mitsubishi Marine Insurance and Meiji Fire Insurance. Business grew in WWII, but wartime destruction left Tokio with nothing to insure and no money to pay claims.

After the war Tokio slowly recovered and resumed overseas operations. Although the US had dismantled the *zaibatsu* during occupation, Tokio Marine allied once again with Mitsubishi when Japan's government rebuilt most of the old groups as *keiretsu*.

During the 1950s and 1960s, the company grew its personal lines, adding homeowners coverage. Domestic business slowed during the 1970s and 1980s, and Tokio boosted operations overseas. It added commercial property/casualty insurer Houston General Insurance (a US company sold in 1997), Tokio Reinsurance, and interests in insurance and investment management firms.

In the 1980s the firm invested heavily in real estate through *jusen* (mortgage companies). Japan's overheated real estate market collapsed in the early 1990s, dumping masses of nonperforming assets on *jusen* and their investors (the country's major banks and insurers, including Tokio Marine).

Deregulation began in 1996, and economic recession soon followed. In 1998 Tokio Marine joined other members of the Mitsubishi group, including Bank of Tokyo-Mitsubishi and Meiji Life Insurance, to form investment banking, pension, and trust joint ventures. The firm also formed its own investment trust and allied with such foreign financial companies as BANK ONE and United Asset Management to develop new investment products. Brokerage Charles Schwab Tokio Marine Securities, a joint venture, was launched in 1999. That year Tokio consolidated its foreign reinsurance operations into Tokio Marine Global Re in Dublin, Ireland, and kicked off a business push that included reorganizing its agent force and planning for online sales.

Millea Holdings was created in 2002 as the holding company for the merger between Tokio Marine and Nichido Fire and Marine. The two were combined and renamed Tokio Marine & Nichido Fire Insurance, a subsidiary of Millea Holdings. During 2005 Millea negotiated the acquisition of Nisshin Fire and Marine Insurance Company. By early 2006 the acquisition was complete and Nisshin Fire was a separately operated subsidiary.

EXECUTIVES

President and Board Member; President, Tokio Marine & Nichido: Kunio Ishihara, age 63
Senior Managing Director and Board Member: Toshiro Yagi, age 58
Managing Director and Board Member: Tomohiro Kotani, age 62
President, Tokio Marine & Nichido Life; Board Member: Tomochika Iwashita, age 60
EVP, Tokio Marine & Nichido; Board Member: Morio Ishii, age 59
Managing Director, Tokio Marine & Nichido; Board Member: Hiroshi Amemiya, age 56
President, Nisshin Fire; Board Member: Hiroshi Miyajima, age 56
Managing Director, Tokio Marine & Nichido; Board Member: Takaaki Tamai, age 56
General Manager of Corporate Legal and Risk Management Department: Tetsuya Unno
Group Leader, Corporate Communications and Investor Relations, Corporate Planning Department: Toshihiko Aizawa
Corporate Communications and Investor Relations: Mitsuru Muraki
Auditors: ChuoAoyama PricewaterhouseCoopers

LOCATIONS

HQ: Millea Holdings, Inc.
Tokyo Kaijo Nichido Building Shinkan 9F, 1-2-1 Marunouchi, Chiyoda-ku, Tokyo 100-0005, Japan
Phone: +81-3-6212-3333   **Fax:** +81-3-6212-3711
Web: www.millea.co.jp

Millea Holdings has operations in about 30 countries.

PRODUCTS/OPERATIONS

2006 Premiums

	% of total
Voluntary auto	44
Fire & allied lines	16
Compulsory auto	15
Personal accident	8
Marine — hull, cargo & transit	5
Other	12
Total	**100**

Selected Subsidiaries

Real Seguros S.A. (Brazil)
The Tokio Marine and Fire Insurance Company (Hong Kong) Limited
The Tokio Marine and Fire Insurance Company (Singapore) Pte. Ltd
Tokio Marine Asset Management Company, Limited
Tokio Marine Financial Solutions Ltd. (Cayman Islands)
Tokio Marine & Nichido Life Insurance Co., Ltd.
Tokio Millennium Re (Bermuda)

COMPETITORS

AIG
Aioi
Allianz
Aviva
HCC Insurance
ING
Mitsui Sumitomo Insurance
Nippon Life Insurance
Nipponkoa
Sompo Japan Insurance

HISTORICAL FINANCIALS

Company Type: Public

Income Statement

FYE: March 31

	ASSETS ($ mil.)	NET INCOME ($ mil.)	INCOME AS % OF ASSETS	EMPLOYEES
3/06	131,887	1,334	1.0%	19,761
3/05	119,923	855	0.7%	18,910
3/04	115,904	977	0.8%	19,779
3/03	90,415	3,138	3.5%	21,235
3/02	63,761	1,212	1.9%	6,700
Annual Growth	19.9%	2.4%	—	31.0%

2006 Year-End Financials

Equity as % of assets: 28.6%   Long-term debt ($ mil.): 9,712
Return on assets: 1.1%   Sales ($ mil.): 22,403
Return on equity: 3.8%

Net Income History

NASDAQ (GS): MLEA

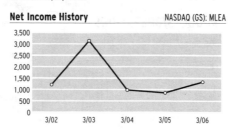

Mitsubishi

In Japanese *mitsubishi* means "three diamonds," but Mitsubishi Corporation claims six jewels. The *sogo shosha*, or trading company, operates through six main business groups: living essentials (agricultural products, food and beverages, textiles, and construction materials); metals (ferrous and nonferrous); machinery (power generation equipment, electrical systems, automobile parts); energy (liquefied natural gas, crude oil); chemicals (petrochemicals, fertilizers, plastics); and a new business initiatives unit, which offers software, logistics, telecommunications, and other services.

Mitsubishi Corporation is part of the Mitsubishi *keiretsu*, a network of affiliated companies that has no official status as a group, but within which there is some cross-ownership and considerable business activity. Other affiliates include Mitsubishi Heavy Industries, The Bank of Tokyo-Mitsubishi, Mitsubishi Electric, Mitsubishi Motors, and Nikon.

Along with the rest of the Mitsubishi companies, Mitsubishi Corporortion has been hurt in recent years by Japan's persistent economic slump. The company restructured and reduced its workforce; it has divided the operations of its former information technology and electronics business between two other groups. It plans to focus on its energy and natural resources, independent power production, and food distribution businesses.

In February 2004 the company announced plans to form a food-distribution joint venture with five Japanese food wholesalers, comprising national wholesaler Meidi-ya and four regional companies. The joint venture, called Alliance Network, is one of Japan's largest food wholesalers. Mitsubishi has a 51% stake in Alliance Network. Later in 2004 Mitsubishi acquired the food, beverage additive, and pharmaceutical active and excipient businesses of Ashland Distribution.

In 2006 Mitsubishi announced plans to acquire more than 40% of Isuzu from General Motors. Later that year Mitsubishi announced plans to buy the Avon Automotive subsidiary of Avon Rubber in a deal worth $120 million.

HISTORY

Yataro Iwasaki's close ties to the Japanese government (along with subsidies and monopoly rights) ensured the success of his shipping and trading company, Mitsubishi. Founded in 1870, Mitsubishi diversified into mining (1873), banking (1885), and shipbuilding (1887); it began to withdraw from shipping in the 1880s. During the next decade it invested in Japanese railroads and property.

In 1918 the Mitsubishi *zaibatsu* (conglomerate) spun off its central management arm, Mitsubishi Trading (the forerunner of Mitsubishi Corporation). By WWII the group was a huge amalgam of divisions and public companies. During the war it made warplanes, ships, explosives, and beer.

The *zaibatsu* were dissolved by US occupation forces, and Mitsubishi was split into 139 entities. After the occupation, the Japanese government encouraged many of the former business groups to reunite around the old *zaibatsu* banks. In 1954 Mitsubishi Trading became the leader of the Mitsubishi Group and established Mitsubishi International (US), which became a leading exporter of US goods.

The 1964 merger of three Mitsubishi companies created Mitsubishi Heavy Industries, a top Japanese maker of ships, aircraft, plants, and heavy machinery. Mitsubishi Kasei, separated from Asahi Glass and Mitsubishi Rayon by a US fiat, became Japan's #1 chemical concern. Mitsubishi Electric emerged as one of the country's leading electrical equipment and electronics manufacturers. In 1971 Chrysler invested in Mitsubishi Motors, which began making cars for the US automaker. That year Mitsubishi Trading was renamed Mitsubishi Corp.

Through the 1980s Japan seemed economically invincible. Then its "bubble economy" burst. The group fell behind in electronics and autos in the US, consumer demand dried up at home, and Mitsubishi Bank was left with a heavy burden of bad loans. Group members, which traditionally provided materials, supplies, and sales outlets for each other, began loosening old *keiretsu* ties during Japan's recession of the 1990s.

In 1993 Chrysler sold its stock in Mitsubishi Motors, and two years later the companies severed production ties. This loss and declining demand in the US for Mitsubishi cars hurt auto sales.

Mitsubishi Bank merged with Bank of Tokyo in 1996 to form the biggest bank in the world, The Bank of Tokyo-Mitsubishi (BTM). In 1997 several Mitsubishi companies admitted paying off a corporate racketeer, setting off a wave of executive resignations.

By 1999 BTM had tumbled from the top spot and was unable to keep the money freely flowing to fellow Mitsubishi members.

Hit hard by the Asian economic crisis, all the struggling Mitsubishi companies had to look outside of the *keiretsu* for help. In 1999 Mitsubishi Motors found a foreign partner, Volvo, for its truck making operations. Mitsubishi Oil merged with an outsider, Nippon Oil, to form Nippon Mitsubishi Oil (later renamed Nippon Oil). In 2000 DaimlerChrysler acquired a controlling stake in Mitsubishi Motors for $2.1 billion.

Executives at Mitsubishi Motors were charged in 2001 after they allegedly kept the lid on thousands of reported defects in Mitsubishi cars instead of issuing recalls. Stung by this and the after-effects of scandals from the previous decade, Mitsubishi unveiled a new corporate philosophy as part of a strategy to revive the group's reputation.

In 2003 Mitsubishi disbanded its information technology and electronics business unit. The unit's operations were divided between the new business and machinery groups. In 2004 the company formed an alliance with GE Yokogawa Medical Systems (GEYMS) to provide GEYMS with help in developing its presence in the Japanese diagnostic imaging market.

EXECUTIVES

Chairman: Mikio Sasaki
President, CEO, Chief Innovation Officer, Internal Audit, and Board Member: Yorihiko Kojima
SEVP and Board Member; Assistant to the President, Resources and Energy Officer, Chief Compliance Officer, and CIO: Yukio Masuda
SEVP and Board Member; Regional CEO, Kansai Block, and General Manager, Kansai Branch: Yukio Ueno
SEVP and Board Member; Chief Information Security Officer and Chief Regional Officer: Hidetoshi Kamezaki
SEVP and Board Member; Group CEO, Chemicals and Regional Officer, China: Takeru Ishibashi
EVP and Board Member; Group CEO, Living Essentials: Takeshi Inoue
EVP and Board Member; Group CEO, Machinery: Masao Miyamoto
EVP; Group COO, Machinery Group: Hajime Katsumura
EVP; Chief Representative China, President Mitsubishi Corporation (China) Investment Co., General Manager Bejing Branch: Katsutoshi Takeda
EVP and Board Member; Group CEO, Energy Business Group: Hisanori Yoshimura
EVP, CFO, and Board Member: Ichiro Mizuno
EVP and Board Member; Group CEO, New Business Initiative: Haruo Matsumoto
EVP and Board Member; Regional CEO, Chubu Block and General Manager, Nagoya Branch: Yoshikuni Kanai
EVP and Board Member; Group CEO, Metals Group: Mutsumi Kotsuka
EVP; Group COO, Energy Business Group: Masatoshi Nishizawa
EVP; Group COO, Foods (Products), Living Essentials Group: Tsunao Kijima
SVP; Regional CEO, North America, and President, Mitsubishi International: Ryoichi Ueda
SVP and Treasurer: Hideshi Takeuchi
SVP; Corporate Functional Officer, Human Resources, Administration Corporate Secretariat, and Legal: Tsuneo Iyobe
Auditors: Deloitte Touche Tohmatsu

LOCATIONS

HQ: Mitsubishi Corporation
(Mitsubishi Shoji Kabushiki Kaisha)
6-3, Marunouchi 2-chome, Chiyoda-ku,
Tokyo 100-8086, Japan
Phone: +81-3-3210-2121   **Fax:** +81-3-3210-8583
US HQ: 655 3rd Ave., New York, NY 10017
US Phone: 212-605-2000   **US Fax:** 212-605-2486
Web: www.mitsubishi.co.jp

In addition to more than 200 sites in Japan, Mitsubishi Corporation operates in 80 other countries around the world.

2006 Sales

	% of total
Japan	82
US	5
Thailand	3
Other countries	10
Total	**100**

PRODUCTS/OPERATIONS

2006 Sales

	% of total
Living Essentials	25
Energy	24
Metals	22
Machinery	18
Chemicals	10
New Business Initiative	1
Total	**100**

Selected Products and Services

Living Essentials
  Apparel
  Canned foods
  Ceramic materials
  Cigarettes
  Coffee beans, coffee and beverages
  Confections and snacks
  Contract food services
  Dairy foods and processed foods
  Fabrics
  Feedstuffs
  Fresh and frozen foods
  Grains and agricultural products
  Marine products
  Meat and livestock
  Mineral water
  Oils and fats
  Photosensitized materials
  Pulp, paper, and packaging materials
  Soft drinks
  Sweeteners
  Textiles for industrial use
  Textile raw materials
  Tires
  Wood, wood products, and construction materials
Energy
  Carbon materials and products
  Crude oil
  LNG
  LPG
  Orimulsion
  Petroleum products
Metals
  Bullion and metals futures
  Fabricated steel structures
  Metallurgical and thermal coal
  Nonferrous metals
  Nonferrous metal products
  Nuclear fuel and components
  Precious metals
  Raw materials for steel
  Semifinished products
  Steel materials
  Specialty steel
Machinery
  Automobiles
  Commercial aviation
  Defense systems and equipment
  Electronics products
  Industrial, agricultural, construction, and other general machinery
  Plant and machinery for power generation, electricity, oil/gas/chemicals, steel/cement, and environmental protection
  Project development and construction
  Satellite communications
  Ships
  Space systems
  Transportation systems
Chemicals
  Fertilizers
  Fine and specialty chemicals
  Inorganic chemicals
  Petrochemicals
  Plastics
New Business Initiative
  Commerce services
  Consumer services
  Financial services
  Information technology services
  Logistics
  Telecommunications systems and services

COMPETITORS

ITOCHU
Marubeni
Mitsui
Samsung Group
Sime Darby
Sumitomo
TOMEN

HISTORICAL FINANCIALS

Company Type: Public

Income Statement

FYE: March 31

	REVENUE ($ mil.)	NET INCOME ($ mil.)	NET PROFIT MARGIN	EMPLOYEES
3/06	41,048	—	—	53,738
3/05	38,548	—	—	51,381
3/04	15,094	—	—	49,219
3/03	12,273	—	—	47,370
3/02	9,737	—	—	44,034
Annual Growth	43.3%	—	—	5.1%

Revenue History

Pink Sheets: MSBHY

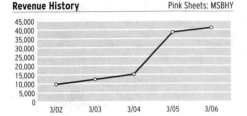

Mitsubishi UFJ Financial Group

Ladies and gentlemen, the big banks are back. Mitsubishi Tokyo Financial Group and UFJ Holdings merged in a 2005 mega deal, resulting in Mitsubishi UFJ Financial Group (MUFG) and giving industry giants HSBC and Citigroup a run for their money. One of the world's biggest banks, the group provides deposit, lending, leasing, investment advice, and trust services in Japan and more than 40 other countries. MUFG is a member of the Mitsubishi group, a mélange of about 30 different companies — active in manufacturing, transportation, insurance, and other industries — that shared common ownership before World War II, but have been operated autonomously since.

MUFG's main operating subsidiaries include Bank of Tokyo-Mitsubishi UFJ, Mitsubishi UFJ Securities, and Mitsubishi UFJ Trust and Banking; it also owns some 60% of UnionBanCal, parent to Union Bank of California. With the formative merger finally complete, the group hopes the new transaction ushers in a new era of economic vitality for Japan (the country's banks have been mired in bad credit and debt problems over the years). The creation of Mitsubishi UFJ Financial Group establishes the number of Japan's major banking groups at three; MUFG is at the top of the heap in Japan, ahead of Mizuho Financial Group and Sumitomo Mitsui Financial Group. In 2006 the company announced it will enter the investment banking fray in the US. It is investing some $100 million in Perella Weinberg Partners, a boutique investment bank founded by former Morgan Stanley vice chairman Joseph Perella and Peter Weinberg, a former Goldman Sachs executive.

HISTORY

Mitsubishi Bank emerged from the exchange office of the original Mitsubishi *zaibatsu* (industrial group) in 1885. It evolved into a full-service bank by 1895 and became independent in 1919, though its primary customers were Mitsubishi group companies. The bank survived WWII, but a US fiat dismantled the *zaibatsu* after the war. Mitsubishi Bank reopened as Chiyoda Bank in 1948. After reopening offices in London and New York, the bank readopted the Mitsubishi name.

In the 1950s Mitsubishi Bank became the lead lender for the reconstituted Mitsubishi group (*keiretsu*). In the 1960s it followed its Mitsubishi partners overseas, helping finance Japan's growing international trade. In 1972 it acquired the Bank of California and began doing more business outside the group.

Japan's overinflated real estate market of the 1980s devastated many of the country's banks, including Nippon Trust Bank Ltd., of which Mitsubishi owned 5%. Japan's Ministry of Finance (MoF) urged Mitsubishi to bail Nippon out; as a reward for raising its stake in Nippon to 69% and assuming a mountain of unrecoverable loans, the MoF allowed Mitsubishi to begin issuing debt before other Japanese banks. In 1995 Mitsubishi Bank and Bank of Tokyo agreed to merge.

Bank of Tokyo (BOT) was established in 1880 as the Yokohama Specie Bank; the Iwasaki family, founders of the Mitsubishi group, served on its board. With links to the Imperial family, the bank was heavily influenced by government policy. With Japan isolated after the Sino-Japanese War, its international operations suffered greatly even before WWII. Completely dismantled after WWII, the bank was re-established in 1946 as the Bank of Tokyo, a commercial city bank bereft of its foreign exchange business. During the 1950s the government restored it as a foreign exchange specialist, but regulations limited its domestic business.

BOT evolved into an investment bank in the 1970s; its reputation as the leading foreign exchange bank brought in international clients and successful derivatives trading and overseas banking. By the time BOT and Mitsubishi Bank agreed to merge, BOT had 363 foreign offices (only 37 in Japan) with more foreign than Japanese employees.

The two banks merged in 1996 to form The Bank of Tokyo-Mitsubishi (BTM); Mitsubishi was the surviving entity. Their California banks merged to create Union Bank of California (UnionBanCal). The next year BTM reorganized its operations but had problems assimilating its disparate corporate cultures.

In 1998 Japanese banking regulators doled out nearly $240 billion to the industry to prop up failing banks and to strengthen healthier ones. Also that year BTM was fined for bribing MoF officials with entertainment gifts and posted a huge loss after writing off $8.4 billion in bad debt. Losses continued in 1999, and the bank responded by reorganizing operationally, cutting jobs and offices, and selling stock in UnionBanCal.

In 2000 BTM announced plans to form a financial group with Mitsubishi Trust Bank and Nippon Trust Bank. The following year the three banks unified and formed Mitsubishi Tokyo Financial Group. Before rolling into Mitsubishi Trust Financial Group, BTM paid back the money showered upon it by the Japanese government in 1998.

In 2004 MTFG introduced a new organizational structure that focuses on its three core markets — retail, corporate, and trust asset businesses. The company hopes to unify business within each division and to improve decision-making company-wide. The group also introduced a new executive officer system with the idea of separating company oversight and business execution. A mechanism for credit risk control was also added.

It was all to change in October 2005, however. During this time, Mitsubishi Tokyo Financial Group merged with UFJ Holdings, emerging (at that time) as the world's largest bank by assets. As a result of the merger, the group was renamed Mitsubishi UFJ Financial Group (MUFG).

EXECUTIVES

Chairman; Deputy Chairman, Bank of Tokyo-Mitsubishi UFJ: Ryosuke Tamakoshi
Deputy Chairman and Chief Audit Officer; President, Mitsubishi UFJ Trust and Banking: Haruya Uehara
President, CEO, and Director; President, Bank of Tokyo-Mitsubishi UFJ: Nobuo Kuroyanagi
Deputy President and Director; Deputy President, Bank of Tokyo-Mitsubishi UFJ: Katsunori Nagayasu, age 58
Senior Managing Director and CFO: Hajime Sugizaki
Senior Managing Director and Chief Risk Management Officer: Yoshihiro Watanabe
Senior Managing Director and Chief Planning Officer: Toshihide Mizuno
Corporate Auditor: Setsuo Uno, age 64
Corporate Auditor: Haruo Matsuki
Corporate Auditor: Takeo Imai, age 64
Corporate Auditor, Mitsubishi UFJ Financial Group and Bank of Tokyo-Mitsubishi UFJ: Tsutomu Takasuka
Corporate Auditor: Kunie Okamoto, age 62
Managing Officer: Takamune Okihara
Managing Officer: Toshio Goto
Managing Officer and General Manager, Retail Business Planning; Managing Director, Bank of Tokyo-Mitsubishi UFJ: Tetsuya Wada
General Manager, Public Relations: Hideaki Fujizuka
Auditors: Deloitte Touche Tohmatsu

LOCATIONS

HQ: Mitsubishi UFJ Financial Group, Inc.
7-1 Marunouchi 2-chome, Chiyoda-ku,
Tokyo 100-8330, Japan
Phone: +81-3-3240-8111   **Fax:** +81-3-3240-8203
Web: www.mufg.jp

2006 Sales

	% of total
Domestic	61
Foreign	
US	21
Europe	10
Asia/Oceania	2
Other areas	6
Total	**100**

PRODUCTS/OPERATIONS

2006 Sales

	% of total
Interest	
Loans, including fees	44
Investment securities	13
Deposits in other banks	4
Other	4
Fees & commissions	26
Other	9
Total	**100**

Selected Subsidiaries

Banco de Tokyo-Mitsubishi UFJ Brasil S/A (99%, Brazil)
Bank of Tokyo-Mitsubishi UFJ (Canada)
Bank of Tokyo-Mitsubishi UFJ (Holland) N.V. (Netherlands)
Bank of Tokyo-Mitsubishi UFJ (Luxembourg) S.A. (99.99%)
Bank of Tokyo-Mitsubishi UFJ (Malaysia) Berhad

Bank of Tokyo-Mitsubishi UFJ (Mexico) S.A.
Bank of Tokyo-Mitsubishi UFJ Trust Company (US)
The Bank of Tokyo-Mitsubishi UFJ, Ltd
BOT Lease Co., Ltd.(21%)
BTMU North America International, Inc. (US)
DC Card Co., Ltd. (45%)
Defined Contribution Plan Consulting of Japan Co., Ltd. (70%)
The Master Trust Bank of Japan, Ltd. (46%)
Mitsubishi UFJ Asset Management Co., Ltd.
Mitsubishi UFJ Factors Limited (76%)
Mitsubishi UFJ Home Loan Credit Co., Ltd. (99.99%)
Mitsubishi UFJ Research and Consulting Ltd. (69%)
Mitsubishi UFJ Securities (HK) Holdings, Limited (China)
Mitsubishi UFJ Securities (USA), Inc.
Mitsubishi UFJ Securities Co., Ltd. (63%)
Mitsubishi UFJ Securities International plc (UK)
Mitsubishi UFJ Trust & Banking Corporation (U.S.A.)
Mitsubishi UFJ Trust and Banking Corporation
Mitsubishi UFJ Trust International Limited (UK)
Mitsubishi UFJ Wealth Management Bank (Switzerland), Ltd.
MU Investments Co., Ltd.
MU Strategic Partner Co., Ltd.
NBL Co., Ltd. (90%)
PT U Finance Indonesia (95%)
The Senshu Bank, Ltd. (68%)
UFJ NICOS Co., Ltd. (69%)
Union Bank of California, N.A. (63%, US)
UnionBanCal Corporation (63%, US)

COMPETITORS

Aozora Bank
BNP Paribas Bangkok
Citigroup
HSBC Holdings
Ito-Yokado
Japan Post
Mitsui Trust
Mizuho Financial
Mizuho Trust & Banking Ltd
ORIX
Resona
Shinsei Bank
Sony
Sumitomo Mitsui

HISTORICAL FINANCIALS

Company Type: Public

Income Statement

FYE: March 31

	ASSETS ($ mil.)	NET INCOME ($ mil.)	INCOME AS % OF ASSETS	EMPLOYEES
3/06	1,582,865	3,090	0.2%	80,000
3/05	1,008,326	3,861	0.4%	43,900
3/04	985,160	7,811	0.8%	43,600
3/03	801,213	1,687	0.2%	44,500
Annual Growth	25.5%	22.3%	—	21.6%

2006 Year-End Financials

Equity as % of assets: 5.1%
Return on assets: 0.2%
Return on equity: 5.2%
Long-term debt ($ mil.): 151,605
Sales ($ mil.): 33,323

Net Income History

NYSE: MTU

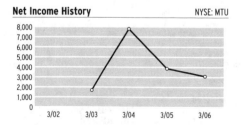

Mitsui & Co.

Part of a network of companies that was founded by a samurai centuries ago, Mitsui & Co. battles to make money. Mitsui & Co., a leading Japanese *sogo shosha* (general trading firm), has more than 700 subsidiaries in a wide range of industries. The company has reorganized its business units into eight main classifications: chemical; energy (liquefied natural gas); food and retail; logistics and financial markets; machinery and infrastructure; lifestyle, consumer service, electronics, and information (power plants, aircraft leasing, IT services); iron and steel products; and iron and steel ores and nonferrous metals. The Master Trust Bank of Japan holds a 10% stake in Mitsui.

Mitsui & Co. is part of Mitsui Group, one of Japan's largest *keiretsu* (companies loosely connected through cross-ownership). The company's largest revenue generators are its trading activities in the energy and chemical sectors. The company invested about $2.8 billion during 2005 and 2006 to expand its iron ore and core interests in Australia, acquire new non-ferrous metal interests, and expand its LNG and oil operations. Mitsui is also investing $950 million to strengthen and develop its Consumer Service, Foods and Retail, Lifestyle, and Motor Vehicle related business units.

In an effort to expand its metal products and minerals segment, Mitsui has created a joint venture company with Posco, named Posco Terminal, which is responsible for the transportation, storage, and distribution of coal, iron ore, and ferroalloy. The company has also acquired a 15% stake in Valepar, a holding company of Brazilian-based iron ore producer Companhia Vale do Rio Doce. In an effort to boost coal production, Mitsui plans to buy a stake in the Moranbah North coal mine in Australia.

The company is working to build its biotechnology and IT businesses. It has created TM Cell Research, a 35% owned biotechnology joint venture created with Toyobo. Mitsui has also developed five nanotechnology research institutes in an effort to capture a stake of the market in Japan. Its other activities include antibody research, DNA chips, DNA computing, DNA expression analysis, nucleic acid testing, and protein analysis research.

HISTORY

In the 17th century unemployed samurai (warrior nobleman) Sokubei Mitsui opened a sake and soy sauce brewery at the urging of his wife, Shuho. After parental encouragement, their youngest son, Hachirobei, went to Edo (now Tokyo) and opened a dry goods store in 1673. Breaking with Japanese retailing tradition, the store offered merchandise at fixed prices on a cash-and-carry basis.

Hachirobei in 1683 opened a currency exchange that evolved into Mitsui Bank. The bank became the Osaka government's official money changer in 1691 and was the first bank to offer money orders in Japan. Before his death in 1694, Hachirobei drafted a unique succession plan to hand down control of the company to every related family, not just the eldest son's side.

The shogun's government called upon Mitsui in the mid-1800s to help finance its war against rebels. The family hired Rizaemon Minomura, an outsider with influence in the government, to protect the company from increasing demands for money. Mitsui became the bank of the Meiji government after Minomura astutely switched support to the winning rebels. Government industrialization pushed Mitsui into textiles, paper goods, and machinery. Minomura emphasized foreign trade and banking, creating Mitsui Bussan (now Mitsui & Co.) and Mitsui Bank in 1876. In the late 1800s Mitsui Bussan profited from a Japanese military buildup, formed a shipping line to take on Mitsubishi's monopoly, and bought coal mines. The Mitsui family withdrew from Mitsui Bussan management in 1936, following attacks by right-wing terrorists who opposed its democratic leanings.

Mitsui prospered during the 1930s as Japan's military prepared for war. After the defeat, occupation forces disbanded Japan's *zaibatsu* industrial groups, slicing Mitsui into more than 200 separate entities. By 1950 more than two dozen leaders of the former Mitsui companies began gathering the Mitsui Group back together. Trading firm Mitsui & Co. was established in 1959. The oil crises of the 1970s stalled the oil-dependent Japanese economy, prompting Mitsui companies to expand operations overseas and move into industries such as technology and aluminum.

The mammoth Sakura Bank was formed in 1990 with the merger of Mitsui Bank and Taiyo Kobe Bank. Other major ventures were to follow: In 1992 Mitsui & Co. joined with Marathon and Royal Dutch Shell and others to search for oil and gas off Russia's Sakhalin Island; and Mitsui & Co. and other Japanese traders were enlisted by Oman in 1993 for a $9 billion liquefied natural gas transport venture. As cable TV emerged in Japan, Mitsui & Co. teamed up the next year with National Media Corp. to launch a home-shopping network.

In anticipation of deregulation in Japan's financial markets, four Mitsui Group firms' pension funds — Sakura Bank, Mitsui Marine & Fire Insurance, Mitsui Mutual Life Insurance, and Mitsui Trust and Banking — were linked in 1998. The next year Sakura Bank set aside old loyalties and agreed to merge with Sumitomo Bank, the Sumitomo *keiretsu's* main bank; the deal closed in 2001. The group's Mitsui Trust and Banking merged with Chuo Trust and Banking to form Chuo Mitsui Trust and Banking, part of Mitsui Trust Holdings.

Mitsui & Co. was implicated in bid-rigging and bribery scandals in 2002, and the company's chairman and CEO resigned. In 2003, the company moved into the German pesticide market by acquiring an 80% stake in Spiess-Urania Chemical, a subsidiary of Norddeutsche Affinerie. Later that year, it entered the biotechnology market by creating TM Cell Research, a 35% owned joint venture created with Toyobo. The company also entered the telecommunications market by acquiring a 30% stake in Shineedotcom from Shin Corp.

In 2003 Mitsui turned its focus back to the expansion of its current operations. It acquired a 15% stake in Valepar, a holding company of Brazilian-based iron ore producer Companhia Vale do Rio Doce. Mitsui and International Power completed the acquisition of the 1,200 MW gas-fired Saltend Power plant in the UK from Calpine Corporation. In 2005 Mitsui acquired a stake in Global in Gás Participações (Gaspart), a Brazil-based gas distribution company.

EXECUTIVES

Chairman: Nobuo Ohashi, age 68
President and CEO: Shoei Utsuda, age 63
EVP and CFO: Tasuku Kondo, age 64
EVP: Katsuo Momii, age 63
Executive Director: Yushi Nagata, age 60
EVP and COO, Asia Business Unit: Gempachiro Aihara, age 63
Senior Executive Managing Officer: Tetsuya Matsuoka, age 61
EVP; Headquaters Director, Mitsui & Co., Europe PLC, Mitsui & Co., Middle East Ltd.: Masataka Suzuki, age 62
Senior Executive Managing Officer, Chief Compliance Officer; Chief Privacy Officer; Environmental Matters; Deputy Chief Operating Officer, Business Process Re-Engineering Project Headquarters: Yasunori Yokote, age 60
EVP: Hiroshi Tada, age 61
Executive Managing Officer; COO, Energy Business Unit: Yoshiyuki Kagawa, age 59
Executive Managing Officer; COO, Financial Markets Business Unit: Osamu Mori, age 57
Executive Managing Officer; COO, Iron and Steel Products Business Unit: Satoru Miura, age 59
Senior Executive Managing Officer; COO, Americas Business Unit: Motokazu Yoshida, age 58
Senior Executive Managing Officer, Chief Financial Officer, Deputy Chief Operating Officer, Business Process Re-Engineering Project Headquarters; Executive Director: Kazuya Imai, age 60
Managing Officer; General Manager, Legal Division: Hideyo Hayakawa
Managing Officer; General Manager, Human Resources and General Affairs Division: Seiichi Tanaka
Auditors: Deloitte Touche Tohmatsu

LOCATIONS

HQ: Mitsui & Co., Ltd.
(Mitsui Bussan Kabushiki Kaisha)
2-1, Ohtemachi 1-chome, Chiyoda-ku,
Tokyo 100-0004, Japan
Phone: +81-3-3285-1111   **Fax:** +81-3-3285-9819
US HQ: 200 Park Ave., New York, NY 10166
US Phone: 212-878-4000   **US Fax:** 212-878-4800
Web: www.mitsui.co.jp

Mitsui & Co. operates through offices in 79 countries.

2006 Trading Transactions

	% of total
Japan	57
US	9
China	5
UK	1
Other countries	28
Total	**100**

PRODUCTS/OPERATIONS

2006 Sales

	% of total
Energy	33
Chemicals	22
Iron & steel	13
Foods	10
Machinery	9
Electronics & information	4
Property & service business	4
Non-ferrous metals	2
General merchandise	2
Textiles	1
Total	**100**

Selected Business Units

Chemical
    Organic Chemicals
    Plastics and Inorganic Chemicals
Consumer Products and Services
    Consumer Service
    Foods and Retail
    Lifestyle

Energy
Logistics and Financial Markets
    Financial Markets
    Transportation Logistics
    Machinery, Electronics, and Information
    Information, Electronics, and Telecommunication Machinery
    Power, Transportation, and Plant Products
Metal Products and Minerals
    Iron and Steel Products
    Iron and Steel Raw Materials and Non-Ferrous Metals

COMPETITORS

ITOCHU	Samsung Group
Kanematsu	Sojitz
Komatsu	Sumitomo
Marubeni	TOMEN
Mitsubishi Corporation	

HISTORICAL FINANCIALS

Company Type: Public

Income Statement

FYE: March 31

	REVENUE ($ mil.)	NET INCOME ($ mil.)	NET PROFIT MARGIN	EMPLOYEES
3/06	34,982	1,721	4.9%	40,993
3/05	32,951	1,132	3.4%	38,210
3/04	28,657	658	2.3%	39,735
3/03	4,829	264	5.5%	37,734
3/02	4,166	416	10.0%	36,116
Annual Growth	**70.2%**	**42.6%**	**—**	**3.2%**

2006 Year-End Financials

Debt ratio: 173.5%
Return on equity: 13.9%
Cash ($ mil.): 9,189
Current ratio: 1.35
Long-term debt ($ mil.): 24,743

Net Income History

NASDAQ (GS): MITSY

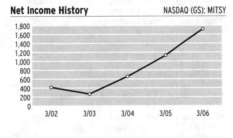

Mittal Steel

Many metal makers lack the mettle of Mittal Steel. Mittal was forged in 2004 when publicly traded Ispat International (of which the Mittal family owned 70%) purchased LNM Holdings (wholly owned by the Mittals) for $13.3 billion. When the dust settled, the combined entity stood as the largest steel company in the world, with annual steel production of 50 million tons. The company manufactures flat rolled and long steel products using direct-reduced iron, which is cheaper than using iron ore or scrap iron. CEO and founder Lakshmi Mittal controls Mittal Steel. In 2006 it agreed to buy rival Arcelor for about $34 billion to create Arcelor Mittal.

By early 2006, Mittal no longer was content to be merely the world's largest steel producer; it wanted to dominate the market. The company announced an offer to the shareholders of Arcelor to buy that company. Arcelor, and seemingly half the governments of Western Europe, initially fought the attempt. The combined company, to be called Arcelor Mittal, will be 43% owned by the Mittal family and have production of 120 million tons of steel annually. After a few months of a transitional management team arrangement, Lakshmi Mittal took over as CEO of the combined company toward the end of 2006.

Mittal Steel had established its hold on the world steel market through its 2005 purchase of the US-based International Steel Group (ISG) for about $4.5 billion. The purchase made the company the largest steel producer in the US (ahead of U.S. Steel and Nucor). In 2006 Mittal and Arcelor merged their laser-welding steel activities with Noble International, a leader in the niche industry. The resulting company will be 40%-owned by Arcelor Mittal.

Mittal Steel, which operates through subsidiaries in Europe, Africa, and the Americas, has laid plans for Asian expansion as well. In 2005 it paid the Valin Group more than $300 million for a 37% stake — the largest for a non-Chinese company — in Hunan Valin Steel Tube & Wire. (Its stake was subsequently lowered to 29%.) It then agreed to construct a 12 million ton plant in India. The company had been eyeing Lakshmi Mittal's native country for a while, and late in 2005 announced that Mittal Steel would begin construction of the plant with hopes for it to come online in about four years. (In 2006 the company announced it would construct the plant in the Indian state Orissa, a region rich in iron ore.) Late in 2005 it was also reported that Mittal was seeking a 49% stake in China's Baotou Iron & Steel Co. Ltd.

Also in 2005 Mittal Europe acquired a 93% stake in Ukrainian state-run steel company KryvorizhStal with the winning $4.84 billion bid in an auction held by the Ukrainian government.

The company has recently begun to broaden its portfolio outside the steel industry, dipping its toe into the energy business. In mid-2005 Mittal formed two joint ventures with India's government-controlled Oil & Natural Gas Corporation: one to buy stakes in foreign oil and gas projects, the other involved in oil and gas trading and shipping.

HISTORY

Mittal Steel Company is the product of decades of steelmaking by India's Mittal family. In 1967 patriarch Mohan Mittal unsuccessfully tried to open a steel mill in Egypt. He and his four younger brothers then set up a steel company in India, but squabbles pushed Mohan to chart his own course, eventually giving rise to an empire that flourished under the Ispat name. Mohan's son Lakshmi began working part-time at the family steel mill while in school; he started full-time at 21, after graduating in 1971.

Mohan set up an operation in Indonesia in 1975 (Ispat Indo) and put Lakshmi in charge. The next year, fueled by ambitions and held back by government regulations in India, Lakshmi formed Ispat International in Jakarta, Indonesia, to focus on expansion through acquisitions. He spent the next decade strengthening the Indonesian operations and perfecting the minimill process using direct-reduced iron (DRI).

Ispat took advantage of the recessionary late 1980s and early 1990s by making a string of acquisitions. In 1988 it took over the management of Trinidad and Tobago's state steel companies (bought 1994; renamed Caribbean Ispat).

In 1992 Ispat bought Mexico's third-largest (albeit bankrupt) steel and DRI producer. Two years later it acquired Canada's Sidbec-Dosco steelmaker. Also that year Lakshmi took exclusive control of international operations, leaving his brothers Pramod and Vinod to control the Indian divisions.

The mid-1990s brought more acquisitions: In 1995 Ispat bought Germany's Hamburger Stahlwerks and a mill in Kazakhstan. The next year it purchased Ireland's only steelmaker, Irish Steel. Lakshmi moved to London in 1996 and purchased a home on Bishops Avenue, known as "millionaire's row." (Saudi Arabia's King Fahd was a neighbor.) In 1997 the company bought the long-product (wire rod) division of Germany's Thyssen AG (renamed Ispat Stahlwerk Ruhrort and Ispat Walzdraht Hochfeld). It also completed a $776 million IPO — the steel industry's biggest, outside of privatizations.

Ispat acquired Chicago-based Inland Steel in 1998 (and renamed it Ispat Inland), including the steel-finishing operations of I/N Tek (60% Inland-owned joint venture with Nippon Steel) and I/N Kote (50% Inland-owned joint venture with NSC).

In 1999 Ispat formed a joint venture with Mexican steelmaker Grupo Imsa to make flat-rolled steel to sell throughout most of the Americas. That year Ispat Inland became the target of a US federal criminal grand jury investigation and a related civil lawsuit for allegedly defrauding the Louisiana Highway Department. (The case was settled for $30 million, with the cost split between Ispat Inland and Contech Construction Products Inc. of Ohio.)

In 2000 the company responded to a downturn in the steel industry by starting a Web-based joint venture with Commerce One to connect buyers and sellers in the worldwide metals market. It also offered to buy VSZ, Slovakia's #1 steelworks, but was outbid by U.S. Steel.

In 2002, the company's 51%-owned pipe making subsidiary, Productura Mexicana de Tuberia, sold almost all of its production assets.

Late in 2004 the Mittal family combined its steel holdings into one company when Ispat International (at the time 70%-owned by the family) purchased Antilles-based LNM Holdings (then privately held by the Mittals) for about $13.3 billion.

EXECUTIVES

Chairman and CEO: Lakshmi N. Mittal, age 56
EVP, Finance and Corporate Treasurer: Sudhir Maheshwari, age 42
EVP, Finance and Corporate Controller: Bhikam C. Agarwal, age 53
CTO: Greg Ludkovsky, age 57
CIO: Leon V. Schumacher
Chairman, Arcelor Mittal: Joseph Kinsch, age 73
CEO, Arcelor Mittal: Roland Junck, age 51
CFO, Arcelor Mittal: Aditya Mittal, age 30
SEVP, Shared Services, Arcelor Mittal: Davinder K. Chugh, age 49
SEVP, Flat Products Europe, Arcelor Mittal: Michel Wurth, age 52
SEVP, Long Products and Distribution, Arcelor Mittal: Gonzalo Urquijo, age 45
SEVP, Stainless, Mining, Asia, and Africa, Arcelor Mittal: Malay Mukherjee, age 58
CEO, Mittal Steel Europe: Roeland Baan, age 49
CEO, Mittal Steel USA: Louis (Lou) Schorsch, age 56
Director, Investor Relations: Julien Onillon
Manager, North American Investor Relations: Thomas A. (Tom) McCue
Director, Human Resources: Inder Walia, age 47
Secretary: Henk Scheffer, age 43
General Counsel: Simon Evans, age 42
General Manager, Corporate Communications: Nicola Davidson
Auditors: Deloitte Accountants B.V.

LOCATIONS

HQ: Mittal Steel Company N.V.
Hofplein 20, 15th Fl.,
3032 Rotterdam, The Netherlands
Phone: +31-10-217-8800   **Fax:** +31-10-217-8850
US HQ: 1 S. Dearborn, Chicago, IL 60603
US Phone: 312-899-3440
Web: www.mittalsteel.com

Based in the Netherlands and run from its London headquarters, Mittal Steel has steelmaking operations in Algeria, Bosnia, Canada, the Czech Republic, France, Germany, Kazakhstan, Macedonia, Mexico, Poland, Romania, South Africa, Trinidad and Tobago, and the US.

2005 Sales and Operating Income

	Sales $ mil.	Sales % of total	Operating Income $ mil.	Operating Income % of total
Americas	12,467	42	1,423	30
Europe	9,762	33	976	20
Asia & Africa	7,683	25	2,265	48
Others & adjustments	(1,780)	—	82	2
Total	**28,132**	**100**	**4,746**	**100**

PRODUCTS/OPERATIONS

Selected Products

Direct reduced iron (DRI)
Flat steel
  Cold-rolled sheet and slab
  Hot-rolled sheet and slab
Long steel
  Bars
  Pipes
  Structural
  Wire (products and rod)

Selected Subsidiaries

LNM Marketing (United Arab Emirates)
Mittal Canada
Mittal Steel Annaba (Algeria)
Mittal Steel Galati (Romania)
Mittal Steel Gandrange (France)
Mittal Steel Hamburg (Germany)
Mittal Steel Hochfeld (Germany)
Mittal Steel Hunedoara (Romania)
Mittal Steel Iasi (Romania)
Mittal Steel Kryviy Rih (Ukraine)
Mittal Steel Lázaro Cárdenas (Mexico)
Mittal Steel Ostrava (Czech Republic)
Mittal Steel Point Lisas (Trinidad and Tobago)
Mittal Steel Poland
Mittal Steel Roman (Romania)
Mittal Steel Ruhrort (Germany)
Mittal Steel Skopje (Macedonia)
Mittal Steel South Africa
Mittal Steel Tebessa (Algeria)
Mittal Steel Temirtau (Kazakhstan)
Mittal Steel USA
Mittal Steel Zenica (Bosnia and Herzegovina)
RZR Ljubija (Bosnia and Herzegovina)
Tréfileurope (France)

COMPETITORS

AK Steel Holding Corporation	Nippon Steel
Algoma Steel	Nucor
Arcelor	Oregon Steel Mills
BlueScope Steel	POSCO
Chaparral Steel	Severstal North America
Corus Group	Shanghai Baosteel
Dofasco	Stelco Hamilton
Gerdau AmeriSteel	ThyssenKrupp
Highveld Steel and Vanadium	United States Steel
JFE Holdings	Vallourec
	Worthington Industries

HISTORICAL FINANCIALS

Company Type: Public

Income Statement

FYE: December 31

	REVENUE ($ mil.)	NET INCOME ($ mil.)	NET PROFIT MARGIN	EMPLOYEES
12/05	28,132	3,365	12.0%	224,286
12/04	22,197	4,701	21.2%	164,393
12/03	5,441	66	1.2%	14,811
12/02	4,889	49	1.0%	15,400
Annual Growth	**79.2%**	**309.5%**	**—**	**144.2%**

2005 Year-End Financials

Debt ratio: 92.0%
Return on equity: 42.1%
Cash ($ mil.): 2,149
Current ratio: 2.09
Long-term debt ($ mil.): 9,335
No. of shares (mil.): —
Dividends
  Yield: 0.9%
  Payout: 4.5%
Market value ($ mil.): —

Stock History

NYSE: MT

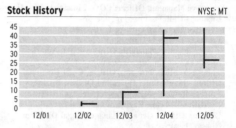

	STOCK PRICE ($) FY Close	P/E High	P/E Low	PER SHARE ($) Earnings	PER SHARE ($) Dividends
12/05	26.33	9	5	4.89	0.22
12/04	38.65	6	1	7.31	—
12/03	8.87	17	4	0.53	—
12/02	2.20	8	3	0.40	—
Annual Growth	**128.7%**	**—**	**—**	**130.4%**	

Mizuho Financial

Mizuho means "golden ears of rice" in Japanese, but in the banking world it means the first bank with a trillion dollars in assets. Since surpassed by the likes of HSBC and Citigroup, Mizuho Financial Group is the parent of Mizuho Bank (retail banking), Mizuho Corporate Bank (commercial financial services), Mizuho Securities (investment and brokerage services), and Mizuho Trust & Banking. All told, the company has approximately 700 branches, sub-branches, and agencies across Japan. Mizuho Financial Group was formed by the 2002 merger of The Dai-Ichi Kangyo Bank, Fuji Bank, and Industrial Bank of Japan (IBJ).

More than 85% of the company's revenue comes from its home market, but it also operates in the US, Europe, Oceania, and other parts of Asia. Mizuho is expanding into Hong Kong and mainland China to profit from Chinese growth and the export of Japanese production facilities from their home market. The bank also plans to expand its nascent securities, investment, trust, and asset management activities by making these services available at most of its bank branches.

HISTORY

Of the three banking institutions that formed Mizuho Holdings, Industrial Bank of Japan (IBJ) is the youngest, founded in 1902. Fuji Bank started in 1880 and Dai-Ichi Kangyo's roots reach back to 1872.

By the late 1990s Japanese banks faced the challenges of a fossilized banking system, chained together by the *keiretsu* cross-shareholding system that hindered companies' agility in the marketplace. Other economic stresses included the Asian financial crisis, which left banks holding thousands of bad loans. In 1997 the Big Bang of banking reform was supposed to free lending institutions to restructure for greater competition, with presumably sounder business models. The industry's reliance on government-sponsored bailouts underscored the need for change.

IBJ, Dai-Ichi Kangyo Bank, and Fuji Bank (none of them excessively chummy within their respective *keiretsu*) saw an opportunity to consolidate, strengthen their business through combined forces, and streamline their operations by closing redundant branches, agencies, and divisions.

Mizuho Holdings was formed in 1999 and placed atop the three banks as their new parent company. While Mizuho's $1.3 trillion in assets made it the largest bank in the world at the time, its copious debts weren't to be ignored, either (though the bank waived the nearly $1 billion in debt of troubled retailer Sogo in 2001).

Also in 2001, other Japanese banks followed the lead of IBJ, Dai-Ichi Kangyo, and Fuji by joining with peers in the quest for size. Sumitomo Bank and Sakura Bank merged to form Sumitomo Mitsui Financial Group; and Sanwa Bank, Tokai Bank, and Toyo Trust and Banking combined to create UFJ Holdings.

Initially, the CEOs of the three banks that comprised Mizuho were tapped as co-CEOs of the company, but they resigned in 2002 after the banks' consolidation was marred by PR gaffes and computer glitches that caused customers to be double-billed, created a logjam of money transfers, and crashed thousands of ATMs. Terunobu Maeda was named the sole CEO of Mizuho later that year.

EXECUTIVES

President, CEO, and Director: Terunobu Maeda, age 61
Deputy President and Head of Internal Audit Group (Chief Auditor); Director: Shunichi Asada, age 57
Managing Director, Head of Financial Control and Accounting Group, and CFO: Satoru Nishibori, age 53
Managing Director, Head of Strategic Planning Group and IT, Chief Strategic Officer, and CIO: Tetsuji Kosaki, age 54
Managing Executive Officer, Head of Risk Management Group, Head of Human Resources Group, Chief Risk Officer, Chief Compliance Officer, and Chief Human Resources Officer: Masayuki Saito, age 53
Executive Officer and General Manager, Corporate Planning: Hiroshi Kiyama, age 52
Executive Officer and General Manager, Corporate Communications: Yoshiaki Ohashi, age 52
Executive Officer and Managing Executive Officer, Mizuho Research Institute, Ltd.: Tetsuro Sugiura, age 52
Executive Officer and General Manager, Administration: Tsuneo Morita, age 52
Executive Officer and General Manager, Human Resources: Shuzo Haimoto, age 52

Corporate Auditor: Yoshiaki Sugita, age 60
Corporate Auditor: Junichi Iwabuchi, age 54
President and CEO, Mizuho Bank; Director: Seiji Sugiyama, age 59
President and CEO, Mizuho Corporate Bank; Director: Hiroshi Saito, age 62
Auditors: Ernst & Young ShinNihon

LOCATIONS

HQ: Mizuho Financial Group, Inc.
1-5-5, Otemachi, Chiyoda-ku,
Tokyo 100-0004, Japan
Phone: +81-3-5224-1111 **Fax:** +81-3-3215-4616
Web: www.mizuho-fg.co.jp

PRODUCTS/OPERATIONS

2006 Sales

	% of total
Interest	
Loans & bills discounted	29
Securities	12
Receivables under resale agreements	7
Other	4
Noninterest	
Fee & commission income	17
Other operating income	9
Trading income	6
Other income	16
Total	**100**

COMPETITORS

Bank of Yokohama
BNP Paribas Bangkok
Citigroup
Mitsubishi UFJ Financial Group
Mitsui Trust
Shinsei Bank
Shizuoka Bank
Sumitomo Mitsui
Sumitomo Trust and Banking

HISTORICAL FINANCIALS

Company Type: Public

Income Statement

	ASSETS ($ mil.)	NET INCOME ($ mil.)	INCOME AS % OF ASSETS	EMPLOYEES
3/06	1,272,307	5,527	0.4%	45
3/05	1,330,323	5,833	0.4%	22,827
3/04	1,303,942	3,853	0.3%	26,575
3/03	1,118,369	(19,835)	—	27,900
3/02	1,140,744	(7,358)	—	30,262
Annual Growth	2.8%	—	—	(80.4%)

FYE: March 31

2006 Year-End Financials

Equity as % of assets: —
Return on assets: 0.4%
Return on equity: —
Long-term debt ($ mil.): —
Sales ($ mil.): 32

Net Income History

NYSE: MFG

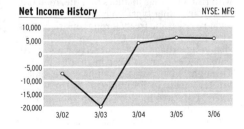

MOL

The downstream operations of MOL Magyar Olaj-és Gázipari Rt. (Hungarian Oil and Gas Company, or MOL) have moved it up to become Hungary's biggest company and one of Central Europe's top refiners. MOL's refineries produce 101,300 barrels of oil equivalent per day, and it operates 812 gas stations in the Czech Republic, Hungary, Poland, Romania, Slovakia, Slovenia, and Ukraine. It is aiming to have 1,500 gas stations by 2010. Other activities include exploration and production in Hungary, Russia, and areas of Central and Eastern Europe. In 2005 the company's proved reserves stacked up to 310.6 million barrels of oil equivalent.

The company has acquired a 36% stake in Slovnaft, Slovakia's sole refiner, and holds a 23% stake in TVK, Hungary's largest petrochemical producer. With Russian companies moving into the region, MOL has been in talks with Polish energy company PKN ORLEN to form alliances. In 2005 MOL acquired the Romanian subsidiary of Royal Dutch Shell, including the purchase of 59 Shell filling stations that the company plans to modernize immediately. Royal Dutch Shell also sold MOL its Romania-based lubricants, aviation, and commercial businesses.

In addition to expanding its refining and marketing operations across Central Europe, the company has restructured its exploration and production activities to focus on the development of oil fields in Russia.

In 2003 MOL concluded a long-term crude oil supply agreement with Russian oil giant YUKOS.

The company agreed in 2004 to sell its gas businesses to E.ON Ruhrgas for about $1 billion. After much scrutiny by Hungarian and EU regulators, the deal was completed in 2006.

HISTORY

The oil refining industry in Hungary dates to the 1880s, when refineries were opened in Fiume (1882) and Budapest (1883). By 1913 Hungary had 28 plants.

Following Hungary's defeat in WWI, the country's refining industry fell into decline, as new national boundaries placed most of its former oil refineries and oil-producing regions outside its borders. By 1921 Hungary had only six operational refineries.

British and American investors set up the European Gas and Electric Company (EUROGASCO) in the US in 1931 to acquire oil and gas concessions in Central Europe and build power plants. By 1937 EUROGASCO (controlled by Standard Oil of New Jersey) was producing oil. A year later Standard Oil set up the Hungarian-American Oil Industry Shareholding Co. (MAORT) to develop the fields, and in 1940 MAORT's production was meeting all of Hungary's oil needs.

During WWII, MAORT requisitioned all oil assets. The oil industry boomed as Hungary served as a major supplier for the German war machine. But by 1944, with German armies in retreat from the Eastern Front, much of Hungary's oil machinery and plants were dismantled. The remaining plants suffered heavy bombing from Allied forces or had equipment confiscated by Russian and Romanian troops.

After the war the Hungarian Soviet Crude Oil Co. began rebuilding Hungary's oil industry and started drilling on the Great Hungarian

Plain in 1946. MAORT also ramped up oil production in the Trans-Danubian fields. In 1949, following charges of sabotage against MAORT managers, MAORT was nationalized and broken up into five national companies, which re-merged in 1952 with Hungarian Soviet Oil Co. (successor to Hungarian Soviet Crude Oil Co.).

In 1957 all operations of the Hungarian crude oil industry were consolidated under Crude Oil Trust, which took over the gas industry by 1960. That year the company was renamed National Crude Oil and Gas Trust (OKGT), and the focus of exploration soon shifted from Trans-Danubian fields to the Great Plain. By 1970 the Great Plain accounted for 67% of oil production and 96% of natural gas production.

Hungary began allowing foreign gasoline distributors to compete in domestic markets during the 1980s. Moving toward privatization, the Hungarian government founded MOL in 1991 as the successor to OKGT, which comprised nine oil and gas enterprises. In 1993 the socialist government sold 8% of MOL to the public. By 1998 the government had sold all but 25% of MOL.

During the 1990s the company also expanded in Central Europe. With Austria's OMV in 1994 it began building a 120-km pipeline linking Austria and Hungary, which gave it access to natural gas from Western Europe for the first time. MOL also opened up service stations in neighboring countries, beginning with one in Romania in 1996. By 2000 the company was operating about 80 stations in Romania, 18 in Slovakia, three in Ukraine, and two in Slovenia, in addition to its 330 stations in Hungary. MOL also acquired about 20% of chemical processor TVK in 1999 and upped the stake to nearly 33% by 2000. That year MOL also acquired 36% of Slovnaft, Slovakia's only oil refiner and its major retailer.

EXECUTIVES

Executive Chairman: Zsolt Hernádi, age 45
Vice Chairman: Sándor Csányi, age 52
Group CEO: György Mosonyi, age 56
Group CFO: József Molnár, age 49
Group Chief Strategy Officer:
 Michel-Marc Delcommune, age 57
Managing Director Exploration and Production Division: Zoltán Áldott, age 36
Managing Director Natural Gas Division:
 Sándor Fasimon, age 39
Managing Director Refining and Marketing Division:
 Ferenc Horváth, age 44
Managing Director Petrochemical Division:
 Vratko Kassovic, age 62
Chief Legal Counsel: Ilona Bánhegyi, age 35
Investor Relations Director: Rupert Foster
Human Resources Director: József Simola
Enterprise Relations: László Miklós
Corporate Communications: Szabolcs Ferencz
Internal Auditor: Zoltán Jancsurák
Security and Protection: Frigyes Bozsik
Managing Director, Lubes Division: Ferenc Dénes
Managing Director, Health, Safety and Environmental Protection Division: Bela Cseh

LOCATIONS

HQ: MOL Magyar Olaj-és Gázipari Rt.
 Október huszonharmadika u.18,
 H-1502 Budapest, Hungary
Phone: +36-1-209-0000 **Fax:** +36-1-464-1335
Web: www.mol.hu

MOL Magyar Olaj-és Gázipari explores for and produces oil and gas in Hungary, Russia, and other areas of Central and Eastern Europe, and owns and operates service stations in Croatia, Hungary, Poland, Romania, Slovakia, Slovenia, and Ukraine. It has refineries at Százhalombatta, Tiszaujvaros, and Zalaegerszeg in Hungary.

PRODUCTS/OPERATIONS

2005 Sales

	% of total
Refining & marketing	62
Natural gas	26
Petrochemicals	11
Exploration & production	1
Total	**100**

COMPETITORS

BG Group
BP
CEPSA
Eni
Hellenic Petroleum
Norsk Hydro
OMV
PKN ORLEN
Repsol YPF
Royal Dutch Shell
TOTAL

HISTORICAL FINANCIALS

Company Type: Public

Income Statement				FYE: December 31
	REVENUE ($ mil.)	NET INCOME ($ mil.)	NET PROFIT MARGIN	EMPLOYEES
12/05	11,505	1,162	10.1%	14,660
12/04	10,839	1,160	10.7%	15,465
12/03	7,318	479	6.5%	15,932
12/02	5,173	289	5.6%	15,268
12/01	4,029	5	0.1%	14,253
Annual Growth	30.0%	300.9%	—	0.7%

Net Income History Budapest: MOL

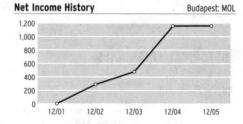

Munich Re

Some companies live with risk. Münchener Rückversicherungs-Gesellschaft Aktiengesellschaft (Munich Re), on the other hand, *thrives* with risk. Coverage includes fire, life, motor, liability, and other types on both facultative (individual risks) and treaty (groups of risks) bases. The firm owns about 90% of ERGO Versicherungsgruppe, putting it second only to Allianz in Germany's direct insurance market. Through American Re, Munich Re enjoys greater access to US markets. As the world's largest reinsurer, the company operates in some 160 countries.

Europe is its biggest market (about 75% of premiums) and the company plans expansion through acquisitions there.

As insurance clients seek less expensive ways to manage risk, reinsurance markets have stagnated. In response, Munich Re moved into direct insurance. Continuing its expansion, Munich Re has

also entered the asset management game, forming MEAG Munich ERGO AssetManagement, a joint venture with ERGO.

Uber-insurer Allianz AG owns about 15% of Munich Re, which in turn owns about 15% of Allianz. Other major shareholders include some of Germany's top banks: HypoVereinsbank and Dresdner Bank. Deutsche Bank has sold its stake in the company.

The company is hoping to continue the growth of its primary insurance segment (more than 80% of business comes from Germany), focusing on personal lines.

In 2005 Munich Re took a nearly 75% hit on its profit margin due to re-investment in its American Re subsidiary, whose internal reserves required a $1.6 billion injection for expected claims related to asbestos and environmental claims on policies mostly written between 1997 and 2002.

HISTORY

Investors Carl Thieme and Theodor Cramer-Klett founded Munich Re in 1880. Within a month Munich Re opened offices in Hamburg, Berlin, Vienna, and St. Petersburg, establishing treaties with German and Danish insurers. In 1888 Munich Re went public; two years later, it opened an office in London and helped finance the creation of Allianz, which would soon come to dominate the German insurance industry. In 1892 the firm opened a branch in the US (it incurred severe losses from the 1906 San Francisco earthquake).

WWI interrupted Munich Re's UK and US operations. The company recovered after 1918, only to be hobbled again by the Great Depression. In 1933 Munich Re executive Kurt Schmitt became minister of economic affairs for the Nazis. Objecting to the evolving policies of National Socialism, he left after a year, returning to Munich Re, where he became chief executive in 1938.

Hitler's ignition of WWII wasn't quite the boom Munich Re needed; its international business was again disrupted. After the war, the Allies further limited overseas operations. Because of his involvement with the Nazi government, Schmitt was replaced by Eberhard von Reininghaus in 1945. The division of Germany further hampered the company's recovery.

Jump-started by the Marshall Plan in 1950, the West German *Wirtschaftswunder* (economic miracle) kicked into high gear, as the devastated country rebuilt. Relaxation of occupation-era trading limits also helped as the company rebuilt its foreign business. By 1969, Munich Re's sales topped DM 2 billion. Amid the global oil crisis and a rash of terrorist acts in Germany, the firm reported its first-ever reinsurance loss in 1977.

German reunification in 1990 provided new markets for Munich Re, but advantages from new business in the East were wiped out by claims arising from that year's harsh winter.

In 1992 an investigation by the German Federal Cartel Office prompted a realignment in the insurance business — Allianz ceded its controlling interests in three life insurers (Hamburg-Mannheimer Versicherungs, Karlsruher Lebensversicherung, and Berlinische Lebensversicherung) to Munich Re, bringing it into direct insurance. Munich Re took over Deutsche Krankenversicherung (DKV) in 1996. Also that year Munich Re acquired American Re. During the 1990s, reinsurance sales dwindled as competition increased, forcing lower premiums, and alternatives to insurance and reinsurance became more common. Munich Re looked to direct insurance, particularly individual property/casualty and life insurance, to compensate. In 1997 it merged Hamburg-Mannheimer and DKV with another insurer, Victoria AG, to form ERGO Versicherungsgruppe. Within a year, ERGO's insurance income accounted for half of all revenues.

Munich Re and ERGO launched asset management firm MEAG Munich ERGO Asset-Management in 1999. That year Munich Re experienced its worst year ever after natural disasters hit its reinsurance business hard. To recoup its losses, the next year the firm expanded both its reinsurance and primary insurance operations into key markets in Europe, North and South America, and Asia. Also in 2000, Munich Re bought CNA Financial's life reinsurance operations. Together with Swiss Re, the company launched Inreon, an online reinsurance exchange, in 2001.

As one of the companies hit hardest financially by the World Trade Center tragedy, Munich Re paid out some $2 billion in claims.

EXECUTIVES

Chairman, Supervisory Board: Hans-Jürgen Schinzler, age 66
Deputy Chairman, Supervisory Board: Herbert Bach
Chairman, Board of Management:
Nikolaus von Bomhard, age 50
Member Board of Management, Accounting, Controlling, Taxes, and Investor Relations:
Jörg Schneider, age 48
Member Board of Management, Corporate Underwriting/Global Clients: Stefan Heyd, age 61
Member Board of Management, Finance, General Services, Organisational Design and Development:
Heiner Hasford, age 54
Member Board of Management, Life and Health and Human Resources: Detlef Schneidawind, age 62
Member Board of Management, Special and Financial Risks and Information Technology: Torsten Jeworrek, age 45
Member Board of Management, Asia, Australasia, and Africa: Karl Wittmann, age 61
Member Board of Management, Europe 1 and Corporate Communications: Christian Kluge, age 65
Member Board of Management, Europe 2 and Latin America: Georg Daschner, age 57
Member Board of Management, North America; Chairman and CEO, American Re: John P. Phelan, age 59
Company Spokesperson: Rainer Küppers
Media Relations: Ursula Jenne-Lindenberg
Auditors: KPMG Bayerische Treuhandgesellschaft AG

LOCATIONS

HQ: Münchener Rückversicherungs-Gesellschaft Aktiengesellschaft
Königinstrasse 107, D-80802 Munich, Germany
Phone: +49-89-38-91-0 **Fax:** +49-89-39-90-56
US HQ: American Re Corporation, 555 College Rd. East, Princeton, NJ 08543
US Phone: 609-243-4200 **US Fax:** 609-243-4257
Web: www.munichre.com

Munich Re operates in some 150 countries worldwide.

PRODUCTS/OPERATIONS

2005 Sales

	% of total
Premiums	75
Investment income	24
Other	1
Total	**100**

Selected Subsidiaries

Asset management
  MEAG MUNICH ERG
Direct insurance
  ERGO Versicherungsgruppe AG (92%)
    D.A.S. Deutscher Automobil Schutz Allgemeine
  Europäische Reiseversicherung AG
  Karlsruher Lebensversicherung AG (54%)
  Rechtsschutz-Versicherungs-AG (62%)
    D.A.S. Deutscher Automobil Schutz Versicherungs-AG (62%)
    DAS Legal Expenses Insurance Company Limited (62%, UK)
    D.A.S. Nederlandse Rechtsbijstand Verzekeringsmaatschappij N.V. (39%, The Netherlands)
  DKV Deutsche Krankenversicherung AG (63%)
  dkv International S.A. (63%, Belgium)
  Hamburg-Mannheimer Versicherungs-AG (63%)
    Hamburg-Mannheimer Sachversicherungs-AG (63%)
  VICTORIA Lebensversicherung AG (63%)
    VICTORIA Krankenversicherung AG (63%)
    VICTORIA MERIDIONAL Compañía Anónima de Seguros y Reaseguros, S.A. (61%, Spain)
    VICTORIA-Seguros de Vida, S.A. (62%, Portugal)
    VICTORIA-Seguros S.A. (62%, Portugal)
    VICTORIA-VOLKSBANKEN Versicherungs-AG (46%, Austria)
Reinsurance
  American Re Corporation (US)
  American Re-Insurance Company (US)
  Great Lakes Reinsurance (UK) PLC
  Münchener Rück Italia S.p.A.
  Munich American Reassurance Company (US)
  Munich Reinsurance Company of Africa Limited (South Africa)
  Munich Reinsurance Company of Australasia Limited (Australia)
  Munich Reinsurance Company of Canada
  New Reinsurance Company (Switzerland)

COMPETITORS

Allianz	General Reinsurance UK
AXA	Hannover Re
Bâloise-Holding	Nippon Life Insurance
Converium Reinsurance	RGA
Everest Re	Swiss Re
GE Insurance Solutions	Transatlantic Holdings
General Re	Winterthur

HISTORICAL FINANCIALS

Company Type: Public

Income Statement

FYE: December 31

	ASSETS ($ mil.)	NET INCOME ($ mil.)	INCOME AS % OF ASSETS	EMPLOYEES
12/05	258,934	3,163	1.2%	37,953
12/04	292,975	2,500	0.9%	40,962
12/03	262,819	(545)	—	41,431
12/02	205,890	1,133	0.6%	41,396
12/01	178,979	221	0.1%	38,317
Annual Growth	**9.7%**	**94.4%**	**—**	**(0.2%)**

2005 Year-End Financials

Equity as % of assets: —
Return on assets: 1.1%
Return on equity: —
Long-term debt ($ mil.): —
Sales ($ mil.): 57,430

Net Income History

German: MUV

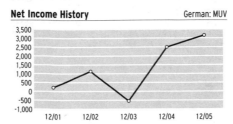

National Australia Bank

National Australia Bank (NAB) is down under, up over, and all around. One of Australia's Big Four banks, NAB operates through four businesses: The Australia region, comprising the NAB and MLC brands; the UK region, which includes Clydesdale and Yorkshire banks; New Zealand, through the Bank of New Zealand; and Institutional Markets & Services, its international group that offers financial management, debt financing, and other services. The company also offers wealth management services through its MLC subsidiary. National Australia Bank also has significant life insurance operations and owns Bank of New Zealand.

NAB is streamlining its UK operations, trimming staff, closing branches, and simplifying its product range while revamping other branches and building the banks' online capabilities, with an emphasis on attracting small business and private banking clients.

This strategy dovetails with the company's reorganization along regional lines (Australia, Europe, and New Zealand) and the alignment of its banking and wealth management operations to better cross-sell financial products to customers. The bank is mulling whether it should sell its credit card division, which has been losing market share, to better focus on its other operations.

HISTORY

Formed in 1858 in Melbourne, National Bank of Australasia (NBA) just missed the peak of the Victoria gold rush. The bank expanded across the territory and was one of the first to lend to farmers and ranchers using land deeds as security. In the late 1870s, drought imperiled Victoria. Seeking greener pastures, NBA entered New South Wales in 1885, then headed into Western Australia. Economic instability continued; in 1893 the bank experienced its first panic and was shuttered for eight weeks. NBA reopened only to close a quarter of its branches between 1893 and 1896.

During the Australian commonwealth's early years, Western Australia was the bank's salvation as the economies in Victoria and South Australia stagnated. NBA helped fund Australia's WWI efforts through public loans. A postwar consolidation wave in banking swept up NBA, which made acquisitions in 1918 and 1922.

Overdue farm and ranch loans weakened the bank during the Depression. As WWII raged, the Commonwealth Bank (established in 1912) took greater control of Australia's banks. With competition among banks primarily limited to branch growth, NBA acquired Queensland National Bank in 1948 and Ballarat Banking Co. in 1955. The bank diversified into consumer finance through acquisition. In the 1960s Australia experienced an economic boom as immigration and industrialization grew. The boom went bust in the 1970s as the world sunk into recession. Still under the Commonwealth Bank's tight control, the banks watched business that had once been theirs lost to building societies, merchant banks, and credit unions.

The 1980s brought banking deregulation. To vie with foreign banks entering Australia, NBA in 1981 merged with Commercial Banking Co. of Sydney and became the National Commercial Banking Corp. of Australia in 1982. (It took its present name in 1984.) Throughout the 1980s the bank diversified and moved into the US and Japan. It invested in property and made loans to foreign countries. All too quickly, though, property values sank and countries defaulted on loans.

To fight recession, NAB looked abroad for opportunities. In 1987 it bought Clydesdale Bank, Northern Bank, and National Irish Bank from Midland Bank Group (now part of HSBC Holdings). Three years later, NAB bought Yorkshire Bank, then turned the four banks around by linking them and tightening loan operations. In 1992 it bought the troubled Bank of New Zealand, again tightening loan operations. Three years later NAB claimed Michigan National in the US.

After the mid-1990s economic recovery, NAB bought HomeSide to try to adapt the US mortgage firm's efficient operations for all its banks.

NAB in 2000 bought Lend Lease's MLC fund management group. It also announced plans to launch a separate stock for its European businesses, fueling speculation it might be on the prowl to buy or merge with a large UK bank. The Australian Competition and Consumer Commission that year accused NAB of credit card transaction price-fixing; the bank faces a possible fine of nearly $6 million.

In 2001 NAB sold US-based Michigan National Bank to ABN AMRO and sold mortgage lender HomeSide International to Washington Mutual the following year. In fiscal year 2002, the bank cut some 2,000 jobs, mostly in back-office operations.

During fiscal year 2003 the company booked pre-tax losses of some $360 million due to unauthorized trading in the company's foreign currency options department. By the end of March 2004, chairman Charles Allen, chief executive Frank Cicutto, and the heads of global markets and foreign exchange had resigned. Three more executives and at least five traders were fired. The fallout continued the next year as the company struggled to regroup.

NAB sold its Irish banks — National Irish Bank and Northern Bank — to Danske Bank in 2005. It retained its UK banks, Yorkshire Bank (England) and Clydesdale Bank (Scotland).

EXECUTIVES

Chairman: Michael A. Chaney, age 55
Managing Director, CEO, and Executive Director: John M. Stewart, age 57, $3,717,322 pay
Group CFO and Executive Director: Michael J. Ullmer, age 54
Group Chief Risk Officer: Michael Hamar, age 59, $740,961 pay
Executive General Manager, Group Development: Cameron A. Clyne, age 37, $722,606 pay
Deputy Group CFO: Gordon Lefevre, age 44
Executive General Manager, Institutional Markets and Services: John Hooper, age 44, $1,429,506 pay
Executive General Manager, People and Culture: Elizabeth Hunter
CEO, Australia and Executive Director: Ahmed Fahour, age 39, $3,322,300 pay
CEO, Bank of New Zealand: Peter L. Thodey, age 55, $961,190 pay
CEO, Europe: Lynne M. Peacock, age 52, $2,293,556 pay
Chief General Counsel: David M. Krasnostein, age 51
Company Secretary: Michaela Healey, age 37
Head of Group Investor Relations: Callum Davidson
Head of Operational Integration: Kevin Turnbull
Group Manager, External Relations: Brandon Phillips
CFO, Australia: Ewen Stafford
CIO, Australia: Michelle Tredenick
Head of Corporate Banking and Head of Institutional Markets and Services, Australia: Paul Orton
Group Communications Adviser: Samantha Evans
Head of Media Relations, Australia: Geoff Lynch
Auditors: Ernst & Young

LOCATIONS

HQ: National Australia Bank Limited
    500 Bourke St., 24th Fl., Melbourne 3000, Australia
Phone: +61-3-8641-3500   **Fax:** +61-3-9208-5695
US HQ: 245 Park Ave., 28th Fl., New York, NY 10167
US Phone: 212-916-9500   **US Fax:** 212-983-1969
Web: www.nabgroup.com

2006 Sales

	% of total
Australia	70
UK	15
New Zealand	6
Other	9
Total	**100**

PRODUCTS/OPERATIONS

2006 Sales

	% of total
Interest	
Loans & advances	67
Due from customers on acceptances	9
Marketable debt securities	4
Due from banks	3
Other	2
Other	
Fees & commissions	5
Banking fees	3
Other	7
Total	**100**

2006 Assets

	% of total
Cash & equivalents	3
Trading securities & derivatives	6
Securities	1
Investments relating to life insurance business	11
Loans & advances	58
Other	21
Total	**100**

Selected Subsidiaries

Bank of New Zealand
Clydesdale Bank PLC
MLC Limited
National Australia Financial Management Limited
Yorkshire Bank PLC.

COMPETITORS

Abbey National
Allied Irish Banks
Australia and New Zealand Banking
Bank of Ireland
Barclays
Commonwealth Bank of Australia
HBOS
HSBC Holdings
Lloyds TSB
Northern Rock
RBS
St.George Bank
Westpac Banking

HISTORICAL FINANCIALS

Company Type: Public

Income Statement

FYE: September 30

	ASSETS ($ mil.)	NET INCOME ($ mil.)	INCOME AS % OF ASSETS	EMPLOYEES
9/06	360,415	3,161	0.9%	38,433
9/05	229,853	3,250	1.4%	38,933
9/04	299,658	1,969	0.7%	43,517
9/03	270,306	2,390	0.9%	45,206
9/02	206,682	1,902	0.9%	46,642
Annual Growth	**14.9%**	**13.5%**	**—**	**(4.7%)**

2006 Year-End Financials

Equity as % of assets: 5.3%   Long-term debt ($ mil.): 68,484
Return on assets: 1.1%   Sales ($ mil.): 24,189
Return on equity: 16.8%

Net Income History

NYSE: NAB

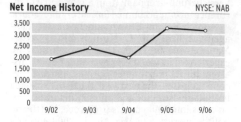

NEC

NEC has three arms and plenty of muscle. The company's IT Solutions business makes high-end computers (servers and supercomputers) and peripherals (monitors and projectors), and it wrestles with Fujitsu for the top spot among Japanese PC makers. Its Electron Devices division makes electronics ranging from transistors to display modules, and competes with Toshiba for the second spot among semiconductor makers (both companies trail Intel). The company sells broadband and wireless networking equipment through its Network Solutions group.

The company has restructured its operations numerous times in recent years. In 2004 NEC took its DRAM joint venture, Elpida Memory, public, thereby reducing its stake in the company and the volatile memory sector. NEC also sold its plasma display business to Pioneer in 2004. Early in 2005 it dissolved its monitor joint venture with Mitsubishi and took full ownership of the unit (NEC Display Solutions). In 2006 it spun off BIGLOBE, one of Japan's largest Internet service providers, as a separate subsidiary and sold more than 20% of its stake in the unit to Sumitomo, Daiwa Securities, and other investors. It also sold its European PC operations, Packard Bell, to Lap Shun "John" Hui, a co-founder of eMachines, in 2006.

HISTORY

A group of Japanese investors, led by Kunihiko Iwadare, formed Nippon Electric Company (NEC) in a joint venture with Western Electric (US) in 1899. Starting as an importer of telephone equipment, NEC soon became a maker and a major supplier to Japan's Communications Ministry. Western Electric sold its stake in NEC in 1925. The company became affiliated with the Sumitomo *keiretsu* (industrial group) in the 1930s and went public in 1949.

After Nippon Telegraph and Telephone (NTT) was formed in 1952, NEC became one of its four leading suppliers. The post-WWII need to repair Japan's telephone systems and the country's continuing economic recovery resulted in strong demand from NTT for NEC's products. In the 1950s and 1960s NTT business represented over 50% of sales, even though NEC had expanded overseas, diversified into home appliances, and formed a computer alliance with Honeywell (US). ITT (US), which had begun acquiring shares in the company decades earlier and owned as much as 59% of NEC, sold its stake in the 1960s.

In the 1970s Honeywell's lagging position in computers hurt NEC; the company recovered through in-house development efforts and a mainframe venture with Toshiba. In 1977 CEO Koji Kobayashi articulated his revolutionary vision of NEC's future as an integrator of computers and communications through semiconductor technology.

NEC invested heavily in R&D and expansion, becoming the world's largest semiconductor maker in 1985. Despite its proprietary operating system, NEC garnered over 50% of the Japanese computer market in the 1980s. NEC entered into a mainframe computer partnership with Honeywell and France's Groupe Bull in 1987.

By the early 1990s NEC had lost its status as world's largest semiconductor maker to Intel. NEC bought 20% of US computer maker Packard Bell in 1995. The following year NEC merged most of its PC business outside Japan with that company, creating Packard Bell NEC. Also in 1996 NEC created US subsidiary Holon Net Corp. to make hardware and software for Internet and intranet markets.

NEC took control of Packard Bell NEC in 1998, upping its stake to 53%. A sluggish Japanese economy and slumping memory prices contributed to NEC's drop in income for fiscal 1998. A defense contract scandal involving overbilling and improper hiring by an NEC unit forced the resignation of chairman Tadahiro Sekimoto and, later, president Hisashi Kaneko.

New president Koji Nishigaki, the first at NEC without an engineering background, led a sweeping reorganization to cut 10% of the company's workforce — 15,000 employees — over three years. He revamped NEC operations around Internet application hardware, software, and services. In 1998 NEC formed a rare pact with a Japanese rival, allying with Hitachi to consolidate memory chip operations. The restructuring of Packard Bell NEC (NEC by then owned 88%) helped cause a $1.3 billion loss for fiscal 1999, NEC's worst-ever drop. NEC folded up its Packard Bell NEC division later that year, imposing layoffs of about 80% of its staff, divesting it from the US retail market, and excising the historic Packard Bell brand name.

NEC restructured again in 2000, splitting into more autonomous units and streamlining its PC operations. That year the company launched an aggressive spending program in a move to lead the broadband mobile networking market. In early 2001 NEC ended a long-running dispute with Cray, investing $25 million in the company and granting distribution rights to its vector supercomputers in North America — a deal contingent upon Cray's dropping an antidumping suit that led to heavy import taxes being placed on NEC supercomputers sold in the US.

In 2002 NEC announced plans to spin off its semiconductor operations and form joint ventures for other divisions comprising its NEC Electron Devices business.

EXECUTIVES

Chairman: Hajime Sasaki, age 70
Vice Chairman: Akinobu Kanasugi, age 65
President: Kaoru Yano, age 62
SEVP: Toshiro Kawamura
EVP: Kazuhiko Kobayashi
EVP: Shunichi Suzuki
SVP, Broadband Solutions Business Unit:
 Saburo Takizawa
SVP, Domestic Sales Business Unit: Kazumasa Fujie
SVP, Infrastructure Solutions Business Unit and Mission Critical Systems Business Unit:
 Masatoshi Aizawa
SVP, Mobile Business Unit: Tsutomu Nakamura
SVP, Computers Platform Business Unit:
 Masahiko Yamamoto
SVP, Software Business Unit: Koichi Ikumi
SVP, Industrial Solutions Business Unit:
 Iwao Fuchigami
Auditors: Ernst & Young ShinNihon

LOCATIONS

HQ: NEC Corporation
 (Nippon Denki Kabushiki Kaisha)
 7-1, Shiba 5-chome, Minato-ku,
 Tokyo 108-8001, Japan
Phone: +81-3-3454-1111   **Fax:** +81-3-3798-1510
Web: www.nec.com

2006 Sales

	% of total
Japan	72
Other countries	28
Total	**100**

PRODUCTS/OPERATIONS

Selected Products

IT Solutions
 PCs
  Desktop
  Handheld
  Notebook
 Peripherals
  CD-ROMs
  Monitors
  Projectors
 Servers
 Supercomputers
Network Solutions
 Broadcasting equipment
 Control servers
 Fiber-optic devices
 Gateways
 Lasers
 Mobile networking and communications devices
 Multiplexers
 Network management applications
 Postal automation systems
 Routers and switches
 Satellite systems
Electron Devices
 Application-specific components
 Discrete devices
 Flat-panel displays
 Integrated circuits
 Memory
 Microprocessors
 Optoelectronics
 Radio-frequency and microwave devices

COMPETITORS

Acer	Mitsubishi Electric
Alcatel-Lucent	Motorola
AMD	Nokia
Apple Computer	Nortel Networks
Canon	Oki Electric
CASIO COMPUTER	Philips Electronics
Cisco Systems	Ricoh
Dell	Samsung Electronics
EDS	Samsung Group
Epson	SANYO
Ericsson	Sharp
Fujifilm	Siemens AG
Fujitsu	Sony
Hewlett-Packard	STMicroelectronics
Hitachi	Sun Microsystems
IBM	Terabeam Inc
Intel	Texas Instruments
Matsushita	Toshiba
Micron Technology	Unisys
Microsoft	

HISTORICAL FINANCIALS

Company Type: Public

Income Statement

FYE: March 31

	REVENUE ($ mil.)	NET INCOME ($ mil.)	NET PROFIT MARGIN	EMPLOYEES
3/06	41,239	—	—	154,180
3/05	45,650	—	—	147,800
3/04	48,120	—	—	143,393
3/03	40,244	—	—	145,807
3/02	39,086	—	—	142,000
Annual Growth	**1.3%**	—	—	**2.1%**

Revenue History

NASDAQ (GS): NIPNY

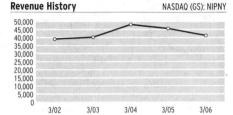

Nestlé

With instant coffee, baby formula, and bottled water in the mix, Nestlé crunches more than just chocolate. The world's #1 food company in terms of sales, Nestlé is the world leader in coffee (Nescafé). It is also one of the world's largest bottled water (Perrier) and baby-food makers. Its 2001 purchase of Ralston Purina made it a top player in the pet food business. Ranging from kitty kibble to pasta, chocolate, and dairy products, its most well-known global brands include Buitoni, Friskies, Maggi, Nescafé, Nestea, and Nestlé. In addition to food products, Nestlé owns about 75% of Alcon Inc. (ophthalmic drugs, contact-lens solutions, and equipment for ocular surgery) and about 28% of cosmetics giant L'Oréal.

The company has a joint venture with L'Oréal (Galderma) that makes nutritional supplements aimed at improving skin, hair, and nails; and another joint venture with Colgate-Palmolive, which develops and markets functional confectionery. Other joint ventures include Cereal Partners Worldwide with General Mills, and Beverage Partners Worldwide with Coke.

Nestlé has long been an international company. Many of its brands are unique to particular countries, with products tailored to local tastes. Seeking to further strengthen its position in the worldwide ice cream market, in 2003 Nestlé acquired the ice cream and related products of the Mövenpick Group, a Swiss food company. The acquisition brought Nestlé licensing agreements with companies in Egypt, Finland, Germany, Norway, Sweden, and Saudi Arabia.

In keeping with its strategy to concentrate on value-added products, during 2006 Nestlé sold its cocoa processing facilities in Germany and the UK to Cargill. Adding to its dominance in the European ice cream sector, the company acquired Finnish dairy company Valid's Valiojäätelö's ice cream business and Greece's Delta Ice cream, which has operations in Bulgaria,

Greece, Macedonia, Montenegro, Romania, and Serbia. Later that year, Nestlé bought the Australian breakfast cereal, snack, and soup operations of Uncle Tobys from Burns Philp for $670 million. The cereal portion was integrated into Cereal Partners Worldwide. In another streamlining move, the company agreed to sell its canned liquid milk businesses in Southeast Asia to Singapore-based Fraser and Neave.

Hedging its bets considering its food products (candy bars, ice cream) are on the opposite end of the waistline wars, Nestlé acquired Jenny Craig for $600 million in 2006.

HISTORY

Henri Nestlé purchased a factory in Vevey, Switzerland, in 1843 that made products ranging from nut oils to rum. In 1867 he developed a powder made from cow's milk and wheat flour as a substitute for mother's milk. A year earlier Americans Charles and George Page had founded the Anglo-Swiss Condensed Milk Company in Cham, Switzerland, using Gail Borden's milk-canning technology.

In 1875 Nestlé sold his eponymous company, then doing business in 16 countries. When Anglo-Swiss launched a milk-based infant food in 1878, Nestlé's new owners responded by introducing a condensed-milk product. In 1905, a year after Nestlé began selling chocolate, the companies ended their rivalry by merging under the Nestlé name.

Hampered by limited milk supplies during WWI, the company expanded into regions less affected by the war, such as the US. In 1929 it acquired Cailler, the first company to mass-produce chocolate bars, and Swiss General, inventor of milk chocolate.

An investment in a Brazilian condensed-milk factory during the 1920s paid an unexpected dividend when Brazilian coffee growers suggested the company develop a water-soluble "coffee cube." Released in 1938, Nescafé instant coffee quickly became popular.

Other new products included Nestlé's Crunch bar (1938), Quik drink mix (1948), and Taster's Choice instant coffee (1966). Nestlé expanded during the 1970s with acquisitions such as Beringer Brothers wines (sold in 1995), Stouffer's, and Libby's.

Moving beyond foods in 1974, Nestlé acquired a 49% stake in Gesparal, a holding company that controls the French cosmetics company L'Oréal. It acquired pharmaceutical firm Alcon Laboratories three years later.

Helmut Maucher was named chairman and CEO in 1981. He began beefing up Nestlé's global presence. Boycotters had long accused Nestlé of harming children in developing countries through the unethical promotion of infant formula, and Maucher acknowledged the ongoing boycott by meeting with the critics and setting up a commission to police adherence to World Health Organization guidelines.

Nestlé bought Carnation in 1985. Maucher doubled the company's chocolate business in 1988 with the purchase of UK chocolate maker Rowntree (Kit Kat). Also in the 1980s Nestlé acquired Buitoni pastas.

The company expanded in the 1990s with the purchases of Butterfinger and Baby Ruth candies, Source Perrier water, Alpo pet food, and Ortega Mexican foods. Company veteran Peter Brabeck-Letmathe succeeded Maucher as CEO in 1997. He cleaned out Nestlé's pantry by selling non-core businesses. In 1999 Nestlé merged its US novelty ice-cream unit with operations of Pillsbury's Häagen-Dazs to form Ice Cream Partners USA.

In 2000 Nestlé purchased snack maker PowerBar. In 2001 Nestlé bought Ralston Purina for $10.3 billion, making it the world's largest pet food maker. To win FTC approval, the companies agreed to sell Meow Mix and Alley Cat dry cat food brands to Hartz Mountain. In a deal that gives Nestlé a 99-year license to use the Häagen-Dazs brand in the US, the company agreed to pay $641 million to General Mills (which has bought Pillsbury from Britain's Diageo) for the other half of Ice Cream Partners.

Later that same year CEO Peter Brabeck-Letmathe announced he was considering reducing the number of outside directorships that he holds because of increased demands as the leader of Nestlé. At the time Brabeck-Letmathe sat on the boards of Alcon, Credit Suisse, Dreyer's Grand Ice Cream, L'Oréal, Roche Holdings, and "Winterthur" Swiss Insurance Company. (He has since left the "Winterthur" board.) And later that year, in a tangle with a French union over retirement benefits, Nestlé threatened to sell Perrier or produce its popular water from another source. However, the company reached a settlement with the union and the production of Perrier continued.

Long-time chairman Rainer Gut retired in 2005 and Brabeck-Letmathe replaced him.

In 2006 Nestlé became the owner of more than 90% of Dreyer's as the result of an exercise of a Put Right whereby Nestlé was required to purchase certain shareholders' Class A Callable Puttable Common Stock (or Class A shares). As a result of this "short form merger," Dreyer's ceased trading on the Nasdaq stock exchange.

EXECUTIVES

Chairman and CEO: Peter Brabeck-Letmathe, age 62
EVP, Asia, Oceania, Africa, and Middle East: Frits van Dijk, age 59
EVP, Finance, Control, Legal, Tax, Purchasing, Export: Paul Polman
EVP, Pharmaceutical and Cosmetic Products, Liaison with L'Oreal, Human Resources, and Corporate Affairs: Francisco Castañer, age 61
EVP, Strategic Business Units and Marketing: Lars Olofsson, age 54
EVP, Technical, Production, Environment, and Research and Development: Werner J. Bauer, age 55
EVP, Nestlé Europe: Luis Cantarell, age 54
EVP, US, Canada, Latin America, and Caribbean: Paul Bulcke
EVP and Chairman and CEO, Nestlé Waters: Carlo Maria Donati, age 59
Deputy EVP, GLOBE Programme, Information Systems, Strategic Supply Chain, eNestlé, and Group Information Security: Chris Johnson, age 45
Deputy EVP and CEO, Nestlé Nutrition: Richard T. Laube, age 49
SVP and Group General Counsel Worldwide: Hans Peter Frick
Chairman and CEO, Nestlé USA: Brad Alford
Head, Investor Relations: Roddy Child-Villiers
General Secretary to Board: Bernard Daniel
Auditors: KPMG Klynveld Peat Marwick Goerdeler SA

LOCATIONS

HQ: Nestlé S.A.
Avenue Nestlé 55, CH-1800 Vevey,
Vaud, Switzerland
Phone: +41-21-924-21-11   **Fax:** +41-21-924-48-00
US HQ: 800 N. Brand Blvd., Glendale, CA 91203
US Phone: 818-549-6000   **US Fax:** 818-549-6952
Web: www.nestle.com

2005 Sales

	% of total
The Americas	41
Europe	38
Asia, Oceania & Africa	21
Total	**100**

PRODUCTS/OPERATIONS

2005 Sales

	% of total
Beverages	26
Milk products, nutrition & ice cream	26
Prepared dishes & cooking aids	18
Chocolate, confectionery & biscuits	12
Pet care	12
Pharmaceutical products	6
Total	**100**

Selected Products and Brands

Bouillons, soups, seasonings, pasta, and sauces
  Buitoni
  Maggi
  Thomy
  Winiary

Chocolate, confectionery, and biscuits
  Butterfinger
  Crunch
  Galak/Milkybar
  Kit Kat
  Nestlé
  Polo
  Smarties

Coffee
  Bonka
  Loumidis
  Nescafé
  Nespresso
  Ricoré, Ricoffy
  Taster's Choice
  Zoégas

Frozen foods (prepared dishes, pizzas)
  Buitoni
  Hot Pockets
  Lean Cuisine
  Maggi
  Stouffer's

Ice cream
  Dreyer's
  Drumstick/Extrême
  Edy's
  Häagen Dazs
  Parar

Infant nutrition
  Beba
  Cérélac
  Good Start
  Lactogen
  Nan
  Neslac
  Nestlé

Other beverages
  Carnation
  Libby's
  Milo
  Nescau
  Nesquik
  Nestea

Performance nutrition
  PowerBar
  Pria

Petcare
  Alpo
  Cat Chow
  Dog Chow
  Fancy Feast
  Gourmet
  Pro Plan
  Purina
  Tidy Cats

Refrigerated products (cold meat products, dough, pasta, pizzas, sauces)
  Buitoni
  Herta
  Nestlé
  Toll House
Shelf-stable products
  Carnation
  Coffee-Mate
  La Lechera
  Milkmaid
  Moça
  Molico
  Nido
  Svelty
Water
  Al Manhal
  Arrowhead
  Deer Park
  Nestlé Aquarel
  Nestlé Pure Life
  Ozarka
  Perrier
  Poland Spring
  S.Pellegrino
  San Bernardo
  Vittel

COMPETITORS

Abbott Labs	Kerry Group
Atkins Nutritionals	Kraft Foods
Bally Total Fitness	Kraft Foods International
Barilla	Kraft Foods North America
Bausch & Lomb	L A Weight Loss
Beverly Hills Weight Loss	Lindt & Sprüngli
Brach's	Mars
Cadbury Schweppes	Medifast
Campbell Soup	Novartis
Charoen Pokphand Group	NutriSystem
Colgate-Palmolive	PepsiCo
ConAgra	Procter & Gamble
Danone	Revlon
eDiets Europe	Russell Stover
eDiets.com	Sara Lee
Ferrara Pan Candy	Slim-Fast
Fit America	Suntory Ltd.
General Mills	TCHIBO Holding
GNC	Unilever
Goya	Unilever NV
Heinz	Unilever PLC
Hershey	United Biscuits
HMG	Weight Watchers
Kellogg	Weight Watchers Ltd.
Kent Gida	World's Finest Chocolate

HISTORICAL FINANCIALS

Company Type: Public

Income Statement				FYE: December 31
	REVENUE ($ mil.)	NET INCOME ($ mil.)	NET PROFIT MARGIN	EMPLOYEES
12/05	69,208	6,075	8.8%	253,000
12/04	76,660	5,935	7.7%	247,000
12/03	70,823	5,002	7.1%	253,000
12/02	64,258	5,451	8.5%	254,199
12/01	50,624	3,993	7.9%	229,765
Annual Growth	8.1%	11.1%	—	2.4%

2005 Year-End Financials

Debt ratio: 16.4%
Return on equity: 16.8%
Cash ($ mil.): 13,217
Current ratio: 1.17
Long-term debt ($ mil.): 6,195

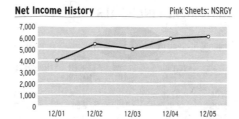

Net Income History Pink Sheets: NSRGY

Nikon

Paul Simon may still have a Nikon camera and still love to take a photograph, but Nikon's focus extends far wider than that. Though well-known for its cameras, lenses, and other consumer optical products, Nikon vies with national rival Canon and Netherlands-based ASML Holding to be the world's top producer of photolithography steppers — crucial equipment used to etch circuitry onto semiconductor wafers and LCD panels. The company makes a broad range of other products, including binoculars, eyewear, surveying instruments, microscopes, industrial equipment, and electronic imaging equipment. Nikon is part of the huge Mitsubishi *keiretsu*, a group of businesses linked by cross-ownership.

Serving the microelectronics industry, Nikon is a leader in manufacturing lithography equipment and boasts more than 7,600 exposure systems installed worldwide.

Nikon has adjusted operations in an effort to become more nimble in the face of a notoriously volatile chip market. It has reorganized into more-autonomous divisions, an arrangement under which the parent corporation serves as a holding company.

The range of Nikon's products offers a snapshot of the optical world. Its cameras have caught images from every manned space flight since Apollo 13. Its microscopes are used in schools and cell biology research laboratories, and its eye examination equipment and prescription glasses and sunglasses are fixtures in opticians' offices worldwide.

HISTORY

Lensmaker Nippon Kogaku KK formed in 1917 with the merger of three large Japanese optical glassmakers. Nippon Kogaku started selling binoculars in 1921; the company introduced its first microscope four years later.

In 1932 the company adopted the brand name Nikkor for its lenses, which were attached to other manufacturers' cameras. By WWII the company had diversified into cameras, microscopes, binoculars, surveying equipment, measuring instruments, and eyeglass lenses. During this time the Japanese government bought nearly all of the company's products. Nippon Kogaku began using the Nikon brand name on its cameras in 1946.

The company introduced its first commercially available pocket camera in the early 1950s, but few of Nikon's cameras made it out of Japan. The world would not begin to appreciate the quality of Nikon's products until photojournalists began using them in the Korean War.

Continuing a European expansion in the 1960s, the company opened subsidiaries in Switzerland (1961) and the Netherlands (1968). The company, in conjunction with undersea explorer Jacques Cousteau and a partner, introduced an underwater camera system in 1963. The 1970s were years of further development: The company introduced high-precision coordinate measuring instruments (1971) and sunglasses (1972), among other products. During the late 1970s Canon passed Minolta and Nikon as the world's top seller of cameras, setting off a battle that has seesawed ever since.

In 1980 the company developed its first stepper system for the semiconductor industry. By 1984 Nikon controlled 53% of the Japanese stepper market. Nippon Kogaku changed its name in 1988 to Nikon Corporation.

The company further broadened its geographic scope in the early 1990s, opening subsidiaries in South Korea (1990), Thailand (1990), Hungary (1991), Italy (1993), and Singapore (1995). When demand for chips dropped in the early 1990s, so did Nikon's sales: the company lost money in fiscal 1993 and fiscal 1994. It restructured its unprofitable camera division, cutting staff by a third to save cash.

In 1997 Shoichiro Yoshida, a Nikon designer since the 1950s who became a proponent of the company's stepper business, was named president, replacing Shigeo Ono, who became chairman. A slumping Asian market and declining prices for chips caused demand for steppers to fall and left the company with slack earnings for fiscal 1998 and 1999. Rebounds in the markets for digital cameras and semiconductor equipment led Nikon back into the black in 2000.

In 2001 the company expanded its semiconductor equipment offerings by entering the market for chemical mechanical polishing (CMP) equipment. In June of that year Ono retired as chairman; Yoshida replaced him.

EXECUTIVES

President, CEO, COO, and Director: Michio Kariya
EVP, CFO, and Director: Ichiro Terato
Senior Managing Director; President, Imaging Company; and Director: Makoto Kimura
Senior Managing Director; President, Core Technology Center; General Manager, Production Technology Headquarters; General Manager, Glass Division; and Director: Kyoichi Suwa
Managing Director; President, Corporate Strategy; General Manager, Information System Management; President, Business Administration; and Director: Mamoru Kajiwara
Managing Director; Divisional President, Office of Management Strategy; and Director: Norio Miyauchi
Managing Director; VP, Imaging Company; and Director: Naoki Tomino
Managing Director; President, Precision Equipment; and Director: Kazuo Ushida
Managing Director; VP, Precision Equipment Company; General Manager, Production Headquarters, Precision Equipment Company; and Director: Yoshimichi Kawai
President, Instruments Company and Director: Hidetoshi Mori

VP, Core Technology Center; General Manager, Optical Technology Headquarters, Core Technology Center; and Director: Yutaka Ichihara
VP, Core Technology Center and General Manager, Intellectual Property Headquarters, Core Technology Center: Takao Watanabe
VP, Corporate Strategy Center: Hideshi Hirai
VP, Precision Equipment Company: Masami Kumazawa
General Manager, Development Management Department, Imaging Company: Tetsuro Goto
VP, Business Administration Center: Koji Morishita
General Manager, LCD Equipment Division, Precision Equipment Company: Jun Iwasaki
President and CEO, Nikon Inc.: Toshiyuki Masai
Auditors: Deloitte Touche Tohmatsu

LOCATIONS

HQ: Nikon Corporation
Fuji Bldg., 2-3 Marunouchi 3-chome, Chiyoda-ku, Tokyo 100-8331, Japan
Phone: +81-3-3214-5311   **Fax:** +81-3-3216-1454
US HQ: 1300 Walt Whitman Rd., Melville, NY 11747
US Phone: 631-547-4200   **US Fax:** 631-547-0362
Web: www.nikon.com

Nikon has operations in Canada, China, the Czech Republic, France, Germany, Hong Kong, Hungary, Italy, Japan, Malaysia, the Netherlands, Poland, Singapore, South Korea, Sweden, Switzerland, Taiwan, Thailand, the UK, and the US.

2006 Sales

	% of total
Asia/Pacific	
Japan	52
Other countries	14
North America	19
Europe	15
Total	**100**

PRODUCTS/OPERATIONS

2006 Sales

	% of total
Imaging Products	54
Precision Equipment	32
Instruments	7
Other	7
Total	**100**

Selected Products

Imaging Products
  Camera lenses
  Compact cameras
  Digital cameras
  Film scanners
  Single-lens reflex (SLR) cameras

Precision Equipment
  Semiconductor and liquid crystal display (LCD) steppers

Instruments
  Biological and industrial microscopes
  Inspection equipment
  Measuring instruments
  Medical imaging systems
  Ophthalmic instruments

Other
  Binoculars
  Eyeglasses
  Sunglasses
  Surveying instruments
  Telescopes

COMPETITORS

ASML	Fujifilm
Canon	Olympus
Carl Zeiss	Pentax
Eastman Kodak	Ultratech
FSI International	

HISTORICAL FINANCIALS

Company Type: Public

Income Statement

FYE: March 31

	REVENUE ($ mil.)	NET INCOME ($ mil.)	NET PROFIT MARGIN	EMPLOYEES
3/06	6,216	246	4.0%	18,725
3/05	5,937	225	3.8%	16,758
3/04	4,793	23	0.5%	13,636
3/03	3,913	(68)	—	13,184
3/02	3,641	(45)	—	14,328
Annual Growth	**14.3%**	—	—	**6.9%**

Net Income History

Exchange: Tokyo

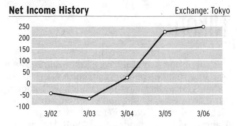

Nintendo

It's not a game, boy, it's serious business, and Nintendo knows it. One of the Big Three videogame console makers, Nintendo makes the GameCube console, which battles with Microsoft's Xbox for second place in its industry (Sony's PlayStation 2 is the world's top game system). In the handheld console segment, however, Nintendo's Game Boy system remains the leader. The firm debuted a videogame player called Nintendo DS (Nintendo Double Screen) in 2004, the Game Boy Micro in late 2005, and the DS Lite in 2006. Its Wii, pronounced "we," videogame system arrived in time for 2006 holiday sales.

Nintendo is also the game software market leader and has sold more than 2 billion games since 1985; hit series include *Pokémon*, *Super Mario Brothers*, and *The Legend of Zelda*.

Nintendo (which, loosely translated, means "leave luck to heaven") once ruled the golden age of the video game industry until more powerful machines introduced by SEGA (in 1989) and Sony (in 1994) pared down its kingdom (SEGA has since stopped making console systems). Microsoft entered the gaming hardware market in 2001, leaving Nintendo with a shrinking piece of the pie.

The company plans to broaden its previous focus on kids and concentrate its efforts on its games, in contrast to competitors Sony and Microsoft, which are developing increasingly complex multimedia systems. The introduction of the Nintendo DS system is a competitive move designed to counter the launch of Sony's PlayStation Portable. The company launched Nintendo Wi-Fi Connection, a free service that will allow DS system players to play other users simply by connecting to a wireless network.

Nintendo introduced a new game console, named Wii (pronounced "we"), in time for the 2006 holiday selling season. The system follows its competitors' new offerings — Microsoft's Xbox 360 and Sony's PlayStation 3 (within the same week). Unlike those two offerings Wii is a game console first and foremost and not a digital entertainment hub. The company hopes that its Wii system, priced at about half of what Sony's Playstation 3 sells for depending on features, will woo game players and make gaming a family activity.

In a bold move that signals a strong focus on just gaming, Wii does not play DVDs and requires an add-on unit to do so. In addition to being backwards compatible with GameCube titles, players also have access to an online library of popular classic Nintendo titles dating back to 1985.

Nintendo owns a majority stake in the Seattle Mariners baseball team, which it purchased for $125 million in 1992.

HISTORY

Nintendo Co. was founded in 1889 as the Marufuku Company to make and sell *hanafuda*, Japanese game cards. In 1907 the company began producing Western playing cards. It became the Nintendo Playing Card Company in 1951 and began making theme cards under a licensing agreement with Disney in 1959.

During the 1950s and 1960s, Hiroshi Yamauchi took the company public and diversified into new areas (including a "love hotel"). The company took its current name in 1963. Nintendo began making toys at the start of the 1970s and entered the budding field of video games toward the end of the decade by licensing Magnavox's Pong technology. Then it moved into arcade games. Nintendo established its US subsidiary, Nintendo of America, in 1980; its first hit was *Donkey Kong* ("silly monkey") and its next was *Super Mario Bros.* (named after Nintendo of America's warehouse landlord).

The company released Famicom, a technologically advanced home video game system, in Japan in 1983. With its high-quality sound and graphics, Famicom was a smash, selling 15.2 million consoles and more than 183 million game cartridges in Japan alone. Meanwhile, in 1983 and 1984, the US home game market crashed, sending pioneer Atari up in flames. Nintendo persevered, successfully launching Famicom in the US in 1986 as the Nintendo Entertainment System (NES).

To prevent a barrage of independently produced, low-quality software (which had contributed to Atari's demise), Nintendo established stringent licensing policies for its software developers. Licensees were required to have approval of every game design, buy the blank cartridges from the company, agree not to make the game for any of Nintendo's competitors, and pay Nintendo royalties for the honor of developing a game.

As the market became saturated, Nintendo sought new products, releasing Game Boy in 1989 and the Super Family Computer game system (Super NES in the US) in 1991. The company broke with tradition in 1994 by making design alliances with companies like Silicon Graphics. After creating a 32-bit product in 1995, Nintendo launched the much-touted N64 game system in 1996. Price wars between the top contenders continued in the US and Japan.

In 1998 Nintendo released *Pokémon*, which involves trading and training virtual monsters (it had been popular in Japan since 1996), in the US. The company also launched the video game *The Legend of Zelda: Ocarina of Time*, which sold 2.5 million units in about six weeks.

Nintendo announced in 1999 that its next-generation game system, Dolphin (later renamed

GameCube), would use IBM's PowerPC microprocessor and Matsushita's DVD players.

In September 2001 Nintendo launched its long-awaited GameCube console system (which retailed at $100 less than its console rivals, Sony's PlayStation 2 and Microsoft's XBox); the system debuted in North America in November. In addition, the company came out with Game Boy Advance, its newest handheld model with a bigger screen and faster chip.

Nintendo formed a business alliance with game software developer Namco in May 2002 for the development and sales of games for the GameCube platform. In October the European Union fined Nintendo $165 million for colluding with seven of its distributors to limit the cross-border flow of its products in a scam to raise prices.

In April 2003 the company cut its royalty rates (charged to outside game developers), in an effort to enhance its video game titles portfolio. Later in the year Nintendo bought a stake (about 3%) in game developer and toy maker Bandai, a move expected to solidify cooperation between the two companies in marketing game software.

EXECUTIVES

President: Satoru Iwata
Senior Managing Director; General Manager, Corporate Analysis and Administration Division: Yoshihiro Mori
Senior Managing Director; General Manager, Licensing Division: Shinji Hatano
Senior Managing Director; General Manager, Entertainment Analysis and Development Division: Shigeru Miyamoto
Senior Managing Director; General Manager, Integrated Research and Development Division: Genyo Takeda
Senior Managing Director; General Manager, Research and Engineering Division: Nobuo Nagai
Managing Director; General Manager, Finance and Information Systems Division: Masaharu Matsumoto
Managing Director; General Manager, General Affairs Division: Eiichi Suzuki
Director; General Manager, Tokyo Branch Office: Kazuo Kawahara
Director; Chairman and CEO, Nintendo of America: Tatsumi Kimishima
Director; General Manager, Manufacturing Division: Takao Ohta
Director; General Manager, Personnel Department: Kaoru Takemura
Auditors: ChuoAoyama PricewaterhouseCoopers

LOCATIONS

HQ: Nintendo Co., Ltd.
11-1 Kamitoba hokotate-cho, Minami-ku, Kyoto 601-8501, Japan
Phone: +81-75-662-9600   **Fax:** +81-75-662-9620
US HQ: 4820 150th Ave. NE, Redmond, WA 98052
US Phone: 425-882-2040   **US Fax:** 425-882-3585
Web: www.nintendo.co.jp

Nintendo Co. has offices and plants in Japan and major subsidiaries in Australia, Canada, France, Germany, the Netherlands, Spain, and the US.

2006 Sales

	$ mil.	% of total
Americas	1,796	42
Japan	1,328	31
Europe	1,105	25
Other regions	98	2
Total	**4,327**	**100**

PRODUCTS/OPERATIONS

Game Consoles and Hardware

Game Boy
Game Boy Advance
Game Boy Player
GameCube
Nintendo DS
Super Nintendo Entertainment System (Super NES)
Wavebird

Selected Games

Donkey Kong series
Pokémon series
Star Wars Episode I Racer
Spider-Man series
Super Mario series
Yoshi series
Zelda series

COMPETITORS

Atari	Namco Bandai
Editis	Radica Games
Electronic Arts	SEGA
LucasArts	Sony
Microsoft	Take-Two
Midway Games	

HISTORICAL FINANCIALS

Company Type: Public

Income Statement

FYE: March 31

	REVENUE ($ mil.)	NET INCOME ($ mil.)	NET PROFIT MARGIN	EMPLOYEES
3/06	4,327	837	19.3%	3,840
3/05	4,788	813	17.0%	3,840
3/04	4,869	314	6.5%	—
3/03	4,203	561	13.4%	2,977
3/02	4,183	803	19.2%	3,073
Annual Growth	0.8%	1.0%	—	5.7%

Net Income History

Pink Sheets: NTDOY

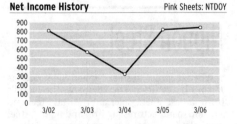

Nippon Life Insurance

Nippon Life Insurance, also known as Nissay, is one of Japan's biggest life insurers (along with Dai-Ichi Mutual Life and Meiji Yasuda Life). A door-to-door sales corps peddles its plain-vanilla products, including individual and group life and annuity products, and the company has nearly 11 million policyholders and 300,000 corporate customers. Deregulation has allowed the company to move into such areas as corporate lending. Other activities include real estate development and management and a variety of educational and philanthropic projects. The company's overseas activities traditionally focus on providing coverage to Japanese companies and citizens abroad.

As the Japanese economy struggles to recover, Nippon Life has grappled with declining individual sales as consumers cut back on expenditures. To attract customers, the company continues to broaden its sales channels, adding Internet and telephone sales and allowing customers to access loans directly through ATMs. The company has also started to target female customers more heavily as potential customers. Since deregulation in the financial services industry has boosted competition, the company has expanded its offerings to include nursing/medical services and a 401(k)-like pension plan. Nippon Life has also partnered with such firms as Deutsche Bank and Putnam to offer investment trusts, investment advisory, and other services. Other business lines include property/casualty insurance (the company merged its Nissay General subsidiary with Dowa Fire & Marine) and information technology services for other insurers.

HISTORY

Nippon Life, known as Nissay, was a product of the modernization that began after US Commodore Perry opened Japan's ports to foreigners in 1854. Industry and trade were Japan's first focus, but financial infrastructure soon followed. The country's first insurer (Meiji Mutual) opened in 1881. In 1889 Osaka banker Sukesaburo Hirose founded Nippon Life as a stock company. It grew and opened branches in Tokyo (1890) and Kyushu (1895).

In the 20th century, the company developed a direct sales force and began lending directly to businesses. Lending remained the backbone of its asset strategy through most of the century. The insurance market in Japan grew quickly until the late 1920s but had already slowed by the eve of the Depression.

After WWII the company reorganized as a mutual and began mobilizing an army of women to build its sales of installment-premium, basic life policies. In 1962 the company began automating its systems and established operations in the US (1972) and UK (1981).

As interest rates rose in the wake of oil price hikes in the 1970s, the company began offering term life and annuities and slowly moved to diversify its asset holdings from mostly government bonds (whose yields declined as rates rose) to stocks. This movement accelerated in the 1980s, as the businesses that traditionally borrowed from Nippon Life turned directly to capital markets to raise money through debt issues. Seeking to replace its shrinking lending business, the company began investing in US real estate and businesses whose values rose in the mid-1980s. The company reached its zenith in 1987; it owned about 3% of all the stocks on the Tokyo Exchange, held more real estate than Mitsubishi's real estate units, and had bought 13% of US brokerage Shearson Lehman from American Express.

By the end of the year, thanks to the US stock market crash, the value of the Shearson investment had fallen 40%. But the company felt confident enough of its importance as the world's largest insurance company (by assets) to crow its intentions to strong-arm Japan's Ministry of Finance into letting it diversify into trust and securities operations.

Then its bubble burst. In 1989 real estate crashed, and the stock market lost more than half its value. Japan's economy failed to improve, and Nippon Life was left struggling with nonperforming loans and assets whose value had declined.

The company suffered further from policy cancellations and from the Ministry of Finance's focus on buoying banks. In 1997 the ministry asked Nippon Life to convert its subordinated debt from Nippon Credit Bank (now Aozora Bank) to stock. That year Nippon Life formed an alliance with Marsh & McLennan's Putnam Investments subsidiary to help manage its assets; the relationship deepened in 1998 when they began developing investment trust products.

The next year Nippon Life faced a shareholder lawsuit over its involvement in the collapse of Nippon Credit Bank; the company claims the Ministry of Finance tricked it into bailing out the bank, even though it was beyond rescue. In 2001 the company merged its Nissay General subsidiary with Dowa Fire & Marine, creating nonlife insurer Nissay Dowa.

In 2003 joint venture Nissay-SVA Life Insurance was formed with consumer electronics manufacturer SVA (Group) Ltd.

EXECUTIVES

Chairman: Ikuo Uno, age 71
Vice Chairman: Mitsuhiro Ishibashi, age 64
President: Kunie Okamoto, age 62
EVP: Eitaro Waki, age 61
EVP: Takao Arai, age 58
Senior Managing Director: Takashi Minagawa, age 59
Senior Managing Director: Tetsuro Taki, age 57
Senior Managing Director: Sadao Kato, age 57
Senior Managing Director: Keizo Tsutsui, age 58
Senior Managing Director: Shunsuke Wada, age 58
Managing Director: Kiyoshi Ujihara
Managing Director: Chiaki Hamaguchi
Managing Director: Akito Kuwabara
Managing Director: Yoichi Fujita
Managing Director: Yoshikazu Takeda
Auditors: Tohmatsu & Co.

LOCATIONS

HQ: Nippon Life Insurance Company
(Nippon Seimei Hoken Kabushiki Kaisha)
3-5-12, Imabashi, Chuo-ku, Osaka 541-8501, Japan
Phone: +81-6-6209-5525   **Fax:** +81-3-5533-5282
US HQ: Nippon Life Insurance Company of America,
521 5th Ave., New York, NY 10175
US Phone: 212-682-3000   **US Fax:** 212-682-3002
Web: www.nissay.co.jp

Nippon Life has operations in China, Germany, Japan, the Philippines, Singapore, Thailand, the UK, and the US.

PRODUCTS/OPERATIONS

2006 Sales

	% of total
Premiums	70
Investment income	25
Other	5
Total	**100**

Selected Subsidiaries and Affiliates

Nippon Life Insurance Company of America (97%, US)
Nippon Life Insurance Company of the Philippines, Inc. (50%)
Nissay Asset Management Corporation (90%)
Nissay Capital Co., Ltd.
Nissay Card Service Co., Ltd.
Nissay Computer Co., Ltd. (45%)
Nissay Credit Guarantee Co., Ltd. (18%)
Nissay Dowa General Insurance Co., Ltd. (36%)
Nissay Information Technology Co., Ltd. (75%)
Nissay Leasing Co., Ltd. (51%)
Nissay-SVA Life Insurance Co., Ltd. (50%)
NLI Commercial Mortgage Fund, LLC (US)
NLI Properties Central, Inc. (US)
NLI Properties East, Inc. (US)
NLI Properties West, Inc. (US)

COMPETITORS

Aflac	Gibraltar Life Insurance
Allianz	ING
Asahi Mutual Life	Meiji Yasuda Life
AXA Life Insurance	Millea Holdings
Daido Life	Mitsui Life
Dai-ichi Mutual Life	Sumitomo Life
Fukoku Mutual	Taiyo Life

HISTORICAL FINANCIALS

Company Type: Mutual company

Income Statement

FYE: March 31

	ASSETS ($ mil.)	NET INCOME ($ mil.)	INCOME AS % OF ASSETS	EMPLOYEES
3/06	432,269	1,745	0.4%	66,437
3/05	434,942	1,885	0.4%	67,116
3/04	430,631	1,880	0.4%	70,073
3/03	366,426	943	0.3%	72,784
3/02	343,097	2,100	0.6%	72,895
Annual Growth	**5.9%**	**(4.5%)**	**—**	**(2.3%)**

2006 Year-End Financials

Equity as % of assets: —   Long-term debt ($ mil.): —
Return on assets: 0.4%   Sales ($ mil.): 58,885
Return on equity: —

Net Income History

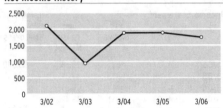

Nippon Steel

When it comes to steel, Nippon Steel rates as Japan's heavy lifter. The company, the world's third-largest steel maker after Mittal Steel and Arcelor, manufactures pig iron and ingots, steel bars, plates, sheets, pipes, and tubes, as well as specialty, processed, and fabricated steel products. Nippon Steel's annual crude steel output is roughly 33 million tons. The company's operations include engineering, construction, chemicals, nonferrous metals, ceramics, electricity supply, information and communications, and urban development (theme parks and condominiums). Nippon Steel also provides energy, finance, and insurance services.

The company has experienced steady growth in its overall business due to an increase in exports primarily to East Asia and more specifically, China. The rising demand for steel has brought its own challenges, such as bottlenecked production, that Nippon Steel plans to resolve by improving its integrated production process.

Part of the strategy calls for alliances with other major steel makers, including one with POSCO, where Nippon Steel has transferred its direct-melting gasification technology. Nippon Steel has also formed an alliance with Kobe Steel to acquire equity stakes in East Asia United Steel, which will share semifinished products. Baosteel-NSC/Arcelor Automotive Steel Sheets is a joint venture among Nippon Steel, Arcelor, and Baoshan Iron & Steel that began operations in 2004. Nippon Steel and Sumitomo Metal Industries integrated their building products units (structural steel sheet) and civil engineering materials operations, creating two new joint ventures. The new companies will be majority-owned by Nippon Steel, with Sumitomo taking 25% and 15% stakes, respectively.

Nippon Steel also plans to acquire the interest it doesn't already own in its key distributors, Nippon Steel Logistics (59%) and Seitetsu Unyu (80%), and then form a holding company that will integrate the three companies.

HISTORY

As Japan prepared for war, the government in 1934 merged Yawata Works, its largest steel producer, and other Japanese steelmakers into one giant company — Japan Iron & Steel. During postwar occupation, Japan Iron & Steel was ordered to dissolve. Yawata Iron & Steel and Fuji Iron & Steel emerged from the dissolution, and with Western assistance the Japanese steel industry recovered from the war years. In the late 1960s Fuji Steel bought Tokai Iron & Steel (1967), and Yawata Steel took over Yawata Steel Tube Company (1968).

Yawata and Fuji merged in 1970 and became Nippon Steel, the world's largest steelmaker. In the 1970s the Japanese steel industry was criticized in the US; American competitors complained that Japan was "dumping" low-cost exports. Meanwhile, Nippon Steel aggressively courted China.

The company diversified in the mid-1980s to wean itself from dependence on steel. It created a New Materials unit in 1984, retraining "redundant" steelworkers to make silicon wafers and forming an Electronics Division in 1986. Nippon Steel began joint ventures with IBM Japan (small computers and software), Hitachi (office workstations), and C. Itoh (information systems for small and midsized companies) in 1988 as increased steel demand for construction and cars in Japan's "bubble economy" took the company to new heights.

In an atmosphere of economic optimism, the company spent more than four times the expected expense to build an amusement park capable of competing with Tokyo Disneyland. The company plowed ahead, spending more than ¥15 billion on the park. Space World amusement park opened on the island of Kyushu in 1990. The company's bubble burst that year.

In response, Nippon Steel cut costs and intensified its diversification efforts by targeting electronics, information and telecommunications, new materials, and chemicals markets. Seeking to remake its steel operations, the company began a drastic, phased restructuring in 1993 that included a step most Japanese companies try to avoid — cutting personnel. A semiconductor division was organized that year as part of the company's diversification strategy.

Upgrading its steel operations, Nippon Steel and partner Mitsubishi in 1996 introduced the world's first mass-production method for making hot-rolled steel sheet directly from smelted stainless steel. Profits were hurt that year by a loss-making project in the information and communications segment and by a steep decline in computer memory-chip prices.

The company began operation of a Chinese steelmaking joint venture, Guangzhou Pacific Tinplate, in 1997. The next year its Singapore-based joint venture with Hitachi, Ltd., began mass-producing computer memory chips in hopes of stemming semiconductor losses. But falling prices convinced Nippon Steel to get out of the memory chip business and in 1999 it sold its semiconductor subsidiary to South Korea's United Microelectronics.

That year the US imposed antidumping duties on the company's steel products. The next year Nippon Steel agreed to form a strategic alliance with South Korea-based Pohang Iron and Steel (POSCO), at that time the world's #1 steel maker. The deal calls for the exploration of joint ventures, shared research, and joint procurement, as well as increased equity stakes in each other (at 2%-3%). Also in 2000 Nippon Steel agreed to provide Sumitomo Metal Industries and Nisshin Steel Co. with stainless steel products.

Early in 2001 Nippon Steel formed a cooperative alliance — focused on automotive sheet products — with French steel giant Usinor (now a part of Arcelor). At the end of the year, Nippon Steel decided to form an alliance with Kobe Steel to pare down costs and share in distribution and production facilities. In 2002 the company continued its series of comprehensive alliances by forming alliances with Japanese steelmaker Nippon Metal Industry to exchange its semi-finished stainless steel technologies and with POSCO to build environment-related businesses.

The company reported a loss of ¥51.69 billion for fiscal 2003 due to securities valuation losses and group restructuring charges. In 2004 Nippon Steel formed a joint venture with Baoshan Iron & Steel and Arcelor to manufacture high-grade automotive steel sheets.

EXECUTIVES

Chairman and Representative Director: Akira Chihara, age 71
President and Representative Director: Akio Mimura, age 66
EVP and Representative Director: Nobuyoshi Fujiwara, age 61
EVP and Representative Director: Makoto Haya, age 61
EVP and Representative Director: Naoki Okumura, age 61
EVP and Representative Director: Kazuo Nagahiro, age 61
EVP: Hideaki Sekizawa, age 61
EVP and Representative Director: Shoji Muneoka, age 60
Managing Director: Toshio Ochiai, age 63
Managing Director: Hideki Furuno, age 62
Managing Director: Hiroshi Shima, age 59
Managing Director: Mitsuo Kitagawa, age 60
Managing Director: Koichi Nakamura, age 60
Managing Director: Tetsuo Imakubo, age 60
Managing Director: Kiichiroh Masuda, age 58
Managing Director: Hidemi Ohta, age 58
Managing Director: Katsutoshi Kurikawa, age 58
Managing Director: Junji Ohta, age 58
Auditors: ChuoAoyama PricewaterhouseCoopers

LOCATIONS

HQ: Nippon Steel Corporation
(Shin Nippon Seitetsu Kabushiki Kaisha)
6-3 Otemachi 2-chome, Chiyoda-ku,
Tokyo 100-8071, Japan
Phone: +81-3-3242-4111   **Fax:** +81-3-3275-5607
US HQ: 780 Third Ave., 34th Fl., New York, NY 10017
US Phone: 212-486-7150   **US Fax:** 212-593-3049
Web: www.nsc.co.jp

Nippon Steel has operations in the Americas, Asia, Australia, and Europe. Its principal subsidiaries are in Australia, Brazil, China, Germany, Singapore, Thailand, and the US.

PRODUCTS/OPERATIONS

Selected Products and Services

Steelmaking and Steel Fabrication
  Fabricated and processed steels
  Pig iron and ingots
  Pipes and tubes
  Plates and sheets
  Sections
  Specialty sheets
Chemicals, Nonferrous Metals, and Ceramics
  Aluminum products
  Ammonium sulfate
  Cement
  Ceramic products
  Coal tar
  Coke
  Ferrite
  Metallic foils
  Semiconductor bonding wire
  Silicon wafers
  Slag products
  Titanium products
  Transformers
Engineering and Construction
  Building construction
  Civil engineering
  Marine construction
  Plant and machinery
  Technical cooperation
Urban Development
  Condominiums
  Theme parks
Electronics, Information/Communications, and LSIs
  Communications services
  Computers and equipment
  Data processing
  Systems development and integration
Other Operations
  Services
    Energy services
    Financial services
    Insurance services
  Transportation
    Loading and unloading
    Marine and land transportation
    Warehousing

COMPETITORS

Arcelor
Bechtel
BlueScope Steel
Corus Group
Fluor
Hitachi
JFE Holdings
Kobe Steel
Marubeni
Mitsubishi Corporation
POSCO
ThyssenKrupp
United States Steel
Vale do Rio Doce
Yamato Kogyo

HISTORICAL FINANCIALS

Company Type: Public

Income Statement

FYE: March 31

	REVENUE ($ mil.)	NET INCOME ($ mil.)	NET PROFIT MARGIN	EMPLOYEES
3/06	33,219	2,925	8.8%	15,212
3/05	31,514	2,051	6.5%	46,451
3/04	27,696	393	1.4%	46,233
3/03	22,940	(431)	—	49,400
3/02	19,461	(214)	—	50,463
Annual Growth	14.3%	—	—	(25.9%)

Net Income History

Exchange: Tokyo

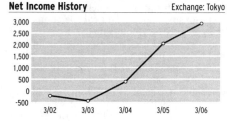

Nissan

Nissan Motor, Japan's #2 auto manufacturer after Toyota and just ahead of Honda, is enjoying one of the car industry's most dramatic turnarounds in recent memory. Nissan's models include Maxima and Sentra cars, Altima and Infiniti upscale sedans, Frontier pickups, the 350Z sports car, and Xterra and Pathfinder SUVs. In 1999 French automaker Renault took a 37% stake in Nissan, and installed president and CEO Carlos Ghosn (nicknamed "Le Cost Killer" based on his talent for turning red ink black) who has since returned the company to profitability. Renault now owns almost 45% of Nissan.

Under the watchful eye of Ghosn, Nissan has gone from a doubtful future to a corporate success story in just a few years. Nissan not only managed to erase automotive debt, it now has cash reserves of about $1.65 billion.

Nissan hit its first series of speed bumps in 2006 after a long stretch of smooth road. Sales hiccups in Japan, the US, and Europe have prompted a few tweaks. After a surge of new products in 2005 Nissan rode out the product in-between time in the US until freshened versions of the Altima and Sentra were unveiled in late 2006. Nissan is also making production adjustments at its plants in the US and Japan.

Late in 2006 Nissan announced plans to introduce a hybrid based on Nissan-developed technology in fiscal 2010. The plan also calls for bringing clean diesel engines to Europe in fiscal 2007 (with the US, China, and Japan getting them sometime after April 2010). The company also plans to expand the availability of flex-fuel vehicles (capable of burning gasoline and ethanol-derived E85) in 2007 with the debut of a flex-fuel Armada (the flex fuel Titan was introduced in 2004).

Nissan is also increasing its investment in R&D and is expanding its presence in emerging markets such as China, Russia, and India.

HISTORY

In 1911 US-trained Hashimoto Masujiro established Tokyo-based Kwaishinsha Motor Car Works to repair, import, and manufacture cars. Kwaishinsha made its first car, sporting its DAT ("fast rabbit" in Japanese) logo, in 1913. Renamed DAT Motors in 1925 and suffering from a strong domestic preference for American cars, the company consolidated with ailing Jitsuyo Motors in 1926. DAT introduced the son of DAT in 1931 — the Datsun minicar ("son" means "damage or loss" in Japanese, hence the spelling change).

Tobata Casting (cast iron and auto parts) bought Datsun's production facilities in 1933. Tobata's Yoshisuke Aikawa believed there was a niche for small cars, and the car operations were spun off as Nissan Motors that year.

During WWII the Japanese government limited Nissan's production to trucks and airplane engines; Nissan survived postwar occupation, in part, due to business with the US Army. The company went public in 1951 and signed a licensing agreement the next year with Austin Motor (UK), which put it back in the car business. A 40% import tax allowed Nissan to compete in Japan even though it had higher costs than those of foreign carmakers.

Nissan entered the US market in 1958 with the model 211, using the Datsun name; it established Nissan Motor Corporation in Los Angeles in 1960. Exports rose as factory automation led to higher quality and lower costs. In the 1970s Nissan expanded exports of fuel-efficient cars such as the Datsun B210. The company became the leading US car importer in 1975.

The company's name change in the US from Datsun to Nissan during the 1980s confused customers and took six years to complete. In 1986 Nissan became the first major Japanese carmaker to build its products in Europe. It launched its high-end Infiniti line in the US in 1989.

Nissan and Japanese telecom firm DDI Corporation set up cellular phone operations in 1992. Japan's recession resulted in a $450 million loss the next year. The company cut costs in 1993 and sold $200 million in real-estate holdings in 1994.

Nissan suffered its fourth straight year of losses, posting an $834 million loss for 1996. Fiscal 1997 brought profits for Nissan — its first since 1992 — in part the result of cost-cutting moves, sales to countries with currencies stronger than the yen, and the launching of new models. In 1998 Nissan made plans to cut production in Japan by 15% over five years, and it received an $827 million loan from the government-owned Japan Development Bank to restructure its debt.

Suffering under an estimated $30 billion in debt in 1999, Nissan invited major carmakers to buy into the company. Renault took a 37% stake and a 15% stake (later increased to 23%) in affiliate Nissan Diesel Motor for $5.4 billion. The stake gave Renault veto power and enabled it to install its chief cost-cutter, Carlos Ghosn, as chief operating officer. Ghosn began plans to slash the number of suppliers, close five plants, and cut its workforce by 14% by 2002.

In 2000 Nissan sold its stake in Fuji Heavy Industries. That year Ghosn became president of Nissan; Nissan's former president, Yoshikazu Hanawa, remained as CEO and chairman. Nissan also announced that it was developing a full-sized truck for the US market and that it and Renault were combining their European sales and marketing operations. Late in the year the company announced plans to build a $930 million manufacturing plant in the US.

Ghosn was named CEO (in addition to president) in 2001. Later in 2001 Nissan announced it would take a 15% stake in Renault while the French carmaker would increase its stake in Nissan to 44%. These steps, along with the French government's decision to reduce its interest in Renault from 44% to 25%, are aimed at further strengthening the bond between the two companies. In 2002 Nissan and Renault completed their planned equity swap.

In mid-2005 Nissan announced that it had selected its assembly plant in Tennessee for production of its first hybrid vehicle.

The following year Nissan began talks with AB Volvo and the Chinese authorities for the sale of Nissan's 50% stake in Dongfeng Motor Co. Ltd. — China's largest maker of commercial trucks.

Later in 2006 billionaire General Motors investor Kirk Kerkorian (who owns about a 10% stake in GM) proposed that the beleaguered US automaker should form a three-way alliance with Nissan and Renault. The three companies' boards subsequently held hasty meetings to ponder the idea. The companies later announced they'd decided there would be no alliance.

Also in 2006, Nissan sold its remaining 6% stake in Nissan Diesel Motor to AB Volvo for about $69 million.

EXECUTIVES

Co-Chairman, President, CEO, Representative Board Member, and Member of the Executive Committee; President and CEO, Nissan North America: Carlos Ghosn, age 52

Co-Chairman, EVP, Administration for Affiliated Companies, External and Government Affairs, Intellectual Asset Management, Industrial Machinery, and Marine, Representative Board Member, and Member of the Executive Committee: Itaru Koeda, age 65

Vice Chairman, External and Government Affairs and Intellectual Asset Management Office: Takeshi Isayama

COO; Japan Operations, General Overseas Markets Operations, China Operations, Global Marketing and Sales, Global Aftersales and Conversion Business, Corporate Quality Assurance and Customer Service, Human Resources, and Treasury, Representative Director and Member of the Executive Committee: Toshiyuki Shiga

EVP, Design, Corporate Planning, Product Planning, Market Intelligence, and LVC Business, Board Member and Member of the Executive Committee: Carlos Tavares

EVP, European Operations and Purchasing, Board Member and Member of the Executive Committee: Hiroto Saikawa, age 53

EVP, Manufacturing, Supply Chain Management, and Global IS, Board Member and Member of the Executive Committee: Tadao Takahashi

EVP, Research, Technology and Engineering Development, Cost Engineering, Board Member and Member of the Executive Committee: Mitsuhiko (Mike) Yamashita

SVP, Alliance Coordination Office, Security Office, Legal Department, Organization Development, Process Re-Engineering, and Secretary; CEO and COO, Global Motorsports: Bernard Rey

SVP, Corporate Quality Assurance and Customer Service Division: Eiji Imai

SVP, Cost Reduction Promotion Office; Manufacturing and Industrial Engineering Division, Oppama Plant, Tochigi Plant, Kyushu Plant, Yokohama Plant, Iwaki Plant; and Overseas Parts Logistics Control Division: Hidetoshi Imazu

SVP, Global Aftersales Division, Aftersales Division (Japan), General Overseas Markets Aftersales Division, and Conversion Business: Junichi Endo

SVP, Global Controller, and Member of the Executive Committee: Alain-Pierre Raynaud

SVP, Global Sales Management Department, Marketing and Sales Brand Management Office, Global Marketing Department, and Global Infiniti Support Department: Steven Wilhite

SVP, Human Resources Department and Diversity Development Office: Hitoshi Kawaguchi

SVP, Integrated System Planning Office, Environmental and Safety Engineering Department, Technology Planning Department, Materials Engineering Department, Materials Engineering Division, and Electronics Engineering Division: Minoru Shinohara

SVP, Japan Marketing and Sales, MC Dealer, Dealer Network Division, and Fleet Business Division: Kazuhiko Toida

SVP, Powertrain Engineering Division: Yo Usuba

SVP, Vehicle Design Engineering Division Number 5, Vehicle Performance Development Department, Body Engineering Department, Advanced Vehicle Engineering Department, and Interior and Exterior Trim Engineering Department: Kimiyasu Nakamura

SVP, Vehicle Production Engineering Division: Sadao Sekiyama

SVP, Design: Shiro Nakamura

Auditors: Ernst & Young ShinNihon

LOCATIONS

HQ: Nissan Motor Co., Ltd.
(Nissan Jidosha Kabushiki Kaisha)
17-1, Ginza 6-chome, Chuo-ku,
Tokyo 104-8023, Japan
Phone: +81-3-3543-5523   **Fax:** +81-3-5565-2228
US HQ: 18501 S. Figueroa St., Gardena, CA 90248
US Phone: 310-771-5631   **US Fax:** 310-516-7967
Web: www.nissan-global.com

Nissan Motor Co. has major manufacturing subsidiaries in China, France, Japan, Mexico, Spain, Taiwan, Thailand, the UK, and the US.

2006 Unit Sales

	% of total
US	30
Japan	24
Europe	15
Other regions	31
Total	**100**

PRODUCTS/OPERATIONS

Selected Products

Nissan	Infiniti
350 Z	FX
Altima	G35 coupe
Armada	G35 sedan
Frontier	I
Maxima	M
Murano	Q
Pathfinder	QX
Quest	
Titan	
Sentra	
Xterra	

COMPETITORS

BMW	Land Rover
Brunswick	Lockheed Martin
DaimlerChrysler	Mazda
Deere	NACCO Industries
Fiat	Peugeot
Ford	Saab Automobile
Fuji Heavy Industries	Suzuki Motor
GE	Toyota
General Motors	Volkswagen
Honda	Volvo
Isuzu	Yamaha Motor
Kia Motors	

HISTORICAL FINANCIALS

Company Type: Public

Income Statement

FYE: March 31

	REVENUE ($ mil.)	NET INCOME ($ mil.)	NET PROFIT MARGIN	EMPLOYEES
3/06	80,178	4,406	5.5%	183,356
3/05	79,742	4,763	6.0%	183,607
3/04	70,087	4,752	6.8%	123,748
Annual Growth	7.0%	(3.7%)	—	21.7%

Net Income History

NASDAQ (CM): NSANY

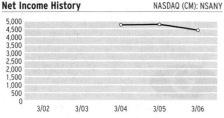

	3/02	3/03	3/04	3/05	3/06

Nokia

Wireless wizard Nokia has cast a spell on the mobile phone market. The company is the world's #1 maker of cell phones (ahead of such rivals as Motorola and Samsung, among others). Nokia is also aiming for the top of the nascent mobile Internet market. The company's products are divided primarily between four divisions: mobile phones (wireless voice and data devices for personal and business uses), multimedia (home satellite systems, and mobile gaming devices), networks (wireless switching and transmission equipment used in carrier networks), and enterprise solutions (wireless systems for businesses). It has agreed to combine its network equipment business with that of Siemens in a joint venture.

The joint venture, to be called Nokia Siemens Networks, would be the #3 player in telecom networking equipment providers after Ericsson and Alcatel-Lucent. Rival Motorola will fall to fourth in the global networking line-up. The Nokia-Siemens deal, valued at more than $30 billion, partly is a reaction to continuing consolidation in the telecom industry, including those of major carriers such as AT&T, Verizon, and Sprint Nextel. It is also an effort to stay ahead of burgeoning newcomers, particularly Asian firms like Huawei Technologies and ZTE.

Nokia's historically robust mobile phone unit also has introduced new products across a range of market niches and managed to pick up market share in the process; the company commands nearly 40% of the global cell phone market. Nokia rolled out new business and consumer models with color screens worldwide and also delivered a unit capable of English and Chinese text recognition to be sold by vendors in China. The company also introduced the N-Gage mobile gaming device. A plan to team up with rival Sanyo Electric to develop advanced mobile handsets was scrapped in mid-2006, only months after it was announced.

HISTORY

Nokia got its start in 1865 when engineer Fredrik Idestam established a mill to manufacture pulp and paper on the Nokia River in Finland. Although Nokia flourished within Finland, the company was not well known to the rest of the world until it attempted to become a regional conglomerate in the early 1960s. French computer firm Machines Bull selected Nokia as its Finnish agent in 1962, and Nokia began researching radio transmission technology. In 1967, with the encouragement of Finland's government, Nokia merged with Finnish Rubber Works (a maker of tires and rubber footwear, formed in 1898) and Finnish Cable Works (a cable and electronics manufacturer formed in 1912) to form Nokia Corporation.

The oil crisis of 1973 created severe inflation and a large trade deficit for Finland. Nokia reassessed its heavy reliance on Soviet trade and shifted its focus to consumer and business electronics. Nokia's basic industries — paper, chemicals, electricity, and machinery — were modernized and expanded into robotics, fiber optics, and high-grade tissues.

The company acquired a 51% interest in the state-owned Finnish telecom company in 1981 and named it Telenokia. The next year Nokia designed and installed (in Finland) the first European digital telephone system. Also in 1982 Nokia acquired interests in Salora, Scandinavia's largest maker of color televisions, and Luxor, the Swedish state-owned electronics and computer firm.

Nokia acquired control of Sahkoliikkeiden, Finland's largest electrical wholesaler, in 1986. It then created the largest information technology (IT) group in Scandinavia, Nokia Data, by purchasing Ericsson's Data Division in 1988. Sales soared, but profits plunged because of stiff price competition in consumer electronics.

To raise cash, the company sold Nokia Data to IT services company ICL in 1991 and bought UK mobile phone maker Technophone, which had been #2 in Europe, after Nokia. Under the leadership of Jorma Ollila (appointed CEO in 1992 and chairman in 1999), Nokia intensified its focus on telecommunications and sold its non-core power (1994), televisions, and tire and cable machinery (1995) units.

It also began selling digital phones at the end of 1993. The company expected to sell 400,000; it shipped 20 million in 1995. The company rode the phones' success to a billion-dollar profit in 1997.

Nokia sold more than 40 million mobile phones in 1998 to surpass Motorola and became the world's #1 mobile phone company. In 1999 Nokia penned deals to put its wireless application protocol (WAP) software into Hewlett-Packard's and IBM's network servers.

The company, which also unveiled several WAP-enabled phones designed to access the Internet, widened its lead as the world's top seller of mobile phones, and made several acquisitions to strengthen its Internet protocol networks business.

Although Nokia was leaps and bounds ahead of its rivals with digital phones and dominated the European global system for mobile communications (GSM) market, it lagged in the US market, where many big carriers adopted QUALCOMM's CDMA standard. Nokia in 2000 began to cover the bases for the third generation by offering products to bridge the gap between generations.

In 2001 Nokia added Internet security appliances to its product line-up with the acquisition of Ramp Networks. Later that year, as part of an initiative to build up its line of network infrastructure products, the company bought US-based router maker Amber Networks. Nokia began working with other equipment makers and wireless service providers that year to develop a global standard for 3G phone software.

In an effort to jumpstart slowing handset sales as the cell phone market in the West and Japan flirted with saturation, Nokia in 2003 teamed with other phone makers and wireless service providers to develop a common global standard for 3G phone software. The effort was also backed by Motorola, Sony Ericsson, and Japan's NTT DoCoMo. After inking several new deals in Europe and Asia, Nokia was a supplier to half of the world's commercial 3G networks by the end of 2003.

The mobile phone unit introduced new products in 2003 across a range of market niches and the company rolled out new business and consumer models and introduced a unit capable of English and Chinese text recognition to be sold by vendors in China. The company also introduced the N-Gage mobile gaming device.

In 2004 the company expanded its focus beyond the traditional mobile phones and networks and reorganized its business units.

EXECUTIVES

Chairman: Jorma Ollila, age 56
Vice Chairman: Paul J. Collins, age 70
President and CEO: Olli-Pekka Kallasvuo, age 53
EVP and CFO: Richard A. (Rick) Simonson, age 48, $1,298,042 pay
EVP and CTO: Tero Ojanperä, age 40
EVP; General Manager, Enterprise Solutions: Mary T. McDowell, age 42
EVP; General Manager, Mobile Phones: Kai Öistämö, age 42
EVP; General Manager, Multimedia: Anssi Vanjoki, age 50, $1,415,115 pay
EVP; General Manager, Networks: Simon Beresford-Wylie, age 48
EVP, Corporate Relations and Responsibility: Veli Sundbäck, age 60
EVP, Customer and Market Operations: Robert Andersson, age 46
EVP, Human Resources: Hallstein Moerk, age 53
EVP, Technology Platforms: Niklas Savander, age 44
SVP; General Manager, CDMA: Soren Petersen
SVP, Core Networks, Networks: Juha Äkräs
SVP, Imaging: Juha Putkiranta
SVP, Games: Ilkka Raiskinen
SVP, Enterprise Mobility Systems: John Robinson
SVP, Global Sales and Marketing, Nokia Enterprise Solutions: Greg Shortell
VP, Communications: Arja Suominen
VP, Investor Relations: Ulla James
Manager, Investor Relations, US: Will Davis
Auditors: SVH Pricewaterhouse Coopers Oy

LOCATIONS

HQ: Nokia Corporation
Keilalahdentie 4, FIN-00045 Espoo, Finland
Phone: +358-7180-08000   **Fax:** +358-7180-38226
US HQ: 6000 Connection Dr., Irving, TX 75039
US Phone: 972-894-5000   **US Fax:** 972-894-5050
Web: www.nokia.com

Nokia sells its products in more than 130 countries. The company has manufacturing plants in 10 countries and research and development centers in 15 countries.

2005 Sales

	% of total
Europe	42
Asia/Pacific	18
Middle East & Africa	13
China	11
North America	8
Latin America	8
Total	**100**

PRODUCTS/OPERATIONS

2005 Sales

	% of total
Mobile phones	61
Networks	19
Multimedia	17
Enterprise solutions	3
Total	**100**

Selected Operations

Mobile phones
- Analog mobile cellular phones
- Digital mobile cellular phones
- Handheld telephone/personal organizers
- Phone accessories (batteries, cases, chargers)

Networks
- Base station site products
- Corporate network products
  - Base stations
  - Messaging platforms
  - Wireless local-area network (LAN) systems
  - Wireless access systems
- Fault-tolerant network routers
- Fixed network switching systems
- Internet protocol (IP) network switching systems
- Microwave radios
- Mobile radio systems
- Network, messaging, and multimedia services and software
- Radio base station controllers
- Radio network controllers
- Wireless network nodes, gateways, switches, and servers

Multimedia (services for advanced mobile devices)
- Convergence products
- Enhancements
- Entertainment
- Imaging

Enterprise solutions
- Business-optimized mobile services

COMPETITORS

Alcatel-Lucent	Pace Micro
BenQ (IT)	Panasonic Mobile
BenQ Mobile	Communications
Cisco Systems	Philips Electronics
ECI Telecom	Pioneer
Ericsson	QUALCOMM
Fujitsu	Robert Bosch
GE	SAFRAN
Harris Corp.	Samsung Electronics
Kyocera	Samsung Group
Microsoft	SANYO
Mitsubishi Electric	Scientific-Atlanta
Motorola	Siemens AG
NEC	Sony Ericsson Mobile
Nortel Networks	telent
Oki Electric	Tellabs
Openwave Systems	Toshiba

HISTORICAL FINANCIALS

Company Type: Public

Income Statement

FYE: December 31

	REVENUE ($ mil.)	NET INCOME ($ mil.)	NET PROFIT MARGIN	EMPLOYEES
12/05	40,496	4,243	10.5%	58,874
12/04	39,932	4,561	11.4%	55,505
12/03	36,987	5,145	13.9%	51,359
12/02	31,466	3,777	12.0%	51,748
12/01	27,635	1,686	6.1%	53,849
Annual Growth	**10.0%**	**25.9%**	**—**	**2.3%**

2005 Year-End Financials

Debt ratio: —
Return on equity: 24.4%
Cash ($ mil.): 11,737
Current ratio: 1.96
Long-term debt ($ mil.): —
No. of shares (mil.): —
Dividends
 Yield: 2.0%
 Payout: —
Market value ($ mil.): —

NYSE: NOK

Stock History

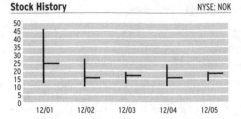

	STOCK PRICE ($) FY Close	P/E High	P/E Low	PER SHARE ($) Earnings	PER SHARE ($) Dividends
12/05	18.30	—	—	0.00	0.36
12/04	15.67	—	—	—	0.31
12/03	17.00	—	—	—	0.26
12/02	15.50	60	23	0.45	0.20
12/01	24.53	—	—	—	0.21
Annual Growth	**(7.1%)**	—	—	**—**	**14.4%**

Nomura Holdings

Nomura Holdings is the parent company of Nomura Securities, Japan's leading brokerage house. The company performs trading, equity and bond underwriting, asset management, and mergers and acquisitions (M&A) advisory services. It also makes private equity and venture capital investments. Nomura's largest segment is domestic retail, which provides investment consulting and brokerage services to consumers in its home market. Nomura Holdings has operations in more than 20 countries. Nomura Securities International is the company's US trading and investment banking unit.

Nomura has shaken off bribery and racketeering scandals that rocked the firm earlier in the decade. Thanks to the recovery of the Japanese economy and an increase in investment by Japanese consumers with an eye toward retirement, Nomura has seen its income from commissions rise. The company has also benefited from an uptick in M&A and IPO activity in Japan.

Nomura, which manages some 50 trillion yen on behalf of its clients, has the ambitious goal of doubling its assets under management by 2009.

The company is buying US-based electronic institutional brokerage Instinet.

HISTORY

Tokushichi Nomura started a currency exchange, Nomura Shoten, in Osaka in 1872 and began trading stock. His son, Tokushichi II, took over and in 1910 formed Nomura's first syndicate to underwrite part of a government bond issue. It established the Osaka Nomura Bank in 1918. The bond department became independent in 1925 and became Nomura Securities. The company opened a New York office in 1927, entering stock brokerage in 1938.

The firm rebuilt and expanded retail operations after WWII. It encouraged stock market investing by promoting "million ryo savings chests," small boxes in which people saved cash (ryo was an old form of currency); when savings reached 5,000 yen, savers could buy into investment trusts. Nomura distributed more than a million chests in 10 years.

Nomura followed clients overseas in the 1960s, helping to underwrite a US issue of Sony stock and opening a London office. It became Japan's leading securities firm after a 1965 stock market crash decimated rival Yamaichi Securities. The firm grew rapidly in the 1970s, ushering investment capital in and out of Japan and competing with banks by issuing corporate debt securities.

As the Japanese economy soared in the 1980s, the company opened Nomura Bank International in London (1986) and bought 20% of US mergers and acquisitions advisor Wasserstein Perella (1988, sold 2001).

Then the Japanese economic bubble burst. Nomura's stock toppled 70% from its 1987 peak and underwriting plummeted. In 1991 and 1992, amid revelations that Nomura and other brokerages had reimbursed favored clients' trading losses, the firm was accused of manipulating stock in companies owned by Japanese racketeers. Nomura's chairman and president — both named Tabuchi — resigned, admitting no wrongdoing.

The firm trimmed staff and offices and focused on its most efficient operations. From 1993 to 2000, it seesawed from red to black and back again.

Junichi Ujiie became president after the payoff scandal; he restructured operations to prepare for Japan's financial deregulation. Nomura invested in pub chain Inntrepreneur and William Hill, a UK betting chain. It also created an entertainment lending unit to lend against future royalties or syndication fees, and spun off a minority stake in its high-risk US real estate business, which ceased lending altogether the next year.

In 1998 Nomura was dealt a double blow when Asian economies collapsed and Russia defaulted on its debts; incurring substantial losses, the firm refocused on its domestic market and reduced overseas operations. That year it teamed with Industrial Bank of Japan for derivatives sales in the UK and pension plan consulting in Japan.

In 1999 Nomura bailed out its ailing property subsidiary Nomura Finance, crippled by the sinking Japanese real estate market. It also invested heavily in UK real estate and bought 40% of the Czech beer market with South African Breweries.

The next year the firm agreed to buy the business services arm of Welsh utilities firm Hyder; it also bought 114,000 flats in Germany with local government authorities, its first European deal outside the UK. Also in 2000 Nomura sold its assets in pachinko parlors and "love" hotels, Japanese cultural traditions with less-than-sparkling reputations. British authorities that year fined Nomura traders in relation to charges of trying to rig Australia's stock market in 1996.

The company made two big deals in the UK in 2001, buying hotel chain Le Méridien and becoming the nation's largest pub owner via the purchase of some 1,000 locations from Bass. Also that year Nomura bought a stake in Thomas Weisel Partners to increase its participation in M&A action between US and Japanese firms. The following year, the company decided to sell the network of more than 4,100 pubs to a consortium of private investors for almost $3 billion.

Chairman: Junichi Ujiie, age 61
President, CEO, and Director: Nobuyuki Koga, age 56
Deputy President and Co-COO: Hiroshi Toda, age 55
Deputy President and Co-COO: Kazutoshi Inano, age 53
Senior Managing Director and CFO: Masafumi Nakada
Executive Managing Officer: Masanori Itatani
Executive Managing Officer and CIO:
  Akihiko Nakamura
**Head of Global Merchant Banking and President and
  CEO, Nomura Principal Finance Co., Ltd.; Senior
  Managing Director, Nomura Securities Co., Ltd.:**
  Akira Maruyama
Head of Global Corporate Communications: Tetsu Ozaki
Head of Global Equity: Hiromasa Yamazaki
Head of Global Fixed Income: Shigesuke Kashiwagi
**Head of Global Investment Banking and Deputy
  President, Nomura Securities Co., Ltd.:**
  Takashi Yanagiya, age 55
Head of Asset Finance: Atsuo Sakurai
Head of Asset Management: Takumi Shibata
Head of Global Markets: Yasuo Agemura
Head of Domestic Retail: Kenichi Watanabe, age 54
Head of Global Corporate Strategy: Akihito Watanabe
Head of Global Fixed Income: Zenji Nakamura
**Senior Managing Director and Regional Manager,
  Americas:** Hideyuki Takahashi
Auditors: Ernst & Young ShinNihon

LOCATIONS

HQ: Nomura Holdings, Inc.
  1-9-1, Nihonbashi, Chuo-ku, Tokyo 103-8645, Japan
Phone: +81-3-3211-1811   **Fax:** +81-3-3278-0420
US HQ: 2 World Financial Center, Bldg. B,
  New York, NY 10281
US Phone: 212-667-9300   **US Fax:** 212-667-1058
Web: www.nomura.com

PRODUCTS/OPERATIONS

2006 Sales

	$ mil.	% of total
Interest & dividends	5,906	38
Commissions	3,033	20
Net gain on trading	2,590	17
Investment banking fees	926	6
Asset management & portfolio service fees	874	6
Private equity entities product sales	751	5
Gain on investments in equity securities	576	4
Other	605	4
Total	**15,261**	**100**

COMPETITORS

Bank of America	Deutsche Bank
Barclays	Goldman Sachs
Bear Stearns	HSBC Holdings
Boom Securities	Lehman Brothers
Charles Schwab	Merrill Lynch
Citigroup	Nikko Cordial
Daiwa Securities	UBS Financial Services

HISTORICAL FINANCIALS

Company Type: Public

Income Statement

FYE: March 31

	REVENUE ($ mil.)	NET INCOME ($ mil.)	NET PROFIT MARGIN	EMPLOYEES
3/06	15,261	2,590	17.0%	14,668
3/05	10,504	884	8.4%	14,344
3/04	10,554	1,654	15.7%	13,987
3/03	7,594	1,016	13.4%	14,385
Annual Growth	26.2%	36.6%	—	0.7%

2006 Year-End Financials

Debt ratio: 665.7%   Current ratio: —
Return on equity: 14.8%   Long-term debt ($ mil.): 116,911
Cash ($ mil.): 83,712

Net Income History

NYSE: NMR

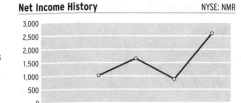

Norsk Hydro

Norsk Hydro is at home in Norwegian waters. Norway's largest publicly traded industrial company, Norsk Hydro has aluminum and energy operations. The two segments are virtually equal in size, with each accounting for nearly half the company's sales. The aluminum segment is strong throughout Asia, Europe, and North America. Its oil and energy operations boast more than 2 billion barrels of reserves and are focused on its home turf. The company also has a much smaller petrochemicals business. In 2004 Norsk Hydro spun off its agrochemical unit (called Yara International) and then sold its remaining ownership to UBS Limited for about $570 million. The Norwegian government owns close to 45% of Norsk Hydro.

Norsk Hydro's aluminum unit is split into three divisions. The first, Primary Metals and Metal Products, produces primary aluminum and processes scrap and ingot. The second unit is Rolled Products and operates cold rolling mills in Europe. The last is Hydro's Extrusion and Automotive unit, which is focused on the building, construction, and automotive industries. Norsk Hydro is the world's #3 aluminum company behind Alcoa and Alcan.

The energy segment explores primarily on the Norwegian continental shelf, but it also has operations off the coasts of Angola and Canada as well as in Russia, Libya, and the Gulf of Mexico. The company has refining operations and markets its products through a network of more than 1,500 stations in Sweden, Norway, Denmark, and the Baltics. (The non-Swedish service stations are operated through a joint venture with Chevron that Norsk Hydro has agreed to sell to retailer Reitan Servicehandel for about $160 million.)

Yet another, this time much larger, move in the direction of boosting its energy business was the 2005 acquisition of Spinnaker Exploration for about $2.45 billion. Spinnaker is an oil and gas production company that explores in the Gulf of Mexico and off the coast of West Africa.

The company has made a deal with Comalco, a subsidiary of Rio Tinto, to purchase alumina (the raw material to make aluminum) beginning with 300,000 tonnes in 2005 and increasing to 500,000 tonnes in 2006-2030. This deal is Norsk Hydro's largest ever alumina supply contract. Norsk Hydro is also investing about $240 million to expand production at its Brazilian-based Alunorte (alumina) plant, in which the company has a 35% stake.

HISTORY

Norwegian entrepreneurs Sam Eyde and Kristian Birkeland began Norsk Hydro-Elektrisk Kvaelstofaktieselskap (Norwegian Hydro-Electric Nitrogen Corp.) in 1905. The company used electricity generated from waterfalls to extract nitrogen from the air to produce fertilizer.

After WWII the Norwegian government seized German holdings in Norsk Hydro and took a 48% stake in the company. It grew to be the largest chemical firm in Scandinavia. In 1965, when Norway granted licenses for offshore petroleum exploration, the company formed partnerships with foreign companies. These included Phillips Petroleum, which spurred the North Sea boom in 1969 when its drilling rig Ocean Viking struck oil in the giant Ekofisk field, and Elf Aquitaine, which oversaw the Frigg discovery in 1971. The Norwegian state increased its share of Norsk Hydro to 51% in 1972.

The company also branched out with hydroelectric-powered aluminum processing at its Karmoy Works (1967) and with a fish-farming subsidiary, Mowi (1969). During much of the 1970s, it focused on oil and gas development, which added to the treasury and helped finance growth, often through acquisitions.

Norsk Hydro pushed into the European fertilizer market by buying Dutch company NSM in 1979; during the 1980s it acquired interests in fertilizer operations in France, Sweden, and the UK. In petrochemicals it expanded by buying two British PVC makers. Norsk Hydro-controlled Hydro Aluminum merged with ASV, another Norwegian aluminum company, in 1986, and the company consolidated its aluminum holdings two years later.

Hydro served as operator in the Oseberg field, which began production in 1988 and grew rapidly to become a major source of oil and gas. In 1990 it bought 330 Danish gasoline stations from UNO-X; in 1992 it purchased Mobil Oil's Norwegian marketing and distribution system. Two years later Norsk Hydro merged its oil and marketing operations in Norway and Denmark with Texaco's.

A weak world economy and increased competition limited its revenues in 1992 and 1993. The company countered slumping sales by selling noncore subsidiaries, including pharmaceutical unit Hydro Pharma (1992) and chocolate maker Freia Marabou (1993).

Norsk Hydro expanded further during the early 1990s, acquiring fertilizer plants in Germany, the UK, and the US, as well as W. R. Grace's ammonia plants in Trinidad and Tobago. The firm acquired Fisons' NPK fertilizer business in 1994. The company agreed to an asset swap with Petro-Canada in 1996, becoming a partner in oil and gas fields off the east coast of Canada. That year Norsk Hydro bought UNO-X's Swedish gas station operations.

The Norwegian government's stake in Norsk Hydro was reduced from 51% to about 45% in 1999 when the company and state-owned Statoil made a deal to take over Saga Petroleum, Norway's leading independent oil producer, to keep it out of foreign hands.

In light of major losses in 1999 by Hydro Agri, the company made plans in 2000 to close several European nitrogen fertilizer operations. However, it agreed to modernize and expand its Hydro Aluminum Sunndal facility, to make it the largest aluminum plant in Europe. That year the company also sold Saga UK (North Sea assets) to Conoco, and its fish-farming unit to Dutch company Nutreco. In 2001 the company acquired a stake in Soquimich, an industrial minerals company in Chile, and majority control of Slovakian aluminum producer Slolvalco.

The new decade brought with it a new focus; the company began to make aluminum and oil and energy its primary business lines. Toward that end Norsk Hydro bought VAW Aluminum from E.On AG for $2.8 billion in a deal that enabled it to expand its product base in Europe and the US, especially to key customers in the automobile industry. It then sold its flexible packaging unit to Alcan for about $545 million in 2003. Furthering the same goal, the company announced in 2003 and then followed through on a spin-off of its agrochemical unit the following year. The resultant company is called Yara International.

EXECUTIVES

Chairman: Jan Reinås, age 59
Deputy Chairman: Borger A. Lenth, age 67
President and CEO: Eivind Reiten, age 53
EVP and CFO: John Ove Ottestad, age 57
EVP, Leadership and Culture: Hilde Aasheim, age 46
EVP and Head of Aluminum Metal:
Torstein Dale (Dale) Sjøtveit
EVP, Aluminium Products: Svein Richard Brandtzæg, age 48
EVP, Oil and Energy: Tore Torvund, age 54
SVP and General Counsel: Odd I. Biller, age 57
SVP, Investor Relations: Idar Eikrem, age 44
SVP, Communications: Cecilie Ditlev-Simonsen, age 43
SVP, Corporate Finance: Ida Helliesen, age 59
SVP, Corporate Internal Audit: Espen Uvholt, age 43
SVP, Operations: Torgeir Kydland, age 50
SVP, Projects: Morten Ruud, age 53
SVP and Head of Human Resources and Organization, Hydro Aluminum: Karin Våland Sandvold
SVP, Corporate Portfolio Strategy: David W. Nunn
SVP, Exploration: Lars Christian Alsvik
SVP, Finance: Helge Vatn
SVP, Industrial Relations: Arild Andreassen, age 57
SVP, Markets: Hilde Myrberg
SVP, Oil Marketing: Bengt Göran Markeborn, age 61

LOCATIONS

HQ: Norsk Hydro ASA
Drammensveien 264, N-0283 Oslo 2, Norway
Phone: +47-22-53-81-00　　**Fax:** +47-22-53-27-25
US HQ: 1200 Smith St., Ste. 800, Houston, TX 77002
US Phone: 713-759-1770　　**US Fax:** 713-753-1339
Web: www.hydro.com

Norsk Hydro sells its products in Europe, including Norway, and in Asia, North America, and other regions. It has oil and gas exploration and production operations along the Norwegian continental shelf, as well as in Angola, Canada, Iran, Libya, Russia, and the UK.

2005 Sales

	% of total
Europe	
EU	
UK	20
Germany	10
France	5
Sweden	5
Italy	4
The Netherlands	4
Spain	3
Denmark	1
Other EU countries	8
Norway	14
Switzerland	4
Other countries	1
Americas	
US	8
Canada	2
Other countries	5
Asia	4
Australia & New Zealand	1
Africa	1
Total	**100**

PRODUCTS/OPERATIONS

2005 Sales

	% of total
Hydro Oil & Energy	
Energy & Oil Marketing	38
Exploration & Production	10
Hydro Aluminum	
Metals	21
Extrusion & Automotive	15
Rolled Products	11
Other	5
Total	**100**

Selected Operations

Hydro Oil & Energy
　Hydro Energy
　Hydro Exploration and Development Norway
　Hydro Exploration and Production International
　Hydro Oil Marketing
　Hydro Operation and Production Norway
　Hydro Technology and Projects
Hydro Aluminum
　Hydro Aluminum Automotive
　Hydro Aluminum Extrusion
　Hydro Aluminum Metal Products
　Hydro Aluminum Rolled Products and Wire Rod
　Hydro North America
　Hydro Primary Metals
Other
　Hydro Petrochemicals

COMPETITORS

Alcan
Alcoa
BASF AG
Bayer
BayWa
BHP Billiton
BP
Devon Energy
Eni
Exxon Mobil
Occidental Petroleum
PDVSA
PEMEX
PETROBRAS
Repsol YPF
Royal Dutch Shell
SEPI
Statoil
ThyssenKrupp
TOTAL

HISTORICAL FINANCIALS

Company Type: Public

Income Statement

FYE: December 31

	REVENUE ($ mil.)	NET INCOME ($ mil.)	NET PROFIT MARGIN	EMPLOYEES
12/05	25,695	2,307	9.0%	32,765
12/04	25,707	2,077	8.1%	34,600
12/03	25,613	1,635	6.4%	42,911
12/02	23,478	1,263	5.4%	50,000
Annual Growth	**3.1%**	**22.2%**	**—**	**(13.1%)**

2005 Year-End Financials

Debt ratio: 24.8%
Return on equity: 16.3%
Cash ($ mil.): 2,113
Current ratio: 1.32
Long-term debt ($ mil.): 3,499

No. of shares (mil.): —
Dividends
　Yield: 5.2%
　Payout: 58.2%
Market value ($ mil.): —

Stock History

NYSE: NHY

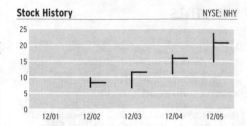

	STOCK PRICE ($) FY Close	P/E High	P/E Low	PER SHARE ($) Earnings	PER SHARE ($) Dividends
12/05	20.64	13	8	1.84	1.07
12/04	15.74	—	—	—	0.28
12/03	11.48	—	—	—	0.26
12/02	8.25	—	—	—	0.21
Annual Growth	**35.8%**	**—**	**—**	**—**	**72.1%**

Nortel Networks

Nortel Networks is one of telecom's North (American) stars. The company, which operates through its Nortel Networks Limited subsidiary, is one of the top global makers of telecom equipment in North America. It makes core network switching, wireless, and optical systems for customers worldwide. Nortel's wireline and enterprise network equipment includes systems for digital voice and data switching, routing, and call center communications. Wireless products include cellular base stations and controllers. The company makes such long-haul fiber optic products as multiplexers and optical switches. Clients include global communications carriers; regional, local, and wireless phone carriers; and corporations.

To boost its efforts to expand operations in developing telecom markets, Nortel acquired a stake in Indian communication software firm Sasken Communication Technologies, in a 2005 deal valued at $10 million. It also bought IT services contractor PEC Solutions in a deal valued at $448 million in 2005. Nortel has created a US-based subsidiary, known as Nortel Government Solutions (formerly Nortel PEC Solutions) from the Fairfax, Virginia-based company.

Nortel in early 2006 agreed to pay nearly $2.5 billion in cash and stock to settle class-action lawsuits that alleged securities laws violations. The settlement stems from alleged violations that also led to the terminations in 2004 of former executives including then-CEO Frank Dunn, CFO Douglas Beatty, controller Michael Gollogly, and several other top financial managers amid an SEC investigation into accounting problems dating back several years. The company installed director Bill Owens as its new chief; Owens previously held the top spot at Teledesic LLC and was the president of SAIC prior to that. Late in 2005, GE and Motorola veteran Mike Zafirovski succeeded Owens.

In early 2005, the company released its 2003 financial statements, nearly a year late, following a massive accounting investigation that uncovered billions in overstated revenues for the years 1999 and 2000. The company also filed a lawsuit against Dunn, Beatty, and Gollogly in an unprecedented attempt to reclaim $10.4 million in bonuses paid to the three executives who, the company claims, were "unjustly enriched at the expense of Nortel."

After Zafirovski took over, the company announced plans to relocate its corporate headquarters to Toronto.

HISTORY

Nortel Networks traces its lineage to 1880, when Bell Telephone Company of Canada was established in Montreal four years after the invention of the telephone. In 1882 the Northern Electric and Manufacturing Co. was founded to produce Bell Canada's mechanical equipment. Northern Electric pooled its resources with electrical wire maker Imperial Wire & Cable to form the Northern Electric Co. in 1914. AT&T's manufacturing subsidiary Western Electric owned 44% of the company.

During the 1930s the company created an electronics division and purchased a majority interest in Amalgamated Electric (1932).

In the mid-1950s, the US Justice Department forced Western Electric to sell its interest in Northern Electric, and Bell Canada purchased most of the shares. In 1958 the company formed Northern Electric Laboratories to push research and development. During the 1960s Northern Electric began supplying switching gear overseas. In 1971 the company merged its Northern Electric Laboratories with Bell Canada's R&D unit to form Bell Northern Research. (Northern Electric retained 70% ownership, while Bell Canada owned the remaining 30%.)

Northern Electric remained wholly owned by Bell Canada until 1973, when that company began reducing its stake. In 1976 Northern Electric changed its name to Northern Telecom and became the first equipment company to introduce a digital switch. When AT&T approved use of the switch in its equipment in 1981, Northern Telecom's growth took off.

Paul Stern became CEO in 1989 as the company thrived on its digital switch sales. The former IBM executive focused on cutting costs in lieu of technical advancement, and customer dissatisfaction built as the company failed to develop the software in its switching systems. Directors forced Stern out and replaced him with Jean Monty as CEO in 1992, just before Northern Telecom suffered a loss of nearly $900 million for 1993.

Monty acted quickly, calming customers, revamping the software, and selling underused divisions and factories. The next year Monty was succeeded by COO John Roth, who began to lead Nortel down a path to expansion.

In 1998 Northern Telecom bought Bell Canada's 30% stake in Bell Northern Research, which had been renamed Nortel Technology Limited. Also that year the company boosted its networking expertise through such acquisitions as Bay Networks. The Bay Networks deal, worth $6.7 billion, led to a loss that year and prompted the 1999 name change to Nortel Networks.

The change was pivotal for the company, transforming it from a staid seller of simple telephone equipment to a fast-moving Internet supplier. As sales of telecom gear slowed industry-wide in 2000 Nortel made moves to focus its unwieldy operations; it outsourced some semiconductor operations, a large part of its manufacturing, and its information technology services. Bell Canada parent BCE distributed to its shareholders most of its 40% stake in Nortel in 2000.

In 2001, amid an economic downturn, Nortel laid off 30,000 employees and scaled back its digital subscriber line operations. Frank Carlucci (chairman since March 2000) stepped down that year. CFO Lynton Wilson took the chair and Roth stepped down as CEO in late 2001. Former CFO Frank Dunn was named CEO and Roth assumed the vice chairman role. Nortel decided that year to cut an additional 20,000 employees.

In 2003 Nortel sold its fixed wireless network access equipment product line, known as Proximity, to Airspan in a continued effort to focus on core businesses. Slipping wireless sales in Europe and North America caused Nortel to look increasingly to developing areas like China for new business.

In 2004, the company outsourced all of its manufacturing operations to Singapore-based Flextronics in a deal valued at more than $2 billion annually. Nortel also fired CEO Dunn as well as the company's CFO that year amid an accounting scandal; director Bill Owens assumed the top spot. Late in 2005, veteran high-tech executive Mike Zafirovski succeeded Owens.

EXECUTIVES

Chairman: Harry J. Pearce, age 64
President, CEO, and Director: Mike S. Zafirovski, age 52, $252,381 pay
EVP and CFO: Peter W. Currie, age 55, $1,377,500 pay
EVP, Corporate Operations: Dennis J. Carey, age 59
SVP, Business Transformation:
  William J. (Bill) Donovan, age 49
SVP, Global Operations and Quality: J. Joel Hackney Jr., age 36
VP, Financial Planning and Analysis: John M. Doolittle, age 41
VP, Global Manufacturing Services: Don McKenna
VP, Chief Architect, and Interim Chief Research Officer: Peter Carbone
VP, Lean Six Sigma and Global Quality: Ellen Bovarnick
CTO: John J. Roese, age 33
CIO: Albert R. Hitchcock, age 41
Chief Compliance Officer: Robert J. (Bob) Bartzokas, age 55
Chief Legal Officer: David W. Drinkwater, age 57
Chief Marketing Officer: Lauren P. Flaherty, age 48
Chief Strategy Officer: George A. Riedel, age 48
Chief Procurement Officer: John Haydon
Senior Advisor: Pascal Debon, age 59, $590,000 pay (prior to title change)
Chairman, LG-Nortel JV and President, LG-Nortel Business Unit: Peter D. MacKinnon, age 44
President and CEO, Greater China: Robert Y. L. Mao, age 62
President, Nortel Asia: Michael Pangia
President, Nortel Greater China: Zhensheng Wu
President, North America: Dion C. Joannou, age 40, $624,817 pay
Auditors: Deloitte & Touche LLP

LOCATIONS

HQ: Nortel Networks Corporation
  8200 Dixie Rd., Ste. 100,
  Brampton, Ontario L6T 5P6, Canada
Phone: 905-863-0000   **Fax:** 905-863-8408
US HQ: 2221 Lakeside Blvd., Richardson, TX 75082
US Phone: 972-684-1000
Web: www.nortel.com

2005 Sales

	$ mil.	% of total
US	5,206	50
Europe, Middle East & Africa	2,725	26
Asia/Pacific	1,405	13
Central & Latin America	611	6
Canada	576	5
Total	**10,523**	**100**

PRODUCTS/OPERATIONS

2005 Sales

	$ mil.	% of total
GSM & UMTS	2,799	27
Circuit & packet voice	2,748	26
CDMA	2,321	22
Data networking & security	1,321	13
Optical networking	1,186	11
Other	148	1
Total	**10,523**	**100**

Selected Products

Wireless
  Base station transceivers and controllers
  Core networking equipment
  Gateway support nodes
  Home location registers
  Mobile switching centers
Enterprise
  Call center communications systems (Symposium)
  Digital telephone switching systems (Meridian, Norstar)
  Interactive voice response systems (Directory Assistance, Periphonics)
  Network management software (Preside, Optivity)
Wireline
  Circuit to packet voice network systems
    Voice and data communications systems for service providers and large enterprises (Succession)
  Packet switching and routing
    Data network access aggregation nodes (Shasta)
    Data routers (Bay)
    Data switching platforms for Internet-based virtual private networks (Contivity)
    Ethernet data switches (Baystack, Business Policy)
    Multi-service switches (Passport)
    Voice and data communications systems for small to mid-sized businesses (Business Communications Manager)
Optical and long-haul
  Dense wavelength division multiplexing equipment
  Repeaters
  Transmission terminals
  Network management software (Preside)
  Optical Ethernet (OPTera)
  Optical networking components
  Optical switching equipment
  Synchronous optical transmission systems
    SDH-based products (TN-X line)
    SONET-based products (SDMS TransportNode)
    SONET/SDH (OPTera Connect DX)

COMPETITORS

3Com	Genesys
ADC Telecommunications	Harris Corp.
ADVA	Hitachi
Agere Systems	Huawei Technologies
Alcatel-Lucent	JDS Uniphase
Allied Telesis	Juniper Networks
Amdocs	Motorola
Avaya	NEC
BroadSoft	Nokia
Ciena	Panasonic Mobile
Cisco Systems	Communications
Corning	Redback Networks
Enterasys	Samsung Group
Ericsson	Siemens AG
Extreme Networks	Sonus Networks
Foundry Networks	Sycamore Networks
Fujitsu	telent

HISTORICAL FINANCIALS

Company Type: Public

Income Statement

FYE: December 31

	REVENUE ($ mil.)	NET INCOME ($ mil.)	NET PROFIT MARGIN	EMPLOYEES
12/05	10,523	(2,575)	—	35,370
12/04	9,828	(51)	—	34,150
12/03	10,193	434	4.3%	35,160
12/02	10,569	(3,266)	—	36,960
12/01	17,511	(27,302)	—	53,600
Annual Growth	(12.0%)	—	—	(9.9%)

2005 Year-End Financials

Debt ratio: 310.3%
Return on equity: —
Cash ($ mil.): 3,028
Current ratio: 1.10
Long-term debt ($ mil.): 2,439

No. of shares (mil.): —
Dividends
Yield: —
Payout: —
Market value ($ mil.): —

Stock History

NYSE: NT

	STOCK PRICE ($) FY Close	P/E High/Low		PER SHARE ($) Earnings	Dividends
12/05	3.55	—	—	(0.59)	—
12/04	4.16	—	—	(0.01)	—
12/03	5.49	65	17	0.10	—
12/02	2.52	—	—	(0.85)	—
12/01	74.60	—	—	(8.56)	—
Annual Growth	(53.3%)	—	—	—	—

Novartis

Although it's based in neutral Switzerland, Novartis has been aggressive in attacking illnesses. The company's prescription drugs include treatments for nervous system and ophthalmic disorders, cardiovascular diseases, and cancer. Its Sandoz generics subsidiary produces finished dosage products as well as active pharmaceutical ingredients for other generics companies to manufacture. Novartis' consumer health unit includes such brands as Ex-Lax, Maalox, and Theraflu. Novartis is also the proud parent of the Gerber baby. CIBA Vision makes eye drops, contact lenses (Focus), and contact lens solutions. Its animal health unit offers parasite control products (Sentinel) and pharmaceuticals for pets and farm animals.

Prescription drugs account for 60% of Novartis' revenues; its blockbusters include the top antiotensin-receptor blocker (ARB); high blood pressure treatment Diovan ($3.7 billion); leukemia drug Gleevec ($2.2 billion); Zometa ($1.2 billion), an intravenous treatment for bone tumors caused by prostate, lung, and breast cancers; single-dose high blood pressure drug Lotrel ($1.1 billion); and antifungal Lamisil ($1.1 billion). Only one, Lamisil, is facing increased competition from generic formulations

and Zometa enjoys a comfortable 75% market share in the US. Other strong products include Femara, used to treat postmenopausal women with early and advanced breast cancer, and irritable bowel syndrome drug Zelnorm.

Recognizing the preference for generics by many US health plans and some US consumers, Novartis consolidated its 14 generic drug brands under the visible and respected Sandoz name; the segment accounted for 15% of Novartis' revenues in 2005. Acquisitions have helped expand the division; Sandoz is the largest manufacturer of generic drugs in the world, ahead of powerhouse Teva Pharmaceuticals.

During 2006 Novartis spent $5.1 billion to acquire struggling vaccine and biopharmaceuticals products maker Chiron, despite Chiron's board rebuffing an earlier offer. Novartis then created a Vaccine and Diagnostics division composed of its existing vaccine operations, and Chiron's diagnostic.

Novartis also boasts a healthy drug pipeline to support its prescription drug business with more than 50 candidates in late-stage development, which grows ever more important as Novartis, like so many other big pharmas, faces patent expirations on key products. Drugs awaiting approval in the US and EU include diabetes treatment Galvus and hypertension drug Rasilez.

The FDA required Novartis in early 2005 to place extra warnings on its epilepsy drug, Trileptal, warning consumers of serious skin reactions such as Stevens-Johnson syndrome and toxic epidermal nerolysis after receiving nearly 20 reports (including one fatality) of these reactions in patients taking the drug.

In mid-2006, Novartis announced it intends to acquire NeuTec Pharma, a UK-based biopharmaceutical company with two drug candidates which target otherwise drug-resistant "superbugs."

HISTORY

Johann Geigy began selling spices and natural dyes in Basel, Switzerland, in 1758. A century later the Geigy family began producing synthetic dyes. About that time Alexander Clavel also entered the synthetic dye trade in Basel, forming the Gesellschaft fur Chemische Industrie Basel (Ciba). Ciba was Switzerland's #1 chemical firm at century's end.

After WWI, Ciba, Geigy, and Sandoz (a Basel synthetic dye maker founded in 1886) formed the Basel AG cartel to compete with German rival I.G. Farben. Basel used its profits to diversify into pharmaceuticals and other chemicals and to gain a foothold in the US. In 1929 Basel merged with German and, later, French and British counterparts, but WWII shattered the so-called Quadrapartite Cartel in 1939, leaving only Basel AG intact.

Basel scientist Paul Muller won a Nobel Prize in 1948 for inventing DDT. Basel AG voluntarily dissolved itself back into its component parts in 1951.

Ciba, Geigy, and Sandoz continued to diversify. Finding new markets in agricultural chemicals, Geigy had passed Ciba in sales by 1967. That year Sandoz bought the Wander group of companies (dietetic products). Ciba and Geigy merged in 1970 and began a series of US acquisitions, including Funk Seeds in 1974. Sandoz bought Minneapolis-based Northrup, King & Co. (1976) and Dutch seed company Zaadunie (1980).

Ciba-Geigy and US biotech company Chiron started a joint venture in 1986 to produce and

market genetically engineered vaccines (Ciba-Geigy acquired 50% of Chiron in 1994). Sandoz also bought shares in US biotechnology companies, including Genetic Therapy and SyStemix, in 1991. It bought Gerber (founded 1927) in 1994.

Ciba-Geigy and Sandoz rejoined to form Novartis in 1996. Sandoz's Daniel Vasella became CEO of the new company. Novartis spun off its specialty chemicals unit in 1997 and bought Merck's insecticide and fungicide operations.

To boost its market share, CIBA Vision bought colored contact lens maker Wesley Jessen VisionCare in 2000. Novartis spun off its crop protection and seed units, merging them with AstraZeneca's Agrochemicals unit to create Syngenta.

Novartis Ophthalmics split off from the CIBA Vision division to become a separate eye health care unit under the Pharmaceutical Division of Novartis in 2001. The firm's joint venture with BioTransplant successfully cloned genetically altered pigs whose organs would be more suitable for human transplants.

Novartis engineered one of the largest deals in European pharma in 2004, when it acquired the rights to a prospective inhaled chronic obstructive pulmonary disease (COPD) treatment from UK drug concerns Arakis and Vectura Group, both of which will, as part of the licensing deal, reap a share of the revenues if the drug is approved for sale.

In a move to bolster its consumer offerings, the company purchased the US and Canadian consumer products division of Bristol-Myers Squibb, which brought headache remedy Excedrin, cold and flu treatment Comtrex, and Keri moisturizers into the company's consumer products stable in 2004.

In 2005, the firm acquired Hexal AG, one of Germany's top generics makers, and a controlling stake in Hexal's sister firm Eon Labs, a US generics manufacturer.

EXECUTIVES

Chairman and CEO: Daniel L. Vasella, age 52, $2,279,700 pay
Vice Chairman: Hans-Jörg Rudloff, age 65
CFO: Raymond Breu, age 60, $791,563 pay
CEO, Novartis Consumer Health: Paul Choffat, age 56, $894,150 pay
CEO, Novartis Pharma: Thomas Ebeling, age 47, $1,780,699 pay
CEO, Novartis Vaccines and Diagnostics: Jörg Reinhardt
CEO, Gerber: Kurt T. Schmidt, age 48
CEO, CIBA Vision: Michael E. Kehoe, age 49
CEO, Sandoz: Andreas Rummelt, age 49
President, Novartis Institutes for BioMedical Research: Mark C. Fishman, age 55, $883,928 pay
Head of OTC, Novartis Consumer Health: Larry Allgaier, age 47
Head of Legal and Tax Affairs: Urs Bärlocher, age 63, $620,585 pay
Head of Human Resources: Juergen Brokatzky-Geiger, age 53, $591,667 pay
Head of Oncology, Novartis Pharma: David Epstein, age 44
Head of Medical Nutrition: Michel Gardet, age 49
Head of Animal Health, Novartis Consumer Health: George Gunn, age 55
Head of Corporate Research: Paul L. Herrling, age 59
Head of Pharma Development, Novartis Pharma AG: James S. Shannon
Head of Transplantation and Immunology: Giacomo Di Nepi, age 52
Head of Ophthalmics: Nicholas Franco, age 43
Head of Corporate Communications: Ann Bailey
Corporate Secretary: Bruno Heynen
General Counsel: Thomas Werlen
Auditors: PricewaterhouseCoopers AG

LOCATIONS

HQ: Novartis AG
Lichtstrasse 35, CH-4056 Basel, Switzerland
Phone: +41-61-324-11-11   **Fax:** +41-61-324-80-01
US HQ: 608 5th Ave., New York, NY 10020
US Phone: 212-307-1122   **US Fax:** 212-246-0185
Web: www.novartis.com

Novartis has operations in more than 140 countries.

2005 Sales

	% of total
Americas	47
Europe	37
Asia, Africa & Australia	16
Total	**100**

PRODUCTS/OPERATIONS

2005 Sales

	% of total
Pharmaceuticals	63
Consumer Health	22
Sandoz	15
Total	**100**

Selected Products

Animal Health
　Agita (fly control)
　Atopica (atopic dermatitis management)
　Dermaxx (pain relief)
　Milbemax/Interceptor (intestinal and heart worm control)
　Tiamutin (antimicrobial)
Branded Pharmaceuticals
　Comtan (treatment for Parkinson's disease)
　Diovan (hypertension drug)
　Elidel (eczema treatment)
　Exelon (treatment of Alzheimer's disease)
　Famvir (antiviral treatment for herpes)
　Femara (advanced breast cancer treatment)
　Foradil (asthma drug)
　Gleevec (leukemia and gastrointestinal tumor treatment)
　Lamisil (antifungal)
　Lescol (cholesterol drug)
　Lotrel (hypertension drug)
　Miacalcic (osteoporosis treatment)
　Neoral (transplant rejection preventative; also treatment for rheumatoid arthritis and psoriasis)
　Ritalin (attention deficit hyperactivity disorder drug)
　Sandostatin LAR (acromegaly, cancer treatment)
　Tegretol (epilepsy, acute mania, and bipolar affective disorders drug)
　Trileptal (epilepsy drug)
　Visudyne (wet age-related macular degeneration drug)
　Voltaren (antirheumatic)
　Zelmac/Zelnorm (irritable bowel syndrome treatment)
　Zometa (cancer treatment)
CIBA Vision
　AQuify Multi-Purpose Solution (contact lens cleaning solution)
　Clear Care (contact lens cleaning system)
　Focus (contact lenses)
　Focus Dailies (disposable contact lenses)
　FreshLook (tinted contact lenses)
　NIGHT & DAY (continual wear contact lenses)
　O2OPTIX (high oxygen contact lenses)
Consumer Health
　Bufferin (systemic analgesic)
　Excedrin (systemic analgesic)
　Ex-Lax (laxative)
　Gas-X (antacid)
　Keri (skin care)
　Lamisil AT Cream (athlete's foot treatment)
　Maalox (antacid)
　No-Doz (stimulant)
　Nicotinell (smoking cessation patch)
　Theraflu (flu treatment)
　Triaminic (cough and cold remedy)
　Voltaren Emulgel (topical analgesic)

Generic Pharmaceuticals
　Atenolol (hypertension drug)
　Amoxicillin/clavulanic acid (antibiotic)
　Citalopram (anti-depressant)
　Enalapril (ACE inhibitor)
　Lisinopril (ACE inhibitor)
　Loratadine (allergy drug)
　Metformin (diabetes drug)
　Metoprolol (hypertension drug)
　Omeprazole (ulcer and acid reflux drug)
　Penicillin (antibiotic)
　Ranitidine (ulcer drug)
　Terazosin (hypertension drug)
Gerber
　Gerber (baby food, care, and wellness products)
　Gerber Life (insurance)
　NUK (baby care products)
Medical Nutrition
　Boost (nutritional supplement drink)
　Compat (enteral products)
　Impact (immuno-booster nutritional products)
　Nutrisource (high-calorie/malnutrition products)
　Resource (oral nutritional supplements)

COMPETITORS

Abbott Labs	Johnson & Johnson
Allergan	Merck
Altana	Milnot
AstraZeneca	Perrigo
Bausch & Lomb	Pfizer
Bayer	Roche
Bristol-Myers Squibb	Sanofi-Aventis
Eli Lilly	Schering
Essilor International	Schering-Plough
Genentech	Wyeth
GlaxoSmithKline	

HISTORICAL FINANCIALS

Company Type: Public

Income Statement

FYE: December 31

	REVENUE ($ mil.)	NET INCOME ($ mil.)	NET PROFIT MARGIN	EMPLOYEES
12/05	32,526	5,190	16.0%	90,924
12/04	28,247	4,989	17.7%	81,392
12/03	24,864	3,788	15.2%	78,541
12/02	23,151	4,218	18.2%	72,877
12/01	19,070	2,799	14.7%	71,116
Annual Growth	**14.3%**	**16.7%**		**6.3%**

2005 Year-End Financials

Debt ratio: 3.4%
Return on equity: 13.6%
Cash ($ mil.): 10,933
Current ratio: 1.40
Long-term debt ($ mil.): 1,319

No. of shares (mil.): —
Dividends
　Yield: 1.4%
　Payout: 28.6%
Market value ($ mil.): —

Stock History

NYSE: NVS

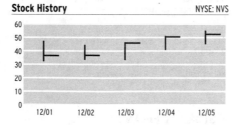

	STOCK PRICE ($) FY Close	P/E High/Low		PER SHARE ($) Earnings	Dividends
12/05	52.48	21	17	2.62	0.75
12/04	50.54	—	—	—	0.66
12/03	45.89	—	—	—	0.60
12/02	36.73	26	20	1.71	0.46
12/01	36.50	41	29	1.13	0.42
Annual Growth	**9.5%**	—	—	**23.4%**	**15.6%**

Novo Nordisk

Novo Nordisk can tell diabetics where to stick it. One of the world's leading producers of insulin, Novo Nordisk also makes insulin analogues, injection devices, and diabetes education materials. Its products include insulin analogues Levemir and NovoLog and the FlexPen, a pre-filled insulin injection tool. In addition to its diabetes products, Novo Nordisk has interests in several other therapeutic areas, including hemostasis management (blood clotting), human growth hormone, and hormone replacement therapy. The not-for-profit Novo Nordisk Foundation, through its Novo A/S subsidiary, owns about 25% of the shares and controls about 70% of the voting power in Novo Nordisk.

Novo Nordisk's non-diabetic products include Activelle (hormone replacement), NovoSeven (hemostasis management), and Norditropin (human growth hormone). The company has also begun research programs in the areas of cancer and inflammation.

The company markets its products in some 180 countries; the US, Japan, and Europe are its major markets, with Europe generating about 40% of sales. However, several key emerging markets — particularly Brazil, China, and India — are contributing to the company's growth.

As with most biopharmaceutical enterprises, Novo Nordisk engages in alliances with medical institutions and other drug companies to further its research and marketing activities. Its partners include Medtronic (to develop pre-filled cartridges for insulin pumps), the Mayo Clinic, Neose Technologies, and Genaissance Pharmaceuticals. Additionally, the company owns about one-third of ZymoGenetics, a Seattle-based biotechnology company.

HISTORY

Novo Nordisk was formed by the 1989 merger of Danish insulin producers Novo and Nordisk.

Soon after Canadian researchers extracted insulin from pancreas of cattle, Danish researcher August Krogh (winner of the 1920 Nobel Prize in physiology) and physician Marie Krogh, his wife, teamed up with H. C. Hagedorn, also a physician, to found Nordisk Insulinlaboratorium. One of their lab workers was an inventor named Harald Pedersen, and in 1923 Nordisk hired Pedersen's brother, Thorvald, to analyze chemicals. The relationship was unsuccessful, however, and the brothers left the company.

The Pedersens decided to produce insulin themselves and set up operations in their basement in 1924. Harald also designed a syringe that patients could use for their own insulin injections. Within a decade their firm, Novo Terapeutisk Laboratorium, was selling its product in 40 countries.

Meanwhile, Nordisk introduced a slow-acting insulin in 1936. NPH insulin, launched in the US in 1950, soon became the leading longer-acting insulin. Nordisk later became a major maker of human growth hormone.

During WWII Novo produced its first enzyme, trypsin, used to soften leather. It began producing penicillin in 1947 and during the 1950s developed Heparin, a trypsin-based drug used to treat blood clots. The company unveiled more industrial enzymes in the 1960s.

In 1981 Novo began selling its insulin in the US through a joint venture with E. R. Squibb (now part of Bristol-Myers Squibb). The next year Novo was the first to produce human insulin (actually a modified form of pig insulin), and in 1983 Nordisk introduced the Nordisk Infuser, a pump that constantly released small quantities of insulin. Two years later Novo debuted the NovoPen, a refillable injector that looked like a fountain pen.

Novo was the world's #2 insulin maker (and the world's largest maker of industrial enzymes) when it merged with #3, Nordisk, in 1989. By combining their research and market share, they were better able to complete globally with then-#1 Eli Lilly. After the merger, Novo Nordisk introduced the NovoLet, the world's first prefilled, disposable insulin syringe.

Novo Nordisk introduced drugs for depression (Seroxat, 1992), epilepsy (Gabitril, 1995), and hemophilia (NovoSeven, 1995). The company entered a joint marketing alliance with Johnson & Johnson subsidiary LifeScan, the world's #1 maker of blood glucose monitors, in 1995. It also began working with Rhône-Poulenc Rorer on estrogen replacement therapies.

Eli Lilly raised a new challenge in 1996 with the FDA approval of Humalog (the US's first new insulin product in 14 years), which is absorbed faster, giving users more flexibility in their injection schedule. (Novo Nordisk's own fast-acting insulin product, NovoLog, received FDA approval four years later.) A 1998 marketing pact with Schering-Plough signaled Novo Nordisk's desire to boost sales of its diabetes drugs in the US, where Eli Lilly has historically dominated.

In 2000 Novo Nordisk split its health care and enzymes businesses; the split left Novo Nordisk with all the health care operations, while a new company, Novozymes, was formed to carry out the enzyme business. It bought out the remaining shares in its Brazilian subsidiary, Biobrás, in 2001. The following year the company spun off its US-based biotechnology firm, ZymoGenetics; though it retained a significant minority stake in the company.

Novo Nordisk divested its 29% stake in Ferrosan, a Danish consumer health care and medical devices company, in 2005.

EXECUTIVES

Chairman: Sten Scheibye, age 55
Vice Chairman: Göran A. Ando, age 57
President and CEO: Lars Rebien Sørensen, age 52, $1,124,640 pay
EVP and CFO: Jesper Brandgaard, age 43, $570,240 pay
EVP and COO: Kåre Schultz, age 45, $601,920 pay
EVP and Chief Science Officer: Mads Krogsgaard Thomsen, age 45, $475,200 pay
EVP and Chief of Staffs: Lise Kingo, age 45, $554,400 pay
Member, Senior Management Board, Devices and Sourcing: Kim Tosti
Member, Senior Management Board, Preclinical and CMC Supply: Jesper Bøving
Member, Senior Management Board, Diabetes Finished Products: Eric Drapé
Member, Senior Management Board, Diabetes Research Unit: Peter Kurtzhals
Member, Senior Management Board, Europe: Klaus Ehrlich
Member, Senior Management Board, International Operations: Jesper Høiland
Member, Senior Management Board, International Marketing: Jakob Riis
Member, Senior Management Board, Japan and Oceania: Roger Moore
Member, Senior Management Board, Corporate Legal: Ole Ramsby
Member, Senior Management Board, North America: Martin Soeters

Member, Senior Management Board, Global Development: Lars Guldbæk Karlsen
Member, Senior Management Board, Quality: Mariann Strid Christensen
Member, Senior Management Board, Corporate Finance: Lars Green
Member, Senior Management Board, Corporate People and Organisation: Lars Christian Lassen
Auditors: PricewaterhouseCoopers

LOCATIONS

HQ: Novo Nordisk A/S
   Novo Allé, 2880 Bagsværd, Denmark
Phone: +45-4444-8888   **Fax:** +45-4449-0555
US HQ: 100 College Rd. West, Princeton, NJ 08540
US Phone: 609-987-5800   **US Fax:** 609-921-8082
Web: www.novonordisk.com

Novo Nordisk has production facilities in Brazil, China, Denmark, France, Japan, and the US.

2005 Sales

	% of total
Europe	40
North America	28
Japan & Oceania	14
Other regions	18
Total	**100**

PRODUCTS/OPERATIONS

2005 Sales

	% of total
Diabetes care	71
Biopharmaceuticals	
Hemostasis management	15
Human growth hormone	8
Hormone replacement therapy	5
Other	1
Total	**100**

Selected Products

Diabetes products
   Glucagen HypoKit (hypoglycemia treatment)
   NovoMix (insulin analogue)
   NovoRapid/NovoLog (insulin analogue)
   Levemir (insulin analogue)
   Mixtard (insulin)
   Actrapid (insulin)
   Insulatard (insulin)
Biopharmaceuticals
   NovoSeven (recombinant hemophilia therapy)
   Norditropin (human growth hormone)
   Activelle (hormone replacement therapy)
   Vagifem (hormone replacement therapy)

COMPETITORS

Abbott Labs	Medtronic MiniMed
Akzo Nobel	Merck
Amylin Pharmaceuticals	Novartis
Baxter	Pfizer
Bayer	Roche
BD	Sankyo Co
Bristol-Myers Squibb	Sanofi-Aventis
Eli Lilly	Schering-Plough
Forest Labs	Wyeth
GlaxoSmithKline	

HISTORICAL FINANCIALS

Company Type: Public

Income Statement

FYE: December 31

	REVENUE ($ mil.)	NET INCOME ($ mil.)	NET PROFIT MARGIN	EMPLOYEES
12/05	5,351	776	14.5%	22,000
12/04	5,324	859	16.1%	20,285
12/03	4,408	820	18.6%	18,800
Annual Growth	**10.2%**	**(2.7%)**	**—**	**8.2%**

2005 Year-End Financials

Debt ratio: 4.6%
Return on equity: 17.0%
Cash ($ mil.): 796
Current ratio: 1.85
Long-term debt ($ mil.): 198
No. of shares (mil.): —
Dividends
Yield: 1.1%
Payout: 26.4%
Market value ($ mil.): —

Stock History

NYSE: NVO

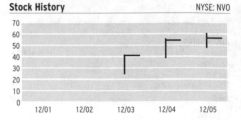

	STOCK PRICE ($) FY Close	P/E High	P/E Low	PER SHARE ($) Earnings	PER SHARE ($) Dividends
12/05	56.28	26	20	2.35	0.62
12/04	54.26	22	15	2.53	0.52
12/03	40.96	17	11	2.38	0.38
Annual Growth	**17.2%**	**—**	**—**	**(0.6%)**	**27.7%**

NTT

Nippon Telegraph and Telephone (NTT) has executed an AT&T-style breakup into two local carriers and a long-distance provider — but unlike Ma Bell's gang, this family is sticking together. The world's #1 telecommunications firm, NTT is a holding company for regional local phone companies NTT East and NTT West, which enjoy *de facto* monopolies in their markets, and long-distance carrier NTT Communications, which faces growing competition. NTT also operates a leading ISP and it owns 62% of Japan's dominant cellular carrier, NTT DoCoMo. The firm has made international investments, too, throughout the Pacific Rim and the US. NTT remains 43%-owned by the state.

While the Japanese government has restructured this telecom Godzilla, the telecom market has worked other changes. Combined sales from data transport, Internet services, and mobile phone operations have eclipsed conventional wireline voice revenue; in contrast to the high-growth cellular market, NTT's number of fixed-line subscribers (about 30 million) is on the decline. Still, the company has announced plans to spend $47 billion in enhancing the fixed-line network. The effort includes replacing traditional phone lines with fiber-optic lines. The company also has announced a new business unit, NTT Resonant, that focuses on the development of video communications and broadband portal services.

The company's international holdings include Hong Kong's HKNet, a 15% stake in Philippine Long Distance Telephone, and Australia-based Davnet Telecommunications (Davtel), which it has renamed NTT Australia. In the US, NTT owns Web-hosting company Verio.

HISTORY

In 1889 the Japanese Ministry of Communications began telephone service, operated as a monopoly after 1900. In 1952 the ministry formed Nippon Telegraph and Telephone Public Corporation (NTT). Regulated by the Ministry of Posts and Telecommunications, NTT was charged with rebuilding Japan's war-ravaged phone system. Another company, Kokusai Denshin Denwa (now KDD), was created in 1953 to handle international phone service.

Japanese authorities cast NTT in the image of AT&T but prohibited it from manufacturing to encourage competition among equipment suppliers. Nonetheless, NTT bought most equipment from favored Japanese vendors. By the late 1970s NTT was a large bureaucracy, perceived as inefficient and corrupt. NTT's president quipped that the only equipment the firm would buy overseas was telephone poles and mops, but in 1981 NTT was forced to allow US companies to bid. The phone firm spent heavily in the 1980s, installing a nationwide fiber-optic network and high-speed ISDN lines.

In 1985 Japan privatized NTT as a precursor to deregulation. At its IPO, NTT became the world's most valuable public company. NTT International was established to provide overseas telecom engineering, and NTT Data Communications Systems, Japan's largest systems integrator, was formed in 1988.

As Japan's stock market bubble burst in 1990, NTT chose AT&T, Motorola, and Ericsson to develop a digital mobile phone system and the next year formed NTT Mobile Communications Network (NTT DoCoMo) as its mobile carrier. Following the deregulation of Japan's cellular market, NTT launched its Personal Handyphone Service (PHS) in 1995.

The Japanese government unveiled a plan to break up NTT in 1996, a year before the World Trade Organization spearheaded a historic agreement to open international telecom markets. Meanwhile, the government forced NTT to allow rivals to connect to its new, all-digital systems. Overseas, NTT made its first significant investment in the US by buying a 12.5% stake in local carrier Teligent (later reduced).

In 1998 tiny Tokyo Telecommunications Net (a Tokyo Electric Power affiliate) offered discount phone rates, spurring NTT to do the same. NTT spun off DoCoMo in the world's largest IPO at the time.

NTT lost its 1999 bidding war with the UK's Cable and Wireless for International Digital Communications. That year NTT split into three carriers, two near-monopoly regional local phone providers — NTT East and NTT West — and a long-distance and international carrier called NTT Communications. Unlike AT&T's breakup in 1984, this split featured a holding company — the new NTT — that owns the three carriers. Criticized for continuing to promote last-generation ISDN as the key to high-speed Internet access, NTT in 1999 began to test higher-speed digital subscriber line (DSL) service and planned to cut 21,000 jobs at NTT West and NTT East over three years.

The company pressed forward with international investments, taking a 49% stake in HKNet of Hong Kong and a 49% stake in Davnet Telecommunications, a subsidiary of Australia's Davnet Limited (both were later increased to 100%). In 2000 the Japanese government said it would sell another 6% of NTT. That year NTT paid $5.5 billion for the 90% of US Web-hosting firm Verio that it didn't already own.

But as a result of the economic downturn, NTT took a write-down of around $4.5 billion on its Verio acquisition in 2001 and shifted more than 25% of its workers to lower-paying positions.

EXECUTIVES

President, CEO, and Director: Norio Wada, age 66
SEVP, CFO, Director of Corporate Management Strategy Division, and Board Member: Satoshi Miura, age 62
SEVP, Technical Strategy and Resonant Promotion, and Director: Ryuji Yamada, age 58
SVP, Intellectual Property, Director of Department III, and Board Member: Yuji Inoue, age 58
SVP, Director of Department II, and Board Member: Shin Hashimoto, age 57
SVP, Director of Department IV, and Board Member: Hiroo Unoura, age 57
SVP, Director of Department IV, and Board Member: Ken Yagi, age 58
SVP, Corporate Management Strategy, and Director: Akira Arima, age 57
SVP, Director of Department I, and Board Member: Kiyoshi Kousaka, age 55
President, NTT East: Toyohiko Takabe, age 59
President, NTT West: Shunzo Morishita, age 58
President, NTT Communications: Hiromi Wasai, age 60
President and CEO, NTT DATA: Tomokazu Hamaguchi, age 62
President, NTT DoCoMo, Inc.: Masao Nakamura, age 62
Auditors: KPMG AZSA & Co.

LOCATIONS

HQ: Nippon Telegraph and Telephone Corporation (Nippon Denshin Denwa Kabushiki Kaisha) 3-1, Otemachi 2-chome, Chiyoda-ku, Tokyo 100-8116, Japan
Phone: +81-3-5205-5581 **Fax:** +81-3-5205-5589
US HQ: 101 Park Ave., 41st Fl., New York, NY 10178
US Phone: 212-661-0810 **US Fax:** 212-661-1078
Web: www.ntt.co.jp

Nippon Telegraph and Telephone operates principally in Japan. The company also operates or has investments in operations throughout the Pacific Rim — including in Australia, Hong Kong, Malaysia, the Philippines, Singapore, and Taiwan — as well as in Europe, Latin America, and the US.

PRODUCTS/OPERATIONS

2006 Sales

	% of total
Fixed voice services	32
Mobile voice services	29
IP, packet communications services	18
System integration	9
Sales of telecom equipment	5
Other services	7
Total	**100**

Selected Subsidiaries and Affiliates

Internet Initiative Japan Inc. (32%)
Nippon Telegraph and Telephone East Corporation (NTT East, regional telecommunications)
Nippon Telegraph and Telephone West Corporation (NTT West, regional telecommunications)
NTT Australia IP Pty Ltd (formerly Davnet Telecommunications Pty Ltd. (Davtel), Australia)
NTT Communications Corporation (long-distance and international telecommunications)
HKNet Company Limited (ISP, Hong Kong)
NTT DATA Corporation (54%, systems integration and network services)
NTT DoCoMo, Inc. (63%, mobile telecommunications)
NTT Resonant Inc. (development of video communications and broadband portal services)
Philippine Long Distance Telephone (PLDT, 15%)
Verio Inc. (corporate Internet services, US)

COMPETITORS

Asia Netcom	KDDI
AT&T	Microsoft
BT	NEC
BT Infonet	SOFTBANK
Cable & Wireless	SOFTBANK MOBILE
Equant	Telstra
Fujitsu	Tokyo Electric
Internet Initiative Japan	Tokyo Telecommunication
Kansai Electric	

HISTORICAL FINANCIALS

Company Type: Public

Income Statement

FYE: March 31

	REVENUE ($ mil.)	NET INCOME ($ mil.)	NET PROFIT MARGIN	EMPLOYEES
3/06	91,805	4,262	4.6%	199,000
3/05	100,990	6,637	6.6%	201,486
3/04	105,672	6,132	5.8%	205,288
3/03	91,026	1,945	2.1%	207,363
3/02	86,734	(6,276)	—	213,062
Annual Growth	**1.4%**	**—**	**—**	**(1.7%)**

2006 Year-End Financials

Debt ratio: 59.6%
Return on equity: 7.0%
Cash ($ mil.): 12,536
Current ratio: 1.07
Long-term debt ($ mil.): 34,563

Net Income History

NYSE: NTT

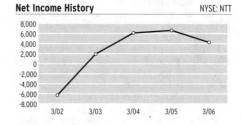

NTT DoCoMo

The Japanese yen for mobility means business for NTT DoCoMo. Formerly NTT Mobile Communications Network, the wireless spin-off of Nippon Telegraph and Telephone (NTT), the mobile phone carrier has more than 51 million subscribers to its digital network (a 56% market share). It is one of the world's largest wireless network operators by subscribers, behind #1 Vodafone. More than 46 million customers subscribe to NTT DoCoMo's i-mode service, which provides mobile Internet services. The company also offers maritime and in-flight phone services and sells handsets. NTT owns 62% of NTT DoCoMo.

DoCoMo means "anywhere" and NTT DoCoMo is everywhere in the Japanese market for mobile communication services. Besides scoring big with the rollout of its popular i-mode service, the company was the first to offer third-generation (3G) mobile phone service (called FOMA) with a 2001 debut in Tokyo.

NTT DoCoMo is exporting i-mode like it was cheap electronics, building an i-mode presence in Europe first through a partnership with Italy's Telecom Italia Mobile (now part of Telecom Italia). It has since licensed the technology to the telecom unit of French construction group Bouygues, to Italy's Wind, and to Telefónica

Móviles in Spain, among others. It has i-mode licensing agreements with more than a dozen GSM network operators in Europe, including Russia and Greece, and in the Asia/Pacific region.

NTT DoCoMo had staked its claim in the US, too, by paying $9.8 billion (in 2001) for a 16% stake in AT&T Wireless. However, AT&T Wireless was the subject of a takeover bidding war in 2004 won by rival Cingular Wireless in a deal valued at $41 billion and NTT DoCoMo sold its stake.

NTT DoCoMo takes an active role in advancing mobile communication technologies. It has a US-based venture investment firm, DoCoMo Capital. The company also has teamed up with Nippon Television Network (NTV) in 2006 to develop content and services and is in a joint venture with Sony focusing on the development of handsets equipped with Sony's smart-card technology. It also is expanding through a 10% stake in KT Freetel, the Korean mobile carrier, and through the purchase of both Guam Cellular & Paging and Guam Wireless Telephone.

But failed expectations have led the company to sell its 20% stake in Hutchison 3G UK to Hutchison Whampoa in a deal valued at €120 million.

HISTORY

Formed in 1952 by the Japanese Ministry of Communications to rebuild Japan's war-ravaged phone system, Nippon Telegraph and Telephone (NTT) enjoyed a monopoly on phone services for more than four decades.

NTT first went into mobile communications with a maritime phone service in 1959, and in 1968 the company began offering paging services. Other telecommunications services followed: car phone service (1979), in-flight phone service (1986), and mobile phone service (1987).

In 1991 NTT established a subsidiary to adopt these wireless segments: It launched operations in 1992 as NTT Mobile Communications Network under the leadership of NTT executive Kouji Ohboshi. The firm quickly took on the DoCoMo nickname. The year closed with slightly more than a million analog mobile phone users in Japan — a market DoCoMo shared with upstart telecom companies DDI and IDO (later bought by DDI). Paging service was more popular, and DoCoMo won more than 3 million customers.

DoCoMo in 1993 launched digital mobile phone service based on a scheme called PDC (personal digital cellular) — a system incompatible with the digital standards that would take root in Europe and the US. Liberalization of the cellular phone market in 1994 triggered unexpected growth: Customers who previously had to lease mobile phones from the network operators could now buy them at retail stores. Further competition emerged in 1995 with the launch of personal handyphone services, or PHS (parent company NTT was among the companies providing PHS), but DoCoMo's subscriber count passed 3.5 million mobile phone users — about half the market.

DoCoMo's pager business peaked in 1996 before commencing a long-term decline; the mobile phone market, where DoCoMo had more than 8 million subscribers, overtook it. The company launched a satellite-based mobile phone system that year to serve customers beyond the range of cell sites, reaching ships and mountainous regions.

Financial crises rocked the Pacific Rim in 1997, and Japan's Fair Trade Commission rocked NTT by ordering it to cut its 95%-ownership of

DoCoMo. Customers continued to flock to mobile phones despite economic turmoil, and DoCoMo passed the 15 million-subscriber mark. In 1998 DoCoMo gave hope to Japan's low-flying market when it left the nest: Its mammoth IPO raised more than $18 billion.

Meanwhile, DDI (now KDDI) had become the first Japanese carrier to launch a digital mobile phone network based on CDMA (code division multiple access) technology. Though DoCoMo still used PDC, it redoubled its efforts to help develop and standardize a next-generation, wideband version of CDMA.

In 1999 DoCoMo took over NTT's unprofitable PHS unit and rolled out a high-speed data service over the PHS network. That year it acquired a 19% stake in the telecom unit of Hong Kong's Hutchison Whampoa.

The next year the company adopted NTT DoCoMo as its corporate name. To promote its new data services, NTT DoCoMo launched a joint venture in Japan with Microsoft (Mobimagic). It took the i-mode service international in 2001 when the company teamed up with Telecom Italia Mobile to introduce the 3G service in Europe. The next year NTT DoCoMo became the largest shareholder in America Online Japan (it sold its stake to America Online in 2003).

The company in 2002 took full ownership of its eight majority-owned regional operating subsidiaries and began consolidating operations. The company also has liquidated several other subsidiaries including an operating unit in Brazil and it has reorganized its European holdings under a single subsidiary, DoCoMo Europe Ltd.

It also continued to advance digital wireless technologies through partnerships that include an alliance (formed in 2000) with Hutchison Whampoa and Dutch mobile phone company KPN Mobile to bid on European operating licenses. It also paid $4.5 billion for a 15% stake in KPN's wireless unit, KPN Mobile (the stake was reduced to 2% then sold back to parent firm KPN. An i-mode affiliation continues, however).

EXECUTIVES

President, CEO, and Director: Masao Nakamura, age 62
SEVP; CFO; Managing Director, Global Business Division; and Director: Masayuki Hirata, age 59
SEVP, Managing Director, Network Division, and Director: Kunio Ishikawa, age 58
SEVP and Director: Seijiro Adachi, age 62
EVP and CTO; Managing Director, Research and Development Division; and Director: Takanori Utano, age 57
EVP and Deputy Managing Director, Corporate Marketing Division; Managing Director, Corporate Marketing Department I: Seiji Tanaka, age 64
EVP; Managing Director, Marketing Division; and Director: Takashi Sakamoto, age 57
EVP; Managing Director, Corporate Marketing Division; Managing Director, Corporate Marketing Promotion Department; and Director: Shuro Hoshizawa, age 57
EVP; Managing Director, Products and Services Division; and Director: Kiyoyuki Tsujimura, age 56
EVP; Managing Director, Human Resources Management Department; and Director: Harunari Futatsugi, age 55
EVP; Managing Director, General Affairs Department; and Director: Kenji Ota, age 57
SVP and Managing Director, Public Relations Department: Masatoshi Suzuki, age 55
SVP, Managing Director Marketing Division and Director: Bunya Kumagai, age 54
Auditors: KPMG AZSA & Co.

LOCATIONS

HQ: NTT DoCoMo, Inc.
Sanno Park Tower, 11-1 Nagatacho-2-chome, Chiyoda-ku, Tokyo 100-6150, Japan
Phone: +81-3-5156-1111 **Fax:** +81-3-5156-0271
Web: www.nttdocomo.com

PRODUCTS/OPERATIONS

2006 Sales

	$ mil.	% of total
Wireless services	36,566.7	90
Equipment sales	4,000.8	10
Total	**40,567.5**	**100**

2006 Sales

	$ mil.	% of total
Mobile phone business	39,862.1	98
PHS business	355.3	1
Other	350.1	1
Total	**40,567.5**	**100**

Selected Services

Cellular
i-mode (wireless Internet access)
In-flight telephone
Mobile multimedia
Personal Handyphone System (PHS, wireless voice and data transmission service)
Satellite mobile communications
Third-generation (3G) wireless (W-CDMA)
World Call (direct international calling)

Regional Operating Subsidiaries

NTT DoCoMo Chugoku, Inc.
NTT DoCoMo Hokkaido, Inc.
NTT DoCoMo Hokuriku, Inc.
NTT DoCoMo Kansai, Inc.
NTT DoCoMo Kyushu, Inc.
NTT DoCoMo Shikoku, Inc.
NTT DoCoMo Tohoku, Inc.
NTT DoCoMo Tokai, Inc.

Selected Subsidiaries and Affiliates

DoCoMo Capital, Inc. (advanced mobile communications technologies venture investments, US)
DoCoMo Europe Ltd.
Far EasTone Telecommunications Co., Ltd. (5%, Taiwan)
KG Telecommunications Co. (Taiwan)
Hutchison Telephone Company Ltd. (24%, Hong Kong)

COMPETITORS

BT
China Mobile
Cingular Wireless
Deutsche Telekom AG
France Telecom
KDDI
Optus
Orange
SK Telecom
SOFTBANK MOBILE
Telstra
Verizon Wireless
Vodafone
WILLCOM

HISTORICAL FINANCIALS

Company Type: Public

Income Statement

FYE: March 31

	REVENUE ($ mil.)	NET INCOME ($ mil.)	NET PROFIT MARGIN	EMPLOYEES
3/06	40,568	5,197	12.8%	21,646
3/05	45,184	6,972	15.4%	21,527
3/04	47,957	6,175	12.9%	21,241
3/03	40,731	1,800	4.4%	23,310
3/02	38,939	(876)	—	19,700
Annual Growth	**1.0%**	**—**	**—**	**2.4%**

2006 Year-End Financials

Debt ratio: 14.8%
Return on equity: 14.7%
Cash ($ mil.): 7,592

Current ratio: 1.41
Long-term debt ($ mil.): 5,095

Net Income History

NYSE: DCM

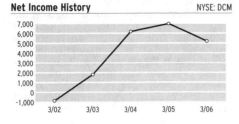

| | 3/02 | 3/03 | 3/04 | 3/05 | 3/06 |

Oki Electric

Oki Electric Industry is plugged into a variety of products. The company's core businesses include information systems, telecommunication systems, semiconductors, and printers. Its information products include facsimile machines offered through its Oki Data subsidiary, as well as automated teller machines, terminals, banking systems, and security systems. The company's electronics operations (represented by Oki Semiconductor in the US) produce integrated circuits, microprocessors, and audiovisual products. Oki's telecom products include network equipment, switching systems, and computer telephony integration systems.

In order to combat a slumping telecommunications market and worldwide downturn in information technology spending, Oki Electric has realigned its operations. Its restructuring efforts include a shift away from hardware sales to broader service offerings such as network design, installation, and maintenance.

Oki acquired the driver chip business for large TFT-LCDs from Texas Instruments Japan in early 2005. TFT-LCD drive chips are used in notebook computers, monitors, and TVs.

HISTORY

Engineer Kibataro Oki founded Meikosha in Tokyo in 1881 to produce telephones (only five years after they were invented). Meikosha was soon producing telegraphs, bells, and medical equipment. Its main factory adopted the name Oki Electric Plant in 1889, and the marketing division began operating under the name Oki & Company in 1896.

In 1907, a year after the founder's death, the Oki groups were united as a limited partnership. Divided again in 1912, they were recombined in 1917 as Oki Electric Co. Oki continued to expand its product line to include automatic switching equipment (1926) and electric clocks (1929).

The manufacturer produced communications equipment for the Japanese military during WWII, but after the war it started working on the teleprinter and added consumer goods such as portable stoves. The company adopted its present name, Oki Electric Industry Company, in 1949.

Oki entered the semiconductor and computer industries in the 1950s, joining Fujitsu, Hitachi, Mitsubishi, Nippon Electric Co., and Toshiba as one of Japan's Big Six electronics makers by 1960. It then began developing overseas businesses, particularly in Latin America, where it built communications networks in Honduras (1962) and Bolivia (1966) and radio networks in Brazil (1971).

In 1970 Oki formed a computer software unit. The company was a major telecommunications equipment supplier for the Japanese government until the mid-1970s, when the government increased its purchases from other companies. Former Nippon Telegraph and Telephone executive Masao Miyake took over as president, initiating a dramatic reorganization into 15 business units.

Oki started building PCs in 1981. It consolidated its US operations as Oki America in 1984. A new financial crisis followed in the mid-1980s when the bottom fell out of the semiconductor market — Oki's earnings plummeted into the red in 1986. However, by the end of the decade Oki had become a major provider of automated teller machines (ATMs) and bank computer systems; growth in the Japanese financial industry sparked a ninefold increase in Oki's sales in 1989. In 1994 Oki established subsidiary Oki Data Corp. to handle printer and fax machine operations.

Plunging memory prices and higher taxes stymied Oki's recovery in fiscal 1998, so the company halted mass random-access memory (RAM) production and closed an assembly and testing facility. Oki shifted its semiconductor focus to large-scale integrated circuits, and placed more emphasis on its information systems segment, which had seen increasing sales.

Further battered by a weak Asian economy, Oki restructured in 1999. That year the company bought Toshiba's ATM operations. It also launched an access control system that uses a person's iris for identification and payment services.

In 2000 Oki announced plans to establish (along with NTT Data, NTT DoCoMo, Microsoft and others) Payment First Corporation, an Internet payment company.

Responding to poor market conditions, Oki announced in 2001 that it would reduce its workforce by about 10% over two years. The company also sold its automotive electronics division to Keihin Corporation.

EXECUTIVES

President, CEO, and Board Member: Katsumasa Shinozuka
EVP, CFO, Chief Compliance Officer, and Board Member: Kazuo Tanaka
EVP; Chairman, Systems Network Business Group; General Manager, China Business Promotion Division; Board Member: Yutaka Maeda
SVP and Board Member: Tadao Murase
SVP, CIO, and Board Member: Nobuhide Hara
SVP; Group Operating Officer, Systems Network Business Group; and Board Member: Takashi Hattori
SVP and Board Member: Naoki Sato
SVP, CTO, and Board Member: Harushige Sugimoto
General Manager, Marketing Promotion Division; Board Member: Hideichi Kawasaki
Senior Operating Officer, Systems Network Business Group; Acting General Manager, Strategic Planning Office: Kazushige Matsui
Group Operating Officer, Semiconductor Business Group: Hironori Kitabayashi
General Manager, Accounting and Control Division: Keiichi Fukumura
Senior Operating Officer, System Network Business Group; Acting General Manager, Network Application Division: Masayoshi Matsushita
Executive Officer: Masataka Sase
Senior Operating Officer, Systems Network Business Group; Deputy General Manager, Marketing Promotion Division: Yutaka Asai
Senior Operating Officer, Systems Network Business Group; Acting President, Financial Solutions Company: Shigeru Yamamoto
Senior Operating Officer, Semiconductor Business Group; Acting General Manager, Strategic Planning Office: Kiyoharu Miyatake
Senior Operating Officer, Semiconductor Business Group; Acting President, Silicon Solutions Company: Akira Kamo
Senior Operating Officer, Systems Network Business Group; Acting President, Network Systems Company: Masao Miyashita
Auditors: Ernst & Young ShinNihon

LOCATIONS

HQ: Oki Electric Industry Company, Limited
(Oki Denki Kogyo Kabushiki Kaisha)
7-12, Toranomon 1-chome, Minato-ku,
Tokyo 105-8460, Japan
Phone: +81-3-3501-3111 **Fax:** +81-3-3581-5522
US HQ: 785 N. Mary Ave., Sunnyvale, CA 94085
US Phone: 408-720-1900 **US Fax:** 408-720-1918
Web: www.oki.com

2006 Sales

	% of total
Asia	
Japan	73
Other countries	5
Europe	12
North America	10
Total	**100**

PRODUCTS/OPERATIONS

2006 Sales

	% of total
Info-Telecom systems	50
Printers	24
Semiconductors	22
Other	4
Total	**100**

Selected Products

Information Systems
Automated teller machines
Point-of-sale terminals
Printers
Terminals
Video delivery software

Electronic Devices
Large-scale integrated circuits
Memory chips
Microprocessors
Optical components
Telecommunications and voice synthesis circuits

Telecommunications Systems
ATM (asynchronous transfer mode) switches
Computer telephony integration
ISDN terminals
Key telephone systems
Fiber-optic communications products
Modems
PBX systems
Radio equipment
Teleconferencing systems
Video/audio encoders/decoders

COMPETITORS

Canon	MICROS Systems
CASIO COMPUTER	Mitsubishi Electric
Cisco Systems	NCR
Dell	NEC
Diebold	NTT DATA
Epson	Ricoh
Fuji Xerox	Samsung Group
Fujitsu	SANYO
Hewlett-Packard	Sharp
Hitachi	Siemens AG
IBM	Sony
Konica Minolta	Symbol Technologies
Kyocera	VeriFone
Lexmark	Wincor Nixdorf
Matsushita	Xerox

HISTORICAL FINANCIALS

Company Type: Public

Income Statement

FYE: March 31

	REVENUE ($ mil.)	NET INCOME ($ mil.)	NET PROFIT MARGIN	EMPLOYEES
3/06	5,855	43	0.7%	21,175
3/05	6,402	104	1.6%	20,410
3/04	6,193	13	0.2%	20,960
3/03	4,885	(55)	—	22,520
3/02	4,558	(257)	—	23,597
Annual Growth	6.5%	—	—	(2.7%)

Net Income History

Exchange: Tokyo

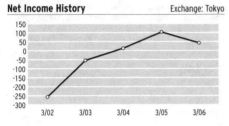

OMV

Oil and chemicals group OMV is Austria's largest industrial company. It explores for natural gas and crude oil, refines crude oil, and imports, transports, and stores gas. A leading oil and gas company in Central and Eastern Europe, OMV has proved reserves of 1.4 billion barrels of oil equivalent. With petroleum products marketed through OMV gas stations and direct distributors, OMV has a 14% retail market share in Central and Eastern Europe. The company also makes plastics (it owns geotextile producer Polyfelt) and chemicals (fertilizers and melamine). OMV's largest shareholders are Austrian state holding company ÖIAG (31.5%) and the International Petroleum Investment Company (IPIC) of Abu Dhabi (17.6%).

OMV has exploration activities in Austria as well as internationally (including Australia, Libya, Pakistan, and the UK).

The bulk of OMV's sales comes from refining and marketing. It has two refineries and a total refining capacity of 380,000 barrels of oil equivalent per day. Petroleum products are marketed through more than 1,780 OMV filling stations and direct distributors. Its natural gas network, serving about 90% of Austria's natural gas demand, draws gas supplies from Russia, Norway, and Germany, as well as from domestic reserves.

Subsidiary Agrolinz Melamin is the Austrian leader in plant nutrients and the world's #2 producer of melamine (a synthetic resin used to manufacture flooring and furniture) behind DSM Chemicals North America. OMV also makes nonwoven geotextiles for engineering materials through its Polyfelt unit and owns 35% of Danish polyolefin producer Borealis.

Austria's gas market, now dominated by OMV, is slated for full competition, and OMV is among state-controlled companies set for full privatization. Meanwhile, the company's expansion eastwards into Romania is supporting its eventual goal: Russia. In 2006 Russian energy giant Gazprom signed long-term contracts for gas deliveries with OMV.

In a major consolidation move, in 2006 OMV agreed to buy Austrian power firm Verbund for $17 billion, but the move was rebuffed by government regulators.

HISTORY

Oil exploration began in Austria in the 1920s, largely as joint ventures with foreign firms such as Shell and Socony-Vacuum. Full-scale production did not get underway until 1938, when the Anschluss (the absorption of Austria by Germany) paved the way for Germany to exploit Austria's natural resources to fuel its growing war machine. In the division of spoils following WWII, Russia gained control of Austria's oil reserves.

The Russian-administered oil assets were transferred to the new Austrian government in 1955, which authorized the company Österreichische Mineralölverwaltung (ÖMG) in 1956 to control state oil assets. ÖMG, state-controlled by the Austrian Mineral Oil Administration, set about building a major refinery in 1960 and acquiring marketing companies Martha and ÖROP in 1965.

In 1968 ÖMG became the first Western firm to sign a natural gas supply contract with Russia. In 1974 the company commissioned the Trans-Austria Gas Pipeline, which enabled the supply of natural gas to Italy. That year ÖMG changed its named to ÖMV Aktiengesellschaft (ÖMV became OMV in 1995 for international markets).

During the 1970s OMV expanded its crude supply arrangements, tapping supplies from Iran, Iraq, Libya, and other Middle Eastern countries. It moved into oil and gas exploration in the mid-1980s, forming OMV Libya (acquiring 25% of Occidental's Libyan production) and OMV UK.

With Austria moving toward increasing privatization, in 1987 about 15% of OMV's shares were sold to the public. The government sold another 10% two years later. In 1989 OMV acquired PCD Polymere. With the aim of merging state-owned oil and chemical activities, OMV acquired Chemie Linz in 1990. The company also opened its first OMV-branded service station that year. In 1994 OMV reorganized itself as an integrated oil and gas group based in Central Europe, with international exploration and production activities, and with other operations in the chemical and petrochemical sectors.

In 1995 OMV acquired TOTAL-AUSTRIA, expanding its service stations by 59. The company introduced OMV lubricants to the Greek market in 1996. It also expanded its OMV service station network in Hungary to 66 stations after acquiring 31 Q8 (Kuwait) sites. In 1997 the Stroh Company's retail network in Austria was merged into OMV.

Expanding its retail network even farther, OMV acquired BP's retail network in the Czech Republic, Slovakia, and Hungary in 1998. It also sold its stake in Chemie Linz and acquired a 25% stake in major European polyolefin producer Borealis, which in turn acquired PCD Polymere. In 1999 the company pushed its retail network into Bulgaria and Romania. That year OMV also acquired Australian company Cultus Petroleum.

OMV and Shell agreed to develop North Sea fields together in 2000. That year OMV also formed a joint venture with Italy's Edison International to explore in Vietnam, and acquired more than 9% of Hungarian rival MOL. It upped that stake to 10% in 2001. The company also made a bid that year for 18% of Poland's largest refiner, PKN Orlen.

In 2002 OMV opened its first gas station in Serbia and Montenegro. It also increased its German gas station count from 79 to 151 with the purchase of 32 units from Royal Dutch Shell and 40 stations from Martin GmbH & Co.

In 2003 the company acquired Preussag Energie's exploration and production assets for $320 million. That year the company moved into Bosnia-Herzegovina, opening nine gas stations.

During 2004 the company bought up 51% of Romania's Petrom, making it the top oil and gas producer in Central Europe. As part of the deal, OMV chose to divest itself of its quarter-chunk of Rompetrol.

EXECUTIVES

Chairman, Supervisory Board: Rainer Wieltsch, age 62
Deputy Chairman, Supervisory Board: Mohamed Nasser Nekhaira Nasser Al Khaily, age 40
Deputy Chairman, Supervisory Board: Peter Michaelis, age 60
Chairman and CEO, Executive Board: Wolfgang Ruttenstorfer, age 56, $1,277,860 pay
Deputy Chairman, Executive Board; VP Refining, Marketing, and Petrochemicals: Gerhard Roiss, age 54, $1,140,481 pay
CFO: David C. Davies, age 51, $984,153 pay
VP Exploration and Production; Managing Director, OMV Exploration and Production: Helmut Langanger, age 56, $1,003,102 pay
Investor Relations: Ana-Barbara Kuncic

LOCATIONS

HQ: OMV Aktiengesellschaft
Otto-Wagner-Platz 5, A-1090 Vienna, Austria
Phone: +43-1-40-440-0   **Fax:** +43-1-40-440-20091
Web: www.omv.com

OMV has marketing operations across Central and Eastern Europe, including Austria, Bulgaria, the Czech Republic, Germany, Hungary, Romania, Serbia, Slovakia, and Switzerland. The company operates refineries in Austria and Germany, and has chemicals and plastics plants in Austria, Italy, and Malaysia.

PRODUCTS/OPERATIONS

2005 Sales

	% of total
Refining & marketing	74
Petrom	17
Gas	5
Exploration & production	3
Chemicals	1
Total	**100**

Selected Subsidiaries

Agrolinz Melamine International GmbH
BIDIM Geosynthetics S.A.
Petrom S.A.
POLYFELT Gesellschaft m.b.H.

COMPETITORS

BP
DSM
Eni
Exxon Mobil
Hellenic Petroleum
MOL
PKN ORLEN
Royal Dutch Shell
Unipetrol

HISTORICAL FINANCIALS

Company Type: Public

Income Statement

FYE: December 31

	REVENUE ($ mil.)	NET INCOME ($ mil.)	NET PROFIT MARGIN	EMPLOYEES
12/05	18,450	1,772	9.6%	49,919
12/04	18,237	876	4.8%	6,232
12/03	9,595	493	5.1%	6,137
12/02	7,420	338	4.6%	5,828
12/01	6,853	338	4.9%	5,659
Annual Growth	28.1%	51.3%	—	72.3%

Net Income History

Pink Sheets: OMVKY

Otto GmbH & Co

Otto GmbH & Co KG (formerly Otto Versand) has the mail-order business in the bag. The world's largest mail-order company sells merchandise in about 20 countries through more than 100 subsidiaries. Customers order through more than 600 print catalogs, as well as through CD-ROM catalogs and the Internet. The firm sells products ranging from clothing to appliances to sporting goods. Otto also owns a majority stake in the Euromarket Designs (a.k.a. Crate & Barrel) housewares chain, and it owns travel agencies in Germany. The family of executive board chairman Michael Otto owns the majority of the company; in 2005 it sold off its longstanding controlling interest in US catalog company Spiegel (now Eddie Bauer Holdings).

The company controls Actebis Holding, a major computer distributor in Europe.

The Otto Group has grown largely through its acquisitions and diversification tactics (entering non-mail-order businesses). The firm does about 50% of its business in Germany, and customers there can get same-day delivery of many of Otto's wares.

HISTORY

East German refugee Werner Otto founded Otto Versand (German for "dispatch") in Hamburg, West Germany, in 1949. It distributed its first catalog in 1950; 300 hand-bound copies offered only shoes, but in 28 styles. Instead of being required to pay upon delivery, customers received bills with their orders; this was new for mail orders. By 1956 the firm employed 500 people; by 1958 the catalog had expanded to 200 pages, offering low-cost women's fashions and other products to 200,000 potential customers.

In 1963 Otto Versand began taking phone orders. Its catalog grew to 800 pages and one million copies by 1967. The following year it published the Post Shop Magazine, its first special-interest catalog, which targeted fashion-conscious youth. In 1969 Otto Versand formed Hanseatic Bank to offer customers monthly payment plans; three years later it formed the Hermes Express Package delivery service.

The firm began a shopping spree in the 1970s by investing in mail-order companies 3 Suisses International (France, 1974), Heinrich Heine (luxury clothes and household goods, West Germany, 1974) and Hanau (West Germany, 1979).

Werner's son Michael succeeded him as chairman in 1981, and in 1982 he led the acquisition of low-cost women's apparel firm Spiegel. Michael immediately revamped Spiegel into an upscale retailer. The ownership of Spiegel was restructured in 1984, but the Otto family remained in control of the US company.

Throughout the 1980s the firm continued investing in European companies (entering the UK in 1986 and Austria in 1988) and began Otto-Sumisho in Japan (a joint venture, 1986). Its combined catalog circulation reached 200 million in 1987.

Otto Versand launched 24-hour delivery service in 1990; that year it expanded to the Polish market by forming joint venture Otto-Epoka. In 1991 it began 24-hour phone sales and acquired a majority stake in Grattan (the UK's fourth-largest mail-order firm). Acquisitions continued during the early and mid-1990s, including Margareta (Hungary), Postalmarket (Italy's largest mail-order firm), and Otto-Burlingtons (Germany-India joint venture).

Otto Versand acquired a majority stake in Reiseland's 60 travel agencies in 1993 and bought two UK collection agencies in 1994. In 1994 it became Germany's first mail-order firm to offer an interactive CD-ROM catalog.

The firm bought a majority stake in US housewares retailer Crate & Barrel in 1998 and bought German computer wholesaler Actebis Holding. It then formed Zara Deutschland, a joint venture in Germany (with Spain's Inditex), to sell clothing in a new chain of outlets. Otto Versand added to its travel business (about 140 locations) in 1998 with the purchase of 25 offices from American Express Germany. It closed Postalmarket that year because of problems with the Italian postal service.

In 1999 Otto Versand acquired the Freemans catalog business (nearly $900 million in 1998 sales) from the UK's Sears PLC. The deal nearly doubled the company's UK mail-order market share, from 8% to 15%. In late 1999 the firm formed a joint venture with Harrods to sell fancy English goods online.

In early 2000 Otto Versand set up a joint venture with America Online (now part of Time Warner) and Deutsche Bank 24 to offer online banking, Internet service, and PCs. In October 2001 the company entered into a joint venture with US Internet travel service provider Travelocity.com to form Travelocity Europe.

In 2003 Otto Versand changed its name to Otto GmbH & Co KG.

EXECUTIVES

Supervisory Board Chairman: Hans Jörg Hammer
Executive Board Chairman and Chief Executive Officer, Otto Group: Michael Otto, age 63
CEO: Gordon Segal, age 65
COO: Peer Witten, age 59
CFO: Juergen Schulte-Laggenbeck, age 39

General Manager, Marketing, Sales, E-Commerce OTTO: Rainer Hillebrand
General Manager, International Procurement Otto Group: Diethard Gagelmann
General Manager, Merchandise (Textiles): Gert Rietz, age 55
General Manager, Human Resources and Planning and Controlling: Winfried Zimmermann
General Manager, Development and Strategy Otto Group: Peter Gelsdorf
General Manager, Merchandising OTTO: Hans-Otto Schrader, age 49
CIO; General Manager of IT and Logistics Otto Group: Wolfgang Linder, age 56
CEO, Otto Doosan Mail Order: Hyung-Suk Kwon, age 63
Chairman and CEO, 3 Suisses International: Pierre Zucchini
CEO, ACTEBIS Holding: Dirk Hauke, age 41
CEO, Baur Versand: Richard Krekeler, age 63
CEO, Hanseatic Bank: Torsten Brandes, age 51
CEO, Hermes Logistik Group: Hanjo Schneider, age 41
CEO, KG EOS Holding: Hans-Werner Scherer, age 51
CEO, oHG Fegro/Selgros Gesellschaft für Großhandel: Rüdiger Strein, age 65
CEO, SCHWAB VERSAND: Rolf Schäfer, age 59
Chairman and CEO, Otto Sumisho: Hiroki Hachiya
Chief Human Resources Officer: Alexander Birken
VP, Corporate Communications: Thomas Voigt
Auditors: KPMG Deutsche Treuhand-Gesellschaft AG

LOCATIONS

HQ: Otto GmbH & Co KG
Wandsbeker Strasse 3-7, 2217 Hamburg, Germany
Phone: +49-40-64-61-0   **Fax:** +49-40-64-61-85-71
Web: www.ottogroup.com

PRODUCTS/OPERATIONS

2006 Sales

	% of total
Retail	64
Wholesale	26
Financial services	8
Other services	2
Total	**100**

Selected Subsidiaries

3 Suisses France
Actebis Holding
Crate & Barrel (majority stake)
Grattan
Handelsgesellschaft Heinrich Heine GmbH
Hanseatic Bank GmbH
Otto-Sumisho (51%)
Reiseland GmbH (100%)

COMPETITORS

Amazon.com
Bed Bath & Beyond
Blair
Direct Marketing
Fast Retailing
Federated
Hammacher Schlemmer
Hanover Direct
J. C. Penney
Karstadt
Lands' End
Lillian Vernon
Linens 'n Things
Littlewoods
L.L. Bean
Maxeda
METRO AG
Pier 1 Imports
PPR
Provell
Schickedanz
Williams-Sonoma

HISTORICAL FINANCIALS

Company Type: Private

Income Statement

FYE: Last day in February

	REVENUE ($ mil.)	NET INCOME ($ mil.)	NET PROFIT MARGIN	EMPLOYEES
2/06	18,533	244	1.3%	55,116
2/05	19,096	248	1.3%	54,428
2/04	17,879	136	0.8%	55,406
2/03	15,083	141	0.9%	65,854
2/02	12,461	125	1.0%	79,137
Annual Growth	10.4%	18.3%	—	(8.6%)

Net Income History

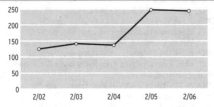

Pearson

There's nothing fishy about information from Pearson, home of salmon-colored newspaper *The Financial Times*. The media giant provides financial information and business news with such titles as *The Financial Times* (known locally as the "Pink 'Un"), the 50%-owned *The Economist,* and its 62% stake in US-based Interactive Data Corporation. The company's Pearson Education unit is the world's top educational publisher through imprints Pearson Scott Foresman, Pearson Addison Wesley, and Pearson Prentice Hall. Pearson's Penguin Group (Penguin, Putnam, Viking) publishes trade books. The company sold its Recoletos Grupo de Comunicacion containing its Spanish media holdings in 2005.

In addition to printed works, the company is making strides with its Internet investments, including the *Financial Times* Web site (FT.com) and online educational services. The company has announced plans to merge its print and online divisions at *Financial Times* in a restructuring that may result in the elimination of about 50 positions.

Under CEO Marjorie Scardino, Pearson has shed many of its non-media assets — which once included The Tussaud Group's wax museums — and is moving to strengthen its printed content brands. Its FT Group (business information holdings) ailed for several years with a shortage of advertising due to an economic turndown, but has seen improvements in recent years. The company has denied that it will sell off the FT unit amid rampant speculation.

Shareholders have been pressuring Scardino to focus more on the company's education unit, which has exceeded expectations and already accounts for two-thirds of the company's sales.

In 2006 the company acquired professional testing unit Promissor from Houghton Mifflin. Pearson plans to combine the unit with its testing unit, Pearson VUE. Later in the year it bought Mergermarket Group, a news and data firm, for $191 million.

HISTORY

In 1844 Samuel Pearson became a partner in a small Yorkshire building firm. When he retired in 1879 his grandson Weetman took over, moving the company to London in 1884. The business enjoyed extraordinary success — building the first tunnel under New York's Hudson River and installing Mexico City's drainage system. By the 1890s the company (incorporated as S. Pearson & Son in 1897) was the world's #1 contractor.

In the 1920s the company bought newspapers and engaged in oil exploration. Weetman died in 1927, and so did the construction business. His heirs then bought into several unrelated businesses. Pearson bought control of *The Financial Times* newspaper in 1957, a deal that also brought it 50% of *The Economist* (*The Financial Times* had acquired half of *The Economist* in 1928). The company later added stakes in vintner Chateau Latour (1963, sold 1988) and publisher Longman (1968). The firm went public in 1969.

During the 1970s Pearson bought Penguin Books (1971) and Madame Tussaud's (1978). In 1989 it added Addison-Wesley (educational publisher, US) and Les Echos (financial newspaper publisher, France).

Concentrating on media interests, the company bought Thames Television in 1993 and Grundy Worldwide (game shows and soap operas) in 1995. It acquired HarperCollins Educational Publishing from News Corp. in 1996, as well as US publisher Putnam Berkley from MCA, gaining such authors as Tom Clancy and Amy Tan. By the mid-1990s, however, Pearson's holdings still lacked focus, and earnings were depressed. Marjorie Scardino, a Texan who had been CEO of The Economist Group since 1992, replaced Frank Barlow in 1997, becoming the first woman to lead a major UK company. She rounded out Pearson's TV holdings with the purchase of All American Communications that year.

In 1998 Pearson bought Simon & Schuster's reference and educational publishing divisions from Viacom (now CBS Corporation) for $4.6 billion and sold Tussaud's amusement business. In 1999 Pearson shed $58 million in college textbooks and instructional programs to John Wiley & Sons.

As part of a long-term plan to build *The Financial Times* brand online, Pearson bought 60% of Data Broadcasting Corporation (now called Interactive Data Corporation) in 2000. It began to cross-promote the FT.com Web site with MarketWatch.com (Data Broadcast sold its 34% stake in the now-called MarketWatch to Pearson in 2001) as part of a $35 million marketing campaign. MarketWatch was later sold to Dow Jones & Company in 2005. Pearson bought troubled UK publisher Dorling Kindersley for nearly $500 million and later combined the firm with its Penguin unit. It also launched a German version of *The Financial Times* with Bertelsmann's Gruner + Jahr.

Later in 2000, Pearson combined its TV operations with CLT-Ufa, co-owned by German media company Bertelsmann and Audiofina, into a new publicly traded broadcasting firm called RTL Group. Pearson took a 22% stake in RTL. In addition, Pearson bought educational test processing firm National Computer Systems (later called NCS Pearson before being integrated into operations). In 2001 Pearson expanded its educational operations, announcing plans for a joint venture with Telefónica to distribute online educational content in Latin America. That year the company also formed a joint venture with an arm of Chinese state television to produce programming for a Chinese audience. In late 2001 Pearson sold its stake in RTL to Bertelsmann. Spain's Telefónica divested its 5% stake in the company in late 2004.

Pearson sold its 79% stake in Spanish media company Recoletos in 2005 to Retos Cartera. In 2005 the company acquired special needs publisher AGS Publishing from WRC Media.

EXECUTIVES

Chairman: Glen Moreno, age 62, $182,362 pay (partial-year salary)
Chief Executive: Dame Marjorie M. Scardino, age 59, $3,007,259 pay
CFO: Robin Freestone
Director People; Chairman, Financial Times Group: Sir David C. M. Bell, age 59, $1,642,982 pay
Director Global Communications: Luke Swanson
Chairman and CEO, Pearson Education: Peter Jovanovich, age 55, $70,536 pay
Chairman and CEO, The Penguin Group: John C. Makinson, age 51, $1,787,496 pay
Chief Executive, Financial Times Group: Rona A. Fairhead, age 44
VP Marketing, Pearson Digital Learning: Kelly Goodrich
Auditors: PricewaterhouseCoopers LLP

LOCATIONS

HQ: Pearson plc
80 Strand, London WC2R ORL, United Kingdom
Phone: +44-20-7010-2000   **Fax:** +44-20-7010-6060
US HQ: 1330 Avenue of the Americas, New York, NY 10019
US Phone: 212-641-2400   **US Fax:** 212-641-2500
Web: www.pearson.com

2005 Sales

	% of total
North America	66
Europe	24
Asia/Pacific	7
Other regions	3
Total	**100**

PRODUCTS/OPERATIONS

2005 Sales

	% of total
School	31
Penguin	21
Higher Education	19
FT Group	15
Professional	14
Total	**100**

Selected Operations

Pearson Education
  Early Learning
  Elementary education
    Pearson Learning Group
    Pearson Scott Foresman
  Secondary education
    Globe Fearon
    Prentice Hall
  Higher education
    Pearson Addison Wesley
    Pearson Allyn & Beacon
    Pearson Prentice Hall College
  Pearson Educational Measurement

Financial Times Group
  Business Day & Financial Mail (50%; South Africa)
  The Economist Group (50%)
    CFO
    The Economist
    The Journal of Commerce
    Roll Call
    The Financial Times
    Financial Times Deutschland (with Gruner + Jahr)
  FT asset Management
  FT.com (financial news)
  FTSE International (market indices, with London Stock Exchange)
  Interactive Data Corp. (62%; US)
  Les Echos (France)
Penguin Group
  Avery   Penguin
  Berkley Books   Penguin Business
  Dorling Kindersley   Penguin Classics
  Dutton   Penguin Reference
  Frederick Warne   Plume
  Hamish Hamilton   Puffin
  Ladybird   Viking
  Michael Joseph

COMPETITORS

1mage
Compass Learning
Daily Mail
Dow Jones
Editis
Educational Testing Service
Gruner + Jahr
HarperCollins
Houghton Mifflin
John Harland
John Wiley
Laureate Education
Learning Tree
McGraw-Hill
Moody's
Mounte LLC
New Horizons Worldwide
New York Times
News Corp.
PLATO Learning
Prometric
ProQuest
Random House
Reader's Digest
Reed Elsevier Group
Reuters
Scholastic
Simon & Schuster
Thomson Corporation
Time
Touchstone Applied Science
Georg von Holtzbrinck
Washington Post
Wolters Kluwer

HISTORICAL FINANCIALS

Company Type: Public

Income Statement

FYE: December 31

	REVENUE ($ mil.)	NET INCOME ($ mil.)	NET PROFIT MARGIN	EMPLOYEES
12/05	7,048	707	10.0%	32,203
12/04	7,995	351	4.4%	33,389
12/03	7,199	326	4.5%	30,868
12/02	6,931	318	4.6%	30,359
12/01	6,228	(2,177)	—	29,027
Annual Growth	3.1%	—	—	2.6%

2005 Year-End Financials

Debt ratio: 44.9%
Return on equity: 11.0%
Cash ($ mil.): 1,559
Current ratio: 2.00
Long-term debt ($ mil.): 2,968

No. of shares (mil.): —
Dividends
  Yield: 4.0%
  Payout: —
Market value ($ mil.): —

Stock History

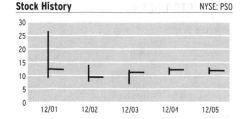

NYSE: PSO

	STOCK PRICE ($) FY Close	P/E High/Low		PER SHARE ($) Earnings	Dividends
12/05	11.87	—	—	—	0.47
12/04	12.16	—	—	—	0.44
12/03	11.21	—	—	—	0.38
12/02	9.35	—	—	—	0.34
12/01	12.28	—	—	—	0.31
Annual Growth	(0.8%)	—	—	—	11.0%

Pernod Ricard

Pernod Ricard, one of the world's largest spirits firms, feathers its nest with the help of Wild Turkey bourbon, but its global brand is its premium Scotch whisky Chivas Regal. The beverage firm also sells spirits ranging from anise drinks and liqueurs (Pernod, Ricard, Zoco) to clear spirits (Wyborova vodka, Havana Club Cuban rum, Beefeater and Seagram's gins). In addition, Pernod Ricard offers Jameson Irish whiskey, Martell cognac, and Jacob's Creek wine. The company in 2005 allied with Fortune Brands to buy UK competitor Allied Domecq (which had been #2 in spirits) and provide stiffer competition for #1 drinks company Diageo.

Pernod Ricard had already boosted its stable of brands through the 2000 purchase of nearly 40% of Seagram's spirits business, but by early 2005 was back in the shopping mood again. To help allay anti-competitive concerns, Pernod Ricard enlisted the help of Fortune Brands for its friendly bid for Allied Domecq. As part of the deal, Fortune ended up with Pernod Ricard's Larios gin, as well as several brands from Allied Domecq (including Canadian Club whisky, Clos du Bois wine, Courvoisier cognac, Maker's Mark bourbon, and Sauza tequila). Pernod Ricard paid about $14 billion for its former chief competitor Allied Domecq, whose holdings included Dunkin' Donuts and Baskin-Robbins ice cream in addition to its alcoholic beverages; Fortune anted up about $5 billion for its part of the acquisition.

A rival bid from Constellation Brands (in cooperation with Blackstone, Brown-Forman, and Lion Capital) had threatened Pernod Ricard's acquisition of Allied Domecq, but Constellation Brands ultimately withdrew from the bidding group, clearing the path for Pernod Ricard.

Pernod Ricard in 2006 sold the Dunkin' Donuts and Baskin-Robbins lines to a consortium of buyers that included Bain Capital, Carlyle Group, and Thomas H. Lee Partners. Other investors also bid on the food companies. As part of the juggling that took place in the Allied Domecq acquisition, Pernod Ricard also sold its Bushmills Irish whisky to competitor Diageo, and its Braemar, Glen Grant, and Old Smuggler brands to Campari.

The company claims that the US Patent and Trademark Office supports the position that Pernod Ricard is the rightful owner of the Havana Club trademark in the US. Bacardi challenges this claim. Pernod Ricard markets its Havana Club rum through a joint venture with the Cuban government.

The Ricard family controls some 15% of Pernod Ricard's voting rights.

HISTORY

Henri-Louis Pernod inherited Pernod Fils, an absinthe distillery, from his father-in-law in 1805 and immediately moved it to Pontarlier, France, to avoid stiff French import taxes. Demand for absinthe, a potent liqueur, spread quickly, and by the 1870s the liqueur was the toast of Paris. It was even featured in the Impressionist paintings, and rumor has it that Vincent Van Gogh's psychosis might have been caused by it.

In the late 1800s serious competition for the absinthe market emerged from distiller Pernod Avignon, run by Jules Pernod (no relation to Henri-Louis). In 1906 Switzerland banned absinthe and France followed suit in 1915. In 1926 Henri-Louis joined with another anise distiller, Aristide Hemard, and formed Etablissements Hemard et Pernod Fils. Jules joined them in 1928. The resulting company was named Pernod.

Four years later the ban on pastis was lifted by the French government, and Paul Ricard, who made pastis illegally beforehand, began selling it openly. The licorice-flavored drink became popular in France. His company, Ricard, became a successful spirits maker and went public in 1962. Ricard acquired the Biscuit cognac brand in 1966.

Pernod and Ricard merged in 1975 to form Pernod Ricard. The company's operations included Campbell (scotch), SEGM (spirits exporter), and JFA Pampryl (fruit juice). In 1976 the group acquired CDC (Cinzano, Dubonnet). Two years later Patrick Ricard, son of Paul, became chairman and CEO.

Expanding through acquisitions in the 1980s, Pernod Ricard bought US-based Austin Nichols (Wild Turkey) from du Ligget Group in 1980 and acquired control of both Sias-MPA (fruit preparations) in 1982 and Compagnie Francaise des Produits Orangina (soft drinks) in 1984. The next year the firm added Ramazzotti (spirits, Italy) and IGM (distribution, Germany) to its mix, and in 1988 it bought Irish Distillers (whiskey), Yoo-Hoo Industries (US), and BWG (distribution, Ireland; sold in 2002). Australia's Orlando Wyndham Wines was added to the company's wine list in 1989 and merged with Pernod Ricard's Wyndham Estate winery the following year.

The group also acquired Spain's Larios gin, the Czech Republic's Becherovka liqueurs, and Italcanditi, a fruit preparations firm. Pernod Ricard added Mexican distillery Tequila Viuda de Romero (Real Hacienda tequila) to its liquor cabinet in January 2000.

Pernod Ricard later teamed up with liquor giant Diageo to bid on Seagram's spirits and wine business. Their collective bid of $8.2 billion (with Pernod Ricard paying $3.2 billion) was accepted in December 2000, with Pernod Ricard agreeing to acquire such brands as Chivas Regal, Glenlivet, and Glen Grant (which was sold to Campari in 2006).

In July 2001 the company agreed to pay $71 million for 80% of Polmos Poznan, maker of one of Poland's top vodka brands, Wyborowa in a deal including export rights. In October the company sold its soft-drink business in Continental Europe, North America, and Australia to Cadbury Schweppes for about $640 million to help finance the Seagram's deal. After months of delay, the company finalized its deal to buy a part of Seagram's drinks business from Vivendi Universal after finally gaining FTC approval in December 2001. Pernod Ricard's 2000 deal with Seagram's added Chivas and a number of other brands to the company's portfolio and improved its presence in Asia, Latin America, and North America. To help fund the Seagram's acquisition, Pernod Ricard sold its soft-drink business (Pampryl fruit juice, Orangina soft drinks, Yoo-Hoo chocolate drink, and cider) in North America, Europe, and Australia to Cadbury Schweppes for $640 million.

In 2002 Pernod Ricard and brand co-owner Diageo licensed Seagram's nonalcoholic mixers to The Coca-Cola Company. Also that year, Pernod Ricard sold Polish juice-making subsidiary Agros Fortuna.

EXECUTIVES

Chairman and CEO: Patrick Ricard, age 61, $2,678,888 pay
Deputy CEO and Director: Pierre Pringuet, age 56, $1,781,215 pay
VP, Finance: Emmanuel Babeau, age 38
Adviser to General Management: Bernard Cazals
VP, Human Resources Group: Yves Flaissier
VP, Marketing: Jean-Paul Richard
Chairman and CEO, Martell Mumm Perrier-Jouët: Lionel Breton
Chairman and CEO, Pernod: Pierre Coppéré
CEO, Irish Distillers Group: Paul Duffy, age 39
Chairman and CEO, Pernod Ricard Pacific: Laurent Lacassagne, age 41
Chairman and CEO, Chivas Brothers: Christian Porta, age 41
Chairman and CEO, Ricard: Philippe Savinel, age 47
Chairman and CEO, Pernod Ricard Europe: Thierry Billot
President and CEO, Pernod Ricard Americas: Michel Bord
Chairman and CEO, Pernod Ricard Asia: Philippe Dréano
Chairman and CEO, Pernod Ricard Central and South America: Francesco Taddonio
Chairman and CEO, Pernod Ricard South Asia: Param Uberoi
VP, Corporate Legal Affairs and General Counsel: Ian Fitzsimons
VP, Corporate Communications: Francisco de la Vega
VP, Investor Relations: Patrick de Borredon
Manager, Press Relations: Florence Taron
Auditors: Deloitte Touche Tohmatsu; Mazars & Guérard

LOCATIONS

HQ: Pernod Ricard SA
12, place des États-Unis, 75116 Paris, France
Phone: +33-1-41-00-41-00   **Fax:** +33-1-41-00-41-41
US HQ: 777 Westchester Ave., White Plains, NY 10604
US Phone: 914-539-4500   **US Fax:** 914-539-4777
Web: www.pernod-ricard.com/fr

Pernod Ricard has operations in the Americas, Asia, and Europe.

2006 Sales

	% of total
Europe	
France	11
Other countries	33
Americas	28
Asia & other regions	28
Total	**100**

PRODUCTS/OPERATIONS

Selected Brands

Ballantine's	Malibu
Beefeater	Martell
Chivas Regal	Mumm
The Glenlivet	Perrier-Jouët
Havana Club	Ricard
Jacob's Creek	Wyborowa
Jameson	
Kahlua	

COMPETITORS

Bacardi	Foster's Wine Estates
Beam	Gallo
Blavod Extreme Spirits	Rémy Cointreau
Brown-Forman	Sidney Frank Importing
Cabo Wabo	Skyy
Constellation Brands	Suntory Ltd.
Diageo	V&S
Fortune Brands	William Grant & Sons

HISTORICAL FINANCIALS

Company Type: Public

Income Statement

FYE: June 30

	REVENUE ($ mil.)	NET INCOME ($ mil.)	NET PROFIT MARGIN	EMPLOYEES
6/06	7,612	841	11.0%	17,600
6/05*	6,329	777	12.3%	12,304
12/03	4,436	582	13.1%	12,254
12/02	5,068	433	8.5%	12,526
12/01	4,035	317	7.9%	13,090
Annual Growth	**17.2%**	**27.6%**	—	**7.7%**

*Fiscal year change

Net Income History

Exchange: Euronext Paris

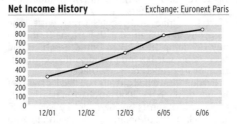

PETROBRAS

PETRÓLEO BRASILEIRO (PETROBRAS) isn't brash, but it is Brazil's largest industrial company. It engages in exploration for oil and gas and in production, refining, purchasing, and transportation of oil and gas products. The company has proved reserves of 14.9 billion barrels of oil equivalent. It operates 14,000 wells, 16 refineries, 25,000 miles of pipeline, and more than 6,900 gas stations. Subsidiary Petrobras Distribuidora is Brazil's leading retailer of oil products and fuel alcohol. Petrobras Energía Participaciones is a leading Argentine oil company. Other units produce petrochemicals and natural gas. The Brazilian government owns 32% of PETROBRAS and 56% of its voting shares.

Petrobras Internacional, also known as Braspetro, conducts exploration worldwide, including in Angola, Kazakhstan, Nigeria, the UK, the US, and across Latin America.

Although most of PETROBRAS' wells are onshore, the bulk of its production comes from offshore operations; the company is recognized as a leader in offshore drilling technology and deepwater wells. To boost its natural gas operations, PETROBRAS is investing $2 billion to build a pipeline from gas fields in Bolivia to Brazil. The company also plans to triple production outside Brazil to 300,000 barrels per day and is eyeing a major acquisition to boost its Gulf of Mexico assets. In 2006 the company acquired a 50% stake in a deepwater block in Equatorial Guinea from a private group of companies for an undisclosed sum.

HISTORY

"O petróleo é nosso!"

"The oil is ours!" proclaimed the Brazilian nationalists' slogan in 1953, and President Getúlio Vargas approved a bill creating a state-run monopoly on petroleum discovery, development, refining, and transport. The same year that PETRÓLEO BRASILEIRO (PETROBRAS) was created, a team led by American geologist Walter Link reported that the prospects of finding petroleum in Brazil were slim. The report outraged Brazilian nationalists, who saw it as a ploy for foreign exploitation. PETROBRAS proved it could find oil, but Brazil continued to import crude oil and petroleum products. By 1973 the company produced about 10% of the nation's needs.

When oil prices soared during the Arab embargo, the government, instead of encouraging exploration for domestic oil, pushed PETROBRAS into a program to promote alcohol fuels. The company was forced to raise gasoline prices to make the more costly gasohol attractive to consumers. During the 1979 oil crunch the price of gasohol was fixed at 65% of gasoline. But during the oil glut of the mid-1980s, PETROBRAS' cost of making gasohol was twice what it cost to buy gasoline — in other words, PETROBRAS lost money.

PETROBRAS soon began overseas exploration. In 1980 it found an oil field in Iraq, an important trading partner during the 1980s. The company also drilled in Angola and, through a 1987 agreement with Texaco, in the Gulf of Mexico.

In the mid-1980s PETROBRAS began production in the deepwater Campos basin off the coast of Rio de Janeiro state. Discoveries there in 1988, in the Marlim and Albacora fields, more than tripled its oil reserves. It plunged deep into the thick Amazon jungle in 1986 to explore for oil, and by 1990 Amazon wells were making a significant contribution to total production. That year, to ease dependence on imports, PETROBRAS launched a five-year, $16.9 billion plan to boost crude oil production. It also began selling its mining and trading assets.

Before the invasion of Kuwait, Brazil relied heavily on Iraq, trading weapons for oil. After the invasion spawned increases in crude prices, PETROBRAS raised pump prices but, yielding to the government's anti-inflation program, still did not raise them enough to cover costs. It lost $13 million a day.

The company sold 26% of Petrobras Distribuidora to the public in 1993 and privatized several of its petrochemical and fertilizer subsidiaries. A 1994 presidential order, bent on stabilizing Brazil's 40%-per-month inflation, cut the prices of oil products. In 1995 the government loosened its grip on the oil and gas industry and allowed foreign companies to enter the Brazilian market. In the wake of this reform, PETROBRAS teamed up with a Japanese consortium to build Brazil's largest oil refinery.

In 1997 PETROBRAS appealed a $4 billion judgment from a 1992 shareholder lawsuit; the suit alleged PETROBRAS had undervalued shares during the privatization of the loss-making Petroquisa affiliate. (The appeal was granted in 1999.)

As part of an effort to boost oil production, PETROBRAS also began to raise money abroad in 1999. The next year PETROBRAS and Spanish oil giant Repsol YPF agreed to swap oil and gas assets in Argentina and Brazil in a deal worth more than $1 billion.

In 2000 the company announced plans to change its corporate name to PETROBRAX, but fierce political and popular reaction forced the company to abort this plan in 2001. In an even greater public relations disaster that year, one of PETROBRAS' giant rigs sank off of Brazil and 10 workers were killed. In 2001 PETROBRAS announced that it was going to spend as much as $3 billion to buy an oil company in order to increase its production in the Gulf of Mexico.

In 2002 the company expressed an interest in buying Argentina's major oil company (YPF) from Spanish/Argentine energy giant Repsol YPF. That year PETROBRAS bought control (59%) of Argentine energy company Perez Companc in a deal valued at $1 billion. PETROBRAS also reported its first oil find in Argentina in 2002.

EXECUTIVES

Chairman: Dilma Vana Rousseff, age 58
President and CEO: José Sérgio Gabrielli de Azevedo, age 57
CFO and Director Investor Relations:
Almir Guilherme Barbassa
Director Exploration and Production:
Guilherme de Oliveira Estrella, age 64
Director Gas and Energy: Ildo L. Sauer, age 52
Director International: Nestor C. Cervero, age 55
Director Services: Renato de Souza Duque, age 51
Director Downstream: Paulo Roberto Costa, age 52
Auditors: Ernst & Young Auditores Independentes S/C

LOCATIONS

HQ: PETRÓLEO BRASILEIRO S.A. - PETROBRAS
Avenida República do Chile 65, sala 401 E,
20035-900 Rio de Janeiro, Brazil
Phone: +55-21-2534-1510   **Fax:** +55-21-2534-6055
US HQ: 750 Lexington Ave., 43rd Fl.,
New York, NY 10022
US Phone: 212-829-1517   **US Fax:** 212-832-5300
Web: www.petrobras.com.br

PETROBRAS explores for oil and gas in Brazil, as well as in Angola, Argentina, Bolivia, Colombia, Cuba, Ecuador, Equatorial Guinea, Kazakhstan, Nigeria, Peru, Trinidad and Tobago, the UK, and the US.

PRODUCTS/OPERATIONS

Selected Subsidiaries

Downstream Participações S.A. (asset exchanges between Petrobras and Repsol-YPF)
Petrobras Comercializadora de Energia Ltda
Petrobras Distribuidora SA (BR; distribution and marketing of petroleum products, fuel alcohol, and natural gas)
Petrobras Energía Participaciones (59%; oil and gas, Argentina)
Petrobras Gás SA (Gaspetro, management of the Brazil-Bolivia pipeline and other natural gas assets)
Petrobras Internacional SA (Braspetro; overseas exploration and production, marketing, and services)
Petrobras International Finance Company PIFCO (oil imports)
Petrobras Negócios Eletrônicos S.A.
Petrobras Química SA (Petroquisa, petrochemicals)
Petrobras Transporte SA (Transpetro, oil and gas transportation and storage)

COMPETITORS

Ashland	Lyondell Chemical
BHP Billiton	Marathon Oil
BP	Norsk Hydro
Chevron	Occidental Petroleum
Devon Energy	PDVSA
Eni	PEMEX
Exxon Mobil	Royal Dutch Shell
Imperial Oil	Sunoco
Koch	TOTAL

HISTORICAL FINANCIALS

Company Type: Public

Income Statement

FYE: December 31

	REVENUE ($ mil.)	NET INCOME ($ mil.)	NET PROFIT MARGIN	EMPLOYEES
12/04*	37,452	6,190	16.5%	53,666
12/03	42,690	6,559	15.4%	48,798
12/02	32,987	2,311	7.0%	49,049
12/01	34,145	3,491	10.2%	38,483
Annual Growth	3.1%	21.0%	—	11.7%

*Most recent year available

2004 Year-End Financials

Debt ratio: 99.3%
Return on equity: 38.8%
Cash ($ mil.): 7,244
Current ratio: 1.46
Long-term debt ($ mil.): 17,613

No. of shares (mil.): —
Dividends
Yield: 2.6%
Payout: 18.1%
Market value ($ mil.): —

Stock History

NYSE: PBR

	STOCK PRICE ($) FY Close	P/E High/Low		PER SHARE ($) Earnings	Dividends
12/04*	39.78	7	4	5.65	1.02
12/03	29.24	5	2	5.98	1.16
12/02	14.94	—	—	—	0.72
12/01	23.30	—	—	0.00	1.47
Annual Growth	19.5%	—	—	—	(11.5%)

*Most recent year available

Petróleos de Venezuela

American motorists rely on Petróleos de Venezuela S.A. (PDVSA), one of the top exporters of oil to the US. The state-owned company has proved reserves of 77.2 billion barrels of oil — the most outside the Middle East — and about 150 trillion cu. ft. of natural gas. PDVSA's exploration and production take place in Venezuela, but the company also has refining and marketing operations in the Caribbean, Europe, and the US. Subsidiary CITGO Petroleum supplies gasoline to some 13,000 US retail outlets. PDVSA also makes Orimulsión, a coal alternative made from bitumen.

Outside of Venezuela, PDVSA refines, markets, and transports its petroleum products in Belgium, the Caribbean, Germany, Sweden, the UK, and the US.

On the domestic front, PDVSA's BITOR subsidiary mines Venezuela's extensive bitumen reserves, turning the tarlike ooze into Orimulsión, a patented fuel marketed as an alternative to coal for electric generating plants.

In a move that requires foreign investment, PDVSA is expanding its production of petrochemicals, gas, and Orimulsión. However, investors will step carefully: Venezuelan President Hugo Chávez's tightening state control over the oil company's operations has led to management unrest and major political instability.

In 2003 the government threatened to split the company in two as a way to break the striking managers' hold on the company, and to restore full production. The strike led to a third of the workforce being laid off by February 2003.

HISTORY

Invited by dictator Juan Vicente Gómez, Royal Dutch Shell looked for oil in Venezuela just before WWI. After the war US companies plunged in. Standard Oil of Indiana began Creole Petroleum in 1920 to explore in Venezuela, selling the company in 1928 to Standard of New Jersey.

When the Venezuelan government threatened to nationalize its oil industry in 1938, the foreign oil companies agreed to pay more taxes and royalties. But in 1945 Venezuela set a pattern for the rest of the world's oil-rich nations when it decreed it was a 50% partner in all oil operations. Venezuela was pivotal to OPEC's creation in 1960, and the next year the government created the Venezuelan Petroleum Corporation (CVP). CVP was granted the nation's unassigned petroleum reserves. By the early 1970s CVP produced about 2% of the nation's oil.

President Carlos Andrés Pérez nationalized oil holdings in 1975, paying only $1 billion for foreign-owned oil assets and creating Petróleos de Venezuela S.A. (PDVSA) to hold the properties. Venezuela formed stand-alone PDVSA subsidiaries: Shell operations became Maraven, Creole became Lagoven, and smaller companies combined into Corpoven. (All units were merged into PDVSA in 1998.)

Free of debt and buoyed by high crude prices in the late 1970s and early 1980s, PDVSA formed ventures (Ruhr Oel) with Germany's Veba Oel and Sweden's Nynas Petroleum. In the US, PDVSA bought 50% of CITGO, the former refining and marketing arm of Cities Service Co., from Southland in 1986 (and the rest in 1990). PDVSA also bought a 50% stake in a Unocal refinery in 1989 to create joint venture UNO-VEN.

After the 1991 Gulf War, Venezuela increased its own production despite OPEC oil quotas. The next year PDVSA opened some marginal fields to foreign investment for the first time since the industry's 1975 nationalization.

Venezuelan President Rafael Caldera named Luis Giusti president of the company in 1994, and the next year Venezuela's oil industry was opened to foreign investment. In 1996 PDVSA began building a $1.5 billion plastics plant with Mobil (later Exxon Mobil). PDVSA and Unocal finally ended UNO-VEN the next year when UNO-VEN CEO David Tippeconnic took over as head of CITGO.

The rush for Venezuelan oil rights was on by 1997; one week's worth of bidding brought in $2 billion from top international oil companies. Meanwhile, PDVSA searched for facilities to refine the heavy crude, striking deals with Phillips

Petroleum (later renamed ConocoPhillips) in 1997 and Amerada Hess (later renamed Hess Corporation) in 1998.

PDVSA's profits took a hit in 1998 when oil prices fell to record lows. Concerns arose about the firm's direction that year after populist Hugo Chávez was elected as Venezuela's president. Chávez and his allies sought to retain state control over PDVSA's resources and to keep a closer check on foreign partners.

In 1999 PDVSA, suffering from a devastated domestic economy, decided to expand its downstream operations globally. As part of that plan, it formed a Houston-based crude and products marketing firm, PDVSA Trading.

Tightening his control of the company, in 2000 Chávez appointed army generals to head up both PDVSA (Gen. Guaicaipuro Lameda) and CITGO (Gen. Oswaldo Contreras Maza). The appointments followed a management shake-up and an oil workers' strike.

In 2001 PDVSA with other oil partners announced that it had secured $1.1 billion in funding to develop an extra-heavy crude production project in the Hamaca region of the Orinoco basin.

Tightening his control on the company, in 2002 Chávez replaced Lameda as PDVSA's top executive with banker Gaston Parra. However, growing management discontent with Chávez's board of directors led to a major strike and a serious disruption of the company's oil production.

The strike spread into other industries and led to violence and a revolt by some military leaders. Pedro Carmona, president of Venezuela's top business association, was appointed to lead a civilian junta in the run-up to national elections. But Chávez refused to step down, and within a few days loyalist troops brought him back to power. In a move to make peace with PDVSA managers, Chávez removed Parra and other controversial appointees from the company's board. He then announced that he would appoint Alí Rodríguez, the former oil minister and head of OPEC, to take over the reins at PDVSA. Venezuela's energy minister (Álvaro Silva Calderón) was appointed to complete Rodríguez's term as OPEC's top executive.

However, continued political turmoil led to another major strike in 2002.

Energy and mines minister Rafael Ramírez became PDVSA's new president in November 2004.

EXECUTIVES

President and CEO: Rafael Ramírez Carreño, age 42
CFO and VP, Finance and Planning:
 José Alejandro Rojas
VP: Alejandro Granado, age 50
VP: Luis Vierma, age 51
Managing Internal Director and Director:
 Eudomario Carruyo, age 59
Managing Internal Director, Commerce and Supply;
 President, PDV Marina and BITOR: Asdrúbal Chávez, age 50
Managing Internal Director and Director; President,
 PDVSA-CVP: Eulogio Del Pino, age 48
Managing Internal Director; President, CIED:
 Déster Rodríguez, age 43
Managing Internal Director and Director:
 Jesús Villanueva, age 56
Auditors: KPMG Alcaraz Cabrera Vázquez

LOCATIONS

HQ: Petróleos de Venezuela S.A.
 Edificio Petróleos de Venezuela, Avenida Libertador,
 La Campiña, Apartado 169,
 Caracas 1010-A, Venezuela
Phone: +58-212-708-4111   **Fax:** +58-212-708-4661
US HQ: 1 Warren Place, 6100 S. Yale Ave.,
 Tulsa, OK 74136
US Phone: 918-495-4000   **US Fax:** 918-495-4511
Web: www.pdvsa.com.ve

PRODUCTS/OPERATIONS

Selected Subsidiaries and Affiliates

Bitúmenes Orinoco, SA (BITOR, bitumen and
 Orimulsión)
Carbozulia, SA (coal)
CIED
CITGO Petroleum Corp. (refining, marketing, and
 petrochemicals; US)
CVP
Deltaven
Intevep, SA (research and support)
Palmaven, SA (agricultural assistance and conservation
 projects)
PDV Marina
PDVSA Gas
PDVSA Petróleo
PDVSA Trading (crude oil and products marketing, US)
Pequiven, SA (petrochemicals)

COMPETITORS

BHP Billiton
BP
Chevron
ConocoPhillips
Devon Energy
Eni
Exxon Mobil
Harvest Natural Resources
Imperial Oil
Koch
Lyondell Chemical
Marathon Oil
Nigerian National Petroleum Corporation
NIOC
Norsk Hydro
Occidental Petroleum
PEMEX
PETROBRAS
Royal Dutch Shell
Saudi Aramco
Sunoco
TOTAL

HISTORICAL FINANCIALS

Company Type: Government-owned

Income Statement

FYE: December 31

	REVENUE ($ mil.)	NET INCOME ($ mil.)	NET PROFIT MARGIN	EMPLOYEES
12/04	63,200	—	—	—
12/03	46,589	—	—	—
12/02	42,580	—	—	45,683
12/01	46,250	—	—	46,425
12/00	53,680	—	—	45,520
Annual Growth	4.2%	—	—	0.2%

Revenue History

Petróleos Mexicanos

Petróleos Mexicanos (PEMEX) not only fuels Mexico's automobile engines, the state-owned oil company also fuels the nation's economy, accounting for some one-third of the Mexican government's revenues and 7% of its export earnings. The integrated company's operations, spread throughout Mexico, range from exploration and production to refining and petrochemicals. Its P.M.I. Comercio Internacional subsidiary manages trading operations outside the country. PEMEX has estimated proved reserves of 16.4 billion barrels of oil equivalent.

PEMEX's refining operations convert crude oil into gasoline, jet fuel, diesel, fuel oil, asphalts, and lubricants. In 2002 PEMEX-Refining produced 1.28 million barrels per day of refined products, up from 1.27 million barrels per day in 2001. PEMEX's Gas and Basic Petrochemicals unit processes natural gas and natural gas liquids, and ships and sells natural gas and liquefied petroleum gas throughout Mexico. It also produces several basic petrochemical feedstocks.

Long recognized as the tangible expression of Mexican nationalism, PEMEX has faced popular opposition in its bid to follow other Latin American state oil companies and privatize some operations. PEMEX is, however, working to become more responsive to market conditions and expand its international scope.

HISTORY

Histories of pre-colonial Mexico recount the nation's first oil business: Natives along the Tampico coast gathered asphalt from naturally occurring deposits and traded with the Aztecs.

As the 20th century began, Americans Edward Doheny and Charles Canfield struck oil near Tampico. Their success was eclipsed in 1910 by a nearby well drilled by British engineer Weetman Pearson, leader of the firm that became Pearson PLC.

President Porfirio Díaz had welcomed foreign ownership of Mexican resources, but revolution ousted Díaz, and the 1917 Constitution proclaimed that natural resources belonged to the nation. Without enforcing legislation, however, foreign oil companies continued business as usual until a 1925 act limited their concessions. During a bitter labor dispute in 1938, President Lázaro Cárdenas expropriated foreign oil holdings — the first nationalization of oil holdings by a non-Communist state. Subsequent legislation created Petróleos Mexicanos (PEMEX).

Without foreign capital and expertise, the new state-owned company struggled, and Mexico had to import petroleum in the early 1970s. But for many Mexicans, PEMEX remained a symbol of national identity and economic independence. That faith was rewarded in 1972 when a major oil discovery made PEMEX one of the world's top oil producers again. Ample domestic oil supplies and high world prices during the Iranian upheaval in the late 1970s fueled a boom and a government borrowing spree in Mexico. Between 1982 and 1985 PEMEX contributed more than 50% of government revenues.

When oil prices collapsed in 1985, Mexico cut investment in exploration, and production dropped. To decrease its reliance on oil, Mexico began lowering trade barriers and encouraging manufacturing, even allowing some foreign ownership of petrochemical processing.

Elected in 1988, President Carlos Salinas de Gortari began to reform PEMEX. Labor's grip on the company was loosened in 1989 when a union leader was arrested and jailed after a gun battle. In 1992, after a PEMEX pipeline explosion killed more than 200 people in Guadalajara, four of its executives and several local officials were sent to prison, amid public cries for company reform.

President Ernesto Zedillo appointed Adrián Lajous Vargas head of PEMEX in 1994. Under the professorial Lajous, PEMEX began to adopt modern business practices (such as trimming its bloated payroll), look for more reserves, and improve its refining capability. Lajous tried to sell some petrochemical assets in 1995, but had to modify the scheme the next year after massive public protests by the country's nationalists. Still, PEMEX began selling off natural gas production, distribution, and storage networks to private companies.

Though oil prices were dropping, in 1998 Mexico finally upped PEMEX's investment budget and PEMEX dramatically increased exploration and production. In spite of 2000's looming national election (elections traditionally had caused bureaucrats to keep a low profile to protect their jobs), Lajous again fanned the flames of the opposition: In 1998 he signed a major deal to sell Mexican crude to Exxon's Texas refinery, and in 1999 a four-year-old PEMEX/Shell joint venture announced it would expand its US refinery.

In 1999 Lajous resigned and was replaced by Rogelio Montemayor, a former governor. The next year Vicente Fox was elected as Mexico's new president, the country's first non-Institutional Revolutionary Party (PRI) leader in seven decades. He announced plans to replace PEMEX's politician-staffed board with professionals — Montemayor was among the casualties — and modernize the company, but he ruled out privatizing PEMEX as politically unfeasible.

Fox subsequently appointed Raúl Muñoz, formerly with Dupont Mexico, to lead PEMEX.

EXECUTIVES

Chairman: Fernando Elizondo Barragán, age 57
CEO: Luis Ramirez Corzo
Director Corporate Finance: José Juán Suárez Coppel
Managing Director, Finance and Treasury:
Octavio Ornelas Esquinca
Deputy Director of Programming and Budget:
Martha Alicia Olvera Rodríguez
Deputy Director of Financial Information Systems:
Victor Manuel Cámara Peón
Corporate Director of Operations:
José Antonio Ceballos Soberanis
Corporate Director of Administration:
Octavio Aguilar Valenzuela
General Counsel: Juan Carlos Soriano Rosas
Auditors: PricewaterhouseCoopers

LOCATIONS

HQ: Petróleos Mexicanos
Avenida Marina Nacional 329, Colonia Huasteca,
11311 México, D.F., Mexico
Phone: +52-55-1944-2500   **Fax:** +52-55-1944-8768
Web: www.pemex.com

2005 Sales

	% of total
Mexico	54
Other countries	45
Other revenues	1
Total	**100**

PRODUCTS/OPERATIONS

2005 Sales

	% of total
Exploration & production	38
Refining	21
Gas & basic petrochemicals	11
Petrochemicals	2
Corporate & subsidiaries	28
Total	**100**

Major Subsidiaries

PEMEX Exploración y Producción (petroleum and natural gas exploration and production)
PEMEX Gas y Petroquímica Básica (natural gas, liquids from natural gas, and ethane processing)
PEMEX Petroquímica (petrochemical production)
PEMEX Refinación (refining and marketing)
P.M.I. Comercio Internacional (international trading)

COMPETITORS

Ashland	Marathon Oil
BHP Billiton	Norsk Hydro
BP	Occidental Petroleum
Chevron	PDVSA
Devon Energy	PETROBRAS
Eni	Royal Dutch Shell
Exxon Mobil	Sunoco
Imperial Oil	TOTAL
Koch	

HISTORICAL FINANCIALS

Company Type: Government-owned

Income Statement

FYE: December 31

	REVENUE ($ mil.)	NET INCOME ($ mil.)	NET PROFIT MARGIN	EMPLOYEES
12/05	87,279	(7,079)	—	139,171
12/04	70,110	(2,278)	—	137,722
12/03	55,927	(3,619)	—	138,215
12/02	45,944	(2,910)	—	137,134
12/01	46,249	(3,519)	—	134,852
Annual Growth	**17.2%**	**—**	**—**	**0.8%**

Net Income History

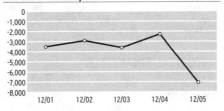

Peugeot

PSA Peugeot Citroën enjoys its space under L'Arc de Triomphe, besting rival Renault to claim the top spot in the battle for auto sales in France. The best-selling auto brand in its home country, Peugeot is #2 behind Volkswagen in passenger car and commercial vehicle sales in Europe. Peugeot makes cars and light commercial vehicles under the Peugeot and Citroën brands. It also offers parts (Faurecia), transportation and logistics (Gefco), and financial services (Banque PSA Finance) for dealers and customers. Other products include motorbikes, scooters, and light-armored vehicles. The Peugeot family controls more than 45% of the voting stock.

Peugeot is experiencing many of the same problems as its European and North American peers. The company has been affected by stagnant European markets, high materials costs, and the compliance costs associated with the new Euro IV environmental standards, and most significant — intense competition from Asian rivals.

Despite a few setbacks, Peugeot has faith in its basic two-brand strategy. The company focuses on efficiently building almost all of its vehicles on one of three basic platforms. This keeps the new models rolling out while keeping development and production costs under control.

A bright spot in 2005 was Peugeot's success in acheiving more sales outside Western Europe. For the first time Peugeot sold more than one million units outside its traditional market, or 30% of total sales. Large gains were made in South America, and even more so in China.

Like every other car maker in the world, Peugeot is scrambling to get its share of the explosive growth in China. To that end the company is expanding its operations in the city of Wuhan. In 2006 Peugeot announced it would build a new manufacturing facility in Wuhan in addition to the plant it already has in the inland Chinese city. The new plant, to be part of Peugeot's existing joint venture with Dongfeng Motor, will help Peugeot in its stated goal of reaching 300,000 in annual Chinese capacity by 2008. The two Wuhan facilities will eventually have an annual capacity of 450,000 units.

HISTORY

In 1810 brothers Frédéric and Jean-Pierre Peugeot made a foundry out of the family textile mill in the Alsace region of France and invented the cold-roll process for producing spring steel. Bicycle production began in 1885 at the behest of avid cyclist Armand Peugeot, Jean-Pierre's grandson.

Armand turned to automobiles and built Peugeot's first car, a steam-powered three-wheeler, in 1889. A gas-fueled Peugeot finished in a first-place tie in the 1894 Paris-Rouen Trials, the earliest auto race on record. That year the budding carmaker built the first station wagon, followed by the first compact, the 600-pound "Le Bébé," in 1905.

Peugeot built factories in France, including one in Sochaux (1912) that remains the company's main plant. It made the first diesel passenger car in 1922. The 1929 introduction of the reliable 201 model was followed by innovations such as synchromesh gears in 1936. The company suffered heavy damage in WWII, but quickly bounced back and began expanding overseas after the war.

In 1954 CEO Roland Peugeot rebuffed a board proposal calling for global expansion that would place the company in competition with US automakers. By 1976 the French government had persuaded Peugeot to merge with Citroën.

André Citroën founded his company in 1915, and in 1919 it became the first in Europe to mass-produce cars. Citroën hit the skids during the Depression and in 1934 handed Michelin a large block of stock in lieu of payment for tires. Citroën never fully recovered, though by 1976 the company's line ranged from the 2CV minicar (discontinued in 1990) to limousines.

In 1978 Peugeot bought Chrysler's aging European plants and withering nameplates, including Simca (France) and Rootes (UK). Peugeot changed the nameplates to Talbot but sales continued to slide. It lost nearly $1.2 billion from 1980 to 1984.

Jacques Calvet took over as CEO in 1984. He cut 30,000 jobs and spent heavily on modernization. Aided by the strong launch of the 205 superminicar, Peugeot returned to profitability in 1985, and by 1989 had halved its production break-even point. In the 1980s Peugeot inked production deals with Renault (industrial vehicles, motors, gearboxes) and Fiat (light trucks) and introduced a reasonably priced electric van in 1990.

Peugeot withdrew from the US in 1991 after five years of declining sales. A year later Renault and Peugeot developed electric cars and set up servicing centers throughout France. Citing an economic slump in 1993, Peugeot suffered its first loss ($239 million) since 1985. A French government incentive to replace cars over 10 years old boosted 1994 sales.

Peugeot and rival Renault together introduced a V6 engine in 1996. Jean-Martin Folz replaced Calvet as chairman and CEO in 1997; restructuring charges contributed to company losses that year. In 1998 the company began building Peugeots and Citroëns in the same plants and created its Faurecia unit when its ECIA subsidiary merged with car parts maker Bertrand Faure. In an effort to capitalize on the growing South American car market, the company purchased more than 80% of Argentina's Sevel, and built a plant in Brazil. In 1999 the company sold its flight systems supplier, SAMM, to TRW's Lucas Aerospace unit.

With demand for its cars falling steeply in South America due to the region's continuing economic crisis, Peugeot restructured its Brazil operations in 2000 and formed a new subsidiary, Citroën do Brasil.

In 2001 Peugeot announced that it was building a new engine plant in Brazil and agreed to produce a subcompact car for the European market with Toyota. The following year Peugeot formed an alliance with BMW to develop and build a line of small diesel engines for use in vehicles made by both companies.

EXECUTIVES

Chairman of the Supervisory Board: Thierry Peugeot, age 49

Chairman of the Managing Board and Member of the Executive Committee: Jean-Martin Folz, age 59

Chairman of the Managing Board: M. Christian Streiff, age 49

EVP, Citroën Marque and Member of the Managing Board and Executive Committee: Claude Satinet

EVP, Employee Relations and Human Resources and and Member of the Managing Board and Executive Committee: Jean-Luc Vergne

EVP, Finance, Control, and Performance and Member of the Managing Board and Executive Committee: Yann Delabrière, age 56

EVP, Group Strategy and Products and Member of the Managing Board and Executive Committee: Jean-Marc Nicolle

EVP, Innovation and Quality and Member of the Managing Board and Executive Committee: Robert Peugeot

EVP, Manufacturing and Components and Member of the Managing Board and Executive Committee: Roland Vardanega

EVP, Peugeot Marque and Member of the Managing Board and Executive Committee: Frédéric Saint-Geours

EVP, Platforms, Technical Affairs, and Purchasing and Member of the Managing Board and Executive Committee: Gilles Michel

VP, Corporate Communications: Liliane Lacourt
VP, Legal Affairs: Jean-Claude Hanus, age 59
VP, Public Relations: Xavier Fels
VP, Purchasing: Jean-Phillippe Collin, age 48
Head of Investor Relations: Valérie Magloire
Auditors: PricewaterhouseCoopers

LOCATIONS

HQ: PSA Peugeot Citroën S.A.
    75, avenue de la Grande-Armée, 75116 Paris, France
Phone: +33-1-40-66-55-11   **Fax:** +33-1-40-66-54-14
US HQ: 150 Clove Rd., Little Falls, NJ 07424
US Phone: 973-812-4444   **US Fax:** 973-812-2280
Web: www.psa-peugeot-citroen.com

PSA Peugeot Citroën has manufacturing operations in Argentina, Brazil, China, the Czech Republic, France, Italy, Portugal, Slovakia, Spain, and the UK.

2005 Sales

	$ mil.	% of total
Europe		
Western Europe	54,576.1	82
Other countries	3,211.8	5
Latin America	2,546.3	4
Other regions	6,302.8	9
Total	**66,637.0**	**100**

PRODUCTS/OPERATIONS

2005 Sales

	$ mil.	% of total
Automobile	53,377.6	73
Automotive equipment	13,001.2	18
Transportation & logistics	3,552.9	5
Finance	1,961.2	3
Other	839.7	1
Adjustments	(6,095.6)	—
Total	**66,637.0**	**100**

COMPETITORS

BMW	Mazda
Bridgestone	Nissan
Caterpillar	Renault
DaimlerChrysler	Renco
Fiat	Saab Automobile
Ford	Suzuki Motor
General Motors	Toyota
Honda	Volkswagen
Isuzu	Yamaha Motor
Kia Motors	

HISTORICAL FINANCIALS

Company Type: Public

Income Statement

FYE: December 31

	REVENUE ($ mil.)	NET INCOME ($ mil.)	NET PROFIT MARGIN	EMPLOYEES
12/05	66,637	—	—	208,500
12/04	77,800	—	—	207,200
12/03	68,292	—	—	199,910
12/02	57,233	—	—	198,600
12/01	45,951	—	—	192,500
Annual Growth	**9.7%**	**—**	**—**	**2.0%**

Revenue History

OTC: PEUGY

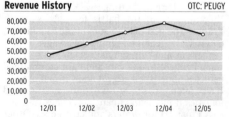

Philips Electronics

Royal Philips Electronics has its royal fingers in lots of different pies. The company makes consumer electronics, including TVs, VCRs, DVD players, phones, and fax machines. But it also makes light bulbs (#1 worldwide), electric shavers (#1) and other personal care appliances, picture tubes, medical systems, and silicon systems solutions. Consumer electronics and appliances account for about a third of the company's sales. Philips has been dumping noncore businesses, such as its stake in music giant PolyGram and its chip unit, and acquiring and forming joint ventures in its core sectors, including medical equipment financing, thin film LCD panels, and digital rights management.

Philips Electronics sold 80% of its semiconductor division to a group of private equity firms, including Kohlberg Kravis Roberts & Co., Silver Lake Partners, and AlpInvest Partners, for about $4.3 billion. The deal, which closed in late 2006, created a stand-alone company called NXP (for Next Experience), based in Eindhoven, the Netherlands. NXP supplies chips to improve the performance of next-generation consumer devices, including digital TVs and cell phones, rather than personal computers.

Philips' medical systems unit is now among the leaders in worldwide medical imaging and monitoring equipment (along with General Electric and Siemens). The company continued to invest in its medical systems in 2006. Europe's largest maker of consumer electronics acquired Intermagnetics General Corporation, a US manufacturer of magnetic resonance imaging (MRI) scanners, for about $1.3 billion in cash. The deal, which closed in November 2006, allows Philips to flex its muscle in the MRI niche of the medical imaging and equipment industry. The acquisition also gives the company a leg up in the fast-growing radio frequency coils area. The coils are sold to hospitals and imaging centers.

In a joint venture with Neusoft Group (software and medical systems), Philips built a medical-imaging equipment manufacturing plant in China.

The Consumer Health and Wellness unit agreed in early 2006 to purchase personal emergency response service Lifeline Systems. Philips rolled the Lifeline operations into its medical systems unit. In addition, Philips is paying about $863 million to buy UK baby care products maker Avent.

In a transaction valued at $2 billion, Philips sold its computer monitor manufacturing operations and a portion of its flat-screen TV business to Hong Kong-based TPV Technology, producer of CRT and LCD displays, in September 2005, making that company the world's largest manufacturer of PC monitors.

Philips has joined several other technology companies to develop software that will prevent music and films from being illegally copied. The alliance, named Coral, includes such companies as Hewlett-Packard, Samsung, and Sony.

HISTORY

Gerard Philips (later joined by brother Anton) founded Philips & Co. in the Dutch city of Eindhoven in 1891. Surviving an industry shakeout, Philips prospered as a result of Gerard's engineering and Anton's foreign sales efforts. The company had become Europe's #3 light bulb maker by

1900. It adopted the name Philips Gloeilampen-fabrieken (light bulb factory) in 1912.

The Netherlands' neutrality during WWI allowed Philips to expand and integrate into glass manufacturing (1915) and X-ray and radio tubes (1918). The company set up its first foreign sales office in Belgium in 1919; it started building plants abroad in the 1930s to avoid trade barriers and tariffs.

During WWII Philips created US and British trusts to hold majority interests in North American Philips (NAP) and in Philips' British operations. Following the war, the company established hundreds of subsidiaries worldwide. It repurchased its British businesses in 1955; NAP operated independently until it was reacquired in 1987.

The company started marketing televisions and appliances in the 1950s. Philips introduced audiocassette, VCR, and laser disc technology in the 1960s but had limited success with computers and office equipment. Despite its development of new technologies, in the 1970s Philips was unable to maintain market share against an onslaught of inexpensive goods from Japan. Meanwhile, NAP acquired Magnavox (consumer electronics, US) in 1974. NAP also purchased GTE Television in 1981 and Westinghouse's lighting business in 1983. In 1986 it provided $60 million in seed money to start Taiwan Semiconductor Manufacturing with the Taiwanese government.

Philips' successful PolyGram unit (formed in 1972) went public in 1989 and bought record companies Island (UK) that year and A&M (US) the next. In 1991 the company changed its name to Royal Philips Electronics.

Ill-timed product introductions contributed to huge losses in the early 1990s. Philips cut some 60,000 jobs and sold money-losing businesses, including its computer business. Cor Boonstra, a former Sara Lee executive, was named chairman and president in 1996. The company sold its cellular communications business in 1996 to AT&T and merged its systems integration unit with BSO/Origin to form Origin B.V. Continuing to focus on core businesses, it sold its 75% stake in PolyGram to Seagram and bought US-based medical instruments maker ATL Ultrasound in 1998.

In 1999 Philips launched a hostile takeover of microchip maker VLSI Technology and, after negotiations, bought VLSI for nearly $1 billion. It also bought a 50% stake in LG LCD, a subsidiary of LG Group, for $1.6 billion; it was renamed LG.Philips LCD Co. In 2000 Philips divested its 24% stake ($3.8 billion) in semiconductor equipment maker ASML Holding.

In April 2001, amid a large decline in profits, Philips announced plans to trim its semiconductor spending by up to 50%. Also that month Boonstra retired and COO Gerard Kleisterlee became chairman and president. In August 2001 Philips completed its acquisition of the Healthcare Solutions Group of Agilent Technologies for $1.7 billion. Since 2001, Philips has cut more than 35,000 jobs; the reductions are the result of support staff job eliminations and the sale of noncore businesses.

Frits Philips, son of founder Anton Philips and the last member of the Philips family to manage the company (he retired in 1977) and who helped develop audio cassettes and the compact disc, died in 2005 at the age of 100.

EXECUTIVES

President and CEO: Gerard Kleisterlee
EVP and CFO: Pierre-Jean Sivignon, age 48
EVP: Gottfried Dutiné, age 52
SVP and Chief Marketing Officer; CEO, Philips Domestic Appliances and Personal Care: Andrea Ragnetti, age 44
SVP and Chief Procurement Officer: Barbara Kux, age 50
SVP and CIO: Daniel Hartert, age 46
SVP and Human Resources Management: Tjerk Hooghiemstra, age 48
SVP, Secretary, and Chief Legal Officer: Arie Westerlaken, age 58
SVP; President and CEO, Philips Consumer Electronics: Rudy Provoost, age 47
SVP; President and CEO, Philips Lighting: Theo van Deursen, age 60
President, Philips Consumer Electronics, North America: Reinier Jens, age 46
CTO: Rick Harwig
SVP; President and CEO, Philips Semiconductors: Frans A. van Houten, age 46
CEO, Philips Consumer Health and Wellness: Ivo Lurvink
CEO, Philips FIMI: Franco Martegani
CEO, Philips Medical Systems: Stephen H. (Steve) Rusckowski, age 49
President, Philips France: Jöel Karecki, age 52
Chairman and CEO, Singapore: Mourad Mankarios, age 62
Head, Lighting Division, ASEAN: Paul Peeters, age 43
Head of Healthcare M&A: Vivek Jain
Head of Media Relations: Gerd Götz
President, Philips France: Alain Le Corvec
Auditors: KPMG Accountants N.V.

LOCATIONS

HQ: Royal Philips Electronics N.V.
(Koninklijke Philips Electronics N.V.)
Breitner Center, Amstelplein 2,
1096 BC Amsterdam, The Netherlands
Phone: +31-20-59-77-777   **Fax:** +31-20-59-77-070
US HQ: 1251 Avenue of The Americas,
New York, NY 10020
US Phone: 212-536-0500   **US Fax:** 212-536-0827
Web: www.philips.com

Royal Philips Electronics has about 135 manufacturing sites in 35 countries; it has sales and service operations in about 150 countries.

2005 Sales

	% of total
Europe & Africa	42
Asia/Pacific	26
North America	26
Latin America	6
Total	**100**

PRODUCTS/OPERATIONS

2005 Sales

	% of total
Consumer electronics	34
Medical systems	21
Lighting	16
Semiconductors	15
Domestic appliances & personal care	7
Other	7
Total	**100**

Selected Products

Consumer electronics
  Audio
  Consumer communications
  Display
  Licenses
  Peripherals and accessories
  Video

Medical systems
  Asset management services
  Cardiac and monitoring systems
  Computed tomography
  Customer financing
  Dictation and speech recognition systems
  Document management services
  Magnetic resonance
  Medical IT
  Nuclear medicine
  Personal health care
  Ultrasound
  X-ray
Lighting
  Automotive and special lighting
  Lamps
  Lighting electronics
  Luminaires
Semiconductors
  Assembly and test
  Communications
  Consumer systems
  Foundries
  Mobile display systems
  Multi-market semiconductors
Domestic appliances and personal care
  Food and beverage
  Home environment care
  Oral health care
  Shaving and beauty
Miscellaneous
  Corporate investments
  Navigation technology
  Optical storage
  Shared services
  Technology and design

COMPETITORS

AMD
Fujitsu
GE
GE India
Gillette
Harman International
LG Electronics
Matsushita
Mitsubishi Electric
Motorola
Nokia
OSRAM
Pioneer
Samsung Group
SANYO
Sharp
Siemens AG
Siemens Corp
Sony
Spectrum Brands
Texas Instruments
THOMSON
Toshiba

HISTORICAL FINANCIALS

Company Type: Public

Income Statement			FYE: December 31
	REVENUE ($ mil.)	NET INCOME ($ mil.)	NET PROFIT MARGIN	EMPLOYEES
12/05	36,000	3,397	9.4%	159,226
12/04	41,367	3,869	9.4%	161,586
12/03	36,462	873	2.4%	164,438
12/02	33,357	(3,361)	—	170,087
12/01	28,868	(2,193)	—	188,643
Annual Growth	5.7%	—	—	(4.1%)

2005 Year-End Financials

Debt ratio: 19.9%   No. of shares (mil.): —
Return on equity: 17.0%   Dividends
Cash ($ mil.): 6,269   Yield: 2.8%
Current ratio: 1.46   Payout: 32.5%
Long-term debt ($ mil.): 3,932   Market value ($ mil.): —

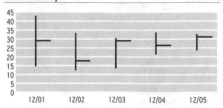

	STOCK PRICE ($) FY Close	P/E High/Low		PER SHARE ($) Earnings	Dividends
12/05	31.10	12	9	2.71	0.88
12/04	26.50	11	7	3.02	0.37
12/03	29.09	—	—	—	0.65
12/02	17.68	—	—	—	0.27
12/01	29.11	—	—	(1.71)	0.27
Annual Growth	1.7%	—	—	—	34.4%

Pioneer

Pioneer takes you on a journey of sight and sound. A leading maker of consumer and commercial electronics, about 40% of its sales come from car electronics (stereos, speakers, navigation systems), which are sold to retailers and automobile manufacturers. Pioneer also makes video equipment (projection TVs, DVD players and DVD recorders, plasma displays) and audio products (stereo components, stereo systems). It also sells products to business customers (plasma displays, AV systems, factory automation systems) and, through Discovision Associations (US-based subsidiary), it generates revenue from licensing optical disc technologies. Pioneer has more than 30 manufacturing facilities worldwide.

A dive in profitability in its core home electronics business has led Pioneer to shake up its top management and restructure its business to devote more resources to its most profitable products, such as car electronics, and to develop high-value-added consumer products. The company has been hurt by falling prices and profits for its core products, including plasma display TVs and DVD players. Pioneer is also focusing efforts on its car navigation systems, a category which has grown to become a major revenue and profit source for the company.

Also as part of its restructuring, Pioneer is selling some of its properties, including its plant in Tokorozawa City, and consolidating some of its operations at new facilities currently under construction in Kawasaki City.

Pioneer acquired NEC's plasma display manufacturing business in September 2004; this turned out to be an ill-advised move, as prohibitively high production costs are driving the company to produce fewer product lines in the former NEC factory.

The company — Pioneer Kabushiki Kaisha in Japanese — was the first to give us the laser disc (LD), car CD players, and car navigation devices that use a satellite-based global positioning system (GPS).

HISTORY

Nozomu Matsumoto, son of a Christian missionary, first heard high-fidelity speakers in 1932; nothing made in Japan compared in quality. In 1938 he founded Fukuin Shokai Denki Seisakusho (Gospel Electric Works) in Osaka to repair radios and speakers. It later began making these items. Matsumoto designed the company's trademark — a tuning fork overlaying the symbol for the ohm (a unit for measuring electrical resistance) — and chose the brand name Pioneer to reflect the company's spirit.

The firm introduced turntables and amplifiers in 1955 and hi-fi receivers in 1958. By the 1960s Pioneer Electronic was Japan's #1 audio equipment maker. It introduced the world's first stereo with speakers separate from the control unit in 1962 and the world's first car stereo in 1963. Subsidiaries opened in the US and Europe in 1966.

Convinced that laser disc (LD) technology was the wave of the future, Pioneer started work on a LD video player in 1972. Pioneer was listed on the NYSE four years later. It partnered with Discovision Associates (DVA, a partnership between IBM and Music Corporation of America) in 1977 to form Universal Pioneer Corporation (UPC). Home LD players appeared in the US in 1980 and in Japan in 1981. But consumers wanted machines that could record, not just play, and demand for LDs remained sluggish.

Matsumoto's eldest son, Seiya, became president in 1982. Two years later Pioneer introduced the world's first car CD system; it also created a LD/CD player, perhaps hoping customers would react better to LD products if they were combined with other features. Pioneer branched into office automation, introducing the Write-Once Read-Many (WORM) optical memory disk in 1985. In 1989 it bought DVA, by then a leading optical-disk research firm with more than 1,400 patents. Also that year it formed Pioneer Trimble with US-based Trimble Navigation to develop a computerized car navigation system.

Pioneer sold record company Warner-Pioneer, a joint venture, to partner Warner — now Time Warner — in 1989, but it took another stab at the US entertainment business the next year when it bought 10% of theatrical filmmaker Carolco Pictures (*Basic Instinct*). But like many high-profile Japanese investments in the US, Carolco turned sour: It filed for Chapter 11 bankruptcy protection in 1995, leading Pioneer to write off its investment.

With sales not meeting expectations, in 1996 Pioneer replaced Seiya as president with his in-law Kaneo Ito (former head of Pioneer's Europe sales network); Seiya became chairman and his brother Kanya was made vice chairman. The company reentered the entertainment business with the 1996 launch of Pioneer Music Group. In 1997 Pioneer restructured itself into three separate operating units: Home Entertainment, Mobile Entertainment, and Business Systems; it added a Display Products unit the following year.

In 1999 the company opted for a simpler moniker, removing the word "electronic" from its name. Chairman Seiya died that year and was replaced by brother Kanya. With price wars and slow sales in its software business eroding profits, Pioneer announced in 1999 a three-year plan to cut more than 2,500 jobs. In 2000 Pioneer started making TV set-top boxes for digital cable. In 2001 Pioneer established two production subsidiaries in China to generate DVD pickups (the lens that converts the laser reflection into digital info), DVD-R/RW drives, and car electronics products.

Pioneer decided to exit the software and music business, opting to focus on hardware; in 2003 it sold subsidiaries Pioneer LDC and Pioneer Entertainment (USA) to Japanese advertising agency Dentsu.

At the beginning of 2005, the company restructured its operations into two divisions, home entertainment and mobile entertainment, abolishing its plasma display OEM business to concentrate on only manufacturing Pioneer-branded displays.

As the company failed to increase its stake in the consumer electronics market and faced losses estimated at $200 million for the 2006 fiscal year, president and CEO Kaneo Ito and chairman Kanya Matsumoto stepped down at the end of 2005. In January 2006, EVP Tamihiko Sudo replaced Ito as president of the company. Also in 2006 the company sold its 100% stake in Pioneer Digital Technologies, a software developer for cable TV set-top boxes in the US, in a management buyout valued at $6.4 million. Other discontinued businesses include Pioneer Precision Machinery Corp. and its subsidiaries.

EXECUTIVES

President and Representative Director: Tamihiko Sudo, age 59
Senior Managing Director, Japanese Domestic Subsidiaries and Representative Director: Akira Niijima, age 62
Senior Managing Director; General Manager, Research and Development Group and Corporate Research and Development Laboratories: Osamu Yamada, age 62
Senior Managing Director, Coporate Management and Export Management and Representative Director: Hajime Ishizuka, age 59
Senior Managing Executive Officer; General Manager, International Business Group: Kazunori Yamamoto, age 64
Managing Director, Production Management and Coordination Division: Tadahiro Yamaguchi, age 60
Managing Director; General Manager, Environmental Preservation Group: Satoshi Matsumoto, age 52
Managing Director; General Manager, Procurement Group: Koichi Shimizu, age 62
Managing Director; General Manager, Mobile Entertainment Business Group: Akira Haeno, age 57
Managing Director: Shinji Yasuda, age 61
Senior Executive Officer; President, Solutions Business: Kiyoshi Uchida, age 55
Senior Executive Officer; General Manager, Intellectual Property Division, Research and Development Group: Seiichiro Kurihara, age 63
Senior Executive Officer; General Manager, Corporate Branding and Communications Division: Masao Kawabata, age 58
Senior Executive Officer; General Manager, Finance and Accounting Division: Hideki Okayasu, age 56
Executive Officer; General Manager, Personnel Division: Osamu Takada, age 58
Auditors: Deloitte Touche Tohmatsu

LOCATIONS

HQ: Pioneer Corporation
4-1, Meguro 1-chome, Meguro-ku,
Tokyo 153-8654, Japan
Phone: +81-3-3495-6774   **Fax:** +81-3-3495-4301
US HQ: 2265 E. 220th St., Long Beach, CA 90810
US Phone: 310-952-2000   **US Fax:** 310-952-2199
Web: www.pioneer.co.jp

2006 Sales

	% of total
Japan	46
North America	16
Europe	12
Other regions	26
Total	**100**

PRODUCTS/OPERATIONS

2006 Sales

	% of total
Home electronics	45
Car electronics	42
Patent licensing	1
Other	12
Total	**100**

Selected Products

Home Electronics Products
 Digital broadcast set-top boxes
 DVD players
 DVD recorders
 DVD-ROM drives
 Equipment for cable-TV systems
 Plasma displays
 Projection TVs
 Recordable DVD drives
 Stereo components
 Stereo systems
 Telephones
Car Electronics Products
 Car AV systems
 Car navigation systems
 Car speakers
 Car stereos
Patent Licensing (related to optical disc technologies)
Other Products (business-use electronics)

COMPETITORS

Bose
Clarion
Harman International
Kenwood
LG Electronics
Matsushita
Philips Electronics
Robert Bosch Corp.
SANYO
Scientific-Atlanta
Sony
THOMSON
Victor Company of Japan

HISTORICAL FINANCIALS

Company Type: Public

Income Statement

FYE: March 31

	REVENUE ($ mil.)	NET INCOME ($ mil.)	NET PROFIT MARGIN	EMPLOYEES
3/06	6,348	(723)	—	38,826
3/05	6,822	(82)	—	39,362
3/04	6,635	235	3.5%	36,360
3/03	5,943	134	2.3%	34,656
3/02	5,043	61	1.2%	31,220
Annual Growth	5.9%	—	—	5.6%

Net Income History

Exchange: Tokyo

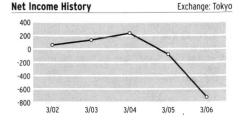

Pirelli & C.

Pirelli products travel the freeway, but may be exiting the information superhighway. After one reorganization Pirelli had four core businesses: tires, energy cables, real estate, and telecommunication cables, but the company has sold off the cable businesses in an effort to direct resources back toward its tire business. Pirelli makes tires for cars, industrial and commercial vehicles, motorcycles, and farm machinery, and the company has revved more than a few motors with its famous calendars. Its real estate sector invests in real estate companies and provides financing services. Italian holding company Camfin owns about a quarter of Pirelli.

Other members of the company's controlling shareholder pact include Banca Intesa, Capitalia, Edizione Holding (parent company of the Benetton Group), and Mediobanca.

Pirelli's two cable divisions sold in 2005 included energy (low-, medium-, and high-voltage power cables and building wire products) and telecommunications (cable assemblies and hardware and fiber-optics). The company sold the divisions to Goldman Sachs in a deal worth about $1.6 billion (€1.3 billion) including debt, and they are now known as Prysmian Cables & Systems. Pirelli still has some tech-related operations, through Pirelli Broadband Solutions and Pirelli Labs.

Although demand for Pirelli-brand tires has dropped in South America (particularly Brazil), the company expects the trend to change. The company plans to attempt to gain market share in the US by promoting its high performance tires, and also has plans to expand its market-share in eastern Europe and Asia. To this end Pirelli has formed a joint venture in China and is exploring its options in India.

In a bid to capitalize on the company's cache, Pirelli has launched a line of clothing, footwear, and accessories under the PZero brand. The items are produced under license by clothing firm IN.CO.M SpA and sold in the US and at more than 1,000 other locations around the world.

HISTORY

After fighting for Italian unification with Garibaldi in the 1860s, Giovanni Battista Pirelli observed that France, not Italy, was providing rubber tubes for an Italian ship salvage attempt. The young patriot reacted by founding Pirelli & Co. in Milan, Italy, in 1872 to manufacture rubber products. In 1879 Pirelli began making insulated cables for the rapidly growing telegraph industry, and by 1890 he was making bicycle tires. Pirelli introduced his first air-filled automobile tire in 1899.

Foreign expansion began when Pirelli opened cable factories in Spain (1902), the UK (1914), and Argentina (1917). The company set up Societe Internationale Pirelli (SIP) in Switzerland in 1937 and consolidated all non-Italian operations within it. After WWII the group expanded along with the growth in worldwide auto sales. Pirelli began production in Turkey and Greece in 1962, and six years later it set up cable plants in Peru.

Pirelli's first radial tires (early 1970s) backfired when they wore out too quickly. In 1971 the company swapped stock with tire maker Dunlop (UK). Although the firms engaged in joint research and development (R&D), they never consolidated production.

Pirelli S.p.A., the Italian operating company, and SIP became holding companies in 1982 by transferring their operating units into jointly owned Pirelli Societe Generale (Switzerland). Also that year Pirelli started producing fiber-optic cables.

Heavy spending on R&D and new equipment bolstered the newly unified tire business, and the 1986 purchase of Metzeler Kautscuk (Germany) made Pirelli one of the world's largest motorcycle tire manufacturers.

Pirelli S.p.A. became an operating company in 1988 when it bought SIP's Pirelli Societe Generale holdings. It launched a hostile bid for Firestone through Pirelli Tyre, but was outbid by Bridgestone. Pirelli settled for the much smaller Armstrong Tire. In 1989 Pirelli sold nearly 24% of Pirelli Tyre to the public.

In 1990 Pirelli proposed an unusually complex and convoluted merger with Continental AG (Germany) designed to leave Pirelli in control. Continental declined, but negotiations continued throughout 1991 until Continental terminated the talks after learning of Pirelli's deteriorating financial condition.

Pirelli became a top power-cable maker with operations in more than 20 countries in 1998 by acquiring Germany-based Siemens' power cable unit in a $277 million deal.

In 1999 Pirelli agreed to ally with Cooper Tire and Rubber, including an arrangement whereby Cooper would distribute and sell Pirelli tires for passenger cars and light trucks in the US, Canada, and Mexico. In return, Pirelli agreed to sell Cooper tires in South America. Additionally, Pirelli Cables Australia acquired Metal Manufacturers Ltd's energy cable business to strengthen its market share down under.

In 1999 Pirelli unveiled a compact, computerized manufacturing system designed to cut the cost of tire production about 25%, while raising tire quality. In 2000 Pirelli sold its terrestrial optical systems business to Cisco Systems for about $2.15 billion; Cisco agreed to invest $100 million in Pirelli's optical components and undersea cable transmissions divisions. Also in 2000 the company sold its fiber-optic telecommunications business to Corning for about $3.6 billion.

In 2001 the company separated energy cables and systems from its telecom business to focus on new growth and reached an alliance agreement with Alloptic to develop network fiber-optic solutions for commercial and home markets. In a surprise July announcement, Pirelli announced that it and the Benetton family had agreed to buy the 23% controlling stake in Olivetti — controlled by Roberto Colaninno, the CEO of both Olivetti and Telecom Italia. Pirelli sold its enameled wire holdings in late 2002 to Investitori Associati, an Italy-based investment group. After merging its operating company (Pirelli SpA) and holding company (Pirelli & C. SapA) in 2003, the company changed its name to Pirelli & C. SpA. The following year Pirelli sold its interest in Afcab, a South Africa-based cable manufacturer.

EXECUTIVES

Honorary Chairman: Leopoldo Pirelli
Chairman: Marco Tronchetti Provera, age 58
Deputy Chairman: Alberto Pirelli
Deputy Chairman: Carlo Alessandro Puri Negri
Managing Director; General Manager, Finance and Administration; Board Member: Carlo O. Buora, age 60
General Manager, Administration and Control: Claudio De Conto
General Manager, Finance: Luciano Gobbi
General Manager, Tires Sector: Francesco Gori

CIO: Dario Scagliotti
President and CEO, Pirelli, North America:
  Kevin Riddett
CEO, Pirelli Labs Optical Innovation: Giorgio Grasso
Director, PZero: Antonio Gallo
Secretary: Carlo Montagna
Head, Investor Relations: Alberto Borgia
Corporate Communications: Ivan Dompé
Investor Relations: Massimiliano Cominelli
VP, Advertising, Public Relations and Motorsports,
  Pirelli Tire North America: Peter Tyson
Creative Director, PZero: Gigi Vezzola
Auditors: PricewaterhouseCoopers SpA

LOCATIONS

HQ: Pirelli & C. SpA
  V.le Sarca, 222, 20126 Milan, Italy
Phone: +39-02-64421   **Fax:** +39-02-6442-4686
US HQ: 100 Pirelli Dr., Rome, GA 30162
US Phone: 706-235-3786   **US Fax:** 706-368-5832
Web: www.pirelli.com

Pirelli has cable and tire manufacturing facilities around the globe.

2005 Sales

	$ mil.	% of total
Europe		
Italy	1,703.9	32
Other countries	1,928.0	36
Central & South America	916.6	17
Oceania, Africa & Asia	455.4	8
North America	379.5	7
Total	**5,383.4**	**100**

PRODUCTS/OPERATIONS

2005 Sales

	$ mil.	% of total
Tires	4,302.4	80
Real estate	829.2	16
Broadband	132.9	2
Environment	72.8	1
Other	46.1	1
Total	**5,383.4**	**100**

Selected Products

Tires
  Automobile (passenger car, SUV, and truck)
  Motorcycle
Real Estate
  Investment funds
  Real estate companies

COMPETITORS

Ansell	Kumho Tire
Bandag	Marangoni
Bridgestone	Michelin
Continental AG	Sime Darby
Falken Tire	Sumitomo Rubber
Fieldens	Watts Industrial Tyres
Goodyear	

HISTORICAL FINANCIALS

Company Type: Public

Income Statement

FYE: December 31

	REVENUE ($ mil.)	NET INCOME ($ mil.)	NET PROFIT MARGIN	EMPLOYEES
12/05	5,383	473	8.8%	26,827
12/04	9,704	374	3.9%	37,154
12/03	8,374	5	0.1%	36,337
12/02	6,615	(640)	—	36,079
12/01	6,652	73	1.1%	39,127
Annual Growth	**(5.2%)**	**59.6%**	**—**	**(9.0%)**

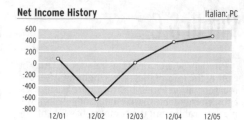

Net Income History   Italian: PC

PKN ORLEN

Crudely moving into the private market, Polski Koncern Naftowy ORLEN (PKN) is the largest refiner and distributor of oil in Poland. Two former state monopolies, Petrochemia Plock (Poland's largest refinery) and Centrala Produktow Naftowych (Poland's #1 petroleum distributor), merged in 1999 to create PKN. The company also owns stakes in two other refineries (its total capacity is 600,000 barrels per day) and has some 1,900 retail sites, about a third of Poland's gas stations. PKN owns a 75% stake in chemical maker Anwil and has holdings in several other Polish companies. Outside Poland, the company has nearly 500 gas stations in Germany, and controls Czech refiner and retailer Unipetrol.

The company also manufactures liquefied propane-butane gas (LPG) for use at industrial plants and for heating public buildings. Other PKN products include polyvinylchloride plastics used in foils, containers, bottles, cable insulation, and auto parts; nitric fertilizers; asphalts for construction of roads, airports, and sports facilities; and basic industrial and engine oils.

Its Eko subsidiary burns hazardous waste, while its ORLEN Transport division handles the distribution of fuel to its gas stations. Its Solino holdings (70%) produces salt and brine, and uses salt caverns for underground storage of petroleum and fuels.

HISTORY

The merger between Petrochemia Plock, Poland's largest refiner and petrochemicals maker, and CPN (Centrala Produktow Naftowych), the nation's largest motor fuel distributor, created Polski Koncern Naftowy (PKN) in 1999.

Poland's oil industry stretches back to the late 1800s, when five refineries were built in the nation's southern region. The Polish Oil Monopoly was formed in 1944 to oversee the country's oil distribution operations; it assumed the CPN name a year later.

While the rest of the world increasingly turned to oil as an energy source after WWII, Poland continued to rely on coal, and its oil industry grew slowly. CPN was split up into 17 regional branches in 1955. The branches controlled local operations, and the head office in Warsaw handled pricing and purchasing.

In the late 1950s the Soviet Union began building the Friendship pipeline to deliver crude oil to East Germany and Poland. The Polish government responded by forming Petrochemia to develop a refinery next to the pipeline in the city of Plock.

The Petrochemia refinery began producing refined products in 1964; four years later it began

processing crude oil to make fuels, lubricants, and bitumen. The refinery also began making products such as detergents and plastics from processed refinery gases and other hydrocarbons. It added petrochemicals in 1970.

Because of the oil industry's slow growth in Poland, the country managed to avoid some of the impact of the 1970s energy crisis. (Even as late as 1995, oil accounted for only 17% of Poland's energy consumption.) But it was forced to pay higher prices for Russian crude. In 1975 the government decided to expand its refining operations and created a second major refiner, Rafineria Gdanska, to focus on motor fuels.

Locked behind the Iron Curtain, Poland was not able to build its oil operations until the early 1990s. In 1992 Petrochemia began expanding its refinery facilities to reach a production capacity of 820,000 barrels per day within 10 years.

After Communism's demise, the Polish government began planning the privatization of its oil operations. After several plans were adopted and discarded in the early 1990s, the government finally decided in 1996 to split CPN up among the nation's refineries. Holding company Nafta Polska was formed that year to own 75% stakes in Poland's refineries and in CPN and carry out the privatization process.

In 1997 CPN was stripped of its fuel depots and rail transport operations, which were placed under the Nafta Polska umbrella. Displeased with the plan to carve up CPN, the distributor's management rallied against the government's plan. The Polish government gave in and went back to the drawing board.

A successful plan was formed in 1998: to merge Petrochemia and CPN. The companies were combined in 1999, and 30% of the new PKN was floated on the Warsaw and London stock exchanges. The next year the government spun off an additional 42% stake and the company added ORLEN to its name (combining the Polish words for eagle and energy). Also in 2000 the government began preparing to float Refineria Gdanska. PKN hoped to get a piece of its regional rival, but the state left PKN out of the bidding to encourage competition.

To meet German antitrust regulations for its merger with Veba Oel, in late 2002 BP sold some 494 gas stations in Germany to PKN. In 2004 PKN purchased 63% of Unipetrol; the European Commission's Competition Directorate granted approval of the purchase in mid-2005.

EXECUTIVES

Chairman: Jacek Bartkiewicz, age 50
President and CEO: Igor A. Chalupec, age 40
VP and COO: Janusz Wisniewski, age 46
CFO: Pawel Szymanski, age 32
VP and Head of Retail & Wholesale Operations:
  Wojciech Heydel, age 44
VP and Chief Human Resources Officer:
  Andrzej Ernest Macenowicz, age 58
VP, Head of Cost Management & IT: Jan Maciejewicz,
  age 49
VP and Chief Investment Officer:
  Cezary Smorszczewski, age 40
Head of Management Systems & Group Restructuring:
  Dariusz Witkowski
Auditors: Ernst & Young

LOCATIONS

HQ: Polski Koncern Naftowy ORLEN SA
ul. Chemików 7, 09-411 Plock, Poland
Phone: +48-24-365-00-00   **Fax:** +48-24-365-40-40
Web: www.orlen.pl

Polski Koncern Naftowy ORLEN has a major refinery in
Plock, Poland; stakes in two refineries in southern Poland;
and a network of gas stations in Poland and Germany.

2005 Sales

	% of total
Poland	51
Germany	24
Czech Republic	17
Other	8
Total	**100**

PRODUCTS/OPERATIONS

2005 Sales

	% of total
Refining & marketing	81
Petrochemicals	16
Other	3
Total	**100**

Selected Subsidiaries

Inowroclawskie Kopalnie Soli "Solino" (70%, salt
   production)
Petrolot Sp. z o.o. (51%, distribution of aviation fuels)
Petroprofit Sp. z o.o. (85%; distribution of fuels, radiator
   fluids, and plastics)
Rafineria Nafty Jedlicze SA (75%, refining)
Rafineria Trzebinia SA (77%, refining)
Zaklady Azotowe Anwil SA (75%, chemical
   manufacturing)

COMPETITORS

BP
Exxon Mobil
LUKOIL
MOL
OMV
Royal Dutch Shell
Statoil

HISTORICAL FINANCIALS

Company Type: Public

Income Statement

FYE: December 31

	REVENUE ($ mil.)	NET INCOME ($ mil.)	NET PROFIT MARGIN	EMPLOYEES
12/05	12,606	1,403	11.1%	21,825
12/04	10,193	799	7.8%	14,296
12/03	6,499	263	4.0%	15,133
12/02	4,398	110	2.5%	17,818
12/01	4,278	94	2.2%	17,582
Annual Growth	31.0%	96.4%	—	5.6%

2005 Year-End Financials

Debt ratio: 20.4%
Return on equity: 31.2%
Cash ($ mil.): 345
Current ratio: 1.47
Long-term debt ($ mil.): 1,042

Net Income History

Warsaw: PKNA

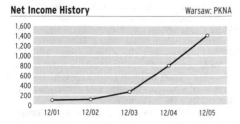

Porsche

Perhaps second only to Harley-Davidson as
the premier cure for a mid-life crisis, Porsche is
still going strong a century after its founder
began designing autos. Porsche's lineup includes
four model lines: the Boxster, the 911 models,
the Cayenne SUV, and the new Cayman S two-
seater coupe. Can't afford a new Cayenne?
Porsche also offers watches, luggage, and tennis
rackets bearing its name. In addition, Porsche offers consulting services to other companies involved in auto and furniture manufacturing,
mechanical and electronic engineering, and construction. Descendants of the founding family
control Porsche.

While other carmakers toil over cash incen-
tives, 0% financing gimmicks, market share, and
strategies for the Chinese market, Porsche has
quietly transformed itself from serious money-
loser into one of the most profitable car companies in the world. The company has nearly
quadrupled its annual unit sales in just under a
decade, all without the costs and risks of constantly rolling out new products. The most recent debuts have been the Cayenne, which has
been hugely successful, and the Cayman S. The
company plans to stick with the winning formula of long product life cycles, and growing
unit sales year over year.

Porsche has sold subsidiary CTS Fahzeug-
Dachsysteme GmbH (roof systems manufacturer) to Magna International for about
$200 million in an all cash deal. In 2006 Porsche
also sold Porsche Engineering Services to Magna
for an undisclosed sum.

Porsche has acquired nearly 20% of Volkswagen (VW) in a deal initially valued at $3.6 billion.
The deal makes Porsche the largest shareholder
of VW. Porsche later raised its VW holdings to
about 27% and has plans to further boost its
stake to about 30%.

HISTORY

Ferdinand Porsche was 25 when a battery-
powered car with a motor he had designed was
unveiled at the Paris Exposition in 1900. Six
years later, Porsche was hired by Daimler Motor.
During his rise to chief engineer at Daimler, he
designed the famous Mercedes-Benz S-series.

Frustrated by the conservative nature of his
employer, Porsche quit and opened an engine-
design company bearing his name in 1931. The
next year Josef Stalin offered to make Porsche
the head of the Soviet Union's auto industry.
Porsche turned Stalin down.

In 1933 Hitler announced his intention to
build a widely affordable "volkswagen" (people's
car). Soon Porsche was designing the vehicle
that would become the Volkswagen Beetle. During WWII Porsche continued work on the Volkswagen project and also provided advice on
increasing Germany's factory production. After
the war, Ferdinand and his son Ferry were imprisoned for two years in France for allegedly
abusing French laborers. Father and son were
compelled to work on the Renault line of automobiles. After his release, Ferdinand reportedly
burst into tears and exclaimed, "My Beetle!"
when he saw his Volkswagen cars populating the
streets in Germany.

By 1948 Ferdinand and Ferry had developed a
Porsche sports-car prototype based on the Volkswagen. It was named the 356 because it was the

356th project undertaken at the Porsche design
office. In 1950 the first Porsche 356 rolled off the
assembly line in Stuttgart. Ferdinand Porsche
lived just long enough to see his sports cars become highly sought by the rich and famous. He
died in 1951.

In 1952 Ferry designed the Porsche emblem,
which combined the Porsche name and the
Stuttgart and Wurttemberg coats of arms.
Porsches won hundreds of races during the
1950s, and the car's popularity grew. (James
Dean was driving his brand-new Porsche when
he was killed in 1955.)

By the 1960s Ferry Porsche decided to build an
entirely new Porsche model that didn't rely so
heavily on the Beetle's design. The company unveiled the Type 911 Porsche in 1964 and discontinued the 356 the next year. In 1973 the company
went public under the Porsche AG name.

The company flourished in the 1980s, due
largely to its cars' popularity in the US. By 1986
Porsche was producing almost 50,000 cars a year,
with about 60% of them destined for the US market. Models introduced in the late 1980s included
the 912, the 924, and the 928.

Porsche's fortunes crashed in the early 1990s,
when the company faced tough competition
and a recession priced many consumers out of
the sports-car market. In 1992 the company
sold only 23,060 cars — 4,100 of those in the
US. That year Wendelin Wiedeking, an engineering and manufacturing expert, was
brought in as CEO. He cut costs, in part, by
convincing most workers to reduce the number
of hours they worked each day and eliminating
overtime. Wiedeking also updated the 911 and
initiated development of the Boxster.

Introduced in 1996, the $40,000 Boxster was
an instant hit — its first year of production sold
out in advance. In 1998 the company initiated
plans to produce a luxury SUV in partnership
with Volkswagen. Porsche launched the Boxster
S, featuring a 250-hp engine, in 1999. The next
year Porsche announced that its Cayenne SUV —
which shares a platform with Volkswagen's SUV
— would hit the market in 2003.

Early in 2002 Porsche announced its next
product launch — the Carrera GT. Production of
the Carrera GT began the following year.

EXECUTIVES

Chairman of the Executive Board, President, and CEO:
Wendelin Wiedeking, age 53
**Member of the Executive Board, Finance and
Controlling:** Holger P. Härter
**Member of the Executive Board, Production and
Logistics:** Michael Macht
**Member of the Executive Board, Research and
Development:** Wolfgang Dürheimer, age 48
Member of the Executive Board, Sales and Marketing:
Klaus Berning, age 49
**Member of the Executive Board, Human Resources and
Labor Relations:** Harro Harmel
**Member of the Executive Board, Human Resources and
Labor Relations:** Thomas Edig, age 45
President and CEO, Porsche Cars North America:
Peter Schwarzenbauer
Managing Director, Porsche France: Detlev van Platen
Managing Director, Porsche Germany: Bernhard Maier
Managing Director, Porsche Cars Great Britain:
Andrew Goss
Managing Director, Porsche Iberica: Joachim Lamla
Managing Director, Porsche Italia: Loris Casadei
Head of Financial Press and Investor Relations:
Frank Gaube, age 45
Head of Press and Public Relations: Anton Hunger
Auditors: Ernst & Young

LOCATIONS

HQ: Dr. Ing. h.c. F. Porsche AG
Porscheplatz 1, D-70435 Stuttgart, Germany
Phone: +49-711-911-0   **Fax:** +49-711-911-5777
US HQ: 980 Hammond Dr., Ste. 1000, Atlanta, GA 30328
US Phone: 770-290-3500   **US Fax:** 770-290-3706
Web: www.porsche.com

Porsche operates main production facilities in
Zuffenhausen, Germany, and in Finland.

2005 Sales

	% of total
Europe	
Germany	34
Other countries	24
North America	34
Other regions	8
Total	**100**

PRODUCTS/OPERATIONS

2005 Sales

	% of total
Vehicles	95
Financial services	5
Total	**100**

2005 Unit Sales

	No.	% of total
Cayenne	41,884	47
911	27,826	32
Boxster	18,009	20
Carrera GT	660	1
Total	**88,379**	**100**

Selected Vehicles

Boxster
Boxster S
Carrera GT
Cayenne
Cayenne S
Cayenne Turbo
Cayenne Turbo S
Cayman S
911 Carrera
911 Carrera 4
911 Carrera 4 Cabriolet
911 Carrera 4S
911 Carrera 4S Cabriolet
911 Carrera Cabriolet
911 Carrera Cabriolet S
911 Carrera S

COMPETITORS

BMW	Nissan
DaimlerChrysler	Peugeot
Fiat	Renault
Ford	Saab Automobile
General Motors	Saleen
Honda	Volkswagen
Mazda	

HISTORICAL FINANCIALS

Company Type: Public

Income Statement

FYE: July 31

	REVENUE ($ mil.)	NET INCOME ($ mil.)	NET PROFIT MARGIN	EMPLOYEES
7/05	7,972	949	11.9%	11,878
7/04	7,645	727	9.5%	11,668
7/03	6,331	640	10.1%	10,699
7/02	4,776	509	10.7%	10,143
7/01	3,883	236	6.1%	9,752
Annual Growth	**19.7%**	**41.5%**	**—**	**5.1%**

2005 Year-End Financials

Debt ratio: 58.2%   Current ratio: 3.97
Return on equity: 27.4%   Long-term debt ($ mil.): 2,407
Cash ($ mil.): 2,128

Net Income History   OTC: PSEPF

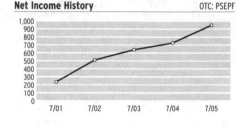

POSCO

POSCO steeled itself against unfavorable market conditions in its neck of the woods, but things are looking up. The company makes hot- and cold-rolled steel products (plate steel, stainless steel, electrical steel, and wire rods), which it sells to the auto and shipbuilding industries. It produces about 30 million tons of steel a year, making it the world's #3 steel maker behind the combined Arcelor Mittal and Nippon Steel. Subsidiaries include POSCO Engineering & Construction (which builds steel plants, steel-related infrastructure, and energy facilities) and POSDATA (systems integration). The South Korean government privatized its stake in POSCO in 2001, ending the company's 30-year steelmaking monopoly.

Unfortunately for POSCO, South Korea has little native iron ore, and the company has had to look for iron elsewhere. It purchases its iron ore and coal from Australia, Brazil, Canada, China, India, and Russia from the likes of CVRD, Rio Tinto, and BHP Billiton. To that end, POSCO has developed about 18 joint ventures, including six in China and others in Australia, Brazil, Canada, Indonesia, Myanmar, South Africa, Thailand, the US, and Venezuela. The company said it would cut steel production by 300,000 tons in 2005 due to low demand.

India sits predominantly in POSCO's expansion sights, as the company announced plans in 2005 to join BHP Billiton in setting up a steelworks in the country capable of an annual capacity of more than 10 million tons. In the summer of that year the company agreed to launch what could be the largest foreign investment ever in India — a $12 billion steel plant in the eastern state of Orissa. (A move since copied and rivaled by Mittal, which has announced similar plans.) Work is expected to begin on Posco's facility in 2007.

China is also on the radar: POSCO submitted plans to the Chinese government for another 10-million-metric-ton plant. The country is POSCO's largest export market; Korea represents around 70% of total steel sales volume.

POSCO's hot-rolled products are used in the construction of automobile chassis, buildings and bridges, industrial pipes and tanks, and railway rolling stocks. The company's cold-rolled products such as cold-rolled coils and galvanized cold-rolled products are used in the automotive industry to manufacture car body panels and for other uses like household goods, electrical appliances, and engineering and metal parts.

POSCO has also formed an alliance with long-time rival Nippon Steel and plans to establish agreements with other steelmakers in China and Europe. The company also intends to diversify into the energy distribution business, bioscience, and other emerging high-tech areas.

HISTORY

After the Korean War, South Korea, the US, and its allies wanted to rebuild South Korea's infrastructure as quickly as possible. Steel was given a high priority, and before long about 15 companies were making various steel products. Quality was a problem, though, as the companies used dated production processes.

With the backing of South Korean president Chung Hee Park, momentum for a large steel plant grew in the late 1960s. In 1967 the South Korean government and Korean International Steel Associates (KISA) — a consortium of seven Western steelmakers — signed an agreement that called for the completion of an integrated mill by 1972. Pohang Iron & Steel Co. (POSCO), the operating company, was incorporated in 1968. Efforts to raise the necessary capital failed, however, and KISA was dissolved in 1969.

Undaunted, the South Koreans turned to the Japanese, who arranged loans covering most of the mill's costs and the early phases of planning and construction. The Japanese also transferred the technology needed to run such a plant. Slow and deliberate planning resulted in a plant far away from Seoul (part of a plan to locate industries throughout the country) and a design that lent itself to future expansion. The first stage, including a blast furnace and two steel converters, was completed in 1973. By the time the fourth stage of construction began in 1979, the Koreans had gained enough confidence to take over many of the tasks. When the last stage was completed in 1981, the plant had an annual capacity of 8.5 million tons.

To ensure steel of acceptable quality, POSCO focused first on plain high-carbon steel for general construction, rather than on specialized (and difficult to produce) varieties. The company gradually broadened its specialized offerings.

In 1985 POSCO began construction on a second integrated steel plant located in Kwangyang. That plant was also built in four stages; its annual production capacity, when it was completed in 1992, was 11.4 million tons. By 1987 POSCO was exporting almost 3 million tons of steel a year and using its knowledge to assist in plant construction projects in other countries.

By the mid-1990s POSCO was exporting 6 million tons of steel annually. The South Korean government sold a 5% stake in POSCO to the public in 1998 and vowed to open up the primary steelmaking industry to competition. However, facing a severe downturn in steel demand that year because of sluggishness in Asian and domestic markets, the company canceled two projects in China and suspended two in Indonesia. In 1999 POSCO merged its two subsidiaries, Pohang Coated Steel and Pohang Steel Industries, to create Pohang Steel Co. That same year POSCO Machinery & Engineering, POSEC-HAWAII, and P.T. Posnesia Stainless Steel Industry were joined to form POSCO Machinery Co. The South Korean government continued selling off its 13% stake in 1999.

In 2000 POSCO sold its 51% stake in telecommunications company Shinsegi Telecom to SK Telecom in exchange for cash and a 6.5% stake in SK Telecom. It also formed a strategic alliance exploration of joint ventures, shared research, and joint procurement — with Nippon Steel, the world's #1 steel maker. The deal also calls for each to take increased equity stakes (2% or 3%) in the other. After about 30 years of government control, the South Korean government sold its remaining shares of POSCO in 2001.

In June 2002 Chairman Yoo was indicted for influencing POSCO subsidiaries and contractors to buy inflated shares of Tiger Pools International (South Korea's sole sports lottery business) for Kim Hong-Gul, the third son of South Korean President Kim Dae-Jung. That same year Pohang Iron & Steel Co. officially changed its company name to POSCO to try and strengthen brand recognition.

In 2003 Yoo resigned ahead of the company's shareholder meeting amid his possible involvement in illegal stock transactions.

EXECUTIVES

Chairman and CEO: Lee Ku-Taek, age 58
President: Kang Chang-Oh, age 61
CFO and Director: Lee Dong-Hee, age 57
SEVP: Choi Kwang-Woong, age 59
SEVP, Corporate Communications and Secretary: Yoon Seok-Man, age 54
SEVP, General Superintendent, Pohang Works: Ryoo Kyeong-Ryul, age 55
SEVP, POSCO China President: Kim Dong-Jin, age 57
SEVP, Stainless Steel Division Manager, Stainless Steel Raw Materials Procurement Department: Lee Youn, age 56
EVP, Cold Rolled Steel Sales, Automotive Flat Panel Sales Dept., and Coated Steel Sales: Choi Jong-Doo, age 57
EVP, Corporate Strategic Planning, and Director: Cho Soung-Sik, age 56
EVP, General Administration, Human Resources, and Labor and Welfare: Choi Jong-Tae, age 54
EVP, General Superintendent, Gwangyang Works: Chung Joon-Yang, age 55
EVP, General Superintendent, Technology Research Center: Hur Nam-Suk, age 53
EVP, Legal Affairs: Kim Sang-Ho, age 50
SVP, Coal Procurement, Iron Ore Procurement, Steel Raw Material Procurement, and Stainless Steel Raw Material Procurement: Kwon Young-Tae, age 53
SVP, Corporate Communications: Kim Sang-Young
SVP, Corporate Ethics and Audit: Park Han-Yong, age 53
SVP, European Union Office: Kwon Oh-Joon, age 53
SVP, General Superintendent, Human Resources Development Center: Kim Chang-Ho, age 57
SVP, Marketing Strategy, Market Development, Sales, and Production Planning: Oh Chang-Kwan, age 51
Auditors: Samil Pricewaterhousecoopers

LOCATIONS

HQ: POSCO
POSCO Center, 892 Daechi-4-dong, Kangnam-ku, Seoul, South Korea
Phone: +82-2-3457-0114   **Fax:** +82-54-220-6000
US HQ: 2 Executive Dr., Ste. 805, Fort Lee, NJ 07024
US Phone: 201-585-3060   **US Fax:** 201-585-6001
Web: www.posco.co.kr

POSCO operates subsidiary companies throughout the world.

2005 Sales

	% of total
Asia	
South Korea	71
China	12
Japan	5
Other countries	6
North America	2
Other regions	4
Total	**100**

PRODUCTS/OPERATIONS

2005 Production

	Tons (thou.)	% of total
Cold-rolled	10,468	34
Hot-rolled	10,330	33
Plates	3,194	10
Wire rods	2,367	8
Stainless steel	1,919	6
Silicon steel sheets	737	2
Other	2,100	7
Total	**31,115**	**100**

COMPETITORS

Bechtel
Corus Group
Fluor
Hitachi
JFE Holdings
Kobe Steel
Marubeni
Mittal Steel Company
Nippon Steel
Samsung Group
Shanghai Baosteel
ThyssenKrupp

HISTORICAL FINANCIALS

Company Type: Public

Income Statement

FYE: December 31

	REVENUE ($ mil.)	NET INCOME ($ mil.)	NET PROFIT MARGIN	EMPLOYEES
12/05	26,041	3,972	15.3%	28,853
12/04	23,973	3,460	14.4%	27,919
12/03	14,924	1,675	11.2%	27,415
12/02	11,484	815	7.1%	27,100
Annual Growth	**31.4%**	**69.6%**	**—**	**2.1%**

2005 Year-End Financials

Debt ratio: 5.8%
Return on equity: 22.4%
Cash ($ mil.): 4,077
Current ratio: 1.98
Long-term debt ($ mil.): 1,120

No. of shares (mil.): —
Dividends
  Yield: 0.8%
  Payout: —
Market value ($ mil.): —

Stock History

NYSE: PKX

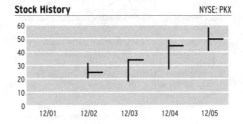

	STOCK PRICE ($) FY Close	P/E High/Low		PER SHARE ($) Earnings	Dividends
12/05	49.51	—	—	—	0.40
12/04	44.53	—	—	0.00	1.61
12/03	33.97	—	—	—	1.06
12/02	24.73	—	—	—	0.59
Annual Growth	**26.0%**	**—**	**—**	**—**	**(12.2%)**

PPR

PPR (formerly Pinault-Printemps-Redoute) might have its roots in timber, but its branches are now firmly in the retail arena. The company axed its timber and building materials business, electrical equipment supplier Rexel, and its consumer credit unit to focus on its retail businesses, which include catalogs (Redcats) and luxury goods (Gucci and Yves Saint Laurent). PPR has become the world's third-largest luxury group via its 99% stake in Italian luxury goods company Gucci Group, and several perfume lines. More than 50% of PPR's sales are generated outside its home country France. Founder François Pinault's investment firm, Artémis, owns 43% of PPR. The company changed its name to PPR in 2005.

The firm has transformed itself from a conglomerate to a focused luxury retail group. The "New PPR," as the company likes to call itself, also has new leadership: François-Henri Pinault, the son of the company's founder, joined the company as its new CEO in March 2005, replacing longtime chief Serge Weinberg.

In addition to Gucci and Yves Saint Laurent, PPR's stable of luxury brands includes Alexander McQueen, Balenciaga, Bottega Veneta, and the Stella McCartney brands, among others. As part of its strategy to focus on its luxury business, PPR recently sold its Paris-based department store chain Printemps.

The retail group includes the world's #3 catalog merchant, Redcats, with distribution in the US and Europe. The division also operates Conforama, France's #1 appliance retailer with about 245 stores in France and seven other countries in Europe; and Fnac book and music stores. Fnac operates more than 110 stores (40-plus outside of France) in five European countries and Brazil. Fnac is considered the next likely target for disposal following PPR's sale of its Printemps department store chain in 2006.

To fund its transformation, PPR sold Guilbert and Pinault Bois & Matériaux (lumber and building supplies) to shore up its balance sheet and fund its offer for the rest of Gucci in 2004.

Self-made billionaire and founder François Pinault has a cache of prestigious businesses, including auction house Christie's.

HISTORY

Sixteen-year-old François Pinault left school in 1952 to join the family timber business. He took over the firm when his father died in 1963; that year the company was renamed Pinault Group. Pinault diversified the company into wood importing and retailing, eventually building a flourishing enterprise. In 1973 Pinault began to show his talent for the art of the deal. Sensing the demand for timber was peaking, he sold 80% of the business, buying it back two years later at an 85% discount.

During the 1970s Pinault bought struggling timber businesses and turned them around. (He was helped, in part, by a policy of the French government that subsidized purchases of failing companies in order to preserve jobs.) Pinault purchased bankrupt wood panel manufacturer Isoroy in 1986 for a token fee. In 1987 he bought ailing paper company Chapelle Darblay, selling it three years later at a 40% profit.

By 1988, when it filed to go public on the Paris exchange, Pinault Group was a vertically integrated timber manufacturing, trading, and distribution company.

Pinault began to diversify outside the timber industry in the 1990s. It acquired electrical equipment distributor CFAO (Compagnie Française de l'Afrique Occidentale) in 1990, the Conforama furniture chain in 1991, and Au Printemps (owner of Printemps stores and 54% of catalog company Redoute) in 1992. The firm then became the Pinault-Printemps Group. The purchase of Au Printemps left the company heavily in debt, and it sold some of its noncore assets during the early 1990s.

In 1993 Pinault-Printemps bought a majority stake in Groupelec and merged it with electrical equipment subsidiary CDME, forming Rexel. In 1994 the company completed its acquisition of Redoute. After renaming itself Pinault-Printemps-Redoute (PPR), it bought a majority stake in French book and music retailer Fnac (buying the rest in 1995). In 1995 Rexel head Serge Weinberg took over the company after CEO Pierre Blayau ran afoul of Pinault over strategy. PPR added West African pharmaceuticals distributor SCOA in 1996. While Rexel gobbled up 11 companies in Europe and the US that year, PPR launched a new chain of women's lingerie stores called Orcanta and started its own venture capital fund.

PPR acquired Becob, France's #3 building materials distributor, in 1997. Expanding globally, Redcats (Redoute's new name) launched the Vertbaudet (children's wear) and Cyrillus (sportswear) catalogs in the UK that year.

In 1998 PPR bought a majority stake in Guilbert, the European leader in office supplies and furniture, and a 44% stake in Brylane (renamed Redcats USA in 2004), the US's #4 mail-order company. PPR bought the remainder of Brylane in 1999. Later that year, PPR sparked a string of legal battles between it and LVMH when it purchased 42% of luxury goods maker Gucci. (The move thwarted LVMH's efforts to take over Gucci by diluting LVMH's stake in the firm.) In 2000 PPR bought France's largest computer retailer, Surcouf.

In March 2001 a Dutch court granted a request by LVMH and ordered an investigation into the legality of the alliance of PPR and Gucci. In a deal to end years of litigation, PPR purchased LVMH's stake in Gucci for $806.5 million in October 2001, increasing its ownership to 53.2%.

The company sold Yves Saint Laurent's haute couture division to French dressmaking company SLPB Prestige Services in March 2002. Guilbert's mail-order business was sold to US office supplies retailer Staples in October of that year for $815 million. (The rest of Guilbert was later sold to Office Depot in May 2003.) In June 2003, PPR's timber wholesale business, Pinault Bois & Matériaux, was sold to the UK's Wolseley plc. In December PPR sold 14.5% of Finaref and Finaref Nordic to Agricole. Also in 2003, PPR increased its stake in Gucci to 67.58%.

In 2005 François-Henri Pinault, the son of the company's founder, joined the company as its new CEO, succeeding Serge Weinberg. During his 10 years at the helm, Weinberg oversaw the transformation of the company from a business-to-business concern to a focused luxury retail group. That year the company changed its name to PPR from Pinault-Printemps-Redoute.

In 2006, as part of its strategy to focus on its luxury business, PPR sold its Paris-based department store chain Printemps to Italy's La Rinascente for about $1.3 billion. The divestiture included all of the chain's 17 stores.

EXECUTIVES

Chairman and CEO: François-Henri Pinault, age 44
CFO: Jean-François Palus, age 44
Chairman and CEO, CFAO: Alain Viry, age 57
Chairman and CEO, Conforama: Christophe Cuvillier, age 43
Chairman and CEO, Fnac: Denis Olivennes, age 45
Chairman and CEO, France-Printemps: Laurence Danon, age 50
Chairman, President, and CEO, Gucci Group: Robert Polet, age 50
Chairman and CEO, Redcats: Thierry Falque-Pierrotin, age 42
Director, Communications: Laurent Claquin, age 35
Director, Human Resources: Alain Luchez, age 54
Director, External Relations: Peggy Nahmany, age 37
Head of Corporate Social Responsibility: Estelle Kistner-L'Hour, age 36
Corporate Secretary: Gérard Mothe, age 53
Press Officer Manager: Catherine Malek
Auditors: Deloitte Touche Tohmatsu; KPMG Audit

LOCATIONS

HQ: PPR SA
  10, Avenue Hoche, 75381 Paris, France
Phone: +33-1-45-64-61-00   **Fax:** +33-1-44-90-62-25
Web: www.ppr.com

2005 Sales

	% of total
Europe	
France	49
Other countries	24
Americas	11
Africa	9
Asia	6
Oceania	1
Total	**100**

PRODUCTS/OPERATIONS

2005 Sales

	% of total
Retail	83
Luxury goods	17
Total	**100**

Operations

Luxury Goods
  Gucci Group N.V. (99.39%, leather goods and apparel)
Retail
  CFAO (distribution of automobiles, motorcycles, pharmaceuticals, and consumer goods in Africa and French territories)
  Conforama (furniture and appliances; Croatia, France, Italy, Luxembourg, Portugal, Spain, and Switzerland)
  Fnac (electronics, books, music; Belgium, Brazil, France, Italy, Monaco, Portugal, Spain, Switzerland, and Taiwan)
  Redcats (catalogs, including Brylane, Daxon, Ellos, and Redoute)

COMPETITORS

Amazon.com
Burberry
C&A
Carrefour
Casino Guichard
Galeries Lafayette
IKEA
LVMH
METRO AG
Otto
Pier Import Europe
Virgin Group
Vivarte

HISTORICAL FINANCIALS

Company Type: Public

Income Statement

FYE: December 31

	REVENUE ($ mil.)	NET INCOME ($ mil.)	NET PROFIT MARGIN	EMPLOYEES
12/05	21,040	679	3.2%	84,316
12/04	33,026	1,283	3.9%	95,397
12/03	30,578	809	2.6%	102,381
12/02	28,692	1,666	5.8%	113,453
12/01	24,624	667	2.7%	115,935
Annual Growth	**(3.9%)**	**0.5%**	**—**	**(7.7%)**

Net Income History

Euronext Paris: PP

Pricewaterhouse-Coopers

Not merely the firm with the longest one-word name, PricewaterhouseCoopers (PwC) is also one of the world's largest accounting firms, formed when Price Waterhouse merged with Coopers & Lybrand in 1998, passing then-leader Andersen. The accountancy has some 770 offices in 149 countries around the world, providing clients with services in three lines of business: Assurance (including financial and regulatory reporting), Tax, and Advisory. The umbrella entity for the PwC worldwide organization (officially PricewaterhouseCoopers International) is one of accounting's Big Four, along with Deloitte Touche Tohmatsu, Ernst & Young, and KPMG. PwC serves some of the world's largest businesses, as well as smaller firms.

PwC puts its heft to good use: Non-North American clients make up nearly two-thirds of the firm's sales. Its bottom line, though, changed significantly in 2002, when PwC sold its consulting arm to IBM. A separation had been under consideration for years in light of SEC concerns about conflicts of interest when firms perform auditing and consulting for the same clients. The collapse of Enron and concomitant downfall of Enron's auditor and PwC's erstwhile peer Andersen undoubtedly hastened plans to spin off PwC's consultancy via an IPO, which was scrapped in favor of the IBM deal. PwC has expanded in developing economies, including Brazil, China, India, and Russia; business also got a temporary boost from the implementation of such new regulatory and financial reporting rules as the International Financial Reporting Standards and the Sarbanes-Oxley Act. Like the other members of the Big Four, PwC picked up business and talent as scandal-felled Andersen was winding down its operations in 2002. The former Andersen organization in China and Hong Kong joined PwC, accounting for about 70% of the approximately 3,500 Andersen alumni that came aboard. The company endured a two-month suspension in Japan in 2006 after three partners of its firm there were implicated in a fraud investigation involving a PwC client, Kanebo. To distance itself from the scandal PwC's existing Japanese firm was renamed and a second firm was launched.

HISTORY

In 1850 Samuel Price founded an accounting firm in London and in 1865 took on partner Edwin Waterhouse. The firm and the industry grew rapidly, thanks to the growth of stock exchanges that required uniform financial statements from listees. By the late 1800s Price Waterhouse (PW) had become the world's best-known accounting firm.

US offices were opened in the 1890s, and in 1902 United States Steel chose the firm as its auditor. PW benefited from tough audit requirements instituted after the 1929 stock market crash. In 1935 the firm was given the prestigious job of handling Academy Awards balloting. It started a management consulting service in 1946. But PW's dominance slipped in the 1960s, as it gained a reputation as the most traditional and formal of the major firms.

Coopers & Lybrand, the product of a 1957 transatlantic merger, wrote the book on auditing. Lybrand, Ross Bros. & Montgomery was formed in 1898 by William Lybrand, Edward Ross, Adam Ross, and Robert Montgomery. In 1912 Montgomery wrote *Montgomery's Auditing,* which became the bible of accounting.

Cooper Brothers was founded in 1854 in London by William Cooper, eldest son of a Quaker banker. In 1957 Lybrand joined up to form Coopers & Lybrand. During the 1960s the firm expanded into employee benefits and internal control consulting, building its technology capabilities in the 1970s as it studied ways to automate the audit process.

Coopers & Lybrand lost market share as mergers reduced the Big Eight accounting firms to the Big Six. After the savings and loan debacle of the 1980s, investors and the government wanted accounting firms held liable not only for the form of audited financial statements but for their veracity. In 1992 the firm paid $95 million to settle claims of defrauded investors in MiniScribe, a failed disk-drive maker. Other hefty payments followed, including a $108 million settlement relating to the late Robert Maxwell's defunct media empire.

In 1998 Price Waterhouse and Coopers & Lybrand combined PW's strength in the media, entertainment, and utility industries, and Coopers & Lybrand's focus on telecommunications and mining. But the merger brought some expensive legal baggage involving Coopers & Lybrand's performance of audits related to a bid-rigging scheme involving former Arizona governor Fife Symington.

Further growth plans fell through in 1999 when merger talks between PwC and Grant Thornton International failed. The year 2000 began on a sour note: An SEC conflict-of-interest probe turned up more than 8,000 alleged violations, most involving PwC partners owning stock in their firm's audit clients. As the SEC grew ever more shrill in its denunciation of the potential conflicts of interest arising from auditing companies that the firm hoped to recruit or retain as consulting clients, PwC saw the writing on the wall and in 2000 began making plans to split the two operations. As part of this move, the company downsized and reorganized many of its operations.

The following year PwC paid $55 million to shareholders of MicroStrategy Inc., who charged that the audit firm defrauded them by approving the client firm's inflated earnings and revenues figures.

The separation of PwC's auditing and consulting functions finally became a reality in 2002, when IBM bought the consulting business. (The acquisition took the place of a planned spinoff.) In 2003 former client AMERCO (parent of U-Haul) sued PwC for $2.5 billion, claiming negligence and fraud in relation to a series of events that led to AMERCO restating its results. The suit was settled for more than $50 million the following year.

In 2005 PwC was ranked among the Top 10 companies in the US for working mothers by *Working Mother* magazine.

EXECUTIVES

Global CEO and Global Board Member:
Samuel A. (Sam) DiPiazza Jr., age 54
Global Managing Partner, Advisory and Tax:
Eugene (Gene) Donnelly
Global Managing Partner, Assurance:
Robert (Rob) Ward
Global Managing Partner, Markets and Operations:
Paul Boorman
Global Co-Leader, People: Richard L. Baird
Global Managing Partner, Markets: Willem L. J. Bröcker
Global Managing Partner, Risk and Quality:
Michael O. (Mike) Gagnon
Global General Counsel; Acting US General Counsel:
Lawrence W. Keeshan
Global Leader, Industries: Alec N. Jones
Global Leader, Regulatory and Public Policy:
Richard R. Kilgust
Senior Partner and CEO, Australia:
Anthony P.D. Harrington
CEO and Senior Partner of PricewaterhouseCoopers LLP, Canada: Christie J. B. Clark
Territory/Regional Leader, Central and Eastern Europe:
John K. Heywood
Chairman, Asia 7 Leadership Team; Executive Chairman, PricewaterhouseCoopers Singapore:
Gautam Banerjee
Chairman, UK: Kieran C. Poynter
Chairman and Senior Partner US: Dennis M. Nally
Global Leader, Entertainment and Media Practice:
R. Wayne Jackson
Global Co-Leader, Human Capital:
Marie-Jeanne Chèvremont-Lorenzini
Senior Managing Director, Global Public Relations:
Peter Horowitz

LOCATIONS

HQ: PricewaterhouseCoopers International Limited
1177 Avenue of the Americas, New York, NY 10036
Phone: 646-471-4000   **Fax:** 646-471-3188
Web: www.pwcglobal.com

PricewaterhouseCoopers has more than 770 offices in 149 countries.

2006 Sales

	% of total
Europe	
Western Europe	41
Central & Eastern Europe	2
North America & Caribbean	38
Asia	10
Australasia & Pacific Islands	4
Middle East & Africa	3
South & Central America	2
Total	**100**

PRODUCTS/OPERATIONS

2006 Sales by Industry

	% of total
Industrial Products	17
Banking & Capital Markets	11
Retail & Consumer	11
Investment Management	10
Technology	9
Professional Services	9
Energy, Utilities & Mining	8
Insurance	5
Entertainment & Media	5
Infocomm	4
Automotive	3
Health Care	3
Government	3
Pharmaceuticals	2
Total	**100**

2006 Sales

	% of total
Assurance	54
Tax	25
Advisory	21
Total	**100**

Selected Products and Services

Audit and Assurance
  Actuarial services
  Assistance on capital market transactions
  Corporate reporting improvement
  Financial accounting
  Financial statement audit
  IFRS reporting
  Independent controls and systems process assurance
  Internal audit
  Regulatory compliance and reporting
  Sarbanes-Oxley compliance
  Sustainability reporting
Crisis Management
  Business recovery services
  Dispute analysis and investigations
Human Resources
  Change and program effectiveness
  HR management
  International assignments
  Reward
Performance Improvement
  Financial effectiveness
  Governance, risk, and compliance
  IT effectiveness
Tax
  Compliance
  EU direct tax
  International assignments
  International tax structuring
  Mergers and acquisitions
  Transfer pricing
Transactions
  Accounting valuations
  Advice on fundraising
  Bid support and bid defense services
  Commercial and market due diligence
  Economics
  Financial due diligence
  Independent expert opinions
  Mergers and acquisitions advisory
  Modeling and business planning
  Post deal services
  Private equity advisory
  Privatization advice
  Project finance
  Public company advisory
  Structuring services
  Tax valuations
  Valuation consulting

COMPETITORS

Bain & Company	H&R Block
Baker Tilly International	Hewitt Associates
BDO International	KPMG
Booz Allen	Marsh & McLennan
Boston Consulting	McKinsey & Company
Deloitte	Towers Perrin
Ernst & Young	Watson Wyatt
Grant Thornton	

HISTORICAL FINANCIALS

Company Type: Partnership

Income Statement

FYE: June 30

	REVENUE ($ mil.)	NET INCOME ($ mil.)	NET PROFIT MARGIN	EMPLOYEES
6/06	21,986	—	—	142,162
6/05	18,998	—	—	130,203
6/04	16,283	—	—	122,471
6/03	14,683	—	—	122,820
6/02	13,800	—	—	124,563
Annual Growth	12.3%	—	—	3.4%

Revenue History

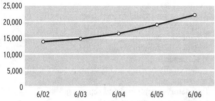

Prudential

The Man from the Pru now surfs the Internet. The company is known for its iconic Man from the Pru agent, now relegated to memory after being supplanted by other sales channels. Prudential is the UK's second-largest insurer (after Aviva); it also has significant operations in Asia and the US. In addition to insurance, Prudential's UK businesses include its banking division; products include pensions, investment bonds, and personal loans. In Asia, the company sells life insurance, savings, and investment products through its Prudential Corporation Asia unit. In the US, Prudential owns Jackson National Life, which offers annuities and life insurance. Other businesses include fund manager M&G.

In early 2006 Prudential rejected a takeover offer from larger rival Aviva valued at nearly $30 billion. Prudential's formerly publicly listed Egg subsidiary offers telephone and Internet banking services, as well as mortgages and VISA credit cards, and is expanding into online brokerage. Overhauling its UK operations, Prudential abolished its direct sales force (some 2,000 people) and is concentrating on sales by phone and through the Internet. It began divesting noncore assets to concentrate on life insurance, group pensions, and with-profit bonds. The consolidation drive also saw Prudential dropping its Scottish Amicable products, which were rebranded under the Prudential name. Late in 2006 Prudential said it was toying with the possibility of further consolidation, including integrating Egg with its life insurance operations,

and then offloading the whole unit. How do you say Pru in Mandarin? The company is well into an expansion strategy in the world's largest marketplace. It is the first European life insurer to gain licenses to operate in ten cities in China through its CITIC Prudential joint venture with China's CITIC Group.

HISTORY

Actually, prudence almost killed Prudential before it ever got started. Founded in 1848 as Prudential Mutual Assurance Investment and Loan Association, the firm initially insured middle-class customers. The Dickensian conditions of the working poor made them too risky for insurers. Unfortunately the company found few takers of the right sort, and by 1852 Prudential was in peril.

Two events saved Prudential: The House of Commons pressed for insurance coverage for all classes, and Prudential's own agents pushed for change. The company expanded into industrial insurance, a modest coverage for the working poor. In 1864, to quell criticism of the insurance industry, Prudential brought in independent auditors to confirm its soundness. This soon became a marketing tool and business took off. The Pru, as it came to be known, became the leading industrial insurer by the 1880s. It covered half the country's population by 1905. The firm's salesmen were known for making personal visits to customers (the "Man from the Pru" became a ubiquitous icon in the 1940s and was revived in 1997).

During the two world wars Prudential boosted its reputation by honoring the policies of war victims when it could have legally denied them. Between wars the company added fire and accident insurance in Europe.

In 1969 it bought Mercantile and General Reinsurance Company from Swiss Re.

In 1982, under the direction of CEO Brian Corby, the Pru reorganized product lines and in 1985 entered the real estate business. In 1986 it entered the US market by buying US-based Jackson National Life. The 1980s were volatile for insurance companies, especially in the wake of Britain's financial deregulation in 1986.

Prudential, which had considered selling Mercantile and General Reinsurance in the early 1990s, sold the reinsurer back to Swiss Re in 1996. It also formed Prudential Bank and created an Asian emerging-market investment fund that year.

In 1997 Prudential bought Scottish Amicable. Insurance regulators reprimanded the company for mis-selling financial products that year.

In 1998 Jackson National bought a California savings and loan, enabling it to sell investment products in the US. Also that year the Pru sold its Australian and New Zealand businesses, and Prudential Bank launched its pioneering Internet bank Egg. In 1999 Prudential bought investment manager M & G Group and to reduce costs it announced plans to cut more than 5,000 jobs in the subsequent three years.

The company changed its name to Prudential plc and began talks with the Prudential Insurance Company of America to resolve confusion of their similar names as they expanded into new markets. The Pru in 1999 joined forces with the Bank of China to offer pension and asset management in Hong Kong.

In 2000 the company announced plans to sell a chunk of its institutional fund management business as well as its traditional balanced pension business to Deutsche Bank. That year the company spun off 20% of Egg. Also in 2000 the company agreed to start an insurance joint venture in China with state-owned investment vehicle CITIC Group.

Entering the Japanese life insurance market, Prudential bought Orico Life in 2001. Prudential's hopes of capturing the lucrative annuities market by acquiring American General were dashed in 2001; American General instead embraced American International Group, leaving the Pru with a $600 million break-up fee.

To consolidate operations in 2001, the firm sold its general insurance business to Swiss insurer Winterthur (a subsidiary of Credit Suisse) and dropped its Scottish Amicable products, which were rebranded under the Prudential name.

EXECUTIVES

Chairman: Sir David C. Clementi, age 57, $837,897 pay
Group Chief Executive and Board Member: Mark Tucker, age 47
Group Finance Director and Board Member: Philip Broadley, age 45, $1,444,650 pay
Chief Executive, The M&G Group, and Board Member: Michael McLintock, age 44, $3,305,359 pay
Chief Executive, Prudential Corporation of Asia: Barry Stowe, age 48
President and CEO, Jackson National Life, and Board Member: Clark P. Manning Jr., age 46, $2,825,736 pay
Chief Executive, Prudential UK and European Insurance Operations, and Board Member: Nicholas E. T. (Nick) Prettejohn, age 45
Group Human Resources Director: Jane Kibbey
Group Communications Director: Rebecca Burrows
Group Legal Services Director and Secretary: Peter Maynard
Group Corporate Relations Director: Geraldine Davies
Head of Business Development Services: Pamela (Pam) Aurbach
EVP, Information Technology: J. George Napoles
EVP, Corporate Development: Jim Sopha
CEO, Egg plc: Ian Kerr
Vice Chairman and COO, Jackson National Life: Mike Wells
EVP and Chief Distribution Officer, Jackson National Life: Clifford J. Jack
Auditors: KPMG Audit Plc

LOCATIONS

HQ: Prudential plc
Laurence Pountney Hill,
London EC4R 0HH, United Kingdom
Phone: +44-20-7220-7588 **Fax:** +44-20-7548-3699
US HQ: Jackson National Life, 1 Corporate Way,
Lansing, MI 48951
US Phone: 517-381-5500 **US Fax:** 517-706-5517
Web: www.prudential.co.uk

PRODUCTS/OPERATIONS

Selected Subsidiaries and Affiliates

Egg plc
Egg Banking plc
Jackson National Life Insurance Company (US)
M&G Investment Management Limited
PCA Life Assurance Company Limited (99%, Taiwan)
Prudential Annuities Limited
Prudential Assurance Company Singapore (Pte) Limited
Prudential Retirement Income Limited
The Prudential Assurance Company Limited

HISTORICAL FINANCIALS

Company Type: Public

Income Statement

FYE: December 31

	ASSETS ($ mil.)	NET INCOME ($ mil.)	INCOME AS % OF ASSETS	EMPLOYEES
12/05	360,294	2,051	0.6%	23,248
12/04	335,340	175	0.1%	21,500
12/03	290,920	1,183	0.4%	21,012
12/02	246,068	(573)	—	21,930
12/01	225,952	(592)	—	23,047
Annual Growth	12.4%	—	—	0.2%

2005 Year-End Financials

Equity as % of assets: 3.4%
Return on assets: 0.6%
Return on equity: 17.2%
Long-term debt ($ mil.): 30,162
No. of shares (mil.): —
Dividends
Yield: 3.0%
Payout: —
Market value ($ mil.): —
Sales ($ mil.): 70,453

Stock History

NYSE: PUK

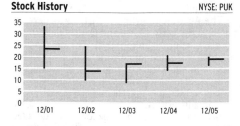

	STOCK PRICE ($) FY Close	P/E High/Low		PER SHARE ($) Earnings	Dividends
12/05	19.10	—	—	—	0.58
12/04	17.40	511	360	0.04	1.07
12/03	17.05	—	—	—	0.74
12/02	13.87	—	—	—	0.76
12/01	23.43	—	—	(0.30)	0.71
Annual Growth	(5.0%)	—	—	—	(4.9%)

Publicis

Advertising is *la joie de vivre* for Publicis. One of the world's largest advertising and media services conglomerates, the company provides a wide range of corporate communication and media services, including creative advertising, media and campaign planning, marketing, and public relations. Its flagship advertising networks include Leo Burnett Worldwide, Publicis Worldwide, and Saatchi & Saatchi; Publicis' Starcom MediaVest and ZenithOptimedia units are among the world's largest media planning enterprises. The company serves such clients as Cadbury, Coca-Cola, General Mills, and Procter & Gamble through offices in about 110 countries.

Publicis is the leading provider of advertising and marketing services in Europe and ranks behind only Omnicom, WPP Group, and Interpublic in worldwide revenue. Its media services operations rank #2 behind WPP Group's MindShare and Mediaedge:cia in total worldwide billings. In addition, its Specialized Agencies and Marketing Services division provides marketing and communications services through a number of agencies, including Arc Worldwide (relationship marketing); Burrell Communications (multicultural advertising); and Manning, Selvage & Lee (public relations).

The company has been working to consolidate many of its operating units following a string of acquisitions, including its $3 billion purchase of Bcom3 in 2002. In the US it folded Publicis Sanchez & Levitan into Bromley Communications to form America's top Hispanic ad agency, while it combined several marketing firms (including Frankel and Semaphore Partners) to form Arc Worldwide. Publicis' acquisition of Bcom3 cemented its worldwide standing and gave the company a large foothold in the US, adding Leo Burnett and Starcom MediaVest to its holdings.

In July 2006 Publicis bought France-based BOZ Group, a specialist in health care communications. BOZ joins Medicus Paris and Saatchi & Saatchi Healthcare Paris in the Publicis Healthcare Communications Group (PHCG). Zeroing in on the Asian market, Publicis acquired events management group Emotion in October the same year. Emotion owns offices in Bangkok, Beijing, Manila, Seoul, Shanghai, Tokyo, and Singapore.

Elisabeth Badinter, daughter of late founder Marcel Bleustein-Blanchet, controls about 10% of Publicis. Japanese advertising giant Dentsu has a 9% stake in the company.

HISTORY

In 1926 Marcel Bleustein, then 19 years old, started France's first advertising agency, which he called Publicis (a takeoff on "publicity" and "six"). He launched his own radio station, Radio Cite, after the French government banned all advertising on state-run stations, and by 1939 he had expanded into film distribution and movie theaters. With the outbreak of WWII, Bleustein fled to London to serve with the Free French Forces.

Having adopted the name Bleustein-Blanchet, he returned to France following the liberation and revived his advertising business. In 1958 he bought the former Hotel Astoria on the Champs-Elysées and opened the first Le Drugstore. The original structure burned in a 1972 fire, and legend has it that Bleustein-Blanchet tapped Maurice Lévy to lead the company after he found Lévy salvaging records amid the ruins.

To expand its business, Publicis formed an alliance — Chicago-based Foote, Cone & Belding Communications (FCB) — in 1988. The partnership soured five years later, however, when Publicis acquired France's Groupe FCA. (FCB claimed the acquisition was a breach of contract and countered by establishing a new holding company for itself, True North Communications.) Bleustein-Blanchet died in 1996, and his daughter, Elisabeth Badinter, was named chair of the supervisory board.

In 1997 Publicis and True North divided their joint network, Publicis Communications, with True North getting the European offices and Publicis getting Africa, Asia, and Argentina. Later that year Publicis attempted a $700 million hostile bid for the 81.5% of True North it didn't already own to stop True North's acquisition of Bozell, Jacobs, Kenyon & Eckhardt. The bid failed, and Publicis' stake in True North was reduced to 11%. (True North was later acquired by Interpublic Group in 2001.)

The company gained new ground in the US through its acquisitions of Hal Riney & Partners and Evans Group in 1998. That year Lévy helped sooth a bitter feud among the descendants of Marcel Bleustein: Elisabeth Badinter had battled with her sister Michele Bleustein-Blanchet over Bleustein-Blanchet's desire to sell her stake in Publicis' holding company. Lévy's solution allowed Bleustein-Blanchet to sell her shares and left Badinter with control of the company.

Continuing its US expansion, in 1999 Publicis bought a 49% stake in Burrell Communications Group (one of the largest African-American-owned ad agencies in the US).

In 2000 the company bought advertising outfit Fallon McElligott (now Fallon Worldwide), marketing firm Frankel & Co., and media buyer DeWitt Media (which was merged into Optimedia). Publicis capped off the year by acquiring Saatchi & Saatchi for about $1.9 billion. Along with the deal, it inherited Saatchi's 50% of media buying unit Zenith Media (jointly owned by Cordiant Communications). In 2001 it merged Optimedia and Zenith, with Publicis owning 75% of the new business.

2002 was a big year for Publicis and the ad industry in general; the decision to acquire Bcom3 catapulted the company into the really big leagues and created a distinct size difference between the top four advertising conglomerates and everyone else.

From 2002 to 2005, the company worked on integrating Bcom3 and Saatchi & Saatchi into its operational infrastructure, as well as making small but selective acquisitions in order to maximize debt reduction.

EXECUTIVES

Chairperson, Supervisory Board: Elisabeth Badinter, age 62
Chairman, Management Board, and CEO: Maurice Lévy, age 64
Chairman, Fallon Worldwide: Patrick (Pat) Fallon
Chairman, Public Relations and Corporate Communications Group: Louis (Lou) Capozzi
Chairman, Publicis Groupe Media: Jack Klues, age 51
Chairman, Saatchi & Saatchi Worldwide and Director, Supervisory Board: Robert L. (Bob) Seelert, age 64
Chairman, Publicis Worldwide: Olivier Fleurot, age 54
Chairman and CEO, Leo Burnett Worldwide; CEO, Leo Burnett USA: Thomas (Tom) Bernardin, age 52

Chairman and CEO, Médias & Régies Europe and
 Director, Supervisory Board: Simon Badinter, age 38
Chairman and CEO, Publicis USA: Susan M. Gianinno,
 age 55
Chairman and CEO, Publicis Network France;
 Chairman and CEO, Saatchi & Saatchi France:
 Philippe Lentschener, age 49
Chairman and Worldwide Creative Director, Bartle
 Bogle Hegarty: John Hegarty
President and CEO, Specialized Agencies and
 Marketing Services: John Farrell
CEO, Saatchi & Saatchi Worldwide and Director,
 Management Board: Kevin J. Roberts, age 57
EVP and CFO: Jean-Michel Etienne, age 54
EVP Operations: Jean-Yves Naouri, age 46
EVP, Publicis Worldwide and Director, Management
 Board: Bertrand Siguier, age 65
General Secretary: Fabrice Fries, age 46
Director of Investor Relations: Pierre Bénaich
Corporate Communications: Eve Magnant
Auditors: Ernst & Young Audit; Mazars & Guérard

LOCATIONS

HQ: Publicis Groupe S.A.
 133, avenue des Champs-Elysées,
 75008 Paris, France
Phone: +33-1-44-43-70-00   Fax: +33-1-44-43-75-25
US HQ: 950 6th Ave., New York, NY 10001
US Phone: 212-279-5550   US Fax: 212-279-5560
Web: www.publicis.fr/corporate/en

Publicis has about 180 offices in more than 100
countries.

2005 Sales

	% of total
North America	43
Europe	40
Other regions	17
Total	**100**

PRODUCTS/OPERATIONS

Selected Operations and Agencies

Advertising
 Bartle Bogle Hegarty (49%)
 Beacon Communications (66%, Japan)
 Fallon Worldwide (US)
 Kaplan Thaler Group (US)
 Leo Burnett Worldwide (US)
 Publicis Worldwide
 Saatchi & Saatchi (US)

Media Services
 Denuo
 Médias & Régies Europe
 Starcom MediaVest Group (US)
 ZenithOptimedia (UK)

Specialized Agencies and Marketing Services Group
 (SAMS)
 Arc Worldwide (relationship marketing and
  promotional campaigns)
 Bromley Communications (49%, multicultural
  advertising, US)
 Lápiz (multicultural marketing, US)
 Manning, Selvage & Lee (public relations, US)
 Medicus Group (health care marketing, US)
 Nelson Communications (health care marketing, US)
 Publicis Dialog (sales promotion and direct marketing)
 Rowland Companies (public relations, US)

COMPETITORS

Aegis Group
Dentsu
Hakuhodo
Havas
Interpublic Group
Omnicom
WPP Group

HISTORICAL FINANCIALS

Company Type: Public

Income Statement

FYE: December 31

	REVENUE ($ mil.)	NET INCOME ($ mil.)	NET PROFIT MARGIN	EMPLOYEES
12/05	4,888	468	9.6%	38,610
12/04	5,219	472	9.0%	36,000
12/03	4,851	195	4.0%	35,166
12/02	3,122	(15)	—	35,681
12/01	2,157	(573)	—	20,592
Annual Growth	**22.7%**	**—**		**17.0%**

2005 Year-End Financials

Debt ratio: 93.1%
Return on equity: 13.3%
Cash ($ mil.): 2,345
Current ratio: 1.03
Long-term debt ($ mil.): 3,389
No. of shares (mil.): —
Dividends
 Yield: 0.9%
 Payout: —
Market value ($ mil.): —

Stock History

NYSE: PUB

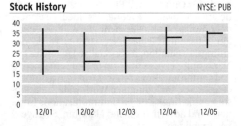

	STOCK PRICE ($) FY Close	P/E High/Low		PER SHARE ($) Earnings	Dividends
12/05	34.75	—	—	0.00	0.30
12/04	32.73	20	13	1.88	0.27
12/03	32.42	—	—		0.23
12/02	20.96	—	—		0.18
12/01	26.00	—	—		0.14
Annual Growth	**7.5%**	**—**	**—**		**21.0%**

Qantas Airways

Some Australians go on walkabout; others fly
about on Qantas Airways, Australia's #1 airline.
Qantas flies to more than 140 destinations (including some served by code-sharing partners) in
about 40 countries. Besides Qantas, which provides both domestic and international service,
the company's operations include an Australian
regional carrier, QantasLink, and a low-fare carrier, Jetstar. Overall, the company's fleet includes
about 215 aircraft. Qantas is part of the Oneworld
global marketing and code-sharing alliance,
which is led by British Airways and American Airlines. In 2006 an investment group led by Macquarie Bank and Texas Pacific Group offered
$8.6 billion to buy the company; Qantas rejected
the offer.

The potential buyout offer suggests that Qantas, which has been consistently profitable, has
been making the right moves in an always-
challenging industry environment.

The company simplified its branding in 2006
by rebadging its Australian Airlines unit, which
catered to international leisure travelers. Australian Airlines routes have been picked up by
Qantas and by Jetstar, which is expanding its
low-fare model beyond Australia's borders. Qantas concentrates on international business travel

and premium leisure routes, and Jetstar focuses
on other leisure destinations.

Besides its primary passenger transportation
business, Qantas generates revenue from aircraft
maintenance, cargo, catering, and tourism operations. In October 2006, the company launched
a new cargo unit, Express Freighters Australia.

HISTORY

Ex-WWI pilots Wilmot Hudson Fysh and Paul
McGinness and stockman Fergus McMaster
founded Queensland and Northern Territory
Aerial Services (Qantas) in 1920 to provide an air
link between Darwin in the Northern Territory
and the railheads in Queensland. In 1922 Qantas began carrying airmail over a 577-mile route
between Charleville and Cloncurry, and by 1930
it covered northeastern Australia with air
routes. Qantas moved its headquarters to Sydney in 1938.

Qantas and Imperial Airways (predecessor of
British Airways, or BA) formed Qantas Empire
Airways in 1934 to fly the last leg of a London-to-
Australia mail route (Singapore to Brisbane). Qantas bought the British share of Qantas Empire in
1947 (when Qantas made its first Sydney-London
flight) and was subsequently nationalized.

By 1950 the airline served most major cities
in the Pacific Rim. Qantas inaugurated a route
to Johannesburg (1952) and opened the Southern Cross route, previously operated by British
Commonwealth Pacific Airlines, to San Francisco and Vancouver via Honolulu (1953).

In 1958 Qantas offered the first complete
round-the-world service. (Pan Am had started a
similar service in 1957 but was barred by the US
government from crossing North America.) It
bought 29% of Malayan Airways in 1959 and
added several European destinations in the 1960s,
including Frankfurt (1966) and Amsterdam
(1967). Founder Fysh retired as chairman in 1966,
and the airline took its present name in 1967.

Tourism in Australia boomed in the 1970s.
Competition from foreign (especially US) airlines initially hurt Qantas, contributing to a
$4 million loss in 1971 (its second since 1924).
But in 1973 annual boardings jumped 28%. Qantas' Aussie passengers flew some 4,217 miles per
journey — the longest average trip of any airline.

In 1987 Qantas bought a stake in Fiji's Air Pacific. Later acquisitions included Australia-Asia
Airlines (1989) and 20% of Air New Zealand
(1990; sold 1997). Qantas enjoyed record profits
in 1989, but a strike by domestic pilots paralyzed
Australia's tourist industry that year, hurting
Qantas in 1990.

The Australian airline industry was deregulated in the early 1990s, and Qantas formed regional carrier Airlink in 1991. The next year it
merged with Australia Airlines, and in 1993 the
Australian government sold BA a 25% stake in
Qantas. Still, the airlines' 1994 attempt to set
prices and services together was rejected by Australian authorities.

Because Australian privatizations had deluged
the stock exchange with issues, Qantas delayed
its IPO until 1995. Also that year Qantas and BA
got approval for a joint service agreement that
allowed them to operate some facilities together.

The carrier began code-sharing with American
Airlines in 1995; three years later Qantas joined
the Oneworld global marketing alliance, led by
American and BA. In 1998 and 1999 Qantas and
BA began combining their operations in Hong
Kong, Indonesia, Malaysia, Singapore, and Thai-
land. The airline expanded its code-sharing with

affiliate Air Pacific in 2000, even as it braced for competition at home from Virgin Atlantic's new Australian low-fare carrier.

Unable to gain regulatory approval, Qantas dropped its bidding war with rival Ansett to acquire regional carrier Hazelton Airlines in 2001. That year Qantas agreed to acquire Impulse Airlines, an ailing Australian low-fare carrier. The company also entered negotiations with Air New Zealand to buy Ansett, but Qantas decided against a purchase of its troubled Australian rival. Air New Zealand subsequently shut down Ansett's operations.

The next year Qantas began negotiations to acquire a stake in Air New Zealand, but Qantas' offer to acquire a 23% stake in the smaller airline was rejected in 2003 by regulators in Australia and New Zealand. The airlines planned to appeal the decision the following year, but were once again denied.

In April 2006 Qantas reached a code-sharing deal with Air New Zealand designed to reduce capacity in the market for flights between Australia and New Zealand. Regulators expressed opposition, however, and the carriers withdrew their applications for approval of the code-sharing plan in November 2006.

EXECUTIVES

Chairman: Margaret A. Jackson, age 52
CEO and Director: Geoff Dixon
CFO, Executive General Manager Strategy, and Director: Peter Gregg
Executive General Manager Qantas: John Borghetti
Executive General Manager People: Kevin Brown
Executive General Manager Qantas Engineering: David Cox
Executive General Manager Associated Businesses: Grant Fenn
Group General Manager Customer Product and Service: Lesley Grant
Group General Manager Strategy and Fleet: Simon Hickey
CEO Jetstar: Alan Joyce
CEO Jetstar Asia: Chong Phit Lian
Chief Risk Officer: Rob Kella
Deputy CFO: Colin Storrie
General Counsel and Company Secretary: Brett Johnson
Assistant Company Secretary: Cassandra Hamlin
Auditors: KPMG

LOCATIONS

HQ: Qantas Airways Limited
Qantas Centre, Level 9, Bldg. A, 203 Coward St., Mascot, New South Wales 2020, Australia
Phone: +61-2-9691-3636   **Fax:** +61-2-9691-3339
US HQ: 300 Continental Blvd., Ste. 350, El Segundo, CA 90245
US Phone: 800-682-6017   **US Fax:** 310-535-1057
Web: www.qantas.com.au

2006 Sales

	% of total
Passenger, freight & other services	
Australia	57
Americas & the Pacific	7
UK & Europe	7
Japan	3
New Zealand	3
Southeast Asia & Northeast Asia	3
Other regions	2
Tours & travel	5
Contract work	4
Other	9
Total	**100**

PRODUCTS/OPERATIONS

2006 Sales

	% of total
Qantas	89
Qantas Holidays	5
Jetstar	5
Qantas Flight Catering	1
Total	**100**

COMPETITORS

Air France-KLM	Delta Air
Air New Zealand	Lufthansa
All Nippon Airways	Northwest Airlines
Cathay Pacific	SAS
China Eastern Airlines	Singapore Airlines
China Southern Airlines	UAL
Continental Airlines	Virgin Blue

HISTORICAL FINANCIALS

Company Type: Public

Income Statement

FYE: June 30

	REVENUE ($ mil.)	NET INCOME ($ mil.)	NET PROFIT MARGIN	EMPLOYEES
6/06	9,961	350	3.5%	34,832
6/05	9,632	580	6.0%	38,000
6/04	7,832	448	5.7%	33,862
6/03	7,585	229	3.0%	34,872
6/02	6,380	241	3.8%	33,044
Annual Growth	**11.8%**	**9.8%**	**—**	**1.3%**

Net Income History

Australian: QAN

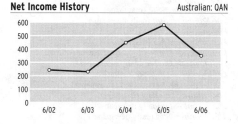

Quebecor

Getting the word out through print, broadcast, and cable is all in a day's work at Quebecor. Subsidiary Quebecor World is one of the world's top commercial printers, primarily producing books, catalogs, direct mail, directories, magazines, and retail inserts. The company's Quebecor Media group owns book stores, cable TV companies, magazines, music stores, newspapers, publishing houses, and broadcast stations. Its Sun Media newspaper unit produces daily newspapers as well as more than 180 regional papers and magazines. Its Vidéotron ltée subsidiary is one of Canada's largest cable companies. The founding Péladeau family controls a 67% voting stake in Quebecor.

The company's TVA Group subsidiary owns the dominant French-language TV network in Quebec. Quebecor Media also has operations in book publishing (Éditions CEC, among others) and music retail (Archambault superstores). In the Internet realm, the company operates a Web portal (canoe.com), as well as several other Web sites. The company has also made a foray into radio with several station acquisitions.

Printing accounts for more than two-thirds of Quebecor's sales, but revenue from the business has dropped. Quebecor World has launched an ambitious program of consolidating facilities and investing in new equipment in an effort to improve its results.

HISTORY

In 1950 law student Pierre Péladeau borrowed $1,500 from his mother so he could buy a small Montreal newspaper called *Le Journal de Rosemont*. This became the base for Péladeau's publishing empire. Within a few years he had established five other weekly newspapers and his first printing firm.

Péladeau seized the opportunity presented to him in 1964 by a strike at the major Montreal paper *La Presse*. He assembled a team from his various weeklies and, according to company legend, had the tabloid *Le Journal* on the streets within three days.

Quebecor went public in 1972 and expanded beyond Quebec, branching out into a variety of communication concerns. But by the late 1980s, the company had refocused on its core printing businesses.

Quebecor purchased printing plants in New Jersey and Michigan in 1985. Péladeau teamed with Robert Maxwell in 1987 to form Mircor to buy a stake in forestry concern Donohue. The company took a major step into the international arena when it bought the printing group BCE PubliTech in 1988, making the company the #1 commercial printer in Canada.

In 1990 Maxwell sold his US printing plants (with state-of-the-art printing presses) to Péladeau, who formed Quebecor Printing (USA) around the new assets. Maxwell subsequently bought a 26% stake in the new company for $100 million.

Maxwell died mysteriously in 1991 followed by revelations of deceptive finances and shady business dealings by the Maxwell empire. This allowed Péladeau to buy back all of Maxwell's shares in Quebecor at bargain-basement prices.

In the 1990s Quebecor continued expanding, buying a bookbinding and publishing company in Mexico (Gráficas Monte Alban, 1991), three US printing plants (1993), France's largest commercial printer (Group Jean Didier, 1995), and a UK printer (1995). Quebecor Printing went public in 1995, which reduced the parent company's interest to less than 50%. Quebecor also set up its multimedia unit and expanded it by acquiring 50% of Sierra Creative Communications and 25% of multimedia software publisher MicroIntel (1996).

A Quebecor-controlled consortium in 1997 acquired Télévision Quatre Saisons, which operates three Canadian TV stations and the Quatre Saisons TV network license. (The company sold the network and related stations in 2001.) Péladeau died from heart failure that year.

In 1999 Quebecor bought Sun Media, which made the company the #2 Canadian newspaper publisher. It later sold a 30% stake in Sun Media to a group of private investors for $260 million. In 1999 Quebecor Printing acquired World Color Press. Also that year Pierre Karl Péladeau, the founder's second son, took over as president and CEO. Péladeau family members have filed a flood of lawsuits against one another and the executor of Pierre Péladeau's estate in a battle for control of family assets, including the company.

Quebecor sold its controlling stake in market pulp, lumber, and newsprint producer Donohue to rival Abitibi-Consolidated in 2000. Also that year the company restructured into two operating units: Quebecor Printing (later Quebecor World) and Quebecor Media. Later in 2000 Quebecor and Caisse de Dépôt et Placement du Québec (Quebec's public-pension agency) won a bidding war with Rogers Communications for the acquisition of Le Groupe Vidéotron, Canada's #3 cable TV operator, with an offer of $3.6 billion. Le Groupe Vidéotron's broadcasting company TVA Group was part of the deal, but was not finalized until 2001 after Quebecor completed the sale of its TQS network, which had been required by regulators.

In 2001 the company bought the 30% of Sun Media that it didn't already own. That year it also bulked up its Latin American holdings with the purchase of Grupo Serla, a school book text printer in Mexico, and 75% of Grafica Melhoramentos, a Brazilian book publisher.

Quebecor bought the European printing facilities of Hachette Filipacchi Médias in 2001 and 2002. Also in 2002, the company merged its Publicor and TVA Publishing operations under the TVA Publishing name.

EXECUTIVES

Chairman: Jean Neveu
EVP and Vice Chairman: Érik Péladeau
President, CEO, and Director: Pierre Karl Péladeau
EVP and CFO: Jacques Mallette
EVP, Corporate Affairs: Luc Lavoie
SVP, Legal Affairs and Corporate Secretary: Louis Saint-Arnaud
VP and Corporate Controller: Denis Sabourin
VP, Human Resources: Julie Tremblay
VP, Internal Audit: Roger Martel
VP, Taxation: Michel Éthier
Chairman, Quebecor Media: Serge Gouin, age 63
President and CEO, Nurun: Jacques-Hervé Roubert
President and CEO, Sun Media: Pierre Francoeur
President and CEO, TVA Group: Pierre Dion, age 42
President and CEO, Vidéotron: Robert Dépatie
President and General Manager, Archambault Group: Natalie Larivière
President, Les Publications TVA: Jocelyn Poirier
President, Le SuperClub Vidéotron ltée and President, Music and Retail Group, Quebecor Media: Richard Soly
VP, Advertising Convergence, Quebecor Media: Jean-Francois Richard
VP, Interactive Media, Quebecor Media and President and CEO, Canoë: Bruno Leclaire
Senior Manager, Corporate Services and Assistant Corporate Secretary: Claudine Tremblay
Senior Manager, Legal Affairs: Frédéric Despars
Auditors: KPMG LLP

LOCATIONS

HQ: Quebecor Inc.
612 Saint-Jacques St.,
Montreal, Quebec H3C 4M8, Canada
Phone: 514-954-0101 **Fax:** 514-954-9624
Web: www.quebecor.com

2005 Sales

	% of total
North America	
US	50
Canada	33
Europe	14
Latin America	3
Total	**100**

PRODUCTS/OPERATIONS

2005 Sales

	% of total
Quebecor World	
Printing	73
Quebecor Media	
Cable television	10
Newspapers	9
Broadcasting	4
Leisure & entertainment	2
Business telecommunications	1
Other	1
Total	**100**

Selected Operations

Quebecor Media Inc.
   Archambault Group Inc. (music and book stores, music recording and distribution)
   Books Segment (general literature and textbook publishing and distribution)
   Netgraphe Inc. (portals and e-commerce sites)
   Nurun Inc. (Web development and e-commerce consulting)
   Sun Media Corporation (newspaper publishing)
   TVA Group Inc. (broadcasting)
      TVA Publishing (magazine publishing)
   Vidéotron ltée (cable operator)
      Le SuperClub Vidéotron ltée (video rental chain)
Quebecor World Inc.
   Distribution
   Pre-media
   Printing (books, catalogs, direct mail, directories, magazines, retail inserts)

Selected Publications

The Calgary Sun (daily newspaper)
Cool! (magazine)
Décoration Chez-Soi (magazine)
The Edmonton Sun (daily newspaper)
Femmes (magazine)
Filles d'aujourd'hui (magazine)
Le Journal de Montréal (daily newspaper)
Le Journal de Québec (daily newspaper)
Les idées de ma maison (magazine)
The London Free Press (daily newspaper)
The Ottawa Sun (daily newspaper)
The Toronto Sun (daily newspaper)
The Winnipeg Sun (daily newspaper)

COMPETITORS

Banta	Dai Nippon Printing
BCE	Hachette Filipacchi Médias
Bell Globemedia	Hollinger
Cadmus Communications	Quad/Graphics
Cancom	Rogers Cable
CanWest Global	Rogers Communications
CBC	R.R. Donnelley
COGECO Inc.	Shaw Communications
Courier	Toppan Printing

HISTORICAL FINANCIALS

Company Type: Public

Income Statement

FYE: December 31

	REVENUE ($ mil.)	NET INCOME ($ mil.)	NET PROFIT MARGIN	EMPLOYEES
12/05	8,755	60	0.7%	45,800
12/04	9,115	93	1.0%	47,400
12/03	8,668	51	0.6%	49,000
12/02	7,619	58	0.8%	50,000
12/01	7,312	(152)	—	54,000
Annual Growth	4.6%	—	—	(4.0%)

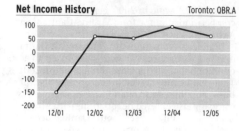

Net Income History — Toronto: QBR.A

Rallye

Retail giant Rallye musters its businesses around not just the French flag, but around flags worldwide. Rallye's Casino Guichard-Perrachon subsidiary operates about 10,000 hypermarkets, supermarkets, and convenience stores in Europe (mostly France), Asia, and Latin America. Rallye has merged two subsidiaries into Groupe Go Sport: Go Sport (France's #2 sporting goods retailer) with about 150 stores and Courir (France's #1 sports and leisure footwear retailer) with more than 200. The company is also active in real estate development, banking, and a variety of investment vehicles. Finatis, through The Euris Group (founded by Rallye Chairman Jean-Charles Naouri), owns about 80% of Rallye.

Rallye's Casino subsidiary is a leading supermarket chain in France and operates in about 20 countries worldwide. Store banners include Casino, Franprix, Géant, and Leader Price. Casino is the #1 convenience store operator in France with stores under the Eco Service, Petit Casino, Spar, and Vival names. Casino has grown by purchasing stakes in supermarket, hypermarket, and convenience store companies with international locations. It plans to continue this global expansion.

While Rallye exited the footwear retail business in the US with its sale of The Athlete's Foot, the company plans to continue to expand Groupe Go Sport in Europe.

Rallye has increased its e-commerce activities through its majority stake of Cdiscount.com, a French online retailer of CDs, videos, and more. Cdiscount belongs to the non-food group, which also includes recent IPO Mercialys (retail real estate development), Casino Cafeteria (corporate cafeterias), and Banque Casino (consumer lending).

HISTORY

Rallye has its roots in Casino Guichard-Perrachon, which was formed after Geoffroy Guichard took over his father-in-law's general store in 1892.

In the early 1920s the company, which would later become a Rallye holding, opened factories to produce items that included food and soap. In 1924 Rallye was formed as a food retailer. Also that year a food distribution group that would become an important acquisition for Rallye in the 1990s, Genty, was founded (renamed Genty Cathiard in 1959).

By WWII Casino had 215 branches. During the war Casino's troubles included 70 stores leveled and 450 damaged in bomb attacks.

The firm launched its first supermarket (Grenoble) in 1960 and its first cafeteria in 1967.

It expanded to Géant hypermarkets (Marseille) in 1970 and formed Casino USA in 1976.

Rallye entered sporting goods in 1981 through the purchase of France's 11-unit Athletic Attic chain and the acquisition of a minority stake of US sports footwear and apparel retailer The Athlete's Foot Group. Rallye then acquired majority control of Athlete's Foot in 1984.

Rallye's sales reached $4.4 billion in 1989. The next year it acquired the food distribution group Genty Cathiard, which included retail units Go Sport (sporting goods) and Courir (sports footwear). The acquisition moved Rallye from #8 to #5 in French supermarket groups.

By 1991 Rallye operated 51 hypermarkets and 227 supermarkets. That year Euris, headed by Jean-Charles Naouri, bought a stake in Rallye, which had heavy debt after borrowing funds to acquire Genty Cathiard. Rallye traded its food retail operations (close to 300 hypermarkets and supermarkets) with food giant Casino in exchange for a 29.5% stake in Casino in 1992.

Rallye merged with subsidiary Genty Cathiard in 1993, when the company went public. Also in 1993 Rallye began a major restructuring for Go Sport that lasted until 1996.

French supermarket chain Promodès made a hostile takeover attempt on Casino and Rallye in 1997, which would have made Promodès France's largest retailer. Rallye (which still had 29% of Casino and about 36% of voting rights) made a friendly counter bid; Promodès backed out and Rallye took control of Casino. By 1998 The Athlete's Foot Group had grown to more than 260 US outlets (company-owned) and more than 400 franchises (about 180 in the US).

Franchises were also located in 38 countries, including Australia, Canada, France, and Hong Kong. Go Sport operated 80 outlets in France and six in Belgium, and there were more than 100 Courir stores (France) by the beginning of 1998. Rallye spun off 22% of Courir in 1999.

Casino expanded its international markets in 1999 by acquiring stakes in food retailing companies in countries that included Brazil, Colombia, Thailand, and Venezuela. Go Sport grew in 1999 by launching new stores in France, Belgium, and Poland — a new market.

In 2000 Casino bought a 51% stake in French online CD retailer Cdiscount.com. Although Rallye as a whole nearly doubled its net profit in 2000, Athlete's Foot suffered a loss of almost $29 million that year and began a three-year restructuring plan that included the closure of 84 unprofitable stores. However, 100 new Athlete's Foot franchises opened in 2001, including the first stores in Mexico and Hungary.

In June 2002, Casino acquired a 39% stake in Laurus, a leading retailer in the Netherlands.

In December 2003, Rallye sold its interest in The Athlete's Foot (TAF) to the chain's managers in a management-led buyout for an undisclosed sum. Accounting for less than 1% of Rallye's sales, TAF had closed nearly 100 branches since 2001 but was still unprofitable.

François de Montaudouin resigned as managing director or Rallye in January 2004 and was succeeded by Chairman Jean-Charles Naouri.

In 2005 the company held an initial public offering for its shopping center real estate development company, Mercialys.

EXECUTIVES

Chairman, President, and CEO:
Jean-Charles Henri Naouri, age 57
Vice Chairman: André Crestey, age 67
Deputy Managing Director: Didier Carlier, age 54
CFO: Jean-Marie Grisard, age 63
Auditors: Barbier Frinault & Autres; KPMG Audit

LOCATIONS

HQ: RALLYE S.A.
83, rue du Faubourg-Saint-Honoré,
75008 Paris, France
Phone: +33-1-44-71-13-62   **Fax:** +33-1-44-71-13-60
Web: www.rallye.fr

2005 Sales

	% of total
Europe	
France	75
Other countries	4
North America	7
South America	7
Asia	5
Indian Ocean	2
Total	**100**

PRODUCTS/OPERATIONS

2005 Sales

	% of total
Food & general retailing	97
Sporting goods retailing	3
Total	**100**

COMPETITORS

ALDI
Auchan
Carrefour
E.Leclerc
Galeries Lafayette
Guyenne et Gascogne
Intersport International Cooperation
ITM Entreprises
METRO AG
PPR
Primisteres Reynoird
Royal Ahold
Tesco
Wal-Mart

HISTORICAL FINANCIALS

Company Type: Public

Income Statement — FYE: December 31

	REVENUE ($ mil.)	NET INCOME ($ mil.)	NET PROFIT MARGIN	EMPLOYEES
12/05	27,873	340	1.2%	147,520
12/04	32,511	75	0.2%	124,223
12/03	29,834	535	1.8%	124,143
12/02	24,820	384	1.5%	122,040
12/01	20,252	303	1.5%	113,444
Annual Growth	**8.3%**	**2.9%**	**—**	**6.8%**

Net Income History — Euronext Paris: RAL

Rank Group

Leisure is highly rated by this company. The Rank Group owns a portfolio of hospitality and leisure businesses around the world. The company has UK gaming holdings, including nearly 120 Mecca Bingo clubs and more than 30 Grosvenor Casinos. It also offers two casinos in Belgium and 11 bingo clubs in Spain, and the online gaming and betting Web site Blue Square. In addition to its gaming businesses, Rank owns the Hard Rock Cafe franchise of restaurants, entertainment venues, and hotels, which it is selling. Rank sold its Deluxe Film and other media operations in 2006; it is seeking buyers for the remaining assets of Deluxe Media Services. Rank is focusing exclusively on its UK gaming operations.

The company's Hard Rock division has been hit by the slump in tourism while its UK gaming businesses, especially those located in the London area, have continued to remain popular. The firm is selling its Hard Rock chain to The Seminole Tribe of Florida for $965 million.

While Rank had received criticism in the past for its wide-ranging, and seemingly incongruent, holdings, the company's diversity saved it from at least some of the ravages of a weak economy. Its film services business at Deluxe achieved success owing to the slate of blockbusters passing through its labs, including *Star Wars: Episode III*, *Spider-Man 2*, and *Die Another Day*. However, after Rank's media business contributed a $228 million loss to its parent's balance sheet in 2004, the company decided to sell the unit.

In 2006 it sold one piece of the business — Deluxe Film — to MacAndrews & Forbes Holdings for approximately $750 million. It later sold its UK DVD replication and distribution business to a subsidiary of Sony DADC. The disposal of the rest (Deluxe Media Services) is still on deck.

Citing the rising cost of compliance with US regulations concerning stock listings, Rank Group in 2005 terminated its listing in that country. CEO Mike Smith retired from Rank Group in early 2006. He was replaced by former hotel executive Ian Burke.

HISTORY

The Rank Group grew out of a sense of strong conviction. Joseph Arthur Rank was a devout Methodist who saw films as a way to spread the message of his religion. Leaving the successful family milling business, he started a production company in 1934 called British National Films. Later Rank acquired General Film Distributors, Pinewood Studios, and the Odeon theater chain. By 1941, Rank's entertainment holdings were so vast that many saw him as a monopolist. But after WWII the British film business deteriorated as American films flooded into the country. Television and an emerging leisure industry also took their toll in the 1950s.

With the holding company recast as The Rank Organisation in 1955, J. Arthur Rank and his managing director, John Davis, set about searching for alternative businesses. Rank formed a joint venture with the Haloid Company (now Xerox) in 1956 to market photocopying equipment. Later called Rank Xerox, the joint venture eventually dwarfed the profits of Rank's other operating units. Davis became chairman in 1962 (Rank died in 1972) and invested in a diverse but underperforming group of businesses, including bingo parlors, hotels, and dance halls. The pitiful results of his efforts were exposed in the late 1970s as Rank Xerox's earnings receded under growing competition in the copier market. Investors forced Davis to step down in 1977.

Michael Gifford was installed as chief executive in 1983 and immediately began cutting overhead and dumping businesses, which increased profits. Rank joined with MCA to create the Universal Studios Florida theme park (now part of Universal Parks & Resorts) in 1988 and acquired Mecca Leisure Group's bingo parlors, casinos, hotels, and clubs in 1990. It also bought the rights to a number of Hard Rock Cafes (originally established in London in 1971).

Rank named former ICI chief Sir Denys Henderson as its new chairman in 1994, and two years later Andrew Teare became Rank's new CEO. Teare led Rank's buyout of Hard Rock cofounder Peter Morton that year and installed former schoolteacher Jim Berk as Hard Rock's CEO. Teare also restructured Rank into four divisions (Film and Entertainment Services, Hard Rock, Holidays, and Leisure) and changed its name to The Rank Group. The company sold its Rank Xerox stake back to Xerox for about $1.5 billion in 1997. After reporting more disappointing results, however, Teare left the company the next year. Mike Smith, former head of gaming firm Ladbrokes, came in as CEO in 1999. Peter Beaudrault replaced Berk at Hard Rock that year.

Smith's restructuring efforts led to the sale of Rank's nightclub business to Northern Leisure in 1999. The Odeon theater chain went to UK buyout specialist Cinven for $450 million and Pinewood Studios was sold for about $100 million in 2000. Rank later sold its 50% stake in Universal Studios Orlando to Blackstone Capital Partners for $275 million, while its UK holiday resorts went to Bourne Leisure for $1 billion. In 2001 Henderson stepped down as chairman; former Avis Europe chairman Alun Cathcart was tapped as his replacement. (Cathcart announced his retiring in 2006.)

Rank expanded its gaming business in 2003 when it acquired online betting site Blue Square for about $100 million. That same year the company formed a joint venture with resort operator Sol Meliá to develop new luxury Hard Rock hotels. The effort, backed by $1 billion from Becker Ventures, came after a boardroom row that ended in the abrupt departure of Hard Rock chief Peter Beaudrault.

Beaudrault left his post at Hard Rock as the theme restaurant chain posted declining sales. He was replaced by Hamish Dodds the following year. Also in 2004 Rank sold its Rank Leisure Machine Services and Rank Seasonal Amusements businesses, which included 35,000 gaming machines, to Gamestec Leisure Limited for £30 million.

In the early part of 2006, Rank completed the sale of Deluxe Film to MacAndrews & Forbes Holdings, the first disposal in a planned exit from the media business entirely. In addition, Smith retired as CEO of the company later that year. Former hotel executive Ian Burke took over the CEO post.

EXECUTIVES

Chairman: W. Alun Cathcart, age 63, $674,397 pay
Deputy Chairman: Peter W. Johnson, age 59
Chief Executive and Director: Ian Burke, age 50
Group Finance Director and Board Member:
Peter R. Gill, age 51, $538,485 pay
Group Human Resources Director: Christine Ray, age 58

President and CEO, Hard Rock Cafe: Hamish Dodds, age 49
President, Deluxe Media Services: Tom Vale
Managing Director, Blue Square: Martin Belsham
Managing Director, Gaming: David Boden, age 49, $535,045 pay
Managing Director, Grosvenor Casinos: Peter McCann
Managing Director, Mecca Bingo: Simon Wykes
Managing Director, Top Rank Espana: Valentin Coruna
Company Secretary: Pamela Coles, age 45
Director Investor Relations: Dan Waugh
Auditors: PricewaterhouseCoopers LLP

LOCATIONS

HQ: The Rank Group Plc
6 Connaught Place,
London W2 2EZ, United Kingdom
Phone: +44-20-7706-1111 **Fax:** +44-20-7262-9886
Web: www.rank.com

2005 Sales

	% of total
UK	44
North America	43
Europe	13
Total	**100**

PRODUCTS/OPERATIONS

2005 Sales

	% of total
Gaming	
Mecca	38
Grosvenor	27
Blue Square	3
Hard Rock	32
Total	**100**

Selected Operations

Gaming
Blue Square (Internet and phone gambling)
Grosvenor Casinos (Belgium and UK)
Mecca Bingo (Spain and UK)
Hard Rock
Hard Rock Cafes
Hotels & Casinos
Hard Rock Casino (London)
Hard Rock Hotel (Bali, Indonesia)
Hard Rock Hotel (Orlando, Florida)
Hard Rock Hotel (Pattaya, Thailand)
Hard Rock Hotel & Casino (Las Vegas)

COMPETITORS

Camelot
Harrah's Entertainment
HOB Entertainment
Ladbrokes
MGM MIRAGE
Planet Hollywood
Stanley Leisure
William Hill

HISTORICAL FINANCIALS

Company Type: Public

Income Statement

FYE: December 31

	REVENUE ($ mil.)	NET INCOME ($ mil.)	NET PROFIT MARGIN	EMPLOYEES
12/05	1,394	219	15.7%	24,323
12/04	3,763	(155)	—	25,159
12/03	3,425	140	4.1%	24,003
12/02	2,367	264	11.2%	21,862
12/01	1,997	458	23.0%	20,955
Annual Growth	**(8.6%)**	**(16.8%)**	**—**	**3.8%**

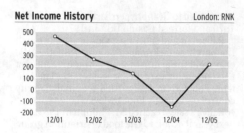

Net Income History London: RNK

Reckitt Benckiser

With a cart full of products, Reckitt Benckiser (rhymes with "freezer") is cleaning up. It's one of the largest household cleaning products makers worldwide. The firm's brands include air fresheners (Airwick), household cleaners (Lysol, Easy-Off), laundry products (Woolite), furniture polishes (Old English), and dishwashing detergents (Electrasol). It also makes over-the-counter pharmaceuticals such as analgesics, antiseptics, flu remedies, and gastrointestinal medications, and offers products for hair removal, denture cleaning, and pest control (d-Con). Reckitt Benckiser also makes French's mustard. The company bought Boots Healthcare International, the consumer health care division of Alliance Boots, in 2006.

The deal was valued at about £1.9 billion and added Nurofen (analgesic), Strepsils (cold remedies), and Clearasil (anti-acne) to Reckitt Benckiser's stable of non-prescription products. In a follow-up deal, Reckitt Benckiser acquired former Boots brands — Clearasil, Strepsils, and Sweetez — in India in October 2006.

The company, which was created by the merger of UK-based Reckitt & Colman and The Netherlands' Benckiser, sells products in 180 countries worldwide. Reckitt Benckiser has divested about 75 minor brands, allowing the firm to focus on its key brands in the areas of fabric care, surface care, dishwashing products, health and personal care, and home care.

In late 2002 the company lost a bid for Pfizer's Schick-Wilkinson Sword shaving products (the world's second-largest razor maker behind Gillette) to Energizer Holdings. But in 2006 Reckitt Benckiser was back taking a run at Pfizer's consumer health care division.

Reckitt, admitting that launching entirely new brands in the fast-moving consumer goods niche is risky and expensive, had been looking for acquisition opportunities. The company approached SSL International (the maker of Durex condoms and Dr. Scholl footcare products) in mid-2003 but talks weren't productive.

HISTORY

Reckitt & Colman's roots can be traced to Jeremiah Colman, who bought a flour mill near Norwich, England, in 1804. In 1823 his nephew James joined the company, and their business was incorporated as J. and J. Colman. Jeremiah died in 1851 and James' son, also named Jeremiah, became a partner, taking over the operations when his father died in 1854. The company moved to Carrow that year.

Colman worked to make the Carrow facilities as self-sufficient and waste-free as possible. The factory had its own foundry, print shop, paper mill (to make containers), and fire brigade. By-products from the milling process were sold to farmers for cattle feed and fertilizer. The company continued to expand, adding wheat flour and using the leftover starch from milling operations to make laundry bluing.

In 1903 the mill acquired Keen, Robinson & Co., a manufacturer of spices. J. and J. Colman got a lock on British mustard sales in 1912 when it acquired its only major competitor, Joseph Farrow & Company. A year later it joined another rival, starch maker Reckitt & Sons, in a joint venture in South America. The joint venture between Colman and Reckitt was a success, and in 1921 they pooled their overseas operations.

The two companies created Reckitt & Colman Ltd. in 1938 to manage their operations, although each company maintained a separate listing on the London Stock Exchange. In 1954 they formally merged into a single entity.

Reckitt & Colman formed its US subsidiary in 1977, and during the 1980s it made a number of acquisitions (Airwick air fresheners, Gold Seal bath products) to expand its presence in the US.

In 1990 the firm picked up such brands as Black Flag (insecticide), Woolite (fabric care), and Easy-Off (oven cleaner) when it bought Boyle-Midway from American Home Products.

The company gained the Lysol brand in 1994 when it bought L&F Household from Eastman Kodak. To help finance the $1.6 billion deal, Reckitt & Colman sold its flagship Colman Mustard unit to Unilever. Its French's operations in the US (mustard, Worcestershire sauce) were its only remaining food business.

Michael Colman, the last active family member, stepped down as chairman in 1995. In 1996 it sold its US personal products unit.

In 1998 Reckitt & Colman bought certain cleaning products brands, including Spray'n Wash and Glass Plus, from S.C. Johnson & Son for about $160 million. CEO Vernon Sankey resigned in 1999, and Michael Turrell became the acting chief executive.

Johann A. Benckiser founded Benckiser in 1823 in the Netherlands to make industrial chemicals. The company launched Calgon Water Softener in 1956 and released Calgonit automatic dishwashing detergent in 1964. From 1982 to 1992 a number of acquisitions expanded the company's market in Central Europe and North America. By 1999 Benckiser's products were sold in 45 countries, including Eastern Europe, Asia, and the Middle East.

After the merger in December 1999, Alan Dalby, former chairman of Reckitt & Colman, was named chairman of Reckitt Benckiser (he retired in 2001). Bart Becht, previously CEO of Benckiser, was named CEO of the new company. In 2000 Reckitt Benckiser announced plans to unload 75 brands to focus on more growth-oriented brands.

As part of an effort to expand its presence in the Asia/Pacific region, Reckitt Benckiser bought Korean household products maker Oxy Co. (Oxy Clean fabric treatment) in 2001.

In 2002 the company won FDA approval to market Subutex and Suboxone in the US. Both are drugs for the treatment of opiate dependence. They are available in 24 other countries.

In early 2006 Reckitt Benckiser completed the previously announced acquisition of Boots Healthcare International (BHI) from Boots Group (now Alliance Boots) for about about £1.9 billion. BHI is a leading UK maker of drugs such as Nurofen (ibuprofen) and Strepsils (sore throat remedy).

EXECUTIVES

Chairman: Adrian D. P. Bellamy, age 64
Vice Chairman: Peter Harf, age 60
CEO and Director: Bart Becht, age 49
CFO and Director: Colin Day, age 51
EVP, Category Development: Rakesh Kapoor, age 47
EVP, Developing Markets: Freddy Caspers, age 45
EVP, Europe: Elio Leoni-Sceti, age 40
EVP, North America and Australia; Regional Director, North American Household: Javed Ahmed, age 46
EVP, Supply: Alain Le Goff, age 54
SVP, Human Resources: Frank Ruether, age 53
SVP, Information Services and Director: Gareth Hill, age 39
SVP, Investor Relations and Corporate Communications: Tom Corran
President, Food Products: Elliott Penner
Corporate Controller and Investor Relations Manager: Mark Wilson
Brand Manager, Cattlemen's: Zoe Susice
Company Secretary: Elizabeth (Liz) Richardson
Head, Corporate Communications: Fiona Fong
Financial Dynamics: Tim Spratt
Auditors: PricewaterhouseCoopers

LOCATIONS

HQ: Reckitt Benckiser plc
103-105 Bath Rd., Slough SL1 3UH, England
Phone: +44-1753-217-800   **Fax:** +44-1753-217-899
US HQ: 399 Interpace Pkwy., Morris Corporate Ctr. IV, Parsippany, NJ 07054
US Phone: 973-404-2600   **US Fax:** 973-404-5700
Web: www.reckittbenckiser.com

2005 Sales

	% of total
Europe	51
North America and Australia	31
Developing markets	18
Total	**100**

PRODUCTS/OPERATIONS

2005 Sales

	% of total
Household & health & personal care	95
Food	5
Total	**100**

Selected Brands

Air care	Fabric care
Airwick	Ava
d-Con	Calgon
Haze	Cherie
Mortein	Colon
Pest Control	Dosia
Wizard	Napisan
Dishwashing	Oxy Clean
Calgonit	Resolve
Electrasol	Spray'n Wash
Finish	Vanish
Jet-Dry	Surface care
Health and personal care	Brasso
Dettol	Dettox
Disprin	Easy Off
Gaviscon	Harpic
Immac	Lime-A-Way
Kukident	Lysol
Lemsip	Old English
Steradent	
Veet	

COMPETITORS

Alliance Boots
Alticor
Blyth
Chattem
Church & Dwight
Clorox
Colgate-Palmolive
Henkel
Johnson & Johnson
Procter & Gamble
S.C. Johnson
Unilever

HISTORICAL FINANCIALS

Company Type: Public

Income Statement

FYE: December 31

	REVENUE ($ mil.)	NET INCOME ($ mil.)	NET PROFIT MARGIN	EMPLOYEES
12/05	7,190	1,151	16.0%	20,300
12/04	7,456	1,129	15.1%	19,900
12/03	6,601	869	13.2%	20,400
12/02	5,663	654	11.6%	22,300
12/01	4,990	517	10.4%	22,400
Annual Growth	**9.6%**	**22.2%**	**—**	**(2.4%)**

Net Income History

London: RB

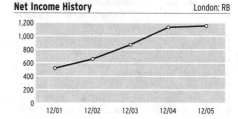

Reed Elsevier

Finding legal, business, scientific, or educational information is a cinch thanks to Reed Elsevier Group plc. Its Reed Business unit publishes business-to-business titles worldwide. Reed Elsevier's legal publishing operations fall under the LexisNexis banner, offering online, CD-ROM, and hard copy legal, corporate, and government information. Reed Elsevier Group also publishes scientific and medical information; its educational materials are published through units including Harcourt Education. Reed Elsevier PLC and Reed Elsevier NV each own 50% of Reed Elsevier Group.

The company also operates event organizer Reed Exhibition Companies.

No slouch in scientific publishing, Reed Elsevier Group issues thousands of scientific and medical journals and millions of research articles through Elsevier Health Sciences and Elsevier Science and Technology. Its Reed Education unit produces the company's educational materials, an area Reed Elsevier Group rapidly expanded through its $4.5 billion acquisition of US-based Harcourt General (now called Harcourt Education). To gain antitrust clearance for the deal Reed Elsevier Group sold Harcourt's higher education, corporate training, and assessment businesses to Canada's Thomson Corporation.

The company has boosted its units with acquisitions: risk management information provider Seisint for $775 million through its LexisNexis unit (2004) and medical publishing business of MediMedia for nearly $340 million (2005).

HISTORY

Newsprint manufacturer Albert E. Reed & Co. was named after its founder in 1894. It went public in 1903. For the next 50 years, Reed grew by buying UK pulp and paper mills. Reed began making packaging materials in the 1930s and added building products in 1954. The company expanded into New Zealand (1955), Australia (1960), and Norway (1962).

Chairman Sir Don Ryder radically altered the company in the 1960s and 1970s, leading Reed into other paper-related products and into the wallpaper, paint, and interior-decorating and do-it-yourself markets. Reed bought International Publishing, Mirror Group Newspapers, and 29% of Cahners Publishing in 1970 (buying the remaining 71% in 1977). By 1978 Ryder's strategy proved flawed. Coordinating so many companies was difficult, and, strapped for cash, Reed dumped most of its Australian businesses.

The company sold the Mirror Group to Robert Maxwell in 1984 and divested the remainder of its nonpaper and nonpublishing companies by 1987 to focus on publishing. It bought Octopus Publishing (1987), the UK's TV Times (1989), News Corp.'s Travel Information Group (1989), and Martindale-Hubbell (1990).

Reed International merged its operations with those of Elsevier, the world's leading scholarly journal publisher, in 1993. Five Rotterdam booksellers and publishers founded Elsevier in 1880. It took its name from a famous Dutch family publishing company, which had operated from the late 16th century to the early 18th century.

Elsevier entered the scientific publishing market in the 1930s, and following WWII diversified into trade journals and consumer manuals. The company made its first US acquisition, Congressional Information Service, in 1979. The company fended off a takeover bid by Maxwell in 1988 by planning a merger with UK publisher Pearson; Maxwell was thwarted, the merger ultimately failed, and Elsevier later sold its Pearson stock. Elsevier bought Maxwell's Pergamon Press in 1991.

Reed and Elsevier were both listed on the NYSE in 1994. Reed Elsevier built its US presence that year with its purchase of Mead's LexisNexis online service. The company acquired Tolley, a UK tax and legal publisher, and a 50% interest in Shepard's, a US legal citation service in 1996. Reed Elsevier sold IPC Magazines (now IPC Media) for $1.4 billion in 1998 to an investment group led by venture capitalists Cinven. Later that year the company bought Matthew Bender and the remaining 50% of Shepard's from Times Mirror.

Crispin Davis, the former head of Aegis Group, became CEO in 1999. The firm reorganized Cahners that year, laying off several hundred employees and consolidating magazine operations. It also boosted its scientific publishing profile by unveiling Web-based scientific information service ScienceDirect. Reed Elsevier purchased educational publisher Harcourt General in 2001 to boost its market share in the US. The company had to sell some of Harcourt's businesses (including the higher education and corporate training operations) to Thomson Corporation in order to ease antitrust concerns.

In 2002 the company's US Cahners Business Information unit changed its name to Reed Business Information US. That year the company also changed its name to Reed Elsevier Group plc.

EXECUTIVES

Chairman: Jan H. M. Hommen, age 63, $274,949 pay (partial-year salary)
CEO and Director: Sir Crispin Davis, age 56, $3,377,735 pay
CFO and Director: Mark H. Armour, age 51, $1,737,585 pay
Director; CEO, Harcourt Education: Patrick J. (Pat) Tierney, age 60, $1,412,491 pay
Director; CEO, Elsevier Division: Erik Engstrom, age 42, $1,783,170 pay
Director; CEO, LexisNexis Division: Andrew Prozes, age 60, $1,941,555 pay
Director; CEO, Reed Business Division: Gerard J. A. van de Aast, age 48, $1,442,970 pay
CEO, Reed Business Information US: Tad Smith, age 40
President and CEO, Holt, Rinehart and Winston: Allen Wheatcroft
Deputy Director, Corporate Relations: Patrick Kerr
Auditors: Deloitte & Touche

LOCATIONS

HQ: Reed Elsevier Group plc
1-3 Strand, London WC2N 5JR, England
Phone: +44-20-7930-7077   **Fax:** +44-20-7166-5799
US HQ: 125 Park Ave., 23rd Fl., New York, NY 10017
US Phone: 212-309-5498   **US Fax:** 212-309-5480
Web: www.reedelsevier.com

Reed Elsevier has offices in Asia, Australia, Canada, Europe, India, Latin America, New Zealand, South Africa, the UK, and the US.

PRODUCTS/OPERATIONS

2005 Sales

	% of total
Elsevier	28
LexisNexis	28
Reed Business	27
Harcourt Education	17
Total	**100**

Selected Operations

Business publishing
  Reed Business

Education publishing and testing
  Harcourt Education

Legal publishing
  LexisNexis

Scientific and medical publishing
  Elsevier Health Sciences
  Elsevier Science and Technology
  ScienceDirect (Web site)

COMPETITORS

Advance Publications	Pearson
American Lawyer Media	Penton Media
Bertelsmann	PRIMEDIA
Cadmus Communications	Reuters
Dow Jones	Thomson Corporation
Editis	Time Warner
IHS	United Business Media
Informa	Georg von Holtzbrinck
John Wiley	VNU
McGraw-Hill	Wolters Kluwer

HISTORICAL FINANCIALS

Company Type: Joint venture

Income Statement

FYE: December 31

	REVENUE ($ mil.)	NET INCOME ($ mil.)	NET PROFIT MARGIN	EMPLOYEES
12/05	8,888	798	9.0%	36,500
12/04	9,269	584	6.3%	35,100
12/03	8,756	594	6.8%	35,600
12/02	8,052	290	3.6%	36,800
12/01	6,617	183	2.8%	34,600
Annual Growth	**7.7%**	**44.6%**	**—**	**1.3%**

2005 Year-End Financials

Debt ratio: 114.9%   Current ratio: 0.75
Return on equity: 20.6%   Long-term debt ($ mil.): 3,895
Cash ($ mil.): 509

Net Income History

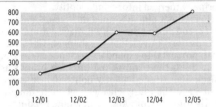

Renault

In Renault's road race against rival Peugeot Citroën to be France's dominant automaker, second place will have to deux. Renault manufactures a range of small to midsize cars (including Clio, Laguna, Megane, Modus, Logan, Espace, Twingo, and Scenic) and light commercial vehicles (Kangoo Express, Traffic, and Master). Like General Motors, Ford, and DaimlerChrysler, Renault is investing heavily in Asia, specifically in Japan. Renault has taken a 44% stake in Japan's #3 automaker, Nissan Motor. The French government has about a 15% stake in Renault.

With the Nissan deal and by taking a 93% stake in Automobile Dacia (Romania's leading automaker), Renault made it clear that it doesn't intend to be left in the international slow lane. The company also has a 70% stake in South Korea-based Renault Samsung Motors (the Samsung Group owns the remaining 30%). Renault sold its Renault V.I. subsidiary and its Mack Trucks unit to Volvo in return for a 20% stake in the Swedish truckmaker. Renault also has a 5% voting stake in Volvo's chief Swedish truck competitor Scania (which Renault has agreed to sell to MAN AG).

Understandably impressed by Nissan's miraculous turnaround (led by Carlos Ghosn), Renault's board named Ghosn CEO of the French automaker in 2005. Loathe to mess with success, Renault has also kept Ghosn behind the wheel at Nissan.

In early 2006 Ghosn made public his plans to revamp Renault. While not in the same precarious position as its North American counterparts General Motors and Ford, Renault's 2005 profits fell by more than 35% from the previous year and its lineup of products is growing stale. Renault has also been pressured by high raw materials costs and higher costs associated with meeting new European emission standards. To head his worries off at the pass Ghosn wants to trim costs without resorting to the painful job cuts and plant closures implemented by his industry peers in the US.

Ghosn aims to cut component, administration, and manufacturing expenses, but his plan to turn Renault around is more aggressive on the product side. Ghosn will push Renault into product markets it traditionally has left untapped. By 2009 Renault plans to introduce 26 new models, half of which will be new to Renault — SUVs, sports cars, and SUV/crossover vehicles. Ghosn will also push Renault up market with the addition of more luxury models in order to reduce the strain on the aging Mélange group of medium-sized cars. The Mélange family of cars generates half of Renault's profits.

HISTORY

In the Paris suburb of Billancourt in 1898, 21-year-old Louis Renault assembled a motorized vehicle with a transmission box of his own design. Louis and his brothers, Marcel and Fernand, established Renault Freres and produced the world's first sedan in 1899. Marcel died in a racing accident (1903) and Fernand left the business (1908), leaving Louis in sole possession of the company. He renamed it La Société Louis Renault in 1908.

In 1914 a fleet of 600 Paris taxis shuttled French troops to fight the Germans in the Battle of the Marne. Renault also built light tanks and airplane engines. Between world wars Renault expanded into trucks, tractors, and aircraft engines. Renault sustained heavy damage in WWII, but Louis Renault operated the remaining Paris facilities for the Germans during their occupation of France. After the liberation of Paris, he was accused of collaboration and died in prison while awaiting trial in 1944. The de Gaulle government nationalized Renault in 1945 and gave the company its present name.

Worldwide economic growth aided Renault's postwar comeback. The company achieved its greatest success in high-volume, low-cost cars such as the 4 CV in the late 1940s and 1950s, the Renault 4 in the 1960s and 1970s, and the Renault 5 in the 1970s and 1980s.

In 1979 Renault acquired 46% of American Motors Corporation (AMC). In the early 1980s AMC fared poorly, and Renault suffered from a worldwide slump in auto sales, an aging product line, and stiff competition from Japanese carmakers. Decreasing sales, an unwieldy bureaucracy, and above-average wages contributed to a $1.5 billion loss in 1984.

Georges Besse took over Renault in 1985, and trimmed employment by 20,000. When Besse was assassinated by terrorists in 1986, Raymond Levy assumed his role and continued his policies, laying off 30,000 more workers and selling AMC to Chrysler (1987).

The French government reduced its share of the firm from 80% to 52% in 1995 and to 44% the following year. In 1997 it shut down a Belgian plant that employed more than 3,000 workers and fired a similar number of employees in France.

In 1999 Renault and Fiat combined their bus-making operations under the name Irisbus and their foundry operations into jointly owned Teksid. Also that year Renault bought a 51% stake in Romanian automaker Automobile Dacia SA, and paid $5.4 billion for a 37% stake in Nissan and a 15% (later increased to 23%) stake in truck affiliate Nissan Diesel Motor.

In 2000 Renault agreed to buy a 70% stake in Samsung Motors' automobile business for around $550 million. It also sold its Mack truck unit to AB Volvo in exchange for a 15% stake in the Swedish truck maker. In 2001 Renault announced plans to further strengthen ties with Nissan. The plan would increase Renault's stake in Nissan to 44% while granting Nissan a 15% stake in Renault. The French Finance Ministry also announced that it would reduce the French government's stake in Renault from 44% to 25% through a future public offering. In 2003 the French government further reduced its stake in Renault from 25% to about 15%.

Early in 2005 Renault sold its 18% stake in Nissan Diesel Motor Co., Ltd. to J.P. Morgan Securities, Ltd., who, in turn, sold the shares on the open market.

The following year Renault called an emergency board meeting to ponder a proposal put forth in writing by billionaire General Motors investor Kirk Kerkorian (he owns about a 10% stake in GM). Kerkorian suggested GM, Renault, and Nissan form a three-way global automotive alliance.

In the midst of the 2006 Paris Auto Show the parties announced there would be no three-way alliance. Later that year Renault announced the forming of a new car manufacturing joint venture with Indian carmaker Mahindra & Mahindra.

EXECUTIVES

Chairman: Louis Schweitzer, age 64
President, CEO, and Director: Carlos Ghosn, age 52
EVP and CFO: Thierry Moulonguet, age 55
EVP, Product and Strategic Planning and Programs: Patrick Pélata, age 51
EVP, Group Human Resources and Corporate Secretary General: Michel de Virville, age 61
EVP, Manufacturing and Powertrain: Michel Gornet, age 59
EVP, Quality and Engineering: Jean-Louis Ricaud, age 54
EVP, Sales and Marketing: Patrick Blain, age 54
SVP and Corporate Controller: Jean-Baptiste Duzan, age 59
SVP, Chairman's Office: Philippe Klein, age 49
SVP Communications: Marie-Françoise Damesin, age 49
SVP, Public Affairs: Luc-Alexandre Ménard, age 62
SVP, Marketing and Strategy: Benoît Marzloff, age 57
CIO: Christian Mardrus, age 47
Chairman and CEO, Renault F1 Team: Alain Dassas, age 60
Chairman and CEO, RCI Banque SA: Philippe Gamba, age 59
Director Engineering: Jacques Lacambre, age 64
Managing Director, Renault Samsung Motors: Jean-Marie Hurtiger, age 55
Auditors: Ernst & Young Audit; Deloitte & Associés

LOCATIONS

HQ: Renault S.A.
13-15 quai Le Gallo,
92109 Boulogne-Billancourt, France
Phone: +33-1-76-84-50-50   **Fax:** +33-1-41-04-51-49
Web: www.renault.com

PRODUCTS/OPERATIONS

2005 Sales

	$ mil.	% of total
Automobiles	46,904.2	95
Sales financing	2,543.9	5
Adjustments	(491.5)	—
Total	**48,956.6**	**100**

Selected Products

Automobiles
Clio	Megane Hatch
Clio Tricorps	Megane Sport Hatch
Espace	Modus
Kangoo 4X4	Scenic
Laguna	Trafic
Logan	Twingo
Megane Cabriolet	Vel Satis
Megane Coupe	

Light Commercial Vehicles
Master
New Kangoo Express
Trafic

COMPETITORS

BMW	Peugeot
DaimlerChrysler	Peugeot Motors of
Fiat	America, Inc.
Ford	Saab Automobile
General Motors	Suzuki Motor
Honda	Tata Group
Isuzu	Toyota
Kia Motors	Volkswagen
Mazda	

HISTORICAL FINANCIALS

Company Type: Public

Income Statement

	REVENUE ($ mil.)	NET INCOME ($ mil.)	NET PROFIT MARGIN	EMPLOYEES
12/05	48,957	—	—	126,584
12/04	55,535	—	—	130,573
12/03	47,101	—	—	130,740
12/02	38,084	—	—	132,351
12/01	32,200	—	—	140,417
Annual Growth	**11.0%**	**—**	**—**	**(2.6%)**

FYE: December 31

Revenue History

Euronext Paris: RNO

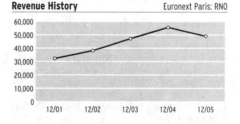

Repsol YPF

The sun shines on Repsol YPF, Spain's largest oil company. A fully integrated oil and gas company, it operates in Latin America, the Middle East, and North Africa. The firm owns YPF, Argentina's #1 oil company, and has operations in more than 28 countries. Repsol YPF operates five refineries in Spain and four in Latin America and produces chemicals, plastics, and polymers. It sells gas under the brands Campsa, Petronor, and Repsol at more than 6,900 service stations in Europe and Latin America. It is one of Spain's largest sellers of liquefied petroleum gas. Repsol YPF had reported proved reserves of 4.9 billion barrels of oil equivalent, but in 2006 announced a 25% cut in this number.

The company acquired its current name and expanded its reserves significantly with the 1999 purchase of YPF, Argentina's leading oil company.

To comply with its agreement with Argentina's government to divest 11% of the company's refining and marketing assets in Argentina, Repsol YPF shed 700 of its stations and a refinery in a $1 billion asset swap with Brazil's Petrobras.

Through 31%-owned affiliate Gas Natural, the company owns about 41% of Spanish natural gas supplier Enagas. Also with Gas Natural, Repsol YPF formed a liquefied natural gas joint venture that will have a marketing capacity of 12 million metric tons and a fleet of more than 10 carriers.

Repsol YPF formed a joint venture with Chevron to develop oil operations in the Orinoco belt of Venezuela.

Altogether Repsol YPF plans to invest more than €21 billion (more than $26 billion) over the next few of years in its operations, particularly in exploration and production, including its Spanish refineries, which will receive an investment of about €4 billion (more than $4 billion).

In 2006 the company acquired BP's 28% stake in the Shenzi field in the Gulf of Mexico.

HISTORY

Repsol YPF, officially created as Repsol in 1987, is actually the result of efforts that began as early as the 1920s to organize Spain's fragmented energy industry.

Following an era of dependency on foreign investment prior to and during Francisco Franco's dictatorship (1939-75), Spain began reorganizing its energy industry. In 1979 it set up the Instituto Nacional de Hidrocarburos, which in 1981 incorporated all public-sector firms involved in gas and oil under one government agency.

Repsol was formed six years later to provide central management to a Spanish oil company that could compete in the unified European market. The government chose the name Repsol, after a well-known brand of Spanish lubricant products. The firm was charged with pursuing a global strategy to bring together all levels of the industry.

In 1989 Repsol offered 26% of the firm on the Madrid and New York stock exchanges, raising over $1 billion. That year Repsol increased its marine fleet with the purchase of the Naviera Vizcaina shipping company and bought Carless Refining & Marketing, a UK business with a chain of 500 service stations operating mainly under the Anglo brand. Although Spain was opening its doors to foreign investment, the Spanish government maintained control over the country's energy industry, including a tightly guarded distribution network under state-controlled Campsa. Campsa oversaw a marketing/logistics system of pipelines, storage terminals, and sales outlets.

The European Community demanded that Spain open its markets to other EC members, forcing Campsa in 1991 to divide its 3,800 gasoline stations among its four major shareholders: Cepsa (Spain's largest private refiner), Petromed, Ertoil, and Repsol. Repsol gained 66% of the logistical network and use of the Campsa brand name.

Repsol and Spanish bank La Caixa merged their interests in natural gas in 1992 to create Gas Natural, a new gas distributor. That year the Spanish government began reducing its majority holding, and by 1996 its stake had dwindled to 10%. (It sold its remaining stock in 1997.)

Expanding its South American operations, Repsol acquired control of Argentinian oil company Astra CAPSA and a Peruvian oil refinery in 1996. That year Repsol purchased a 30% stake in the Tin Fouye Tabankort field in Algeria.

In 1999 Repsol paid $2 billion for a 15% stake in giant oil company YPF, which was auctioned off by Argentina's government. After acquiring another 83% of YPF for $13.2 billion, Repsol changed its name to Repsol YPF. To help pay down debt incurred in the acquisition, Repsol YPF sold its UK North Sea oil and gas operations to US independent Kerr-McGee for $555 million in 2000. That year the company (as part of its commitment to Argentina's government after acquiring YPF) agreed to swap some of its Argentine refining and marketing assets for Brazilian oil and gas operations owned by Petrobras.

In 2002 Repsol YPF sold oil and gas assets in Indonesia to CNOOC for about $585 million.

In 2004 former chairman of Spain's top gas supplier Gas Natural S.A., Antonio Brufau, replaced Alfonso Cortina de Alcocer as chairman of Repsol.

EXECUTIVES

Chairman and CEO: Antonio Brufau Niubó
Vice Chairman: Ricardo Fornesa Ribó
CFO: Luis Mañas Antón
EVP Upstream: Miguel Ángel Remón Gil
Executive Director of Argentina, Brazil, and Bolivia: Enrique Locutura Rupérez
Executive Director of Downstream: Pedro Fernández Frial
Executive Director of Upstream: Nemesio Fernández-Cuesta Luca de Tena
Group Managing Director of Communication and Head of the Chairman's Office: Jaume Giró Ribas
Group Managing Director of Finance and Corporate Services: Fernando Ramírez Mazarredo
Group Managing Director of Human Resources: Jesus Fernández de la Vega
Managing Director of Refining and Marketing in Europe: Jorge Segrelles García
Executive Director of Management and Development Control: Miguel Martinez San Martin
Managing Director of Refining and Marketing Latin America: Pascual Olmos Navarro
Managing Director of RYTTSA: Alfonso Ballestero Aguilar
Director of Chemicals: Juan Pedro Maza Sabalete
Director of External Relations: Antonio Gomis Sáez
Director of Legal Affairs: Rafael Piqueras Bautista
Director of LPG: Manuel Guerrero Pemán
Director of Planning and Control: Pedro Fernández Frial
Secretary and Director: Luis Suárez de Lezo Mantilla
Auditors: Deloitte SL

LOCATIONS

HQ: Repsol YPF, S.A.
　Paseo de la Castellana, 278-280,
　28046 Madrid, Spain
Phone: +34-91-348-80-00　**Fax:** +34-91-348-28-21
Web: www.repsol-ypf.com

Repsol YPF has operations in more than 30 countries in Africa, Asia, the Caribbean, Europe, Latin America, and the Middle East.

2005 Sales

	% of total
Spain	44
Argentina, Bolivia & Brazil	16
Other countries	40
Total	**100**

PRODUCTS/OPERATIONS

2005 Sales

	% of total
Refining & marketing	80
Exploration & production	8
Chemicals	8
Gas & electricity	4
Total	**100**

COMPETITORS

Anadarko Petroleum
Apco Argentina
BHP Billiton
BP
Devon Energy
Endesa
Eni
Exxon Mobil
IBERDROLA
Imperial Oil
Koch
Marathon Oil
Murphy Oil
Noble Energy
Norsk Hydro
Occidental Petroleum
PDVSA
PEMEX
PETROBRAS
Petrobras Energía
Pioneer Natural Resources
Royal Dutch Shell
TOTAL
Unión Fenosa

HISTORICAL FINANCIALS

Company Type: Public

Income Statement

FYE: December 31

	REVENUE ($ mil.)	NET INCOME ($ mil.)	NET PROFIT MARGIN	EMPLOYEES
12/05	60,458	3,389	5.6%	35,909
12/04	56,881	2,651	4.7%	33,337
12/03	46,720	2,412	5.2%	31,121
12/02	38,248	1,348	3.5%	30,110
Annual Growth	**16.5%**	**36.0%**	**—**	**6.0%**

2005 Year-End Financials

Debt ratio: 55.2%　　　　No. of shares (mil.): —
Return on equity: 16.9%　Dividends
Cash ($ mil.): 3,728　　　Yield: 1.8%
Current ratio: 1.26　　　 Payout: —
Long-term debt ($ mil.): 11,514　Market value ($ mil.): —

Stock History

NYSE: REP

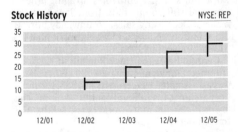

	STOCK PRICE ($) FY Close	P/E High/Low	PER SHARE ($) Earnings	Dividends
12/05	29.41	— —	—	0.53
12/04	26.10	— —	—	0.42
12/03	19.55	— —	—	0.41
12/02	13.08	— —	—	0.15
Annual Growth	**31.0%**	**— —**	**—**	**52.3%**

Reuters

Reuters Group helps you stay informed on the business of business and just about everything else. One of the world's leading providers of news and information, the company provides global access to financial data, news feeds, and corporate information though its operations in more than 120 countries. It culls information from more than 300 stock exchanges and gathers information on more than 40,000 companies worldwide. With nearly some 190 news bureaus, Reuters ranks as the world's largest international news agency, publishing stories in almost 20 languages. It also has a 50% stake in news and information joint venture Factiva with Dow Jones, which it is selling to Dow Jones for about $160 million.

While probably best known for its international news reporting, the company gets just 5% of its revenue from its media operations. Financial data and software tools for traders and sales people, meanwhile, makes up more than 40% of Reuters' business. Almost three-quarters of the company's business comes through subscriptions or other recurring revenue streams.

Reuters has been struggling to get through a difficult recovery period after a near collapse of its business in 2001. Under the leadership of CEO Tom Glocer, the company has slashed headcount and closed down several operations in order to get costs under control. It has also sold off many operations, including two consulting and advisory businesses (TowerGroup and Yankee Group), most of its stake in TIBCO Software, and its Radianz network services business. In 2005 Reuters sold its 62% stake in Instinet to NASDAQ for $1.1 billion. However, the company did acquire Moneyline Telerate, a leading supplier of money market information, for about $145 million in 2005.

To complete its turnaround, though, Reuters is hoping to move beyond its core institutional and enterprise customers and become more of a consumer-oriented business. In 2004 it relaunched its reuters.com Web site as an advertising-supported news and information portal serving a general audience, and in 2005 the company brought in former MSNBC executive Dean Wright to take charge of its consumer products operation. The company has also reduced the amount of news it sells to customers such as Yahoo! and MSN and it is exploring ways to distribute content through subscriptions directly to consumers on mobile devices. Reuters marked another momentous change in 2005 when it left London's Fleet Street, historically the city's home for journalists, and moved into a new headquarters at Canary Wharf.

As a public company with a vested interest in maintaining the objectivity of its news and information, Reuters is ultimately controlled by the Founders Share Company, an organization established in 1984 that is overseen by representatives of four major news organizations.

HISTORY

In 1849 German news correspondent Paul Julius Reuter seized the chance to scoop his competitors by using carrier pigeons to bridge the telegraph gap between Aachen, Germany, and Brussels. He moved to London in 1851 and began telegraphing stock quotes between Paris and London. In 1865 Reuter's Telegram Co. was organized as a limited company.

Reuter ceded management to his son Herbert in 1878 and died in 1899. Herbert made the disastrous decision to establish Reuter's Bank in 1913. Two years later, under the strain of WWI anti-German sentiment and the death of his wife, Herbert committed suicide. Successor Roderick Jones changed the company's name to Reuters Ltd. and took it private in 1916 to avoid a hostile takeover. Reuters advanced into new technology by using radios and teleprinters in the 1920s. By 1925 The Press Association owned a majority of the company; it ousted Jones in 1941, displeased with his relationship to the British government. In an attempt to uphold Reuters' independence, The Reuters Trust was created that year.

Reuters established international bureaus during the 1940s and 1950s, but its owners' focus on the bottom line limited the scale of expansion. The company partnered with Ultronic Systems Corporation in 1964 to launch Stockmaster, a financial data transmission system. Nine years later Reuters introduced its Monitor electronic marketplace to track the foreign exchange market. Monitor Dealing, introduced in 1981, enabled dealers to trade currencies online.

The company went public in 1984 as Reuters Holdings PLC, and with the new capital, it accelerated acquisitions. It bought Visnews (now Reuters Television, 1985), Instinet (1986), TIBCO (1994), and Quotron (1994). The company also acquired a new CEO during this time when Peter Job, a journalist who joined Reuters in 1963, was named to the top spot in 1991. In 1994 the company launched Reuters Television for financial markets. The following year it agreed to make its information available on the Internet via IBM's infoMarket service. In 1997 the FBI began investigating whether Reuters illegally used information from rival Bloomberg (the case was dropped two years later).

With competition from the Internet nipping at its heels, Reuters restructured in 1998 to refocus along product lines (which led to the creation of holding company Reuters Group PLC). In 1999 Reuters and Dow Jones & Company launched a joint venture combining their online news databases.

In 2000 Reuters announced a joint venture with online investment information provider Multex.com (to launch an Internet portal for European investors). It also purchased The Yankee Group from fellow financial information provider Primark.

Job retired as CEO in 2001 and was replaced by Tom Glocer, the second American and first non-journalist (he's a lawyer) to hold the position. During his first week on the job, Glocer announced that the company would cut about 1,800 jobs by the end of 2002. Also in 2001 Reuters took Instinet public (retaining about a 60% stake).

In late 2002 the company purchased foreign exchange transaction technology specialist AVT Technologies. The company reduced its stake in TIBCO Software in 2004 to less than 10%. It also sold The Yankee Group to private investors.

In 2005 Reuters moved into a new headquarters building at Canary Wharf, leaving its Fleet Street offices after 66 years. Late that year the company sold its stake in Instinet to Nasdaq for $1.1 billion.

EXECUTIVES

Chairman: Niall FitzGerald, age 61, $860,200 pay
CEO and Director: Thomas H. (Tom) Glocer, age 46, $2,919,518 pay
COO and Director: Devin N. Wenig, age 39
CFO and Director: David J. Grigson, age 51, $1,307,504 pay
VP Media Sales: Walker Jacobs
VP Mobile and Emerging Media: Stephen Smyth
Chief Technology Officer: Roy Lowrence
CIO: David Lister, age 45
Chief Marketing Officer: Lee Ann Daly
Managing Director, Global Sales and Service Operations: Christopher Hagman, age 47
Global Head of Operations and Technology: Michael (Mike) Sayers, age 51
Chairman, Factiva: Clare Hart, age 45
Interim CEO, Factiva: Claude Green
President, Investment Banking and Brokerage: Isaak Karaev, age 55
President, Reuters Japan: Yuji Takei, age 45
President, Reuters Media: Chris Ahearn
EVP of Marketing, Reuters Media: Janet Scardino
EVP Sales and Training, Reuters America: Michael Steinharter
Group Human Resources Director: Stephen Dando, age 44
Global Head of Corporate Affairs: Simon Walker, age 51
Global Managing Editor and Head of Editorial Operations: David Schlesinger, age 43
Global Head of Public Relations: Stephen Naru
Editor-in-Chief and Global Head of Content; Chairman, Reuters Foundation: Geert Linnebank, age 49
General Counsel and Company Secretary: Rosemary Martin, age 46
Head of Investor Relations: Miriam McKay
Auditors: PricewaterhouseCoopers LLP

LOCATIONS

HQ: Reuters Group PLC
The Reuters Bldg., Canary Wharf,
London E14 5EP, United Kingdom
Phone: +44-20-7250-1122 **Fax:** +44-20-7542-4064
US HQ: 3 Times Sq., New York, NY 10036
US Phone: 646-223-4000 **US Fax:** 646-223-4001
Web: www.reuters.com

Reuters Group has operations in more than 120 countries.

2005 Sales

	% of total
Europe, Middle East & Africa	55
The Americas	27
Asia/Pacific	18
Total	**100**

PRODUCTS/OPERATIONS

2005 Sales

	% of total
Sales & trading	66
Enterprise	16
Asset management & research	11
Media	7
Total	**100**

Selected Products

Enterprise
  Datafeeds
  Risk management
Financial desktop
  Reuters Knowlege family (company and industry-specific research)
  Reuters Trader family (basic sales, trading, and portfolio management)
  Reuters Xtra family (sophisticated sales, trading, and portfolio management)
Media (broadcast news, video, and photographic coverage)

COMPETITORS

Agence France-Presse	Misys
Algorithmics	Moneyline Telerate
Associated Press	Morningstar
Bloomberg	NASD
CSK	NYSE
D&B	Quick Corp.
Dow Jones	S&P
FactSet	SunGard
Financial Times	Telekurs
GL Trade	Thomson Corporation
IBM	TIBCO Software
Interactive Data	UPI
LexisNexis	Value Line

HISTORICAL FINANCIALS

Company Type: Public

Income Statement

FYE: December 31

	REVENUE ($ mil.)	NET INCOME ($ mil.)	NET PROFIT MARGIN	EMPLOYEES
12/05	4,230	681	16.1%	15,300
12/04	5,749	846	14.7%	15,500
12/03	5,686	(68)	—	16,744
12/02	4,805	(204)	—	17,414
12/01	5,792	134	2.3%	19,429
Annual Growth	(7.6%)	50.3%	—	(5.8%)

2005 Year-End Financials

Debt ratio: 52.6%
Return on equity: 59.1%
Cash ($ mil.): 1,170
Current ratio: 1.30
Long-term debt ($ mil.): 638

No. of shares (mil.): —
Dividends
 Yield: 2.5%
 Payout: 114.4%
Market value ($ mil.): —

Stock History

NASDAQ (GS): RTRSY

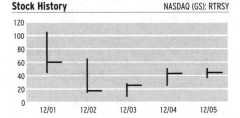

	STOCK PRICE ($) FY Close	P/E High	P/E Low	PER SHARE ($) Earnings	PER SHARE ($) Dividends
12/05	44.35	52	38	0.97	1.11
12/04	42.95	1	1	47.20	1.06
12/03	25.35	—	—	(0.29)	0.94
12/02	17.20	—	—	(0.87)	0.90
12/01	59.99	—	—	—	1.40
Annual Growth	(7.3%)	—	—	—	(5.6%)

Ricoh

Ricoh may be best known for its imaging equipment, but the company is more than just another copycat. One of the world's leading manufacturers of copiers and supplies, Ricoh also makes fax machines, scanners, and printers. Other products from the company, which has more than 400 subsidiaries and affiliates worldwide, include digital cameras, personal computers, servers, semiconductors, printed circuit boards, and optical data storage drives. Among

Ricoh's US-based subsidiaries are office equipment specialists Ricoh Corporation, Lanier Worldwide, and Savin.

Ricoh continues to expand its networked imaging and connectivity products, which include laser printers, copiers, and document management software and systems. The company has also moved beyond its core office products into related services, including systems customization, integration, consulting, and facilities management.

HISTORY

Ricoh began in 1936 as the Riken Kankoshi Company, making photographic paper. With founder Kiyoshi Ichimura at the helm, the company soon became the leader in Japan's sensitized-paper market. It changed its name to Riken Optical Company in 1938 and started making cameras. Two years later it produced its first camera under the Ricoh brand.

By 1954 Ricoh cameras were Japan's #1 sellers and were also popular abroad. The next year the company entered the office machine market with its compact mimeograph machine. Ricoh followed that in 1960 with an offset duplicator.

Ricoh built its business in the 1960s with a range of office machines, including reproduction and data processing equipment and retrieval systems. The company began establishing operations overseas, including US subsidiary Ricoh Industries U.S.A. in 1962. The US unit started marketing cameras but found greener pastures in the copier industry, where Ricoh's products were sold under the Pitney Bowes and Savin brand names. The company changed its name to Ricoh Company in 1963. Two years later Ricoh entered the emerging field of office computers and introduced an electrostatic copier. In 1968 Ichimura died, and Mikio Tatebayashi took over as president for the next eight years.

During the 1970s Ricoh debuted the first high-speed fax machine and began consolidating its network outside Japan. In 1973 Ricoh established a second US subsidiary — Ricoh Electronics — to assemble copier supplies and parts, becoming the first Japanese company to produce copiers in the US. It released a plain-paper copier in 1975, followed the next year by a daisy wheel printer and its first word processor. Tatebayashi died in 1976 and was replaced by Takeshi Ouye as president. Subsidiary Rapicom was established in 1978 in Japan to develop fax products.

Throughout the 1970s Savin and Pitney Bowes continued to brand and sell Ricoh-made products in the US, but in the early 1980s Ricoh started marketing products under its own name. It introduced a PC and its first laser printer in 1983. By the next year Ricoh had 7% of the US copier market. Other products introduced in the 1980s included a color copier, minicomputers developed with AT&T, and (in Japan) a digital copier that could also be used as an input/output station for electronic filing systems. Ricoh's overseas sales continued to grow in the late 1980s and for a while exceeded its domestic sales. In 1983 Ouye turned over leadership of the company to Hiroshi Hamada.

Ricoh founded Tailien Optical (Shenzhen) Co. Ltd. in 1992 to make compact camera parts. As the 1990s progressed, the company increasingly pushed products based on digital technologies.

Ricoh won licensing fees from Samsung Electronics in a 1995 dispute over fax machine patents. Seeking to boost international sales, it bought marketing firms Savin in the US and Gestetner Holdings (later renamed NRG Group)

in Europe that year. The next year Hamada became chairman and CEO, and Masamitsu Sakurai took over as president.

The company's push during the mid-1990s to increase overseas sales paid off. Amid an Asian economic crisis, Ricoh's overall sales remained relatively stable, while sales of its copiers outside Japan increased 20% and 9% for 1998 and 1999, respectively.

In 2000 the company reorganized its US operations and consolidated its European distribution centers. Early the following year Ricoh boosted its push into the US market with its acquisition of office equipment supplier Lanier Worldwide for about $250 million. Despite shaky world economic conditions, in fiscal 2002 Ricoh saw growth in sales and profits, with strong overseas sales making up for slightly lowered revenues from Japan.

In 2004 Ricoh augmented its printer business by acquiring Hitachi Printing Solutions.

EXECUTIVES

President, CEO, and COO: Masamitsu Sakurai, age 64
Deputy President: Tatsuo Hirakawa
Executive Managing Director: Koichi Endo
Executive Managing Director: Masayuki Matsumoto
Executive Managing Director: Katsumi (Kirk) Yoshida
Managing Director: Kazunori Azuma
Managing Director: Makoto Hashimoto
Managing Director: Yuji Inoue
Managing Director: Shiroh Kondoh
Managing Director: Zenji Miura
Managing Director: Takashi Nakamura
Managing Director: Kiyoshi Sakai
Managing Director: Kazuo Togashi
EVP; Chairman and CEO, Ricoh Corporation:
 Susumu (Sam) Ichioka
EVP: Kenji Hatanaka
EVP: Etsuo Kobayashi
EVP: Hideko Kunii
EVP: Hiroshi Kobayashi
EVP: Haruo Nakamura
EVP: Terumoto Nonaka
EVP: Tadatoshi Sakamaki
EVP: Hiroshi Tategami
Auditors: KPMG AZSA & Co.

LOCATIONS

HQ: Ricoh Company, Ltd.
 15-5, Minami-Aoyama 1-chome, Minato-ku,
 Tokyo 107-8544, Japan
Phone: +81-3-3479-3111   **Fax:** +81-3-3403-1578
US HQ: 5 Dedrick Place, West Caldwell, NJ 07006
US Phone: 973-882-2000   **US Fax:** 973-882-2506
Web: www.ricoh.com

Ricoh Company has more than 400 subsidiaries and affiliates worldwide. The company has manufacturing plants in China, France, Hong Kong, Japan, South Korea, Taiwan, the UK, and the US.

2006 Sales

	% of total
Japan	51
Europe	23
The Americas	20
Other	6
Total	**100**

PRODUCTS/OPERATIONS

2006 Sales

	% of total
Office Solutions	
Imaging	76
Network system	10
Industrial products	6
Other	8
Total	**100**

Selected Products

Office Solutions
  Imaging Solutions
    Diazo copiers
    Digital duplicators
    Digital monochrome and color copiers
    Fax machines
    Imaging supplies and consumables
    Wide-format copiers
    Printing systems (laser, multifunction)
    Scanners
  Network System Solutions
    Document management software
    Networking and applications software
    Network systems
    Personal computers
    Servers
    Services and support
Industrial
  Electronic components
  Measuring equipment
  Optical equipment
  Semiconductor devices
  Thermal media
Other
  Digital cameras and other photographic equipment
  Financing and logistics services
  Optical disks

COMPETITORS

3M	Konica Minolta
Brother Industries	Kyocera Mita
Canon	Lexmark
CASIO COMPUTER	Matsushita
Danka	NEC
Eastman Kodak	Nikon
Epson	Océ Imagistics
Fuji Xerox	Oki Data
Fujifilm	Oki Electric
Hewlett-Packard	SANYO
Hitachi	Sharp
IBM	Toshiba
IKON	Xerox

HISTORICAL FINANCIALS

Company Type: Public

Income Statement

FYE: March 31

	REVENUE ($ mil.)	NET INCOME ($ mil.)	NET PROFIT MARGIN	EMPLOYEES
3/06	16,368	830	5.1%	—
3/05	16,954	777	4.6%	—
3/04	17,118	882	5.2%	—
3/03	14,732	615	4.2%	—
3/02	12,574	463	3.7%	—
Annual Growth	6.8%	15.7%	—	—

2006 Year-End Financials

Debt ratio: 20.4%
Return on equity: 10.2%
Cash ($ mil.): 1,613
Current ratio: 1.53
Long-term debt ($ mil.): 1,672

Net Income History

OTC: RICOY

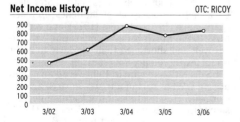

Rio Tinto

Rio Tinto is always on the lookout for pay dirt. Rio Tinto Group, one of the world's largest mining operations, comprises dual-listed sister companies Rio Tinto Limited (in Melbourne) and Rio Tinto plc (in London). Although each company trades separately, the two Rio Tintos operate as one business. Rio Tinto mines coal (about 20% of sales), iron, copper, uranium, industrial minerals (borax, salt, talc), aluminum, gold, and diamonds. The company has operations worldwide, but it operates primarily in Australia and North America (accounting for about 40% each). Mining operations in these areas account for about three-quarters of sales. Subsidiaries include Kennecotts Energy, Exploration, and Copper.

By focusing on large-scale, long-life mining operations, Rio Tinto has weathered commodity prices that have dipped and risen over several years. Like its rivals, the company continues to seek acquisitions as it cuts costs and improves productivity. Rio Tinto's tight-fisted operating style, while providing exceptional margins for its industry, has drawn the ire of unions, which have been critical of the company's employment and environmental records.

Rio Tinto had owned 14% of Lihir Gold but divested its stake in the company. Prior to that decision the company had controlled Lihir and its management. In late 2005, though, Rio Tinto reliquished its management rights and decided to sell its entire stake in Lihir.

HISTORY

Rio Tinto Limited began life as the Zinc Corporation in 1905 to recover zinc from the tailings of the silver and lead mines around Australia's mineral-rich Broken Hill area. The company expanded steadily, extending its operations into a wide range of mining and metallurgical activities, primarily in Australia. By 1914 it had changed its name to Consolidated Zinc Corporation. The company discovered the world's largest deposit of bauxite (1955) and formed Hamersley Holdings with Kaiser Steel (1962) to mine iron ore.

Rio Tinto plc (UK) began with mining operations in Spain in 1873. It sold most of its Spanish holdings in 1954 and branched out to Australia, Africa, and Canada. In 1962 Rio Tinto and Australia's Consolidated Zinc merged to form RTZ. The companies merged their Australian interests as a partially owned subsidiary, CRA (from Conzinc Riotinto of Australia).

In 1968 RTZ bought U.S. Borax, which was built on one of the earth's few massive boron deposits. (The use of boron in cleansers was widespread in the late 19th century.) A 1927 discovery in the Mojave Desert led to development of a large boron mine. Until its Turkish mine was nationalized, RTZ controlled the world's boron supply. It sold U.S. Borax's consumer products operations in 1988.

RTZ opened a large copper mine at Bougainville in Papua New Guinea in 1969. Subsidiary CRA discovered diamonds in Western Australia's Argyle region three years later. CRA then opened Australia's largest thermal-coal development at Blair Athol in 1984.

RTZ bought Kennecott Corporation in 1989 and expanded its copper operations. Kennecott had been formed by Stephen Birch and named for Robert Kennicott (a typo altered the spelling of the company's name); it had begun mining at Bingham Canyon, Utah, in 1904. Kennicott died in Alaska while trying to establish an intercontinental telegraph line. Backed by J.P. Morgan and the Guggenheims, Birch also built a railroad to haul the ore. Kennecott merged its railroad and mine operations in 1915. Kennecott consolidated its hold on Chile's Braden copper mine (1925) and on the Utah Copper Company (1936) and other US mines. When copper prices slumped, British Petroleum's Standard Oil of Ohio subsidiary bought Kennecott (1981). In 1989 RTZ purchased British Petroleum's US mineral operations, including Kennecott.

By the 1990s RTZ and CRA (by then 49% owned by RTZ) were increasingly competing for mining rights to recently opened areas of Asia and Latin America. RTZ sold the last of its non-mining holdings (building products group) in 1993. In 1995 RTZ brought CRA into its operations. Through Kennecott, RTZ purchased US coal mine operators Nerco, Cordero Mining Company, and Colowyo Coal Company. Also in 1995 the company acquired 13% of Freeport-McMoRan Copper & Gold (sold in 2004).

The RTZ and CRA company names were changed to Rio Tinto plc and Rio Tinto Limited, respectively, in 1997. Rio Tinto bought a Wyoming coal mine from Kerr-McGee for about $400 million in 1998. The next year Rio Tinto bought 80% of Kestrel (coal, Australia) and increased its ownership of Blair Athol from 57% to 71% and increased its stake in Comalco (aluminum) to 72%.

In 2000 CEO Leon Davis retired; his position passed to energy group executive Leigh Clifford. In a move that sparked an outcry from union officials, Davis accepted a position as non-executive deputy chairman. Later that year Rio Tinto acquired both North Limited and Ashton Mining. The company also bought Comalco's outstanding shares and the Peabody Group's Australian subsidiaries.

Rio Tinto sold its Norzink Zink Smelter to Outokumpu in 2001. It also increased its holdings in Queensland Alumina, Coal & Allied Industries, and Palabora Mining, and it began developing the Hail Creek Coal Project in Australia, which is based on one of the largest coking coal deposits in the world. In 2003 Rio Tinto sold its 25% stake in Minera Alumbrera (Argentina) and Peak Gold Mine (Australia) to Wheaton River Minerals for around $210 million.

EXECUTIVES

Chairman: Paul D. Skinner, age 62, $1,049,000 pay
CEO and Executive Director: R. Leigh Clifford, age 58, $3,093,000 pay
Director, Group Resources and Executive Director: Tom Albanese, age 49
Finance Director and Executive Director: Guy R. Elliot, age 50, $1,829,000 pay
Chief Executive, Aluminum: Oscar Y. L. Groeneveld, age 52, $1,525,000 pay
Chief Executive, Diamonds: Keith Johnson, age 44, $1,105,000 pay
Chief Executive, Energy: Preston Chiaro, age 52, $930,000 pay
Chief Executive, Industrial Minerals: Andrew Mackenzie, age 48, $1,149,000 pay
Chief Executive, Iron Ore: Sam Walsh, age 56, $1,636,000 pay
Chief Executive, Copper: Bret Clayton, age 44
Managing Director, Rio Tinto Australia: Charles (Charlie) Lenegan, age 53
Secretary, Melbourne: Stephen Consedine, age 44
Secretary, London: Anette Lawless, age 49
Head of Communication and External Relations, London: Andrew Vickerman, age 50

Head of Human Resources, London: Karen McLeod, age 58
Head of Operational and Technical Excellence (OTX), Brisbane: Grant Thorne, age 56
Head of Global Business Services, London: Michael Merton
General Manager, Marketing, Rio Tinto Coal: Kelly Cosgrove
Auditors: PricewaterhouseCoopers; PricewaterhouseCoopers LLP

LOCATIONS

HQ: Rio Tinto Group
    55 Collins St., Level 33, Melbourne 3000, Australia
Phone: +61-3-9283-3333   **Fax:** +61-3-9283-3707
Web: www.riotinto.com

Rio Tinto has mining operations worldwide.

PRODUCTS/OPERATIONS

2005 Sales

	$ mil.	% of total
Iron Ore	5,497	27
Copper	4,839	23
Energy	3,867	19
Aluminum	2,744	13
Industrial Minerals	2,487	12
Diamonds	1,076	5
Other	93	1
Adjustments	(1,570)	—
Total	**19,033**	**100**

Selected Holdings

Iron Ore
    Channar (60%, Australia)
    Corumba (Brazil)
    Hamersley Iron Pty. Ltd. (Australia)
    Iron Ore Co. of Canada (59%)
    Robe River Iron Associates (53%, Australia)
Copper
    Atlantic Copper (13%, Spain)
    Bingham Canyon (US)
    Escondida (30%, Chile)
    Grasberg — Joint Venture (40%, Indonesia)
    Kennecott Utah Copper (US)
    Neves Corvo (49%, Portugal)
    Northparkes (80%, Australia)
    Palabora (49%, South Africa)
Energy
    Bengalla (30%, Australia)
    Blair Athol Coal (71%, Australia)
    Coal & Allied Industries Ltd. (76%, Australia)
    Hail Creek Coal (92%, Australia)
    Hunter Valley Operations (78%, Australia)
    Kennecott Energy (US)
    Kestrel (80%, Australia)
    Mt Thorley (60%, Australia)
    Tarong Coal (Australia)
    Warkworth (42%, Australia)
Aluminum and Bauxite
    Anglesey Aluminium Metal Ltd. (51%, smelting, UK)
    Bell Bay (Australia)
    Boké (4%, Guinea)
    Boyne Island (59%, smelting, Australia)
    Eurallumina (56%, Italy)
    Queensland Alumina Ltd. (39%, Australia)
    Tiwai Point (79%, New Zealand)
    Weipa (Australia)
Industrial Minerals
    Rio Tinto Industrial Minerals
        Rio Tinto Iron & Titanium (titanium dioxide; Canada/SouthAfrica)
        Rio Tinto Minerals (boron, salt, and talc; Argentina/Australia/the US)
Gold
    Barneys Canyon (US)
    Bingham Canyon (US)
    Cortez/Pipeline (40%, US)
    Escondida (30%, Chile)
    Greens Creek (70%, US)
    Lihir (15%, Papua New Guinea)
    Morro do Ouro (51%, Brazil)
    Rawhide (51%, US)

Diamonds
    Argyle Diamond Mines (Australia)
    Diavik (60%, Canada)
    Merlin (Australia)
Other
    Lead
        Greens Creek (70%, US)
        Zinkgruvan (Sweden)
    Nickel
        Empress (56%, Zimbabwe)
    Tin
        Neves Corvo (49%, Portugal)
    Uranium
        Energy Resources of Australia Ltd. (68%)
        Palabora (49%, South Africa)
        Rössing (69%, Namibia)
    Zinc, Lead, and Silver
        Greens Creek (70%, US)
        Norzink (Norway)

COMPETITORS

Alcan
Alcoa
ALROSA
Anglo American
AngloGold Ashanti
ASARCO
Barrick Gold
BHP Billiton
Cleveland-Cliffs
Codelco
CONSOL Energy
De Beers
Freeport-McMoRan
Glencore
Goldcorp
Grupo México
ITOCHU
Kaiser Aluminum
Marubeni
Metaleurop
Newmont Mining
Peter Kiewit Sons'
Phelps Dodge
RAG
Southern Copper
Teck Cominco
Umicore
Vale do Rio Doce

HISTORICAL FINANCIALS
Company Type: Public

Income Statement
FYE: December 31

	REVENUE ($ mil.)	NET INCOME ($ mil.)	NET PROFIT MARGIN	EMPLOYEES
12/05	19,033	4,969	26.1%	32,000

2005 Year-End Financials

Debt ratio: 18.1%
Return on equity: 36.5%
Cash ($ mil.): 2,910
Current ratio: 1.56
Long-term debt ($ mil.): 3,123
No. of shares (mil.): —
Dividends
    Yield: 1.8%
    Payout: 92.0%
Market value ($ mil.): —

Stock History
NYSE: RTP

200					
180					
160					
140					
120					
100					
80					
60					
40					
20					
0	12/01	12/02	12/03	12/04	12/05

	STOCK PRICE ($) FY Close	P/E High/Low		PER SHARE ($) Earnings	Dividends
12/05	182.79	51	30	3.63	3.34

Robert Bosch

Robert Bosch is one of the world's top makers of automobile components. Bosch's automotive offerings include antilock braking and fuel-injection systems, auto electronics, starters, and alternators. The company also makes industrial machinery and hand tools and owns 50% of Bosch-Siemens Hausgerate, a European appliance maker. Bosch's Blaupunkt unit is a major manufacturer of car audio equipment. Subsidiary Bosch Rexroth makes electric, hydraulic, and pneumatic machinery for applications ranging from automotive to mining. The Robert Bosch Stiftung, a charitable organization, controls 92% of the company's voting rights; the Bosch family controls 7%.

Bosch is enjoying healthy growth in the Americas, Asia, and Eastern Europe. To maintain momentum, the company plans to invest in these markets even more. Recent expansions include the 2006 opening of a new automotive electrical component manufacturing plant in Changsha, central China.

However, Robert Bosch faces competitors that move manufacturing operations to low wage regions, and encroach into Bosch's traditional geographic markets. Moving jobs out of Germany is extremely unpopular, so Bosch is struggling with keeping domestic jobs while remaining competitive.

Bosch has offered to take over Pacifica Group Ltd., an Australian brake technology company, for €187 million and the assumption of about €134 million in Pacifica debt. Pacifica had rejected a lower bid earlier from Bosch, as well as a bid in mid-2006 from a party believed to be Bosch. The German company is Pacifica's biggest customer, at 28% of sales, with General Motors accounting for 22%.

About the same time as the Pacifica Group announcement, Bosch acquired TeleAlarm Group, a Swiss maker of alarms and nurse-call systems used in hospitals and nursing homes.

Bosch has also agreed to set up a joint venture with Japan's DENSO Corporation for the manufacture of diesel particulate filters in Eastern Europe. The two companies will each market and sell the filters separately. The move anticipates that particulate filters will become standard equipment for all new diesel cars built in Europe.

HISTORY

Self-taught electrical engineer Robert Bosch opened a Stuttgart workshop in 1886 and the following year produced the world's first alternator for a stationary engine. In 1897 his company built the first automobile alternator. Later electrical automotive product launches included spark plugs (1902), starters (1912), and regulators (1913). Bosch believed in treating employees well and shortened their workday to eight hours (extraordinary for 1906).

US operations begun in 1909 were confiscated during WWI as part of a trade embargo against Germany. Bosch survived the German depression of the 1920s, introduced power tools (1928) and appliances (1933), and bought Blaupunkt (car radios, 1933). Industrial and military demand for the company's products continued from the 1930s until WWII. Bosch died in 1942 and left 90% of his company to charity.

Bosch suffered severe damage in WWII, and its US operations were again confiscated. It rebuilt after the war and enjoyed growing demand for its appliances and automotive products as postwar incomes increased worldwide. In 1963 Hans Merkle took the helm. Believing fuel efficiency and pollution control would be important issues in the future, Bosch invested heavily to develop automotive components that would raise gas mileage and lower emissions. The company made the world's first electronic fuel-injection (EFI) system in 1967. That year Bosch and Siemens formed Bosch-Siemens Hausgerate to make home appliances.

The oil crisis of the 1970s increased awareness of fuel efficiency and benefited sales of EFI systems. Buying a plant in Charleston, South Carolina, Bosch re-entered the US in 1974 to make fuel-injection systems. It introduced the first antilock braking system in 1978.

A 1984 strike against Bosch in Germany disrupted automobile production throughout Europe. In the late 1980s the company developed technology for multiplexing (employing one wire to replace many by using semiconductor controllers) in automobiles, established it as an industry standard, and licensed it to chip makers Intel (US), Philips (the Netherlands), and Motorola (US). Throughout the 1980s and into the 1990s, Bosch acquired various telecommunications companies.

In 1993 Bosch's sales dropped for the first time since 1967. In response, the company cut its workforce. In 1996 Bosch bought Emerson's half of joint venture S-B Power Tool Co., which makes Bosch, Dremel, and Skil brand tools. Further consolidating its position as a world leader in braking systems, Bosch also purchased AlliedSignal's struggling light-vehicle braking unit. The company sold its private mobile radio business to Motorola in 1997 and, to speed its business for mobile phones, bought Dancall Telecom (a maker of mobile-phone handsets) from UK-based Amstrad.

In 1998 the company's Bosch-Siemens Hausgerate joint venture opened a plant in the US and bought Masco's Thermador unit (cooktops, ovens, and ranges). In 1999 Bosch sold its US-based telecom unit to a joint venture of Motorola and Cisco Systems. The next year UK-based General Electric Company (now Marconi) bought the German operations of Bosch's telecom unit.

Early in 2000 the company sold its mobile-phone business to Siemens AG. That year the company's joint venture with Siemens bought Rexroth AG (Atecs Mannesmann AG's automation and packaging technology group) for about $9.2 billion. The new division was named Bosch Rexroth AG. In 2001 Bosch bought out Siemens' stake in Bosch Rexroth and consolidated its operations as a wholly owned subsidiary.

In 2006 Robert Bosch agreed to purchase Telex Communications for $420 million. Telex is a provider of audio, wireless, communications, and safety equipment with applications in large public places including stadiums and airports.

EXECUTIVES

Chairman, Supervisory Council: Herman Scholl
Deputy Chairman, Supervisory Council: Walter Bauer
Chairman, Management Board: Franz Fehrenbach, age 57
Deputy Chairman, Management Board: Seigfried Dais
Director, Management Board: Rudolf Colm
Director, Management Board: Gerhard Kümmel
Director, Management Board: Wolfgang Malchow
Director, Management Board, Automotive Electronics and Energy and Body Systems: Volkmar Denner
Director, Management Board; Chairman of Automotive Technology Business Sector: Bernd Bohr

Director, Management Board, Consumer Goods and Building Technology: Wolfgang Chur
Director, Management Board, North and South American Operations: Peter Marks
Director, Management Board, Worldwide Automotive Original Equipment Sales and Automotive Aftermarket: Peter Tyroller
Auditors: PwC Deutsche Revision AG

LOCATIONS

HQ: Robert Bosch GmbH
  Postfach 106050, D-70049 Stuttgart, Germany
Phone: +49-711-811-0   **Fax:** +49-711-811-6630
US HQ: 2800 S. 25th Ave., Broadview, IL 60155
US Phone: 708-865-5200   **US Fax:** 708-865-6430
Web: www.bosch.com

2005 Sales

	$ mil.	% of total
Europe	32,550.5	66
The Americas	9,333.5	19
Asia	6,405.9	13
Africa & Australia	812.4	2
Total	**49,102.3**	**100**

PRODUCTS/OPERATIONS

2005 Sales

	$ mil.	% of total
Automotive technology	31,162.5	63
Consumer goods & building technology	11,796.8	24
Industrial technology	6,143.0	13
Total	**49,102.3**	**100**

Selected Divisions and Products

Automotive Technology
  Automotive aftermarket
  Automotive electronics
  Car multimedia
  Chassis systems and brakes
  Diesel systems
  Energy and body systems
  Gasoline systems
Consumer Goods and Building Technology
  Household appliances
  Power tools
  Security systems
  Thermotechnology (gas-fired hot water heating systems)
Industrial Technology
  Bosch Rexroth
  Packaging technology

COMPETITORS

American Standard	Magna International
Black & Decker	Motorola
BorgWarner	Nokia
Dana	Pioneer
Delphi	Prestolite Electric
DENSO	Senior
Eaton	Siemens VDO Automotive
Electrolux	Snap-on
Emerson Electric	Stanley Works
Federal-Mogul	Tenneco
GE	Textron
Honeywell International	ThyssenKrupp
Ingersoll-Rand	Valeo
ITT Corporation	Visteon
Johnson Controls	Whirlpool
Key Safety Systems	

HISTORICAL FINANCIALS

Company Type: Private

Income Statement

FYE: December 31

	REVENUE ($ mil.)	NET INCOME ($ mil.)	NET PROFIT MARGIN	EMPLOYEES
12/05	49,102	2,902	5.9%	249,000
12/04	54,570	2,285	4.2%	242,348
12/03	45,635	1,381	3.0%	232,000
12/02	36,659	681	1.9%	224,341
12/01	30,143	576	1.9%	220,999
Annual Growth	13.0%	49.8%	—	3.0%

Net Income History

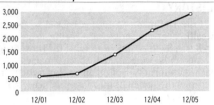

Roche Holding

Roche is on a roll. The company operates two segments: pharmaceuticals and diagnostics. Roche's prescription drugs include cancer therapies Rituxan and Herceptin, antibiotic Rocephin, obesity treatment Xenical, AIDS drug Invirase, acne drug Accutane, and Tamiflu, which is used to prevent and treat influenza, including avian strains. The company markets many of its bestsellers with affiliates Genentech and Chugai Pharmaceutical. Roche's diagnostics arm offers advanced DNA tests, diabetes monitoring supplies, and point-of-care diagnostics used in a variety of health care settings. Descendants of the founding Hoffmann and Oeri families own half of the company. Fellow druggernaut Novartis owns 33% of the company.

To narrow its focus on pharmaceuticals and diagnostics, Roche has steadily dropped non-core operations; it sold its consumer health business, which included vitamins, the analgesic Aleve, and antacid Rennie, to Bayer HealthCare in 2005. Two years prior, the company sold its fine chemicals business to DSM, and in 2000 Roche spun off Givaudan, a leader in fragrances and flavors, and BASILEA Pharmaceutica, its biotech division focused on infectious disease and skin disorder drugs.

Roche owns almost 60% of Genentech, one of the world's largest biotech companies, and has a 51% stake in Japan's Chugai Pharmaceutical. Genentech accounts for 19% of the company's sales, and Chugai contributes 10%.

The bulk of Roche's research and development efforts are aimed at anemia, rheumatoid arthritis, cancer, diabetes, and central nervous system disorders; the company has nearly 110 drugs in development. The company maintains several development alliances with other companies to beef up its pipeline. In 2006 Roche received approval for the application of its cancer drug MabThera (known as Rituxan in the US) in treating rheumatoid arthritis throughout the EU. It also put its post-menopausal osteoporosis treatment Boniva out on the EU and US markets at that time.

In response to the fears of a pandemic of Avian Influenza Virus, Roche is ramping up its production of its antiviral drug Tamiflu and will produce over 300 million doses by 2007. The company is also in talks with a number of generic drug manufacturers and Asian governments to increase inventories through outsourced manufacturing. In mid-2006 it signed a collaborative agreement with Cardinal Health for the production and distribution of Tamiflu. The FDA in late 2006 warned that observers had witnessed side effects of bizarre (violent, erratic) behavior in Japanese children taking Tamiflu to prevent or treat avian flu.

HISTORY

Fritz Hoffmann-La Roche, backed by family wealth, began making pharmaceuticals in a lab in Basel, Switzerland, in 1894. At the time, drug compounds were mixed at pharmacies and lacked uniformity. Hoffmann was not a chemist, but saw the potential for mass-produced, standardized, branded drugs.

By WWI, Hoffman had become successful, selling Thiocal (cough medicine), Digalen (digitalis extract), and other products on four continents. During the war, the Bolsheviks seized the firm's St. Petersburg, Russia, facility, and its Warsaw plant was almost destroyed. Devastated, Hoffmann sold company shares outside the family in 1919 and died in 1920.

As WWII loomed, Roche divided its holdings between F. Hoffman-La Roche and Sapac, which held many of Roche's foreign operations. US operations became more important during the war. Roche synthesized vitamins C, A, and E (eventually becoming the world's top vitamin maker) and built plants and research centers worldwide.

Roche continued to develop such successful products as tranquilizers Librium (1960) and Valium (1963), the world's best-selling prescription drug prior to anti-ulcer successors Tagamet (SmithKline Beecham, now part of GlaxoSmith-Kline) and Prilosec (AstraZeneca). Roche made its first fragrance and flavor buy, Givaudan, in 1963.

In the 1970s, after several governments accused it of price-gouging on Librium and Valium, Roche agreed to price restraints. The company was fined for vitamin price-fixing in 1976. It was also rapped that year for its slow response to an Italian factory dioxin leak that killed thousands of animals and forced hundreds of families to evacuate.

Roche became one of the first drugmakers to sell another's products when it agreed to sell Glaxo's Zantac ulcer treatment in the US in 1982. The move let Roche maintain its large US sales force at the time when Valium went off patent, decimating the company's drug sales.

Roche acquired a product pipeline when it bought a majority stake in genetic engineering firm Genentech in 1990. In 1994 it bought the struggling Syntex, solidifying its position in North America. The company gained Aleve and other products in 1996 when it bought out its joint venture with Procter & Gamble and also acquired Cincinnati-based flavors and fragrances firm Tastemaker.

In its biggest acquisition ever, Roche bought Corange in 1998 for $10.2 billion; its subsidiary Boehringer Mannheim was renamed Roche Molecular Biochemicals. In 1999 Roche announced it had located the gene that causes osteoarthritis. The company began to market anti-obesity pharmaceutical Xenical in the US that year, despite reports of some unpleasant side effects.

Also in 1999 Roche agreed to a record-setting fine to end a US Justice Department investigation into Roche's role in an alleged vitamin price-fixing cartel; in 2000 it agreed to pay out again (to 22 states) to settle a lawsuit regarding the cartel. A related European Union probe the following year also found Roche guilty and levied heavy fines against the firm. In 1999 and 2000 Roche squeezed cash out of its high-flying biotech progeny; it bought the 33% of Genentech it didn't own in 1999, then raised a total of almost $8 billion by reselling 42% of the firm in three offerings in 1999 and 2000.

Influenza drug Tamiflu failed to win European Union approval in 2000, but breast cancer drug Herceptin was OK'd there. Also that year two long-time Roche leaders, chairman Fritz Gerber and CFO Henri Meier, retired; both remained on Roche's board for a brief time thereafter.

In 2001 rival Swiss pharmaceuticals firm Novartis bought a 20% stake in Roche from financier Martin Ebner's BZ Gruppe Holding. Roche sold its vitamins and fine chemicals business in 2003 to narrow its focus.

EXECUTIVES

Chairman and CEO: Franz B. Humer, age 60, $5,342,097 pay
Vice Chairman: Bruno Gehrig, age 59
Vice Chairman: André Sérenus Hoffman, age 48
CFO: Erich Hunziker, age 53, $1,875,053 pay
Medical Director: Salvatore Badalamenti
Head of Corporate Services and Human Resources, and Secretary: Gottlieb A. Keller, age 51, $1,012,500 pay
Head of Global Corporate Communications: Rolf D. Schläpfer, age 50
Head of Global Pharma Development: Eduard E. Holdener, age 61
Head of Global Research: Jonathan K. C. Knowles, age 58, $1,443,810 pay
Head of Pharma Partnering: Peter Hug, age 48
Head of Roche Group Media Office: Daniel Piller
Head of Science Communications: Katja Prowald
Head of the Chairman's Office: Pierre Jaccoud, age 51
Head of the Roche Center for Medical Genomics: Klaus Lindpaintner
CEO, Roche Pharmaceuticals: William M. Burns, age 58, $1,766,767 pay
CEO, Roche Diagnostics: Severin Schwan, age 39
President and CEO, Roche North American Pharmaceuticals Operations and Hoffmann-La Roche: George B. Abercrombie
Head of Human Resources, Roche Diagnostics: Silvia Ayyoubi
Head of Human Resources, Roche Pharmaceuticals: Paul Newton-Syms
Auditors: KPMG Klynveld Peat Marwick Goerdeler SA

LOCATIONS

HQ: Roche Holding Ltd
Grenzacherstrasse 124, CH-4070 Basel, Switzerland
Phone: +41-61-688-11-11   **Fax:** +41-61-691-93-91
US HQ: 340 Kingsland St., Nutley, NJ 07110
US Phone: 973-235-5000   **US Fax:** 973-235-7605
Web: www.roche.com

Roche sells its products in more than 150 countries.

2005 Sales

	% of total
North America	40
Europe	32
Japan	14
Latin America	6
Other	8
Total	**100**

PRODUCTS/OPERATIONS

2005 Sales

	% of total
Roche pharmaceuticals	62
Genentech	24
Chugai	14
Total	**100**

2005 Sales by Therapeutic Area

	% of total
Oncology	40
Virology	15
Transplantation	8
Metabolic disorders	7
Cardiovascular diseases	6
Anemia	6
Central nervous system	5
Infectious diseases	4
Inflammatory diseases/bone diseases	2
Dermatology	1
Other	6
Total	**100**

COMPETITORS

Abbott Labs
Amgen
AstraZeneca
Bristol-Myers Squibb
Chiron
Dade Behring
Diagnostic Products
Eli Lilly
GlaxoSmithKline
Johnson & Johnson
Merck
Novartis
Pfizer
Sanofi-Aventis
Schering-Plough
Wyeth

HISTORICAL FINANCIALS

Company Type: Public

Income Statement

	REVENUE ($ mil.)	NET INCOME ($ mil.)	NET PROFIT MARGIN	EMPLOYEES
12/05	26,985	4,398	16.3%	68,218
12/04	27,630	5,867	21.2%	64,703
12/03	25,132	2,471	9.8%	65,357
12/02	21,423	(2,902)	—	69,659
12/01	15,638	2,210	14.1%	63,717
Annual Growth	**14.6%**	**18.8%**	**—**	**1.7%**

FYE: December 31

2005 Year-End Financials

Debt ratio: 26.7%   Current ratio: 3.75
Return on equity: 17.1%   Long-term debt ($ mil.): 7,084
Cash ($ mil.): 15,871

Net Income History
OTC: RHHVF

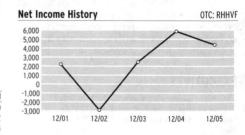

280

Rogers Communications

Canada is tuned in to Rogers Communications. As the nation's #1 cable TV operator, it has some 2.3 million subscribers throughout eastern Canada. The company's Rogers Wireless subsidiary is Canada's largest mobile phone outfit with more than 6 million subscribers on its GSM-based network. Rogers Telecom is a facilities-based alternative fixed-line phone carrier with nationwide services. The Rogers Media unit has interests in broadcasting and publishing and it holds the company's stake in Blue Jays Holdco, with interests in the Toronto Blue Jays major league baseball team and Rogers Centre sports complex. CEO Ted Rogers controls about 91% of the firm's voting power. Microsoft holds a minority stake in the company.

The company formerly operated in British Columbia, but this Mr. Rogers moved neighborhoods when it swapped its western cable systems for Shaw Communications' eastern cable operations. Rogers is looking to become a one-stop communications shop for many of its neighbors.

Rogers' cable unit provides broadband Internet access to more than 1 million customers and voice over cable phone service to nearly 50,000 customers. The cable networks are being upgraded for telephony services, and the company is poised to become a major player in that area now that it owns the former Sprint Canada. Rogers also offers a video-on-demand service, Rogers on Demand, which is able to reach almost 2 million homes.

After winning spectrum licenses in all major areas of Canada, Rogers Wireless has upgraded its network and converted it to the GSM (global system for mobile communications) standard. The wireless unit markets its services under the Rogers Wireless and Fido brands

Rogers Media owns more than 40 radio and three TV broadcast stations. It also produces 70 consumer magazines, trade publications, and directories. In addition to magazines and its radio and TV stations, Rogers Media also owns a regional sports network (Rogers Sportsnet), a home shopping network (The Shopping Channel), 50% of production and distribution firm Dome Productions, and numerous Internet holdings.

HISTORY

Edward Rogers, at age 21, transmitted Canada's first radio signal across the Atlantic in 1921. He invented the first alternating current (AC) radio tube in 1925, which revolutionized the home-receiver industry.

Son of a wealthy businessman, Rogers founded Rogers Majestic in Toronto in the mid-1920s to make his radio tubes. He also established several radio stations, including CFRB ("Canada's First Rogers Batteryless"), which later commanded the country's largest audience.

In 1931 Rogers won the first experimental license to broadcast TV, but his businesses were sold when he died in 1939. His son Ted Rogers Jr. was only five at the time, but even as a youngster he showed business acumen, buying up shares of Standard Broadcasting. In his twenties he bought CHFI, a Toronto radio station that pioneered FM broadcasting.

Rogers moved into cable TV and in 1967 was awarded licenses for Toronto, Brampton, and Leamington. Rogers Cable TV expanded when it bought Canadian Cablevision (1979) and Premier Cablevision (1980). With the takeover of UA-Columbia Cablevision in 1981, Rogers became Canada's largest cable operator.

The firm also began pushing cellular phone service through subsidiary Rogers Cantel in 1985. (The carrier won a license for nationwide coverage in 1992.) In 1986 all of Rogers' holdings were combined to form Rogers Communications.

Rogers acquired a stake in telecom company Unitel in 1989. When it received permission to sell long-distance in 1992, Unitel geared up to take on monopoly Bell Canada. However, the venture wasn't successful, and Rogers walked away from its 32% stake in 1995.

Meanwhile, in 1994 Rogers acquired rival cable TV and publishing firm Maclean-Hunter. The next year it acquired Shaw Communications' Vancouver cable system and began providing Internet access. After selling its 62% stake in Toronto Sun Publishing to management in 1996, Rogers extended its Internet content operations, including a partnership with Intuit to develop a financial Web site. (The company shuttered or reorganized many of its Internet operations in 2001.)

Expenses related to cable network upgrades and Cantel's development created operating losses for several years. To raise cash, in 1998 Rogers sold subsidiary Rogers Telecom to local phone startup MetroNet Communications and sold its home-security unit to Protection One. That year it turned its first profit in the 1990s.

In 1999 Microsoft paid $400 million for a 9% stake in the company; Rogers agreed to use Microsoft set-top box software and offer Microsoft's Web services to its customers. Also in 1999 AT&T and British Telecommunications (now BT Group) together bought a 33% stake in Cantel; Rogers' stake fell to 51%.

The next year Rogers agreed to buy Quebec cable operator Videotron. But media firm Quebecor, backed by pension fund manager Caisse, weighed in with a rival bid, and Rogers collected a breakup fee of about $160 million when Videotron terminated the companies' deal. Soon thereafter, the company announced the creation of Rogers Telecom (reusing the name), a unit set up to enter the telephone market.

Also in 2000 Rogers purchased an 80% stake in the Toronto Blue Jays baseball team for $112 million (it later acquired the remaining 20%). The next year Rogers gained another 75,000 cable subscribers with the acquisition of Cable Atlantic.

In 2001, AT&T Wireless bought out British Telecom's stake in Rogers Wireless, raising their ownership to a third. The same year, Rogers Communications offered to buy up the remaining shares of Rogers Wireless held by the public, but shareholders rejected the deal.

When in 2004 Rogers Communications raised $250 million in capital after having tried for up to $500 million, speculation abounded that the company would once again try to purchase AT&T Wireless' stake in Rogers Wireless, which later proved true. Rogers Communications has since bought all of the company that it didn't already own in early 2005. Later that year the firm made another major purchase, this time the $264 million acquisition of Call-Net Enterprises, owner of Sprint Canada. (After the deal, Rogers rechristened Call-Net as Rogers Telecom.)

EXECUTIVES

Chairman: Alan D. Horn, age 54
Vice Chairman; VP, Rogers Cable: Philip B. (Phil) Lind, age 62
President and CEO; Chairman, Rogers Wireless and Rogers Cable; Vice Chairman, Rogers Media, and President and CEO, Rogers Telecommunications: Edward S. (Ted) Rogers, age 72, $2,988,048 pay
CFO: William W. (Bill) Linton
EVP Consumer Sales and Service: James S. (Jim) Lovie
EVP Corporate Marketing and Convergence: Stephen Graham
SVP and Chief Human Resources Officer: Kevin P. Pennington
SVP Communications Group; President, Rogers Business Solutions: Randall J. (Randy) Reynolds
SVP Communications Group; President, Rogers Wireless, and Rogers Cable: Robert W. (Rob) Bruce, $1,212,822 pay (partial-year salary)
SVP Customer Care: Donald E. (Don) Moffatt
SVP Media; President and CEO, Rogers Media: Anthony P. (Tony) Viner, $1,474,721 pay
VP Communications: Jan L. Innes
VP Controller: Sarah Burcher
VP Investor Relations: Bruce M. Mann
VP Treasurer, Rogers Communications, Rogers Wireless, and Rogers Cable: M. Lorraine Daly
VP, General Counsel, and Secretary, Rogers Communications, Rogers Cable, and Rogers Wireless: David P. Miller, $815,573 pay
President and CEO, Publishing, Rogers Media: Brian Segal
President and COO, Communications Division; and Director: Nadir H. Mohamed, age 49, $2,558,508 pay
President, Rogers Broadcasting Limited: Rael Merson
President, Rogers Cable; Director: Edward S. Rogers, age 36
President, Rogers Sportsnet: Douglas Beeforth
President, Toronto Blue Jays: Paul V. Godfrey, age 67
Auditors: KPMG LLP

LOCATIONS

HQ: Rogers Communications Inc.
333 Bloor St. East, 10th Fl.,
Toronto, Ontario M4W 1G9, Canada
Phone: 416-935-7777   **Fax:** 416-935-3597
Web: www.rogers.com

PRODUCTS/OPERATIONS

2005 Sales

	$ mil.	% of total
Wireless		
Services		
Post-paid voice & data	2,902.3	45
Prepaid	179.8	3
One-way messaging	16.8	—
Equipment sales	338.0	5
Cable		
Services		
Cable TV	1,114.3	17
Internet	378.2	6
Rogers Home Phone	4.2	—
Video store operations	280.6	4
Adjustments	(3.5)	—
Media		
Advertising	432.3	7
Retail	216.0	3
Blue Jays Holdco	127.6	2
Circulation & subscription	117.7	2
Other	47.6	—
Telecom		
Business	235.8	4
Consumer	127.8	2
Adjustments	(95.8)	—
Total	**6,419.7**	**100**

Selected Operations

Cable
  Cable television
  Broadband Internet access
Media
  Radio
  TV broadcasting
  Televised shopping
  Publishing
Telephone
  Dial-up Internet access
  Local access
  Long-distance
  Teleconferencing
Wireless Communications
  Cellular service
  Data service
  Digital PCS
  Paging

COMPETITORS

Alliance Atlantis	Corus Entertainment
Communications	Fundy Communications
Astral Media	MTS Allstream
Axia NetMedia	Persona
BCE	Quebecor
Bell Aliant	Shaw Communications
Bell Globemedia	Sprint Nextel
Cancom	Telemedia
CanWest Global	Tele-Metropole
CBC	TELUS
Cogeco Cable	Transcontinental
COGECO Inc.	

HISTORICAL FINANCIALS

Company Type: Public

Income Statement

FYE: December 31

	REVENUE ($ mil.)	NET INCOME ($ mil.)	NET PROFIT MARGIN	EMPLOYEES
12/05	6,420	(268)	—	21,000
12/04	4,657	(225)	—	18,057
12/03	3,746	(44)	—	15,027
12/02	2,743	222	8.1%	14,900
12/01	2,460	(284)	—	13,500
Annual Growth	27.1%	—	—	11.7%

2005 Year-End Financials

Debt ratio: 278.7%   No. of shares (mil.): —
Return on equity: —   Dividends
Cash ($ mil.): —   Yield: 0.2%
Current ratio: 0.65   Payout: —
Long-term debt ($ mil.): 7,071 Market value ($ mil.): —

Stock History

NYSE: RG

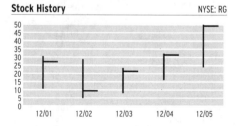

	STOCK PRICE ($) FY Close	P/E High	P/E Low	PER SHARE ($) Earnings	PER SHARE ($) Dividends
12/05	49.20	—	—	(1.08)	0.10
12/04	31.44	—	—	(1.13)	0.08
12/03	21.34	—	—	(0.19)	0.08
12/02	9.38	36	7	0.78	—
12/01	27.12				
Annual Growth	16.1%	—	—	—	11.8%

Rolls-Royce

Rolls-Royce plc doesn't make luxury cars — BMW owns those operations — but it *can* provide serious horsepower. The company is the second-largest aircraft engine maker in the world, behind General Electric's GE Aircraft Engines division. Rolls-Royce's aerospace business makes commercial and military gas turbine engines for military, airline, and corporate aircraft customers worldwide. In the US, the company makes engines for regional and corporate jets, helicopters, and turboprop aircraft. Rolls-Royce also constructs and installs power generation systems and is one of the world's largest makers of marine propulsion systems.

Sales and profits at Rolls-Royce are flying high. Some key wins include nearly 250 civil aircraft engine orders. On the defense side Rolls-Royce won a service contract valued at more than $260 million for navies in the UK, France, Belgium, and the Netherlands. The company also made strides in its share of the work on the upcoming F-35 Joint Strike Fighter project (officially named Lightning II).

Geographically, Rolls-Royce is making particular headway in Asia as a result of the air travel boom in the region. But it's not just planes that are driving Rolls-Royce's success in Asia. As economies develop in the region, sectors served by Rolls-Royce from shipbuilding to energy production are growing at a breakneck pace. In 2005 sales in Asia grew by 18%, and orders booked increased by 70%.

Moving forward, Rolls-Royce is focused on three initiatives. First the companys want to maintain momentum by bringing new and innovating products to market. Next, Rolls-Royce aims to keep costs down by tightening its supply chain, increasing productivity, and purchasing from more low-cost suppliers. Lastly, the company aims to continually grow its aftermarket services division.

Rolls-Royce shares its name with the luxury auto, but the two parted ways when the British government split them in 1971. German carmaker BMW owns about 9% of Rolls-Royce.

HISTORY

In 1906 automobile and aviation enthusiast Charles Rolls and engineer Henry Royce unveiled the Silver Ghost, an automobile that earned Rolls-Royce a reputation as maker of the best car in the world.

A year after Rolls' 1910 death in a biplane crash, Royce suffered a breakdown. From his home Royce continued to design Rolls-Royce engines such as the Eagle, its first aircraft engine, in 1914, and other engines used to power airplanes during WWI — but management of the company fell to Claude Johnson, who remained chief executive until 1926.

Although the company returned to primarily making cars after WWI, its engines were used in several history-making flights and, in 1931, set world speed records for land, sea, and air. Rolls-Royce bought the Bentley Motor Company that year. In 1933 it introduced the Merlin engine, which powered the Spitfire, Hurricane, and Mustang fighters of WWII. Rolls-Royce began designing a jet engine in 1938 and over the years it pioneered the turboprop engine, turbofan, and vertical takeoff engine.

Realizing that it had to break into the lucrative US airliner market to stay alive, Rolls-Royce bought its main British competitor, Bristol-Siddley Engines, in 1966. With Bristol-Siddley came its contract to build the engine for the Anglo-French Concorde in 1976 and a US presence. Lockheed ordered the company's RB211 engine for its TriStar in 1968, but Rolls-Royce underestimated the project's technical and financial challenges and entered bankruptcy in 1971. The British government stepped in and nationalized the aerospace division and sold the auto group. The RB211 entered service on the TriStar in 1972 and on the Boeing 747 in 1977.

Rolls-Royce was reprivatized in 1987. In a diversification effort two years later, the company bought mining, marine, and power plant specialist Northern Engineering Industries. In the early 1990s the aerospace market was hurt by military spending cutbacks and a recession; the company cut over 18,000 jobs.

A joint venture with BMW launched the BR710 engine for Gulfstream and Canadair's long-range business jets in 1990. The company bought Allison Engine in 1995.

Rolls-Royce sold Parsons Power Generation Systems to Siemens in 1997. Also that year it won a contract to supply Trent 892 engines for Boeing 777 jets being built for American Airlines in a deal worth $1 billion.

In 1998 the British government approved a repayable investment of about $335 million in the company to develop a new model of Trent aircraft engines. Narrowing its focus, the company sold its power transmission and distribution business to Austria-based VA Technologie.

Rolls-Royce pumped up its gas and oil equipment business in 1999 by buying the rotating compression equipment unit of Cooper Cameron (now Cameron International), and it became one of the world leaders in marine propulsion by acquiring Vickers. The company then bought the aero and industrial engine repair service of First Aviation Services and took full control of its aircraft-engine joint venture with BMW; in return BMW received a 10% stake in Rolls.

In 2000 subsidiary Rolls-Royce Energy Systems India Private was awarded its first order: producing a Bergen gas engine for Garden Silk Mills for powering a textile plant in India. That year Rolls-Royce won a contract to supply engines for Israel's El Al airline's Boeing 777s. Late in 2000 it was reported that the company would cut about 5,000 jobs over three years.

Early in 2001 Rolls-Royce sold most of its Vickers Turbine Components business. In October the company cut about 11% of its workforce in response to the worldwide crisis in the commercial jet business.

In 2002 the company announced that it had inked a 10-year, $2 billion deal to supply engines to Gulfstream Aerospace. That year Rolls-Royce sold its Vickers Defence Systems unit, which made tanks and armored vehicles, to Alvis Plc. In 2003 Sir Ralph Robins, who had been executive chairman for more than a decade, retired from his post. Early in 2004 Rolls-Royce and GE Aircraft Engines were picked to supply engines for Boeing's upcoming 787 Dreamliner. Rolls-Royce was also selected to supply engines for Airbus' upcoming behemoth A380.

EXECUTIVES

Non-Executive Chairman: Simon M. Robertson, age 65
Chief Executive: Sir John E. V. Rose, age 53
COO: John P. Cheffins, age 57
Finance Director: Andrew B. Shilston, age 50
Director, Engineering and Technology:
  Michael G. (Mike) Howse, age 62
Director, Human Resources: John R. Rivers, age 56
Director, Procurement: Chris J. Hole, age 57
President and CEO, Rolls-Royce North America:
  James M. Guyette, age 61
President, Civil Aerospace: Mike Terrett, age 47
President, Corporate & Regional Aircraft, Rolls-Royce
  North America Inc.: Ian C. Aitken
President, Defence Aerospace: Colin H. Green, age 58
President, Energy: E. Thomas (Tom) Curley, age 48
President, Helicopters, Rolls-Royce North America:
  Stuart Mullan, age 40
President, Marine: Saul Lanyado
President and CEO, Rolls-Royce Deutschland:
  Michael Haidinger
Chairman, Rolls-Royce Deutschland: Axel Arendt,
  age 57
COO, Rolls Royce Corporation: Steven F. (Steve) Dwyer
Director, Gas Turbine Operations: Mike Lloyd
Director, Services: Miles A. Cowdry
Company Secretary and Director of Government
  Relations: Charles E. Blundell, age 53
Auditors: KPMG Audit Plc

LOCATIONS

HQ: Rolls-Royce plc
  65 Buckingham Gate,
  London SW1E 6AT, United Kingdom
Phone: +44-20-7222-9020   **Fax:** +44-20-7227-9178
US HQ: 14850 Conference Center Dr.,
  Chantilly, VA 20151
US Phone: 703-834-1700   **US Fax:** 703-709-6087
Web: www.rolls-royce.com

Rolls-Royce has operations in about 15 different
countries and sells its products around the world.

2005 Sales

	% of total
North America	
US	37
Canada	3
Europe	
UK	13
Other countries	16
Asia	23
Africa	2
Australasia	1
Other regions	5
Total	**100**

PRODUCTS/OPERATIONS

2005 Sales

	% of total
Civil Aerospace	53
Defence	21
Marine	17
Energy	8
Financial Services	1
Total	**100**

Selected Products and Services

Aircraft engines
Diesel engines
Engine support services
Gas turbine systems
Industrial power plants
Marine equipment
Nuclear submarine propulsion systems
Overhaul and repair services
Ship engines
Shiplift systems

COMPETITORS

AAR	Hitachi
ABB Inc.	Honeywell International
Bechtel	Ishikawajima-Harima
Cummins	Kawasaki Heavy Industries
DaimlerChrysler	Marubeni
Emerson Electric	McDermott
Fiat	Peter Kiewit Sons'
Fluor	Pratt & Whitney
GE Aircraft Engines	SAFRAN
GE Aircraft Engines UK	Siemens AG
GE Honda Aero Engines	Textron
Halliburton	Volvo

HISTORICAL FINANCIALS

Company Type: Public

Income Statement

FYE: December 31

	REVENUE ($ mil.)	NET INCOME ($ mil.)	NET PROFIT MARGIN	EMPLOYEES
12/05	12,718	—	—	35,600
12/04	11,440	—	—	35,200
12/03	10,036	—	—	36,100
12/02	9,283	—	—	39,200
12/01	9,182	—	—	43,300
Annual Growth	**8.5%**	—	—	**(4.8%)**

Revenue History

OTC: RYCEY

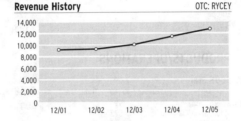

Royal Ahold

A tattered prince of global food retailing, Royal Ahold owns or has interests in about 3,450 supermarkets, hypermarkets, discount stores, and specialty stores in Europe and the US. It is one of the world's largest grocery retailers (behind Wal-Mart, Carrefour, and METRO AG), as well as a leading supermarket operator in the US (mainly on the East Coast under names such as Giant Food, Stop & Shop, and Tops Markets), and also owns food distributor U.S. Foodservice. Royal Ahold runs Albert Heijn, the #1 food retailer in the Netherlands; and Schuitema, a Dutch retailer and food distributor (73%-owned). Other interests include online food retailer Peapod and a majority stake in Scandinavian food seller ICA.

The global grocery chain plans to divest U.S. Foodservice and appoint separate European and US chief operating officers. Royal Ahold will also divest Tops Markets and its retail operations in Poland (to France's Carrefour) and Slovakia and sell its holding in Jerónimo Martins Retail. Cost cutting is also on the agenda with the goal of reducing debt and returning about $2.5 billion to shareholders. Ahold has been under pressure from investors Centaurus Capital of the UK and Paulson & Co. of the US, which together own more than 6% of Ahold, to split up the company.

In the Netherlands, the company owns or franchises about 710 Albert Heijn supermarkets, as well as nearly 300 Gall & Gall liquor stores, and

some 200 Etos health and beauty care stores. Its other European holdings include Swedish food retailer and wholesaler ICA AB, which operates in Sweden, Norway, and the Baltic states (through a joint venture).

Often working with local partners, Ahold developed grocery chains in Indonesia, Malaysia, and Thailand. But a massive accounting scandal, most of it at U.S. Foodservice, and economic weakness in Latin America caused the global food retailer to retreat by selling its Asian and Latin American holdings — among others — to reduce debt and focus on more-stable markets.

While the company is shedding assets overseas, it is in buying mode closer to home. It recently acquired 27 Konmar stores in the Netherlands from Laurus N.V. Also, Ahold acquired 56 Julius Meinl supermarkets in the Czech Republic.

HISTORY

Albert Heijn and his wife took over his father's grocery store in Ootzaan, Netherlands, in 1887. By the end of WWI, the company had 50 Albert Heijn grocery stores in Holland, and at WWII's end it had almost 250 stores. In 1948 the company went public.

It opened its first self-service store in 1952 and its first supermarket in 1955. Growing into the #1 grocer in the Netherlands, Albert Heijn opened liquor and cosmetic stores in 1973. (It changed its name to Ahold that year to better reflect its range of businesses.) Ahold expanded outside the Netherlands in 1976 when it found supermarket chain Cadadia in Spain (sold 1985).

Ahold entered the US in 1977 by purchasing BI-LO and furthered its expansion in 1981 by adding Pennsylvania-based Giant Food Stores. In 1987, in honor of its 100th anniversary, Ahold was granted the title Koninklijke (Dutch for "royal"). In 1988 it bought a majority stake in Dutch food wholesaler Schuitema.

The company added New York-based Tops Markets in 1991. That year Royal Ahold founded food retailer and distributor Euronova (now called Ahold Czech Republic). In 1993 Cees van der Hoeven was promoted to chief executive and Royal Ahold was listed on the NYSE.

Other acquisitions included New England grocery giant The Stop & Shop Companies in 1996. That year saw the beginning of several Asian joint ventures that gave Royal Ahold stores in Singapore, Malaysia, and Thailand. In 1998 Royal Ahold added Maryland-based grocer Giant Food Inc. (unrelated to Royal Ahold's Giant Food Stores). Royal Ahold's moves in 1999 included the acquisition of several Spanish supermarket chains (with a total of about 200 stores), the purchase of Dutch institutional food wholesaler Gastronoom, and the acquisition of 50% of Sweden's top food seller, ICA AB.

In 2000 Royal Ahold acquired Spanish food retailer Kampio, and #2 and #4 US foodservice distributors U.S. Foodservice and PYA/Monarch. In 2001 the firm acquired online grocer Peapod. The retailer also expanded its bricks-and-mortar US presence in 2001 by purchasing Alliant Exchange, parent of Alliant Foodservice, which distributes food to more than 100,000 customers.

Royal Ahold reported its first net loss in nearly 30 years in the second quarter of 2002. In February 2003 CEO Cees van der Hoeven resigned following an announcement that the grocery giant would restate its financial results because of accounting irregularities at U.S. Foodservice.

(van der Hoeven is facing charges by Dutch prosecutors in connection with the scandal at U.S. Foodservice.) Chairman Henny de Ruiter became acting CEO of the company. In May 2003 IKEA veteran Anders Moberg became acting CEO; de Ruiter remained chairman.

Adding to its woes, in July the public prosecutor in Amsterdam launched a criminal investigation into possible falsification of accounts by the company. In September the board of directors of Royal Ahold approved the appointment of Moberg as CEO.

In October 2003 Royal Ahold published its 2002 results revealing a $1.27 billion loss, which the retailer attributed to special charges related to overstated profits at U.S. Foodservice.

At a shareholders meeting in March 2004, Ahold placed the blame for the accounting scandal, which had nearly bankrupted the company in 2003, squarely on the shoulders of Jim Miller, the former CEO of U.S. Foodservice. In September, Ahold reached a settlement with the Dutch public prosecutor in which the company agreed to pay €8 million. In October the company reached a settlement with the US Securities and Exchange Commission that imposed no fines on Royal Ahold due, in part, to its "extensive cooperation" with the investigation.

In 2005 the company settled a US class action lawsuit by paying $1.1 billion to shareholders. Concurrently, the company reached an agreement to settle litigation with the Dutch Shareholders' Association.

In 2006 a Dutch court found former CEO Cees van der Hoeven and former CFO Michael Meurs guilty of fraud. Van der Hoeven and Meurs were accused of improperly booking sales from four subsidiaries in Scandinavia, Argentina, and Brazil. Both men were fined and given suspended sentences. Former executive board member Jan Andreae, who headed Ahold's European operations, was sentenced to four months in jail, suspended for two years, and fined.

EXECUTIVES

Chairman: René Dahan, age 65
Vice Chairman: Jan H. M. Hommen, age 63
President and CEO: Anders C. Moberg, age 56, $3,481,842 pay
Acting EVP and CFO: John Rishton, age 48
SVP and Chief Accounting Officer: Joost L.M. Sliepenbeek, age 43
EVP, Chief Corporate Governance Counsel: Peter N. Wakkie, age 58, $1,332,337 pay
SVP, Chief Business Controlling Officer: Brian W. Hotarek, age 60
SVP and CIO: David B. (Dave) McNally, age 51
SVP and Chief Human Resources Officer: James G. (Jim) Lawler, age 47
SVP, Chief Treasury and Tax Officer: Kimberly Ross, age 41
Corporate Secretary: Norbert L. J. (Nol) Berger, age 53
SVP, Finance and Fiscal Affairs: André Buitenhuis, age 59
SVP, Legal Affairs and General Counsel: A. H. P. M. (Ton) van Tielraden, age 51
SVP, Corporate Communications: Kerry Underhill, age 46
President and CEO, Giant Food Stores/Tops Markets: Anthony (Tony) Schiano
President and CEO, U.S. Foodservice: Lawrence S. (Larry) Benjamin, age 51
President, Peapod: Andrew B. Parkinson
Director, Investor Relations: Henk Wurfbain
Auditors: Deloitte & Touche AB

LOCATIONS

HQ: Royal Ahold N.V.
(Koninklijke Ahold N.V.)
Piet Heinkade 167 - 173,
1019 GM Amsterdam, The Netherlands
Phone: +31-20-509-51-00   **Fax:** +31-20-509-51-10
US HQ: 1385 Hancock St., Quincy Center Plaza,
Quincy, MA 02169
US Phone: 781-380-8000   **US Fax:** 617-770-8190
Web: www.ahold.com

Royal Ahold operates or has interest in supermarkets and specialty stores in Europe (the Baltic republics, Belgium, the Czech Republic, Denmark, the Netherlands, Norway, Poland, Portugal, Slovakia, and Sweden), and the US.

2005 Stores

	No.
Europe	2,615
US	840
Total	**3,455**

2005 Sales

	% of total
US Retail	41
US Foodservice	33
Europe Retail	26
Total	**100**

2005 Sales

	% of total
US	74
Europe	26
Total	**100**

PRODUCTS/OPERATIONS

2005 Stores

	Company-owned	Franchised	Associated
Albert Heijn	994	657	—
Stop & Shop/Giant-Landover	573	—	—
Central Europe	499	3	—
Giant-Carlisle/Tops	262	5	—
Schuitema	105	—	357
Total	**2,433**	**665**	**357**

2005 Sales

	% of total
Retail	67
Foodservice	33
Total	**100**

Selected Operations

Retail
  Central and South America
    CARHCO (33%; discount supermarkets; Costa Rica, Honduras, Nicaragua)
    Disco S.A. (supermarkets, Argentina)
  Europe
    Albert (supermarkets, Czech Republic)
    Albert Heijn (supermarkets)
    Etos (health and beauty stores)
    Feira Nova (hypermarkets, Portugal)
    Gall & Gall (liquor stores)
    Hypernova (hypermarkets, Czech Republic and Poland)
    ICA AB (60%, supermarkets, Scandinavia)
    Jerónimo Martins (49%, supermarkets and hypermarkets, Portugal)
    Max (supermarkets, Poland)
    Pingo Doce (supermarkets, Portugal)
    Prima (mini-hypermarkets, Czech Republic)
    Schuitema (73%, wholesale supplier)
    Sesam (supermarkets, Poland)
  US
    Giant-Carlisle (supermarkets)
    Giant-Landover (supermarkets)
    Stop & Shop (supermarkets)
    Tops (supermarkets)

Foodservice
  PYA/Monarch (US)
  U.S. Foodservice
Other
  Ahold Real Estate (real estate development; the Netherlands, US)
  Peapod (online grocery shopping, US)
  Statoil (50%, gasoline stations, Scandinavia)

COMPETITORS

A&P
Albertsons
ALDI
Auchan
Carrefour
Casino Guichard
Delhaize
Eroski
Golub
Hannaford Bros.
IGA
ITM Entreprises
Kooperativa Förbundet
Kroger
Laurus
Lidl & Schwarz Stiftung
Meijer
METRO AG
NorgesGruppen
Red Apple Group
Safeway
Shaw's
SYSCO
Tengelmann
Tesco
Wal-Mart

HISTORICAL FINANCIALS

Company Type: Public

Income Statement

FYE: Sunday nearest December 31

	REVENUE ($ mil.)	NET INCOME ($ mil.)	NET PROFIT MARGIN	EMPLOYEES
12/05	52,223	(11)	—	167,801
12/04	70,543	149	0.2%	206,441
12/03	69,693	(929)	—	257,140
12/02	65,466	(4,520)	—	341,909
12/01	59,002	140	0.2%	404,453
Annual Growth	(3.0%)	—	—	(19.7%)

2005 Year-End Financials

Debt ratio: 48.4%
Return on equity: —
Cash ($ mil.): 2,638
Current ratio: 1.07
Long-term debt ($ mil.): 5,764
No. of shares (mil.): —
Dividends
  Yield: —
  Payout: —
Market value ($ mil.): —

Stock History

NYSE: AHO

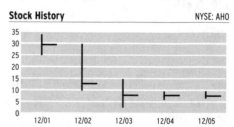

	STOCK PRICE ($) FY Close	P/E High/Low	PER SHARE ($) Earnings	PER SHARE ($) Dividends
12/05	7.53	— —	—	—
12/04	7.77	— —	—	—
12/03	7.76	— —	—	0.68
12/02	12.73	— —	(4.88)	0.52
12/01	29.39	— —	—	0.44
Annual Growth	(28.9%)	— —	—	24.3%

Royal Bank of Canada

Royal Bank of Canada sits enthroned as Canada's banking monarch. Also known as RBC Financial Group — and Canada's largest financial institution — the bank operates in three segments: a Canadian consumer unit, which includes banking, investments, and insurance; an international consumer unit (banking and investments in the US and abroad); and a global wholesale unit (capital markets and corporate and commercial banking). In addition to more than 1,300 domestic locations, the bank has about 40 offices in the Caribbean and more in some 30 countries. Its US operations include RBC Centura Banks, which operates in the Southeast, and brokerage firm RBC Dain Rauscher.

RBC is merging Dain Rauscher with its sister firm, investment bank RBC Dominion Securities (aka RBC Capital Markets). The move lets the company combine all of its US securities businesses into a single entity.

Other subsidiaries include Canadian discount brokerage RBC Action Direct and RBC Insurance. In 2006 the company boosted its brokerage activities when it said that it would buy the electronic brokerage business of New York boutique Carlin Financial Group. The move will give RBC better access to hedge fund traders and other professional traders who like Carlin's speed and efficiency.

RBC Centura has been purchasing community banks and other small financial services in the South and plans to add more branches in Georgia, Florida, and the Carolinas. To that end, it bought Flag Financial, which has some 20 branches in the South. However, the company is re-evaluating many of its other US operations. It sold Houston-based home lender RBC Mortgage to New Century Financial in 2005.

The company moved into the US trust business in 2006 when it acquired American Guaranty & Trust, a unit of National Life Insurance Company.

Beyond North America, RBC provides foreign exchange services and import/export services for Canadian and multinational clients. The bank has set out to become a leader in wealth management, acquiring and adding services to attract high-net-worth clients (and the fees it can charge them for handling their assets). To that end, it acquired private bank Abacus Financial Services Group, which has five offices in the UK and another in Amsterdam. RBC has paired with Belgium-based bank Dexia to form a joint venture called RBC Dexia Investor Services, which will provide investment administration services to institutional clients.

HISTORY

Royal Bank of Canada (RBC) has looked south of the border ever since its 1864 creation as Merchants Bank in Halifax, Nova Scotia, a port city bustling with trade spawned by the US Civil War. After incorporating in 1869 as Merchants Bank of Halifax, the bank added branches in eastern Canada. Merchants opened a branch in Bermuda in 1882. Gold strikes in Canada and Alaska in the late 1890s pushed it into western Canada.

Merchants opened offices in New York and Cuba in 1899 and changed its name to Royal Bank of Canada in 1901. RBC moved into new Montreal headquarters in 1907 and grew by purchasing such banks as Union Bank of Canada (1925). In 1928 it moved into the 42-story Royal Bank Building, then the tallest in the British Empire.

The bank faltered during the Depression but recovered during WWII. After the war RBC financed the expanding minerals and oil and gas industries. When Castro took power in Cuba, RBC tried to operate its branches under communist rule but sold out to Banco Nacional de Cuba in 1960.

RBC opened offices in the UK in 1979 and in West Germany, Puerto Rico, and the Bahamas in 1980. As Canada's banking rules relaxed, RBC bought Dominion Securities in 1987. The US Federal Reserve approved RBC's brokerage arm for participation in stock underwriting in 1991.

In 1992 the bank faced a $650 million loss after backing the Reichmann family's Olympia & York property development company, which failed under the weight of its UK projects. The next year an ever-diversifying RBC bought Royal Trustco, Canada's #2 trust company, and Voyageur Travel Insurance, its largest retail travel insurer. A management shakeup in late 1994 ended with bank president John Cleghorn taking control of the company.

In 1995 RBC listed on the New York Stock Exchange and the next year joined with Heller Financial (an affiliate of Japan's Fuji Bank) to finance trade between Canada and Mexico. It began offering PC home banking in 1996 and Internet banking in 1997. That year RBC became one of the world's largest securities-custody service providers with its acquisition of The Bank of Nova Scotia's institutional and pension custody operations.

The company and Bank of Montreal agreed to merge in 1998, but Canadian regulators, fearing the concentration of banking power seen in the US, rejected the merger. In response, the bank trimmed its workforce and orchestrated a sale-leaseback of its property portfolio (1999).

In the late 1990s RBC grew its online presence by purchasing the Internet banking operations of Security First Network Bank (now Security First Technologies, 1998), the online trading division of Bull & Bear Group (1999), and 20% of AOL Canada (1999). It also bought several trust and fiduciary services businesses from Ernst & Young.

In 2000 it acquired US mortgage bank Prism Financial and the Canadian retail credit card business of BANK ONE. RBC also sold its commercial credit portfolio to U.S. Bancorp. The company agreed to pay a substantial fine after institutional asset management subsidiary RT Capital Management came under scrutiny from the Ontario Securities Commission for alleged involvement in illegal pension-fund stock manipulation. RBC ended up selling RT Capital to UBS AG the following year.

Also in 2001 RBC made another US purchase: North Carolina's Centura Banks (now RBC Centura Banks). It sold Bull & Bear Securities to JB Oxford Holdings of Los Angeles.

EXECUTIVES

Chairman: David P. O'Brien, age 64
President, CEO, and Director: Gordon M. Nixon, age 48, $3,398,000 pay
COO: Barbara G. Stymiest, $1,699,000 pay
CFO: Janice R. Fukakusa, $339,800 pay

Group Head, Canadian Personal and Business Clients: W. James (Jim) Westlake, $1,614,050 pay
Group Head, Global Capital Markets; President and CEO, RBC Dominion Securities: Charles M. (Chuck) Winograd, $2,700,249 pay
Group Head, Global Technology and Operations: Martin J. (Marty) Lippert, $2,527,263 pay
Group Head, Human Resources and Transformation: Elisabetta Bigsby
Group Head, US and International: Peter Armenio
EVP and General Counsel: David R. Allgood
EVP, Corporate Treasury: James B. (Jim) Archer-Shee
EVP, Corporate Treasury: Ian MacKay
EVP, Government Affairs and Business Development: Charles S. (Charlie) Coffey
EVP, RBC Global Services; CEO, RBC Dexia Investor Services: José Placido
EVP, Sales; President and CEO, Royal Mutual Funds: Anne Lockie
SVP, Investor Relations: Nabanita Merchant
VP and Secretary: Carol J. McNamara
VP and Chief Economist: Craig Wright
Chairman, RBC Dain Rauscher: Irving (Irv) Weiser
Chairman, RBC Dominion Securities: Anthony S. (Tony) Fell, age 67
Chairman and CEO, RBC Centura Banks: Scott M. Custer, age 49
Ombudsman: Wendy Knight
Auditors: Deloitte & Touche LLP

LOCATIONS

HQ: Royal Bank of Canada
Royal Bank Plaza, 200 Bay St.,
Toronto, Ontario M5J 2J5, Canada
Phone: 800-769-2599
US HQ: 1 Liberty Plaza, New York, NY 10006
US Phone: 212-858-7100   **US Fax:** 212-428-2329
Web: www.rbc.com

PRODUCTS/OPERATIONS

2005 Sales

	% of total
Interest	
Loans	37
Securities	16
Other	5
Noninterest	
Insurance premiums, investment & fee income	11
Trading revenue	5
Investment management & custodial fees	4
Securities brokerage commissions	4
Service charges	4
Underwriting & other advisory fees	4
Other	10
Total	**100**

2005 Sales

	% of total
Personal banking	28
Global insurance	26
Wealth management	18
Business & commercial	16
Cards & payment solutions	12
Total	**100**

2005 Assets

	% of total
Cash & equivalents	2
Trading account securities	27
Other securities	7
Derivative-related amounts	8
Residential mortgages	19
Personal loans	9
Business & credit card loans	13
Assets purchased under reverse repurchase agreements	9
Other	6
Total	**100**

COMPETITORS

Bank of America	Goldman Sachs
Barclays	HSBC Holdings
BB&T	JPMorgan Chase
BCE	Laurentian Bank
Bear Stearns	Mellon Financial
BMO Financial Group	Merrill Lynch
CIBC	National Bank of Canada
Citigroup	Nomura Securities
Citigroup Global Markets	Scotiabank
Deutsche Bank	TD Bank
First Citizens BancShares	UBS
FMR	UBS Financial Services

HISTORICAL FINANCIALS

Company Type: Public

Income Statement

FYE: October 31

	ASSETS ($ mil.)	NET INCOME ($ mil.)	INCOME AS % OF ASSETS	EMPLOYEES
10/05	399,140	2,970	0.7%	60,012
10/04	367,502	2,331	0.6%	57,795
10/03	313,693	2,308	0.7%	60,812
10/02	243,940	1,851	0.8%	59,549
Annual Growth	**17.8%**	**17.1%**	**—**	**0.3%**

2005 Year-End Financials

Equity as % of assets: 4.1%
Return on assets: 0.8%
Return on equity: 19.4%
Long-term debt ($ mil.): 44,340
Sales ($ mil.): 24,996

Net Income History

NYSE: RY

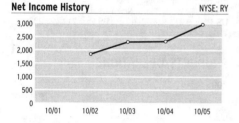

Royal Bank of Scotland

It only seems like some banks print their own money — Royal Bank of Scotland (RBS) really does. In fact, it has been producing its own banknotes for nearly three centuries. Operating as Royal Bank of Scotland, NatWest, and Ulster Bank, the company has approximately 2,500 locations that offer such services as deposit accounts, credit cards, and mortgages to commercial and personal clients in Scotland, England, Wales, and Ireland. RBS also sells insurance and investment products over the telephone through its Direct Line subsidiary, and provides private banking through The Coutts Group and Adam & Company. In the US it owns Citizens Financial and RBS Lynk (formerly Lynk Systems).

Citizens Financial is one of the largest foreign-owned banks in the US, with more than 1,500 branches in the Northeast, where it operates as Citizens Bank, and the Midwest, where it operates as Charter One. RBS bought Lynk Systems, an Atlanta-based payment processing firm, for some $525 million in cash in 2004.

RBS has organized its business into eight divisions: Corporate Banking and Financial Markets, Retail Banking (Royal Bank and NatWest), Retail Direct, Manufacturing (operations support for the customer-facing businesses), Wealth Management, RBS Insurance (including Churchill Insurance), Ulster Bank, and Citizens Financial.

Some of the divisions are busy growing through acquisitions. In 2004 Ulster Bank bought First Active and Citizens Financial bought Cleveland-based Charter One Financial. Its leasing arm, Lombard, owns one of the UK's largest car dealerships, Dixon Motors.

In 2004 RBS paid about $360 million for the credit card business of Connecticut-based People's Bank, a deal that beefed up the bank's presence in the US credit card market.

RBS has established a strong presence in China by buying a stake in, and forming a strategic partnership with, Bank of China, one of the country's largest banks. Together the two banks offer credit cards and will be offering insurance products.

If you have overdraft protection for your checking account, you can thank RBS, which invented the service in 1728.

HISTORY

Royal Bank of Scotland was founded in 1727, but its roots go back to the Darien Company, a merchant expedition that was established to set up a Scottish trading colony in Panama. The Darien expedition ended disastrously in 1699. In 1707 England voted to compensate Scottish creditors for the colony's failure (in part because England had promised support, then reneged, contributing to the collapse), and a small industry sprang up around paying creditors and loaning them money. In 1727 the Equivalent Company, the combined entity of these organizations, was granted a banking charter and became Royal Bank of Scotland.

In 1826 the Parliament voted to take away Scottish banks' right to issue banknotes for less than five pounds, which would have required banks to use gold or silver. Few banks had such reserves, and the move sparked an outcry. Novelist Sir Walter Scott's *The Letters of Malachi Malagrowther,* which defended the Scottish one-pound note, helped shoot down the proposal.

RBS expanded throughout Scotland over the next 50 years. It opened a London branch in 1874; it didn't establish a branch outside London until it bought Williams Deacon's Bank, which had a branch network in North England. RBS continued to use the Williams Deacon's name, as it did with Glyn, Mills & Co., which it purchased in 1939.

In 1968 RBS took on its modern persona as a public company when it merged with National Commercial Bank. The company moved overseas during the 1970s, establishing offices in Hong Kong and major US cities.

RBS spent the next 20 years trying to achieve another merger of the same scale as National Commercial. In 1981 the bank was wooed by Standard Chartered Bank and Hongkong and Shanghai Bank (now part of HSBC Holdings), but British regulators denied both suitors.

The bank moved into telephone operations in 1985, when it set up Direct Line for selling car insurance. In 1988 RBS bought New England bank Citizens Financial. In 1989 the company entered into an alliance with Banco Santander (now Santander Central Hispano), Spain's largest banking group. The alliance created a cross-pollination of ideas and strategies that boosted both banks' operations. The first fruit of the alliance came in 1991 with the launch of Interbank On-line Systems (IBOS), which connected several European banks and allowed for instantaneous money transfers.

In the 1990s RBS was linked with a variety of partners. It even made a bid for the much larger bank Barclays, in a move regarded as cheeky, but was rebuffed. In 1997 it announced a joint venture with Richard Branson's Virgin Group called Virgin Direct to offer personal banking. The company also bought Angel Trains Contract, a rolling stock leasing company, and established a transatlantic banking transfer system (similar to IBOS) with US bank CoreStates (now owned by First Union).

In 1999 RBS opened a branch in Frankfurt as a base for European activities. The next year Citizens Financial bought UST Corp., making it the #2 bank in New England next to FleetBoston.

The next year RBS acquired NatWest after a prolonged takeover battle with rival Bank of Scotland (now part of HBOS plc). The bank sold Gartmore Investment Management, its fund management unit, to Nationwide Mutual Insurance Company. Royal Bank also sold the assets of NatWest's Equity Partners unit and launched NatWest Private Banking to target wealthy investors.

EXECUTIVES

Chairman: Sir Thomas F. W. (Tom) McKillop, age 62
Executive Chairman, Retail Markets: Gordon Pell, age 56, $2,711,350 pay
Group Chief Executive and Executive Director: Sir Frederick A. (Fred) Goodwin, age 47, $2,850,000 pay
Group Finance Director and Executive Director: Guy Whittaker, age 49
Chief Executive, Corporate Markets: Johnny A. N. Cameron, age 51
Chief Executive, Manufacturing and Executive Director: Mark Fisher, age 46
Executive Director; Chairman and CEO, Citizens Financial Group: Lawrence K. (Larry) Fish, age 61, $4,254,550 pay
Chief Executive, RBS Insurance: Annette Court
CEO, RBS Insurance: Chris Sullivan
Chief Executive, Ulster Bank Group: Cormac McCarthy
Group Secretary and General Counsel: Miller R. McLean, age 56
Group Director, Communications: Howard Moody
Group Director, Human Resources: Neil Roden
Head of Group Communications: Carolyn McAdam
Chief Economist: Andrew McLaughlin
Head of Group Secretariat: Hew Campbell
Head of Investor Relations: Richard O'Connor
CEO, RBS National Bank, Citizens Financial Group: Joseph A. (Joe) Hoffman
Auditors: Deloitte & Touche LLP

LOCATIONS

HQ: The Royal Bank of Scotland Group plc
36 St Andrew Square,
Edinburgh EH2 2YB, United Kingdom
Phone: +44-131-556-8555   **Fax:** +44-131-557-6140
US HQ: 1 Citizens Plaza, Providence, RI 02903
US Phone: 401-456-7000   **US Fax:** 401-456-7819
Web: www.rbs.com

PRODUCTS/OPERATIONS

Selected Subsidiaries

Adam & Company (private banking)
Citizens Financial Group, Inc (banking, US)
Coutts & Co (private banking)
Coutts Bank Ltd (private banking, Switzerland)
Direct Line Insurance plc
Greenwich Capital Markets, Inc. (broker dealer, US)
Lombard North Central PLC (banking, credit finance, and leasing)
National Westminster Home Loans Limited

National Westminster Bank Plc
RBS Life Holdings Limited (life assurance)
The Royal Bank of Scotland International Limited
  (Channel Islands)
The Royal Bank of Scotland plc
Ulster Bank Limited

COMPETITORS

Abbey National	Irish Life
Alliance & Leicester	JPMorgan Chase
Allied Irish Banks	Lloyds TSB
Bank of America	London Scottish Bank
Bank of Ireland	PNC Financial
Barclays	Standard Chartered
Citigroup	Standard Life
HBOS	Virgin Group
HSBC Holdings	Woolwich
ING Direct UK	

HISTORICAL FINANCIALS

Company Type: Public

Income Statement				FYE: December 31
	ASSETS ($ mil.)	NET INCOME ($ mil.)	INCOME AS % OF ASSETS	EMPLOYEES
12/05	1,345,013	7,888	0.6%	137,000
12/04	1,215,877	8,099	0.7%	136,600
12/03	577,018	3,220	0.6%	—
12/02	664,023	6,756	1.0%	—
12/01	538,630	4,125	0.8%	—
Annual Growth	25.7%	17.6%	—	0.3%

2005 Year-End Financials

Equity as % of assets: 5.1%   Long-term debt ($ mil.): 372,548
Return on assets: 0.6%   Sales ($ mil.): 64,212
Return on equity: 11.4%

Net Income History   London: RBS

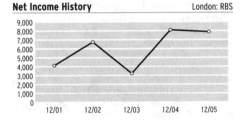

Royal Dutch Shell

Royal Dutch Shell (formerly Royal Dutch/Shell Group) sits on an oil and gas throne that is only slightly lower than those of Exxon Mobil and BP. The company has worldwide proved reserves of 11.5 billion barrels of oil equivalent. It also produces bitumen, refined products, and chemicals; transports natural gas; trades gas and electricity; develops renewable energy sources; and owns 45,000 gas stations. Revelations of overestimated oil reserves in 2004 prompted a push for greater transparency in the company's organizational structure. This led to the 2005 merger of former publicly traded owners Royal Dutch Petroleum and The "Shell" Transport and Trading Company into a new publicly traded Royal Dutch Shell.

The Anglo-Dutch entity has restructured to stay competitive. Gone are the decentralized committees that ruled the company's once Byzantine bureaucracy; they have been replaced by divisional chiefs who report to the CEO. Most

of the oil giant's crude is produced in Nigeria, Oman, the UK, and the US. Royal Dutch Shell owns or has interests in about 50 refineries worldwide. The company has announced, however, that it will invest some $12 billion (in addition to the $2.6 billion already spent) in offshore projects near Dubai. Royal Dutch Shell has also pledged to infuse $600 million into its joint venture with PetroChina for the development of develop wells and to cover day-to-day operating expenses.

In 2004 the company reported that it had overestimated its reserves by 24%. The bad news resulted in the ouster of the Royal Dutch Shell's chairman and CFO.

Searching for new oil assets, in 2006 the company acquired a large swath of oil sands acreage in Alberta, Canada, and made a bid to buy the 22% of Shell Canada that it did not already own.

That year the company agreed to give control of the $22 billion Sakhalin-2 project to Russian gas giant Gazprom.

HISTORY

In 1870 Marcus Samuel inherited an interest in his father's London trading company, which imported seashells from the Far East. He expanded the business and, after securing a contract for Russian oil, began selling kerosene in the Far East.

Standard Oil underpriced competitors to defend its Asian markets. Samuel secretly prepared his response and in 1892 unveiled the first of a fleet of tankers. Rejecting Standard's acquisition overtures, Samuel created "Shell" Transport and Trading in 1897.

Meanwhile, a Dutchman, Aeilko Zijlker, struck oil in Sumatra and formed Royal Dutch Petroleum in 1890 to exploit the oil field. Young Henri Deterding joined the firm in 1896 and established a sales force in the Far East.

Deterding became Royal Dutch's head in 1900 amid the battle for the Asian market. In 1903 Deterding, Samuel, and the Rothschilds created Asiatic Petroleum, a marketing alliance. With Shell's non-Asian business eroding, Deterding engineered a merger between Royal Dutch and Shell in 1907. Royal Dutch shareholders got 60% control; "Shell" Transport and Trading, 40%.

After the 1911 Standard Oil breakup, Deterding entered the US, building refineries and buying producers. Shell products were available in every state by 1929. Royal Dutch/Shell joined the 1928 "As Is" cartel that fixed prices for most of two decades.

The post-WWII Royal Dutch/Shell profited from worldwide growth in oil consumption. It acquired 100% of Shell Oil, its US arm, in 1985, but shareholders sued, maintaining Shell Oil's assets had been undervalued in the deal. They were awarded $110 million in 1990.

After the 1990-91 Persian Gulf crisis, Shell sold a major California refinery to Unocal (1991) and its US coal mining unit to Zeigler Coal (1992).

Management's slow response to two 1995 controversies — environmentalists' outrage over the planned sinking of an oil platform and human rights activists' criticism of Royal Dutch/Shell's role in Nigeria — spurred a major shakeup. It began moving away from its decentralized structure and adopted a new policy of corporate openness.

In 1996 Royal Dutch/Shell and Exxon formed a worldwide petroleum additives venture. Shell Oil joined Texaco in 1998 to form Equilon Enterprises, combining US refining and marketing

operations in the West and Midwest. Similarly, Shell Oil, Texaco, and Saudi Arabia's Aramco combined downstream operations on the US's East and Gulf coasts as Motiva Enterprises.

In 1999 Royal Dutch/Shell and the UK's BG plc acquired a controlling stake in Comgas, a unit of Companhia Energética de São Paulo and the largest natural gas distributor in Brazil, for about $1 billion.

In 2000 the company sold its coal business to UK-based mining giant Anglo American for more than $850 million. To gain a foothold in the US power marketing scene, Royal Dutch/Shell formed a joint venture with construction giant Bechtel (called InterGen). The next year the company agreed to combine its German refining and marketing operations with those of RWE-DEA. Royal Dutch/Shell tried to expand its US natural gas reserves in 2001 by making a $2 billion hostile bid for Barrett Resources, but the effort was withdrawn after Barrett agreed to be acquired by Williams for $2.5 billion.

In 2002, in connection with Chevron's acquisition of Texaco, Royal Dutch/Shell acquired ChevronTexaco's (now Chevron) stakes in the underperforming US marketing joint ventures Equilon and Motiva. That year the company, through its US Shell Oil unit, acquired Pennzoil-Quaker State for $1.8 billion. Also that year Royal Dutch/Shell acquired Enterprise Oil for $5 billion, plus debt. In addition, it purchased RWE's 50% stake in German refining and marketing joint venture Shell & DEA Oil (for $1.35 billion).

In 2004 the Group signed a $200 million exploration deal with Libya, signaling its return to that country after a more than decade-long absence. Plans to build a $7 billion LNG plant in Qatar were announced in early 2005. In the same year the company's Shell Chemicals subsidiary announced plans sell its 50% stake in Basell, one of the world's largest polyolefin makers. Royal Dutch/Shell became Royal Dutch Shell after the merger of Royal Dutch Petroleum and The "Shell" Transport and Trading Company.

EXECUTIVES

Non-Executive Chairman: Jorma Ollila, age 56
Deputy Chairman and Senior Independent Non-Executive Director: John Kerr (Lord of Kinlochard), age 64
Chief Executive and Director: Jeroen van der Veer, age 59
Executive Director, Exploration and Production: Malcom Brinded, age 53
Executive Director, Downstream — Oil Products & Chemicals: Rob J. Routs, age 60
Executive Director, Gas and Power: Linda Z. Cook, age 48
CFO and Director: Peter R. Voser, age 48
Group Director, Human Resources: John D. Hofmeister
Group Director, International Directorate: Hugh Mitchell
Group Legal Director: Beat Hess, age 57
Group Director, Strategic Planning, Sustainable Development, and External Affairs: Adrian Loader
Chairman, Shell Nigeria and CEO, Shell EP Africa: Chris Finlayson, age 48
President and CEO Shell Canada: Clive Mather, age 59
CEO, Shell Renewables; President, Shell Hydrogen: Graeme Sweeney
Chief Executive, Renewables: Karen de Segundo, age 60
Chief Executive, Shell Hydrogen: Jeremy B. Bentham
Chief Executive, Shell Consumer: Charles Harrison
CEO, Shell EP Americas: Raoul Restucci
President, Shell Trading: Mike Warwick
Head of Contracting and Procurement: Kees Linse
Company Secretary: Michiel Brandjes, age 51
Auditors: PricewaterhouseCoopers LLP

LOCATIONS

HQ: Royal Dutch Shell plc
Carel van Bylandtlaan 30,
2596 HR The Hague, The Netherlands
Phone: +31-70-377-9111 **Fax:** +31-70-377-3115
US HQ: 630 Fifth Ave., Ste. 3166, New York, NY 10111
US Phone: 212-218-3113 **US Fax:** 212-218-3114
Web: www.shell.com

Royal Dutch Shell operates in more than 145 countries.
It has major oil and gas interests in Argentina, Australia,
Bangladesh, Brunei, Canada, China, Colombia,
Denmark, Egypt, Gabon, Germany, Kazakhstan,
Malaysia, the Netherlands, New Zealand, Nigeria,
Norway, Oman, Pakistan, Peru, the Philippines, Russia,
Syria, the UK, the United Arab Emirates, the US, and
Venezuela.

2005 Sales

	$ mil.	% of total
Eastern Hemisphere		
Europe	122,684	40
Other regions	61,388	20
Western Hemisphere		
US	101,308	33
Other countries	21,351	7
Total	**306,731**	**100**

PRODUCTS/OPERATIONS

2005 Sales

	$ mil.	% of total
Oil products (refining & marketing)	237,210	77
Chemicals	31,018	10
Exploration & production	23,970	8
Gas & power	13,766	5
Corporate & other	767	—
Total	**306,731**	**100**

COMPETITORS

7-Eleven
Ashland
BHP Billiton
BP
Celanese AG
Chevron
Dow Chemical
DuPont
Eastman Chemical
Eni
Exxon Mobil
FEC Resources
Hess
Huntsman
Imperial Chemical Industries
Imperial Oil
Koch
Lyondell Chemical
Marathon Oil
Norsk Hydro
Occidental Petroleum
PDVSA
PEMEX
PETROBRAS
PetroKazakhstan
Repsol YPF
Sinopec Shanghai Petrochemical
Sunoco
TOTAL

HISTORICAL FINANCIALS

Company Type: Public

Income Statement

FYE: December 31

	REVENUE ($ mil.)	NET INCOME ($ mil.)	NET PROFIT MARGIN	EMPLOYEES
12/05	306,731	26,261	8.6%	109,000

RWE

RWE doesn't stand for Runs With Electricity,
but it could. Through its subsidiaries, the energy
conglomerate provides electricity, gas, water, and
environmental services to residential and business customers, primarily in Europe and North
America. RWE is one of Germany's top two electricity suppliers (along with E.ON); it also owns
two major UK-based utilities: #3 global water
provider RWE Thames Water (which it has
agreed to sell) and domestic electricity and gas
supplier RWE npower. RWE owns oil and gas exploration and production company RWE-DEA;
other businesses include companies engaged in
gas transportation and storage, power generation, energy trading, information technology,
and coal mining.

In 2006 the company agreed to sell RWE
Thames Water to Kemble Water Limited, a consortium led by Macquarie Bank's European Infrastructure Funds unit.

Overall, RWE serves 20 million electricity customers and 10 million gas customers. Its core
markets are Germany, central Eastern Europe,
the UK, and the US.

As Germany's old industrial controls continue
to tumble like Berlin's famous wall in the face of
European Union-wide deregulation, RWE is
doing its best to cope with the chaos of a new
order by restructuring its regional energy businesses. The company's former German utility
unit, RWE Energie, lost its regional monopoly
status because of deregulation, and RWE has responded by splitting its domestic power generation, distribution, and supply operations into
new units.

HISTORY

Founded at the end of the 19th century, RWE
mirrored the industrialization of Germany in its
growth. It was formed as Rheinisch-Westfalisches
Elektrizitatswerk in 1898 by Erich Zweigert, the
mayor of Essen, and Hugo Stinnes, an industrialist from Mulheim, to provide electricity to Essen
and surrounding areas. The company began supplying power in 1900.

Stinnes persuaded other cities — Gelsen-
kirchen and Mulheim — to buy shares in RWE
in 1905. In 1908 RWE and rival Vereinigte Elektrizitatswerk Westfalen (VEW) agreed to divide
up the territories that each would supply.

Germany's coal shortages, caused by WWI,
prompted RWE to expand its coal operations,
and it bought Rheinische Aktiengesellschaft für
Braunkohlenbergbau, a coal producer, in 1932.
RWE also built a power line network, completed
in 1930, to connect populous northern Germany
with the south. By 1939, as WWII began, the
company had plants throughout most of western
Germany. However, the war destroyed much of
its infrastructure, and RWE had to rebuild.

The company continued to rely on coal for
most of its fuel needs in the 1950s, but in 1961
RWE and Bayern Atomkraft sponsored the construction of a demonstration nuclear reactor, the
first of several such projects, at Gundremmingen. The Gundremmingen plant was shut down
in 1977, and to replace it RWE built two 1,300-
MW reactors that began operation in 1984.

RWE began to diversify, and in 1988 it acquired Texaco's German petroleum and petrochemical unit, which became RWE-DEA. By
1990 RWE's operations also included waste management and construction. RWE reorganized,
creating RWE Aktiengesellschaft as a holding
company for group operations.

RWE-DEA acquired the US's Vista Chemical in
1991, and RWE's Rheinbraun mining unit
bought a 50% stake in Consolidation Coal from
DuPont. (The mining venture went public in
1999 as CONSOL Energy.) RWE led a consortium that acquired major stakes in three Hungarian power companies in 1995.

Hoping to play a role in Germany's telecommunications market, RWE teamed with VEBA
in 1997 to form the o.tel.o joint venture, and
RWE and VEBA gained control of large German
mobile phone operator E-Plus. The nation's telecom market was deregulated in 1998, but Mannesmann and former monopoly Deutsche
Telekom proved to be formidable competitors. In
1999 RWE and VEBA sold o.tel.o's fixed-line
business (along with the o.tel.o brand name) and
cable-TV unit Tele Columbus. The next year the
companies sold their joint stake in E-Plus.

Faced with deregulating German electricity
markets, RWE Energie had begun restructuring
as soon as the market opened up in 1998. It
agreed to buy fellow German power company
VEW in a $20 billion deal that closed in 2000.
RWE also joined with insurance giant Allianz
and France's Vivendi in a successful bid for a
49.9% stake in state-owned water distributor
Berliner Wasserbetriebe (Vivendi later spurned
an RWE offer to buy its energy businesses).

After taking advantage of deregulating markets in Germany, RWE moved to pick up other
European utilities: It acquired UK-based Thames
Water (later renamed RWE Thames Water) in
2000 and bought a majority stake in Dutch gas
supplier Intergas the next year. In 2002 the company issued an exchange offer to acquire UK electricity supplier Innogy (later renamed RWE
npower) for a total of about $4.4 billion in cash
and $3 billion in assumed debt. It also completed
a $3.7 billion purchase of Czech Republic gas
supplier Transgas.

In a move to further streamline operations,
RWE sold its 50% stake in refinery and service station subsidiary Shell & DEA Oil to Deutsche Shell
and Shell Petroleum. To do battle in an increasingly competitive utility industry, RWE is acquiring stakes in other European utilities. In 2003
RWE also acquired North American utility American Water Works, which was combined with the
US operations of RWE Thames Water, for $4.6 bil-
lion in cash and $4 billion in assumed debt.

EXECUTIVES

Chairman: Thomas R. Fischer, age 59
Deputy Chairman: Frank Bsirske
President and CEO; Chairman, RWE Energy and RWE
 Thames Water: Harry J. M. Roels, age 58
EVP and CFO: Klaus Sturany, age 60
EVP Human Resources and Law: Jan Zilius, age 60
EVP; President and CEO, RWE Energy:
 Berthold Bonekamp
CEO, RWE Dea Aktiengesellschaft: Georg Schöning,
 age 54
CEO, RWE Thames Water: William J. (Bill) Alexander,
 age 59
CEO, RWE npower: Andrew J. (Andy) Duff, age 47
Head of Investor Relations: Ingo Alphéus
Head of Press Department: Bill McAndrews
Auditors: PricewaterhouseCoopers AG

LOCATIONS

HQ: RWE Aktiengesellschaft
Opernplatz 1, 45128 Essen, Germany
Phone: +49-201-12-00   **Fax:** +49-201-12-15199
Web: www.rwe.com

RWE operates in Europe and the Americas.

2005 Sales

	% of total
Europe	
Germany	55
UK	21
Other countries	18
Americas	5
Asia, Africa & Australia	1
Total	**100**

PRODUCTS/OPERATIONS

2005 Sales

	% of total
RWE Energy	59
RWE Power	16
RWE npower	15
RWE Thames Water	10
Total	**100**

Selected Divisions and Subsidiaries

RWE Energy (domestic and continental European
   downstream energy operations)
   RWE Net AG (electricity transmission and distribution
      system operations)
   RWE Solutions AG (industrial services)
RWE Power (upstream energy operations)
   RWE-DEA AG (oil and gas exploration, production,
      and storage)
   RWE Rheinbraun AG (coal mining and coal-fired
      power generation)
RWE npower (formerly RWE Innogy, electricity and gas
   supply, UK)
RWE Thames Water (water and waste water services, UK
   and international)

COMPETITORS

BASF AG
BP
Cegedel
Centrica
Electricité de France
EnBW
Endesa
Enel
E.ON
E.ON UK
European Minerals
Exxon Mobil
Royal Dutch Shell
Severn Trent
SUEZ
UES of Russia
United Utilities
Vattenfall
Vattenfall Europe Berlin
Veolia Environnement

HISTORICAL FINANCIALS

Company Type: Public

Income Statement

FYE: December 31

	REVENUE ($ mil.)	NET INCOME ($ mil.)	NET PROFIT MARGIN	EMPLOYEES
12/05	47,986	2,642	5.5%	85,928
12/04	55,919	2,915	5.2%	97,777
12/03	53,686	1,196	2.2%	127,028
12/02	45,579	1,101	2.4%	131,765
12/01	26,592	550	2.1%	155,634
Annual Growth	15.9%	48.0%	—	(13.8%)

Net Income History   Pink Sheets: RWEOY

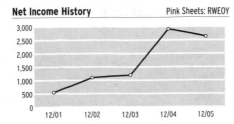

SABMiller

It's Miller time at South African Breweries.
SAB's 2002 purchase of Miller Brewing earned it
a new name, SABMiller plc, and made it the
world's third-largest brewer, behind InBev and
Anheuser-Busch. The company, which has operations in more than 60 countries, dominates
South African brewing on the strength of Africa's
best-selling beer, Castle Lager. It brews other regional brands, including Hansa Pilsener.
SABMiller also makes wines, spirits, and fruit
drinks as well as bottling Coca-Cola products.
Miller's former parent Altria Group owns almost
30% of SABMiller.

Apartheid kept SABMiller from investing overseas in the 1980s, so it grew by purchasing a diverse range of businesses at home. After
sanctions were lifted in the early 1990s, the company bulked up on foreign breweries. It now has
major operations in Africa, China, India, Central
Europe, and Central America. The company produces the popular Snow beer brand in China
through a 49% joint venture with China Resources Snow Breweries (CR Snow).

In 2005 SABMiller acquired almost 97% of
Bavaria S.A., the second largest brewer in South
America. Bavaria's brands include Águila, Atlas,
Cristal, and Pilsener. In 2006 it announced a
joint venture with Vietnam Dairy Products Joint
Stock Company (Vinamilk) to establish a brewery in Vietnam. It also acquired citrus-flavored
malt beverage Sparks and lager Steel Reserve
from contract brewer McKenzie River Corporation for $215 million. SAB's Colombian sub-
sidiary Bavaria in 2006 agreed to sell its fruit
juice business to beverage company Postobón,
also located in Colombia. Later that year the
company struck a deal with Coca-Cola Amatil to
sell and distribute imported beer in Australia.

As beer sales slow, SABMiller has increased
its concentration on energy drinks, flavored alcohol, and bottled water in its core South
African Market.

HISTORY

British sailor Frederick Mead purchased the
Castle Brewery in Johannesburg in 1892, about
15 years after gold was discovered in South
Africa. Mead took his brewing operation public
as South African Breweries (SAB) in 1895. The
company launched its flagship Castle Lager three
years later and survived the Anglo-Boer War
(1899-1902) as South Africa's fastest-growing
non-industrial firm. Mead died in 1915.

The brewer acquired the Grand Hotel in Cape
Town in 1921 and a stake in Schweppes (carbon-
ated drinks) in 1925. In the late 1940s SAB began
an extensive expansion program involving its
breweries, small hotels, and pubs. In 1951 it acquired the Hotel Victoria in Johannesburg. An
increase in beer taxes during the 1950s led SAB
to start producing liquors. With beer demand
slackening, South Africa's three largest brewers
— SAB, Ohlsson's, and United Breweries —
merged in 1956. The new company, which took
the SAB name, controlled about 90% of the beer
market. Beer taxes continued to pressure sales,
and in 1960 SAB acquired control of Stellen-
bosch Farmers' Winery to extend its product
range. In 1962 the restriction prohibiting alcohol consumption by blacks was lifted, opening an
enormous market. SAB continued to extend its
range of beer brands during the 1960s by adding
licenses to brew Amstel and Carling Black Label.

Further diversifying, SAB formed Barsab (an
investment venture with Thomas Barlow &
Sons) in 1966. The company launched its hotel
division, Southern Sun Hotels, three years later
by merging its hotels with those owned by the
Sol Kerzner family. The Barsab venture was dissolved in 1973, leaving SAB with furniture and
footwear businesses. The following year it acquired the South African bottling business of
Pepsi (converted to Coca-Cola in 1977). The
company added the beer interests of the Rem-
brandt Group and a 49% stake in Appletiser, a
fruit drinks company, in 1979. (It gained control
of it in 1982.)

SAB moved into apparel retailing with its purchase of the Scotts Stores (1981) and Edgars
(1982). After forming a joint venture with Ceres
Fruit Juices (1986), SAB made a number of investments in South Africa, including Lion Match
Company (1987), Da Gama Textiles (1989), and
Plate Glass (1992).

In the 1990s, the company expanded internationally. It acquired stakes in breweries in Hungary (1993), Tanzania and China (1994), and
Poland and Romania (1996). Graham Mackay
(now CEO) became managing director in 1996.

Before moving its main listing to the London
Stock Exchange in 1999, SAB sold its Amalgamated Retail unit (furniture, appliances), Lion
Match Company, and a large stake in Edgars. It
then bought controlling interests in Czech brewers Pilsner Urquell and Radegast to become the
largest brewer in Central Europe and sold its 68%
interest in Plate Glass to Dibelco (a D' Ieteren and
Copeba joint venture). Bevcon (a consortium of
three South African companies) sold its 27% interest in SAB in 1999.

The continuing woes of the South African
economy in 2000 fueled SAB's desire to continue
expanding its international base. In 2001 SAB
announced its China Resources Breweries Ltd
joint venture in the Sichuan province of China.
It also became the first international brewer with
a presence in Central America, spending more
than $500 million on breweries in Honduras and
El Salvador.

In 2002 SAB bought Miller Brewing from
Philip Morris (now Altria Group) for $5.6 bil-
lion, making it the world's second-largest brewer
at the time. SAB then changed its name to
SABMiller plc. SABMiller moved into Western
Europe in 2003 with the $270 million purchase
of Italian brewer Birra Peroni.

Similar to rival Anheuser-Busch, SABMiller is particularly interested in growing its base in China, which has the world's largest market for alcohol. SABMiller has invested heavily in China Resources Breweries. It had hoped to purchase control of the Harbin Brewery Group but was spurned by Anheuser-Busch, which successfully outbid SABMiller for control of the brewery in 2004. Several months later, SABMiller and China Resources Breweries purchased the Chinese brewing assets of Lion Nathan Limited.

EXECUTIVES

Chairman: Meyer Kahn, age 66, $269,623 pay
CEO and Director: Ernest A. (Graham) Mackay, age 56, $3,913,876 pay
CFO and Director: Malcolm I. Wyman, age 59, $1,887,358 pay
SVP, Investor Relations: Gary Leibowitz
President, Grupo Empresarial Bavaria: Karl Lippert
President and CEO, Miller Brewing Company: Tom Long, age 47
President and CEO, SABMiller Americas: Norman J. Adami, age 51
President, SABMiller South America: Barry Smith, age 55
Managing Director, Kompania Piwowarska: Mark J. Bowman
Managing Director, Miller Brands (UK): Gary Whitlie
Managing Director, SABMiller Africa and Asia: André C. Parker, age 55
Managing Director, SABMiller Central America: Trent Odgers
Managing Director, SABMiller Europe: Alan Clark, age 46
Managing Director, SABMiller India: Jean-Marc Delpon de Vaux
Managing Director, The South African Breweries: Tony van Kralingen, age 48
General Director, TransMark and Kaluga Brewing: James Wilson
Company Secretary and General Counsel: John Davidson
Group Marketing Director: Nick Fell
Director, Corporate Affairs: Sue Clark, age 42
Director, Human Resources: Johann Nel, age 49
Communications Executive: Briony Gilbert
Auditors: PricewaterhouseCoopers LLP

LOCATIONS

HQ: SABMiller plc
1 Stanhope Gate, London W1K1AF, United Kingdom
Phone: +44-20-7659-0100 **Fax:** +44-20-7659-0111
Web: www.sabmiller.com

SABMiller has operations in more than 60 countries worldwide.

2006 Sales

	% of total
North America	32
South Africa	25
Europe	21
Latin America	14
Africa & Asia	8
Total	**100**

PRODUCTS/OPERATIONS

Selected Brands

Beer

North America
Hamm's
Henry Weinhard's
Leinenkugel's
Miller
Milwaukee's Best
Miller Genuine Draft
Miller High Life
Olde English
Port Royal
Suprema

Africa
Amstel (license)
Carling Black Label
Castle (Draught, Lager, Lite, Milk Stout)
Fusion
Hansa Pilsener
Lion Lager (license)
Redd's
Rhino
Vita Malt
X-Cape

Europe
Dog In The Fog
Dorada
Dreher
Frisco
Gambrinus
Holsten
Keller
Miller
Peroni
Redd's
Saris
Timisoreana
Tyskie
Wührer
Zolotaya
ubr

Asia
Haywards
Knock Out
Royal Challenge
Snow

Soft drinks
Appletiser
Coca-Cola (license)
Grapetiser

Wines and spirits
Distell

COMPETITORS

AmBev
Anheuser-Busch
Asahi Breweries
Asia Pacific Breweries
Brau Union
Carlsberg
CBR Brewing
Constellation Brands
Diageo
Foster's
Grolsch

Heineken
InBev
Kirin Brewery Company
Lion Nathan
Molson Coors
PepsiCo
Pyramid Breweries
Suntory Ltd.
Tsingtao
Yanjing

HISTORICAL FINANCIALS

Company Type: Public

Income Statement

FYE: March 31

	REVENUE ($ mil.)	NET INCOME ($ mil.)	NET PROFIT MARGIN	EMPLOYEES
3/06	15,307	—	—	53,772
3/05	12,901	—	—	40,892
3/04	11,366	—	—	39,571
3/03	8,295	—	—	42,402
3/02	3,185	—	—	33,230
Annual Growth	**48.1%**	**—**	**—**	**12.8%**

Revenue History

Pink Sheets: SBMRY

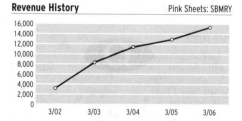

Saint-Gobain

Compagnie de Saint-Gobain is in a glass by itself. The materials mega-group, the world's #2 glass producer after Nippon Sheet Glass, controls more than 1,000 companies in five sectors: Building Distribution (40% of sales; building materials and ceramic tile distribution), Construction products (insulation, gypsum, pipe, and other products), Flat Glass (including glass products for the automotive and specialty glass markets), Packaging (glass bottles for the perfume, beauty, and cleaning products segments), and High-Production Materials. Saint-Gobain dates to the 1660s, when it provided glass for Versailles; today it makes 30 billion glass containers a year and provides insulation for 20% of all US homes.

Saint-Gobain acquired dozens of companies in 2004. New distribution division acquisitions included some 30 companies in France, Germany, and the UK — in addition to the acquisition of Sweden-based building products distribution company Dahl International. Saint-Gobain also acquired 11 distribution sector companies in emerging countries. Non-distribution acquisitions included flat glass operations in China, construction products companies in China and the Czech Republic, and performance materials investments in China, Russia, and Romania.

Saint-Gobain expects more than $100 million in savings over the first two years following its 2006 acquisition of UK drywall and building materials maker BPB.

In 2006 the company sold its CALMAR packaging unit to MeadWestvaco for $710 million. That year the company formed a joint venture with Owens Corning to merge their reinforcements and composites businesses. The new venture will have sales of about $1.8 billion; Saint-Gobain will own 40%.

Saint-Gobain teamed up with Alghanim Industries in another joint venture to buy Turkish insulation maker Izocam from Koç Holdings.

In keeping with this trend of teamwork, the company is looking for a partner for its specialty bottle maker Desjonqueres.

HISTORY

Originally called Dunoyer, Saint-Gobain (named after the factory location) was founded in 1665 by order of the Sun King, Louis XIV, who needed mirrors to adorn his palaces. Because Venice had the monopoly on glass, Louis lured Venetian artisans to Paris. Some were poisoned by Italian assassins, but enough remained to teach Parisians their secrets. Saint-Gobain glass decorates the Palace of Versailles' Hall of Mirrors.

With its decreed glass monopoly in France, the company grew steadily until the French Revolution interrupted its prosperity. By the early 1800s, however, Saint-Gobain was shining again. It set up a sales office in New York in 1830 and its first foreign subsidiary in Germany in 1857. Under chemist Joseph Gay-Lussac's direction, Saint-Gobain began dabbling in chemicals in the mid-1800s.

Expanding to Italy (1889) and Spain (1904), the firm was Europe's leading glassmaker by 1913. Saint-Gobain pioneered the production of tempered security glass in the 1920s; it diversified into glass fiber in the 1930s.

Pilkington, a UK competitor, developed a glassmaking method in 1959 that obviated the need for polishing and therefore slashed production costs. Saint-Gobain refit its factories to use the Pilkington method to keep its 50% EC market share. In 1968 the shareholding Suez Group forced Saint-Gobain to merge with Pont-à-Mousson (now Saint-Gobain Canalisation), then the world's leading iron pipe maker. The merger led to a much-needed restructuring that included selling Saint-Gobain's chemical interests.

The company acquired a majority interest in US building-material maker CertainTeed in 1976. In 1982 it was forced to divest some of its interests when it was nationalized by France's new socialist government. Despite nationalization the company grew steadily during the 1980s, investing in Compagnie Générale des Eaux, the world's largest drinking-water distributor.

In 1986, after a change in France's political climate, Saint-Gobain became the first company to be reprivatized. Three years later it purchased Générale Française de Céramique (clay tile) and controlling interest in Vetri (glass containers, Italy).

Saint-Gobain bought Norton (the world's leader in abrasives) and UK glassmaker Solaglas in 1990. With the 1991 purchases of German glassmakers GIAG and Oberland, Saint-Gobain became the world's #1 glass manufacturer within a year.

After the recession of the early 1990s, Saint-Gobain sold its paper and packaging interests to Jefferson Smurfit in 1994, raising more than $1 billion for acquisitions. With Ball Corporation, it formed a glass container joint venture, Ball-Foster Glass, in 1995; the next year it bought Ball's stake. Acquisitions in 1997 included industrial ceramics firms in Germany and France and UK abrasives maker Unicorn International. In 1998 Saint-Gobain bought Bird Corp. (roofing materials, US) and CALMAR (plastic pump sprayers, US). The next year it bought US-based Furon, which was absorbed into a new unit, Saint-Gobain Performance Plastics.

In 2000 Saint-Gobain acquired Meyer International (a UK building materials supplier), Raab Karcher (a German building materials distributor), and US-based polymer specialist Chemfab. The following year Saint-Gobain bolstered its ceiling systems operations with the acquisition of the Maars Group's metal ceiling-grid business. In 2002 Saint-Gobain acquired the 25% of France-based Lapeyre SA (doors, windows, cabinetry) stock it didn't own.

The company's most notable deal of 2004 was the €686 million acquisition of Swedish plumbing products distributor Dahl International. Early in 2005 Saint-Gobain raised its stake in Hankuk Glass Industries, a Korean glass maker with sales of more than $250 million, from 46% to more than 80%.

In August 2005, the company made a hostile $6.5 billion bid for UK drywall/plasterboard maker BPB plc after friendly overtures were rejected. BPB, which operates about 90 factories, rejected Saint-Gobain's initial offer as too low. Saint-Gobain came back with a sweetened $6.68 billion bid, which BPB accepted. The transaction closed in 2006.

EXECUTIVES

Chairman and CEO: Jean-Louis Beffa, age 65
COO and Director: Pierre-André de Chalendar, age 47, $607,940 pay
CFO: Benoît Bazin
SVP: Jean-Claude Breffort
SVP: Jean-François Phelizon
SVP and President, Building Distribution Sector: Philippe Crouzet
SVP and President, Construction Products Sector: Claude Imauven
SVP and President, Flat Glass Sector: Jacques Aschenbroich
SVP and President, High-Performance Materials Sector: Roberto Caliari
SVP and President, Packaging Sector: Jérôme Fessard
VP, Construction Products Sector, North America: Peter R. Dachowski
VP, Corporate Planning: Guillaume Texier
VP, Research: Didier Roux
VP, External Relations: Nicole Grisoni-Bachelier
Auditors: KPMG Audit; PricewaterhouseCoopers Audit

LOCATIONS

HQ: Compagnie de Saint-Gobain
Les Miroirs, 18 Avenue d'Alsace,
92400 Courbevoie, France
Phone: +33-1-47-62-30-00   **Fax:** +33-1-47-78-45-03
US HQ: 750 E. Swedesford Rd., Valley Forge, PA 19482
US Phone: 610-341-7000   **US Fax:** 610-341-6824
Web: www.saint-gobain.com

Saint-Gobain has more than 1,000 subsidiaries in nearly 50 countries.

2005 Sales

	% of total
Western Europe	
France	31
Other countries	41
North America	16
Asia/Pacific & emerging countries	12
Total	**100**

PRODUCTS/OPERATIONS

2005 Sales

	% of total
Building distribution	40
Construction products	26
Flat glass	12
High-performance materials	12
Packaging	10
Total	**100**

Selected Segments and Products

Housing products
  Building materials distribution
    Industrial carpentry
    Materials for new construction and renovation
  Building materials
    Composite materials and mortars
    Concrete products
    PVC siding
    Roofing products
  Pipe
    Ductile cast iron pipe
    Pipe systems
Glass
  Flat glass (clear, colored, and layered)
    Automotive glass
    Construction materials glass
    Specialty glass
  Containers
    Bottles and jars
    Flasks
    Plastic pumps and dispensers
  Insulation and reinforcements
    Glass threads
    Glass wool
    Insulating foam
    Processing (glass, carbon, polyester glass grids and fabrics)
    Rock wool

High-performance materials
  Abrasives
    Coated abrasives
    Grinding wheels
    Superabrasives
    Thin grinding wheels
  Ceramics and plastics
    High-performance ceramics
    Industrial ceramics
    Specialty ceramics

COMPETITORS

3M
Anchor Glass
AptarGroup
Asahi Glass
Ball Corporation
Cookson Group
CRH
DuPont
Georgia-Pacific Corporation
Gerresheimer Glas
Glaverbel
Guardian Industries
Hanson Aggregates UK
James Hardie
Johns Manville
Knauf Insulation
Kyocera
Morgan Crucible
Nippon Electric Glass
Nitto Boseki
Owens Corning Sales
Owens-Illinois
Pilkington
Pochet
PPG
Rexam
RHI
Royal Ceramic Industry
Royal Group Technologies
Schott
Toshiba
Travis Perkins
Uralita
Vitro
Wienerberger
Wolseley

HISTORICAL FINANCIALS

Company Type: Public

Income Statement

FYE: December 31

	REVENUE ($ mil.)	NET INCOME ($ mil.)	NET PROFIT MARGIN	EMPLOYEES
12/05	41,581	1,497	3.6%	199,630
12/04	43,682	1,477	3.4%	181,228
12/03	37,141	1,304	3.5%	172,811
12/02	31,730	1,090	3.4%	172,357
12/01	26,920	1,005	3.7%	173,329
Annual Growth	**11.5%**	**10.5%**	**—**	**(3.6%)**

Net Income History

Euronext Paris: SGO

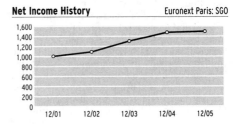

Samsung

Samsung Group has reason to sing. The *chaebol* (family-controlled conglomerate) has surpassed its former archrival, the erstwhile Hyundai Group, to become the #1 business group in South Korea. Samsung's flagship unit is Samsung Electronics, which is the world's top maker of dynamic random-access memory (DRAM) and other memory chips, as well as a global heavyweight in all sorts of electronic gear, including LCD panels, DVD players, and cellular phones. Other affiliated companies include credit-card unit Samsung Card, Samsung General Chemicals, Samsung Life Insurance, Samsung Securities, and trading arm Samsung Corporation.

Forced into action by the Korean economic crisis of the late 1990s, Samsung has whittled away at its debt and shed non-core operations. While the group's holdings have fallen from 61 affiliates to about 35, it still spans many diverse business niches, including advertising, textile production, amusement parks, hotels, and professional baseball. Meanwhile, Samsung announced in November 2005 a $44.9 billion R&D investment over the next five years that would focus on such core business sectors as semiconductors, displays, and mobile communications.

Lee Kun-Hee, son of Samsung's founder, has dissolved much of the central management structure, including his post as the group's chairman, in his revamp of the group. In April 2005 he announced he would step down as director of eight Samsung affiliates, including the holding company, but remain chairman of Samsung Electronics. However, in response to the South Korean government's aims to restrict the voting rights of *chaebol*, Samsung Group filed suit against the government in June 2005 over the legitimacy of current antitrust actions.

The group broke ground on its largest overseas facility yet in early 2006 — a mobile phone production and research base in Tianjin, China. Samsung Telecom Technology boosted its investment in the base from $29 million to $197 million since the first of the year, with plans to boast a production capacity of 17.7 million mobile phone sets upon completion.

HISTORY

In 1936 Japan-educated Lee Byung-Chull began operating a rice mill in Korea, then under Japanese rule. By 1938 Lee had begun trading in dried fish and had incorporated as Samsung (Korean for "three stars"). WWII left Korea fairly unscathed, and by war's end Samsung had transportation and real-estate adjuncts.

The Korean War, however, destroyed nearly all of Samsung's assets. Left with a brewery and an import business for UN personnel, Lee reconstructed Samsung in South Korea. He formed the highly profitable Cheil Sugar Company, then the country's only sugar refiner, in 1953. Textile, banking, and insurance ventures followed.

A 1961 political coup brought Park Chung Hee to power in South Korea. Lee, wealthy and tied to the former government, was accused of illegal profiteering. A 1966 smuggling case involving one of Lee's sons led to another scandal, but charges were dropped when Lee gave the government an immense fertilizer plant. Despite the political change, Samsung still grew, diversifying into paper products, department stores, and publishing.

In 1969, with help from SANYO, Lee established Samsung Electronics, which benefited from the government's export drive and low wage rates. By disassembling Western-designed electronics, Samsung Electronics figured out how to produce inexpensive black-and-white TVs and, later, color TVs, VCRs, and microwave ovens. It manufactured these products under private labels for corporations including General Electric and Sears. In concert with the government's industrialization push, the *chaebol* also began making ships (1974), petrochemicals (1977), and aircraft engines (1977). By the 1980s Samsung was exporting electronics under its own name.

When Lee died in 1987, his son Lee Kun-Hee assumed control. After years of importing technology and spending freely on R&D, in 1990 Samsung became a world leader in chip production. Encouraged by the government, Samsung agreed to cooperate with fellow *chaebol* Goldstar (now LG Group) to obtain foreign technology to develop liquid crystal displays. In 1994 Lee, a longtime car lover, announced plans to form Samsung Motors.

In 1996 Lee was caught in a corruption scandal and got a two-year suspended sentence for bribery. The next year Asian financial markets crashed. To lessen its debt, the group sold Samsung Heavy Industries' construction-equipment business to Sweden's Volvo and sold Samsung Electronics' power-device unit to Fairchild Semiconductor in 1998. Also that year the South Korean government fined several *chaebol*, including Samsung, a collective $93 million for illegally funneling money to weaker subsidiaries.

The early 21st century saw the group surge as its flagship unit Samsung Electronics racked up big wins in semiconductors, cell phones, high-end televisions, and other consumer electronics.

News surfaced in July 2005 that Samsung Group had attempted to acquire Kia Motors in 1997. Conversations between a Samsung official and the former head of a daily newspaper were allegedly intercepted and recorded by the country's National Intelligence Service. The group apologized over the conversation, which also allegedly centered on illegal political donations during the 1997 presidential election.

Meanwhile, Lee arrived in the US in September 2005 to reportedly receive medical treatment. That didn't stop the Korean National Assembly's finance and economy committee from summoning Lee to question him over unpaid debts left by the group's bankrupt Samsung Motors (Lee subsequently didn't appear). Korean President Roh Moo-Hyun simultaneously blasted Lee and the group, saying it sought to sidestep corporate governance reform. Led by main creditor Seoul Guarantee Insurance, 15 creditors planned to push ahead with a lawsuit over the unpaid debts — potentially the country's biggest lawsuit in financial terms.

Two executives — Her Tae-hak, former chief of Samsung Everland, and Park Ro-bin, current Samsung Everland president — were sentenced to prison in October 2005 on charges of helping Lee transfer wealth to his son in illicit bond deals a decade earlier. That month the Korean Supreme Court ordered Lee and nine former and current Samsung Electronics executives to pay $18.7 million (19 billion won) for instigating heavy losses to the company.

EXECUTIVES

Chairman, Samsung Electronics: Kun-Hee Lee, age 64
Vice Chairman and CEO, Samsung Advanced Institute of Technology: Lee Yun-Woo, age 60
Vice Chairman and CEO, Samsung Electronics: Yun Jong-Yong, age 62
Vice Chairman, Corporate Restructuring Headquarters: Lee Hak-Soo
EVP, Samsung Human Resources Development Center: Kim Sookeun
President and CEO, Cheil Communications: Bai Dong-Man
President and CEO, Cheil Industries; President and CEO, Samsung BP Chemicals: Ahn Bok-Hyun
President and CEO, Samsung Corning: Song Yong-Ro
President and CEO, Samsung Corporation: Pae Chong-Yeul
President and CEO, Samsung Electro-Mechanics: Kang Ho-Moon
President and CEO, Samsung Engineering: Jung Yeon-Joo
President and CEO, Samsung EVERLAND: Park Ro-Bin
President and CEO, Samsung Fine Chemicals: Lee Yong-Soon
President and CEO, Samsung Fire and Marine Insurance: Lee Soo-Chang
President and CEO, Samsung Heavy Industries: Kim Jing-Wan
President and CEO, Samsung Networks: Park Yang-Gyu
President and CEO, Samsung Petrochemical: Her Tae-Hak
President and CEO, Samsung Securities: Bae Ho-Won
CEO and VP, Samsung Lions: Kim Euong-Yong

LOCATIONS

HQ: Samsung Group
     250, 2-ga, Taepyung-ro, Jung-gu,
     Seoul 100-742, South Korea
Phone: +82-2-727-7114   **Fax:** +82-2-727-7985
US HQ: 105 Challenger Rd., Ridgefield Park, NJ 07660
US Phone: 201-229-4000   **US Fax:** 201-229-4110
Web: www.samsung.com

Samsung Group has operations in more than 50 countries around the world.

PRODUCTS/OPERATIONS

Selected Operations

Chemicals
  Samsung Fine Chemicals Co., Ltd.
  Samsung General Chemicals Co., Ltd.
  Samsung Petrochemical Co., Ltd.
Electronics
  Samsung Corning Co., Ltd. (TV picture-tube glass)
  Samsung Electro-Mechanics Co., Ltd. (electronic components)
  Samsung Electronics Co., Ltd. (semiconductors, consumer electronics)
  Samsung SDI Co. Ltd.
  Samsung SDS Co., Ltd. (systems integration, telecommunications)
Financial and Insurance
  Samsung Capital Co., Ltd.
  Samsung Card Co., Ltd. (loans, cash advances, financing)
  Samsung Fire & Marine Insurance Co., Ltd.
  Samsung Life Insurance Co., Ltd.
  Samsung Life Investment Trust Management Co., Ltd.
  Samsung Securities Co., Ltd.
  Samsung Venture Investment Co., Ltd.

Other
  - Cheil Communications, Inc. (advertising)
  - Cheil Industries Inc. (textiles)
  - S1 Corporation (security systems)
  - Samsung Advanced Institute of Technology
  - Samsung Corporation (general trading)
  - Samsung Engineering Co., Ltd.
  - Samsung Everland Inc. (amusement parks)
  - Samsung Heavy Industries Co., Ltd. (machinery, vehicles)
  - Samsung Lions (pro baseball team)
  - Samsung Techwin Co., Ltd. (fine machinery including semiconductor equipment)
  - The Shilla Hotels & Resorts Co., Ltd.

COMPETITORS

ABB
BenQ (IT)
Daewoo International
DuPont
Ericsson
Fujitsu
Gree Electrical Appliances
Haier Electronics
Hitachi
Hyundai Corporation
IBM
ITOCHU
Kyobo Life Insurance
LG Group
Marubeni
Matsushita
Matsushita Electric Works
Micron Technology
Millea Holdings
Mitsui
Motorola
NEC
Ningbo Bird
Nokia
Nortel Networks
Northrop Grumman
Philips Electronics
SANYO
Sharp
Siemens AG
SK Group
Sony
Ssangyong
TDK
telent
Toshiba

HISTORICAL FINANCIALS

Company Type: Group

Income Statement

FYE: December 31

	REVENUE ($ mil.)	NET INCOME ($ mil.)	NET PROFIT MARGIN	EMPLOYEES
12/05	141,421	9,483	6.7%	229,000
12/04	133,135	12,954	9.7%	222,000
12/03	101,459	5,632	5.6%	195,000
12/02	121,735	9,229	7.6%	175,000
12/01	98,700	4,500	4.6%	175,000
Annual Growth	9.4%	20.5%	—	7.0%

Net Income History

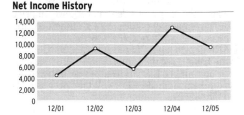

San Miguel

Filipinos filling out their grocery lists often turn to San Miguel — they don't have much other choice. San Miguel Corporation (SMC) is the largest beverage and food firm in the Philippines, selling more than 200 product lines made in more than 100 area factories. The company brews and distributes beer, including San Miguel Pale Pilsen and Red Horse, and controls more than 90% of the Philippine beer market. It enjoys similar dominance of the soft-drink market, thanks to its 65% stake in bottler Coca-Cola Philippines (The Coca-Cola Company owns the remaining 35%) and its 2001 purchase of the Cosmos Bottling Corporation. Wrapping things up is San Miguel's can, bottle, and container business.

SMC's food and agribusiness subsidiaries make a variety of meat products, animal feeds, coconut products, and dairy goods, while its packaging operations produce glass containers, aluminum cans, corrugated cartons, metal caps, and crowns. It also manages real estate. The company says it plans to expand into Australia, China, Indonesia, Japan, Malaysia, Taiwan, Thailand, and Vietnam. SMC snapped up a majority stake in Singapore-based ice-cream producer King's Creameries in February 2005 and obtained full control of National Foods for $1.45 billion (A$1.9 billion) in June 2005. The company had been locked in a tight bidding race for the Australian dairy company with Fonterra Co-operative Group (Fonterra removed its offer only days after San Miguel's increased bid in April).

Chairman Eduardo Cojuangco says he owns less than 10% of the company; however, others report he owns as much as 20% of SMC and controls the voting rights of another 27% through the United Coconut Planters Bank. These shares are under government sequestration (but still controlled by Cojuangco); some Filipino government officials contend the shares were gained through corrupt use of a levy imposed on farmers during the presidential administration of Ferdinand Marcos.

HISTORY

Don Enrique Barretto y de Ycaza opened La Fabrica de Cerveza de San Miguel, a brewery, in Manila in 1890. By 1900 the European-styled beers of San Miguel were outselling imported brands five to one. The company became a corporation in 1913. By WWI the brewery was selling beer in Hong Kong, Shanghai, and Guam.

Andres Soriano y Roxas joined San Miguel in 1918 and in the 1920s established the Royal Soft Drinks Plant (1922), the Magnolia Ice Cream Plant (1925), and the first non-US national Coca-Cola bottling and distribution franchise (1927). After WWII, the company added additional facilities and factories as it modernized and expanded.

In the 1960s the firm changed its name to San Miguel Corporation (SMC). After the death of Andres in 1964, his son Andres Soriano Jr. became president. He decentralized operations into product segments. SMC continued to diversify in the 1970s.

A family feud erupted in 1983 when members of the controlling Soriano and Zobel families engaged in a proxy battle. Realizing he couldn't win the proxy fight, Enrique Zobel sold all of his shares (about 20% of SMC) to Eduardo Cojuangco, a Ferdinand Marcos ally and president of United Coconut Planters Bank. Upon death in 1984, Cojuangco became chai

Cojuangco's estranged cousin Corazo won the 1986 national election, and her government claimed assets associated with Marcos and his followers, including Cojuangco's share of SMC. Cojuangco left the country with Marcos, and Andres Soriano III became CEO. Cojuangco returned to the Philippines in 1989 to reclaim his share of the company. In mid-1998, immediately following Cojuangco-backed Joseph Estrada's election as president of the Philippines, Andres Soriano III stepped down, and Cojuangco returned to SMC's helm.

SMC sold Coca-Cola Bottlers Philippines to Sydney-based Coca-Cola Amatil (CCA) in 1995 in exchange for a 25% stake in CCA. Four years later SMC flirted with plans to sell its interest in CCA, and then went on a buying binge. SMC and a company it majority owns, La Tondeña Distillers, jointly bought Filipino juice maker Sugarland. SMC then bought Australian brewer J. Boag & Son in June 2000.

Estrada announced the government's plan to sell a 27% stake in SMC, but those plans were altered dramatically after Estrada's ouster in early 2001. His successor, President Gloria Arroyo, said the government would seize 47% of the company's shares controlled by United Coconut Planters Bank (27%) and Cojuangco (20%).

Meanwhile, company expansion continued. San Miguel agreed to buy the Philippines' largest processed-meat maker, Pure Foods. The company bought 65% of bottler Coca-Coca Philippines from CCA in July, giving up its stake in CCA as part of the deal. In August 2001, SMC then acquired 83% of rival RFM's Cosmos Bottling, the Philippines' #2 soft drink company, further consolidating its domestic beverage dominance. In September the company transferred its 49% stake in Sugarland to La Tondeña Distillers, which then became the sole owner of the juice maker.

In 2002 Japanese brewer Kirin paid $530 million for 15% of San Miguel. Following an announced expansion plan into Asia, San Miguel purchased a Thailand industrial complex for $20 million in September 2003 and Thai Amarit Brewery Ltd. in April 2004.

EXECUTIVES

Chairman and CEO: Eduardo M. Cojuangco Jr.
Vice Chairman, President, and COO: Ramon S. Ang
CFO and Treasurer: Ferdinand K. Constantino
SVP, Corporate Human Resources: David S. Santos
SVP, Corporate Marketing: M.L. Menlou B. Bibonia
SVP, Corporate Planning and Development:
  Maria Belen C. Buensuceso
SVP, Corporate Quality Management:
  Alberto A. Manlapit
SVP, Corporate Technical Services:
  Lubin B. Nepomuceno
SVP, Group Audit: Veneranda M. Tomas
President, Coca-Cola Bottlers Philippines:
  Roberto N. Huang
President, Ginebra San Miguel: Danilo C. Navarro
President, San Miguel Beer Division:
  Faustino F. Galang
President, San Miguel Packaging Products:
  Alberto O. Villa-Abrille Jr.
President, San Miguel Properties Inc.:
  Jeronimo U. Kilayko
President, San Miguel Pure Foods Company:
  Enrique A. (Ricky) Gomez Jr.
President Director, P.T. Delta — Djakarta:
  Manuel M. Moreno
CEO, Berri, Limited: Alison Watkins
Corporate Secretary and General Counsel:
  Francis H. Jardeleza
Auditors: SyCip Gorres Velayo & Co.

LOCATIONS

HQ: San Miguel Corporation
40 San Miguel Ave., Mandaluyong,
Metro Manila 1550, Philippines
Phone: +63-2-632-3000   **Fax:** +63-2-632-3099
Web: www.sanmiguel.com.ph

San Miguel Corporation has manufacturing plants in
China, Hong Kong, Indonesia, the Philippines, Vietnam,
and other countries in Southeast Asia. The company's
beers are sold in some 20 countries in the Americas,
Asia, and Australia.

2004 Sales

	% of total
Philippines	87
China	4
Australia	4
Indonesia	2
Vietnam	1
Other countries	2
Total	**100**

PRODUCTS/OPERATIONS

2004 Sales

	% of total
Beverage	64
Food	33
Packaging	3
Total	**100**

Selected Products and Brands

Beverages
  Beer (Multinational)
    Ander Bir (licensed)
    Blue Ice
    Cerveza Negra
    Gold Eagle
    Miller Genuine Draft (licensed)
    Red Horse
    San Miguel Light
    San Miguel (Draft Beer, Pale Pilsen, Super Dry)
  Beer (Regional)
    China (Blue Star, Double Happiness Beer, Dragon
      Beer, Guang's Draft, Kirin, Pineapple Beer, Valor)
    Hong Kong (Bruck, Eagle High, Knight, Lowenbrau
      — licensed, San Miguel Dark)
    Indonesia (Anker Stout — licensed, Carlsberg —
      licensed)
    Vietnam (Bock)
  Bottled water
    Distilled drinking water (FIRST, Wilkins)
    Mineral water (VIVA!)
  Juice drinks
    Cordial lime juice
    Magnolia (Fruit Drinks, FunChum, Junior Juice, Ice
      Tea)
    Zip juice
  Nonalcoholic malt beverages
    Cali (Shandy, 10, Ice)
    Guang's Pineapple Shandy (China)
    San Miguel NAB
    Shanta Super Shandy (Indonesia)
  Wines and spirits
    Gin (Ginebra San Miguel, Oxford London Dry Gin —
      licensed)
    Rum (Añejo, Tondeña, San Miguel)
Food and Agribusiness
  Dairy
    Dari Creme
    Star
  Meat (beef, chicken, pork)
    Longanisa
    Magnolia
    Moby
    Valiente

Real Estate
  Bel Adea
  Buenavista Homes
  Country Mile Homes
  The Enterprise Center
  Greenwoods
  HOC Realty Inc.
  HQ Business Centers
  The Legacy
  Lexington
  Maravilla
  Primavera Hills
  San Miguel Properties Corp.
  Villa de Calamba
  Wedge Woods

COMPETITORS

Amcor
Anheuser-Busch
Asahi Breweries
Asia Brewery
Bacardi USA
Benguet
Cadbury Schweppes
Cargill
Carlsberg
CBR Brewing
ConAgra
Danone
Diageo
Foster's
Heineken
InBev
International Paper
Kirin Brewery Company
Lion Nathan
Mercian
Nestlé
PepsiCo
Tsingtao
Tyson Foods

HISTORICAL FINANCIALS

Company Type: Public

Income Statement

FYE: December 31

	REVENUE ($ mil.)	NET INCOME ($ mil.)	NET PROFIT MARGIN	EMPLOYEES
12/04*	3,106	144	4.6%	26,427
12/03	2,666	132	5.0%	26,420
12/02	2,536	124	4.9%	27,259
12/01	2,353	125	5.3%	26,697
12/00	1,771	137	7.7%	14,864
Annual Growth	**15.1%**	**1.3%**	**—**	**15.5%**

*Most recent year available

2004 Year-End Financials

Debt ratio: 24.7%   Current ratio: 1.61
Return on equity: 7.5%   Long-term debt ($ mil.): 479
Cash ($ mil.): 479

Net Income History

OTC: SMGBY

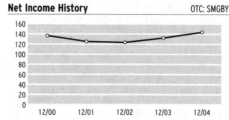

Sanofi-Aventis

Sanofi-Aventis helps docs treat its sneezy patients without making them sleepy, grumpy, or dopey. The company specializes in allergy, cardiovascular, central nervous system, oncology, and internal medicine formulations; its other top sellers include Lovenox (deep vein thrombosis), Plavix (thrombosis), Taxotere (breast cancer), and Eloxatin (colorectal cancer). The company was formed by the 2004 marriage of two French drugmakers, Sanofi-Synthélabo and Aventis; the deal formed the world's third largest pharmaceutical company, behind only Pfizer and GlaxoSmithKline.

Other bestselling prescription drugs in the company's portfolio include insomnia drug Ambien (for which the US FDA approved a children's extended-release version in late 2006) and antihistamine Allegra. Allegra lost patent protection in 2006, along with other breadwinners Amaryl, Arava, and DDAVP.

Sanofi-Aventis is also a major player in the human vaccine market and sales have remained strong after Chiron's inability to deliver flu shots in late 2004. Sales of Sanofi-Aventis' own flu vaccine rose 25% in 2004, and nearly 30% in 2005.

The company has built a 130-drug pipeline, with more than half of the candidates in clinical trials, and also has about 20 new vaccines in development. Sanofi-Aventis also partners with smaller firms, such as Immuno-Designed Molecules, to increase its potential products while keeping costs down.

Like any drug company, Sanofi-Aventis' candidates only receive attention when they either succeed or fail spectacularly. Its antibiotic Ketek has been approved for use in adults, but due to reports of liver failure in patients, the FDA is considering calling for the company to halt its clinical trials on children. Critical investigations of the Ketek clinical trials uncovered improprieties, some data from other trials were discarded as substandard, and charges of fraud.

In Europe, which generates 44% of the company's sales, Sanofi-Aventis is focusing on its generic drug business. It also makes OTC analgesic products for the European market. The company in 2006 received EU approval for the use of its weight-loss drug rimonabant, which entered the market under the brand name Acomplia (the company anxiously awaits FDA approval for US distribution).

In 2006 generics manufacturer Apotex challenged Sanofi-Aventis and Bristol-Myers Squibb's collaborative marketing effort for chart topper Plavix by introducing its generic version for roughly a quarter of the cost while Sanofi-Aventis' patent was challenged in the US courts over a 180-day period. Apotex was able to flood the market to the degree that, despite intervention by the US courts, Sanofi-Aventis was forced to keep the drug at the generic's equivalent price for the remainder of the patent's efficacy, costing the company millions in proceeds.

Chairman and CEO Jean-François Dehecq, who has steered the company over three decades, has announced that his head of research and development Gérard Le Fur will take over as CEO in early 2007.

HISTORY

The Sanofi group got its start in 1973 when French oil conglomerate Elf Aquitaine merged several health care, cosmetics, and animal nutrition companies into one subsidiary. In 1977 Sanofi set up a Japanese subsidiary, through which it developed joint ventures with Japan's Meiji Seika Kaisha and Taisha Pharmaceutical firms. In 1979 Elf spun off Sanofi, although it retained ownership of more than half of the company. Almost from its founding Sanofi grew through acquisitions and alliances. During the 1980s, it used a massive war chest to buy stakes and set up joint ventures, such as one with American Home Products (now Wyeth) in 1982.

The company bought *couturier et parfumier* Nina Ricci in 1988; such well-known fragrances as L'Air du Temps put it among the industry's top perfume houses. But Sanofi overreached the next two years and was outbid by American Home Products for AH Robins (the drug firm bankrupted by lawsuits over deaths from its Dalkon Shield IUD) and by Rhône-Poulenc (now part of Aventis) for Rorer. A chastened Sanofi and Kodak subsidiary Sterling Drug in 1991 entered into an alliance that didn't involve an exchange of cash.

In 1993 Sanofi made a splash when it bought the perfume business of fashion designer Yves Saint-Laurent. The next year it bought out much of the pharmaceutical joint venture with Kodak. Sanofi began divesting such noncore businesses as veterinarian and biotech operations in 1995. After suffering a loss in its perfume and beauty division in 1996, it sold Nina Ricci. The rest of its beauty division was sold in 1999 in preparation for the Synthélabo merger.

Synthélabo was founded in 1970 when drug firms Laboratoires Dausse and Laboratoires Robert et Carriere merged. In 1973 it became a 53%-owned subsidiary of L'Oréal. In 1980 drug firm Metabio-Jouillie became a part of Synthélabo, making it the #3 drug company in France. In 1983 Synthélabo and US drugmaker Searle created Lorex to market the French firm's products in the UK. (Synthélabo bought Searle's interest 10 years later.)

Throughout the 1980s Synthélabo acquired, merged, and formed joint ventures, including some in Japan with Mitsubishi Chemical, Fujisawa Pharmaceutical (1985), and Tanabe Seiyaku (1987). The company continued its acquisitive ways in the 1990s, buying several French rivals.

In 1996 Synthélabo entered an alliance with Genset to research cancer-causing genes; it also signed on with SmithKline Beecham (now GlaxoSmithKline) and Human Genome Sciences to fund genetic research.

The next year Synthélabo bought Pharmacia & Upjohn's German generic drug subsidiary Sanorania Pharma. As Synthélabo and Sanofi merged in 1999, the new company's concentration on pharmaceuticals dictated several changes, including the sale of the company's interests in joint venture Pasteur Sanofi Diagnostics, as well as its beauty division, home to such well-known perfume lines as Yves Saint Laurent.

Sanofi-Synthélabo made good on its plans to target the US in 2000, expanding its sales force there. But the merger wasn't without its problems: Former Synthélabo CEO Hervé Guérin was ousted as vice-chairman and COO of Sanofi-Synthélabo after he and Chairman Jean-François Dehecq butted heads. In 2002 the company boosted its pipeline by entering into an alliance

with Immuno-Designed Molecules, a biotechnology firm focusing on cancer drugs. Also that year the FDA approved the firm's colorectal cancer drug, Eloxatin, in record time.

EXECUTIVES

Chairman and CEO: Jean-François Dehecq, age 66, $3,647,644 pay
Vice Chairman: Jürgen Dormann, age 66
SEVP; EVP, Scientific and Medical Affairs; Director: Gérard Le Fur, age 55
EVP, Pharmaceutical Operations: Hanspeter Spek, age 56
SVP, Legal Affairs and General Counsel; Advisor to the Chairman: Jean-Pierre Kerjouan, age 66
SVP, Audit and Internal Control Assessment: Marie-Hélène Laimay, age 47
SVP, Business Development: Olivier Jacquesson, age 56
SVP, Commercial Operations, USA: Pascal Soriot, age 45
SVP, Communication: Nicole Cranois, age 58
SVP, Corporate Affairs: Philippe Peyre, age 55
SVP, Corporate Human Resources: Jean-Claude Armbruster, age 61
SVP, Finance and CFO: Jean-Claude Leroy, age 54
SVP, Global Marketing: Pierre Chancel, age 49
SVP, Industrial Affairs: Gilles Lhernould, age 50
SVP, Pharmaceutical Operations, Europe (excluding France and Germany): Gilles Brisson, age 54
SVP, Pharmaceutical Operations, France: Christian Lajoux, age 58
SVP, Pharmaceutical Operations, Germany: Heinz-Werner Meier, age 54
SVP, Pharmaceutical Operations, Intercontinental: Antoine Ortoli, age 52
SVP, Pharmaceutical Operations, USA: Timothy G. Rothwell, age 54
SVP, Vaccines: David J. (Dave) Williams, age 56
Investor Relations: Sanjay Gupta
Auditors: Ernst & Young Audit; PricewaterhouseCoopers Audit

LOCATIONS

HQ: Sanofi-Aventis
174 avenue de France, 75013 Paris, France
Phone: +33-1-53-77-40-00   **Fax:** +33-1-53-77-42-96
US HQ: 300-400 Somerset Corporate Blvd., SC4-310A, Bridgewater, NJ 08807
US Phone: 908-243-6000   **US Fax:** 908-243-6483
Web: www.sanofi-aventis.com

Sanofi-Aventis has about 75 manufacturing plants worldwide, located in Brazil, France, Germany, Hungary, India, Italy, Japan, Mexico, Morocco, Singapore, the UK, and the US.

2005 Sales

	% of total
Europe	44
US	35
Other regions	21
Total	**100**

PRODUCTS/OPERATIONS

2005 Sales

	% of total
Pharmaceuticals	92
Human vaccines	8
Total	**100**

Selected Pharmaceutical Products

Actonel (osteoporosis)
Allegra/Telfast (allergies)
Amaryl (diabetes)
Ambien (sleep disorders)
Aprovel/Avapro (hypertension)
Arava (rheumatoid arthritis)
Copaxone (multiple sclerosis)
Cordarone (anti-arrhythmic)
Corotrope (acute congestive heart failure)
Delix/Tritace (cardiovascular conditions)
Depakine (anti-epileptic)

Dogmatil (psychosomatic disorders)
Eloxatin (colorectal cancer)
Fasturtec/Elitek (hyperuricemia)
Insuman (insulin for diabetes mellitus)
Kerlone (hypertension)
Ketek (antibiotic)
Lantus (long-acting insulin)
Lovenox/Clexane (cardiovascular conditions)
Nasacort (nasal congestion relief)
Plavix (atherothrombosis)
Solian (schizophrenia)
Stilnox (hypnotic for insomnia)
Targocid (anti-infective)
Tavanic (anti-infective)
Taxotere (breast and ovarian cancer)
Ticlid (thrombosis)
Tildiem (angina and hypertension)

Selected Subsidiaries

Aventis, Inc. (US)
Aventis Pharmaceuticals Inc. (US)
Lorex Pharmaceuticals Inc. (US)
Sanofi-Synthélabo Inc. (US)
Sanofi-Synthélabo Recherche

COMPETITORS

Abbott Labs	GlaxoSmithKline
Amgen	Johnson & Johnson
AstraZeneca	Merck
Bayer	Novartis
Bristol-Myers Squibb	Novo Nordisk
Chiron	Pfizer
Eli Lilly	Schering
GE Healthcare Bio-Sciences	Wyeth

HISTORICAL FINANCIALS

Company Type: Public

Income Statement

	REVENUE ($ mil.)	NET INCOME ($ mil.)	NET PROFIT MARGIN	EMPLOYEES
FYE: December 31				
12/05	33,771	2,608	7.7%	97,181
12/04	20,525	(5,001)	—	96,439
12/03	10,106	2,342	23.2%	33,086
12/02	7,808	1,719	22.0%	32,436
12/01	5,863	1,052	17.9%	—
Annual Growth	**54.9%**	**25.5%**	**—**	**44.2%**

2005 Year-End Financials

Debt ratio: 10.2%
Return on equity: 4.7%
Cash ($ mil.): 1,848
Current ratio: 0.92
Long-term debt ($ mil.): 5,607
No. of shares (mil.): —
Dividends
  Yield: 1.4%
  Payout: 32.0%
Market value ($ mil.): —

Stock History

NYSE: SNY

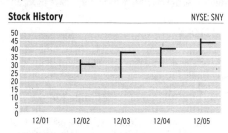

	STOCK PRICE ($) FY Close	P/E High/Low		PER SHARE ($) Earnings	Dividends
12/05	43.90	24	19	1.94	0.62
12/04	40.05	—	—	—	0.51
12/03	37.75	—	—	—	0.42
12/02	30.40	—	—	—	—
Annual Growth	**13.0%**			**—**	**21.5%**

SANYO Electric

"Sanyo" means "three oceans" in Japanese, and when it comes to consumer and commercial electronics, SANYO covers the waterfront. The electronics powerhouse has more than 170 subsidiaries worldwide. From electric bicycles to semiconductors, SANYO manufactures products both innovative and prosaic. Its companies make a variety of electrical devices and appliances, including industrial and commercial equipment (refrigerated supermarket cases), audio and video equipment (DVD players, TVs, digital cameras), semiconductors, communications equipment (cellular phones, computers), batteries, and home appliances (microwave ovens, air conditioners).

Japan accounts for almost half of the company's sales. SANYO is focused on developing environment-friendly products such as solar cells, rechargeable batteries, and CFC-free refrigerators and air-conditioning units. The company also is placing particular emphasis on developing multimedia products, such as digital cameras and liquid-crystal displays (LCDs).

To remain competitive in the explosive high-tech environment, SANYO is forming alliances with leading technology developers, including a five-member consortium to address 3-D technology (ITOCHU, NTT DATA, Sharp, and Sony) and an initiative with Samsung (home-use air conditioners). SANYO also embarked on a joint venture with International Rectifier. In 2004 Seiko Epson and SANYO merged its LCD businesses. The new company, called Sanyo Epson Imaging Devices, began operations in October 2004. A month later Sanyo Epson announced plans to shift its focus to making TFD (thin-film diode) panels. As a result of this decision, the company moved part of its LCD panel manufacturing operations to China.

Sanyo entered the European mobile phone market in 2004 by supplying wireless handsets to London-based Orange SA. The company also joined forces with Robert Bosch, a German manufacturer of car parts, to create rechargeable batteries for cars that run on both gasoline and battery power. Sanyo Electric has a similar agreement with DaimlerChrysler.

In further efforts to cut costs, the company announced plans to cut 15% of its staff worldwide and close or sell 20% of its factory space in Japan.

HISTORY

Toshio Iue, SANYO's first CEO, had the "three oceans" (Pacific, Atlantic, and Indian) in mind — he wanted to turn the company into an international enterprise. SANYO was formed after WWII when the Allies broke Matsushita Electric into two companies. Toshio, brother-in-law to Matsushita founder Konosuke Matsushita, took charge of SANYO, which then made bicycle lamps.

By 1949 the company was producing radios, and in the 1950s it diversified into refrigerators, fans, and washing machines. In 1953 a Japanese household appliances rush began, and SANYO led washing machine sales. By the end of the decade, the company was Japan's leading exporter of transistor radios.

To raise money, in 1959 SANYO created Tokyo SANYO Electric, in which it took a 20% stake. The company established its first factory abroad, in Hong Kong, in 1961 and created Cadnica, a durable rechargeable battery.

The 1970s oil crisis drew SANYO into alternative energy development, and the company continued its energy research when the crisis had passed. In 1973 SANYO joined forces with Emerson Electric (US) to bail out Emerson's Fisher electronics subsidiary. (SANYO bought Fisher in 1978.) SANYO began shifting its focus from appliances to high-tech products in the mid-1970s. It started making color TVs in the US in 1976. Although sales slowed when SANYO initially opted to develop VCRs using the ill-fated Betamax format, they rose tremendously in the 1970s, from $71 million in 1972 to $855 million in 1978.

SANYO and Tokyo SANYO Electric merged in 1986. A high yen forced the company to move much of its manufacturing outside Japan; that year it made more products abroad than any other Japanese company. By then the country's leading TV maker, SANYO formed a joint venture with Sears to manufacture TVs. SANYO also developed the world's first CFC-free refrigeration system, a version of which was installed in New York's Guggenheim Museum.

In 1993 SANYO set a world record for solar-energy conversion efficiency. The company strengthened its electronic components and solar businesses two years later by establishing SANYO Electronic Components and SANYO Solar Industries. In 1997 SANYO introduced the highest-output home-use solar cells, capable of producing 160 watts of electricity.

In 1998 the company formed a pact with IBM to make semiconductors using Big Blue's energy-saving copper-circuit technology. The next year SANYO allied with Philips to develop semiconductors and related products. Weakness in the Asian economy, a slowdown in US sales, and overall decreased demand hammered SANYO's earnings for fiscal 1999.

Also in 1999 SANYO teamed up with Eastman Kodak to develop flat-panel displays based on next-generation organic electroluminescent technology. The company announced several product developments, including an advanced battery for hybrid-fuel vehicles and an air-conditioning and refrigeration compressor that uses carbon dioxide instead of Freon.

Amid charges of knowingly selling defective solar cell systems, president Sadao Kondo resigned in 2000. He was replaced by Yukinori Kuwano. In 2001 SANYO acquired Toshiba's nickel metal hydride battery business, solidifying its position as one of the world's leading battery manufacturers.

In 2002 the company formed an alliance with China's largest consumer electronics maker, Haier Group, whereby SANYO sells its products through Haier's outlets and service centers and, in turn, selected Haier goods are sold in Japan.

In 2003 SANYO and Eastman Kodak agreed to jointly fund production of full-color organic light-emitting diode (OLED) displays; OLED displays feature full-motion images viewable from very wide angles. Also in 2003 SANYO turned wholly owned SANYO Electric Software Co. into a 50/50 joint venture with NTT DATA.

The company shook up its management ranks in 2005, electing former newscaster Tomoyo Nonaka as chairman. Toshimasa Iue, the grandson of Sanyo's founder, became president.

EXECUTIVES

Chairman: Tomoyo Nonaka
President and Director: Toshimasa Iue
EVP and Director: Koichi Maeda
EVP and Director: Tetsuo Naraha
EVP and Director: Kazuhiko Suruta

Executive Officer: Satoshi Inoue
Executive Officer: Osamu Kajikawa
Executive Officer: Hiroshi Ono
Executive Officer: Akira Kan
Executive Officer and Director: Mitsuru Honma
Senior Officer: Teruo Tabata
Senior Officer: Toshiaki Iue
Senior Officer: Takenori Ugari
Senior Officer: Tadao Shimada
Senior Officer: Yoshio Iwasa
Senior Officer: Yoshihiro Nishiguchi
Auditors: ChuoAoyama PricewaterhouseCoopers

LOCATIONS

HQ: SANYO Electric Co., Ltd.
  (San'yo Denki Kabushiki Kaisha)
  5-5 Keihan-Hondori, 2-chome, Moriguchi,
  Osaka 570-8677, Japan
Phone: +81-6-6991-1181   **Fax:** +81-6-6992-0009
US HQ: 2055 Sanyo Ave., San Diego, CA 92154
US Phone: 619-661-1134   **US Fax:** 619-661-6795
Web: www.sanyo.co.jp

SANYO Electric has more than 170 subsidiaries worldwide, and operates manufacturing facilities in more than 20 countries (located primarily in Asia, as well as in North America and Europe).

2006 Sales

	% of total
Asia	
Japan	48
Other countries	26
North America	15
Europe	8
Other regions	3
Total	**100**

PRODUCTS/OPERATIONS

2006 Sales

	% of total
Consumer	45
Component	39
Commercial	10
Other	6
Total	**100**

Selected Products

A/V information and communications equipment
  Automotive stereo components
  CDs
  CD-R/RW systems
  Cellular phones
  Color TVs
  Cordless phones
  Digital cameras
  Digital memory players
  DVD players
  DVD-ROM systems
  Fax machines
  High-definition plasma TVs
  High-definition TV systems
  Liquid crystal display (LCD) projectors
  Medical computer systems
  Optical pickups
  Personal Handyphone System (PHS, phones and base stations)
  Portable navigation systems
  VCRs
  Video cameras
Batteries
  Alkaline batteries
  Lithium batteries
  Lithium-ion rechargeable batteries
  Manganese batteries
  Nickel-cadmium rechargeable batteries
  Nickel-metal-hydride rechargeable batteries
  Solar cells
  Solar-cell power systems

Electronic devices
  CCD
  Electronic components
  Laser diodes
  LCDs
  LEDs
  MOS-LSIs
  Thick-film integrated circuits (ICs)
  Transistors and diodes
Home appliances
  Air conditioners
  Air purifiers
  Automatic tablet-wrapping machines
  Clothes dryers
  Compressors for freezers, refrigerators, and air
    conditioners
  Dehumidifiers
  Dishwashers and dryers
  Electric and kerosene heating equipment
  Electric fans
  Electronic and electric products for bicycles
  Freezers
  Home-use pumps
  Massage loungers
  Medical sterilizing equipment
  Medical-use refrigerators
  Microwave ovens
  Motor-assisted bicycles
  Refrigerators
  Small kitchen appliances (toasters, rice cookers,
    electromagnetic cookers)
  System kitchens
  Ultralow-temperature freezers
  Vacuum cleaners
  Washing machines
  Waste disposers
Industrial and commercial equipment
  Absorption chillers and heaters
  Automatic chip mounters
  Beverage dispensers
  Commercial freezers and refrigerators
  Gas-engine heat-pump air conditioners
  Golf cart systems
  Ice makers
  Package air conditioners
  Prefabricated freezers
  Refrigerated/freezer/supermarket showcases
  Water coolers

COMPETITORS

AMD	Mitsubishi Electric
Apple Computer	Motorola
BenQ Mobile	National Semiconductor
Canon	NEC
CASIO COMPUTER	Ningbo Bird
Daewoo Electronics	Nokia
Dell	Oki Electric
Electrolux	Philips Electronics
Energizer Holdings	Pioneer
Epson	Pitney Bowes
Fujitsu	Ricoh
GE	Samsung Electronics
Gillette	Sharp
Hewlett-Packard	Siemens AG
Hitachi	Sony
IBM	Sony Ericsson Mobile
Intel	THOMSON
Kyocera	Toshiba
LG Electronics	United Technologies
Matsushita	Whirlpool

HISTORICAL FINANCIALS

Company Type: Public

Income Statement

FYE: March 31

	REVENUE ($ mil.)	NET INCOME ($ mil.)	NET PROFIT MARGIN	EMPLOYEES
3/06	21,805	(1,758)	—	106,389
3/05	24,480	(1,603)	—	96,023
3/04	13,083	42	0.3%	82,337
Annual Growth	29.1%	—	—	13.7%

HOOVER'S HANDBOOK OF WORLD BUSINESS 2007

2006 Year-End Financials

Debt ratio: 159.5%   Current ratio: 1.36
Return on equity: —   Long-term debt ($ mil.): 4,277
Cash ($ mil.): 4,815

Net Income History   Pink Sheets: SANYY

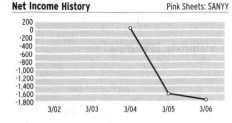

SAP

SAP's plans to dominate the software world are more than a little enterprising. The company is the leading provider of enterprise resource planning (ERP) software used to integrate back-office functions such as distribution, accounting, human resources, and manufacturing. More than 27,000 companies in over 120 countries use its software. SAP continues to shift its huge customer base to its mySAP products, which are Web-based software platforms used for a variety of enterprise functions. SAP has leveraged its prominent position in the ERP market to expand into related fields, including supply chain and customer relationship management (CRM).

SAP has methodically transitioned towards incorporating Web-based capabilities into its product lines. While the company's huge installed base of customers provides a steady stream of recurring licensing and service revenue, SAP has come under pressure from investors to pursue new areas of growth. With its legacy ERP software industry maturing, the company has intensified its efforts in the CRM software arena.

Following Oracle's acquisition of ERP rival PeopleSoft, SAP acquired TomorrowNow, a support firm for PeopleSoft, in an effort to lure customers away from Oracle. Early in 2005 SAP agreed to acquire retail software specialist Retek, but it was eventually outbid by Oracle. Later in the year SAP acquired point-of-sale software provider Triversity, as well as KhiMetrics, a developer of pricing and forecasting software for the retail market.

Partially in response to Microsoft's expanding presence in the enterprise software market, SAP has also released a scaled-down version of its software designed specifically for small and midsized businesses, as well as new software development tools and services for its strategic partners in Europe. The company has also announced plans to expand its ERP business in fledgling, unsaturated markets in Latin America and Asia (with a particular emphasis on China). SAP announced a reorganization of its operations in the Americas early in 2006. The company is combining its North American units (SAP America and SAP Canada) with its Latin American units (South America, Mexico, Central America, and the Caribbean) to form a single organization called SAP Americas.

SAP has also introduced its NetWeaver technology and application platform, which is designed to increase the interoperability between enterprise data and SAP's software products.

Three of SAP's founders — Hasso Plattner, Dietmar Hopp, and Klaus Tschira — control about 32% of the company.

HISTORY

Former IBM software engineers Hasso Plattner, Hans-Werner Hector, Dietmar Hopp, Claus Wellenreuther, and Klaus Tschira started SAP in 1972 when the project they were working on was moved to another unit.

While rival software firms made many products to automate the various parts of a company's operations, these engineers decided to make a single system that would tie a corporation together. In 1973 they launched an instantaneous accounting transaction processing program called R/1. By 1979 they had adapted the program to create R/2, mainframe software that linked external databases and communication systems.

The company went public in 1988. That year Plattner began a project to create software for the computer network market. In 1992, as sales of its R/2 mainframe software lagged, SAP introduced its R/3 software.

In 1996 Hector decided to sell holdings amounting to about 10% of SAP's stock, a move that possibly undermined hostile-takeover barriers; he left the company after a dispute with Hopp.

In 1998 SAP listed its stock on the NYSE; longtime executive Henning Kagermann was named co-chairman along with Plattner. In 1999 the company expanded on the Internet, unveiling a Web-based exchange (mySAP.com) supporting online transactions and other services. The company's long-standing resistance to employee stock options weakened in 2000 when SAP approved an option program to offset the loss of more than 200 key US managers in an 18-month period.

Later that year SAP launched a US subsidiary (SAP Markets) and increased its minority stake in software maker Commerce One.

In 2001 SAP acquired enterprise portal software provider Top Tier Software, renaming it SAP Portals. It also invested additional money in Commerce One, raising its ownership stake to about 20%.

The company reabsorbed its SAP Portals and SAP Markets subsidiaries in 2002, integrating their offerings into its mySAP product family.

In 2003 Plattner stepped down, leaving Kagermann in sole control of the chairman and CEO positions.

The next year SAP announced it was acquiring the public stake in SAP SI as part of a plan to fold that company into its services operations.

EXECUTIVES

Chairman, Executive Board and CEO:
  Henning Kagermann, age 58
CFO and Member, Executive Board: Werner Brandt, age 52
President, Customer Solutions and Operations and Member, Executive Board: Leo Apotheker, age 53
President, Product and Technology Group and Member, Executive Board: Shai Agassi, age 37
Chief Human Resources Director and Member, Executive Board: Claus E. Heinrich, age 50
Member, Executive Board, Global Service and Support: Gerhard Oswald, age 52
Member, Executive Board, Research and Breakthrough Innovation: Peter Zencke, age 56
Extended Management Board: Leslie Hayman
Extended Management Board, Global Marketing: Martin Homlish
Extended Management Board, Strategic Research and Development: Peter J. Kirschbauer

EVP, SAP NetWeaver, Product and Technology Group:
  Klaus Kreplin
**EVP; General Manager, Suite Optimization and
  Program Office:** Doug Merritt
EVP, Platform Ecosystem Development: Zia Yusuf
SVP, Active Global Support: Karl-Heinz Hess
SVP, Enterprise Information Management:
  Nimish Mehta
SVP, Global Communications: Anne M. McCarthy
SVP, Industry Solutions Marketing: Richard Campione
SVP, User Experience, Product and Technology Group:
  Dan Rosenberg
President, Global Small and Midsize Enterprises:
  Hans-Peter Klaey
President and CEO, SAP America:
  William R. (Bill) McDermott, age 44
Auditors: KPMG Deutsche Treuhand-Gesellschaft AG

LOCATIONS

HQ: SAP Aktiengesellschaft
  Neurottstrasse 16, 69190 Walldorf, Germany
Phone: +49-6227-74-7474   **Fax:** +49-6227-75-7575
US HQ: 3999 West Chester Pike,
  Newtown Square, PA 19073
US Phone: 610-661-1000   **US Fax:** 610-355-3106
Web: www.sap.com

2005 Sales

	% of total
Europe, Middle East & Africa	
Germany	21
Other countries	32
Americas	
US	27
Other countries	8
Asia/Pacific	
Japan	5
Other countries	7
Total	**100**

PRODUCTS/OPERATIONS

2005 Sales

	% of total
Services	
Maintenance	37
Consulting	25
Training	4
Software	33
Other	1
Total	**100**

2005 Software Sales

	% of total
Enterprise resource planning	42
Customer relationship management	22
Supply chain management	18
Product lifecycle management	6
Supplier relationship management	6
Other	6
Total	**100**

2005 Sales by Industry Sector

	% of total
Discrete	23
Service	23
Process	21
Consumer	17
Public	9
Financial	7
Total	**100**

Selected mySAP Software

Customer relationship management
Enterprise resource planning
Product life cycle management
Supplier relationship management
Supply chain management

Selected Services

Application hosting
Business consulting
Implementation and training
Maintenance

COMPETITORS

Epicor Software	Microsoft
i2 Technologies	Oracle
IBM	salesforce.com
Intentia	SSA Global
Lawson Software	

HISTORICAL FINANCIALS

Company Type: Public

Income Statement

FYE: December 31

	REVENUE ($ mil.)	NET INCOME ($ mil.)	NET PROFIT MARGIN	EMPLOYEES
12/05	10,082	1,772	17.6%	34,550
12/04	10,253	1,788	17.4%	32,802
12/03	8,872	1,357	15.3%	30,251
12/02	7,771	533	6.9%	29,374
12/01	6,544	517	7.9%	28,878
Annual Growth	**11.4%**	**36.1%**		**4.6%**

2005 Year-End Financials

Debt ratio: 0.5%
Return on equity: 27.0%
Cash ($ mil.): 4,054
Current ratio: 12.56
Long-term debt ($ mil.): 37

No. of shares (mil.): —
Dividends
  Yield: 0.6%
  Payout: 4.7%
Market value ($ mil.): —

Stock History

NYSE: SAP

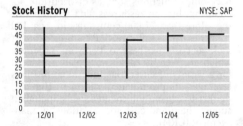

	STOCK PRICE ($) FY Close	P/E High/Low		PER SHARE ($) Earnings	Dividends
12/05	45.07	8	6	5.72	0.27
12/04	44.21	—	—	—	0.19
12/03	41.56	—	—	—	0.14
12/02	19.50	—	—	—	0.10
12/01	31.93	—	—	—	0.09
Annual Growth	**9.0%**	—	—	—	**31.6%**

SAS

Airline group SAS carries passengers throughout Scandinavia — and well beyond. Half of the company's sales come from its Scandinavian Airlines operations, which include units that operate in Denmark (Scandinavian Airlines Danmark), Norway (SAS Braathens), and Sweden (Scandinavian Airlines Sverige), as well as Scandinavian Airlines International, which serves destinations in Europe, North America, and Asia. SAS extends its reach as a member of the global Star Alliance, a marketing and code-sharing partnership led by Lufthansa and UAL's United Airlines. Additional SAS businesses include other airlines, airline support businesses, and hotel manager Rezidor SAS Hospitality.

Carriers outside the Scandinavian Airlines system generate about 20% of SAS sales and have become increasingly important contributors to the parent company's revenue mix. Subsidiaries

and affiliates include Spanair, Spain's #2 carrier (behind Iberia); Widerøe, a Norway-based regional airline; Finnish carrier Blue1; airBaltic; and Estonian Air.

The group's airline support businesses, which account for another 20% of sales, include ground handling and aircraft maintenance units, as well as freight hauler SAS Cargo. Rezidor SAS Hospitality, one of Europe's leading hotel operators, oversees some 215 hotels in nearly 50 countries, mainly in Scandinavia and northern Europe.

SAS has been selling non-core businesses to focus on its airline operations, however, and in 2006 the company announced plans for an IPO of its 75% stake in Rezidor SAS. SAS sold a 25% interest in Rezidor SAS to Carlson Hotels Worldwide in 2005. Other divestments that year included European Aeronautical Group, a provider of charting and navigational data, which was sold to Canada-based Navtech.

In the midst of the strategy shift, SAS chief Jørgen Lindegaard stepped down in 2006 after five years at the helm. Mats Jansson, the CEO for Swedish food importer and retailer Axel Johnson AB, was announced as the new president and CEO, effective January 2007. In the meantime, EVP Gunnar Reitan was named acting president and CEO.

The Swedish government owns 21% of SAS, and the governments of Denmark and Norway each own 14%. The ownership structure was adopted in 2001, when the former Scandinavian Airlines System, a consortium made up of three companies controlled by the governments of Denmark, Norway, and Sweden, respectively, was restructured into a single, publicly traded company, SAS AB.

HISTORY

The national airlines of Sweden (ABA), Norway (DNL), and Denmark (DDL) first met in 1938 to negotiate joint service to New York. The plan was delayed by WWII but kept alive in Sweden, where banker Marcus Wallenberg founded Svensk Interkontinental Luftrafik (SILA), a private airline that in 1943 replaced ABA as Sweden's international carrier. With SILA's financial backing, the yet-to-be-formed Scandinavian Airlines System (SAS) obtained the necessary landing concessions to open a Stockholm-New York air route in 1945. SAS was formed in 1946.

After opening service to South America (1946), Southeast Asia (1949), and Africa (1953), SAS inaugurated the world's first commercial polar route in 1954. It formed charter airline Scanair in 1961 and Danish domestic carrier Danair, through a joint venture, in 1971.

Deregulation of US airlines (1978) signaled the demise of nationally protected airlines. SAS seemed ill-equipped to adapt and reported its first loss in 18 years in 1980. Jan Carlzon, former head of Swedish airline Linjeflyg, became SAS's president in 1981. By targeting businessmen as the airline's most stable market and substituting an economy-rate business class for first-class service on European flights, Carlzon turned SAS's losses into profits by the end of 1982.

The company bought about 25% of Airlines of Britain Holdings in 1988, gaining a foothold at London's Heathrow Airport. Another purchase that year brought SAS nearly 10% of Continental Airlines Holdings. In 1989 the airline signed agreements that provided route coordination and hub-sharing with Swissair, Finnair, LanChile, and Canadian Airlines International.

SAS tried in the early 1990s to merge with KLM, Swissair, and Austrian Airlines to create a new international carrier, but that effort failed in 1993, leading to the replacement of Carlzon. New CEO Jan Stenberg consolidated the group, shed noncore businesses, and cut 15,000 jobs. By late 1994 SAS had sold SAS Service Partner (catering, its largest nonairline unit), Diners Club Nordic, and most of the SAS Leisure Group. By spinning off its 42% stake in LanChile and creating a new Latvian airline with Baltic International, SAS focused its air routes in Scandinavia, Western Europe, and the Baltic region.

The SAS trading subsidiary was folded into the airline unit in 1994. Through its hotel unit, SAS allied itself with Radisson Hotels to expand its presence in Europe, the Middle East, and Asia. In 1997 the company joined UAL's United Airlines, Lufthansa, VARIG, and others to form the Star Alliance. In 1998 SAS acquired Finland's Air Botnia (later renamed Blue1).

New code-sharing agreements in 1999 included deals with Singapore Airlines and Icelandair. SAS agreed to sell half its 40% stake in British Midland to Lufthansa, paving the way for British Midland to join the Star Alliance.

SAS boosted its cargo services in 2000 when it partnered with giants Lufthansa Cargo and Singapore Airlines to harmonize their cargo handling and information technology services.

The SAS consortium was restructured into a single publicly traded company, SAS AB, in 2001. That year SAS and Danish carrier Maersk Air were fined by the European Commission for agreeing not to compete on certain Scandinavian routes. SAS EVP Vagn Sørensen accepted responsibility for the illegal agreement and resigned. A month later SAS's board of directors also resigned, and a new board was elected at an extraordinary shareholders' meeting held later that year. At that time Jørgen Lindegaard took over the CEO position.

Also in 2001 a Scandinavian Airlines flight crashed while attempting to take off from Milan's Linate airport, killing all 110 on board. The following year SAS joined with Deutsche Lufthansa and Singapore Airlines to form WOW, a global cargo alliance.

Jørgen Lindegaard stepped down in 2006 after five years at the helm. Mats Jansson, the CEO for Swedish food importer and retailer Axel Johnson AB, was announced as the new president and CEO, effective in January 2007. In the meantime, EVP Gunnar Reitan was named acting president and CEO.

EXECUTIVES

Chairman: Egil Myklebust, age 64
Vice Chairman: Jacob Wallenberg, age 51
Acting President and CEO: Gunnar Reitan, age 52
President and CEO: Mats Jansson, age 54
EVP and CFO: Gunilla Berg, age 50
EVP Corporate Administration and Support:
Bernhard Rikardsen
EVP Scandinavian Airlines Businesses:
John S. Dueholm, age 55
SVP: Hans-Otto Ollongren

CEO, Scandinavian Airlines Danmark: Susanne Larsen
CEO, Scandinavian Airlines Sverige: Anders Ehrling
CEO, Scandinavian Airlines International:
Lars Lindgren
CEO, SAS Cargo Group: Kenneth Marx, age 40
CEO, Widerøe's Flyveselskap: Per Arne Watle
CEO, SAS Ground Services: Hans-Otto Halvorsen
CEO, Flight Academy: Olof Bärve
CEO, SAS Media: Lennart Löf-Jennische
CEO, Rezidor SAS: Kurt Ritter
CEO, Blue1: Stefan Wentjärvi
CEO, SAS Technical Services: Peter Möller
CEO, Spanair: Lars Nygaard
General Counsel and Secretary: Mats Lönnkvist
Human Resources Services: Patric Dahlqvist-Sjöberg
Auditors: Deloitte & Touche AB

LOCATIONS

HQ: SAS AB
Frösundaviks Allé 1, Solna,
S-195 87 Stockholm, Sweden
Phone: +46-8-797-00-00   **Fax:** +46-8-797-16-03
Web: www.sasgroup.net

PRODUCTS/OPERATIONS

2005 Sales

	% of total
Scandinavian Airlines	50
Airline support	20
Subsidiary & affiliate airlines	20
Hotels	8
Airline-related businesses	2
Total	**100**

COMPETITORS

Accor	Finnair
Aer Lingus	Hilton
Air France	Hyatt
Air Portugal	Iberia
Alitalia	KLM
AMR Corp.	Marriott
A.P. Møller - Mærsk	Penauille Servisair
British Airways	Ryanair
Choice Hotels	Starwood Hotels & Resorts
DHL	Virgin Atlantic Airways
easyJet	

HISTORICAL FINANCIALS

Company Type: Public

Income Statement

FYE: December 31

	REVENUE ($ mil.)	NET INCOME ($ mil.)	NET PROFIT MARGIN	EMPLOYEES
12/05	7,773	32	0.4%	32,363
12/04	8,781	(283)	—	32,481
12/03	7,970	(195)	—	34,544
12/02	7,423	(15)	—	35,506
12/01	4,866	(101)	—	30,972
Annual Growth	**12.4%**	**—**	**—**	**1.1%**

Net Income History

Stockholm: SAS

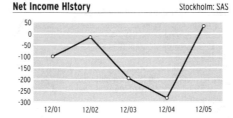

Schneider Electric

If you're building something and are hungry for power, this company could help. Schneider Electric is one of the world's largest manufacturers of equipment for electrical distribution and for industrial control and automation. The company helps power generators distribute electricity; designs automation systems for the automobile and water-treatment industries; builds infrastructure for airports, road and rail networks, and port facilities; and manages electric power in residential, industrial, and commercial buildings. Schneider has agreed to acquire American Power Conversion (APC) for about $6.1 billion in cash, widening the company's portfolio in uninterruptible power supply systems.

Schneider's brands include Merlin Gerin and Square D (electrical distribution products), as well as Telemecanique (automation and control).

Other Schneider operations include MGE UPS Systems (power supplies), Kavlico (sensors and transducers), TAC (building automation and security controls), and Dinel (optoelectronic sensors and amplifiers). Schneider sells its products to the construction, electric power, industrial, and infrastructure markets.

Schneider has equipped the Ras Laffan refinery in Qatar, operated by Qatargas. Schneider and TAC outfitted the Ambi Mall shopping center near New Delhi, India. The company has provided distribution equipment in the form of 72 electrical substations and 2,000 starters for the control panels of swimming pools at Jumeirah (The Palm), the artificial-island resort in Dubai.

After buying the European and Middle Eastern operations of Invensys Building Systems in 2005, Schneider has acquired the Asian and US operations of Invensys Building Systems for nearly $300 million (about €231 million) in cash.

Schneider has bought the Napac subsidiary of L'Air Liquide. The French firm makes intelligent remote management products for the infrastructure market, allowing engineers and operators to run refineries, water systems, refrigerated warehouses, power plants, and other facilities from a distance. Napac will be integrated into Schneider's Sorhodel Bardin subsidiary.

The company has agreed to acquire GET Group, a UK manufacturer of wiring devices and other electrical products.

HISTORY

Schneider Electric's predecessor was founded in 1782 to make industrial equipment. After the upheavals of the French Revolution and the Napoleonic Wars, the firm came under the control of brothers Adolphe and Eugene Schneider in 1836. Within two years they had built the first French locomotive (the country's first rail line had opened in 1832).

Schneider became one of France's most important heavy-industry companies, branching into a variety of machinery and steel operations. However, the country's industrial development continued to trail that of Britain and Germany due to recurrent political strife, including the revolution of 1848 and the Franco-Prussian War. France also possessed fewer coal and iron deposits.

During WWI Schneider was a key part of France's war effort. It entered the electrical contracting business in 1929 and fought off nationalization attempts in the mid-1930s.

The blitzkrieg of 1939 brought much of France under Nazi occupation, and the Schneider factories that were not destroyed were commandeered by the Germans. The company rebuilt after the war, aided by the French government. It was restructured as a holding company, and its operating units were split into three subsidiaries: civil and electrical engineering, industrial manufacturing, and construction. Charles Schneider, the last family member to lead the company, died in 1950.

In 1963 Schneider concluded an alliance with the Empain Group of Belgium, and by 1969, three years after Schneider went public, the two companies merged to become Empain-Schneider. It was a period when the company made numerous non-core acquisitions, entering such fields as ski equipment, fashion, publishing, and travel.

Schneider began reorganizing in 1980. The effort entered its final phase in 1993 with a major recapitalization that saw the merger of its former parent company, Société Parisienne d'Entreprises et de Participations, with Schneider SA and the issue of new stock to existing stockholders. The company also streamlined operations. Merlin Gerin (acquired 1975) and Télémécanique (1988) became Schneider Electric in Europe, and their North American operations were merged into Square D after its acquisition in 1991.

Schneider's 1994 takeover of two Belgian subsidiaries led Belgium's government to charge then-CEO Didier Pineau-Valencienne with fraud in the valuation of the stock. (A Belgian newsmagazine reported in 1997 that the government turned down an offer to settle out of court.)

In 1996 Schneider established the Schneider Electric (China) Investment Co. in Beijing, China's first totally French-owned firm. The next year the company sold Spie Batignolles, its electrical contracting subsidiary.

In 1999 Schneider agreed to pay $1.1 billion for Lexel, a joint venture owned by Finland's Ahlstrom and Denmark's NKT Holding, to broaden its electrical equipment offerings for the household. That year the company changed its name to Schneider Electric and its main subsidiary's name to Schneider Electric Industries.

Looking to add more machinery makers as customers, Schneider in 2000 acquired Crouzet Automatismes, based in France, and Positec, based in Switzerland.

Although Schneider announced in early 2001 that it would buy Legrand (a deal valued at about $6.4 billion), EU regulators blocked the acquisition in October. As part of the UN's "Oil for Food" program, Schneider received an order from Iraq in 2002 for nearly 16,000 circuit breakers to be used in that country's power grid. In early 2003 the company's North American division and US-based Leviton Manufacturing inked a joint technology agreement to develop prototype voice-data-image products.

In 2004 Schneider acquired the Kavlico sensor business of Solectron for nearly $200 million and the US-based Andover Controls (building automation and security controls) from Balfour Beatty for about $400 million. Schneider continued with the purchase of France-based optoelectronics maker Dinel later that year.

The following year Schneider acquired electronic sensor specialist BEI Technologies for about $562 million.

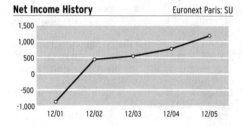
Scottish Power

Scottish Power is a local hero in the UK's deregulated energy market. One of the largest multi-utilities in the country, the company supplies electricity and natural gas to more than 5.2 million customers and generates 6,200 MW of capacity (primarily fossil-fueled) through its UK Division, which also markets and trades energy. Scottish Power's Infrastructure Division operates the company's regulated domestic power transmission and distribution assets. Subsidiary PPM Energy, formerly a part of divested US unit PacifiCorp, markets and trades energy, operates renewable energy projects, and provides related services in the US. In 2006 Scottish Power agreed to be acquired by Iberdrola for $22.5 billion.

The company has made itself a target for a takeover since divesting noncore assets, including its water utility, telecommunications, and appliance retailing businesses. In 2006 Scottish Power sold PacifiCorp, which generates and distributes electricity to 1.6 million customers in the western US, to MidAmerican Energy Holdings.

Scottish Power is focused on growing its renewable generation portfolio in the UK and the US. It is also working to improve its traditional generation and infrastructure assets, as well as to expand its retail supply customer base in the UK.

HISTORY

The UK power industry was nationalized in 1947, and two regional state-controlled boards were charged with generating, transmitting, and distributing electricity in Scotland. The two monopolies were the North of Scotland Hydro-Electric Board (formed 1943) and the South of Scotland Electricity Board (SSEB, formed 1955). In keeping with the deregulation trend that swept the UK in the 1980s, Scottish Power was formed in 1989 to assume the non-nuclear operations of SSEB, and Hydro-Electric (now part of Scottish and Southern) took the northern board's assets. Scottish Power had to prepare for competition, which began in a limited form in 1990.

Scottish Power's initial assets included six coal, gas, and hydropower plants that served southern Scotland, including Glasgow and much of the Scottish industrial base, and England's Northumberland county. The company, which went public in 1991, also inherited 73 retail outlets that sold consumer electronic and electrical goods. It expanded this retail business across the UK in the 1990s.

The company teamed with SeaWest of the US and Japan's Toman in the early 1990s to set up Europe's largest wind farm, in Wales. It set up other wind-energy plants in Northern Ireland, Scotland, and England; by the mid-1990s Scottish Power was the largest wind-farm operator in the UK.

In 1993 the company moved into telecommunications. Running fiber-optic lines alongside its high-voltage power lines between Glasgow and Edinburgh, the company's Scottish Telecom unit (established 1994) provided high-speed voice and data services to several major businesses.

With opportunities for growth limited by the relatively small population base in southern Scotland, the company sought to expand through geographic and business diversification. In 1995 it became the first UK power firm to buy a rival when it acquired Manweb, a regional electricity company that served northwestern England and North Wales. The next year the company became the first British electricity firm to buy a water company when it acquired Southern Water, a water supply and wastewater services firm based on England's South Coast. Scottish Power disposed of many of Southern Water's noncore businesses in 1997.

In 1998 Scottish Power boosted its telecom business with the purchase of Demon Internet, then the UK's largest independent ISP. That year, after merger talks with two US electric utilities failed, Scottish Power agreed to acquire PacifiCorp, a major utility in the US Pacific Northwest. The deal was completed in 1999.

With the BBC, Scottish Telecom launched a free Internet service, Freebeeb.net, in 1999. That year Scottish Telecom's name was changed to Thus, and the company floated a 49.9% stake in the unit. Scottish Power also announced a restructuring plan that would cut jobs and divest noncore businesses. In 2000 it announced plans to join the Royal Bank of Scotland in offering bundled services, including banking, utilities, and telecommunications. The company also divested PacifiCorp's Powercor Australia unit.

In 2001 Scottish Power agreed to sell its retail appliance business to Powerhouse Retail. It also restructured into three business units: UK power generation and supply, infrastructure (asset management and water supply), and US operations (PacifiCorp). Later that year the company announced plans to spin off its remaining stake in Thus; the transaction was completed in 2002.

Scottish Power also sold its Southern Water unit to First Aqua, a private investment firm backed by the Royal Bank of Scotland, for $2.9 billion in 2002. Ian Russell left his position as chief executive in early 2006; Philip Bowman assumed Russell's CEO duties.

EXECUTIVES

Chairman: Charles Miller Smith, age 65
CEO and Board Member: Philip Bowman, age 53
Executive Director, Finance and Strategy:
 Simon Lowth, age 43, $454,833 pay
 (prior to promotion)
Secretary and Group Director, Commercial and Legal:
 James Stanley, age 50
President and CEO, Energy Networks:
 David Rutherford, age 41
Group Company Secretary: Andrew Mitchell, age 53
President, Energy Retail: Willie MacDiarmid
President, Energy Wholesale: John Campbell
President and CEO, PPM Energy: Terry F. Hudgens, age 50
VP, Investor Relations: Bob Hess
Head of Media Relations: Colin McSeveny
Media Relations Manager: Simon McMillan
Media Relations Manager, Wales and North West England: Anne Benson
Head of UK Community Affairs and Manweb:
 Gaynor Kenyon
Director, Investor Relations: Jennifer Lawton
Manager, Investor Relations: David Ross
Assistant Company Secretary: Donald McPherson
Public Relations Executive: Jane Holmes
Assistant Secretary: Alan McCulloch
Group Director, Human Resources and Communications: Stephen Dunn
Auditors: PricewaterhouseCoopers LLP

LOCATIONS

HQ: Scottish Power plc
 1 Atlantic Quay, Glasgow G2 8SP, United Kingdom
Phone: +44-141-248-8200   **Fax:** +44-141-248-8300
Web: www.scottishpower.plc.uk

Scottish Power primarily operates in the UK and the US.

PRODUCTS/OPERATIONS

2006 Sales

	% of total
UK	
Energy Retail & Wholesale	75
Energy Networks	15
US (PPM Energy)	10
Total	**100**

Selected Subsidiaries

Infrastructure Division
 Scottish Power UK plc
  SP Distribution Limited (operates as SP Transmission & Distribution, regulated distribution assets)
  SP Manweb plc (operates as SP Transmission & Distribution, regulated distribution assets)
  SP Power Systems Limited (PowerSystems, network management and maintenance)
  SP Transmission Limited (operates as SP Transmission & Distribution, regulated transmission assets)
PPM Energy, Inc. (formerly PacifiCorp Power Marketing, wholesale power generation and marketing, US)

UK Division
 ScottishPower Energy Management (Agency) Limited (formerly ScottishPower Energy Trading (Agency), wholesale electricity and gas marketing and trading)
 ScottishPower Energy Management Limited (formerly ScottishPower Energy Trading, wholesale electricity and gas marketing and trading)
 ScottishPower Energy Retail Limited (retail electricity and gas supply)
 ScottishPower Generation Limited (power production)
 SP Dataserve Limited (data management, metering, and billing)

COMPETITORS

British Energy	PG&E
Centrica	Portland General Electric
EDF Energy	Premier Power
Edison International	Puget Energy
Electricity Supply Board	Questar
E.ON UK	Scottish and Southern
Green Energy (UK)	Energy
International Power	United Utilities
MidAmerican Energy	Viridian Group
National Grid	Western Power
National Grid Gas	Distribution
npower	

HISTORICAL FINANCIALS

Company Type: Public

Income Statement

				FYE: March 31
	REVENUE ($ mil.)	NET INCOME ($ mil.)	NET PROFIT MARGIN	EMPLOYEES
3/06	9,475	1,888	19.9%	9,793
3/05	12,869	(930)	—	16,142
3/04	10,587	1,354	12.8%	14,821
3/03	8,347	1,243	14.9%	13,825
Annual Growth	4.3%	15.0%	—	(10.9%)

2006 Year-End Financials

Debt ratio: 64.4%   Current ratio: 2.22
Return on equity: 21.1%   Long-term debt ($ mil.): 5,719
Cash ($ mil.): 7,781

Net Income History

NYSE: SPI

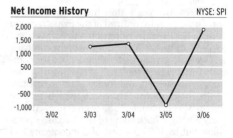

Securitas

Securitas profits from the lack of caritas in human nature. The world's #1 security services company provides security guards to banks, retailers, large corporations, small businesses, and residential customers in more than 20 countries, mainly in North America and Europe. Securitas' purchase of US security firms Pinkerton's and Burns International Services, now included in its Security Services USA subsidiary, has given it a dominant position in the US security-guard services market. The acquisitive company has been busy expanding in Europe and the US. Swedish firm Säkl controls about 17% of Securitas, which was founded in 1934.

To squeeze more value out of its operations, Securitas is forming three new companies by spinning off some of its security businesses to shareholders. Two companies have already been created: Securitas Direct offers security services to consumers and small business, and Securitas Systems provides security products and services to large companies. The company's Cash Handling Services, which includes subsidiary Loomis, Fargo & Co., will be spun off and renamed Loomis.

These moves allow Securitas to focus on its guarding operations in Europe and the US. (After the creation of Loomis in 2007, Securitas will consist of the two guarding operations: Security Services USA and Security Services Europe.)

Recent additions to the company's Security Services Europe holdings include the 2006 acquisitions of security firms Renful Flugverkehr Services GmbH (Germany), DAK Güvenlik (Turkey), and Paneuropea de Seguridad Integral (Spain). Also in 2006 the Canadian operations within Security Services USA acquired Sécurité St. Germain in Quebec, Canada.

HISTORY

Securitas established its first outpost in 1934, in Helsingborg, Sweden, when Erik Philip-Sörensen bought Hälsingborgs Nattvakt and renamed it Securitas. Erik was following in the footsteps of his father, who in 1901 had established a small Danish guard company as part of the ISS Group of security companies. Securitas was housed within ISS as well.

Sörensen spent the next two decades establishing and acquiring more Swedish firms and adding them to the Securitas family. He also added to his own family two sons, Sven and Jörgen, who would figure into Securitas' future. Jörgen began establishing new branches in Belgium and the UK in the late 1950s. The companies were combined into one company, Group 4, in 1968.

In 1974, two years after the Securitas name was finally branded onto all of the firm's security companies, the elder Sörensen retired. Sven and Jörgen bid against ISS for control of the company and won. Seven years later they divided the company equally: Sven took half of the Securitas operations in Sweden, and Jörgen assumed control of the international businesses (which became Group 4 Securitas). In 1983 Sven sold Securitas. Jörgen bought back some of the Swedish operations, but by 1985 the rest of the company had ended up in the hands of Swedish investment firm Investment AB Latour (now chaired by Gustaf Douglas, also vice chairman of Securitas).

The new owners trimmed away all companies that weren't directly related to guard services and alarm systems. Securitas then began an acquisition rampage in 1988 with the purchase of Swedish lock manufacturer Assa. Not content with the lovely lakes and mountains of Sweden, Securitas bought companies in Denmark, Norway, and Portugal and set up new operations in Hungary.

Securitas went public in 1991 and soon bought US lock maker Arrow; it also began cutting a wider swath through Europe. With its 1992 purchase of security firm Protectas, Securitas gained operations in Austria, France, Germany, and Switzerland; it bought more firms in Spain in 1992 and in Finland the next year. To streamline further, Securitas merged its lock manufacturing operations with those of Finland's Metra, creating Assa-Abloy. It spun off the new company in 1994 but retained a 45% stake. Securitas made more acquisition raids in Estonia, Poland, and the UK in 1996.

In 1997 Securitas created Securitas Direct to handle its domestic and small-scale alarms business; the division quickly became active throughout Scandinavia, as well as in France, Spain, and Switzerland. That year the company made more acquisitions in France and Sweden. In 1998 Securitas made two significant purchases: Raab Karcher Sicherheit, the market leader in industrial guarding services in Germany, and Proteg, France's security market leader (Securitas sold Proteg's fire protection divisions to Williams PLC in 1999).

The grand-daddy of acquisitions was still to come. In early 1999 Securitas bought 150-year-old US security firm Pinkerton's in a bid to create the largest security firm in the world. Securitas took over Pinkerton's operations in the Czech Republic, Germany, Portugal, and the UK. The next year Securitas made several US acquisitions, including the purchase of Burns International Services for $650 million.

Securitas' takeover of US companies didn't stop with Pinkerton's and Burns. In 2001 the company became the second-largest cash-handling services provider in the US when it bought the remaining 51% of Loomis, Fargo & Co. (Securitas had previously acquired 49% of Loomis as part of the Burns deal).

Securitas continued expanding in 2002, but this time the company focused outside the US, buying security companies in the Netherlands and Canada. In 2003 it returned its focus to the US by acquiring Lincoln Security, a security-guard service provider operating in California, Nevada, and Oregon. It also acquired Armored Motor Services of America. Later that year Securitas expanded its Security Services Europe offerings through the acquisition of Spanish-based Ebro Vigilancia & Seguridad and Netherlands-based VNV.

The company acquired UK security alarm firm Bell Group in 2004 as a platform for Securitas Systems' UK & Ireland business.

The following year the Company sold its cash-handling services activities in the Czech Republic, Poland, and Hungary to Brink's.

In 2006 Securitas spun off two of its divisions into independent specialized security companies: Securitas Direct AB and Securitas Systems AB. It also announced plans to spin off its cash handling operations, which will be renamed Loomis. The divestitures mark the company's shift to focus exclusively on its security guard operations.

EXECUTIVES

Chairman: Melker Schörling, age 58
Vice Chairman: Gustaf Douglas, age 67
President, CEO, and Director; Chairman, Securitas Direct: Thomas Berglund, age 53
President and CEO: Alf Göransson, age 48
EVP and CFO: Håkan Winberg, age 49
SVP Investor Relations: Henrik Brehmer
President and CEO, Security Systems: Juan Vallejo, age 48
CEO, Securitas Cash Handling Division; Divisional President, Loomis Cash Handling Services: Håkan Ericson, age 43
Divisional President, Direct: Dick Seger, age 52
Divisional President, Mobile Services: Morten Rønning, age 45
Divisional President, Security Services Europe: Tore K. Nilsen, age 49
Regional President, Security Services North America: Brad Van Hazel, age 48
Divisional President, Security Services North America: Santiago Galaz, age 46
COO, Security Services North America: William N. (Bill) Barthelemy, age 51
Manager Investor Relations: Linda Wallgren
Auditors: PricewaterhouseCoopers AB

LOCATIONS

HQ: Securitas AB
Lindhagensplan 70, SE-102 28 Stockholm, Sweden
Phone: +46-8-657-74-00   **Fax:** +46-8-657-70-72
US HQ: 2 Campus Dr., Parsippany, NJ 07054
US Phone: 973-267-5300   **US Fax:** 973-397-2681
Web: www.securitasgroup.com

Securitas has operations in Argentina, Austria, Belgium, Canada, the Czech Republic, Denmark, Estonia, Finland, France, Germany, Hungary, Ireland, Mexico, the Netherlands, Norway, Poland, Portugal, Spain, Sweden, Switzerland, the UK, and the US.

2005 Sales

	% of total
Europe	
Nordic region	15
Other countries	46
US	37
Other regions	2
Total	**100**

PRODUCTS/OPERATIONS

2005 Sales

	% of total
Security Services Europe	37
Security Services USA	32
Cash Handling Services	17
Securitas Systems	9
Direct	4
Other	1
Total	**100**

COMPETITORS

Allied Security
Brink's
Command Security
Group 4 Securicor
Initial Security
Prosegur
TransNational Security
Tyco Fire and Security
UTC Fire & Security
Wackenhut

HISTORICAL FINANCIALS

Company Type: Public

Income Statement   FYE: December 31

	REVENUE ($ mil.)	NET INCOME ($ mil.)	NET PROFIT MARGIN	EMPLOYEES
12/05	8,291	341	4.1%	217,000
12/04	9,025	222	2.5%	206,153
12/03	8,121	171	2.1%	210,700
12/02	7,508	170	2.3%	203,070
12/01	5,710	112	2.0%	207,799
Annual Growth	**9.8%**	**32.1%**	**—**	**1.1%**

Net Income History   Stockholm: SECUB

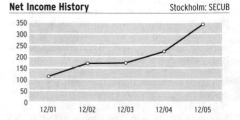

Seiko Epson

Seiko Epson looked at its watch and saw that times have changed. Also referred to just as Epson, the company is a manufacturing arm of Seiko Group, the internationally known watchmaker. The Seiko Epson product portfolio includes IT products such as desktop and portable computers; electronic devices and components, including semiconductors; and a variety of other products, such as lenses, motors, and magnets. A top printer manufacturer, Seiko Epson produces dot matrix, ink jet, laser, and thermal printers, as well as printer components. Heirs of Seiko's founder, Kitaro Hattori, control the company.

Although watches and precision products constitute the company's smallest segment (about 5% of sales), Seiko Epson has no plans to wind down its oldest business. The skills gleaned from watchmaking, including miniaturization and precision timing, have given rise to the company's other, more profitable lines, including LCDs, semiconductor products, and other parts for mobile phones.

In 2004 Seiko Epson combined its liquid crystal display (LCD) manufacturing operations with those of Sanyo Electric to form Sanyo Epson Imaging Devices Corporation.

HISTORY

In 1881, 21-year-old Kitaro Hattori, who had begun working in the jewelry trade at age 13, opened a Tokyo watch shop and called it K. Hattori & Co. In 1892 Hattori started a factory in Seikosha to manufacture wall clocks and, later, watches and alarm clocks. K. Hattori & Co. went public in 1917. In 1924 it began using the Seiko brand on its timepieces. Kitaro's son Ganzo formed Daini Seikosha Co., precursor of Seiko Instruments, in 1937.

The company formed Daiwa Kogyo Ltd., a maker of mechanical watches, in 1942; it would later become Seiko Epson. Developments included self-winding watches (1955) and transistorized table clocks (1959).

A big break came for the company in 1964, when it developed crystal chronometers and printing timers for the Tokyo Olympics' official timekeepers. It was the first time a precision timepiece and a printer had been combined. Based on that technology, in 1968 Seiko Epson debuted the EP-101, the first commercially successful miniature printer (used primarily with calculators).

During the late 1960s Seiko Epson entered the semiconductor field when it began developing LSIs (large-scale integrated circuits) for its watches. The company introduced the world's first quartz watch in 1969 and the first quartz digital watch in 1973. It soon expanded into liquid crystal display (LCD) technology. It formed its US affiliate, Epson America, in 1975. With the advent of the PC in the 1970s, Seiko Epson also began working on computer printers. It released its first dot matrix model in 1978. The next year the company introduced the Alba and Pulsar watch brands.

The company's European headquarters, in the Netherlands, opened in 1980. Seiko Epson debuted the first laptop computer, the HX-20, in 1982; a high-quality daisy wheel printer and LCD color TV in 1983; and an ink jet printer in 1984. In 1985 it began making contact lenses. Reijiro Hattori, grandson of the company's founder, took the helm in the late 1980s.

In 1990 Seiko baptized the Scubamaster, a computerized diver's watch featuring a dive table. The next year it introduced a wristwatch/pager. That year it added color printers to its line. Seiko Epson unveiled digital cameras for use with PCs and Macs in 1996. The next year Lattice Semiconductor invested $150 million with Seiko Epson to build a new semiconductor wafer factory.

In 1998 the company made its US semiconductor manufacturing subsidiary, Epson Electronics America, an independent firm. It also formed an ink jet printer joint venture in China. That year the company entered the personal digital assistant (PDA) market with a line of PDAs that use the satellite-based Global Positioning System.

In 1999 Seiko Epson acquired Pacific Metals Co.'s metal powder operations, a complement to its metal injection molding subsidiary Injex.

With profit margins from its printers shrinking, in 2000 the company announced plans to consolidate its printer operations in China, Indonesia, and Singapore, and to expand its LCD products line. The following year Seiko Epson agreed to form a joint venture with IBM to produce logic chips for cell phones, handheld computers, and other devices.

EXECUTIVES

Chairman and CEO: Saburo Kusama
Vice Chairman: Yasuo Hattori
EVP, CFO, and Board Member: Toshio Kimura
President, COO, and Board Member: Seiji Hanaoka
EVP, CIO, and Board Member: Norio Niwa
Senior Managing Director and Board Member: Masayuki Morozumi
Managing Director and Board Member: Yasumasa Otsuki
Managing Director and Board Member: Masao Akahane
Managing Director and Board Member: Torao Yajima
Managing Director and Board Member: Kenji Kubota
Managing Director and Board Member: Hiroshi Komatsu
Chief Executive, Imaging and Information Products Operations Division; Board Member: Seiichi Hirano
Chief Executive, Visual Instruments Operations Division; Board Member: Kenji Uchida
Chief Executive, TFT Operations Division: Hideaki Iwano
President, Sanyo Epson Imaging Devices Corporation: Shuji Aruga
Auditors: ChuoAoyama PricewaterhouseCoopers

LOCATIONS

HQ: Seiko Epson Corporation
3-3-5 Owa, Suwa, Nagano 392-8502, Japan
Phone: +81-266-52-3131   **Fax:** +81-266-53-4844
US HQ: 3840 Kilroy Airport Way, Long Beach, CA 90806
US Phone: 562-981-3840   **US Fax:** 562-290-5220
Web: www.epson.com

Seiko Epson has operations in Japan, as well as manufacturing and sales operations in Australia, China, France, Germany, Hong Kong, Indonesia, Italy, Malaysia, the Netherlands, the Philippines, Singapore, South Korea, Spain, Taiwan, the UK, and the US.

PRODUCTS/OPERATIONS

2006 Sales

	% of total
Information-related equipment	60
Electronic devices	33
Precision products	5
Other	2
Total	**100**

Selected Products

Information-related equipment
 Computers
 LCD projection TVs
 Printers
 Projectors
 Scanners
Electronic devices
 Crystal devices
 LCDs
 Semiconductors
Precision products
 Optical devices
 Watches

COMPETITORS

Acer	LSI Logic
Bausch & Lomb	Matsushita
Canon	NEC
CASIO COMPUTER	Océ
Citizen Watch	Oki Electric
Dell	Ricoh
Fujitsu	Samsung Group
Hewlett-Packard	SANYO
Hitachi	Sharp
IBM	Sony
Intel	Swatch
Kyocera	Toshiba
Lexmark	Xerox

HISTORICAL FINANCIALS

Company Type: Public

Income Statement

FYE: March 31

	REVENUE ($ mil.)	NET INCOME ($ mil.)	NET PROFIT MARGIN	EMPLOYEES
3/06	13,178	(152)	—	90,701
3/05	13,759	518	3.8%	85,647
3/04	13,378	360	2.7%	84,899
3/03	11,035	104	0.9%	73,797
3/02	9,606	(139)	—	68,786
Annual Growth	**8.2%**	**—**		**7.2%**

Net Income History

Exchange: Tokyo

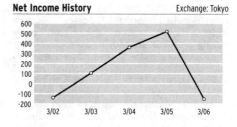

Sharp

Sharp's business is pointed at the electronics market. Best known for its consumer electronics, the company is a leading maker of electronic components and computer hardware and peripherals. Its flagship components business makes LCDs (used in everything from airplane cockpits to PCs to pinball machines), flash memory, integrated circuits, and laser diodes used in optical data drives. Sharp also makes PCs, printers, and cell phones; consumer audio and video products, such as CD and DVD players and video cameras; and a variety of appliances, such as air conditioners, refrigerators, and vacuum cleaners.

Sharp has targeted such products as LCD televisions, next-generation phone handsets, and home networking gear for growth. On the components side, the company sees demand for advanced LCDs increasing as new handheld devices come into the mainstream. Sharp has shifted the focus of its television business from traditional tube TVs to flat-panel LCDs. In 2005 it acquired Fujitsu's LCD subsidiary, Fujitsu Display Technology.

Sharp is spending about ¥6 billion (around €44 million or more than $50 million) on building an LCD module assembly plant in Poland. The facility is scheduled to begin production in early 2007, providing LCD modules for TVs being sold into European markets.

Electrolux and Sharp, which previously collaborated on microwave ovens, have agreed to work together on refrigerator technology. Models from the joint R&D will be made at a Sharp factory in Thailand.

Sharp recalled 28,000 battery packs made by Sony for laptop computers in the Japanese market because the lithium-ion batteries are at risk of overheating and catching fire. Fujitsu and other PC makers have also recalled the Sony-made batteries.

HISTORY

Tokuji Hayakawa got started in manufacturing in 1912 when he established Hayakawa Electric Industry to make a type of belt buckle he had designed. Three years later he invented the first mechanical pencil, named the Ever-Sharp, which was a commercial success. After an earthquake leveled much of Tokyo in 1923, including Hayakawa's business, he moved to Osaka and sold the rights to his pencil to finance a new factory. He introduced Japan's first crystal radio sets in 1925 and four years later debuted a vacuum tube radio.

Following WWII, Hayakawa Electric developed an experimental TV, which it began mass-producing in 1953. The company was ready with color TVs when Japan initiated color broadcasts in 1960. Hayakawa Electric grew tremendously during the 1960s, introducing microwave ovens (1962), solar cells (1963), the first electronic all-transistor-diode calculator (1964), and the first gallium arsenide LED (1969). The firm opened a US office in 1962.

In 1970 the company began to make its own semiconductor devices and changed its name to Sharp Corporation, a nod to the name of its first product. It began mass production of LCDs in 1973. Sharp later introduced the first electronic calculator with an LCD (1973), solar-powered calculators (1976), and a credit card-sized calculator (1979).

The company began producing VCRs in the early 1980s, and in 1984 Sharp introduced its first color copier. That year the firm introduced a fax machine and began concentrating its marketing efforts on small businesses (while its competitors were scrambling for large corporate accounts). Haruo Tsuji became president in 1986. He restructured the company and concentrated research on LCDs. Sharp blitzed the market with a new line of creative products in the late 1980s, including a high-definition LCD color TV (1987) and a notebook-sized PC (1988).

Sharp introduced a cordless pocket telephone in 1992 that operated continuously for over five hours, as well as a low-cost high-definition television (HDTV). That year the company announced strategic alliances with Apple to build the Newton personal digital assistant (which flopped) and with the Shanghai Radio and Television to make air conditioners, fax machines, copiers, and printers (Shanghai Sharp Electronics began production in 1994). During the mid-1990s Sharp's ViewCam camcorder and Zaurus personal digital assistant were both big sellers.

In 1996 Sharp formed partnerships with Alcatel, Advanced Micro Devices, Fujitsu, Intel, and Nanjing Panda Electronics (China's second-largest TV maker).

Katsuhiko Machida became president in 1998 as the company attempted to pump younger blood into its veins; Tsuji became company adviser. A downturn in the global economy and competitive pricing in the LCD business put Sharp's profits under pressure in 2001, prompting the company reduced its workforce.

Also in 2001 Sharp introduced its AQUOS flat-panel TV, which became a popular model among consumers; it had made 10 million AQUOS TVs by mid-2006. It set plans to build its Mihara Plant for manufacturing electronic components, and agreed to collaborate on home appliances with SANYO Electric.

In 2002 Sharp built a plant for large-screen LCD TVs in Kameyama City, in Japan's Mie prefecture. It began production of system LCDs at the Tenri Plant. Later that year Sharp broke ground on a new plant in Kameyama.

The following year the company began production of system LCDs at the Mie Plant No. 3. Sharp joined with eight other manufacturers of consumer electronics in forming the Blu-ray Disc Founders (later the Blu-ray Disc Association), an industry organization promoting a next-generation technology format for DVDs. SAP and Sharp agreed on partnering for mobile business applications. The company initiated production of photovoltaic modules in Europe.

Sharp launched an online music distribution service, Any Music, in 2004. The company built a printed circuit board manufacturing facility at the Mihara Plant, and set plans to construct a second plant and technical center in Wuxi, China. IBM Japan and Sharp collaborated on developing an IC card with a new operating system. Sharp and Sony Ericsson started working together on a 3G FOMA mobile phone for the Japanese market.

Construction finally began on Plant No. 2 in Kameyama in mid-2005; about a year later, the plant started turning out LCD panels for flat-screen TVs. Later that year Sharp and the University of Tokyo established Todai-Sharp Laboratories for advanced R&D on flexible electronics.

EXECUTIVES

President: Katsuhiko Machida
SEVP; Chief General Administration Officer: Hiroshi Saji
Senior Executive Director; Group General Manager, Human Resources Group: Akihiko Kumagai
Senior Executive Director; Group General Manager, International Business Group: Toshishige Hamano
Senior Executive Director; Group General Manager, Domestic Sales and Marketing Group: Masaaki Ohtsuka
Senior Executive Director and Chief Environmental Protection Officer: Akira Mitarai
Senior Executive Director; Group General Manager, Sales and Marketing Group, Electronic Components and Devices: Shigeo Nakabu
Senior Executive Director and CTO: Kenji Ohta
Senior Executive Director, Information and Communication Systems Group: Masafumi Matsumoto

Executive Director; Group General Manager, Digital Document Systems Group: Yoshiaki Ibuchi
Executive Director, LCD Business: Mikio Katayama
Executive Director; Group General Manager, Tokyo Branch: Toshio Adachi
Director; General Manager, Management Planning Board: Takashi Nakagawa
Director; Group General Manager, Corporate Accounting and Control Group: Tetsuo Ohnishi
Director; Group Deputy General Manager, International Business Group; Chairman and President, Sharp Electronics: Toshihiko Fujimoto
Director; Group General Manager, Corporate Research and Development: Toru Chiba
Auditors: KPMG AZSA & Co.

LOCATIONS

HQ: Sharp Corporation
22-22 Nagaike-cho, Abeno-ku,
Osaka 545-8522, Japan
Phone: +81-6-6621-1221   **Fax:** +81-6-6627-1759
US HQ: Sharp Plaza, Mahwah, NJ 07430
US Phone: 201-529-8200   **US Fax:** 201-529-8425
Web: www.sharp.co.jp

Sharp operates in more than 25 countries around the world.

2006 Sales

	% of total
Asia	
Japan	62
Other countries	7
Europe	11
Americas	10
Other regions	10
Total	**100**

PRODUCTS/OPERATIONS

2006 Sales

	% of total
Consumer/information products	
Audio-Visual & communication equipment	39
Information equipment	15
Home appliances	8
Electronic components	
LCDs	23
ICs	5
Other	10
Total	**100**

Selected Products

Consumer/Information products
Audio-visual and communication equipment
Audio amplifiers
Compact disc players
Digital cameras
DVD players
High-definition televisions
Liquid crystal display DVD televisions
Liquid crystal display televisions
Liquid crystal display video projectors
Mobile phones
Video cameras
Home appliances
Air conditioners
Microwave ovens
Refrigerators
Vacuum cleaners
Washing machines
Information equipment
Calculators
Digital copiers
Fax machines
Mobile business tools
Personal computers
Printers
Electronic components
Flash memory
Integrated circuits
Laser diodes and other optoelectronic devices
Radio-frequency components
Satellite broadcasting components
Solar cells and other photovoltaic devices

HISTORICAL FINANCIALS

Company Type: Public

Income Statement				FYE: March 31
	REVENUE ($ mil.)	NET INCOME ($ mil.)	NET PROFIT MARGIN	EMPLOYEES
3/06	23,787	754	3.2%	46,872
3/05	23,616	715	3.0%	46,751
3/04	21,367	575	2.7%	46,164
3/03	16,715	272	1.6%	46,633
3/02	13,599	85	0.6%	46,518
Annual Growth	15.0%	72.4%	—	0.2%

Net Income History   OTC: SHCAY

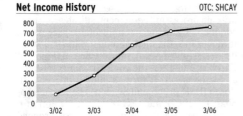

Shiseido

If your face is a canvas, Shiseido wants to be the paint. Shiseido, Japan's largest cosmetics maker, makes makeup and skin care products for men and women. It also makes toiletries, sun care products, fragrances, professional salon hair care products, pharmaceuticals, and fine chemicals. Upscale brands include Shiseido and Clé de Peau Beauté. Mid- and mass-market brands include Ayura and Aquair. Other interests include specialty fragrance, hair, and skin care salons. About three-quarters of Shiseido's sales come from Japan. Shinzo Maeda, general manager of corporate planning, became president and CEO in mid-2005. Morio Ikeda took the title of chairman.

Faced with growing competition in the Japanese cosmetics industry, Shiseido has been touching up business for its chain stores by using information from point-of-sale terminals and consultants' personal display assistants. It's also continuing to grow overseas. Shiseido opened its first store in Shanghai and opened more stores in China in 2005.

The company is also adding brands with the introduction of the Integrate makeup line and the Elixir Superieur skincare brand set, which launched in August and September 2006, respectively. Shiseido anticipates generating some $260 million in sales revenue for the two brands by March 2007. Since August 2005 the company has launched four noteworthy brands in Japan — Aqua Label, Maquillage, Tsubaki, and Uno.

To specifically target the Chinese market, Shiseido in late 2006 launched a cosmetics brand named Urara. The company planned to boost the number of specialty stores that carry its products from more than 1,000 to some 1,700 by the end of 2006.

Shiseido closed two of its six primary plants in Japan (specifically, Tokyo and Kyoto) in June 2006. It closed its Shiseido Beautech and Haramachi Paper divisions in 2005.

As Shinzo Maeda replaced Morio Ikeda as chief executive in mid-2005, he made plans to continue Shiseido's makeover begun by Ikeda in 2001. Maeda also anticipates growth amid increased competition.

Shiseido Malaysia Sdn. Bhd., a joint venture, was formed in early 2005 through a partnership with Warisan TC Holdings Berhad. Since 1977 a division of Warisan, Tung Pao Sdn. Bhd., has distributed Shiseido brands in Malaysia.

The firm has an Institute of Beauty Sciences which researches the relationship between "cosmetic behavior" and psychology.

HISTORY

Yushin Fukuhara, former head pharmacist for the Japanese admiralty, established Japan's first modern drugstore, Shiseido Pharmacy, in 1872. Attracted by the store's Western-style products and format, the customers were the nobility and the rich. Shiseido manufactured Japan's first toothpaste in 1888 and introduced its first cosmetics product (Eudermine, a skin lotion) in 1897. Fukuhara opened the country's first soda fountain in 1902.

Yushin's son, Shinzo, created Shiseido's first extensive makeup lines, introducing flesh-toned face powder in 1906 and a fragrance line in 1918. Under Shinzo's influence, cosmetics replaced drugs as Shiseido's mainstay.

Shiseido began franchise operations in 1923 and business boomed. The firm went public that year; in 1927 Shinzo became president. During WWII the company couldn't make cosmetics, only medicines, and many of Shiseido's factories were destroyed. This led to near-bankruptcy in 1945, but Shiseido rebounded the next year, thanks to nail enamel.

In 1951 it introduced its de Luxe high-end cosmetics line, and by 1956 it had become the #1 Japanese cosmetics firm. With a 1962 move into Hong Kong, Shiseido began overseas operations. It steadily expanded its international business by setting up subsidiaries across the world (including one in New York City in 1965).

In the 1970s Shiseido failed at marketing its products in the US, and at home its market share was slipping. Seen as being out of touch with the young, it was also hampered by strict product development laws that caused delays in getting products to market. In the mid-1980s it developed a successful US marketing strategy that included selling exclusive product lines in high-end department stores such as Macy's; it also made several acquisitions, including Zotos (hair products, US, 1988).

The firm's first prescription-only drug, an ophthalmological treatment used in certain types of cataract surgery and cornea transplants, was launched in 1993. In 1996 it announced a biological compound that retards skin aging by preventing oxidization. The company bought the Helene Curtis salon hair care business in the US and Canada from Unilever that year. In 1997 Shiseido bought Helene Curtis Japan salon hair operations and a New Jersey factory, which more than doubled its North American production.

Also in 1997 Akira Gemma (a Shiseido veteran of nearly four decades) became CEO, and the company expanded to Croatia, the Czech Republic, Hungary, and Vietnam. It bought the professional salon products business of the US's Lamaur Corporation in 1998.

Shiseido opened a New York City flagship store in 1998 and began selling cosmetics in Russia in 1999. It also began selling soap, shampoo, and baby powder in 1999 under the wildly popular Hello Kitty name, licensed from Japanese media firm Sanrio. Late that year Shiseido introduced Clé de Peau Beauté to international markets as its top-of-the-line beauty brand.

Looking to expand its foreign brands portfolio, in June 2000 Shiseido bought the Sea Breeze line of facial products from Bristol-Myers Squibb; it also acquired 75% of French cosmetics firm and aromatherapy specialists Laboratoires Decléor. In September the company announced an agreement with Intimate Brands (owner of Victoria's Secret and Bath & Body Works) to develop a new prestige beauty products line.

In June 2001 Morio Ikeda took over for Gemma as president and CEO; Gemma was named chairman.

In 2002 Shiseido, together with Limited Brands, introduced a new retail beauty company called aura science. One of 10 outlets planned to open in major US cities, the first aura science store was opened in Columbus, Ohio, in April of that year.

In the fall of 2003 the introduction of two new fragrances under the brand name FCUK (French Connection United Kingdom) by Shiseido's Zirh International subsidiary was met with vocal protest from some consumers. Shiseido reorganized its operations in China in 2004.

EXECUTIVES

Chairman: Morio Ikeda
President, CEO, and Director: Shinzo Maeda, age 57
Corporate Senior Executive Officer and Chief Area Managing Officer of China: Tadakatsu Saito
Corporate Executive Officer and Chief Area Managing Officer of Chugoku/Shikoku Area: Takashi Hibino
Corporate Executive Officer and Chief Area Managing Officer of Tokyo/West Kanto Area: Kohei Mori
Corporate Executive Officer, Basic Research and New Business Development: Michihiro Yamaguchi
Corporate Executive Officer, Production Business, Logistics, and Technical: Masami Hamaguchi
Corporate Executive Officer, R&D Strategy, Product Development, and Patents: Yoshimaru Kumano
Corporate Officer, Boutique Business and Chief Officer, Professional Business Operations: Kyoichiro Sato
Corporate Officer, Non-Shiseido Brand Business and General Manager, Beauty Consultant Training, Cosmetics Business: Kazuko Ohya
Corporate Officer, Pharmaceutical Business and Fine Chemicals Business and General Manager, Pharmaceutical Business: Eiji Yano

Chief Officer, Cosmetics Business; President and CEO,
  Shiseido Sales: Toshimitsu Kobayashi
General Manager, America's Department: Tosio Negami
President and CEO, Shiseido Cosmetics America Ltd.:
  Heidi Manheimer
General Manager, Personnel: Kazutoshi Satake
General Manager, Technical: Kiyoshi Nakamura
Senior Corporate Auditor: Kazunari Moriya
Auditors: KPMG AZSA & Co.

LOCATIONS

HQ: Shiseido Company, Limited
  5-5, Ginza 7-chome, Chuo-ku,
  Tokyo 104-0061, Japan
Phone: +81-3-3572-5111   **Fax:** +81-3-3289-1235
US HQ: 900 3rd Ave., New York, NY 10022
US Phone: 212-805-2300   **US Fax:** 212-688-0109
Web: www.shiseido.co.jp

2006 Sales

	% of total
Asia & Oceania	
Japan	71
Other countries	9
Europe	13
Americas	7
Total	**100**

PRODUCTS/OPERATIONS

2006 Sales

	% of total
Cosmetics	80
Toiletries	9
Other	11
Total	**100**

Selected Brands and Operations

Mass Market
  Aquair
  SuperMild
Middle Market
  Aspril
  Ayura
  Uno
Prestige
  Aupres
  Carita
  Shiseido
High Prestige
  Clé de Peau Beauté
Other Operations
  Chromatography products (chemical analysis
    equipment)
  Fine chemicals (photochromic titanium dioxide
    pigment)
  Laboratoires Decléor (French cosmetics and
    aromatherapy products)
  Shiseido Pharmaceutical Co., Ltd.
  Zotos International, Inc. (research and development
    facilities)

COMPETITORS

Alberto-Culver	Kao
Alticor	L'Oréal
Avon	Mary Kay
Bath & Body Works	Procter & Gamble
Beiersdorf	Revlon
Body Shop	Revlon
Chanel	Shu Uemura
Colgate-Palmolive	Unilever
Estée Lauder	Wella
Henkel	Yves Saint-Laurent
Inter Parfums	

HISTORICAL FINANCIALS

Company Type: Public

Income Statement

	REVENUE ($ mil.)	NET INCOME ($ mil.)	NET PROFIT MARGIN	EMPLOYEES
3/06	5,706	123	2.2%	25,781
3/05	5,949	(82)	—	24,184
3/04	5,909	261	4.4%	24,839
3/03	5,184	204	3.9%	25,202
3/02	4,448	(172)	—	25,021
Annual Growth	**6.4%**	**—**		**0.8%**

FYE: March 31

Net Income History

OTC: SSDOY

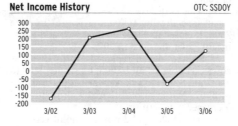

Siemens

Thinking globally and acting locally is more than semantics for Siemens. The company is Europe's largest electronics and electrical engineering firm and has operations worldwide in the industrial automation and control, information and communications, lighting, medical, power transmission, and transportation sectors. Siemens is a leading global manufacturer of telecom network equipment, which it provides through its Siemens Communications Group. The company supplies computer products through a joint venture called Fujitsu Siemens. Its financial services unit offers corporate financing, fund management, insurance, and risk management services. Its US-based holding company is called Siemens Corporation.

Siemens acquired Diagnostic Products Corporation (DPC), a maker of immunodiagnostic systems, for about $1.9 billion in 2006. On the heels of the DPC announcement the company made plans to further bolster its medical unit, agreeing to acquire the diagnostics division of Bayer for more than $5 billion. It is integrating both companies into its Siemens Medical Solutions unit.

Siemens purchase of Diagnostic Products follows a string of acquisitions made in 2005. It bought medical-imaging equipment maker CTI Molecular Imaging in a deal valued at about $1 billion; it bolstered its financial services division, especially in the medical equipment financing sector, with the acquisition of UK-based financial services firm Broadcastle; and it purchased Flender Holding, a German supplier of gear systems, from a unit of Citigroup in a deal valued at $1.5 billion.

The company sold its minority stake in chip maker Infineon Technologies in 2006.

Also in 2006 the company announced that it was combining its mobile network operations with those of Nokia, creating a joint venture called Nokia Siemens Networks. Each company will own 50% of the joint venture, which will combine Nokia's network business group and Siemens' carrier-related operations.

HISTORY

In 1847 electrical engineer Werner von Siemens and craftsman Johann Halske formed Siemens & Halske. The firm's first major project linked Berlin and Frankfurt with the first long-distance telegraph system in Europe (1848). In 1870 it completed a 6,600-mile telegraph line from London to Calcutta, India, and in 1874 it made the first transatlantic cable, linking Ireland to the US.

The company's history of firsts includes Europe's first electric power transmission system (1876), the world's first electrified railway (1879), and one of the first elevators (1880). In 1896 it patented the world's first X-ray tube and completed the first European subway, in Budapest, Hungary.

By the next century it had formed light-bulb cartel OSRAM with German rivals AEG and Auer (1919) and created a venture with Furukawa Electric called Fuji Electric (1923). It developed radios and traffic lights in the 1920s and began producing electron microscopes in 1939.

Siemens & Halske played a critical role in Germany's war effort in WWII and suffered heavy losses. During the 1950s it recovered by developing data processing equipment, silicates for semiconductors, and the first implantable pacemaker. It moved into the nuclear industry in 1959 when its first reactor went into service at Munich-Garching. In 1966 the company reincorporated as Siemens AG. It formed joint ventures with Bosch (BSH Bosch und Siemens Hausergäte, appliances, 1967) and AEG (Kraftwerk Union, nuclear power, 1969), among others. AEG dropped out of Kraftwerk Union (now Siemens Power Generation) in 1977.

In 1981 Karlheinz Kaske became the first CEO from outside the von Siemens family. Under his lead the firm entered joint ventures with Philips, Intel, and Advanced Micro Devices. In 1988 and 1989 it made several buys, including Bendix Electronics (US), and was a willing buyer when IBM wanted to unload Rolm (then the #1 maker of PBXs). It had acquired all of Rolm's businesses by 1992. That year Heinrich von Pierer replaced Kaske as CEO.

The 1990s saw more consolidation: Siemens and German computer maker Nixdorf combined computer businesses to form Siemens Nixdorf Informationssysteme (SNI, 1990); the firm acquired Sylvania's North American lamp business from GTE and merged it with the OSRAM companies in North America to form OSRAM Sylvania (1993).

The Asian economic crisis combined with other factors to make 1998 the worst year in the company's 150-year history. That year Siemens sold its defense electronics operations to British Aerospace (now BAE SYSTEMS) and Daimler-Benz (now DaimlerChrysler) and bought CBS's power generation business (formerly Westinghouse Electric).

In 1999 Siemens held an IPO for its passive components and electron tubes unit. It spun off its semiconductor operations into Infineon Technologies, but kept a 71% stake after Infineon's IPO in 2000. In 2000 BSH paid $9.2 billion for the engineering and automotive parts unit Atecs Mannesmann. Also that year Siemens boosted its IT Service unit in the US by purchasing information services company ENTEX, and it agreed to merge its nuclear business with Framatome's.

Siemens shares began trading on the New York Stock Exchange in 2001. The company bought Dallas-based Efficient Networks for $1.5 billion that year. The slump in the telecommunications industry hurt Siemens that year, and the company cut 9,700 jobs.

Late in 2001 Siemens cut its stake in Infineon Technologies to less than 50%, and in 2002 it announced an additional 6,500 jobs to be cut from its telecom unit. It continued to trim its information and communications holdings with the 2002 sale of Unisphere Networks to Juniper Networks. Later that year, the company sold seven noncore subsidiaries (including Mannesmann Plastics Machinery, Demag Cranes & Components, and Gottwald Port Technology) to buyout firm Kohlberg Kravis Roberts for $1.7 billion.

Siemens in 2004 bought the equipment, treatment, and technology components of US Filter for more than $990 million in cash as part of its expansion into the US. The purchase was intended to strengthen its presence in the industrial water treatment and supply equipment market and to help it better compete against General Electric.

In early 2005, CEO von Pierer was named chairman and stepped down as chief executive. Klaus Kleinfeld, CEO of US subsidiary Siemens Corporation, was named to the top spot at Siemens AG.

EXECUTIVES

Chairman of the Supervisory Board:
Heinrich von Pierer, age 65, $848,137 pay
Second Deputy Chairman of the Supervisory Board:
Josef Ackermann, age 58
First Deputy Chairman of the Supervisory Board:
Ralf Heckmann, age 57
President, CEO, Member of the Corporate Executive Committee, and Member of the Management Board:
Klaus Kleinfeld, age 49, $2,069,992 pay
EVP, Member of the Corporate Executive Committee, and Member of the Managing Board:
Prof Edward G. Krubasik, age 62, $1,597,288 pay
EVP, Chief Personnel Officer, Member of the Corporate Executive Committee, and Member of the Managing Board: Jürgen Radomski, age 65, $1,597,288 pay
EVP, Member of the Corporate Executive Committee, and Member of the Managing Board: Uriel J. Sharef, age 62, $1,597,726 pay
EVP, Member of the Corporate Executive Committee, and Member of the Managing Board: Klaus Wucherer, age 62, $1,597,288 pay
EVP, Member of the Corporate Executive Committee, and Member of the Managing Board:
Johannes Feldmayer, age 50, $1,597,288 pay
CFO and Member of the Corporate Executive Committee: Joe Kaeser, age 48
Group President, Communications Group:
Eduardo Montes Pérez, age 54
Group President, Siemens VDO Automotive AG:
Wolfgang Dehen
EVP, Member of the Corporate Executive Committee, and Member of the Managing Board:
Rudolf (Rudi) Lamprecht, age 58, $1,597,288 pay
SVP, Member of the Managing Board; Group President, Siemens Medical Solutions: Erich R. Reinhardt, age 60, $1,242,683 pay
Group President, Industrial Solutions and Services:
Joergen-Ole Haslestad

Group President, Transportation Systems:
Hans M. Schabert
Group President, Power Generation: Klaus Voges
Member, Management Board and CTO:
Hermann Requardt, age 51
Corporate Information Office: Volkhart P. Matthäus
Management Consulting Personnel: Karl-Heinz Sämann
Corporate Communications: Janos Gönczöl
Auditors: KPMG Deutsche Treuhand-Gesellschaft AG

LOCATIONS

HQ: Siemens AG
Wittelsbacherplatz 2, D-80333 Munich, Germany
Phone: +49-89-636-00   **Fax:** +49-89-636-52-000
US HQ: Citicorp Center, 153 E. 53rd St.,
New York, NY 10022
US Phone: 212-258-4000   **US Fax:** 212-767-0580
Web: www.siemens.com

2006 Sales

	% of total
Europe	
Germany	19
Other countries	31
Americas	
US	20
Other countries	6
Asia/Pacific	15
Africa, Middle East & former Soviet republics	9
Total	**100**

PRODUCTS/OPERATIONS

2006 Sales

	% of total
Communications	15
Automation & Drives	13
Power Generation	12
Siemens VDO Automotive	11
Medical Solutions	9
Industrial Solutions & Services	9
Power Transmission & Distribution	7
Siemens Building Technologies	5
OSRAM	5
Transportation Systems	5
Siemens Business Services	4
Other	5
Total	**100**

COMPETITORS

ABB	Intel
Abbott Labs	Invensys
Accenture	Johnson Controls
Affiliated Computer	MAN
Alcatel-Lucent	Matsushita
ALSTOM	McKesson
AREVA	Microsoft
Avaya	Mitsubishi Electric
Beckman Coulter	Motorola
Bombardier	NEC
Capgemini	Nokia
Cerner	Nortel Networks
Cisco Systems	Philips Electronics
CIT Group	Phonak
Computer Sciences Corp.	Robert Bosch
Dade Behring	Roche Diagnostics
Danfoss Turbocor	Rockwell Automation
Delphi	SAP
Deutsche Telekom AG	Schneider Electric
Dresser-Rand	Shell Solar
EDS	Starkey Laboratories
Emerson Electric	Texas Instruments
Ericsson	Toshiba
GE	Tyco
Hewlett-Packard	United Technologies
Hitachi	UTStarcom
Hologic	Varian Medical Systems
Honeywell ACS	Visteon
Huawei Technologies	Wavecom
IBM	ZTE
Infineon Technologies	

HISTORICAL FINANCIALS

Company Type: Public

Income Statement

FYE: September 30

	REVENUE ($ mil.)	NET INCOME ($ mil.)	NET PROFIT MARGIN	EMPLOYEES
9/06	110,798	3,848	3.5%	475,000
9/05	90,896	2,708	3.0%	461,000
9/04	92,688	4,199	4.5%	424,000
9/03	86,088	2,836	3.3%	411,000
9/02	82,437	2,548	3.1%	426,000
Annual Growth	7.7%	10.9%	—	2.8%

2006 Year-End Financials

Debt ratio: 45.7%   Current ratio: 1.32
Return on equity: 11.0%   Long-term debt ($ mil.): 17,001
Cash ($ mil.): 13,716

Net Income History

NYSE: SI

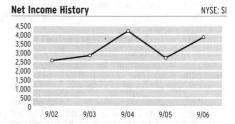

Sime Darby Berhad

Malaysia's oldest and largest conglomerate, Sime Darby started in rubber and stretched out. Its core business activities include the distribution of autos (BMW, Ford, Land Rover) and heavy equipment (Caterpillar); tire manufacturing; oil palm and rubber plantations; production of edible oils; residential and commercial property development; and the construction and operation of power plants. The general trading arm distributes products such as advanced composite materials, auto parts, and sealants. It also has stakes in hotels, hypermarkets, and medical facilities. Germany-based tire manufacturer Continental AG has acquired a 30% stake in Sime Darby's tire operations with an option to purchase a larger share.

Amid continued economic weakness in many of the Asian nations in which it does business, Sime Darby has worked to control costs and to limit acquisitions to companies that operate in its core business areas. It has also sought to expand in Australia.

In 2005 the group also revealed its plan to expand its Indonesian plantation operations and auto assembly business. It opened talks to purchase up to 65,000 hectares of palm oil plantation land on Borneo island. On the auto front, Sime Darby announced it would assemble the Hyundai Getz, a compact car, at a Malaysian plant within the year. It also acquired Special Brand, an importer and distributor of vehicles, in December 2005.

In February 2006 Sime Darby said it would buy out minority shareholders of Hyundai-Sime Darby and transform it into a wholly owned subsidiary.

HISTORY

William Sime, a 37-year-old Scottish adventurer, convinced Henry Darby, a wealthy 50-year-old English banker, that money could be made in rubber, a product that had just been introduced to Malaya from Brazil. Together they established Sime, Darby & Co., Ltd., in 1910 to manage about 500 acres of rubber estates in the jungles of Malacca, Malaya. To overcome local hostility to their venture, the pair maintained close links with the Chinese business community.

Riding a rubber boom, Sime, Darby became a managing agent for other plantations before moving into general trading. In 1915 it set up a branch office in Singapore and formed a London office for marketing. To clear jungle and meet growing demand for rubber, in 1929 Sime, Darby bought Sarawak Trading, which held a franchise for Caterpillar earth-moving equipment. In 1936 Sime, Darby moved its headquarters to Singapore.

In 1958 Sime Darby Holdings Ltd. was incorporated in England as successor to Sime, Darby & Co., Ltd. When demand for rubber softened in the 1960s, it was one of the first plantations to diversify into palm oil and cocoa production. It acquired the Seafield Estate and Consolidated Plantations in the 1970s, becoming a dominant force in Malaysian plantations while it started processing crops into finished products. Success of the switch to oil palms allowed the conglomerate's autocratic British CEO, Denis Pinder, to gobble up numerous firms. In 1973 allegations appeared in newspapers about improprieties at "Slime Darby." Pinder ended up in Changi prison on misdemeanor charges. The mysterious death of Sime Darby's outside auditor, found stabbed in his bathtub, was ruled a suicide.

After Pinder's successor upset Malaysians by investing in unsuccessful European ventures, Pernas (the Malaysian government trading corporation) bought Sime Darby shares on the London Stock Exchange and demanded an Asian majority be placed on the board. Outmaneuvered, the British lost control of Sime Darby in 1976. The only man acceptable as chairman to both Asian and British board members was Tun Tan Siew Sin, a former Malaysian finance minister and son of Tun Tan Cheng Lock, one of Malaysia's founding fathers. The firm, reincorporated in Malaysia as Sime Darby Berhad in 1978, moved its head office to Kuala Lumpur in 1979.

Sime Darby acquired the tire-making operations of B.F. Goodrich Philippines in 1981 and the Apple Computer franchise for southeast Asia in 1982. It bought an interest in United Estates, a Malaysian property development firm, two years later. In 1989 Sime Darby bought Dur-A-Vend, a UK condom wholesaler marketing a product called Jiffy with the slogan "Do it in a Jiffy." Sime Darby moved into tourism in 1991, acquiring Sandestin Resorts in Florida.

Expanding its financial portfolio in 1996, Sime Darby acquired control of United Malayan Banking (breaking it up into Sime Bank and SimeSecurities). The next year it consolidated its travel-related holdings into its Sime Wings unit. Hurt by regional financial turmoil, Sime Darby in 1999 sold Sime Bank and SimeSecurities to Malaysian financier Tan Sri Rashid Hussain.

In 1999 it divested Sandestin Resorts, LEC Refrigeration, and its 7% stake in British chemical firm Elements. Despite its streamlining, the firm could not resist picking up power generation assets as the power industry restructured. In 2000 it increased its stake in Port Dickson Power to

60%. Sime Darby also sold its insurance operations that year.

In 2003 Sime Darby sold a 30% stake in its tire business to Continental AG. Continental has an option to purchase an additional 21% in the future.

EXECUTIVES

Chairman: Tan Sri Dato' Seri Ahmad Sarji bin Abdul Hamid, age 67
Deputy Chairman: Tunku Tan Sri Dato' Seri Ahmad bin Tunku Yahaya, age 76
Group Chief Executive and Director: Dato' Ahmad Zubair Ahmad Zubir Bin Haji Murshid, age 48
Group CFO: Sekhar Krishnan
Director of Business Development: Martin G. Manen
Managing Director, Consolidated Plantations Berhad and Divisional Director, Plantations Division: YBhg Datuk Syed Tamin Syed Mohamed
Managing Director, Hastings Deering (Australia) and Divisional Director, Heavy Equipment Distribution: Scott Cameron
Managing Director, Sime Engineering Services and Divisional Director, Energy: Mohamad Shukri bin Baharom
Managing Director, Sime UEP Properties and Divisional Director, Property Development: Jauhari bin Hamidi
Managing Director, Tractors Malaysia Holdings Berhad and Divisional Director, Heavy Equipment Distribution: Azhar Bin Abdul Hamid
Divisional Director, Allied Products and Services: Tuan Haji Mohamed Ja'far bin Abdul Carrim
Divisional Director, Motor: Yip Jon Khiam
Group Secretary and Tax Controller: Nancy P. Y. Yeoh
Auditors: PricewaterhouseCoopers

LOCATIONS

HQ: Sime Darby Berhad
Wisma Sime Darby, 21st Fl., Jalan Raja Laut, 50350 Kuala Lumpur, Malaysia
Phone: +60-3-2691-4122   **Fax:** +60-3-2698-7398
Web: www.simenet.com

2006 Sales

	% of total
Malaysia	31
China	21
Australia	20
Singapore	14
Other countries	14
Total	**100**

PRODUCTS/OPERATIONS

2006 Sales

	% of total
Motor vehicles	41
Heavy equipment	28
Energy & utilities	9
Plantations	7
Property	4
General trading, services & other	11
Total	**100**

COMPETITORS

Ansell
Bridgestone
Cummins
DaimlerChrysler
General Motors
Goodyear
Hopewell Holdings
HSBC Holdings
Hutchison Whampoa
Jardine Matheson
Joy Global
Komatsu
Marubeni
Michelin
Swire Pacific

HISTORICAL FINANCIALS

Company Type: Public

Income Statement

FYE: June 30

	REVENUE ($ mil.)	NET INCOME ($ mil.)	NET PROFIT MARGIN	EMPLOYEES
6/06	5,474	304	5.6%	28,770
6/05	4,906	211	4.3%	24,916
6/04	3,923	242	6.2%	24,405
6/03	3,612	213	5.9%	27,484
6/02	3,164	202	6.4%	26,384
Annual Growth	**14.7%**	**10.7%**	**—**	**2.2%**

Net Income History

Pink Sheets: SIDBY

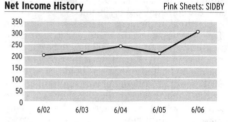

Singapore Airlines

For people in Singapore, traveling very far means traveling by air, and that means Singapore Airlines (SIA). The carrier flies to more than 60 cities in about 35 countries, primarily in the Asia/Pacific region but also in Europe and North America. It boasts a fleet of about 90 aircraft. SIA extends its network via code-sharing with fellow members of the Star Alliance marketing partnership, such as Lufthansa. Besides its main passenger transportation business, SIA units include regional carrier SilkAir and SIA Cargo, which operates about 15 freighters. In addition, SIA owns a 49% stake in UK-based Virgin Atlantic Airways. The Singapore government owns 56% of SIA through Temasek Holdings.

Airline operations account for some 95% of SIA's sales. The company's other businesses include Singapore Airport Terminal Services (SATS), which provides catering, security, and cargo handling to SIA and other airlines, and SIA Engineering, which offers aircraft maintenance and repair.

SIA is adding destinations to its network, mainly in Asia, and increasing the frequency of service on high-demand routes. In addition, the company is preparing to add the Airbus A380 superjumbo jet to its fleet.

HISTORY

Singapore Airlines (SIA) was formed as Malayan Airways in 1937 but did not begin scheduled service until 1947, when the Mansfield & Co. shipping line used it to link Singapore with other Malayan cities. The airline added service to Vietnam, Sumatra, and Java by 1951 and opened routes to Borneo, Brunei, Burma, and Thailand by 1958.

Meanwhile, British Overseas Airways Corporation (BOAC, predecessor of British Airways) bought 10% of Malayan in 1948 and raised its stake to 30% in 1959. Australia's Qantas Airways also took a 30% stake in Malayan that year. In 1963 the governments of Singapore, Malaya,

Sarawak, and Sabah merged to form Malaysia, inspiring Malayan to change its name to Malaysian Airways. Singapore seceded from the federation in 1965 but joined Malaysia to buy control of the airline from BOAC and Qantas in 1966, changing the name to Malaysia-Singapore Airlines.

The carrier extended service to Bombay, Melbourne, Rome, and London in 1971 and then to Osaka, Athens, Zurich, and Frankfurt in 1972. That year managerial disagreements led Malaysia and Singapore to dissolve the company to form two separate national airlines: The domestic network went to the Malaysian Airline System, and international routes went to SIA. Joe Pillay of Singapore's ministry of finance became SIA's first chairman. The government owned 82%, and employees held 17%.

SIA initiated such now well-known amenities as free drinks, hot towels, and headsets in 1972, thereby gaining a reputation for outstanding service. By 1974 it served 25 cities worldwide. It added flights to Auckland and Paris in 1976, Tehran and Copenhagen in 1977, and San Francisco, its first US destination, in 1978.

In 1985 the government reduced its stake in SIA to 63%. The company joined Cathay Pacific and Thai International in 1988 to form Abacus, a computer reservation system for Asia/Pacific carriers. The next year SIA bought stakes in Delta Air Lines and Swissair; the three created a route network reaching 82 countries. The Singapore airline also snagged a 40% stake in Royal Air Cambodge from the Cambodian government in 1993. In 1995 SIA ordered 77 Boeing 777s for delivery between 1997 and 2004.

The US and Singapore governments signed an "open skies" agreement in 1997 (the first between the US and an Asian nation), allowing unlimited flights between the two countries, but SIA canceled its alliance with Delta and Swissair in favor of one with Germany's Lufthansa.

A December 1997 crash of a new SilkAir 737 killed all 104 people on board; investigators speculated that the crash was an act of suicide by the pilot. (Two years later SIA agreed to pay each family settlements of up to $195,000.) The Asian crisis added to the airline's woes, but SIA was able to cut costs when the government reduced contributions to the national pension plan and the Singapore airport lowered landing fees.

In 1999 SIA implemented code-sharing with SAS, and soon SIA announced it would join SAS in the global Star Alliance marketing network. After failed attempts to buy into South African Airways and Australia Ansett, SIA bought a 49% stake in UK carrier Virgin Atlantic for some $960 million, acquired 25% of Air New Zealand (reduced to 7% in 2001), and joined the Star Alliance in 2000. Also that year 82 passengers died when Singapore Airlines flight SQ006 crashed into debris on an out-of-service runway.

SIA spun off its cargo operations, SIA Cargo, in 2001. Later in the year SIA Cargo formed an alliance with Lufthansa Cargo, SAS, and Deutsche Post.

In the airline industry downturn that followed the September 11, 2001, attacks on the US, SIA was forced to tighten its belt. By the next year, however, nearly all of the service that the carrier had suspended had been restored.

The airline trimmed its schedule and cut jobs in 2003 because of decreased demand for air travel to Asia, which stemmed in part from fears of the SARS virus.

SIA sold its remaining stake in Air New Zealand in 2004.

EXECUTIVES

Chairman: Stephen Ching Yen Lee
CEO and Director: Chew Choon Seng
SEVP, Operations and Services: Bey Soo Khiang
EVP, Marketing and the Regions: Huang Cheng Eng
SVP, Cabin Crew: Tan Pee Teck
SVP, Corporate Services: Teoh Tee Hooi
SVP, Engineering: Mervyn Sirisena
SVP, Europe: Theong Tjhoen Onn
SVP, Finance: Chan Hon Chew
SVP, Flight Operations: Gerard Yeap Beng Hock
SVP, Human Resources and Company Secretary: Loh Meng See
SVP, North Asia: Ng Kian Wah
SVP, Planning: Mak Swee Wah
SVP, Product and Services: Yap Kim Wah
SVP, Southeast Asia, Korea, and Japan: Teh Ping Choon
SVP, Special Projects: Hwang Teng Aun
SVP, West Asia and Africa: Tan Chik Quee
Regional VP, Americas: Subhas Menon
VP, Marketing USA: Ken Bright
President and CEO, SIA Engineering Company: William S. K. Tan
President and CEO, Singapore Airport Terminal Services: Ng Chin Hwee
President, Singapore Airlines Cargo: Goh Choon Phong
Chief Executive, SilkAir: Mike Barclay
Auditors: Ernst & Young

LOCATIONS

HQ: Singapore Airlines Limited
Airline House, 25 Airline Rd., 819829, Singapore
Phone: +65-6541-4885   **Fax:** +65-6542-3002
US HQ: 5670 Wilshire Blvd., Ste. 1800,
Los Angeles, CA 90036
US Phone: 323-934-8833   **US Fax:** 323-934-4482
Web: www.singaporeair.com

2006 Airline Operations Revenue

	% of total
East Asia	44
Europe	15
Southwest Pacific	12
America	8
West Asia & Africa	7
Non-scheduled services & other	14
Total	**100**

PRODUCTS/OPERATIONS

2006 Sales

	% of total
Airline operations	95
Airport terminal services	3
Engineering services	2
Total	**100**

Selected Subsidiaries and Affiliates

SIA Engineering Company Limited (87%, engine maintenance and repair)
SIA Properties (Pte) Ltd. (building services)
SilkAir (Singapore) Private Limited (regional airline)
Singapore Airlines Cargo Private Limited (SIA Cargo)
Singapore Airport Terminal Services Limited (87%)
    SATS Airport Services Pte. Ltd.
    SATS Catering Pte. Ltd.
    SATS Security Services Private Ltd.
Singapore Aviation and General Insurance Company (Pte) Limited
Singapore Flying College Pte. Ltd.
Virgin Atlantic Limited (49%, holding company for Virgin Atlantic Airways, UK)

COMPETITORS

Air France-KLM	Delta Air
AMR Corp.	Garuda Indonesia
British Airways	Japan Airlines
Cathay Pacific	Korean Air
China Airlines	Malaysian Airlines
China Eastern Airlines	Northwest Airlines
China Southern Airlines	Qantas
Continental Airlines	

HISTORICAL FINANCIALS

Company Type: Public

Income Statement

FYE: March 31

	REVENUE ($ mil.)	NET INCOME ($ mil.)	NET PROFIT MARGIN	EMPLOYEES
3/06	8,234	808	9.8%	28,558
3/05	7,271	841	11.6%	28,146
3/04	5,796	504	8.7%	29,734
3/03	5,934	601	10.1%	30,243
3/02	5,123	343	6.7%	29,316
Annual Growth	**12.6%**	**23.9%**	**—**	**(0.7%)**

Net Income History

Singapore: SIA

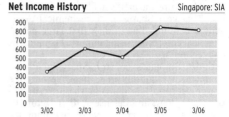

Sinopec Shanghai Petrochemical

China's own entry into the world of giant chemical companies, Sinopec Shanghai Petrochemical Company, is one of that country's largest producers of ethylene, a crucial ingredient in the manufacture of synthetic fibers, resins, and plastics. It also makes petroleum-based fuels and oils and other intermediate petrochemicals such as benzene. The company, which operates primarily within China (most of its revenues are from eastern China), has joint ventures with UK company BP, US firm Dow Chemical, and Japan's ITOCHU Corporation. China Petroleum & Chemical (Sinopec), which is controlled by the Chinese government, owns about 55% of Shanghai Petrochemical.

Throughout the first half of the decade more and more foreign chemical companies have gained entrance into the Chinese petrochemical market, increasing competition for Shanghai Petrochemical. Thus far the company isn't overly concerned about the trend, as the opening of the market has substantially increased its customer base and demand for its products.

In anticipation of China's admission to the World Trade Organization, Shanghai Petrochemical Company began to overhaul its production facilities. The upgrades have enabled the company to process 10 million tons of crude oil per year, along with 1 million tons of ethylene and other synthetic fiber materials. The current quality of Chinese ethylene is generally inferior to that produced in developed countries. The upgrades have allowed the company to produce world-class polyethylene and polypropylene, which it can use domestically and sell on the world market.

HISTORY

The Mao-inspired Cultural Revolution of the 1960s restored the aging leader's political grip, but it also caused immense economic disruptions in China, including a virtual shutdown of foreign trade. In the early 1970s party reformists led by Zhou Enlai and Deng Xiaoping advocated improved contact with the outside world and the restoration of foreign trade, giving the Chinese economy access to much-needed technology. In 1972, the year President Nixon's visit to China restored Sino-US ties, China began contracting for plant and equipment imports, especially in the petrochemical areas of chemical fertilizers for agriculture and artificial fibers for industrial use. That year Shanghai Petrochemical Company was founded as China's first large petrochemical enterprise, using imported equipment and technology.

Under Sinopec's control, Shanghai Petrochemical fit squarely into the government's Four Modernizations policy (agriculture, industry, technology, and defense). Other factors in the firm's growth were the booming economies of the coastal cities in the east and south, made possible by economic liberalization policies that encouraged foreign investment. The Guangdong province in the south led the way as Hong Kong enterprise migrated there in the 1980s in search of lower wages and overhead. The expansion of industrial output there and in other provinces resulted in greatly increased demand for petrochemicals.

Emboldened by growth and further reforms in the oil industry, Sinopec restructured Shanghai Petrochemical in 1993 and listed it on the Hong Kong and New York stock markets. (It was the first Chinese company listed on the New York Stock Exchange.) The company formed a joint venture with US-based agribusiness giant Continental Grain in 1995 to build a liquid petroleum gas plant and teamed up with British Petroleum (now BP) to build an acrylonitrile plant. The company entered a joint venture with Union Carbide (purchased by Dow Chemical) in 1996 to build a polymer emulsion plant in China. Shanghai Petrochemical increased its market share for acrylics with its 1997 purchase of the Zhejiang Acrylic Fibre Plant, then a producer of about 40% of China's total acrylic-fiber output. Annual production grew to 130,000 tons by 1999.

Three broad-reaching events have hammered the company's profits: the Asian economic crisis, the decrease of Sinopec's subsidy on crude oil, and a global oversupply of petrochemicals. In 1997 Shanghai Petrochemical's product-mix adjustments, combined with cost cutting, offset some of the increased crude costs and lower prices. The company announced in 1998 that the Chinese government planned to crack down on the smuggling of foreign petrochemicals and help the domestic market. The firm remains vulnerable to policy changes, however. Additionally, consolidation of the Chinese petrochemical industry could translate into lost jobs. The company continued to modernize its facilities and increase its capacity in 2000 when it moved to upgrade operations in order to become a world-class production base for petrochemicals and derivatives.

EXECUTIVES

Chairman: Lu Yiping, age 59
Vice Chairman and President: Rong Guangdao, age 49
Vice Chairman: Du Chongjun, age 50
CFO and Director: Han Zhihao, age 53
VP: Tang Chengjian, age 49
VP and Director: Wu Haijun, age 42
VP: Zhang Jianping, age 42
VP: Yin Jihai, age 47
VP: Shi Wei, age 45
VP: Zhang Zhiliang, age 51
Executive Director: Gao Jinping, age 38
Company Secretary: Zhang Jingming, age 47
Auditors: KPMG

LOCATIONS

HQ: Sinopec Shanghai Petrochemical Company Limited (Sinopec Shanghai Shiyou Huagong Gufen Youxien Gongsi)
48 Jinyi Rd., Jinshan District,
Shanghai 200540, China
Phone: +86-21-5794-1941   **Fax:** +86-21-5794-2267
Web: www.spc.com.cn

Sinopec Shanghai Petrochemical Company operates primarily in China.

PRODUCTS/OPERATIONS

2005 Sales

	% of total
Intermediate petrochemicals	31
Petroleum products	31
Resins & plastics	22
Synthetic fibers	7
Other	9
Total	**100**

Selected Products

Intermediate Petrochemicals
  Benzene
  Butadiene
  Ethylene
  Ethylene glycol
  Ethylene oxide
Petroleum Products
  Diesel
  Gasoline
  Jet oil
  Residual oil
Resins and Plastics
  LDPE film and pellets
  Polyester chips
  PP pellets
  PVA
Synthetic Fibers
  Acrylic staple
  Acrylic top
  Polyester filament-POY
  Polyester staple
  PP fiber
  PVA fiber

COMPETITORS

BASF AG
DuPont
ExxonMobil Chemical
Formosa Plastics
Jilin Chemical
Marubeni
Shell Chemicals
Sinopec Beijing Yanhua Petrochemical

HISTORICAL FINANCIALS

Company Type: Public

Income Statement

FYE: December 31

	REVENUE ($ mil.)	NET INCOME ($ mil.)	NET PROFIT MARGIN	EMPLOYEES
12/05	5,678	232	4.1%	25,481
12/04	4,761	501	10.5%	28,451
12/03	3,502	190	5.4%	31,008
12/02	2,641	136	5.1%	31,489
Annual Growth	**29.1%**	**19.4%**	**—**	**(6.8%)**

2005 Year-End Financials

Debt ratio: 7.8%
Return on equity: 10.1%
Cash ($ mil.): 255
Current ratio: 1.22
Long-term debt ($ mil.): 183
No. of shares (mil.): —
Dividends
  Yield: 6.4%
  Payout: 74.8%
Market value ($ mil.): —

Stock History

NYSE: SHI

	STOCK PRICE ($) FY Close	P/E High/Low		PER SHARE ($) Earnings	Dividends
12/05	38.00	14	9	3.22	2.41
12/04	37.30	—	—	—	0.97
12/03	46.26	—	—	—	0.60
12/02	14.95	—	—	—	—
Annual Growth	**36.5%**	**—**		**—**	**100.4%**

SNCF

France's state-owned railway company, Société Nationale des Chemins de Fer Français (SNCF), is still blazing a trail as the nation's primary provider of local and long-distance passenger and freight service. Passenger transportation accounts for a majority of the company's sales. SNCF's Eurostar joint venture shuttles passengers between Paris and London via the Channel Tunnel, and Thalys links Paris with other European capitals. SNCF's high-speed TGV passenger trains travel at up to 250 mph. In addition, the company carries about 50 billion ton-km of freight annually. SNCF owns stakes in dozens of other passenger and freight transportation companies.

Holdings managed by the rail company's main investment arm, SNCF-Participations, include stakes in Keolis (45%), a French bus operator that also has operations in Canada and Germany; Geodis, one of France's largest transport and logistics groups; and Seafrance, a ferry operator.

To be a major player in Europe's increasingly deregulated road and rail transport network, SNCF is forging cross-border alliances: Transnational ventures have included working with Deutsche Bahn to design a European high-speed rail system, operating a bus and rail joint venture with UK-based Go-Ahead Group, and joining the UK's FirstGroup in bidding for a UK rail franchise.

HISTORY

France's first railway line, opened in 1827, was used to haul coal from Saint-Etienne to the port of Andrezieux. Four years later the first steam locomotives and passenger service were introduced between Saint-Etienne and Lyon. Paris opened its first rail line in 1837. Although the early railway companies were under private ownership, the state controlled the network of rail lines through licensing. Under Napoleon III's Second Empire (1852-1870), the government encouraged an expansion of railway lines that linked Paris to every major town and city in France. By 1870 the main routes of France's modern railway system had been laid; in 1914 the network system had grown to nearly 40,000 km.

After the devastation of WWI, railway companies invested heavily in rebuilding. Burdened by debt, the rail network was forced to seek government intervention for its survival. In 1938 the government set up Société Nationale des Chemins de Fer Français to unify the five largest railway systems: Compagnie de l'Est, Compagnie du Midi, Compagnie du Nord, Compagnie du Paris-Lyon-Méditerranée, and Compagnie du Paris-Orléans.

Although WWII destroyed the French railway system for a second time, the massive rebuilding enabled postwar French governments to adopt modern innovations. In 1950 SNCF began a systemwide electrification of its tracks; a decade later 7,600 km of its major lines were powered by electricity.

SNCF also pioneered the development of fast trains. Following an overhaul of SNCF in the early 1970s, the company continued to develop high-speed trains to stay competitive with airlines. In 1981 the company's TGV (*train à grande vitesse*) hit a record speed of 380 kph (236 mph). TGVs entered commercial service that year. By 1987 some 43 cities were connected to Paris by TGVs.

To add to its European logistics and freight services, SNCF acquired 20% of Spanish trucking firm TRANSFESA in 1993. In 1995 it launched Eurostar, a London-Paris service using the newly opened Channel Tunnel. Partners in the joint venture were Belgian National Railroads (Société Nationale des Chemins de Fer Belges) and European Passenger Services, the British Rail unit later spun off as Eurostar (UK). That year SNCF saw its operations disrupted by a nationwide rail strike that lasted three weeks. In 1995 SNCF also created road transport and logistics group Géodis, which it privatized a year later.

Diversifying further, SNCF also entered telecommunications in 1996 and set up a communications network to lease spare capacity. That year the company's chairman resigned following charges of corruption related to his tenure at an oil company. SNCF, also plagued by debts and strikes, decided to get back on track. It began restructuring and appointed former Aerospatiale chief Louis Gallois to head the company. In 1997 it shifted most of its debt load to Réseau Ferré de France, which was created to manage France's rail infrastructure.

In 1999 SNCF acquired Via-GTI, France's largest privately owned public transport company, which was in a joint venture with UK transport group Go-Ahead to operate the Thameslink train franchise. That year SNCF acquired Swiss rolling stock group Ermewa; it also sold its hotel interests to Accor but formed an alliance with the hotelier to offer discount lodging.

SNCF and German railway Deutsche Bahn agreed in 2000 to collaborate on developing a new generation of high-speed trains.

SNCF's rail operations were hampered by labor unrest in 2003, capped by a strike in May and June of that year. The company responded by cutting costs.

After a decade at SNCF, Gallois left the company in 2006 to serve as co-CEO of defense group EADS.

EXECUTIVES

CEO: Guillaume Pepy, age 48
Chief Financial and Information Officer: Jean-Pierre Menanteau
Deputy Managing Director, Operations: Jacques Couvert
Deputy Managing Director, Freight: Marc Véron
Director, Communications: Bernard Emsellem
Director, Human Resources: Pierre Izard
Director, Strategy: Elisabeth Borne
Director, Voyages France Europe: Mireille Faugère
Chairman, SNCF-Participations: Claire Dreyfus-Cloarec
Secretary General: Paul Mingasson
Auditors: Ernst & Young Audit; Mazars & Guérard

LOCATIONS

HQ: Société Nationale des Chemins de Fer Français
34 rue du Commandant Mouchotte,
75699 Paris, France
Phone: +33-1-53-25-60-00   **Fax:** +33-1-53-25-61-08
Web: www.sncf.fr

COMPETITORS

Air France
Arriva
British Airways
FirstGroup
National Express Group
Stagecoach
Veolia Environnement
Virgin Group

HISTORICAL FINANCIALS

Company Type: Government-owned

Income Statement

	REVENUE ($ mil.)	NET INCOME ($ mil.)	NET PROFIT MARGIN	EMPLOYEES
12/04	30,089	441	1.5%	229,877
12/03	28,271	14	0.0%	243,944
12/02	23,243	66	0.3%	242,163
12/01	17,830	(124)	—	220,700
12/00	18,680	167	0.9%	216,605
Annual Growth	12.7%	27.5%	—	1.5%

2004 Year-End Financials

Debt ratio: 422.1%
Return on equity: 10.9%
Cash ($ mil.): 2,367

Current ratio: 0.54
Long-term debt ($ mil.): 18,541

Net Income History

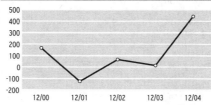

Sodexho Alliance

Sodexho Alliance has a lot of mouths to feed. The company is the world's #2 contract foodservice provider (after Compass Group), with operations in more than 75 countries. Its clients include corporations, colleges, hospitals, and public institutions. Besides foodservice, Sodexho Alliance also provides facilities management (grounds keeping, laundry), service vouchers, remote site management (including offshore rigs), and river pleasure cruises. In 2001 Sodexho Alliance bought Sodexho Marriott Services (one of the largest foodservice companies in the US) to serve as its North American subsidiary and renamed the firm Sodexho, Inc. Chairman Pierre Bellon and his family own about 37% of the company.

The company's client list spans the globe, and includes France's Peugeot and Total Fina, Sweden's Ericsson, the UK's Unilever, and Germany's Ministry of Foreign Affairs. Foodservice operations account for some 98% of the company's business. Sodexho Alliance is the largest such operator in North America through Sodexho, Inc. Its North American operations generate more than 40% of sales.

Through its Sodexho Pass subsidiary, the company's service vouchers (passes, coupons, and smart cards for food, transportation, medical care, and employee and social benefits) are used in Europe and Latin America. It operates a fleet of boats for river and harbor dinner cruises in cities such as Boston, Chicago, London, New York, Paris, Philadelphia, Seattle, and Washington, DC.

HISTORY

The Bellon family had been luxury ship hospitality specialists since the turn of the century, 60 years before Pierre Bellon founded Sodexho in 1966. By 1971 Bellon had his first contract outside France to provide food service to a Brussels hospital. Sodexho continued to expand its services into the late 1970s, entering remote site management in Africa and the Middle East in 1975 and starting its service vouchers segment in Belgium and Germany in 1978.

Sodexho jumped the pond in 1980, expanding its businesses into North and South America. The company went public on the Paris Bourse exchange in 1983. Two years later it bought Seiler, a Boston vending machine company-turned-restaurateur. Sodexho then bought San Francisco's Food Dimensions in 1987. After beefing up its American operations with four other US acquisitions, the company merged Food Dimensions and Seiler in 1989. Sodexho's US river cruise company, Spirit Cruises — an echo of the Bellon family's original calling — was also included in the merger. The merged US companies were renamed Sodexho USA in 1993.

The 1990s proved an era of growth and acquisitions for Sodexho. The company expanded into Japan, Africa, Russia, and five Eastern European countries in 1993. The company acquired a 20% stake in Corrections Corporation of America the following year and virtually doubled its size with the acquisition of the UK's Gardner Merchant in 1995. The largest catering company in that region, Gardner Merchant had holdings that spanned Australia, Asia, northern Europe, the UK, and the US — generally markets where Sodexho did not have a strong presence. That year the company also acquired Partena, a Swedish security and care company, from Volvo's Fortos.

Gardner Merchant's US business was officially merged with Sodexho USA in 1996 to make it the #4 foodservice company in the US. Also that year Sodexho acquired Brazilian service voucher company Cardapio. After a year of legal wrangling, Sodexho also lost a fight for control of Accor's Eurest France to rival caterer Compass Group and sold off its minority interest. The next year Sodexho acquired 49% of Universal Ogden Services, renamed Universal Services, an American remote site manager. To signify its efforts to maintain the individuality of the companies it acquires, Sodexho changed its name to Sodexho Alliance in 1997.

Marriott International merged its foodservice branch with Sodexho's North American foodservice operations in 1998. With a 48% stake, Sodexho Alliance became the largest shareholder; former Marriott International stockholders took the rest, with the Marriott family controlling 9%. Before the merger, Sodexho USA was less than one-fourth the size of Marriott International's foodservice division. Sodexho acquired GR Servicios Hoteleros in 1999, thereby becoming the largest caterer in Spain. The following year it agreed to merge its remote site management operations with Universal Services and rename it Universal Sodexho.

In 2001 its initial $900 million bid to buy the 52% of Sodexho Marriott Services it didn't already own was rebuffed by its subsidiary's shareholders. Sodexho Alliance made a better offer (about $1.1 billion) and finally reached an agreement to purchase the rest of Sodexho Marriott Services. The deal was completed later that year and Sodexho Marriott Services changed its name to Sodexho, Inc. Also that year the company agreed to pay some $470 million for French rival Sogeres and US-based food management firm Wood Dining.

In 2002 the company announced it had detected accounting and management errors in its UK operations, causing the value of its stock to fall by nearly one-third. In addition, the company replaced its UK management team because of poor performance there. Founder and chairman Bellon announced in 2004 that he intended to pass the title of CEO to group president and COO Michel Landel on September 1, 2005.

Admitting no wrongdoing, Sodexho settled an $80 million race-bias law suit just before it was to go to trial in 2005. The suit, brought by the African-American employees of its American subsidiary, Sodexho, Inc., charged that African-Americans were routinely passed over for promotions and were segregated within the company. In addition to paying the monetary award, Sodexho agreed to increase company diversity through promotion incentives, monitoring, and training.

In 2005 Bellon, 75, stepped down as company CEO but remained chairman. The CEO position was filled by Sodexho veteran Landel.

EXECUTIVES

Chairman: Pierre Bellon, age 76, $593,827 pay
Vice Chairman: Remí Baudin, age 76, $47,421 pay
CEO: Michel Landel, age 55, $2,104,630 pay
Group COO and CEO, Continental Europe and South America Food Management Services: Jacques Petry, age 52
Group COO and CEO, UK and Ireland Food Management Services: Philip Jansen, age 39
Group COO and CEO, Service Voucher and Cards: Pierre Henry, age 54

Group COO and President and COO, Sodexho North America: Richard (Dick) Macedonia, age 63
Group COO, CEO, Universal Sodexho Remote Sites; and CEO, Asia and Australia Food Management Services: Nicholas Japy, age 50
Group CFO: Siân Herbert-Jones, age 46
Group EVP, Marketing: Damien Verdier, age 49
Group SVP, Corporate Communications and Sustainable Development: Clodine Pincemin, age 54
Group SVP, Human Resources: Elisabeth Carpentier, age 52
Chairman, Sodexho Canada: Garry C. Knox
Group SVP, Strategic Planning: Vincent Hillenmeyer, age 40
President, Sodexho Canada: Gregory E. (Greg) Nordal, age 49
President, Sodexho/Spirit Cruises: Lorna Donatone
Investor Relations: Jean-Jacques Vironda
Auditors: PricewaterhouseCoopers

LOCATIONS

HQ: Sodexho Alliance, SA
3, avenue Newton,
78180 Montigny-le-Bretonneux, France
Phone: +33-1-30-85-75-00   **Fax:** +33-1-30-43-09-58
US HQ: 9801 Washingtonian Blvd., Ste. 1234,
Gaithersburg, MD 20878
US Phone: 301-987-4431   **US Fax:** 301-987-4444
Web: sodexho.com

Sodexho Alliance has operations in more than 76 countries.

2005 Sales

	% of total
Europe	
Continental Europe	34
UK/Ireland	12
North America	44
Other regions	10
Total	**100**

PRODUCTS/OPERATIONS

2005 Sales

	% of total
Food & management services	98
Service vouchers & cards	2
Total	**100**

COMPETITORS

Accor
American Express
ARAMARK
Aramark Uniform and Career Apparel
Autogrill
Carnival
Chartwells
Cintas
Compass Group
Creative Host Services
Crothall Services
Culinaire International
Delaware North
Expedia
First Choice
HDS Services
Healthcare Services
HMSHost
Hogg Robinson
Host America
MyTravel
priceline.com
Star Cruises
Sunlight Service
Thompson Hospitality
TQ3 Travel
TRAVIZON

HISTORICAL FINANCIALS

Company Type: Public

Income Statement

	REVENUE ($ mil.)	NET INCOME ($ mil.)	NET PROFIT MARGIN	EMPLOYEES
				FYE: August 31
8/05	14,269	190	1.3%	324,446
8/04	13,902	204	1.5%	312,975
8/03	12,905	162	1.3%	308,385
8/02	12,475	134	1.1%	315,141
Annual Growth	**4.6%**	**12.4%**	**—**	**1.0%**

2005 Year-End Financials

Debt ratio: 122.3%   Current ratio: 1.73
Return on equity: 9.6%   Long-term debt ($ mil.): 2,372
Cash ($ mil.): 1,670

Net Income History

NYSE: SDX

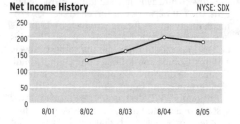

SOFTBANK

SOFTBANK's investment strategy is anything but soft. Full-throttle investing by founder, president, and CEO Masayoshi Son has molded SOFTBANK through aggressive investments in a variety of ventures. Under Son's leadership (he is hailed by many as the Bill Gates of Japan), the company has extended its investment reach across e-commerce, Internet infrastructure, telecommunications, information technology-related distribution services, publishing, marketing, and technology services. SOFTBANK complemented its 2003 purchase of Japan Telecom (now Softbank Telecom) with acquisition of the Japanese business of mobile phone company Vodafone (renamed Softbank Mobile) in 2006. Son owns more than 30% of SOFTBANK.

The company is cobbling together its holdings in telephone, broadband, and Internet services (its control of Yahoo! Japan and its minority stake in Yahoo! are the bedrock of its Internet holdings) to create a rock-solid technology front. After spending nearly $16 billion to buy Softbank Mobile, SOFTBANK said it would inject some $2 billion into the company. Through its Softbank Telecom, SOFTBANK is also taking on Japanese telecom giant NTT, offering a discounted landline phone service. Son assumed leadership of Softbank Mobile and Softbank Telecom in 2006. In an attempt to create a larger domestic market for its e-commerce and Internet companies, SOFTBANK moved aggressively into the broadband Internet connection market, providing asymmetric digital subscriber line (ADSL) services. Even though SOFTBANK still has stakes in more than 130 companies, it has been pruning some of its less-profitable holdings to reduce debt and to fund acquisitions and its high-speed Internet access business in Asia. A stock market darling during the "Internet bubble" of the late 1990s, SOFTBANK saw its stock price decline — along with its bottom line — after the bubble burst. The company ventured into such areas as banking, purchasing a major chunk of what is now Aozora Bank, which it sold in 2003. SOFTBANK regained its footing again later, though, and embarked upon its present strategy. Despite its soft spot for all things technological, SOFTBANK also shops outside the wired world: The company acquired the Fukuoka Daiei Hawks (now the Fukuoka Softbank Hawks), a professional baseball team, in 2005.

HISTORY

Ethnic Korean Masayoshi Son grew up in Japan using the name Yasumoto to conform with the Japanese policy of assimilation. In the early 1970s, the 16-year-old came to the US and began using his Korean name. Son entered the University of California at Berkeley and, while there, invented the prototype for the Sharp Wizard handheld organizer.

Bankrolled by the nearly $1 million that Sharp paid him for his patent, Son returned to Japan and founded software distributor SOFTBANK in 1981. The company got its first big break when it inked a distribution agreement with Joshin Denki, one of Japan's largest consumer electronics retailers, that year. Son used this agreement to gain exclusive distribution rights for much of the software he distributed.

SOFTBANK went public in 1994. That year, as part of an evolving plan to control digital data delivery, Son bought the trade show division of Ziff-Davis Publishing, augmenting it in 1995 with the purchase of COMDEX, the trade show operations of the Interface Group. The next year SOFTBANK bought the rest of Ziff-Davis. It also bought 80% of Kingston Technology (sold 1999) and a stake in Yahoo! — which laid the cornerstone for its Internet empire.

SOFTBANK accelerated its Internet investment pace in 1997, taking stakes in dozens of Web companies. That year it filed suit against Yell Publishing, a Japanese firm that published a book accusing SOFTBANK of issuing phony financial statements, among other improprieties.

In 1998 the firm moved into financial services, entering a joint venture with E*TRADE to offer online stock trading in Japan. SOFTBANK also took Ziff-Davis public (it retained a majority stake).

Internal changes marked 1999 when SOFTBANK merged with MAC, Son's private asset management company, and transformed itself into a holding company focused on Internet-related companies. It teamed with the National Association of Securities Dealers to create a Japanese version of the Nasdaq stock market (launched in 2000; closed in 2002). SOFTBANK also partnered with Microsoft and Tokyo Electric Power to launch SpeedNet, a Japanese Internet service provider.

In 2000 the nearly decimated Ziff-Davis announced it would transform its online arm, ZDNet, from a tracking stock into a stand-alone company and adopt the ZDNet name; later CNET Networks bought both companies instead. That year SOFTBANK formed venture capital funds focusing on areas such as Latin America, Japan, Europe, the UK, and emerging markets.

The company reorganized in 2000 and placed most of its non-Japan-based holdings under a new unit called SOFTBANK Global Ventures. Sharpening its focus on Internet investments, SOFTBANK sold its stake in antivirus software maker Trend Micro. Branching into banking,

SOFTBANK headed a consortium that paid $932 million for Japan's failed Nippon Credit Bank. SOFTBANK's share of the bank (renamed Aozora) stood at nearly 49%. The firm's stock price tumbled in 2000, and it considered taking several holding companies public.

In 2001 Cisco bought a nearly 2% stake in SOFTBANK in exchange for the firm's 12% stake in the hardware company's Japanese unit. The company also sold its SOFTBANK Forums Japan, an Internet trade show company, to MediaLive International. In 2002 Nasdaq Japan announced its plans to close, after two loss-making years. SOFTBANK owned 43%.

EXECUTIVES

President and CEO; Chairman, Yahoo Japan; Chairman, President, and CEO, Vodafone: Masayoshi Son, age 49
Director; President and Vice Chairman, SOFTBANK Holdings: Ronald D. (Ron) Fisher, age 58
Director; President and CEO, Yahoo Japan: Masahiro Inoue, age 49
Chairman and CEO, M.P. Technologies: Masuo Yoshimoto
Director; EVP and COO, SOFTBANK BB: Ken Miyauchi
President and CEO, SoftBank IDC: Yutaka Shinto
Corporate Auditor: Mitsuo Sano
Auditors: ChuoAoyama PricewaterhouseCoopers

LOCATIONS

HQ: SOFTBANK CORP.
1-9-1 Higashi Shinbashi, Minato-ku, Tokyo 105-7303, Japan
Phone: +81-3-6889-2000 **Fax:** +81-3-5543-0431
US HQ: 300 Delaware Ave., Wilmington, DE 19801
US Phone: 302-576-2713
Web: www.softbank.co.jp

PRODUCTS/OPERATIONS

2006 Sales

	% of total
Fixed-line telecommunications	31
e-Commerce	25
Broadband infrastructure	23
Internet culture	14
Other	7
Total	**100**

Selected Holdings

All About, Inc. (36%, specialized Internet information guides)
ALPS MAPPING K.K. (online map planning and production)
AtWork Corporation (personnel outsourcing services)
Club iT Corporation (67%, content distribution)
cyber communications inc. (26%, Internet advertising agency)
E-Book Systems K.K. (34%, electronic publishing licensing)
EC Architects Corp. (96%, consultation and design services)
Firstserver, Inc. (65%, server rentals and domain registration)
Fukuoka Softbank Hawks Corp. (professional baseball team)
Fukuoka Softbank Hawks Management (baseball stadium management and marketing)
IMX, Inc. (25%, electronic distribution of broadcasts and films)
IP Revolution, Inc.(fixed-line fiber optic, ultrahigh-speed Internet)
ITmedia Inc. (72%, IT information site)
M.P. Technologies, Inc. (33%, Internet infrastructure)
MOVIDA SOLUTIONS, Inc. (formerly E-Cosmos Inc., 60%, technical support and consulting)
TV Bank Corporation (video content services)
ValueCommerce Co., Ltd. (49.8%, Internet advertising)
Vector Inc. (58%, software sales)
Yahoo Japan Corporation (41%, Internet services)
Yahoo! Inc. (4%, Internet services)

COMPETITORS

3i Group
Accel Partners
Alloy Ventures
Benchmark Capital
CSK
Fujitsu
Hummer Winblad
Internet Capital
Internet Initiative Japan
Kleiner Perkins
Safeguard Scientifics
Sequoia Capital
Shikoku Electric
Trinity Ventures

HISTORICAL FINANCIALS

Company Type: Public

Income Statement

FYE: March 31

	REVENUE ($ mil.)	NET INCOME ($ mil.)	NET PROFIT MARGIN	EMPLOYEES
3/06	9,428	489	5.2%	14,182
3/05	7,083	(557)	—	—
3/04	4,898	(1,014)	—	6,662
3/03	3,395	(834)	—	6,170
3/02	3,056	(669)	—	5,706
Annual Growth	32.5%	—	—	25.6%

Net Income History

Exchange: Tokyo

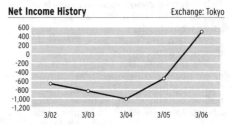

Sojitz

Sojitz Corporation is trading in all kinds of places. Formerly called Sojitz Holdings, the company's 500 subsidiaries trade in a wide array of businesses, ranging from steel and automobile parts to apparel, making it one of the largest trading houses in Japan. Sojitz's other major businesses include aerospace, foods, oil and gas, chemicals and plastics, retail property development, and construction materials. Asia and North America (through its Sojitz Corporation of America unit) are major contributors to its overseas trading operations. Sojitz was formed by the 2003 merger of two Japanese trading powerhouses, Nissho Iwai and Nichimen Corporation.

As part of its cost restructuring to reduce debt, Sojitz has been on a tear to sell off its low performing business divisions and additional real estate holdings. The company then reorganized into five business units: machinery and aerospace, energy and mineral resources, chemicals and plastics, real estate development and forest products, and consumer lifestyle business. It also formed a subsidiary in China to enter key businesses such as the automotive, ball bearing, textiles, and plastics industries.

HISTORY

The Nissho and Iwai companies got their acts together as Nissho Iwai in 1968, but each company dates back to the middle of the 19th century. In 1863, Bunsuke Iwai opened a shop in Osaka to sell imported goods such as glass, oil products, silk, and wine. The Meiji government, which came to power in 1868, encouraged modernization and industrialization, a climate in which Iwai's business flourished. In 1877 Iwajiro Suzuki established a similar trading concern, Suzuki & Co., that eventually became Nissho.

After cotton spinning machines were introduced in Japan in the 1890s, both Iwai and Suzuki imported cotton. Iwai began to trade directly with British trader William Duff & Son (an innovation in Japan, where the middleman, or *shokan*, played the paramount role in international trade). Iwai became the primary agent for Yawata Steel Works in 1901 and was incorporated in 1912. Meanwhile, Suzuki, solely engaged in the import trade, emerged as one of the top sugar brokers in the world and established an office in London.

To protect itself from foreign competition, Iwai established a number of companies to produce goods in Japan, including Nippon Steel Plate (1914) and Tokuyama Soda (1918). Stagnation after WWI forced Suzuki to restructure. In 1928 the company sold many of its assets to trading giant Mitsui and reorganized the rest under a new name, Nissho Co.

Both Iwai and Nissho subsequently grew as they helped fuel Japan's military expansion in Asia in the 1930s. But Japan's defeat in WWII devastated the companies. When the occupation forces broke up Mitsui and other larger trading conglomerates, both companies took advantage of the situation to move into new business areas. In 1949 Nissho established Nissho Chemical Industry, Nissho Fuel, and Nijko Shoji (a trading concern). It also opened its US operations, Nissho American Corp., in 1952.

Poor management by the Iwai family led the company into financial trouble in the 1960s and prompted the Japanese government to instruct the profitable Nissho to merge with Iwai in 1968.

In 1979 Nissho Iwai was accused of funneling kickbacks from US aircraft makers to Japanese politicians. The scandal led to arrests, the resignation of the company's chairman, and the suicide of another executive. Nissho Iwai exited the aircraft marketing business in 1980.

Despite Japan's recession in the 1990s, Nissho Iwai managed to make some significant investments. In 1991 the company teamed up with the Russian government to develop a Siberian oil refinery. A year later Nissho acquired a stake in courier DHL International, and in 1995 it set up a unit to process steel plates in Vietnam.

However, in the late 1990s rough economic conditions caught up with the firm. It dissolved its NI Finance unit (domestic financing) in 1998 after its disastrous performance. The large trading firm, or *sogo shosha*, also began a major restructuring effort to get back on track.

In 1999 Nissho Iwai sold its headquarters, its 5% stake in DHL International, and its stake in a Japanese ISP, Nifty. CEO Masatake Kusamichi resigned. He was replaced by Shiro Yasutake, who took charge of the firm's restructuring. In 2000, the company's ITX Corp. acquired five IT-related affiliates of Nichimen Corp.

As part of the group's streamlining efforts, in 2001 Nissho Iwai spun off its nonferrous marketing unit (Alconix) and agreed to merge the group's LNG operations with Sumitomo's LNG

business. The next year Hidetoshi Nishimura replaced Yasutake as CEO.

In 2003 Nissho Iwai merged with the smaller Nichimen Corp. to form Nissho Iwai-Nichimen Holdings. Hidetoshi Nishimura, president and CEO of Nissho Iwai, and Toru Hambayashi, president of Nichimen, became co-CEOs of the new holding company. In 2004 the company changed its name from Nissho Iwai-Nichimen Holdings to Sojitz Holdings Corporation.

As part of its ongoing reorganization in 2005 the firm renamed itself again when it merged the holding company into Sojitz Corporation.

EXECUTIVES

President and CEO: Akio Dobashi
EVP: Yutaka Kase
EVP: Masaki Hashikawa
SVP, Energy and Mineral Resources: Shuhei Inoue
SVP, Machinery and Aerospace: Michiharu Katsura
SVP, Machinery and Aerospace: Kazuhiko Nakajima
Senior Managing Executive Officer, New Business Development: Yasuyuki Fujishima
Senior Managing Executive Officer, Risk Management: Katsuhiko Kobayashi
Managing Executive Officer: Keisuke Ishihara
Managing Executive Officer and CFO: Yoji Sato
Director: Shigeo Muraoka
Director: Yoshihiko Miyauchi, age 71
President and CEO, Europe and Africa: Yasushi Hoshika
President, Energy and Mineral Resources: Hiroyuki Tanabe
President and CEO, Asia: Hiroshi Kanematsu
President, Machinery and Aerospace: Kazunori Teraoka
President, Americas: Jun Matsumoto
President, Chemicals and Plastics: Joji Suzuki
President, China: Yoshimi Ota
President, Consumer Lifestyle Business: Taichi Yonemura
President, Real Estate Development and Forest Products: Masao Ichishi
CIO: Shinichi Taniguchi
Auditors: KPMG AZSA & Co.; Ernst & Young ShinNihon

LOCATIONS

HQ: Sojitz Corporation
1-20 Akasaka 6-chome, Minato-ku,
Tokyo 107-8655, Japan
Phone: +81-3-5446-3600   **Fax:** +81-3-5446-1542
US HQ: 1211 Avenue of the Americas, 44th Fl.,
New York, NY 10036
US Phone: 212-704-6500   **US Fax:** 212-704-6947
Web: www.sojitz.com

2006 Sales

	% of total
Japan	76
Asia & Oceania	12
North America	7
Europe	4
Other regions	1
Total	**100**

PRODUCTS/OPERATIONS

2006 Sales

	% of total
Energy & Mineral Resources	24
Machinery & Aerospace	19
Consumer Lifestyle Business	18
Overseas subsidiaries	15
Chemicals & Plastics	13
Real Estate Development & Forest Products	8
Other	3
Total	**100**

COMPETITORS

Chori	Mitsui
ITOCHU	Sekisui House
Kanematsu	Sumitomo
Marubeni	TOMEN
Mitsubishi	Toyota Tsusho

HISTORICAL FINANCIALS

Company Type: Public

Income Statement

FYE: March 31

	REVENUE ($ mil.)	NET INCOME ($ mil.)	NET PROFIT MARGIN	EMPLOYEES
3/06	42,282	372	0.9%	17,213
3/05	43,477	(3,835)	—	16,419
3/04	55,487	(318)	—	14,600
Annual Growth	(12.7%)	—	—	8.6%

2006 Year-End Financials

Debt ratio: —
Return on equity: —
Cash ($ mil.): 4,292
Current ratio: —
Long-term debt ($ mil.): 4,656

Net Income History

Exchange: Tokyo

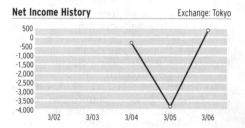

Sony

All eyes are on Sony — or, more likely, on its high-profit PlayStation home video game systems. PlayStation 2 dominates the game console market with about 70% of global sales (Nintendo's GameCube and Microsoft's Xbox control about 15% each). Sony, one of the world's top consumer electronics firms, also makes a host of other products, including PCs, digital cameras, Walkman stereos, and semiconductors; these products account for more than 60% of the company's sales. Sony's entertainment assets include recorded music and video (Epic and Columbia), motion pictures (Sony Pictures Entertainment, Sony Pictures Classics), DVDs (Sony Pictures Home Entertainment), and TV programming (Columbia TriStar). In addition Sony sells mobile phones via Sony Ericsson, its joint venture with Ericsson. Sony also owns an 8% stake in music club Columbia House.

Though the PlayStation still dominates the game machine scene, sales of other electronics (DVD recorders, TVs, and computers) and music have seen a drop. Weak consumer demand, price wars, and increased competition from Apple Computer's iPod, which has clobbered Sony's CD and mini disk Walkman products and Samsung's consumer electronics lines, have cut into Sony's TV sales (its biggest market). To boost sagging sales, Sony is emphasizing high-definition products for consumers and broadcasters, integrated mobile video, music, and gaming products, and semiconductors (aimed at improving product innovation).

Sony went through a major management shake-up in 2005, bringing Sir Howard Stringer on board as chairman and CEO in June. Stringer, who served as head of the company's US and electronics divisions, is the first non-Japanese CEO to head the company. Nobuyuki Idei stepped down as chairman and CEO and serves as a corporate advisor for the company.

Stringer's reorganization plans build off Sony's last restructuring effort, which began in 2004 and was to reduce the company's headcount by 20,000 and shift component sourcing to low-cost markets such as China. Stringer's plans call for cutting 10,000 jobs, shuttering 11 manufacturing plants, and reducing the company's electronics product lines by 20%.

Sony's PlayStation 3 was released in November 2006 (pushed back from its original spring release date). Like the Xbox 360, the PlayStation 3 is more of a multimedia entertainment hub than a video game system; its computing power allows users to play a game, chat online and listen to music all at the same time, but also it's able to render film-quality animations at a resolution that's equivalent to that of a cinematic digital projector.

Sony joined forces with other companies (including Matsushita and Samsung) to establish the Blu-ray optical disc format as the post-DVD standard for optical storage media. Games designed for the PlayStation 3 will be the first mass utilization of the Blu-ray format.

In an effort to combat losses in a weakening music industry, Sony merged its music division with BMG; the new company (Sony BMG Music Entertainment) is now the #2 player (after Universal Music). Sony led a consortium of companies (including cable company Comcast and several investment firms) that bought movie studio MGM in early 2005.

HISTORY

Akio Morita, Masaru Ibuka, and Tamon Maeda (Ibuka's father-in-law) started Tokyo Telecommunications Engineering in 1946 with funding from Morita's father's sake business. The company produced the first Japanese tape recorder in 1950. Three years later Morita paid Western Electric (US) $25,000 for transistor technology licenses, which sparked a consumer electronics revolution in Japan. His firm launched one of the first transistor radios in 1955, followed by the first Sony-trademarked product, a pocket-sized radio, in 1957. The next year the company changed its name to Sony (from "sonus," Latin for "sound," and "sonny," meaning "little man"). It beat the competition to newly emerging markets for transistor TVs (1959) and solid-state videotape recorders (1961).

Sony launched the first home video recorder (1964) and solid-state condenser microphone (1965). Its 1968 introduction of the Trinitron color TV tube began another decade of explosive growth. Sony bet wrong on its Betamax VCR (1976), which lost to rival Matsushita's VHS as the industry standard. However, 1979 brought another success, the Walkman personal stereo.

Pressured by adverse currency rates and competition worldwide, Sony used its technology to diversify beyond consumer electronics and began to move production to other countries. In the 1980s it introduced Japan's first 32-bit workstation and became a major producer of computer chips and floppy disk drives. The purchases of CBS Records in 1988 ($2 billion) and Columbia Pictures in 1989 (a $4.9 billion deal, which included TriStar Pictures) made Sony a major force in the rapidly growing entertainment industry.

The firm manufactured Apple's PowerBook, but its portable CD player, Data Discman, was successful only in Japan (1991). In the early 1990s Sony joined Nintendo to create a new kind of game console, combining Sony's CD-ROM drive with the graphic capabilities of a workstation. Although Nintendo pulled out in 1992, Sony released PlayStation in Japan (1994) and in the US (1995) to great success.

In 1998 Sony shipped its first digital, high-definition TV to the US, folded TriStar into Columbia Pictures, and merged its Loews Theatres unit with Cineplex Odeon. Philips, Sun Microsystems, and Sony formed a joint venture in early 1999 to develop networked entertainment products. Also in 1999 Nobuyuki Idei became CEO.

Adverse market conditions in 2001, aggravated by the September 11 attacks, led Sony Pictures Entertainment to consolidate its two domestic television operations, folding Columbia TriStar Network Television into Columbia TriStar Domestic Television (CTDT).

In 2002 an investment group led by Onex Corporation acquired its Loews Theatres unit (which filed for bankruptcy in February 2001).

Sony unveiled the Vaio Pocket in 2004, a portable music player designed to compete with Apple's iPod; Vaio Pocket debuted in the US later that year. Sony also introduced a similar product, Network Walkman — its first Walkman with a hard drive — in 2004. In October 2004 the company launched a music download system in Japan dubbed MusicDrop.

To manage its financial units (Sony Life Insurance Company, Sony Assurance, and Sony Bank), it created Sony Financial Holdings in 2004. The company announced in 2005 that Idei would be succeeded by foreigner Howard Stringer, who had been in charge of Sony's entertainment unit.

EXECUTIVES

Chairman and CEO: Sir Howard Stringer, age 64
President and Director; CEO, Electronics Business Group; Officer In Charge Of Technology Development Group: Ryoji Chubachi, age 59
Executive Deputy President and Director; President, TV and Video Business Group and Digital Imaging Business Group: Katsumi Ihara, age 57
Executive Deputy President: Yutaka Nakagawa
Executive Deputy President and Sony Group China Representative: Shizuo Takashino, age 63
EVP and Corporate Executive in Charge of Electronics Marketing; Senior General Manager, Global Marketing Division: Hideki (Dick) Komiyama
EVP and CFO: Nobuyuki Oneda, age 61
EVP and General Counsel: Nicole Seligman, age 50
EVP; President, B&P Business Group: Mitsuru Ohki, age 62
EVP; President, Personal Solutions Business Group: Eiji Kishi
EVP, Corporate Laboratories: Katsuaki Tsurushima, age 64
EVP; President, Core Component Business Unit: Akira Kubota
EVP; President, Semiconductor Business Unit: Kenshi Manabe
EVP, Electronics Marketing: Fujio Nishida, age 58
EVP, Technology Strategy; President, Technology Development Group: Keiji Kimura, age 54
SVP, Corporate Communications and External Relations: Naofumi Hara
SVP, Group Human Resources: Kunitaka Fujita
SVP, Investor Relations: Takao Yuhara, age 60
Chairman and CEO, Sony Computer Entertainment: Ken Kutaragi
President and CEO, Sony Computer Entertainment America: Jack Tretton

Chairman and CEO, Sony Music Entertainment: Andrew R. (Andy) Lack, age 59
Chairman and CEO, Sony Pictures Entertainment: Michael M. Lynton, age 45
Chief Marketing Officer: Andrew House
Auditors: ChuoAoyama PricewaterhouseCoopers

LOCATIONS

HQ: Sony Corporation
6-7-35, Kitashinagawa, Shinagawa-ku, Tokyo 141-0001, Japan
Phone: +81-3-5448-2111   **Fax:** +81-3-5448-2244
US HQ: 550 Madison Ave., New York, NY 10022
US Phone: 212-833-6800   **US Fax:** 212-833-6956
Web: www.sony.net

Sony's primary manufacturing plants are located in Japan, as well as in China, Malaysia, Mexico, Spain, the UK, and the US; it sells its products worldwide.

2006 Sales

	% of total
Japan	29
US	26
Europe	23
Other regions	22
Total	**100**

PRODUCTS/OPERATIONS

2006 Sales

	% of total
Electronics	64
Games	12
Financial services	10
Pictures	10
Other	4
Total	**100**

2006 Electronics Sales

	% of total
Video	21
Televisions	20
Information & communications	18
Components	14
Audio	11
Semiconductors	5
Other	11
Total	**100**

Selected Products

Electronics
  Video
    Digital cameras
    DVD and video players
    Set-top boxes
    Video cameras
  TVs and monitors
    Computer displays
    LCD TVs
    Projection TVs
    Plasma TVs
  Information and communication
    PCs
    PDAs
    Professional-use audio and video equipment
    Printers
  Audio
    Car audio
    Car navigation systems
    Home audio
    Portable audio
  Semiconductors
    CCDs
    LCDs
Pictures
  Digital production
  Home entertainment acquisition and distribution
  Motion picture production, acquisition, and distribution
  Online distribution and broadband services
  Studio facilities
  Television broadcasting
  Television production, acquisition, and distribution

Games (hardware and software)
  PlayStation 2
  PlayStation Portable (PSP)
Financial services
  Insurance policy underwriting (life insurance)
  Internet banking (personal loans, mortgage loans, investment trusts)
  Leasing and credit financing
  Non-life insurance products (auto and medical insurance)
Music
  CDs
  CD-ROMs
  DVDs
  DVD-ROMs
  MDs
  Recorded music and music videos
  Super Audio CDs

COMPETITORS

Apple Computer
Bertelsmann
Dell
Disney
Eastman Kodak
Fujitsu
Hewlett-Packard
IBM
Intel
Kyocera
LG Electronics
Matsushita
Microsoft
Motorola
Nintendo
Nokia
Philips Electronics
Pioneer
Samsung Group
SANYO
Sharp
THOMSON
Universal Studios
Victor Company of Japan

HISTORICAL FINANCIALS

Company Type: Public

Income Statement   FYE: March 31

	REVENUE ($ mil.)	NET INCOME ($ mil.)	NET PROFIT MARGIN	EMPLOYEES
3/06	63,541	1,051	1.7%	158,500
3/05	66,584	1,524	2.3%	151,400
3/04	71,216	841	1.2%	162,000
3/03	62,031	959	1.5%	161,100
3/02	56,837	115	0.2%	168,000
Annual Growth	2.8%	73.9%	—	(1.4%)

2006 Year-End Financials

Debt ratio: 23.9%
Return on equity: 3.9%
Cash ($ mil.): 10,541
Current ratio: 1.18
Long-term debt ($ mil.): 6,502

Net Income History   NYSE: SNE

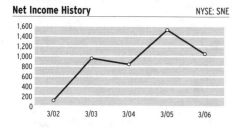

Statoil

Statoil (formerly Den norske stats oljeselskap) is Norway's oil and gas exploration, production, transport, refining, and marketing giant. Statoil operates in 29 countries, focusing its upstream activities on the Norwegian continental shelf, the North Sea, the Caspian Sea, Western Africa, and Venezuela. It has proved reserves of nearly 4.3 billion barrels of oil equivalent. Statoil has a retail network of about 2,000 gas stations (including a chain of 200 automated outlets) in nine north European countries. Statoil sold its 50% stake in petrochemicals venture Borealis in 2005. The Norwegian government, which has been divesting shares in Statoil, still owns 70% of the group.

The company manages the state's direct financial interest (known as SDFI) in oil and gas partnerships active on the Norwegian continental shelf. It also owns the world's largest offshore gas platform, the Aasgard B off Norway's west coast. In addition, Statoil supplies electricity in Norway and Sweden.

Statoil is not only Norway's largest oil and gas group, it is also one of the largest international exploration and production companies. However, to focus on its core areas, Statoil has divested its US exploration and production operations, although the US is still a major market for the company's exports: Statoil ships about 500,000 barrels of oil per day to the US and Canada. It is also a major exporter to Asia. However the company has agreed to acquire the Gulf of Mexico interests of Canada-based EnCana Corp. for about $2 billion. The assets include a 25% working interest in a Tahiti discovery operated by Chevron, as well as interests in five other discoveries now under appraisal.

The company is also considering the sale of its Ireland-based retail, commercial, and industrial businesses so that it can focus on its Scandinavian and Eastern European operations. In early 2006 it sold its 30% stake in the Ringsend gas power plant in Dublin to RBS Power Investments.

Statoil has a production target for 2007 of 1.4 million barrels of oil equivalent per day, and it plans to obtain most of its production from the Norwegian continental shelf (1.1 million boe per day). The group has submitted a plan to develop and operate the Tyrihans field in the Norwegian Sea to Norway's Ministry of Petroleum and Energy. Statoil has a nearly 47% stake in the field.

In 2006 the company acquired three oil prospects in the Gulf of Mexico from Plains Exploration & Production for $700 million. It also agreed to buy offshore assets in Gulf of Mexico from Anadarko Petroleum for $901 million.

HISTORY

To exert greater control over exploration and production of the Norwegian continental shelf (NCS), the government of Norway set up Den norske stats oljeselskap (Statoil) in 1972.

A decade earlier three geologists had visited Norway on behalf of Phillips Petroleum (later renamed ConocoPhillips) to apply for sole rights to explore on the NCS. The government initially refused drilling rights to foreign companies, and in 1963 Norway claimed sovereignty over the NCS. Two years later the government began allowing exploration. Phillips' major discovery in the Ekofisk field in 1969 prompted Norway to set up its own oil company. After Statoil's formation

in 1972, the company garnered funds to expand through taxation of multinationals, production limits, leasing contracts, and other measures.

In 1974 a giant discovery was made in the North Sea's Statfjord field, and Statoil was given a 50% stake. A year later Statoil began exploring for oil and gas, exporting oil, and commissioning its first subsea oil pipeline, the Norpipe, which extended to the UK. In 1986 Statoil's gas pipeline system, the Statpipe, began transporting gas from the North Sea to the mainland.

Moving into retailing, Statoil acquired Esso's service stations and other downstream operations in Sweden and Denmark in 1985 and 1986. The next year, cost overruns stemming from the extension of Statoil's Mongstad oil refinery led to the ousting of the company's first president, Arve Johnsen, and many of his deputies. Harald Norvik was appointed CEO in 1988.

In 1990 Statoil and BP teamed up to develop international operations, and in 1992 Statoil acquired BP's service stations in Ireland. Statoil and Neste Chemicals (later part of Industri Kapital) formed the Borealis petrochemicals group in 1994.

The company in 1995 acquired Aran Energy, moving into exploration offshore Ireland and the UK. Statoil brought its field projects in China and Azerbaijan onstream in 1997. That year Statoil spun off its shipping operations as Navion, partly owned by Norway's Rasmussen group. It also contracted with Kvaerner to build a giant offshore gas platform for Aasgard field in the Norwegian Sea.

The Aasgard field project resulted in cost overruns in 1999, again leading to a Statoil board shakeup and CEO resignation. Norvik, who had advocated partial privatization of Statoil, was replaced by Olav Fjell, former head of Norway's Postbanken (who resigned in 2003). That year Statoil helped Norsk Hydro take over rival Saga in return for some of Saga's assets.

As part of a major restructuring in 2000, Statoil sold most assets of US unit Statoil Energy. Political opposition that year postponed Statoil's plans for partial privatization, but the government proceeded with an IPO in 2001, raising about $3 billion.

In 2002 Statoil sold its oil and gas assets in the Danish North Sea to Dong, the Danish state oil company, for about $120 million. That year the company also acquired the Polish unit of Sweden's Preem Petroleum, which owned 79 gas stations in Poland.

In 2003 Statoil sold its Navion unit to shipping group Teekay, for about $800 million. That year it also acquired two Algerian natural gas projects from BP for $740 million. A bribery scandal involving an Iranian oil contract forced the resignation of the chairman, CEO, and another top executive in 2003.

EXECUTIVES

Chairman: Jannik Lindbæk, age 66
Deputy Chair: Kaci Kullmann Five, age 53
President and CEO: Helge Lund, age 42
EVP and CFO: Eldar Sætre, age 50
EVP Communication: Reidar Gjærum, age 44
EVP Exploration and Production Norway: Terje Overvik, age 53
EVP Health, Safety, and Environment (HSE): Nina Udnes Tronstad, age 47
EVP Natural Gas: Rune Bjørnson, age 45
EVP International Exploration and Production: Peter Mellbye, age 57
EVP Manufacturing and Marketing: Jon A. Jacobsen, age 48

EVP Technology and Projects: Margareth Øvrum, age 48
EVP Human Resources: Jens R. Jenssen, age 53
SVP Corporate Audit: Svein Andersen
SVP Health, Safety, and the Environment: Stig Bergseth
SVP Information and Communication Technology: Ole A. Jørgensen
SVP Country Analysis and Social Responsibility: Rolf M. Larsen
SVP Legal Affairs: Jacob S. Middelthon
SVP Corporate Services: Randi G. Olsen
SVP Exploration, Exploration and Production Norway: Tim Dodson
VP Public Affairs: Wenche Skorge
Head of Research and Technology Development: Morten Loktu, age 46
Investor Relations, US: Geir Bjørnstad
Auditors: Ernst & Young AS

LOCATIONS

HQ: Statoil ASA
Forusbeen 50, N-4035 Stavanger, Norway
Phone: +47-51-99-00-00   **Fax:** +47-51-99-00-50
US HQ: 1055 Washington Blvd., 7th Fl.,
Stamford, CT 06901
US Phone: 203-978-6900   **US Fax:** 203-978-6952
Web: www.statoil.com

Statoil has offices in 29 countries worldwide.

PRODUCTS/OPERATIONS

2005 Sales

	% of total
Manufacturing & marketing	68
Exploration & production	
Norway	19
International	4
Natural gas	9
Total	**100**

COMPETITORS

BP
Exxon Mobil
Norsk Hydro
OMV
Royal Dutch Shell
TOTAL

HISTORICAL FINANCIALS

Company Type: Public

Income Statement

	REVENUE ($ mil.)	NET INCOME ($ mil.)	NET PROFIT MARGIN	EMPLOYEES	FYE: December 31
12/05	58,012	4,533	7.8%	25,644	
12/04	50,649	4,121	8.1%	23,899	
12/03	37,182	2,468	6.6%	19,326	
12/02	35,060	2,422	6.9%	17,115	
12/01	26,139	1,907	7.3%	16,686	
Annual Growth	22.1%	24.2%	—	11.3%	

2005 Year-End Financials

Debt ratio: 30.6%
Return on equity: 30.4%
Cash ($ mil.): 2,045
Current ratio: 0.99
Long-term debt ($ mil.): 4,819
No. of shares (mil.): —
Dividends
Yield: 1.8%
Payout: 20.1%
Market value ($ mil.): —

HOOVER'S HANDBOOK OF WORLD BUSINESS 2007

Stock History

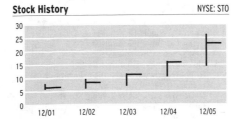

NYSE: STO

	STOCK PRICE ($) FY Close	P/E High	P/E Low	PER SHARE ($) Earnings	PER SHARE ($) Dividends
12/05	22.96	12	7	2.09	0.42
12/04	15.88	—	—	—	0.36
12/03	11.30	—	—	0.00	0.37
12/02	8.27	1	1	7.78	0.30
12/01	6.55	—	—	—	—
Annual Growth	36.8%	—	—	(35.5%)	11.9%

STMicroelectronics

The list of European chip makers starts with ST. STMicroelectronics (ST) is one of the world's largest and most respected semiconductor companies; it is the #1 Europe-based chip maker (ahead of Infineon) and vies with Texas Instruments to be the top maker of analog chips. ST makes many types of discrete devices (such as transistors and diodes) and integrated circuits (ICs), including microcontrollers, memory chips, and application-specific and custom ICs. It sells to manufacturers in the telecommunications, computer, consumer electronics, industrial, and automotive markets. (ST chips are in half of all cars on the road.) Top clients include Nokia, Robert Bosch, Schlumberger, Scientific-Atlanta, and Sony.

ST focuses on intensive product development, especially in close concert with key long-term strategic allies such as Alcatel-Lucent, Nokia, and Seagate Technology. It joined memory chip maker Hynix in a venture to build a multibillion-dollar chip factory in China. The company has also expanded its product range through a series of small, complementary acquisitions. Its product breadth lends to its expertise in SoC (system-on-a-chip) ICs, which integrate disparate functions onto a single device.

The company, which employs a highly decentralized organizational structure that reflects its global reach, has also won many awards for its commitments to manufacturing quality, environmental responsibility, and employee satisfaction. Its top-flight management has been credited with helping ST to avoid the dismal losses and big layoffs experienced by many chip makers during the brutal industry downturn of 2001-2003.

ST reorganized its product groups at the beginning of 2007. Among the moves was the creation of a stand-alone Flash Memory Group; there are rumors that the company may sell the flash business, packaging it with the flash memory business of Intel and fobbing it off on a consortium of private equity investment firms. Intel and ST have previously partnered on R&D in flash memory technology.

Other product lines in the company's former Memory Products Group are being bundled into a new Industrial & Multisegment Sector, contained within the new Microcontrollers, Memories & Smartcards Group. That group also comprises ST's microelectromechanical systems (MEMS) business.

Remaining product lines are swept into the Application Specific Groups, which include the existing Automotive Product Group and Computer Peripherals Group, along with the newly created Mobile, Multimedia & Communications Group and the Home Entertainment & Displays Group.

HISTORY

SGS-THOMSON was formed through the 1987 merger of SGS Microelettronica, a state-owned Italian chip maker, and the nonmilitary electronics arm of Thomson-CSF (now Thales). Included in the deal were two US operations: SGS Semiconductor in Phoenix and Texas-based Thomson Components-Mostek (acquired by Thomson in 1986 from United Technologies).

Microelettronica was part of Finmeccanica, formed in 1948 as the engineering subsidiary of the (now liquidated) Italian state industrial holding company IRI.

Thomson SA got its start shortly before the turn of the century, when a group of French businessmen acquired patents from General Electric predecessor Thomson-Houston Electric and created Compagnie Française Thomson-Houston to produce power generation equipment.

Both Thomson and Microelettronica were struggling at the time of their merger. Pasquale Pistorio, a Motorola veteran who became head of SGS in 1980, was named president of the new company. To jump-start the organization, he closed and sold factories, trimmed management, and shifted jobs to the Mediterranean and Asia.

SGS-THOMSON lost $300 million in its first two years of operation, made a small profit in 1989, then stumbled again as recession spread across Europe. To secure the company's market presence, Pistorio began making acquisitions and forging alliances with major chip buyers such as Alcatel, Hewlett-Packard, and Sony. By 1993 SGS-THOMSON had become the world's #1 maker of erasable programmable read-only memories (EPROMs). Profits soared to $160 million, and the company bought Tag Semiconductors, a maker of low-cost chips, from US conglomerate Raytheon. SGS-THOMSON went public in 1994.

Thomson sold off its stake in the company in 1997 and SGS-THOMSON changed its name to STMicroelectronics (ST) in 1998. The company formed development deals with Philips Electronics (for advanced chip manufacturing processes) in 1997 and with Mitsubishi (for flash memory chips) in 1998.

In 1999 ST bought Adaptec's Peripheral Technology Solutions group, which makes chips for disk drives; Vision Group, a developer of image sensors; and Arithmos, a maker of ICs for digital displays.

In 2000 ST acquired the Canada-based semiconductor fabrication operations of Nortel Networks for about $100 million. The deal included a six-year supply agreement worth at least $2 billion. The following year, though, ST announced that a sluggish chip industry would lead it to close the former Nortel fab as part of an overall reduction in its capital spending; ST later closed a fab in California as well.

Early in 2002 the company announced that it planned to sell its small PC graphics chip business. Later that year ST bought Alcatel Microelectronics from French telecom giant Alcatel (now Alcatel-Lucent) for about $345 million. In a related transaction, ST resold Alcatel's mixed-signal chip business to AMI Semiconductor (the operating unit of AMIS Holdings).

Pistorio retired early in 2005; company veteran Carlo Bozotti was designated as his successor. That year ST decided to exit the DSL chip business, a market it entered when it acquired Alcatel Microelectronics.

EXECUTIVES

Chairman: Gérald Arbola, age 57
Vice Chairman: Bruno Steve, age 64
President and CEO: Carlo Bozotti, age 53
COO: Alain Dutheil, age 61
EVP and CFO: Carlo Ferro, age 45
EVP and General Manager, Advanced System Technology and Chief Strategic Officer: Andrea Cuomo, age 52
EVP and General Manager, Home, Personal, Communication Groups: Philippe Geyres, age 54
EVP, European Region and External Technological Coordination: Enrico Villa, age 64
EVP, Front-End Technology and Manufacturing: Laurent Bosson, age 63
VP and CEO, Asia/Pacific Region: Jean-Claude Marquet, age 64
VP; CEO, Asia Pacific: Francois Guibert, age 53
VP and Treasurer: Piero Mosconi, age 66
VP, Corporate Communications: Carlo E. Ottaviani, age 62
VP, Human Resources: Patrice Chastagner, age 59
VP, Investor Relations: Stanley March
VP, North America: Reza Kazerounian, age 48
Chairman, STMicroelectronics K.K.: Keizo Shibata, age 69
Chief Economist: Jean-Philippe Dauvin
Auditors: PricewaterhouseCoopers SA

LOCATIONS

HQ: STMicroelectronics N.V.
39 Chemin du Champ des Filles, Plan-Les-Ouates, 1228 Geneva, Switzerland
Phone: +41-22-929-29-29   **Fax:** +41-22-929-29-00
US HQ: 1310 Electronics Dr., Carrollton, TX 75006
US Phone: 972-466-6000   **US Fax:** 972-466-8387
Web: www.st.com

STMicroelectronics has operations in more than 30 countries.

2005 Sales

	$ mil.	% of total
Asia/Pacific		
Japan	307	3
Other countries	4,063	46
Europe	2,789	31
North America	1,141	13
Other regions	582	7
Total	**8,882**	**100**

PRODUCTS/OPERATIONS

2005 Sales

	$ mil.	% of total
Application-specific product group	4,991	56
Memory product group	1,948	22
Micro, linear & discrete product group	1,882	21
Other	61	1
Total	**8,882**	**100**

Selected Products

Telecommunications, Peripherals, and Automotive
Telecommunications
Wireless telecommunications
Baseband devices
Multimedia processors
Radio-frequency signal semiconductors
Wireline telecommunications
Datacom ICs (packet switching, Ethernet)
Line cards (subscriber line interface circuits, or SLICs)
Modem ICs and boards
Telephone set ICs (speech circuits, line interfaces)
Peripherals and automotive
Audio and automotive
Audio power amplifiers, audio processors, and graphic equalizer ICs
Air bag controls
Antiskid braking system ICs
Ignition circuits
Injection circuits
Microcontrollers
Smart valves for motor control
Data storage
Disk drive actuators, controllers, host interfaces, and micromachinery
Industrial and power supplies
Battery chargers for portable electronic systems
Industrial automation system ICs
Power ICs for motor controllers and read/write amplifiers
Printers
Head drivers, motor drivers, and pen chips for ink jet printers and color copiers
Memory
Electrically erasable programmable read-only memories (EEPROMs)
Erasable programmable read-only memories (EPROMs)
Flash memory
Nonvolatile random-access memories (NVRAMs)
Smart card ICs
Consumer and Microcontrollers
Consumer electronics
DVD (decoder/host processor chips)
Imaging and display (modules and sensors for flat-panel displays, monitors, and video cameras)
Set-top box (decoders and integrated tuner/demodulator/error correction chips)
TV (application-specific microcontrollers)
Microcontrollers (8- and 16-bit)
Discrete and Standard ICs
Discrete power devices
Power transistors
Radio-frequency (RF) products (used in avionics, telecom, and television broadcasting equipment)
Standard linear and logic ICs

COMPETITORS

Agere Systems	International Rectifier
AMD	LSI Logic
Analog Devices	Maxim Integrated Products
Atmel	National Semiconductor
Avago Technologies	NEC Electronics
Broadcom	NXP
Cypress Semiconductor	ON Semiconductor
Fairchild Semiconductor	QUALCOMM
Freescale Semiconductor	Renesas
Fujitsu	Samsung Electronics
IBM Microelectronics	Sharp
Infineon Technologies	Texas Instruments
Intel	Toshiba

HISTORICAL FINANCIALS

Company Type: Public

Income Statement

FYE: December 31

	REVENUE ($ mil.)	NET INCOME ($ mil.)	NET PROFIT MARGIN	EMPLOYEES
12/05	8,882	266	3.0%	50,000
12/04	8,760	601	6.9%	49,500
12/03	7,238	253	3.5%	45,700
12/02	6,318	429	6.8%	43,170
12/01	6,357	257	4.0%	40,300
Annual Growth	**8.7%**	**0.9%**	**—**	**5.5%**

2005 Year-End Financials

Debt ratio: 3.2%
Return on equity: 3.0%
Cash ($ mil.): 2,027
Current ratio: 1.70
Long-term debt ($ mil.): 269
No. of shares (mil.): —
Dividends
Yield: 1.0%
Payout: 62.1%
Market value ($ mil.): —

Stock History

NYSE: STM

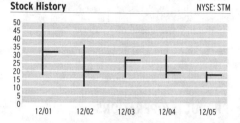

	STOCK PRICE ($) FY Close	P/E High/Low		PER SHARE ($) Earnings	Dividends
12/05	18.00	67	48	0.29	0.18
12/04	19.32	46	25	0.65	0.09
12/03	27.01	106	62	0.27	0.06
12/02	19.51	75	23	0.48	0.03
12/01	31.67	168	62	0.29	0.03
Annual Growth	**(13.2%)**	**—**	**—**	**0.0%**	**56.5%**

Stora Enso Oyj

Forest products company Stora Enso Oyj's roots reach back more than 700 years. Stora Enso is the #1 producer of newsprint and sawn softwood timber in Europe and is a global leader in the production of a wide range of paper and wood products such as magazine paper, newsprint, fine papers, packaging boards, and sawn timber. The company also manufactures graphic products, office papers, and wallpaper base. Its publication paper products segment comprises more than 30% of Stora Enso's total sales, while the European market is the company's strongest, bringing in nearly a quarter of total sales. The Finnish government and Sweden's Knut and Alice Wallenberg Foundation each control about 24% of Stora Enso.

Stora Enso owns and operates facilities in more than 40 countries worldwide; Stora Enso North America is one of the company's strongest subsidiaries. The company has announced plans to integrate its North American division into its global product divisions in order to streamline operations. The move is not expected to significantly impact its US operations.

Having identified China as a growth area, Stora Enso has announced joint ventures with Chinese companies Shandong Huatai Paper and

Gaofeng Forest. Current projects in China also include further development of eucalyptus plantations and expansion of the product range and capacity of Stora Enso's Suzhou Mill operations.

Stora Enso continues to focus on its core paper (magazine, newsprint, fine) and timber businesses (packaging boards, lumber) while divesting peripheral businesses such as specialty paper, off-site energy generation, and packaging paper. In 2006 it announced plans to sell its pulp subsidiary Celulose Beira Industrial (a.k.a. Celbi) to Portugal-based Altri.

Stora Enso bought German paper wholesaler Schneidersöhne for $588 million (€450 million) in 2005. In addition, Stora Enso has announced plans to acquire the 29% interest in Corenso United (coreboard, cores, and tubes) that it does not own from UPM-Kymmene. Stora Enso is also expanding its operations in Russia. Likewise, it has acquired a Brazil-based coated papers unit from International Paper for $420 million (€333 million).

In Finland, which accounts for more than a third of Stora Enso's production, labor disputes shut down all of the company's paper mills in that country in 2005, overshadowing reported sales and profit improvements. The labor disputes stemmed from disagreements over plant shutdowns for mid-summer and Christmas holidays, as well as outsourcing. Strikes by workers have been followed by lockouts (one lasting more than a month) by employers, which temporarily crippled the country's paper industry and affected the chemical and transportation sectors as well. Stora Enso has announced plans to eliminate about 2,000 jobs, close five plants in Europe and the US, and sell another six mills in Europe, as part of a nearly $400 million restructuring program.

HISTORY

Stora Enso's ancestors were mining Kopperberg Mountain in Sweden as long ago as 1288. The mountain housed a copper mine that Swedish nobles and German merchants managed as a cooperative. By the 17th century King Karl IX instituted German mining methods to increase production. Copper became Sweden's largest export, at one point accounting for 60% of the country's gross national product.

Copper production slowed after two cave-ins in 1655 and 1687, and exploitation of the region's timber and iron ore resources began. By the early 1800s the company was producing pig and bar iron. In 1862 all of the company's activities were combined to form Stora Kopparbergs Bergslag. The role of copper became less important as the company consolidated its iron works and ventured into forest products. The firm reorganized as a limited liability company in 1888.

By 1915 Stora Kopparbergs had firmly established pulp and paper mills, as well as iron and steel works concentrated along the Dalalven River Basin. The company's activities revolved around these facilities for the next 60 years.

During the 1960s Stora Kopparbergs was hurt by low bulk commodity prices and increased competition. The company, feeling the crunch of the oil crisis, sold its holdings in steel and mining between 1976 and 1978. With its purchase of Billerud (forestry), the company became Sweden's largest industrial concern in 1984. Stora Kopparbergs shortened its name to Stora, meaning "great" or "large" in Swedish, to commemorate the event.

Stora went on a shopping spree in the late 1980s and early 1990s to compete with its giant US rivals. In 1998 Stora established operations in China through a joint venture. The company also merged with Finnish forest products company Enso Gutzeit Oyj to form Stora Enso Oyj that year.

Hans Gutzeit founded a sawmill in 1872 on the Finnish island of Kotka. Gutzeit's company bought Utra Wood Co. to eliminate competition and incorporated in Finland as Aktiebolaget W. Gutzeit & Co. in 1896. The company constructed a pulp mill to use waste wood from the Kotka sawmill.

In 1917 the Russian Revolution marked the disappearance of a major market; at the same time, Finland's declaration of independence from Norway halted production. Gutzeit's Norwegian shareholders sold the company to the new Finnish state in 1919. In 1924 the company was renamed Enso-Gutzeit.

Russia attacked Finland in 1939; in the armistice that followed, Finland ceded land on which Enso-Gutzeit had many of its operations. However, postwar devastation in the former Russia created Soviet demand for the company's building products. In the 1950s and 1960s the company added a paper mill, a box factory, bleaching plants, and pulp mills.

The company merged with Veitsiluoto in 1996 to form Enso Oy. Two years later Enso Oy merged with Stora to form Stora Enso.

Stora Enso bought US-based Consolidated Papers (now Stora Enso North America) for $4.9 billion in 2000. The acquisition moved Stora Enso past International Paper as the world's #1 paper and board producer. The next year Stora Enso dissolved its pulp division by reallocating the mills to divisions that use pulp in their operations. In 2002 the company sold 300,000 acres of forestland, primarily in Wisconsin and Michigan, to paper maker Plum Creek Timber Company for about $140 million.

In 2004 Stora Enso acquired Netherlands-based Scaldia Paper from International Paper as it moved to strengthen its presence in Europe.

EXECUTIVES

Chairman: Claes Dahlbäck, age 59
Vice Chairman: Ilkka Niemi, age 60
CEO and Director: Jukka Härmälä, age 60
CEO: Jouko Karvinen, age 49
SEVP, Finance and Strategy and CFO:
  Hannu Ryöppönen, age 54
SEVP, Market Services: Jussi Huttunen, age 52
SEVP, Information Technology, Human Resources, and Business Excellence; Country Manager, Sweden:
  Christer Agren, age 52
SEVP, Stora Enso Fine Paper: Pekka Laaksonen, age 50
SEVP, Publication Paper: Bernd Rettig, age 50
SEVP, Stora Enso North America: Lars Bengtsson, age 61
SEVP, Stora Enso Packaging Boards; Country Manager, Finland: Kai Korhonen, age 55
EVP, Corporate Technology and Asia/Pacific: Markku Pentikäinen, age 53
EVP, Consumer Brands: Niilo Pöyhönen, age 53
EVP, Corporate Communications: Kari Vainio, age 60
EVP, Corporate Strategy, Investments, and Business Planning: Magnus Diesen, age 62
EVP, Timber: Peter Kickinger, age 42
EVP, Corporate Human Resources and Business Excellence: Gary Parafinczuk
SVP and Director, Environment: James D. Weinbauer
SVP and Group Treasurer, Financial Services:
  Markus Rauramo, age 36
SVP, Investor Relations: Keith B. Russell, age 48
SVP, Legal Affairs: Jyrki Kurkinen, age 58
President and Regional Manager, North America: John Gillen
VP, Investor Relations, North America: Scott A. Deitz
Auditors: PricewaterhouseCoopers Oy

LOCATIONS

HQ: Stora Enso Oyj
  Kanavaranta 1, FIN-00101 Helsinki, Finland
Phone: +358-20-46-131   **Fax:** +358-20-46-214-71
US HQ: 231 1st Ave. North, Wisconsin Rapids, WI 54495
US Phone: 715-422-3111   **US Fax:** 715-422-3469
Web: www.storaenso.com

Stora Enso Oyj operates through hundreds of mills and offices in more than 30 countries in Asia, Europe, and the Americas.

2005 Sales

	% of total
Europe	72
North America	17
Other regions	11
Total	**100**

PRODUCTS/OPERATIONS

2005 Sales

	% of total
Publication paper	33
Packaging boards	23
Fine paper	18
Wood products	11
Merchants	9
Other	6
Total	**100**

Selected Products

Book paper
Business forms
Cartonboards
Coreboards and tubes
Corrugated boxes
Digital papers
Directory paper
Document papers
Envelope papers
Fluff pulp
Food service boards
Graphic board
Graphic paper
Kraft papers
Laminated papers
Liquid packaging boards
Magazine paper
Newsprint
Paper-grade pulp
Sawn boards
Scholastic paper

COMPETITORS

Abitibi-Consolidated
Iggesund Paperboard
International Paper
Myllykoski Paper
NewPage
Norske Skog
OfficeMax
Smurfit-Stone Container
UPM-Kymmene
Weyerhaeuser

HISTORICAL FINANCIALS

Company Type: Public

Income Statement				FYE: December 31
	REVENUE ($ mil.)	NET INCOME ($ mil.)	NET PROFIT MARGIN	EMPLOYEES
12/05	15,799	(193)	—	46,664
12/04	17,176	504	2.9%	43,779
12/03	15,416	294	1.9%	44,264
12/02	14,935	(349)	—	42,461
Annual Growth	1.9%	—	—	3.2%

2005 Year-End Financials

Debt ratio: 59.2%
Return on equity: —
Cash ($ mil.): 416
Current ratio: 1.24
Long-term debt ($ mil.): 5,187

No. of shares (mil.): —
Dividends
Yield: 3.1%
Payout: —
Market value ($ mil.): —

Stock History

NYSE: SEO

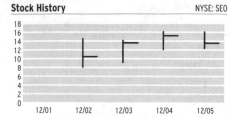

	STOCK PRICE ($) FY Close	P/E High/Low		PER SHARE ($) Earnings	Dividends
12/05	13.52	—	—	—	0.41
12/04	15.21	—	—	—	0.39
12/03	13.56	—	—	—	0.41
12/02	10.46	—	—	—	0.34
Annual Growth	8.9%	—	—	—	6.4%

Suzuki

Suzuki Motor Corporation is Japan's #1 minicar producer as well as its #3 motorcycle manufacturer (behind Honda and Yamaha). Suzuki's US cars and SUVs include the Aerio, Forenza, Reno, and the Grand Vitara; motorcycles include the V-Strom, Hayabusa, and Boulevard. Suzuki's nonvehicle products include generators, outboard marine engines, and prefabricated housing. The company operates in more than 190 countries. Suzuki has partnered to make cars with General Motors and builds cars in India with local partner Maruti Udyog.

General Motors sold almost all of its 20% stake in Suzuki to raise cash for its own beleaguered operations in early 2006. GM now holds only about a 3% stake in the company — although it has an informal agreement with Suzuki to buy back the stake within one year.

GM Daewoo Auto & Technology (formerly Daewoo Motor) GM, Suzuki, and Shanghai Automotive Industry Corp. together control 67% of GM Daewoo. The deal is aimed at giving GM and Suzuki a better footing in the Asian market.

Suzuki's long-standing Indian carmaking partner Maruti Udyog is that nation's leading carmaker, but the partnership's dominance is being threatened by another alliance. In 2006 Renault and Maruti rival Mahindra & Mahindra (M&M) struck up a partnership to build jeeps, trucks, and passenger cars on a brand new assembly line in India. The deal will also see M&M importing Renault's popular Logan model cars for sale in India.

HISTORY

In 1909 Michio Suzuki started Suzuki Loom Works in Hamamatsu, Japan. The company went public in 1920 and continued producing weaving equipment until the onset of WWII, when it began to make war-related products.

Suzuki began developing inexpensive motor vehicles in 1947, and in 1952 it introduced a 36cc engine to motorize bicycles. The company changed its name to Suzuki Motor and launched its first motorcycle in 1954. Suzuki's entry into the minicar market came in 1955 with the Suzulight, followed by the Suzumoped (1958), a delivery van (1959), and the Suzulight Carry FB small truck (1961).

Suzuki's triumph in the 1962 50cc-class Isle of Man TT motorcycle race started a string of racing successes that brought international prominence to the Suzuki name. The company established its first overseas plant in Thailand in 1967.

In the 1970s Suzuki met market demand for motorcycles with large engines. Meanwhile, a mid-1970s recession and falling demand for low-powered cars in Japan led the minicar industry there to produce two-thirds fewer minicars in 1974 than in 1970. Suzuki responded by beginning auto exports and expanding foreign distribution. In 1975 it started producting motorcycles in Taiwan, Thailand, and Indonesia.

Suzuki boosted capacity internationally throughout the 1980s through joint ventures. Motorcycle sales in Japan peaked in 1982, then tapered off, but enjoyed a modest rebound in the late 1980s. In 1988 the company agreed to handle distribution of Peugeot cars in Japan.

Suzuki and General Motors began their long-standing relationship in 1981 when GM bought a small stake in Suzuki. The company began producing Swift subcompacts in 1983 and sold them through GM as the Chevy Sprint and, later, the Geo Metro. In 1986 Suzuki and GM of Canada jointly formed CAMI Automotive to produce vehicles, including Sprints, Metros, and Geo Trackers (Suzuki Sidekicks), in Ontario; production began in 1989.

Although sales via GM increased through 1990, US efforts with the Suzuki nameplate faltered shortly after Suzuki formed its US subsidiary in Brea, California, in 1986. A 1988 *Consumer Reports* claim that the company's Samurai SUV was prone to rolling over devastated US sales. The next year Suzuki's top US executives quit, apparently questioning the company's commitment to the US market.

Suzuki established Magyar Suzuki, a joint venture with Hungarian automaker Autokonszern Rt., C. Itoh & Co., and International Finance Corporation in 1991 to begin producing the Swift sedan in Hungary. The company expanded a licensing agreement with a Chinese government partner in 1993, becoming the first Japanese company to take an equity stake in a Chinese carmaking venture. The next year Suzuki introduced the Alto van, Japan's cheapest car, at just over $5,000, and the Wagon R miniwagon, which quickly became one of Japan's top-selling vehicles.

In a case that was later overturned, a woman was awarded $90 million from Suzuki after being paralyzed in a Samurai rollover in 1990. The company sued Consumers Union, publisher of *Consumer Reports,* in 1996, charging it had intended to fix the results in the 1988 Samurai testing.

GM raised its 3% stake in Suzuki to 10% in 1998. The company teamed up with GM and Fuji Heavy Industries (Subaru) in 2000 to develop compact cars for the European market. It was also announced that GM would spend about $600 million to double its stake in Suzuki to 20%. In 2001 Suzuki announced that it had agreed to cooperate with Kawasaki in the development of new motorcycles, scooters, and ATVs. The next year Suzuki agreed to take control of Maruti Udyog Ltd., the state-owned India-based car manufacturer, in an $80 million rights issue deal.

EXECUTIVES

Chairman and CEO: Osamu Suzuki
President and COO: Hiroshi Tsuda
Senior Managing Director: Takahira Kiriyama
Senior Managing Director: Shinzo Nakanishi
Senior Managing Director: Takashi Nakayama
Senior Managing Director: Shunichi Wakuda
Managing Director: Takao Hirosawa
Managing Director: Sadayuki Inobe
Managing Director: Akio Kosugi
Managing Director: Akihiro Sakamoto
Managing Director: Takeo Shigemoto
Managing Director: Kazuo Suzuki
Auditors: Seimei Audit Corporation

LOCATIONS

HQ: Suzuki Motor Corporation
   300 Takatsuka, Hamamatsu,
   Shizuoka 432-8611, Japan
Phone: +81-53-440-2061   **Fax:** +81-53-440-2776
US HQ: 3251 E. Imperial Hwy., Brea, CA 92821
US Phone: 714-996-7040   **US Fax:** 714-524-8499
Web: www.globalsuzuki.com

Suzuki Motor Corporation operates major subsidiaries in Australia, Austria, Cambodia, Canada, Colombia, France, Germany, Hungary, India, Indonesia, Italy, Myanmar, New Zealand, Pakistan, the Philippines, Poland, Spain, Thailand, the UK, and the US. It distributes its products in more than 190 countries.

2006 Sales

	$ mil.	% of total
Asia		
Japan	15,463.4	54
Other countries	5,159.7	18
Europe	4,184.4	15
North America	3,341.1	12
Other regions	359.1	1
Adjustments	(5,151.9)	—
Total	**23,355.8**	**100**

PRODUCTS/OPERATIONS

2006 Sales

	$ mil.	% of total
Automobiles	18,027.9	77
Motorcycles	4,773.4	21
Other products	554.5	2
Total	**23,355.8**	**100**

Selected Products

Cars, Minicars, and SUVs
   Aerio Sedan
   Forenza
   Forenxa wagon
   Grand Vitara
   Reno
   SX4
   XL-7
Motorcycles
   Boulevard C90
   Boulevard M109R
   DR650SE
   DR-Z250
   DR-Z400E
   DR-Z400S
   DR-Z125L
   GSX-R600
   GSX-R750
   GSX-R1000
   GZ250
   Hayabusa 1300
   RM85
   RM125
   RM250
   SV650
   V-Strom 650
All Terrain Vehicles
   Eiger 400 4X4
   Eiger 400 Automatic 4X4
   Ozark 250
   QuadSport Z400
   Vinson 500 4X4

Other Products
- Electro-scooters
- General-purpose engines
- Generators
- Motorized wheelchairs
- Outboard motors
- Prefabricated houses

Selected Overseas Subsidiaries and Affiliates
- American Suzuki Motor Corp.
- Cambodia Suzuki Motor Co. Ltd.
- Magyar Suzuki Corp. (Hungary)
- Maruti Udyog Ltd. (54%, India)
- Pak Suzuki Motor Co., Ltd. (Pakistan)
- Suzuki Motorcycles Pakistan Ltd.
- Thai Suzuki Motor Company., Ltd. (Thailand)

COMPETITORS

Bajaj Auto
BMW
Bombardier
Brunswick
DaimlerChrysler
Dover
Ek Chor China Motorcycle
Fiat
Ford
General Motors
Harley-Davidson
Honda
Hyundai
Invacare
Isuzu
Kawasaki Heavy Industries
Kohler
Lion Group
Mahindra
Mazda
Nissan
Peugeot Motors of America, Inc.
Piaggio
Remy
Renault
Saab Automobile
Tata Motors
Toyota
Triumph Motorcycles
Volkswagen
Volvo
Yamaha Motor

HISTORICAL FINANCIALS

Company Type: Public

Income Statement

FYE: March 31

	REVENUE ($ mil.)	NET INCOME ($ mil.)	NET PROFIT MARGIN	EMPLOYEES
3/06	23,356	561	2.4%	14,180
3/05	21,995	563	2.6%	13,760
3/04	20,816	415	2.0%	13,700
3/03	16,816	259	1.5%	13,920
3/02	12,577	169	1.3%	14,260
Annual Growth	16.7%	35.0%	—	(0.1%)

Net Income History

OTC: SZKMF

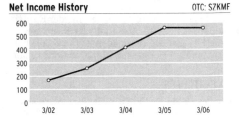

Swatch

Swatch is worth watching. The Swatch Group (formerly Société Suisse de Microélectronique & d'Horlogerie) is the world's second-largest watchmaker (after Citizen Watch). Its 18 watch brands range from low-priced, collectible Swatch and Flik Flak to premium-priced Blancpain, Brequet, and Omega brands. Swatch watches are sold at some 15,000 retailers worldwide, plus at more than 500 Swatch stores, about 1,000 shop-in-shops, and some 140 kiosks. The company supplies nearly all the components for its own watches and is a supplier to other watchmakers. Its Dress Your Body subsidiary designs and makes jewelry for the Swatch Group brands. Chairman Nicolas Hayek's family controls about 37% of The Swatch Group.

The Swatch Group holds about 25% of the world's watch market.

The company, which has more than 100 subsidiaries and affiliated units, also makes watch components and private-label watches. In addition, it makes semiconductors, quartz oscillators, and industrial lasers, among other items, for industries such as telecommunications and medical electronics. The company's EM-Microelectronic subsidiary is the leading producer of radio frequency identification (RFID) technology that is taking hold in the retail industry. Swatch also provides timing and scoring services at major sporting events such as the Olympic Games.

In April 2006 the company formed a retail partnership with Tourneau, the world's largest watch store, to open watch stores in high-end outlet malls across the US.

In 2004 Swatch unveiled the Paparazzi, a watch it made in collaboration with MSN Direct (a division of Microsoft) which can link to updated international news, weather forecasts, and lottery results. All that, and it tells the time.

HISTORY

The Swatch Group was first established when watchmakers ASUAG and SSIH were merged in 1983. ASUAG was founded in 1931 in Switzerland to make watches. By the late 1970s ASUAG had acquired some 100 family-owned companies, many of which were operating independently and inefficiently. When it merged with SSIH, ASUAG owned the Longines and Rado brands and made watch components.

Watchmaker SSIH was formed in 1930 with the merger of brands Tissot and Omega (which traced its history to 1848). SSIH and other Swiss watchmakers were struggling by the late 1970s. The market was flooded with cheaper watches made in Japan and Hong Kong that used quartz technology (a technology invented — but ignored — by the Swiss). SSIH had licensed out its prestigious Omega brand to other manufacturers in various countries, hurting that brand's reputation.

With both ASUAG and SSIH on the verge of bankruptcy, Swiss banks named Nicolas Hayek (then the CEO of consulting firm Hayek Engineering) to advise the companies on their futures. He recommended that ASUAG and SSIH merge and then mass-produce a low-cost watch and sell it globally at a set price. The two companies merged in 1983, forming SMH (Société Suisse de Microélectronique & d'Horlogerie); its headquarters were ASUAG's in Biel, Switzerland.

SMH had sales of about $1.1 billion with losses of some $124 million in 1983. That year it introduced the Swatch watch amid some resistance and objections that the watch would ruin the Swiss image of makers of high-quality, premium-priced watches. But Swatch watches became fashion statements and pop-culture icons in the 1980s and Hayek, who spearheaded the turnaround, became a Swiss business hero. Hayek and a group of investors bought a controlling 51% stake of SMH, and he became CEO in 1985.

In 1992 the company bought Blancpain (luxury watches) and Frederic Piguet (luxury watch components). By 1993 SMH had expanded into semiconductor chips, pagers, and telephones. The next year it formed a joint venture (19%-owned by SMH) called Micro Compact Car (MCC) with Daimler-Benz to make a battery- and gasoline-powered Swatchmobile.

Because of difficulty in translating its name into other languages, the company changed its name in 1998 to The Swatch Group. That year it also sold its 19% stake in MCC to Daimler-Benz. In 1999 Swatch bought Groupe Horloger Breguet, a manufacturer of mechanical timepieces since 1775, and Swiss watch case maker Favre & Perret. In 2000 the growing company pocketed German luxury watchmaker Glashütter, among others. Acquisitions in 2001 included two Greek companies, Aliki Perri and Alikonia. Swatch bought Swiss watch dial maker Rubattel & Weyermann in 2002. Later that year Hayek retired as CEO, but remained chairman; his son Nicolas became CEO.

In October 2006 the company acquired watch dial maker MOM Le Prélet SA of Switzerland.

EXECUTIVES

Chairman: H. C. Nicolas G. Hayek Sr.
Vice Chairman: Peter Gross
President: G. Nicolas (Nick) Hayek Jr.
President Swatch Group Japan and South Korea; President, Léon Hatot, cK watch & jewelry, and Dress Your Body: Arlett Emch
President, Swatch Group France, Swatch Group France Les Boutiques, Swatch Group Italy, Swatch Group Spain, Flik Flak: Florence Ollivier-Lamarque
President, EM Microelectronic, Micro Crystal, Renata, Microcomponents, Sokymat Automotive, Oscilloquartz, Omega Electronics, Lasag: Mougahed Darwish
CFO and Executive Management Board, Controlling/Finance, Quality Assurance, Investor Relations, Swatch Group UK: Edgar Geiser
Executive Management Board, Blancpain, Swatch Group Middle East, Panama: Marc A. Hayek
Executive Management Board, Legal, Licences, Strategic Projects, Real Estate (except Engineering), Patents (ICB), Swatch Group Greece, Swatch Group Poland: Hanspeter Rentsch
Extended Group Management Board; President, Rado: Roland Streule
Extended Group Management Board, Hamilton, Endura, and Swatch Group Mexico: Matthias Breschan
Extended Group Management Board, Frédéric Piguet, Valdar, and Universo: Edmond Capt
Extended Group Management Board, Asulab: Rudolf Dinger
Extended Group Management Board, Longines: Walter von Känel
Extended Group Management Board, Balmain: Jerry Simonis
Extended Group Management Board; President, Omega: Stephen Urquhart
Corporate Treasurer: Thomas Dürr
Head of Media Relations: Beatrice Howald
Auditors: PricewaterhouseCoopers AG

LOCATIONS

HQ: The Swatch Group Ltd.
Seevorstadt 6, CH-2501 Biel, Bern, Switzerland
Phone: +41-32-343-68-11   **Fax:** +41-32-343-69-11
US HQ: 1200 Harbor Blvd., Weehawken, NJ 07086
US Phone: 201-271-1400   **US Fax:** 201-558-5042
Web: www.swatchgroup.com

The Swatch Group sells its products worldwide. It has more than 150 manufacturing facilities, plus other operations in 50 countries throughout the world.

2005 Sales

	% of total
Europe	48
Asia	37
Americas	12
Oceania	2
Africa	1
Total	**100**

PRODUCTS/OPERATIONS

2005 Sales

	% of total
Watches & jewelry	76
Watch production	12
Electronic systems	12
Total	**100**

Selected Products and Brands

Watches
  Basic Range
    Flik Flak
    Swatch
  High Range
    Longines
    Rado
  Middle Range
    Calvin Klein
    Certina
    Hamilton
    Mido
    Pierre Balmain
    Tissot
  Prestige
    Blancpain
    Breguet
    Glashüte Original/Union
    Jaquet-Droz
    Léon Hatot
    Omega
    Paparazzi
  Private Label
    Endura
Jewelry
  Dress Your Body
Retailing
  Les Boutiques

Selected Electronic Systems Operations

EM Microelectronic-Marin SA (microelectronics)
Lasag AG (lasers for industrial applications)
Microcomponents AG (components for the automobile industry)
Omega Electronics SA (sports timing equipment, information displays system)
Oscilloquartz SA (high-stability frequency sources)

COMPETITORS

Armitron	Loews
Benetton	LVMH
Bulgari	Movado Group
Bulova	Richemont
CASIO	Rolex
Citizen Watch	Seiko
Fossil	Tiffany
Guess	Timex
Hermès	

HISTORICAL FINANCIALS

Company Type: Public

Income Statement

FYE: December 31

	REVENUE ($ mil.)	NET INCOME ($ mil.)	NET PROFIT MARGIN	EMPLOYEES
12/05	3,262	—	—	20,650
12/04	3,517	—	—	20,949
12/03	3,095	—	—	20,700
12/02	2,835	—	—	20,327
12/01	2,420	—	—	19,665
Annual Growth	**7.8%**	—	—	**1.2%**

Revenue History

Pink Sheets: SWGAF

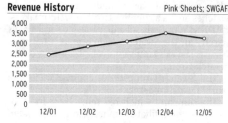

Swire Pacific

Swire Pacific has holdings on land, at sea, and in the air. The *hong* (general trading company) holds some 20 million sq. ft. of developed and undeveloped commercial and residential real estate in Hong Kong, China, and the US. Swire Pacific's interests also include marine services for the oil and gas industry; it has a 50-vessel fleet. The company owns 46% of Cathay Pacific Airways, to which it sold Chinese carrier Dragonair in 2006. Other interests include paint manufacturing (in a joint venture with ICI), sporting goods, and sugar; it is a major Coca-Cola bottler in southern China. The firm is controlled by its founding family through UK-based John Swire & Sons, which owns more than 65% of Swire Pacific.

Despite regional economic turmoil, Swire Pacific is committed to building new office space in Hong Kong. Not wanting to be shut out when the UK gave up control of Hong Kong, Swire Pacific over the years has assiduously allied itself with Chinese interests through joint ventures in Hong Kong and Taiwan and on the mainland.

HISTORY

John Swire began a Liverpool trading company in 1816. By the time he died in 1847 John Swire & Sons derived much of its revenues from the US cotton trade. One of Swire's sons, John Samuel Swire, refocused the company on Chinese tea and textiles during the US Civil War. Unhappy with his representatives in Asia, Swire went to Shanghai and in 1866 partnered with customer Richard Butterfield. Butterfield & Swire (B&S) took *Taikoo* ("great and ancient") as a Chinese name. Butterfield soon left, but his name lived on with the company until 1974.

By 1868 B&S had offices in New York and Yokohama, Japan; it added a Hong Kong office two years later. The firm created China Navigation Company in 1872 to transport goods on the Yangtze River; by the late 1880s, the shipping line served all the major Pacific Rim ports. Hong Kong-based Taikoo Sugar Refinery began operations in 1884.

The third John Swire took over B&S in 1898 and built the Taikoo Dockyard in Hong Kong. The company's Chinese operations were eventually devastated by the Japanese attack on China in 1937, World War II, and the Communist takeover in 1949. However, the company rebuilt in Hong Kong, and in 1948 it bought control of Cathay Pacific, a Hong Kong airline with six DC-3s.

In the 1950s and 1960s the Swire family expanded the airline and established airport and aircraft service companies. Swire Pacific, the holding company for most of the family's Hong Kong interests, went public in 1959. It won the Coca-Cola bottling franchise for Hong Kong in 1965. The fifth generation of Swires, John and Adrian, took command of parent company John Swire & Sons in 1968 (Adrian became chairman in 1987). The Taikoo Dockyard merged its business with Hongkong & Whampoa Dockyard in 1972.

The 1984 agreement to return Hong Kong to Chinese control in 1997 plunged the colony into uncertainty. Capital flight and free-falling real estate values gave Swire an opportunity to pick up properties at bargain prices.

Meanwhile, Cathay Pacific had become a major Pacific carrier. In 1987 Swire sold about 12% of the airline to CITIC, China's state-owned overseas investment company. (CITIC later increased its share.) Three years later Swire bought 35% of Hong Kong's Dragonair, also partly owned by CITIC, and gave it Cathay Pacific's Shanghai and Beijing routes.

In the 1990s Swire's financial results and property values fluctuated along with confidence about the consequences of China's takeover. In 1997 Swire expanded its Chinese operations, acquiring the rights to distribute Volvo cars in China and Hong Kong. As Asian financial markets collapsed, Swire sold its insurance-underwriting businesses to focus on core operations. Adrian Swire stepped down that year, relinquishing the John Swire & Sons chairmanship to a nonfamily member, Edward Scott.

To expand its dwindling undeveloped property base a Swire-led consortium bought a reclaimed waterfront site on Hong Kong Island in 1998. Reflecting a rebounding economy, in 1999 the company sold more than 274,000 sq. ft. of Hong Kong office space to Time Warner and Cable & Wireless HKT.

In 2000 Swire sold health care and medical products trading unit Swire Loxley to CITIC Pacific. The next year Swire Properties announced plans to build a major retail, office, and hotel project in Guangzhou in a joint venture with the Guangzhou Daily Group.

That year Swire sold its 49% stake in Carlsberg Brewery Hong Kong Ltd., in order to focus on its growing regional soft drinks operations. The company sold its 49% stake in Schneider Swire Ltd. to joint venture partner Schneider Electric Industries in 2002. Also that year Swire agreed to sell its controlling stake in its Coca-Cola bottling plant in Dongguan, China, to Coca-Cola.

EXECUTIVES

Chairman, Swire Pacific, Cathay Pacific Airways, and Hong Kong Aircraft Engineering: David M. Turnbull, age 49, $797,349 pay
Finance Director: M. Cubbon, age 48, $577,146 pay
Executive Director; Chairman, Taiwan Operations: Davy C. Y. Ho, age 57, $2,868,000 pay
Executive Director: Christopher D. Pratt, age 49

Property Director; Chairman, Swire Properties:
Keith G. Kerr, age 53, $8,997,000 pay
Chairman, John Swire & Sons:
James W. J. Hughes-Hallett, age 56
Managing Director, Beverages Division: John R. Slosar, age 49
Secretary: Yat Hung (David) Fu
Auditors: PricewaterhouseCoopers

LOCATIONS

HQ: Swire Pacific Limited
35th Fl., 2 Pacific Place, 88 Queensway, Hong Kong
Phone: +852-2840-8098   **Fax:** +852-2526-9365
Web: www.swirepacific.com

2005 Sales

	% of total
Asia	
Hong Kong	41
Other countries	30
North America	21
Shipping	8
Total	**100**

PRODUCTS/OPERATIONS

2005 Sales

	% of total
Property investment & trading	33
Trading & industrial	32
Beverages	27
Marine services	8
Total	**100**

Selected Subsidiaries

Aviation
  Cathay Pacific Airways Limited (46%)
  Hong Kong Air Cargo Terminals Limited (20%, cargo handling service)
  South China Aero Technology Limited (60%)
  Vogue Laundry Service Limited (46%)

Beverages
  Swire Beverages Holdings Limited
  Swire Coca-Cola Beverages Hefei Limited (60%, China)
  Swire Coca-Cola HK Limited (88%)
  Swire Coca-Cola USA
  Xian BC Coca-Cola Beverages Limited (75%, China)

Marine Services
  Honkong Salvage & Towage
  Hongkong United Dockyards Limited (50%)
  Pacific Manning Company Pty Limited (ship personnel management)
  Shekou Container Terminals Limited (17%)
  Swire Pacific Offshore Limited (management services, Bermuda)
  Swire Pacific Ship Management Limited (ship personnel management)

Properties
  Swire Properties Limited (holding company)
  Swire Properties, Inc. (US)

Trading and Industrial
  Beldare Motors Limited
  Crown Beverage Cans Hong Kong Limited (45%)
  ICI Swire Paints (China) Limited (36%)
  Intermarket Agencies (Far East) Limited (70%, sports and casual apparel)
  Swire Resources (sports shoes and apparel)
  Swire SITA Waste Services Limited (50%)
  Taikoo Motors Offshore Limited
  Taikoo Sugar Limited (branded food products)
  Waylung Waste Services Limited

COMPETITORS

AMR Corp.	Lai Sun Development
China Southern Airlines	Marks & Spencer
Henderson Land	Northwest Airlines
Development	PepsiCo
Hopewell Holdings	Qantas
HSBC Holdings	Sime Darby
Hutchison Whampoa	Singapore Airlines
ITOCHU	UAL
Japan Airlines	WBL Corporation
Jardine Matheson	Wing Tai
Kumagai Gumi	

HISTORICAL FINANCIALS

Company Type: Public

Income Statement

FYE: December 31

	REVENUE ($ mil.)	NET INCOME ($ mil.)	NET PROFIT MARGIN	EMPLOYEES
12/05	2,443	407	16.7%	63,500
12/04	2,357	842	35.7%	60,400
12/03	2,263	634	28.0%	56,700
12/02	1,951	693	35.5%	58,000
12/01	1,948	528	27.1%	55,000
Annual Growth	**5.8%**	**(6.3%)**	**—**	**3.7%**

Net Income History

OTC: SWRAY

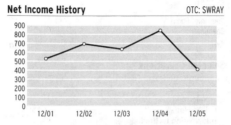

Tata Group

Founded as a textile trader more than a century ago, the Tata Group now includes enough businesses to blanket India. The nation's largest industrial conglomerate, Tata runs more than 90 companies in seven main business sectors: chemicals, communications and IT, consumer products, energy, engineering, materials, and services. Two of its largest operations are steelmaking, through Tata Steel, and vehicle manufacturing (Tata Motors). Tata Tea is one of the largest tea producers in the world and owns the venerable Tetley brand. Tata Steel has agreed to acquire Corus Group for £4.1 billion, which would create the sixth-largest steel company in the world. The group is managed through holding company Tata Sons.

The Tata family owns about 3% of Tata Sons. Much of the rest is held by charitable trusts established by the family; more than 60% of Tata Sons' profits are channeled into philanthropic trusts. Tata Sons generally holds only minority stakes in the group's companies but maintains control with the support of other investors, including state-owned financial institutions. However, Tata is restructuring its cross-holding structure. The company plans to increase its stakes in all of its group companies via the creeping acquisition route, beginning with Tata Tea. It expects to eventually own more than 50% of the company.

In 2006 the company agreed to make investments in Bangladesh totalling about $3 billion, including a steel plant, urea factory, and coal-powered energy plants. That year Tata Motors and the Brazilian truck chassis manufacturer Marcopolo formed a joint venture to make buses and coaches for India and other countries. Tata Motors also agreed to a joint venture with the venerable automaker Fiat to build cars for the Indian and export markets.

Tata moved into drug development with its joint venture Advinus Therapeutics, which it started with former Ranbaxy research director Rashmi Barbhaiya.

The group's hotel subsidiary is buying the Boston Ritz-Carlton Hotel for $170 million. It is its second hotel acquisition in the US (it also bought the Pierre Hotel in Manhattan in 2005).

HISTORY

Jamsetji Tata, a Parsi (Zoroastrian) from Bombay, started a textile trading company in 1868. He began in textile manufacturing, then embarked on a mission to industrialize India. Before his death in 1904 Tata had built the Taj Mahal Hotel in Bombay and set in motion plans to create a hydroelectric power plant, a forum for technical education and research in India, and a steel mill to supply rapidly expanding railroads.

Jamsetji's son Dorabji carried on. Dorabji found a jungle site for the steel mill, renamed the area Jamshedpur after his father, and in 1907 established Tata Iron and Steel Company (Tisco). Three years later Tata Hydro-Electric Power went on line. By 1911 Jamsetji's plans were realized when the Indian Institute of Science opened.

The British chairman of the Railway Board promised "to eat every pound of steel rail" Tata made. Tata shipped 1,500 miles of rail to British troops in Mesopotamia during WWI.

Six years after Dorabji's death in 1932, J. R. D. Tata, the son of Dorabji's cousin, took over the family empire. India's first licensed pilot, J. R. D. had started Tata Airlines, later nationalized as Air India. He founded Tata Chemicals in 1939. After WWII and Indian independence, the government built a state-owned steel industry but allowed Tata's mills to operate through a grandfather clause. Inefficient government operations led to high fixed prices for steel, and Tata profited.

Tata Engineering & Locomotive Co. (Telco), founded in 1945 to make steam locomotives, entered truck production in 1954 by collaborating with Daimler-Benz (now DaimlerChrysler). With help from Swiss firm Volkart Brothers, the company also started the Voltas manufacturing conglomerate. In 1962 Tata joined James Finlay of Scotland to create Tata-Finlay, now Tata Tea.

For a long time India's socialist government and unwieldy bureaucracy hampered Tata. The group was reluctant to pay bribes for licenses to enter new fields, and red tape and trade restrictions discouraged expansion abroad. A 1970 antitrust law ended the "managing agency" system, in which Tata Sons had held interests in subsidiaries and Tata Industries managed them for a fee; the subsidiaries became independently managed.

J. R. D. retired as chairman in 1991, and his nephew Ratan Tata took control of the company. In 1994 Tata formed a major alliance with Daimler-Benz to assemble cars. A Tata IBM joint venture in 1997 launched the first computer operating system in Hindi, India's national language (Tata sold its IBM stake in 1999).

In 2000 Tata Tea bought UK tea bag maker Tetley, an acquisition that made Tata the world's largest tea producer. In 2001 Tata made plans to sell its pharmaceuticals unit (Rallis India) and float 10% of its information technology unit (TCS).

In 2002 Tata acquired a 25% stake in telecom giant Videsh Sanchar Nigam Ltd. (VSNL) from the Indian government. Tata said it would combine its Tata Teleservices unit with VSNL. In 2003 Tata International formed an alliance with Turbo Power Systems Inc. to develop and distribute generational products and solutions used in the power generation industry. Tata Coffee signed an agreement with Starbucks to supply it with premium coffee beans starting in 2004.

Although a recessionary economy hurt India's heavy industries, Tata offset downturns with operations such as IT unit Tata Consultancy Services (TCS), which the group spun off in 2004 while still retaining 80% ownership.

Early the next year the group bought Singapore's National Steel, which boosted Tata's capacity by 2 million tons and greatly enhanced its position in the Asia/Pacific region.

Working to expand its telecommunications businesses, in 2006 Tata's IT and telecom companies joined forces with China's Huawei Technologies to bid for the telecom business of the Goa government. That year, it sold its 48% stake in Idea Cellular to Aditya Birla Group.

Tata Tea bought the Eight O'Clock coffee brand in 2006 for $220 million. That year Tata and Tata Tea bought a 30% stake in Energy Brands, the maker of health products.

Other deals were not so easy, however. Facing growing resistance in Europe to foreign ownership, in 2006 Tata subsidiary Tata Power dropped its bid for Siemens' hydropower business in Austria.

EXECUTIVES

Chairman: Ratan N. Tata, age 69
Member, Group Executive Office and Group Corporate Centre; Executive Director, Tata Sons; Chairman, Rallis India; Vice Chairman, Tata Chemicals: R. Gopalakrishnan, age 61
Member, Group Executive Office and Group Corporate Centre, and Finance Director; Finance Director, Tata Sons: Ishaat Hussain, age 59
Member, Group Executive Office and Group Corporate Centre; Managing Director, Tata Industries: Kishor A. Chaukar, age 58
Member, Group Executive Office and Group Corporate Centre; Executive Director, Tata Sons: Arunkumar R. (Arun) Gandhi
Member, Group Executive Office and Group Corporate Centre; Executive Director, Tata Sons: Alan Rosling
Member, Group Corporate Centre; Vice Chairman, Tata Sons and Tata Investment Corporation: Noshir A. Soonawala, age 71
Member, Group Corporate Centre; Chairman, Tata Refractories and TRF; Director, Tata Sons, Tata Industries, Tata Motors, and Tata International: Jamshed J. (J. J.) Irani, age 70
Member, Group Corporate Centre; Chairman Tata Coffee and Asian Coffee; Vice Chairman, Tata Tea and Indian Hotels: R. K. Krishna Kumar
Director, Tata Sons and Tata Industries; Chairman, Tata AIG Life Insurance, Tata AIG General Insurance, Tata Asset Management, and Tata Projects: Farrokh K. Kavarana, age 61
Chairman, Tata International, Tata Elxsi, Tata BP Solar India, and TCE Consulting Engineers: Syamal Gupta
Dean, Finance and Corporate Governance, Tata Management Training Centre (TMTC): Pratip Kar
EVP Human Resources: Satish Pradhan

SVP Corporate Affairs: Romit Chaterji
VP Learning and Director: Radhakrishnan Nair, age 44
VP Public Affairs: Sanjay Singh
VP Group Corporate Social Responsibility: Anant G. Nadkarni
Group General Counsel: Bharat Vasani
Manager, Information Technology: Berjes E. Shroff
Chief Economist: Siddhartha Roy
President, Tata International: Ram Balasubramaniam
Chief Archivist: H. Raghunath

LOCATIONS

HQ: Tata Group
Tata Sons Limited, Bombay House, 24, Homi Mody St., Mumbai 400 001, India
Phone: +91-22-5665-8282 **Fax:** +91-22-5665-8160
US HQ: 1700 N. Moore St., Ste. 1005, Arlington, VA 22209
US Phone: 703-243-9787
Web: www.tata.com

PRODUCTS/OPERATIONS

2006 Sales

	% of total
Engineering	32
Materials	23
Communications & information systems	20
Services	9
Energy	7
Consumer Goods	5
Chemicals	4
Total	**100**

Selected Operations

Communications and IT
 Control systems
  Nelco
  Tata Honeywell
 Information technology
  Nelito Systems
  Tata Consultancy Services (TCS, 80%)
   Tata Infotech
  Tata Elxsi
  Tata Interactive Systems
  Tata Technologies
 Telecommunications
  Tata Cellular
  Tata Internet Services
  Tata Telecom
  Tata Teleservices
  VSNL
Engineering
 Automotive
  Tata Auto Component Systems
  Tata Cummins
  Tata Engineering
  Telco Construction Equipment Co.
  Tata Holset
 Engineering products
  TAL Manufacturing Solutions
  TRF
  Voltas
 Engineering services
  Stewarts and Lloyds of India
  Tata Construction and Projects
  Tata Korf Engineering Services
  Tata Projects
  TCE Consulting Engineers
Materials
 Composites
  Tata Advanced Materials
 Metals
  Tata Steel (Tisco)
  Tata Metaliks
  Tata Refractories
  Tata Ryerson
  Tata Sponge Iron
  Tata SSL
  Tinplate Company of India
Energy
 Tata BP Solar India
 Tata Electric Companies

Consumer Products
 Tata Ceramics
 Tata Coffee Limited
 Tata McGraw Hill Publishing Company
 Tata Tea
 Tata Tetley
 Titan Industries
 Trent
Services
 Hotels and property development
  Indian Hotels Company (Taj Group)
  Information Technology Park
  Tata Housing Development Company
 Financial services
  Tata-AIG General Insurance
  Tata-AIG Life Insurance
  Tata-AIG Risk Management
  Tata Investment Corporation
 International operations
  Tata International
 Other services
  Tata Economic Consultancy Services
  Tata Services
  Tata Strategic Management Group
Chemicals
 Rallis India
 Tata Chemicals
 Tata Pigments

COMPETITORS

Accor	Infosys
Bechtel	James Finlay
Birla	Nippon Steel
BlueScope Steel	POSCO
Caterpillar	Procter & Gamble
Corus Group	Reliance Industries
Essar Group	Ritz-Carlton
Fluor	RPG
Ford	Steel Authority of India
Four Seasons Hotels	Suzuki Motor
GE	Toyota
General Motors	Unilever PLC
Hilton	United States Steel
Hindustan Lever	Wipro
Hyatt	Yamato Kogyo
Indian Oil	

HISTORICAL FINANCIALS

Company Type: Group

Income Statement

FYE: March 31

	REVENUE ($ mil.)	NET INCOME ($ mil.)	NET PROFIT MARGIN	EMPLOYEES
3/06	21,676	—	—	202,713
3/05	17,878	—	—	215,873
3/04	13,921	—	—	220,219
3/03	10,943	—	—	210,443
3/02	9,816	—	—	218,443
Annual Growth	21.9%	—	—	(1.9%)

Revenue History

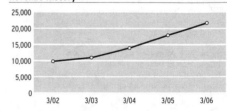

Tate & Lyle

Consumers get a rush from the business of Tate & Lyle — a sugar rush, that is. The company is one of the world's largest producers of white and raw sugar, including leading consumer brands Tate & Lyle (UK), Redpath (Canada), and Alcântara (Portugal). Headquartered in London, Tate & Lyle also makes sugar by-products such as molasses used in animal feed and citric acid, glutamate, and starches used in foodstuffs and packaging. The company is also the world's supplier of sucralose, the low-calorie sweetener sold under the name SPLENDA. Serving multiple sectors, Tate & Lyle's customers include those in the food, beverage, pharmaceutical, cosmetic, paper, packaging, and building industries.

With demand for SPLENDA at an all time high (it is used in more than 4,000 foods, beverages, and pharmaceuticals worldwide), Tate & Lyle doubled its production at its Alabama plant. Another sucralose plant in Singapore is scheduled to begin operations in 2007.

Continuing its growth strategy, in 2005 the company acquired Italian ingredients-maker Cesalpinia Foods; in 2006 it acquired Netherlands-based biodegradable-plastic company Hycail BV; and US specialty-food-ingredient operation Custom Continental Ingredients.

Some of the company's patents on SPLENDA expired in 2006, which puts the brand at risk of having to compete with possible generic versions of the product. Tate & Lyle, however, maintains that it is difficult to manufacture sucralose on a large scale and only it is equipped to do so. Determined to keep SPLENDA the only game in the sucralose town the company filed a suit in US Federal District Court in Illinois against one Chinese sucralose manufacturer and six importers.

During 2006 consumer groups in the US called for the FDA to revoke its approval of sucralose, saying health concerns such as skin rashes, headaches, and gastrointestinal problems had been ignored by the agency.

Sweet is not Tate & Lyle's only game. The company uses grains, wheat, and corn to make ethanol (used as an alternative fuel), citric acids (used in foods and beverages), starches (used in foodstuffs and packaging), and sweeteners (corn syrup, fructose, and others used in beverages, baked goods, and pharmaceuticals).

In reaction to America's increasing energy woes, in 2006 Tate & Lyle announced a $260 million investment in building a new wet-corn mill in Fort Dodge, Iowa. The mill will double the company's ethanol-production capacity.

Archer Daniels Midland sold its 6% share of Tate & Lyle in 2005. British bank Barclays owns 12% and French insurance giant AXA owns approximately 11%.

HISTORY

Henry Tate founded Henry Tate & Sons in 1869 and the next year began building a sugar refinery in Liverpool. Tate was noted for his philanthropy, and in 1896 he provided the money to found the Tate Gallery. When he died three years later, he left the business to his sons. In 1903 William Henry Tate took the company public, although only 17 investors, primarily family members, put up money for the company.

Abram Lyle founded his sugar company in 1881 when he bought Odam's and Plaistow Wharves, on the River Thames, to build a sugar

refinery. While Tate focused on sugar cubes, Lyle concentrated on a sugary concoction called Golden Syrup.

WWI saw an interruption in raw beet sugar imports from Germany and Austria, and in 1918 the two companies began discussing a merger. Although they combined, creating Tate & Lyle in 1921, they kept separate sales organizations into the 1940s. Seeking new sources of sugar, Tate & Lyle began investing abroad. In 1937 it created the West Indies Sugar Company and built a processing plant in Jamaica.

Although WWII brought sugar rationing (1940) and both of Tate & Lyle's London factories were severely damaged by bombs, there was great demand for the company's inexpensive syrup. Following the war, a movement to nationalize Tate & Lyle failed. In the 1950s Tate & Lyle expanded, buying Rhodesian Sugar Refineries (1953, now ZSR) and Canada & Dominion Sugar Company (1959, later Redpath Industries). It added United Molasses in 1965.

Tate & Lyle acquired the only other independent British cane refiner, Manbre and Garton, in 1976. That year it entered the US market when it bought Refined Sugars. The company added Portuguese sugar refiner Alcântara in 1983; US beet refiner Great Western Sugar Company in 1985; and Staley Continental (now A E Staley Manufacturing), a major producer of high-fructose corn syrup, in 1988. It sold Staley's food service business to SYSCO that year and bought Amstar Sugar Corporation (which became Domino Sugar). Tate & Lyle launched Sucralose, a low-calorie sweetener, in 1991 in cooperation with Johnson & Johnson. The company began investing millions in emerging markets in 1990 through acquisitions and joint ventures, including Mexico's Occidente in 1995.

Larry Pillard became CEO in 1996. Sucralose was approved for use in the US in 1998. Also in 1998 Tate & Lyle purchased the food ingredients division of Bayer Group's Haarmann & Reimer unit, renaming it Tate & Lyle Citric Acid. The deal made Tate & Lyle the only global producer of citric acid.

In 2001 Tate & Lyle sold off the Domino brand to a group of investors. As US sugar prices remained weak, during 2002 the company sold its Western Sugar business to Rocky Mountain Sugar Growers Cooperative. It also exited the sugar business in China with the sale of Well Pure to a group of Chinese investors.

As part of its strategy to jettison noncore or underperforming businesses, in 2002 Tate & Lyle sold its French monosodium glutamate production unit, Orsan S.A., to Ajinomoto. The next year the company sold United Molasses Co. and UM Canada to Westway Holdings.

In 2004 Tate & Lyle became the sole manufacturer of SPLENDA brand of sucralose, when it renegotiated its alliance with McNeil Nutritionals. Under the agreement, Tate produces SPLENDA and is responsible for its worldwide sales to food manufacturers; and McNeil is responsible for retail and foodservice sales. Later that same year Tate & Lyle formed a joint venture with DuPont to make an ingredient made from renewable sources such as corn to replace petrochemicals in the manufacture of clothing, plastics, and textiles.

In the largest food antitrust class-action suit in US history, parent Tate & Lyle paid $100 million in 2004 to settle a lawsuit concerning sweeteners used by Coke and Pepsi. The suit alleged that Tate & Lyle conspired to fix prices of high-fructose corn syrup.

EXECUTIVES

Chairman: Sir David Lees, age 69, $492,279 pay
CEO and Director: Iain Ferguson, age 50, $1,998,686 pay
COO and Director: Stanley Musesengwa, age 53, $1,360,290 pay
Corporate Development Director and Board Member: Stuart Strathdee, age 54, $530,548 pay
Group Finance Director: John Nicholas, age 49
Group Human Resources Director: Corry Wille, age 45
SVP Industrial Ingredients: Peter Boynton
Chief Executive, Amylum Group: Frank Karsbergen
Chief Executive, Food and Industrial Ingredients, Europe: Clive Rutherford
Chief Executive, Sugars, Europe: Ian Bacon, age 51
Group President, Manufacturing and Technology: Loren Luppes
President, Global Food Ingredients Group: Mark White
President, Food and Industrial Ingredients, Americas: D. Lynn Grider
President, Sucralose: Austin Maguire
President, Sugars, Americas: Silvio Allamandi
President, Support and Efficiency Services: Pat Mohan
Company Secretary and General Counsel: Robert (Rob) Gibber, age 43
Director Corporate Communications: Rowan Adams
Manager Community Relations: Michael Grier
Head of Global Research and Development: Robert (Bob) Schanefelt
Head of Investor Relations: Mark Robinson
Auditors: PricewaterhouseCoopers LLP

LOCATIONS

HQ: Tate & Lyle PLC
   Sugar Quay, Lower Thames St.,
   London EC3R 6DQ, United Kingdom
Phone: +44-20-7626-6525   **Fax:** +44-20-7623-5213
US HQ: 2200 E. El Dorado St., Decatur, IL 62525
US Phone: 217-421-4230   **US Fax:** 217-421-3167
Web: www.tate-lyle.co.uk

Tate & Lyle has more than 65 manufacturing and production sites in 29 countries, mainly in the Americas, Europe, and Southeast Asia.

2006 Sales

	% of total
North America	40
Europe	23
UK	18
Other regions	19
Total	**100**

PRODUCTS/OPERATIONS

2006 Sales

	% of total
Food & industrial ingredients	50
Sugars	46
Sucralose	4
Total	**100**

Selected Brands

Alcântara (Portugal)
Amylum (Europe)
Rebalance (Europe)
Redpath (Canada)
SPLENDA (worldwide)
Tate & Lyle (UK)

Selected Products

Animal feed (molasses)
Corn sweeteners (dextrose, fructose, glucose, high fructose corn syrup, maltodextrin)
Fermentation products (amino acid, citric acid, ethanol, monosodium glutamate, polyols, potable alcohol)
Starches and starch derivatives
Sugar (beet, cane, raw, white)

Selected Joint Ventures

Amylum Romania SA (49.7%, cereal sweeteners and
    starches)
DuPont Tate & Lyle Bio-Products Company LLC (50%,
    industrial ingredients)
IDEA SpA (blending, Italy)
Mexama, SA de CV (65%, citric acid, Mexico)
Orsan Guangzhou Gourmet Powder Company Limited
    (80%, glutamate producer, China)
Tapioca Development Corporation (33%, starch,
    Thailand)
United Molasses (Ireland) Ltd. (50%, molasses)

COMPETITORS

ADM	Kerry Group
Ag Processing	Kerry Ingredients
American Crystal Sugar	Merisant Worldwide
Associated British Foods	National Starch
C&H Sugar	NutraSweet
Cargill	Onex
Connell Company	Penford
Corn Products	PPB
CSM	Roquette Frères
Cumberland Packing	Südzucker
Danisco a/s	Sterling Sugars
Florida Crystals	Tereos
Greencore	Tongaat-Hulett
Imperial Sugar	U.S. Sugar

HISTORICAL FINANCIALS

Company Type: Public

Income Statement			FYE: March 31
	REVENUE ($ mil.)	**NET INCOME** ($ mil.)	**NET PROFIT MARGIN**	**EMPLOYEES**
3/06	6,471	—	—	9,349
3/05	6,279	—	—	11,200
3/04	5,782	—	—	11,500
3/03	4,985	—	—	9,500
3/02	5,623	—	—	8,503
Annual Growth	3.6%	—	—	2.4%

Revenue History Pink Sheets: TATYY

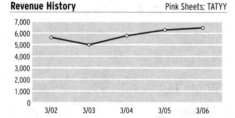

Tatung

Tatung can make sure you stay connected, stay
cool, and cook a perfect bowl of rice. The company
manufactures computer products (LCD monitors,
tablet computers), appliances (air conditioners,
refrigerators, rice cookers), industrial goods
(cable and wire, transformers, motors), and medical devices (blood pressure monitors, electrical
massage devices, thermometers). The company
also offers product development, prototyping, and
logistics services. The family-run company maintains a close relationship with Tatung University
and Tatung Senior High School, institutions en-
dowed by Tatung's founder, Shan-Chih Lin.

Tatung has subsidiaries in more than a dozen
countries. Taiwan-based subsidiaries include

Tatung OTIS Elevator (a joint venture with US-
based elevator maker Otis Elevator), Chunghwa
Picture Tubes (cathode-ray tube and LCD products), San Chih Semiconductor (silicon wafers),
and Taiwan Telecommunication Industry (videoconferencing and phone products). Its US operations include Tatung Company of America
(displays and appliances).

HISTORY

Shan-Chih Lin founded a construction company, the Shan-Chih Business Association, in
1918. Projects during its 30-year lifespan included
the Taiwanese government's Building of the Executive Yuan, which houses the country's ministry offices.

The company entered heavy industry in 1946
when it began repairing railway cars. It diversified into electric products in 1949 with fans,
which it started exporting five years later. In
1950 the company changed its name to Tatung
("great harmony").

Because he believed strongly in the importance of education, when Lin retired in 1942, he
donated 80% of his assets to the Hsieh-Chih Association for the Development of Industry, which
went on to administer scholarships, awards, the
Tatung Institute of Technology, and the Hsieh-
Chih Industrial Publishing Company. The phil-
anthropist's bequest established the Tatung
Schools-Company, made up of the Institute of
Technology and Tatung High School. This
education-industry cooperative provides hands-
on training in Tatung factories and offices. The
Institute of Technology was founded in 1956.

During the 1960s Tatung expanded further into
home appliances and electronics, adding refrigerators (1961), air conditioners (1964), and televisions (1964) to its product line. Taiwan
Telecommunication was formed in 1966.

Lin died in 1971. In 1972 Lin's grandson, Lin
Weishan (W. S.) was named president; he began
expanding Tatung's operations overseas. Tatung
established US subsidiary Tatung Co. of America
that year, initially to make electric fans. In 1973
Tatung formed a joint venture with Japanese
computer maker Fujitsu. Tatung would go on
that decade to establish offices in Japan (1975)
and South Korea (1979).

The company's joint venture with US company
Otis Elevator was formed in 1983. Tatung continued to expand overseas during the 1980s, establishing subsidiaries in the UK (1981) and
Germany (1985). During that period the company
continued to move production overseas, shipping
the finished goods back to Taiwan as imports.

Tatung's profits slipped in the early 1990s as
Taiwan's economy slowed, but the company rebounded, signing a deal with Packard Bell (folded
into NEC) in 1991 to supply the computer marketer with 100,000 PCs a month. In 1994 the
company formed an alliance with telecommunications company QUALCOMM to develop cellular phone systems for Taiwan.

The following year Tatung subsidiary Chunghwa Picture Tubes began making large picture
tubes for Toshiba. Tatung started making computer motherboards in 1996.

To keep pace with Internet use, the company
in 1997 introduced an Internet access set-top
box. Sales were down that fiscal year, a result of
the Asian economic crisis and falling cathode-
ray tube prices. In 1998 Tatung unveiled a DVD
player and its PC Cinema, a PC combining TV,
computer, and telephone functions with Internet access.

In 1999 Chunghwa Picture Tubes opened Taiwan's first factory to build thin-film transistor
LCDs. The subsidiary's chairman was indicted
later that year for allegedly investing foreign capital to manipulate parent Tatung's stock
(Chunghwa itself went public on the Taipei exchange in 2001). In 2000 Tatung spun off its information and communications department as a
separate company, Tatung System Technologies.

Tatung jumped on the mobile computing
bandwagon in 2001, introducing a tablet PC.
Bucking the downsizing trend in the electronics
industry, the company expanded its production
capacity in China and Europe the next year.

In 2003 Tatung System Technologies won the
build-operate-transfer contract for the National
Taiwan Science Education Center.

2004 was a year for new operating units.
Tatung established SeQual Technologies (oxygen generators for therapeutic and home health
care uses), Tatung Compressors (Zhongshan) of
China, and Toes Opto-Mechatronics.

The company in 2005 set up another Chinese
subsidiary, Tatung Wire & Cable Technology
(Wujiang). That same year Tatung combined its
Desktop PC business unit with Elitegroup Computer Systems (ECS), becoming the largest
shareholder in ECS.

Lin Weishan (W. S.) was elected chairman of
Tatung in 2006.

EXECUTIVES

Chairman: Lin Tingsheng
President: Lin Weishan
EVP: W. T. Lin
Marketing Director: Greg Hwang
Production Director: H. H. Lin
Managing Director, Tatung (UK) Ltd.: C. T. Lin
President, Tatung Science and Technology: Kam Chan
European Manager, Tatung Server Europe: Andre Hu
UK Sales Manager, Tatung Server: Mark Burnett
Sales Manager: Shawn Chang

LOCATIONS

HQ: Tatung Co.
    22 Chungshan North Rd., Sec. 3, Taipei, Taiwan
Phone: +886-22-592-5252   **Fax:** +886-22-592-1813
US HQ: 2850 El Presidio St., Long Beach, CA 90810
US Phone: 310-637-2105   **US Fax:** 310-637-8484
Web: www.tatung.com.tw

Tatung has operations in Canada, China, the Czech
Republic, Japan, Mexico, the Netherlands, Singapore,
Taiwan, Thailand, the UK, the US, and Vietnam.

PRODUCTS/OPERATIONS

Selected Products

Computers and Communications
    Monitors
    Peripherals
    Silicon wafers

Consumer Products
    Air conditioners and dehumidifiers
    Compressors
    Microwave ovens
    Refrigerators
    Rice cookers
    Office furniture and office furniture systems
    Televisions and video displays

Industrial Equipment
    Copper rods
    Cyclos
    Elevators
    Industrial castings
    Motors
    Switch gears
    Transformers
    Varnishes and varnish thinners
    Wire and cable

COMPETITORS

Acer
CASIO COMPUTER
Dell
Dover
Electrolux
Emerson Electric
Fuji Electric
Fujitsu
GE
Hewlett-Packard
Hitachi
IBM
Kyocera
Lennox
Lenovo
LG Group
Marubeni
Matsushita
Mitsumi Electric
Nam Tai
NEC
Oki Electric
Philips Electronics
Pioneer
Quanta Computer
Samsung Group
SANYO
Sharp
Siemens AG
Sony
Sumitomo Electric
Sun Microsystems
Taiwan Semiconductor
telent
Toshiba
United Microelectronics
United Technologies
Whirlpool
Yamaha
Zenith

TDK

While TDK may be best known for blank audiotapes and CDs, the company actually records most of its sales from the sale of manufactured electronic materials and components. The company, which pioneered the use of the magnetic substance ferrite in the 1930s, is a major supplier of such products as ferrite magnets, transformer and inductor cores, and multilayer chip capacitors. Other components include voltage-controlled oscillators, noise reduction filters, and magnetic recording heads used inside computer disk drives. TDK decided to end manufacturing of recordable CDs and DVDs in early 2006, closing a plant in Luxembourg.

Consistently looking overseas for expansion of its business, the company derives more than 70% of sales from outside of Japan. Like many manufacturers, TDK has set up operations in China to take advantage of lower production costs and to gain entree to the world's largest consumer market.

In 2005 TDK sold its semiconductor business in order to focus on core product lines. It continues to make capacitors, ferrite cores, inductors, and high-frequency components. Also that year, the company acquired the Lambda power supply systems business of Invensys.

HISTORY

Kanzo Saito, who had previously raised rabbits for their fur, took out a patent in 1935 on ferrite, a type of ceramic made mainly from iron oxide that held promise for electronics applications. (Japan's Yogoru Kato is credited with inventing the material.) Saito founded Tokyo Denkikagaku Kogyo K.K. (TDK) to pioneer the mass production of ferrite and output rose quickly as developers found countless new uses for the substance. Saito handed over the presidency of the company in 1946 to Teiichi Yamazaki, who expanded TDK's portfolio into products such as magnetic recording tape (1952).

The company's global thrust began when it opened a Los Angeles office in 1959. Two years later it was listing shares on the Tokyo Stock Exchange. TDK branched into cassette tapes in 1966 and electromagnetic wave absorbers in 1968, the year the company opened its first overseas manufacturing center in Taiwan.

During the 1970s TDK launched operations in Australia, Europe, and South America. It began listing its shares on the New York Stock Exchange in 1982. That year the company also introduced a solar battery. In 1983 TDK officially changed its name to TDK Corporation.

In 1987 Hiroshi Sato was appointed president of the company. TDK bought integrated circuit maker Silicon Systems in 1989 (sold in 1996 to Texas Instruments) as Sato began to modernize the company's offerings and organization. With a conservative management style, he'd often wait to see how other companies fared in new markets before committing TDK, prompting the industry to label him the "gambler who follows someone else." During his tenure, Sato gave the company solid footholds in niches such as optical disks, high-density heads, and cellular phone components.

To reverse falling profits in 1992, Sato made plans to eliminate managers by playing on the Japanese sense of honor — he asked them to accept pay cuts and work on standby at home until their retirement, expecting that they would simply resign. Sato was forced to scuttle the plan amid international outcries and depleted morale.

The company revamped its organization in 1994 around four operating divisions. That year it began producing high-end magnetic heads in China, but poor demand and a weakened yen hurt sales and profits. Meanwhile, TDK had become the global leader in magnetic tape manufacturing.

The company bought UK-based communications equipment maker Grey Cell Systems in 1997, thereby gaining a European presence in the data transmission market. In 1998 Sato and Yamazaki retired; Hajime Sawabe was tapped as president and CEO. After a sluggish Japanese economy caused earnings to decline in 1999, TDK restructured its product lines again the next year and acquired California-based Headway Technologies, a maker of giant magnetoresistive heads used in computer disk drives.

TDK, like other high-tech firms, suffered the ravages of the deep slump in the electronics market during the early 21st century. Sales of components fell off as manufacturers reacted to weak demand for PCs, mobile phones, and other electronics gear.

Competitive pricing in the CD-R market led to losses for TDK's recording media business in 2001, prompting the company to close many of its manufacturing plants and outsource its blank tape and CD manufacturing. Meanwhile, price pressures from competitors in China and Taiwan,

especially in the recordable media sector, added to TDK's woes and contributed to losses in 2002.

The company in 2003 sold subsidiary TDK Mediactive, which makes video games for PCs and game consoles, to Take-Two Interactive.

In 2004 TDK joined the Blu-ray Disc Founders (now known as the Blu-ray Disc Association), a trade organization of electronics manufacturers embracing an advanced DVD format originally established by Sony. An opposing format, HD-DVD, has been put forward by Toshiba and NEC, and endorsed by multiple manufacturers. Some companies are making products for both formats.

The company opened the TDK History Museum in Akita prefecture in 2005, on the 70th anniversary of TDK's founding.

Hajime Sawabe was named chairman and CEO in 2006, while EVP Takehiro Kamigama was promoted to president and COO.

EXECUTIVES

Chairman and CEO: Hajime Sawabe, age 64
President and COO: Takehiro Kamigama, age 48
SEVP: Kiyoshi Ito, age 61
EVP: Jiro Iwasaki, age 60
SVP and General Manager, Electronic Components Sales and Marketing: Shinji Yoko, age 58
SVP and General Manager, Intellectual Properties Center, Materials Research Center, and Information Technology Research Center: Takeshi Nomura, age 54
SVP: Michinori Katayama, age 59
Chairman, TDK China: Raymond Leung, age 50
Corporate Officer and General Manager, Network Devices Business: Yukio Hirokawa, age 59
Corporate Officer and General Manager, Recording Media and Solutions Business: Masatoshi Shikanai, age 56
Corporate Officer and General Manager, Corporate Research and Development Center: Kenryo Namba, age 59
Corporate Officer, General Manager, Capacitors Group, and Deputy General Manager, Circuit Devices Business Group: Takaya Ishigaki, age 53
Corporate Officer and General Manager, Sensors and Actuators Business: Minoru Takahashi, age 58
Corporate Officer; General Manager, Finance and Accounting Department; and CFO: Seiji Enami, age 59
Corporate Officer: Shinichi Araya
Corporate Officer: Shiro Nomi
Corporate Officer: Shunji Itakura
Auditors: KPMG AZSA & Co.

LOCATIONS

HQ: TDK Corporation
1-13-1 Nihonbashi, Chuo-ku,
Tokyo 103-8272, Japan
Phone: +81-3-5201-7102   **Fax:** +81-3-5201-7114
US HQ: 901 Franklin Ave., Garden City, NY 11530
US Phone: 516-535-2600   **US Fax:** 516-294-8318
Web: www.tdk.co.jp

TDK has manufacturing facilities in China, Hong Kong, Hungary, Israel, Japan, Malaysia, the Philippines, South Korea, Taiwan, Thailand, the UK, and the US, with sales offices around the world.

2006 Sales

	$ mil.	% of total
Asia/Pacific		
Japan	1,484	22
Other countries	3,861	57
Americas	771	11
Europe	648	10
Middle East & Africa	32	—
Total	**6,796**	**100**

PRODUCTS/OPERATIONS

2006 Sales

	$ mil.	% of total
Electronic materials & components		
Recording devices		
Electronic materials	1,545	23
Electronic devices	1,322	19
Other electronic components	311	4
Recording media & systems	918	14
Total	**6,796**	**100**

Selected Products

Data Storage
Magnetic heads (hard disk drives)
Thermal printing heads
Electronic Components
Anechoic chambers
Capacitors
Converters
Cores and magnets
Ferrite
Metal
Rubber and plastic
Electrodes
Ferrite electromagnetic wave absorbers
Inductors and coils
Noise filters
Optical isolators
Oscillators
Power supplies
PTC/NTC thermistors
Sensors
Transformers
Uninterruptible power systems (UPS)
Varistors
Recording Media and Systems
Audio tape
Computer-aided instruction software
Magnetic tape (computers)
MiniDiscs
PC cards and peripherals
Video tape
Other
Factory automation systems
MPEG-4 based streaming server software
Organic EL displays
Solar cells

COMPETITORS

AVX	Pioneer
EPCOS	Samsung Group
Fujifilm	Sanken Electric
Fujitsu	Solectron
Hitachi	Sony
Imation	Toshiba
KEMET	Tyco Electronics
Kyocera	Vicor Corporation
Matsushita	Vishay Intertechnology
Murata Manufacturing	Yamaha
Philips Electronics	

HISTORICAL FINANCIALS

Company Type: Public

Income Statement

FYE: March 31

	REVENUE ($ mil.)	NET INCOME ($ mil.)	NET PROFIT MARGIN	EMPLOYEES
3/06	6,796	377	5.5%	53,923
3/05	6,148	311	5.1%	37,115
3/04	6,216	397	6.4%	36,804
3/03	5,102	100	2.0%	31,705
Annual Growth	**10.0%**	**55.5%**	**—**	**19.4%**

2006 Year-End Financials

Debt ratio: 0.1%
Return on equity: 6.3%
Cash ($ mil.): 2,043

Current ratio: 3.34
Long-term debt ($ mil.): 3

Net Income History

NYSE: TDK

Telecom Italia

Former state monopoly Telecom Italia is changing with the times. Following through on a reorganization plan started in 2001, the company now operates through four divisions. The Operations side of the company includes its wireline unit, Italy's #1 telephone operator, and international wireline holdings (metro broadband network services in France, Germany, and the Netherlands and wholesale network operations in Europe and South America). It also includes its domestic and international (Brazilian) mobile businesses. Its remaining two divisions, considered Business Units, consist of its Media holdings (news, TV production, and Web content) and Olivetti, its specialized applications provider.

Like other telecommunications companies, Telecom Italia is embracing convergence as the future of the industry. Evidence of the company's commitment to this strategy is its elimination of the separate wireline and wireless division in favor of a "one company" strategy of integrated management. The effort simplified a complicated management structure and reduced debt at the same time. The company's Telecom Italia Mobile, or TIM, subsidiary, Italy's #1 wireless provider, has been merged into Telecom Italia.

The company's Telecom Italia Media unit includes leading ISP Nuova Tin.it, which includes the assets of Virgilio purchased in 2005. It also includes MTV Italia, La7 Televisioni, and TM News, which distributes Associated Press news and other content to media and corporate subscribers. Telecom Italia sold its nearly 62% stake in directories unit SEAT Pagine Gialle to an investor group in a deal valued at $3.55 billion.

Telecom Italia also provides office products and the development and production of products using silicon technology, such as ink-jet printer heads) through Olivetti, a former rival that once controlled 55% of Telecom Italia before a complex merger and reorganization.

HISTORY

After gaining political power in Italy, Benito Mussolini began a program of nationalization, focusing first on three major banks and their equity portfolios. Included were three local phone companies that became the core of Societa Finanziaria Telefonica (STET), created in 1933 to handle Italy's phone services under the state's industrial holding company, Istituto per La Ricostruzione Industriale (IRI).

Germany and Italy grew closer in the years leading up to WWII, and Italian equipment makers entered a venture with Siemens to make phone equipment. STET came through the war

with most of its infrastructure intact and a monopoly on phone service in Italy. Siemens' properties, along with those of other equipment makers, were taken over by another company, TETI, which was nationalized and put under STET's control in 1958. This expanded STET's monopoly to include equipment manufacturing.

Italy's industries were increasingly nationalized under IRI. Companies within the IRI family forged alliances with each other and with independent companies, which frequently were absorbed into STET.

STET's scope expanded during the 1960s and 1970s to include satellite and data communications, but its monopoly was undermined by new technologies such as faxes, PCs, and teleconferencing. In the technology race among equipment makers, STET fell behind. And in a satellite communications era, STET's status as a necessary long-distance carrier was threatened. Despite these pressures, change did not come easily to STET. State monopolies maintained popular support, not only on nationalistic grounds but also because of labor's strong anticompetitive stance.

Anticipating privatization, however, IRI reorganized STET in 1994 and poured new capital into the company. STET's five telecom companies — SIP (domestic phone operator), Italcable (intercontinental), Telespazio (satellite), SIRM (maritime), and Iritel (domestic long distance) — were merged into one, Telecom Italia. Its mobile phone business was spun off as Telecom Italia Mobile (TIM) in 1995.

To end political feuding, the government abruptly replaced the heads of STET and Telecom Italia in 1997. Telecom Italia was merged with STET, which took the Telecom Italia name and was privatized that year. Berardino Libonati became chairman, and Franco Bernabe, formerly CEO of oil company ENI, took the helm as CEO. The company had begun taking stakes in foreign telecom companies, including Mobilkom Austria, Spanish broadcaster Retevision, and — as European Union competition began in 1998 — Telekom Austria.

Erstwhile rival Olivetti launched a hostile takeover bid for Telecom Italia in 1999. Though Telecom Italia tried to fend off the smaller firm with various maneuvers, including a proposed merger with Deutsche Telekom, Olivetti gained 55% of Telecom Italia. Olivetti CEO Roberto Colaninno took over as chairman and CEO.

In 2001 Colaninno and several other Telecom Italia officials were named as suspects in an investigation of whether the company had violated accounting, conflict-of-interest, and share-manipulation laws. Colaninno was replaced when tire maker Pirelli and Edizione Holding, the parent company of the Benetton Group, acquired a 23% stake in Olivetti.

Telecom Italia teamed up with Rupert Murdoch's News Corp. to develop the Stream pay TV joint venture, renamed Sky Italia. The venture gained a kick-start when the two companies teamed to buy Italian pay-TV business Telepiu from Vivendi Universal in a cash and debt assumption deal that was valued at $871 million. Telecom Italia then sold a 30% stake in the venture to News Corp. It retained a 20% share with News Corp. controlling 80%.

Once the subsidiary, Telecom Italia became the parent company after the 2003 merger with former parent Olivetti. The reorganization simplified a corporate structure that was at best confusing. Because Telecom Italia accounted for more than 95% of the revenues of Olivetti, the reorganization also kept the focus on the core business.

The company began selling some international fixed-line assets and putting some wireless operations outside Italy on the market. Disposals included Digitel, the Venezuelan wireless carrier, to Oswaldo Cisneros' Telvenco in a deal valued at about $425 million. It also sold its 81% stake in Greek wireless carrier Hellas Telecommunications, to US-based private equity firms Texas Pacific Group and Apax Partners in a deal valued at $1.4 billion.

The company also sold its nearly 62% stake in directories unit SEAT Pagine Gialle to an investor group in a deal valued at $3.55 billion.

EXECUTIVES

Chairman: Guido Rossi, age 75
Deputy Chairman: Gilberto Benetton, age 65
CEO and Director: Carlo O. Buora, age 60
Operations CEO and Director: Riccardo Ruggiero, age 46
Head of Finance, Administration, and Control; Head of Internet and Media Business Unit; Managing Director, Telecom Italia Media: Enrico Parazzini, age 62
Head of Human Resources and Organization: Gustavo Emanuele Bracco, age 58
Head of Purchasing: Germanio Spreafico, age 54
Head of Mobile Business Unit and Director; Managing Director, Telecom Italia Mobile: Marco De Benedetti, age 44
Head of Communication and Image: Gian Carlo Rocco di Torrepadula
Head of Corporate and Legal Affairs: Aldo Cappuccio, age 57
Head of Telecom Italia Latin America: Paolo Dal Pino, age 43
Head of Internal Audit: Armando Focaroli, age 61
Head of Mergers and Acquisitions: Francesca Di Carlo, age 43
Head of Public and Economic Affairs: Riccardo Perissich, age 64
Head of International Affairs: Giampaolo Zambeletti
Head of IT Governance: Marco Forneris
Head of International and Legal Affairs: Nicola Verdicchio
Head of Investor Relations: Valeria Leone
Head of Security: Giovanni Penna
General Counsel: Francesco Chiappetta, age 46
Brand Enrichment Manager: Andrea Kerbaker, age 46
Chairman and CEO, Olivetti Tecnost S.p.A.: Giovanni Ferrario
Auditors: Reconta Ernst & Young S.p.A.

LOCATIONS

HQ: Telecom Italia S.p.A.
Corso d'Italia 41, 00198 Rome, Italy
Phone: +39-06-36-881   **Fax:** +39-06-36-882-965
Web: www.telecomitalia.it

2005 Sales

	$ mil.	% of total
Europe		
Italy	28,768.2	79
Other countries	2,753.6	8
Central & South America	3,804.3	11
North America	434.8	1
Australia, Africa & Asia	471.0	1
Total	**36,231.9**	**100**

PRODUCTS/OPERATIONS

2005 Sales

	$ mil.	% of total
Wireline	19,782.6	55
Mobile	15,362.3	42
Olivetti	471.0	1
Media	217.4	1
Other revenues	398.6	1
Total	**36,231.9**	**100**

2005 Sales

	$ mil.	% of total
Services		
Traffic	18,863.8	52
Subscription charges	9,712.2	27
Fees	437.2	1
Other services	4,325.7	12
Sales		
Telephone products	2,363.8	7
Other sales	438.4	1
Revenue on construction contracts	90.8	—
Total	**36,231.9**	**100**

Selected Subsidiaries and Affiliates

Wireline
  BBNed N.V. (96%, telecommunications services, The Netherlands)
  HanseNet Telekommunikation GmbH (broadband network operator, Germany)
  Liberty Surf Group
  Loquendo S.p.A.
  Matrix S.p.A. (Internet services)
  Nuova Tin.it S.r.l. (Internet services)
  Path. Net S.p.A. (99.9%, networking systems and telecommunications)
  Telecontact Center S.p.A.
  Telecom Italia Deutschland GmbH
  Telecom Italia Sparkle Group (development of international services for heavy users such as fixed-line operators, ISPs, and international companies)
Mobile
  TIM Brasil Group
    TIM Celular S.A.
      Blah! S.A.
      CRC — Centro de relacionamento com clientes Ltda
  TIM Participaçoes Group
  TIM Italia
Media
  Telecom Italia Media S.p.A.
    Holding Media e Comunicazione S.p.A. (TV licenses for La7 and MTV Italia)
    TM News
Olivetti Group
  Olivetti S.p.A. (formerly Olivetti Tecnost)
    Olivetti I-Jet S.p.A.
    Olivetti International B.V. (The Netherlands)
    Wirelab S.p.A. (10%)

COMPETITORS

BT	Océ Imagistics
Cable & Wireless	Ricoh
Canon	SFR
Danka	Swisscom
Deutsche Telekom AG	Telefónica
FastWeb	Tiscali
France Telecom	Vodafone Omnitel
Hewlett-Packard	Wind Telecomunicazioni
Hutchison Whampoa	Xerox
IBM	

HISTORICAL FINANCIALS

Company Type: Public

Income Statement

FYE: December 31

	REVENUE ($ mil.)	NET INCOME ($ mil.)	NET PROFIT MARGIN	EMPLOYEES
12/05	36,232	2,297	6.3%	85,484
12/04	43,050	2,103	4.9%	91,365
12/03	39,172	2,312	5.9%	93,187
12/02	32,319	868	2.7%	106,620
Annual Growth	**3.9%**	**38.3%**	**—**	**(7.1%)**

2005 Year-End Financials

Debt ratio: 96.5%
Return on equity: 4.6%
Cash ($ mil.): 13,277
Current ratio: 1.05
Long-term debt ($ mil.): 51,006

No. of shares (mil.): —
Dividends
  Yield: 3.6%
  Payout: —
Market value ($ mil.): —

Stock History

NYSE: TI

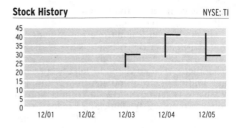

45				
40				
35				
30				
25				
20				
15				
10				
5				
0	12/01	12/02	12/03	12/04	12/05

	STOCK PRICE ($) FY Close	P/E High/Low		PER SHARE ($) Earnings	Dividends
12/05	29.21	—	—	—	1.04
12/04	40.87	—	—	—	0.92
12/03	29.70	—	—	—	—
Annual Growth	**(0.8%)**	**—**	**—**	**—**	**13.0%**

Telefónica

Spain's onetime phone monopoly, Telefónica, is still the telecommunications *jefé* among Spanish- and Portuguese-speaking populations worldwide. Through Telefónica de España, the company is the leading fixed-line operator in Spain with more than 16 million lines in service. It has more than 41 million total fixed lines in service including operations in Latin America through subsidiary Telefónica Latinoamérica and in the Czech Republic through Telefónica O2 Czech Republic (formerly the Cesky Group). Telefónica Móviles, its 93%-owned wireless unit (it is buying the rest), has 20 million subscribers in Spain among 135 million overall. The company is merging its operations with those of Telefónica Móviles.

Spain's dominant phone company is like a latter-day conquistador. The company's most recent victory is the acquisition of UK-based mobile phone operator O2. The deal, valued at more than $31 billion, gives Telefónica a strong presence in the UK, including Ireland, and in Germany. The Spanish operator did not yet have operations in those regions and the deal is a major step in European expansion. To help pay the costs the company is considering the sale of its 60% stake in phone directory business Telefónica Publicidad e Información (TPI).

Telefónica also is seeking fortune in Latin America where it has made acquisitions and formed partnerships to extend its holdings in both fixed-line and wireless operations (Latin American holds more than half the company's assets and accounts for more than 40% of its revenue). Through its Telefónica Móviles unit, the company agreed to acquire the assets of BellSouth Latin America Group, which has holdings in 10 South and Central American countries, in a deal valued at more than $5.8 billion. When completed, the deal will make Telefónica the region's largest telecom operator. Telefónica is also building an undersea fiber-optic cable to connect the US and Latin America.

At home, the company's domestic operations provide phone and data transmission services. Telefónica also provides pay-TV services in Spain, as well as in Peru. In addition, the company has acquired a 51% stake in Ceský Telecom from the

Czech government with the intention of taking full ownership in the company.

Although it's a leading telecom provider in some Latin American markets, such as Brazilian and Mexican mobile telecommunications, Telefónica has fallen victim to volatile currency and political issues in others. In addition, the company is facing increased competition at home, prompting Telefónica de España to cut nearly a third of its workforce by 2008. The company also is straightening out its media holdings by selling its Antena 3 broadcast TV station. It also has sold its Vía Digital pay-TV service to rival Sogecable.

Banco Bilbao Vizcaya Argentaria (BBVA) and La Caixa are Telefónica's largest shareholders (owning about 7% and 5%, respectively).

HISTORY

When a 1923 military coup brought General Miguel Primo de Rivera to power in Spain, the government-run phone system was in shambles. More than half of the country's 90,000 lines did not work. With little cash in the government coffers, Primo de Rivera sought foreign assistance.

Supported by National City Bank (now Citigroup), US-based ITT bought three private Spanish phone companies, later combining them to form Compañía Telefónica Nacional de España. The ITT unit gained the state phone concession in 1924, and the government agreed not to reclaim the system for 20 years. But when Franco came to power in 1939, he froze Telefónica's assets. ITT tried to sell the company to German buyers in 1941 but backed out when the US State Department objected. The Spanish government nationalized Telefónica in 1945, keeping 41% of its shares.

Long-distance service was introduced in 1960, satellite communications in 1967, and international service in 1971. Still, when Spain entered the European Union (EU) in 1986, Telefónica was unprepared for the increase in demand for services, and complaints rose.

The firm purchased a minority stake in Compañía de Teléfonos de Chile in 1990, and a Telefónica-led consortium won a bid to manage the southern half of ENTEL, Argentina's former state phone system. The company acquired a majority stake in Peru's telecom monopoly in 1994 and a year later joined Unisource, a European telecom consortium.

The Spanish government at first defied the EU's directive to break up its telecom monopoly. But in 1994 the government announced it would meet the EU's 1998 deadline for opening telecom markets; in exchange Telefónica won permission to begin new businesses when competition arrived.

Flamboyant former investment banker Juan Villalonga took over as chairman in 1996. The boyhood friend of Spain's prime minister began expanding Telefónica's presence in Latin America with several acquisitions in 1997. They included 35% of Brazil's Companhia Riograndense de Telecomunicações (CRT); a large stake in Multicanal, Argentina's #1 cable company (sold in 1998 to Grupo Clarín); and 35% of satellite TV service Vía Digital.

The Spanish government had finished divesting its interest in the company in 1997 (retaining a golden share), and competition came to Spain the next year. The company cut 10,000 jobs and became Telefónica S.A. It also won fixed-line phone company Telesp and a cellular company in Brazil's auction of the former national phone company,

Telebras. In 1999 Telefónica sold to the public part of its Internet unit, Terra Networks. The next year it took near-total ownership of four of its Latin American units: Telefónica de Argentina, Telefónica del Perú, Telesp, and Tele Sudeste Celular.

To expand its multimedia offerings, Telefónica bought Netherlands-based independent TV producer Endemol for $5.3 billion in 2000 and formed Telefónica Media. After dropping out of the UK wireless license auction, the company teamed up with Finland's Sonera (later acquired by Telia) to win a license in the German auction. But when merger talks with Dutch telecom carrier KPN broke down, Villalonga resigned over disagreements on the direction of the company.

In 2001 Telefónica combined its Brazilian mobile telephone holdings with those of Portugal Telecom to form market leader Brasilcel. Telefónica then spent $2.7 billion in Mexico in 2001 and 2002 to buy four wireless operators and a 65%-stake in a fifth (Pegaso PCS) to achieve #2 in that market.

EXECUTIVES

Executive Chairman and CEO: César Alierta Izuel, age 60
Vice Chairman: Isidro Fainé Casas, age 62
CFO and General Manager of Finance and Corporate Development: Santiago Fernández Valbuena, age 46
General Manager, Development, Planning, and Regulation, and Director: Luis Lada Díaz, age 56
General Manager, Corporate Communication: Luis Abril Pérez, age 57
General Manager, Auditing and Management Resources: Calixto Ríos Pérez, age 60
General Director, Human Resources: Óscar Maraver Sánchez-Valdepeñas
General Director, Sponsorships and External Relations: Francisco de Bergia González, age 55
General Manager, Commercial Development and Subsidiaries: Guillermo Fernández-Vidal, age 58
General Manager, Corporate Development: Angel Vilá Boix
General Manager, Purchasing: Alberto M. Horcajo Aguirre
General Manager, Institutional Relations and the Telefónica Foundation: Javier Nadal Ariño, age 55
General Manager, Planning and Management Control: Alfonso Alonso Durán
General Manager, Coordination, Business Development, and Synergies, and Director: Julio Linares López, age 59
General Secretary: Ramiro Sanchez de Lerin Garcia-Ovies
Legal Services: Juan Carlos Ros
Chairman, Telefónica de España: Luis Lada
Auditors: Ernst & Young, S.L.

LOCATIONS

HQ: Telefónica, S.A.
Gran Vía 28, 28013 Madrid, Spain
Phone: +34-91-584-0306   **Fax:** +34-91-584-9347
Web: www.telefonica.com

In addition to Spain, Telefónica's areas of operation include more than 40 countries in Africa, Asia, Europe, Latin America, and North America.

2005 Sales

	% of total
Europe	
Spain	52
Other	5
Latin America	42
Other regions	1
Total	**100**

PRODUCTS/OPERATIONS

2005 Sales

	$ mil.	% of total
Telefónica Móviles	18,515.2	40
Telefónica de España	13,540.1	29
Telefónica Latinoamérica	9,709.5	21
Telefónica Contenidos	1,537.4	3
Cesky Group	1,272.0	3
Directories business	687.6	1
Atento	471.7	1
Other revenues	813.9	2
Total	**46,547.4**	**100**

COMPETITORS

Amena
América Móvil
América Telecom
Auna
Cableuropa
France Telecom
Jazztel
Portugal Telecom
Spantel
Telecom Italia
Teleconnect
Telmex
uni2
Vodafone
Vodafone España

HISTORICAL FINANCIALS

Company Type: Public

Income Statement

FYE: December 31

	REVENUE ($ mil.)	NET INCOME ($ mil.)	NET PROFIT MARGIN	EMPLOYEES
12/05	46,547	4,908	10.5%	207,641
12/04	42,584	3,517	8.3%	173,554
12/03	36,520	3,373	9.2%	148,288
12/02	30,845	(5,466)	—	152,845
Annual Growth	**14.7%**	**—**	**—**	**10.8%**

2005 Year-End Financials

Debt ratio: 134.3%
Return on equity: 21.8%
Cash ($ mil.): 4,419
Current ratio: 0.62
Long-term debt ($ mil.): 30,583

No. of shares (mil.): —
Dividends
Yield: 3.7%
Payout: 152.8%
Market value ($ mil.): —

Stock History

NYSE: TEF

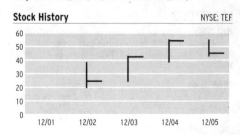

	STOCK PRICE ($) FY Close	P/E High/Low		PER SHARE ($) Earnings	Dividends
12/05	45.02	51	40	1.08	1.65
12/04	54.33	77	54	0.71	1.32
12/03	42.49	22	13	1.94	1.14
12/02	24.56	—		—	—
Annual Growth	**22.4%**	**—**	**—**	**(25.4%)**	**20.3%**

Telefonica Chile

Once a telecom dictator, Compañía de Teleco-municaciones de Chile is now battling to keep its top ranking in a highly competitive market. Operating as Telefonica Chile (formerly Telefónica CTC Chile), the former state monopoly provides local phone access and long-distance services through subsidiaries Telefónica Mundo 188 and Globus (formerly VTR Larga Distancia). It also provides data transmission, directory services, and public phones. It has sold its 35% stake in Sonda, Chile's largest information systems provider, and it has sold its subsidiary, Telefónica Móvil, the largest wireless provider in Chile, to Telefónica Móviles in a deal valued at $1 billion. Spain's Telefónica controls about 40% of the company.

Telefonica Chile continues to control 70% of the local phone access market and handles more than a third of the long-distance market. Having one of the world's first all-digital networks, the company is well equipped to handle Chile's telecom needs, though competition is fierce.

In 2006 the company changed its operating name to Telefonica Chile.

HISTORY

Telecommunications in Chile began in 1880, four years after Alexander Graham Bell's invention of the telephone, with the establishment of Compañía de Teléfonos de Edison in Valparaiso.

The International Telephone and Telegraph Corporation (ITT) bought the company's 26,205 phones in 1927. Three years later the Compañía de Teléfonos de Chile S.A. (CTC) was formed to acquire local phone companies. CTC became ITT's largest phone company in South America by gaining a 50-year concession that controlled 92% of Chile's phones. CTC became very valuable to ITT; by 1962 it provided about 12% of ITT's total profits. CTC was ITT's last phone property in South America to escape nationalization. In 1970 ITT CEO Harold Geneen, fearing that the election of Marxist Salvador Allende as president would lead to CTC's nationalization, met clandestinely with CIA officials to discuss how to prevent Allende's inauguration.

Allende won the election. The Chilean government assumed management control of CTC in 1971 but to delay having to compensate ITT, did not formally expropriate CTC. During sensitive negotiations over compensation, internal ITT memos that discussed the anti-Allende plans came to light. Allende offered a mere $12 million for CTC, about $141 million less than CTC was worth.

Allende was killed in a 1973 coup led by General Augusto Pinochet, who was to run Chile under a cruel military dictatorship for the next 17 years. Pinochet agreed to pay ITT's price for CTC, and in 1974 the Corporación de Fomento de la Producción (CORFO, or Corporation for the Promotion of Production) bought the 80% of the company that had been owned by ITT.

CORFO sold 30% of its CTC shares to Bond Corporation Chile in 1988. A subsidiary of Telefónica de España (today Telefónica), the Spanish telephone monopoly, bought Bond Chile stock in 1990 and changed Bond Chile's name to Telefónica Internacional Chile. Later that year CTC became the first South American company to be listed on the NYSE.

In 1994 Chile became the first Latin American country to allow all comers to offer fixed-line phone service. Although deregulation increased competition and slashed long-distance prices in 1994, other regulatory changes expanded CTC's protected local calling areas. CTC increased local call prices as much as 70%. That year CTC acquired 80% of Intercom, Chile's largest cable TV company.

The company changed its name to Compañía de Telecomunicaciones de Chile S.A. in 1995 and won the right to expand service to all regions of Chile. In 1996 CTC merged its cable operations with those of Metropolis to form Metropolis-Intercom, a cable TV company with over 40% of the market; it also merged its cellular operations with those of VTR-Celular, forming Startel, to achieve national coverage. That year CTC joined a Telefónica-led consortium that won a 35% stake in telecom company Companhia Riograndense de Telecomunicações in Brazil's first privatization auction.

In 1998, the year Pinochet retired, CTC received government approval to acquire VTR Larga Distancia, Chile's #4 long-distance carrier, despite regulatory concerns over the possible stifling of competition. A year later CTC sold its Internet division to Telefónica (as part of that company's Terra Networks subsidiary) and acquired 60% of Sonda, Chile's largest information systems provider. It also began using the brand name Telefónica CTC Chile. The next year the company announced the sale of its cable TV assets. In 2001 CTC created a new subsidiary to explore opportunities with fixed wireless local loop technology.

Restructuring in the face of the telecom slump, the company in 2002 cut 900 jobs and reorganized into three main business units: consumer and small business customers, major business, and mobile services. It also sold a 25% stake in Sonda to Sonda founder Andres Navarro in a deal valued at $37.5 million. Navarro later exercised an option to acquire the remaining 35% stake held by CTC.

EXECUTIVES

Chairman: Emilio G. López, age 64
Deputy Chairman: Narcís S. Serra, age 61, $131,212 pay
CEO: José Moles Valenzuela
Corporate Manager, Operations, and CTO: Franco Faccilongo, age 49
Corporate Manager, CFO, and General Manager, t-gestiona: Julio Covarrubias, age 47
Corporate Manager, Small and Medium Business and Professionals: Luis F. de Godoy, age 41
Corporate Manager, Residential Communications: Rafael Zamora, age 39
General Counsel and Secretary: Cristián Aninat, age 49
Corporate Manager, Regulation: Humberto Soto, age 46
Corporate Manager, Strategy and Business Development: Nicolás Domínguez, age 35
Corporate Manager, Management Control: Diego Martínez-Caro, age 35
Corporate Manager, Internal Auditing: Jesús García, age 38
Corporate Manager, Human Resources: Mauricio Malbrán, age 50
General Manager, Telefónica Empresas: Ricardo Majluf, age 58
Head of Investor Relations: Sofía Chellew
Auditors: Deloitte & Touche

LOCATIONS

HQ: Compañía de Telecomunicaciones de Chile S.A.
Avenida Providencia 111, Piso 2, Santiago, Chile
Phone: +56-2-691-2020   **Fax:** +56-2-691-7881
Web: www.telefonicachile.cl

PRODUCTS/OPERATIONS

2005 Sales

	% of total
Fixed-line telecommunications	
Basic services	76
Long-distance	10
Corporate customer communications & data	13
Other revenues	1
Total	**100**

Selected Services

Data transmission
Directory advertising
Domestic and international long distance
Equipment sales
Fixed wireless communications
Interconnections
Line installations and connections
Local phone service
Public telephones
Radio trunking

Selected Subsidiaries and Affiliates

Compañía de Telecomunicaciones de Chile — Equipos y Servicios de Telecomunicaciones S.A. (99.9%; equipment maintenance, line installation and services, and public phones)
Compañía de Teléfonos de Chile — Transmisiones Regionales S.A. (188 Telefónica Mundo, 99%, long-distance services)
Globus 120 S.A. (99.9%, long-distance services)
Tecnonáutica S.A. (Internet products and services)
Telefónica Empresas CTC Chile S.A. (99.9%, corporate telecommunications services)
Telefónica Gestión de Servicios Compartidos Chile S.A. (T-Gestiona, 99.9%, professional services)
Telefónica Móvil S.A. (Telefónica Móvil, 99.9%, wireless communications)

COMPETITORS

Chilesat Corp
Entel
TELECOM (Colombia)

HISTORICAL FINANCIALS

Company Type: Public

Income Statement

	REVENUE ($ mil.)	NET INCOME ($ mil.)	NET PROFIT MARGIN	EMPLOYEES
				FYE: December 31
12/05	1,103	87	7.9%	3,910
12/04	1,265	36	2.9%	3,774
12/03	1,382	48	3.5%	6,817
12/02	1,208	41	3.4%	4,571
Annual Growth	(3.0%)	28.8%	—	(5.1%)

2005 Year-End Financials

Debt ratio: 44.4%
Return on equity: 5.6%
Cash ($ mil.): 203
Current ratio: 0.97
Long-term debt ($ mil.): 680

No. of shares (mil.): —
Dividends
Yield: 7.4%
Payout: —
Market value ($ mil.): —

NYSE: CTC

	STOCK PRICE ($) FY Close	P/E High/Low	PER SHARE ($) Earnings	Dividends
12/05	8.80	— —	—	0.65
12/04	11.24	— —	—	10.01
12/03	14.95	— —	—	0.10
12/02	9.59	— —	—	0.01
Annual Growth	(2.8%)	— —	—	302.1%

Teléfonos de México

Teléfonos de México (Telmex) is no longer a monopoly, but it's still Mexico's #1 fixed-line telecom operator with more than 18 million access lines in service and over 70% of the market. Telmex has spun off its Telcel subsidiary (Mexico's leading wireless carrier) and most of its international investments to form América Móvil, which in turn owns a stake in Latin American wireless joint venture América Telecom. Carso Global Telecom, a holding company controlled by Mexican billionaire Carlos Slim Helú, owns a controlling 71% voting stake in Telmex.

Telmex also owns a stake in Spanish-language portal Prodigy MSN (formerly T1msn), a partnership with Microsoft.

The company's 2004 acquisition of AT&T Latin America, in a cash-and-debt deal valued at $207 million, expanded Telmex's operations in Argentina, Brazil, Chile, Colombia, and Peru. Telmex executives said it would invest $50 million in the bankrupt company's network technology and use the assets to expand business with corporate clients in the region. The company also has acquired 40% of long-distance carrier Chilesat, and said it would acquire the rest.

Through purchases made in 2004 and 2005, Telmex also has taken control of Brazilian telecom provider Embratel by buying the stake formerly held by MCI in a deal valued at $400 million. In a separate deal, the company sold its stake in MCI to Verizon Communications in a cash deal valued at $1.1 billion.

Telmex also has acquired a controlling 30% stake in Net Serviços de Comunicação, the #1 cable TV operator in Brazil. As part of its continued plan to expand into the television business, it bought Colombian companies TV Cable and Cable Pacifico in late 2006.

Long-time chairman Carlos Slim Helú stepped down in 2004, appointed with the title of honorary lifetime chairman of the board of directors. He was replaced as chairman by his son, Carlos Slim Domit. US-based AT&T Inc. (formerly known as SBC Communications) owns a nearly 8% stake in Telmex.

HISTORY

Mexican Telephone and Telegraph, backed by investors allied with AT&T Corp., received a government concession to operate in Mexico City in 1903. Two years later a Swedish consortium led by equipment maker Ericsson also won a concession, and it became Empresa de Teléfonos Ericsson in 1909.

In 1915 Mexican Telephone and Telegraph was nationalized. The company languished after WWI, but the Ericsson enterprise thrived. In 1925 International Telephone and Telegraph (ITT), led by telecom pioneer Sosthenes Behn, won the concession to operate Mexican Telephone and Telegraph. ITT expanded operations nationwide and linked to AT&T's system in the US. In 1932 ITT won control of Ericsson.

Teléfonos de México (Telmex) was created after WWII to buy the ITT and Ericsson subsidiaries in Mexico. Private investors bought Telmex in 1953, but it remained under close state regulation until the government bought 51% of the voting shares in 1972. Phone service grew slowly, and the government continually raised the long-distance tax until it accounted for half of Telmex's revenues. By the 1980s the government was using Telmex funds for unrelated programs.

The 1985 earthquakes heavily damaged Telmex's facilities, and it was forced to modernize and expand in the rebuilding stage. To improve the inefficient enterprise, President Carlos Salinas announced in 1989 that Telmex would be privatized. The following year a consortium that included Grupo Carso, SBC Communications (now known as AT&T Inc.), and France Telecom won voting control of Telmex. (France Telecom sold its stake in 2000.)

Telmex bought a 49% stake in Empresas Cablevision's Mexican cable business in 1995, and the next year it teamed with Sprint to offer business telecom services in the US and Mexico. After long-distance competition began in 1997, Telmex surrendered about a quarter of its market share. Many customers, angered over years of unexplained hang-ups and incorrect billings, switched providers. Also that year Telmex and Sprint formed another venture to resell long-distance service to Mexican Americans. However, the venture had to gain approval from the FCC, and regulators insisted that Telmex lower the high termination fees charged to US long-distance providers. Telmex agreed to do so, and the venture won approval in 1998. Telmex also invested in former US ISP Prodigy in 1998.

Meanwhile, Telmex maintained a de facto monopoly over local service until 1999 when MAXCOM, backed by Grupo Radio Centro, entered the market. Telmex gained strength in other communications arenas, receiving additional radio spectrum for mobile and PCS wireless services, joining SBC to buy Cellular Communications of Puerto Rico, and buying Miami-based Topp Telecom (prepaid cellular service) and Dallas-based CommSouth (prepaid local service). It bought out Sprint's share of their joint venture and took a 1% stake ($100 million) in Williams Communications Group (now WilTel Communications), the US-based fiber-optic firm. It also began managing Guatemalan phone company TELGUA and the next year acquired a controlling stake.

Also in 2000 Telmex and Microsoft introduced T1msn, a Spanish-language Internet portal (T1msn acquired the Spanish-language portal Yupi in 2001). Telmex also formed a joint venture with Bell Canada International and SBC to expand operations in South America.

EXECUTIVES

Honorary Chairman: Carlos Slim Helú, age 66
Co-Chairman: Jaime Chico Pardo, age 56
Co-Chairman: Carlos Slim Domit, age 39
Vice Chairman: Juan Antonio Pérez Simón, age 65
CEO: Héctor Slim Seade
CFO: Adolfo Cerezo Pérez
President, TELMEX International:
Oscar Von Hauske Solís
Secretary and General Counsel:
Sergio F. Medina Noriega
Director, Commercial — Corporate Market:
Isidoro Ambe Attar
Director, Commercial — Retail Markets:
Patricio (Patrick) Slim Domit
Director, Human Resources: Jaime Pérez Gómez
Director, Regulation and Legal:
Javier Mondragón Alarcón
Director, Investments and Strategic Development:
Andrés R. Vazquez del Mercado Benshimol
Director, Strategic Alliances, Communication, and Institutional Relations: Arturo Elías Ayub
Director, Technical and Long-distance:
Eduardo Gómez Chibli
Dean of Inttelmex: Javier Elguea Solís
Auditors: Mancera, S.C.

LOCATIONS

HQ: Teléfonos de México, S.A. de C.V.
Parqué Vía 198, oficina 701, Colonia Cuauhtémoc, 06599 México, D.F., Mexico
Phone: +52-55-5703-3990   **Fax:** +52-55-5545-5550
Web: www.telmex.com.mx

Teléfonos de México (Telmex) has operations in Argentina, Brazil, Chile, Colombia, Mexico, Peru, and the US.

2005 Sales

	$ mil.	% of total
Mexico	11,593.0	77
Brazil	3,212.7	21
Other countries	348.5	2
Total	**15,154.2**	**100**

PRODUCTS/OPERATIONS

2005 Sales

	$ mil.	% of total
Local service	5,440.4	36
Long-distance		
Domestic	3,424.8	23
International	1,227.5	8
Corporate networks	1,713.1	11
Interconnections	1,710.6	11
Internet	1,030.5	7
Other revenues	607.3	4
Total	**15,154.2**	**100**

Selected Services

Calling cards
Internet access
Local fixed-line access
National and international fixed-line long-distance
Network engineering
Pay phones
Telephone directories
Wireless data networking

Selected Subsidiaries and Affiliates

Controladora de Servicios de Telecomunicaciones, S.A. de C.V. (holding company)

Alquiladora de Casas, S.A. de C.V. (phone equipment installations)

Anuncios en Directorios, S.A. de C.V. (phone directories)

Compañía de Teléfonos y Bienes Raíces, S.A. de C.V. (phone equipment installation)

Consorcio Red Uno, S.A. de C.V. (telecom and IT systems integration services)

Teléfonos del Noroeste, S.A. de C.V. (Telnor, regional fixed-line telecom services)

Telmex USA, L.L.C. (long-distance services, US)

Uninet, S.A. de C.V. (ISP)

Embratel Participaçoes, S.A. (97%, long-distance holding company, Brazil)

Empresa Brasileira de Telecomunicaçoes S.A. (Embratel, 96%, long-distance operating company, Brazil)

PrimeSys Soluções Empresariais S.A. (96%, value-added services provider, Brazil)

Star One S.A. (77%, satellite services provider, Brazil)

Net Serviços de Comunicação S.A. (31%, cable TV, broadband Internet, and local phone services, Brazil)

Telmex do Brasil, Ltda. (97%, enterprise telecom services, Brazil)

Metrored Telecomunicaciones, S.R.L. (83%, data transmission services, Argentina)

Techtel-LMS Comunicaciones Interactivas, S.A. (93%, corporate telecom services, Argentina)

Telmex Argentina, SA. (corporate telecom services)

Telmex Chile Holding, S.A. (telecom services)

Telmex Colombia, S.A. (corporate telecom services)

Telmex Corp, S.A. (99.3%, formerly Chilesat Corp S.A., long-distance)

Telmex Perú (corporate telecom services)

Grupo Telvista, S.A. de C.V. (45%, telemarketing services between the US and Mexico, US)

COMPETITORS

Alestra
Avantel
IMPSAT
Iusacell
Movil@ccess
NextiraOne Europe
Quepasa
Telefónica Móviles

HISTORICAL FINANCIALS

Company Type: Public

Income Statement

FYE: December 31

	REVENUE ($ mil.)	NET INCOME ($ mil.)	NET PROFIT MARGIN	EMPLOYEES
12/05	15,154	2,516	16.6%	75,484
12/04	12,451	2,533	20.3%	76,683
12/03	10,411	1,934	18.6%	62,103
12/02	10,944	1,722	15.7%	63,775
12/01	12,140	2,212	18.2%	67,550
Annual Growth	5.7%	3.3%	—	2.8%

2005 Year-End Financials

Debt ratio: 77.7%
Return on equity: 29.2%
Cash ($ mil.): 2,164
Current ratio: 1.24
Long-term debt ($ mil.): 7,102
No. of shares (mil.): —
Dividends
 Yield: 3.5%
 Payout: 781.8%
Market value ($ mil.): —

Stock History

NYSE: TMX

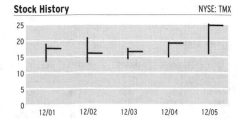

	STOCK PRICE ($) FY Close	P/E High/Low		PER SHARE ($) Earnings	Dividends
12/05	24.68	227	145	0.11	0.86
12/04	19.16	92	71	0.21	0.59
12/03	16.51	—	—	—	0.55
12/02	15.99	—	—	—	0.56
12/01	17.51	—	—	—	0.49
Annual Growth	9.0%	—	—	(47.6%)	15.1%

Televisa

With its television, radio, and publishing interests, Grupo Televisa is *número uno* in the Latin media world. The firm is Mexico's #1 TV broadcaster with four networks and almost 260 affiliated stations. It also has a 51% stake in cable joint venture Cablevisión and a 60% stake in SKY direct-to-home digital satellite television system. The company's publishing unit, Editorial Televisa, is a leading producer of Spanish-language magazines. Televisa also owns three soccer teams, a sports stadium, and 50% of 17 Mexican radio stations. Through a trust, chairman and CEO Emilio Azcárraga Jean owns 49% of Televisa.

The company's dominance in the Mexican television market was evidenced by the successful launch of Mexico's first reality TV program, *Big Brother* (produced by Televisa's new television partnership with Europe's Endemol), as well as its *La Madrasta*, the highest-rated telenovela in Mexico in 2005.

Televisa has cut some costs by selling its music recording operations to US-based Hispanic broadcaster Univision Communications (in which Televisa has a 10% stake), and 50% stake in its radio operations to Grupo Prisa. The company has announced it will sell its Univision stake.

Looking beyond TV broadcasting, the company launched a new Web content platform in 2006 that allows users to download content for a fee. It also plans to sell phone service in 2007.

HISTORY

Credited with launching the Golden Age of Mexican cinema in the 1940s via his Churrubusco Studios, Emilio Azcárraga Vidaurreta was a radio pioneer who also owned one of Mexico's first TV channels. He joined fellow TV channel owners Rómulo O'Farrill (a newspaper publisher) and Guillermo Camarena (an inventor) to form one network, Telesistema Mexicana, in 1954. When Azcárraga Vidaurreta died in 1972, his son Emilio Azcárraga Milmo took the reins of the company, dubbed it Grupo Televisa,

and began his long stint as chairman. His aggressive style earned him the nickname "El Tigre" (The Tiger).

Azcárraga Milmo saw Mexican television as an escape for the nation's middle and lower classes. He nurtured stars for soap operas (called *telenovelas*) and variety shows and insisted upon the actors' loyalty in return. Grupo Televisa started producing feature films for markets in Mexico and abroad in 1978. It also ran cable TV and music recording businesses and a regional TV network that it bought in 1982. The company used its news programs to support Mexico's Institutional Revolutionary Party (PRI).

A 1990 attempt to start a sports newspaper in the US (*The National*) met with failure (it closed after a year, leaving the company with heavy debts). Azcárraga Milmo bought out the other principal investors in 1990 and reorganized Televisa into a holding company, taking it public in 1991. The company launched its Skytel paging service in Mexico in 1992 and bought a minority stake in US-based Univision. The Mexican government privatized the Televisión Azteca network in 1993, giving Televisa its first taste of competition in the TV broadcast market.

Televisa joined Brazil's Organizações Globo and TCI (now AT&T Broadband) in 1995 to develop direct-to-home (DTH) satellite television. (News Corp. joined the venture, now called SKY, in 1997.) The company also pared its staff by 12% and divested some of its lesser operations, including the sale of 49% of its cable TV businesses to telephone giant Teléfonos de México (Telmex).

A month before his death in 1997, Azcárraga Milmo installed his 29-year-old son, Emilio Azcárraga Jean, as president and CEO of the company. The company sold half of its stake in Univision the next year and slashed more jobs. Holding company Grupo Televicentro sold a 9% stake in Televisa in 2000 and used the proceeds to pay off debt. It also sold its newspaper, *Ovaciones*, in 2000. Later that year Televisa consolidated its ownership of publishing unit Editorial Televisa.

A plan to merge its radio stations with those of Grupo Acir was foiled when Mexican competition authorities ruled against it. But the next year the company was able to strike a deal to sell 50% of its radio station subsidiary to Grupo Prisa. Also that year the company eliminated 730 jobs in response to falling advertising revenue. It again increased its stake in Univision from 6% to 15%. The company agreed to form a television production company in a joint venture with Endemol in 2001.

In 2002 Televisa sold its Fonovisa Records regional music label to Univision for $210 million.

EXECUTIVES

Chairman, President, and CEO: Emilio Azcárraga Jean, age 38

Vice Chairwoman: María A. Aramburuzabala Larregui, age 43

CFO: Salvi Folch Viadero, age 39

EVP: Bernardo Gómez Martínez, age 39

EVP: Alfonso de Angoitia, age 44

VP and Controller: Jorge Lutteroth Echegoyen, age 53

VP, Administration: Rafael Carabias Príncipe, age 62

VP, Internal Auditing: Juan F. Calvillo Armendáriz, age 64

VP, Legal, Corporate General Counsel, and Secretary: Juan Sebastian Mijares, age 47

VP, Newscasts: Leopoldo G. González Blanco, age 47

VP, Operations, Technical Service, and Television Production: Maximiliano Arteaga Carlebach, age 64

VP, Production: Jorge E. Murguía Orozco, age 56
VP, Sales and Marketing: Alejandro Quintero Iñíguez, age 56
VP, Tax: José A. Lara del Olmo, age 36
VP, Television: José A. Bastón Patiño, age 38
CEO, Cablevision: Jean Paul Broc Haro, age 44
CEO, Editorial Televisa: Eduardo Michelsen Delgado, age 35
CEO, Innova: Alexandre M. Penna da Silva, age 51
CEO, Sistema Radiopolis: Raúl Rodríguez Gonzáles, age 47
VP, Legal and General Counsel, Television Division: Joaquín Balcarcel Santa Cruz, age 37
Director of Investor Relations: Michel Boyance
Auditors: PricewaterhouseCoopers

LOCATIONS

HQ: Grupo Televisa, S.A.
Avenida Vasco de Quiroga, No. 2000,
Colonia Santa Fe, Delegación Álvaro Obregón,
01210 México, D.F., Mexico
Phone: +52-55-5261-2445   **Fax:** +52-55-5261-2494
Web: www.televisa.com

PRODUCTS/OPERATIONS

2005 Sales

	% of total
Television broadcasting	55
Sky Mexico	18
Publishing	8
Programming exports	6
Cable television	4
Pay television networks	3
Publishing distribution	1
Radio	1
Other	4
Total	**100**

Selected Operations

Cable Television
  Cablevision (51%)
Pay Television Networks (24 pay-TV networks under 13 different brands)
Programming Exports
  Bailando por un Sueño
  La Madrastra
Publishing
  Magazines
    Tele Guía (television program guide)
    TV y Novelas (weekly entertainment magazine)
Radio (50%, 17 stations throughout Mexico)
Sky Mexico (60%, satellite TV)
Television Broadcasting
  Channel 2
  Channel 4
  Channel 5
  Channel 9
Other
  Azteca Stadium (Mexico City)
  Esmas.com (Internet portal)
  OCESA Entretenimiento (40%, Mexican live-entertainment promoter)
  Soccer teams
    America
    Necaxa
    Real San Luis
  Univision (10%, US)
  Videocine (film production and distribution)

COMPETITORS

Bertelsmann
CIE
Cisneros Group
MVS
Radio Center Group
Satmex
Telemundo
Time Warner
TV Azteca

HISTORICAL FINANCIALS

Company Type: Public

Income Statement

FYE: December 31

	REVENUE ($ mil.)	NET INCOME ($ mil.)	NET PROFIT MARGIN	EMPLOYEES
12/05	3,021	635	21.0%	15,100
12/04	2,630	312	11.8%	14,100
12/03	2,100	250	11.9%	12,300
12/02	2,087	(109)	—	12,600
Annual Growth	**13.1%**	**—**	**—**	**6.2%**

2005 Year-End Financials

Debt ratio: 68.2%
Return on equity: 26.3%
Cash ($ mil.): 1,374
Current ratio: 1.58
Long-term debt ($ mil.): 1,797
No. of shares (mil.): —
Dividends
  Yield: 3.1%
  Payout: —
Market value ($ mil.): —

Stock History

NYSE: TV

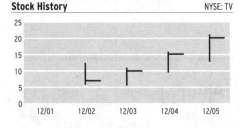

	STOCK PRICE ($) FY Close	P/E High/Low	PER SHARE ($) Earnings	Dividends
12/05	20.13	— —	—	0.62
12/04	15.13	— —	—	0.39
12/03	9.97	— —	—	0.09
12/02	6.98	— —	—	
Annual Growth	**42.3%**	**— —**	**—**	**162.5%**

TeliaSonera

An expert at cold calling, TeliaSonera (formerly Telia) offers telecom services primarily in the chilly Nordic and Baltic regions. The company has become the leading telecom company in these regions, with more than 8 million fixed lines and about 15 million mobile phone subscribers. It also has more than 2 million Internet customers. Facing growing competition since Sweden deregulated its telecom industry in 1993, TeliaSonera has responded by traveling abroad. Its network facilities reach the European continent, the Americas, and Asia. It is expanding in growth markets such as Russia and Eurasia. The Kingdom of Sweden owns 45% of TeliaSonera; the Republic of Finland owns nearly 14%.

The company is organized into five business areas: mobile, international carrier, networks, Internet services, and equity holdings. It also is expanding into other countries with carrier services, using its fiber-optic network to reach the European continent and the US. The company's Internet protocol (IP) backbone connects Europe, the Americas, and Asia; TeliaSonera has investments in telecom ventures in nearly 30 countries, but the company has said it considers its international operations as financial assets rather than core business elements.

Although in 2005 TeliaSonera agreed to pay $3.1 billion to the Çukurova Group to buy another 27% of Turkish telecom Turkcell, which would have increased its stake to more than 63%, the company was outbid by Russian holding company Alfa Group. TeliaSonera has filed for breach of contract with Çukurova.

At home in Sweden and Finland, where it is the largest mobile operator, the group is building out its GSM networks, along with technology upgrades to quadruple the speed for mobile data services and increase its coverage to more than 90% of the land area. Most of TeliaSonera's growth is driven by its mobile phone services. It provides wireless phone services in Denmark, Finland, Norway, and Sweden. It also has mobile subsidiaries in the GSM markets of Azerbaijan, Georgia, Kazakhstan, and Moldolva. It has mobile and broadband operations through its 2004 acquisition of Omnitel. In addition, it has a stake in Russian mobile operator MegaFon.

In 2006 TeliaSonera acquired an 82% stake in NextGenTel Holding, the #2 broadband provider (via DSL) in Norway. The publicly listed company will continue to operate independently under its own brand. TeliaSonera is pulling its wireless customers online using SMS (short messaging service) and WAP (wireless application protocol) technologies, and it has teamed up with Microsoft to offer e-mail access via mobile phones. TeliaSonera is the leading ISP in the Baltic and Nordic regions.

Following the merger that created TeliaSonera, the company said it would eliminate as many as 1,500 jobs.

HISTORY

Telia's wires go back to 1853 when the Swedish government created Kongl. Elektriska Telegraf-Verket to operate a telegraph line linking Stockholm and Uppsala. The next year it opened a line that reached the main European continent; the company became Telegrafverket in 1860.

Just a year after the telephone was invented in 1876, the firm installed its first phone line. The 1880s saw private phone companies sprout up in Sweden's larger cities, and by 1900 Telegrafverket had installed some 62,000 telephones. Even though Sweden was open to telecom competition, the company became a de facto monopoly in 1918 when it bought the country's largest exchange, Stockholms Allmanna Telefon. In 1921 Telegrafverket began laying its first long-distance cable.

Telegrafverket began automating its phone systems in the 1930s. After WWII, the company entered a major growth period: More than 110,000 new telephone users were connected in 1947 alone. Also in the mid-1940s, Telegrafverket launched one of the world's first mobile phone networks (closed radio).

Renamed Televerket, the firm continued to grow rapidly in the 1960s and 1970s and introduced data communications services in 1965. It teamed up with equipment maker Ericsson in 1970 to form Ellemtel, an R&D concern that developed the first all-digital public switching system. (Ellemtel ceased operations in 1999.) Televerket began moving into satellite services in 1970, when INTELSAT installed an earth station in the Nordic region. In the early 1980s it rolled out several new services, including cable TV, cellular, and international packet switching.

Meanwhile, the company began losing its monopoly status in the 1980s and lost its government funding in 1984. Fearing competition from giants such as AT&T and British Telecom (now BT Group), the company in 1991 joined the Netherlands' Royal KPN to form Unisource, a global telecommunications provider; Swisscom joined the group two years later. Sweden's telecom deregulation was completed in 1993, and the firm became Telia. That year it ventured into the Baltic states.

AT&T teamed up with Unisource in 1994 to provide services to multinationals. Moving into the Americas in 1997, Telia led a consortium that secured rights to offer cellular service in Brazil.

Unisource never took off, and, after AT&T jumped ship in 1998, Telia and its partners began divesting the venture's assets. After Telia's proposed merger with Norway's Telenor fell through in 1999, the company began tweaking its strategy to become a strong global player. But conditions within the telecom industry forced the company to revamp its international carrier strategy, cut 400 jobs within the unit, and trim its operations.

In 2000 the Swedish government floated 30% of Telia. A restructuring in 2001 created five new business areas. Telia did acquire Norwegian mobile phone operator NetCom ASA. In 2002 Telia acquired Nordic competitor Sonera and the two companies were combined to form TeliaSonera.

In 2004 the group acquired the Danish operations of Orange, the wireless unit of France Telecom. The acquisition improved TeliaSonera's market position in Denmark, moving it from fourth- to third-largest mobile operator. In 2004 it sold its Sonera Zed unit, an aggregator and reseller of digital content to mobile phone users, to Spanish interactive media group Wisdom Entertainment. It also unloaded its stake in satellite company Eutelsat.

TeliaSonera Sweden launched live TV broadcasts on its mobile phones in 2005, in collaboration with TV4 News and entertainment channels The Voice TV and Start.

EXECUTIVES

Chairman: Tom von Weymarn, age 62
Vice Chairman: Carl Bennet, age 54
President and CEO: Anders Igel, age 55
EVP and CFO: Kim J. Ignatius, age 50
Group VP, Corporate Human Resources: Rune Nyberg, age 57
Group VP, Corporate Legal Affairs, and General Counsel: Jan Henrik Ahrnell, age 47
Group VP, Corporate Networks and Technology: Lars-Gunnar Johansson, age 62
President, TeliaSonera Norway, Denmark, and the Baltic Countries: Kenneth Karlberg, age 52
Head, Corporate Communications: Ewa Lagerqvist
Head, Large Corporate Segment: Esa Korvenmaa
President, TeliaSonera Finland: Juho Lipsanen, age 45
President, TeliaSonera Sweden: Anders Bruse, age 51
Head of Corporate Marketing, Products, and Services: Terje Christoffersen, age 54
Media Relations: Marianne Laurell
Media Relations: Charlotte Zuger
Auditors: PricewaterhouseCoopers AB

LOCATIONS

HQ: TeliaSonera AB
Sturegatan 1, SE-106 63 Stockholm, Sweden
Phone: +46-8-504-550-00   **Fax:** +46-8-504-550-01
US HQ: 2201 Cooperative Way, Ste. 302,
Herndon, VA 20171
US Phone: 703-546-4000   **US Fax:** 703-546-4125
Web: www.teliasonera.com

2005 Sales

	% of total
Nordic region	
Sweden	43
Finland	18
Norway	8
Denmark	8
Baltic region	10
Eurasia region	7
Other regions	6
Total	**100**

PRODUCTS/OPERATIONS

Selected Subsidiaries and Affiliates

AB Lietuvos Telekomas (60%, fixed-line telecommunications, Lithuania)
AS Eesti Telekom (49%, fixed-line telecommunications, Estonia)
　EMT (formerly AS Eesti Mobiltelefon, 49%, mobile telecommunications, Estonia)
FinturHoldings B.V. (74%, mobile telecommunications holdings, The Netherlands)
　Azercell (51%, mobile telecommunications, Azerbaijan)
　Geocell (83%, mobile telecommunications, Georgia)
　KCell (51%, mobile telecommunications, Kazakhstan)
　Moldcell (mobile telecommunications, Moldova)
Latvijas Mobilais Telefons SIA (60%, mobile telecommunications, Latvia)
NetCom AS (telecommunications services, Norway)
NextGenTel Holdings ASA (82%, broadband provider, Norway)
OAO MegaFon (44%, mobile telecommunications, Russia)
Sonera Carrier Networks Oy (Finland)
Sonera Mobile Networks Oy (Finland)
Svenska UMTS-nät AB (50%, mobile telecommunications, UMTS joint venture with Tele2)
Telia Communications AB
TeliaSonera Finland Oyj
TeliaSonera Holding (holding company for noncore investments)
　Auria Group (home electronics retail outlets)
　Infonet Serices Corporation (20%, data communications services, US)
　Telefos AB (49%, holding company)
　　Swedia Networks AB (telecom construction services)
　　Validation AB (testing and integration services)
　Unite AB (security services)
TeliaSonera International Carrier AB (Internet protocol-based data transport)
TeliaSonera International Carrier Inc. (US)
TeliaSonera International Carrier UK Ltd.
TeliaSonera Sverige AB (IT services)
Tilts Communications A/S
　Lattelekom SIA (49%, fixed-line telecommunications, Latvia)
Turkcell Iletisim Hizmetleri A.S. (37%, mobile telecommunications, Turkey)
UAB Omnitel (mobile telecommunications, Lithuania)

COMPETITORS

BT
Cable & Wireless
COLT Telecom
Deutsche Telekom AG
Elisa
Equant
France Telecom
Global Crossing
KPN
Level 3 Communications
Sprint Nextel
TDC
TDC Song
Tele2
Telenor
Vodafone

HISTORICAL FINANCIALS
Company Type: Public

Income Statement

FYE: December 31

	REVENUE ($ mil.)	NET INCOME ($ mil.)	NET PROFIT MARGIN	EMPLOYEES
12/05	11,019	556	5.0%	28,175
12/04	12,405	1,861	15.0%	29,082
12/03	11,383	1,254	11.0%	26,694
12/02	6,805	(1,139)	—	29,173
12/01	5,411	177	3.3%	17,149
Annual Growth	19.5%	33.1%	—	13.2%

2005 Year-End Financials

Debt ratio: 19.8%　　Current ratio: 1.34
Return on equity: 3.6%　Long-term debt ($ mil.): 2,579
Cash ($ mil.): 2,116

Net Income History

Pink Sheets: TLSNF

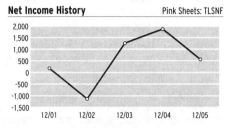

Telstra

With Telstra's telecommunications services, Matilda can stay connected, even while waltzing. As Australia's #1 carrier, this former monopoly provides traditional fixed-line phone services to 10 million access lines in service. Telstra also has more than 8 million mobile phone customers and it is the country's leading ISP (BigPond) with 3 million broadband subscribers. Dancing in the international stage, Telstra has teamed up with PCCW to form a pan-Asian Internet protocol backbone network (REACH). The company may spin off or sell its Sensis directory services unit. The Australian comonwealth owns 52% of Telstra. It has considered selling the stake, which has been valued at about $20 billion.

Telstra operates a digital GSM (global system for mobile communications) network and a second digital network based on CDMA (code division multiple access) technology for wireless communications. Online, the carrier provides Internet access to more than 1.5 million subscribers and has developed remote access via satellite. The firm also owns 50% of pay TV operator Foxtel and it acquired Australia-based Trading Post Group in a deal valued at nearly $484 million that bolstered the company's advertising and publishing operations. Telstra also bought technology services provider Kaz Group in a deal valued at $252 million.

The company's Telstra International unit oversees Telstra's operations in Australasia. Telstra International has telecom facilities in Hong Kong, Singapore, and in New Zealand (through TelstraClear). Its 50-50 joint venture with PCCW, known as REACH, is Asia's largest international carrier of voice, private line, and Internet protocol data services; it attained nominal profits but was forced to seek a debt restructuring deal.

Telstra had halted its Asian expansion efforts to improve investor relations, but it's back exploring its options. The company has announced plans to buy competitor New World Mobile Holdings, merge its Hong Kong operations with theirs, and possibly take the merged entity public. Telstra also has sales and service operations in Europe and in the US, where it has opened offices in Chicago, Dallas, and Los Angeles.

Telstra provides wholesale services to some 50 licensed operators. With competition in every arena, it has focused on the Internet and mobile phone markets.

HISTORY

When Australia gained independence in 1901, telecommunications were assigned to the new state-owned Postmaster-General's Department (PMG). Engineer H. P. Brown, who had managed the UK's telegraph and telephone system, became head of PMG in 1923. He set up research labs that year, oversaw the first overseas call to London in 1930, and streamlined operations until his reign ended in 1939.

During WWII Australia quickly expanded its communications infrastructure to assist the Allied Front in the South Pacific. Following the war, the government formed the Overseas Telecommunications Commission (OTC) in 1946 to handle international operations independent of PMG.

Even as new technology connected the continent and boosted the productivity of PMG, postal operations steadily recorded losses in the postwar era. In 1974 a Royal Commission recommended that postal and telecom services be split. Australian Telecommunications Commission (Telecom Australia) was launched in 1975 (OTC retained overseas services); it turned a profit in its first year.

Looking to connect residents in the outback, the firm signed Japan's Nippon Electric (now NEC) in 1981 to set up a digital radio transmission system; by the next decade it connected some 50,000 outback users. Also in 1981 Telecom Australia took a 25% stake in government-owned satellite operator AUSSAT and launched nationwide paging and mobile phone service in Melbourne and Sydney.

Renamed Australian Telecommunications in 1989, the carrier got its first whiff of competition as others were allowed to provide phone equipment. Two years later Optus Communications began competing with Telecom Australia; for the privilege it was forced to buy the unsuccessful AUSSAT. Long-distance competition began in 1991, and mobile phone competition began the following year. In response, Telecom Australia merged with OTC to become the Australian and Overseas Telecommunications Corporation (AOTC). AT&T's Frank Blount became CEO to lead the transition.

AOTC became Telstra Corporation in 1993 and launched a digital wireless GSM-based network. It joined with Rupert Murdoch's News Corp. to form pay TV operator Foxtel in 1995.

That year Telstra teamed with Microsoft to create ISP On Australia. Microsoft dropped out in 1996, but Telstra kept the service (Big Pond) and its portal (renamed Telstra.com in 1999). The government fully deregulated telecommunications and sold a third of Telstra to the public in 1997.

Kerry Packer's Publishing and Broadcasting bought a 25% stake in Foxtel in 1998. The next year Telstra posted an Australian record-setting profit, former Optus CEO Ziggy Switkowski succeeded Blount, and the government floated an additional 17% stake.

Telstra combined its New Zealand operations with those of cable TV operator Austar United to form Telstra Saturn in 1999. Two years later it bought Clear Communications, the New Zealand unit of BT Group (formerly British Telecommunications), in a deal worth about $182 million and merged it with Telstra Saturn to form TelstraClear.

In 2004 former chairman Bob Mansfield resigned his post after conflicts with the board of directors over the proposed acquisition of publisher John Fairfax Holdings. Mansfield supported the acquisition. Late the same year CEO Ziggy Switkowski was sacked by the board after holding the position for six years, during which time the company's share price dropped considerably. The company hired former Orange SA CEO Sol Trujillo in his place.

EXECUTIVES

Chairman: Donald G. (Don) McGauchie, age 55
CEO and Board Member: Solomon D. (Sol) Trujillo, age 54
COO: Greg Winn
CFO and Group Managing Director, Finance and Administration: John Stanhope, $792,596 pay
CIO: Fiona Balfour
Group Managing Director, BigPond: Justin Milne
Group Managing Director, Infrastructure Services: Michael Rocca, $877,546 pay
Group Managing Director, Public Policy and Communications: Phil Burgess
Group Managing Director, Small to Medium Enterprises: Deena Shiff
Group Managing Director, Strategic Marketing; Interim Director, Mergers and Acquisition: William J. (Bill) Stewart
Group Managing Director, Telstra Business and Government: David Thodey, $893,308 pay
Group Managing Director, Telstra Consumer and Marketing; President, International: David Moffatt, age 40, $1,051,985 pay
Group Managing Director, Telstra Country Wide: Geoff Booth, age 51
Group Managing Director, Telstra Media Services and CEO, Sensis: Bruce J. Akhurst, $1,105,137 pay
Group Managing Director, Telstra Wholesale: Kate McKenzie
General Manager, Investor Relations: David Anderson
SVP, Sales and Global Accounts, Telstra Incorporated: Andrew Morawski
Company Secretary: Douglas Gration
Director, Media Relations: Andrew Maiden
Auditors: Ernst & Young; Auditor General of Melbourne

LOCATIONS

HQ: Telstra Corporation Limited
   242 Exhibition St., Melbourne 3000, Australia
Phone: +61-3-9634-6400   **Fax:** +61-3-9634-1189
Web: telstra.com.au

2006 Sales

	% of total
Australia	92
Other countries	8
Total	**100**

PRODUCTS/OPERATIONS

2006 Sales

	% of total
Consumer marketing & channels	39
Enterprise & government	20
Business	13
Wholesale	12
Sensis	8
International	6
Operations	1
Other	1
Total	**100**

Selected Services

Advertising and directory services
Audio, video, and Internet conferencing
Broadband ISP
Cable TV
Data transmission
E-mail
Enhanced fax products and services
Freecall (toll-free 1-800 phone service)
Information technology (IT) services
Internet access
Mobile phone service
Prepaid telephony
Satellite transmission

COMPETITORS

Asia Netcom
Hutchison Whampoa
NTT
Optus
Pacific Internet
PowerTel
Telecom Corporation of New Zealand
Vodafone

HISTORICAL FINANCIALS

Company Type: Public

Income Statement

FYE: June 30

	REVENUE ($ mil.)	NET INCOME ($ mil.)	NET PROFIT MARGIN	EMPLOYEES
6/06	16,631	1,806	10.9%	49,443
6/05	16,891	3,179	18.8%	46,336
6/04	14,315	953	6.7%	41,941
6/03	13,732	2,311	16.8%	42,064
6/02	11,310	2,183	19.3%	44,977
Annual Growth	10.1%	(4.6%)	—	2.4%

2006 Year-End Financials

Debt ratio: 104.8%   Current ratio: 0.67
Return on equity: 18.5%   Long-term debt ($ mil.): 9,032
Cash ($ mil.): 503

Net Income History

NYSE: TLS

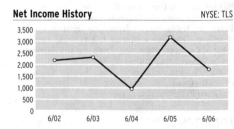

Tengelmann

American shoppers know the Tengelmann Group best through its majority-owned A&P (Great Atlantic & Pacific Tea Company) supermarkets. More than 400 A&P-owned stores in the US make up only part of Tengelmann, one of Europe's leading food retailers (along with German rivals ALDI Group, METRO AG and REWE-Zentral). The group has more than 7,500 supermarkets, drugstores, and general merchandise stores in 15 countries (mostly in Europe) under such names as Tengelmann and Kaiser's (supermarkets and drugstores) in Germany, Obi (do-it-yourself supply stores), Plus (a discount food chain), and KiK (apparel and general merchandise stores). The sons of chairman and former CEO Erivan Haub now run the company.

The youngest son, Christian, runs the group's struggling A&P business, and the eldest, Karl-Erivan, leads Tengelmann's European operations.

With the sale of its A&P Canada operation in 2005 and continued losses in the US, Tengelmann has chosen to concentrate on expanding its businesses in Europe, especially in the continent's south and east. To that end, it has sold its Obi DIY chain in China to UK home improvement giant B&Q. Plus recently expanded into Greece and Romania and is planning to enter markets in Croatia, Ukraine, and Bulgaria. The international divisions of the company's Plus, Obi, and textile discounter KiK chains are growing rapidly.

While Tengelmann is expanding its Plus and Obi chains in Europe, the company has closed or sold at least 600 of its Tengelmann and Kaiser's supermarkets, lessening its dependence on food retailing. The German retailer sold the last of its Kd chemist's shops to beauty retail chain Dirk Rossmann in 2005.

The company's Gubi manufacturing business operates meat processing plants, a bakery, and plant nursery to supply its retail chains. Another Tengelmann operation, Ligneus, makes interior fixtures for hotels and restaurants.

HISTORY

William and Louise (Scholl) Schmitz founded Wilh. Schmitz Scholl in Mülheim, Germany, in 1867, importing goods and processing coffee. In 1893 the Schmitzes' sons opened their first retail store, selling groceries, sweets, coffee, tea, and cocoa. The family called the store Tengelmann, after employee Emil Tengelmann, to avoid the social stigma then attached to grocers in Germany.

The company rebuilt after WWII left many of its stores in ruins. The man who would guide the company through much of its growth was still a youngster at the time. In 1952 Erivan Haub, the great-grandson of William and Louise Schmitz, was 20 when he was sent to the US for three years to learn the ropes at supermarkets in California and Illinois. He saw that US grocery stores, unlike most in Germany, let consumers serve themselves. Haub passed this practice along to his relatives, and Tengelmann Group opened its first self-serve stores in Germany soon afterward. Haub developed a fondness for the US during this trip that has not faded: His children were born in America to give them citizenship;

St. Joseph's University in Philadelphia named its business school after Haub to recognize the family's contributions.

Haub took over as head of the company in 1969 after his uncle's death. First on his shopping list was acquisitions. He bought Kaiser's Kaffee-Geschäft, a troubled German supermarket chain, two years later, then converted some of the stores into the discount Plus format. Tengelmann adopted the role of rescuer again in 1979 when it agreed to buy more than half of the troubled US supermarket chain Great Atlantic & Pacific Tea Company (A&P). Haub turned the grocer around by focusing on acquisitions and revamping older store formats.

International expansion marked the tone of Tengelmann in the 1990s. Using its Plus discount chain as a vehicle, Tengelmann branched out into East Germany and other countries once part of the communist bloc, such as Hungary and Poland. Germany, with its stiff competition and strict laws limiting acquisitions and requiring shops to close early on weeknights, paled in comparison as a growth opportunity to the hungry environments in the East.

Tengelmann enraged Holocaust survivors in 1991 when it proposed building a Kaiser's supermarket on part of the Ravensbrück Nazi concentration camp site, where approximately 92,000 women and children had been killed. The company canceled its plans after worldwide protests, although the local community, in need of jobs, had supported the idea.

Heavy competition among German retailers hammered profits in 1995. Haub announced plans to cut costs and restructure the company. The changes included modifying the Plus store format from discounter to neighborhood convenience store; Haub continued to back new deep-discount chain Ledi. Tengelmann entered a partnership in 1998 with the Pam group of Venice, merging its Italian supermarkets with Pam's. It also bought 165 German Tip discount stores from competitor Metro. The youngest Haub son, Christian, was promoted to CEO of A&P in 1998. He is also chairman of A&P's board of directors.

In the midst of a restructuring, in 2000 the company announced its would sell or close at least 600 of the poorly performing Tengelmann and Kaiser's stores. Meanwhile, it is extending its Obi do-it-yourself stores into Latvia, Slovakia, and Finland.

In 2002 Tengelmann restructured its troubled A&P operations, which posted a $72 million loss for the fiscal year ending in February 2002. After 33 years as the sole managing partner of the Tengelmann Group, Erivan Haub turned the management of the company over to his sons Karl-Erivan and Christian in 2002.

After 97 years in the chocolate business, Tengelmann sold its chocolate subsidiary Wissoll to German confectionery group Van Netten GmbH in 2003.

Tengelmann entered the Russian market in 2004, opening two Obi stores in Moscow.

2005 was a year marked by retrenchment in several markets for Tengelmann. The Kd Kaiser's drugstore chain was sold to Dirk Rossmann in May. In July the company withdrew from its partnership with the Haier Group to open Obi stores in China. In August the company sold its profitable A&P Canada division to METRO INC. It also disposed of its 22 Interfruct Cash & Carry stores in Hungary and Slovenia.

EXECUTIVES

Chairman, Executive Board: Bernd Ahlers
Chairman of Holding Management Board; CEO, Europe: Karl-Erivan W. Haub
Chairman, President and CEO, A&P: Christian W. E. Haub
CFO: Jens-Jürgen Böckel, age 63
CEO, Plus: Michael Hürter
CEO, Kaiser's Tengelmann AG: Bernd Ahlers
CEO and Managing Partner, KiK: Stefan Heinig
CEO, Obi: Sergio Giroldi
Secretary: Melanie Markmann
Head of Public Relations Department: Sieglinde Schuchardt
Auditors: KPMG Deutsche Treuhand-Gesellschaft AG

LOCATIONS

HQ: Tengelmann Warenhandelsgesellschaft KG
Wissollstraße 5-43,
45478 Mülheim an der Ruhr, Germany
Phone: +49-208-5806-7601   **Fax:** +49-208-5806-7605
Web: www.tengelmann.de

Tengelmann has stores in Austria, Bosnia and Herzegovina, the Czech Republic, Germany, Hungary, Italy, Poland, Portugal, Russia, Slovakia, Slovenia, Spain, Switzerland, and the US.

2005 Stores

	No.
Europe	
Germany	5,388
Other countries	1,426
North America	689
Total	**7,503**

2005 Sales

	% of total
Germany	51
Other countries	49
Total	**100**

PRODUCTS/OPERATIONS

2005 Stores

	No.
Plus	3,826
KiK	1,751
Kaiser's Tengelmann	718
A&P	689
Obi	497
Interfruct Cash & Carry	22
Total	**7,503**

Selected Store Operations

Plus (grocery and goods discount store chain)
KiK (discount clothing and textile stores)
Kaiser's (grocery and drugstore chain)
The Great Atlantic & Pacific Tea Company (56%, A&P grocery store chain)
Obi (do-it-yourself supply, hardware, and appliance retailer)
Tengelmann (grocery store chain)

COMPETITORS

ALDI	Lidl & Schwarz Stiftung
A.S. Watson	Maxeda
AVA AG	METRO AG
Carrefour	Praktiker
Casino Guichard	REWE-Zentral
Delhaize	Royal Ahold
Edeka Zentrale	Schlecker
Home Depot	SPAR Handels
ITM Entreprises	Tesco
Kingfisher	Wal-Mart

HISTORICAL FINANCIALS

Company Type: Private

Income Statement

FYE: April 30

	REVENUE ($ mil.)	NET INCOME ($ mil.)	NET PROFIT MARGIN	EMPLOYEES
4/05	33,840	—	—	183,050
4/04	32,104	—	—	184,046
4/03*	29,511	—	—	183,638
6/02	28,227	—	—	183,396
6/01	22,626	—	—	186,000
Annual Growth	10.6%	—	—	(0.4%)

*Fiscal year change

Revenue History

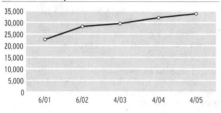

Tesco

Tesco is proof of the good a little dressing up can do. The company runs more than 2,700 supermarkets, supercenters, and convenience stores in the UK (where it is the #1 retailer), and in Ireland, Central Europe, Asia, and soon, the US. Built on the "pile it high and sell it cheap" philosophy of founder Sir Jack Cohen, Tesco abandoned its discount format, with its down-market image, for a variety of dressier midmarket formats. Its operations include convenience and gasoline retailing (Tesco Express), small urban stores (Tesco Metro), supercenters (Tesco Extra), and financial services through Tesco Personal Finance. Tesco.com covers 98% of the UK and is the leading Internet delivery service there.

In addition to groceries, Tesco.com also offers books and music, health tips, and even legal advice (do-it-yourself wills and divorce kits).

While about 75% of Tesco's sales are generated in the UK, the retailer is expanding faster away from home, particularly in Central Europe and Asia. Its 2003 acquisition of C Two-Network (C2), a small Japanese convenience store operator, marked its entry into the world's second-largest consumer market. In 2004 Tesco acquired a 50% stake in Ting Hsin International's Hymall business, for about £145 million. Tesco announced plans in late 2006 to increase its Hymall stake to 90% to boost growth into three regions, particularly Beijing. Hymall operates 44 hypermarkets in Shanghai and in northeastern China. The company plans to open 15 to 20 new stores in Malaysia where it currently operates about a dozen outlets. In South Korea, Tesco has made a deal to increase its ownership share in Homeplus, a retail joint venture with Samsung, from 89% to 99% by 2011.

Looking to further its global ambitions, Tesco has set its sights on the US, where the company plans to launch a new convenience store chain called Fresh & Easy. At least 100 stores are slated to open in Las Vegas, Los Angeles, and Phoenix in 2007.

Tesco's rapid growth has earned the company a 20% share and a 7% share of the UK grocery and non-food markets, respectively. Although food has been the cornerstone of Tesco's operations, the company is actively expanding its non-food offerings, including clothing, gasoline, music, travel, financial services (through a joint venture with the Royal Bank of Scotland), and even residential phone and Internet service. The company opened its first in a planned chain of stand-alone, nonfood stores — called Tesco Homeplus — in October 2005. The stores offer apparel, beauty supplies, electronics, and other general merchandise.

HISTORY

With WWI behind him, in 1919 Jack Cohen invested his serviceman's gratuity in a grocery stall in London's East End. He introduced his first private-label product, Tesco Tea, in 1924 — the name was the combination of the initials of his tea supplier (T. E. Stockwell) and the first two letters of Cohen's last name. By the late 1920s Cohen had several stalls, and in 1929 he opened his first store, under the Tesco name, in Edgeware, London.

Cohen founded Tesco Stores Limited in 1932. During the rest of the decade, the company added more than 100 stores, mainly in London. Cohen visited the US in 1935, studying its self-service supermarkets, and returned to England with a plan of using a similar "pile it high and sell it cheap" format. Delayed by WWII, Tesco opened its first American-styled store in 1947 and went public that year as Tesco Stores Holdings. By 1950 the company ran 20 self-service stores.

Tesco grew primarily through acquisitions during the 1950s and 1960s, adding about 600 stores. By the early 1970s, however, competition and a recession battered Tesco. Managing director Ian MacLaurin initiated radical changes, including abandoning trading stamps and, to shed its down-market image, refurbishing stores with a more upscale decor. A price-slashing initiative in 1977 dramatically increased Tesco's market share within a year. Because cheap brands were best-sellers, Tesco began creating its own private-label brands. The company also started closing unprofitable stores while opening superstores, some with gas stations.

In 1979, the year Sir Jack Cohen died, Tesco entered Ireland by buying Three Guys (abandoning the effort in 1986). In 1983 the company became Tesco, and two years later it named MacLaurin as chairman. By 1991 Tesco was the UK's largest independent gasoline retailer.

Looking for new opportunities, in 1992 Tesco introduced small urban stores called Tesco Metro and the next year began expanding outside England, acquiring stores in France and Scotland. In 1994 it acquired an initial 51% stake in Global, a 43-store grocery chain in Hungary.

Tesco acquired 31 Stavia stores in Poland in 1995; a year later it added 13 Kmart stores in the Czech Republic and Slovakia. Tesco returned to Ireland in 1997 by acquiring 109 Associated British Food stores. It also launched its financial services division that year and named John Gardiner as chairman (replacing the retiring MacLaurin) and Terry Leahy as CEO.

By 2000, Tesco's profitable online shopping business was one of the world's most successful, and the company made it a separate subsidiary, Tesco.com. To build on that success, Tesco bought a 35% stake in GroceryWorks, a subsidiary of the US Safeway grocery chain, in 2001.

In March 2002, Tesco acquired the travel company First Class Leisure and renamed the business Tesco Freetime. Tesco became the market leader in the fragmented Polish food retailing arena by acquiring German hypermarket operator HIT in2002. In January 2003 Tesco completed the acquisition of the British convenience store chain T&S Stores for £519 million.

In April 2004, David Reid became non-executive chairman, replacing Gardiner, who retired from Tesco. In August, Tesco sold the Dillons chain of newsstands to TM Retail for an undisclosed amount. Tesco had acquired Dillons when it purchased T&S Stores.

In 2005, Tesco transferred some 770 back-office jobs from the UK to Bangalore, India, where it opened a software development and accounting office. Tesco also opened its first Kipa store in Turkey since it acquired the Turkish chain in 2003. The 50,000-sq.-ft. store brought Tesco's store count in Turkey to six.

In 2006 the company bought 27 small stores from Edeka in the Czech Republic. In the fall it launched a higher-end, 30-piece apparel line for men and women called F&F Collection by Lee Rees-Oliviere (Tesco's head designer recruited from Marks and Spencer). In October Tesco sold its 38% stake in Internet grocer GroceryWorks to Safeway, its partner in the venture.

EXECUTIVES

Non-Executive Chairman: David E. Reid, age 59, $1,034,018 pay
Chief Executive and Board Member: Terry P. Leahy, age 50, $2,115,995 pay
Commercial and Trading Director and Board Member: Richard W. P. Brasher, age 44
International and Information Technology Director and Board Member: Philip A. (Phil) Clarke, age 46, $1,252,715 pay
Finance and Strategy Director and Board Member: Andrew T. Higginson, age 48, $1,254,633 pay
Finance Services Director: Martin Brown
Group Marketing Director, CEO, USA, and Board Member: Tim J. R. Mason, age 48
Retail and Logistics Director and Board Member: David T. Potts, age 47, $1,187,490 pay
Category Director, Produce: Peter Durose
Corporate and Legal Affairs Director and Secretary: Lucy Neville-Rolfe, age 53
Human Resources Director, Tesco Stores Ltd.: Clare M. Chapman, age 45
Information Technology Director, UK: Colin Cobain
International Corporate Affairs Director: Peter Bracher
Investor Relations Director: Steve Webb, age 43
Personnel Director: David Fairhurst
Chairman, Tesco Mobile: Matthew Key, age 43
Chief Executive, Tesco.com: Laura Wade-Gery, age 38
Chief Executive, UK Convenience Stores: Colin P. Holmes
Chief Executive, Clothing: Terry Green, age 51
Investor Relations: Steve N. Butler
Auditors: PricewaterhouseCoopers LLP

LOCATIONS

HQ: Tesco PLC
Tesco House, Delamare Rd., Cheshunt, Hertfordshire EN8 9SL, United Kingdom
Phone: +44-1992-632-222   **Fax:** +44-1992-630-794
Web: www.tesco.com

2006 Sales

	% of total
Europe	
UK	76
Other countries	13
Asia	11
Total	**100**

	No.
Europe	
UK	1,898
Poland	105
Ireland	91
Hungary	87
Slovakia	37
Czech Republic	35
Turkey	8
Asia	
Thailand	219
Japan	111
South Korea	62
China	39
Malaysia	13
Taiwan	6
Total	**2,711**

PRODUCTS/OPERATIONS

Selected Subsidiaries and Joint Ventures

Ek-Chai Distribution System Co. Ltd. (99%, Lotus stores, Thailand)

Tesco Global Aruhazak (99%, Kaposvar and Tesco stores, Hungary)

One Stop Stores Ltd. (100%, One Stop convenience stores, England and Wales)

Samsung Tesco. Co. Limited (89%, Homeplus stores, South Korea)

Tesco Ireland Limited

Tesco Kipa (93%, hypermarkets, Turkey)

Tesco Personal Finance Group Limited (credit cards, savings accounts, loans, online banking, insurance)

Tesco Polska Sp. Z o.o. (Czestochowa stores, Poland)

Tesco Stores CR a.s. (Czech Republic)

Tesco Stores SR a.s. (Slovakia)

Tesco.com (online sales)

COMPETITORS

ALDI	METRO AG
Alliance Boots	Musgrave Budgens-Londis
ASDA	Netto Foodstores
BP	NEXT
Carphone Warehouse	Primark
Carrefour	Royal Ahold
Co-operative Group	Royal Dutch Shell
Dunnes Stores	Somerfield
Exxon Mobil	SPAR Handels
First Quench	T.K. Maxx
Gap	Waitrose
J Sainsbury	Wm Morrison
John Lewis	Supermarkets
Marks & Spencer	Woolworths Group
Matalan	

HISTORICAL FINANCIALS

Company Type: Public

Income Statement

FYE: Last Saturday in February

	REVENUE ($ mil.)	NET INCOME ($ mil.)	NET PROFIT MARGIN	EMPLOYEES
2/06	68,701	2,744	4.0%	237,024
2/05	65,176	2,621	4.0%	335,750
2/04	57,564	2,055	3.6%	310,411
2/03	41,615	1,495	3.6%	270,800
2/02	33,575	1,178	3.5%	247,374
Annual Growth	**19.6%**	**23.5%**	—	**(1.1%)**

Net Income History

OTC: TSCDY.PK

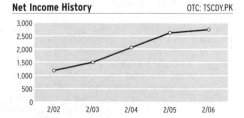

Thomson

Niche information is The Thomson Corporation's niche. The company provides specialized information (such as business, legal, and financial data) online and through CD-ROMs, computer software, and print products. Thomson has divested almost all of its traditional media assets in favor of electronic products. It sold most of its 130 daily and non-daily newspapers, as well as its 20% stake in Canadian media giant Bell Globemedia, a firm it founded with telecommunications company BCE. It bought several Harcourt General businesses (after Harcourt was sold to Reed Elsevier Group) and also owns legal information firm Westlaw. The Thomson family, through their Woodbridge investment company, owns about 63% of Thomson.

Thomson groups its information businesses into four main categories: legal and regulatory; learning; finance; and scientific and health care. The largest unit is the legal sector (40% of sales), which provides information to law schools, law firms, and government institutions. It includes such brands as LIVEDGAR, FindLaw, and Foundation press. Other well known products in the company's other divisions include Thomson Gale and Prometric in the learning division, the finance group's Datastream and TradeWeb, and the Physicians' Desk Reference in the scientific and health care group.

Thomson's makeover into an new media information provider has been costly, but ultimately it has made the firm more technologically advanced than it was in previous incarnations. Thomson has increased the amount of revenues it gains from Internet-related and other electronic services (almost 70% of total sales). The strategy also proved to be a highly acquisitive one for the company, rather than relying heavily on in-house technology development. However, Thomson greatly reduced the number of company purchases it made in 2005 (down to 35 buys totaling almost $290 million versus more than 55 acquisitions for $1.3 billion in 2004), and focused on integrating its previous acquisitions.

Branding has also become very important for the company, and it has been striving to increase the profile of the Thomson name by prominently displaying it on its subsidiary websites and other marketing materials.

A string of deals over the years has cemented Thomson's presence in North America (including the buys of former rival Primark, investor research firm Carson Group, and NewsEdge, which it folded into its Dialog business).

In 2006 the company announced plans to sell its Thomson Medical Education unit and its IOB Brazilian regulatory business. In addition, it said it would implement a new business plan called THOMSONplus to save the business more than $300 million by 2009. Later that year reports surfaced that its Thomson Learning division would be up for sale.

HISTORY

Having failed at farming and auto parts distribution, Roy Thomson left Toronto for the hinterlands of Ontario and started a radio station in 1930. He purchased the *Timmons Press*, a goldmining town newspaper, in 1934. Thomson bought other town papers, venturing outside Ontario in 1949 and into the US in 1952.

The Thomson Newspaper empire grew rapidly during the 1950s. In 1953 Thomson moved to the UK, where he bought the *Scotsman* (Edinburgh). When commercial TV broadcasting began in the UK, Thomson started Scottish Television (1957) and merged it with the UK's Kemsley Newspapers, publisher of the *Sunday Times*, to create the International Thomson Organization in 1959.

International Thomson bought the *Times* of London (1967) and entered the travel business. The next year J. Paul Getty invited International Thomson into a North Sea oil drilling venture. The consortium struck oil in 1973, just as the OPEC oil embargo took hold. Oil accounted for the bulk of International Thomson's profits by 1976, when Thomson died. His son, Kenneth, took over as chairman. In 1978 a public holding company was created to house International Thomson's operations.

Using oil earnings to expand and diversify its publishing interests, the company sold the *Times* in 1981 and began shopping for specialty publishers with subscription-based revenues, which would be less vulnerable to recession. Purchases included American Banker and Bond Buyer (financial publications, 1983), Gale Research (library reference materials, 1985), and several online information providers. The company then completed the sale of its oil and gas holdings.

Thomson Newspapers and International Thomson merged to become The Thomson Corporation in 1989, and in 1991 it bought Maxwell's Macmillan Professional and Business Reference Publishing. The company grouped its newspapers in regional clusters.

The firm bought law and textbook publisher West Publishing in 1996. Continuing its selective divestment of newspapers, the company sold 43 daily papers in the US and Canada in 1996.

In 1998 Thomson veteran Richard Harrington became CEO. Also that year Thomson bought tax return software maker Computer Language Research as well as a pair of tax and law publishing units from UK's Pearson. It also bought Knight Ridder's Technimetrics financial information unit and spun off its travel group business.

In 2000 Thomson announced it would sell its newspapers to focus on the Internet. The company bought Sylvan Learning Systems' Prometric division, which provides computer-based testing services, and Wave Technologies International, a provider of multimedia instructional products. Thomson also bought the online data services division of Dialog, and it acquired rival financial data provider Primark for $1 billion.

Thomson joined forces in 2001 with Canadian telecommunications giant BCE to create media firm Bell Globemedia, with Internet, newspapers, and broadcasting assets worth about $2.7 billion. (It sold its interest in the company two years later.) Also that year it bought the higher education and corporate training businesses of Harcourt General from Reed Elsevier Group plc (formerly Reed Elsevier plc) and acquired business content provider NewsEdge.

Thomson started trading on the New York Stock Exchange in mid-2002. Later that year it beefed up its Internet education group with the purchase of certain e-learning assets from McGraw-Hill. In 2003 the company purchased Elite Information Group, a maker of law firm practice software, for more than $100 million.

In 2006 Kenneth Thomson died at the age of 82.

EXECUTIVES

Chairman: David K. R. Thomson
Deputy Chairman: W. Geoffrey Beattie, age 45
President, CEO, and Director:
 Richard J. (Dick) Harrington, age 59
EVP, CFO, and Director: Robert D. (Bob) Daleo, age 57
EVP and Director: David H. (Dave) Shaffer, age 62
EVP Human Resources: Robert B. Bogart
**EVP and Corporate Chief Technology and Operations
 Officer:** Michael E. Wilens, age 52
EVP; President and CEO, Thomson Learning:
 Ronald H. Schlosser, age 53
**EVP; President and CEO, Thomson Legal and
 Regulatory:** Brian H. Hall, age 54
**EVP; President and CEO, Thomson Scientific and
 Healthcare:** Robert C. Cullen
SVP and CIO: Carl Urbania, age 63
SVP and Corporate Chief Strategy Officer:
 Richard Benson-Armer, age 42
SVP and General Counsel: Deirdre Stanley, age 37
SVP and Strategic Sourcing Officer:
 Barbara E. Scarcella
SVP and Treasurer: Stephane Bello, age 40
SVP Corporate Communications:
 Gustav D. (Gus) Carlson
SVP Technology: Joe Rhyne
VP, Corporate Controller, and Chief Accounting Officer:
 Linda J. Walker
VP Investor Relations: Frank J. Golden, age 46
Secretary: David W. Binet
Auditors: PricewaterhouseCoopers LLP

LOCATIONS

HQ: The Thomson Corporation
 Toronto-Dominion Bank Tower, 66 Wellington
 Street West, Toronto, Ontario M5K 1A1, Canada
Phone: 416-360-8700   **Fax:** 416-360-8812
US HQ: Metro Center, 1 Station Place,
 Stamford, CT 06902
US Phone: 203-539-8000   **US Fax:** 203-539-7734
Web: www.thomson.com

2005 Sales

	$ mil.	% of total
US	6,890	79
Europe	1,058	13
Asia/Pacific	367	4
Canada	300	3
Other regions	88	1
Total	**8,703**	**100**

PRODUCTS/OPERATIONS

2005 Sales

	$ mil.	% of total
Legal & regulatory	3,491	40
Learning	2,319	26
Financial	1,897	22
Scientific & health care	1,018	12
Adjustments	(22)	—
Total	**8,703**	**100**

Selected Operations

Thomson Financial
 AutEx (global securities market tracking)
 BETA (back office data processing)
 Datastream (current and historical economic and
  financial information, UK)
 First Call Wire (corporate news and stock)
 Thomson ONE Wealth Management (electronic
  financial information)
 TradeWeb (online fixed income securities trading)
Thomson Learning
 Thomson Course Technology (information technology
  learning materials)
 Thomson Gale (academic and business reference
  material)
 Thomson NETg (information technology training)
 Thomson Prometric (computer based testing
  development)
 Thomson Wadsworth (higher education textbooks)
 Universitas 21 Global (online university)

Thomson Legal and Regulatory
 FindLaw (Web portal of legal resources)
 Foundation Press (law school publications)
 HubbardOne (online legal resources)
 NewsEdge (news and market research)
 Thomson Elite (law firm management software)
 Thomson West (online and print legal book
  publishing)
Thomson Scientific and Healthcare
 Derwent World Patents Index (patent and scientific
  data)
 Dialog DataStar (scientific and business information)
 Micromedex (drug information)
 Thomson Pharma (pharmaceutical information)
 Physician's Desk Reference
 Web of Science (global research online)

COMPETITORS

Addison-Wesley	LexisNexis
American Lawyer Media	McGraw-Hill
Berkshire Hathaway	Pearson
Bloomberg	ProQuest
Comtex News	Reed Elsevier Group
D&B	Reuters
Dow Jones	Scholastic Library
Encyclopædia Britannica	Publishing
IHS	Solucient
infoUSA	United Business Media
John Wiley	Wolters Kluwer
Kaplan	W.W. Norton

HISTORICAL FINANCIALS

Company Type: Public

Income Statement

FYE: December 31

	REVENUE ($ mil.)	NET INCOME ($ mil.)	NET PROFIT MARGIN	EMPLOYEES
12/05	8,703	947	10.9%	40,500
12/04	8,098	1,016	12.5%	39,550
12/03	7,606	846	11.1%	39,000
12/02	7,756	438	5.6%	42,000
12/01	7,237	552	7.6%	44,000
Annual Growth	**4.7%**	**14.4%**	**—**	**(2.1%)**

2005 Year-End Financials

Debt ratio: 41.8%
Return on equity: 10.0%
Cash ($ mil.): 407
Current ratio: 0.97
Long-term debt ($ mil.): 3,983

No. of shares (mil.): —
Dividends
Yield: 2.0%
Payout: 55.6%
Market value ($ mil.): —

Stock History

NYSE: TOC

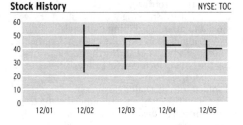

	STOCK PRICE ($) FY Close	P/E High/Low		PER SHARE ($) Earnings	Dividends
12/05	39.66	32	22	1.42	0.79
12/04	42.27	—	—	—	0.75
12/03	47.08	36	19	1.31	0.73
12/02	42.00	88	35	0.65	0.81
12/01	48.35	69	0	0.84	1.09
Annual Growth	**(4.8%)**	**—**	**—**	**14.0%**	**(7.7%)**

ThyssenKrupp

How do you say "giant engineering and steel company" in German? Try "ThyssenKrupp." The company is one of the world's largest steel producers and getting larger. ThyssenKrupp operates worldwide in three business areas: steel, capital goods, and services. The steel unit concentrates on carbon steel and stainless steel, while the capital goods unit consists of two segments: elevators and technologies (machine tools, large-diameter bearings, and industrial doors). The services sector provides tailor-made materials, environmental services, mechanical engineering, and scaffolding services. The former automotive segment of the capital goods unit was disbanded and sold off in pieces in 2006.

ThyssenKrupp is a product of the 1999 merger of Thyssen AG, (pronounced "TISS-in") and Fried. Krupp AG Hoesch-Krupp. Although its combined interests range from elevators to shipbuilding, the company relies heavily on the cyclical steel market; hence, ThyssenKrupp has put on hold its plans to spin off the steel unit.

The company's steel unit is investing nearly $800 million throughout its global operations. ThyssenKrupp's largest investment has gone toward its tinplate manufacturing business, which supplies the food and beverage industries. To take full advantage of China's fast-paced economy, ThyssenKrupp's Shanghai stainless steel venture with Shanghai Baosteel is multiplying its cold strip mill production capacity by five in 2006. It also submitted a bid for Dofasco, initiating a bidding war with Arcelor for Canada's largest steel company. ThyssenKrupp's $4.1 billion bid, coming in late 2005, was designed to strengthen the company's position in the North American auto market. The company pulled out of the contest for Dofasco in early 2006, deciding the price was too high. The company still has a hope of gaining control of Dofasco, though. After Mittal Steel's hostile takeover attempt of Arcelor proved successful, it pledged to sell Dofasco to ThyssenKrupp. (The deal is held up due to a prior arrangement Arcelor had made concerning ownership of Dofasco in an attempt to fend off Mittal.)

Also in 2006 the company gained majority control of German submarine maker Atlas Elektronik when it bought a 60% stake from BAE Systems. The French aerospace company EADS went in on the deal with ThyssenKrupp and owns the remaining 40%.

Krupp Foundation owns 20% of the company.

HISTORY

Formed separately in the 1800s, both Thyssen and Krupp flourished in their early years under family control. Friedrich Krupp opened his steel factory in 1811. He died in 1826 and left the nearly bankrupt factory in the hands of his 14-year-old son Alfred, who turned the business around. At the first World's Fair in 1851, Alfred unveiled a steel cannon far superior to earlier bronze models.

Twenty years later, August Thyssen founded a puddling and rolling mill near Mulheim. He bought small factories and mines, and by WWI, he ran Germany's largest iron and steel company. During the world wars the resources of both companies were turned toward war efforts.

Post-WWII years were tough for both companies. Thyssen was split up by the Allies, and when it began production again in 1953, it consisted of one steel plant. In the Krupp camp, Alfred's great-grandson Alfried was convicted in 1948 of using slave labor during WWII. Released from prison in 1951, Alfried rebuilt Krupp. After near ruin following WWII, both companies emerged and enjoyed a resurgence, along with the German economy, in which they prospered and expanded during the 1950s.

By the 1980s Thyssen's businesses included ships, locomotives, offshore oil rigs, specialty steel, and metals trading and distribution. Krupp continued to grow, and in 1992 it took over engineering and steelmaking concern Hoesch AG. (Eberhard Hoesch had begun making railroad tracks in the 1820s. The company grew and expanded into infrastructure and building products.)

The new Fried. Krupp AG Hoesch-Krupp bought Italian specialty steelmaker Acciai Speciali Terni, chemical plant builder Uhde, and South African shipper J.H. Bachmann. Its automotive division formed a joint venture in Brazil and added production sites in China, Mexico, Romania, and the US. In 1997 Thyssen expanded in North America with its $675 million acquisition of Giddings & Lewis (machine tools, US) and the purchase of Copper & Brass Sales (metals processing and distributing).

Krupp attempted a hostile takeover of Thyssen in 1997. The takeover failed, but the companies soon agreed to merge their steel operations to form Thyssen Krupp Stahl. Bigger plans were in the works, and in 1998 the two companies agreed to merge. That year Thyssen sold its Plusnet fixed-line phone business to Esprit Telecom Group.

In 1999 Krupp's automotive division (Krupp Hoesch Automotive) bought Cummins' Atlas Crankshaft subsidiary. Thyssen also bought US-based Dover's elevator business for $1.1 billion. Krupp and Thyssen completed their merger in 1999. The company planned to spin off its steel operations, but held off due to its success in 2000. ThyssenKrupp did, however, sell its Krupp Kunststofftechnik unit (plastic molding machines) for about $183 million. To speed corporate decision-making, the company made plans to scrap its dual-management structure in 2001.

Early in 2001 ThyssenKrupp agreed to buy 51% of Fiat unit Magneti Marelli's suspension-systems and shock-absorbers business. It also has the option of buying the remainder after 2004. In 2002 the company formed alliances with NKK and Kawasaki Steel to share its steel sheet making technologies while expanding its business with Japanese automotive makers in Europe. ThyssenKrupp's joint venture with Chinese steelmaker ANSC Angang New Steel, known as TAGAL, began producing galvanized coil of which about 80% will be used in China's burgeoning automotive industry.

In 2004 ThyssenKrupp sold its residential real estate unit for around $2.8 billion to a consortium of real estate funds operated by Morgan Stanley and Corpus-Immobiliengruppe.

EXECUTIVES

Chairman, Supervisory Board: Gerhard Cromme, age 63
Chairman, Executive Board: Prof Ekkehard D. Schulz, age 65, $2,911,095 pay
Vice Chairman, Executive Board, Controlling and Mergers and Acquisitions: Ulrich Middelmann, age 61
Member, Executive Board; Chairman, Executive Board, ThyssenKrupp Steel: Karl-Ulrich Köhler, age 50
Member, Executive Board; Chairman, Executive Board, ThyssenKrupp Elevator and ThyssenKrupp Services: Edwin Eichler, age 48

Member, Executive Board; Vice Chairman, Executive Board, ThyssenKrupp Technologies: Wolfram Mörsdorf, age 58
Member, Executive Board; Chairman, Executive Board, ThyssenKrupp Technologies: Olaf Berlien, age 44
NAFTA Representative and Chairman, ThyssenKrupp (national holding company in the US): Gary Elliott, age 62
Member, Executive Board and CFO: A. Stefan Kirsten, age 45, $1,764,300 pay
Member, Executive Board, Personnel and Social Policy: Ralph Labonte, age 53, $1,764,300 pay
Member, Executive Board; Chairman, Executive Board, ThyssenKrupp Stainless: Jürgen H. Fechter, age 44
Corporate Communications, Strategy, and Executive Affairs: Jürgen Claassen
Auditors: KPMG Deutsche Treuhand-Gesellschaft AG

LOCATIONS

HQ: ThyssenKrupp AG
August-Thyssen-Strasse 1,
40211 Düsseldorf, Germany
Phone: +49-211-824-0   **Fax:** +49-211-824-36000
US HQ: 3155 W. Big Beaver Rd., Troy, MI 48007
US Phone: 248-643-3929   **US Fax:** 248-643-3518
Web: www.thyssenkrupp.com

ThyssenKrupp operates worldwide; it has current operations centered in Europe and North America.

2005 Sales

	% of total
EU	
Germany	33
Other countries	31
US	21
Asia	7
Other regions	8
Total	**100**

PRODUCTS/OPERATIONS

2005 Sales

	% of total
Steel	33
Services	28
Automotive	17
Technologies	13
Elevator	9
Total	**100**

COMPETITORS

Acerinox	MAN
Bechtel	Marubeni
Corus Group	Mittal Steel Company
Descours & Cabaud	Nippon Steel
GEA Group	POSCO
Ingersoll-Rand	Qingdao Iron and Steel
ITOCHU	Schindler Holding
JFE Holdings	Sumitomo Metal Industries
Kobe Steel	United States Steel
Magna International	United Technologies

HISTORICAL FINANCIALS

Company Type: Public

Income Statement

FYE: September 30

	REVENUE ($ mil.)	NET INCOME ($ mil.)	NET PROFIT MARGIN	EMPLOYEES
9/05	50,658	1,227	2.4%	183,729
9/04	48,489	1,114	2.3%	187,678
9/03	41,897	594	1.4%	190,102
9/02	36,001	212	0.6%	191,254
9/01	34,572	605	1.7%	193,516
Annual Growth	10.0%	19.3%	—	(1.3%)

2005 Year-End Financials

Debt ratio: 36.2%   Current ratio: 2.06
Return on equity: 11.8%   Long-term debt ($ mil.): 3,822
Cash ($ mil.): 5,570

Net Income History   German: TKA

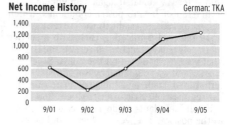

Tokyo Electric Power

Japan Inc. would grind to a halt without Tokyo Electric Power Company (TEPCO), which supplies power to 27.7 million customers in Tokyo, Yokohama, and the rest of the Kanto region. One of the world's largest electric utilities, TEPCO's 190 power plants have the generating capacity of approximately 63,000 MW, primarily produced by thermal, nuclear, and hydroelectric power sources. Through interests in telecom businesses, the company offers telephony and Internet services; it also has international consulting and power generation operations. Other businesses include construction, real estate, and transportation companies.

Although public confidence has been shaken by a rash of accidents within Japan's nuclear industry, the company promotes the use of nuclear power as an earth-friendly energy source. TEPCO currently operates three power plants. However, the company has struggled to restore its credibility after the Japanese government shut down TEPCO's 17 nuclear reactors due to safety concerns, prompted by the company's admittance of falsifying safety data to cover up faults at several of its nuclear facilities in 2002.

TEPCO is diversifying its operations in the face of further deregulation. In 2005 the company's liberalization of the retail electric power market has resulted in about 60% of TEPCO's revenues coming from retail sales. The company also owns a majority stake in telecommunications firm POWEREDCOM, which offers data communications services through TEPCO and other Japanese utilities' fiber-optic networks; TEPCO increased its stake in POWEREDCOM to 84% in 2004. POWEREDCOM has absorbed local and long-distance phone company Tokyo Telecommunication Network (TTNet), in which TEPCO held a 39% stake.

In 2006 Mirant agreed to sell its power plants in the Philippines to TEPCO and Marubeni for $3.4 billion.

HISTORY

The Tokyo Electric Power Company (TEPCO) descended from Tokyo Electric Light, which was formed in 1883. In 1887 the company switched on Japan's first power plant, a 25-KW fossil fuel generator. Fossil fuels were the main source of electricity in Japan until 1912, when long-distance transmission techniques became more efficient, making hydroelectric power cheaper.

In 1938 Japan nationalized electric utilities, despite strong objections from Yasuzaemon Matsunaga, a leader in Japan's utility industry and former president of the Japan Electric Association. After WWII Matsunaga championed public ownership of Japan's power companies, which helped in 1951 to establish the current system of 10 regional companies, each with a service monopoly. Tokyo Electric Power was the largest. That year it was listed on the Tokyo Stock Exchange and was regulated by the Ministry of International Trade and Industry. (The ministry has regulated electric utilities since 1965.)

Fossil fuel plants made a comeback in Japan in the postwar era because they could be built more economically than hydroelectric plants. When the OPEC oil embargo of the 1970s demonstrated Japan's dependence on foreign oil, TEPCO increased its use of liquefied natural gas (LNG) and nuclear energy sources. (It brought its first nuke online in 1971.) In 1977 it formed the Energy Conservation Center to promote conservation and related legislation.

To further reduce its oil dependence TEPCO joined other US and Japanese firms in building a coal gasification plant in California's Mojave Desert in 1982. Two years later TEPCO announced it would begin building its first coal-burning generator since the oil crisis. It established Tokyo Telecommunication Network (TTNet), a partnership to provide telecommunications services, in 1986 and TEPCO Cable TV in 1989.

As part of its interest in alternative energy systems, TEPCO established a global environment department in 1990 to conduct R&D on energy and the environment. Its environmental program has included reforestation and fuel cell research.

Liberalization in 1995 allowed Japan's electric utilities to buy power from independent power producers; TEPCO quickly lined up 10 suppliers. The company proceeded with energy experimentation in 1996, trying a 6,000-KW sodium-sulfur battery at a Yokohama transformer station. The next year the company announced that it would become the first electric utility to sell liquefied natural gas as part of its energy mix, and finished building the world's largest nuclear plant.

To gain experience in deregulating markets, TEPCO invested in US power generating company Orion Power in 1999. (It agreed to sell its 5% stake to Reliant Energy in 2001.) At home the firm joined Microsoft and SOFTBANK to form SpeedNet, which provides Internet access over TTNet's network. In 2000 TEPCO got its first taste of deregulation when large customers (accounting for about a third of the market) began choosing their electricity suppliers. Also in 2000 TEPCO joined a group of nine Japanese electric companies to create POWEREDCOM.

In 2001 TEPCO joined up with Sumitomo and Electricité de France to build Vietnam's first independent power plant.

EXECUTIVES

Chairman: Shigemi Tamura
President: Tsunehisa Katsumata
EVP, General Accounting, Planning, and International: Katsutoshi Chikudate
EVP: Hisao Naito
EVP: Yoshihisa Morimoto
EVP: Takashi Hayashi
EVP: Susumu Shirakawa
EVP: Takuya Hattori

Managing Director: Yuichi Hayase
Managing Director: Katsumi Mizutani
Managing Director: Masataka Shimizu
Managing Director: Ichiro Takekuro
Managing Director: Norio Tsuzumi
Managing Director: Takashi Fujimoto
Managing Director: Akio Nakamura
Managing Director: Shigeru Kimura
Auditors: Ernst & Young ShinNihon

LOCATIONS

HQ: The Tokyo Electric Power Company, Incorporated
(Tokyo Denryoku Kabushiki Kaisha)
1-3, Uchisaiwai-cho 1-chome, Chiyoda-ku,
Tokyo 100-8560, Japan
Phone: +81-3-4216-1111   **Fax:** +81-3-4216-2539
US HQ: 1901 L St. NW, Ste. 720, Washington, DC 20036
US Phone: 202-457-0790   **US Fax:** 202-457-0810
Web: www.tepco.co.jp

The Tokyo Electric Power Company provides electricity in Japan's Kanto region, which includes Tokyo and Yokohama. It also has independent power projects, consulting operations, and other investments in Asia, Australia, Europe, the Middle East, North America, and South America.

PRODUCTS/OPERATIONS

2006 Sales

	% of total
Electricity	93
Information & telecommunications	3
Energy & environment	2
Other	2
Total	**100**

Selected Subsidiaries

TEPCO CABLE TELEVISION Inc. (85%, cable television)
TEPCO SYSTEMS CORPORATION (information software and services)
Toden Kogyo Co., Ltd. (facilities construction and maintenance)
Toden Real Estate Co., Inc. (property management)
Tokyo Densetsu Service Co., Ltd. (facilities construction and maintenance)
Tokyo Electric Power Environmental Engineering Company, Incorporated (facilities construction and maintenance)
Tokyo Electric Power Services Company, Limited (facilities construction and maintenance)

COMPETITORS

Chubu Electric Power	Korea Electric Power
Chugoku Electric Power	Kyushu Electric Power
Hokkaido Electric Power	NTT
Hokuriku Electric Power	Osaka Gas
Internet Initiative Japan	Shikoku Electric
Jinpan International	Tohoku Electric Power
Kansai Electric	Tokyo Gas
KDDI	

HISTORICAL FINANCIALS

Company Type: Public

Income Statement

FYE: March 31

	REVENUE ($ mil.)	NET INCOME ($ mil.)	NET PROFIT MARGIN	EMPLOYEES
3/06	41,632	2,640	6.3%	38,235
3/05	44,609	2,103	4.7%	53,380
3/04	45,946	1,416	3.1%	51,694
3/03	41,045	1,379	3.4%	52,322
3/02	39,358	1,521	3.9%	40,725
Annual Growth	**1.4%**	**14.8%**	**—**	**(1.6%)**

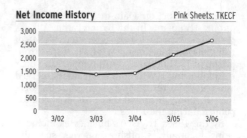

Net Income History   Pink Sheets: TKECF

Tokyo Electron

Let me tell you about TEL. Tokyo Electron Limited (TEL) is the world's #2 manufacturer of semiconductor production equipment — well behind #1 Applied Materials, but well ahead of other contenders. TEL's chip-making systems include chemical vapor deposition, thermal processing, etching, cleaning, and probing equipment. The company also makes flat-panel display (FPD) production equipment, and distributes other companies' chip-making equipment, computer systems, networking products, and software in Japan. Subsidiary Tokyo Electron Device distributes chips, boards, and software made by companies including Advanced Micro Devices, Agilent, Motorola, and Microsoft.

Chip production equipment accounts for nearly three-quarters of TEL's sales, and customers outside Japan account for nearly two-thirds of sales.

Like its customers and competitors, TEL suffered through a dismal time during the chip industry slump of 2001-2003. To counter these conditions, and to give itself more flexibility for future market ups and downs, TEL restructured its operations. Among other measures, it merged production plants, closed field offices, and let go many of its contract workers. It has also sold its physical vapor deposition (PVD) product line to Metron Technology, which sold its assets to Applied Materials in late 2004.

HISTORY

Frustrated by the unreliable semiconductor production equipment their employer, Nissho Trading Co. (now Sojitz), was importing from the US, Tokuo Kubo and Toshio Kodada quit their jobs at Nissho in 1963 and founded Tokyo Electron Laboratories (TEL). Tokyo Broadcasting System provided some initial backing.

At first about half of the company's sales came from importing US semiconductor equipment. The other half came from exporting Japanese electronics, such as car radios. In 1968 TEL and US-based diffusion furnace maker Thermco Systems (later acquired by Allegheny International) formed TEL-Thermco Engineering Co. TEL followed with other joint ventures, paying royalties to manufacture other companies' products in Japan.

The company's US unit, TEL America (now Tokyo Electron America), was established in 1972. In 1978 Tokyo Electron Laboratories was renamed Tokyo Electron Limited (also TEL).

TEL went public in 1980. In 1981 the company formed a joint venture with GenRad (later acquired by Teradyne) to make test systems in the

US. In 1988 TEL acquired Thermco's stake in their joint venture.

The company began a major international expansion in 1993, setting up shop in South Korea. In the following years it expanded into Germany, Italy, the UK, and Taiwan. In 1996 TEL managing director Tetsuro Higashi was named president. (He is now chairman and CEO.)

In 1997 TEL delivered the first of its 300mm wafer production equipment. The next year the company acquired the semiconductor equipment division (now part of Tokyo Electron Arizona) of Sony's Material Research Corp. Also in 1998 TEL formed Tokyo Electron EE Limited to refurbish and upgrade semiconductor manufacturing equipment.

The company formed its French subsidiary in 1999. That year TEL and AlliedSignal (now Honeywell International) formed a joint venture to develop chip-making equipment. Also in 1999 rival Tegal won a permanent injunction against TEL to stop US sales of some of TEL's wafer etching equipment; legal wrangling over patent issues continued between the two companies through 2000.

In 2000 TEL acquired US-based Supercritical Systems, a maker of semiconductor cleaning devices. The next year the company bought Timbre Technologies, a US-based maker of metrology tools used in chip production.

In 2002 the company expanded its reach into China when it opened a support office there. TEL finally prevailed over Tegal in the long-running patent infringement case, with the US Court of Appeals for the Federal Circuit finding for the Japanese company.

That same year TEL agreed with Dainippon Screen and Ebara on forming a joint venture to develop an electron-beam lithography system, using technology from Toshiba. The company also became involved in the Albany NanoTech project, supporting advanced semiconductor R&D in cooperation with researchers at the University at Albany, in the state capital of New York.

Kiyoshi Sato was promoted to president and CEO in 2003, succeeding Tetsuro Higashi, who became chairman. The company marked its 40th anniversary. TEL and Nikon agreed on joint development of liquid immersion exposure systems for semiconductor manufacturing. The company consolidated its service and support division as Tokyo Electron BP Ltd. that year.

Continuing the trend of cooperative relations with other vendors of semiconductor manufacturing equipment, TEL partnered with Mattson Technology in 2004. Later in the year it created a new American holding company, Tokyo Electron US Holdings, to oversee such subsidiaries as Tokyo Electron America, Tokyo Electron Massachusetts, TEL Technology Center America, and Tokyo Electron Arizona.

TEL made management changes at the outset of 2005, following a series of restructuring moves for the corporation. Tetsuro Higashi reclaimed the CEO post, while Kiyoshi Sato remained as president and COO.

The company went through a sweeping reorganization in early 2006, with the semiconductor production equipment division divided into four product-specific divisions. A new Sales & Services division was created, organized on a customer basis. Later in the year, the company created TEL Venture Capital, a firm that will make seed and early-stage investments in promising technology ventures, emulating similar investment firms established by competitors Applied Materials and Novellus Systems.

EXECUTIVES

Chairman and CEO: Tetsuro (Terry) Higashi
Vice Chairman: Tetsuo (Tom) Tsuneishi
President and COO: Kiyoshi (Ken) Sato
SVP, Technology and Development: Masao Kubodera
SVP, FPD and General Manager, FPD Division: Mitsuru Onozato
SVP, Business Development and Account Management and General Manager, Business Development and Account Management, Japan: Makoto Mizokuchi
SVP, Corporate Strategic Planning: Hiroki Takebuchi
SVP, Technology: Ben Tsai
VP; General Manager, Administration: Yoshiteru Harada
VP; General Manager, Marketing: Yoichi Ishikawa
VP; General Manager, Human Resources and Finance: Yutaka Nanasawa
VP; General Manager, Business Development and Account Management, North America and Europe; and Director: Yukio Sunahara, age 69
President and COO, Tokyo Electron U.S. Holdings: Barry R. Mayer
Auditors: Masatoshi Yoshino, Eiji Miyashita, Fumihiko Sugiura

LOCATIONS

HQ: Tokyo Electron Limited
TBS Broadcast Center, 3-6 Akasaka 5-chome, Minato-ku, Tokyo 107-8481, Japan
Phone: +81-3-5561-7000   **Fax:** +81-3-5561-7400
US HQ: 2400 Grove Blvd., Austin, TX 78741
US Phone: 512-424-1000   **US Fax:** 512-424-1001
Web: www.tel.com

Tokyo Electron has operations in China, France, Germany, Ireland, Israel, Italy, Japan, the Netherlands, South Korea, Taiwan, the UK, and the US.

2006 Sales

	% of total
Asia/Pacific	
Japan	39
Taiwan	22
South Korea	12
US	14
Other regions	13
Total	**100**

PRODUCTS/OPERATIONS

2006 Sales

	% of total
Industrial electronic equipment	
Semiconductor production	72
FPD production	12
Computer network equipment	3
Electronic equipment	13
Total	**100**

Selected Products

Production Equipment
Liquid crystal displays
Coater/developers
Plasma etcher/ashers
Semiconductors
Carrierless cleaners
Coater/developers
Metal chemical vapor deposition (CVD) systems
Oxidation/diffusion furnaces and LP-CVD systems
Plasma etchers
Scrubbers
Spin-on dielectric coaters
Wafer probers
Wafer-level burn-in and test systems
Distributed Products
Data management software
Film metrology tools
Lithography process management software
Semiconductor manufacturing yield management software
Semiconductors and board-level products
Storage area network (SAN) equipment
Wafer inspection systems

COMPETITORS

AIXTRON	Future Electronics
Amtech Systems	Hitachi
Applied Materials	Lam Research
ASM International	Novellus
Aviza Technology	Semitool
Dainippon Screen	Tegal
Electroglas	ULVAC
FEI	Veeco Instruments
FSI International	

HISTORICAL FINANCIALS

Company Type: Public

Income Statement

FYE: March 31

	REVENUE ($ mil.)	NET INCOME ($ mil.)	NET PROFIT MARGIN	EMPLOYEES
3/06	5,729	408	7.1%	8,950
3/05	5,911	573	9.7%	8,864
3/04	5,014	79	1.6%	8,870
3/03	3,843	(347)	—	10,053
3/02	3,150	(150)	—	10,171
Annual Growth	**16.1%**	**—**	**—**	**(3.1%)**

Net Income History

Exchange: Tokyo

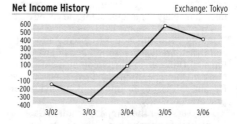

Tomkins

Not so long ago, whether you wanted to pack some heat or merely pack some lunch, multinational conglomerate Tomkins had a subsidiary that could make your day. But the company has sold its food manufacturing operations and subsidiary Smith & Wesson in order to reshape itself as a global engineering group. Tomkins companies make and distribute automotive products, industrial power systems, plumbing components, windows, doors, valves, and other construction products. In the US, Tomkins' brand divisions include Gates (automotive belts and hoses) and Trico (wiper blades), and Stant (automotive caps, seals, and gaskets).

Tomkins fortunes improved somewhat in 2005 despite the automotive sector doldrums in North America and Europe. The company plans to stay competitive by focusing on core products and keeping an eye out for acquisitions that offer a complementary and profitable fit.

Meanwhile, Tomkins is well positioned to take advantage of the explosive growth of the automotive industry in China. The company already leads the Chinese market for transmission belts. The company added to its China presence in 2005 with the opening of two new facilities there — bringing Tomkins' number of Chinese facilities to seven. Tomkins also added an automotive components facility in India in 2005.

HISTORY

Tomkins was founded in 1925 as the F. H. Tomkins Buckle Company, a maker of buckles and fasteners. Tomkins continued to develop within this niche market for the next six decades. In 1983 Gregory Hutchings acquired a 23% stake in the company. Hutchings, who at age 24 had started his own construction business, had won a reputation as a go-getter when he caught the eye of Lords Hanson and White; he was hired by the Hanson Group in 1980 as its chief acquisition scout. In 1984 Hutchings became Tomkins' CEO and set about acquiring manufacturing companies in the UK and the US.

The company acquired Ferraris Piston Service (auto components) and Hayters (a garden tool manufacturer) that year, followed by Pegler-Hattersley (plumbing fixtures) in 1986, Smith & Wesson (guns) in 1987, and Murray Ohio (lawn mowers and bicycles) the next year. In 1992 the company acquired Rank Hovis McDougall, a leading UK baker and food manufacturer.

Tomkins made only eight major purchases between 1983 and 1993, as Hutchings worked to put his acquisitions on a sound financial footing, upgrading plants and equipment and giving each company the autonomy to become efficient.

In 1994 Tomkins bought Outdoor Products and Dynamark Plastics from Noma Industries of Canada: Outdoor Products complemented the Murray Ohio operations, and injection molder Dynamark Plastics fit into Tomkins' industrial products portfolio.

Two years later the company acquired Gates, a US maker of belts and hoses, with operations in 15 countries; the move gave Tomkins access to new markets in Latin America and Southeast Asia. That year Tomkins acquired the hose operations of Nationwide Rubber Enterprises, making Gates the leading manufacturer of curved hose in Australia. In 1997 Tomkins acquired US firm Stant Corp., a leading maker of windshield wipers, fuel tank caps, and other auto accessories, to further complement Gates' product lines.

Besides acquisitions, Tomkins regularly disposed of companies that no longer fit its strategic plan. It sold Inchbrook Printers in 1996 and Ferraris Piston Service, the first business purchased by Tomkins under Hutchings' leadership, in 1997. In a symbolic break with its past, Tomkins sold F. H. Tomkins Buckle in 1998.

That year Tomkins made another automotive equipment acquisition when it bought US-based Schrader-Bridgeport; it also bought Martine Spécialités, a supplier of frozen patisserie products. In 1999 the company acquired ACD Tridon, a Canadian manufacturer of automotive parts.

In 2000 Smith & Wesson settled more than a dozen lawsuits with US cities attempting to collect damages for handgun violence cases. Breaking rank with other handgun makers, the company agreed to install child-safety locks on its guns and ensure that gun sellers conduct background checks.

Tomkins moved to exit the food manufacturing business in 2000, selling Red Wing and agreeing to sell the European operations of Ranks Hovis McDougall. Hutchings resigned that year in the midst of an investigation of his spending practices (including his use of corporate jets and the presence of Hutchings' wife and housekeeper on the company payroll), and chairman David Newlands took over. That year the company sold its bicycle, snowblower, and mowing machinery businesses (Hayter and Murray). In 2001 Tomkins sold Smith & Wesson to US-based Saf-T-Hammer, a manufacturer of gun safety equipment, for $15 million.

In 2002 Tomkins sold its Gates Consumer and Industrial (GCI) division to the Rutland Fund for about $35 million in cash. GCI's products include carpet padding and accessories, diving suits, and commercial rubber compounds. Also that year Jim Nicol took over as CEO. The following year Tomkins sold its Milliken Valve Company, Inc. subsidiary to the Henry Pratt Company for $7.3 million in cash.

In 2006 Tomkins acquired chimney and vent pipe manufacturer Selkirk, L.L.C. Selkirk became a Tomkins subsidiary within its Air Systems Components business.

EXECUTIVES

Non-Executive Chairman: David B. Newlands, age 59, $562,571 pay
CEO and Director: Jim Nicol, age 52, $215,377 pay
CFO and Director: Ken Lever, age 52, $395,176 pay
EVP: David J. (D.J.) Carroll, age 49
EVP, Human Resources: Malcolm T. Swain, age 52
VP, Corporate Development: John Zimmerman, age 43
President, Air Systems Components Division: Terry J. O'Halloran, age 58
President, Dexter Axle Company: W.M. Jones, age 56
President, The Gates Rubber Company: Richard Bell, age 57
Secretary: Norman C. Porter, age 54
General Counsel: G.S. Pappayliou, age 52
Auditors: Deloitte & Touche

LOCATIONS

HQ: Tomkins plc
East Putney House, 84 Upper Richmond Rd., London SW15 2ST, United Kingdom
Phone: +44-20-8871-4544   **Fax:** +44-20-8877-9700
Web: www.tomkins.co.uk

2005 Sales

	$ mil.	% of total
US	3,854	67
Europe		
UK	296	5
Other countires	567	10
Other regions	1,059	18
Total	**5,776**	**100**

PRODUCTS/OPERATIONS

2005 Sales

	% of total
Industrial & Automotive	
Power transmission	31
Fluid power	11
Fluid systems	7
Wipers	7
Other	16
Building products	
Air systems components	15
Other	13
Total	**100**

Subsidiaries and Affiliates

Industrial and Automotive
Dexter Axle (axles and wheels for trailers, US)
Gates Corporation (automotive belts, hoses, pulleys; US)
Schrader Bridgeport (automotive electronics, tire valves and gauges; US)
Schrader Electronics Ltd. (remote tire pressure measuring systems, US)
Stackpole Limited (belts, pulleys, tensioners, engine modules, and electromechanical drive systems; Canada)
Standard-Thomson Corporation (automotive thermostats, US)
Stant Manufacturing Inc. (gas caps, closure caps; US)
Trico Products Corporation (wiper systems, signal flashers; US)

Building Products
Aquatic Whirlpools (whirlpool baths, US)
Hart & Cooley (heating, ventilation, and air-conditioning components; US)
Lasco Bathware (fiberglass and acrylic baths and whirlpools, US)
Lasco Fittings (PVC pipe fittings, US)
Philips Products (aluminum and vinyl windows, vinyl-clad steel doors, ventilation devices; US)
Ruskin Air Management Ltd (air handling products and louvers, US)
Ruskin Company (air, fire, and smoke dampers; louvers and fiberglass products; US)

COMPETITORS

Applied Industrial Technologies
Bridgestone
Continental AG
Goodyear
Tenneco
United Technologies

HISTORICAL FINANCIALS

Company Type: Public

Income Statement

	REVENUE ($ mil.)	NET INCOME ($ mil.)	NET PROFIT MARGIN	EMPLOYEES
12/05	5,776	313	5.4%	37,324
12/04	5,356	378	7.1%	36,720
12/03	5,650	476	8.4%	39,328
12/02*	3,365	124	3.7%	39,596
4/02	4,924	218	4.4%	40,670
Annual Growth	**4.1%**	**9.4%**	**—**	**(2.1%)**

*Fiscal year change

FYE: December 31

2005 Year-End Financials

Debt ratio: 36.7%
Return on equity: 13.1%
Cash ($ mil.): 406
Current ratio: 2.00
Long-term debt ($ mil.): 921
No. of shares (mil.): —
Dividends
Yield: 7.3%
Payout: —
Market value ($ mil.): —

Stock History

NYSE: TKS

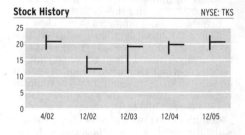

	STOCK PRICE ($) FY Close	P/E High/Low		PER SHARE ($) Earnings	Dividends
12/05	20.61	—	—	—	1.51
12/04	19.79	—	—	—	0.90
12/03	19.15	—	—	—	0.80
12/02*	12.22	—	—	—	0.73
4/02	20.61	—	—	—	—
Annual Growth	**0.0%**			**—**	**27.4%**

*Fiscal year change

Toronto-Dominion Bank

The Toronto-Dominion Bank wants to score financial TDs at home and abroad. Also known as TD Bank or TD Financial Group, Canada's second-largest bank by assets provides retail banking services under the TD Canada Trust banner, including deposits, loans, credit cards, and mortgages. The company also offers financial and advisory services to businesses. Other operations include TD Insurance, TD Asset Management (mutual funds), and TD Securities (investment banking, equities, and foreign exchange). TD Bank bought a majority stake in US-based Banknorth (now TD Banknorth) in early 2005. It sold the US operations of online discount brokerage TD Waterhouse to Ameritrade (now TD Ameritrade) in early 2006.

TD Waterhouse continues to operate in Canada and the UK.

Frustrated by limited growth opportunities at home, TD Bank decided to venture south of the border with its purchase of Banknorth. TD Bank paid about $4.8 billion in cash and stock for a 51% stake, with the option to raise its position to two-thirds. TD Bank hopes to use the acquisition as a springboard for further southward expansion, such as the possible purchase of a mortgage lender. Additionally, the company assumed about a 32% stake in TD Ameritrade as part of the sale of TD Waterhouse.

Looking for new ways to increase earnings outside of its core business of retail banking in Canada — a mature market with limited growth potential and several large competitors — TD Bank is buying subprime auto lender VFC.

HISTORY

The Bank of Toronto was established in 1855 by flour traders who wanted their own banking facilities. Its growth encouraged another group of businessmen to found the Dominion Bank in 1869. Dominion emphasized commercial banking and invested heavily in railways and construction.

As the new nation expanded westward, both banks established branch networks. They helped fund Canada's primary industries — dairy, mining, oil, pulp, and textiles. True to its pioneering spirit, a Bank of Toronto official claimed to be the first to have set up a branch office with the help of aviation (in Manitoba in the 1920s).

The demand for agricultural products and commodities dropped after WWI, but production continued full throttle, creating a world grain glut that helped trigger the stock market crash of 1929. Both the Bank of Toronto and Dominion Bank contracted during the 1930s. After growing during and subsequent to WWII, The Bank of Toronto and Dominion Bank decided to increase their capital base, merging into a 450-branch bank in 1955.

In the 1970s TD Bank opened offices in Bangkok, Beirut, and Frankfurt, among other cities abroad. During the 1980s it was active in making loans to less-developed countries. After the deregulation of the Canadian securities industry in 1987, CEO Richard Thomson reduced international lending and began focusing on brokerage activities. The strategy paid off when several Latin American countries fell behind on their loans in the late 1980s.

As the North American economy slowed in the early 1990s, TD Bank's nonperforming loans increased and, with it, its loan loss reserves. The bank still made acquisitions, including Central Guaranty Trust (1993) and Lancaster Financial Holdings (1995, investment banking). It worked to build its financial services, expanding its range of service offerings and geographic coverage and buying New York-based Waterhouse Investor Services (1996); 97% of Australia-based Pont Securities (1997); and California-based Kennedy, Cabot & Co. (1997). In 1998 the bank sold its payroll services to Ceridian, and its Waterhouse Securities unit bought US discount brokerage Jack White & Co.

That year the government nixed TD Bank's merger with Canadian Imperial on the same day it voided the Royal Bank of Canada/Bank of Montreal deal. The banks believed the consolidation necessary to stave off foreign banks' encroachment into Canada, but the government had domestic antitrust concerns: Though Canada has one-tenth the population of the US, its five top banks all ranked in the top 15 in North America.

In 1999 TD Bank bought Trimark Financial's retail trust banking business and spun off part of Waterhouse Investor Services, which would become part of TD Waterhouse Group. That year the bank ramped up its focus on Internet banking.

Not giving up on acquisition-fueled growth, in 2000 the company bought CT Financial Services (now TD Canada Trust) from British American Tobacco. As a condition for government approval, TD Bank had to sell its MasterCard credit portfolio (sold to Citibank Canada) and a dozen southern Ontario branches (to Bank of Montreal).

The company's plans to hitch a ride on the Wal-Mart gravy train derailed in 2001. Arrangements to open bank branches in some US-based Wal-Mart stores were squelched by regulators enforcing the banking and commerce barrier. TD Bank later closed all of its existing branches (more than 100 in all) inside Canadian Wal-Marts as part of a broader restructuring.

TD Bank suffered its first-ever annual loss during fiscal year 2002. Write-downs on loans to telecommunications, technology, and energy firms contributed mightily to the dismal results.

EXECUTIVES

Chairman: John M. Thompson, age 63
Deputy Chair: Rt. Hon. Frank J. McKenna, age 58
President, CEO, and Director: W. Edmund (Ed) Clark, age 58, $2,701,440 pay
Vice Chair and Group Head, US Personal and Commercial Banking; Chairman, President, and CEO, TD Banknorth: William J. (Bill) Ryan, age 61, $1,146,983 pay
Vice Chair and Group Head, Wholesale Banking; Chairman and CEO, TD Securities: Robert E. (Bob) Dorrance, age 49, $1,716,272 pay
Vice Chair and Chief Risk Officer: Bharat B. Masrani, age 49
Vice Chair, Corporate Operations: Fredric J. Tomczyk, age 50, $1,202,893 pay
Vice Chair; President, TD Canada Trust: Andrea S. Rosen
EVP and Group Head, Business Banking and Insurance; Co-Chair, TD Canada Trust: Bernard T. (Bernie) Dorval, age 51
EVP and Group Head, Personal Banking; Co-Chair, TD Canada Trust: Timothy D. (Tim) Hockey, age 41
EVP and Group Head, Wealth Management: William H. (Bill) Hatanaka
EVP and CFO: Colleen M. Johnston
EVP and Chief Investment Officer: Robert F. MacLellan
EVP, Corporate Development: Daniel A. Marinangeli, age 55, $900,480 pay
EVP and General Counsel: Christopher A. Montague
EVP, Human Resources: Theresa L. Currie
EVP; President, TD Securities: Michael W. (Mike) MacBain
EVP, TD UK Brokerage: Michael A. Foulkes

EVP, Commercial Banking, Canadian Personal and Commercial Banking Group: Paul C. Douglas
EVP, Discount Brokerage and Financial Planning, Wealth Management Group: John G. See
EVP, Risk Management and Chief Risk Officer: Mark R. Chauvin
SVP and Chief Information Officer: Steven L. Tennyson
SVP and Chief Marketing Officer: Dominic J. Mercuri
SVP, Corporate and Public Affairs: Kerry A. Peacock
Auditors: Ernst & Young LLP

LOCATIONS

HQ: The Toronto-Dominion Bank
Toronto-Dominion Centre, King St. West and Bay St., Toronto, Ontario M5K 1A2, Canada
Phone: 416-982-8222   **Fax:** 416-982-5671
US HQ: 31 W. 52nd St., New York, NY 10019
US Phone: 212-827-7000   **US Fax:** 212-827-7248
Web: www.td.com

PRODUCTS/OPERATIONS

2006 Sales

	% of total
Interest	
Loans	49
Securities	16
Dividends	4
Deposits with banks	1
Noninterest	
Investments & securities services	10
Insurance, net of claims	4
Service charges	4
Credit fees	2
Loan securitizations	1
Other	9
Total	**100**

2006 Assets

	% of total
Trading securities	20
Loans	
Consumer installment & other personal	16
Residential mortgage	13
Business & government	10
Credit card	1
Investment securities	12
Securities purchased under reverse repurchase agreements	8
Trading derivatives' market revaluation	7
Cash & equivalents	3
Other	10
Total	**100**

COMPETITORS

BMO Financial Group	FMR
Caisses Desjardins	Laurentian Bank
Charles Schwab	Morgan Stanley
CI Financial Income	National Bank of Canada
CIBC	Power Financial
E*TRADE Financial	RBC Financial Group
Edward Jones	Scotiabank

HISTORICAL FINANCIALS

Company Type: Public

Income Statement

				FYE: October 31
	ASSETS ($ mil.)	NET INCOME ($ mil.)	INCOME AS % OF ASSETS	EMPLOYEES
10/06	357,470	4,121	1.2%	51,147
10/05	316,021	1,823	0.6%	50,991
10/04	260,631	1,544	0.6%	42,843
10/03	215,499	884	0.4%	41,934
10/02	184,929	(61)	—	51,000
Annual Growth	17.9%	—	—	0.1%

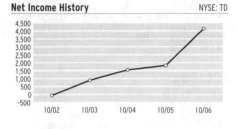

Net Income History — NYSE: TD

	10/02	10/03	10/04	10/05	10/06

Toshiba

Toshiba products play an active role, be it in computing, controlling, powering, or communicating — transporting, cooking, playing, or even elevating. The company's portfolio includes personal and professional computers (notebook PCs, servers), telecommunications and medical equipment (mobile phones, X-ray machines), industrial machinery (power plant reactors, elevators), consumer appliances (microwaves, DVD players), electronic components (electron tubes, batteries), and semiconductors. Its portfolio also includes air traffic control and railway transportation systems.

Toshiba's ongoing restructuring efforts have resulted in cost-cutting measures and a shift in emphasis to more profitable segments such as consumer electronics and components. Toshiba has pulled out of the commodity DRAM (dynamic random-access memory) business, and is instead focused on specialty memory products. The company has cut costs in its PC operations by increasing its outsourcing agreements with contract manufacturers in Taiwan and mainland China. Toshiba sells about 70% of its products in Asia.

Toshiba has used partnerships (often with competitors) to fuel product development. It merged its LCD operations with those of Matsushita, forming Toshiba Matsushita Display Technology. The company formed an alliance with rival Fujitsu that will focus on system-on-chip (SOC) operations, leaving the door open for wider semiconductor product integration in the future. Toshiba has partnered with Canon to develop surface conduction electron emitter display (SED) panels, which it views as the successor to LCD televisions. It also joined with Sony and IBM to develop new microprocessors.

Early in 2006 Toshiba agreed to acquire nuclear power plant equipment and service provider Westinghouse Electric for $5.4 billion. Toshiba plans to sell minority stakes in the company, eventually reducing its ownership to 51%.

HISTORY

Two Japanese electrical equipment manufacturers came together in 1939 to create Toshiba. Tanaka Seizo-sha, Japan's first telegraph equipment manufacturer, was founded in 1875 by Hisashige Tanaka, the so-called Edison of Japan. In the 1890s the company started making heavier electrical equipment such as transformers and electric motors, adopting the name Shibaura

Seisakusho Works in 1893. Seisakusho went on to pioneer the production of hydroelectric generators (1894) and X-ray tubes (1915) in Japan.

The other half of Toshiba, Hakunetsusha & Company, was founded by Ichisuke Fujioka and Shoichi Miyoshi as Japan's first incandescent lamp maker (1890). Renamed Tokyo Electric Company (1899), the company developed the coiled filament lightbulb (1921), Japan's first radio receiver and cathode-ray tube (1924), and the internally frosted glass lightbulb (1925). In 1939 it merged with Shibaura Seisakusho to form Tokyo Shibaura Electric Company (Toshiba).

Toshiba was the first company in Japan to make fluorescent lamps (1940), radar systems (1942), broadcasting equipment (1952), and digital computers (1954). Production of black-and-white televisions began in 1949. Even so, through the 1970s the company was considered an also-ran, trailing other Japanese business groups, known as *keiretsu*, partly because of its bureaucratic management style.

Electrical engineer Shoichi Saba became president in 1980. Saba invested heavily in Toshiba's information and communications segments. The company became the first in the world to produce the powerful one-megabit DRAM chip (1985). That year it unveiled its first laptop PC. In the meantime Saba (named chairman 1986) pushed Toshiba into joint ventures to exchange technology with companies such as Siemens and Motorola.

But in 1987 Toshiba incurred the wrath of the US government. A subsidiary sold submarine sound-deadening equipment to the USSR, resulting in threats of US sanctions and a precipitous decline in its stock price and in US sales. Chairman Saba and president Sugichiro Watari resigned in shame.

Toshiba in 1992 bought a $500 million stake in Time Warner (the stake was reduced in 1998). In 1996 the company appointed marketing and multimedia specialist Taizo Nishimuro as president, breaking its tradition of filling the position with an engineer from its heavy electrical operations.

In 1997 Toshiba and IBM formed joint venture Dominion Semiconductor to develop memory chips. (IBM sold its stake to Toshiba in 1999.) The next year the company looked to boost earnings by cutting its workforce and allying with other manufacturers such as GE and Fujitsu in development deals. But continued semiconductor price declines, and sluggish demand in Japan, caused the company to record its first annual loss in more than two decades.

Nishimuro made plans to cut 5,000 jobs, and streamlined Toshiba's 15 divisions to eight in-house companies. Toshiba in 1999 agreed to take a $1 billion charge to settle a class-action lawsuit alleging some manufacturers supplied potentially corrupt disk drives in its portable computers — even though no Toshiba customer complaints were filed.

In 2000 Nishimuro stepped down as CEO. SVP and Information and Industrial Systems and Services subsidiary president Tadashi Okamura assumed the post. Nishimuro filled the vacant chairman's seat. Toshiba announced another restructuring effort in 2001, which included plans to reduce its workforce, shift manufacturing to overseas plants, and withdraw from unprofitable businesses. The following year it sold its DRAM manufacturing plant, Dominion Semiconductor, to Micron Technology.

EXECUTIVES

Chairman: Tadashi Okamura
President, CEO, and Director: Atsutoshi Nishida
SEVP and Director: Shigeo Koguchi
SEVP and Director: Masao Niwano
SEVP and Director: Yoshiaki Sato
SEVP and Director: Toshio Yonezawa
EVP and Director: Tsuyoshi Kimura
EVP and Director: Fumio Muraoka
EVP: Makoto Azuma
EVP: Masashi Muromachi
Auditors: Ernst & Young

LOCATIONS

HQ: Toshiba Corporation
    1-1, Shibaura 1-chome, Minato-ku,
    Tokyo 105-8001, Japan
Phone: +81-3-3457-4511   **Fax:** +81-3-3455-1631
US HQ: 1251 Avenue of the Americas, 41st Fl.,
    New York, NY 10020
US Phone: 212-596-0600   **US Fax:** 212-593-3875
Web: www.toshiba.co.jp

2006 Sales

	% of total
Asia	
Japan	53
Other countries	18
North America	15
Europe	11
Other regions	3
Total	**100**

PRODUCTS/OPERATIONS

2006 Sales

	% of total
Digital products	37
Social infrastructure	27
Electronic devices	20
Home appliances	10
Other	6
Total	**100**

Selected Products

Digital products
  Digital Media Network Company
    Digital cameras
    Digital tuners
    DVD players and recorders
    Hard disk drives
    Industrial and surveillance cameras
    Optical disk drives
    Projectors
    Televisions
  Mobile Communications Company
    Mobile phones
  Personal Computer & Network Company
    Handheld computers
    Notebook computers
    Servers
Social infrastructure
  Industrial and Power Systems & Services Company
    Boiling water reactor plants
    Building energy management systems
    Control and measurement system devices
    Industrial computers
    Nuclear fuel reprocessing plants
    Power generating equipment (hydroelectric,
      thermal, geothermal)
    Railway station service systems
    Superconducting magnets
    Transportation management systems
    Water supply and sewage monitoring systems
  Social Network & Infrastructure Systems Company
    Air traffic control and navigation aid systems
    Automatic letter processing systems
    Banknote processing machines
    Broadcasting systems
    Face recognition security systems

Electronic devices
  Semiconductor Company
    LSI systems
    Memory
    Microprocessors
Home appliances
  Air conditioners
  Batteries
  Lighting
  Microwaves
  Refrigerators
  Washing machines

COMPETITORS

ABB
Acer
Alcatel
ALSTOM
Apple Computer
Canon
CASIO COMPUTER
Dell
Electrolux
Emerson Electric
Ericsson
Fujifilm
Fujitsu
Fujitsu Siemens
Gateway
GE
Hewlett-Packard
Hitachi
IBM
Ingersoll-Rand
Intel
Kyocera
Lenovo
Lucent
Matsushita
Motorola
NEC
Nokia
Oki Electric
Philips Electronics
Pioneer
Ricoh
Samsung
SANYO
Seiko
Sharp
Siemens AG
Sony
Sony Ericsson Mobile
Spansion
Sun Microsystems
Texas Instruments
Unisys

HISTORICAL FINANCIALS

Company Type: Public

Income Statement

FYE: March 31

	REVENUE ($ mil.)	NET INCOME ($ mil.)	NET PROFIT MARGIN	EMPLOYEES
3/06	53,945	665	1.2%	172,000
3/05	54,264	428	0.8%	165,000
3/04	52,816	273	0.5%	166,651
3/03	47,192	154	0.3%	165,776
3/02	40,666	(1,915)	—	176,398
Annual Growth	7.3%	—	—	(0.6%)

Net Income History

Pink Sheets: TOSBF

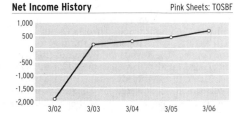

TOTAL

TOTAL does it all. One of the world's largest integrated oil companies, it explores for, develops, and produces crude oil and natural gas; refines and markets oil; and trades and transports both crude and finished products. Operating in more than 130 countries, the company has reserves of 11.4 billion barrels of oil equivalent. It operates 27 refineries and almost 17,000 TOTAL and Elf-branded gas stations, mostly in Europe and Africa. The company is also a major producer of chemicals. TOTAL FINA was formed in 1999 when France's TOTAL bought Belgium-based PetroFina. It became TOTAL FINA ELF in 2000 with the acquisition of French rival Elf Aquitaine. The company renamed itself as TOTAL S.A. in 2003.

TOTAL's chemical units produce petrochemicals, monomers, polymers, and specialty chemicals such as adhesives, inks, paints, resins, and rubbers. In 2006 the company spun off its (Arkema) unit, which produces chlorochemicals, intermediates, and performance polymers.

HISTORY

A French consortium formed the Compagnie Française des Pétroles (CFP) in 1924 to develop an oil industry for the country. Lacking reserves within its borders, France had a 24% stake in the Turkish Petroleum Company (TPC), acquired from Germany in 1920 as part of the spoils from WWI. When oil was discovered in Iraq in 1927, the TPC partners (CFP; Anglo-Persian Oil, later BP; Royal Dutch Shell; and a consortium of five US oil companies) became major players in the oil game.

In 1929 France acquired a 25% stake in CFP (raised to 35% in 1931) but ensured the company's independence from government control. CFP began establishing refining and transporting capabilities, and by the start of WWII it was a vertically integrated petroleum company.

With France's occupation by Germany during WWII, CFP was effectively blocked from further expansion, and its stake in Iraq Petroleum (formerly the TPC) was held by its partners until the end of the war. In 1948, over French protests, the US partners ended the "Red Line" agreement, a pact that limited members' competition in that Middle Eastern region.

After WWII, CFP diversified its sources for crude, opening a supply in 1947 from the Venezuelan company Pantepec and making several major discoveries in colonial Algeria in 1956. It also began supplying crude to Japan, South Korea, and Taiwan in the 1950s. To market its products in North Africa and France and other European areas, it introduced the brand name TOTAL in 1954. It began making petrochemicals in 1956.

Algeria in 1971 became North Africa's first major oil-producing country to nationalize its petroleum industry. This was not as dire a blow to CFP as it could have been; by that time the company got only about 20% of its supplies from Algeria. Exploration had paid off, with discoveries in Indonesia in the 1960s and, in the early 1970s, the North Sea.

CFP joined Elf Aquitaine in 1980 to buy Rhône-Poulenc's petrochemical segment. Ten years later it purchased state-owned Orkem's coating business (inks, resins, paints, and adhesives).

In 1985 the company had adopted its brand name as part of its new name, TOTAL Compagnie Française des Pétroles, shortened in 1991 to TOTAL. The firm was listed on the NYSE that year. The French government began reducing its stake in TOTAL in 1992 (ultimately to less than 1%). The company expanded reserves with stakes in fields in Argentina, the Caspian Sea, and Colombia.

In 1995, the year Thierry Desmarest became CEO, TOTAL contracted to develop two large oil and gas fields in Iran, despite US pressure not to do business there. The next day TOTAL led a consortium (including Russia's Gazprom and Malaysia's Petronas) in a $2 billion investment in Iran's gas sector, just days after selling its 55% stake in its North American arm, Total Petroleum, to Ultramar Diamond Shamrock — insulating TOTAL from the threat of US sanctions.

TOTAL bought Belgium's Petrofina, an integrated oil and gas company, for $11 billion in 1999 and became TOTAL FINA. Within days the new TOTAL FINA launched a $43 billion hostile bid for rival Elf Aquitaine. Elf made a counterbid, but TOTAL FINA wound up acquiring 95% of Elf in 2000 for $48.7 billion and became TOTAL FINA ELF. The new company gained control of the remainder of Elf later that year.

In 2001 the company, in collaboration with Pertamina and Unocal Indonesia, agreed to invest $500 million to boost its production of liquefied gas in Indonesia by 14%. That year the company also acquired generating assets in Argentina from AES for $370 million. Also that year an explosion in a TOTAL FINA ELF subsidiary's petrochemical and fertilizer plant in southern France killed 29 people and injured 2,500. In 2003 a number of former Elf executives and state officials were named in a corruption scandal that implicated the former French oil giant in influence peddling and bribery in the early 1990s.

EXECUTIVES

Chairman and CEO: Thierry Desmarest, age 60
EVP and Director; President, Exploration and Production; CEO-Elect: Chrisophe de Margerie, age 54
EVP; President, Gas and Power; President-Elect, Exploration and Production: Yves-Louis Darricarrère, age 55
EVP and CFO: Robert Castaigne, age 60
EVP; President, Refining and Marketing: Jean-Paul Vettier, age 61
EVP; President, Strategy and Risk Assessment: Bruno Weymuller, age 57
SVP Executive Career Management: Michel Bonnet
SVP Human Resources and Corporate Communications: Jean-Jacques Guilbaud
SVP; President, Trading and Shipping: François Groh
SVP Administration, Refining and Marketing Division: Pierre Klein
SVP Northern Europe, Exploration and Production Division: Michel Bénézit
SVP Africa, Exploration and Production Division: Jean Privey
SVP Industrial and Safety, Strategy and Risk Assessment Division: Pierre Guyonnet
SVP Marketing Europe, Refining and Marketing Division: Eric De Menten
SVP Marketing France, Refining and Marketing Division: André Tricoire
SVP North America; ATOFINA General Representative in the US, Organic Peroxides and Additives: Jean-Pierre Seeuws, age 59

LOCATIONS

HQ: TOTAL S.A.
  2 place de la Coupole, La Défense 6,
  92400 Courbevoie, France
Phone: +33-1-47-44-58-53   **Fax:** +33-1-47-44-58-24
US HQ: 444 Madison Ave, 42nd Fl., New York, NY 10022
US Phone: 212-922-3065   **US Fax:** 212-922-3074
Web: www.total.com

TOTAL has operations in more than 130 countries.

2005 Sales

	% of total
Europe	
France	24
Other countries	39
North America	13
Africa	6
Asia & other regions	18
Total	**100**

PRODUCTS/OPERATIONS

2005 Sales

	% of total
Downstream	70
Chemicals	16
Upstream	14
Total	**100**

COMPETITORS

Akzo Nobel
Anglo American
Ashland
BASF AG
BHP Billiton
BP
Chevron
ConocoPhillips
Devon Energy
DuPont
Eni
Exxon Mobil
Imperial Oil
Lyondell Chemical
MOL
Norsk Hydro
Occidental Petroleum
Pakistan State Oil
PDVSA
PEMEX
PETROBRAS
PPG
Royal Dutch Shell
Statoil

HISTORICAL FINANCIALS

Company Type: Public

Income Statement

FYE: December 31

	REVENUE ($ mil.)	NET INCOME ($ mil.)	NET PROFIT MARGIN	EMPLOYEES
12/05	145,229	13,736	9.5%	112,877
12/04	167,412	9,852	5.9%	111,401
12/03	131,412	7,664	5.8%	110,783
12/02	109,362	6,567	6.0%	121,469
12/01	93,312	4,670	5.0%	122,025
Annual Growth	**11.7%**	**31.0%**	**—**	**(1.9%)**

2005 Year-End Financials

Debt ratio: 18.6%	No. of shares (mil.): —
Return on equity: 15.7%	Dividends
Cash ($ mil.): 5,118	Yield: 9.7%
Current ratio: 1.31	Payout: 15.7%
Long-term debt ($ mil.): 16,076	Market value ($ mil.): —

Stock History

NYSE: TOT

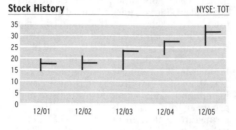

	STOCK PRICE ($) FY Close	P/E High	P/E Low	PER SHARE ($) Earnings	PER SHARE ($) Dividends
12/05	31.67	2	1	19.64	3.08
12/04	27.52	—	—	—	3.72
12/03	23.18	—	—	—	1.99
12/02	17.91	—	—	—	1.48
12/01	17.60	—	—	—	1.20
Annual Growth	**15.8%**	**—**	**—**	**—**	**26.6%**

Toyota

Toyota Motor Corporation, Japan's #1 carmaker, has a driving ambition to become greener. The company makes a hybrid-powered (gas and electric) sedan — the Prius — that is being snapped up in US and European markets. Its gas-powered cars, pickups, minivans, and SUVs include such models as Camry, Corolla, 4Runner, Land Cruiser, Sienna, the luxury Lexus line, the new Scion brand, and a full-sized pickup truck, the V-8 Tundra. Toyota also makes forklifts and manufactured housing, and offers consumer financial services. Once a darkhorse in the global automotive game, Toyota has begun to close the gap on General Motors and DaimlerChrysler, and has already passed Ford Motor.

While most of its North American and European competitors are contracting their operations due to falling demand and overcapacity, Toyota is growing to meet increased global demand.

The company has an expressed plan of gaining a global 10% share of the automotive market by the early 2010s. To do this, Toyota feels it must build the cars where, or very near where, they will be bought. To this end Toyota opened new vehicle plants in the Czech Republic in 2005 and is scheduled to open its 11th US plant in San Antonio, Texas in 2006.

The greatest focus of Toyota's overseas strategy is currently in China, a country that is expected to become the second-largest car market (behind the US) by 2010. By that year Toyota wants to have a 10% market share in China. Like its competitors, Toyota is beefing up its Chinese operations by joining forces with local automotive players. With its Chinese partner China FAW Group Corporation, Toyota builds Land Cruisers and Corollas in China. Through another agreement with Guangzhou Automobile Group, Toyota began jointly developing engines in 2005. Also in association with Guangzhou Automobile, in 2006 the first

Chinese-built Camry rolled off the assembly line in Nansha near Hong Kong. The Camry is the best-selling car in the US and has been a leading import in China. The Chinese-built Camrys are priced to move in an effort to quickly boost Toyota's market share.

While growing its worldwide production base, Toyota has committed itself to leading the charge toward the development of more efficient, environmentally friendly vehicles, primarily powered by hybrid gasoline-electric technology. The company says it wants to build 1 million hybrids by the early 2010s. In addition to the Prius, Toyota currently offers hybrid versions of the Highlander SUV and the venerable Camry.

Late in 2006 Toyota bought a 5.9% stake in Isuzu Motors. The two companies plan to cooperate on engine technologies with Isuzu concentrating on small diesel engines and diesel emission controls while Toyota will focus on environmental improvements for gasoline engines and alternative fuels. The move marks the second time in as many years that Toyota has taken advantage of a broken GM alliance with a Japanese partner. Toyota bought an 8.7% stake in Fuji Heavy Industries from GM in 2005.

HISTORY

In 1926 Sakichi Toyoda founded Toyoda Automatic Loom Works. In 1930 he sold the rights to the loom he invented and gave the proceeds to his son Kiichiro Toyoda to begin an automotive business. Kiichiro opened an auto shop within the loom works in 1933. When protectionist legislation (1936) improved prospects for Japanese automakers, Kiichiro split off the car department, took it public (1937), and changed its name to Toyota.

During WWII the company made military trucks, but financial problems after the war caused Toyota to reorganize in 1950. Its postwar commitment to R&D paid off with the launch of the four-wheel-drive Land Cruiser (1951); full-sized Crown (1955); and the small Corona (1957).

Toyota Motor Sales, U.S.A., debuted the Toyopet Crown in the US in 1957, but it proved underpowered for the US market. Toyota had better luck with the Corona in 1965 and with the Corolla (which became the best-selling car of all time) in 1968. By 1970 Toyota was the world's fourth-largest carmaker.

Toyota expanded rapidly in the US. During the 1970s the oil crisis caused demand for fuel-efficient cars, and Toyota was there to grab market share from US makers. In 1975 Toyota displaced Volkswagen as the US's #1 auto importer. Toyota began auto production in the US in 1984 through NUMMI, its joint venture with GM. The Lexus line was launched in the US in 1989.

Because of the European Community's restrictions on Japanese auto imports until the year 2000, Toyota's European expansion slowed. Toyota responded in 1992 by agreeing to distribute cars in Japan for Volkswagen and also by establishing an engine plant (later moved to full auto production) in the UK.

The sport utility vehicle (SUV) mania of the 1990s spurred Toyota's introduction of luxury minivans and light trucks. Hiroshi Okuda, a 40-year veteran with Toyota and the first person from outside the Toyoda family to run the firm, succeeded Tatsuro Toyoda as president in 1995.

In 1997 Toyota introduced the Prius, a hybrid electric- and gas-powered car. The next year Toyota boosted its stake in affiliate Daihatsu (minivehicles) to about 51% and started Toyota Mapmaster (51%-owned), to make map databases for car navigation systems.

Okuda became chairman in 1999, replacing Shoichiro Toyoda, and Fujio Cho became president. Also that year Toyota announced plans to invest $800 million to boost US auto production by 16% (200,000 vehicles) to about 1.45 million.

In 2000 Toyota also bought a 5% stake in Yamaha (the world's #2 motorcycle maker). International developments included Toyota's agreement with the Chinese government to produce passenger cars for sale in China.

Early in 2001 Toyota opened a new plant in France. Later that year the company formed an agreement with PSA Peugeot Citroën to begin joint car production in Europe (production began in 2005). Toyota also increased its stake in truck maker Hino Motors to 50%.

In 2004 Toyota announced that it would establish 14 Lexus dealerships in China. Later in 2004 Toyota forged a joint venture agreement with Guangzhou Automobile Group Co., Ltd. to build engines in China.

In 2005 Toyota bought just under 9% of General Motors' 20% stake in Fuji Heavy Industries — the Japanese maker of Subaru passenger vehicles. Early the following year the two companies announced Toyota Camrys will be built at Fuji Heavy Industry's under-utilized Subaru of Indiana plant.

EXECUTIVES

Honorary Chairman and Member of the Board:
Shoichiro Toyoda, age 80
Chairman: Fujio Cho, age 69
Vice Chairman: Katsuhiro Nakagawa, age 63
President and Member of the Board:
Katsuaki Watanabe, age 63
EVP and Member of the Board: Mitsuo Kinoshita, age 59
EVP, Product Development and Vehicle Engineering and Member of the Board: Kazuo Okamoto, age 61
EVP and Member of the Board: Akio Toyoda, age 49
EVP, Powertrains and Quality and Member of the Board: Masatami Takimoto, age 59
EVP and Member of the Board: Yoshimi Inaba, age 59
EVP and Member of the Board: Takeshi Uchiyamada, age 58
EVP and Member of the Board: Tokuichi Uranishi, age 63
EVP and Member of the Board: Kyoji Sasazu, age 61
Senior Managing Director, Finance and Accounting Group and Member of the Board: Takeshi Suzuki, age 57
Senior Managing Director and Member of the Board: Atsushi (Art) Niimi, age 57
Chairman and CEO; Toyota Motor Sales, and Toyota Motor North America, Inc.: Yukitoshi (Yuki) Funo, age 59
Senior Managing Director; President, Toyota Motor Engineering and Manufacturing Europe S.A./N.V., and Member of the Board: Shinichi Sasaki, age 58
Senior Managing Director, Vehicle Engineering Group, Future Project Division, and Motor Sports Division, and Member of the Board: Tetsuo Hattori, age 58
Senior Advisor, Member of the Board: Hiroshi Okuda, age 72
Managing Officer; President, Toyota Motor Sales USA: James E. Press, age 59
Managing Officer; President and CEO, Toyota Motor Manufacuring North America: Seiichi Sudo
General Manager, Public Affairs Division: Masayuki Nakai
Auditors: PricewaterhouseCoopers Audit

LOCATIONS

HQ: Toyota Motor Corporation
(Toyota Jidosha Kabushiki Kaisha)
1, Toyota-cho, Toyota, Aichi 471-8571, Japan
Phone: +81-565-28-2121   **Fax:** +81-565-23-5800
US HQ: 9 W. 57th St., Ste. 4900, New York, NY 10019
US Phone: 212-223-0303   **US Fax:** 212-759-7670
Web: www.toyota.co.jp

Toyota Motor operates more than 50 manufacturing facilities in 27 countries throughout the world.

2006 Sales

	$ mil.	% of total
Asia		
Japan	65,847	37
Other countries	15,637	9
North America	63,470	35
Europe	21,912	12
Other regions	12,217	7
Total	**179,083**	**100**

2006 Unit Sales

	No. (thou.)	% of total
Asia		
Japan	2,364	30
Other countries	881	11
North America	2,556	32
Europe	1,023	13
Other regions	1,151	14
Total	**7,975**	**100**

PRODUCTS/OPERATIONS

2006 Sales

	$ mil.	% of total
Automotive	164,622	90
Financial services	8,486	5
Other	10,133	5
Adjustments	(4,158)	—
Total	**179,083**	**100**

Selected Products

Selected Automobile Brands and Models
Lexus
  ES
  GS
  GS Hybrid
  GX
  IS
  LS
  LX
  RX
  RX Hybrid
  SC
Scion
  tC
  xA
  xB
Toyota
  Cars
    Avalon
    Camry
    Camry Hybrid
    Camry Solara
    Corolla
    Matrix
    Prius
    Yaris
  SUVs and Vans
    4Runner
    FJ Cruiser
    Highlander
    Highlander Hybrid
    Land Cruiser
    RAV4
    Sequoia
    Sienna
  Trucks
    Tacoma
    Tundra
Other Products
  Factory automation equipment
  Forklifts and other industrial vehicles
  Housing products

Selected Investments
Daihatsu Motor (51%, motor vehicles)
Hino Motors Ltd. (50%, trucks)

COMPETITORS

BMW	Kubota
Caterpillar	Land Rover
DaimlerChrysler	Marubeni
Deere	Mazda
Fiat	Nissan
Ford	Peugeot
Fuji Heavy Industries	Renault
General Motors	Saab Automobile
Honda	Saturn
Ingersoll-Rand	Suzuki Motor
Isuzu	Volkswagen
Kia Motors	Volvo
Komatsu	

HISTORICAL FINANCIALS
Company Type: Public

Income Statement
FYE: March 31

	REVENUE ($ mil.)	NET INCOME ($ mil.)	NET PROFIT MARGIN	EMPLOYEES
3/06	179,083	11,681	6.5%	285,977
3/05	172,749	10,907	6.3%	265,753
3/04	163,637	10,995	6.7%	264,410
3/03	128,965	6,247	4.8%	264,096
Annual Growth	**11.6%**	**23.2%**	**—**	**2.7%**

2006 Year-End Financials
Debt ratio: 53.4%
Return on equity: 13.4%
Cash ($ mil.): 19,193
Current ratio: 1.07
Long-term debt ($ mil.): 48,016

Net Income History
NYSE: TM

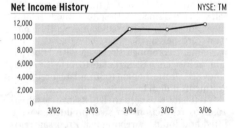

TUI

Once a steel and mining conglomerate, TUI (formerly Preussag) now makes a living on the road. Its tourism business, which is the largest in Europe, serves about 18 million customers and accounts for almost 75% of the company's sales. TUI operates more than 3,500 travel agencies, more than 275 hotels, and about 80 tour operators, as well as more than 100 aircraft through six airlines. TUI's service division provides various support services for travelers, including airport reception, medical support, and departure assistance. The firm is also a significant marine transportation concern through Hapag-Lloyd, which has more than 140 containerships.

To reposition itself as a tourism company, TUI sold its operations in such areas as building engineering, metals trading, and real estate. In early 2004 TUI announced a divestment program which would have involved the public flotation of Hapag-Lloyd, all while Hapag-Lloyd was unloading all non-shipping and tourism business including VTG-Lehnkering and the sale of its two-thirds stake in French building company Algeco. TUI later abandoned the plan to spin off Hapag-Lloyd, but the disposition of the other Hapag-Lloyd assets was still a good move and has simplified TUI's operations (tourism now accounts for almost 75% of total revenues). The company later expanded its marine transportation business even further with the 2005 purchase of Canadian shipping firm CP Ships for almost $2 billion. The operations of CP Ships were integrated with those of Hapag-Lloyd, making Hapag-Lloyd one of the world's largest container carriers.

Also in 2004 TUI acquired the 49% stake, previously held by Kuoni Reisen Holding AG, in its Swiss joint venture TUI Suisse (the third-largest travel company in Switzerland). It also entered the Russian travel market by forming a joint venture, TUI Mostravel Russia, with Russian tour operator Mostravel. TUI holds a 34% stake in the joint venture.

TUI Travel Solutions GmbH sold 50% of its stake in TQ3 Travel Solutions to Navigant International in 2004, thereby turning TQ3 into a global joint venture company. It continued to operate globally under the TQ3 Travel Solutions brand, while in the US and Canada it was branded TQ3Navigant. In early 2006, TUI sold Navigant the rest of TQ3 and no longer has any stake in the brand or company.

HISTORY

TUI was founded in Berlin in 1923 as Preussische Bergwerks-und Hutten-Aktiengesellschaft (Prussian Mine and Foundry Company) to operate former state-owned mining companies, saltworks, and smelters. Despite outmoded equipment and a war-shattered economy, the company prospered. So in 1929 the Prussian parliament combined Preussag with Hibernia and Preussischen Elektrizitats to form the state-run VEBA group, hoping to stimulate foreign investment. It didn't.

WWII left Preussag a shell of its former self. In 1952, as restrictions on steel production were lifted and industry rebounded, Preussag relocated to Hanover. After taking steps to reestablish itself, Preussag made a public offering in 1959; VEBA kept about 22%.

A worldwide steel glut that lasted through the 1960s forced Preussag to diversify. Acquisitions included railroad tank car and transport agent VTG and shipbuilding and chemical companies. The company also formed oil exploration unit Preussag Energie in 1968. In 1969 VEBA finally sold its remaining stake in Preussag to Westdeusche Landesbank (WestLB).

When the 1970s oil crisis drove up steel costs, Preussag began international ventures to counter falling revenues at home. But the 1980s brought PR disasters. The European Commission fined Preussag and five other zinc producers for antitrust violations in 1984.

In 1989 Preussag reorganized into a holding company with four independent units: coal, oil, natural gas, and plant construction. But it was about to take a sharp business turn. Michael Frenzel, who had managed WestLB's industry holdings, became CEO in 1994 in the midst of another steel recession. Frenzel was determined to shift Preussag away from its rusting past and toward services and technology. In 1997 it acquired container shipping and travel firm Hapag-Lloyd, which had a 30% stake in Touristik Union

International (TUI). By the end of 1998 it was Europe's top tourism group after buying the rest of TUI, First Reisebuero Management, and a 25% stake in the UK's Thomas Cook (raised to 50.1% in 1999).

As part of its restructuring, Preussag traded its plant engineering units and half of its shipbuilding unit (HDW) to Babcock Borsig for a 33% stake in that company in 1999. Preussag then made plans to transfer another 25% of HDW to Sweden's Celsius in a deal (along with Babcock Borsig) to merge Celsius' Kockums submarine shipyards with HDW. That year Hapag-Lloyd and TUI were merged into Hapag Touristik Union (renamed TUI Group in 2000); VTG merged with Lehnkering, a 126-year-old freight forwarding group, becoming VTG-Lehnkering.

The group also acquired a stake in French package tour leader Nouvelles Frontières and sold a metals trading unit, W. & O. Bergmann, to Enron. By 2002 the company had sold off most of its non-tourism operations, changed its name to TUI, and restructured its business to focus primarily on tourism.

In 2004 TUI sold a division of its VTG-Lehnkering logistics operation to investors for an undisclosed amount. In March 2004 TUI Travel Solutions GmbH sold 50% of its stake in TQ3 Travel Solutions to Navigant International. It sold the rest of TQ3 to Navigant two years later.

WestLB surrendered its majority shareholding of TUI in 2004, freeing up 90% of the company's shares for free float.

EXECUTIVES

Chairman, Executive Board: Michael Frenzel, age 59
Chairman, Supervisory Board: Jürgen Krumnow
Executive Director, Airline Sector: Christoph Müller
Executive Director, Central Europe Sector: Volker Böettcher
Executive Director, Controlling: Sebastian Ebel, age 43
Executive Director, Finance: Rainer Feuerhake, age 62
Executive Director, Hotels and Resorts Sector: Karl J. Pojer
Executive Director, Human Resources and Legal Affairs: Peter Engelen, age 50
Executive Director, Shipping: Adolf Adrion, age 66
Executive Director, Shipping: Michael Behrendt, age 55
Executive Director, Tourism; CEO, TUI Northern Europe: Peter Rothwell, age 47
Executive Director, Western European Sector: Eric Debry
Head of the Group Controlling Department and Board Member: Olaf Seifert
Director, Investor Relations: Björn Beroleit, age 37
Director, Logistics/Holdings: Helmut Stodieck, age 67
Auditors: PricewaterhouseCoopers

LOCATIONS

HQ: TUI AG
Karl-Wiechert-Allee 4, D-30625 Hanover, Germany
Phone: +49-511-566-00   **Fax:** +49-511-566-1901
Web: www.tui-group.com

PRODUCTS/OPERATIONS

2005 Sales

	% of total
Tourism	72
Shipping	20
Other	8
Total	**100**

2005 Tourism Division Sales

	% of total
Central Europe	41
Northern Europe	34
Western Europe	20
Destinations	4
Other tourism	1
Total	**100**

COMPETITORS

Accor	Kuoni Travel
American Express	Mitsui O.S.K. Lines
A.P. Møller - Mærsk	MyTravel
BTI Canada	Neptune Orient
Carlson	REWE-Zentral
Carnival	Royal Caribbean Cruises
Club Med	Thomas Cook AG
First Choice	

HISTORICAL FINANCIALS

Company Type: Public

Income Statement

	REVENUE ($ mil.)	NET INCOME ($ mil.)	NET PROFIT MARGIN	EMPLOYEES	FYE: December 31
12/05	23,234	—	—	61,559	
12/04	24,615	—	—	57,716	
12/03	24,119	—	—	64,257	
12/02	22,710	—	—	70,299	
12/01	21,080	—	—	69,550	
Annual Growth	**2.5%**	**—**	**—**	**(3.0%)**	

Revenue History

German: TUI

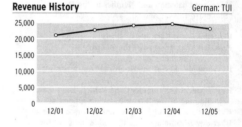

UBS

One of the largest investment managers in the world, UBS has offices in some 50 nations — primarily in Europe and North America — that provide financial services through three major segments. Its Global Wealth Management & Business Banking, Investment Bank, and Global Asset Management divisions serve institutional investors and high-net-worth individuals by offering mutual funds, asset management, corporate finance, and estate planning. UBS Investment Bank provides securities underwriting, mergers and acquisitions advice, fixed-income products, and foreign exchange. The company also provides traditional banking services in its home country of Switzerland.

UBS is eyeing foreign investments and in 2006 was rated one of the top issuers of private equity in Asia (not including Japan). The bank has stakes in Bank of China and midsized brokerage Beijing Securities. It is also buying Brazilian investment bank Banco Pactual for $1 billion up front and additional payments totalling another $1.6 billion if certain milestones are met. The move gives UBS a foothold in the volatile yet growing Brazilian private equity market — Banco Pactual is the #2 investment bank there — and allows it to match investments that rival Credit Suisse has made in the country.

In 2006, with the commodities market at a fever pitch, UBS bought ABN AMRO's futures and commodities trading business for an estimated $400 million. The bank is said to be eyeing German Commerzbank's investment banking unit as well, in an attempt to establish more of a footprint in Germany.

The banking company ran afoul of US sanctions on Iran and Iraq after it was discovered that UBS illegally supplied US banknotes to both countries.

HISTORY

Businessmen in Winterthur, Switzerland, formed the Bank of Winterthur in 1862 to serve trading interests, finance railroads, and operate a warehouse. In 1912 the bank merged with the Bank of Toggenburg (formed in 1863) to create Schweizerische Bankgesellschaft — Union Bank of Switzerland (UBS).

It expanded in Switzerland, buying smaller banks and adding branches. After growing in the post-WWI era, it was hit hard by the Depression. UBS benefited from Switzerland's neutrality in WWII, gaining deposits from both Jews and Nazis. In 1946 the bank opened an office in New York. Expansion in Switzerland continued after the war with the purchase of Eidgenossische Bank of Zurich.

UBS continued its acquisitions in the 1950s; by 1962 it had 81 branches. Other purchases included Interhandel, a cash-rich Swiss financial concern (1967), and four savings banks (1968). In 1967 it opened a full-service office in London, and during the 1970s established several securities underwriting subsidiaries abroad.

International financial markets became supercharged in the 1980s, and UBS resolved to catch up with its domestic peers in international operations. As London prepared for financial deregulation in 1986, UBS bought brokerage house Phillips & Drew.

The firm's UK brokerage business was hit hard by the 1987 US stock market crash; over the next two years losses continued, prompting an overhaul of the London operations. Then its US operations were jarred by the collapse of the junk bond market in 1990. The next year UBS set up offices in Paris, Singapore, and Hong Kong and took over Chase Manhattan's (now J.P. Morgan Chase) New York money management unit.

Meanwhile, the firm continued to expand within Switzerland, buying five more banks to boost market share and fill in gaps in its branch network. These buys left UBS with overlapping operations and a bloated infrastructure when recession hit. Falling real estate values left the bank with a heavy load of nonperforming loans.

In 1994 profits plummeted. Stockholder Martin Ebner, dissatisfied with the performance of president Robert Studer, tried to wrest control of UBS; failing that, he sought to have Studer charged with criminal fraud. In 1996 he almost thwarted Studer's election to the chairmanship.

UBS launched a multiyear reorganization in 1994 by consolidating its consumer credit operations. The next year it joined with Swiss Life/Rentenanstalt to offer insurance products through its bank network.

In 1996, after rebuffing Credit Suisse Group's merger bid, UBS began an even more draconian reorganization, cutting domestic branches and

writing down billions of francs in bad loans, leading to UBS' first loss ever (with another the next year). In 1998 the company merged with Swiss Bank Corp. then cut 23% of its staff. Later that year the bank lost $1.6 billion in the stumbling Long-Term Capital Management hedge fund, prompting chairman Mathis Cabiallavetta to resign.

As UBS struggled to swallow Swiss Bank in 1999, it retreated somewhat from riskier markets, began selling some $2 billion in real estate, and sold its 25% stake in Swiss Life/Rentenanstalt. Looking to bulk up, the firm that year bought Bank of America's European and Asian private banking operations and Allegis Realty Investors, a US real estate investment management firm.

In 2000 UBS reorganized yet again and bought US broker Paine Webber (now UBS Paine Webber). UBS's integration of Paine Webber continued into the next year. Also in 2001 chairman Marcel Ospel was criticized for UBS's handling of Swissair's cash crisis, which resulted in the air fleet's grounding.

The bank came under computer attack in 2002 when a disgruntled PaineWebber employee set off a "logic bomb" in UBS's computer system. Despite the deletion of 1,000 files across the company network and $3 million in damages, UBS and its stock price weathered the attack.

Continuing to target the mass affluent around the planet, UBS also acquired the South American wealth management operations of Dresdner Bank and the North American wealth management business of Julius Baer in 2004. It sold some of its private banking business in Switzerland to Julius Baer the following year.

In late 2004 UBS bought SoundView (now UBS Capital Markets), the capital markets and specialist business of US company Charles Schwab, for $265 million in cash. UBS integrated the operations into the equities business of its investment bank, making the unit one of the top market makers of Nasdaq stock.

In 2006 UBS picked up the private client services business of Piper Jaffray Companies for $875 million in cash and debt.

EXECUTIVES

Chairman: Marcel Ospel, age 56
Vice Chairman: Peter Böckli, age 70
Executive Vice Chairman: Stephan Haeringer, age 60
Executive Vice Chairman and Group Chief Credit Officer: Marco Suter, age 48
President and CEO: Peter A. Wuffli, age 49
Deputy Group CEO; Chairman and CEO, Global Wealth Management and Business Banking: Marcel Rohner, age 42
CFO: Clive Standish, age 53
Chairman and CEO, Americas: Mark B. Sutton, age 52
Chairman and CEO, UBS Global Asset Management: John A. Fraser, age 55
Vice Chairman, Business Banking: Eugen Haltiner
Vice Chairman, Wealth Management: Carlo Grigioni
CEO, Alternative and Quantitative Investments, Global Asset Management: Joe Scoby
CEO, Dillon Read Capital Management; Chairman, UBS Investment Bank: John P. Costas, age 49
Chairman and CEO, UBS Investment Bank: Huw Jenkins, age 48
Chairman, UBS Investment Bank, Americas; Global COO, UBS Investment Bank: Robert Wolf
Corporate Secretary: Luzius Cameron
CTO: Scott G. Abbey
Group Chief Credit Officer: Philip J. Lofts
Group Chief Risk Officer: Walter H. Stürzinger, age 51

Chief Communication Officer: Thomas R. (Tom) Hill, age 44
Group Head of Human Resources: Thomas Hammer
Group General Counsel: Peter Kurer, age 57
Managing Director and Chief Administrative Officer, Prime Services: John Laub
Auditors: Ernst & Young Ltd.

LOCATIONS

HQ: UBS AG
Bahnhofstrasse 45, CH-8098 Zurich, Switzerland
Phone: +41-44-234-41-11   **Fax:** +41-44-234-34-15
US HQ: 1285 Avenue of the Americas, 2nd Fl., New York, NY 10019
US Phone: 212-713-2000   **US Fax:** 212-713-2099
Web: www.ubs.com

PRODUCTS/OPERATIONS

2005 Sales

	% of total
Interest	59
Fees & commissions	21
Industrial holdings	11
Trading income	8
Other	1
Total	**100**

2005 Assets

	% of total
Cash & equivalents	14
Reverse repurchase agreements	20
Trading portfolio	24
Positive replacement values	16
Loans	13
Other	13
Total	**100**

COMPETITORS

Bank of America
Barclays
CIBC
Citigroup
Coutts Group
Credit Suisse
Deutsche Bank
Goldman Sachs
HSBC Holdings
JPMorgan Chase
Julius Baer
Merrill Lynch
Mitsubishi UFJ Financial Group
Mizuho Financial
Morgan Stanley
RBC Financial Group
Sal. Oppenheim Jr. & Cie.
Smith Barney
UniCredit
Wachovia Securities

HISTORICAL FINANCIALS

Company Type: Public

Income Statement

FYE: December 31

	ASSETS ($ mil.)	NET INCOME ($ mil.)	INCOME AS % OF ASSETS	EMPLOYEES
12/05	1,566,202	10,665	0.7%	69,569
12/04	1,549,012	7,794	0.5%	67,424
12/03	1,235,296	5,245	0.4%	65,929
12/02	935,481	4,000	0.4%	69,061
12/01	786,021	1,933	0.2%	69,985
Annual Growth	**18.8%**	**53.3%**	**—**	**(0.1%)**

2005 Year-End Financials

Equity as % of assets: 2.5%   Dividends
Return on assets: 0.7%   Yield: —
Return on equity: 24.8%   Payout: —
Long-term debt ($ mil.): 621,364   Market value ($ mil.): —
No. of shares (mil.): —   Sales ($ mil.): 76,292

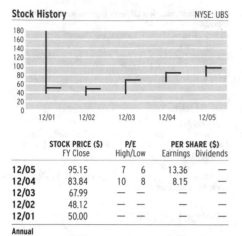

	STOCK PRICE ($) FY Close	P/E High/Low		PER SHARE ($) Earnings	Dividends
12/05	95.15	7	6	13.36	—
12/04	83.84	10	8	8.15	—
12/03	67.99	—	—	—	—
12/02	48.12	—	—	—	—
12/01	50.00	—	—	—	—
Annual Growth	**17.5%**	—	—	**63.9%**	—

Unilever

One is a lonely number, unless you're Unilever. One of the largest producers of some 400 packaged consumer goods, Unilever operates in nearly all countries in Asia, Africa, North America, the Middle East, Western Europe, and Latin America. The company's brand names for fragrances, frozen foods, soap, and tea include Calvin Klein, Birds Eye, Axe, Dove, and Lipton. Unilever is part of the Unilever Group owned by the Netherlands-based Unilever N.V. and UK-based Unilever PLC. Unilever has two global divisions, Home & Personal Care and Food. The company sold its Unilever Cosmetics International unit to Coty in 2005 for about $800 million.

Unilever foods account for more than half of the firm's sales. Brands range from the widely recognized, such as Hellmann's mayonnaise (acquired in the $24 billion purchase of Bestfoods in 2000), to locally marketed products, such as Italy's Findus frozen foods. The Unilever line of home and personal care products includes deodorants (Axe, Degree), hair care products (Suave, ThermaSilk), prestige fragrances (Calvin Klein), men's fragrances (Axe), and skincare (Lever 2000, Pond's). Its other familiar goods include Q-Tips, Vaseline, and laundry and cleaning products such as all, Wisk, and Surf.

The early 2005 announcement that The Procter & Gamble Company (P&G) would acquire The Gillette Company — making P&G the largest consumer products maker in the world, ahead of Unilever — put pressure on the company to quickly fine-tune its restructuring. A couple of weeks later, amid reports of a flat year for growth, Unilever announced sweeping changes in its leadership organization and that it would abandon its dual chairman/CEO structure that has been in place for decades. In April 2005 Antony Burgmans became chairman and Patrick Cescau took the title of CEO.

In mid-2004 Unilever announced that it would invest some $500 million to develop and expand its share of the food, beverage, and cosmetics markets in Indonesia throughout the next 10 years.

HISTORY

After sharpening his sales skills in the family wholesale grocery business, Englishman William Lever formed a new company in 1885 with his brother James. Lever Brothers introduced Sunlight, the world's first packaged, branded laundry soap. Sunlight was a success in Britain, and within 15 years Lever Brothers was selling soap worldwide. Between 1906 and 1915 the company grew mostly through acquisitions. Needing vegetable oil to make soap, the company established plantations and trading companies worldwide. During WWI Lever began using its vegetable oil to make margarine.

Rival Dutch butter makers Jurgens and Van den Berghs were pioneers in margarine production. In 1927 they created the Margarine Union, a cartel that owned the European market. The Margarine Union and Lever Brothers merged in 1930, but for tax reasons formed two separate entities: Unilever PLC in London and Unilever N.V. in Rotterdam, the Netherlands.

Despite the Depression and WWII, Unilever expanded, acquiring US companies Thomas J. Lipton (1937) and Pepsodent (1944). Unilever benefited from the postwar boom in Europe, the increasing use of margarine, new detergent technologies, and the growing use of personal care products.

Although product development fueled some growth, acquisitions (at one time running at the rate of one per week) played a major role in shaping Unilever. These included Birds Eye Foods in the UK (1957) and, in the US, Good Humor (1961), Lawry's Foods (1979), Ragu (1986), Chesebrough-Ponds (1987), Calvin Klein Cosmetics (1989, now Unilever Cosmetics International), Faberge/Elizabeth Arden (1989), and Breyers ice cream (1993).

In 1995 Unilever began cutting its global workforce by 7,500. The following year it bought hair care and deodorant maker Helene Curtis. Unilever shed its specialty chemicals operations in 1997. In 1998 the company sold its Plant Breeding International Cambridge (PBIC) business to Monsanto.

In 2000 Unilever bought US weight-management firm Slim-Fast Foods for $2.3 billion and ice-cream maker Ben & Jerry's. As part of its previously announced brand-reduction strategy, Unilever also that year sold its European bakery supplies business to CSM. Later that same year, the company bought Bestfoods for $24 billion, which would result in putting Bestfoods' US baking business (Entenmann's, Oroweat bread) up for sale. George Weston's offer of $1.77 billion won the bidding war for Bestfoods' US baking business. Unilever also owns the rights to the game show Wheel of Fortune.

Unilever sold its Elizabeth Arden fragrance and skin care business to French Fragrances in 2001. Also that year, it sold its North American seafood businesses (the Gorton's brand in the US and BlueWater in Canada) to seafood conglomerate Nippon Suisan Kaisha. The company sold Unipath, which produces the Clearblue home pregnancy test, to Inverness Medical Innovations in December 2001.

In 2002 Unilever sold its retail dry cleaning and laundry-related business to ZOOTS-The Cleaner Cleaner and its institutional and industrial cleaning business, DiverseyLever, to Johnson Wax Professional. It also sold 19 of its North American food brands (including Mazola corn oil, Argo and Kingsford cornstarches, Karo corn syrup, and Henri's salad dressings) to a subsidiary of Associated British Foods plc. The company sold its Iberia

Foods business to the Brooklyn Bottling Group. It also sold its international specialty oils and fats business Loders Croklaan Group.

In 2003 Unilever sold its French frozen-products company Fridedoc to home-vending company Toupargel. Unilever sold its Brut brand of male personal care products, including fragrance, antiperspirant, and deodorant products, to Helen of Troy. The agreement gives Helen of Troy ownership of the brand in the Americas, Canada, Mexico, Puerto Rico, and elsewhere in Latin America; Unilever retains ownership in Europe, Africa, Australia, Asia, and the Middle East.

Unilever sold the rest of its Mazola brand, an operation in Mexico, to the Mexican subsidiary of Associated British Foods in early 2004, along with its Capullo cooking oil and Inca brand butter. ABF had acquired the US Mazola brand in 2002.

Acquired from Helene Curtis in 1996, the Finesse brand was purged by Unilever in early 2006 alongside its Aqua Net brand, which it had purchased from Chesebrough-Ponds in 1988.

EXECUTIVES

Chairman: Antony Burgmans, age 59, $2,704,469 pay (prior to promotion)
Vice Chairman, Unilever N.V and Unilever PLC, and Director: Bertrand P. Collomb, age 63
Group Chief Executive: Patrick J. Cescau, age 57, $2,105,770 pay (prior to promotion)
CFO: Rudy Markham, age 60, $1,732,443 pay (prior to promotion)
Chairman, Unilever Israel: Ron Gutman
Chairman and CEO, Unilever Philippines: Howard Belton
President and CEO, Unilever Canada: Jeffrey Allgrove, age 50
President and CEO, Unilever Cosmetics International: Fergus Balfour, age 51
President, Africa Business Group: Douglas (Doug) Baillie, age 49
President, Americas and President, Slim Fast Worldwide: John Rice, age 53
Chairman, Hindustan Lever: Harish Manwani, age 51
Chairman, Unilever Japan: Arun Adhikari
President, Europe: Kees van der Graaf, age 55
President, Global Foods: M. S. (Vindi) Banga, age 50
President, Global Foodsolutions: Diego Bevilacqua, age 51
Chief Human Resources Officer: Sandy Ogg, age 51
Group VP, Unilever US: Michael B. (Mike) Polk, age 44
Joint Secretary and General Counsel: Stephen G. (Steve) Williams, age 57
Marketing Director, Dove, North America: Philippe Harousseau
Group Treasurer: Pascal Visée, age 43
Corporate Communications: Paul Wood
Investor Relations: Leigh Ferst
Auditors: PricewaterhouseCoopers

LOCATIONS

HQ: Unilever PLC
Unilever House, Blackfriars,
London EC4P 4BQ, United Kingdom
Phone: +44-20-7822-5252 **Fax:** +44-20-7822-6191
HQ: Unilever N.V.
Weena 455, 3000 DK Rotterdam, The Netherlands
Phone: +31-10-217-4000 **Fax:** +31-10-217-4798
US HQ: 700 Sylvan Ave., Englewood Cliffs, NJ 07632
US Phone: 201-894-4000 **US Fax:** 201-871-8257
Web: www.unilever.com

Sales

	% of total
Europe	41
The Americas	33
Asia/Africa	26
Total	**100**

PRODUCTS/OPERATIONS

Sales

	% of total
Foods	55
Home & personal care	44
Other operations	1
Total	**100**

Selected Brands

Ades beverage
Culinary (Calvé, Colmans, Hellman's, Knorr, Lipton Cup-a-Soup, Ragu, Skippy)
Carb Options (low carb Ragu, Wish-Bone, Skippy, Lipton, and Lawry's)
Deodorants (Axe, Brut, Degree, Dove, Rexona)
Fragrances (Brut, Calvin Klein, House of Cerruti, House of Valentino, Lagerfeld)
Frozen foods (Birds Eye, Findus)
Hair care (Organics, Suave, SunSilk, ThermaSilk)
Household care (Cif, Domestos)
Ice cream (Ben & Jerry's, Breyers, Good-Humor, Klondike, Magnum, Popsicle, Solero)
Laundry (all, Ala, Comfort, Omo, Snuggle, Surf, Wisk)
Personal wash (Dove, Lever 2000, Lux, Pond's, Q-tips, Vaseline)
Professional cleaning (DiverseyLever)
Salad dressing (Wish-Bone)
Spreads and cooking products (Becel, Country Crock, I Can't Believe It's Not Butter!, Promise, Rama)
Tea-based beverages (Lipton)
Weight management (Slim-Fast)

COMPETITORS

Alberto-Culver	Johnson & Johnson
Alticor	Kao
Atkins Nutritionals	Kraft Foods
Avon	L'Oréal
Beiersdorf	LVMH
Campbell Soup	Mars
Church & Dwight	McBride
Clorox	MedPointe
Coca-Cola	Nestlé
Colgate-Palmolive	PepsiCo
ConAgra	Procter & Gamble
Dairy Farmers of America	Reckitt Benckiser
Danone	Revlon
Del Monte Foods	Sara Lee Household
Dial	S.C. Johnson
Estée Lauder	Shiseido
General Mills	Tata Group
Gillette	Uniq
Inter Parfums	

HISTORICAL FINANCIALS

Company Type: Joint venture

Income Statement

FYE: December 31

	REVENUE ($ mil.)	NET INCOME ($ mil.)	NET PROFIT MARGIN	EMPLOYEES
12/04	54,413	2,541	4.7%	223,000
12/03	53,674	3,472	6.5%	234,000
12/02	50,698	2,236	4.4%	247,000
12/01	45,914	1,638	3.6%	279,000
12/00	44,813	1,041	2.3%	261,000
Annual Growth	**5.0%**	**25.0%**	**—**	**(3.9%)**

2004 Year-End Financials

Debt ratio: 127.6%
Return on equity: 34.8%
Cash ($ mil.): 2,150
Current ratio: 0.83
Long-term debt ($ mil.): 9,337

Net Income History

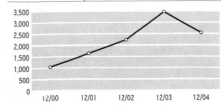

Veolia Environnement

Veolia Environnement holds water — as well as waste management, energy, and transportation — operations. The company's Veolia Water unit, which provides water and wastewater services to more than 108 million people, is the world's largest water company, ahead of Suez. Subsidiary Onyx, one of the world's leading waste management companies, treats nearly 53 million tons of waste per year. Majority-owned energy unit Dalkia operates global cogeneration facilities and heating and cooling systems, and Veolia Transport (formerly Connex) is a top European provider of bus, light-rail, and rail transport.

Veolia Environnement has been selling off its noncore businesses. In 2004 the company sold the assets of its former USFilter unit, a leading water-treatment equipment manufacturer, as well as its US-based Culligan water-treatment business. Also divested was Veolia Environnement's stake in Spanish construction group Fomento de Construcciones y Contratas (FCC).

Today's Veolia Environnement consists of the water, waste, energy, and transport businesses of the former Vivendi group. The group spun off Veolia Environnement (then called Vivendi Environnement), sold a minority stake to the public, and renamed itself Vivendi Universal in 2000 (and Vivendi in 2006). To raise cash, Vivendi Universal reduced its stake in the environmental services company from 63% to about 20% in 2002. Vivendi Universal sold a 15% stake in Veolia Environnement in 2004, leaving Vivendi Universal with a 5% stake in its former subsidiary. It finally sold the last of its holdings in Veolia in the summer of 2006, offering the shares on the open market. Vivendi expected to gain more than $1 billion from the sale.

The former Vivendi Environnement changed its name to Veolia Environnement in 2003 to signify the break with Vivendi Universal. The name Veolia is derived from Aeolus, the keeper of the winds in Greek mythology.

HISTORY

What is now Veolia Environnement originated in 1853 as Compagnie Générale des Eaux in Paris. The company irrigated farmlands and subsequently supplied water. By 1860 Paris had granted the company a 50-year contract to provide the city's water. In 1880 it moved beyond France to provide water in Venice, Italy. Operations in Turkey (Istanbul) and Portugal (Oporto) followed.

Compagnie Générale des Eaux extended its water network in 1924, and by WWII it supplied half of all urban households in France. After the war the company expanded into household waste collection (1953) and operation of household waste incineration and compost plants (1967). Wastewater treatment activities began in 1972.

In the next decade Compagnie Générale des Eaux dove into diversification. It increased its holding in energy-conversion systems operator Compagnie Générale de Chauffe to 100% (making it France's leading energy company) in 1980. That year it merged its wastewater treatment subsidiaries to create Omnium de Traitement et de Valorisation (OTV). Its waste operations were further augmented through the takeover of Compagnie Générale d'Entreprises Automobiles (CGEA), a transport and waste management firm. The company also ventured into telecommunications, pay-TV, and construction (it gained a controlling stake in builder SGE in 1988 but disposed of its interest in the firm, later known as VINCI, in 2000).

CGEA bid for and won control of several former British Rail lines in 1996 when the UK's railway system was privatized. Operating under the name Connex, the company began to run trains throughout southeastern England, the UK's largest commuting area.

In 1998 CGEA changed its name to Vivendi. The group (which came to include mobile phone provider Cegetel and a stake in the Havas media company) transferred the Compagnie Générale des Eaux name to its water business. Vivendi also organized its Compagnie Générale de Chauffe and Sithe Energies (now a part of Dynergy) subsidiaries into a single energy division, named Dalkia. In 1999 Sithe Energies bought 23 thermal power plants from US utility GPU (later FirstEnergy) and became the leading independent power producer in the northeastern US.

Vivendi continued its charge into the US that year. The group acquired waste services company Superior Services (then the US's fourth-biggest solid waste company). Its purchase of USFilter transformed Vivendi into the world's largest water company and marked the biggest acquisition of a US firm by a French company.

The ever-evolving Vivendi transformed into a global media company and renamed itself Vivendi Universal in 2000. It bought Seagram and French pay-TV provider CANAL+ and spun off its water, waste management, transportation, and energy operations (Vivendi Environnement) after turning down German utility RWE's $28 million offer to buy the business.

Vivendi Environnement's waste operations grew after snapping up operations in Brazil, Hong Kong, and Mexico from Waste Management. In 2001 the company merged its Dalkia energy operations with the energy services operations of Electricité de France (EDF).

In 2002 Vivendi Universal reduced its stake in Vivendi Environnement from 63% to about 20%; the next year Vivendi Environnement changed its name to Veolia Environnement. Vivendi finally divested all of its interest in Veolia in the middle of 2006.

EXECUTIVES

Chairman and CEO: Henri Proglio, age 57
SEVP, Deputy Managing Director, and CFO:
Jérôme Contamine, age 47
EVP, Human Resources: Eric Marie de Ficquelmont,
age 50
EVP and Head, Energy Services Division:
Olivier Barbaroux, age 49
EVP and Head, Transportation Division:
Stéphane Richard, age 44
EVP and Head, Waste Management Division:
Denis Gasquet, age 51
EVP and Head, Water Division: Antoine Frérot, age 46
Investor Relations: Nathalie Pinon
US Investor Relations: Brian Sullivan
Auditors: Barbier Frinault & Autres; Salustro Reydel

LOCATIONS

HQ: Veolia Environnement SA
36-38, avenue Kléber, 75116 Paris, France
Phone: +33-1-71-75-00-00   **Fax:** +33-1-71-75-10-45
US HQ: 14950 Heathrow Forest, Ste. 200,
Houston, TX 77032
US Phone: 281-985-5479   **US Fax:** 713-302-1059
Web: www.veoliaenvironnement.com

2005 Sales

	% of total
Europe	
France	49
Germany	7
UK	6
Other countries	19
North America	
US	9
Oceania	3
Asia	2
Other regions	5
Total	**100**

PRODUCTS/OPERATIONS

2005 Sales

	% of total
Water	51
Waste management	27
Energy services	16
Transportation	6
Total	**100**

Selected Operations

Water
   Compagnie Générale des Eaux
   Veolia Water S.A.
Waste Management
   CGEA Onyx
   Renosol
   Société d'Assainissement Rationnel et de Pompage
      (SARP)
   SARP Industries
   Veolia Environmental ServicesNorth America Corp.
Energy
   Dalkia (66%)
Transport
   CGEA Connex
   Connex Transport Ltd (formerly Connex Rail Ltd, UK)

COMPETITORS

Alpheus	Severn Trent
American States Water	Shanks
AWG plc	SNCF
Bouygues	Stagecoach
Electricité de France	SUEZ
Electricité de Strasbourg	SUEZ Environnement
Elyo	ThermoEnergy
Kelda	United Utilities
Northumbrian Water	Vattenfall
Pennon	Waste Management
RWE Thames Water	Waste Recycling
SABESP	Welsh Water
Scottish Power	

Company Type: Public

Income Statement   FYE: December 31

	REVENUE ($ mil.)	NET INCOME ($ mil.)	NET PROFIT MARGIN	EMPLOYEES
12/05	29,900	658	2.2%	271,153
12/04	33,664	293	0.9%	251,584
12/03	35,917	(2,294)	—	309,563
12/02	31,532	(2,085)	—	302,283
12/01	20,640	159	0.8%	295,286
Annual Growth	**9.7%**	**42.7%**	**—**	**(2.1%)**

2005 Year-End Financials

Debt ratio: 489.9%   No. of shares (mil.): —
Return on equity: 20.2%   Dividends
Cash ($ mil.): 3,294   Yield: 1.6%
Current ratio: 0.98   Payout: —
Long-term debt ($ mil.): 16,436 Market value ($ mil.): —

Stock History   NYSE: VE

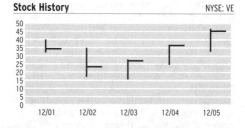

	STOCK PRICE ($) FY Close	P/E High/Low	PER SHARE ($) Earnings	Dividends
12/05	45.30	— —	—	0.70
12/04	36.45	— —	—	0.57
12/03	27.00	— —	—	0.53
12/02	23.31	— —	—	—
12/01	34.25	— —	—	—
Annual Growth	**7.2%**			**14.9%**

VINCI

Veni, vidi, vici . . . VINCI. Formerly Société Générale d'Enterprises (SGE), VINCI, through its VINCI Construction unit, is one of the world's largest building, civil engineering, and maintenance contractors. VINCI Energies is a French leader in electrical engineering and information technology. Eurovia (the major operating unit of the VINCI Roads division) is a top European roadworks and urban redevelopment company. VINCI Concessions, one of the world's largest concessions companies, builds and operates car parks, toll roads, and airports. VINCI Park manages parking facilities in about a dozen countries. VINCI's home base of France accounts for more than 60% of the company's sales by region.

VINCI's core construction operations generate more than 40% of total sales. Subsidiary Sogea performs general contracting and engineering. The group, whose major projects include restoring the Strasbourg cathedral and the fountains of Place de la Concorde in Paris, has agreed to manage the restoration of the Château de Versailles Hall of Mirrors and contribute its technical expertise to the project.

VINCI Energies (formerly GTIE, or Générale de Travaux et d'Installation Électrique) is a top electrical engineering group in France, as well

as a major European player in information and communication technologies. The unit also focuses on power supply infrastructure and public lighting systems. It acquired Imhoff, a French environmental controls company, in 2006. The move is expected to boost its HVAC business.

In addition to being one of Europe's top roadworks and urban redevelopment companies, Eurovia is a leader in the road construction materials, demolition, and waste recycling markets. The company operates in 17 countries, including Chile, Canada, and the US. In the US Eurovia owns two southeastern highway contractors, Orlando, Florida-based Hubbard Construction and Charlotte, North Carolina-based Blythe Construction. Eurovia has won a contract to replace cobblestones at the Place de L'Etoile in Paris, near the Arc de Triomphe. The cobblestones have not been replaced since 1947.

Eurovia has been investing heavily in raw ingredients for its roadbuilding. In 2006 it agreed to buy German gravel quarry operator Sutter; it also took a 52% stake in Belgian quarry company Carrieres Unies de Porphyre with the understanding it would buy the rest of the shares as well.

The company has been marked by unrest in the board room, as chairman Antoine Zacharias reportedly wanted to oust CEO Xavier Huillard in favor of Nexity CEO Alain Dinin. Zacharias was the one who ended up resigning. However, VINCI and Nexity are exploring a joint venture or other alliance of their real estate businesses, and Dinin has expressed interest in buying the real estate unit outright. At the end of 2006, Dinin resigned from VINCI's board.

HISTORY

VINCI's origins lie with French conglomerate Vivendi (now Vivendi Universal), which was founded in 1853 as Compagnie Générale des Eaux. Its mission was to irrigate French farmland and supply water to towns. The company won contracts to serve Lyons (1853), Nantes (1854), Paris (1860), and Venice (1880). Générale des Eaux moved into construction in 1972, building an office tower (and later hotels and houses) in Paris. The company also entered communications in the 1980s.

In 1988 Générale des Eaux acquired control of construction and civil engineering giant Société Générale d'Entreprises. SGE subsidiaries included Campenon Bernard SGE (part of Générale des Eaux since 1981), Sogea, Freyssinet, Cochery Bourdin Chaussé, Saunier Duval, Tunzini, Lefort Francheteau, and Wanner. SGE traces its construction roots to 1910. It became a subsidiary of Générale d'Electricité in 1966. Glassmaker Saint-Gobain acquired control of SGE in 1984.

Under Générale des Eaux, SGE enhanced its European profile through acquisitions, including British builder Norwest Holst (1989), German road builder VBU (1991), and German pipe and duct maker MLTU (1992).

Générale des Eaux acquired publisher Havas in 1998 and took the name Vivendi — representing vivacity and mobility. Its purchase of US Filter in 1999 made Vivendi the world's largest water company. Vivendi's SGE unit (renamed VINCI) agreed to acquire the construction arm of rival conglomerate Suez's GTM unit in 2000.

Groupe GTM traces its roots to Société Lyonnaise des Eaux et de L'Eclairage, a leading French water utility. Formed in 1880, Lyonnaise des Eaux built up its French and international operations to include water distribution, as well as gas and electricity production and distribution.

A century later the company had diversified into such businesses as heating (Cofreth), waste management (Sita), and communications, acquiring a stake in Lyonnaise Communications (now Lyonnaise Câble) in 1986.

In 1990 Lyonnaise des Eaux acquired construction firm Dumez, whose subsidiary GTM-Entrepose was France's largest car park manager. Four years later Dumez-GTM was formed to consolidate the construction and civil engineering businesses of Dumez and GTM-Entrepose. In 1997 Lyonnaise des Eaux and Compagnie de Suez merged to create a leading provider of private infrastructure services, Suez Lyonnaise des Eaux (which shortened its name to Suez in 2001). Compagnie Universal du Canal Maritime de Suez, the builder of the Suez Canal, was founded in 1858 and became Financière de Suez in 1958. In 1967 Financière de Suez acquired control of Lyonnaise des Eaux.

SGE changed its name to VINCI in 2000. That year, as part of their strategy to rationalize operations and focus on core businesses, Vivendi and Suez agreed to a friendly takeover of GTM by VINCI. Suez emerged as the combined company's largest shareholder, but by the following year both Suez and Vivendi Universal had exited most of VINCI's capital, leaving no core stockholder.

The company expanded its concessions holdings even more in 2002 by hooking up with construction group Eiffage to grab a 17% stake in Europe's second-largest toll road operator, ASF, which was floated that year by the French government. In 2003 the group won the contract to manage the restoration of the historic Hall of Mirrors. It also won the concession contract to operate, along with joint venture partner Keolis, the International Airport of Grenoble.

In 2006 chairman Antoine Zacharias resigned after an attempt to oust CEO Xavier Huillard failed. He was replaced by Yves-Thibault de Silguy, formerly of French utility company Suez.

EXECUTIVES

Chairman: Yves-Thibault de Silguy, age 57
Vice Chairman: Bernard Huvelin, age 68
Vice Chairman; Chairman, VINCI Concessions: Bernard Val, age 63
CEO and Director: Xavier Huillard, age 52
SEVP; Chairman and CEO, Eurovia (VINCI Roads): Roger Martin
EVP; Chairman and CEO, VINCI Construction: Philippe Ratynski, age 46
EVP and CFO: Christian Labeyrie, age 49
EVP, Corporate Communications, Human Resources, and Synergies: Pierre Coppey, age 42
VP Business Development: Jean-Luc Pommier
Chairman and CEO, GTM Construction: Robert Hosselet
Chairman and CEO, Freyssinet: Bruno Dupety
Chairman, Sogea Construction: Jean Rossi
Chairman, VINCI Construction: Richard Francioli, age 46
Chairman and CEO, Cofiroute: Henri Stouff
Director: Jean-Pierre Marchand-Arpoumé
Chairman and CEO, VINCI Park: Denis Grand
Chairman and CEO, VINCI plc: John Stanion
CEO, VINCI Concessions: David Azema, age 45
Co-COO, Eurovia: Jean-Louis Marchand
Chairman and CEO, VINCI Energies: Jean-Yves Le Brouster, age 58
EVP, Eurovia France and Europe: Guy Vacher
EVP, Eurovia International: Daniel Roffet
EVP, VINCI Energies; Operating Officer, VINCI Assurances: Patrick LeBrun
Managing Director, CFE: Renaud Bentegeat
Deputy Managing Director, VINCI Energies: Philippe Touyarot
Auditors: Deloitte Touche Tohmatsu — Audit; RSM Salustro Reydel; Deloitte & Associés; Salustro Reydel

LOCATIONS

HQ: VINCI
1 cours Ferdinand-de-Lesseps,
92851 Rueil-Malmaison, France
Phone: +33-1-47-16-35-00 **Fax:** +33-1-47-51-91-02
Web: www.groupe-vinci.com

VINCI has operations in more than 100 countries.

2005 Sales

	% of total
Europe	
France	62
UK	8
Germany	7
Central & Eastern Europe	7
Rest of Europe	7
North America	4
Other regions	5
Total	**100**

PRODUCTS/OPERATIONS

2005 Sales

	% of total
Construction	43
Roads	30
Energy	16
Concessions & services	9
Other operations	2
Total	**100**

Selected Subsidiaries

VINCI Construction
  Campenon Bernard Construction
  Compagnie d'Entreprises CFE (45%, Belgium)
  Dumez-GTM
  Freyssinet
  GTM Construction
  Janin Atlas (Canada)
  Les Travaux du Midi
  VINCI Bautec (Germany)
  VINCI plc (formerly Norwest Holst Group PLC, UK)
  SKE SSI (US)
  Sogea Construction
VINCI Roads
  Blythe (US)
  Eurovia
  Hubbard (USA)
  Ringway Ltd. (91%, UK)
  SSZ (92%, Czech Republic)
VINCI Energies (Energy and Information)
  Emil Lundgren (Sweden)
  Saga Enterprises
  Santerne Exploitation
VINCI Concessions
  Autopista del Bosque (83%, Chile)
  Cofiroute Participations (65%)
  Gestipark (50%, Canada)
  Société Concessionnaire de l'Aéroport de Pochentong (70%, Cambodia)
  Sogeparc France
  VINCI Airports US
  VINCI Park

COMPETITORS

AMEC	FCC Barcelona
Autostrade	Halliburton
Avionic Services	HOCHTIEF
Bechtel	Louis Berger
Bilfinger Berger	Schneider Electric
Bouygues	Skanska
Bovis Lend Lease	WS Atkins
EIFFAGE	

HISTORICAL FINANCIALS

Company Type: Public

Income Statement

FYE: December 31

	REVENUE ($ mil.)	NET INCOME ($ mil.)	NET PROFIT MARGIN	EMPLOYEES
12/05	25,513	1,032	4.0%	133,513
12/04	26,626	998	3.7%	128,000
12/03	22,733	680	3.0%	127,513
12/02	19,331	501	2.6%	140,000
12/01	16,115	402	2.5%	129,000
Annual Growth	12.2%	26.6%	—	0.9%

Net Income History Euronext Paris: DG

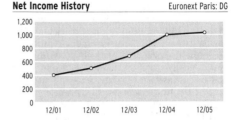

Virgin Group

Led by adventurous founder, chairman, and owner Sir Richard Branson, Virgin Group gets around. The group's travel operations, led by 51%-owned Virgin Atlantic Airways, are among its biggest breadwinners. Virgin Atlantic is complemented by its pan-European and Australian low-fare cousins, Virgin Express and Virgin Blue. Virgin Group also operates two UK rail franchises and sells tour packages. The group's Virgin Megastores sell music, videos, and computer games. Other Virgin Group operations include balloon flights, beverages, bridal stores, cosmetics, financial services, health clubs, Internet services, mobile phone services, publishing, and a record label.

Branson has made Virgin Group's name one of the most recognizable brands in the world by plastering it on everything from airplanes to cola. The group continues to look for new growth opportunities to balance against the airline industry's ups and downs.

In addition, Branson has announced plans to raise cash by selling stakes in several group companies. Virgin Blue and telecom provider Virgin Mobile Holdings have already gone public. In 2006, UK cable operator NTL bought Virgin Mobile, which will continue to operate under the Virgin brand. The deal was valued at nearly $1.7 billion.

Virgin Group's latest airline venture, Virgin America, plans to take to the skies in 2006. Another low-fare affair, Virgin America will operate out of San Francisco using a leased fleet of more than 100 Airbus jets.

The group is also looking at expanding into the Indian airline services market. Branson has initiated talks to acquire stakes in several unspecified Indian airlines as part of an effort to establish the Virgin brand in that country.

HISTORY

Always one to revel in competition, Richard Branson got his start in the business world at the age of 17, dropping out of boarding school to pursue his magazine, *Student,* in 1968. Two years later he was on to a new challenge when he started Virgin — a mail-order record company named for his lack of experience at such things. After a postal strike the next year put a damper on that enterprise, Branson opened the first Virgin record store. Continued success led to a recording studio and record label that went on to sign several popular British rock bands in the 1970s, including the Sex Pistols, Genesis, and the Rolling Stones.

With his entertainment businesses flourishing in the early 1980s, Branson sought a new adventure and found it in the airline industry, another business he knew very little about. Virgin Atlantic Airways took off in 1984 with one plane and one transatlantic route. Growing steadily, Virgin Atlantic became one of the world's most profitable airlines in the 1980s. The company added Virgin Holidays (tours) to its travel group in 1985.

Branson collected all his businesses (except the travel operations) into a new company called Virgin Group and took it public in 1986. Despite the company's continued growth and profits, the market slashed its value after the crash of 1987, and a frustrated Branson bought it all back the following year. Virgin sold its smaller UK record stores in 1988 to focus on the development of its Megastores concept. It also entered the hotel business that year.

Virgin started Britain's first national commercial rock radio station in 1992. Branson sold the Virgin Music Group (a decision he still regrets) to THORN EMI that year for about $1 billion. He used the proceeds to build Virgin Atlantic. By the early 1990s the airline had added to its fleet and had new routes, including flights to Asia. It also took on British Airways and won a libel suit in 1993.

The company debuted Virgin Cola in 1994 and bought 25% of the Our Price record store chain with WH Smith (it purchased the rest in 1998). Virgin acquired MGM Cinemas (the UK's largest theater operator) and introduced its financial services business in 1995. Meanwhile it added dozens of new Megastores around the world in the mid-1990s. Virgin got back into the recording business in 1996 when it launched the V2 record label. It also bought low-fare Euro Belgian Airlines (renamed Virgin Express).

Virgin looked to keep itself on the right track in 1997 when it got into the rail business. Realizing that the right track might be the Internet, Branson has pushed the group towards the age of e-commerce and online services with Virgin.com. Mobile phone sales (at its existing retail locations) entered the company's cornucopia in 1999. In late 1999 Virgin agreed to sell its cinema chain to Vivendi (now Vivendi Universal), raising funds for other online and retail ventures. It launched a major Australian airline (Virgin Blue) in 2000.

That year Branson's bid to wrest the operation of UK's national lottery from current contract holder Camelot Group came up short. The National Lottery Commission extended Camelot's contract for seven years. Later in 2000 the company sold 49% of Virgin Atlantic to Singapore Airlines.

In 2001 Virgin agreed to sell Virgin Sun (package holidays) to rival travel firm First Choice Holidays. Also that year the company sold its 16 French Megastores, as well as some international rights to the Virgin brand, to France's Lagardère.

Virgin Mobile in 2002 began offering prepaid wireless service in the US in conjunction with Sprint PCS.

EXECUTIVES

Chairman: Sir Richard Branson, age 56
Chief Executive: Stephen Murphy
Director Financial Control: Susannah Parden
Group Brand Marketing Director: Ashley Stockwell
IT Services Director: Gareth Lewis
Group General Counsel: Josh Bayliss
Auditors: KPMG

LOCATIONS

HQ: Virgin Group Ltd.
120 Campden Hill Rd.,
London W8 7AR, United Kingdom
Phone: +44-20-7229-1282   **Fax:** +44-20-7727-8200
Web: www.virgin.com

Virgin Group has operations in Africa, Asia, Australia, Europe, and North America.

PRODUCTS/OPERATIONS

Major Operations

Virgin Active (45%, health clubs)
Virgin Arcadia Productions (video production)
Virgin Airship & Balloon company (commercial hot air balloon for advertising and other contracts)
Virgin Atlantic Airways (51%, international airline)
Virgin Balloon Flights (passenger balloons)
Virgin Biz Net (Web site creation and other online services for small businesses)
Virgin Blue (Australian low-fare airline)
Virgin Books (book publishing)
Virgin Bride (bridal emporium)
Virgin Cars (car purchasing Web site)
Virgin Cola (beverage brands)
Virgin Cosmetics (more than 500 products for men and women available in the UK)
Virgin Direct (financial services)
Virgin Energy (25%, utility bill payment program)
Virgin Express (pan-European low-fare airline)
Virgin Holidays (UK-based tour operator)
Virgin Limobike (motorcycle passenger service)
Virgin Limousines (Northern California limo service)
Virgin Megastores (retail music, movies, and computer games)
Virgin Mobile (mobile phone services)
Virgin Money (financial information)
Virgin Net (online entertainment, sports and leisure service)
Virgin One (banking services)
Virgin Student (online community)
Virgin Trains (passenger trains)
Virgin Travelstore (online travel agency)
Virgin Vouchers (voucher program)
V2 Music (record label)
V.SHOP (entertainment stores)

COMPETITORS

Accor	Marriott
Air France	MyTravel
AMR Corp.	News Corp.
Bertelsmann	Pearson
British Airways	PepsiCo
Coca-Cola	Rank
Disney	Sony
EMI Group	Starwood Hotels & Resorts
HMV	Time Warner
Japan Airlines	Tower Records
KLM	UAL
Lufthansa	Vivendi

HISTORICAL FINANCIALS

Company Type: Private

Income Statement

	ESTIMATED REVENUE ($ mil.)	NET INCOME ($ mil.)	NET PROFIT MARGIN	EMPLOYEES
3/04*	8,100	—	—	35,000
1/03	7,000	—	—	36,000
1/02	6,500	—	—	34,000
1/01	6,000	—	—	32,000
1/00	5,200	—	—	30,000
Annual Growth	11.7%	—	—	3.9%

FYE: March 31

*Fiscal year change

Revenue History

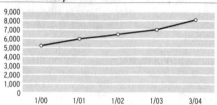

Vivendi

Vivendi (formerly known as Vivendi Universal) is the bright sun at the center of a solar system of market-leading media and telecommunications holdings. The company's telecom holdings include the 56%-owned SFR, France's #2 wireless carrier that also owns a 35% stake in alternative fixed-line operator Neuf Cegetel. Vivendi's media assets include Universal Music Group, the leading music publishing and recording company, and Vivendi Games, its subsidiary that develops, publishes, and distributes interactive entertainment. Vivendi also owns CANAL+ Group, the #1 pay-TV provider in France and a leading producer and distributor of pay-TV and films.

In 2006, the company, through Universal Music Group, agreed to acquire BMG Music Publishing in a deal valued at $2.1 billion. The deal, which advances Universal Music's lead in the music industry — it already has a greater than 25% market share — faces scrutiny from regulators but is expected to be completed by year's end. The company beat out several leading rivals in the highly publicized bidding process including Viacom and Warner Music Group.

Vivendi also has acquired the nearly 8% stake in Universal Studios Holding from Matsushita Electric Industrial. The deal, valued at nearly $1.2 billion, gives it 100% ownership in the holding company that owns Universal Music Group, Universal Interactive, and 20% of NBC Universal in an effort to boost the company's revenues.

The company also has agreed to combine its CANAL+ unit with rival French pay-TV provider Television Par Satellite (TPS) in a deal that gives Vivendi control over the new group.

Citing a desire to further reduce costs, the company in 2006 said it will end its listing on the New York Stock Exchange. It dropped Universal from its name — and became simply Vivendi — also in 2006 as part of its agreements with General Electric that created NBC Universal.

HISTORY

Authorized by an imperial decree, Compagnie Générale des Eaux was founded in 1853 by investors such as the Rothschild family and Napoleon III's half-brother to irrigate French farmland and supply water to towns. It won contracts to serve Lyons (1853), Nantes (1854), Paris (1860), and Venice (1880).

After WWI Générale des Eaux created water engineering firm Société Auxiliaire de Distribution d'Eau (Sade, 1918) and extended its water distribution network to several areas of France. By 1953 the company had added trash collection to its services. In the 1960s it began managing district heating networks and waste incineration/composting plants. The company moved into construction in 1972. By the time Guy Dujouany became chairman in 1976, water distribution accounted for less than half of the company's sales.

Dujouany began an expansion drive. In 1980 Générale des Eaux became France's #1 private energy management firm when it bought Générale de Chauffe. Also that year it expanded its wastewater and waste management businesses and moved into transportation, buying Compagnie Générale d'Entreprises Automobiles (CGEA). The company also entered communications in the 1980s: it took a 15% stake in pay-TV provider CANAL+ (1983) and it created mobile phone unit Société Francaise de Radiotelephonie (SFR, 1987).

Générale des Eaux took its water services global in the 1990s. Dujouany stepped down in 1996, and was succeeded by Jean-Marie Messier, who immediately dumped some businesses. In 1997 the company launched telecom provider Cegetel and increased its stake in publisher Havas to 30%. In 1998 the firm bought the rest of Havas, increased its ownership in CANAL+, and took the name Vivendi to represent "vivacity" and "mobility." Its purchase of USFilter in 1999 made it the world's largest water company.

Bulking up its media holdings, it acquired US educational software and games firm Cendant Software and bought French film producer Pathé. It sold most of Pathé's assets but kept stakes in BSkyB and CANAL+'s CanalSatellite digital-TV unit.

In 2000, in a $34 billion deal that set the stage for Vivendi's transformation into a global conglomerate, the company bought Seagram and the portion of CANAL+ that it didn't already own. The combined company became Vivendi Universal (VU). To gain European Commission approval for the Seagram acquisition, VU had to unload its stake in BSkyB. VU also sold Seagram's liquor business for $8.1 billion to Diageo and Pernod Ricard, which split up the various Seagram's brands between them.

In 2001 the company struck the biggest deal in its history by agreeing to buy the entertainment assets of USA Networks (now named InterActiveCorp). The deal closed the following year and VU combined Universal Studios with the USA business — which included film and TV production and cable channels — into a new company called Vivendi Universal Entertainment (VUE).

But in 2002 VU posted a roughly $25 billion loss, the largest one-year loss in French corporate history, and Messier's reputation took on some tarnish. He was forced to resign after the board of directors, following months of squabbling, withdrew support for his leadership. VU's buying spree led to crippling debt and the board doubted Messier had the ability to turn the company around. He was replaced by Jean-René Fourtou, the former vice chairman of drug maker Aventis (now Sanofi-Aventis).

Adding insult to injury, the US SEC accused Messier and other executives, including finance director Guillaume Hannezo, of accounting irregularities. Messier was fined $1 million, barred from being an officer or director of a public US company for 10 years, and denied a $25 million "golden parachute" deal. He was later fined €1 million by France's market regulators for inaccurate financial reporting.

At the end of 2002 VU completely exited the publishing business by selling Vivendi Universal Publishing (now named Editis) to Lagardère for $1.2 billion, and Houghton Mifflin to Thomas H. Lee and Bain Capital for $1.6 billion.

In 2004 VU saw its Hollywood aspirations fade to black. A prominent part of Fourtou's debt reduction plan was the sale of 86%-owned VUE, with the exception of Universal Music Group, to GE. In the deal that included Universal Studios, cable TV channels, and theme parks and created NBC Universal, VU received $3.8 billion in cash and retained a 19% stake in the new company.

In 2005 Fourtou stepped down as CEO of the company and turned the reins over to former COO Jean-Bernard Lévy. Fourtou became chairman of the supervisory board.

The company changed its name in 2006 to Vivendi, dropping the Universal, as part of the agreements creating NBC Universal.

EXECUTIVES

Chairman of the Supervisory Board:
Jean-René Fourtou, age 67
Chairman of the Management Board and CEO:
Jean-Bernard Lévy, age 50
Member of the Management Board and CFO:
Jacques Espinasse, age 63
Member of the Management Board; SEVP Human Resources; Chairman, Vivendi Universal Games:
René Pénisson, age 64
Member of the Management Board; Chairman, CANAL+ Group; Chairman and CEO, Canal Plus SA:
Bertrand Méheut, age 54
Member of the Management Board; Chairman and CEO, Universal Music Group: Douglas (Doug) Morris, age 67
Member of the Management Board; Chairman, Groupe SFR Cegetel: Frank Esser, age 48
Member of the Management Board; Chairman of the Management Board, Maroc Telecom:
Abdeslam Ahizoune, age 51
SEVP, Strategy and Development: Robert de Metz, age 54
EVP, Mergers and Acquisitions: Régis Turrini, age 47
EVP, General Counsel, and Secretary to the Supervisory and Management boards: Jean-François Dubos, age 60
EVP, Communications and Public Affairs:
Michel Bourgeois, age 56
EVP, Investor Relations: Daniel Scolan
Deputy CFO: Sandrine Dufour, age 37
Head, Internal Audit and Special Projects:
Vincent Vallejo, age 43
CEO, Vivendi Universal Games: Bruce Hack
Auditors: RSM Salustro Reydel

LOCATIONS

HQ: Vivendi
    42 avenue de Friedland, 75380 Paris, France
Phone: +33-1-71-71-10-00   **Fax:** +33-1-71-71-10-01
US HQ: 800 Third Ave., New York, NY 10022
US Phone: 212-572-7000   **US Fax:** 212-753-9301
Web: www.vivendi.com

2005 Sales

	$ mil.	% of total
Europe		
France	14,968	63
Other countries	2,368	10
US	2,958	12
Morocco	2,172	9
Other countries	1,407	6
Total	**23,873**	**100**

PRODUCTS/OPERATIONS

2005 Sales

	$ mil.	% of total
Telecommunications		
SFR	10,644	44
Maroc Telecom	2,279	10
Media		
Universal Music Group	5,995	25
CANAL+ Group	4,230	18
Vivendi Universal Games	785	3
Adjustments	(60)	—
Total	**23,873**	**100**

Selected Subsidiaries and Affiliates

CANAL+ Group
  CANAL+ Group
    Canal Plus SA (49%, pay TV operations)
    CanalSatellite S.A. (66%, direct broadcast satellite TV)
    MultiThématiques (cable TV)
    StudioCanal S.A. (film production and distribution)
Universal Music Group
  Universal Studios Holding I Corp. (USHI, 92%)
    NBC Universal (18%, media holdings, US)
    Universal Interactive
    Universal Music Group (music production and distribution, US)
Vivendi Universal Games (interactive entertainment software)
SFR Cegetel Group
  SFR (56%, wireless telecom services)
  Neuf Cegetel (35%, fixed-line telecom services)
Maroc Telecom S.A. (51%, telecom services, Morocco)
Other
  Vivendi Telecom International S.A.
    Elektrim Telekomunikacja Holding (49%, Poland)
    Polska Telefonia Cyfrowa (PTC, 48%, mobile telecommunications, Poland)

COMPETITORS

AOL
Bouygues
CompleTel
Eidos
Electronic Arts
EMI Group
France Telecom
ITV
Orange
Sony BMG
Tele2
Tiscali
Virgin Group
Warner Music

HISTORICAL FINANCIALS

Company Type: Public

Income Statement

FYE: December 31

	REVENUE ($ mil.)	NET INCOME ($ mil.)	NET PROFIT MARGIN	EMPLOYEES
12/05	23,873	3,045	12.8%	34,031
12/04	29,236	3,985	13.6%	37,906
12/03	31,998	(1,705)	—	55,451
12/02	60,959	(46,594)	—	61,815
12/01	45,835	(1,038)	—	381,504
Annual Growth	(15.0%)	—	—	(45.3%)

2005 Year-End Financials

Debt ratio: 26.8%
Return on equity: 14.9%
Cash ($ mil.): 3,572
Current ratio: 0.83
Long-term debt ($ mil.): 5,667

Net Income History

Euronext Paris: VIV

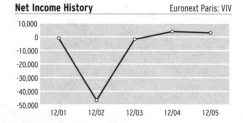

Vodafone Group

Customers have voted with their phones to make Vodafone Group the world's #2 wireless phone services provider (by subscribers) with nearly 187 million customers (trailing only China Mobile). Vodafone Group has grown rapidly through acquisitions and has advanced toward its goal of creating a pan-European wireless network. The company, formerly known as Vodafone AirTouch, owns stakes in wireless carriers around the globe. Vodafone companies are leading mobile phone operators in the US (45%-owned Verizon Wireless), Germany (D2), and the UK (Vodafone). The company is uniting its far-flung affiliates under the Vodafone brand.

Owing to investor pressures, the Vodafone Group has reportedly considered the sale of its stake in Verizon Wireless but more recent word from the company said it has no plans to do so. The company has sold its 98%-owned Vodafone Japan unit to SOFTBANK in a deal valued at nearly $16 billion. It continues in partnership with SOFTBANK.

Besides leading the mobile carrier market in the UK, the company has teamed up with BT Group to supply the UK incumbent carrier with mobile network services. Vodafone Group's other acquisitions include Germany's Mannesmann, which had controlled the #1 network in Germany (D2) and the #2 network in Italy (Omnitel). Vodafone also owns stakes in wireless carriers in several other European countries, including France, the Netherlands, and Spain. The company also has acquired a 79% stake in Romanian mobile operator MobiFon and all of Oskar Mobil, the Czech Republic wireless carrier, from Telesystem International Wireless in a cash deal valued at $3.5 billion that increases Vodafone Group's holding to 99% of MobiFon. Vodafone is also assuming

$950 million in debt with the transaction. Vodafone has agreed to acquire Telsim, the number two mobile service operator in Turkey, for about $4.6 billion.

On the other side of the Atlantic, Vodafone Group has combined its US wireless operations (acquired when the company bought AirTouch in 1999) with those of Bell Atlantic and GTE to form Verizon Wireless, the #1 US wireless provider. Verizon Wireless is 45%-owned by Vodafone Group and 55%-owned by Verizon Communications (formed when Bell Atlantic bought GTE). In 2004 Vodafone Group lost out in a bidding war with Cingular Wireless over the acquisition of AT&T Wireless.

Vodafone Group has announced plans to consolidate its holdings both in Asia and Europe, including the acquisition of outstanding stakes in wireless subsidiaries in Japan, Portugal, and the Netherlands. It has sold its 74% stake in Mexico's Grupo Iusacell, held jointly with Verizon Communications, to Movilccess in a deal valued at $7.4 million. It also is selling its 21% stake in Indian regional operator RPG Cellular Services and has sold its operations in Sweden (Europolitan Vodafone) to Telenor.

HISTORY

Vodafone was formed in 1983 as a joint venture between Racal Electronics (a UK electronics firm) and Millicom (a US telecom company), and was granted one of two mobile phone licenses in the UK. It launched service in 1985 as a Racal subsidiary. Vodafone and Cellnet, the other licensee, were swamped with demand. In 1988 Racal offered 20% of Vodafone to the public; three years later the rest of the firm was spun off to become Vodafone Group.

Vodafone moved beyond the UK in the 1990s. By 1993 it had interests in mobile phone networks in Australia, Greece, Hong Kong, Malta, and Scandinavia.

For a time Vodafone and Cellnet, a joint venture of British Telecom (now BT Group) and Securicor, enjoyed a duopoly in the UK. Regulators elected not to impose price controls, and the pounds rolled in. But in 1993 a new wireless provider, One 2 One, launched a digital network in London. Vodafone countered that year with its own GSM (global system for mobile communications) digital network.

With increasing competition at home, Vodafone continued to expand in 1994. It launched or bought stakes in operations in Fiji, Germany, South Africa, and Uganda.

Digital service took on a larger role in Vodafone's UK business, and by 1997 some 85% of new subscribers were opting for digital GSM. In 1998 Vodafone sold its French service provider, Vodafone SA, and bought digital cellular carrier BellSouth New Zealand. It also expanded into Egypt by buying a minority stake in Misrfone, marking the largest British investment in Egypt since the Suez Canal.

In 1999 Vodafone prevailed in a brief bidding war with Bell Atlantic (now Verizon) to buy AirTouch Communications for about $60 billion. Vodafone's Chris Gent took over as CEO of the new company, Vodafone AirTouch. The prize for Vodafone: entry into the lucrative US market, plus the opportunity to consolidate minority interests in European wireless carriers.

Vodafone AirTouch moved to significantly boost its European footprint in 1999 by launching a $131 billion hostile takeover bid for Germany's Mannesmann. The company acquired

Mannesmann for about $180 billion in stock in 2000 and agreed to sell the conglomerate's engineering operations and its UK mobile phone unit, Orange. (France Telecom bought Orange for $37.5 billion later that year.) Vodafone AirTouch also announced plans for an IPO for Italian fixed-line carrier Infostrada, acquired in the Mannesmann deal, but the company instead agreed to sell Infostrada to Italian utility giant Enel. (The deal closed in 2001.)

Also in 2000 Vodafone AirTouch expanded its presence in the US, buying CommNet Cellular for $1.4 billion, then combining its US wireless operations with those of Bell Atlantic and GTE to form Verizon Wireless.

That year the company dropped AirTouch from its name and became Vodafone Group once again. It also continued its expansion push, investing in China Mobile (Hong Kong) and agreeing to buy Irish mobile phone operator Eircell (now Vodafone Ireland) in a deal that was completed in 2001. Also in 2001 Vodafone expanded its stakes in Japan Telecom Holdings (now Vodafone Holdings K.K.) and its J-Phone mobile phone operations (now Vodafone K.K.) by buying out rival BT Group; it also bought BT's remaining interest in Spain's Airtel.

In 2003 the company agreed to buy UK-based Project Telecom in a deal valued at about $250 million. It also reached an agreement to buy Singlepoint, the fast-growing UK independent service provider, from Caudwell Holdings, in a deal valued at $650 million.

EXECUTIVES

Chairman: Sir John R. H. Bond, age 64
Deputy Chairman: John G. S. Buchanan, age 63
CEO and Director: Arun Sarin, age 51, $2,207,473 pay
CEO, Europe and Deputy CEO: Vittorio A. Colao, age 45
Group CFO and Director: Andrew N. (Andy) Halford, age 46
Group Corporate Affairs Director: Simon Lewis, age 46
Group Human Resources Director: J. Brian Clark, age 56
Group Strategy and Business Integration Director: Alan Harper, age 48
Group General Counsel and Company Secretary: Stephen R. Scott, age 51
Director of External Relationships: Matthew Kirk, age 45
Group Treasurer; CFO, Vodafone Group Services Limited: Gerry Bacon
CEO, Central Europe, Middle East, Asia/Pacific, and Affiliates: Paul Donovan
CEO, New Businesses and Innovation and Director: Thomas Geitner, age 50, $679,000 pay (prior to title change)
CEO, Vodafone UK: Nicholas (Nick) Read
Chief Executive, Americas Region: Gavin Darby, age 50
Interim CEO, Europe; Chief Executive, Vodafone Germany: Friedrich P. (Fritz) Joussen, age 43
Chief Executive, Vodafone Italy: Pietro Guindani, age 48
Chief Executive, Vodafone Libertel N.V.: Guy Laurence
Executive Chairman and Chairman of the Board, Vodafone K.K.: Shiro Tsuda, age 61
CTO: Tim Miles, age 47
Chief Marketing Officer: Frank Rovekamp
Director of Corporate Responsibility: Charlotte Grezo
Manager, Other Vodafone Subsidiaries: Hans Kuropatwa, age 47
Head of Group Media Relations: Bobby Leach
Group Investor Relations Director: Charles Butterworth
Auditors: Deloitte & Touche LLP

LOCATIONS

HQ: Vodafone Group Plc
Vodafone House, The Connection, Newbury,
West Berkshire RG14 2FN, United Kingdom
Phone: +44-1635-33-251   **Fax:** +44-1635-45-713
Web: www.vodafone.com

2006 Sales

	% of total
Mobile telecommunications	
Europe	
Germany	19
UK	17
Italy	15
Spain	13
Other mobile	31
Other operations	
Germany	4
Other revenues	1
Total	**100**

PRODUCTS/OPERATIONS

2006 Sales

	$ mil.	% of total
Mobile telecommunications	39,609	95
Other operations	1,885	5
Adjustments	(175)	—
Total	**41,319**	**100**

2006 Sales

	% of total
Services	93
Equipment & other	7
Total	**100**

COMPETITORS

Belgacom	Orange
China Mobile	Swisscom
Cingular Wireless	Telefónica Móviles
Hutchison Whampoa	Telekom Austria
KPN	Telstra
NTT DoCoMo	T-Mobile International
O2	Virgin Mobile Telecoms

HISTORICAL FINANCIALS

Company Type: Public

Income Statement				FYE: March 31
	REVENUE ($ mil.)	NET INCOME ($ mil.)	NET PROFIT MARGIN	EMPLOYEES
3/06	41,319	(23,081)	—	60,000
3/05	78,018	(25,896)	—	57,378
3/04	61,285	(14,842)	—	60,109
3/03	47,962	(14,298)	—	66,667
3/02	32,554	(23,780)	—	70,800
Annual Growth	6.1%	—	—	(4.1%)

2006 Year-End Financials

Debt ratio: 19.3%   Current ratio: 0.49
Return on equity: —   Long-term debt ($ mil.): 29,133
Cash ($ mil.): 5,024

Net Income History

NYSE: VOD

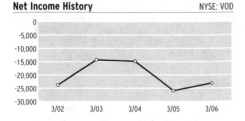

Volkswagen

With cars named for Scottish sports and cutesy insects, Volkswagen (VW) leads the Continent as Europe's #1 carmaker. Along with Golf and the New Beetle, VW's annual production of 5 million cars, trucks, and vans includes such models as Passat, Jetta, Rabbit, and Fox. VW also owns a garage full of luxury carmakers — AUDI, Lamborghini, Bentley, and Bugatti. Other makes include SEAT (family cars, Spain) and SKODA (family cars, the Czech Republic). VW operates plants in Africa, the Americas, the Asia/Pacific region, and Europe. It also holds 34% of the voting rights in Swedish truck maker Scania. VW also offers consumer financing.

The company has admitted it suffers from a triple threat of high costs, products with inflated sticker prices, and flagging quality. To turn the company around former DaimlerChrysler master hatchet-man Wolfgang Bernhard (now head of the VW brand group) plans to squeeze $8.4 billion in savings from VW's operations by 2010.

VW's global markets are suffering. Sales in the US are falling through the floor while its new models are selling sluggishly in Europe. Meanwhile its once dominant position in China is seriously threatened by General Motors. VW's 2005 losses in the US were more than $1 billion. In fact, it lost more money per car than GM — a dubious distinction indeed.

To win, VW has to cut wage costs, trim jobs, and cut way back on its current overcapacity of 30%. Early in 2006 Volkswagen announced it planned to cut 20,000 jobs at its Volkswagen brand over the course of three years.

About half of those 20,000 workers are employed making components. VW makes about 40% of its components, more than any other European competitor. VW is talking with European labor unions regarding the fate of those plants which include selling them off, operating them as joint ventures with parts suppliers, or closing them outright.

In late 2006 VW bought a 15% stake in German truckmaker MAN AG as a way of expressing its desire for a three-way truck alliance between VW, MAN, and Scania.

The German state of Lower Saxony controls about 14% of Volkswagen (or 18% of the voting rights). Fellow German automaker Porsche has taken about a 27% stake in VW (and has plans to increase it stake to nearly 30%).

Late in 2006 VW announced VW boss Bernd Pischetsrieder would step down at the end of that year and would be replaced by Audi chief Martin Winterkorn. The management shake-up was attributed to an internal power struggle between supervisory board chairman Ferdinand Piëch and Pischetsrieder.

HISTORY

Since the early 1920s auto engineer Ferdinand Porsche (whose son later founded the Porsche car company) had wanted to make a small car for the masses. He found no backers until he met Adolf Hitler in 1934. Hitler formed the Gesellschaft zur Vorbereitung des Volkswagens (Company for the Development of People's Cars) in 1937 and built a factory in Wolfsburg, Germany.

No cars were delivered during WWII, as the company produced military vehicles using slave labor of Jews and Russian prisoners of war.

Following WWII British occupation forces oversaw the rebuilding of the bomb-damaged plant and initial production of the odd-looking "people's car" (1945). The British appointed Heinz Nordhoff to manage Volkswagen (1948) and then turned the company over to the German government (1949).

In the 1950s VW launched the Microbus and built foreign plants. Although US sales began slowly, by the end of the decade acceptance of the little car had increased. Advertising that coined the name "Beetle" helped carve VW's niche in the US.

VW sold stock to the German public in 1960. In 1966 it purchased Auto Union (AUDI) from Daimler-Benz. The Beetle became a counterculture symbol in the 1960s, and US sales took off. By the time of Nordhoff's death in 1968, the Beetle had become the best-selling car in history.

In the 1970s the Beetle was discontinued in every country except Mexico. VW lost heavily during the model-changeover period.

VW agreed to several deals in the 1980s, including a car venture in China (1984), the purchase of 75% of SEAT (1986; it bought the rest in 1990), and the merger of its suddenly faltering Brazilian unit with Ford's ailing Argentine operations to form Autolatina (1987). In 1990 the company began building China's largest auto plant and acquired a 70% stake in Czech auto company Skoda. After suffering a $1.1 billion loss, the company put Ferdinand Piech in the driver's seat in 1993. Under his leadership the company cut costs and boosted sales by resuscitating the SEAT and Skoda brands and launching a bigger, more luxurious Passat sedan in 1997.

VW acquired Rolls-Royce Motor Cars, Vickers' Cosworth auto engines subsidiary, Italian sportscar maker Bugatti, and Italy's Automobili Lamborghini — all in 1998. Although less luxurious than VW's other pursuits, the New Beetle helped boost US sales that year. Also in 1998 VW established a $12 million fund to compensate the surviving 2,000 concentration-camp inmates forced to work as slave labor during WWII. However, the company was hit with a class-action lawsuit filed on behalf of Holocaust survivors anyway.

In 1999 chairman Ferdinand Piëch announced an end to VW's acquisition binge, saying that growth would be driven from within; VW announced it would pour $31.5 billion into modernizing its factories through 2004. VW hoped to tap the market in China after getting approval in 1999 to sell a newly developed minicar there. That year it announced plans to invest $1 billion in its Mexico plant over the next five years.

Volkswagen expanded into heavy commercial vehicles in 2000 by purchasing a 34% stake in Swedish truck maker Scania (from holding company Investor). That year it also bought the 30% of Skoda that it didn't already own. Anticipating China's entry into the World Trade Organization, Volkswagen announced in 2001 that it would invest $1.7 billion in China and the Asia/Pacific region over the next five years. Later in the year — and half a world away — 12,500 workers at the company's Mexico plant went on strike for 19 days over a pay dispute.

In April 2002 former BMW head Bernd Pischetsrieder succeeded Piëch as CEO. The following year, in July, the final classic Beetle rolled off the VW assembly line in Mexico. The final Beetle concluded a 70-year run of constant production. Also in 2003, BMW took control of the Rolls-Royce brand from Volkswagen.

EXECUTIVES

Chairman of the Supervisory Board:
Ferdinand K. Piëch, age 67
Deputy Chairman of the Supervisory Board:
Jürgen Peters, age 60
COO: Matthias Seidl
Chairman of the Board of Management:
Martin Winterkorn, age 59
**Member of the Board of Management, Finance and
Controlling:** Hans Dieter Pötsch, age 53
**Member of the Board of Management, Labor and
Human Resources:** Horst Günter Neumann
**Member of the Board of Management, Procurement
and South America:** Francisco Javier Garcia Sanz
**Member of the Board of Management, Product
Manufacturing:** Dirk Große-Loheide, age 42
**Member of the Board of Management, Controlling and
Finance:** Frank Fiedler, age 43
**Member of the Board of Management, Sales and
Marketing:** Harald Schomburg, age 46
Chairman, Automobili Lamborghini: Werner Mischke
President and CEO, VW Brazil: Thomas Schmall, age 42
General Representative; President, VW South America:
Viktor Klima, age 59
**Member of the Board of Management; Chairman of the
Board of Management, Commerical Vehicles Brand:**
Stephan Schaller, age 49
**Member of the Board of Management, Finance and
Corporate Strategy:** Carsten Isensee, age 46
Chairman, Volkswagen Financial Services:
Burkhard Breiing
Chairman of the Executive Committee, SEAT:
Andreas Schleef
CEO, gedas AG: Axel Knobe, age 57
CEO, VW China: Winfried Vahland
Managing Director, South Africa: David Powels, age 44
Director, Design: Murat Günak
Director, Product Strategy: Stefan Liske
Head, Product Development: Wolfgang Schreiber,
age 48
Head, Human Resources: Jochen Schumm, age 57
Auditors: PwC Deutsche Revision AG

LOCATIONS

HQ: Volkswagen AG
Brieffach 1848-2, 38436 Wolfsburg, Germany
Phone: +49-53-61-90   **Fax:** +49-53-61-92-82-82
US HQ: 3800 Hamlin Rd., Auburn Hills, MI 48326
US Phone: 248-340-5000
Web: www.volkswagen.de

2005 Sales

	$ mil.	% of total
Europe		
Germany	31,143.6	28
Other countries	50,998.3	45
North America	16,253.3	14
Asia/Oceania	6,230.6	6
South America	5,869.4	5
Africa	2,330.7	2
Total	**112,825.9**	**100**

PRODUCTS/OPERATIONS

2005 Sales

	$ mil.	% of total
Automotive	101,084.7	90
Financial services	11,363.4	10
Other	377.8	—
Total	**112,825.9**	**100**

2005 Sales

	$ mil.	% of total
Volkswagen Brand Group	58,770.9	52
Audi Brand Group	33,672.0	30
Commercial vehicles	8,641.8	8
Financial services	11,363.4	10
Other	377.8	—
Total	**112,825.9**	**100**

Selected Makes and Models

AUDI
 A3
 A4
 A6
 A8
 Q7
 RS
 S4
 TT Coupe
 TT Roadster
Bentley
 Arnage
 Continental Flying Spur
 Continental GT Coupe
Bugatti
 EB 110
Lamborghini
 Gallardo
 Gallardo Spyder
 Murcièlago LP640
 Murcièlago Roadster
SEAT
 Alhambra
 Altea
 Cordoba
 FR Series
 Ibiza
 Leon
 Toledo
Skoda
 Fabia
 Fabia Pratik
 Octavia
 Superb
Volkswagen Passenger Vehicles
 Fox
 Gol
 Golf
 Lupo
 Multivan
 New Beetle
 New Beetle Cabriolet
 Jetta/Bora
 Parati
 Passat/Santana
 Phaeton
 Polo
 Sharan
 Touareg
 Touran

COMPETITORS

BMW	Mazda
DaimlerChrysler	Nissan
Fiat	Peugeot
Ford	Porsche
Fuji Heavy Industries	Renault
General Motors	Saab Automobile
Honda	Suzuki Motor
Isuzu	Toyota

HISTORICAL FINANCIALS

Company Type: Public

Income Statement

FYE: December 31

	REVENUE ($ mil.)	NET INCOME ($ mil.)	NET PROFIT MARGIN	EMPLOYEES
12/05	112,826	1,326	1.2%	344,902
12/04	121,346	923	0.8%	342,502
12/03	109,394	1,374	1.3%	336,843
12/02	91,130	2,708	3.0%	324,892
12/01	78,429	2,582	3.3%	322,070
Annual Growth	9.5%	(15.3%)	—	1.7%

2005 Year-End Financials

Debt ratio: 131.4%   Current ratio: 1.09
Return on equity: 4.4%   Long-term debt ($ mil.): 36,730
Cash ($ mil.): 9,431

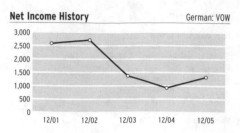

Net Income History   German: VOW

Volvo

Despite the fact that the name "Volvo" conjures up more visions of soccer moms than of burly truck drivers, AB Volvo has parked its car business. The company is now a leading maker of trucks, buses, and construction equipment as well as marine (Volvo Penta), aircraft (Volvo Aero), and industrial engines. The company's most widely known business — auto making — has been sold to US-based carmaker Ford Motor Company. The sale enabled Volvo to focus on its remaining units, particularly trucks. Its other interests include full control of the famous Mack Trucks brand in North America and Renault Trucks in Europe.

Volvo is enjoying the benefits of a global cyclical upswing in worldwide demand for commercial vehicles — particularly heavy-duty trucks. The company's construction equipment and aerospace components businesses also enjoyed record profits in 2005, and Volvo's bus business posted a second year of modest profitability after a few tough years. To boost its presence in Asia, in early 2006 Volvo acquired a 13% stake in Nissan Diesel Motor for a reported $195 million. Later that year Volvo bought another 6% of Nissan Diesel Motor from Nissan Motor, bringing its stake up to 19%. Also in 2006, the company entered talks with Nissan and the Chinese government to purchase Nissan's 50% stake in Dongfeng Motor Co., Ltd. — China's largest maker of commercial trucks.

In response to new emissions standards that go into effect in late 2006 in Europe and the beginning of 2007 in North America, Volvo has been sprucing up the operations of its Mack and Renault brands. The move is in step with Volvo's other truck operations which also have been revamped to comply with the new standards.

Volvo expects European demand for heavy-duty trucks to continue its upward trend in response to rapid growth in Eastern Europe, and the North American market is expected to grow as aging fleets are updated. Fleet replacement ahead of the new emissions stardards is also driving sales.

Early in 2006 Volvo announced it had developed at hybrid heavy-duty truck engine that will increase fuel efficiency by up to 35%. Trucks outfitted with the new technology will be available starting in 2009.

HISTORY

Swedish ball bearing maker SKF formed Volvo (Latin for "I roll") as a subsidiary in 1915. It began building cars in 1926, trucks in 1928, and bus chassis in 1932 in Gothenburg. Sweden's winters and icy roads made the company keenly attentive to engineering and safety. Volvo bought an engine maker in 1931. In 1935 Volvo became an independent company led by Assar Gabrielsson and Gustaf Larson.

Sweden's neutrality during WWII allowed Volvo to grow and move into component manufacturing and tractor production. Output in 1949 exceeded 100,000 units, 80% of which were sold in Sweden. The purchase of Bolinder-Munktell (farm machinery, diesel engines; Sweden; 1950) enhanced Volvo's position in the Swedish tractor market. Volvo introduced turbocharged diesel truck engines and windshield defrosters and washers in the 1950s. By 1956 car production had outstripped truck and bus output.

Aware that it was too small to compete in global markets, Volvo diversified (energy, industrial products, food, finance, and trading). Volvo increased its market share by purchasing several trucking and construction equipment companies that included White Motors' truck unit (US, 1981) and Leyland Bus (UK, 1986). In the 1980s Volvo acquired drug and biotechnology concern Pharmacia (now Pfizer) and Custos (investments, Sweden). The company consolidated its food and drug units with state-controlled holding company Procordia in 1990.

At that time, however, Volvo was facing stagnant sales. It embarked on the largest industrial undertaking in Swedish history, spending more than $2 billion to modernize plants and develop a series of high-performance family sedans, which it introduced in 1991. Still, high costs and persistent recession in Europe kept the company in the red during the early 1990s.

Adding to its troubles, there was public outcry against a planned merger with French automaker Renault. The plan was abandoned in 1993, and the company sold its drug and consumer product interests (which had landed back in Volvo's lap when the government divested Procordia in 1993). These sales brought Volvo back into the black.

In 1997 Volvo sold its 11% stake in Renault left over from the abandoned merger. The next year the company strengthened its line of excavators and its Far Eastern presence by buying Samsung Heavy Industries' construction equipment unit. Volvo also bought Mexico's bus maker Mexicana de Autobuses and GM's share in Volvo GM Heavy Truck (now Volvo Trucks North America).

Anticipating a lower demand for cars, Volvo closed an assembly plant in Canada in 1998, and in 1999 Volvo acquired a 13% stake (later upped to 25%) in rival truck maker Scania. To pay for its new focus on making heavy trucks, Volvo sold its auto brand and manufacturing operations in Sweden, Belgium, and the Netherlands to Ford Motor Company for $6.45 billion in 1999. Volvo then agreed to take a 20% stake in the truck and construction equipment operations of Japan's Mitsubishi Motors.

In 2000 Volvo boosted its stake in Scania to 46%, but its hope of acquiring a majority interest died when the EU rejected the $7.53 billion deal. Volvo then turned to France's Renault, and bought the company's Mack truck unit in exchange for a 15% stake in Volvo. Later in the year Volvo entered into talks with Volkswagen AG concerning the possible sale of Volvo's stake in Scania. The EU later thwarted the proposed deal, citing anti-competitive issues.

DaimlerChrysler bought out Volvo's 3.3% stake in Mitsubishi in 2001. Volvo's Renault Trucks subsidiary inked a technology transfer deal in 2002 with Chinese truckmaker Dongfeng Motors. The agreement cleared the road for Dongfeng to equip its heavy- and medium-duty trucks with Renault engines. In 2003 Volvo became the first Western truck manufacturer to produce vehicles under its own name in Russia. The following year Volvo opened a new truck factory in China with its partner China National Heavy Truck Corporation; the factory can produce up to 1,200 trucks per year. Also in 2004 Volvo Construction Equipment (Volvo CE) sold its line of compact motor graders to Champion LLC, a company headed up by Gary Abernathy, a former manager at Volvo CE. Volvo acquired the remaining 50% of bus manufacturer Prévost Car from Henlys Group in late 2004.

EXECUTIVES

Chairman: Finn Johnsson, age 60
President, CEO, and Director: Leif Johansson, age 55
Deputy CEO, EVP, China: Jorma Halonen, age 58
SVP and CFO: Pär Östberg, age 44
SVP: Per Löjdquist, age 57
SVP, Secretary, General Counsel, and Director: Eva Persson, age 53
SVP, Strategic Planning and Business Development: Ricard Fritz
SVP, Human Resources: Stefan Johnsson, age 47
President, Mack Trucks: Paul L. Vikner, age 57
President, Renault Trucks: Stefano Chmielewski, age 54
President, Volvo Bus: Håkan Karlsson, age 45
SVP, Public and Environmental Affairs: Jan-Eric Sundgren, age 55
President, Volvo Aero: Olaf Persson, age 41
President, Volvo Construction Equipment: Tony Helsham, age 52
President, Volvo Financial Service: Salvatore L. Mauro, age 46
President, Volvo Trucks: Staffan Jufors, age 55
President, Volvo Penta: Göran Gummeson, age 59
President, Volvo Powertrain: Lars-Göran Moberg, age 63
President, Volvo Trucks North America: Peter Karlsten
Head, Investor Relations: Christer Johansson
Corporate Communications, North America: Marjorie A. Meyers
Auditors: PricewaterhouseCoopers AB

LOCATIONS

HQ: AB Volvo
S-405 08 Gothenburg, Sweden
Phone: +46-31-660000   **Fax:** +46-31-54-57-72
US HQ: 570 Lexington Ave., 20th Fl.,
New York, NY 10022
US Phone: 212-418-7400   **US Fax:** 212-418-7435
Web: www.volvo.com

2005 Sales

	% of total
Europe	
Western Europe	47
Eastern Europe	5
North America	29
Asia	9
South America	5
Other regions	5
Total	**100**

PRODUCTS/OPERATIONS

2005 Sales

	% of total
Trucks	65
Construction equipment	14
Buses	7
Volvo Penta	4
Financial services	3
Volvo Aero	3
Other	4
Total	**100**

Selected Products and Brand Names

Trucks
  Mack
  Renault
  Volvo
Construction Equipment
  Articulated haulers
  Backhoe loaders
  Excavators
  Motor graders
  Skid steer loaders
  Wheel loaders
Buses
  City buses
  Coaches
  Intercity buses
Financial Services
  Customer financing
  Insurance
Volvo Penta
  Marine engines (luxury and work boats)
  Industrial engines (forklifts and construction equipment)
Volvo Aero
  Aircraft engines
  Engine components

COMPETITORS

Cummins
Cummins Westport
DaimlerChrysler
Deere
Fiat
Freightliner
Fuji Heavy Industries
General Motors
Hino Motors
Honda
International Truck and Engine
Isuzu
MAN
Mitsubishi Motors
Navistar
Nissan
Nissan Diesel
Oshkosh Truck
PACCAR
Penske
Rolls-Royce
Scania
Suzuki Motor
Terex
Toyota
Yamaha Motor

HISTORICAL FINANCIALS

Company Type: Public

Income Statement

FYE: December 31

	REVENUE ($ mil.)	NET INCOME ($ mil.)	NET PROFIT MARGIN	EMPLOYEES
12/05	30,238	1,433	4.7%	81,078
12/04	31,855	2,183	6.9%	78,196
12/03	25,313	550	2.2%	75,740
12/02	21,301	(717)	—	71,160
12/01	17,915	(377)	—	70,921
Annual Growth	**14.0%**	**—**	**—**	**3.4%**

2005 Year-End Financials

Debt ratio: 54.8%   Current ratio: 1.30
Return on equity: 13.6%   Long-term debt ($ mil.): 5,475
Cash ($ mil.): 4,644

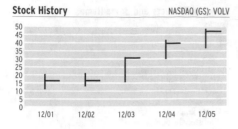

Stock History   NASDAQ (GS): VOLV

	STOCK PRICE ($) FY Close	P/E High/Low		PER SHARE ($) Earnings	Dividends
12/05	47.09	—	—	—	1.50
12/04	39.59	8	6	5.21	2.86
12/03	30.62	—	—	—	0.65
12/02	16.55	—	—	—	0.55
12/01	16.40	—	—	—	0.54
Annual Growth	30.2%	—	—	—	29.1%

Wal-Mart de México

Just call it Wal-Mex. Formerly known as Cifra, Wal-Mart de México is the numero uno retailer in Mexico, with 780-plus stores and restaurants. These include Bodega food and general merchandise discount stores and Superama supermarkets; Suburbia apparel stores; and Vips and El Portón restaurants. It also runs about 175 Wal-Mart Supercenters and SAM'S CLUB warehouses, which generate about 55% of the company's sales. Its stores are located in 100 cities throughout Mexico, although more than half are in and around Mexico City. Wal-Mart Stores first grabbed a stake in the company when it combined its Mexican stores (a joint venture with Cifra) with Cifra's stores. Wal-Mart Stores owns about 62% of Wal-Mart de México.

Wal-Mart has shaken up Mexico's grocery and department store sectors since entering the country in the 1990s. Now the country's largest supermarket operator and private employer, Wal-Mart de México operates more stores than any of its parent company's other international divisions and contributes more than 25% of its international sales.

But success has sparked a backlash; Mexican antitrust regulators launched an investigation into Wal-Mex's purchasing practices in May 2002, and the retailer has quit the country's supermarket and department store trade group because of the group's opposition to comparative advertising. Three of Mexico's largest supermarket chains — Grupo Gigante, Soriana, and Comerci — have formed purchasing and other alliances to better compete with Wal-Mex, which accounts for about 40% of the retail market in Mexico. Nevertheless, the country's top mass merchandiser spent about $635 million to open about 90 stores and restaurants in 2005, including about 40 Bodega Aurrera stores in more rural areas. Wal-Mex is opening stores in Monterrey, the country's most affluent city, and throughout northern Mexico, where its Texas rival H. E. Butt Grocery is well established.

A newly completed Bodega Aurrera store near the site of the ancient ruins of Teotihuacan, 25 miles northeast of Mexico City, Mexico has attracted criticism and support from local residents.

In its bid to become the ultimate supplier to small business, SAM'S CLUBs in Mexico have begun selling fully-stocked convenience store stands to independent entrepreneurs. The "Mi Tiendita" (Spanish for "My Little Store") package includes shelving, some 200 products, a cash register, and even training for would-be convenience store operators. Wal-Mex is also testing a new smaller format, called MercaMas, designed for poorer neighborhoods on the fringes of big cities.

HISTORY

Spanish-born Jerónimo Arango Arias studied art and literature at several American universities without graduating. In his twenties he wandered around Spain, Mexico, and the US. He struck upon an idea after seeing a crowd waiting in line at the E. J. Korvette discount department store in New York City. Jerónimo called his two brothers, Plácido and Manuel, and convinced them to join him in a new business venture.

Borrowing about $250,000 from their father, a Spanish immigrant to Mexico successful in textiles, the three brothers opened their first Aurrerá Bolivar discount store in downtown Mexico City in 1958. Offering goods and clothing well below manufacturers' list prices, the store was an immediate hit with consumers but encountered hostility from competing Mexico City retailers. When local retailers threatened to boycott the Arangos' suppliers, the company turned to suppliers in Guadalajara and Monterrey.

In 1965 the Arango brothers formed a joint venture with Jewel Cos. of Chicago to open new Aurrerá stores. Jewel bought a 49% interest in the business a year later. Plácido and Manuel left the business with their portion of the money, but Jerónimo stayed as head of the company, taking it public in 1976.

By 1981 almost a third of Jewel's earnings came from its operations in Mexico. But the next year the peso crashed, obliterating its earnings there. American Stores took over Jewel in 1984, and Jerónimo bought back Jewel's stake in the company (which was renamed Cifra that year).

With the Mexican economy staggering from the peso devaluation, weak oil markets, and a huge debt crisis, Jerónimo was taking a major risk. Although no new stores were opened, none were closed. Employees were expected to work longer, and those who left were not replaced. With Mexico's middle class hit hard, Jerónimo emphasized the Bodega Aurrerá no-frills warehouses, which discounted all kinds of nonperishable merchandise, from canned chili to VCRs.

Cifra and Wal-Mart Stores formed a joint venture in 1991 to open Club Aurrerá membership clubs similar to Sam's Club outlets. The two companies expanded the venture the next year to include the development of Sam's Club and Wal-Mart Supercenters in Mexico.

Remodeling began on Cifra's stores in 1992. The work was completed two years later, and the company was poised to take advantage of Mexico's much-improved economy.

However, devaluation struck again late in 1994. The resulting contraction of credit and rise in prices hit Mexican consumers hard, and Cifra's 1995 sales declined 15%. But again it kept on as many employees as possible, transferring them to new stores that had been in development. Despite the hard times, Cifra opened 27 new stores (including 15 restaurants).

Wal-Mart consolidated its joint venture into Cifra in 1997 in exchange for about 34% of that company; Wal-Mart later raised its stake to 51%.

In early 2000 Cifra was renamed Wal-Mart de México. Shortly thereafter, Wal-Mart upped its stake in Wal-Mart de México to about 61%.

In November 2002 Eduardo Castro-Wright was promoted from COO to CEO of Wal-Mart de México, succeeding Cesareo Fernandez who retained the chairman's title.

In March 2003 Mexico's Federal Competition Commission closed an investigation of Wal-Mex's purchasing practices, citing a lack of evidence that the retailer violated competition laws. Overall in 2003, Wal-Mex entered nine new cities in Mexico and added 46 new outlets.

In January 2005 Fernandez stepped down as chairman and was succeeded by Ernesto Vega. A month later, CEO Eduardo Castro-Wright left Wal-Mex to become executive vice president and COO of the Wal-Mart Stores Division in the US. He was succeeded by Eduardo Solorzano, formerly COO of Wal-Mex. Also that year Wal-Mex acquired the Mexican assets of French retailer Carrefour. Carrefour, which operated 29 hypermarkets in Mexico, restructured its operations and left the Mexican market.

EXECUTIVES

Chairman: Ernesto Vega
President, CEO, and Director: Eduardo Solorzano, age 48
EVP and CFO, Director: Rafael Matute, age 45
EVP and COO: Scot Rank, age 45
EVP, People Division, Logistics and Loss Prevention: José Angel Gallegos, age 55
SVP, General Counsel: Jose Luis Rodriguezmacedo, age 49
SVP, Real Estate: Xavier del Río, age 58
VP, Bodega Aurrera: Jose Luis Torres, age 47
VP, Corporate Affairs: Raul Argüelles, age 42
VP, Financial Services: Herbert Pelka, age 51
VP, Food and Consumables, Self-Service Division: David Dager, age 47
SVP, Self-Service Division: Joaquin Gonzalez-Varela, age 40
VP, Fresh Merchandising, Self-Service Division: Francisco Casado, age 53
VP, General Merchandise and Apparel, Self-Service Division: Victoria Alvarez, age 54
VP, Internal Audit: Eduardo Juárez, age 57
VP, Logistics: Rodolfo Von Der Meden, age 42
VP, Marketing: Demetrio Ruiz, age 45
VP, People Division: Ruben Camarena, age 49
VP, SAM'S CLUB: Simona Visztova, age 38
VP, Specialty Divisions, Self-Service Division: Alberto Ebrard, age 44
VP, Suburbia: Alejandro Bustos, age 54
VP, Superama: Mario Sanchez, age 47
VP, Systems: Maria del Carmen Valencia, age 38
VP, Vips: Gian Carlo Nucci, age 36
VP, Wal-Mart Supercenter: Miguel Baltazar, age 53
Director, Finance: Federico Casillas
Manager, Investor Relations: Mariana Rodríguez
Auditors: Mancera, S.C.

LOCATIONS

HQ: Wal-Mart de México, S.A. de C.V.
    Blvd. Manuel Avila Camacho 647, Delegación
    Miguel Hidalgo, 11220 México, D.F., Mexico
Phone: +52-55-5283-0100   **Fax:** +52-55-5387-9240
Web: www.walmartmexico.com.mx

Wal-Mart de México operates 780-plus stores and restaurants in 103 cities throughout Mexico.

PRODUCTS/OPERATIONS

2005 Stores

	No.
Restaurants	298
Bodega Aurrera	203
Wal-Mart Supercenters	105
SAM'S CLUB	69
Superama	55
Suburbia	53
Total	**783**

2005 Sales

	% of total
Bodega Aurrera	31
SAM'S CLUB	28
Wal-Mart Supercenters	27
Superama	6
Suburbia	5
Restaurants	3
Total	**100**

Selected Stores

Bodega Aurrera (large, limited assortment discount warehouses)
El Portón (restaurants)
SAM'S CLUB (membership-only warehouse outlets)
Suburbia (apparel stores)
Superama (supermarkets)
Vips (restaurants)
Wal-Mart Supercenters (discount hypermarkets)

COMPETITORS

Chedraui
Comerci
Costco Wholesale
El Puerto de Liverpool
Gigante
Grupo Carso
H-E-B
Safeway
Sanborns
Soriana

HISTORICAL FINANCIALS

Company Type: Public

Income Statement

FYE: December 31

	REVENUE ($ mil.)	NET INCOME ($ mil.)	NET PROFIT MARGIN	EMPLOYEES
12/05	15,315	879	5.7%	124,295
12/04	12,549	700	5.6%	109,057
12/03	10,729	486	4.5%	99,881
12/02	10,097	472	4.7%	92,708
12/01	9,642	457	4.7%	84,607
Annual Growth	12.3%	17.8%	—	10.1%

2005 Year-End Financials

Debt ratio: 0.0%
Return on equity: 19.5%
Cash ($ mil.): 1,314
Current ratio: 1.17
Long-term debt ($ mil.): 0

Net Income History

OTC: WMMVY

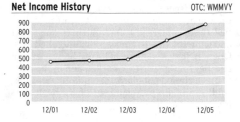

Waterford Wedgwood

Waterford Wedgwood is (gently) toasting its position as the world's premier maker of luxury crystal and fine china. The company's Waterford Crystal Group produces handcrafted crystal stemware, lamps, and giftware under the Waterford and Stuart brands. The Wedgwood Group makes fine bone china giftware and tableware under the Wedgwood brand. The company owns German ceramics makers Rosenthal. In 2004 it sold its US premium cookware maker, All-Clad, to SEB to reduce debt. Chairman Tony O'Reilly and his brother-in-law, deputy chairman Peter Goulandris, increased their control of the company in 2005 to about 51% of the company.

Not every company has a great-great-great-great-grandson of its founder sitting on the board of directors. And although Waterford Wedgwood has just that in Alan Wedgwood, it's former Heinz ketchup king Tony O'Reilly who has given the firm its luster.

O'Reilly helped turn the company around after years of losses in the late 1980s and early 1990s. He outsourced product lines to cheaper manufacturers and licensed the company's popular brands to makers of products such as linens and writing instruments. Most of Waterford Wedgwood's sales are through department stores and specialty retailers.

In August 2004 New York State Attorney General Eliot Spitzer alleged that The May Department Stores and Federated Department Stores conspired to pressure Waterford Wedgwood into backing out as the planned anchors of Bed Bath & Beyond's new tableware division. Though the four companies admitted no wrongdoing in the antitrust case, they paid a total of $2.9 million in civil penalties.

The company's shares tumbled in value in the first quarter of 2005 when CFO Paul D'Alton resigned after less than a year of duty. A few weeks later, the company was buoyed by the announcement of Waterford Wedgwood's restructuring plan, which included closure of its Waterford Crystal plant in Dungarvan, Ireland and its Rosenthal division in Germany. In total approximately 1,800 jobs were lost in the process.

Later in 2005 Waterford Wedgwood was delisted from the Nasdaq stock exchange because it was trading at such a low price and level for an extended period of time.

To boost profitability the company is selling under-utilized assets; mostly property. To that end, Waterford Wedgwood is exploring the development of its 36-acre site in Kilbarry, Co. Waterford by real estate developer Ballymore Homes.

HISTORY

Waterford Wedgwood traces its roots back to two companies more than 200 years old. Josiah Wedgwood, an 18th-century English artisan, got his start as a potter bridging the gap between wooden bowls for the common people and fine porcelain for the rich. He developed a method of making ordinary clay look like porcelain and later developed fine ceramic ware incorporating neoclassical figures applied in a white cameo relief on a colored background — which became the signature product of Josiah Wedgwood and Sons.

Wedgwood operated as a family business for the next 176 years and may have indirectly contributed to Darwin's theory of evolution. Charles Darwin married into the Wedgwood clan and thus gained the financial security to pursue his scientific research on a full-time basis. Wedgwood did not have a non-family director on its board until 1945.

Around the same time that Wedgwood was gaining recognition in England, Quakers George and William Penrose founded a crystal glassmaking business in 1783 in the Irish port city of Waterford. The two companies shared a reputation for quality and for exquisite craftsmanship. However, they both experienced the vagaries of fashion and financial difficulties.

Waterford went bankrupt in 1851 and remained inactive until its revival, aided by WWII refugees. With this new base of skilled artisans from Central Europe, it started operations again in 1947. The company quickly re-established the Waterford reputation. Profits rose steadily in the 1970s and early 1980s, with the US emerging as Waterford's primary market. In addition to consumer products, Waterford glassware has been used for the Boston Marathon Trophy and to hold the late President Reagan's jelly beans.

In 1986 Waterford borrowed heavily to acquire Wedgwood for $360 million, a move designed to allow both companies to cut costs by sharing marketing operations and by streamlining production. Waterford Wedgwood was still struggling in 1990 when Tony O'Reilly (the Irish-born then-chairman of US-based H.J. Heinz) and Morgan Stanley bought a 30% stake worth $125 million. That year the company launched its first new brand of crystal in 200 years, Marquis by Waterford. The line was a success, and by 1993 Waterford Wedgwood had returned to profitability.

The company acquired Stuart & Sons, the leading UK maker of premium crystal, in 1995 and introduced a best-seller, its Cornucopia fine bone china pattern. In 1996 Waterford Wedgwood also launched new licensed gift lines — pens and linens — and formed a strategic alliance with German luxury ceramics maker Rosenthal, in which it owned a 26% stake. In 1997, in a departure from tradition, the company introduced a line of china under the Waterford name.

In 1998 Waterford Wedgwood increased its stake in Rosenthal to nearly 85%, making it the world's #1 producer of fine porcelain, and cut 1,500 jobs to reduce costs. In 1999 the company purchased US cookware-maker All-Clad for $110 million. Also in 1999 the company bought a 15% stake in ceramics maker Royal Doulton. Expanding its European presence, the company acquired German ceramics brand Hutschenreuther in August 2000 (and integrated operations into the Rosenthal business in 2003). In 2002 Waterford Wedgwood bought another 15% of Rosenthal, increasing its stake to nearly 90%, and also acquired Ashling Corporation, a maker of luxury linens. The same year Waterford Wedgwood laid off nearly 15% of its workforce amid a worldwide economic downturn and diminished interest in luxury goods.

In 2003 Waterford Wedgwood acquired the Spring premium cookware business (Switzerland) and Cashs, a catalog and mail-order business (Ireland). Also that year the company cut more than 1,000 jobs by closing two British factories and moving production to China. In addition, Waterford Wedgwood upped its stake in Royal Doulton to nearly 22%. The next year Wedgwood sold its US premium cookware maker, All-Clad, to SEB for $250 million.

EXECUTIVES

Chairman: Sir Anthony O'Reilly, age 70
Deputy Chairman; Chairman, Waterford Wedgwood UK:
 Peter John Goulandris, age 58
CEO and Director: Peter B. Cameron, age 59
CFO, Company Secretary, and Director:
 Patrick J. Dowling, age 58
Creative Director: Georgina Godley
**Director; CEO, Waterford; CEO, Waterford Crystal
 Limited:** John Foley, age 55
Director; CEO, Rosenthal AG: Ottmar C. Küsel, age 54
**Chief Marketing and Brand Officer; President,
 Rosenthal USA:** Lou Scala
CEO, Wedgwood: Moira Gavin, age 48
Managing Director, Wedgwood Europe: Nick Robinson
Auditors: PricewaterhouseCoopers

LOCATIONS

HQ: Waterford Wedgwood plc
 Embassy House, Herbert Park Ln., Ballsbridge,
 Dublin 4, Ireland
Phone: +353-1-607-0166 **Fax:** +353-1-607-0177
US HQ: 1330 Campus Pkwy., Wall, NJ 07719
US Phone: 732-938-5800 **US Fax:** 732-378-2120
Web: www.waterfordwedgwood.com

2006 Sales

	% of total
Europe	
UK	17
Other	28
North America	40
Asia/Pacific	10
Other regions	5
Total	**100**

PRODUCTS/OPERATIONS

2006 Sales

	% of total
Ceramics	68
Crystal	27
Linens & premium cookware	5
Total	**100**

Selected Operations

Rosenthal
 Hutschenreuther
 Rosenthal Studio-Line
 Thomas — The Trend Factory
Waterford Crystal
 Marquis by Waterford Crystal
 Stuart Crystal
 Waterford
Wedgwood
 Coalport
 Franciscan
 Johnson Brothers
 Masons Ironstone

COMPETITORS

ARC International	Noritake
Belleek	Oneida
Brown-Forman	Pagnossin
Carlsberg	Richard-Ginori 1735
CRISAL	Royal Doulton
Fitz and Floyd, Silvestri	Société du Louvre
Guy Degrenne	Syratech
Homer Laughlin	Taittinger
Lancaster Colony	Tiffany
Lenox Group	Villeroy & Boch
Newell Rubbermaid	WKI Holding

HISTORICAL FINANCIALS

Company Type: Public

Income Statement

FYE: March 31

	REVENUE ($ mil.)	NET INCOME ($ mil.)	NET PROFIT MARGIN	EMPLOYEES
3/06	933	(228)	—	9,606
3/05	946	(206)	—	8,536
3/04	1,013	(60)	—	8,059
3/03	1,027	2	0.2%	8,935
Annual Growth	**(3.1%)**	**—**	**—**	**2.4%**

Net Income History

London: WTFU

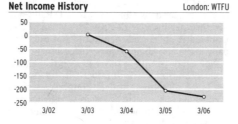

Whitbread

Whitbread wins the award for being one of the UK's leading hospitality and leisure groups. Whitbread, which sponsors a prestigious book award, has operations ranging from restaurants to hotels to fitness clubs. Its dining operations include about 380 pub restaurants (Brewers Fayre and Beefeater), more than 430 Costa coffee shops, and about 50 T.G.I. Friday's locations (franchised from US-based Carlson Restaurants Worldwide). Whitbread also operates more than 470 Premier Travel Inn budget hotels and the David Lloyd Leisure chain of fitness clubs with about 60 locations.

Once a highly diversified holding company, Whitbread has been steadily paring away assets and operations to focus its efforts on pubs, restaurants, budget hotels, and other leisure properties. In 2005 it sold a portfolio of Marriott hotels into a joint venture with Marriott International, which sold the properties to Royal Bank of Scotland the following year for $1.7 billion. The deal marked the end of the company's involvement in full-service hotels, allowing it to focus on expanding the Premier Travel Inns chain. The company also sold its historic Chiswell Street brewery site in 2005 and disposed of a 23% stake in Britvic.

With some of its found cash from divestitures, Whitbread plans to expand its budget hotel business by 50% over the next few years. The company plans to develop new pubs in conjunction with its expanding portfolio of hotels. New marketing efforts have been launched to continue expanding the membership rolls at its David Lloyd Leisure clubs, and an expanded menu at Costa has helped boost business for the coffee shop chain.

Meanwhile, Whitbread is making further divestments to trim operations. In 2006 it sold its 50% stake in Pizza Hut (UK) to US-based YUM! Brands for about $210 million, including the assumption of about $25 million in debt. The former joint venture operates and franchises more than 660 pizza joints. Whitbread also sold about

240 freestanding pub locations to Mitchells & Butlers for more than $900 million that year. The company is studying a possible sale of its T.G.I. Friday's locations.

Leading all of these developments is chief executive (and former hotels head) Alan Parker, who succeeded longtime chief executive David Thomas after the latter's retirement in 2004.

HISTORY

Samuel Whitbread became a brewer's apprentice in 1734 and learned his lessons well; in 1742 he began brewing beer at his own brewery. By 1750 he had built a new brewery and began producing porter in bulk. Whitbread had a head for business as well as beer, acquiring other breweries and investing in new brewing techniques to increase the quality of his beers. The company prospered despite an unlucky venture into politics by Samuel II; he opposed the war with Napoleon and committed suicide after Waterloo.

In the 1880s beer drinking declined, and Whitbread began buying up sinking pubs. But by WWI, the company started to concentrate on bottled beer sales in order to reduce its dependence on the tied pubs.

In 1944 W. H. Whitbread became chairman (the first Whitbread since founder Samuel) and took advantage of the aftermath of WWII to snap up less-robust rivals. The company first absorbed smaller breweries into its production and distribution operations but later made a living from taking over breweries and keeping their tied houses. The company went public in 1948 and had 10,000 pubs by 1970.

In the 1970s beer consumption fell yet again, and Whitbread started streamlining operations. It closed its original brewery in 1976. The company also began its shift from beer to other businesses, including acquiring a Pizza Hut franchise. It sold its wines and spirits business at the end of the 1980s.

The company continued to remake itself the next decade under the leadership of CEO Peter Jarvis. As more Britons began to eat out instead of going to the local pub for entertainment, Whitbread shifted with them, buying and developing restaurant concepts including its Beefeater Restaurant and Pub and family-friendly Brewers Fayre (complete with Charlie Chalk Fun Factories for kids). In 1995 Whitbread went shopping, buying David Lloyd Leisure and 16 Marriott hotels (even as it divested 400 underperforming pubs). The company later sold its Australian and Canadian Keg steak houses in 1995 and 1996, respectively, and expanded its Pizza Hut chain.

In 1997 Jarvis stepped down and was succeeded by David Thomas. A renewed focus on its core business that year also prompted the company to dispose of all pubs that served beer not brewed by Whitbread. In 1998 Whitbread and Allied Domecq agreed to merge their retail beer and wine stores into a new company called First Quench. It also sold one of its five breweries, put another brewery on the market, and in the wake of the declining popularity of old-fashioned pubs, sold 253 of its pubs and 40 of its Beefeaters Restaurant & Pubs.

Whitbread's attempt to buy more than 3,500 UK pubs and restaurants from Allied Domecq for $3.8 billion failed in 1999. (Rival Punch Taverns had the winning bid.) In early 2000 the company bought Swallow Group, a hotel and pub operator, with plans to convert the Swallow locations to the Marriott brand. That same year Whitbread sold its brewery business to Interbrew (now InBev).

The company unloaded all 3,000 of its pubs in 2001, selling them to Deutsche Bank's Morgan Grenfell equity fund for $2.3 billion. During 2002 the company rebranded about two dozen of its Swallow hotels but sold the remaining 13 properties to REIT Asset Management the following year.

In 2004 the company acquired Premier Lodge, the UK's #3 budget-hotel chain, from Spirit Group (a managed pubs business once owned by Texas Pacific Group but later sold to Punch Taverns) and merged the chain with its Travel Inn hotels to form Premier Travel Inn. Thomas retired that year and was replaced as CEO by Alan Parker, who formerly served as head of Whitbread's hotels business. The following year the company formed a joint venture with Marriott International to sell its full-service hotels. (Royal Bank of Scotland bought the properties in 2006 for $1.7 billion.)

In 2006 the company continued divesting certain assets, selling its 50% stake in Pizza Hut (UK) to US-based YUM! Brands for more than $205 million, including the assumption of more than $25 million in debt. The company also sold about 240 freestanding pubs to Mitchells & Butlers for more than $900 million.

EXECUTIVES

Chairman: Anthony J. (Tony) Habgood, age 59
Chief Executive and Director: Alan Parker, age 59, $721,405 pay
Group Commercial Director: Paula Vennells
Group Finance Director:
Christopher C. B. (Chris) Rogers, age 46
Group Human Resources Director: Angie Risley, age 47, $359,845 pay
Managing Director, Costa: John Derkach, age 46
Managing Director, David Lloyd Leisure: Mike Tye, age 50
Managing Director, Premier Travel Inn:
Patrick Dempsey, age 45
Managing Director, Pub Restaurants: Mark Phillips
Managing Director, TGI Friday's: Tim Hammond, age 44
Company Secretary and Legal Affairs Director:
Simon Barratt
Communications Director: Anna Glover
Group IT Director: Ben Wishart
Commercial Director, Marriott Hotels, Whitbread Hotel Company: Tony Dangerfield
Finance Director, David Lloyd Leisure: Eric Dodd, age 34
Information Technology Director, Whitbread Restaurants: Ann Fraser
Director of Communications, Hotels: Abigail Langan
Communications Manager, Restaurants:
Beverley Wilkins
Corporate Affairs Manager: Dan Waugh
Corporate Public Relations Manager: Julie Weldon
PR Manager, David Lloyd Leisure: Karl Johnson
PR Manager, Hotels and Pub Restaurants:
Dionne Parker
Auditors: Ernst & Young LLP

LOCATIONS

HQ: Whitbread PLC
Whitbread House, Park Street West,
Luton LU1 3BG, United Kingdom
Phone: +44-15-8242-4200   **Fax:** +44-15-8288-8844
Web: www.whitbread.co.uk

2006 Sales

	% of total
UK	98
Other countries	2
Total	**100**

PRODUCTS/OPERATIONS

2006 Sales

	% of total
Pub restaurants	38
Premier Travel Inn	26
High Street restaurants	15
David Lloyd Leisure	14
Other	7
Total	**100**

Selected Operations

Pub restaurants
  Brewers Fayre
  Beefeater
Premier Travel Inn (hotel)
High Street restaurants
  Costa
  T.G.I. Friday's
David Lloyd Leisure (health and fitness club)
Other
  Touchbase (business centers)

COMPETITORS

Accor
Bannatyne Fitness
Best Western
Compass Group
Days Inn
De Vere Group
Enterprise Inns
Esporta
First Leisure
Gondola
Greene King
InterContinental Hotels
J D Wetherspoon
Mitchells & Butlers
Punch Taverns
Restaurant Group
Travelodge Hotels (UK)
Wolverhampton & Dudley
Wyndham

HISTORICAL FINANCIALS

Company Type: Public

Income Statement

FYE: Thur. nearest Mar. 1

	REVENUE ($ mil.)	NET INCOME ($ mil.)	NET PROFIT MARGIN	EMPLOYEES
2/06	2,758	460	16.7%	45,000
2/05	3,516	339	9.6%	53,483
2/04	3,341	307	9.2%	52,437
2/03	2,835	241	8.5%	55,315
2/02	2,859	(75)	—	61,470
Annual Growth	**(0.9%)**	**—**	**—**	**(7.5%)**

Net Income History

London: WTB

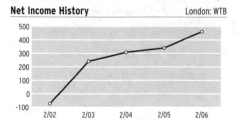

Wipro

You might say this company has really cleaned up in the technology services business. Wipro is one of India's leading providers of system integration and outsourcing services, but it also manufactures a variety of consumer products, including hand soap. Operating in about 35 countries, its Wipro Technologies division offers software development and business process outsourcing (BPO) services, as well as management consulting and product engineering. Its Wipro Infotech unit focuses on providing IT services for customers in India and the Asia/Pacific region. Wipro's consumer products operation makes detergent, soap, and talcum powder along with light bulbs. Chairman Azim Premji owns more than 80% of the company.

Once highly diversified, Wipro has focused on expanding its technology services businesses, which now account for about 90% of its revenue. Wipro Technologies has benefited from cost-conscious companies, particularly in the US (which accounts for more than half its business), looking to outsourcing as a way to drive profits. Wipro has continued to maintain its position as a leading consumer products maker in India, however; it ranks #1 or #2 in several product categories, including shampoos, baby care products, and light bulbs.

In addition to technology and consumer products, Wipro manufactures hydraulic parts and equipment primarily for the automotive market through Wipro Fluid Power. It also provides support services for users of General Electric medical devices though Wipro GE Medical Systems, a joint venture 51% owned by GE.

The company's Wipro Technologies unit formed another joint venture in 2006 with Motorola. WMNetServ is focused on the delivery of outsourced telecom services.

Premji, whose stake in Wipro has made him the richest person in India and one of the wealthiest in the world, took his father's post as head of the company in 1968. A self-taught businessman who shuns publicity, he is known as a man who values integrity over extreme wealth: Wipro has suffered power outages and import confiscations in the past for its refusal to offer or accept bribes.

HISTORY

In 1947 M. H. Hasham Premji turned down an offer from the prime minister of Pakistan to migrate from India and become finance minister. Premji cited his loyalty to India as well as to his business, Western Indian Vegetable Products (Wipro), founded in 1946 to sell cooking oil. Wipro went public in 1947.

Like any proper Indian industrialist, Premji eventually diversified into other markets, including bath soap and hydraulic fluid. Instead of employing the customary tactic of courting Indian bureaucrats to help grow his business, Premji focused on customers. He kept costs low by branding generic products and selling directly to retailers instead of middlemen. When Premji died of a heart attack in 1966, he left behind a $2 million business.

Premji's 21-year-old son, Azim, who had only three months left in his engineering degree program at Stanford, returned home and took the reins in 1968. Although he had little idea how to run a business, he took a cue from his father's success and continued diversifying into new markets. India ordered computing giant IBM to leave the country in 1977 after a dispute over investment and intellectual property, opening the door for Wipro to tackle computer manufacturing and distribution. Instead of plucking away ex-IBM employees, Premji hired managers from a truck maker and a refrigeration company, who together helped turn Wipro computers into a leading national brand.

In 1980 Wipro began offering information technology services in India. Three years later the company moved into software, offering branded products in the same market as US upstart Microsoft. Wipro entered the toilet soap and dot matrix printer markets in 1985.

It was in the late 1980s that Wipro finally discovered its growth business, software services (it abandoned software sales in 1990). The company's reputation as a software integrator was secured in 1989 when Wipro and General Electric, whose business model Premji admired and followed very carefully, formed Wipro GE Medical Systems as a joint venture. Possessing GE as a partner and long-term client over the next decade attracted scores of research and development contracts from blue-chip clients in the US (Cisco Systems), Japan (Hitachi), and Europe (Alcatel).

During the early 1990s Wipro began transitioning away from costly onsite software projects in the US to more profitable offshore development in India. It also entered the lighting business in 1992. With Taiwan-based Acer, Wipro formed a joint venture in 1995 to manufacture and sell computers and other peripherals in India.

The company reorganized in 1999 into four companies, each run separately: software, hardware and systems, consumer care and lighting, and hydraulic fluid. Wipro Net was also formed to offer e-commerce implementation services. In 2000 Wipro listed on the New York Stock Exchange, gaining an international investment audience for what few shares Premji didn't already own. The move caused his personal wealth to soar.

In 2002 Wipro launched genetic data software division Healthcare and Life Sciences. Also that year the company bought Indian call center operator Spectramind for $90 million and American Management Systems' global energy practice for $24 million to form Wipro BPO Solutions. The following year, though, it reorganized its operations, folding Wipro BPO into its global IT services division, Wipro Technologies, along with the technology-oriented parts of its HealthSciences unit.

EXECUTIVES

Chairman, CEO, and Managing Director:
Azim H. Premji, age 60, $465,666 pay
COO and President, Technology Services:
A. Lakshman Rao, age 57, $169,113 pay
EVP, Finance and CFO: Suresh C. Senapaty, age 49, $174,890 pay
EVP, Human Resources: Pratik Kumar, age 40, $137,362 pay
SVP, Human Resources Development: Ranjan Acharya, age 48, $112,278 pay
VP and General Counsel: Madhu Khatri, age 43
VP, Mission Quality: Jagdish Ramaswamy, age 42
VP, Corporate Communication, Brand, and Community Initiatives: Vijay Gupta, age 48
VP, Corporate Taxation: P. V. Srinivasan, age 46
Head, Energy and Utilities: Tamal Dasgupta, age 55, $118,071 pay
President, Wipro Consumer Care & Lighting:
Vineet Agrawal, age 44, $147,637 pay
President, Wipro Infotech; President, Global IT Service Lines, Wipro Technologies: Suresh Vaswani, age 46, $174,345 pay

President, Embedded & Product Engineering Solutions, Wipro Technologies: Ramesh Emani, age 50, $170,337 pay
President, Enterprise Solutions, Wipro Technologies: Sudip Banerjee, age 46, $154,392 pay
President, Banking, Finance, and Insurance Vertical, Wipro Technologies: Girish S. Paranjpe, age 48, $158,259 pay
VP, Marketing, Wipro Consumer Care & Lighting: Kumar Chander, age 38
VP, Sales, Wipro Consumer Care & Lighting: Anil Chugh, age 42
Company Secretary: V. Ramachandran
Treasurer: Lakshminarayana Lan
Manager, Corporate Communication: Sandhya Ranjit
Investor Relation Officer: Sridhar Ramasubbu
Auditors: KPMG

LOCATIONS

HQ: Wipro Limited
Doddakannelli, Sarjapur Rd.,
Bangalore, Karnataka 560035, India
Phone: +91-80-2844-0011   **Fax:** +91-80-2844-0056
US HQ: 1300 Crittenden Ln., 2nd Fl.,
Mountain View, CA 94043
US Phone: 650-316-3555   **US Fax:** 650-316-3468
Web: www.wiprocorporate.com

Wipro has operations throughout India. Its technology services divisions have operations in more than 35 countries.

2006 Sales

	$ mil.	% of total
US	1,203.3	50
Europe	547.0	23
India	490.6	21
Other regions	146.5	6
Total	**2,387.4**	**100**

PRODUCTS/OPERATIONS

2006 Sales

	$ mil.	% of total
Global IT		
IT services & products	1,643.9	69
BPO services	172.4	7
India & Asia/Pacific IT		
Products	233.6	10
Services	137.2	6
Consumer care & lighting	126.6	5
Other	73.7	3
Total	**2,387.4**	**100**

Selected Operations

Wipro Consumer Care & Lighting (consumer products manufacturing)
Wipro Fluid Power (hydraulic equipment manufacturing)
Wipro GE Medical Systems (49%, medical equipment support services)
Wipro Infotech (technology services, India and Asia/Pacific)
Wipro Technologies (global technology services)

Selected Technology Services

Business process outsourcing (BPO)
Enterprise information technology
Application development and re-engineering
Business intelligence and data warehousing
Consulting
Enterprise application integration
Research and development
Embedded systems
Hardware design and development
Internet access devices
Software design and development
Telecommunications and networking
Technology infrastructure support

Selected Products

Consumer care
Chandrika (soap)
Glucovita (vitamins)
Milk & Roses (soap)
Safewash (laundry detergent)
Santoor (soap)
Santoor Chandan (soap)
Santoor Talc
Wipro Active Talc
Wipro BabySoft
Wipro Shikakai (shampoo)
Lighting
Wipro Smartlite
Wipro Longlite
Office furniture
Vibrant
Wipro Sterling

COMPETITORS

Accenture
BearingPoint
Capgemini
Cognizant Tech Solutions
Computer Sciences Corp.
Convergys
Deloitte Consulting
EDS
GE
HCL Technologies
Hindustan Lever
Hitachi
HP Technology Solutions Group
Hyundai
IBM Global Services
Infosys
Johnson & Johnson
Keane
Komatsu
Perficient
Perot Systems
Philips Electronics
Procter & Gamble
Satyam
Sauer-Danfoss
Siemens Medical
Tata Consultancy
TeleTech
Unilever

HISTORICAL FINANCIALS

Company Type: Public

Income Statement

	REVENUE ($ mil.)	NET INCOME ($ mil.)	NET PROFIT MARGIN	EMPLOYEES
3/06	2,387	456	19.1%	53,700
3/05	1,863	363	19.5%	46,500
3/04	1,346	230	17.1%	32,000
3/03	900	170	18.9%	23,300
3/02	696	171	24.5%	13,800
Annual Growth	36.1%	27.9%	—	40.5%

FYE: March 31

2006 Year-End Financials

Debt ratio: —
Return on equity: 29.7%
Cash ($ mil.): 882
Current ratio: 3.40
Long-term debt ($ mil.): —

Net Income History

NYSE: WIT

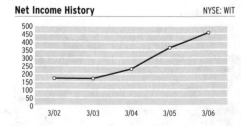

Wolters Kluwer

This publisher is focused on the basics in life: death and taxes. One of Europe's leading professional publishers, Wolters Kluwer disseminates information on tax and legal affairs, business information, medical and scientific data, and education through print and electronic formats. Its operations include CCH Publishing, Ovid Technologies, Pharma Solutions, and Wolters-Noordhoff. The company has divested the businesses that made up its professional training division. Wolters Kluwer has operations in more than 25 countries, primarily in Europe and North America.

Under the direction of CEO Nancy McKinstry, the company is attempting to regain its financial health after battling a multi-year advertising slump. In 2003 McKinstry announced a three-year plan to turn the company around by focusing on key customer segments. Wolters Kluwer went on to cut some 1,500 jobs at the company as part of the restructuring. McKinstry said the company is on track to meet its goals by the end of 2006.

Wolters Kluwer has made a number of acquisitions to expand into new professional publishing market segments. Acquisitions in 2005 included Italian publishers De Agostini Professionale and Utet Professionale as well as Romanian legal publisher EON. In 2006 the company acquired ProVation Medical, a provider of medical documentation, coding, and workflow tools.

The company has received approval to open a bookstore for professional publications in China. The store will be operated in partnership with Chinese firm China Law Press. Wolters Kluwer estimated that it doubled its customers in China in 2005 and sees plenty of room for growth.

HISTORY

A pioneer of the Dutch publishing industry, J. B. Wolters founded his publishing house in 1836 to provide instructional material for Netherlands schools. The company later merged with educational publisher Noordhoff (founded in 1858). J. B. Wolters had no children, so the business went to his brother-in-law E. B. Horst in 1860. Dutch academic Anthony Schepman took over the management of Wolters-Noordhoff in 1917 and led the business' expansion. In 1920 it opened an office in the Dutch colony of Indonesia.

Wolters-Noordhoff and Information and Communication Union (ICU) merged in 1972. ICU had been formed by the merger in 1970 of Samson (founded by Nicholaas Samson in 1883 to print government publications) and publisher A. W. Sijthoff. After the Wolters-Noordhoff-ICU merger, the resulting company initially took the ICU name, but in 1983 it became the Wolters Samson Group. That year it began exploring a merger with Kluwer.

Abele Kluwer, a former assistant schoolteacher, became a publisher in 1889. His publishing house specialized in educational products and children's books. The company expanded its range in the 1920s with a growing number of up-to-date publications regarding new laws, regulations, court decisions, and scholarly texts. Kluwer hired its first non-family managing director, J. M. Gorter, in 1957 and went public in 1967.

Reed Elsevier (now called Reed Elsevier Group plc) made a bid to acquire Kluwer in 1987, buying a minority stake in the company. The Anglo-Dutch concern was rebuffed by the subsequent merger of Wolters Samson with Kluwer that year, however, and was left with about a third of the shares in the new Wolters Kluwer. Despite Reed Elsevier's repeated advances to work closely with Wolters Kluwer, the company pursued an independent growth strategy. In 1990 it acquired J.B. Lippincott, a US health care publisher. That year Reed Elsevier sold its stake in the firm.

In the early 1990s Wolters Kluwer began acquiring several medium-sized European companies and in 1995 bought Commerce Clearing House (with roots dating back to 1892). In 1997 it agreed to an $8.8 billion acquisition deal from Reed Elsevier; however, the deal fell apart the following year. (Both companies blamed regulatory hurdles for the pact's failure.) Meanwhile, Wolters Kluwer bought Waverly (medical and scientific books and magazines) and Plenum Publishing (scientific and technical trade books and journals). It also bought Ovid Technologies, a provider of electronic information retrieval services to the academic, medical, and scientific markets.

The following year Wolters Kluwer acquired US professional information publisher Bureau of Business Practice and search and retrieval service Accusearch. In late 1999 internal candidate Casper van Kempen replaced C.J. Brakel as chairman; he was out six months later, having clashed with the board over the company's Web strategy. Deputy chairman Robert Pieterse was tapped to replace him. Also in 2000 Wolters Kluwer announced that it would invest some $240 million in Internet-related operations. The company divested itself of its professional training business that year. In 2001 the company bought Cutter Environment, a unit of Cutter Information, which was folded into its Aspen Publishers unit. Wolters Kluwer sold the health care book division of its Aspen Publishing unit in late 2002 to Jones and Bartlett Publishers. In addition, Wolters Kluwer sold its academic publishing unit (Kluwer Academic Publishers) for $582 million to two London-based equity firms. The company bought US financial services and information firm GainsKeeper Inc. in 2002.

Pieterse left the company in 2003 and was replaced by board member Nancy McKinstry. The company made two acquisitions in 2003: CEDAM, an Italian legal publisher, and TyMerix, a legal e-billing service in the US. In 2004 the company's corporate and financial services unit acquired software maker Summation Legal Technologies.

In 2005 the company announced it would group all of its financial businesses under the name Wolters Kluwer Financial Services.

EXECUTIVES

Chairman of the Supervisory Board: Adri Baan, age 64
Deputy Chairman of the Supervisory Board:
 Harry Pennings
Chairman of the Executive Board and CEO:
 Nancy McKinstry, age 47, $1,667,494 pay
Executive Board Member and CFO:
 Boudewijn L. J. M. Beerkens, $1,050,474 pay
Executive Board Member: Jean-Marc Detailleur, $898,884 pay
EVP and General Counsel, North America:
 Deidra D. Gold, age 50

SVP Accounting and Control: Matthijs Lusse
SVP Business Development: Jack Lynch
SVP Human Resources: Kathy Baker
SVP Operational Auditor: Paul Kooijmans
SVP Planning and Analysis: Ann Riposanu
SVP Strategy: Andres Sadler
VP, Company Secretary, and General Counsel:
 Martin Thompson
VP Content and Platform Management, North America:
 Paul Jensen
VP Corporate Communications: Caroline Wouters
VP Corporate Treasury: George Dessing
VP Investor Relations: Oya Yavuz
VP Mergers and Acquisitions (Europe): Jheroen Muste
VP Risk Management: Mahdy de Groot
VP Tax Management: Rinus Kwakkel
Auditors: KPMG Accountants N.V.

LOCATIONS

HQ: Wolters Kluwer nv
 Apollolaan 153, P.O.Box 75248,
 NL-1070 AE Amsterdam, The Netherlands
Phone: +31-20-60-70-400   **Fax:** +31-20-60-70-490
Web: www.wolterskluwer.com

2005 Sales

	% of total
Europe	52
North America	44
Asia/Pacific	3
Other countries	1
Total	**100**

PRODUCTS/OPERATIONS

2005 Sales

	% of total
Legal, Tax & Regulatory Europe	38
Health	20
Tax, Accounting & Legal	18
Corporate & Financial Services	15
Education	9
Total	**100**

2005 Sales

	% of total
Print	48
Electronic	
Software/CD-ROM	20
Internet/Online	19
Services	13
Total	**100**

COMPETITORS

Advanstar
American Lawyer Media
Bertelsmann
Blackwell Publishing
Bureau of National Affairs
Cadmus Communications
Editis
IHS
John Wiley
McGraw-Hill
Pearson
Reed Elsevier Group
Thomson Corporation
Verlagsgruppe Georg von Holtzbrinck
VNU

Income Statement

FYE: December 31

	REVENUE ($ mil.)	NET INCOME ($ mil.)	NET PROFIT MARGIN	EMPLOYEES
12/05	3,996	309	7.7%	17,419
12/04	4,448	184	4.1%	18,393
12/03	4,313	(87)	—	19,689
12/02	4,082	344	8.4%	20,833
12/01	3,399	124	3.6%	19,766
Annual Growth	4.1%	25.7%	—	(3.1%)

Net Income History   OTC: WTKWY

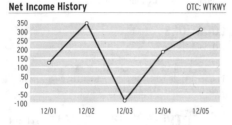

Woolworths

Chow down under with Australia's #1 food retailer, Woolworths (aka "Woolies"). The company operates about 2,385 supermarkets, general merchandise, and electronics stores throughout Australia. (Its 700-plus supermarkets and nearly 575 liquor stores account for about 80% of sales.) In addition, Woolworths sells gasoline and leverages its distribution network to provide wholesale merchandise for third-party supermarkets. Australia's #2 retailer (after Coles Myer), Woolworths' general merchandise discount stores operate under the Big W name. The company also runs over 200 Dick Smith Electronics stores and 18 Dick Smith Electronics PowerHouse superstores, and about 120 company-owned Tandy consumer electronics shops.

Woolworths (which has no relation to the five-and-dime chain once operated in the US) is trying not to choke on its own success, but it's hard to be humble. It has added gas pumps and banking to some supermarket locations, has opened Woolworths Metro (convenience stores), and acquired 72 Franklins supermarkets in 2001 (from a rival chain owned by Hong Kong-based Dairy Farm International Holdings). In a bid to fend off rival Coles Myer's entry into the food-and-fuel market, Woolworths has formed a joint venture with Caltex Australia to expand its network of discount fuel outlets to 450. Also, the retailer has overhauled its supply chain operations to become a low-cost operator after studying systems at US retail giant Wal-Mart and the UK's Tesco. To that end, the company sold its distribution centers to Australian Prime Property Fund for about $626 million in a leaseback deal that will reduce debt and increase supply chain flexibility.

Woolworths has about 20% of Australia's take-home liquor market, compared to Coles Myers' 16% share. In a bid to increase liquor sales — which are growing faster than general merchandise or grocery sales — Woolworths and millionaire pubs owner Bruce Mathieson recently beat out Coles in a takeover battle for Australia's

biggest pub operator, Australian Leisure & Hospitality (ALH), which has 263 liquor outlets, 154 of them in pubs, and a 5% share of the country's take-home liquor market.

In 2005 Woolworths completed the takeover of ALH and now operates its retailing activities, leaving the pubs and gaming operations to Mathieson.

Roger Corbett retired as CEO in 2006. He was succeeded by Michael Luscombe, the company's long-serving director of supermarkets.

HISTORY

Harold Percival Christmas first tried a mail-order dress business before opening the popular Frock Salon retail store. Christmas and his partners opened a branch store in the Imperial Arcade in Sydney in 1924, renaming it "Woolworths Stupendous Bargain Basement" and luring customers with advertisements calling it "a handy place where good things are cheap . . . you'll want to live at Woolworths." The company borrowed the name from Frank Woolworth's successful US chain, after determining that chain had no plans to open stores in Australia. Woolworths was listed on the Australian stock exchange in 1924.

Food sales came more than 30 years later. Woolworths opened its first freestanding, full-line supermarket in 1960, then diversified into specialty retail, buying the Rockmans women's clothing store chain the next year (sold, 2000). It expanded into discounting with the Big W chain in 1976 and further diversified when it bought 60% of the Dick Smith Electronics store chain in 1981 (buying the remainder in 1983).

The purchase of the Safeway grocery chain (the Australian operations of the US-based chain) put Woolworths on the top of the supermarket heap in 1985. But the company was hurting (it lost $13 million in 1985-86) because of a restructuring in the early 1980s that had weakened management by bulking up the front offices and dividing responsibilities. Woolworths got a shot in the arm from Paul Simons, who returned to the company in 1987 after running competitor Franklins. Simons cleaned house in the front offices, closed unprofitable stores, and began the successful "Fresh Food People" marketing strategy.

Industrial Equity Limited (IEL) bought the company in 1989; IEL then became part of Adelaide Steamship group, which spun off Woolworths as a public company in 1993.

The following year career Woolworths manager Reg Clairs took over as CEO, following the untimely death (on a golf course) in 1993 of Harry Watts, who was being groomed for the job. As a result, the company has an unwritten rule of avoiding CEOs older than 60.

Clairs took the company in a variety of new directions. Woolworths began supplying fresh food to neighbor Asia in 1995. The company added Plus Petrol outlets adjacent to Woolworths Supermarkets in 1996. It also started a superstore concept for its Dick Smith Electronics chain (Power House) that year.

Clairs (who was turning 60 in 1999) stepped down in late 1998 and Roger Corbett took over as CEO. Woolworths also began offering banking services to its customers and bought Dan Murphy, a Victoria-based liquor chain, in 1998. It divested its Chisholm Manufacturing meat plants in 2000.

In 2001 Woolworths acquired two liquor store chains (Liberty Liquor, Booze Bros), more than 200 Tandy Electronics stores, and 72 Franklins supermarkets from Hong Kong-based Dairy Farm International Holdings. In June 2002 Woolworths exited the New Zealand market when it sold its supermarkets group there to Foodland Associated for $690 million.

Supermarket division chief Bill Wavish resigned in May 2003 (he is staying on as a consultant into 2004) and was replaced by former chief general manager of supermarket operations Tom Flood. Wavish was considered one of the top candidates to replace CEO Corbett. Also in 2003 the company discontinued its Australian Independent Wholesalers (AIW) operations. Flood resigned abruptly in 2004. Flood, like Wavish, was considered a likely successor to Corbett.

In the fall of 2004, the board of directors of Australia's biggest pub owner, Australian Leisure & Hospitality (ALH), recommended the company accept a $985 million takeover bid by Woolworths and The Bruce Mathieson Group. Previously, the duo had acquired a 16% stake in ALH. In mid-2005 the company acquired the New Zealand supermarkets of Foodland Associated and 22 Action stores in Western Australia, Queensland, and New South Wales for about $1.8 billion.

In September 2006 the company announced it had purchased a 10% stake in New Zealand's The Warehouse retail chain.

EXECUTIVES

Chairman: James A. Strong, age 58
CEO and Director: Michael Luscombe
CFO and Director: Tom Pockett, $761,870 pay
Director of Business Development: Marty Hamnett, $646,216 pay
Chief Logistics and Information Officer: Steve Bradley, $717,160 pay
Director of Corporate Marketing: Bernie Brookes, $704,988 pay
Director of Supermarkets: Naum J. Onikul
General Manager, Human Resources: Julie Coates
General Manager, BIG W: Greg Foran
General Manager, Woolworths Academy: Judy Howard
General Manager, Corporate Services and Secretary: Rohan K. S. Jeffs
General Manager, Dick Smith Electronics: Alvin Ng
General Manager, Supermarket Operations: Peter Smith
General Manager, Property: Peter Thomas
General Manager, Freestanding Liquor Operations: Grant O'Brien
General Manager, Mercury Program: Penny Winn
General Manager, Asset Development: Barry Neil
General Manager, Business Development: Gary Reid
General Manager, Petrol: Ramik Narsey
Auditors: Deloitte Touche Tohmatsu

LOCATIONS

HQ: Woolworths Limited
1 Woolworths Way, Bella Vista,
New South Wales 2153, Australia
Phone: +61-2-8885-0000
Web: www.woolworths.com.au

PRODUCTS/OPERATIONS

2006 Sales

	% of total
Australian food & liquor	68
Petrol	12
Big W	8
New Zealand supermarkets	7
Consumer electronics	3
Hotels	2
Total	**100**

Selected Operations

Food stores
Safeway
Woolworths Metro
Woolworths Supermarkets

General merchandise stores
BIG W

Liquor stores
BWS (neighborhood stores)
Dan Murphy's (destination outlets)
First Estate (fine wine stores)
Woolworths Liquor (attached to supermarkets)

Specialty retail
Dick Smith Electronics
Dick Smith Electronics PowerHouse
Tandy Electronics

Other
Caltex/WOW Petrol (gas stations)
GreenGrocer.com.au (online grocery store)
Woolworths Ezy Banking
Woolworths HomeShop (online grocery and liquor store)

COMPETITORS

ALDI	Harvey Norman Holdings
BP	Metcash
Coles Group	Pick'n Pay
Foodland Associated	Royal Dutch Shell
Harris Scarfe Holdings	

HISTORICAL FINANCIALS

Company Type: Public

Income Statement

FYE: June 30

	REVENUE ($ mil.)	NET INCOME ($ mil.)	NET PROFIT MARGIN	EMPLOYEES
6/06	27,542	749	2.7%	175,000
6/05	23,875	602	2.5%	145,000
6/04	19,269	504	2.6%	140,000
6/03	17,551	434	2.5%	145,000
6/02	13,791	317	2.3%	145,000
Annual Growth	18.9%	24.0%	—	4.8%

Net Income History

Australian: WOW

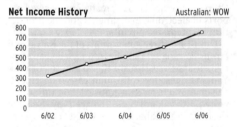

WPP Group

Marketing and advertising services bind this group together. WPP Group is the world's second-largest media and communications services conglomerate (behind Omnicom Group), with operations in more than 100 countries. Its flagship advertising agency networks, including Grey Worldwide, JWT, Ogilvy & Mather, and Young & Rubicam, offer creative campaign development and brand management services. WPP's holdings also include public relations firms, media buying and planning agencies, and many specialized marketing and communications units. In addition, its Kantar Group division is one of the world's leading market research organizations. WPP was founded in 1958 under the name Wire and Plastic Products.

Having weathered a challenging recession, WPP is looking to position itself for growth in both the near- and long-term future. It completed a $1.75 billion acquisition of US-based rival Grey Global Group in 2005, beating out bids from private equity players (including Kohlberg Kravis Roberts & Co.) and rival advertising firm Havas. In addition to expanding the overall size of the company, the acquisition carried with it another important asset, Grey's long-standing relationship with Procter & Gamble. Soon after P&G's mega-merger with Gillette closed in 2005, however, the consumer products giant shifted about $800 million in media services assignments from WPP's Mindshare to Starcom MediaVest (a unit of Publicis).

The company is also keeping its eye open for additional acquisitions as it races to overtake Omnicom. WPP has long been speculated as a leading candidate to snatch up media planning and buying conglomerate Aegis Group. Other rumored acquisition targets include both of France's leading advertising companies, Havas and Publicis. In a smaller but potentially important deal, WPP in 2006 invested in online game publisher WildTangent. Advertising on video games is seen as a key emerging market. Also that year, WPP acquired the Dewey Square Group, an advertising and PR firm with several US offices, and invested in advertising and marketing agencies in China, India, and South Korea.

WPP spent the last half of 2005 and early part of 2006 integrating the various operations of Grey into the rest of the holding company. It plans to build upon those foundations going forward. Other strategies for the future include bolstering its international revenue as well as augmenting the amount of revenue its marketing services segment brings in.

HISTORY

WPP Group began as Wire and Plastic Products, a maker of grocery baskets and other goods founded in 1958 by Gordon Sampson (who retired from the company in 2000). Investors led by former Saatchi & Saatchi advertising executive (and current WPP CEO) Martin Sorrell bought the company in 1985 and began acquiring marketing firms under the shortened name of WPP. In 1987 Sorrell used revenue from these businesses (and a sizable loan) to buy US advertising warhorse J. Walter Thompson (now JWT).

JWT was founded by William James Carlton as the Carlton & Smith agency in 1864. The New York City-based firm was bought by James Walter Thompson in 1877 and was later responsible for Prudential Insurance's Rock of Gibraltar symbol (1896). It began working for Ford (which is still a client) in 1943. JWT went public in 1969.

Following its acquisition of JWT, WPP formed European agency Conquest in 1988. The company (and its debt) grew the next year when it bought the Ogilvy Group (founded by David Ogilvy in 1948) for $860 million, making WPP the world's largest advertising company. But its acquisition frenzy also positioned the company for a fall in 1991, when depressed economies in the US and the UK slowed advertising spending. Saddled with debt, WPP nearly went into receivership before recovering the next year.

WPP began a period of controlled growth with no major acquisitions in 1993. It expanded internationally in 1994, opening new offices in South America, Europe, the Middle East, and Asia. Winning IBM's $500 million international advertising contract that year also aided WPP's financial recovery. However, this led to the loss of business from IBM's rivals, including AT&T, Compaq's European division (Compaq was purchased by Hewlett-Packard in 2002), and Microsoft.

By 1997 the company was again ready to flex its acquisition muscle. The firm bought 21 companies that year, including a stake in IBOPE (a market research firm in Latin America) and a share of Batey Holdings (the majority owner of Batey Ads, a prominent ad agency in the Asia/Pacific region). That year WPP also created its media planning unit MindShare.

More acquisitions followed in 1998, including a 20% stake in Asatsu (the #3 advertising agency in Japan). The next year the company bought Texas-based market research firm IntelliQuest Information Group, which was merged with WPP's Millward Brown unit. Along with its acquisitions, WPP snagged some significant new accounts in 1998 and 1999, lining up business with Kimberly-Clark, Merrill Lynch, and the embattled International Olympic Committee.

In 2000 the company bought US-based rival Young & Rubicam for about $4.7 billion — one of the largest advertising mergers ever. The move catapulted WPP to the top spot among the world's advertising firms. As if that wasn't enough, its MindShare unit later snagged the $700 million media planning account of consumer products giant Unilever. WPP also took a 49% stake in UniWorld Group, the largest African-American-owned ad agency in the US.

Hamish Maxwell, chairman since 1996, retired in 2001 and was replaced by Philip Lader, the former US ambassador to the UK. That year, however, WPP's top ranking was stolen away by Interpublic Group following its acquisition of True North Communications. It later sparked a bidding war with Havas Advertising when it offered $630 million to buy UK media services firm Tempus Group. WPP grudgingly completed its acquisition of Tempus in 2002. The following year the company acquired Cordiant Communications.

In 2005 WPP made another big splash in the industry when it acquired Grey Global Group for $1.75 billion.

EXECUTIVES

Chairman: Philip Lader, age 60
COO: Tro Piliguian
EVP Public Relations and Public Affairs: Howard G. Paster, age 62
Group Strategy Director and Director: Mark Read, age 39
Group Communications Director: Feona McEwan
Chief Talent Officer: Mark Linaugh
Executive Chairman, Mediaedge:cia: Charles Courtier, age 41
Chairman, BKSH: Charlie Black
Chairman, BPRI: Jonathan Shingleton
Chairman, Chime Communications: Lord Tim Bell, age 64
Chairman and CEO, Brierley & Partners: Harold (Hal) Brierley
Chairman, Banner Corporation: Roderick (Rod) Banner
Chairman and CEO, The Voluntarily United Group of Creative Agencies: Andy Berlin
Chairman, Fitch: Rodney Fitch
Chairman and CEO, Grey Global Group: Edward H. (Ed) Meyer, age 79
Chairman and CEO, Grey Worldwide: James R. (Jim) Heekin III, age 57

LOCATIONS

HQ: WPP Group plc
27 Farm St., London W1J 5RJ, United Kingdom
Phone: +44-20-7408-2204   Fax: +44-20-7493-6819
US HQ: 125 Park Ave., New York, NY 10017
US Phone: 212-632-2200   US Fax: 212-632-2222
Web: www.wpp.com

WPP Group has operations in more than 100 countries.

2005 Sales

	% of total
North America	39
Europe	
UK	15
Other countries	26
Asia/Pacific, Latin America & Middle East	20
Total	**100**

PRODUCTS/OPERATIONS

2005 Sales

	% of total
Advertising & media services	49
Branding & health care communications	26
Market research & consulting	15
Public relations & public affairs	10
Total	**100**

COMPETITORS

Aegis Group
Dentsu
GfK
GfK NOP
Havas
Interpublic Group
Ipsos
Omnicom
Publicis
Taylor Nelson
VNU

HISTORICAL FINANCIALS

Company Type: Public

Income Statement				FYE: December 31
	REVENUE ($ mil.)	NET INCOME ($ mil.)	NET PROFIT MARGIN	EMPLOYEES
12/05	9,247	433	4.7%	74,631
12/04	37,758	288	0.8%	59,932
12/03	33,118	196	0.6%	54,324
12/02	28,925	86	0.3%	49,439
12/01	5,838	115	2.0%	51,009
Annual Growth	**12.2%**	**39.3%**	**—**	**10.0%**

2005 Year-End Financials

Debt ratio: 46.1%
Return on equity: 5.8%
Cash ($ mil.): 1,919
Current ratio: 0.84
Long-term debt ($ mil.): 3,725

Stock History   NASDAQ (GS): WPPGY

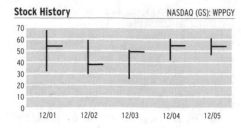

	STOCK PRICE ($) FY Close	P/E High/Low		PER SHARE ($) Earnings	Dividends
12/05	54.00	39	30	1.57	0.26
12/04	54.67	5	3	12.90	—
12/03	49.30	—	—	—	—
12/02	37.88	—	—	—	—
12/01	53.90	—	—	—	—
Annual Growth	**0.0%**	**—**		**(87.8%)**	**—**

Yamaha

This company doesn't produce records, but it does help people make plenty of music. Yamaha is the world's leading maker of musical instruments, including pianos, electronic keyboards, and synthesizers. It also manufactures and distributes a wide variety of wind and percussion instruments, as well as guitars, violins, and other string instruments. Yamaha also is a leading manufacturer of home audio and video equipment and makes a line of professional audio gear. In addition, the company makes semiconductors and other electronic components. Yamaha owns more than 20% of Yamaha Motor Co., Japan's #2 motorcycle manufacturer.

While musical instruments has traditionally been Yamaha's largest businesses segment (accounting for more than half of revenue), its components business has been the top performer in terms of profits. Sales of digital signal processing chips for use in mobile phones has been the big driver in this segment, but Yahama is expanding into new applications for its chips, including automobile components and amusement equipment. Still, musical instruments remain at the core of the company's identity and growth plans. Beyond increased spending for marketing and product development, Yamaha continues to invest in its music instruction schools as a way to create future consumers for its products.

The company is also expanding beyond its manufacturing roots to become a leader in new digital content markets. It operates ringtone downloading services for mobile phone users in about a dozen countries, and it has launched Web sites that allow music fans to hear songs from up-and-coming artists. Yamaha is also leading the development of networked karaoke equipment that can download songs from the Internet and offer uploading features. To strengthen its position in the music-creation market, Yamaha acquired Steinberg Media Technologies (a division of Pinnacle Systems) in late 2004.

One segment that has struggled, though, is Yamaha's leisure business. Its six resorts across Japan have been impacted by adverse weather and a slowdown in domestic tourism spending. Yamaha continues to invest in upgraded facilities and marketing efforts while it evaluates a potential sale of the resort properties.

HISTORY

Torakusu Yamaha first repaired medical instruments. But while repairing a broken organ, he decided he could make his own. His first attempt did not have good sound, but continuous work over a four-month period led to a new organ — completed in 1887 — that was highly praised. He established Yamaha Organ Manufacturing Company in 1889. In 1897, as production grew, Yamaha incorporated the company as Nippon Gakki (Japan Musical Instruments). Nippon Gakki began producing upright pianos in 1900 and grand pianos in 1902.

In 1920 the company diversified into the production of wooden airplane propellers (based on woodworking skills used in making pianos) and added pipe organs (1932) and guitars (1946) to its line of musical instruments. Genichi Kawakami, whose father had managed the company since 1927, took over in 1950.

The company formed its first overseas subsidiary, Yamaha de Mexico, in 1958. Under Kawakami's leadership, Nippon Gakki became the world's largest producer of musical instruments, developing Japan's first electronic organ, the Electone, in 1959. Kawakami conducted the company's movements into wind instruments (1965), stereos (1968), microchips (1971), and furniture (1975). He established the Yamaha Music Foundation in 1966 to oversee the company's music schools. By 1982 people in the Americas, Europe, and Asia could buy Yamaha-brand products locally.

Nippon Gakki undertook further diversification, particularly into customized chips for CD players. In 1983 it introduced a powerful, but affordable synthesizer. The company changed its name to Yamaha in 1987. It opened a facility in China two years later. Yamaha emphasized exports of electronic instruments and the production of integrated circuits.

Until 1992 three generations of the Kawakami family dominated Yamaha. After a failed attempt by heir apparent Hiroshi Kawakami to cut back Yamaha's workforce through early retirement, the manufacturer's in-house labor union revolted. Kawakami was replaced by Seisuke Ueshima, a Yamaha veteran who set out to work on a combination of product innovation and corporate restructuring. Ueshima made a pact with the unions to keep most factory workers, lay off 30% of its Japanese administrative staff, and cut overseas employees.

In 1997 the company launched a joint licensing program with Stanford University for the Sondius-XG sound synthesis technology; the two institutions agreed to share royalties from the technology, which provides realistic sound quality for musical instruments and computer games.

Undergoing sluggish sales of electronic parts, in 1999 Yamaha stopped producing magnetic heads for hard disk drives, shut down a semiconductor plant, and trimmed its workforce by giving 11% of its employees early retirement. In 2000 the company introduced a bamboo guitar that could help slow the depletion of hardwoods and debuted its Super "Melo-Ring" for cellular phone users. That same year, Shuji Ito was named president of Yamaha. The company launched a high-resolution projector for home theater use in

2001. Genichi Kawakami, the 90-year-old former president of Yamaha, died in 2002.

In early 2003 the company decided to exit from the CD recorder market to focus more on high-end home theater systems. Also that year Yamaha's Electronics Marketing Corporation began operations and the Hangzhou Yamaha Musical Instruments Co. was founded in China.

EXECUTIVES

Chairman: Katsuhiko Kishida, age 65
President and Director: Shuji Ito, age 64
Managing Director, Digital Content, Digital Media, Development, and Technology Planning and Board Member: Hirokazu Kato, age 62
Managing Director, Coporate Planning, Personnel, and Information Systems and Board Member: Tsuneo Kuroe, age 60
Director of General Administration and Environmental Management and Board Member: Shinya Hanamoto, age 60
Director of Accounting and Finance, Auditing, and Golf Products Division and Board Member: Tokihisa Makino, age 56
Director of Car Parts, Production Engineering, and Quality Assurance Divisions and Board Member: Yasushi Yahata
General Manager, Audio Visual and Information Technology Business Group: Hiroshi Sekiguchi
General Manager, Europe; President, Yamaha Music Holding Europe: Motoki Takahashi
General Manager, HG Piano Development Division: Hajime Hayashida
General Manager, Innovative Technology Group: Koji Niimi
General Manager, Legal and Intellectual Property Division: Kosuke Kamo
General Manager, Musical Instruments Group: Mitsuro (Mick) Umemura
General Manager, Pro Audio and Digital Musical Instruments Division: Katsuhiro Tokuda
General Manager, Product Design Laboratory: Yasuhiro Kira
General Manager, Public Relations Division: Yoshikazu Tobe
General Manager, Purchasing and Logistics Division: Tsutomu Sasaki
General Manager, Semiconductor Design: Tatsumi Ohara
General Manager, Sound Life Marketing and Development Laboratory: Takuya Tamaru
President, Yamaha Corporation of America and Yamaha Commercial Audio Systems: Yoshihiro (Yoshi) Doi
Auditors: Ernst & Young ShinNihon

LOCATIONS

HQ: Yamaha Corporation
10-1, Nakazawa-cho, Hamamatsu,
Shizuoka 430-8650, Japan
Phone: +81-53-460-2800   **Fax:** +81-53-460-2802
US HQ: 6600 Orangethorpe Ave., Buena Park, CA 90620
US Phone: 714-522-9011   **US Fax:** 714-522-9961
Web: www.global.yamaha.com

2006 Sales

	% of total
Japan	57
North America	18
Europe	16
Asia & other regions	9
Total	**100**

PRODUCTS/OPERATIONS

2006 Sales

	% of total
Musical Instruments	59
Audio visual & information technology	14
Electronic equipment & metal products	11
Lifestyle-related products	8
Recreation	3
Other	5
Total	**100**

Selected Products and Services

Musical instruments
  Digital and electronic musical instruments
    Electronic pianos
    Portable keyboards
    Synthesizers
  Digital content distribution
  Educational musical instruments
  Educational services
    English schools
    Music schools
  Percussion instruments
  Pianos
  Pro audio equipment
  Soundproofing and acoustical design
  String instruments (guitars, violins)
  Wind instruments
Consumer audio visual and information technology products
  CD players
  DVD players
  Digital cinema projectors
  Home theater systems
  PC speakers
  Routers
  Stereo receivers
  Stereo speakers
  Video projectors
Electronic equipment and metal products
  Electronic devices
  Electronic alloys and other specialty metals
  Large-scale integration chips (LSIs)
  Semiconductors
  Thermoelectric materials
Lifestyle-Related Products
  Bathtubs and washstands
  Furniture
  System kitchens
Recreation
  Golf courses
  Leisure facilities
  Sightseeing facilities
  Ski resorts
Other
  Automobile interior components
  Golf equipment
  Industrial robots
  Metallic molds and components

COMPETITORS

CASIO COMPUTER
Creative Technology
Epson
Fender Musical Instruments
Gibson Guitar
Harman International
Hoshino Gakki
Kawai
Matsushita
Philips Electronics
Pioneer
Roland
Samick
Samsung Electronics
Sharp
Sony
Steinway
TDK
TEAC
Toshiba
Victor Company of Japan
Young Chang

HISTORICAL FINANCIALS

Company Type: Public

Income Statement

FYE: March 31

	REVENUE ($ mil.)	NET INCOME ($ mil.)	NET PROFIT MARGIN	EMPLOYEES
3/06	4,542	239	5.3%	25,298
3/05	4,966	183	3.7%	23,828
3/04	5,107	412	8.1%	23,903
3/03	4,379	150	3.4%	23,563
3/02	3,803	(78)	—	23,020
Annual Growth	**4.5%**	**—**	**—**	**2.4%**

Net Income History

Pink Sheets: YAMCY

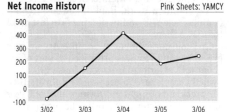

YPF

The largest company in Argentina answers to a Spanish parent: Integrated oil company YPF is 99%-owned by Repsol YPF, Spain's largest oil concern (formerly Repsol). YPF has proved reserves of about 1.2 billion barrels of oil, and 8 trillion cubic feet of natural gas. It produces, refines, and markets petroleum, natural gas, and petrochemicals. The company's three Argentine refineries have an annual capacity of about 116 million barrels, 51% of Argentina's total refining capacity. YPF distributes oil to its approximately 1,900 service stations in Argentina. Subsidiary YPF International has production interests in Indonesia and develops US oil and gas properties.

YPF also produces electricity and distributes LPG through interests in Bolivia, Brazil, Chile, Peru, and Russia.

Before its acquisition by Repsol, YPF had transformed itself from an inefficient state-owned firm into a streamlined international player. It has benefited from the Mercosur agreement, which set up an economic union in South America to promote regional trade.

HISTORY

An Argentine government team discovered oil while drilling for water in 1907. Determined to keep the oil under Argentine control, the government formed the world's first state-owned oil company, Direccion Nacional de los Yacimientos Petroliferos Fiscales (YPF), in 1922 to operate the newly discovered field. However, YPF lacked drilling equipment, capital, and staff; it found that the only way to increase domestic oil production was to allow in foreign oil companies. Although YPF's activities ebbed in the 1920s, it made major oil discoveries across Argentina in the 1930s.

A major turning point came with Juan Peron's rise to power in 1945. Peron extended state control over broad sections of the economy, including oil. He nationalized British and

US oil holdings and gave YPF a virtual monopoly. In 1945 YPF accounted for 68% of the country's oil production; by 1955 it produced 84% of the national total. The company discovered a huge gas field two years later in western Argentina, making YPF — and Argentina — a major gas producer.

However, YPF's production failed to keep pace with the demands of the growing economy, and imports still dominated Argentina's oil market. Over the next 30 years, YPF experienced radical swings in government policy as ultranationalist military regimes alternated with liberal, reformist governments. YPF grew into a bloated and inefficient conglomerate. Between 1982 and 1989, despite a World Bank-financed program to modernize YPF's refineries, the firm lost more than $6 billion.

In 1989 Carlos Menem became Argentina's president, and YPF was privatized as part of his economic reform plan to cut loose 50 state-owned companies. To prepare YPF for its IPO, the president brought in a former head of Baker Hughes, Jose Estenssoro, to draft a plan for privatization. The plan was so impressive that Menem gave him the job as CEO of the company in 1990. Estenssoro cut 87% of YPF's staff and sold off $2 billion of noncore assets. By 1993 YPF was profitable and went public as YPF Sociedad Anonima, selling 45% of its shares to raise $3 billion.

A year later YPF began expanding beyond Argentina by shipping crude oil to Chile through a new 300-mile pipeline. It bought woebegone Texas oil company Maxus Energy in 1995 and turned it around at great expense. Estenssoro and three other YPF executives died in a plane crash that year; in 1997 YPF selected Roberto Monti, who had headed Maxus, to serve as its CEO.

In 1997 YPF and Astra C.A.P.S.A. — in which Spanish oil firm Repsol had a controlling stake — jointly purchased a 67% stake in Mexpetrol Argentina (an affiliate of Mexican state oil company PEMEX). Repsol was aggressively moving overseas. In 1998 Repsol lobbied hard to buy part of YPF; Spain's King Juan Carlos himself phoned up Menem to promote Repsol's interests.

A year later the Argentine government auctioned off a 15% stake in YPF to Repsol for $2 billion; Repsol then bought another 83% of the company for $13.2 billion. Repsol became Repsol YPF, and its chairman, Alfonso Cortina, took over as chairman and CEO of YPF, while Monti was named VC and COO.

Monti retired the next year, after Repsol YPF increased its stake in YPF from 98% to 99%.

EXECUTIVES

Chairman: Antonio Brufau Niubo
CEO: Enrique Locutura
CFO and Director: Carlos A. Olivieri
General Manager and Director: Jose Maria Ranero Diaz
Director of External Relations: Fabian Falco
Director of General E&P, Argentina, Bolivia, and Brazil: Gonzalo López Fanjul
Director of Human Resources: Matteo Llurba
Director of Legal Affairs: Alejandro Quiroga Lopez
Director of Trading, Latin America: Alejandro Luchetta
Director of General Refining and Marketing, Latin America: Pascual Olmos
Director of LPG, Latin America: Alfredo Pochintesta
Controller: Gabriel Leiva

LOCATIONS

HQ: YPF, S.A.
Avenida Presidente Roque Sáenz Peña 777,
C. 1035 ACC Buenos Aires, Argentina
Phone: +54-11-4329-2000   **Fax:** +54-11-4329-2113
Web: www.repsol-ypf.com/eng/home/home.asp

YPF's oil and gas interests are primarily located in Argentina, Indonesia, and the US.

PRODUCTS/OPERATIONS

2005 Sales

	% of total
Refining & marketing	51
Exploration & production	42
Chemicals	6
Other	1
Total	**100**

COMPETITORS

BP
COPEC
Exxon Mobil
Imperial Oil
PDVSA
PEMEX
PETROBRAS
Petróleo Ipiranga
Pioneer Natural Resources
Royal Dutch Shell
TOTAL

HISTORICAL FINANCIALS

Company Type: Public

Income Statement

FYE: December 31

	REVENUE ($ mil.)	NET INCOME ($ mil.)	NET PROFIT MARGIN	EMPLOYEES
12/05	7,546	1,694	22.5%	10,574
12/04	6,709	1,409	21.0%	9,583
12/03	7,222	1,513	20.9%	9,395
12/02	5,815	1,038	17.8%	8,946
Annual Growth	**9.1%**	**17.7%**	**—**	**5.7%**

2005 Year-End Financials

Debt ratio: 13.0%
Return on equity: 21.4%
Cash ($ mil.): 175
Current ratio: 1.52
Long-term debt ($ mil.): 1,035
No. of shares (mil.): —
Dividends
Yield: 8.2%
Payout: —
Market value ($ mil.): —

Stock History

NYSE: YPF

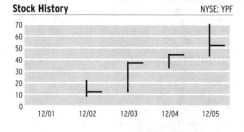

	STOCK PRICE ($) FY Close	P/E High/Low		PER SHARE ($) Earnings	Dividends
12/05	51.99	—	—	—	4.26
12/04	44.00	—	—	—	4.70
12/03	37.02	—	—	—	2.67
12/02	12.17	—	—	—	1.12
Annual Growth	**62.3%**	**—**	**—**	**—**	**56.1%**

Zurich Financial Services

It's a wonder anyone would leave Zürich, nestled as it is in the beautiful Swiss Alps. But the business interests of Zurich Financial Services (Zurich) have crossed the mountains and spread to all but cover the globe. With operations in more than 50 countries worldwide, the company is the second-largest provider of general corporate insurance (after AIG). Focused on markets in Europe and in the US (through its North America Commercial unit), the company's General Insurance segment offers property/casualty and specialty insurance, while its Life Insurance segment offers life insurance, annuities, and other investment policies. The company was founded in 1872.

A strategic reorganization begun in 2004 has sought to consolidate Zurich's business under a single brand and refocus on its two principal segments — General Insurance and Life Insurance. The company operates through five divisions. Its Global Corporate unit focuses on risk management for large international and domestic clients. The Europe General Insurance division provides property/casualty and specialty lines for businesses and individuals; key markets are Germany, Italy, Spain, and Switzerland. The International Businesses unit has operations focused in Latin America, the Asia/Pacific region, China, Southern Africa, and other emerging markets.

In the US, Zurich serves business customers through its North America Commercial division, which includes Zurich American Insurance Company and its subsidiaries. Its Farmers Group operates the Farmers Management Services providing management to the Farmers Insurance Group, which provides auto and homeowners insurance. Zurich manages the Farmers Exchanges but holds no ownership stake.

The company's reorganization and efforts to refocus on its principal lines of business, as well as its expansion into markets deemed "underrepresented," have led to a financial turnaround.

HISTORY

The roots of Zurich Financial Services (ZFS) stretch back to the 1872 founding of a reinsurer for Switzerland Transport Insurance. The company soon branched out into accident, travel, and workers' compensation insurance and in 1875 it changed its name to Transport and Accident Insurance plc Zurich to reflect the changes. It then expanded into Berlin (the jumping-off point for its expansion into Scandinavia and Russia) and Stuttgart, Germany. The company exited marine lines in 1880; it later left the reinsurance business and expanded into liability insurance; in 1894 it changed its name to Zurich General Accident and Liability Insurance.

In 1912 Zurich crossed the Atlantic, expanding operations into the US. It agreed in 1925 to provide insurance for Ford cars at favorable terms. Zurich's business was hard hit during the war years of the late 1930s and 1940s. In 1955 the company changed its name to Zurich Insurance.

Starting in the 1960s, Zurich began buying other insurers, including Alpina (1965, Switzerland), Agrippina (1969, Germany), and Maryland Casualty Group (1989, US). It also bought the property liability operations of American General.

In the early 1990s the company shifted its strategy, expanding into what it deemed underrepresented markets in the UK and the US. Being big wasn't enough; Zurich needed to find a focus. It also jettisoned such marginal or unprofitable business lines as commercial fire insurance in Germany.

In 1995 Zurich bought struggling Chicago-based asset manager Kemper and in 1997 bought lackluster mutual fund manager Scudder Stevens & Clark, forming Scudder Kemper. That year it also bought failed Hong Kong investment bank Peregrine Investment Holdings.

In 1998 Zurich merged with the financial services businesses of B.A.T Industries, formerly known as the British-American Tobacco Co., created in 1902 as a joint venture between UK-based Imperial Tobacco and American Tobacco. As public disapproval of smoking grew in the 1970s, British-American Tobacco began diversifying; it changed its name to B.A.T Industries in 1976 and moved into insurance. In 1984 it rescued UK insurer Eagle Star from a hostile offer by German insurance giant Allianz. The next year it bought Hambro Life Assurance, renaming it Allied Dunbar. Moving into the large US market in 1988, B.A.T bought Farmers Insurance Group.

While B.A.T battled the antismoking army of the 1990s, the insurance industry struggled with stagnant growth. In 1997 Europe's largest insurance firms were named as defendants in class action lawsuits that sought recovery for unpaid claims on Holocaust-era insurance policies. In 1998 Zurich became a founding member of the International Commission on Holocaust Era Insurance Claims (ICHEIC).

Also in 1998 Zurich and B.A.T's insurance units merged to create Zurich Financial Services. The firm reshuffled some of its holdings and sold Eagle Star Reinsurance. In 1999 Zurich spun off its real estate holdings into PSP Swiss Property and, at the turn of the century, it focused on expansion, buying the new business of insurer Abbey Life, which it merged into Allied Dunbar. In 2000, the holding companies formed to own Zurich (Zurich Allied and Allied Zurich) were merged into the firm.

In 2002 Zurich completed the spin off of reinsurance unit Zurich Re, which became Converium. It also sold troubled asset manager Zurich Scudder to Deutsche Bank and acquired the bank's life insurance operations in Italy, Spain, and Portugal. It also acquired life insurance firm Deutsche Herold, as well as German financial services provider Bonnfinanz and mutual fund distributor DGV. Zurich also sold a large holding in its US-based Zurich Life to BANK ONE and sold its operations in Hungary, Poland, and Slovakia, to Italian insurer Generali.

The write off of assets and strengthening of non-life reserves resulted in Zurich posting a $3.4 billion loss for 2002. Rolf Hüppi, Zurich's legendary chairman and CEO, stepped down while the company's asset management unit tumbled and investors pulled out. James Schiro, previously with PricewaterhouseCoopers, was named as the new chief executive and has guided a turnaround at the company. Zurich has seen growth in net income every year since 2002.

Zurich has paid out some $900 million in claims related to the September 11 terrorist attacks in the US.

EXECUTIVES

Chairman: Manfred Gentz, age 63, $56,992 pay
Vice Chairman: Philippe O. Pidoux, age 63, $68,660 pay
COO: Peter Eckert, age 61
Group Finance Director: Patrick H. O'Sullivan, age 57
Chief Administrative Officer: Richard P. Kearns, age 56
Chief Information Technology Officer:
  Michael Paravicini, age 45
General Counsel and Company Secretary:
  Monica Mächler-Erne, age 50
CEO, Europe General Insurance: Dieter Wemmer, age 49
CEO, General Insurance: John Amore, age 58
CEO, Global Corporate Business:
  Geoffrey (Geoff) Riddell, age 50
CEO, Global Life Insurance: Paul van de Geijn, age 60
CEO, Zurich Advice Network: Stephen J. Leaman
CEO, Zurich North America Commercial:
  Axel P. Lehmann, age 47
CEO, Farmers Insurance Group: Paul N. Hopkins, age 50
CEO, Switzerland: Markus Hongler
Head, Investor Relations and Rating Agencies:
  Seraina Maag-Gubler
Chief Economist and Head, Media and Public Relations: Daniel M. Hofmann
Group Head, Human Resources: Peter Goerke, age 44
Chief Investment Officer: Martin Senn, age 49
Chief Risk Officer: Wayne Fisher, age 60
Group Chief Actuary: Steve Wilson, age 39
Global Chief Underwriting Officer:
  Timothy (Tim) Mitchell, age 55
Group Chief Marketing Officer and Head, Corporate Communications: E. Randall Clouser, age 47
Auditors: PricewaterhouseCoopers AG

LOCATIONS

HQ: Zurich Financial Services
  Mythenquai 2, 8022 Zurich, Switzerland
Phone: +41-44-625-25-25   **Fax:** +41-44-625-26-41
US HQ: North America Commercial, Zurich Towers,
  1400 American Ln., Schaumburg, IL 60196
US Phone: 847-605-6000   **US Fax:** 847-413-5187
Web: www.zurich.com

2005 Sales

	$ mil.	% of total
Europe	42,751	62
North America	17,572	25
International businesses	3,506	5
Centrally managed businesses	4,603	8
Adjustments	(1,246)	—
Total	**67,186**	**100**

PRODUCTS/OPERATIONS

2005 Assets

	$ mil.	% of total
Investments		
Debt securities	125,297	37
Equity securities	90,314	27
Cash & cash equivalents	23,482	7
Real estate held for investment	12,702	4
Policyholders' collateral and other loans	11,987	4
Mortgage loans	9,307	3
Investments in associates	580	—
Other investments	3,624	1
Reinsurers' share of reserves for insurance contracts	20,494	6
Receivables	11,283	3
Deferred policy acquisition costs	11,179	3
Deferred tax assets	4,393	1
Mortgage loans given as collateral	3,064	1
Deposits made under assumed reinsurance contracts	2,450	1
Accrued investment income	2,390	1
Derivative assets & other assets	1,787	—
Fixed assets	1,729	—
Deferred origination costs	690	—
Goodwill	605	—
Other intangible assets	2,255	1
Total	**339,612**	**100**

2005 Sales

	$ mil.	% of total
Net earned premiums & policy fees	40,457	60
Net capital gains on investments & impairments	13,382	20
Net investment income	9,765	15
Management fees	2,058	3
Net loss on divestments of businesses	(2)	—
Other income	1,526	2
Total	**67,186**	**100**

2005 Sales

	$ mil.	% of total
General insurance	31,056	45
Life insurance	28,729	42
Other business	5,345	8
Farmers management services	2,210	3
Corporate & other	1,686	2
Adjustments	(1,840)	—
Total	**67,186**	**100**

COMPETITORS

AIG
Allianz
Aviva
AXA
CNA Financial
Generali
The Hartford
St. Paul Travelers
Winterthur

HISTORICAL FINANCIALS

Company Type: Public

Income Statement

FYE: December 31

	ASSETS ($ mil.)	NET INCOME ($ mil.)	INCOME AS % OF ASSETS	EMPLOYEES
12/05	339,612	3,214	0.9%	52,010
12/04	346,083	2,587	0.7%	53,246
12/03	317,876	2,120	0.7%	62,000
12/02	285,856	(3,430)	—	67,824
12/01	231,605	(387)	—	70,000
Annual Growth	**10.0%**	**—**	**—**	**(7.2%)**

2005 Year-End Financials

Equity as % of assets: —   Long-term debt ($ mil.): —
Return on assets: 0.9%   Sales ($ mil.): 67,186
Return on equity: —

Net Income History

Swiss: ZURN

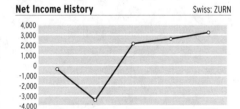

Hoover's Handbook of

World
Business

The Indexes

Index by Industry

AEROSPACE & DEFENSE

Aerospace & Defense Parts Manufacturing
BAE SYSTEMS 52
Rolls-Royce 282

Aircraft Manufacturing
Airbus 29
Bombardier 70
EADS (European Aeronautic Defence and Space Company EADS N.V.) 116

AUTOMOTIVE & TRANSPORT

Sime Darby Berhad 307

Auto Manufacturing
BMW (Bayerische Motoren Werke AG) 67
DaimlerChrysler 103
Fiat S.p.A. 129
Honda 153
Hyundai 158
Koç Holding 184
Mazda 213
Nissan 233
Peugeot (PSA Peugeot Citroën S.A.) 253
Porsche (Dr. Ing. h.c. F. Porsche AG) 259
Renault 272
Suzuki 320
Toyota 348
Volkswagen 359

Auto Parts Manufacturing
DENSO 107
Magna International 207
Robert Bosch 278
Tomkins 343

Truck, Bus & Other Vehicle Manufacturing
Isuzu 170
MAN 209
Volvo 360

BANKING

Banking – Asia & Australia
Bank of China 55
Mitsubishi UFJ Financial Group 219
National Australia Bank 225

Banking – Canada
Bank of Montreal 56
Canadian Imperial Bank of Commerce 83
Royal Bank of Canada 285
Toronto-Dominion Bank 345

Banking – Europe
Allied Irish Banks 39
BBVA (Banco Bilbao Vizcaya Argentaria, S.A.) 61
Crédit Agricole 98
Dexia 113
Espírito Santo 128
HBOS 147
Lloyds TSB 199
Royal Bank of Scotland 286
UBS 350

Money Center Banks
ABN AMRO 21
Banco Santander Central Hispano 54
Barclays 57
BNP Paribas 68
Credit Suisse 99
Deutsche Bank 110
HSBC Holdings 156
Mizuho Financial 222

BEVERAGES

Alcoholic Beverages
Bacardi & Company 51
Carlsberg 87
Diageo 114
Foster's Group 132
Heineken 148
InBev 164
Kirin Brewery 182
Pernod Ricard 249
SABMiller 289
San Miguel 293

Nonalcoholic Beverages
Cadbury Schweppes 82

BUSINESS SERVICES

Advertising & Marketing
Dentsu 108
Publicis 265
WPP Group 369

Commercial Printing
Dai Nippon Printing 101
Quebecor 267

Staffing
Adecco 24

CHEMICALS

Agricultural Chemicals
Agrium 27
Koor Industries 186

Basic and Intermediate Chemical & Petrochemical Manufacturing
BASF 58

Sinopec Shanghai Petrochemical 309

Paints, Coatings & Other Finishing Product Manufacturing
Akzo Nobel 31
Imperial Chemical 161

Plastic & Fiber Manufacturing
Bayer 60
Formosa Plastics 130

COMPUTER HARDWARE

NEC 226
Toshiba 346

Computer Peripherals
Canon 84
Oki Electric 245
Ricoh 276
Seiko Epson 303

Personal Computers
Acer 23

COMPUTER SERVICES

Information Technology Services
Atos Origin 45
Capgemini 86
Fujitsu 137
Infosys Technologies 167
Wipro 365

COMPUTER SOFTWARE

Enterprise Resource Planning Software
SAP 297

CONSTRUCTION

Construction & Design Services
Bouygues 71
Hopewell Holdings 154
Tata Group 323
VINCI 354

Construction Materials
Hanson 145
Lafarge 194
Saint-Gobain (Compagnie de Saint-Gobain) 290

CONSUMER PRODUCTS MANUFACTURERS

Apparel
adidas 25
LVMH 206

Index by Headquarters

ARGENTINA
Buenos Aires
YPF 371

AUSTRALIA
Bella Vista
Woolworths 368

Mascot
Qantas Airways 266

Melbourne
BHP Billiton 66
National Australia Bank 225
Rio Tinto 277
Telstra 335

Southbank
Foster's Group 132

Sydney
AMP Limited 40

Tooronga
Coles Group 95

AUSTRIA
Vienna
OMV 246

BELGIUM
Brussels
Dexia 113
Fortis 131

Leuven
InBev 164

BERMUDA
Pembroke
Bacardi & Company 51

BRAZIL
Rio de Janeiro
PETROBRAS (PETRÓLEO
BRASILEIRO S.A. -
PETROBRAS) 250

CANADA
Aurora
Magna International 207

Brampton
Loblaw 200

Calgary
Agrium 27
Imperial Oil 162

Montreal
Alcan 32
BCE 62
Bombardier 70
Quebecor 267

Toronto
Bank of Montreal 56
Canadian Imperial Bank of
Commerce 83
George Weston 142
Hollinger 152
Inco (CVRD Inco Limited) 166
Nortel Networks 238
Rogers Communications 281
Royal Bank of Canada 285
Thomson 339
Toronto-Dominion Bank 345

CHILE
Santiago
Telefonica Chile (Compañía de
Telecomunicaciones de Chile
S.A.) 331

CHINA
Beijing
Bank of China 55

Shanghai
Sinopec Shanghai Petrochemical 309

DENMARK
Bagsværd
Novo Nordisk 241

Billund
LEGO 197

Copenhagen
A.P. Møller — Mærsk 42

Valby
Carlsberg 87

ENGLAND
London
Reed Elsevier 271

Slough
Reckitt Benckiser 270

FINLAND
Espoo
Nokia 235

Helsinki
Stora Enso Oyj 318

FRANCE
Blagnac
Airbus 29

Boulogne-Billancourt
Renault 272

Clermont-Ferrand
Michelin (Compagnie Générale des
Établissements Michelin) 215

Clichy
L'Oréal 202

Courbevoie
Saint-Gobain 290
TOTAL 347

Montigny-le-Bretonneux
Sodexho Alliance 311

Paris
Alcatel-Lucent 33
Atos Origin 45
AXA 49
BNP Paribas 68
Capgemini 86
Carrefour 88
Club Méditerranée 93
CNP Assurances 94
Crédit Agricole 98
Danone 104
Electricité de France 117
France Telecom 134
Gaz de France 139
Lafarge 194
Lagardère 195
LVMH 206
Pernod Ricard 249
Peugeot (PSA Peugeot Citroën
S.A.) 253
PPR 261
Publicis 265
Rallye 268
Sanofi-Aventis 294
SNCF (Société Nationale des Chemins
de Fer Français) 310
Veolia Environnement 353
Vivendi 356

Roissy
Air France 28

Rueil-Malmaison
Schneider Electric 299
VINCI 354

Saint-Etienne
Casino Guichard-Perrachon 89

Saint-Quentin-en-Yvelines
Bouygues 71

Villeneuve d'Ascq
Auchan 46

Évry
Accor 22

GERMANY
Berlin
Axel Springer 50
Deutsche Bahn 109

Bonn
Deutsche Post 111
Deutsche Telekom 112

Cologne
Lufthansa (Deutsche Lufthansa
AG) 204

Düsseldorf
E.ON 124
Henkel 149
METRO 214
ThyssenKrupp 340

Essen
ALDI 35
Karstadt Quelle 179
RWE 288

Frankfurt am Main
Deutsche Bank 110

Gütersloh
Bertelsmann 65

Hamburg
Otto GmbH & Co 247

Hanover
TUI 349

Herzogenaurach
adidas 25

Leverkusen
Bayer 60

Ludwigshafen
BASF 58

Munich
Allianz 38
BMW (Bayerische Motoren Werke
AG) 67
MAN 209
Munich Re (Münchener
Rückversicherungs-Gesellschaft
Aktiengesellschaft) 224
Siemens 306

Index of Executives

A

Aasheim, Hilde 238
Abat, Jean-Raymond 49
Abbey, Scott G. 351
Abe, Hisamasa 136
Abercrombie, George B. 280
Abiteboul, Jean 139
Abramsky, Jenny 78
Abreu Aguiar, José A. 122
Abril Pérez, José María 61
Abril Pérez, Luis 330
Acharya, Ranjan 366
Achleitner, Paul 38
Ackermann, Josef 111, 307
Ackling, Kevin 80
Adachi, Seijiro 244
Adachi, Toshio 304
Adachi, Yoroku 85
Adam, Philippe 23
Adami, Norman J. 290
Adams, George 181
Adams, Paul 76
Adams, Ralph G. 106
Adams, Rowan 325
Adhikari, Arun 352
Adrion, Adolf 350
Aelick, Ronald C. 166
Agarwal, Bhikam C. 222
Agassi, Shai 297
Agemura, Yasuo 237
Agius, Marcus 58
Agnelli, Roger 166
Agnellini, Victor 34
Agon, Jean-Paul 203
Agrawal, Vineet 366
Agren, Christer 319
Agrusti, Raffaele 142
Aguilar, Alfonso Ballestero 274
Ahearn, Chris 275
Ahizoune, Abdeslam 357
Ahlers, Bernd (Tengelmann) 337
Ahlers, Bernd (Tengelmann) 337
Ahmed, Javed 271
Ahn Bok-Hyun 292
Ahn, Kyung-Soo 137
Ahrnell, Jan Henrik 335
Ahuja, Sanjiv 134
Aihara, Gempachiro 221
Aiken, Philip S. 67
Aimono, Minoru 37
Airey, Dawn 79
Aitken, Ian C. 283
Aizawa, Masatoshi 227
Aizawa, Toshihiko 217
Akahane, Masao 303
Akamatsu, Yoshio 172
Akhavan, Hamid 113
Akhurst, Bruce J. 336
Akikusa, Naoyuki 137
Akiyama, Kotaro 44
Akiyama, Masaki 212
Äkräs, Juha 235

Al Khaily, Mohamed Nasser Nekhaira Nasser 246
Alangoya, Emine 184
Alary, Pierre 70
Albanese, Tom 277
Albrecht, Karl 35
Albrecht, Theo (ALDI) 35
Albrecht, Theo Jr. (ALDI) 35
Áldott, Zoltán 224
Alejandro Rojas, José 252
Alekperov, Vagit Y. 205
Alexander, Anthony 164
Alexander, Ralph C. 73
Alexander, William J. 288
Alexandre, Patrick 29
Alfaia de Carvalho, António P. 122
Alford, Brad 228
Algermissen, Alex 198
Alierta Izuel, César 330
Allamandi, Silvio 325
Allan, John (Kingfisher) 181
Allan, John Murray (Deutsche Post) 112
Allavena, Jean-Luc 195
Allen, David C. 73
Allen, Sharon L. 106
Allert, Richard H. 96
Allgaier, Larry 240
Allgood, David R. 285
Allgrove, Jeffrey 352
Almassy, Stephen E. 127
Almond, Stephen 106
Alonso Durán, Alfonso 330
Alphandéry, Edmond 94
Alphéus, Ingo 288
Alsvik, Lars Christian 238
Altavilla, Alfredo 129
Altemark, Lars 198
Alvarez, José A. 54
Alvarez, Victoria 362
Alves Pereira, Carlos 122
Ambe Attar, Isidoro 332
Ambroso, Augusto 129
Ambrus, Mary Lou 34
Amemiya, Hiroshi 217
Amore, John 373
Ananenkov, Alexander Georgievich 140
Andersen, Jørgen 88
Andersen, Kurt 64
Andersen, Lars Norman 198
Andersen, Nils S. 88
Andersen, Svein 317
Andersen, Thomas Thune 43
Andersen, Ulrik 88
Anderson, Brad 98
Anderson, David 336
Anderson, James 120
Anderson, Matthew 79
Anderson, Ruth 188
Anderson, Stephanie E. 166
Anderson, Toby 174
Anderson, William D. 63
Andersson, Bengt 119
Andersson, Robert 235

Ando, Göran A. 242
Andrade, Flávio de 76
Andreassen, Arild 238
Andrews, Steve 80
Andriès, Olivier 30
Andruchow, Al 120
Ang, Ramon S. 293
Angelici, Bruno 45
Angelidis, Emanuele 81
Angulo, Jean Carlos 194
Aninat, Cristián 331
Announ, Pascal 90
Ano, Masatoshi 107
Ansell, Clive R. 80
Antinori, Thierry 204
António, Firmin 23
Anzai, Fujio 171
Aoki, Satoshi 154
Aoki, Yasushi 179
Apotheker, Leo 297
Appel, Frank 112
Ara, Yasuaki 137
Arai, Kazuo 108
Arai, Takao 232
Arakawa, Shoshi 74
Aramaki, Koichiro 182
Aramburuzabala Larregui, María A. 333
Araya, Shinichi 327
Arbola, Gérald 318
Arce, David 54
Archambault, François 203
Archer-Shee, James B. 285
Arena, R. J. 156
Arendt, Axel 283
Argüelles, Raul 362
Argus, Don R. 66
Arima, Akira 243
Arima, Toshio 136
Arlett, Julian 193
Armbruster, Jean-Claude 295
Armenio, Peter 285
Armour, Mark H. 272
Armstrong, Graeme D. 162
Arnault, Bernard 206
Arndt, Frank-Peter 68
Arteaga Carlebach, Maximiliano 333
Aruga, Shuji 303
Asada, Shunichi 223
Asai, Yutaka 245
Asakawa, Osamu 37
Asami, Yasuo 74
Asano, Katsuhiko 182
Aschenbroich, Jacques 291
Ashby, Ian R. 67
Ashcroft, Charles P. 120
Ashton, Lynda 174
Atay, Temel K. 184
Attal, Laurent 203
Auci, Ernesto 129
Auque, François 116
Aurbach, Pamela 264
Avery, Kate 196
Ayuso, Javier 61
Ayyoubi, Silvia 280

Azcárraga Jean, Emilio 333
Azema, David 355
Azuma, Kazunori 276
Azuma, Makoto 346

B

Baan, Adri 367
Baan, Roeland 222
Babeau, Emmanuel 250
Bacardi, Facundo L. 52
Bacardit, Ramón 150
Bach, Herbert 225
Bach, Luis 52
Bacon, Gerry 358
Bacon, Ian 325
Badalamenti, Salvatore 280
Badinter, Elisabeth 265
Badinter, Simon 266
Badke, Michael 180
Bae Ho-Won 292
Baffsky, David 23
Baguley, Peter 174
Bahadur, Harsh 215
Bai Dong-Man 292
Bailby, Marc-Antoine 138
Bailey, Ann 240
Baillie, Douglas 352
Bailly, Jean-Paul 94
Baird, Patrick S. 27
Baird, Richard L. 263
Baker, Kathy 367
Baker, Wendy 199
Balakrishnan, V. 167
Balasubramaniam, Ram 324
Balbinot, Sergio 142
Balcarcel Santa Cruz, Joaquín 334
Balcom, Robert A. 143, 201
Balfour, Fergus 352
Balfour, Fiona 336
Bali, S. Ashish 106
Baltazar, Miguel 362
Bamba, Ryoichi 85
Bandier, Martin N. 120
Bando, Aihiko 44
Banerjee, Gautam 263
Banerjee, Sudip 366
Banga, M. S. 352
Bangle, Chris 68
Bánhegyi, Ilona 224
Banner, Roderick 369
Bannister, C. C. R. 156
Banziger, Hugo 111
Baptista, Michael 22
Barat, Jean-Paul 174
Barbant, Jean-Christophe 194
Barbaroux, Olivier 117, 354
Barber, R. G. 156
Barberis, Joe 96
Barberot, Olivier 134
Barbosa, Fabio C. 22
Barclay, Mike 309
Barker, Ros 193

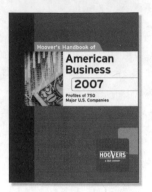

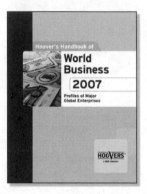